MOON HANDBOOKS®
COSTA RICA

FIFTH EDITION

CHRISTOPHER P. BAKER

W9-CGK-963

AVALON TRAVEL

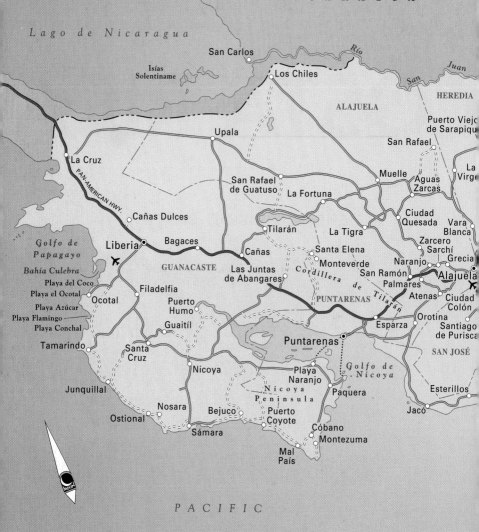

N I C A R A G U A

Lago de Nicaragua

San Carlos

Isías Solentiname

Los Chiles

ALAJUELA

HEREDIA

Puerto Viejo de Sarapiqu

Upala

San Rafael

La Cruz

San Rafael de Guatuso

La Fortuna

Muelle

Aguas Zarcas

La Virge

PAN-AMERICAN HWY.

Cañas Dulces

Ciudad Quesada

Vara Blanca

Tilarán

La Tigra

Zarcero

Sarchí

Golfo de Papagayo

Liberia

Bagaces

Cañas

Santa Elena

Naranjo

Grecia

Bahía Culebra

GUANACASTE

Las Juntas de Abangares

Monteverde

San Ramón

Alajuela

Playa del Coco

Palmares

Playa el Ocotal

Filadelfia

Cordillera

de

Atenas

Ciudad Colón

Playa Azúcar

Ocotal

Puerto Humo

PUNTARENAS

Tilarán

Esparza

Playa Flamingo

Guaitíl

Orotina

Playa Conchal

Santiago de Purisca

Tamarindo

Santa Cruz

Puntarenas

SAN JOSÉ

Nicoya

Golfo de Nicoya

Junquillal

Playa Naranjo

Esterillos

Nicoya Peninsula

Paquera

Nosara

Bejuco

Jaco

Ostional

Puerto Coyote

Sámara

Cóbano

Montezuma

Mal País

P A C I F I C

Isla del Coco

O C E A N

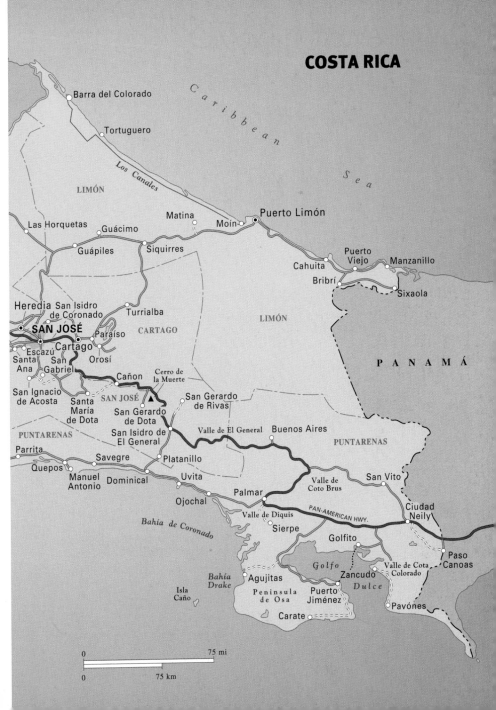

COSTA RICA

Barra del Colorado

Tortuguero

Caribbean Sea

Los Canales

LIMÓN

Las Horquetas
Matina
Moín
Puerto Limón

Guácimo

Guápiles
Siquirres
Puerto Viejo
Manzanillo

Cahuita

Bribrí
Sixaola

Heredia San Isidro de Coronado
Turrialba
LIMÓN

SAN JOSÉ
Paraíso
CARTAGO

Cartago

Escazú San Gabriel
Orosí

Santa Ana

PANAMÁ

San Ignacio de Acosta
Cañon
Cerro de la Muerte

SAN JOSÉ
San Gerardo de Rivas

Santa María de Dota
San Gerardo de Dota

San Isidro de El General
Valle de El General
Buenos Aires

PUNTARENAS
PUNTARENAS

Parrita
Platanillo

Savegre
San Vito

Quepos
Uvita
Valle de Coto Brus

Manuel Antonio Dominical
Palmar

Ojochal
Valle de Diquis
PAN-AMERICAN HWY.
Ciudad Neily

Bahía de Coronado
Sierpe
Paso Canoas

Golfito

Bahía Drake
Agujitas
Golfo
Valle de Cota Colorado

Zancudo

Isla Caño
Península de Osa
Puerto Jiménez
Dulce

Carate
Pavónes

0 _____ 75 mi

0 _____ 75 km

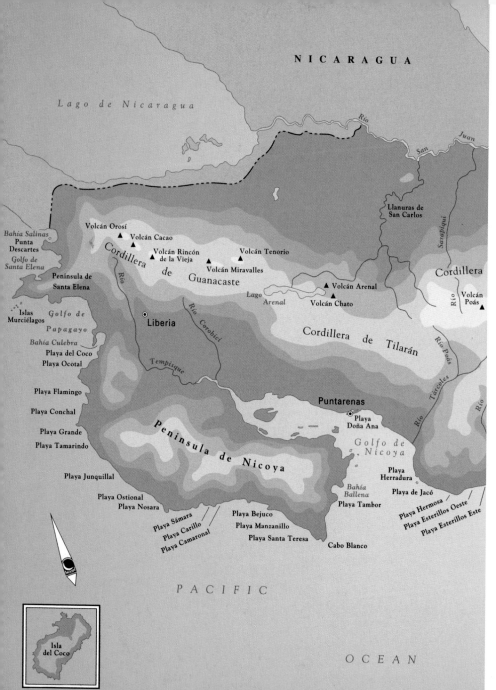

NICARAGUA

Lago de Nicaragua

Río San Juan

Sarapiquí

Llanuras de
San Carlos

Bahía Salinas
Punta
Descartes
Golfo de
Santa Elena

Volcán Orosí
▲ Volcán Cacao
▲

Cordillera
de
Guanacaste

Volcán Rincón
de la Vieja ▲
Volcán Miravalles ▲

Volcán Tenorio ▲

Cordillera

Río

Volcán Arenal ▲
Volcán Chato ▲

Volcán
Poás ▲

Península de
Santa Elena

Río Poás

Islas
Murciélagos

Golfo de
Papagayo

Bahía Culebra
Playa del Coco
Playa Ocotal

Liberia

Río Corobicí

Lago
Arenal

Cordillera   de   Tilarán

Río Tárcoles

Río

Tempisque

Playa Flamingo

Playa Conchal

Playa Grande
Playa Tamarindo

Península
de
Nicoya

Puntarenas
Playa
Doña Ana

Golfo de
Nicoya

Playa Junquillal

Playa Herradura

Bahía
Ballena

Playa de Jacó

Playa Ostional
Playa Nosara

Playa Tambor

Playa Bejuco
Playa Manzanillo

Playa Hermosa
Playa Esterillos Oeste
Playa Esterillos Este

Playa Sámara
Playa Carillo
Playa Camaronal

Playa Santa Teresa

Cabo Blanco

PACIFIC

Isla
del Coco

OCEAN

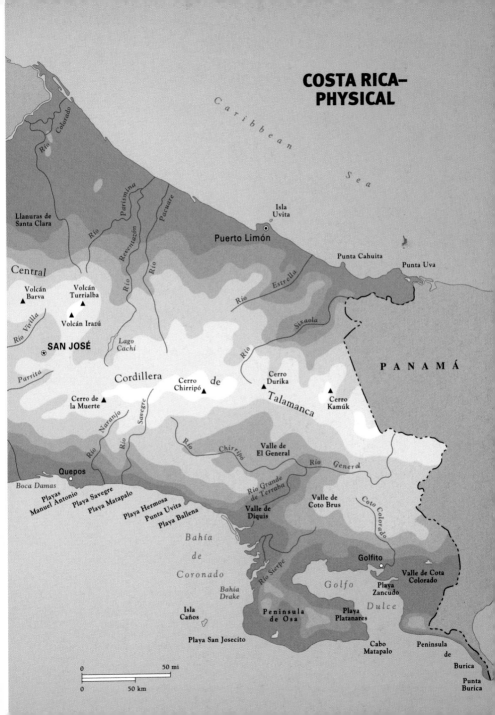

COSTA RICA–
PHYSICAL

Caribbean Sea

Llanuras de
Santa Clara

Río Colorado

Río Parismina

Río Reventazón

Río Pacuare

Isla
Uvita

Puerto Limón

Punta Cahuita

Punta Uva

Central

Volcán
Barva

Volcán
Turrialba

Río

Río Estrella

Volcán Irazú

Río Virilla

SAN JOSÉ

Lago
Cachí

Río Sixaola

PANAMÁ

Parrita

Cordillera

de

Cerro
Chirripó

Cerro
Durika

Cerro
Kamúk

Cerro de
la Muerte

Talamanca

Río Naranjo

Río Savegre

Río

Río Chirripó

Valle de
El General

Río General

Quepos

Boca Damas

Playas
Manuel Antonio

Playa Savegre

Playa Matapalo

*Río Grande
de Terraba*

Valle de
Coto Brus

Coto Colorado

Playa Hermosa

Punta Uvita

Valle de
Diquis

Playa Ballena

Bahía

de

Coronado

Río Sierpe

Golfo

Golfito

Valle de Cota
Colorado

Bahía
Drake

Playa
Zancudo

Dulce

Isla
Caños

Península
de Osa

Playa
Platanares

Playa San Josecito

Cabo
Matapalo

Península
de

Burica

Punta
Burica

0   50 mi

0   50 km

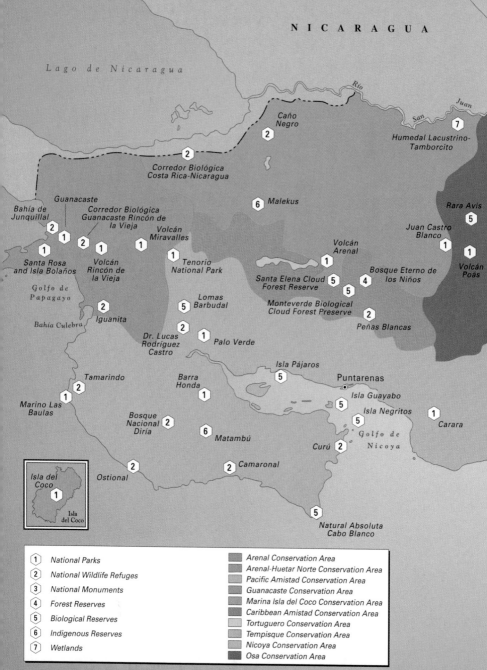

NICARAGUA

Lago de Nicaragua

Caño Negro ②

Río San Juan

⑦ Humedal Lacustrino-Tamborcito

② Corredor Biológica Costa Rica-Nicaragua

⑥ Malekus

Rara Avis ⑤

Guanacaste

Corredor Biológica Guanacaste Rincón de la Vieja

Bahía de Junquillal ②

① ② ① Volcán Miravalles ①

Juan Castro Blanco ①

Volcán Poás ①

① Santa Rosa and Isla Bolaños

Volcán Rincón de la Vieja

① Tenorio National Park

Volcán Arenal ①

Golfo de Papagayo

② Iguanita

⑤ Lomas Barbudal

Santa Elena Cloud ⑤ Forest Reserve ④

Bosque Eterno de los Niños

⑤

Bahía Culebra

Monteverde Biological Cloud Forest Preserve

② Peñas Blancas

② Dr. Lucas Rodríguez Castro

① Palo Verde

Tamarindo ②

Barra Honda ①

Isla Pájaros ⑤

Puntarenas

Isla Guayabo

① Marino Las Baulas

Bosque Nacional Diria ②

⑤ Isla Negritos

① Carara

② Matambú ⑥

Curú ②

Golfo de Nicoya

② Ostional

② Camaronal

⑤ Natural Absoluta Cabo Blanco

Isla del Coco ①

Isla del Coco

① National Parks
② National Wildlife Refuges
③ National Monuments
④ Forest Reserves
⑤ Biological Reserves
⑥ Indigenous Reserves
⑦ Wetlands

Arenal Conservation Area
Arenal-Huetar Norte Conservation Area
Pacific Amistad Conservation Area
Guanacaste Conservation Area
Marina Isla del Coco Conservation Area
Caribbean Amistad Conservation Area
Tortuguero Conservation Area
Tempisque Conservation Area
Nicoya Conservation Area
Osa Conservation Area

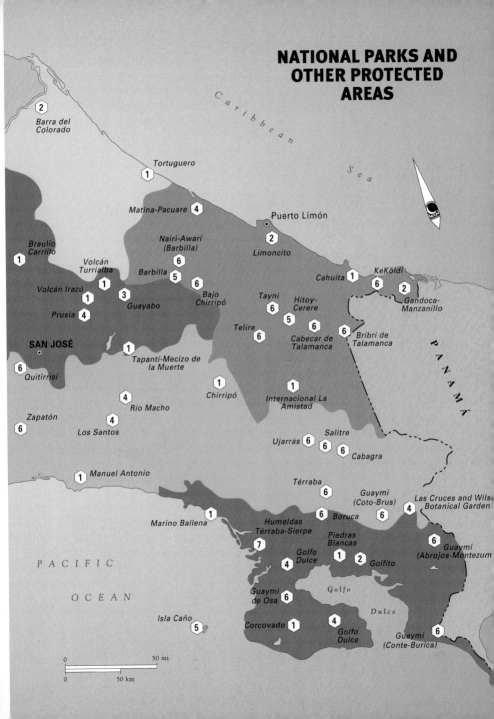

NATIONAL PARKS AND OTHER PROTECTED AREAS

CONTENTS

Discover Costa Rica

Explore Costa Rica

Golfo Dulce and Peninsula de Osa

South-Central Costa Rica

Know Costa Rica

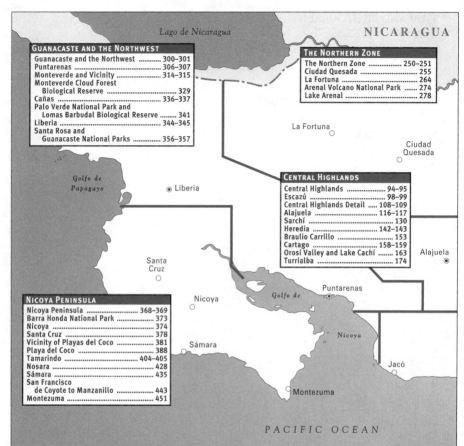

Lago de Nicaragua

NICARAGUA

La Fortuna

Ciudad
Quesada

Golfo de
Papagayo

Liberia

Alajuela

Santa
Cruz

Nicoya

Golfo de

Puntarenas

Nicoya

Sámara

Jacó

Montezuma

PACIFIC OCEAN

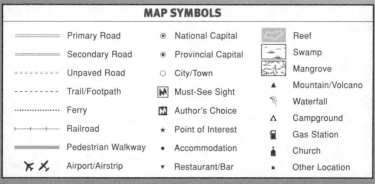

MAP SYMBOLS

═══════ Primary Road	⊛ National Capital	Reef
═══════ Secondary Road	◉ Provincial Capital	Swamp
========= Unpaved Road	○ City/Town	Mangrove
--------- Trail/Footpath	Ⓜ Must-See Sight	▲ Mountain/Volcano
.... Ferry	Ⓜ Author's Choice	⚐ Waterfall
┼──┼──┼ Railroad	★ Point of Interest	Λ Campground
▬▬▬▬ Pedestrian Walkway	• Accommodation	⛽ Gas Station
✕ ✕ Airport/Airstrip	▼ Restaurant/Bar	▲ Church
		▪ Other Location

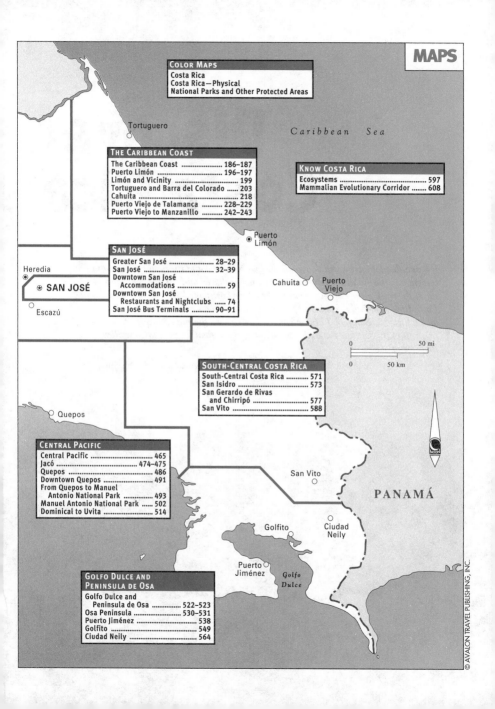

MAPS

Tortuguero

Caribbean   Sea

Puerto Limón

Heredia

SAN JOSÉ

Escazú

Cahuita

Puerto Viejo

0   50 mi

0   50 km

Quepos

San Vito

PANAMÁ

Golfito

Ciudad Neily

Puerto Jiménez

Golfo Dulce

© AVALON TRAVEL PUBLISHING, INC.

Discover
Costa Rica

If San Salvador were hosed down, all the shacks cleared and the people rehoused in tidy bungalows, the buildings painted, the stray dogs collared and fed, the children given shoes, the trash picked up in the parks, the soldiers pensioned off—there is no army in Costa Rica—and all the political prisoners released, those cities would, I think, begin to look a little like San José. In El Salvador I had chewed the end of my pipestem to pieces in frustration. In San José I was able to have a new pipestem fitted . . . [Costa Rica] was that sort of place.

Paul Theroux, The Old Patagonian Express

Paul Theroux portrays a litany of places one might want to avoid in his highly entertaining and incisive book *The Old Patagonian Express,* describing his journey south by rail from Massachusetts to Tierra del Fuego. But Costa Rica is different. One of his characters sums it up. Freshly arrived in San José, the capital city, Theroux finds himself talking to a Chinese man in a bar. The man—a Costa Rican citizen—had left his homeland in 1954 and traveled widely throughout the Americas. He disliked every country he had seen except one. "What about the United States?" Theroux asked. "I went all around it," replied the man. "Maybe it is a good country, but I don't think so. I could not live there. I was still traveling, and I thought to myself, 'What is the best country?' It was Costa Rica—I liked it very much here. So I stayed."

The temptations and appeals of this tiny nation are so abundant that an estimated 40,000 North American citizens and an equal number of other nationals (constituting more than 2 percent of Costa Rica's population) have moved here in recent years and now call Costa Rica home, attracted by financial incentives and a quality of life among the highest in the Western

Hemisphere. Costa Rica isn't simply one of the world's best-kept travel secrets; it's also a great place to live.

For years travelers had neglected this exciting yet peaceful nation, primarily because of a muddled grasp of Central American geopolitics. While its neighbors have been racked by turmoil, Costa Rica has been blessed with a remarkable normalcy—few extremes of wealth and poverty, no standing army, and a proud history as Central America's most stable democracy.

Ticos—as the friendly, warmhearted Costa Ricans are known—pride themselves on having more teachers than policemen, a higher male life expectancy than does the United States, an egalitarianism and strong commitment to peace and prosperity, and an education and social-welfare system that should be the envy of many developed nations. Even the smallest town is electrified, water most everywhere is potable, and the telecommunications system is the best in Latin America. In 1990, the United Nations declared Costa Rica the country with the best human-development index among underdeveloped nations—and in 1992, it was taken off the list of underdeveloped nations altogether. No wonder *National Geographic* called it the "land of the happy medium."

Despite its diminutive size (the country is about as big as Nova Scotia, or as Vermont and New Hampshire put together), Costa Rica proffers more beauty and adventure per acre than any other country on earth. It is in fact a kind of microcontinent unto itself. The diversity of terrain—most of it supremely beautiful—is remarkable. Costa Rica is sculpted to show off the full potential of the tropics. You can journey, as it were, from the Amazon to a Swiss alpine forest simply by starting in a Costa Rican valley and walking uphill. Within a one-hour journey from San José, the capital city, the tableau metamorphoses from dense rainforest to airy deciduous forest, montane cloud forest swathing the slopes of towering volcanoes, dry open savanna, lush sugarcane fields, banana plantations, rich cattle ranches set in deep valleys, rain-soaked jungle, lagoons, estuaries, and swamps teeming with wildlife in the northern lowlands. The verdant rainforest spills down the steep mountains to greet the Pacific and Atlantic Oceans, where dozens of inviting beaches remain unspoiled by footprints, and in places offshore coral reefs open up a world more beautiful than a casket of gems.

Costa Rica's varied ecosystems—particularly its tropical rainforests—are a naturalist's dream. Unlike many destinations, where man has driven the animals into the deepest seclusion, Costa Rica's wildlife seems to love to put on a song-and-dance. Animals and birds are prolific and in many cases relatively easy to spot—sleek jaguars on the prowl, tattered moth-ridden sloths moving languidly among the high branches, scarlet macaws that fall from their perches and go squalling away, coatimundis, toucans, brightly colored tree frogs, and other exotic species in abundance. That sudden flutter of blue is a giant morpho butterfly. That mournful two-note whistle is the quetzal, the tropical birder's Holy Grail. The pristine forests and jungles are full of arboreal sounds that are, according to one writer, "music to a weary ecotraveler's ears." You can almost feel the vegetation growing around you. There is a sense of life at flood tide.

The nation's 12 distinct ecological zones are home to an astonishing array of flora and fauna—approximately 5 percent of all known species on earth in a country that occupies less than 0.003 percent of its land area—including more butterfly species than in the whole of Africa, and more than twice the number of bird species than in the whole of the United States—in colors so brilliant that their North American cousins seem drab by comparison. Stay here long enough and you'll begin to think that with luck you might, like Noah, see examples of all the creatures on earth.

Scuba divers, anglers, golfers, spa addicts, kayakers and white-water rafters, hikers, surfers, honeymoon romantics, and every other breed of escape artist can also find nirvana in Costa Rica. The adventure travel industry here has matured into one of the world's finest.

For better or worse, Costa Rica has also burst into blossom as a contender on the international beach-resort scene. The nation boasts any number of supremely attractive resorts, civilized hotels, and rustic lodges and cabinas where, lazing in a hammock dramatically overlooking the beach, you might seriously contemplate giving up everything back home and settling down to while away the rest of your days enjoying the never-winter climate.

¡Pura vida!

Arranging your visit here takes some forethought. While Costa Rica looks small on a map, it can take a lot longer than you think to get from one place to another, thanks to all the mountains and valleys, and convoluted roads. Many of these roads are unpaved, in appalling condition, or lack road signs (or all of the above). It's best to outline your trip region by region, focusing on destinations that look interesting to you, and plan on spending three or four days in each place. Trying to take in the whole country would occupy at least a month.

The country has a well-developed network of roads, and you can easily drive yourself around (it's best to rent a four-wheel-drive vehicle). If you don't fancy driving, you can get practically everywhere by public bus without breaking the bank. Modern air-conditioned buses serve all major destinations, as do passenger planes, which can also get you speedily between remote destinations otherwise hard to access.

The country's strong suits are nature and active adventures (if you're seeking world-class museums and galleries, or pre-Columbian temples, head elsewhere). The vast majority of visitors to Costa Rica come to see wildlife and/or get their adrenaline kicks in youthful pursuits. The country is a nirvana for active travelers with recreation or a specific adventure in mind: whatever your taste in recreation, Costa Rica has something for you. The most popular activities are horseback riding, scuba diving, sportfishing, surfing, and whitewater rafting.

WHEN TO GO

Costa Rica has distinct seasons, with dry season (December–April) the ideal time to travel. This is the busiest time, however; during Christmas, New Year's, and Easter, many accommodations are booked months in advance. The rainy season—promoted as the "green season" but known locally as *invierno* (winter)—runs from April through November. Prices are often lower, and it is usually easier to find vacant hotels rooms in popular destinations. The highlands can be especially delightful at this time of year. The Golfito and Caribbean lowlands, both of which can be lashed by the whip of tropical storms in the wet season, don't have a distinct dry season anyway.

Dress accordingly.

WHAT TO TAKE

Pack items that work in various combinations—preferably darker items that don't show the inevitable dirt and stains you'll quickly collect on your travels. Dark clothes tend to be hotter than khaki or light clothing. Bright clothing tends to scare off wildlife; pack khakis and subdued greens if you plan on serious nature viewing. Be sure to bring a pair of cargo shorts or pants and a photographer's jacket with heaps of pockets.

If you're going to be in San José and the highlands, or cloud forest destinations such as Monteverde, pack a warm sweater and/or a warm windproof jacket (a light waterproof jacket is also a good idea). The lowlands are humid and hot: you'll want light, loose-fitting shirts and pants, which help protect you against thorns and biting bugs while you're hiking. Denim jeans take forever to dry when wet, so pack light cotton-polyester-blend pants instead; they're cooler and dry quickly. Ideally, everything should be drip-dry, wash-and-wear. For longer visits, pack a regular change of socks and underpants. Wash them frequently to help keep athlete's foot and other fungal growths at bay.

Two T-shirts plus two dressier shirts, a sweatshirt and sweatpants, a polo shirt, a pair of Levi's, "safari" pants, two pairs of shorts, and a "safari" or photographer's jacket with heaps of pockets suffice me. Women may wish to substitute blouses and mid-length skirts. And don't forget your bathing suit. Most travelers will not need dressy clothes. However, many Costa Ricans love to dress up for dinner or the theater, as well as for business functions. You may wish to take a jacket and tie or cocktail dress for dinners in more expensive hotels and restaurants, and for the theater. Otherwise, Costa Ricans dress informally, but always very neatly. Knee-length shorts for men are acceptable almost anywhere. Save your running shorts for the beach.

Visiting in wet season? Eschew raincoats for a breathable Gore-Tex jacket or a hooded poncho, plus a small umbrella (you can buy one in San José).

A comfortable, well-fitting pair of sneakers will work for most occasions. You'll want lightweight canvas hiking boots with ankle protection—good against thorns—for hiking muddy trails.

Space on buses and planes is limited. Limit yourself to one bag (preferably a sturdy duffel bag or internal-frame backpack with plenty of pockets), plus a small day pack or camera bag. Avoid backpacks with external appendages: they catch and easily bend or break. One of the best investments you can make is a well-made duffel bag that can be carried by hand and on the back. A small day pack allows you to pack everything for a one- or two-day journey. Then you can leave the rest of your gear in the storage room of a San José hotel and return frequently as you travel around the country using the capital as a base.

SAN JOSÉ

The cramped and bustling capital city is hardly a sightseeing destination in its own right; its main sites can be done in a day. Pre-Columbian artifacts (notably gold and jade) are exhibited at three small museums; a handful of galleries will satisfy art enthusiasts; and souvenir shoppers are well-served by stores selling quality crafts. It's really a place to pass through, and its central position proves handy as a hub for forays further afield.

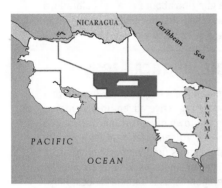

THE CENTRAL HIGHLANDS

Wrapped in gently ascending volcanoes to the north and steep mountains to the south, the densely populated highlands are tremendously scenic, with their crisp springlike climate a further draw. A week's touring isn't too much, although the main sites can be captured in a three- or four-day stay. You can safely skip the town centers without fear of missing anything vital.

The area's main draw is its scenic drives, best enjoyed by ascending Poás and/or Irazú volcanoes (both enshrined as national parks), with stops en route to taste coffee at Café Britt; or to explore the nation's only significant pre-Columbian site at Guayabo National Monument. The region boasts scores of offbeat places of interest for nature lovers, from Flor de Mayo (a breeding center for endangered macaws) to Grecia's World of Snakes. The upper mountain slopes are densely forested and protected within reserves offering birders and hikers access along muddy trails. Two of the nation's premier whitewater runs cascade out of these mountains. You can delight in overnights at a fistful of splendidly upscale boutique hotels.

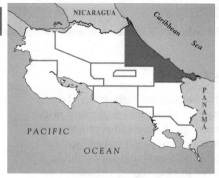

THE CARIBBEAN COAST

This humid zone is notable for its Caribbean—predominantly Jamaican— roots, reflected in Rastafarian culture and spicy cuisine. The southern village of Cahuita and Puerto Viejo draw the surfing, backpacking, and tie-dye crowd seeking an offbeat cultural immersion and laid-back lifestyle. Most visitors settle in for a while and break their lassitude with spells to go snorkeling, ride horses, trek into remote Indian reserves, or gawk at the animals and birds in easily accessed Cahuita National Park. To the north, Tortuguero National Park, accessed by boat or plane, provides premium wildlife viewing; cut through with waterways, this watery world is explored by canal from dedicated nature lodges, many edging right up to a beach where you can witness marine turtles laying eggs. Anglers are gung-ho about Barra del Colorado, a down-at-the-heels place preeminent as a sportfishing center. Allow two or three days each at Tortuguero, Cahuita, and Puerto Viejo.

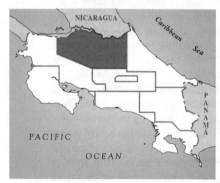

THE NORTHERN ZONE

Costa Rica's northern lowlands are a center for active adventures, centered on the town of La Fortuna, gateway to Arenal Volcano National Park and its eponymous (and very active) volcano. Hiking and horseback riding are popular hereabouts, as is bathing in hot springs. Nearby, inordinately scenic Lake Arenal draws windsurfers and freshwater anglers, while remote Caño Negro National Wildlife Refuge is also a nirvana for anglers and birders. The southern fringe is hemmed by dense montane rainforest most easily accessed by a series of nature lodges, such as Selva Verde and Rara Avis, bordering Braulio Carrillo National Park. This relatively flat, humid region extends north to the Nicaraguan border and is cut through by a trellis of rivers, notably the Río Sarapiquí, a boating thoroughfare popular for nature viewing. Three or four days should prove sufficient.

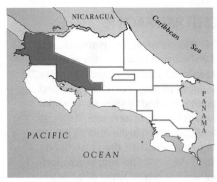

GUANACASTE AND THE NORTHWEST

The nation's northwest region is distinct for both its climate and culture, and is fully deserving of a week's visit. Parched for six months a year, the flatlands are covered in remnants of dry tropical forest attractive for its seasonal flaring of blossoms and for the relative ease with which wildlife can be viewed. Known for its cowboy culture, this is also cattle country, with numerous ranches that double as eco-centers. Guanacaste is limned to the east by a string of volcanoes flanked by lush montane forest. Vast tracts are protected with national parks and nature reserves that offer dramatic scenery and tremendous diversity; all are easily accessed by branch roads off the Pan-Am Highway. The big draw is Monteverde Cloud Forest Biological Reserve, centered on a rural community where a dozen or so key attractions will hold your attention for days. Birding is superb at both Monteverde and Palo Verde National Park, while Santa Rosa National Park combines important historical sites with incredible wildlife viewing and top-notch surfing.

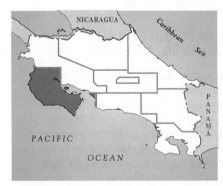

NICOYA PENINSULA

Almost every visitor to Costa Rica sets their sights on the Nicoya Peninsula, known for its white-sand beaches. Surfers are particularly enamored of this hook-shaped region, whose dozens of beaches and coastal attractions are linked by often difficult-to-negotiate dirt roads (a four-wheel drive is essential). Large-scale resort development concentrates at Playa Tamarindo and Playa Flamingo, both centers for sportfishing. Scuba centers offer dives offshore, notably around the Murcielagos Islands. Playa Grande and Ostional are important nesting sites for marine turtles. Other than the community of Guaitíl, where an indigenous pottery tradition is preserved, sites of interest concentrate along the Pacific shore, which grows lusher to the south around Montezuma, Malpaís, and Santa Teresa, the latter surfers' havens bordering the nation's first wildlife reserve. Accommodations run the span from ascetic to sublime inspirations. Exploring the entire peninsula might take two weeks or more at a leisurely pace. Allow at least four days; one week is recommended.

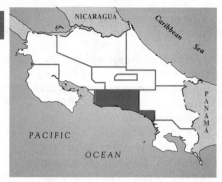

CENTRAL PACIFIC

This region comprises a narrow coastal plain hemmed hard up to the ocean by steep forest-clad mountains. The shore is fringed by long, lonesome gray-sand beaches washed by killer waves world-famous in surfing lore. Jacó, the most developed resort in the country, retains its popularity with the party-hearty crowd despite its ho-hum beach. Surfing beaches extend all the way south to Dominical and, beyond, the Brunca Coast, a once-inaccessible region in the throes of tourist development. To the north, Tárcoles is the nation's foremost site for viewing crocodiles (best done on boat safaris), while nearby Carara National Park offers world-class wildlife viewing. South of Carara, the climate becomes increasingly humid, noticeable in the lush tropical forests of Manuel Antonio National Park, a superlative spot combining splendid beaches, almost-guaranteed close-up encounters with monkeys, and good snorkeling amid one of the nation's few coral reefs. Nearby Quepos is a center for sportfishing. Inland, arduous hikes into the steep coastal mountains lead to waterfalls that feed such rivers as the Naranjo and Savegre, good for rafting. You can pack it all into a five-day visit.

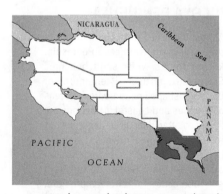

GOLFO DULCE AND THE PENINSULA DE OSA

One of the nation's wettest quarters is centered on a huge gulf enfolded by the Osa Peninsula. The humble port town of Golfito makes a good base for sportfishing, and for forays to remote rainforest lodges, many of them quite deluxe. Many people come to visit Osa's Corcovado National Park, a crown jewel of rainforest biota; here, hikers stand as good a chance as anywhere in the nation of seeing jaguars, harpy eagles, and other endangered species. Zancudo and nearby Puerto Jiménez, gateway to Corcovado, appeal to backpackers and other laid-back travelers. The kilometer-long waves that wash up to Pavones draw surfers from around the world. Remote, tucked-away Drake Bay is good for boat excursions in search of whales and dolphins, and to Caño Island, an erstwhile Indian ceremonial site. Some 500 kilometers southwest of Costa Rica, Cocos Island is off-limits to all but experienced divers, drawn not least by huge schools of sharks. If you only wish to experience Corcovado, budget a two- or three-day stay, arriving and departing by air. But most travelers will want at least a couple of extra days to chill. Budget travelers, and others keen to explore more thoroughly, should plan on one week, minimum.

SOUTH-CENTRAL COSTA RICA

The nation's Cinderella region is finally beginning to appear on the map. Sites of touristic interest are relatively few, highlighted by Wilson Botanical Gardens. But hale and hearty adventure seekers can follow the trail up Chirripó, the nation's highest mountain; the trailhead is accessed by one of several Shangri-la valleys that lead into the rugged and little-explored Talamanca mountains and La Amistad International Peace Park. Indigenous communities exist in isolation. As little as two or three days will suffice here, unless you plan on exploring Chirripó and the Talamancas, in which case you'll need at least three additional days.

It would take months to exhaust the possibilities for a total immersion in Costa Rica. Few visitors have time to explore Costa Rica from tip to toe, unless they've opted to fly to and from distinct locales using San José as a hub (in which case, visiting the "four quarters" is eminently feasible). The typical visitor spends about 10 days in Costa Rica, quite enough to savor a smorgasbord sampler, ideally concentrating on two or three regions. Allow three or four weeks for a more complete itinerary that takes in half a dozen of the best parks plus a potpourri of active adventures.

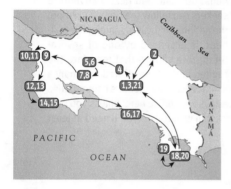

DAYS 5–6:
Transfer to La Fortuna for two days, with hiking at Arenal Volcano National Park; a ride on the Arenal Aerial Tram; and a soak at Tabacón Hot Springs.

DAY 7:
Transfer via Lake Arenal and Tilarán to Monteverde. This afternoon, take in such sites as the Serpentarium and Jewels of the Rainforest Bio-Art Exhibition.

DAY 1:
Arrive at Juan Santamaría International Airport; transfer to a hotel in or near San José.

DAY 8:
You'll want to be up early for a guided hike in Monteverde Cloud Forest Biological Reserve or Santa Elena Cloud Forest Reserve. In the afternoon, enjoy a canopy exploration.

DAY 2:
Take an early-morning flight to Tortuguero National Park for wildlife viewing, including an evening turtle viewing.

DAY 9:
Transfer to Rincón de la Vieja National Park for horseback riding and overnight at a nature lodge.

DAY 3:
After a morning wildlife viewing by canoe or boat, fly to San José for overnight. Take time to explore the capital city.

DAY 4:
Today, an early-morning visit to Poás Volcano National Park is followed by a visit to the La Paz Waterfall & Butterfly Garden.

A tour guide from Tortuga Lodge shows a tropical plant in Tortuguero National Park.

view of main crater, Poás Volcano

DAY 10:
Continue north to **Santa Rosa National Park** for a hike offering great wildlife viewing. You'll overnight nearby at **Hacienda Los Inocentes**.

DAY 11:
Spend a full day horseback riding and wildlife viewing at Hacienda Los Inocentes.

DAY 12:
Today, head to the Nicoya Peninsula and **Tamarindo** for relaxing. This afternoon you might try surfing at **Playa Grande Marine Turtle National Park**.

DAY 13:
Active travelers might try their hand at catching the big one on a half-day sportfishing excursion. Spend the rest of the day sunning on the beach or by the pool. This evening, head to Playa Grande to witness marine turtles laying eggs (in season).

DAY 14:
Transfer to **Nosara** via Ostional Wildlife Refuge. If you're driving, the coast road will prove an adventure! This evening visit the turtle *arribada* (in season).

DAY 15:
Relax at Nosara, where the beach is good for tidepooling, with great beach breaks for surfers.

DAYS 16–17:
This morning, depart Nicoya for the Central Pacific and a crocodile safari on the **Río Tárcoles**. Then continue to **Manuel Antonio** for two days of wildlife viewing, snorkeling, and relaxing in Manuel Antonio National Park.

DAY 18:
Transfer to San José and fly from Pavas airport to **Carate**, on the Osa Peninsula. Overnight at a nearby nature lodge.

DAY 19:
A guided hike in **Corcovado National Park** guarantees sightings of scarlet macaws, monkeys, and plenty of other exotic species.

DAY 20:
Relax at your nature lodge.

DAY 21:
Transfer to San José for your departure flight.

National parks, wildlife refuges, and biological reserves are found throughout the country. These protected reserves range from swamp (good for crocodile viewing) and dry forest environments to lowland rainforests and high-mountain forests smothered in cloud, with enough diversity of terrain and wildlife to keep nature lovers enthralled for weeks. Many reserves are remote, with few services, and require often arduous hiking. Others are visitor friendly; many are mere minutes and thereby easily accessed from major cities. If you're here for the wildlife, plan to visit three or four diverse reserves to get the full range. The most popular and easily explored destinations are Cahuita National Park, Manuel Antonio National Park, Monteverde Cloud Forest Biological Reserve, Poás Volcano National Park, and Tortuguero National Park.

Scores of private facilities make wildlife viewing easy. These range from large reserves (such as La Selva or Selva Verde) that differ only in name from the government-owned national parks they often adjoin; to small breeding centers and zoos such as Flor de Mayo, the World of Snakes, and Zoo Ave.

Good wildlife viewing is ostensibly offered by the many immensely popular canopy tours or treetop adventures, which range from aerial trams and suspension bridges slung between trees to zipline crossings with you slung in harness. Note, however, that the volume of human activity associated with canopy tours has scared away most wildlife from the immediate vicinity. Sure, you'll have fun. But don't expect to see a great deal of wildlife.

If actually *viewing* wildlife in its natural surrounds is the sine qua non of your vacation, sign up for guided natural history excursions and tours. If the group experience isn't your thing, then hire your own local naturalist guide (most major tour operators can make arrangements). You'll see many, many times more critters in the company of an eagle-eyed guide.

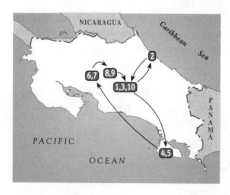

DAY 1:
Arrive at Juan Santamaría International Airport; transfer to a hotel in or near San José.

DAY 2:
Take an early-morning flight to **Tortuguero National Park** and spend the day viewing wildlife. This evening, take a guided turtle-viewing walk on the beach.

DAY 3:
Morning wildlife viewing is followed by an afternoon flight to San José. Time permitting, visit **Flor de Mayo** (by prior arrangement only) and/or **Zoo Ave**.

DAY 4:
Fly to **Corcovado National Park** and transfer to a nature lodge.

DAY 5:
You'll want to spend the day hiking in Corcovado National Park.

DAY 6:
Fly to San José, then transfer to **Monteverde** for two days and two nights, with visits to the Serpentarium, Jewels of the Rainforest Bio-Art Exhibition, and other attractions.

DAY 7:
This morning, hire a guide for a visit to either **Monteverde Cloud Forest Biological Reserve** or the **Santa Elena Cloud Forest Reserve**. Later, you might want to go horseback riding.

DAY 8:
Be sure to explore the forest canopy at Monteverde before departing for the Central Highlands. Consider a short excursion en route to enjoy a crocodile safari on the **Río Tárcoles**.

DAY 9:
The early bird catches the worm today for a visit to **Poás Volcano National Park** followed by hiking at **La Paz Waterfall and Butterfly Garden** or **Selva Verde** private reserve. Return to your hotel near Alajuela.

DAY 10:
Transfer to San José for your departure flight.

© CHRISTOPHER P. BAKER

Playa Corcovado, Corcovado National Park

Costa Rica boasts glorious beaches. Only a few, however, are of the frost-white variety silvering the shore like confectioners' sugar. Such diamond-dust beaches are found along sections of Nicoya, plus Manuel Antonio National Park (the most radiantly white are Playa Conchal and Playa Flamingo). The vast majority are of taupe color, many with the texture of potting soil, the result of sediments washed down from the mountains by rivers. Several beaches are almost black. Virtually all are backed by jungly forest, with slender coconut palms tilting over the shore, so that you can sunbathe in view of sloths and monkeys; it is not unusual to discover jaguar prints in the sand. Miles-long and dramatically scenic, the nation's beaches are an integral part of the nature experience, made more so by the sheer number that serve as nesting sites for marine turtles.

Dozens of beaches are favored by surfers drawn by tubular waves conjured by the breeze from the warm, often murky, water. Swimming requires caution, however, as many unsheltered beaches are known for rip-tides, dangerous undertows that every year kill dozens of swimmers and surfers. Many beaches are at least seasonally littered with tree trunks and driftwood.

DAYS 4–5:

Today, continue to Tamarindo for two nights. Surfers will want to spend time hitting the waves. Active travelers might try their hand at catching the big one on a half-day sportfishing excursion. Spend the rest of the day sunning on the beach or by the pool. This evening, head to Playa Grande to witness marine turtles laying eggs (in season).

DAYS 6–7:

Continue south to Nosara for two days to enjoy tidepooling, and view ridley turtles (in season) at nearby Playa Ostional.

DAY 1:

Arrive at Juan Santamaría International Airport; transfer to a hotel in or near San José.

DAYS 8–9:

This morning, head south to Manuel Antonio for two nights; enjoying wildlife viewing, snorkeling, and/or surfing at Manuel Antonio National Park.

DAYS 2–3:

This morning, transfer to Playa Conchal or Playa Flamingo for two nights, perhaps with time for sportfishing and even scuba diving.

DAY 10:

Today, transfer to the airport for your departure flight.

© CHRISTOPHER P. BAKER

Playa Flamingo

Best Wildlife Beaches

Caribbean: Tortuguero; Cahuita; Gandoca-Manzanillo
Guanacaste: Naranjo
Nicoya: Grande; Ostional; Montezuma
Central Pacific: Manuel Antonio; Barú; Ballena; Piñuela
Southern Pacific: San Josecito; Corcovado; Carate; Platanares; Cativo

Best Surfing Beaches

Caribbean: Cocles
Guanacaste: Playa Naranjo and Potrero Grande (Santa Elena National Park)
Nicoya: Grande; Tamarindo; Langosta; Avellana; Negra; Bejuco; Manzanillo; Santa Teresa
Central Pacific: Jacó; Dominical; Ballena
Southern Pacific: Pavones

Most Beautiful Beaches

Caribbean: Gandoca-Manzanillo
Guanacaste: Blanca
Nicoya: Flamingo; Conchal; Grande; Guiones; Montezuma; Santa Teresa
Central Pacific: Manuel Antonio; Esterillos; Ballena
Southern Pacific: Zancudo

© CHRISTOPHER P. BAKER

Playa Cocles

Dedicated surfers are constantly in search of the perfect wave. For many, the search has ended in Costa Rica, the "Hawaii of Latin American surf." Long stretches of oceanfront provide thousands of beach breaks. Numerous rivers offer quality sandbar rivermouth breaks, particularly on the Pacific coast. The coral reefs on the Caribbean coast, says Costa Rican surf expert Peter Brennan, "take the speed limit to the max." And there are plenty of surf camps.

If the surf blows out or goes flat before you are ready to pack it in for the day, you can simply jump over to the other coast, or—on the Pacific—head north or south. If one break isn't working, another is sure to be cooking. You rarely see monster-size Hawaiian waves, but they're nicely shaped, long, and tubular, and in places never-ending—often nearly a kilometer!

Despite the strong winds that sweep along the coast of the Pacific northwest in summer, ocean windsurfing in Costa Rica has yet to take off. Bahía Salinas, in the extreme northwest, is recommended and has two windsurfing centers. Inland, Lake Arenal is paradise, with 23–35 kph easterly winds funneling through a mountain corridor year-round. Strong winds rarely cease during the dry season (December–April). The lake has acquired an international reputation as one of the best all-year freshwater windsurfing spots in the world, with two dedicated windsurfing centers. If you rent equipment at Arenal, try negotiating to use the same equipment at the coast, where equipment is in short supply.

All the major surf beaches have surf shops where board sales and rentals are offered. Many hotels and car rental companies offer discounts to surfers.

Generally, your double board bag flies free as a second piece of checked luggage on international airlines. Airlines require that you pack your board in a board bag. (Within Costa Rica, Nature Air permits short boards, but not long boards.)

WHERE TO GO

THE CARIBBEAN COAST

The Caribbean has fewer breaks than the Pacific, but still offers great surfing during winter and spring. Waves are short yet powerful rides with sometimes Hawaiian-style radical waves. Occasionally massive swells sweep over the coral reefs, creating demanding tubes.

A 20-minute boat ride from Puerto Limón is Isla Uvita, with a strong and dangerous left. Farther south there are innumerable short breaks at Cahuita. Closing in on the Panamanian border, things really heat up! Puerto Viejo has the biggest rideable waves in Costa Rica (up to seven meters at times, mostly in December), although these legendary waves have diminished in size because of coastal uplift caused by the April 1991 earthquake. One expert recommends avoiding the Tortuguero region, where sharks are abundant.

The best time is late May through early September (hurricane season) and December–March (when Atlantic storms push through the Caribbean, creating three-meter swells).

GUANACASTE AND THE NORTHWEST

The Pacific Northwest offers more than 50 prime surf spots. The best time is during the rainy season

© CHRISTOPHER P. BAKER

with good surf, lively action, and several surf camps.

THE CENTRAL PACIFIC

March through June are good. The best time, however, is during the heart of the rainy season (July–December), when the Caribbean dies down and conditions along the central Pacific create a full spectrum of breaks.

Central Pacific surfing centers on Jacó, though the waves really appeal to beginners and intermediates. Farther south lie Playa Hermosa, which has miles of expert beach breaks and an international contest every August, plus Escondida, Esterillos Este and Oeste, and Boca Damas. The playas are blessed with surf camps. Manuel Antonio has beach breaks, lefts, and rights. What it lacks in consistency it more than makes up for in natural beauty. Farther south lies Playa Dominical, which has "militant" sandbars and long point waves in an equally beautiful and classically tropical setting.

(May–October), when the surf can build to three meters; there are large offshore winds throughout the dry season (November–April), but the waves are smaller.

Hot spots such as Witch's Rock at Playa Naranjo (one of the best beach breaks in the country, with strong offshore winds December–March) require four-wheel drive or boat for access. You can rent a boat from Playa del Coco and other beach resorts for visits to Naranjo and Potrero Grande (also in Santa Rosa National Park).

Tamarindo is the surfing capital and is an excellent jumping-off place for a surf safari south to more isolated beaches. Just north of Tamarindo is Playa Grande, with a five-km-long beach break acclaimed as Costa Rica's most accessible consistent break. There's fine surfing the whole way south from Tamarindo, including at Avellanas and Playa Negra, a narrow beach with fast waves breaking over a coral- and urchin-encrusted shelf—definitely for experts only when the waves are big. Continuing south you'll find Nosara, Sámara, Camaronal, Coyote, Manzanillo, and Mal País, all

GOLFO DULCE AND THE OSA PENINSULA

Golfo Dulce and the Osa Peninsula have many surfing beaches. The cognoscenti head to Zancudo and Pavones, on the southern shore of the Golfo Dulce. On a decent day, the fast, nearly one-kilometer left break (one of the longest in the world) is "so long it will make your legs wobbly," according to Peter Brennan. The waves are at their grandest in rainy season, when the long left point can offer a three-minute ride.

You don't have to be in Limón province's Cahuita or Puerto Viejo more than five seconds to figure that the Caribbean coast draws a high proportion of tattooed, tie-dyed travelers intent on savoring (and contributing to) an offbeat way of life. College-age surfers (predominantly from the USA) and backpacking youth comprise the largest segment of off-the-beaten-path travelers, whose comfort zone resembles a tropical Haight-Ashbury. Regardless of age (Costa Rica draws no shortage of middle-aged and even golden-years hippies), de rigueur clothing, for both males and females, is a bandanna, a pair of well-worn calf-length cargo pants, and plenty of tattoos and piercings.

Budget is everything, as is a more relaxed, freewheeling pace of travel that eschews rigid planning and, ideally, prolongs a visit over many weeks or months. Thus, the offbeat traveler typically relies on Costa Rica's efficient, super-cheap bus service and a plethora of inexpensive accommodations (it's possible to find clean, hospitable lodgings for $5 a night). The offbeat trend is so important that most major towns now cater with a choice of budget hostels. And the coastal capitals of offbeat all have "surfer camps" (some quite sophisticated) run by savvy entrepreneurs catering to surfers and latter-day Beats.

A more sophisticated, even monied, crowd is part of the genre. Yoga camps, spiritual centers, and even communes are springing up like mushrooms on a damp log. Some are quite expensive. One of the beauties of Costa Rica is that it offers options for a pampered, deluxe experience along with the no-frills, budget-oriented offbeat experience, and travelers can mix and match according to whim. Those on a "traditional" itinerary might throw an offbeat experience into the mix by adding an overnight stay with a *campesino* (peasant) or indigenous family.

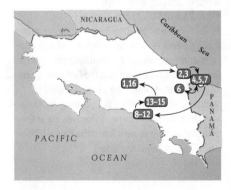

DAY 1:

After arriving at Juan Santamaría International Airport, transfer to the Terminal Caribe for a bus to Cahuita, for two days of relaxing at this lazy Caribbean village.

DAY 2:

Consider a horseback ride along Playa Negra, and snorkeling at Cahuita National Park. Make the most of regional cuisine with dinner at Miss Edith's.

DAY 3:

Take an excursion to Aviarios del Caribe Sloth & Wildlife Refuge, where you can go canoeing through the estuarine swamps in search of crocodile and other exotic wildlife.

DAY 4:

Head to **Puerto Viejo,** where your options include surfing, horseback riding, and hanging out: sunning on the beach by day and kicking it at Puerto Viejo's hip and funky bars by night.

DAY 5:

Surfers will want to tackle Salsa Brava, the local wave. Others might want to explore **Gandoca-Manzanillo Wildlife Refuge,** and even sign up for a kayak trip or dolphin safari.

DAY 6:

Today, journey into the Talamancas for an overnight at **Reserva Indígena Yorku,** which you access by canoe.

DAY 7:

Return to Puerto Viejo for your last evening relaxing on the Caribbean coast.

local children in Cahuita

DAY 8:

Return to San José and take a bus to the surfer's village of **Dominical.**

DAY 9:

Surfers will no doubt want to check out the wave action while others visit nearby **Hacienda Barú,** where you can thrill to a canopy tour.

DAYS 10–12:

Today, head to **Finca Brian y Emilia,** in the Escaleras hills. Here, take a two-day hike into the

Puerto Viejo

mountains to spend a night with a *campesino* (peasant) family.

DAY 13:

Return to Dominical and take a bus to San Isidro and thence to **San Gerardo de Rivas,** a Shangri-la good for spotting quetzals. You'll want to pack some warm clothes.

DAY 14:

Begin your hike in **Chirripó National Park,** accompanied by a guide. You'll overnight near the mountain summit.

DAY 15:

Up early for the hike to the summit of Costa Rica's highest mountain. Congratulations! After time to enjoy the thrill, return to San Gerardo de Rivas, where you can overnight.

DAY 16:

Take a public bus to San Isidro and from there to San José for your flight home.

Catering to kids takes some forethought. Many active sports are suitable only for adults and teens, and younger children are generally less tolerant of the patient waiting in silence required to deliver the delayed gratification of viewing rare wildlife. Below, I offer a suggested itinerary that combines educational and fun options for both adults and children.

DAY 1:

Arrive at Juan Santamaría International Airport; transfer to a hotel in or near San José.

DAY 2:

Today, visit La Paz Waterfall & Butterfly Garden, with time to hike to the waterfalls; then continue to Selva Verde for a nocturnal nature hike and overnight.

DAY 3:

This morning, take a boat excursion on the Río Sarapiquí before transferring to the Rainforest Aerial Tram for a ride through the forest canopy. Both opportunities offer a chance to see lots of wildlife.

DAY 4:

After overnighting in or around San José, transfer to the Orosi Valley for a day of whitewater rafting on the Río Pejibaye. Return to the San José area.

DAY 5:

Today, take the children to Zoo Ave and the World of Snakes, where the kids can even hold snakes. Continue to Los Angeles Cloud Forest Reserve for overnight.

DAY 6:

This morning, take a guided hike in the cloud forest, then continue to the beach resort of Tamarindo.

DAYS 7–8:

Enjoy two days and three nights of relaxing and activities such as horseback riding on the beach, a canopy zipline tour, and a nighttime visit to Playa Grande to see marine turtles laying eggs.

DAY 9:

Today, transfer to San José via the Río Tárcoles for an afternoon crocodile safari.

DAY 10:

Transfer to the airport for your departure flight.

Rainforest Aerial Tram

COURTESY RAINFOREST AERIAL TRAM

Few are the visitors to Costa Rica whose notion of the ideal vacation is doing absolutely nothing and lazing away one's time in a hammock. Statistics show that the vast majority of visitors come to *do* something fun, the more adventurous the better. In fact, the chance to partake of bicycling, golfing, or whitewater rafting is one of the great appeals of Costa Rica. The most popular activities are hiking, horseback riding, scuba diving, sportfishing, surfing, and whitewater rafting.

You don't have to be fresh out of high school to take advantage of Costa Rica's innumerable active adventures. Among the thousands of surfers who flock annually, for example, are no small number of baby boomers holding tight to their youth.

Several new golf courses have recently opened, with mixed success. Less traditional activities, however, have caught on, proving that many visitors to Costa Rican prefer to push the envelope. Options for zipline canopy tours are too numerous to mention. ATV (all-terrain-vehicle) tours by four-wheel motorcycles are increasing in popularity. And waterfall rappelling is coming on strong.

DAY 1:

Following arrival at Juan Santamaría International Airport, transfer to Los Angeles Cloud Forest Reserve or Chachagua Rainforest Lodge, with time for optional hikes.

DAY 2:

After a morning hike in the forest, transfer to La Fortuna. This afternoon, take a horseback ride or enjoy another activity.

DAY 3:

Give today to hiking and mountain biking at and around Arenal Volcano National Park, with time for an invigorating soak at Tabacón Hot Springs.

DAY 4:

You've earned a rest today, with options for windsurfing at Lake Arenal or kayaking on the Peñas Blancas river.

DAY 5:

Transfer to the highlands, stopping en route at San Lorenzo Canopy Tour for a thrilling zipline ride through the forest.

DAY 6:

Today, transfer to the Orosi Valley for an exhilarating whitewater rafting trip on the Pacuare River, a great way to see wildlife. Return to San José in the late afternoon.

DAY 7:

Transfer to San José for your departure flight.

Explore
Costa Rica

San José

San José, the nation's capital, squats on the floor of the Meseta Central, a fertile upland basin 1,150 meters (3,773 feet) above sea level in the heart of Costa Rica. Surrounded by mountains, it's a magnificent setting. The city's central position makes it an ideal base for forays into the countryside, applying the hub-and-spoke system of travel—almost every part of the country is within a four-hour drive.

San José—or "Chepe," as Ticos call it—dominates national life. Two-thirds of the nation's urban population lives in greater (or metropolitan) San José, whose population of 1.3 million represents 30 percent of the nation's total. San José is congested, bustling, and noisy. The cramped city streets grow more choked every year with honking cars, buzzing mopeds, and trucks and gaily painted buses spewing diesel.

Its commercial center is dominated by hotels, offices, ugly modern high-rises, and shops stocked with the latest fashions. Almost every street has its lottery vendors, hawkers, and carts bursting with fruits, leather goods, music cassettes, and miscellaneous knickknacks.

Though the city is not without its share of homeless and beggars, there are few of the ghoulish *tugurios* (slums) that scar the hillsides of so many other Latin American cities. The modest working-class *barrios* (neighborhoods) are mostly clean and well ordered, while the tranquil residential districts such as Sabana Sur, San Pedro, and Rohrmoser are blessed with gracious houses with green lawns and high metal fences.

The city's chaos of architectural styles is part Spanish, part Moorish, and many streets in the older neighborhoods are still lined with

Must-Sees

Look for **M** to find the sights and activities you can't miss and ⋈ for the best dining and lodging.

© CHRISTOPHER P. BAKER

National Theater

M Pre-Columbian Gold Museum: This splendid collection of gold and jade displays a cornucopia of indigenous ornaments and artifacts (page 41).

M National Theater: San José's architectural pride and joy gleams after a recent restoration. Don your duds for a classical performance in season (page 41).

M Fidel Tristan Jade Museum: The world's largest collection of pre-Columbian jade ornamentation is exhibited in creative displays (page 44).

M Parque Nacional: A breath of fresh air in the crowded city, this leafy park is the setting for the **Monumento Nacional** (page 44).

M Central Market: Tuck your wallet safely away to explore this tight-packed warren of stalls and stores selling everything from pig's heads to saddles (page 47).

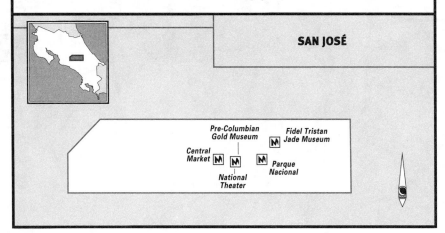

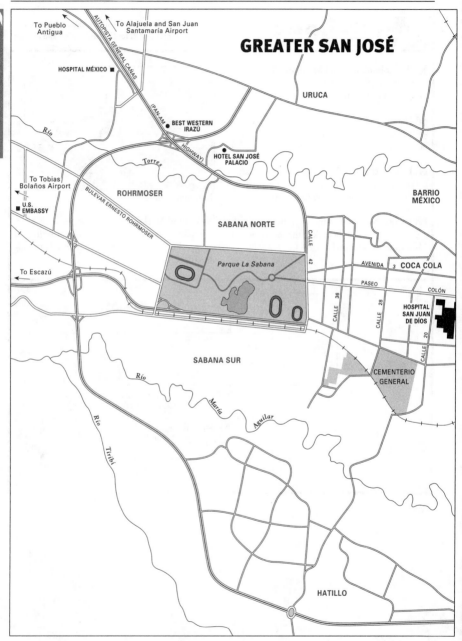

GREATER SAN JOSÉ

To Pueblo Antigua

To Alajuela and San Juan Santamaría Airport

AUTOPISTA GENERAL CAÑAS

HOSPITAL MÉXICO ■

URUCA

(PAN-AM)

BEST WESTERN IRAZÚ

HIGHWAY

Torres

HOTEL SAN JOSÉ PALACIO

To Tobias Bolaños Airport

ROHRMOSER

BULEVAR ERNESTO ROHRMOSER

BARRIO MÉXICO

U.S. EMBASSY ■

SABANA NORTE

CALLE 42

AVENIDA 3   COCA COLA

To Escazú

Parque La Sabana

PASEO

COLÓN

CALLE 36

CALLE 28

HOSPITAL SAN JUAN DE DÍOS

CALLE 20

SABANA SUR

Río

CEMENTERIO GENERAL

Río María

Aguilar

Río Tiribí

HATILLO

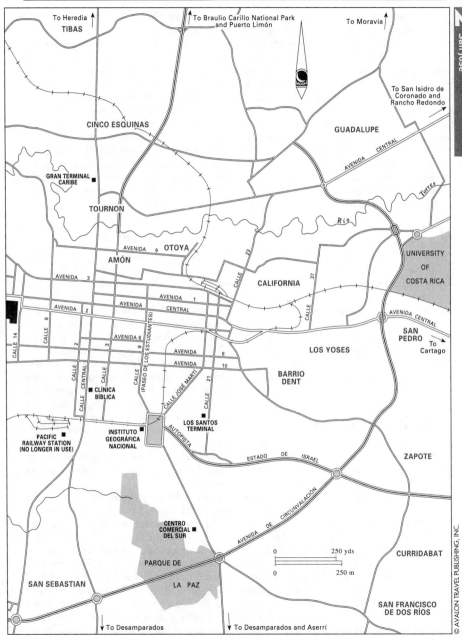

San José

To Heredia
TIBAS

To Braulio Carillo National Park
and Puerto Limón

To Moravia

To San Isidro de
Coronado and
Rancho Redondo

CINCO ESQUINAS

GUADALUPE

AVENIDA CENTRAL

GRAN TERMINAL
CARIBE

TOURNON

Río Torres

AVENIDA 9 OTOYA

AMÓN

CALLE 23

CALIFORNIA

CALLE 37

UNIVERSITY
OF
COSTA RICA

AVENIDA 3

AVENIDA 1

AVENIDA 2

AVENIDA
CENTRAL

AVENIDA CENTRAL

SAN
PEDRO

To
Cartago

CALLE 14

CALLE 8

AVENIDA 6

CALLE 9

CALLE (PASEO DE LOS ESTUDIANTES)

AVENIDA

AVENIDA

CALLE 2

CALLE 3

LOS YOSES

CALLE 8

CALLE 10

BARRIO
DENT

CALLE CENTRAL

CALLE JOSÉ MARTÍ

CALLE 21

CLÍNICA
BÍBLICA

PACIFIC
RAILWAY STATION
(NO LONGER IN USE)

INSTITUTO
GEOGRÁFICA
NACIONAL

LOS SANTOS
TERMINAL

AUTOPISTA

ESTADO DE ISRAEL

ZAPOTE

AVENIDA DE CIRCUNVALACIÓN

CENTRO
COMERCIAL
DEL SUR

CURRIDABAT

0   250 yds

0   250 m

PARQUE DE

SAN SEBASTIAN

LA PAZ

SAN FRANCISCO
DE DOS RÍOS

To Desamparados

To Desamparados and Aserrí

© AVALON TRAVEL PUBLISHING, INC.

one- or two-story houses made of wood or even adobe, with ornamental grillwork abutting the sidewalk and opening onto inner patios in the colonial style. What few older structures remain are of modest interest, however: The city is almost wholly lacking the grand colonial structures of, say, Havana or Mexico City. If it's colonial quaintness you're seeking, skip San José.

Nonetheless, the city offers several first-rate museums and galleries. Despite its working-class tenor, the city is large enough and its middle-class component cosmopolitan enough in outlook to support a vital cultural milieu. Although San José lacks a predominant central square such as Mexico City's Zócalo, the downtown has undergone a facelift in recent years under a Ministry of Culture concerned to improve the city's image. And new pedestrian precincts have been added, along with trees and neoclassical street lamps.

The city has scores of accommodations for every budget, including a new crop of backpackers' hostels and one of the world's preeminent boutique hotels. The restaurant scene is impressive, with dozens of world-class eateries spanning the globe, including some exciting nouvelle options. And night owls will appreciate San José's vivacious nightlife, from modest casinos to raging discos with Latin music hot enough to cook the pork.

PLANNING YOUR TIME

The vast majority of visitors to the country spend one or two days in the capital city, if only to kill time between flights or forays to other parts of the country. Notwithstanding, bona fide tourist attractions can be counted on two hands. After a day or two, it is time to move on.

You'll appreciate basing yourself in a leafy residential district to escape the noise and bustle of downtown, where the major sites of interest are located. Your checklist of must-sees downtown should include the **Teatro Nacional,** San José's late-19th-century belle-epoque theater, and the modest **Catedral Metropolitan,** as well as the **Fidel Tristan Jade Museum** and **Pre-Columbian Gold Museum,** which honor the nation's pre-Columbian legacy with fine displays.

The **National Center of Culture,** also downtown, pays tribute to the works of contemporary artists, as does the **Contemporary Art Museum,** near Sabana Parque. If you enjoy walking, the historic **Barrio Amón** district has been given a facelift and makes for a pleasant stroll. By night, **El Pueblo,** a shopping and entertainment complex north of downtown, will prove fulfilling.

San José's outer-perimeter sites are few. An exception is **Pueblo Antiguo,** where the nation's almost extinct traditional lifestyle is honored in yesteryear recreations. If you enjoy scenic drives, head south into the mountains along the **"Route of the Saints,"** following deep valleys into the heart of coffee country.

SAFETY CONCERNS

Avoid driving in San José. Despite San José's grid system of one-way streets, finding your way around can be immensely frustrating. San José is ideal for walking: Downtown is compact, with everything of interest within a few blocks of the center. However, its sidewalks are in horrendous repair. Watch out for potholes, tilted flagstones, and gaping sewer holes.

Be wary when crossing streets. In the words of *National Geographic:* "Rush hour is a bullfight on the streets, with every car a blaring beast and every pedestrian a *torero.*" Tico drivers do not like to give way to pedestrians, and they give no mercy to those still in the road when the light turns to green. Don't take your eyes off the traffic for a moment. Stand well away from the curb, especially on corners, where buses often mount the curb.

San José has a high crime rate. Be especially wary in and around the "Coca-Cola" bus terminal (avoid the area altogether at night) and the red-light district south of Avenida 2, especially between Calles Central and 10. Be cautious in parks. (An average of five thieves are arrested daily in Parque Central in San José, where the mid-1990s saw an increase in violent youth gangs—*chapulines*—that operated like Fagin's urchins in Dickens' *Oliver Twist.* The name means "grasshoppers," because the gangs swarm their victims like locusts. Fortunately, the city's beefed-up police patrols now include cops on bicycles; downtown they're almost always in sight.) And give a wide berth to Barrio Lomas, in the extreme west of Pavas; this is the city's desperately poor slum area and the domain of violent gangs.

Don't use buses at night, and be alert if you use them by day. Crowded places are the happy hunting grounds of quick and expert crooks.

HISTORY

Until little more than 200 years ago, San José was no more than a few muddy lanes around which clustered a bevy of ramshackle hovels. The village first gained stature in 1737 when a thatched hermitage was built to draw together the residents then scattered throughout the valley. Inauspiciously, the first wholesale influx was composed of Spaniard and Creole smugglers, who, say the Biesanzes in their book *The Ticos* "having rebelled against the royal monopoly of commerce by resorting to contraband, were punished by being 'exiled' from Cartago," the colonial capital city founded in 1564 by Juan Vásquez de Coronado. The new settlement was christened Villa Nueva de la Boca del Monte del Valle de Abra, later shortened to San José in honor of the local patron saint.

San José quickly grew to equal Cartago in size and developed a lucrative monopoly on the tobacco and nascent coffee trades. Tobacco profits funded civic buildings; by the close of the 18th century, San José had a cathedral fronting a beautiful park, a mint, a town council building, and military quarters.

When the surprise news of independence from Spain arrived by mail in October 1821, the councils of the four cities (Alajuela, Cartago, Heredia and San José) met to determine their fate, and a constitution—the Pacto de Concordia—was signed, its inspiration derived from the 1812 Spanish Constitution. Alas, says historian Carlos Monge Alfaro, early Costa Rica was not a unified province but a "group of villages separated by narrow regionalisms." A bloody struggle for regional control soon ensued.

On 5 April 1823, the two sides clashed in the Ochomogo Hills. The victorious republican forces, commanded by an erstwhile merchant seaman named Gregorio José Ramírez, stormed and captured Cartago. San José thus became the nation's capital city. Its growing prominence, however, soon engendered resentment and discontent. In March 1835, in a conciliatory gesture, San José's city fathers offered to rotate the national capital among the four cities every four years. Unfortunately, the other cities had a bee in their collective bonnet. In September 1835, they formed a league, chose a president, and on 26 September attacked San José in an effort to topple the government. The Josefinos won what came to be known as La Guerra de la Liga ("The War of the League"), and the city has remained the nation's capital ever since.

By the mid-1800s the coffee boom was bringing prosperity, culture, and refinement to the once-humble backwater. San José developed a substantial middle class eager to spend its newfound wealth for the social good. Mud roads were bricked over and the streets illuminated by kerosene lamps. Tramways began to appear. The city was the third in the world to install public electric lighting. Public telephones appeared here well ahead of most cities in Europe and North America. By the turn of the century, tree-lined parks and plazas, libraries, museums, the Teatro Nacional, and grand neoclassical mansions and middle-class homes graced the city. Homes and public buildings, too, adopted the French-inspired look of New Orleans and Martinique.

Uncontrolled rapid growth in recent years has spread the city's tentacles until the suburban districts have begun to blur into the larger complex.

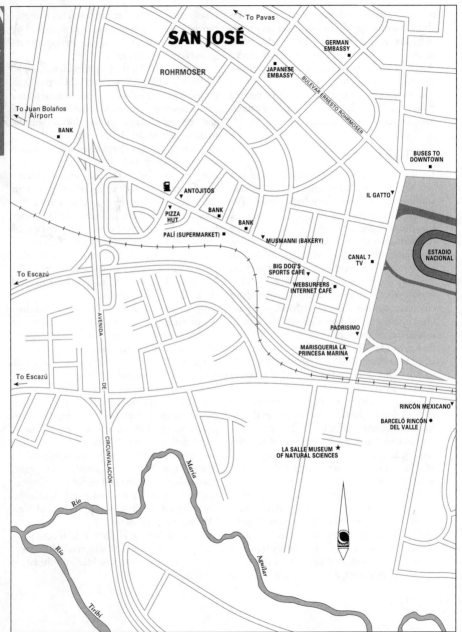

SAN JOSÉ

ROHRMOSER

To Pavas

GERMAN EMBASSY

JAPANESE EMBASSY

BULEVAR ERNESTO ROHRMOSER

To Juan Bolaños Airport

BANK

BUSES TO DOWNTOWN

ANTOJITOS

IL GATTO

PIZZA HUT

BANK

BANK

PALÍ (SUPERMARKET)

MUSMANNI (BAKERY)

ESTADIO NACIONAL

To Escazú

CANAL 7 TV

BIG DOG'S SPORTS CAFÉ

WEBSURFERS INTERNET CAFÉ

AVENIDA

PADRISIMO

To Escazú

MARISQUERIA LA PRINCESA MARINA

DE

RINCÓN MEXICANO

BARCELÓ RINCÓN DEL VALLE

CIRCUNVALACION

LA SALLE MUSEUM OF NATURAL SCIENCES ★

María

Río

Río

Aguilar

Tiribí

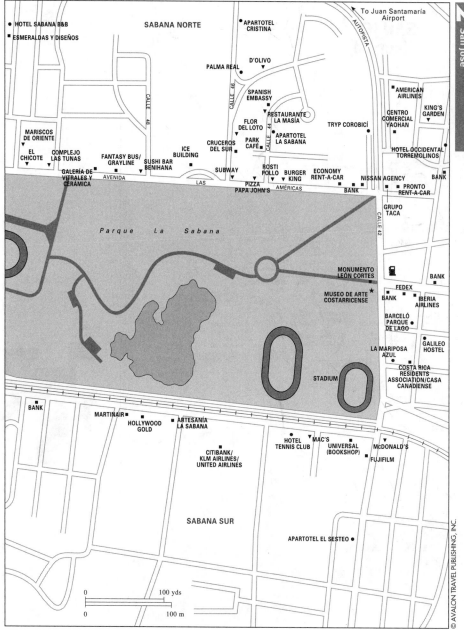

To Juan Santamaría Airport

HOTEL SABANA B&B
ESMERALDAS Y DISEÑOS

SABANA NORTE

APARTOTEL CRISTINA

D'OLIVO

PALMA REAL

SPANISH EMBASSY

AMERICAN AIRLINES

CENTRO COMERCIAL YAOHAN

KING'S GARDEN

FLOR DEL LOTO
RESTAURANTE LA MASÍA

TRYP COROBICÍ

HOTEL OCCIDENTAL TORREMOLINOS

MARISCOS DE ORIENTE

COMPLEJO LAS TUNAS

FANTASY BUS/ GRAYLINE

ICE BUILDING

CRUCEROS DEL SUR

PARK CAFÉ

APARTOTEL LA SABANA

EL CHICOTE

GALERÍA DE VITRALES Y CERÁMICA

SUSHI BAR BENIHANA

SUBWAY

ROSTI POLLO

BURGER KING

ECONOMY RENT-A-CAR

NISSAN AGENCY

PRONTO RENT-A-CAR

BANK

AVENIDA

LAS

AMÉRICAS

PIZZA PAPA JOHN'S

BANK

GRUPO TACA

CALLE 46

CALLE 48

CALLE 44

CALLE 42

Parque   La   Sabana

MONUMENTO LEÓN CORTES

BANK

MUSEO DE ARTE COSTARRICENSE

FEDEX

BANK

IBERIA AIRLINES

BARCELÓ PARQUE DE LAGO

GALILEO HOSTEL

LA MARIPOSA AZUL

STADIUM

COSTA RICA RESIDENTS ASSOCIATION/CASA CANADIENSE

BANK

MARTINAIR

HOLLYWOOD GOLD

ARTESANÍA LA SABANA

HOTEL TENNIS CLUB

MAC'S

UNIVERSAL (BOOKSHOP)

McDONALD'S

CITIBANK/ KLM AIRLINES/ UNITED AIRLINES

FUJIFILM

SABANA SUR

APARTOTEL EL SESTEO

0   100 yds

0   100 m

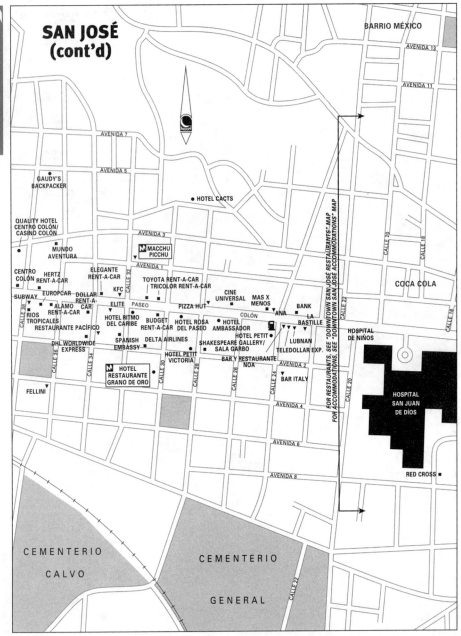

San José

SAN JOSÉ
(cont'd)

BARRIO MÉXICO

AVENIDA 13

AVENIDA 11

AVENIDA 7

AVENIDA 5

GAUDY'S
BACKPACKER

HOTEL CACTS

QUALITY HOTEL
CENTRO COLÓN/
CASINO COLÓN

AVENIDA 3

MACCHU
PICCHU

MUNDO
AVENTURA

AVENIDA 1

CALLE 20

CALLE 18

COCA COLA

CENTRO
COLÓN

HERTZ
RENT-A-CAR

ELEGANTE
RENT-A-CAR

TOYOTA RENT-A-CAR
TRICOLOR RENT-A-CAR

CINE
UNIVERSAL

MAS X
MENOS

KFC

CALLE 32

SUBWAY

EUROPCAR

DOLLAR
RENT-A-
CAR

ELITE

PASEO

PIZZA HUT

COLÓN

ANA

BANK

LA
BASTILLE

CALLE 16

CALLE 38

ALAMO
RENT-A-CAR

RIOS
TROPICALES

RESTAURANTE PACÍFICO

HOTEL RITMO
DEL CARIBE

BUDGET
RENT-A-CAR

HOTEL ROSA
DEL PASEO

HOTEL
AMBASSADOR

HOTEL PETIT

CALLE 22

HOSPITAL
DE NIÑOS

DHL WORLDWIDE
EXPRESS

SPANISH
EMBASSY

DELTA AIRLINES

SHAKESPEARE GALLERY/
SALA GARBO

LUBNAN

TELEDOLLAR EXP.

CALLE 36

CALLE 34

HOTEL
RESTAURANTE
GRANO DE ORO

HOTEL PETIT
VICTORIA

CALLE 30

CALLE 28

BAR Y RESTAURANTE
NOA

CALLE 26

AVENIDA 2

CALLE 24

BAR ITALY

CALLE 20

HOSPITAL
SAN JUAN
DE DÍOS

FELLINI

AVENIDA 4

AVENIDA 6

AVENIDA 8

FOR RESTAURANTS, SEE "DOWNTOWN SAN JOSÉ RESTAURANTS" MAP
FOR ACCOMMODATIONS, SEE "DOWNTOWN SAN JOSÉ ACCOMMODATIONS" MAP

RED CROSS

CEMENTERIO
CALVO

CEMENTERIO

GENERAL

CALLE 32

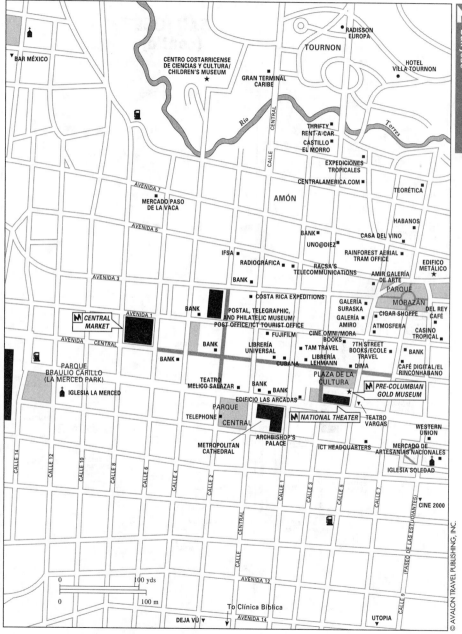

BAR MÉXICO

RADISSON EUROPA

TOURNON

HOTEL VILLA TOURNON

CENTRO COSTARRICENSE DE CIENCIAS Y CULTURA/ CHILDREN'S MUSEUM ★

GRAN TERMINAL CARIBE

Río Torres

CALLE CENTRAL

THRIFTY RENT-A-CAR
CASTILLO EL MORRO

EXPEDICIONES TRÓPICALES
CENTRALAMERICA.COM

TEORÉTICA

AVENIDA 7

MERCADO PASO DE LA VACA

AMÓN

AVENIDA 5

HABANOS

BANK
UNO@DIEZ

CASA DEL VINO

IFSA

RADIOGRÁFICA

RAINFOREST AERIAL TRAM OFFICE

RACSA'S TELECOMMUNICATIONS

AMIR GALERÍA DE ARTE

EDIFICO METÁLICO ★

AVENIDA 3

BANK

COSTA RICA EXPEDITIONS

PARQUE MORAZÁN

M CENTRAL MARKET

AVENIDA 1

BANK

POSTAL, TELEGRAPHIC, AND PHILATELIC MUSEUM/ POST OFFICE/ICT TOURIST OFFICE

GALERÍA SURASKA
GALERÍA AMIRO

CIGAR SHOPPE
ATMOSFERA

DEL REY CAFÉ

CASINO TROPICAL

AVENIDA CENTRAL

BANK

FUJIFILM

CINE OMNI/MORA BOOKS

LIBRERÍA UNIVERSAL

BANK

CUBANA

TAM TRAVEL
LIBRERÍA LEHMANN

7TH STREET BOOKS/ECOLE TRAVEL

DIMA

BANK

PARQUE BRAULIO CARILLO (LA MERCED PARK)

IGLESIA LA MERCED

TEATRO MELICO SALAZAR

BANK
BANK

PLAZA DE LA CULTURA

CAFÉ DIGITAL/EL RINCÓNHABANO

M PRE-COLUMBIAN GOLD MUSEUM

TELEPHONE

PARQUE CENTRAL

EDIFICIO LAS ARCADAS

M NATIONAL THEATER

TEATRO VARGAS

WESTERN UNION

METROPOLITAN CATHEDRAL

ARCHBISHOP'S PALACE

ICT HEADQUARTERS

MERCADO DE ARTESANÍAS NACIONALES

IGLESIA SOLEDAD

CALLE 14
CALLE 12
CALLE 10
CALLE 8
CALLE 6
CALLE 4
CALLE 2
CALLE CENTRAL
CALLE 1
CALLE 3
CALLE 5
CALLE 7
CALLE 9
PASEO DE LAS ESTUDIANTES

CINE 2000

0   100 yds
0   100 m

AVENIDA 12

To Clínica Bíblica

DEJA VÚ ▼
AVENIDA 14

UTOPIA ▼

© AVALON TRAVEL PUBLISHING, INC.

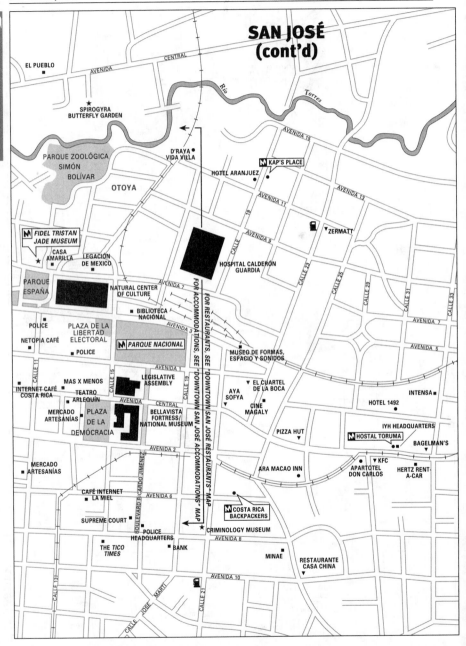

SAN JOSÉ
(cont'd)

San José

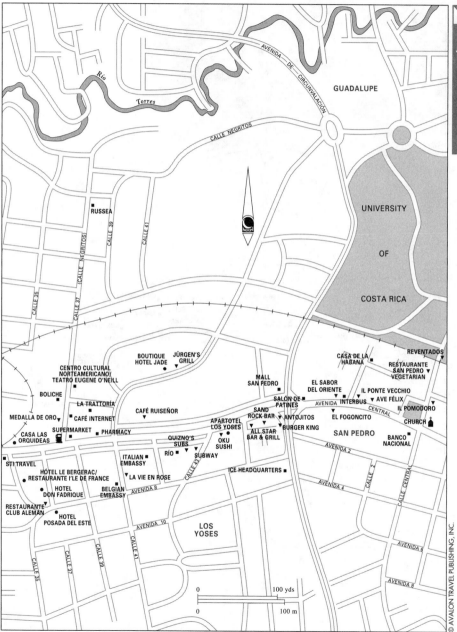

RUSSEA

GUADALUPE

AVENIDA - DE - CIRCUNVALACIÓN

Río Torres

CALLE NEGRITOS

UNIVERSITY

OF

COSTA RICA

CALLE 39
CALLE 41
(CALLE NEGRITOS)
CALLE 37
CALLE 35

REVENTADOS
CASA DE LA HABANA
RESTAURANTE SAN PEDRO VEGETARIAN
BOUTIQUE HOTEL JADE
JÜRGEN'S GRILL
CENTRO CULTURAL NORTEAMERICANO/ TEATRO EUGENE O'NEILL
MALL SAN PEDRO
EL SABOR DEL ORIENTE
IL PONTE VECCHIO
BOLICHE
SALÓN DE PATINES
AVENIDA INTERBUS CENTRAL
AVE FÉLIX
IL POMODORO
LA TRATTORIA
CAFÉ RUISEÑOR
SAND ROCK BAR
ANTOJITOS
EL FOGONCITO
CHURCH
MEDALLA DE ORO
CAFÉ INTERNET
APARTOTEL LOS YOSES
BURGER KING
SAN PEDRO
BANCO NACIONAL
CASA LAS ORQUIDEAS
SUPERMARKET
PHARMACY
QUIZNO'S SUBS
ALL STAR BAR & GRILL
AVENIDA 2
STI TRAVEL
OKU SUSHI
RÍO
SUBWAY
CALLE 33
CALLE CENTRAL
ITALIAN EMBASSY
ICE HEADQUARTERS
HOTEL LE BERGERAC/ RESTAURANTE I'LE DE FRANCE
LA VIE EN ROSE
AVENIDA 4
CALLE 2
HOTEL DON FADRIQUE
BELGIAN EMBASSY
AVENIDA 8
RESTAURANTE CLUB ALEMÁN
HOTEL POSADA DEL ESTE
AVENIDA 10
LOS YOSES
AVENIDA 6
CALLE 35
CALLE 37
CALLE 39
CALLE 41
AVENIDA 8

0   100 yds
0   100 m

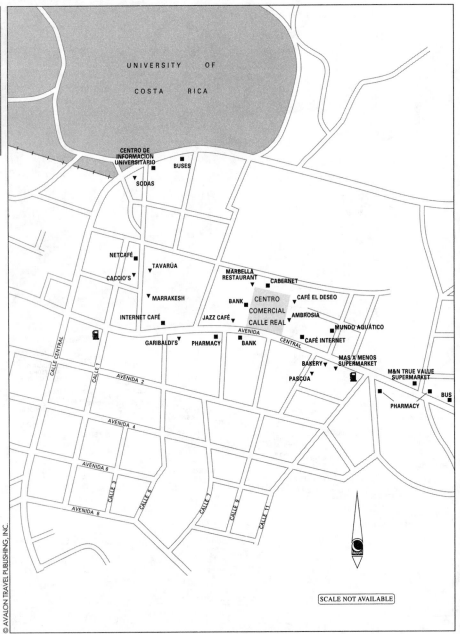

SAN JOSÉ
(SAN PEDRO
CURRIDABAT)

HOTEL MILVIA

JIMÉNEZ Y TANZÍ

BANK

PLAZA DEL SOL

BANK

POP'S

HÄAGENDAZ CAFÉ   To Cartago

FUNDACIÓN NEOTRÓPICA

Sights

Orientation

Streets *(calles)* run north to south; avenues *(avenidas)* run east to west. Downtown San José is centered on Calle Central and Avenida Central (which is closed to traffic between Calles Central and 11), though the main thoroughfare is Avenida 2. To the north of Avenida Central, *avenidas* ascend in odd numbers (Avenida 1, Avenida 3, and so on); to the south they descend in even numbers (Avenida 2, Avenida 4, etc.). West of Calle Central, *calles* ascend in even numbers (Calle 2, Calle 4, etc.); to the east they ascend in odd numbers (Calle 1, Calle 3, and so on).

West of downtown, Paseo Colón runs west 2.5 kilometers to Parque Sabana (Paseo Colón is closed to traffic Sundays). East of downtown, Avenida 2 merges into Avenida Central, which runs through the Los Yoses and San Pedro districts.

Josefinos rarely refer to street addresses by *avenida* and *calle.* Very few streets have street numbers, there are no post codes, and an amazing number of Josefinos have no idea what street they live on! Thus, Costa Ricans use landmarks, not street addresses, to find their way around. They usually refer to a distance in meters *(metros)* from a particular landmark such as, say, a large supermarket or a church. A typical address might be "200 meters east and 425 meters south of the gas station, near the church in San Pedro."

These landmarks have passed into local parlance, so that Josefinos will instinctively know where is meant by "100 meters north and 300 meters west of Auto Mercado," for example. If you state a specific street address, you may receive a confused look. To make matters worse, many reference landmarks still in common use disappeared years ago: the edifice may have disappeared, but the "landmark" remains. For example, the Coca-Cola factory near Avenida Central and Calle 14 long ago disappeared, but the reference is still to "Coca-Cola."

San José

BARRIOS OF SAN JOSÉ

The names of San José's most important neighborhoods—or *barrios*—will come in handy if you plan on extensive sightseeing. Here are the most important:

Barrio Amón
Between Avenidas 3 and 11 and Calles Central and 17, immediately northeast of downtown, this historic neighborhood offers San José's most venerable buildings. It is in the midst of revival after going to seed. It makes for an interesting walking tour—as does the contiguous Barrio Otoya.

Barrio México
To the north of Avenida 7, west of Calle 16, this working-class area provides a slice of local color. Few tourist facilities but an important church. Be cautious at night.

Desamparados
A working-class suburb on the south side of San José, with one of the most impressive churches in the city, plus a museum honoring traditional life in Costa Rica.

Escazú
About three km southwest of San José, this is the most fashionable and ritzy of the capital city's suburbs, replete with upscale residences, shopping malls, restaurants, etc., as well as being the center of North American expat life in Costa Rica. Physically separated from the capital city core, it has its own distinct center and functions almost as a separate entity. As such, and because of its importance, it deserves a separate entry. See *Escazú*, in the *Central Highlands* chapter.

Los Yoses
East of downtown, Avenida Central leads to this bustling residential and commercial center that is off the tourist path yet contains some fine historic bed-and-breakfast hotels, restaurants, and upscale shopping malls.

Moravia
Strictly a separate entity from San José, this quiet residential suburb (officially known as San Vicente de Moravia), six km northeast of downtown, is the undisputed center for art and handicrafts.

Pavas and Rohrmoser
These contiguous residential neighborhoods, due west of Sabana Park, are the setting for fine mansions, a growing number of quality restaurants, and several embassies in Rohrmoser, while Pavas fades to lowly working-class districts.

San Bosco
Although rarely referred to as San Bosco, its main thoroughfare—Paseo Colón—is the vitally important western extension of Avenida Central. A large number of car rental companies and airlines have headquarters here. The area contains several select restaurants and hotels.

San Pedro
Beyond Los Yoses, about three km east of downtown, this hip, upscale residential enclave owes its vitality to the presence of the University of Costa Rica. It offers some fine bed-and-breakfast hotels, trendy restaurants, nightclubs, and shopping malls.

Tibas
About three km north of downtown, this important residential suburb—officially called San Juan de Tibas—is replete with restaurants and nightclubs. It is off the tourist track.

© CHRISTOPHER P. BAKER

looking out over Avenida Central

The initial phase of a plan to introduce regular street numbers for buildings was introduced in spring 2000 by the new, semi-private postal service. Each house will receive a number, and districts will get postal codes. Progress, however, has been slow.

For now, addresses are still written by the nearest street junction. Thus, the Bar Esmeralda, on Avenida 2 midway between Calles 5 and 7, gives its address as "Avenida 2, Calles 5/7." In telephone directories and advertisements, *calle* may be abbreviated as "c," and *avenida* as "a."

Street names are usually hung on buildings at street corners, about five meters off the ground. Many streets have no signs. And although officially buildings have numbers, they're rarely posted and almost never used. Thus, there's no telling which side of the street the building you're seeking is on.

Distances are sometimes expressed in 100 meters *(cien metros)*, which usually refers to one block. *"Cinquenta metros"* (fifty meters) is sometimes used to mean half a block.

PLAZA DE LA CULTURA

San José's unofficial focal point is the Plaza de la Cultura, bordered by Calles 3/5 and Avenidas Central/2. It's a popular hangout for tourists and young Josefinos (as San José residents like to be called) alike. Musicians, jugglers, and marimba bands entertain the crowds. Tourists gather on the southwest corner to absorb the colorful atmosphere while enjoying a beer and food on the open-air terrace of the venerable Gran Hotel, fronted by a little plaza named **Parque Mora Fernandez.**

Pre-Columbian Gold Museum

The Museo del Oro Pre-Columbino (506/ 243-4202, fax 506/243-4220, museooro@racsa .co.cr, 10 A.M.–4:30 P.M. Tues.–Sun. and holidays, $5), in the basement beneath the plaza (the entrance is on Calle 5), is run by the state-owned Banco Central. The more than 2,000 glittering pre-Columbian gold artifacts (frogs, people, etc.) displayed weigh in at over 22,000 troy ounces. A collection of old coins is displayed in an adjoining room, in the **Numismatic Museum** (Museo Numismática) and **Architecture Museum** (Museo de Arquitectura), while a small exhibit hall features works from the bank's art collection. A self-guided audiotape tour costs $2. Free guided tours are presented by bilingual guides Tuesday and Thursday at 2 P.M., and on weekends at 11 A.M. and 2 P.M. Bring identification for the security check upon entry.

National Theater

The nation's architectural showpiece, the Teatro Nacional (Avenida 2, Calles 3/5, tel. 506/221-9417, 9 A.M.–5 P.M. Mon.–Fri., 9 A.M.–12:30 P.M. and 1:30–5 P.M. Saturday, $3), on the south side of Plaza de la Cultura, is justifiably a source of national pride. The theater was conceived in 1890, when a European opera company featuring the prima donna Adelina Patti toured Central America but was unable to perform in Costa Rica

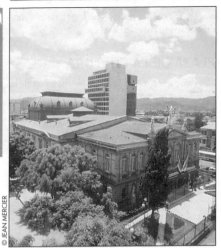

National Theater

because there was no suitable theater. Jilted, the ruling *cafelateros* (coffee barons) voted a tax on coffee exports to fund construction of a theater, and craftsmen from all over Europe were imported. It was inaugurated on 19 October 1897, to a performance of *Faust* by the Paris Opera and its great Corps de Ballet.

Outside, the classical Renaissance facade is topped by statues symbolizing Dance, Music, and Fame. Inside, the foyer, done in pink marble, rivals the best of ancient Rome, with allegorical figures of Comedy and Tragedy, stunning murals depicting themes in Costa Rican life and commerce (if the giant mural showing coffee harvesting looks familiar, it's probably because you've seen it on the old five-*colón* note), and a triptych ceiling supported by six-meter-tall marble columns topped with bronze capitals.

Art and good taste are lavishly displayed on the marble staircase, with its gold-laminated ornaments sparkling beneath bronze chandeliers. A grandiose rotunda painted in Milan in 1897 by Arturo Fontana highlights the three-story auditorium, designed in a perfect horseshoe and seating 1,040 in divine splendor. The ceiling fresco depicts naked celestial deities surrounding a giant crystal chandelier. The auditorium floor was designed to be raised to stage level by a man-

ual winch so that the theater could be used as a ballroom.

Guided tours are offered.

PARQUE CENTRAL

This small, palm-shaded park, between Calles Central/2 and Avenidas 2/4, is San José's main plaza. The unassuming park has a fountain, a bronze statue, hardwood sculptures, and venerable guachipelín, guanacaste, and higueron trees. At its center is a raised platform with a large domed structure supported by arches where the municipal band plays concerts on Sunday. The bandstand—a bit of an ugly duckling—stands over the **Carmen Lyra Children's Library,** named for a Costa Rican writer famous for her children's stories.

Across Avenida 2, the **Teatro Melico Salazar,** dating to the 1920s, has fluted Corinthian columns, high balconies, and gilding providing a study in understated period detail.

The area immediately southwest of the square is best avoided.

Metropolitan Cathedral

Dominating the east side of Parque Central is the city's modest, Corinthian-columned Catedral Metropólitan: whitewashed, with a blue domed roof more reminiscent of a Greek Orthodox church than a Catholic edifice. The original cathedral was toppled by an earthquake in 1821; the current structure dates from 1871. The interior is unremarkable, bar its lofty barrel-arched ceiling, and there is little of the ostentatious baroque influence found in cathedrals elsewhere on the continent. Tucked neatly in its shadow to the south is the **Archbishop's Palace,** dating from the 18th century and one of the few colonial structures of note in San José. The cathedral is open for mass Mon–Sat. 6 A.M.–noon and 3–6 P.M., and Sunday 6 A.M.–9 P.M.

PARQUES ESPAÑA AND MORAZÁN

Parque Morazán is tucked between Calles 5/9 and Avenida 3/5. The park's four quadrants surround the domed **Temple of Music,** supposedly

© CHRISTOPHER P. BAKER

Edificio Metálico

inspired by Le Trianon in Paris. A small Japanese garden lies in the northeast quadrant, which also contains a children's playground.

Parque Morazán merges east into diminutive **Parque España,** a secluded place to rest your feet. Its tall and densely packed trees have been adopted by birds, and their chorus is particularly pleasing just before sunrise and sunset. Note the quaint, colonial-style tiled "pavilion" on the northeast corner, and the busts that form a pantheon of national figures. A life-size statue of a conquistador stands on the southwest corner. On the north side of the park you will see an old, ornately stuccoed, ocher-colored colonial building, **Casa Amarilla,** which once housed the Court of Justice and today is the Chancellery, or State Department (no entry).

The **Edificio Metálico,** between Parque Morazán and Parque España, is one of San José's more intriguing edifices. This ocher-colored prefabricated building is made entirely of metal. Designed by the French architect Victor Baltard (some attribute it to Charles Thirio), who also designed the old Les Halles market in Paris, the structure was shipped piece by piece from Belgium in 1892 and welded together in situ. The facade is dressed with a bust of Minerva, the

"goddess of wisdom." The building is now a school.

National Center of Culture

On the east side of Parque España is the erstwhile Liquor Factory (Fábrica Nacional de Licores), now housing the multifaceted Centro Nacional de Cultura (CENAC, tel. 506/223-4776, 10 A.M.–5 P.M. Tue.–Sat., free admission). Alongside its permanent collection of national art, ceramics, and architecture, the **Museum of Contemporary Art and Design** shows revolving displays by leading Costa Rican artists. Outside, note the old sun clock and exemplary decorative stonework on the west side. The building dates to 1887, and though it's drained of alcohol, relics of the distilling days linger. The museum spans art from throughout Latin America, from perfume bottles and concept cars to print ads for United Colors of Benetton. The National Dance Company, National Theater Company, and **Museum of Iberoamerican Culture** (Casa de la Cultura Iberoamericana), and the College of Costa Rica are housed here, too, in a complex comprising two theaters, three art galleries, a library (8 A.M.–4 P.M. Mon.–Fri.), and live cultural activities.

ⓜ Fidel Tristan Jade Museum

This world-famous Museo de Jade (Calle 9 and Avenida 7, tel. 506/223-5800, 8:30 A.M.–3 P.M. Mon.–Fri., $2), on the 11th floor of the INS (Instituto Nacional de Seguro), displays the largest collection of jade in the Americas, including a panoply of pre-Columbian artifacts (mostly carved adzes and pendants) and reproductions. They're well organized, with some mounted pieces backlit to show off the beautiful translucent colors of the jade. The museum also displays a comprehensive collection of pre-Columbian ceramics and gold miniatures organized by culture and region, as well as special exhibits of jewelry by important national and foreign artists. Humankind's eternal preoccupation with sex is evidenced by the many enormous clay phalluses and figurines of men and women masturbating and copulating. Bring your camera—the museum's 11th-floor vantage point offers splendid panoramic views over the city.

PLAZA DE LA DEMOCRACÍA

This uninspired square, between Avenidas Central/2 and Calles 13/15, was built in 1989 to receive visiting presidents attending the Hemispheric Summit. Dominating the dreary, unkempt plaza is the crenellated historic **Bellavista Fortress,** which today houses the National Museum. On the west side is a bronze statue of **Don "Pepe" Figueres,** etched with some of the former president's favorite sayings. To the south are the buildings of the "Judicial Circuit," including the Supreme Court and Immigration buildings.

The National Museum and Supreme Court are linked by a newly laid pedestrian precinct, **Boulevard Ricardo Jiménez,** known colloquially as Camino de la Corte, with shade trees and wrought-iron lampposts and benches.

Legislative Assembly

The pretty white Asamblea Legislativa (506/243-2547, fax 506/243-2551, rruiz@congreso.aleg .go.cr), housed in a Moorish structure on the north side of the plaza on Calle 15, was originally the Presidential Palace, built in 1912 by presidential candidate Máximo Fernández in anticipation of victory in the 1914 elections. He lost. Nonetheless, he lent his home—known as the Blue Castle (Castillo Azul)—to president-elect Alfredo González Flores as his official residence. The Tinoco brothers (Federico and Joaquín) ousted Flores in a coup in 1917 and took possession of the home. Eventually it was returned to Fernández, who sold it to the U.S. State Department as the site of the U.S. Diplomatic Mission. It was a private residence between 1954 and 1989, when the Costa Rican government bought it. Today it houses the Congress and features a tiny library and history exhibit, open to the public at 9 A.M. Tue.–Thur. only for a 90-minute tour. A dress code applies: no sandals or shorts (for men), nor miniskirts for women.

You can visit the assembly in session, Tue.–Thur. from 4 P.M. Cameras are permitted, without flash.

National Museum

A large collection of pre-Columbian art (pottery, stone, and gold) and an eclectic mix of colonial-era art, furniture, costumes, and documents highlight the Museo Nacional (Calle 17 and Avenida Central/2, tel. 506/257-1433, www .museocostarica.com, 8:30 A.M.–4 P.M. Tues.–Sun., $0.50, students free), in the old Bellavista Fortress on the east side of Plaza de la Democracia. Separate exhibition halls deal with history, archaeology, geology, religion, and colonial life. Only a few exhibits are translated into English. The towers and walls of the fortress are pitted with bullet holes from the 1948 civil war. The museum surrounds a landscaped courtyard featuring colonial-era cannons. The main entrance is on the east side; you may also enter by ascending the steps on the west side.

ⓜ PARQUE NACIONAL

Recently renovated Parque Nacional, the largest and most impressive of the city's central parks, graces a hill that rises eastward between Calles

15/19 and Avenidas 1/3. At the park's center, under towering trees, is the massive **National Monument** (Monumento Nacional), one of several statues commemorating the War of 1856. The statue depicts the spirits of the Central American nations defeating the American adventurer William Walker. The monument originated in France: it was made in the Rodin studios. Avoid the park at night.

Museum of Forms, Space & Sounds

Housed in the ornate, pagodalike former Atlantic Railway Station, built in 1907, the Museo de Formas, Espacios y Sonidos (Avenida 3, Calle 21/23, tel./fax 506/222-9462, mufeso@racsa.co.cr, 9:30 A.M.–3 P.M. Mon.–Fri., $0.75 adults, free to children, students, and elderly) is dedicated to plastic arts, architecture, and sounds. One room is dedicated to sculptures spanning the decades and feature sculptors' tools for carving in stone and wood. Another room features musical instruments from piccolos to tubas. A third shows models of famous buildings, including the ruins of Ujarras, plus a traditional farmstead, Parque Central, and the railway station. It's handicapped equipped. To the rear are vintage rolling stock and an old steam locomotive, Locomotora 59 (or *Locomotora Negra*), imported from Philadelphia in 1939 for the Northern Railway Company. Descriptions are offered in braille.

BARRIO AMÓN AND BARRIO OTOYA

Barrio Amón and Barrio Otoya, north of Parques Morazán and España, form an aristocratic residential neighborhood founded at the end of the last century by a French immigrant, Amón Fasileau Duplantier, who arrived in 1884 to work for a coffee enterprise owned by the Tournón family, which lent its name to an adjacent region. Until recently, it had suffered decline and stood on the verge of becoming a slum. The restoration of Parque Morazán prompted investors to refurbish the neighborhood's grand historic homes. The area is worth an exploratory walk. Of particular

note is the **Bishop's Castle** (Avenida 11, Calle 3), an ornate, Moorish, turreted former home of Archbishop Don Carlos Humberto Rodriguez Quirós.

Avenida 9, between Calle 7 and 3, is lined with beautiful ceramic wall murals depicting traditional Costa Rican scenes.

TeoréTica (Apdo. 4009-1000 San José, Calle 7, Avenidas 9/11, tel./fax 506/233-4881, teoretica@amnet.co.cr, www.teoretica.org, 9 A.M.–6 P.M. Mon.–Fri., 10 A.M.–4 P.M. Saturday), housed in a beautiful mansion, is a local artists' foundation and gallery displaying revolving avantgarde exhibitions. It has a library, and offers workshops.

Costa Rican Science and Cultural Center

The prominent building on the west side of Barrio Amón, at the north end of Calle 4, looks like an old penitentiary, and indeed that's what it was from 1910 until 1979. Today it houses the Centro Costarricense de Ciencias y Cultura (506/238-4929, www.museocr.com, 8 A.M.–4:30 P.M. Tues.–Fri., 10 A.M.–5 P.M. Sat.–Sun.), comprising a library and auditorium, plus the **National Gallery** (not to be confused with the National Gallery of Contemporary Art), dedicated to contemporary art displayed in splendidly lit and airy exhibition halls conjured from former jail cells and watchtowers. Also here is the **Children's Museum** (www.cccc.ed.cr). The Museo de los Niños lets children reach out and touch science and technology, with exhibits that include a planetarium and rooms dedicated to astronomy, planet Earth, Costa Rica, ecology, science, human beings, and communications. *La Sala de Café* is an interactive educational school that teaches youngsters about coffee.

Simón Bolívar Zoo

This 14-acre Parque Zoológico (Calle 7 and Avenida 11, tel. 506/256-0012, 8 A.M.–3 P.M. Mon.–Fri., 9 A.M.–4:30 P.M. weekends and holidays; $2) has steadily improved and can now be recommended, although it still falls short of international par. The native species on display

San José

Costa Rican Science and Cultural Center

includes spider and capuchin monkeys, most of the indigenous cats, and a small variety of birds, including toucans and tame macaws.

Until recently, the zoo was appalling, reflecting a severe shortage of funds that resulted in understaffing and an inability to provide the animals with adequate facilities, nutrition, or veterinary care. The Fundación Pro-Zoológicos (FUNDAZOO, Apdo. 11594, San José 1000, tel. 506/223-1790, fax 506/223-1817, fundazoo@racsa.co.cr) works to improve conditions at the zoo. An excellent Nature Center has been opened, with a video room, library, and work area for schoolchildren. The amphibians and reptiles recently received a new home—the Joyeros del Bosque Húmedos—designed by the Baltimore Aquarium. The alligators and tapirs have a new lagoon, and other beasts will get their own new enclosures in due course.

BARRIO TOURNON

This *barrio* lies north of Barrio Amón, north of the Río Torres, and a hilly, 20-minute walk from the city center.

El Pueblo

Centro Comercial El Pueblo (Avenida 0, tel. 506/221-9434, crpueblo@hotmail.com) is an entertainment and shopping complex designed to resemble a Spanish colonial village. El Pueblo's warren of alleys harbors art galleries, quality craft stores, and restaurants specializing in traditional Costa Rican country meals.

The Calle Blancos bus departs from Calles 1/3 and Avenida 5. Get off half a kilometer after crossing the river. Use a taxi by night. Taxis to and from El Pueblo often overcharge, so settle on a fee before getting into your cab. There's free parking and 24-hour security.

Spirogyra Butterfly Garden

This small butterfly garden and farm (Avenida 0, tel./fax 506/222-2937, parcar@racsa.co.cr, www.infocostarica.com/butterfly, 8 A.M.–5 P.M. daily, $6 adults, $5 students, $3 children) is 100 meters east and 150 meters south of El Pueblo. More than 30 species flutter about in the 350-square-meter garden, which is sheltered by a net. In the center is a small waterfall surrounded by orchids, heliconias, and trees. A separate section, with cages where eggs and caterpillars develop, is protected from nature's predators. The small natural forest is protected as a private botanical garden. Hummingbirds abound! Bilingual tours are offered every half-hour, or you can opt for a 30-minute self-guided tour; an educational video is shown prior to the tour.

WEST-CENTRAL DOWNTOWN
Central Market
The Mercado Central, between Avenidas Central/1 and Calles 6/8, is San José's most colorful market and heady on atmosphere. Everything but the kitchen sink seems on offer within its dark warren of alleyways: baskets, flowers, hammocks, spices, meats, vegetables, and souvenirs. There are fish booths selling octopus, dorado, and shrimp; butchers' booths with oxtails and pigs' heads; flower stalls, saddle shops, and booths selling medicinal herbs guaranteed to cure everything from sterility to common colds. Outside, street hawkers call out their wares sold from brightly colored barrows. Pickpockets thrive in crowded places—watch your valuables. Closed Sunday.

Postal, Telegraphic, and Philatelic Museum
On the second floor of the main post office, the Museo Postal, Telegráfico y Filatélico (Calle 2, Avenidas 1/3, tel. 506/223-6918, 8 A.M.–5 P.M. Mon.–Fri., free admission) features old telephones, philatelic history displays, and postage stamps including Penny Blacks. Costa Rica's oldest stamp—dating from 1863—is also represented. It hosts a stamp exchange the first Saturday of every month in the philatelic office, upstairs.

Parque Braulio Carrillo
This tiny park (not to be confused with Braulio Carrillo National Park), between Avenidas 2/4 and Calles 12/14, is also known to Josefinos as La Merced Park, because it faces Iglesia La Merced church. Highlights include a Gothic arch-shaped fountain to match the arched windows of La Merced church and a monument honoring the astronomer Copernicus.

WEST OF DOWNTOWN
Cementerio General
When you've seen everything else, and before heading out of town, check out the final resting place of Josefinos, with its many fanciful marble mausoleums of neoclassical design. The cemetery, on the south side of Avenida 10 between Calles 20/36, is particularly worth seeing on 1 and 2 November, when vast numbers of people leave flowers at the tombs of their relatives.

National Printing Museum
A motley yet interesting collection of printing presses, typesetting machines, typefaces, and other print-related objects represent the history of printing in Costa Rica over the last 150 years. The Museo de la Empresa Nacional (8 A.M.–3 P.M. Tues.–Fri., free admission) is in the La Uruca district, just behind the Capris S.A. Corporation Complex. Tours are guided.

Parque la Sabana
This huge park, one mile west of the city center, at the west end of Paseo Colón, used to be the national airfield (the old terminal now houses the Contemporary Art Museum). Today, it's a focus for sports and recreation and contains both the National Stadium (on the northwest corner) and the National Gymnasium (southeast corner), which features an Olympic-size swimming pool. There are also basketball, tennis, and volleyball courts, a baseball diamond and a soccer field, and tree-lined paths. A small lake on the south side is stocked with fish, and fishing is permitted. The Sabana-Cementerio bus, which leaves from Calle 7 and Avenida Central, will take you there.

The park is also the setting for the **Contemporary Art Museum** (Museo de Arte Costarricense, tel. 506/222-7155, musarco@racsa.co.cr, www.cr/arte/musearte/musearte.htm, 10 A.M.–4 P.M. Tues.–Sun., $1, free on Sunday), which faces Paseo Colón on the east side. The museum houses a permanent collection of important works, including a diverse collection of woodcuts, wooden sculptures, and 19th- and 20th-century paintings. Revolving exhibitions of contemporary native artists are also shown. The

Golden Hall (Salón Dorado), on the second floor, depicts the nation's history from pre-Columbian times through the 1940s; done in stucco and bronze patina, the resplendent mural was constructed during Costa Rica's "muralist" period by French sculptor Louis Feron. Lovers of chamber music will also appreciate free concerts in the Salón Dorado.

La Salle Museum of Natural Sciences (Museo La Salle de Ciencias Naturales, tel. 506/ 232-1306, 8 A.M.–4 P.M. Mon.–Sat., 9 A.M.– 5 P.M. Sunday, $1), in the old Colegio La Salle on the southwest corner of Sabana Park, is reputed to have one of the most comprehensive collections of Central American flora and fauna in the world and houses more than 22,500 exhibits (mostly stuffed animals and mounted insects) covering zoology, paleontology, archaeology, and entomology. Some of the stuffed beasts have been ravaged by time and are a bit moth-eaten; other displays simulating natural environments are so comical one wonders whether the taxidermist was drunk. A coterie of caimans and crocodiles that live on a small island in the *museo* patio are the only live animals. If it looks closed, ring the buzzer and hope that the curator appears to open the door and switch on the lights. The Sabana-Estadio bus, which departs from the Catedral Metropolitana on Avenida 2, passes Colegio La Salle.

Pueblo Antiguo and Parque de Diversiones

This splendid 12-acre Disney-style attraction (P.O. Box 730, San José 1150, tel. 506/231-2001, fax 506/296-2212, ventas@parquediversiones .com, 9 A.M.–5 P.M. Mon.–Fri., 9 A.M.–9 P.M. weekends, $8.50, or $34 including historic show, $40 with transfers and dinner), three km west of downtown in La Uruca, is the Colonial Williamsburg of Costa Rica. The theme park recreates the locales and dramatizes the events of Costa Rican history. Buildings in traditional architectural styles include a replica of the National Liquor Factory, Congressional Building, a church, a market, a fire station, and the Costa Rican Bank. The place comes alive with oxcarts, horse-drawn carriages, live music, folkloric dances, and actors dramatizing the past. The park has three sections: the capital city, coast (including a replica of the Tortuguero Canals), and country (with original adobe structures moved to the site, including a sugar mill, coffee mill, and milking barn). The venture is operated by the Association for the National Children's Hospital, and profits fund improvements to the hospital. There are craft shops and a restaurant that serves typical Costa Rican cuisine. It hosts "Costa Rican Nights" with traditional entertainment Fri.–Sat. 6–9 P.M. There are no signs; it's about 200 meters east of Hospital México on the road that runs along the west side of the Autopista.

Pueblo Antiguo is part of a theme park (9 A.M.–5 P.M. Wed.–Sat., free admission)—*parque de diversiones*—that features roller coasters, bumper cars, and a ride in an inflatable raft down a massive water slide. Rides cost from $0.65. An all-day pass costs $8.

SOUTH OF DOWNTOWN

Soledad Church (Iglesia Soledad) is a pretty, ocher-colored church fronting a tiny plaza at Avenida 4 and Calle 9, Paseo de los Estudiantes. Paseo runs south two km to the **Peace Park** (Parque de la Paz), a favorite of Josefinos on weekends. It has an artificial lake with boats, plus horseback rides, kite-flying, sports fields, and even horse-drawn carriage rides. To get there, follow Paseo to **Parque Gonzalez Viquez,** then follow Calle 11 south to the park, which is bisected by the *autopista* (the freeway, or ring road, that skirts the city).

Desamparados, a working-class suburb on the southern outskirts of San José, has an impressive church and the **Joaquín García Monge Museum** (tel. 506/259-5072, 1–4 P.M. Mon.–Fri.) dedicated to the eponymous Costa Rican author and intellectual. Nearby is the **Oxcart and Rural Life Museum,** (Museo de las Carretas y Vida Rural, tel. 506/259-7042, 8 A.M.–noon and 2–6 P.M. Tues.–Sun., $1), in a venerable home displaying artifacts profiling the traditional peasant lifestyle, notably rustic oxcarts spanning the decades.

Nearby, **Parque Okayama,** in the suburb of San Francisco de Dos Ríos, features a Japanese garden.

At **Fossil Land** (tel. 506/276-6060, vonbell @racsa.co.cr), two km east of Patarrá, about three km southeast of Desamparados, visitors can witness a fossil dig in the midst of mountains. Activities include rappelling and spelunking, plus there's a canopy adventure, mountain bike route, trails, and a lake stocked with tilapia.

Criminology Museum

Reflecting a national concern with public awareness and responsibility, the ostensible purpose of the Museo Criminologío (Calle 17/19 and Avenida 6, tel. 506/207-5647, 8–noon and 2–4 P.M. Mon.–Fri., free admission), in the Judicial Police headquarters in the Supreme Court Building, is to prevent crime through education. The museum attempts to achieve this by featuring pictures and displays of Costa Rica's more famous crimes, along with weapons involved in the diabolical deeds, a jar containing an embalmed severed hand, and an illegally aborted fetus.

EAST OF DOWNTOWN

The relative upscale *barrios* of Los Yoses and San Pedro sprawl eastward for several kilometers but offer few attractions. North of San Pedro lies the suburb of **Moravia**—properly San Vicente de Moravia (it appears as San Vicente on maps)— about five km northeast of downtown and renowned as the center of handicrafts. The main street is known as "Calle de los Artesanías" for its crafts shops. The town's pretty plaza is sleepily suburban.

University of Costa Rica

The university campus (tel. 506/207-4000, www.ucr.ac.cr), in San Pedro, about two km east of downtown, is a fine place to take in Costa Rica's youthful bohemianism. The *sodas* (outdoor snack-diners, bars, and bookstores nearby hint at Berkeley's famed Telegraph Avenue.

The campus houses the **Entomological Museum** (tel. 506/207-5318, hlezama@cariari.ucr .ac.cr, http://cariari.ucr.ac.cr/~insectos/intro.htm, 1–4:45 P.M. Mon.–Fri., $1 adults, $0.50 children), one of the largest collections of insects in the world. The Museo Entomológico features an immense variety of Costa Rican and Central American insects, including a spectacular display of butterflies. Knowledgeable guides are available, but call ahead to check availability and opening times, which reputedly vary. Inexplicably, it's housed in the basement of the School of Music (Facultad de Artes Musicales). Don't be discouraged if the door is locked. Ring the bell for admission. You can take a bus from the National Theater on Avenida 2 and Calle 5 to the church in San Pedro, from where the Facultad and museum are signposted.

The **Centro de Información Universitario** (tel. 506/207-5535, 7:30 A.M.–5 P.M. Mon.–Fri.), at the northern end of Calle 1, is an information center for students.

Entertainment and Recreation

Whatever your nocturnal craving, San José has something to please. The *Tico Times* and the "Viva" section of *La Nación* have listings of what's on in San José, from classical music and theater to cinema showings, concerts, and discos.

The best online resource is Tico Fiesta, www.ticofiesta.com, featuring listings and interactive links to cafés, bars, nightclubs, restaurants, radio stations, and educational and social events for all ages.

BARS

The local *pulpería* often doubles as a combination of bar, family room, and front porch. Tourist bars are concentrated in "Gringo Gulch" (Calles 5/9, Avenidas Central/3) but many have a salacious component, and care against robbery is advised when walking the streets. Bars in San Pedro are more bohemian, catering to the university crowd and upscale Ticos. Most of the other class acts are in Escazú, about seven km west of town (see the *Central Highlands* chapter).

It's generally quite acceptable for women to drink at bars and nightclubs. Avoid the spit-and-sawdust working men's bars, with their many drunkards seeking a fight.

Downtown

My favorite place hereabouts is the hip **El Cuartel de la Boca del Monte** (Avenida 1, Calles 21/23, tel. 506/221-0327), a popular hangout for young Josefinos and the late-night, post-theater set. The brick-walled bar is famous for its 152 inventive cocktails, often served to wild ceremony and applause. It has live music on Monday and Wednesday. Don't bother before 9 P.M., when folks begin to arrive.

Bongo's Bar, in El Pueblo, sports a tropical jungle motif, and was one of the happenin' spots in town at last visit, with a great singles bar, especially during Happy Hour (6–8 P.M.). It plays everything from '80s pop to Latin tunes, plus live music on weekends ($5 entrance; ladies get in free until 10 P.M.). It's closed Sundays.

The liveliest spot among gringos is the 24-hour **Blue Marlin Bar** (Calle 9, Avenida 1), in the Hotel Del Rey. It's packed day and night. Fishermen gather here to tell each other big tales and trawl for good-time girls soliciting male patrons.

Key Largo (Calle 7, Avenidas 1/3, tel. 506/221-0277), once the most notorious establishment in town, recently received a makeover and, having divested itself of its former reputation, today predominantly serves a Latin clientele. This lively bar, housed in a handsome colonial mansion, has live music (Tuesday, Wednesday, and Friday is pop, Thursday is tropical music, and Saturday has '60s greatest hits), dancing, and cable TVs above the three bars. Open through 5 A.M.

Nashville South (Calle 5, Avenidas 1/3, tel. 506/233-1988) caters to country-and-western fans, and has pool and billiards upstairs.

La Esmeralda (Avenida 2, Calles 5/7, tel. 506/221-0503), a once-lively restaurant and bar that was the informal headquarters of the mariachis' union, was closed at last visit for a total makeover. Hopefully it will reopen in its former role, hosting flamboyantly dressed mariachis who warm up for diners while awaiting calls to serenade on some lover's behalf or to enliven a birthday party or other event. The bands expect tips or will charge a set fee per song. It is perfectly acceptable to decline a song if a band approaches your table.

Farther Afield

West of Downtown, the venerable and lively **Bar México** (Calle 16 and Avenida 13, tel. 506/221-8461) serves excellent *bocas* and margaritas, and has mariachi music. Thursday is Singles Night. Music videos light up a giant screen.

The **Shakespeare Bar** (Avenida 2, Calle 28, tel. 506/257-1288) draws a more intellectual crowd. It has a piano bar and sometimes hosts live jazz. On Sabana Sur, **Mac's** (tel. 506/231-3145, 9 A.M.–2 A.M.) is a TV bar popular with gringos. There's a pool table upstairs. **Big Dog's**

Sports Café (tel. 506/290-0216), on Sabana Oeste, has free margarita shots 6–10 P.M. Thursdays and 5–7 P.M. Mon.–Fri.

East of Downtown, in Los Yoses is **Río** (tel. 506/225-8371), on Avenida Central, a lively place with TVs showing music videos. A hip young crowd gathers, especially for occasional all-day musical events when the street outside is closed and the party spills out onto the road. Often open until the last guest goes home.

In San Pedro, the hip upstairs bar at **El Fogoncito** (see the *Food* section, this chapter) shows music videos on a large screen. Thursday is jazz night. Several club-bars congregate on the southwest side of the San Pedro traffic circle, including the **All Star Bar & Grill,** the **Skaka Boom,** and **Sand Rock Bar** (tel. 506/225-9229).

Calles Central, 3, and 5, north of Avenida Central in San Pedro, are lined with student bars. Favorites include **Pizzería y Pool Marrakesh** (tel. 506/281-3098, 10 A.M.–midnight Mon.–Sat. and 2 P.M.–midnight Sunday), a crowded hangout with video games, table football, and pool; the similar **Caccios** (tel. 506/224-3261; open Mon.–Sat. 11 A.M.–2 A.M.); and **Tavarúa** (tel. 506/225-7249, 11 A.M.–midnight Mon.–Sat.). All three get crowded, but otherwise offer nothing in decor. Nearby, on Calle Central, **Reventados** (tel. 506/224-5124, 11 A.M.–2 A.M. Mon.–Sat.) has male strippers for ladies on Wednesdays.

Further out, **Wazzaap** (tel. 506/236-0100), in Plaza Los Colegios Commercial Center, Moravia, is a modern, totally cool bar playing great music and drawing a hip crowd.

Cigar Rooms

The **Habanos Smoking Club** (tel. 506/224-5227), in the Calle Reál Shopping Center in San Pedro, offers climatized smoking rooms and an elegant bar; open 10 A.M.–2 A.M. Mon.–Sat. The **Casa del Habano** (Calle 4, Avenida 1, tel. 506/280-7931, ccallini@habanoscr.net), also in San Pedro, was under construction at last visit and was to offer two bars, a restaurant, a mini-museum of cigars, plus a large collection of premium smokes. **Jurgen's Grill** (tel. 506/283-2239)

has a tasteful cigar lounge with leather seats. It's attached to a premium restaurant (see *Food,* this chapter).

Gentlemen's Nightclubs

San José has no shortage of gentlemen's clubs. Many are sleazy. Even the most respectable clubs are prone to ripping off patrons with exorbitant charges. *Caveat emptor!*

DISCOS

Many discos stay open until dawn. Most apply some sort of dress code; shorts for males are never allowed.

The in-vogue spot at last visit was **Tabogan** (Calle Blancos, tel. 506/257-3396, Thur.–Sat., $5), on the north side of Centro Comercial El Pueblo, where patrons dance beneath a huge *palenque* (thatched roof). It has live music.

El Pueblo, in Barrio Tournón, boasts about a dozen bars and discos, featuring everything from salsa to Bolivian folk music. The most sophisticated disco is **Cocoloco** (tel. 506/222-8782), which revs things up with two dance floors and live bands on weekdays; open Tue.–Sat. Next door is **Ebony 56 Bar & Grill,** with a choice of three dance floors playing salsa, rock, and Latin sounds. And in the heart of El Pueblo, the **Flubber Club, Jail Club, Joselo's Bar, D-K-Da, Twister Club,** and **Bar Manhattan** crowd together and offer a near-identical theme.

Centro Comercial del Sur (tel. 506/227-1779) offers **Dynasty** (tel. 506/226-5000), playing reggae, soul, and funk classics, and ranging into rap.

For *salsa,* one of the steadfast popular venues is **Disco Salsa 54** (Calle 3, Avenidas 1/3, tel. 506/233-3814), with two discos in one: one favors romantic Latin sounds; the other is world beat and techno.

Some of the hippest spots are east of downtown, drawing a more sophisticated crowd. Try multitiered **Planet Mall** (tel. 506/280-4693, $5), the largest disco in Central America, on the fifth and sixth floors of the Mall San Pedro.

GAY SAN JOSÉ

Accommodations

A U.S. travel agency, Colours Destinations, operates **Colours Oasis Hotel** (tel. 506/296-1880 or 506/232-3504, fax 506/296-1597, colours@racsa.co.cr, www.colours.net; in the U.S., tel. 877/932-6652 or 954/845-0321, fax 954/845-0322, $59 standard, $79 superior, $99 junior suite, $119 suite, $169 studio apartment low season; $79/99/119/139/189 high season), a small gay-owned colonial-style property on the northwest corner of the "Rohrmoser Triangle" in the quiet residential Rohrmoser district. It has exquisite contemporary decor. There's a pool, Jacuzzi, TV room, plus a café, and a restaurant and bar where social events are hosted.

In Barrio Amón is the gay-run and gay-friendly **Joluva Guesthouse** (see *Accommodations,* this chapter). Other gay-friendly hotels include **Hotel Edelweiss, Hotel Fleur de Lys, Hotel Kekoldi,** and **Hotel Santo Tomás.**

Meeting Places

Meeting Places Uno (c/o Diez Tourist Information Center, Calle 1, Avenida 9, tel./fax 506/258-4561, 1en10@amnet.co.cr, www.1en10.com, 9 A.M.–9:30 P.M. Mon.–Sat.) is the best resource and meeting place for gay and lesbian visitors to Costa Rica. It sells sandwiches and pastries. The owners, Johnny and Rafa, offer free reservation services and have an Internet café plus storage room.

Other gay-friendly spots include **Cafe Mundo** (Avenida 9, Calle 15, tel. 506/222-6190) and **Café La Esquina,** in Colours Oasis Hotel. The latter has gay theme parties monthly. Joseph Itiel, author of *¡Pura Vida!: A Travel Guide to Gay & Lesbian Costa Rica* (Orchid House, 1993), strongly advises against "cruising" the parks, where "you can get yourself into real trouble." Transvestites hang out at night around Parque Morazán.

Gay saunas are particularly popular rendezvous, notably at **Sauna Dionisio** (Calle 9, Avenidas 2/4, tel. 506/257-3649) and **Sauna Jano** (Calle 1, Avenidas 4/6, tel. 506/233-3755).

Uno@Diez (Calle 3, Avenidas 5/7, tel. 506/258-4561) is a gay-run Internet café that functions as a gay and lesbian information center.

Entertainment and Events

The **El Bochinche** (Calle 11, Avenidas 10/12, tel. 506/221-0500), a two-story bar and restaurant with an art deco interior, is popular, as are **Puchos** (Avenida 8, Calle 11, tel. 506/256-1147) and **Zona Caliente** (tel. 506/225-4005) in Los Yoses.

Discos: La Avispa (Calle 1, Avenidas 8/10, tel. 506/223-5343) caters to both gays and lesbians with a disco playing mostly techno and Latin music, plus a pool room, a bar, and a big-screen TV upstairs. Drag queens flock on show night. **Los Cuchas** (Avenida 6, Calles Central/1, tel. 506/223-4310) is said to be a fast-paced disco for working-class gays. **Deja Vu Disco** (Calle 2, Avenidas 14/16, tel. 506/223- 3758) is spacious and elegant, and caters to both men and women; don't go wandering alone around the run-down neighborhood.

Coconut Groove (Avenida 12, Calle 11, tel. 506/396-3202, 4 P.M.–2:30 A.M. Tue.–Sat.) is a gay bar, restaurant, and nightclub. Others include **Utopia** (Avenida 14, Calles 7/9, tel. 506/221-3140) and **La Casita** (Calle 11, Avenidas 6/8, tel. 506/223-1537).

In nearby Piedades, **Club Paso Fino** (tel. 506/374-2928) is a bar, restaurant, and nightclub that caters to gays and lesbians each first and third Saturday night. See the *Central Highlands* chapter for more information.

CINEMAS

More than a dozen movie houses show American and other foreign movies—often in English with Spanish subtitles, although many are dubbed into Spanish. (Movies with Spanish soundtracks are advertised as *hablado en Español*.) *La Nación* and the *Tico Times* list current movies. Most movie houses charge $2–6. They are just about the only places in San José where smoking is not permitted.

Sala Garbo (Calle 28 and Avenida 2, tel. 506/222-1034) shows avant-garde international movies.

Other venues include **Cine Colón** (Paseo Colón, Calles 38/40, tel. 506/221-4517); **Cine Magaly** (tel. 506/223-0085), in Barrio California; **Cine Omni** (Calle 3, Avenidas Central/1 tel. 506/221-7903); and **Cines del America** (tel. 506/234-8868), in Mall San Pedro.

THEATER

Theatergoing here is still light-years from Broadway, but San José has a score of professional theaters, including a viable fringe—often called theater-in-the-round—serving controversial fare. Theaters are tiny and often sell out early. Book early. Tickets rarely cost more than $2. Performances normally run Thurs.–Sun. and begin at 7:30 or 8 P.M. Most performances are in Spanish.

The **Little Theater Group** (tel. 506/289-3910), supposedly the oldest English-language theatrical group in Latin America, presents English-language musicals and comedies throughout the year at its own theater in the Bello Horizontes district.

Other key theaters include **Teatro de Bellas Artes** (tel. 506/207-4095), at the University of Costa Rica, in San Pedro; **Teatro Chaplin** (Avenida 12, Calles 11/13, tel. 506/223-2919) for mime; **Teatro de la Comedia** (Avenida Central, Calles 13/15, tel. 506/223-2170) for comedy; **Teatro Eugene O'Neill Theater** (Calle Los Negritos, tel. 506/207-7554), in Barrio Escalante; **Teatro La Máscara** (Calle 13, Avenidas 2/4, tel. 506/365-5368) for alternative theater; and **Teatro**

Melico Salazar (Avenida 2, Calles Central/2, tel. 506/221-1492), for drama and dance.

LIVE MUSIC, DANCE, AND ART

Folklórica

One of the most colorful cabaret shows in town is the **Fantasía Folklórica,** which depicts traditions, legends, and history of Costa Rica's seven provinces. The program blends traditional Costa Rican dances with avant-garde choreography and stunning stage backdrops. Every Tuesday, 8 P.M., at the Melico Salazar Theater.

Pueblo Antigua (tel. 506/231-2001) hosts "Costa Rican Nights" with traditional entertainment Fri.–Sat. 6–9 P.M., with marimba music and folkloric dancing ($40).

Classical

The **National Symphony Orchestra** performs at the Teatro Nacional on Thursday and Friday (8 P.M.) and Sunday mornings (10:30 A.M.), April–December. You can buy tickets for performances at a ticket booth next to the entrance ($2–10). Dress the part: Josefinos treat a night at the National Theater as a distinguished social occasion.

The **North American-Costa Rican Cultural Center** (tel. 506/225-9433) presents the "U.S. University Musicians Series," with concerts each month. The **National Lyric Opera Company** (Compañía de Lírica Nacional), presents operas, June through mid-August, in the Teatro Melico Salazar.

Concerts are also given at the gallery of the Facultad de Bellas Artes (College of Fine Arts), on the University of Costa Rica campus.

Jazz

The nascent jazz scene is now fairly robust. The cognoscenti head to the **Shakespeare Gallery** (Calle 28, Avenida 2), next door to Sala Garbo; and **Jazz Café** (Avenida Central, tel. 506/253-8933, jaaz.cafe@terra.com, 6 P.M.– midnight) in a venerable red-brick building in San Pedro. The latter has two-for-one cover ($2) on Fridays, 5–8 P.M. Otherwise, cover is $2.50–6.

Lukas (tel. 506/233-8145, coretu@racsa.co.cr), in El Pueblo, is a steakhouse offering live music Fri.–Sat. nights.

Dance Classes

Kurubandé (tel. 506/234-0682) offers dance classes in everything from salsa to merengue. It has schools throughout San José and the highlands.

Steps: Centro de Danza (tel. 506/228-8257) specializes in jazz and hip-hop. **Casa de España** (tel. 506/296-2575) offers Spanish dance lessons, Mondays at 5:30 P.M. and Thursdays at 9 A.M. And the **Taller Nacional de Danza** (tel. 506/222-9398) offers dance classes to the public, spanning ballet to flamenco.

Peñas

TeoréTica (Apdo. 4009-1000 San José, Calle 7, Avenidas 9/11, tel./fax 506/233-4881, teoretica @amnet.co.cr, www.teoretica.org), a local artists' foundation and gallery, hosts artists *tertulias* (get-togethers) every second Tuesday at 7 P.M.

CASINOS

If two fiery-throated hummingbirds move roughly in the same line, Costa Rica punters are likely to place a bet on which one will reach a certain point first. Every street corner has two or three touts selling tickets for the national lottery. And every second tourist hotel is home to a small casino where the familiar sounds of roulette, craps, and blackjack continue into the night.

Rummy, canasta (a form of roulette, but with a basket containing balls replacing the roulette wheel), craps, and *tute* (a local variant of poker) are the casino games of choice. Bingo is a favorite pecuniary pursuit in less cosmopolitan terrain. Government oversight remains relatively weak, and house rules and payoffs are stacked far more heavily in the house's favor than they are in the United States.

The upscale casino of **Club Colonial** (Avenida 1, Calles 9/11, tel. 506/258-2807, clubcolo @racsa.co.cr) will evoke images of a Humphrey Bogart movie. The upscale **Horseshoe Casino**

(Avenida 1, Calle 9, tel. 506/233-4383) has a jungle theme. Cater-corner, the casino in the **Hotel Del Rey** (Avenida 1, Calle 9, tel. 506/257-7800) is open 24 hours.

The following hotels also have casinos: Aurola Holiday Inn, Hotel Balmoral, Barceló Amon Plaza, Barceló San José Palacio, Best Western Hotel Irazú, Camino Real, Centro Colón, Gran Hotel, Presidente, Radisson Europa Hotel & Conference Center, Royal Dutch, and Royal Garden. Further out, the Cariari and Herradura hotels also have casinos (see *San Antonio de Belén* and *Escazú*, in the *Central Highlands* chapter).

FESTIVALS

The **Ox-Cart Festival** (Festival de las Carretas), along Paseo Colón, in November, celebrates traditional rural life with a parade of dozens of ox-carts *(carretas)* from throughout the country.

The **Festival of Light** (Festival de la Luz) is a Christmas parade highlighted by the "Parade of Lights" from Parque Sabana along Calle 42, Paseo Colón, and Avenida 2 to Calle 11, with floats trimmed with colorful Christmas lights (6–10 P.M.).

SPORTS AND RECREATION

Sabana Park has baseball diamonds, basketball courts, jogging and walking trails, soccer fields, tennis and volleyball courts, plus an Olympic-size swimming pool (open noon–2 P.M.; $3) and showers. Sabana's trails provide a peaceful, traffic- and pollution-free environment for running. It has showers. Avoid the streets.

Bowling

Boliche (Calle 37, tel. 506/253-5745, 11 A.M.– midnight), in Los Yoses, has 10-pin bowling for $10 per hour.

Gyms and Health Clubs

Most upscale hotels have spa facilities: Hotel Confort Corobicí and Hotel Palma Reál are noteworthy. Most gyms are for private membership only.

Motor Racing

Formula Uno (tel. 506/381-7650, 4–11 P.M. Mon.–Fri. and noon–11 P.M. Sat.–Sun., $2 admission) is an indoor adults-only go-cart track in Alto de Guadelupe, northeast of San José, on the road to Coronado. The go-carts have four-speed 160-cc engines and reach 60 kph. ($6 per 10 minute race). Similarly, **Waterland** (tel. 506/293-2891, www.waterland.cr) has a go-cart track; see the *Ciudad Cariari and San Antonio de Belén* section, in the *Central Highland* chapter.

Rollerblading and Skating

The **Salón Los Patines** (Avenida Central, tel. 506/224-6821, 7–10 P.M. Mon.–Fri., and 1–3:30 P.M., 4–6:30 P.M., and 7–10 Sat.–Sun.,

$3), just east of the San Pedro roundabout, offers roller-skating.

Soccer

You can ask to join in a soccer game in Sabana Park. The San José team plays at the Estadio Nacional (tel. 506/221-7677), in Sabana Park. Its archrival, Saprissa (tel. 506/235-3591), plays in Tibas.

Tennis

You'll find public courts in Sabana Park. You must be a guest to play on hotel courts, or a member to play at private clubs, including the **Tennis Club** (tel. 506/232-1266, crtennis @racsa.co.cr), on Sabana Sur.

Shopping

With the exception of arts and crafts, shopping in San José lacks scope. Shop hours are usually 8 A.M.–6 P.M. Mon.–Sat. Many places close at noon for a siesta; a few stay open until late evening. Most shops close on Sunday, and many on Saturday, too.

BOOKS

7th Street Books (Calle 7 and Avenida Central/1, tel. 506/256-8251, fax 506/258-3302, marroca@racsa.co.cr) has by far the widest variety of books in English, emphasizing travel and nature, but also offering novels and nonfiction. American owner John McCuen is knowledgeable and helpful.

    Librería Internacional (libinter@amnet.co.cr) is one of the best bookstore chains, with locations in Rohrmoser (tel. 506/220-3015) and San Pedro (tel. 506/253-9553). **LibroMax** (tel. 506/280-7192, libromax@amnet.co.cr, www .libromax.com), Costa Rica's answer to Barnes & Noble, has five outlets in town, including in Multiplaza, Mall San Pedro, and Plaza Real Cariari.

    Also check Costa Rica Expeditions' **Travelers Store** (Calle Central, Avenida 3, tel. 506/257-

0766); **Mora Books** (Avenida, Calles 3/5, tel. 506/255-4136), in the Omni Building, which sells used books, plus magazines and maps (open noon–7 P.M.); and **Librería Universal** (Avenida Central and Calles Central/1, tel. 506/222-2222); and its well-stocked store at the junction of Sabana Sur and Calle 42 (tel. 506/296-1010, 10 A.M.–8 P.M. daily).

COFFEE

Every souvenir store sells premium packaged coffee. Make sure the package is marked *puro,* otherwise the coffee may already be laced with enough sugar to make even the most ardent sugar-lover turn green. **La Esquina del Café** (Avenida 9, Calle 3 bis, tel. 506/233-4560, corner@racsa .co.cr, www.laesquinadelcafe.com, 9 A.M.– 5 P.M. Mon.–Sat.), sells a wide variety of gourmet coffees as well as roasters, *chorreadores* (traditional cotton strainers on a wooden frame), and other paraphernalia.

    You can also buy whole beans—albeit not the finest export quality—roasted before your eyes at the Mercado Central. Ask for whole beans (*granos*), or you'll end up with superfine grounds. One pound of beans costs about $1.

HANDICRAFTS

San José is replete with arts and crafts, such as reproduction pre-Columbian gold jewelry, hammocks, wood carvings, Panamanian *molas,* and the famous brightly painted miniature oxcarts. Most tourist hotels have gift stores, notably **Boutique Annmarie** in the Hotel Don Carlos.

Mercado de Artesanías Nacionales (Calle 11, Avenidas 4/6), behind Iglesia Soledad, teems with colorful stalls selling T-shirts, paintings, trinket jewelry, and superb-quality hammocks. Sundays are best.

The **Mercado Central,** on Avenida 1, has a panoply of leather work and other artisans' stalls,

SHOPPING WITH A CONSCIENCE

Think twice before buying something exotic: The item may be banned by U.S. Customs and, if so, you could be fined. Even if legal to import, consider whether your purchase is an ecological sin. In short, shop with a conscience! Don't buy:

- Combs, jewelry, or other items made from tortoise shells.
- Coral, coral items, or shells. Costa Rica's coral reefs are being gradually destroyed. And every shell taken from a beach is one less for the next person to enjoy.
- Jewelry, artwork, or decorated clothes made of feathers. The bird may well have been shot simply for its plumage—and it may well be endangered.
- Furs from jaguars, ocelots, etc. Such furs are illegal. Your vanity isn't worth the life of such magnificent and endangered creatures.
- Think twice, too, about buying tropical hardwood products. Help protect Costa Rica's forests.

For more information, contact the **U.S. Fish and Wildlife Service** (Department of the Interior, Washington, D.C. 20240, www.fws.gov), which puts out a booklet, *Buyer Beware;* or the **U.S. Customs Service** (1301 Constitution Ave., Washington, D.C. 20229, www.customs.treas.gov).

as does **Plaza Esmeralda,** 800 meters south and 50 meters east from Palí in Pavas.

Specialty handicraft stores concentrate on Calle 5, between Avenida 1/5. These include **Atmósfera** (Calle 5, Avenidas 1/3, tel. 506/222-4322), with two floors (a gallery on the second floor displays fantastic indigenous masks, carved fantasy beasts, and paintings); and, next door, **Suríksa Gallery** (tel. 506/222-0129), selling top-quality woodcarvings and furniture, including the works of renowned North American artists/carpenters Barry Biesanz and Jay Morrison.

A handful of handicrafts stores cluster together on two levels at **La Casona** (Calle Central, Avenidas Central/1). The cross-section of crafts includes Guatemalan textiles, woodcrafts from Honduras, and the popular Costa Rican nativity figures and Christmas crèches in ceramics and wood.

Centro Comercial El Pueblo has many high-quality art galleries and crafts stores.

Stained glass, anyone? **Galería de Vitrales y Cerámica** (tel. 506/232-7932, semstudio@hotmail.com), on Sabana Norte, sells beautiful stained-glass art, plus vases, bowls, etc.

The suburb of Moravia, five km northeast of downtown, is a major center for arts and crafts, with a wide array of shops along the main street. A bus departs San José from Avenida 3, Calles 3/5; a microbus departs from Avenida 7, Calle 6.

CLOTHING

If you admire the traditional Tico look, check out the **Mercado Central** (Calle 6 and Avenida 1), where you'll find embroidered *guayabero* shirts and blouses and cotton *campesino* hats. **La Choza Folklórica** (Avenida 3, Calle 1) specializes in replicas of national costumes. You can also buy Costa Rican dresses (bright red, blue, and green designs on white cotton) at **Bazaar Central Souvenir** (Calle Central, Avenida 3).

Costa Rica produces high-quality leather work, including purses, attaché cases, and cowboy boots. The suburb of Moravia is well known for producing leather goods. In town, try **Galería del Cuero** (Avenida 1, Calle 5, tel. 506/223-2034); **Marroquinería Del Río** (Calle 9,

Avenidas Central/2, tel. 506/238-2883); and **Artesanías Malety** (Avenida 1, Calles 1/3, tel. 506/221-1670). Shoemakers abound in San José, and almost everywhere downtown you can come upon rows of boots made from 50 or so different leathers, including dandy two-tones. A bevy of high-quality shoemakers can be found on Paseo Colón and Avenida 3 between Calles 24 and 26.

The best place for upscale clothing is **Mall San Pedro,** replete with brand-name boutiques.

JEWELRY

Artisan markets sell attractive ethnic-style earrings and bracelets. Much of what you'll see on the street is actually gold-washed, not solid gold. Most upscale hotel gift stores sell Colombian emeralds and semiprecious stones, 14-karat-gold earrings and brooches, and more, along with fabulous pre-Columbian re-creations: try **Esmeraldas y Diseños,** next to Hotel Sabana B&B in Sabana Norte; **La Casa del Indio** (Avenida 2, Calles 5/7, tel. 506/223-0306); and **Esmeraldas y Creaciones** (tel. 506/280-0808), in Los Yoses.

The **Gold Museum Shop** (tel. 506/256-9125), beneath the Plaza de la Cultura, sells quality gold reproductions, plus ceramics, books, and other art.

CIGARS

Costa Rica is a prime spot to buy Cuban cigars, with a dozen or so outlets. (U.S. citizens should note that it is illegal to buy Cuban cigars without a license, and even non-U.S. citizens can have them confiscated if in transit home via the U.S.) Alas, the majority of "Cuban" cigars sold in Costa Rica are fakes! Don't be fooled by the genuine-looking boxes and wrappers, even in major stores.

If you want the real thing, try **Habanos de Costa Rica** (tel. 506/383-6835), one block north of Parque Morazán; the **Cigar Shoppe** (Calle 5 and Avenida 3, tel. 506/257-5021), in the foyer of Diana's Inn; the **Habanos Smoking Club** (tel. 506/224-5227), in the Calle Reál Shopping Center in San Pedro; the **Tobacco Shop,** tel. 506/223-0873, in Centro Comercial El Pueblo; plus **El Rincón Habano** (Calle 7, Avenidas Central/1, tel. 506/222-1892, 9 A.M.–6:30 P.M. Mon.–Fri., 9 A.M.–6 P.M. Saturday, 9:30 A.M.–5 P.M. Sunday).

The **Casa del Habano** (Calle 4, Avenida 1, tel. 506/280-7931, ccallini@habanoscr.net), in San Pedro, sells a vast stock of Cuban cigars kept in a huge humidor. It has smoking lounges (in preparation at last visit).

WOODWORK

For stunning colonial furniture, such as wooden doorways, pillars, and chests, check out **Park Café** (Calle 44, tel. 506/290-6324, psitacci @racsa.co.cr), in Sabana Norte. **Antiguedades San José** (Avenida 7, Calle 7, tel. 506/222-8200) also has an eclectic range of antiques.

Guzman Mora conjures classical compositions from wood. His Spanish-style guitars sell for about $80. You can try them out in his showroom—**Aristides Guzman Mora, Ltd.** (tel. 506/223-0682), at Cinco Esquinas, in Tibas.

San José

Accommodations

San José's accommodations run the gamut from budget hovels to charming boutique hotels and large name-brand options. Many super-cheap budget hotels are dark, dirty, and/or dingy and concentrate near the "Coca-Cola" bus station (Calle 16, Avenidas 1/3), and between Calles 6/10 and Avenidas 3/5. Both areas boast plenty of drunks and cheap hookers (many of the hotels themselves are little more than brothels) and are best avoided, not least because of theft problems. (Readers have written to complain about theft in Pension Otoya, for example.) Fortunately, several well-run backpackers hostels have opened in recent years. It's worth noting that many budget accommodations lack hot water. Also, San José is a noisy city; it is always wise to ask for a room away from the street. Hotels are arranged below by price category, then by area.

UNDER $25

Downtown

Number one choice is **M Costa Rica Backpackers** (Avenida 6, Calles 21/23, tel. 506/221-6191, fax 506/223-2406, costaricabackpackers @hotmail.com, www.costaricabackpackers.com, $8 pp dorms, $19 private rooms), run by two friendly and savvy French guys, Stefan and Vincent. This splendid, spotless, secure backpackers' pad is in a large house with small kidney-shaped swimming pool and garden with hammocks and swing chairs. It offers a choice of clean male, female, or mixed dorms, or private rooms, plus heaps of hot water in the shared bathrooms. A huge TV lounge has ripped leather sofas. It has cooking facilities, plus laundry and storage, as well as free 24-hour Internet and coffee and tea, plus a tour-planning room. All dorms have lockers.

Also to consider is the **Pangea Hostel** (Avenida 11, Calle 3 bis, tel. 506/221-1992, email@hostel-pangea.com, www.hostelpangea.com, $9 pp), in a converted old home at the corner of Avenida 13 and Calle 3 bis, in Barrio Amón. It has dorms with clean shared bathrooms with hot water, plus a kitchen, TV lounge, and safes. It offers free storage, free Internet access, and free breakfast.

Nearby, the no-frills, German-run **Tranquilo Backpackers** (Calle 7, Avenida 11, tel. 506/223-3189 or 355-5103, tranquilobackpackers @hotmail.com, www.tranquilobackpackers.com, $7 pp dorms, $11 s, $19 d private rooms), in a converted colonial home with aged wooden floors, has male, female, and mixed dorms, plus 10 well-lit private rooms with roughhewn handmade beds. Furnishings are basic and bare-bones, although the place is kept spotless. It has shared hot showers, Internet, laundry, free coffee and tea, a TV lounge, book exchange, storage, and hammocks in the skylit reception area. It offers sushi, curry, and pasta nights in a small kitchen.

Another good bet is **Casa Ridgeway** (Calle 15 bis, Avenidas 6/8, tel./fax 506/233-6168, friends @sol.racsa.co.cr, www.amigosparalapaz.com, $10 pp dorm, $12 pp private dorm, $24 s/d room). The hostel is attached to the Friends Peace Center (Centro de los Amigos Para la Paz) and has three small well-lit dorms and five private rooms in a relaxed and friendly environment. There's a laundry, a basic kitchen, and shared showers, plus a TV/VCR room and library. No alcohol or smoking.

Nearby, **Casa León** (Avenida 6 bis, Calles 13/15, tel. 506/222-9725, casa_leon_sa@hotmail .com, $10 pp in the dorm, $15 s, $25 d private room with shared bath, $25/30 with private bath) has one clean, simple, well-lit dorm with shared showers with hot water, plus four private rooms (one with private bathroom). Guests have kitchen and laundry privileges, and there's storage.

The **Hotel Cocorí** (Avenida 3, Calle 16, tel. 506/233-0081, fax 506/255-1058, $11 s, $17 d), conveniently close to the bus station, has 26 rooms with simple but adequate furnishings, and private bathrooms with hot water. It has a downstairs TV lounge with leather sofas, plus restaurant and laundry.

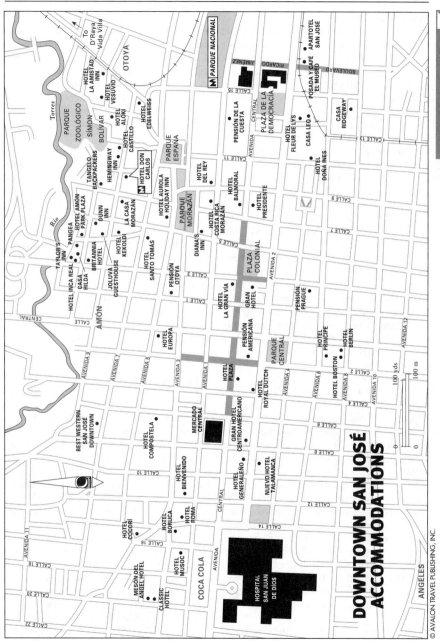

DOWNTOWN SAN JOSÉ
ACCOMMODATIONS

To D'Raya Vida Villa

PARQUE NACIONAL

APARTOTEL SAN JOSÉ

POSADA Y CAFÉ EL MUSEO

BOULEVARD

RICARDO JIMÉNEZ

CALLE 15

HOTEL LA AMISTAD INN

HOTEL VESUVIO

HOTEL ALOKI

PARQUE ZOOLÓGICO SIMÓN BOLÍVAR

HOTEL CASTILLO

HOTEL EDELWEISS

PENSIÓN DE LA CUESTA

PLAZA DE LA DEMOCRACIA

CENTRAL

CASA RIDGEWAY

CALLE 13

AVENIDA

Torres

HOTEL FLEUR DE LYS

CASA LEO

PARQUE ESPAÑA

HOTEL DON CARLOS

HOTEL DEL REY

CALLE 11

HOTEL DOÑA INES

CALLE 9

HEMINGWAY INN

TANGEO BACKPACKERS

PARQUE MORAZÁN

HOTEL AUROLA HOLIDAY INN

HOTEL BALMORAL

HOTEL PRESIDENTE

CALLE 7

Río

HOTEL AMÓN PARK PLAZA

PANGEA

DUNN INN

LA CASA MORAZÁN

HOTEL KEKOLDI

HOTEL COSTA RICA MORAZÁN

TAYLOR'S INN

BRITANNIA HOTEL

HOTEL SANTO TOMÁS

DIANA'S INN

CALLE 5

HOTEL INCA REAL

CASA HILDA

JOLUVA GUESTHOUSE

PENSIÓN OTOYA

CALLE 3

PLAZA COLONIAL

AVENIDA 2

AMÓN

CALLE 1

HOTEL LA GRAN VIA

GRAN HOTEL

PENSIÓN PRAGUE

CENTRAL

CALLE

HOTEL EUROPA

PENSIÓN AMERICANA

PARQUE CENTRAL

HOTEL PRINCIPE

HOTEL BERLIN

AVENIDA 12

AVENIDA 9

AVENIDA 7

AVENIDA 5

AVENIDA 3

AVENIDA 1

HOTEL PLAZA

HOTEL ROYAL DUTCH

AVENIDA 4

AVENIDA 6

HOTEL BOSTON

AVENIDA 8

AVENIDA 10

CALLE 2

100 yds

100 m

BEST WESTERN SAN JOSÉ DOWNTOWN

CALLE 4

CALLE 6

MERCADO CENTRAL

GRAN HOTEL CENTROAMERICANO

CALLE 8

HOTEL COMPOSTELA

CALLE 10

HOTEL BIENVENIDO

HOTEL GENERALEÑO

NUEVO HOTEL TALAMANCA

CALLE 12

CENTRAL

CALLE 14

AVENIDA 11

HOTEL COCORI

CALLE 16

HOTEL BORUCA

HOTEL ROMA

ANGELES

CALLE 18

MESÓN DEL ANGEL HOTEL

HOTEL MUSOC

COCA COLA

AVENIDA

HOSPITAL SAN JUAN DE DIOS

CALLE 20

CLASSIC HOTEL

CALLE 22

West of Downtown

I recommend **Gaudy's Backpackers** (Avenida 5, Calle 36/38, tel. 506/258-2937, gaudys@back packers.co.cr, www.backpacker.co.cr, from $7 pp dorm, from $20 private room), in a beautiful home in a peaceful residential area. You enter to a lofty-ceilinged TV lounge with sofas. It opens to a courtyard with hammocks. There are two co-ed dorms (one with eight bunk beds, another with 12 bunk beds) and three small private rooms; one room upstairs has a tub, another has a balcony. Guests get use of a full kitchen, and there's laundry service ($5), plus free Internet. The place is kept spotless.

La Mariposa Azul (P.O. Box 246-1007 San José, Avenida 4, Calles 40/42, tel. 506/221-7524, www.mariposaazul.co.cr, $11 pp dorm, $25 family room) is another charming middle-class home turned backpackers hostel. Washed by breezes and heaps of light, it has a large TV lounge with sofas that's open to a courtyard. A stone-lined staircase leads to two upstairs dorms (one with 10 beds, the second with 12) that share two spacious bathrooms with hot water. Two family rooms with a TV sleep four people and share two additional bathrooms. It has lockers and a security box, plus common kitchen. Rates include breakfast, laundry, and Internet access.

I like the **Classic Hotel B&B** (Calle 20, Avenidas 3/5, tel. 506/223-4316, fax 506/257-3123, hotelclassic@hotmail.com, $10 pp dorm, $35 s, $45 d private room), advantageously situated adjacent to the bus station. This classy conversion of a colonial home offers pleasant wicker furnishings. It has 24 huge bunk beds in a four-room, separate-sex dorm in the modern annex to the rear, where a garden contains a delightful thatched dining area; the rooms are well-lit and cross-ventilated. Guests get kitchen privileges. The main two-story building offers nine private rooms with ceiling fans, cable TV, telephone, drape curtains, wicker furnishings, and clean, modern private baths with hot water; some rooms have beautiful hardwood floors. It accepts credit cards. Rates include continental breakfast and tax.

Another option is **Galileo Hostel** (Avenida 2, Calle 40, tel. 506/221-8831, galileo@galileohostel .com, www.galileohostel.com, $6 pp dorms, $16–18 private room) in a pleasant colonial-style home with cozy TV lounge with fireplace and small library. Three dorms share three bathrooms. There are four private rooms, but some lack windows, and two are tiny cell-like cubicles. It offers laundry ($5) and has a community kitchen plus courtyard garden with hammocks. Rates include Internet use.

East of Downtown

Headquarters of the Costa Rican Youth Hostel Association, the **N Hostal Toruma** (Avenida Central, Calles 29/31, tel./fax 224-4085, recajhi @racsa.co.cr, www.hicr.org or www.toruma .com, $10 pp IYH cardholders, $15 pp nonmembers) is a beautiful old colonial-style structure with segregated dormitories accommodating 95 beds in 17 well-kept rooms. Family rooms are available ($22 s, $26 d private rooms). There are laundry facilities and a restaurant, plus Internet, cable TV, and parking. It's popular with the backpacking crowd. Advance booking required; book weeks ahead in peak season. It's open 7 A.M.–10 P.M., and you can stay out later with a pass. Rates include breakfast.

$25–50

Downtown

The **Nuevo Hotel Talamanca** (Apdo. 11661, San José 1000, Avenida 2, Calles 8/10, tel. 506/233-5033, fax 506/233-5420, hoteltalamanc @racsa.co.cr, $40 s/d, $50 suite) is an elegant option on the city's main drag. The 46 a/c rooms and four junior suites (with hot tubs and minibars) are tastefully appointed and have TVs and telephones. The four junior suites have been described as "a vision in chrome and black, emphasizing sharp lines and minimalist furnishings." Other rooms are done in cool slate greens. It's popular with Tico businessfolk.

In Barrio Amón is the gay-run and gay-friendly **Joluva Guesthouse** (Calle 3 bis, Avenidas 9/11, tel. 506/223-7961, fax 506/257-7668, joluva @racsa.co.cr, www.joluva.com; in the U.S., tel. 619/294-2418 or 800/296-2418; $25–45 s, $30–50 d). The seven sparsely furnished rooms have wooden floors, cable TV, and small private bathrooms. Rates include continental breakfast.

A newcomer, **Hotel Inca Real** (P.O. Box 5174-1000, San José, Avenida 11, Calles 3/5, tel. 506/222-5318, fax 506/221-1386, info @janesviajes.com, www.janesviajes.com, $39 s, $49 d) is a pleasant conversion of a three-story colonial home with a skylit atrium lobby with sofas, wrought-iron pieces, and planters. It has 33 carpeted rooms with modest hardwood furnishings, cable TVs, telephone, and large showers. Some rooms are huge. I noted a musty smell. It has secure parking, Internet service, and a souvenir store. Rates include breakfast and tax.

Splendidly situated on a corner of Parque Morazán is the no-frills **Diana's Inn** (Calle 5, Avenida 3, tel. 506/223-6542, fax 506/233-0495, dianas@racsa.co.cr, $28 s, $38 d), with a/c rooms with private bath, phone, and color TV. They're basic, as are the public areas, but clean and well lit. The three-story pink building was once home to an ex-president of Costa Rica, but has lost its luster. Rates include tax and breakfast.

The **Pensión de la Cuesta** (Avenida 1, Calles 11/13, tel. 506/256-7946, fax 506/255-2896, ggmnber@racsa.co.cr, www.suntoursandfun.com/ lacuesta, $18–23 s, $28–35 d), is clean, cozy, charmingly eccentric, and ideal for those who like offbeat hotels. This 1930s house, full of antiques and potted plants, is owned by local artists Dierdre Hyde and Otto Apuy, whose original artworks adorn the walls. There are nine rooms plus a furnished apartment (with kitchen) for up to six people. The shared baths are clean. There's a TV room and self-service laundry. Guests get free use of the kitchen. It also has an apartment with kitchen for $22 s, $28 d low season, $25/30 high season.

The **Hotel La Amistad Inn** (Avenida 11, Calle 15, tel. 506/258-0021, fax 506/258-4900, wolfgang@sol.racsa.co.cr, $32 s, $45 d standard, $40 s, $53 d "deluxe") enjoys a quiet location just east of the zoo on the edge of the historic Barrio Otoya district. This restored old mansion has 40 somewhat cramped rooms, each featuring two queen-size beds with orthopedic mattress (some also have a bunk bed), ceiling fan, tele-

phone, cable TV, safe, and black marble bathroom with hairdryer. "Deluxe" rooms are so-defined by virtue of a/c and mini-refrigerators. One reader reports newer rooms downstairs are noisy. Another reports leaking fixtures and no hot water: apparently, the manager had turned off the heater to save money! And the dining room could do with perking up. The hotel has a small garden and an Internet café, plus lockers. It's under multilingual German ownership (the influence is evident in the breakfasts).

Nearby is the adorable **Hotel Kekoldi** (Apdo. 12150, San José, Avenida 9, between Calles 5 and 7, tel. 506/240-0804, fax 506/248-0767, reservations@kekoldi.com, www.kekoldi.com, $45 s, $59 d standard, $70 s/d superior), in Barrio Amón. Relocated to a two-story 1950s house, the conversion offers 10 spacious rooms with hardwood floors, heaps of light and minimal and modest furnishings in tropical colors (a lively blend of yellows, orange, and purples), including wall murals, plus cable TV, fans, and security box. Breakfasts are served in a beautiful garden in Japanese style.

The **Hotel Costa Rica Morazán** (Calle 7, Avenida 1, tel. 506/222-4622, fax 506/233-3329, crmorazan@racsa.co.cr or info@hotel palazamorazan.com) is a popular albeit modest downtown option, with 33 a/c rooms with cable TV. Its bar/restaurant is a popular lunch spot for the city business crowd, and there's a lively bar and casino. Rates: $45 s/d, $75 junior suite, $90 superior year-round. **Hotel Vesuvio** (Avenida 11, Calles 13/15, tel. 506/221-7586, fax 506/221-8325, info@hotelvesuvio.com, www .hotelvesuvio.com, $45 s, $55 d, $75 s/d deluxe) is a modern structure that hints at Spanish colonial. The 20 rooms have spic-and-span, all-pink decor, with TV, safety deposit box, telephone, and private bath. It has an intimate restaurant and a pleasing tiled patio out front for literally watching the world go by. There's private parking. Rates include full American breakfast.

The uninspired **Hemingway Inn** (Calle 9, Avenida 9, tel./fax 506/221-1804, ernest@racsa .co.cr, www.hemingwayinn.com; in the U.S., Interlink 670, P.O. Box 025635, Miami, FL 33102, $36 s, $46 d), in a twin-story colonial-era building in Barrio Amón, has 17 small, sparely furnished rooms with ceiling fans, color TVs, security boxes, and orthopedic mattresses. Some have hardwood walls. The Hemingway Suite has a canopied bed and pleasing maroon decor, plus a spacious bathroom. Full breakfast is served on a small patio that has a Jacuzzi. It charges $7 for parking, and has Internet service. A reader complains of rude service. Rates include breakfast.

The **Hotel Plaza** (Apdo. 2019, San José 1000, Avenida Central, Calles 2/4, tel. 506/222-5533, fax 506/262-2641, hotplaza@sol.racsa.co.cr, $36 s, $42 d), has 40 small, simply furnished but pleasant and clean rooms facing onto the *bulevar* All rooms have cable TV, plus small bathrooms with tiny sinks.

Also worth considering is the small and homey **Hotel Doña Inés** (P.O. Box 1754-1002, San José, Calle 11, Avenidas 2/6, tel. 506/222-7443 or 506/222-7553, fax 506/223-5426, hoteldonaines@racsa.co.cr, www.donaines.com, $35 s, $45 d low season, $40/50 high season), behind the Iglesia la Soledad. It's a good bet, for its luxury bathrooms with full-size tubs, TVs, phones, and reproduction antique furnishings in the 20 carpeted bedrooms. It has added a small and pleasant restaurant for breakfasts and dinner. Rates include breakfast and tax.

The **Hotel Royal Dutch** (Avenida 2, Calle 4, tel. 506/222-1414, fax 506/233-3927, dutchcr@racsa.co.cr, www.royaldutch.com, $33 s, $39 d low season, $45 s, $50 d high season) has 26 modestly furnished, spacious, well-lit, carpeted a/c rooms with fan, cable TV, telephone, security box, and private bath with hot water. There's a small street-front restaurant and a casino.

Pensión Prague (Calle 5, Avenidas 4/6, tel. 506/256-4108, info@praguecolonial.com, www .praguecolonial.com, $25–35 s/d), just two blocks from Plaza de la Cultura, is Czech-run and offers six rooms with modest furniture on colonial-tiled and lacquered hardwood floors, ceiling fans, original paintings, plus VCRs. Three rooms have a king-size bed. Some rooms have shared baths, albeit spacious and beautifully tiled. The single suite opens onto its own patio; another room has French doors onto a

narrow veranda. The dining area features a whirlpool with a waterfall-fountain. Two dark downstairs rooms have no outside windows. Noise from the traffic outside is a drawback. Rates include breakfast.

Looking for self-catering? The modern **Hotel San José** (Apdo. 1500-1002, San José, Avenida 2, Calles 17/19, tel. 506/256-2191, fax 506/221-6684, hsanjose@racsa.co.cr, www.hotel-sanjose .com; in the U.S., tel. 800/575-1253; $30 s, $37 d standard rooms, $40 s, $47 d apartments), facing the National Museum, offers 18 small rooms plus one- and two-bedroom apartment suites with living rooms and fully equipped kitchenettes. All rooms have cable TVs, phones, parquet floors, and clean bathrooms. It has parking.

West of Downtown

The **Hotel Petit** (Paseo Colón, Calle 24, tel. 506/233-0766, fax 506/233-4794, petithotel @yahoo.it, www.costarica1_link.com, $25 s, $35 d) has 15 simple rooms, all with hot showers. Some are light and airy, others dingy; some have electric stoves. There's a kitchen, laundry service, secure parking, and a cable TV in the lounge, plus a bar and café serving full Tico breakfasts. Rooms vary markedly. Rates include breakfast.

The exterior of the **Hotel Petit Victoria** (Calle 28, Avenida 2, tel. 506/255-8488, fax 506/221-6372, victoria@amnet.com, $15 pp) resembles a New England home. The intriguing entrance hall—approached through a Chinese-style circular doorway with intricate woodwork—has fancy colonial tiles and a venerable chandelier. Despite the hotel's popularity, the 13 basically appointed bedrooms are disappointing—made more so by the melancholy blue color scheme, although each has a TV, fan, and small refrigerator, and bathrooms are spacious and airy—and readers have complained about standards. There's a kitchen, a TV lounge, plus a skylit 24-hour café-cum-bar.

The German-Tico run **Hotel Ritmo del Caribe** (Paseo Coló, Calles 32/34, tel./fax 506/256-1636, hotel@ritmo-del-caribe.com, www.ritmo-del-caribe.com, $25 s, $30 d standard, $30/40 "comfort" room) in a 1950s art deco home, bills itself as an "upscale backpackers" place for Europeans. It has 11 rooms (two to six beds each) with orthopedic mattresses, soundproof double-pane windows, wooden floors, and modern art. Some have a TV (by request) and balcony. It rents Suzuki 350 motorcycles and offers motorcycle tours. There's also a small tour desk, plus a bar. Rates include buffet breakfast.

Mesón del Ángel Hotel (Calle 20, Avenidas 3/5, tel. 506/223-7747, fax 506/223-2106, $35 s, $45 d) is a restored two-story, mid-20th-century home with natural stone highlights. The huge lounge with mirrored wall is graced by a hardwood floor and opens to a pleasing dining room and garden courtyard with outside lounging areas. The 21 rooms (some spacious and with floor-to-ceiling windows onto the courtyard) feature tall ceilings, modest but pleasing furnishings, cable TV, security box, and private bathroom. Rooms facing the street get traffic noise. It offers parking and Internet. Rates include breakfast and tax.

The rambling **Hotel Cacts** (Apdo. 379, San José 1005, Avenida 3 bis, Calles 28/30, tel. 506/221-2928, fax 506/221-8616, hcacts@racsa .co.cr, www.tourism.co.cr/hotels/cacts, $37 s, $42 d standard, $47 s, $59 d superior) offers 33 nonsmoking rooms, all with telephone and cable TV, plus private bath with hot water. Some rooms in the new extension are a bit dark and have small bathrooms, although all are kept sparklingly clean. Meals are served refectory style in a rooftop bar-restaurant. It offers a tour agency, provides airport pick-up, and has secure parking plus a swimming pool. Rates include breakfast.

The **Hotel Ambassador** (P.O. Box 10186, San José 1000, Paseo Colón, Calles 26/28, tel. 506/221-8155, fax 506/255-3396, info@hotel ambassador.co.cr, www.hotelambassador.com; in North America, tel. 800/709-2806; $40 s, $45 d standard, $55 s/d junior suite, $85 suite) offers a good location within a 20-minute walk of both the city center and Sabana Park. The 74 a/c rooms are clean and spacious and have minibars, safes, and cable TVs. Amenities include a restaurant, a coffee shop, and a bar with dance floor. Rates include continental breakfast.

Also see **Classic Hotel B&B,** in the Under $25 section above.

East of Downtown

Bamboo and rattan abounds in the **Ara Macao Inn** (Calle 27, Avenidas Central/2, tel. 506/233-2742, fax 506/257-6228, aramacao@hotels.co.cr, www.hotels.co.cr/aramacao.htm; in the U.S., SJO 2290, P.O. Box 025216, Miami, FL 33102-5216; $35 s, $43 d standard, $39 s, $47 d suite low season, $40 s, $50 d standard, $45 s, $55 d suite high season), a recently restored early-20th-century house in Barrio La California. The four sun-filled standards and seven suites have polished hardwood floors, ceiling fans, cable TV, and radios. Some are compact, pleasantly furnished apartments; "suites" have coffee-makers, refrigerators, and microwaves. Rates include tax and breakfast served in a breeze-swept patio corridor.

Readers rave about **M Kap's Place** (Calle 19, Avenidas 11/13, tel. 506/221-1169, fax 506/256-4850, isabel@racsa.co.cr, www.kapsplace.com, $18–28 s, $30 d low season, $25–35 s, $55 d high season), a charming guesthouse with 11 rooms and a fully furnished apartment with kitchen on a tranquil street in Barrio Aranjuez, a 20-minute walk from downtown. All rooms are spic-and-span and beautifully decorated in lively colors, and have cable TV and telephones. Two rooms share a bathroom; two other small rooms are for one person only; one is next to the laundry and has no phone. The rooms and apartment ($50) open to a lovely covered patio with lots of sunlight, and hammocks for enjoying an afternoon siesta. No meals are served, but guests have kitchen privileges. It's run by Karla Arias, an erudite Tica and single mom, who goes out of her way to please guests. She speaks fluent English and French. A 10 percent surcharge applies if paying with credit card. guests at night permitted.

Across the street, the intimate **Hotel Aranjuez** (Apdo. 457, San José 2070, Calle 19, Avenidas 11/13, tel. 506/256-1825 or 506/223-3559, fax 506/223-3528, info@aranjuez.com) has 23 eclectically decorated rooms with cable TV, phones, and hair dryers. It's formed of four contiguous houses, each with its own personality. It was closed for complete refurbishment at last visit.

Hotel y Restaurante Casa Las Orquideas (P.O. Box 1101-2050, San José, tel. 506/283-0095, fax 506/234-8203, casaorquideas@yahoo.com, $12 pp dorm, $35 s, $45 d standard, $80 s/d junior suite), on Avenida Central in Los Yoses, is an attractive option done up in pea-green and tropical murals. The 11 rooms have tile floors and New Mexico–style bedspreads. Upstairs rooms have more light plus king-size beds. One room is a dorm with 10 beds. There's a small yet elegant restaurant, plus secure parking.

$50–100

Downtown
Posada y Café de Museo (Avenida 2, Calle 17, tel. 506/257-9414 or 506/258-1027, juanrey17@hotmail.com, $70 s/d, $100 suite), cater-corner to the Museo Nacional, is a recent conversion of the former 1930-era mansion of the head of the Banco Nacional. It has six rooms (four more are planned) with hardwood ceilings, hardwood and colonial tile floors, and clean modern bathrooms with hot water. Individually styled rooms are modestly yet nicely furnished, with wrought-iron beds, cable TV, Internet hookups, and lots of light. A suite has a large walk-in shower and hefty hardwood furnishings. There's a breakfast room and an art gallery, plus a delightful streetside café. The intellectual Argentinian owners are a delight.

The **Hotel Europa** (Apdo. 72, San José 1000, Calle Central, Avenidas 3/5, tel. 506/222-1222, fax 506/221-3976, europa@racsa.co.cr; in North America, tel. 800/222-7692; $52 s, $58 d) has 72 spacious, paneled, a/c rooms, and two suites with more elegant tones. All have cable TVs, direct-dial telephones, and safes, although the hotel remains frumpy. Four larger "deluxe" rooms have wide balconies at no extra cost. Avoid lower-floor rooms facing onto the noisy street (quieter, inner-facing rooms are more expensive). The tiny pool is for dipping only. The hotel restaurant and efficient service make amends. Rates include breakfast and tax.

The **Gran Hotel** (Apdo. 527, San José 1000, Avenida 2, Calle 3, tel. 506/221-4000, fax 506/221-3501, granncr@racsa.co.cr, www.calypsotours.com, $38 s, $45 d; $80 s, $95 d suites), dating from 1899, has 105 a/c modestly furnished rooms of varying sizes. All have telephones and cable TVs, plus bright art, and older

© CHRISTOPHER P. BAKER

Gran Hotel

tiled baths. Rooms facing the plaza can be noisy. Junior suites are elegant. It has an unsophisticated but lively casino on the ground floor, plus a tour desk, gift shop, and the basement Bufo Dorado Restaurant. The Gran enjoys a superb position in front of the Teatro Nacional, where the hotel's 24-hour Café Parisienne is a favorite hangout for Costa Rica's motley gringo residents.

Another steps-to-everything option is the **Hotel Balmoral** (Apdo. 3344, San José 1000, Avenida Central, Calles 7/9, tel. 506/222-5022, fax 506/221-7826, info@balmoral.co.cr, www .balmoral.co.cr; in the U.S., tel. 800/691-4865; $60–90 s, $70–95 d, $120 s, $125 s suites), one block east of Plaza de la Cultura. The Balmoral offers 120 a/c rooms and four suites with moss-green carpeting, dark wood furniture, cable TVs, and safety deposit boxes. However, rooms are small, bathrooms are very small, and walls are so thin you can hear your next-door neighbor brushing his/her teeth. A sauna and mini-gym, a restaurant and casino, and tour desk and car rental agencies are on the ground floor. It has secure parking. Rates include breakfast.

Opposite the Balmoral on Avenida Central is the **Hotel Presidente** (Apdo. 2922, San José 1000, tel. 506/222-3022, fax 506/221-1205, info@hotel-presidente.com, www.hotel-presidente.com, $60 s, $70 d low season, $65 s, $75 d high season), with 110 a/c rooms, each with a direct-dial telephone and cable TV. Some have a safety-deposit box. The spacious rooms are pleasantly furnished with an understated contemporary elegance. The hotel has a rooftop Jacuzzi and sauna, a casino, and a bar, plus a wonderful street-front restaurant and café. It also has junior suites ($105 s/d) and suites ($129 s/d). Rates include breakfast.

The 24-room **Britannia Hotel** (Calle 3, Avenida 11, tel. 506/223-6667, fax 506/223-6411, britania@sol.racsa.co.cr; in North America, tel. 800/263-2618; $77 s, $89 d standard, $93 s, $105 d deluxe; $106 s, $117 d junior suite) is a neoclassical Victorian-style mansion built in 1910 in Barrio Amón. The five deluxe rooms and five junior suites in the old house boast high ceilings, stained glass, arches, ceiling fans, mosaic tile floors, and English-style furniture. A new

block has 13 standard rooms, all with cable TVs, telephones, safety-deposit boxes, a king-size or two twin beds, plus a private bathroom with tub. The boutique hotel features "tropical courtyards," a restaurant converted from the old cellar, a coffee shop, and room service.

Nearby is the **Hotel Del Rey** (Avenida 1, Calle 9, tel. 506/257-7800, fax 506/221-0096, info @hoteldelrey.com, www.hoteldelrey.com; in the U.S., tel. 888/972-7272; $55 s, $68 d standard, $85 s/d deluxe; $135 suites), a renovated neoclassical building long on history (many of the bullet holes on the face of the Bellavista Fortress were fired from this building in the 1948 revolution). The five-story, 104-room structure is a National Heritage Treasure. Seventeen rooms are deluxe (five with balconies); all rooms, which range from singles to suites for six people, are large, carpeted, and come with king-size beds, cable TV, and handcrafted wooden doors with electronic locks. Those facing the street can be noisy. The Del Rey boasts a boisterous 24-hour casino, 24-hour café/restaurant, full-menu room service, a gift shop, and a sportfishing desk and travel agency. It's run by an English diamond in the rough, Timothy Johnson. The Blue Marlin Bar has a salacious edge. There's secure parking.

The yin to the Del Rey's yang is the U.S.-run **Hotel Santo Tomás** (Avenida 7, Calles 3/5, tel. 506/255-0448, fax 506/222-3950, info@hotelsantotomas.com, www.hotelsantotomas.com, $55 s, $65 d standard, $65 s, $72 superior, $80–90 s/d deluxe), an intimate bed-and-breakfast with 20 nonsmoking rooms in an elegant turn-of-the-century plantation home built from mahogany. The high vaulted ceiling and original hardwood and colonial tile floors are impressive. Rooms vary (some are huge), but all have cable TV and direct-dial phones, queen-size beds with orthopedic mattresses, antique reproduction furniture, throw rugs, and watercolors. There are three separate TV lounges and a full-service tour planning service, library, gift store, and Internet access. Laundry service available. The all-male staff is bilingual. No guests at night. The gracious garden features the delightful Restaurant El Oasis and a solar-heated swimming pool, a Jacuzzi, and water slide and cascade. Rates include breakfast.

Parque Morazán with Hotel del Rey in background

For atmosphere, try the **Hotel Don Carlos** (Calle 9 bis, Avenidas 7/9, tel. 506/221-6707, fax 506/255-0828, hotel@doncarloshotel.com, www. doncarlos.co.cr; in the U.S., SJO 1686, P.O. Box 025216, Miami, FL 33102-5216; $55 s, $65 d standard, $65 s, $75 d superior). Founded by pre-Columbian art expert Don Carlos Balser in an aged colonial-style mansion, the homey, well-run hotel is replete with Sarchí oxcarts and archaeological treasures. Magnificent wrought-iron work, stained-glass windows, stunning art, and bronze sculptures abound—one wall is covered with 272 hand-painted tiles showing San José at the turn of the century. The 36 rooms and suites have been refurbished and upgraded, and the noise of passing vehicles—once a problem—has abated since traffic was rerouted. Colonial rooms are at the back, reached by a rambling courtyard. All rooms have cable TVs, safes, and hair dryers. It has a superb gift shop and there's a full tour service, live marimba music, small gym, sun deck with water cascade and dipping pool, plus an espresso bar, and a restaurant lit by an atrium skylight. It offers free Internet service. Rates include continental breakfast, welcome cocktail, and English-language newspaper.

La Casa Morazán (Calle 7, Avenidas 7/9, tel. 506/257-4187, fax 506/257-4175, anakeith @sol.racsa.co.cr, www.casamorazan.com, $35 s, $45 d low season; $45 s, $55 d high season) is set in a colonial mansion and boasts antique furnishings and modern art, plus original (rather stained) tile floors. The 11 a/c rooms all have cable TV, old-style telephones, large bathrooms, and 1950s furniture. Dowdy, yet possessing its own charm. Breakfast and lunch are served on a small patio. The cook will prepare dinner upon request. Rates include breakfast.

A newcomer, **Hotel Castillo B&B** (Avenida 9, Calle 9, tel. 506/222-3769, fax 506/221-6431, hotelcastillo@racsa.co.cr, www.hotelcastillo.biz, $40 s, $50 d standard, $50/60 superior, $60/70 deluxe) is a cheap conversion of a 1900-era three-story colonial home. It has modern tile floors and is modestly furnished in uninspired fashion. The 12 rooms have almond-wood floors, teak ceilings, and security boxes; some rooms lack windows. The Ambassador Suite has a kitchenette and Roman-style bathtub. Ten more rooms with kitchenettes were to be added. There's Internet access, plus a billiards room with pool table open to a shaded open-air restaurant. The hotel is less upscale than its brochure suggests.

Taylor's Inn (Avenida 13, Calles 13/15, tel. 506/257-4333, fax 506/221-1475, taylor @catours.co.cr, $38 s, $46 d) has nine nonsmoking rooms with cable TV and private bath with hot water. Note the pretty ceramic tiles on the exterior of this 1908 property, and the modern art within. Rates include "tropical" breakfast served in a breezy, skylit courtyard.

Another good option is the Swiss-owned and -operated **Hotel Fleur de Lys** (Calle 13, Avenidas 2/4, tel. 506/223-1206, fax 506/257-3637, florlys@racsa.co.cr, www.hotelfleurdelys.com, $60 s, $70 d standard, $85 junior suite low season, $68 s, $78 d standard, $93 junior suite high season). This marvelously restored mansion offers 31 individually styled rooms, each named for a species of flower. All have sponge-washed pastel walls, tasteful artwork, phones, cable TVs, hair dryers, and wrought-iron or wicker beds with crisp linens. A wood-paneled restaurant serves Italian cuisine, and live music is offered twice weekly in the bar. There's a tour desk and on-site parking. Its enviable location, one block from the National Museum, is a plus. It also has suites ($100–130 low season, $108–135 high season) Rates include breakfast.

The popular **Dunn Inn** (Calle 5, Avenida 11, tel. 506/222-3232, fax 506/221-4596, willpa @sol.racsa.co.cr, www.dunninn.com, $34–45 s/d, $54 suite), in a restored 19th-century home, is operated by Texan Patrick Dunn. Rooms— 13 in the original Spanish-colonial home, 17 in a newer addition—are simple and small but clean, and have cable TV and telephone. Some have a refrigerator. Older brick-lined rooms downstairs have atmosphere, albeit little light. The suite has a Jacuzzi bathtub. The hotel features a hot tub and a skylit patio restaurant lush with greenery. There's a barbershop on site.

The modern **Hotel Villa Tournon** (Apdo. 6606, San José 1000, 200 meters west of El Pueblo, tel. 506/233-6622 or 800/771-5185, fax 506/222-5211, hvillas@racsa.co.cr, www .costarica-hotelvillatournon.com, $71 s, $76 d standard; $82 s, $87 d superior; $96 s, $102 d suite), in Barrio Tournón, 200 meters from El Pueblo, is brimful of contemporary art and sculpture and is a favorite of North American tourists. The 80 mammoth a/c rooms are graciously appointed in autumnal colors with wood furnishings and leather chairs. The restaurant, centered on a massive brick hearth, offers fireside dining. There's a piano bar, and a swimming pool (fed by a cascade from the whirlpool above) in a splendidly decorated garden. Ask for rooms off the street. It offers free Internet and secure parking.

The **Raya Vida Villa** (Apdo. 2209-2100, San José, tel. 506/223-4168, fax 506/223-4157, rayavida@costarica.net, www.rayavida.com; in the U.S., P.O. Box 025216-1638, Miami, FL 33102-5216; $60 s, $80 d low season, $75 s, $95 d high season) is a lovely and lovingly restored two-story antebellum-style (Pre-1860) mansion tucked in a cul-de-sac in Barrio Otoya, behind the tall black gate at the end of Avenida 11 and Calle 17. The live-in owner, Michael Long, rents four rooms, each delightfully done up in individual decor: the Pineapple Room, ideal for honeymooners, has a four-poster bed; the Mask Room features masks from around the world; another room has a king-size bed and limestone floor and opens to a shaded patio with fountain. There's an exquisite TV lounge and reading room with fireplace and chandeliers, plus a TV den, although all rooms have cable TV plus fans. The place is secluded and peaceful and festooned with original artwork, including Toulouse-Lautrec and Salvador Dalí. Rates include full breakfast and airport pickup.

The **Hotel La Gran Vía** (Apdo. 4450, San José 1000, Avenida Central, Calles 1/3, tel. 506/222-7313, fax 506/222-7205, hgranvia @sol.racsa.co.cr, www.granvia.co.cr, $50 s, $65 d) has 32 pleasingly decorated rooms with twin double beds, TV, and safety-deposit box. Some have a/c. Those with balconies overlooking the street can be noisy; inside rooms are quieter. There is a restaurant and coffee shop. Rates include taxes.

Hotel Alóki (Calle 13, Avenida 11, tel. 506/222-6702, fax 506/223-1598; in the U.S., Interlink 610, P.O. Box 025635, Miami, FL

33102, tel. 770/660-1503), in the historic Barrio Otoya district, offers a tranquil setting a stone's throw from downtown. It was closed for restoration under new owners at last visit, and rates had yet to be announced.

Nearby, the 25-room **Hotel Edelweiss** (Avenida 9, Calles 13/15, tel. 506/221-9702 or 506/823-2534, fax 506/222-1241, edelweiss @sol.racsa.co.cr, www.edelweisshotel.com) has been acquired by new owners who were renovating at last visit.

West of Downtown

The **N Hotel Restaurante Grano de Oro** (P.O. Box 1157-1007, San José, Calle 30, Avenida 2, tel. 506/255-3322, fax 506/221-2782, granoro @racsa.co.cr, www.hotelgranodeoro.com $80 s, $85 d standard, $100 s, $105 d superior, $110 s, $120 d deluxe, $145–245 s/d suites), is undisputably the city's finest hotel and my hotel of preference whenever I stay in San José. The guestbook is a compendium of compliments. "What charm! What comfort!"… "The best hotel we've stayed in-ever!"… "We would love to keep it a secret, but we promise we won't." A member of the Small Distinctive Hotels of Costa Rica, the gracious turn-of-the-century mansion, in a quiet residential neighborhood off Paseo Colón, proves that a fine house, like a jewel, is made complete by its setting. Congenial hosts Eldon and Lori Cooke have overseen the creation of a real home away from home in traditional old-world Costa Rican style. In the 36 faultlessly decorated guestrooms (five more were to be added), orthopedic mattresses guarantee contented slumber beneath sturdy beamed ceilings. Each is done up in a tasteful combination of soft grays and regal maroons or deep blues; black rattan and handcrafted iron furniture; Costa Rica fine and folk art on the walls; and king-size canopied beds in some rooms. Gleaming hardwood floors add to the sense of elegant refinement. Cable TV and direct-dial telephones are standard. Extravagant bathrooms are adorned with hand-painted colonial tiles, brass fittings, fluffy towels, torrents of piping-hot water, and cavernous showers and/or deep bathtubs. A downstairs suite features mahogany wall panels, Jacuzzi bathtub, and French doors that open onto a private garden. And the rooftop wood-paneled Vista de Oro suite has a plate-glass window running the full width of one wall, providing views of three volcanoes; it also offers an elevated Jacuzzi, a king-size bed, and regal decor that includes colonial tilework, classical statuary, oriental throw rugs, and sofas lushly decorated in Turkish fabrics. Soothing classical and Spanish guitar music and the sound of trickling water from a fountain in the bromeliad-filled patio waft through the hallways, lounge, and courtyard restaurant lush with foliage. The restaurant—which was due to be expanded at last visit, raising the ante on the competition with an elegant new look—could well be San José's finest. There's a well-stocked gift shop and a rooftop solarium with two Jacuzzis. No request is too much for the mustard-keen, English-speaking, ever-smiling staff.

The **Hotel Rosa del Paseo** (Apdo. 287, San José 1007, Paseo Colón, Calles 28/30, tel. 506/257-3213, fax 506/223-2776, rosadelp @racsa.co.cr, www.online.co.cr/rosa; in the U.S., 2011 N.W. 79th Ave., SJO 1162, Miami, FL 33122; $55 s, $65 d standard, $75 junior suite low season; $60 s, $70 d standard, $85 junior suite high season) has 18 nicely decorated rooms plus one suite in a century-old residence on Paseo Colón. Architectural details combine parquet and tile floors, original artwork, and art-nouveau flourishes with "Victorian Caribbean." All rooms have handsome modern decor, cable TV, safes, and ceiling fans, plus white-tiled private bathrooms with hot water. A master suite has a large Jacuzzi tub, and there's a garden courtyard. It was looking a bit jaded at last visit. Secure parking. Rates include breakfast.

The **Quality Hotel Centro Colón** (Apdo. 433, San José 1007, Avenida 3, Calle 38, tel. 506/257-2580, fax 506/257-2582, info@hotel centrocolon.com, www.hotelcentrocolon.com, $75 s/d standard, $82 superior, $90 junior suite) is in one of the two towers of the Centro Colón complex. The 126 carpeted, a/c rooms (including 42 suites) are "extra-large" and come with cable TVs, safety-deposit boxes, hair dryers, and telephones, plus king-size beds. Some rooms have excellent volcano views. An executive floor offers

Internet links. There's also a business center, restaurant, casino, and a nightclub/bar done up in dazzling eye-popping pink and neon!

The delightful **Hotel Occidental Torremolinos** (Apdo. 114-1107, San José 2000, Avenida 5, Calle 40, tel. 506/222-5266, fax 506/255-3167, torremolinos@racsa.co.cr, www.occidental-hoteles .com, $55 s/d standard, $70 suite low season; $81 s/d standard, $105 suites high season) is entered via a classically elegant lounge and bar opening to a lush garden with shade umbrellas and a pool. Its 84 rooms in contemporary style are modest in size but handsomely furnished, with lots of hardwoods. All have cable TVs, carpeting, alarm clock radios, direct-dial telephones, and hair dryers. Suites have glassed-in balconies. It offers a pool and a Jacuzzi, plus a courtesy bus to downtown and car rental service. The beautiful restaurant El Quijote has hints of Italian and Japanese decor. Rates include breakfast.

Nearby, **Barceló Parque del Lago** (Apdo. 624, San José 1007, Avenida 2, Calles 40/ 42, tel. 506/257-8787, fax 506/223-1617, parquedellago@barcelo.com, www.barcelo.com, $80 s/d standard, $90 junior suite, $115 penthouse suite) is a modern four-story hotel with 40 exquisitely decorated, a/c rooms, plus suites with kitchenettes, all with a maroon-and-green color scheme. Woods, ceramics, plants, and Costa Rican artworks combine to create a nostalgic ambience. Sound-insulated windows, cable TV, direct-dial phone with fax, minibar, coffeemaker, and hair dryer are standard. Suites have kitchenettes. There's a restaurant and bar. The public areas have original colonial tile.

In a similar vein is the stylish **Palma Real** (Apdo. 694-1005, San José, tel. 506/290-5060, fax 506/232-9085, reservas@hotelpalmareal.com, www.hotelpalmareal.com, $86 s, $96 d standard, $106 s, $116 d suite), in a quiet residential area 200 meters north of the ICE in Sabana Norte. This upscale, contemporary boutique hotel, full of marble and autumnal colors, draws a business clientele. It features 65 carpeted, tastefully decorated a/c rooms, with minibars, bathtubs, cable TVs, telephones, huge windows, orthopedic mattresses, and hair dryers in the well-lit marble-lined bathrooms. Two suites have king-size beds and Jacuzzi bathtubs. There's a state-of-the-art gym and a large open-air Jacuzzi, plus a business center, a bar, and elegant restaurant.

The **Barceló Rincón del Valle** (Apdo. 422-1007, San José, tel. 506/231-4927, fax 506/231-5924, rincondelvalle@barcelo.com, www.barcelo .com, $47 s, $51 d standard, $71 s, $82 d superior, $82 s, $93 d junior suite), on the south side of Sabana Park, is a small contempo stunner done up in polished hardwoods, maroons, black, and deep sea greens. The lively decor blends modern with traditional styles. It has 20 carpeted rooms with cable TVs, hair dryers, telephones, and safety-deposit boxes. Some rooms are a bit dingy. There's a 24-hour café, plus restaurant and laundry, and guests have use of nearby tennis courts and swimming pool. Rates include breakfast.

You don't have to be a member or even a tennis fan to check into the **Hotel Tennis Club** (P.O. Box 595-4005, San José, tel. 506/232-1266, fax 506/232-3867, crtennis@racsa.co.cr, $40 s, $50 d standard, $60 s/d superior low season; $45 s, $55 d standard, $70 s/d superior high season), on the south side of Sabana Park. The 27 spacious a/c rooms, each with king-size bed, cable TV, and pleasing bathroom, are complemented by 11 tennis courts, a gym, pool, spa, and sauna. Superior rooms also have minibars and balconies. Hotel guests get free use of sports facilities. Some rooms have kitchenettes. Secure parking; child care includes a children's playground.

The small, family run **Hotel Sabana B&B** (Apdo. 91-1200 Pavas, San José, tel. 506/296-3751, fax 506/232-2876, info@costaricabb.com, www.costaricabb.com, $50 s, $60 d low season; $60 s, $70 d high season), on the north side of Sabana, offers four simple yet cozy rooms with parquet floors, fans, 72-channel cable TVs, and private baths with hot water. Internet and email service is offered, and there's a tour desk, a kitchenette, free tea and coffee, and a terrace and garden. Rates include airport pickup and breakfast.

For self-catering, **Apartotel La Sabana** (P.O. Box 11400-1000 San José, tel. 506/220-2422, fax 506/231-7386, info@apartotel-lasabana .com, www.apartotel-lasabana.com, $45–79 low season, $59–87 high season), on the north side of Sabana Park, has elegantly furnished a/c rooms and apartments with cable TV and telephone, plus a pool and sauna. Rooms vary in size, from doubles to large units for six people. Rates include breakfast.

Nearby, **Apartotel Cristina** (tel. 506/220-0453, fax 506/220-2096, apartcrit@racsa.co.cr, www.apartotelcristina.com, $55 s, $68 d standard, $110 s/d junior suite), 300 meters north of ICE, has 42 modestly furnished one-, two-, and three-bedroom apartments in contemporary vogue; all have cable TVs, security boxes, and kitchens. It has a pool and secure parking.

On the south side of the park is the **Apartotel El Sesteo** (P.O. Box 1205-1007, San José, tel. 296-1805, fax 296-1865, sesteo@racsa.co.cr, www.sesteo.com, $39 rooms, $47/75 one-/two-bedroom units low season; $47 and $55/85 high season), 200 meters south of McDonald's and centered on a beautiful garden with pool. It has 36 simple yet clean, well-maintained one- and two-bedroom units. Twenty feature a kitchen and dining and living areas; the other 16 are hotel-style rooms. All have cable TV and direct-dial telephone. It offers a Jacuzzi, laundry, and secure parking. Rates include continental breakfast.

East of Downtown

Hotel Posada del Este (Avenida 8, Calle 37, tel. 506/283-0101, fax 506/225-3516, yoses @costaricainn.com, www.costaricainn.com, $45 s, $55 d) is a splendid 1950s-style home (once the former Dutch embassy) with a Frank Lloyd Wright feel. It is entered via a marvelous lounge with wall-to-wall and floor-to-ceiling windows overlooking a back garden in need of landscaping at last visit. It offers 12 rooms with hardwood furnishings, cable TV, telephones, security box, and modern bathrooms with hot showers. Alas, the dowdy furnishings (cheap carpeting, ho-hum furniture) don't live up to the home's potential. Rates include full breakfast.

The **Hotel Don Fadrique** (Apdo. 1754-2050, San José, Calle 37, Avenida 8, tel. 506/225-8186, fax 506/224-9746, info@hoteldonfadrique.com, www.hoteldonfadrique.com, $50 s, $60 d low season; $60 s, $70 d high season) claims 20 "lux-uriously furnished rooms" and "lush tropical gardens." The rooms are decorated in tropical pastels (some have Guatemalan bedspreads), with original modern art on the walls (the entire place, in fact, is festooned with contemporary art). Each has parquet wood or tile floor, telephone, cable TV, safety-deposit box, and fan. Take an upstairs room, with heaps of light. There's a lounge with lush sofas, and a charming patio where you can enjoy breakfast beneath the shade of a mango tree. Rates include full breakfast.

L'Hôtel Le Bergerac (Apdo. 1107, San José 1002, Calle 35, Avenida Central, tel. 506/234-7850, fax 506/225-9103, info@bergerac.co.cr, www.bergerachotel.com, $58 s, $68 d standard, $75 s, $85 d superior, $85 s, $95 d deluxe) is a pretty colonial home in Los Yoses on Calle 35, 50 meters south of Avenida Central, with views south toward the Cordillera Talamanca. Exuding French influence, Le Bergerac is a full-service hotel with a deep maroon/rust and gray color scheme and the feel of a bed-and-breakfast. Service is discreet. The hotel has 19 rooms in three buildings (five in the original home, reached via a sweeping spiral staircase), all with cable TVs, direct-dial telephones, Internet access, and safes, plus hardwood floors and classical furniture. Rooms vary in size, and some have bidets and their own patio gardens. It boasts a gourmet restaurant serving recherché French cuisine, along with *bocas* and drinks in the evening. It has secure parking, a travel agency, and a sequestered conference room. Rates include full breakfast.

Hotel Milvia (Apdo. 1660, San Pedro 2050, tel. 506/225-4543, fax 506/225-7801, hmilvia @novanet.co.cr, www.hotelmilvia.com; in the U.S., Costa Rica Connection, 975 Osos St., San Luis Obispo, CA 93401, tel. 805/543-8823 or 800/345-7422, fax 805/543-3626, john @crconnect.com; $70 s, $76 d) offers a discreet charm, with four rooms upstairs in the restored turn-of-the-century wooden home, plus five downstairs rooms in a contemporary add-on built around a tiny garden courtyard (noise from adjoining rooms can be a problem). Hardwood floors glisten downstairs; rooms upstairs are carpeted. The spacious, individually styled rooms are modestly furnished. Bathrooms feature hand-painted decorative tiles. Fans and phones are standard. There's a dining room, lounge with TV and VCR, and boutique. Upstairs, a terrace provides views over the garden full of bright yellow lirios. Follow Avenida Central east from San José, turn left 100 meters beyond Centro Comercial M&N in San Pedro (you'll see the hotel signed here), then take the first right. Rates include taxes and continental breakfast.

The **Hotel 1492** (P.O. Box 4988-1000 San José, Avenida 1 #2985, Calles 31/33, tel. 506/225-3752, fax 506/280-6206, jade@cool .co.cr, www.hotel1492.com, $60 s, $70 d standard, $80 s/d junior suite), in the quiet residential neighborhood of Barrio Escalante, is a beautiful little colonial-style residence boasting 10 simply yet handsomely appointed rooms (three are junior suites). Each room has hardwood floors, private bath, hot water, ceiling fan, telephone, and cable TV. Exquisite *rejas* (turned wooden grills) and tile abound, including in the bathrooms. Most rooms have windows that open to small gardens, and there's a patio garden done up in Tico fashion where a happy hour of wine and cheese is hosted nightly. The handsome lounge has a soaring ceiling and fireplace, the original tile floor, and ceramic mosaics in the walls. Rates include Tico breakfast.

A classy option is the low-rise **Boutique Hotel Jade** (tel. 506/283-2239, fax 506/224-2166, amehotel@racsa.co.cr, www.hotelboutiquejade .com, $83 s, $97 d, $115 suite), in the Barrio Dent district of San Pedro, 300 meters north of the Subaru dealership. It has 29 spacious, carpeted, executive-style rooms with rich and lively decor, handsome fittings, ceiling fans, cable TVs, desks, phones, modems, minibars, plus vanity chairs and sofa, and spacious showers. Six are handicapped equipped, and there are some nonsmoking rooms. Junior suites are truly classy. Murals adorn the corridor walls. There's a small lounge, plus a rear garden with a beautiful swimming pool and fountain, and a café. The highlight, however, is the sophisticated Jürgen's Grill, and there's a cafeteria, gift store, and a brick patio with lap pool.

The **Apartotel Los Yoses** (Apdo. 1597-1000, San José, tel. 506/225-0033, fax 506/225-5595, losyoses@apartotel.com, www.apartotel.com, from $35 s, $45 d), 25 meters east of the Pollos Kentucky, has 23 rooms, swimming pool, free parking, and daily housekeeping.

Farther Afield

The **Best Western Irazú** (Autopista General Cañas, 100 meters south of Centro Comercial San José 2000, tel. 506/232-4811, fax 506/231-6485, bwireservas@grupomarta.com, www .bestwesterncostarica.com; in the U.S., tel. 800/528-1234; in Canada, tel. 800/463-6654; $79 s, $89 d standard, $103 s, $113 d premium) has 350 rooms, including a nonsmoking floor. Most rooms have a balcony overlooking the pool or gardens, plus direct-dial telephone, cable TV, iron and ironing board, and a/c. The hotel features all the amenities of a deluxe property: tennis courts, sauna, swimming pool, restaurant, Costa Rica's largest casino, plus a small shopping mall. It is popular for tour groups. Its out-of-the-way location has little to recommend it, although there's an hourly shuttle bus to downtown.

Casa Conde Apartotel & Suites (tel. 506/226-0808, fax 506/226-1554, www.hotelcasaconde.com, $90 s/d), south of Parque de la Paz, in Desamparados, provides some of the most upscale apartments in town. Each of the 110 graciously furnished deluxe units has a large, modern kitchen. There's an elegant restaurant, a pool, and secure parking.

$100–150
Downtown

Dominating the downtown skyline is the sophisticated **Hotel Aurola Holiday Inn** (P.O. Box 7802-1000, San José, Avenida 5, Calle 5, tel. 506/222-2424, fax 506/255-1171, reservas @aurola-holidays.com, www.aurola-holidayinn .com; in the U.S., tel. 800/465-4329; $125 s/d, $150 junior suite, $250 suite). The modern highrise overlooking Parque Morazán offers 201 a/c rooms featuring regal furnishing, cable TVs, minibars, safes, coffee-makers, work desks, and irons. The 11th floor is smoke-free, an executive floor caters to business travelers, and one room is wheelchair accessible. Topping off the hotel's attractions is the *mirador* restaurant on the 17th floor, adjacent to the casino. The hotel contains a gym, sauna, and indoor pool. However, Gregg Calkin describes it as "a giant hermetically sealed container with windows that don't open."

The handsome **Hotel Amón Plaza** (Apdo. 4192-1000, San José, Avenida 11, Calle 3 bis, tel. 506/257-0191, fax 506/257-0284, ventas @hotelamonplaza.com, www.hotelamonplaza.com, $110 s, $120 d standard, $135 s, $145 d junior suite, $165 s, $175 d deluxe suite, $215 s, $225 d master suite), in the historic Barrio Amón area downtown and newly under the wing of the Barceló chain, is a modern four-story, "neo-Victorian" hotel with 90 rooms, including 24 junior and six deluxe suites. Rooms have a/c, telephones, cable TVs, coffee-makers, safety-deposit boxes, and hair dryers. An unusually elegant marble lobby decorated with artwork hints at the upscale decor throughout. It features an office center with computers, plus conference center, spa and solarium, casino, disco, and underground parking. The Danubio Restaurante is *muy elegante.*

The business-oriented **Radisson Europa Hotel & Conference Center** (Apdo. 538-2120, San José, Calle 3, Avenida 15, tel. 506/257-3257, fax 506/257-8221, eurohot@sol.racsa .co.cr; in North America, tel. 800/333-3333; $130 s, $140 d) is a thoroughly modern five-star hotel with 107 "superior" rooms, six executive suites, and one presidential suite, all with a/c, 24-hour room service, direct-dial telephones, cable TVs, minibars, and safes. It has a restaurant, café, and bar, plus a full-serve business center. It also offers a pool and spa with Jacuzzi, plus a small gym, an art gallery and shops, and the inevitable casino.

West of Downtown

Looking a little like a set from *Star Trek* is the **Tryp Corobicí** (P.O. Box 2443-1000, San José, tel. 506/232-8122, fax 506/231-5834, trypcorobici@sol.melia.com, www.solmelia.com, $120 s/d standard, $130 junior suite, $125 executive suite, $170 suite, $215 master suite), on the northeastern corner of Sabana Park. Its angled exterior is ungainly, but its soaring atrium, with its newly added fountain, a surfeit of marble, and tier upon tier of balconies festooned with ferns, is impressive. The 200 spacious rooms and eight suites boast handsome furnishings. All have a/c, safes, minibars, cable TVs, and plenty of closet space. Suites have kitchenettes. Executive rooms have modem ports. It offers a business center, plus a nightclub and casino for those who don't want to wander far at night. There's a 24-hour cafeteria, and an Internet café, plus Italian and Japanese restaurants. The spa and gym are first-rate. There's a courtesy shuttle to downtown.

Farther Afield

The **Barceló San José Palacio** (P.O. Box 458-1150, San José, tel. 506/220-2034, fax 506/220-2036, sanjosepalacio@barcelo.com, www.barcelo .com, $104 s/d standard, $124–139 suites), five km northwest of the city center, has 254 carpeted, a/c rooms with pleasing decor, TVs, phones, minibars, and safes. It offers a large swimming pool, tennis and racquetball courts, health spa and gym, sauna and whirlpool, plus a casino popular with the San José elite. A lively casino and elegant and reasonably priced restaurant are countered by a drab piano bar with adjacent grill. The hotel is out on a limb, one mile north of Sabana Park on the Autopista General Cañas—an awkward location that necessitates a taxi, despite its proximity to Sabana. The hotel charges for its three-times-a-day shuttle to San José.

Also see *Ciudad Cariari and San Antonio de Belén,* in the *Central Highlands* chapter, for information on the **Meliá Confort Cariari Conference Center & Golf Resort,** the **Hotel Herradura Golf Resort & Conference Center,** and the **Costa Rica Marriott Hotel and Resort.**

Food

Recommended restaurants are listed below according to type and location. Don't neglect the many fine hotel restaurants, such as the Hotel y Restaurante Grano de Oro—for my mind, the best restaurant in San José (it is the only restaurant to be given "five forks" for excellence by *La Nacion* for five years straight). Many of the best restaurants can be found in the suburb of Escazú, within a 15-minute drive of San José (see *Escazú* in the *Central Highlands* chapter).

There's no shortage of U.S. fast-food joints and their local equivalents for those who hanker for a taste of back home.

BREAKFAST

Downtown

My preferred option is **La Criollita** (Avenida 7, Calles 7/9, tel. 506/256-6511, 7 A.M.–8 P.M. Mon.–Fri., 7 A.M.–4 P.M. Saturday), a clean and atmospheric favorite of the business crowd. It serves full American breakfasts ($3.50) plus Tico breakfasts ($3), as well as soups, salads, sandwiches, and tempting entrées such as garlic shrimp ($6), roast chicken ($4.50), plus natural juices. You can choose an airy, skylit indoor setting with contemporary decor, or a shaded garden patio with caged birds.

East of Downtown

One of the best spots is **Bagelmon's** (Avenida 2, Calle 33, tel. 506/224-2432, 7 A.M.–9 P.M.), in Barrio La California. The ambience is pleasing, with dark wood paneling and wrought-iron chairs. It serves reuben, tuna, smoked ham, and other sandwiches ($2–5), as well as bagels (onion, pumpernickel, etc.), muffins, brownies, and cinnamon rolls, plus breakfast specials, from *gallo pinto* to scrambled eggs. **Café Ruiseñor** (Avenida Central, Calles 41/43, tel. 506/225-2562, 7 A.M.–7 P.M. Mon.–Sat., noon–5 P.M. Sunday),

© CHRISTOPHER P. BAKER

Hotel Grano de Oro

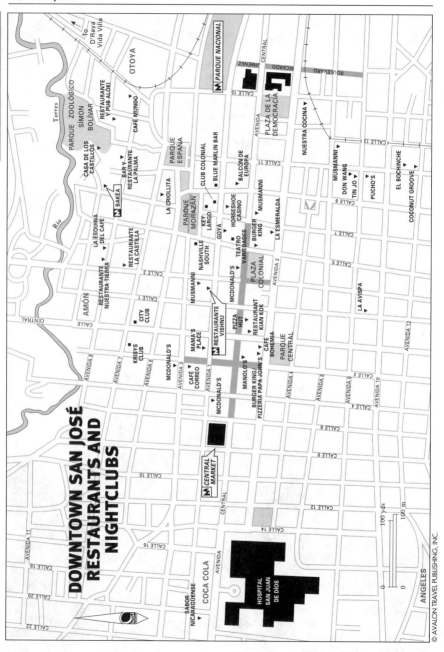

DOWNTOWN SAN JOSÉ
RESTAURANTS AND
NIGHTCLUBS

© AVALON TRAVEL PUBLISHING, INC.

in Los Yoses, does good breakfasts, including a Swiss buffet ($3).

West of Downtown

The **Hotel Grano de Oro** (Calle 30, Avenidas 2/4, tel. 506/255-3322, breakfast 6–11 A.M.) is justifiably popular with both tourists and Tico businessfolk for intimate breakfasts on the outdoor patio. Try the superb gringo or Tico breakfasts (the "Gringo"—a large bowl of granola with bananas, and thick slices of freshly baked whole-wheat toast—should see you through the day).

SODAS

Sodas—cheap snack bars serving typical Costa Rican fare—are a dime a dozen. They serve "working-class" fare, such as tripe soup and rice-and-bean dishes. You can usually fill up for $2–4. They're good for mixing Ticos, notably so at the **Mercado Central** (Avenidas Central/1 and Calles 6/8), which has dozens of inexpensive *sodas*. Closed Sunday.

Downtown

Manolo's (Avenida Central, Calles Central/2, tel. 506/221-2041) is a lively 24-hour bistro with a menu that runs from salads to filet mignon. Try the *churros,* greasy Mexican doughnuts, best enjoyed at the patio open to the pedestrian street. Upstairs you can fill up on sandwiches, seafood, meat dishes, and other fare; the third story is a bit more elegant and double the price. It has a daily special for $2.50.

Another of my favorites is **Mama's Place** (Avenida 1, Calle Central/2, tel. 506/223-2270, 7 A.M.–7 P.M. Mon.–Fri., 7 A.M.–4 P.M. Saturdays), a quintessential mom-and-pop restaurant run by an Italian couple and serving huge portions heavy on the spaghetti. It serves *casados* for $4.50.

West of Downtown

I like **Sabor Nicaragüense** (Calle 20, Avenida Central/1, tel. 506/248-2547, 7 A.M.–9 P.M.), a clean family diner with heaps of light and both indoor and outside dining. It serves *gallo pinto,* roast meats, enchiladas, and Nicaraguan specialties.

COSTA RICAN TRADITIONAL

Downtown

The Centro Comercial El Pueblo, in Barrio Tournón, has several restaurants renowned for traditional Costa Rican fare. **La Cocina de Leña** (tel. 506/256-5353, www.lacocina.co.cr, 11 A.M.–10 P.M. Sun.–Thur., 11 A.M.–11:30 P.M. Fri.–Sat., entrées $10) is one of the best. Here, you'll dine by candlelight, surrounded by the warm ambience of a cozy rural farmhouse. Dishes include Creole chicken, *olla de carne* soup, and square tamales made with white cornmeal, mashed potatoes, and beef, pork, or chicken, wrapped tightly in a plantain leaf. The open-air **Lukas** (tel. 506/233-8145, coretu@racsa.co.cr), in El Pueblo, is a steakhouse with a pleasing aesthetic that stays open until dawn to capture the danced-out patrons of the discos. It serves an executive lunch (noon–3 P.M.) plus such dishes as mixed tacos and *picadillos* (small chopped-vegetable platter), fried pork, mixed meats, and grilled corvina in garlic butter prepared al dente over a large grill.

Roasted chicken and onions are the name of the game at **Nuestra Cocina** (Avenida 2 and Calle 13, tel. 506/222-2137), where you can watch your bird being cooked Tico-style over wood coals. Rustic ambience and tamales, tortillas, and more from a wood-fired stove for less than $4. The old wooden structure is festooned with cloves of garlic and onions.

The **Café Parisienne,** the terrace cafe fronting the Gran Hotel, besides snacks and coffee, serves simple Costa Rican fare—*arroz con pollo* (rice with chicken; $4) and more—at a reasonable price. The hustle and bustle of the *plazuela* out front provides good theater.

The venerable **La Esmeralda** (Avenida 2, Calles 5/7), known for its simple food and mariachis, was closed for a total remodeling at last visit.

NOUVELLE

Downtown

For classy decor head to chic **M Bakéa** (Calle 7, Avenida 1, tel. 506/221-1051, bakea-amon

@terra.com, noon–midnight Tue.–Sat.), which enlivened the dining scene when it opened in 2003. This family-run, tastefully urban hot spot—a conversion of a colonial home retaining its wooden and tile floors—has three small rooms (the "Japanese room" has a glass floor!) and a shaded stone courtyard with Ikea-style metal furnishings and track lighting. Food is presented in artistic fashion but is of hit-and-miss quality. Typical dishes include pumpkin soup with rosemary ($2.75), tilapia with wine and port sauce and braised leeks ($16.50), and sautéed scallops with curry and risotto ($9.50). For desserts, try the tiramisu ($4.50) or homemade ice cream with caramelized figs ($3.25), then espresso or cappuccino.

West of Downtown

I highly recommend the elegant **ⓜ Restaurante Grano de Oro** (Calle 30, Avenidas 2/4, tel. 506/255-3322, 11 A.M.–10 P.M.), where chef Francis Canal has successfully merged Costa Rican into nouvelle. Creative interpretations include poached mahi mahi ($8), tenderloin in green peppercorn sauce ($11), a superb salmon soufflé, and sweet curry chicken sprinkled with coconut ($8). The menu is vast; the prices exceedingly fair. So, too, the specialty cocktails and an array of desserts (you *must* try the sublime Pie Grano de Oro). At last visit, the restaurant was due to be expanded in a new facility with wine cellar, promising even greater delights.

Restaurante Bar Noa (Paseo Colón, Calle 24, tel. 506/221-9570, 7 A.M.–3 P.M. Monday, and 7 A.M.–2 A.M. Tue.–Sun.) specializes in gourmet seafoods and steaks and offers a lunchtime "executive menu" ($3). It doubles as an art gallery and offers live jazz.

I also love dining at **Jürgen's Grill** (tel. 506/283-2239, noon–2:30 P.M. and 6–10:30 P.M. Mon.–Fri., 6–11 P.M. Saturday), in the Boutique Hotel Jade in San Pedro, east of downtown. It has a marvelous aesthetic, with wood-beamed ceiling, bold reds, heavy drapes, oriental rugs, and contemporary art. It serves such nouvelle treats as gazpacho ($4.25), mussels Rockefeller ($11.50), toast Winston (pork beef with white wine sauce, mushrooms, and cheese with salad; $8), shrimp gratin with camembert and jelly ($20), and tilapia with mustard ($12). A bar and cigar lounge offer postprandial pleasure. It has a dress code, soothing music, and exemplary service.

Another hot spot is **El Fogoncito** (Avenida Central and Calle 4, San Pedro, tel. 506/280-0002, 11 A.M.–1 A.M. Sun.–Thur., 11 A.M.–2 A.M. Fri.–Sat.), a lofty-ceilinged, sparsely decorated contemporary stunner with a glazed cement floor and giant fruit sculptures. It has various salons. Downstairs there's a coffee shop with pastries, with a classy bar to the left. The main restaurant serves international nouvelle dishes such as Bombay salad ($6), Mayan salad ($4.50), Brazilian meats cooked to order ($11), and dishes from Scotland to Russia, all around $10.

CONTINENTAL
Downtown

The streetfront **News Café** (tel. 506/222-3022, 6 A.M.–midnight) of the Hotel Presidente is an atmospheric charmer, lent a cozy ambience by wrought-iron furnishings. Its wide-ranging menu runs from soups, salads, and sandwiches to calamari rings ($3.50), fajitas ($6), burgers (from $4), and even rib-eye steak ($13) and garlic tilapia ($8.50). It has lunch specials and scrumptious desserts.

SPANISH AND SOUTH AMERICAN
Downtown

The atmospheric **Goya** (Avenida 1, Calles 5/7, tel. 506/221-3887, 11:30 A.M.–11 P.M. Mon.–Fri., noon–9 P.M. Saturday) provides generous *bocas* as well as excellent Spanish cuisine, including a splendid paella plus rabbit in wine, at moderate prices (entrées begin at about $6). It has live entertainment nightly, including acoustic (Monday), "live sexy dances" (Tuesday and Friday), *trova* (Wednesdays), and karaoke (Thursday).

West of Downtown

The **Restaurante La Masía** (Calle 44, tel. 506/296-3528, 11:45 A.M.–2 P.M. and 6:30–10 P.M. Mon.–Sat.), in Edificio Casa de España, 175 meters west and 175 meters north of the Nissan agency, on Sabana Norte, offers classical elegance plus splendid cuisine. Paellas cost from $9.50 for two people. I thoroughly enjoyed my sea bass *a la vizcaína* with puréed spinach and carrots ($11). Brisk service is offered by waiters in cummerbunds.

East of Downtown

Chef Emilio Machado works wonders at the small but beautifully appointed **Marbella Restaurant** (Centro Comercial de la Calle Real, tel. 506/224-9452, 11:30 A.M.–3 P.M. and 6:30–10:30 P.M. Tue.–Fri., noon–3 P.M. and 7–11:30 P.M. Saturday, and noon–5 P.M. Sunday), in San Pedro. The large selection of seafood dishes includes paella Marbella (shellfish and sea bass) and paella Valenciana (chicken and seafood). The paella Madrilena (rabbit, chicken, and pork) is particularly good. Entrees run $5–15.

FRENCH

West of Downtown

La Bastille (Paseo Colón, Calle 22, tel. 506/255-4994, 11 A.M.–11 P.M. Mon.–Fri., 6–11 P.M. Saturdays) is the oldest French restaurant in San José. Chef Hans Pulfer produces superb French cuisine. It's elegant and expensive.

East of Downtown

Cognoscenti craving classical French head to the Île de France (tel. 506/283-5812, 7 A.M.–10 P.M. Mon.–Sat.), at L'Hôtel Le Bergerac, serving entrées such as pâté de lapin au poivre (rabbit with green peppercorns and cognac; $7), vichyssoise ($4), salon in cream of watercress ($13), and sea bass in thyme sauce ($13). Desserts include profiteroles, and there's a large wine collection.

Nearby, La Vie En Rose (Calle 21, tel. 506/225-0870, noon–3 P.M. and 6:30–10:30 P.M.

Mon.–Sat.) is a fabulous conversion of a 1950s home, now graced by a piano bar and café-restaurant in dark greens. The French owner-chef serves escargots ($8.50) and classics such as rabbit in mustard sauce ($8.50).

Also consider **Le Chandelier** (tel. 506/225-3980, $4 appetizers, $8–15 entrées, closed Sunday), in a restored Mediterranean-style mansion complete with beamed ceiling and fireplace, just behind the high-rise ICE Building in San Pedro. It has 10 separate dining areas, including a sculpture garden. Chef Claude Dubuis conjures up imaginative cuisine, stunning sauces, and his own version of typical Costa Rican fare: roasted heart of palm, cream of *pejivalle* soup, gratin of corvina with avocado. The restaurant is adorned with murals and the chef/owner's own works of art.

ITALIAN

Downtown

The **Balcón de Europa** (Calle 9, Avenidas Central/1, tel. 506/221-4841, below $10, closed Saturday) is a revered culinary shrine where chef Franco Piatti presents moderately priced cuisine from central Italy in an appropriately warm, welcoming setting with wood-paneled walls festooned with historic photos and framed proverbs. Try *pasta a la boscaiola* with tuna, tomatoes, and mushrooms.

West of Downtown

An inexpensive option on Paseo Colón is **Ana** (Paseo Colón, Calles 24/26, tel. 506/222-6153, noon–2:30 P.M. and 6:30–11 P.M. Mon.–Fri., 6:30–11 P.M. Saturday, and noon–4:30 P.M. and 6:30–10 P.M. Sunday), with pleasing ambience and the usual Italian fare of lasagna, spaghetti, and veal. **Fellini** (Avenida 4, Calle 36, tel. 506/222-3520), is recommended for its nouvelle Italian and French cuisine, such as rabbit in *chile*, or lamb with porcini mushrooms. The memorabilia plays up the great Italian film director.

Further west, the elegant **D'Olivo** (tel. 220-0453, $4–10, noon–3 P.M. and 7–10 P.M. Mon.–

Sat.), next to Hotel Palma Real on Sabana Norte, serves pastas and seafood. Nearby, **Il Gatto** (tel. 506/220-4439, www.ilgatto .com.ar), on Sabana Oeste, has a splendid contemporary aesthetic and a huge menu ranging from mozzarella and tomato salad ($3.50), pizzas and raviolis (from $4), fettuccines (from $6), and salmon with spinach ($7), perhaps followed by tiramisu ($2.50) or an ice cream brownie sundae ($2.50). It has a large wine list, plus a kid's menu. Choose indoors, or outside on the broad terrace.

Pizza Bar Italy (Avenida 2, Calle 24, tel. 506/223-4985) serves a range of tasty Italian dishes in a down-home Italian setting. **Pizza Papa John's** (tel. 258-9999), on Sabana Norte, will deliver.

East of Downtown

The **Il Ponte Vecchio** (tel. 506/283-1810, 11:30 A.M.–2:30 P.M. and 5:30–10:30 P.M. Mon.–Sat.), 200 meters west of San Pedro church, serves moderately priced, tasty cuisine cooked with imported Italian ingredients: sun-dried tomatoes, porcini mushrooms, and basil. Pastas are homemade by chef Antonio D'Alaimo. A Roman arch doorway and a mural of Venice's famous Ponte Vecchio add to the ambience.

Il Pomodoro (Calle Central, tel. 506/224-0966, 11:30 A.M.–11 P.M. Sun.–Mon. and Thursday, 11 A.M.–midnight Fri.–Sat.), 100 meters north of San Pedro church, is a popular hangout for university types who favor the pizzas ($4–8).

La Trattoria (Centro Comercial Real, tel. 506/224-7065, noon–10 P.M. Mon.–Thur., noon–11 P.M. Fri.–Sat., and noon–9 P.M. Sunday, $5–8), off Avenida Central in San Pedro, has a pleasant bistro-style ambience, with Italian murals. The menu features gnocchi, large portions of fettuccine, plus spaghettis, and raviolis.

Pasana (Avenida Central, tel. 506/280-2869, noon–midnight Mon.–Thur., noon–1 A.M. Fri.–Sat., noon–10 P.M. Sunday), 50 meters east of Max X Menos, in San Pedro, has a classy Italian atmosphere and specializes in pizzas *a la leña* (from the wood oven).

GERMAN AND SWISS

East of Downtown

The **Zermatt** (Calle 23, Avenida 11, tel. 506/222-0604, $15, closed Saturday) offers its famous fondue Bourguignonne and chicken supreme Zermatt.

Restaurante Club Alemán (Avenida 8, Calles 35/37, tel. 506/225-0366, fax 506/225-2016, clubaleman@racsa.co.cr, www.clubaleman.org, 11 A.M.–3 P.M. and 5–11 P.M. Tue.–Sat., and 11 A.M.–6 P.M. Sunday, $6.50–9), a meeting place for the local German community, is a clean and elegant place with a typical German menu: Bismarck herring, sauerkraut and sauerbraten, pork Cordon Bleu, and peach melba. It also has an outside barbecue and airy shaded deck, and a downstairs German-style bar with pine furniture that's only open 6–8 P.M. Fri.

MEXICAN

Downtown

One of the best options is **Antojitos** (www.losantojitoscr.com, 11:30 A.M.–11 P.M. Mon.–Thur., 11 A.M.–midnight Fri.–Sat., and 11 A.M.–10 P.M. Sunday), inexpensive yet classy, and justifiably popular with Ticos. Meals cost from $4; a grilled tenderloin costs $10. It has four outlets in San José: west of Sabana Park, in Rohrmoser (tel. 506/231-5564); east of downtown in Los Yoses (tel. 506/225-9525), in Centro Comerciál del Sur, in San Pedro (tel. 506/227-4160); and north of town on the road to Tibas (tel. 506/235-3961). It sometimes has mariachi.

West of Downtown

The **Bar México** (Calle 16, Avenida 13, tel. 506/221-8461) is a lively favorite. Live mariachi music forms a backdrop for excellent Mexican cuisine. Generous *bocas* are offered with drinks at the bar.

Rincón Mexicano (tel. 506/220-1865, 8 A.M.–6 P.M. Mon.–Sat.), on Sabana Sur, is a charming family-style café with colorful decor serving Mexican breakfasts, *pollo con mole, tortas,* and homemade baked goods. **Restaurante Padrisimo** (tel. 506/257-6353, 11 A.M.–11 A.M.

Mon.–Thur., 11 A.M.–11:30 P.M. Fri.–Sat.), on Sabana Oeste, is a colorful, eye-pleasing eatery with in-or-out dining, serving ceviche, *flautas* (from $2.50), and burritos (from $2).

Nearby, **Complejo Las Tunas** (tel. 506/231-1802, 11 A.M.–11:30 P.M.), in a large log cabin overlooking Sabana Park, 500 meters west of the ICE Building, in Sabana Norte, is Costa Rica's answer to Tex-Mex for those seeking Tico-Mex fare (tacos, for example, offer shredded beef rolled in a tortilla and deep-fried). Las Tunas has drive-in service.

East of Downtown

The attractive **Garibaldi's** (Avenida Central, tel. 506/280-5739, noon–11 P.M. Monday, Thursday, and Saturday, noon–11:30 P.M. Friday), in San Pedro, has suitably Mexican decor and a full Mexican menu, from quesadillas to tostadas.

ASIAN

Downtown

My favorite Chinese restaurant is **Tin Jo** (Calle 11, Avenidas 6/8, tel. 506/221-7605, 11:30 A.M.–3 P.M. and 5:30–10 P.M. Mon.–Thur. and Sunday, 11:30 A.M.–11 P.M. Fri.–Sat.). The decor is quaintly colonial Costa Rican, but the food is distinctly Asian: tasty Mandarin and Sichuan specialties, plus Thai, Indian, Indonesian, and Japanese food at moderate prices. It even has sushi, satay ($4), samosas ($3), and curries ($6). If you want chopsticks, ask for *palillos*.

Next door is the more homey **Don Wang** (tel. 506/223-6484, 11 A.M.–3 p.m. and 5:30–11 P.M. Mon.–Sat., and 11 A.M.–10 P.M. Sunday), serving generous, reasonably priced portions, although the quality isn't up to par with Tin Jo. It offers Taiwanese dishes and small *bocas,* plus dim sum. Seafood dishes are a particular bargain ($4–6); it also has *platos fuertes* (set meals) for $1.50.

Do's Sushi Bar (Avenida 1, Calles 7/9) is a clean option with contemporary decor; likewise **Josy's Sushi,** in Centro Comercial El Pueblo, in Barrio Tournón.

West of Downtown

The **Flor del Loto** (Calle 46, tel. 506/232-4652, 11 A.M.–3 P.M., 6–11 P.M. Mon.–Fri., 11 A.M.–11 P.M. Saturday, and 11 A.M.–9:30 P.M. Sunday, $7), in Sabana Norte, is the place if you like your Chinese food hot and spicy. Mouth-searing Hunan and Sichuan specialties include *mo-shu-yock* (Shi Chuen–style pork) and *ma po tofu* (vegetables, bamboo shoots, and tofu stir-fried in sizzling hot-pepper oil).

Villa Bonita (tel. 506/232-9855, $8), 100 meters south of the U.S. Embassy, in Pavas, is an upscale Asian restaurant offering a Chinese, Thai, and Indian buffet served in a huge dining room. It's run by Hong Kong natives, who prepare such dishes as tilapia.

Another acclaimed option is **King's Garden** (tel. 506/255-3838), on the second floor of the Centro Comercial Yaohan, opposite the Hotel Corobicí. The head chef is from Hong Kong; the menu features many favorites from the city, as well as Cantonese and Sichuan dishes. A set dinner for two costs about $14. **Mariscos de Oriente** (tel. 506/232-2973, 11 A.M.–3 P.M. and 6–10:30 P.M. Mon.–Fri., 11 A.M.–10:30 P.M. Saturday, and 11 A.M.–9:30 P.M. Sunday, $7), on Sabana Norte, specializes in seafood, such as squid in oyster sauce and abalone with mushrooms, and has suitably Chinese decor.

The cozy **Arirang** (Paseo Colón, Calles 38/40, tel. 506/223-2838, 11:30 A.M.–3 P.M. and 5:30–9:30 P.M. Mon.–Fri., 11:30 A.M.–9:30 P.M. Saturday and holidays), in Centro Colón, caters to those who love grilled eel, *kimch'i, chu'sok,* and other Korean specialties cooked on a hibachi at your table. It also has sushi specials. Most dishes cost less than $10.

Restaurante Pacifico (Calle 24, Paseo Colón/Avenida 2, tel. 506/257-9523, 11:30 A.M.–3 P.M. and 5:30–10:30 P.M. Mon.–Sat., 5–9 P.M. Sunday) is a small family-run Japanese restaurant with a sushi bar. It has a homely, unpretentious atmosphere. Sushi orders come with miso and salad (you can fill up for $15). It also serves the likes of squid in spicy sauce ($9) and breaded shrimp with sweet and sour sauce ($9).

East of Downtown

The **Restaurante Casa China** (Calle 25, Avenida 8/10, tel. 506/257-8392, 8 A.M.–midnight) is the real McCoy and the headquarters for the Asociación China de Costa Rica. This no-frills, refectory-style eatery serves set lunches for $1, and even has ping-pong. You could be in Shanghai!

Medalla de Oro (Calle 37, tel. 506/253-5512, 11 A.M.–3 P.M. and 5–11 P.M. Mon.–Fri., 11 A.M.–11 P.M. Saturdays, and 11:30 A.M.–4 P.M. Sundays, $8), 50 meters north of the gas station in Los Yoses, serves Cantonese and Szechuan dishes, such as steamed corvina in ginger sauce with soybeans and green onion.

Ave Félix (tel. 506/225-3362, 11 A.M.–10:45 P.M. Sun.–Thur., 11 A.M.–midnight Fri.–Sat.), 200 meters west of the San Pedro church, is a popular Chinese restaurant acclaimed for its original sauces: soy sauce spiced with crushed garlic, minced onion, and sesame oil; and sweet-and-sour sauce with lemon juice and the juice of maraschino cherries. The Taiwanese chef conjures more than 100 entrées that include some exotic offerings as well as staples ($4–8) such as bird's nest sliced beef ($6). Portions are huge.

My favorite sushi spot is **Oku Sushi** (tel. 506/364-7894, noon–3 P.M. and 6–10 P.M. Mon.–Thur., noon–3 P.M. and 6–11 P.M. Friday, and noon–11 P.M. Saturday), a contemporary restaurant (it has no bar) with hip minimalist decor. It has live music and all-you-can-drink Fridays 8–11 P.M. ($10). The menu also includes salmon in mushroom sauce with ginger and mashed potatoes ($7.50) and a seafood platter ($7).

SEAFOOD AND STEAKS

Downtown

The **Restaurante y Bar La Palma** (Avenida 9, Calle 9/11, tel. 506/258-4541, 5–11 P.M. Tues.–Sat.) serves seafood and steaks amid atmospheric surrounds, with all dishes around $10. Samples include chicken curry ($10), and sea bass prepared any of half a dozen ways.

I recommend the **Restaurant El Oasis** (Avenida 7, Calles 3/5, tel. 506/255-0448), in the Hotel Santo Tomás, a real charmer with a colonial tiled bar, elegant place settings, ceiling fans, and a courtyard garden with waterfall. It serves shrimp cocktails ($13), salads, filet mignon ($10), sea bass with garlic and white wine ($7), and pastas, and desserts such as banana flambé ($3).

For atmosphere try **Casa de las Costillas** (tel. 506/223-0523, 11 A.M.–2:30 P.M. and 6–10 P.M. Mon.–Fri., noon–11 P.M. Saturday, and noon–5 p.m. Sunday), or "House of Ribs," outside the zoo, and featuring saddles and other horsey decor and a menu offering onion rings, grilled pork loin, ribs, and grilled meats ($3–12).

West of Downtown

My favorite seafood restaurant is **Ⅻ Machu Picchu** (Calle 32, Avenidas 1/3, tel. 506/222-7384, 11 A.M.–3 P.M. and 6–10 P.M. Mon.–Sat.), with delicious authentic Peruvian seafood and *spicy* sauces! Try the superb ceviches ($2.50–5) or the *picante de mariscos* (a seafood casserole with onions, garlic, olives, and cheese), enjoyed in a suitably nautical ambience. Moderately priced (some potato entrées are less than $4; garlic octopus is $5). The pisco sours are powerful. The place is always full of Ticos.

For a cheap meal, check out **Marisquería La Princesa Marina** (tel. 506/232-0481, 11 A.M.–3 P.M., 6–10 P.M. daily, $1–5), on Sabana Oeste. This canteen-like seafood spot is a favorite of Ticos at lunch. It serves from a wide menu and wins no gourmet prizes, but at least you fill up.

Another great spot is **La Fuente de Los Mariscos** (tel. 506/231-0631, 11:15 A.M.–10:30 P.M.), in Centro Comercial San José adjacent to the Hotel Irazú in La Uruca, with seafood at moderate prices.

For meat and seafood, try **El Chicote** (tel. 506/232-0936, 11 A.M.–3 P.M. and 6–11 P.M. Mon.–Fri., 11 A.M.–11 P.M. Sat.–Sun.), 400 meters west of ICE in Sabana Norte; it's noted for its house specialty of baby beef ($13), châteaubriand, shrimp-stuffed tenderloin, and filet mignon basted with honey served with breaded bananas and mashed potatoes. Try the oyster cocktail ($11), New Zealand mussels ($9), or garlic shrimp ($16). Steaks are cooked over a large open fire. Palms and ferns abound, and options for dining include an elegant a/c interior or small shaded patio. It has a drive-in next door.

East of Downtown

At cozy **Ambrosia** (tel. 506/253-8012, 11:30 A.M.–3 P.M. and 6:30–10:30 P.M. Mon.–Sat., 11:30 A.M.–4 P.M. Sunday), 75 meters east of Banco Popular in San Pedro, chef Janie Murray conjures up soufflés, quiches, and other moderately priced dishes, including pastas, ceviche, steaks, and—the house specialty—sea bass prepared eight different ways.

VEGETARIAN

Downtown

The superb **N Restaurante Vishnu** (Avenida 1, Calles 1/3, tel. 506/290-0119, vishnu @racsa.co.cr, 7 A.M.–9:30 P.M. Sunday, 9 A.M.–7:30 P.M. Mon.–Sat.) serves health-food breakfasts, lunches, and dinners. Meals are generous in size and low in price (a *casado* costs $3); the menu includes veggie lasagne, veggie burgers, and fruit salads. Vishnu has 10 other outlets around town, including at Calle 14, Avenida Central/2, and at Calle 1, Avenida 4.

East of Downtown

The small, simple **Restaurante Vegetariano San Pedro** (tel. 506/224-1163, 10 A.M.–6 P.M. Mon.–Fri.), on Calle Central 200 meters north of San Pedro church, has a *casado* with juice for $2, plus soy burgers ($1.75), salads, and pastas ($4).

MIDDLE EASTERN

For a taste of the Levantine, head west of Downtown to **Lubnan** (Paseo Colón, Calles 22/24, tel. 506/257-6071), serving noteworthy Middle Eastern specialties such as shish kebob, falafel, *michi malfuf* (stuffed cabbage), and *kafta naie* (marinated ground beef).

And how about Turkish fare? **Aya Sofya** (Avenida Central, Calle 21, tel. 506/221-7185, 11 A.M.–10:30 P.M. Mon.–Sat.) serves stuffed grape leaves, doner kebab (marinated lamb barbecue), and baklava, all skillfully prepared by Turkish chef Ali Osman Agirkaya and all at reasonable prices.

CAFÉS AND PASTRY SHOPS

Downtown

One of the best coffee shops in town is the **Café Teatro** inside the foyer of the National Theater. Marble-topped tables, magnificent tile, a gilded and mirrored serving counter, classical music, and artwork adorning the walls are topped by tempting desserts. Likewise, **Café Bohemia** (tel. 506/358-8465, 10 A.M.–10 P.M. Mon.–Sat.), formerly Soda Perla, next to Teatro Melica Salazar, is a bistro with classy, romantic ambience serving sandwiches, snacks, plus a *plato ejecutivo* (set lunch; $5 including beer), and mustard chicken ($14), as well as espressos, cappuccinos, etc.

And the **Café Correo** (tel. 506/257-3670, 9 A.M.–5 P.M. Mon.–Fri. , 9 A.M.–7 P.M. Saturday), in the Post Office overlooking Avenida Central, is a little gem. Soft lighting and jazz provide a romantic background for enjoying lattes, espressos, mochas, and pastries such as cheesecakes, chocolate cake, and strawberry tarts ($1–2).

The artsy, Argentinian-run **Café de la Posada** (Avenida 2, Calle 17, tel. 506/257-9414 or 506/258-1027, juanrey17@hotmail.com, 9 A.M.–7 P.M. Mon.–Thur., 9 A.M.–11 P.M. Fri.–Sun.) opens to a pedestrians-only street and appeals to a bohemian crowd. It offers jazz and classical music, and serves espressos, cappucinos, plus quiches, omelettes, and sandwiches (all from $1.50), Argentinian *empeñadas,* and ice creams, chocolate mousse, and other tempting desserts.

A popular option with the business lunch crowd is **Restaurante Nuestra Tierra** (Avenida 9, Calle 3 bis, tel. 506/258-2983, 10:30 A.M.–10:30 P.M.), divided into sections offering rustic country ambience and urban elegance. Menu samples include *chorreado* (ground corn crepes; $1), tortillas ($1.50), tamales, and fajitas served with rice, beans, and plantain ($7). It also serves a wide range of creative entrées, sandwiches, soups, salads, and killer desserts.

The bohemian **Café Mundo** (Avenida 9, Calle 15, tel. 506/222-6190, 11 A.M.–11 P.M. Mon.–Thur., 11 A.M.–midnight Fri.–Sat., 5 P.M.–midnight Sunday) is justifiably popular with businessfolk.

This handsome remake of a colonial mansion has open patios and several indoor rooms. Persian rugs and contemporary art on the walls add to the warm mood. Its eclectic menu spans tempura veggies ($5.50), chicken satay ($5.50), Caesar salad (from $3.50), plus pastas, pizzas, surf and turf (from $8), desserts such as tiramisu, plus cappuccino ($1.75). Portions are generous.

M Spoon has burgeoned over the past decade from a small take-out bakery one block off Avenida Central in Los Yoses (tel. 506/224-0328) into a chain with outlets on Avenida Central near the Plaza de la Cultura (tel. 506/221-6702) and throughout the city. In addition to desserts, Spoon serves sandwiches, salads, lasagna, soups, *empañadas* (pastries stuffed with chicken and other meats), and *lapices,* a Costa Rican equivalent of submarines, all at bargain prices. **Musmanni** (tel. 506/296-5750) is a national *pastelería* chain selling pastries and fresh breads. It has about one dozen outlets in San José.

West of Downtown

The **Pastelería Francesca** (Calle 30, Paseo Colón); and **Pastelería Don Simon** (Calle 28, Paseo Colón) are recommended.

East of Downtown

In Los Yoses I like **Café Ruiseñor** (see *Breakfast,* above), a classy, trendy spot serving a range of coffee drinks including lattes ($1.25), plus soups, salads, and sandwiches ($3), entrées such as curried chicken ($6), sea bass with herbs and white wine ($4), and pepper steak ($7.50), and desserts such as banana splits, German apple tart, and parfaits. It offers open-air dining.

Café Bindi (tel. 506/234-7659, 11 A.M.–8 P.M. Mon.–Fri.), 50 meters north of Iglesia Fatima, has great desserts, plus cappuccinos, espressos, and teas, and an art gallery.

Café el Deseo (Centro Comercial Calle Real #23, tel. 506/283-3381, 10 A.M.–8 P.M. Mon.–Sat.), off Avenida Central, in San Pedro, is a hip contemporary café with black, white, and red decor. It sells stuffed croissants, quiches, crepes, ice creams, and exotic chocolate desserts.

© CHRISTOPHER P. BAKER

entrance to the Mercado Central

Ice cream fans should check out **Häagen-Dazs Café** (Avenida Central, tel. 506/280-5245, 10 A.M.–10 P.M. Sun.–Thur., 10 a.m.–11 P.M. Fri.–Sat.), in San Pedro. This clean, contemporary ice cream parlor serves everyone's favorite ice cream, from cones to special sundaes. It also has espressos and cappuccinos.

MARKETS

Within the warren of the **Mercado Central** (Calles 6/8, Avenidas Central/1, closed Sunday) are stands selling poultry, flowers, meat, fish, medicinal herbs, fresh produce, and coffee. An equally colorful alternative across the way is **Mercado Borbón** (Calle 8, Avenidas 3/5). The **Mercado Paso de la Vaca** (Avenida 7, Calle 6) is a clean produce market selling everything from fresh herbs to meats.

There are dozens of supermarkets.

The **Casa del Vino** (Avenida 7, Calles 5/7, tel. 506/221-2224) is well-stocked with wines, as is **Cabernet** (in the Centro Comercial Real #16, tel. 506/281-2481, mseaward@racsa.co.cr), off Avenida Central, in San Pedro, which sells all things wine-related.

Information and Services

TOURIST INFORMATION

ICT operates a tourist information office booth in at the airport. Its main tourist information office (tel. 506/223-1733, fax 506/223-5452, promoict@tourism.costarica.com), beneath the Plaza de la Cultura on Calle 5, is open 9 A.M.–1 P.M. and 2–5 P.M. Mon.–Fri.; its office in the post office (Calle 2, Avenidas 1/3, tel. 506/223-1733, ext. 336) is open 8 A.M.–4 P.M. Mon.–Fri. The ICT head office is at Avenida 4, Calles 5/7, on the 11th floor. It does not provide tourist information, however, and was scheduled to move at last visit.

TRAVEL AGENCIES

There are dozens of English-speaking travel agencies in San José. They can arrange city tours, one- and multi-day excursions, beach resort vacations, air transportation, and more. I recommend U.S.-run **Costa Rica Expeditions** (Avenida 3, Calle Central, tel. 506/257-0766, fax 506/257-1665, costaric@expeditions.co.cr, www.costaricaexpeditions.com) and **Swiss Travel** (tel. 506/282-4898, fax 506/282-4890, info @swisstravelcr.com, www.swisstravelcr.com). **STI Travel** (Avenida Central, Calle 35, tel. 506/283-8200, stitravel@racsa.co.cr, www.stitravel.com), in Los Yoses, specializes in cheap airfares.

NEWSPAPERS AND MAGAZINES

Most major hotel gift stores sell popular international newspapers and periodicals, as does **7th Street Books.** Most bookstores named above also sell magazines. **La Casa de las Revistas** has outlets at Calle Central, Avenidas 4/6, and Calle 7, Avenidas 1/3, selling a wide range of Spanish- and English-language magazines.

LIBRARIES

The National Library or **Biblioteca Nacional** (Avenida 3, Calles 15/17, tel. 506/221-2436, 8 A.M.–6:30 P.M. Mon.–Fri.) has more than 100,000 volumes. The main index and information desk are upstairs on the second floor. The national newspaper collection is here.

Another useful source is the **Biblioteca Universidad de Costa Rica** (tel. 506/225-7372), at the university in San Pedro. The **Mark Twain Library** (Calle Negritos, tel. 506/207-7573, 9 A.M.–7 P.M. Mon.–Fri., 9 A.M.–noon Saturday), in the Centro Cultural Norteamericano in Los Yoses, has English-language books and reference materials. You must be a member to check books out, but it's open to the public for reference.

MONEY

San José has dozens of banks. For small sums I recommend using your hotel cashier (hotels give the same exchange rates). Bank outlets are listed in the Yellow Pages of the telephone directory.

You'll need your passport and a good deal of patience for bank transactions, especially at the notoriously slow, state-run Banco Nacional. Fortunately, most banks have a separate foreign exchange counter, usually guaranteeing speedier service.

Most banks will give cash advances against your Visa card, and many banks now have **ATM machines** that issue cash advances against Visa. However, very few will grant a cash advance for MasterCard. An exception is the **Banco de San José.**

Credomatic (Calle Central, Avenidas 3/5, tel. 506/257-0155) will assist you with card replacement for Visa/MasterCard.

You can send and receive money by wire transfer via **Western Union** (tel. 506/283-6336), which has offices throughout the city.

POST AND COMMUNICATIONS
Mail

The main post office, or **Correo Central** (Calle 2, Avenidas 1/3, tel. 506/223-9766, 8 A.M.–5 P.M. Mon.–Fri.), has a 24-hour stamp machine. You can also buy stamps and post your mail at front desks at upscale hotels.

To collect incoming mail at the Correo Central, go to window 17 through the entrance nearest Avenida 1. You'll need identification. Mail should be addressed to you using your name as it appears on your passport or other I.D., c/o Lista Correo, Correo Central, San José. There's a small charge (about 25 cents) per letter.

American Express cardholders can have mail sent to them c/o Agencia Super Viajes (tel. 506/290-7309; in the U.S., tel. 800/528-2121), in Pavas.

FedEx (tel. 506/255-4567) is on Paseo Colón between Calles 40/42. **DHL Worldwide Express** (tel. 506/223-1423 or 506/210-

3838) is on Calle 34, between Paseo Colón and Avenida 2.

Telephones

There are plenty of public telephones throughout the city. **KitCom** (Calle 3, Avenidas 1/3, tel. 506/258-0303), on the second floor of the OTEC Building, 175 meters north of the Plaza de la Cultura, has a complete telecommunications office. **TDE Teledollar Express** (tel. 506/256-9190), on Paseo Colón, has international telephone and fax services; it's open 8:30 A.M.–4 P.M. Mon.–Sat. and 8 A.M.–2 P.M. Sunday.

Alternately, use the **ICE** offices on Sabana Norte or south of the San Pedro roundabout; or RACSA's **Telecommunications Center** (Calle 1, Avenida 5, tel. 506/287-0515).

Internet Services

Most tourist hotels now have Internet cafés or access for guests.

Downtown, one of the best Internet cafés is the **Cyber Café** (Avenida 2, tel. 506/233-3310, cybercafe@searchcostarica.com), in the basement of Las Arcadas, 50 meters west of the Teatro Nacional. It has a pleasant outdoor dining area, has international newspapers to read, plus a travel desk, and charges 150 *colones* for 10 minutes, 300 *colones* for 30 minutes, and 500 *colones* for one hour.

Internet Café Costa Rica (incecomp@racsa .co.cr) has several locations offering Web access for 500 *colones* per hour: its downtown office at Avenida Central, Calle 2 (tel. 506/255-0540) is open 8 A.M.–midnight; and its office next to Cine Capri (tel. 506/255-1154) is open 9 A.M.–9 P.M.

Also consider **Netopia Café** (Avenida 1, Calle 11, tel. 506/233-6320, netopia@racsa.co.cr, 9 A.M.–midnight Mon.–Sat., and 10 A.M.–10 P.M. Sunday); **Café Digital** (Calle 7, Avenidas Central/1, tel. 506/248-7033, 8 A.M.–10 P.M. Mon.–Sat., 10 A.M.–10 P.M. Sunday); and **Uno@Diez** (Calle 3, Avenidas 5/7, tel. 506/258-4561, 10 A.M.–9 P.M. Mon.–Sat.).

West of downtown, **Internet Café Costa Rica** (Centro Colón, tel. 506/222-2584) is open 9 A.M.–10 P.M. **Web Surfers Internet**

Café (tel. 506/291-0074, 9 A.M.–9 P.M. Mon.–Sat., noon–8 P.M. Sunday), upstairs in Multicentro Sabana, on Sabana Oeste, charges $1.25 per hour.

East of downtown, choices include **Internet Café Costa Rica** (Avenida Central, Calle Central, tel. 506/224-7382, 24 hours), San Pedro; **Net Café** (Calle 1, 300 meters north of Avenida Central, in San Pedro, tel. 506/234-8200, supernet64 @latinmail.com, 7 A.M.–10 P.M. Mon.–Fri., and 9 A.M.–9 P.M. Sat.–Sun.; and **C@fé Internet** (Calle 37, tel. 506/281-3111, 9 A.M.–9 P.M. Mon.–Fri., and 9 A.M.–6 P.M. Saturday), in Los Yoses.

LAUNDRIES

Most laundromats *(lavanderías)* offer a wash-and-dry service (about $4 per load). Downtown, try **Sixaola** (Avenida 2, Calles 7/9, tel. 506/221-2111 or 506/225-5333), which has outlets throughout San José. **Lavanderías de Costa Rica** (tel. 506/237-6273) will pick up and deliver.

The **CyberCafé** in Edificio Las Arcadas, 50 meters west of the Teatro Nacional, has a small self-service laundromat.

Most hotels can arrange to do your laundry with 24 hours' notice. Many budget hotels have a laundry sink and drying area (don't wash your clothes in the large water tank; instead, draw water from the tank and wash your clothes in the sink).

PHOTOGRAPHY

Fuji (Avenida 1, Calles Central/1, tel. 506/257-0148, fujifilm@universalcr.com) has several outlets selling film and cameras and offering one-hour processing. The major photographic outlet is **Dima** (Avenida Central, Calles 3/5, tel. 506/222-3969), which also offers repair service.

MEDICAL SERVICES

The privately run **Hospital Clínica Bíblica** (tel. 506/257-5252) is the best hospital in town and accepts U.S. Medicare. The following private hospitals provide medical facilities at reasonable rates: **Clínica Católica, Clínica Americana,** and **Clínica Santa Rita**.

The public **Hospital Dr. Calderón Guardia** (tel. 506/257-7922) and **Hospital México** (tel. 506/232-6122) are alternatives, as is the public **Hospital San Juan de Dios** (Paseo Colón, Calle 16, tel. 506/257-6282), the most centrally located medical facility. They provide free emergency health care on the Social Security system. The **Children's Hospital** (Hospital Nacional de Niños, Paseo Colón, tel. 506/222-0122) cares for children. Women are served by the **Hospital de la Mujer** (tel. 506/257-9111).

Getting There and Around

BY AIR

Juan Santamaría International Airport (tel. 506/437-2400 or 506/441-0744) is on the outskirts of Alajuela, 17 km west of San José.
Pavas Airport (Tobías Bolaños, tel. 506/232-2820), about four km southwest of town, is used for most domestic flights, including small charter planes and air-taxis. Bus 14B runs from Avenida 1, Calles 16/18, and stops in Pavas, a short walk from the airport.

Some hotels offer free shuttles into town. If you need to take a **taxi,** pay in advance at an official booth immediately outside the arrivals lounge.

Taxi Aeropuerto (tel. 506/221-6865 or 506/441-1319, fax 506/441-1356, www.taxiaeropuerto .com) operates the taxis between the airport and downtown and accepts 24-hour reservations; they're orange (local San José taxis are red). The legally sanctioned daytime fare into downtown San José is $12 by day and night. It normally takes 20 to 30 minutes to reach downtown, depending on traffic.

Public buses run by **Tuasa** (tel. 506/222-5325) also operate between downtown San José and Alajuela every 10 minutes via the airport, 5 A.M.–10 P.M., and then every 30 minutes 10 P.M.–5 A.M. The fare is 65 *colones* (30 cents).

The driver will make change, but you'll need small bills or change. The journey takes about 30 minutes, and ends downtown at Avenida 2, Calles 12/14. Luggage space is limited. To return for your departure fligh, take the San José–Alajuela bus, which departs from Avenida 2, Calles 12/14, every 10 minutes.

Interbus (tel. 506/283-5573, fax 506/293-7655, interbus@Gostaricapass.com, www.inter busonline.com) offers a 24-hour airport shuttle for $5 per person. **Grayline Fantasy Bus** (tel. 506/232-3681) also has a shuttle linking the airport and nine San José hotels ($6), by reservation. Look for representatives with the Grayline logo on their shirts as you exit Customs.

Several **car-rental companies** have offices immediately beyond Customs; additional offices are about 500 meters east, adjacent to the Hampton Inn. If you plan on spending a few days in San José before heading off to explore the country, you'll be better off using taxis and local buses. Rental cars are in short supply. Make your reservations *before* departing home.

At press time, the **departure tax** for travelers leaving Costa Rica was $26 (payable in dollars or *colones* equivalent). You pay at the booth to the right inside the departure lounge prior to checking in. To avoid long lines, pay your departure tax when you **arrive** in Costa Rica.

A **tourist information booth** is in the baggage claim area, and another immediately beyond Customs. There's a **Banco San José** in the departure terminal, but it will exchange no more than $50 in dollars for *colones*. Change the rest before you arrive at the airport. Taxis accept dollars, so save changing money until you arrive at your hotel. You will need local currency if you plan on taking public transport into San José. There's also a post office, are several duty-free and gift shops, plus a bookshop, and a full-service restaurant and bar beyond immigration.

BY CAR

Westbound from downtown San José, Paseo Colón feeds right onto the Pan-American Highway (Hwy. 1), which leads to the Pacific coast,

Guanacaste, and Nicaragua. A tollbooth just east of the airport charges 60 *colones* (25 cents) per vehicle for westbound traffic only.

Calle 3 leads north from downtown and becomes the Guápiles Highway (Hwy. 32) for Puerto Limón and the Caribbean and Northern Zone. Avenida 2 leads east via San Pedro to Cartago and the southern section of the Pan-Am Highway (Hwy. 2), bound for Panamá. There's a tollbooth (60 *colones*) about three km east of the suburb of San Pedro.

BY TAXI

More than 3,000 taxis serve the city. They're red (taxis exclusively serving the airport are orange); if it's any other color, it's a "pirate" taxi operating illegally. You can travel anywhere within the city for less than $4.

By law taxi drivers (who must display a business card with name, license plate, and other details) must use their meters—*marias*—for journeys of less than 12 kilometers. Still, not everyone does. Always demand that the taxi driver use his meter, otherwise you're gonna get ripped off. Some taxi drivers get commissions from certain hotels: if you're heading to a budget hotel, they may tell you that the place you're seeking is closed, full, etc., and will try to persuade you to go to a hotel they recommend. Don't fall for this! If the cabbie insists, get out and take another cab.

You do not normally tip taxi drivers in Costa Rica, but give your taxi driver any small change.

Finding a taxi is usually not a problem, except during rush hour and when it's raining. One of the best places to find a taxi is Parque Central, where they line up on Avenida 2, and in front of the Gran Hotel and National Theater two blocks east (where taxi drivers not using their meters may charge slightly higher rates).

There are reports of taxi drivers making sexual advances toward single women; this is more likely to happen with pirate taxis, which you should always avoid.

During Christmas, watch for *taxista* Jorge Lietón, who drives around with a complete nativity scene on his roof.

San José

BY BUS

San José has no central terminal. Buses for Puerto Limón and the Caribbean depart from the **Gran Terminál Caribe** on Calle Central, Avenidas 15/17. Most buses to other destinations leave from the area referred to as **Coca-Cola** (centered on Calle 16 and Avenida 1, but spread around many streets; see *Safety*, above). Other buses leave from the bus company office or a streetside bus stop—*parada*. Many street departure points are unmarked: ask the locals.

Buses from San José are particularly crowded on Friday and Saturday. So, too, are those returning to San José on Sunday and Monday.

A Safe Passage/Viaje Seguro (tel. 506/365-9678 or 506/441-7837, rchoice@racsa.co.cr, www.costaricabustickets.com) will make your bus reservations and buy your ticket for you in advance, eliminating your need to visit "Coca-Cola"and taking the hassle out of making bus reservations in San José. Tickets cost $15 single, $25 a pair to anywhere in the nation. It also offers airport transfers.

San José has an excellent network of privately owned local bus services. The ICT publishes a listing of current bus schedules, including the bus company and telephone numbers. While some routes are served by slick new Mercedes, other buses are decrepit old things belching fumes, with wooden, uncushioned seats (many are garishly painted, with improbable names such as *Guerrero del Camino* ("Road Warrior"), *Desert Storm, Tico Tex,* and *Titanic.*

Bus companies include **Atlántico Norte** (tel. 506/256-8963), **Auto-Transportes Caribeños** (tel. 506/221-2596), **Autotransportes Mepe** (tel. 506/758-1572 or 506/798-0282), **Autotransportes San José–San Carlos** (tel. 506/255-4318), **Autotransportes Tilarán** (tel. 506/222-3854), **Empresarios Unidos** (tel. 506/222-0064), **Microbuses Rápidos** (tel. 506/261-0506), **Pulmitán** (tel. 506/222-1650), **SACSA** (tel. 506/230-4271), **Tracopa Alfaro** (tel. 506/222-2666), **Tralapa** (tel. 506/223-5859), **Transportes Morales** (tel. 506/223-5567), **Transtusa** (tel. 506/222-4464), and **Tuasa** (tel. 506/222-5325).

Most buses operate 5 A.M.–10 P.M., with frequency of service determined by demand. Downtown and suburban San José buses leave their principal *paradas* (bus stops) every few minutes. The wait is rarely long, except during rush hours (7–9 A.M. and 5–7 P.M.). Also, buses to outer suburbs often fill up, so it's best to board at their principal downtown *parada,* designated by a sign, Parada de Autobuses, showing the route name and number.

A sign in the windshield tells the route number and destination. Fares are marked by the doors and are collected when you board. Drivers provide change and tend to be scrupulously honest. Buses are ridiculously cheap: about 40 *colones* (15 cents) downtown and under 60 *colones* elsewhere within the metropolitan area (laser bars count passengers as they enter and leave; don't stand between the bars or pass through them more than once, as the driver must pay for any discrepancies between the passenger count and the fares collected).

Many buses take a circular route that can provide a good introductory sightseeing experience. From the west, the most convenient bus into town is the Sabana-Cementerio service (route 2), which runs counterclockwise between Sabana Sur and downtown along Avenida 10, then back along Avenida 3 (past the "Coca-Cola"bus station) and Paseo Colón. The Cementerio-Estadio service (route 7) runs in the opposite direction along Paseo Colón and Avenida 2 and back along Avenida 12. Both take about 40 minutes to complete the circle.

Buses to Los Yoses and San Pedro run east along Avenida 2 and, beyond Calle 29, along Avenida Central. Buses to Coronado begin at Calle 3, Avenidas 5/7; to Guadalupe at Avenida 3, Calles Central/1; to Moravia from Avenida 3, Calles 3/5; and to Pavas from Avenida 1, Calle 18.

Be wary of pickpockets on buses, especially in crowded situations. Be especially suspect of anyone pushing you or pushing against you.

BY CAR

There are about 50 car rental agencies in San José, concentrated along Paseo Colón. However,

San José

BUSES FROM SAN JOSÉ

Destination; Days; Times; Duration; Company; Departure Point

Alajuela (and airport); Daily; every 15 min. 4 A.M.–10 P.M.; 25 mins.; Tuasa; Ave. 2, Calles 10/12

Atenas; Daily; 6 A.M., 9 A.M., 11 A.M., 2 P.M., 4 P.M., 6 P.M., 7 P.M.; Ave.1, Calles16

Arenal Volcano NP (see La Fortuna)

Braulio Carrillo NP (see Guápiles)

Cahuita; Daily; 6 A.M., 10 A.M., 1:30 and 3:30 P.M.; 4 hrs; Calle Central, Ave. 13/15

Cañas; Daily; 8:30 and 10:20 A.M. and 12:20, 1:20, 2:30 P.M., 4:45 P.M., and 4:45 P.M. (Friday and Saturday only); 3.5 hrs; Transportes la Cañera; Calle 16, Ave. 1/3

Caño Negro NP (see Los Chiles)

Carara Biological Reserve (see Jacó)

Cartago; Daily; every 10 min. 5 A.M.–midnight (plus hourly midnight–5 A.M., Friday and Saturday); 45 min.; SACSA; Calle 5, Ave. 18

Chirripó NP (see San Isidro)

Ciudad Quesada (San Carlos); Daily; hourly 7:30 A.M.–7:30 P.M.; 2.5 hrs; Autotransportes San José–San Carlos; Calle 12, Ave. 7/9

Corcovado NP (see Puerto Jiménez)

Dominical; Daily; 7 A.M., 9 A.M., 1:30 and 4 P.M.; 8 hrs; Transportes Muse; Calle 14, Ave. 5

La Fortuna; Daily; 6:15, 8:40 A.M. and 11:30 A.M.; 4.5 hrs; Autotransportes San José–San Carlos; Calle 12, Ave. 7/9.

Golfito; Daily; 7 A.M. and 3 P.M.; 8 hrs; Tracopa; Calle 14, Ave. 5

Guápiles; Daily; every 30 min. 5:30 A.M.–9:45 P.M. (Mon —Fri.), 6 A.M.–9 P.M. (Sat.–Sun.); 60 min.; Atlántico Norte; Gran Terminal Caribe, Calle Central, Calles 13/15.

Guayabo National Monument (see Turrialba)

Heredia; Daily; every 10 min. 5 A.M.–midnight, every 30 min. midnight–4 A.M.; 25 min.; Calle 1, Ave. 7/9, and Calle 4, Avenidas 5/7

Heredia; Daily; every 15 min. 6 A.M.–10 P.M.; 25 min.; Microbuses Rápidos; Ave. 2, Calles 10/12.

Irazú Volcano NP; Saturday and Sunday; 8 A.M.; 90 min.; SACSA; Ave. 2, Calle 1/3

Jacó; Daily; 7:30 and 10:30 A.M. and 3:30 P.M.; 2.5 hrs; Transportes Morales; Calle 18, Ave. 1/3

Liberia; Daily; 6 A.M., 7 A.M., 9 A.M., 10 A.M., and 11:30 A.M. and 1 P.M., 3 P.M. (direct), 4 P.M., 5 P.M. (direct), 6 P.M., and 8 P.M.; 4 hrs; Pulmitán; Calle 14, Ave. 1/3

Los Chiles; Daily; 5:30 A.M. and 3:30 P.M.; 5 hrs; Atláorte; Calle 12, Ave. 1/3

Manuel Antonio (see Quepos)

Manzanillo; Daily; 4 P.M.; 5 hrs; Auto-Transportes Mepe; Terminal Caribe.

Monteverde; Daily; 6:30 A.M. and 2:30 P.M.; 3.3 hrs; Autotransportes Tilarán; Calle 12, Ave. 9.

Nicoya; Daily; 6:30 A.M., 8 A.M. and 10 A.M., and 1:30 P.M., 2 P.M., 3 P.M. and 5 P.M.; 6 hrs; Tracopa Alfaro; Calle 14, Ave. 3/5

Nosara; Daily; 6 A.M.; 6 hrs; Tracopa Alfaro, Calle 14, Ave. 3/5

Orotina; Daily; 5 A.M., 6 A.M., 7 A.M., 10 A.M., and 2 P.M., 4 P.M., 5 P.M., 6 P.M., and 7 P.M.;??; Ave. 1, Calle 16.

Palmar; Daily; 5 A.M., 7 A.M., 8:30 A.M. and 10 A.M. and 1 P.M., 2:30 P.M. and 6 P.M.; 5 hrs; Tracopa; Calle 14, Avenidas 3/5.

Paso Canoas; Daily; 5 A.M., 7:30 A.M., 11 A.M.,

1 P.M., 4:30 P.M., and 6 P.M.; 8 hrs; Trecopa; Ave. 5, Calle 16.

Peñas Blancas; Daily 4:30 A.M., 5 A.M., 7 A.M., and 1:20 P.M., and 4:10 P.M.; 6 hrs

Playa Brasilito (see Playa Flamingo)

Playa Flamingo; Daily; 8 and 10 A.M.; 6 hrs; Tralapa; Avenida 3, Calle 18/20

Playa Hermosa; Daily; 3:20 P.M.; 5 hrs; Tralapa; Calle 12, Ave. 5/7

Playa Junquillal; Daily; 2 P.M.; 5 hrs; Tralapa; Calle 20, Ave. 3

Playa Panamá (see Playa Hermosa)

Playa Potrero; (see Playa Flamingo)

Playas del Coco; Daily; 8 A.M., and 2 P.M.; 5 hrs; Pulmitán; Calle 14, Ave. 1/3

Poás Volcano NP; Daily; 8:30 A.M.; 1.5 hrs; Tuasa; Ave. 2, Calles 12/14

Puerto Jiménez; Daily; 6 A.M. and noon; 8 hrs; Atlántico Norte; Calle 14, Ave. 9/11

Puerto Limón; Daily; 5 A.M., 5:30 A.M., 6:45 A.M., then hourly 7:30–6:30 P.M.; 2.5 hrs; Auto-Transportes Caribeños; Calle Central, Ave. 13/15

Puerto Viejo de Limón (see Cahuita)

Puerto Viejo de Sarapiquí; Daily; 6:30 A.M., 8 A.M., 10 A.M. and 11:30 A.M. and 1:30 P.M.; 3:30 P.M., 4:30 P.M. and 6 P.M. via Braulio Carrillo NP, and 6:30 A.M., noon, and 3 P.M. via Heredia; 4 hrs; Atlántico Norte; Calle 12, Ave. 7/9

Puntarenas; Daily; every 40 min. 6 A.M.–7 P.M.; 2 hrs; Empresarios Unidos; Avenida 12, Calle 16.

Quepos/Manuel Antonio; Daily; 6 A.M., noon, and 6 P.M. direct bus, and 7 A.M., 10 A.M., 2 P.M., and 4 P.M. indirect bus (Quepos only); 3.5 hrs (direct); Transportes Morales; Avenida 3, Calle 18.

Sámara; Daily; 12:30 P.M. and 6:15 P.M.; 6 hrs; Tracopa Alfaro; Calle 14, Ave. 3/5

San Isidro; Daily; every hour, 5:30 A.M. to 5 P.M.; 3 hrs; Transportes Musoc; Avenida 3, Calle 16.

Santa Cruz; Daily; 7 A.M., 9 A.M., 10 A.M., 11 A.M., noon, and 1 P.M., 2 P.M., 4 P.M. and 6 P.M.; 5 hrs; Tracopa Alfaro; Calle 20, Ave. 1/3

Santa María de Dota; Daily; 7:15 A.M., 9 A.M., 11:30 A.M., and 12:30 P.M., 3 P.M., 5 P.M., and 7:30 P.M.; 2.5 hrs

Santa Rosa NP; (see Peñas Blancas)

San Vito; Daily; 5:45 A.M., 8:15 A.M., 11:30 A.M., and 2:45 P.M.; Tracopa Alfaro; Ave. 3, Calle 16.

Sarchí; Daily; every 30 min. 5 A.M.–10 P.M.; 1.5 hrs; Tuan; Calle 18, Ave. 3

Sixaola; 6 A.M., 10 A.M., and 1:30 P.M., and 3:30 P.M.; 5 hrs; Auto-Transportes Mepes; Terminal Caribe.

Tamarindo; Daily; 3:30 P.M.; 5.5 hrs; Tracopa Alfaro; Calle 14, Ave. 5

Tilarán; Daily; 7:30 A.M., 9:30 A.M., and 12:45 P.M., 3:45 P.M., and 6:30 P.M.; 4 hrs; Auto-Transportes Tilarán; Calle 12, Ave. 9/11.

Turrialba; Daily; hourly 5 A.M.–10 P.M.; 1.5 hrs; Transtusa; Calle 13, Ave. 6/8

Uvita; Mon.–Fri. 3 P.M., and Sat.–Sun. 5:30 A.M., and 3 P.M.; 7 hrs; Transportes Morales; Ave. 3, Calles 16/20.

Zarcero; Daily; hourly 5 A.M.–7:30 P.M.; 1.5 hrs; Autotransportes Ciudad Quesada; Calle 16, Ave. 1/3

(For information on **international buses,** see the sidebar *Crossing into Nicaragua and Panamá* in the *Know Costa Rica* section.)

San José

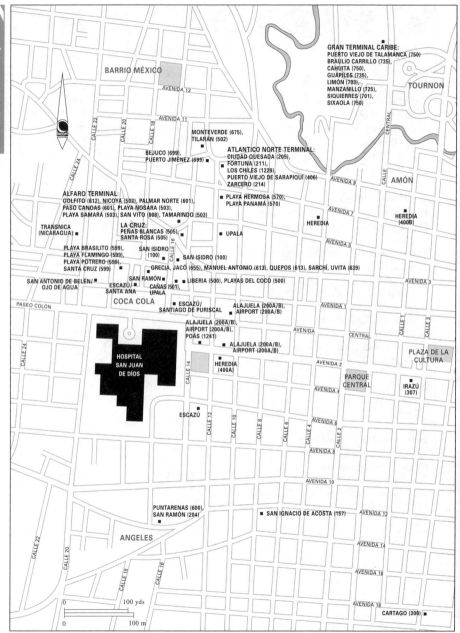

BARRIO MÉXICO

AVENIDA 13

AVENIDA 11

CALLE 22

CALLE 20

CALLE 18

CALLE 24

MONTEVERDE (675),
TILARÁN (502)

GRAN TERMINAL CARIBE:
PUERTO VIEJO DE TALAMANCA (750),
BRAULIO CARRILLO (735),
CAHUITA (750),
GUÁPILES (735),
LIMÓN (703),
MANZANILLO (725),
SIQUIERRES (701),
SIXAOLA (750)

TOURNON

BEJUCO (699),
PUERTO JIMÉNEZ (699)

ATLANTICO NORTE TERMINAL:
CIUDAD QUESADA (205),
FORTUNA (211),
LOS CHILES (1229),
PUERTO VIEJO DE SARAPIQUÍ (406)
ZARCERO (214)

AVENIDA 9

CENTRAL

CALLE

AMÓN

ALFARO TERMINAL:
GOLFITO (612), NICOYA (503), PALMAR NORTE (601),
PASO CANOAS (601), PLAYA NOSARA (503),
PLAYA SAMARÁ (503), SAN VITO (808), TAMARINDO (503)

PLAYA HERMOSA (570),
PLAYA PANAMÁ (570)

AVENIDA 7

HEREDIA

HEREDIA
(400B)

TRANSNICA
(NICARAGUA)

LA CRUZ:
PEÑAS BLANCAS (505),
SANTA ROSA (505)

UPALA

AVENIDA 5

PLAYA BRASILITO (599),
PLAYA FLAMINGO (599),
PLAYA POTRERO (599),
SANTA CRUZ (599)

SAN ISIDRO
(100)

CALLE 16

SAN ISIDRO (100)

GRECIA, JACÓ (655), MANUEL ANTONIO (613), QUEPOS (613), SARCHÍ, UVITA (639)

AVENIDA 3

SAN ANTONIO DE BELÉN/
OJO DE AGUA

SAN RAMÓN

ESCAZÚ/
SANTA ANA

CAÑAS (501),
UPALA

LIBERIA (500), PLAYAS DEL COCÓ (500)

COCA COLA

PASEO COLÓN

CALLE 24

ESCAZÚ/
SANTIAGO DE PURISCAL

ALAJUELA (200A/B),
AIRPORT (200A/B)

AVENIDA 1

CALLE 1

CALLE 3

ALAJUELA (200A/B),
AIRPORT (200A/B),
POÁS (1241)

AVENIDA

CENTRAL

PLAZA DE LA
CULTURA

HOSPITAL
SAN JUAN
DE DÍOS

CALLE 14

ALAJUELA (200A/B),
AIRPORT (200A/B)

HEREDIA
(400A)

AVENIDA 2

AVENIDA 4

PARQUE
CENTRAL

IRAZÚ
(307)

ESCAZÚ

CALLE 12

CALLE 10

CALLE 8

CALLE 6

CALLE 4

CALLE 2

AVENIDA 6

AVENIDA 8

AVENIDA 10

PUNTARENAS (600),
SAN RAMÓN (204)

SAN IGNACIO DE ACOSTA (157)

AVENIDA 12

ANGELES

AVENIDA 14

CALLE 22

CALLE 20

CALLE 18

CALLE 16

AVENIDA 16

AVENIDA 18

CARTAGO (300)

0   100 yds

0   100 m

SAN JOSÉ BUS TERMINALS

Río

Torres

PARQUE ZOOLÓGICA SIMÓN BOLÍVAR

OTOYA

PARQUE MORAZÁN

PARQUE ESPAÑA

CALLE 5

BARRIO MÉXICO/SABANILLO ■

M PARQUE NACIONAL

CALLE 7

CALLE 9

CALLE 11

CALLE 15

RICARDO JIMÉNEZ

PLAZA DE LA DEMOCRACIA

■ TICA (GUATEMALA, HONDURAS, NICARAGUA, PANAMÁ)

■ TURRIALBA (302)

BOULEVARD

SIRCA (NICARAGUA) ■

CALLE 13

© AVALON TRAVEL PUBLISHING, INC.

don't even think about it for travel *within* San José. Too many headaches! Most places are quickly and easily reached by taxi, by bus, or on foot. Note that Paseo Colón is one-way only—eastbound—weekdays 6:30–8:30 A.M.

A peripheral highway *(circunvalación)* passes around the south and east sides of San José. The northern and western extensions completing the circle were almost complete at last visit.

Parking spaces are at a premium, and you could end up having to park so far away you may as well have walked in the first place. Parking meters take five-*colón* coins (30 minutes) as well as tokens *(ficas)*. You can obtain these at the Departamento de Parquémetros, in the administrative offices of the Mercado Central, Calle 6, Avenidas Central/1, second floor; or at the Banco de Costa Rica, at the window where municipal taxes are paid. Private parking lots offer secure 24-hour parking; you must leave your ignition key with the attendant. Never park in a no-parking zone, marked Control por Grúa ("Controlled by tow truck"). Regulations are efficiently enforced.

Break-ins and theft are common (rental cars are especially vulnerable; make sure your insurance covers loss). Never leave anything of value in your car, even in the trunk.

Central Highlands

The beauty of the Central Highlands region owes much to the juxtaposition of valley and mountain. The large, fertile central valley—sometimes called the Meseta Central ("Central Plateau")—is a tectonic depression some 20 km wide and 70 km long. The basin is held in the cusp of verdant mountains that rise on all sides, their slopes quilted with dark green coffee and pastures as bright as fresh limes. Volcanoes of the Cordillera Central frame the valley to the north, forming a smooth-sloped meniscus. To the south lies the massive, blunt-nosed bulk of the Cordillera Talamanca. The high peaks are generally obscured by clouds for much of the "winter" months (May through November). When clear, both mountain zones offer spectacularly scenic drives, including the chance to drive to the very crest of two active volcanoes: Poás and Irazú.

The Meseta Central is really two valleys in one, divided by a low mountain ridge—the Fila de Bustamente (or Cerro de la Carpintera)—which rises immediately east of San José. West of the ridge is the larger valley of the Poás and Virilla Rivers, with flanks gradually rising from a level floor. East of the ridge the smaller Valle de Guarco (containing Cartago) is more tightly hemmed in, and falls away to the east, drained by the Río Reventazón.

Must-Sees

M **Rancho San Miguel:** This stable comes into its own at night when it hosts an Andalusian horse show offering a dramatic display of fine horsemanship (page 112).

M **Flor de Mayo:** Visits are strictly by appointment at this private breeding center for endangered macaws. Serious birders and nature lovers will be enthralled (page 115).

M **La Paz Waterfall Gardens:** The world's largest butterfly garden, hiking trails, and spectacular waterfalls highlight a visit to this nature theme park. It has a fine restaurant and luxurious, *Lord of the Rings*-style accommodations (page 121).

M **Poás Volcano National Park:** Imagine a drive-in volcano! You can park near the summit, then walk to the crater rim of this steaming volcano. As a bonus, you're blessed with stupendous views (page 126).

M **Bosque De Paz Rain/Cloud Forest:** This remote, seldom-visited Shangri-la offers prime birding and wildlife viewing in a rain-soaked mountain setting (page 132).

M **Zoo Ave:** A Noah's Ark-ful of critters are displayed at this well-run zoo offering close-up encounters with many slithering and snapping beasts you may not wish to meet in the wild. All the favorites are here, from monkeys to the big cats, as well as a large collection of snakes (page 134).

M **Los Angeles Cloud Forest Reserve:** There are no quetzals here, but sloths, monkeys galore, and countless bird species inhabit this mountain-crest, mist-shrouded forest with nature trails and a short zipline canopy tour (page 140).

M **Café Britt:** Workers in *campesino* outfits provide an entertaining entrée to the world of coffee, including theatrical skits and ending with your favorite beverage (page 146).

M **Irazú Volcano National Park:** The drive up Volcán Irazú is a scenic switchback made more fun by the anticipation of magnificent views from the summit (page 160).

M **Guayabo National Monument:** Interested in pre-Columbian history? Head to the nation's foremost excavated indigenous village, with stone structures in the heart of the forest (page 177).

M Central Highlands

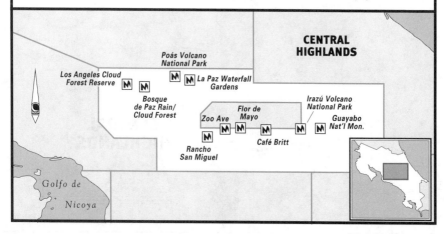

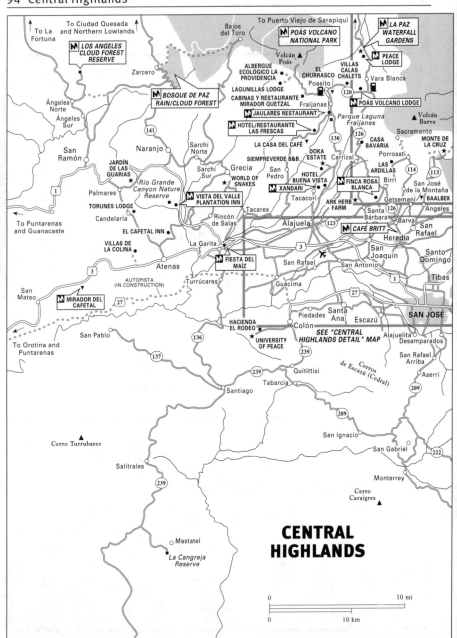

CENTRAL
HIGHLANDS

0 _____ 10 mi

0 _____ 10 km

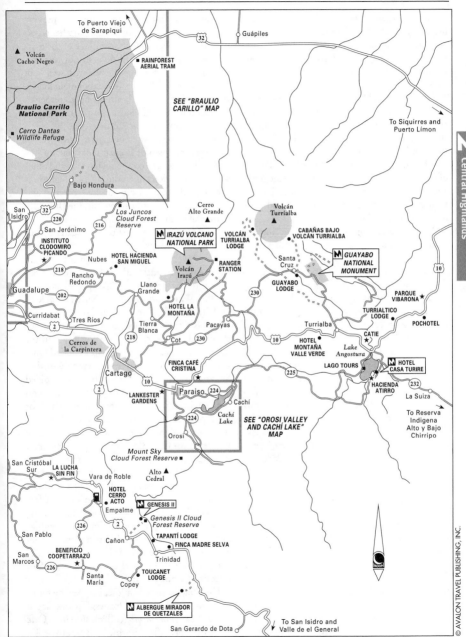

To Puerto Viejo
de Sarapiquí

Guápiles

32

Volcán
Cacho Negro

RAINFOREST
AERIAL TRAM

SEE "BRAULIO
CARILLO" MAP

Braulio Carrillo
National Park

To Siquirres and
Puerto Límon

Cerro Dantas
Wildlife Refuge

Bajo Hondura

San
Isidro

32

220

San Jerónimo

216

Los Juncos
Cloud Forest
Reserve

Cerro
Alto Grande

Volcán
Turrialba

CABAÑAS BAJO
VOLCÁN TURRIALBA

INSTITUTO
CLODOMIRO
PICANDO

218

Nubes

HOTEL HACIENDA
SAN MIGUEL

IRAZÚ VOLCANO
NATIONAL PARK

VOLCÁN
TURRIALBA
LODGE

GUAYABO
NATIONAL
MONUMENT

10

Rancho
Redondo

Santa
Cruz

Guadalupe

202

Llano
Grande

Volcán
Irazú

RANGER
STATION

GUAYABO
LODGE

PARQUE
VIBARONA

230

Curridabat

218

Tres Ríos

HOTEL LA
MONTAÑA

TURRIALTICO
LODGE

POCHOTEL

2

Tierra
Blanca

218

Cot

Pacayas

230

Turrialba

CATIE

Cerros de
la Carpintera

10

HOTEL
MONTAÑA
VALLE VERDE

Lake
Angostura

232

FINCA CAFÉ
CRISTINA

225

LAGO TOURS

HOTEL
CASA TURIRE

Cartago

2

10

Paraiso

224

HACIENDA
ATIRRO

LANKESTER
GARDENS

Cachí

La Suiza

224

Cachí
Lake

SEE "OROSI VALLEY
AND CACHÍ LAKE"
MAP

To Reserva
Indígena
Alto y Bajo
Chirripo

Orosi

Mount Sky
Cloud Forest Reserve

San Cristóbal
Sur

LA LUCHA
SIN FIN

Vara de Roble

Alto
Cedral

HOTEL
CERRO
ACTO

GENESIS II

Empalme

San Pablo

226

Genesis II Cloud
Forest Reserve

Cañón

TAPANTÍ LODGE

San
Marcos

2

BENEFICIO
COOPETARRAZÚ

FINCA MADRE SELVA

226

Santa
María

Trinidad

TOUCANET
LODGE

Copey

ALBERGUE MIRADOR
DE QUETZALES

San Gerardo de Dota

To San Isidro and
Valle de el General

© AVALON TRAVEL PUBLISHING, INC.

Almost 70 percent of the nation's populace lives here, concentrated in the four colonial cities of San José, Alajuela, Cartago, and Heredia, plus lesser urban centers that derive their livelihood from farming. Sugarcane, tobacco, and corn smother the valley floor, according to elevation and microclimate. Dairy farms rise up the slopes to more than 2,500 meters. Small coffee *fincas,* too, are everywhere on vale and slope, the dark green, shiny-leafed bushes often shaded by erythrina trees, which can be planted simply by breaking off a branch and sticking it in the ground. Pockets of natural vegetation remain farther up the slopes and in protected areas such as Braulio Carrillo National Park, Tapantí National Park, and other havens of untamed wildlife.

Though variations exist, an invigorating and salubrious climate is universal (the valley floor has been called a place of perpetual summer and the upper slopes a place of perpetual spring). In the dry season, mornings are clear and the valley basks under brilliant sunshine. In the wet ("green") season, clouds typically form over the mountains in early afternoon, bringing brief showers and often torrential downpours. Temperatures average in the mid-20s C (mid-70s F) year-round in the valley and cool steadily as one moves into the mountains, where coniferous trees lend a distinctly alpine feel. Western-facing slopes have a distinct dry season that roughly corresponds to North America's winter months. The eastern-facing—windward—slopes receive considerably more rainfall any time of year. Braulio Carrillo and Tapantí National Parks, for example, are generally always wet.

PLANNING YOUR TIME

You could well spend two weeks touring the highlands, but for most folks three or four days should prove sufficient. Ideally you'll want your own car, although tour operators in San José offer canned excursions to most destinations of interest. Don't underestimate the time it can take to move between destinations: roads are convoluted and signage is poor.

Touring the highlands en route to another region makes sense; choose your destinations accordingly. For more extensive touring, moving from one overnight destination to another is perhaps the best way to take advantage of the marvelous scenic drives and diversity of terrains. Fortunately, the region is blessed with well-kept budget accommodations, rustic mountain lodges, plus several world-class boutique hotels dispersed throughout the highlands, and you're never far from a worthwhile place to stay.

Some places you will not want to miss. West of San José, the town of **Escazú** melds quaint historical charm with a cosmopolitan vibe and offers some of the nation's finest dining, plus nightspots that draw the youth from San José. Nearby, and long a staple of the tourist circuit, the **Butterfly Farm** will teach you all about flutterby lore, while the Andalusian horse show at **Rancho San Miguel** is breathtaking.

Northwest of San José, two must-sees are **Poás Volcano National Park,** where you can peer into the bowels of a living volcano, and **La Paz Waterfall Gardens Nature Park & Wildlife Park.** The drive up the mountain slopes is a tremendously scenic excursion, although the same can be said for any journey into the mountains. If heading for Ciudad Quesada, Hwy. 141 will deliver you via the **World of Snakes,** the crafts town of **Sarchí** (to be avoided on weekends, when tour buses crowd in), and the delightful village of **Zarcero,** renowned for the topiary in the church plaza. From here, nature lovers might make the sidetrip to **Bosque De Paz Rain Cloudforest Biological Reserve.** Alternately, the fast (perhaps too fast) Hwy. 1 speeds you westward via Palmares, where orchid lovers should call in at **Jardín de Las Guarias.** Be sure to divert at La Garita for a few hours at **Zoo Ave,** the nation's finest zoo. Travelers heading to La Fortuna might consider hiking in **Los Angeles Cloud Forest Reserve** and, if active adventure is your bag, an adrenaline-packed ride through the forest at the **San Lorenzo Canopy Tour.**

Heredia, north of San José, is appealing for its colonial-era cathedral and fortress. To learn about Costa Rica's *grano de oro* (coffee), stop in at **Café Britt** near Heredia. Nearby, **INBioparque** is a worthy place to learn about the nation's diverse ecosystems, while the montane rainforests of **Braulio Carrillo National Park** offer tremendous hiking opportunities for the hale and hearty. The **Rainforest Aerial Tram,** on the eastern side of Braulio Carrillo, is popular and fun, although travelers report seeing little wildlife; you might stop in while en route to the Caribbean.

A less daunting, albeit longer, route to the Caribbean is via **Cartago,** worth a stop only for its Cathedral of Our Lady of the Angels. If you're planning on driving from San José to the summit of Irazú Volcano National Park, I recommend the scenic route via Rancho Redondo. **Guayabo National Monument,** east of Cartago, is a great birding spot and of interest for anyone keen on pre-Columbian culture, while the colorful and varied **Lankester Gardens** thrills everyone fond of gardens. A sojourn in the **Orosi–Cachí Valley** makes a thrilling scenic excursion, as do the rugged journey to the off-the-beaten-track hamlet of **Moravia del Chirripó;** a drive along the **Route of the Saints,** which begins due south of San José; and the daunting drive to **Cerro de la Muerte,** from which you might descend to **San Gerardo De Dota** to view quetzals in this hidden Shangri-la.

Lastly, white-water enthusiasts can get their kicks on the Ríos Reventazón or Pacuare, offering tremendous opportunities for viewing wildlife, as does the easily accessed **Tapantí–Mecizo De La Muerte National Park.**

Few towns have any accommodations of note, although there's no shortage of budget options. Unless you're traveling by bus and have early morning connections that call for overnighting near bus stations, you'll appreciate staying on the outskirts of towns, or further out, in properties that guarantee greater character.

West of San José

ESCAZÚ

Beginning only four km west of San José's Parque Sabana, Escazú is officially part of Metropolitan San José yet is so individualistic that it functions virtually as a sister city. The town, one of the oldest settlements in the country (and also among its most modern), is accessed by the Carretera Prospero Fernández (Hwy. 27), an expressway that passes north of Escazú and continues via Ciudad Colón to the Pacific lowlands.

There are actually three Escazús, each with its own church, patron saint, and character. **San Rafael de Escazú** is the ultramodern, lower town, nearest the freeway. Its once sleepy *campesino-*town ambience has been pushed aside by a wave of modern development, including chic restaurants and nightclubs and ultrachic shopping plazas that have drawn scores of English-speaking expatriates (there's good reason that the U.S. embassy and ambassador's home are here). Dozens of U.S.-style malls, condos, and resort communities have sprung up in recent years, adding to the ever-burdensome congestion. A beautiful old church stands here in colonial counterpoint.

San Rafael merges south to **San Miguel de Escazú,** about one km uphill. San Miguel, the heart of old Escazú, was originally a crossroads on trails between indigenous villages. The indigenous folks gave it its name, Itzkatzu (Resting Place). A small chapel constructed in 1711 became the first public building. Here, time seems to have stood still for a century. The occasional rickety wooden oxcart weighed down with coffee beans comes to town, pulled by stately oxen. Cows wander along the road. And there are still a few cobblestone streets with houses of adobe (sun-dried brick made of mud, cattle blood, egg white, lime, grass, and horse dung), including those around the village plaza with its red-domed church, built in 1799 and painted with a traditional strip of color at the bottom to ward off witches. The church has a new frontage in modern style, with twin towers. It overlooks a new plaza—**Parque República de Colombia**—that caused discontent when built in 2000, replacing the local soccer pitch.

Above San Miguel, the road climbs steadily to **San Antonio de Escazú,** a dairy and agricultural center beyond which the steep slopes are

Central Highlands

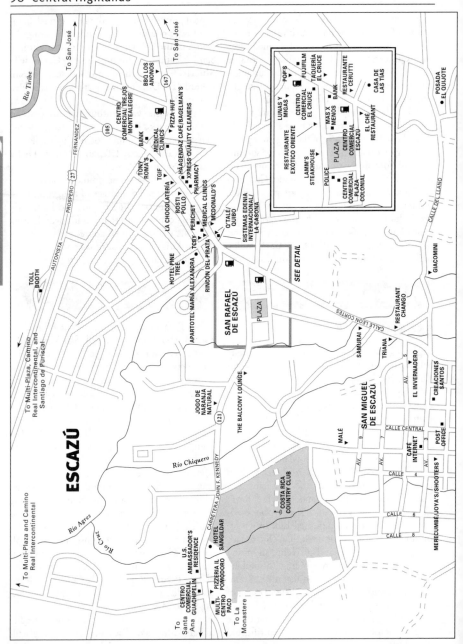

ESCAZÚ

To San José

To San José

Río Tribe

To Multi-Plaza, Camino
Real Intercontinental, and
Santiago de Puriscal

To Multi-Plaza and Camino
Real Intercontinental

Río Agres

Río Cruz

Río Chiquero

TOLL
BOOTH

AUTOPISTA

PROSPERO (27)

FERNANDEZ

(105)

(167)

BBQ LOS
ANONOS

CENTRO
COMERCIAL TREJOS
MONTEALEGRE

BANK

PIZZA HUT

MEDICAL
CLINICS

HAAGENDAZ CAFÉ/BAGELMAN'S

XPRESS QUALITY CLEANERS

TONY
ROMA'S

TGIF

PHARMACY

LA CHOCOLATERÍA

ROSTI
POLLO

TCBY

PERICHET

MEDICAL CLINICS

McDONALD'S

Q'TALÉ/
QUBO

SISTEMAS EDENIA
INTERNACIONAL/
LA CASONA

HOTEL PINE
TREE

APARTOTEL MARIA ALEXANDRA

RINCON DEL PIRATA

SAN RAFAEL
DE ESCAZÚ

PLAZA

SEE DETAIL

GIACOMINI

RESTAURANT
CHANGO

CALLE LEON CORTES

CALLE DE LLANO

SAMURAI

TRIANA

JOGO DE
NARANJA
NATURAL

(121)

THE BALCONY LOUNGE

EL INVERNADERO

CREACIONES
SANTOS

AV. 5

SAN MIGUEL
DE ESCAZÚ

MALÉ

AV. 9

AV. 7

CALLE CENTRAL

CAFÉ
INTERNET

AV. 3

POST
OFFICE

AV. 4

CALLE

CALLE 4

CALLE 6

CALLE 8

MERECUMBE/JOYA'S/SHOOTERS

COSTA RICA
COUNTRY CLUB

CARRETERA JOHN F. KENNEDY

HOTEL
SANGILDAR

U.S.
AMBASSADOR'S
RESIDENCE

PIZZERIA IL
POMODORO

MULTI-
CENTRO
PACO

CENTRO
COMERCIAL
GUACHIPELIN

To
Santa
Ana

To La
Monastere

To La
Monastere

Detail:

LUNAS Y
MIGAS

POP'S

FUJIFILM

TAQUERIA
EL CRUCE

RESTAURANTE
CERUTTI

CASA DE
LAS TIAS

POSADA
EL QUIJOTE

RESTAURANTE
EXÓTICO ORIENTE

MAS X
MENOS

CENTRO
COMERCIAL
EL CRUCE

BANK

CENTRO
COMERCIAL
ESCAZÚ

EL CHÉ
RESTAURANT

PLAZA

LAMM'S
STEAKHOUSE

POLICE

CENTRO
COMERCIAL
PLAZA
COLONIAL

Central Highlands

BELO HORIZONTE

RISCOS DE GUACAMAYA COUNTRY INN

BELLO HOTIZONTE COUNTRY CLUB

Quebrada Herrera

FRUIT VENDOR

BARRY BIESANZ WOODWORKS

Río Agres

CALLE LEÓN

BUS STOP

PLAZA

SAN ANTONIO DE ESCAZÚ

To Pico Blanco Inn

CALLE SAN MIGUEL

Parque

To Tara

To Tara

AV. CENTRAL

Río Chiquero

To Tara

CALLE 5

ESTADIO PLAZA

CALLE 3

MUSMANNI

HOTEL TAPEZCO INN

BUSES

Parque

AV. 12

To Restaurante Tiquicita

TEEN'S CHAT / VIDEO BAD BOY

EL RINCONCITO ARGENTINO

BANK

CALLE

AV. 2

AV. 4

AV. 6

AV. 8

AV. 10

Río Cruz

COSTA VERDE INN

VILLA ESCAZÚ

CALLE MONTE

0.25 mi

0.25 km

© AVALON TRAVEL PUBLISHING, INC.

clad in coffee bushes and cloud forest. Above rises Monte La Cruz (topped by an imposing 15-meter-tall iron cross), Piedra Blanca, Cerro Rabo de Mico (the tallest at 2,455 meters), and Cerro de Escazú, fluted with waterfalls.

Barry Biesanz Woodworks

In the hills of Bello Horizonte is the workshop (P.O. Box 47-1250 Escazú, tel. 506/289-4337, fax 506/228-6184, woodworks@biesanz.com, www.biesanz.com) of one of Costa Rica's leading wood designers and craftsmen ("a burly woodworker," in his own words). Barry Biesanz—who admits to once being "a starving hippie in Marin County, California"—today turns his adopted country's native hardwoods into beautiful bowls, boxes, and furniture. His works are expressive, vital, and strongly Asian, combining classic joinery and simple design. His elegant curves and crisply carved lines seem to bring life to the vivid purples, reds, and greens of purple heart, rosewood, and lignum vitae. Biesanz employs 20 or so Tico carvers (he also offers an informal apprenticeship program for visiting carvers). Through all these hands and guided by Biesanz's creative genius, his craftspeople create subtle, delicate forms from their chosen blocks of wood. His boxes and bowls grace the collections of three U.S. presidents, Pope John Paul II, and assorted European royalty. Biesanz promotes reforesta-

tion by giving away rosewood and other saplings grown at his nursery, on site.

The highlight is a visit to Barry Beisanz's workshop and store, where you can pick up exquisite handcrafted hardwood items. His showroom and store is open Mon.–Fri. 9 A.M.–5 P.M., and by appointment on Saturdays.

Also check out the superb stained-glass windows and wares at **Creaciones Santos** (Avenida 3, Calles 1/3, tel. 506/228-6747, creaciones_santos@yahoo.com), in San Miguel de Escazú.

Looking for quality art? Try **Galería Contemporaneo Kira** (tel. 506/289-4376), in Centro Comercial Trejos Monte.

Escazú Hills Sanctuary

This private reserve (tel. 506/253-3795) south of San Antonio de Escazú ascends to 2,400 meters and includes more than 1,900 hectares of primary cloud forest on a large dairy farm in the El Cedral area of the Escazú Hills. Much of the land has been reforested with trees native to the hills. Cedars, oaks, and laurels—all dominant giants of the mountaintops—tower in splendor, waving beards of Spanish moss. There are stands of jaul, the tall slender coffin tree, and a dense understory of bamboo that protects dozens of large mammal and other species, including sloths and pumas. Another 400 hectares will gradually become part of the reserve, which is slated to receive a new status as the **Escazú Mountains National Park** (Parque Nacional Montañas Escazú).

Horseback rides are available at **Hacienda Cerro Pando** (Apdo. 586, San José 1000, tel./fax 506/253-3795) in Cedral de Acosta.

Entertainment and Events

Escazú is a happening spot for young Josefinos with cash to throw around. They warm up with drinks at **Fandango,** then head next door to **Babu,** a fun, hip-hoppin' place in the Centro Comercial Trejos Montealegro, where other clubs—**Taos, Praukie Go,** and **Bamboleo**—also cater to the hip crowd. I like **Órale** (tel. 506/228-6438), with lively music and an outdoor bar that claims the "best margaritas south of Mexico."

Q'tal (tel. 506/228-4091, $5 admission), by El Cruce, is a classy nightspot where live riffs

---

WITCH CAPITAL OF COSTA RICA

Escazú is famous as the *bruja* (witch) capital of the country. The Río Tiribi, which flows east of Escazú, is said to be haunted, and old men still refuse to cross the Los Anonos Bridge at night for fear of La Zegua and Mico Malo (the magic monkey). Some 60 or so witches are said to still live in Escazú, including Doña Estrella, who says, "Any woman who lives in Escazú long enough eventually becomes a *bruja*." Amorous tourists should beware La Zegua, an incredibly beautiful enchantress. When the (un)lucky suitor gets her to bed, she turns into a horse.

NATIONAL BOYEROS DAY

Held every second Sunday of March since 1983, the *Día de los Boyeros* festival pays homage to the *boyeros,* the men who guide the traditional oxcarts to market. More than 100 *boyeros* from around the country trim their colorful carts and gather for this celebration, which includes an oxcart parade helped along by a supporting cast of women and children in traditional garb, plus a musical accompaniment of *cimarronas,* the traditional instrument mandatory for popular feasts. Lencho Salazar, a local folklorist, regales crowds with tales of *brujas.* Grupo Auténtico Tradicional Tiquicia treats onlookers to much-loved local melodies. And young girls perform ancestral dances.

range from bolero to jazz. Every Wednesday a female dance troupe performs. It has a house band and a dance floor, plus large-screen TV and pool table.

Anba (tel. 506/228-8106), in Pulticentro Paco, on the Santa Ana road, is a wine bar with almost 200 labels. Gourmet appetizers are served. And **The Balcony Lounge** wine-and-martini bar nearby also serves good *bocas.*

Merecumbé (Calle 2, Avenida 3, tel. 506/289-4774), in San Miguel, offers dance classes.

The **Restaurant Chango** hosts live music on Thursday and Friday. And **El Rinconcito Argentino** (tel. 506/228-6691 or 506/228-0140) offers tango lessons daily at 7:30 P.M.

Shooters, in San Miguel, is a down-to-earth bar popular with young Ticos. You can play billiards and bowl at the **Metro Bowl** (tel. 506/288-1122, 2 P.M.–midnight Mon.–Thur., 2 P.M.–1 A.M. Friday, 11 A.M.–1 A.M. Saturday, 10 a.m.–midnight Sunday), 400 meters south of Multiplaza Mall, with a state-of-the-art, 20-lane bowling complex ($10 per hour) and video game rooms.

For movies, head to **Cine Rock,** in Centro Comercial Trejos Montealegre; or the two-screen **Cine Colonial** in Plaza Colonial Escazú.

Held every second Sunday of March, the **National Boyeros Day** (*Día de los Boyeros*) pays

homage to the *boyeros,* the men who guide the traditional oxcarts to market.

On Christmas Day, a hydraulic engine is employed to move singular figures—including a headless priest, the devil spinning a Ferris wheel, the corpse who opens his coffin, and a carousel, all elements of a Nativity celebration—in front of Iglesia San Antonio.

Accommodations

Escazú is known for its fine bed-and-breakfast inns.

$25–50: The **Hotel Tapezco Inn** (P.O. Box 1229-1250, Escazú, tel. 506/228-1084, fax 506/289-7026, info@tapezco-inn.co.cr. $35 s, $45 d), one block south of the main square in San Miguel de Escazú, is a contemporary colonial-style property with 15 charmless, simply furnished rooms, each with hot water, telephone, TV, and fan. It offers a Jacuzzi and sauna, plus a small restaurant. Rates include breakfast and tax.

In the Bello Horizonte hills, **Riscos de Guacamaya Country Inn** (Apdo. 351, Escazú 1250, tel. 506/228-9074, fax 506/289-5776, faberr @racsa.co.cr, $35 s/d shared bath, $50 s/d private bath, $60 suite low season; $50 s/d shared bath, $60 s/d private bath, $75 suite high season), formerly home to renowned fugitive Robert Vesco, is a charming option with one suite, two double rooms (two with shared bath), and three single rooms, most of which have beautiful parquet floors, and all of which have cable TV and private bath with hot water. The huge suite has a double and two single beds and a massive bathroom. There's a restaurant (plus 24-hour room service), and a brick sun deck around a pool with fine views. Rates include breakfast.

The lofty-ceilinged **Costa Verde Inn** (tel. 506/228-4080, fax 506/289-8591, costai @racsa.co.cr, www.costaverdeinn.com; in the U.S., SJO 1313, P.O. Box 025216, Miami, FL 33102-5216; $40 s, $45 d low season; $45 s, $55 d high season) is a beautiful, atmospheric, and peaceful bed-and-breakfast long on creature comforts. Hardwoods abound; walls are adorned with hand-colored historic photos; decor is simple, romantic, and bright, the furnishings tasteful. The lounge has a plump

Central Highlands

leather sofa, an open fireplace, and a large-screen TV. Twelve individually styled bedrooms come with king-size beds, built-in hardwood furniture, and huge, beautifully tiled bathrooms. Room 8 has a bathroom in natural stone with an open pit shower at its center. Outside are a shaded terrace with rough-hewn supports and open fireplace, plus a swimming pool, sun deck with whirlpool, and tennis court. A solid bargain. Rates include breakfast.

$50–100: The **Hotel Pine Tree** (Apdo. 1516-1250, Escazú, tel. 506/289-7405, fax 506/228-2180, pinetree@racsa.co.cr, www.hotelpinetree.com, $40 s, $50 d), in a modestly furnished 1950s home in the heart of San Rafael, has 15 rooms, some with king-size beds and spacious bathrooms; all have parquet floors, cable TVs, telephones, and safety boxes. The inn has a pool and solarium and parking, plus a large lounge with fireplace. Pets are welcome. Rates include breakfast.

My favorite hotel is the **Casa de Las Tías** (tel. 506/289-5517, fax 506/289-7353, casatias @kitcom.net, www.hotels.co.cr/casatias.html; in the U.S., SJO-478, P.O. Box 025216, Miami, FL 33102; $54 s, $65 d, $87 suite); it bills itself as a "country bed-and-breakfast in town." This exquisite yellow-and-turquoise, southern plantation–style wooden home has five airy, wood-paneled rooms, all with polished hardwood floors, wooden ceilings, wicker and antique furniture, ceiling fans, and Latin American art and other tasteful decor. One room has a balcony with chaise longue and rocker. The suite is beautiful and boasts a king-size bed and heaps of light pouring in from wide windows facing the back garden. All have private bath and ceiling fan. Breakfast (featuring wonderful homemade bread) is served on the garden patio full of birdsong. Your delightful hosts, Xavier and Pilar Vela, are planning to convert two garden cottages for rental. Airport pickups with advance notice. Rates include full breakfast.

Villa Escazú (Apdo. 1401, Escazú 1250, tel./fax 506/289-7971, escazu@hotels.co.cr, www.hotels.co.cr/vescazu.htm; $28 s, $49 d standard, $35 s, $60 d deluxe low season; $35 s, $60 d standard, $45 s, $75 d deluxe high season)

boasts stunning hardwood interiors mixed with rustic and tasteful modern decor in a pretty Swiss-style chalet. A "minstrel's gallery" balcony overhangs the lounge, with its fireplace and wide chimney of natural stone. Two bedrooms on both the main and third floors share three bathrooms. A deluxe room has a private bath. And a studio apartment has cable TV, a sofa, kitchenette, and modern bathroom with large walk-in shower ($250 week; one week minimum rental). The solid and superbly crafted house is enhanced by an all-around outside veranda with wicker chairs for enjoying the view. Breakfast is served on a terrace overlooking landscaped lawns that cascade downhill to a fruit orchard. There's an open barbecue at the back, and a stone patio with outdoor seating out front. Villa Escazú is run by friendly Floridian Inez Chapman, who prepare full breakfasts. Guest-friendly dogs abound. Rates include breakfast and tax.

Also recommended is the American-run **Posada El Quijote** (Apdo. 1127, Escazú 1250, tel. 506/289-8401, fax 506/289-8729, quijote @quijote.co.cr, www.quijote.co.cr, $55 s, $65 d standard, $65 s, $75 d superior, $75 s, $85 d deluxe), in the Bello Horizonte hills. This beautiful Spanish colonial home is exquisitely decorated and stocked with modern art. The eight tastefully appointed rooms look out over beautiful gardens, and have queen- or king-size beds, telephones, cable TVs, and private baths with lots of high-pressure hot water. Two superior rooms have a patio. Breakfast is served under an arbor on the intimate patio, and you can order light lunches and dinners, and take a nip at the bar. Room 25 has a bathroom that you won't be able to tear yourself away from. The hotel was for sale at last visit. Add 7 percent for credit card transactions. No children under 12. Rates include full breakfast.

Hotel Sangildar (Apdo. 1511, Escazú 1250, tel. 506/289-8843, fax 506/228-6454, info @hotelsangildar.com, www.hotelsangildar.com; in the U.S., tel. 800/758-7234, $78 s/d low season; $98 high season), set in lush grounds adjoining the Costa Rica Country Club on the western outskirts of Escazú, is a handsome contemporary Spanish-style building named for San Gildar, the Father of Triumph, whose effigy was placed in a private chapel in Escazú in 1834 (today it can be seen in the parish church). Hardwoods and stonework abound, and the 28 luxurious rooms (each with cable TV, plus a telephone in both the bedroom and bathroom, and hair dryer) reflect tasteful decor. Amenities include a swimming pool, a small shop, bar, and the elegant Terraza del Sol restaurant. Airport transfers are provided. Rates include continental breakfast.

Apartotel María Alexandra (Apdo. 3756, San José 1000, tel. 506/228-1507, fax 506/289-5192, apartotel@mariaalexandra.com, www.mariaalexandra.com, $80–$100), a quiet and comfy retreat away from the main road, offers 14 fully furnished, elegant, luxury a/c one- and two-bedroom apartments, each with king-size bed, telephone, cable TV and VCR (with video rentals), and full kitchen, plus private parking. There are also twin-level townhouses that sleep up to five people. I consider them the finest apartments in the region. Facilities include a lounge and restaurant, pool, sauna, and mini-golf. A reader praised the attentive and superlative service. There's a tour and travel operation on site.

In the hills, the **Apartotel Pico Blanco Inn** (Apdo. 900, Escazú 1250, tel. 506/228-1908 or 506/289-6197, fax 506/289-5189, pblanco@costarica.net, $35 s, $45 d standard, $45 s, $55 d suite) is a bed-and-breakfast at the end of a cobbled drive in San Antonio de Escazú. The English owner has stamped a very British imprint: lots of wicker furniture and a cozy Georgian-style bar-cum-restaurant. The 20 comfortable rooms all feature private balconies with fantastic views, plus terra-cotta tile floors, Peruvian wall hangings, carved hardwood headboards, and small bathrooms with hot water. There are also two two-bedroom cottages.

Courtyard Marriott San José (Apdo. 356-1260, San José, tel. 506/208-3000, fax 506/288-0808, courtyard@costarica-marriott.com, www.courtyard.com or www.marriott.com, $79 s/d), on Calle Marginal Norte, in Plaza Itskatzu, combines classic contemporary elegance with a traditional Spanish feel. The 125 rooms feature gorgeous hardwood floors (some rooms are carpeted), colonial-style furniture, minifridge, coffee-maker, security box, and iron and ironing board. Some rooms have a balcony. There's a bar, Internet, and self-service laundry, and a hourly shuttle runs to San José (5 A.M.–10 P.M.).

Nearby, and competing with the Courtyard Marriott, the **Comfort Hotel Real Costa Rica** (tel. 506/204-6700, fax 506/204-6800, www.choicehotels.com, $80 s/d), on the Autopista Prospero Fernández, has 154 modestly furnished, fully equipped rooms.

$100–150: The **Alta** (tel. 506/282-4160, fax 506/282-4162, info@thealtahotel.com, www.thealtahotel.com; in the U.S., Interlink 964, P.O. Box 025635, Miami, FL 33102, tel. 888/388-2582; $135 s/d standard, $155 junior suite, $695 penthouse low season; $155 s/d standard, $185 junior suite, $790 penthouse high season) sits on a hillside three km west of Escazú on the "old road" to Santa Ana. The thoroughly contemporary hotel is lent a monastic feel by its gently curved arches, hand-forged ironwork, whitewashed narrow corridors, and cathedral ceilings. The five-story hotel's 23 deluxe rooms (including four suites and a staggering penthouse suite with three guest rooms) display a fine aesthetic sensibility, with terra-cotta tile floors, hardwoods stained with sienna, and subdued autumn colors. All rooms have Internet access. The splendid bathrooms have tubs inset in Romanesque alcoves. Some rooms proffer modest views from private balconies; others hug the oval, glass-tiled swimming pool in the shade of a spreading guanacaste tree. The top-floor suite is sublime and even has its own library and *mirador* courtyard with fountain. The La Luz restaurant serves nouvelle cuisine. There's a full-service spa with sauna and massage, plus executive services for businessfolk. (Rooms in the Penthouse rent individually for $270 low season, $350 high season.)

$150–250: The **Hotel Real Intercontinental** (tel. 506/289-7000 or 800/521-5753, fax 506/289-8989, costaricaintercontinental@gruporeal.co.cr; in North America, tel. 800/722-6466, $155 s/d standard, $175–205 business, $500 junior suite, $750–1,000 suite), off the Prospero Fernandez Hwy. at Blvd. Camino Real, two km west of Escazú, is a large-scale hotel exuding contemporary opulence. The hotel is set in landscaped grounds including a clover-shaped pool with swim-up bar. Each of the 261 a/c rooms is luxuriously carpeted, with a 25-inch TV, electronic key lock, direct-dial telephone with voice mail, safety box, hair dryer, king-size bed with orthopedic mattress, plus a lounge chair and writing desk. Bathrooms are magnificent—magnesium-bright lighting and marble. Top floor Camino Real Club rooms, including junior suites and a presidential suite, feature bathrobes, daily newspaper, plus concierge service. The hotel—centered on a five-story atrium lobby—has a fully equipped business center and a conference center. It has two restaurants, a health and fitness center, massage parlor, beauty center, stores, car rental agency, and travel agency. A shuttle runs to/from downtown San José. Rates include breakfast.

Rhett and Scarlett would be aghast to find **Tara** (tel. 506/228-6992, fax 506/228-9651, tarasp@racsa.co.cr, www.tararesort.com; in the U.S., Interlink 345, P.O. Box 025635, Miami, FL 33152; $100 s/d room, $125 junior suite, $150–200 suite low season; $130 s/d room, $160 junior suite, $195–250 suite high season) a bed-and-breakfast. But there it is, foursquare on the hill above Escazú. Who said the South's plantation lifestyle has gone with the wind? The somewhat aloof Greek Revival plantation mansion—complete with Corinthian columns, period-piece furnishings, dark hardwoods, and 15 resplendent bedrooms with antique rosewood tester beds and private verandas—also offers 26 two-bedroom villas in classical style, all with fax, printer, and computers with Internet access. A penthouse suite offers a 360-degree view. There's a gym, a pool, a gazebo with Jacuzzi, a barbecue terrace, and a pavilion patio with staggering views over the valley. Guests eat in a formal dining room. Health nuts will love Scarlett's Fountain of Youth Spa, and there's a tennis court and croquet lawn. Spa packages are offered. Rates include continental breakfast.

Food

For breakfast, head to **Bagelman's** (tel. 506/228-4460, 7 A.M.–8 P.M.), resembling Starbucks but also serving bagels (onion, pumpernickel, etc.), muffins, brownies, and cinnamon rolls, plus breakfast specials from *gallo pinto* to scrambled eggs. You can sit in the overly a/c café or outside on a shady patio.

Escazú has several noteworthy delis, including **Wall Street** (tel. 506/228-6422, 10 A.M.–10 P.M.), in Centro Comercial Trejos Monte, serving *bocas,* hams, marinated artichokes, potato salad, etc. My favorite spot is **Lunas y Migas** (tel. 506/288-2774), a clean a/c gourmet deli and bakery run by delightful Argentinian owners who conjure superlative sandwiched, oven-baked *empeñadas* ($1) with spinach or ham and cheese, plus pizzas, fettuccines, croissants, breads, tarts, etc. Try the scrumptious zucchini quiche, followed by cappuccino or espresso.

One of the best options is **Restaurant Chango** (Calle León Cortes, tel. 506/228-1173, noon–midnight), in San Rafael, serving Mediterranean and international cuisine, plus steaks (including baby back ribs, the house special; $11), seafood, and grilled pork dishes (entrées from $8–20). It has live music Thur.–Fri.

For a rustic eatery in the hills, head to Cuesta Grande de San Antonio de Escazú and the **Restaurante y Mirador Tíquicia** (tel. 506/289-5839), where the views are mesmerizing. The hacienda has a glassed-in terrace and an open patio. Your meal is prepared over charcoal. It hosts folkloric dancing on Wednesday evenings ($30 including dinner and shuttle from San José).

The now-hot, now-cool **La Luz** (tel. 506/282-4160, 6 A.M.–3 P.M. and 6–10 P.M. Mon.–Sat., Sunday 6 A.M.–4 P.M. and 6–10 P.M.), in the Hotel Alta, serves fusion cuisine melding Costa Rican ingredients with Pacific rim influences. The setting—a contemporary remake on a Tudor theme—is classy, the views splendid, and the service exemplary. Quality, alas, is never consistent. Try the macadamia nut–crusted chicken in *guaro*-chipotle cream, or fiery garlic prawns in tequila-lime-butter sauce ($12), followed by chocolate macadamia tart ($7). Live jazz is hosted.

The politically and economically advantaged crowd eats at **El Invernadero** (tel. 506/228-0216 or 800/222-2222, www.el-invernadero.com, noon–3 P.M. and 6–10:30 P.M. Mon.–Thur., noon–3 P.M. and 6–midnight Fri.–Sat.), blending traditional decor into a contemporary setting. Real silverware and tall-stemmed glasses set the tone. The name means "winter house," perhaps because the a/c is set at freezing. It serves Italian and Costa Rican nouvelle, such as flambéed shrimp ($21) and a superb tilapia *chile dulce* in red pepper sauce and brandy ($12).

For a classy contemporary ambience try **Quiubo** (tel. 506/228-4091, 11:30 A.M.–11 P.M. Tue.–Thur. and Sunday, 11:30 A.M.–1 A.M. Fri.–Sat.), with a large continental menu ranging from heart of palm salad ($6) and black bean soup ($3.25) to pepper sauce tenderloin ($10.75) and sea bass in mushroom sauce ($10).

The Tara hotel's **Atlanta Restaurant** (tel. 506/228-6992) offers grand elegance, spectacular views, and such dishes as grilled beef with shrimp and béarnaise sauce ($12) and lobster bisque ($5). It has an all-you-can-eat Pasta Night each Sunday, and a Family Fun Sunday brunch (11 A.M.–2 P.M.).

Le Monastère (tel. 506/289-4404, reservations @monastere-restaurant.com, www.monastere-restaurant.com, 7–10 P.M. Mon.–Wed., 7–11 P.M. Thur.–Sat.) has been called a "religious dining experience," not for the cuisine but for the venue— a restored chapel amid gardens in the hills east of town. The waiters dress like monks and Gregorian chants provide background music. The menu includes grilled lamb chops, and *vol au vent* of asparagus. Expect to pay $30 pp. It's signed on the Santa Ana road from Escazú.

The fashionable place for Italian is the handsome, atmospheric **Restaurante Cerutti** (tel. 506/228-4511, noon–2:30 P.M. and 6:30–11 P.M. Wed.–Sun.), 200 meters south of El Cruce, in a charming old home. It offers elegance and such specialties as squid in red wine ($7) and taglioni lobster ($14).

I recommend the elegant **Tutti Li** (tel. 506/289-8768, noon–10:30 P.M. Mon.–Wed. and noon–11 P.M. Thur.–Sat., noon–9 P.M. Sunday), in Plaza Itzkazu, serving salmon carpaccio

or octopus ($6.50), raviolis ($6.50), an excellent risotto ($7.50), 28 types of pizza, and profiteroles ($3.50). Service is first-class.

At **El Ché Restaurant** (tel. 506/228-1598, 11 A.M.–1 A.M. Sun.–Thur., 11 A.M.–1:30 A.M. Fri.–Sat.), you can watch traditional Argentinian delicacies prepared in front of your eyes on an open barbecue rotisserie. A **churasco** costs $10. It also serves a charcoal-grilled corvina al ajillo (sea bass with garlic; $10). El Ché has rustic yet endearing ambience—a piece of the pampas transplanted, but also drawing local Americans and Brits to its unpretentious bar.

Tony Roma's (11 A.M.–11 P.M. Mon.–Thur., 11 A.M.–midnight Fri.–Sat., and 11 A.M.–10 P.M. Sunday) has an outlet in San Rafael, serving ribs.

Café Heliconia (tel. 506/288-0707; 8 A.M.–8 P.M.), 150 meters south of Rolex Plaza, serves soups, salads, sandwiches, and killer desserts. The American-run **Café de Artistas** (tel. 506/228-6045), next door, is another good option.

In San Miguel, **Goya's** (Calle 2, Avenida 3, tel. 506/289-3704, 12:30 P.M.–3 P.M. and 5–10 P.M. Tue.–Sun. and 12:30–10 P.M. Saturday) is a clean, well-lit sushi restaurant, although I prefer **Samurai** (Calle León Corte, tel. 506/228-4124, noon–3 P.M. and 6:30–10 P.M.), with a splendid superchic Japanese aesthetic and in or out dining. It has various rooms, including an hibachi and two tatami rooms.

In San Rafael I like the small, unpretentious **Restaurante Exótico Oriente** (tel. 506/288-0951), on Carretera John F. Kennedy, a homey placed serving Indonesian and Thai food, including classics such as pad thai ($5) and curry vegetables ($5). And the upscale **Taj Majal** (tel. 506/228-0980, closed Monday), in a converted private home one km west of Centro Comercial Paco, on the Santa Ana road, serves tempting Indian dishes.

For Mexican fare, try **Taquería El Cruce,** a pleasing little mom-and-pop place serving the usual Mexican fare, and open-sided to the street at El Cruce. No meal costs more than $3. I like **Malé** (tel. 506/289-217, 11 A.M.–9 P.M. Tue.–Sun., 11 A.M.–10:30 P.M. Fri.–Sat.), on Calle 2 in San Miguel, which offers a marvelous contempo design and lively decor with Mexican music. No meal costs more than $5. It has a special meat plate of ribs on Thur.–Fri. nights.

For the real McCoy, try **El Tapatio,** a kiosk in Plaza Colonial where Lina, from Mexico, makes molés, tacos, and tortillas for pennies.

I hear good reports about two Peruvian restaurants: **Embrujo Limeño,** opposite Hotel María Alexander, and the upscale **Inca Grill,** on the Santa Ana road. Not reviewed.

For *tapas,* try the Spanish-owned **Triana** (tel. 506/288-0793), on Calle León Cortes, and blending contemporary and traditional Costa Rican decor. Samples include garlic mushrooms ($3), spiced octopus in olive oil ($4), and paella ($5.25).

There are two chocolate specialty shops: **La Chocolatería** (tel. 506/289-9637, 8 A.M.–7 P.M. Mon.–Fri. and 10 A.M.–7 P.M. Saturday), and **Giacomini** (tel. 506/288-3381, 10 A.M.–7 P.M. Mon.–Sat.), on Calle de Llano. The latter is a coffee shop with a classy contemporary decor and a garden with waterfalls. It serves paninis ($3.50), croissants, salads, pastries, cappuccinos, espressos, etc., in addition to chocolate delights. And **Häagen-Dazs Café** (tel. 506/228-4260; 10 A.M.–10 P.M. Mon.–Thur. and Sunday, 10 A.M.–11 p.m. Fri.–Sat.) serves excellent ice cream sundaes. And **Pops** sells ice cream (9 A.M.–10 P.M. daily).

You can stock up on groceries at **Mas X Menos,** in San Rafael. **Musmanni,** on the south side of the plaza in San Miguel, sells baked goods. **Lamm's** is a quality butcher in San Rafael.

Services

There's a **Scotiabank** at El Cruce, in San Rafael.

The **post office** (Calle Central, Avenida 1, 8 A.M.–5:30 P.M. Mon.–Fri., 7:30 A.M.–noon Saturday) is in San Miguel.

For Internet service try **Sistema Edenia Internacional** (tel. 506/228-2510, 8 A.M.–6 P.M. Mon.–Fri., 10 A.M.–6 P.M. Saturday), in Centro Comercial La Rambla, which charges $1.25 per hour.

Teens Chat (Calle 2, Avenida Central, tel. 506/288-3623), in San Miguel, is open 9 A.M.–10 P.M. Mon.–Sat., 10 A.M.–9 P.M. Sunday. Upstairs, **Video Bad-Boy** (no tel.), has video games

as well as Internet service and gets noisy. **Café Internet** (Calle 2, Avenida 3) is nearby.

Scarlett's Fountain of Youth Spa (tel. 506/228-6992, tarasp@racsa.co.cr), at Tara, offers complete spa services.

X-Press Quality Cleaners (tel. 506/289-9878, 11 A.M.–8 P.M. Mon.–Fri., 7 A.M.–7 P.M. Saturday) has pick-up and drop-off laundry service costing $1.75 per kilo for wash, dry, fold.

Fujifilm (tel. 506/289-8363) caters to photographic needs.

Getting There

Buses depart San José for Escazú from Avenida 1, Calle 18, every 15 minutes. The "Bebedero" bus departs San José from Calle 14, Avenida 6, for San Antonio de Escazú. And a bus for San Rafael de Escazú departs Calle 16, Avenidas Central/1.

Jaguar Limousine Services (tel. 506/204-7858, www.jaguarlimousineservices.com) uses Lincoln Town Cars.

SANTA ANA TO CIUDAD COLÓN

Santa Ana, about five km west of Escazú, is a sleepy town set in a sunny mountain valley. The church dates from 1870, and there are still many old adobe homes and old wooden houses clad in bougainvillea. Today it is more famous for ceramics and its onions and garlic and locally made honey. Look for braided onions hanging from restaurant lintels and roadside stands. There are some 30 independent pottery shops in the area; many artisans still use an old-fashioned kick-wheel to fashion the pots.

Continuing west you reach **Piedades,** about five km west of Santa Ana. This peaceful village—coffee is important hereabouts—has a beautiful church boasting impressive stained-glass windows.

The road gradually rises to **Ciudad Colón,** a neat little town about eight km west of Santa Ana. Coffee is an important crop here. (Work on the new, much-awaited San José–Puerta Caldera Highway was begun in 2000 and was expected to be completed by 2005; it will pass through Ciudad Colón and drop to Orotina, in the Central Pacific.)

The **Julia and David White Artists' Colony** (Apdo. 102-6100, Ciudad Colón, tel. 506/249-1414, fax 506/249-1831, info@forjuliaanddavid.org, www.forjuliaanddavid.org) offers residential artists courses, May–Nov.

Reserva Forestal el Rodeo

This reserve—in the hills about five km southwest of Ciudad Colón and part of a cattle estate called Hacienda el Rodeo (tel. 506/249-1013, 10 A.M.–6 P.M. Sat.–Sun. and holidays)—protects the largest remaining tract of virgin forest in the Meseta Central. In the late 1970s, Emilio Ramírez Rojas and his uncle Cruz Rojas Bennett donated 350 hectares of primary forest on an untouched part of their estate to the nation. It's popular with Ticos on weekends. The rustic **Restaurante del Abuelo** serves Tico fare.

The family also donated land to the United Nations. From that wellspring came the **University for Peace** (P.O. Box 138-6100, Ciudad Colón, tel. 506/249-1511, fax 506/249-1929, info@upeace.org, www.upeace.org, 8 A.M.–4:30 P.M. Mon.–Fri.), where students from many lands come to pursue disciplines designed to make the world a better place. The 303-hectare facility includes botanical gardens containing busts to famous figures, such as Gandhi and Henry Dunant (founder of the Red Cross). UPeace is charged with the mission of global education and research in support of the peace and security goals of the United Nations and in contributing to building a culture of peace. It offers residential degree courses. Visitors are welcome. It's about one km beyond Hacienda el Rodeo.

Entertainment

The **Club Paso Fino** (tel. 506/374-2928), in Piedades, is a bar, restaurant, and nightclub that caters to gays and lesbians each first and third Saturday night. It has a swimming pool. Open Wed.–Sat. **Macondo Azul** (tel. 506/249-2046), a bar-cum-restaurant on the main road in Ciudad Colón, has heaps of rustic ambience. It features live jazz, rock, **trova,** and dancing, and has a classic jukebox.

Sports and Recreation

A round of golf at **Parque Valle del Sol** (tel. 506/282-9222, fax 506/282-9333, golf@vallesol.com, www.vallesol.com) costs $70 for 18 holes. Club rental is $20. It has a golf academy 6 A.M.–4 P.M. Tue.–Sun. ($27.50 per hour; $170 full day).

Club Hípico La Caraña (tel. 506/282-6106, fax 506/282-6754), a highly regarded equestrian club, offers classes in dressage and jumping, as well as guided horseback tours in the mountains south of Santa Ana. You can also rent horses ($2) at **Rancho Macho** (see *Food,@ above), and at* **Hacienda el Rodeo** ($3 per hour; see above).

Accommodations

Villa Belén (tel. 506/239-4678 or 239-2040, fax 506/239-0740, villabelen@yahoo.com, www.villabelen.com, $65 s/d), about two km north of Santa Ana, on the road to San Antonio de Belén, is an exquisite American-owned historic hacienda-style villa. This charmer is centered on a courtyard with a swimming pool, and is surrounded by acres of tropical gardens. Each of the five rooms is distinct, with dainty furnishings, terra-cotta tile floors, regal drapes, plus cable TVs. A separate two-bedroom apartment is very homey. Facilities include a sauna and colonial-tiled Jacuzzi (defunct at last visit), an outdoor barbecue pit, and a large, cozy lounge. Breakfast is served on the patio. No children. There's also a two-bedroom apartment with kitchen for $250 per week. Rates include continental breakfast.

A few kilometers west of Piedades, in the hillside hamlet of La Trinidad, is **Albergue El Marañon** (tel. 506/249-1271, fax 506/249-1761, cultourica@expreso.co.cr, www.cultourica.com, $35 s, $49 d), surrounded by an orchard and with views toward Poás enjoyed from a terrace. This simple yet tasteful and reclusive place has eight rooms (two triples); four are in the garden with private patios and bathrooms with solar-heated water. Hammocks are slung beneath ranchitas in the garden. There's also a three-room apartment with kitchen for $77. Children welcome. Four cabi-

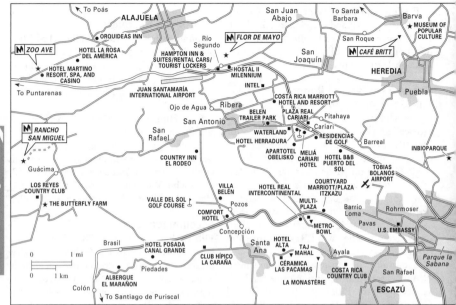

nas and a restaurant were to be added. Your German and Costa Rican hosts, Frank Doyé and Anabelle Contreras Castro, host two-week Spanish-language courses and offer three- to 20-day excursions throughout the country. Rates include breakfast.

Splendid is the word for **Hotel Posada Canal Grande** (Apdo. 84, Santa Ana, tel. 506/282-4089, fax 506/282-5733, canalgra@racsa.co.cr, www.novanet.co.cr/canal, $40 s, $50 d), in the heart of an old coffee *finca*, 800 meters north of the church in Piedades. The two-story villa-hotel is operated by a Florentine art collector and is popular with Italians. The lodge boasts an old terra-cotta tile floor, rustic antique furnishings, plump leather chairs, and a fireplace. The 12 bedrooms have parquet wood floors, exquisite rattan-framed queen-size beds with Guatemalan bedspreads, cable TV, and wide windows offering views toward the Gulf of Nicoya. Italian taste is everywhere, from the ultra-chic furniture and halogen lamps to the classical vases overflowing with flowers, the ceramic bowls full of fruit, and the antique Italian prints gracing the walls.

There's a large pool in grounds mantled in groves of grapefruit, banana, mango, and coffee trees. It has a restaurant, sauna, and tour agency, and massage and horseback rides are offered. Airport transfers provided. Rates include breakfast.

Food

Tony's Ribs (tel. 506/282-5650), at the west end of the Santa Ana shopping center, fires up its grill nightly. Ribs, chicken, seafood, and steaks—and *bocas* with drinks (including exotic cocktails)—are accompanied by music and views of the valley from the open-air terrace.

Rancho Macho (tel. 506/228-7588), in the hills above Santa Ana, serves Tico fare such as sweet fried onion, barbecued chicken *(la plancha de gallo),* and the like, cooked over a coffee-wood fire. Typical meals cost about $6. There's often live music, and always great views from the terrace. (The turnoff is just east of the Red Cross, at the west end of Santa Ana.)

The elegant **Restaurante Canal Grande** at the Hotel Posada Canal Grande serves ambitious Italian fare, such as scallops al vino ($6) and pastas from $5.

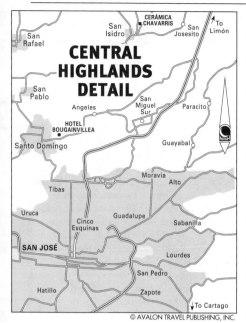

CENTRAL HIGHLANDS DETAIL

San Rafael
San Isidro
CERÁMICA CHAVARRIS
San Josesito
To Limón
San Pablo
Angeles
San Miguel Sur
Paracito
HOTEL BOUGAINVILLEA
Santo Domingo
Guayabal
Moravia
Alto
Tibas
Uruca
Cinco Esquinas
Guadalupe
Sabanilla
SAN JOSÉ
Lourdes
San Pedro
Hatillo
Zapote
To Cartago

© AVALON TRAVEL PUBLISHING, INC.

This remnant indigenous community lives a relatively marginalized life, though members eke out livings as weavers; you may see some of their fine baskets on sale at roadside stalls.

From Santiago you can follow a paved road southwest to **Salitrales,** 18 km west of Santiago. Due west from Santiago, another road snakes through the mountains and descends to Orotina via San Pablo de Turrubares. Salitrales nestles atop the southwesternmost flank of the highlands. By continuing south 11 km beyond Salitrales, and turning east, you arrive at **Rancho Mastatal Environmental Learning Center and Lodge** (Apdo. 185-6000, Puriscal, tel. 506/416-6359, info@ranchomastatal.com, www.ranchomastatal.com), a 219-acre farm and private wildlife refuge adjoining the **La Cangreja National Park.** Rancho Mastatal has seven km of wilderness trails leading through pristine forest that is home to monkeys, parrots, toucans, and countless butterflies. Rancho Mastatal offers environmental workshops and languages courses, and welcomes volunteers. Horses can be rented ($10 with guide).

Getting There

Buses marked "Ciudad Colón" depart San José from Calle 18, Avenidas 1/3, every 15 minutes. Driving, take the Santa Ana exit off the Carretera Prospero Fernandez freeway; or, from Escazú, take the road west from El Cruce in San Rafael (this road has some steep hills and windy bends).

SANTIAGO DE PURISCAL

Santiago de Puriscal (called Puriscal by locals), 20 km west of Ciudad Colón, is an important agricultural town. Santiago's main plaza has lots of monkey puzzle trees (araucaria pine) and is overlooked by a pretty church surrounded by bougainvillea. Nearby, a major conservation and reforestation project—**Arbofilia** (tel. 506/240-7145, www.ticoorganico.com/arbofilia.htm)—can be visited for educational tours.

Midway between Ciudad Colón and Santiago, at Km 30, is the entrance for the **Guayabo Indian Reserve,** protecting the land of the Quitirrisi Indians on the slopes of Cerro Turrubares.

Accommodation

Rancho Mastatal (see above, $15 camping, $20 pp A-frame, from $25 s, $35 d main house, $25 pp Jeanne's House, $125 pp Leo's House) has three rooms in the main century-old farmhouse with shared bathrooms. A porch has hammocks. Jeanne's House has six bamboo bunks and two double beds, a stove, and electricity, indoor and outdoor showers, and shared toilets. Leo's House is a finely built wooden cabin sleeping up to six people. Budget-minded folks can choose to sleep beneath an A-frame bamboo and thatch structure. You can camp if you bring your own tent, or choose to stay with local *campesino* families. Rates include all meals.

Getting There and Around

Buses depart San José for Santiago de Puriscal from Calle 16, Avenidas 1/3 hourly. Bus no. 613 leaves for Quepos from the east side of the church in Santiago.

Jeep-taxis line the south side of the square in Santiago.

Central Highlands

Cariari to La Guácima

CIUDAD CARIARI AND SAN ANTONIO DE BELÉN

Ciudad Cariari is centered on an important junction on the Autopista General Cañas, 12 km west of San José and about five minutes' drive from Juan Santamaría Airport. Here are San José's leading conference center, a major shopping mall, a golf course, and two of the nation's longest standing premium hotels, where many travelers overnight upon arriving in or before departing Costa Rica.

From Ciudad Cariari, the road west leads five km to **San Antonio de Belén,** a small, unassuming town that has taken on new importance since the recent opening nearby of the Marriott Hotel and Intel's microprocessor assembly plant. The road system hereabouts is convoluted.

Sports and Recreation

The heavily wooded, 18-hole championship **Meliá Confort Cariari Conference Center & Golf Resort** (tel. 506/239-0022, www.melia-cariari .com/costa-rica-golf/) was recently completely redesigned by George Fazio.

Waterland (tel. 506/293-2891, www.waterland .cr, 9 A.M.–5 P.M. Tues.–Sun., April–Nov., daily Dec.–Feb., $8 admission adults, $3 children), 500 meters west of the Autopista General Cañas, is a 12-hectare, open-air aquatic amusement complex centered on a massive 1,300-square-meter pool with volleyball, water slides, and rope swing, plus underwater cave. There's also an artificial river, a wave pool, miniature golf, plus kiddies play areas, and horseback riding. A tree-to-tree cable-and-pulley ride costs $3 extra, plus there're go-karts ($1.50) and ATVs ($1.50), and paintball ($8).

Ojo de Agua (tel. 506/441-2808, 8 A.M.–3:30 P.M., $1.50 admission), three km northwest of San Antonio at San Rafael de Alajuela, is a swimming resort *(balneario)* with swimming pools, a children's pool, and a natural lake fed by a subterranean river. There're also picnic areas, sauna, bar and restaurant, and volleyball, tennis,

and soccer facilities. You can hire boats on the lake. Ticos flock here on weekends. Parking costs $1.50.

Accommodations

$25–50: The gringo-owned **Belén Trailer Park** (tel. 506/239-0421, fax 506/239-2578, rga-surf@costarricense.co.cr, $10 RV nightly, $60 weekly, $220 monthly), about one km east of Belén Plaza, is Costa Rica's only fully equipped RV and camper site. It has hookups with electricity and water for 30 vehicles, plus a disposal station, shady lawns for camping, a washing machine, and hot showers (mornings only). It permits camping for $5–8 daily, depending on tent size.

Hotel B&B Puerta del Sol (tel. 506/293-8109, fax 506/239-3733, puertadelsol@racsa.co.cr, www.puertadelsol.co.cr, $55 s, $68 d with fan, $61 s, $75 d a/c), outside Cariari, is run by a friendly Tico family and offers 20 modestly furnished rooms in a two-story modern home. All have fans, TVs, telephones, refrigerators. Second-floor rooms get hot but have a/c. Two are handicap-equipped, and an apartment has a large lounge and king-size bed (it opens to a second bedroom, optional). Breakfast is served on a patio facing the pool with lounge chairs and palms. It offers free Internet access. No smoking. Rates include breakfast and tax.

If you fancy a self-catering option, consider **Apartotel Obelisco** (tel. 506/239-6696, fax 506/239-6701, www.apartotelobelisco.com, $125–150 daily, $570 weekly), hidden away west of Cariari. Oddly shaped rooms come in three types; all are twin-level with hardwood staircases and cool tile floors, plus full kitchen, cable TV, and wonderful bathrooms with spacious shower tub (some have Jacuzzi tubs). Some have a mezzanine office with Internet. A small restaurant serves breakfast only. It has laundry service, grocery, pool and sundeck, and secure parking. It offers free rides to the airport 24 hours. Rates include breakfast.

El Rodeo Country Inn (P.O. Box 49-4005, San Antonio de Belén, tel. 506/293-3909, fax

506/239-3464, rodeoinn@racsa.co.cr, $65 s, $75 d standard, $80 s/d junior suite, $100 suite), about two km south of San Antonio de Belén on the road to Santa Ana, is a contemporary-style hacienda with 29 rooms, all with a/c, cable TV, telephone, safety box, and elegant furnishings. The three spacious junior suites are fabulous, with beautiful hardwood floors, two queen beds, handsome furnishings, and huge bathrooms with marble tile floors and sinks. Three master suites boast king beds and Jacuzzi tubs in bathrooms with Romanesque columns. Facilities include a swimming pool, Jacuzzi, tennis courts, and a splendid restaurant (see *Food,* below). Rates include breakfast and dinner.

Hotel & Country Club Residencias de Golf (P.O. Box 357-2120, San José, tel. 506/239-2272, fax 506/239-2001, reservacions@residenciasdegolf .com, www.residencias-golf.co.cr, $85 s/d standard, $110 s/d superior, $120 suite low season; $105 standard, $120 superior, $140 suite high season), immediately southeast of the Meliá Cariari, is a reclusive complex offering a Jacuzzi, a heated swimming pool, and access to the adjacent Cariari Country Club. It has 90 standards, doubles, and suites, all with fans, a/c, safety box, cable TV, and radio. Most rooms have king-size beds and resemble apartments; some have singles. Suites have kitchenettes. There's a restaurant and bar, plus Jacuzzi, pool, and sauna.

$100–150: The colonial-style **Costa Rica Marriott Hotel and Resort** (tel. 506/298-0000, fax 506/298-0011, costaric@marriott.co.cr, www.marriotthotels.com; in the U.S., tel. 800/831-1000; from $135 s, $145 d), at Ribera de Belén, one km northeast of San Antonio, occupies a 30-acre coffee plantation commanding panoramic views down through lush landscaped grounds to distant mountains. This showy jewel has 252 rooms and seven suites, all exquisitely decorated and with French doors opening to a patio or balcony. The decor fits the bill: in public areas, evocative antiques, distressed timbers, and stone floors, while the large bedrooms boast regal furnishings and fabrics and a full complement of modern amenities. It features a ballroom, golf practice range, horizon swimming pool, three restaurants, three tennis courts, a gym, shops, and a business center.

The **Hotel Herradura Golf Resort & Conference Center** (Apdo. 7-1880, San José 1000, tel. 506/293-0033, fax 506/293-2713, www .hotelherradura.com, $140 s, $150 d standard, $120 s, $130 d superior, $205–300 suites low season; $120 s, $130 d standard, $130 s, $140 d superior, $230–335 suites high season), at Ciudad Cariari, is renowned as a convention hotel. It offers 234 spacious, elegantly furnished, a/c rooms (including 28 suites) accented with dark hardwoods and offering work desks, cable TVs, direct-dial telephones, ample closets, and 24-hour room service. Some have a patio or a balcony. Suites come in five styles. At last visit, rooms were beginning to show their age. The Herradura has several restaurants, including Japanese and Mexican. There is a spa; a large outdoor swimming pool with swim-up bar, faux beach, and mammoth whirlpool; 10 night-lit tennis courts; and impressive entertainment facilities, including the Krystal Casino and a 51,000-square-foot conference center. A shuttle runs to downtown.

$150–250: Immediately south of the Herradura is the **Meliá Confort Cariari Conference Center & Golf Resort** (Apdo. 737-1007, San José, tel. 506/239-0022, fax 506/239-2803, cariari@solmelia.com, www.solmelia.com; in the U.S., tel. 800/336-3542; $150 s/d standard, $155 s/d executive low season; $170 s/d standard, $175 s/d high season; $250 s/d junior suite year-round, $375 master suite year-round), offering deluxe resort facilities, including access to the Cariari Country Club next door and its championship golf course, 10 tennis courts, and Olympic-size pool. The 220 spacious, handsomely appointed, carpeted a/c rooms and 24 suites are arrayed around an outdoor swimming pool with swim-up bar. All have leather-upholstered furniture, TVs, phones, alarm clocks, safes, twin or king beds, tiled combination baths, and garden or pool views. It was being refurbished at last visit. The hotel also has a kiddies' pool, health club, whirlpool, massage service, beauty salon, and playground. Plus, there are two restaurants and a casino.

Food

For traditional Costa Rican fare, head to **El Rodeo** (see above, noon–10:30 P.M. Mon.–Sat., 11:30 A.M.–5 P.M. Sunday), decorated in traditional hacienda style and adorned with saddles and other rodeo-themed miscellany. It serves a wide-ranging menu that includes sliced tongue on corn tortilla ($1), ceviche, and hot jalapeño cream tenderloin ($9).

Antonio Ristorante Italiano & Cigar Room (tel. 506/293-0622 or 506/239-1613, 11:30 A.M.–11 P.M. Mon.–Fri., Sat.–Sun. 4–11 P.M.), 100 meters southeast of the Hotel Herradura, serves exquisite cuisine. Try the melazane (baked eggplant topped with marinara sauce), or gnocchi ($10), or calamari with spaghetti ($11.50). There's an "executive lunch" special ($4). It has a piano bar.

The **Sakura** (tel. 506/239-0033, ext. 33, 11:30 A.M.–3 P.M. and 6–11 P.M. Mon.–Sat., 11 A.M.–10.P.M. Sunday), in the Hotel Herradura, is expensive, but offers superb Teppani-style Japanese cooking and an excellent sushi bar. The Herradura also offers the elegant **Restaurante Sancho Panza** (tel. 506/239-0033, ext. 265, 10 A.M.–midnight) with bullfight posters, lofty beamed ceiling, and a tinkling fountain. I recommend it for a snack lunch (try the turkey sandwich with fries; $8.50). The menu features a shrimp avocado or garlic octopus starter ($8.50), paellas (from $8), pork chops with prunes ($17), and a surf-and-turf skewer ($12.50).

The downstairs food court in **Plaza Real Cariari** has almost a dozen fast-food outlets, including health-food options.

Services

Plaza Real Cariari, on the north side of the freeway, has a bank, pharmacy, bookstore, six-screen cinema, and boutiques.

Getting There

Buses for Ojo de Agua depart San José from Avenida 1, Calles 20/22, hourly on the half hour, every quarter hour on weekends. Buses also depart Alajuela from Calle 10, Avenida Central.

LA GUÁCIMA

The road west from San Antonio de Belén continues to La Guácima, known among socialites for the **Los Reyes Country Club** (tel. 506/438-0004), with a nine-hole golf course (golf@losreyescr.com). On weekends you may settle in with champagne and cucumber sandwiches to watch a chukker or two of polo, a game introduced to Costa Rica in 1898 by the British who came to build the Atlantic Railroad. November through August is polo season, when six national teams compete; the club also hosts international competitions. The social scene here is quite the thing. Pip-pip!

There's a **Pista de Quatrociclismo** (a racecourse for ATV four-wheel motorcycles) four km west of La Guácima.

Rancho San Miguel

This stable and stud farm (tel. 506/220-4060, www.ranchosanmiguel.co.cr), about three km north of La Guácima, raises Andalusian horses and has a tiny museum with *capas,* saddles, and other miscellany relating to horsemanship. The highlight is the nocturnal one-hour dressage and horsemanship show in an enclosed arena to the accompaniment of classical Spanish music. It's a fabulous experience. Although the show is spotlit, it's quite dark, so you'll need fast film or a digital camera to capture the action. The show is offered Tuesday, Thursday, and Saturday at 8 P.M. (and by arrangement for groups). At last visit, the dinner and cocktails weren't up to par, but the hosts were intent on upgrading. The show costs $25, or $37 with dinner, and $42 pp including hotel transfers, cocktail, performance, and dinner.

The stable offers horse-riding lessons for adults and children. There's a botanical garden.

The Butterfly Farm

The Butterfly Farm (Apdo. 2132, Alajuela 4050, tel. 506/438-0300, fax 506/438-0300, www.butterflyfarm.co.cr, 8:30 A.M.–5 P.M.), established in 1983 by Joris Brinkerhoff and María Sabido as the first commercial butterfly farm in Latin America, has grown to be the second-largest ex-

© CHRISTOPHER P. BAKER

A visitor photographs butterflies at the Butterfly Farm in La Guácima.

porter of living pupae in the world. A two-hour visit begins with a video documentary followed by a guided tour through the gardens and laboratory, where you witness and learn all about each stage of the butterfly life cycle. Hundreds of butterflies representing 60 native species flit about in an endless ballet. Photographers should bring a macro lens.

In the wild, butterflies' survival rate to adulthood is estimated to be only 2 percent. Raised under controlled conditions within the netted garden, the survival rate on the farm is 90 percent, ensuring an ongoing supply for the 30,000 pupae exported annually. The guides will show you the tiny eggs and larvae that, you're informed, are coded to "eat and grow, eat and grow." The guide will thrust out a fat, four-inch caterpillar to show the point. If a newborn human baby ate at the same rate, it would grow to the size of a double-decker bus in two months. You'll also see the pupae hanging in stasis and, with luck, witness a butterfly emerging to begin life anew. Although butterfly activity is greatly reduced in late afternoon, that's the time to enjoy the spectacular show of the *Caligo memnon* (giant owl butterfly), which flies only at dawn and dusk. It's also best to visit on a sunny day, as the insects "hibernate" on rainy and cloudy days.

Guided tours (two hours) are offered at 8:45 A.M., 11 A.M., 1 P.M., and 3 P.M. Entrance costs $15 adults, $9 students, $7.50 residents and children (children under four free), and $25 and $12.50 respectively with transportation to your hotel.

Getting There

The Butterfly Farm offers direct bus service from major San José hotels daily (by reservation, tel. 506/438-0400) at 7:30 A.M., 10 A.M., and 2 P.M. Dec.–April and twice daily May–November. Alternately, public buses marked "La Guácima" depart at 11 A.M. and 2 P.M. (except Sunday) from Calle 10, Avenidas 4/6, behind the Merced church in San José. Take the bus until the last stop (about 60 minutes), from where you walk— follow the signs—about 400 meters. The return bus to San José departs at 3:15 P.M.

From Alajuela, buses marked "La Guácima Abajo" depart from Calle 10, Avenida 2, at 8:30 A.M., 9 A.M., 10:30 A.M., and 12:30 P.M., and return at 9:45 A.M., 11:45 A.M., 3:45 P.M., and 5:45 P.M. Ask the driver to stop at La Finca de Mariposas.

Central Highlands

Northwest of San José

ALAJUELA

A mini version of San José, Alajuela (pop. 35,000) sits at the base of Volcán Poás, 20 km northwest of San José and two km north of Juan Santamaría Airport and the Pan-American Highway. First named La Lajuela in 1657, the town is known locally as "La Ciudad de los Mangos" for the mango trees around the main square. Today, Costa Rica's "second city" is a modestly cosmopolitan town with strong links to the coffee industry. Saturday is market day, and hundreds of people gather to buy and sell produce fresh from the farm.

It has the convenience of being close to the airport and hence has plentiful hotel options.

Every 11 April, **Juan Santamaría Day** is cause for celebration, with parades, bands, dancing, and arts-and-crafts fairs. The town also hosts the annual nine-day **Mango Festival** in July.

church with the cathedral in the background, Alajuela

Sights

Memories of Juan Santamaría—or "Erizo" (meaning "hedgehog," referring to Santamaría's bristly hair)—the homegrown drummer-boy hero of the Battle of 1856, figure prominently in Alajuela, notably in the **Museo Cultural y Histórico Juan Santamaría** (Avenida 3, Calles Central/2, tel. 506/441-4775 or 506/442-1838, www.museojuansantamaria.go.cr, 10 A.M.–6 P.M. Tues.–Sun., free admission), housed in the former colonial city jail on the northwest corner of the Parque Central. This small museum tells the story of the War of 1856 against the no-good American adventurer William Walker. The two rooms of permanent exhibits are full of maps, paintings, cannons, and other war-era mementos. Other exhibits include local handicrafts, plus there's a library, and an auditorium where cultural programs are offered. Call ahead to arrange a screening of an English-language film. Guided tours are given 9 A.M.–4:30 P.M. Tues.–Fri.

At the heart of town is **Parque Central,** officially called Plaza del General Tomás Guardia. This hub of social activity is a popular hangout for retired males who sit under the mango trees giving nicknames to the passersby (the old men's presence has inspired local wags to dub the park, with pointed metaphor, El Parque de las Palomas Muertas—Park of the Dead Doves). Some of the park benches have chess sets built into them. Twice weekly, music is played in the domed bandstand. Pretty 19th-century structures with fancy iron grilles surround the park.

The square is backed by a red-domed colonial-era **cathedral,** simple within, where the bodies of ex-presidents Tomás Guardia and León Cortés Castro are buried. It has some impressive religious statuary, including a glass cabinet brimful of eclectic and macabre offerings to La Negrita. **Iglesia de Agonía,** in Greek-orthodox-meets-baroque style, is five blocks east.

Two blocks south of Parque Central is **Parque Juan Santamaría,** a tiny concrete plaza with a statue of the national hero rushing forward

© CHRISTOPHER P. BAKER

Iglesia de Agonía, Alajuela

with flaming torch and rifle to defend the country against William Walker's ragtag army.

◪ Flor de Mayo

At Río Segundo de Alajuela, three km southeast of Alajuela, Richard and Margot Frisius breed green and scarlet macaws for eventual release into the wild. Their home and breeding center, Flor de Mayo (Apdo. 2306-4050, Alajuela, tel./fax 506/441-2658, richmar@racsa.co.cr, www.amigosdelasaves.com, by appointment), features three huge aviaries where pairs of breeding macaws are housed, plus a flyway where they can fly and learn to flock. Dozens of other birds have been welcomed into the Frisiuses' beautiful home, surrounding a lush botanical garden: the estate was owned and landscaped by the famous botanist and orchid lover Sir Charles Lankaster. The Frisiuses run a nonprofit organization—Amigos de las Aves—and have raised hundreds of scarlet and green macaws. The

main breeding and aviaries are on an eight-acre site across the road. Here, adolescent macaws build up muscle and learn to socialize in huge flight cages.

Visitation is strictly by appointment only. Flor de Mayo is hard to find: it's 600 meters east of the Hampton Inn and 100 meters east of the Hostal II Millennium, where you turn north at the traffic light; go 400 meters to a Y-fork, then 200 meters uphill; Flor de Mayo is on the left.

Accommodations

Under $25: The **Hostel Villa Real** (Avenida 3, Calle 1, tel. 506/441-4022, villarealcr@hotmail .com, $9 pp dorm), favored by budget travelers and handily close to the bus station, has six simple rooms with shared bathroom in an old wooden home. Bathrooms have hot water, and there's a basic TV lounge. The owners speak English.

Another good bet, the **Mango Verde Hostel** (Avenida 3, Calles 2/4, tel. 506/441-6330, fax 506/443-5074, miraflores@hotmail.com, $10 s, $20 d shared bath, $15 s, $25 d private bath), has 10 rooms with fans, some private baths with hot water, and a shared kitchen and TV lounge. The old house has terra-cotta tile and wood floors, and a large rear courtyard with hammocks and a basic kitchenette. Internet service is offered.

Hotel El Peñol (Calle Llovet, tel. 506/442-2132, bnbhospenol@racsa.co.cr, www.hospenol costarica.com, $15 s, $20 d shared bath, $20 s, $25 d private bath) is run by a friendly Colombian. Rooms are clean and bright, and bathrooms have hot water. Some rooms have satellite TV. There's a TV lounge plus secure parking, and guests get kitchen privileges. Free airport transfers are offered.

Next door, the **Hotel Cortez Azúl** (Avenida 5, Calles 2/4, tel. 506/443-6145, $11 pp shared bath, $12–15 pp private bath) is a basic budget option. It has five rooms (two with private bathrooms), and there's a communal kitchenette in the back garden.

$25–50: The **Pensión Alajuela** (Calle Central, Avenida 9, tel./fax 506/441-6251, pension @racsa.co.cr, www.pensionalajuela.co, $20 s, $25 d shared bath, from $27 s, $31 d private bath) is

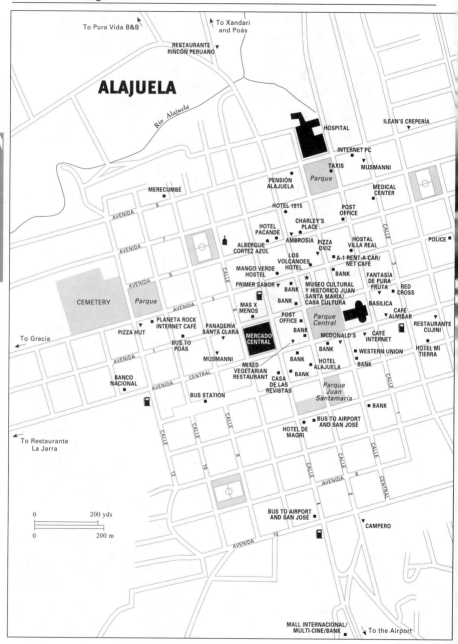

To Pura Vida B&B

To Xandari
and Poás

RESTAURANTE
RINCÓN PERUANO

ALAJUELA

Río Alajuela

ILEAN'S CREPERÍA

HOSPITAL

INTERNET PC

TAXIS
MUSMANNI

Parque

MEDICAL
CENTER

MERECUMBÉ

PENSIÓN
ALAJUELA

HOTEL 1915

POST
OFFICE

CHARLEY'S
PLACE

HOTEL
PACANDÉ

AMBROSIA

PIZZA
OVIZ

HOSTAL
VILLA REAL

POLICE

ALBERGUE
CORTEZ AZUL

LOS
VOLCANOES
HOTEL

A-1 RENT-A-CAR/
NET CAFÉ

AVENIDA 9

AVENIDA 7

MANGO VERDE
HOSTEL

FANTASÍA
DE PURA
FRUTA

RED
CROSS

AVENIDA 5

PRIMER SABOR

BANK

MUSEO CULTURAL
Y HISTÓRICO JUAN
SANTA MARÍA/
CASA CULTURA

BASILICA

CAFÉ
ALMIBAR

MAS X
MENOS

BANK

CEMETERY

Parque

AVENIDA 3

POST
OFFICE

*Parque
Central*

RESTAURANTE
CUJINI

PLANETA ROCK
INTERNET CAFÉ

PANADERÍA
SANTA CLARA

BANK

MCDONALD'S

CAFÉ
INTERNET

HOTEL MI
TIERRA

PIZZA HUT

To Grecia

BUS TO
POÁS

MERCADO
CENTRAL

BANK

WESTERN UNION

AVENIDA 1

MUSMANNI

MIXED
VEGETARIAN
RESTAURANT

BANK

HOTEL
ALAJUELA

BANK

BANCO
NACIONAL

CENTRAL

CASA
DE LAS
REVISTAS

BANK

*Parque
Juan
Santamaría*

BANK

BUS STATION

To Restaurante
La Jarra

HOTEL DE
MAGRI

BUS TO AIRPORT
AND SAN JOSÉ

AVENIDA 8

BUS TO AIRPORT
AND SAN JOSÉ

AVENIDA 2

CAMPERO

AVENIDA 10

| 0 | 200 yds |
| 0 | 200 m |

MALL INTERNACIONAL/
MULTI-CINE/BANK

To the Airport

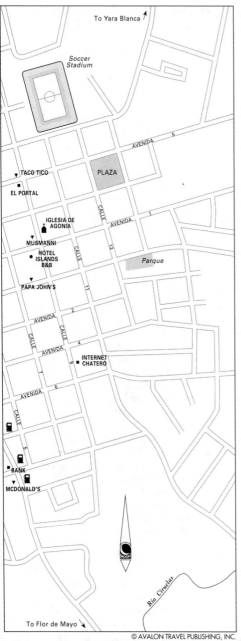

To Yara Blanca

Soccer
Stadium

AVENIDA 5

TACO TICO

EL PORTAL

PLAZA

IGLESIA DE
AGONIA

AVENIDA 1

MUSMANNI

HOTEL
ISLANDS
B&B

Parque

PAPA JOHN'S

AVENIDA 2

AVENIDA 4

INTERNET
CHATERO

AVENIDA 6

BANK

MCDONALD'S

MOON

Rio Ciruelas

To Flor de Mayo

© AVALON TRAVEL PUBLISHING, INC.

Central Highlands

simple yet appealing, with 12 clean rooms with
small, tiled private bathrooms with hot water
(eight rooms have cable TV). There's a snack
bar, book exchange, laundry service, and Internet access.

Hotel Alajuela (Calle 2, Avenidas Central/2,
tel. 506/441-1241, fax 506/441-7912, $20 s,
$30 d shared bath, $35 s, $40 d private bath),
cater-corner to Parque Central, has 50 clean
and nicely furnished rooms, most with private
baths with hot water. Apartment rooms with
kitchens in the old section are dark. It has laundry service but no restaurant.

The family-run **Hotel Pacandé B&B**
(Avenida 5, Calles 2/4, tel. 506/443-8481 or
cellular 506/369-4666, joslazano@uole.com,
www.hotelpacande.com, $10–15 pp dorms, $20
s/d shared bath, $30 s, $35 d private bath), 200
meters north and 50 meters west of the park, is a
handsome 1950s home with eight modestly furnished rooms, including dorms with bunks. Five
rooms share three bathrooms; others have private
bathrooms, all with hot water. Upstairs rooms get
lots of light; cheaper rooms downstairs are ill-lit.
There's Internet, laundry, and secure parking,
plus airport shuttle, Internet, and kitchen privileges. The family also rents a villa outside town.
Rates include breakfast.

The **Hotel Mi Tierra** (Avenida 2, Calles 2/5,
tel. 506/441-1974, hotelmitierra@hotmail.com,
www.hotelmitierra.com, $10 pp dorm, $25 s/d
shared bath, $35 s/d private bath) has nicely
furnished dorm rooms with bunks and fans. It
also offers seven simply furnished rooms in a
pleasant middle-class home. They're clean and
have wooden floors, cable TV, and small shared
bathrooms with hot water. Two have a private
bath (five will eventually have private bath). A
small kidney-shaped pool graces the back garden. It has workout machines. Guests get
kitchen privileges.

Charly's Place (Avenida 5, Calles Central/2,
tel./fax 506/441-0115, $20 s, $25 d shared
bath, $25/35 private bath low season; $25 s,
$40 d shared bath, $30 s, $45 d private bath
high season) has 11 simply yet adequately appointed rooms with hardwood floors and private

baths with hot water. The upstairs rooms are well lit; rooms downstairs are dim. Guests can use the kitchen. There's an attractive patio dining area, plus laundry and secure parking. A reader, however, reports "bad vibes" and "sleazy treatment."

Hotel Islands B&B (Avenida 1, Calles 7/9, tel. 506/442-0573, fax 506/442-2909, islandsbb@hotmail.com, $35 s, $40 d), owned by Davido Quesada, a professional soccer player, is a pleasant little place with eight rooms with private bathrooms and hot water. It has fax service and private parking. Rates include breakfast.

I recommend the **Hotel Los Volcanes** (Aenida 3, Calles Central/2, tel. 506/441-0525, fax 506/440-8006, losvolcanes@racsa.co.cr, www .montezumaexpediciones.com, $25 s, $35 d shared bath, $35 s, $45 d private bath), facing the museum, and a recent addition. Housed in a charming, fully restored 1920s home with lofty paneled ceilings and polished hardwoods, it offers six large, well-lit bedrooms with ceiling fans and pleasing furnishings (wrought-iron and hardwood beds), wooden floors, lofty wooden ceilings, cable TV, and handsome bathrooms (some are shared). Two more elegant rooms are to the rear, where there's a patio with hammocks. It has a small TV lounge, plus laundry, and secure parking. Full Costa Rican breakfasts are served. It also has a four-person apartment ($75). Rates include full breakfast and airport transfers.

The **Hostal II Millenium B&B** (tel./fax 506/441-2365, bbmilenium@racsa.co.cr, www .bbmilleniumcr.com, $12 pp dorm, $35 s, $40 d low season; $40 s, $50 d high season) is a charming and popular bed-and-breakfast in a middle-class home at Río Segundo de Alajuela, 1.5 km from the airport. It has two female dorms with large walk-in shower; two men's dorms; and a mixed-sex dorm. To the rear are five simply furnished private rooms, all with small cable TVs, fans, and private bath with hot water (the private rooms are overpriced). It has a TV lounge with leather sofas and rattan furniture, plus a shaded dining area. Guests get kitchen access. There's parking and a 24-hour airport pick-up service. The owner speaks English and is a delight. Rates include breakfast and tax.

$50–100: I love the family-run **Hotel 1915** (Calle 2, Avenida 5/7, tel./fax 506/441-0495, $45 s, $55 d standard, $65 s/d with a/c), three blocks north of the central plaza. It has 18 clean and homey rooms whose modern bathrooms have large walk-in hot water showers with little gardens attached. It has a huge lounge with fabulous antique hardwood furnishings and earth tones, plus stone and stucco walls, creating a delightful, upscale ambience (upgrade renovations were ongoing at last visit). Breakfast is served in a rear shaded patio with a grill and wood-fired oven. If a taxi driver tells you this place is full, or offers some other excuse not to take you, don't believe him.

The best place and highly recommended is **Pura Vida Bed and Breakfast** (Apdo. 1703, Alajuela, tel./fax 506/441-1157, cell 506/383-2597, info@puravidahotel.com, www.puravidahotel .com, from $55 s, $65 d), an intimate place set in a beautiful one-acre garden and run by Californians Niki and Bernie, delightful new owners. The handsome old timber-beamed home (a former coffee **finca**) has been restored and upgraded with an exciting contempo aesthetic, with hints of Santa Fe in the lounge. Its seven rooms are all themed; some are exquisite. All have splendid bathrooms. The Orchid Room, for example, is done up in whites and reds with a black four-poster metal bed. Four one- and two-bed garden *casitas* have living rooms with calming, eye-pleasing contemporary furnishings; each has kitchenettes, patio, fireplace, and kitchen. It offers baggage storage, Internet access, a small library with TV and stereo system, plus a shaded restaurant facing the lush garden at which gourmet dishes are served (at any time of day or night). There are lots of guest-friendly dogs, plus secure parking. Excursions are offered. Rates include breakfast.

The **Hampton Inn** (Apdo. 962-1000, San José, tel. 506/442-0043 or 800/426-7866, fax 506/442-9532, hamptoninnreservas @grupomarta.com, www.hamptoninn.com, $71 s, $81 d low season; $95 s, $101 d high season), 500 meters east of the airport terminal, is perfect if you have tight flight transfers and don't mind charmless motel-style Americana. The 100 a/c rooms (75 percent nonsmoking) are soundproofed and feature king or two double beds, cable TV with in-room movies, and telephones. It offers a fully accessible room, airport transfers, and runs to nearby restaurants. The hotel claims to guarantee "100 percent satisfaction" or your money back but readers report that the hotel is badly run and doesn't come through on this billing. Rates include continental breakfast and airport transfers.

Adjacent is **Hampton Suites** (tel. 506/442-3320 or 800/478-4857, fax 506/442-2781, hamptonsuites@grupomarta.com, $92 s, $98 d standard, $110 s, $115 d suite), with 28 studio-suites, of which six are handicap-equipped.

The family-run **Hotel de Magri** (tel./fax 506/441-4502, hoteldemagri@go.com, www.hoteldemagri.com, $56 s, $65 d low season, $60/70 high season) is a 19th-century home that was being renovated in contemporary vogue at last visit. It has a dramatic atrium interior and will have 12 a/c carpeted rooms with cable TV, hair dryer, security boxes.

Another B&B option is the modern and delightful **Hotel Brilla Sol** (tel. 506/442-5129, florelo@racsa.co.cr, www.hotelbrillasol.com, $35 s, $45 d), four km west of the airport in the barrio of El Roble. It has a courtyard with swimming pool and parking, plus free parking airport shuttles. Rates include breakfast.

Food

Alajuela's small but lively colony of Peruvians adds a touch of authenticity to the **Rincón Peruano Restaurant** (tel. 506/442-3977), 200 meters north of Avenida 9, along Calle 2. For less than $5 you can feast on Peruvian dishes, including the restaurant's famous *papa relleno*. Dancing on Tuesday.

Jalapeños Comida Tex-Mex (tel. 506/430-4027, 11 A.M.–10 P.M. Mon.–Fri., 10 A.M.–2 P.M. Sat.–Sun.), on the west side of Parque Central, rapidly drew a dedicated clientele of expats after opening in 2003. This cheerful place offers great bargains on eggs ranchero, omelettes, and nachos (made with fresh corn *flautas*). A filling burger with fries and drink costs a mere $2.50. The hosts, Norman and Isabel, are delightful.

Ambrosia (Avenida 5, Calle 2, tel. 506/440-

3440, 9 A.M.–6:30 P.M. Mon.–Sat.), next to Charley's Place, offers pleasant surrounds and a shaded terrace. It has an *almuerzo ejecutivo* (fixed lunch) for $2.25, plus lasagna, pizzas, and sandwiches.

The clean, a/c **Primer Sabor** (Avenida 3, Calles 2/4, tel. 506/441-7082, 11 A.M.–10 P.M. Fri.–Wed.) is the best option for Chinese.

For Italian, try **Restaurante Cujini** (Calle 5, Avenida Central). For pizza, head to **Papa John's** (Calle 9, Avenidas Central/1).

Ileana's Café & Crepería (Avenida 9, Calles 3/7, 9 A.M.–6 P.M. Mon.–Sat.) is a delightful little spot.

Vegetarians are served by the no-frills **Mixed Vegetarian Restaurant** (Avenida Central, Calles 2/4).

You can buy baked goods at **Musmanni** (Calle 8, Avenidas Central/1, and Calle 9, Avenidas 1/3). For ice creams, head to **Fantasía de Pura Frutas** (Avenida 1, Calles 1/3), selling *helados* in a million fruit flavors.

Information

Hospital San Rafael (Avenida 9, Calles Central/1, tel. 506/441-5011) is a full-service hospital. Medical clinics downtown include the **Clínica Medical Juan Santamaría** (Calle 3, Avenidas 5/7, tel. 506/441-6284). There are plenty of pharmacies.

The **police station** is at Avenida 3, Calle 7 (for the local traffic police, call tel. 506/441-7411; for criminal investigation, call the OIJ, tel. 506/437-0442).

Services

There are more than one dozen bank outlets in the town center; see the map.

Western Union (Calle Central, Avenidas Central/2) has an office.

You can make international calls at **ICE** (Avenida 7, Calle 1).

The numerous Internet cafés include **Internet Ch@tero** (Calle 9, Avenidas 4/6, internetchatero @racsa.co.cr), which charges $0.75 cents per hour; **El Portal** (Calle 9, Avenidas 3/5); **A-1 Net Cafe** (Avenida 3, Calles Central/1); and **Internet PC** (Avenida 9, Calles 1/3).

Tourist Lockers (tel. 506/442-3671, 7 A.M.–7 P.M. Mon.–Fri., 8 A.M.–4 P.M. Sat.–Sun.), opposite the Hampton Inn & Suites, rents locker space.

Fujifilm (Calle Central, Avenidas Central/2, tel. 506/441-5251) sells film and cameras.

Getting There

TUASA (tel. 506/222-5325) buses depart San José from Avenida 2, Calle 10/12, every 10 minutes, 5 A.M.–11 P.M. Return buses depart from Calle 8, Avenidas Central/1, in Alajuela. The buses run past the airport.

Major car rental companies that have offices opposite the Hampton Inn & Suites include **Economy, Thrifty, Toyota,** and **Tropical.**

SLOPES OF POÁS VOLCANO

Above Alajuela, the scenic drive up Poás Volcano takes you through quintessential coffee country, with rows of shiny dark-green bushes creating artistic patterns on the sensuous slopes. Farther up, coffee gives way to fern gardens and

© CHRISTOPHER P. BAKER

main crater, Poás Volcano

fields of strawberries grown under black shade netting, then dairy pastures separated by forests of cedar and pine.

There are three routes to Poás Volcano National Park. All lead via **Poasito,** the uppermost village on the mountain and a popular way station for hungry sightseers.

Alajuela to Vara Blanca via Carrizal: From Alajuela, Avenida 7 exits town and turns uphill via Carrizal and Cinco Esquinas to **Vara Blanca,** a village nestled just beyond the saddle between Barva and Poás Volcanoes on the edge of the Continental Divide about 25 km north of Alajuela.

At Vara Blanca, you can turn west for Poás Volcano National Park, or descend northward via the marvelously scenic valley of the Río Sarapiquí to the Northern Zone. There's a toll booth (50 cents, voluntary) at **Cinchona,** about two km north of Vara Blanca (a dirt road leads east to **Colonia Virgen del Socorro,** famous as a premier bird-watching site). A short distance further, you'll pass the hamlet of **Cariblanco,** where a dirt road leads west about nine km to **Laguna Hule,** a lake set in a dormant volcanic crater; four-wheel drive is recommended.

Alajuela to Poasito via San Isidro: From downtown Alajuela, Calle 2 leads north through the heart of coffee country. At **San Isidro de Alajuela,** about seven km above Alajuela, a turn leads four km west to **Doka Estate** (tel. 506/449-5152, fax 506/449-6427, info@kidaestate.com, www.dokaestate.com), at Sabanilla de Alajuela, and a great place to learn about coffee production and processing. This privately owned coffee plantation and mill offers the Doka Coffee Tour, where visitors are taught the age-old techniques of coffee growing, milling, and roasting. There's a coffee-tasting room and gift store, and an open-air restaurant with magnificent views. The tour costs $15; an optional lunch costs $7. Open 9:30 A.M.–1:30 P.M. Mon.–Sat., by reservation on Sunday. The same family also runs **La Casa del Café** (tel. 506/449-6035, 8 A.M.–5 P.M. Mon.–Fri., 8 A.M.–1 P.M. Saturday), perched above the coffee fields three km north of San Isidro de Alajuela, with a wooden balcony from which to admire the views or watch the pickers at work.

coffee fields at the Doka Estate

Alajuela to Poasita via San Pedro: A more common route to Poás is via San José de Alajuela, San Pedro, and Sabana Redondo. **San José de Alajuela,** about three km west of Alajuela, is a village with a historic church at a major junction: west (Hwy. 3) for La Garita (see *La Garita,* below) and northwest to Grecia, Sarchí, and San Ramón. The road to Poás begins at **Cruce de Grecia y Poas,** one km along the road to Grecia. From here it's uphill all the way via the pretty hamlet of **San Pedro,** highlighted by its church.

The road merges with the road via San Isidro at Fraijanes and continues two km uphill to Poasito.

La Paz Waterfall Gardens

This splendid and popular nature and wildlife park (tel. 506/482-2720, wgardens@racsa.co.cr, www.waterfallgardens.com, 8:30 A.M.–5 P.M. daily, $21 admission adults, $10 students and children), at Montaña Azul, about four km north of Vara Blanca, features the largest butterfly garden in the world, enclosed in a soaring hangar-size cage within which butterflies flutter freely. There's also a hummingbird garden, a rainforest wildlife exhibit, and orchid houses, all accessed by well-laid concrete trails that lead along the river to four waterfalls; educational posters line the trails. Standing on the viewing platform at the Templo Fall, you're pummeled by spray blasted from the base of the fall, a testament to its awesome hydraulic power. Continuing downriver, you get to a metal staircase that clings to the cliffside and takes you to the Magía Blanca (the largest cascade), Encantada, and La Paz falls. It's a daunting climb back. A short distance further downhill, at a tight hairpin bend in the road, is La Catarata la Paz—the "Peace Waterfall"—a pencil-thin fall that attracts Ticos en masse on weekends (watch for pedestrians in the road). The restaurant here has a veranda with marvelous views over the valley and forest. Birding tours are led by Dr. Aaron Sekerak, author of *A Travel & Suite Guide to Birds of Costa Rica.* Last admission is 4 P.M.

Accommodations

On the Vara Blanca Road: Budget hounds might try **La Rana Holandesa** (tel./fax 506/483-0816, $18 s, $25 d), one km above Carrizal, about 15 km northeast of Alajuela. Dutch-Tica owners John and Vicky Dekker offer three rooms (two share a large bathroom) with hot water. The larger room with small private bath has two bunks and a single bed. There's laundry service. The Dekkers provide free airport pickup and offer a guided tour for $80. A seven-night package costs $750 d including dinners and four sightseeing trips. Rates include full breakfast on the backyard patio.

Pura Vida Health Spa (P.O. Box 1112-4050, Alajuela, tel. 506/92-8099, fax 506/483-0041; in the U.S., R&R Resorts, P.O. Box 1496, Conyers, GA 30012, tel. 770/483-0238 or 888/767-7375, reservations@puravidaspa.com, www.puravidaspa.com), at Pavas de Carrizal, seven km northeast of Alajuela, offers 50 villas, cabanas, and luxury carpeted chalet tents ("tentalows") with shared bath, amid enchanting gardens with pools, plus two suites with king-size beds in the main house. The deluxe Japanese Pagoda has a sunken living room, king-size bed, Jacuzzi, deck, and outdoor shower. It offers various packages, including "The Relax & Retreat Week," from $1,045 per person double occupancy, including daily yoga, meditation, body work, and eco-adventures. (When driving from Alajuela, turn

sharp left at Salon Apolo 15, and Pura Vida is one km up the dirt road.)

Villa Calas Chalets (tel. 506/239-0234, fax 506/482-2222, $25 s/d small, $31 s/d large), midway between Vara Blanca and Poasito, has seven basic A-frame chalets fronted by a charming garden on the very crest of the saddle in the midst of a dairy farm—a magnificent setting. Four large cabins have loft bedrooms, kitchenettes and dining area, plus small lounge with wood-burning fireplace. All have clean bathrooms with hot water. Alas, the furniture is barebones. It offers trout fishing. A handsome roadside restaurant was being built at last visit.

I adore **N** **Poás Volcano Lodge** (Apdo. 5723, San José 1000, tel. 506/482-2194, fax 506/482-2513, poasvl@racsa.co.cr, www.poasvolcanolodge.com, $45 s, $55 shared bath, $55 s, $75 d private bath, $65 s, $90 d junior suite, $75 s, $115 d suite), on a dairy farm about one km west of Vara Blanca. The magnificent rough stone mountain lodge, stunningly situated amid emerald-green pastures betwixt Poás and Barva Volcanoes, might have been conceived by Frank Lloyd Wright. Actually, it was built as a farmhouse by an English family. The unusual design lends im-

view from Albergue Ecológico la Providencia

mense atmosphere to the lodge, recently enhanced with an upscale appealing aesthetic by new owners. Centerpiece is a timber-beamed lounge with sumptuous sofas chairs in front of a massive open fireplace. French doors open onto a patio with fabulous views over the Caribbean lowlands. The nine bedrooms are rustic yet comfortable, with thick down comforters; some rooms have shared but voluminous baths. The large suite has a stunning bathroom with a fathoms-deep stone bathtub shaped like a pool; the skylit bedroom has its own fireplace, plus a magnificent contemporary four-poster king-size bed. Eight rooms are in an adjacent block. Horseback rides and mountain bikes are offered, and there's a game room with billiards. Trails lead into the forest good for spotting quetzals. The lodge serves filling breakfasts, and dinners by request. Horseback rides cost $15–30. Rates include breakfast.

dairy cows at Poás Volcano Lodge

For the ultimate in luxury, check out  **Peace Lodge,** part of La Paz Waterfall Gardens Nature Park & Wildlife Park (see above, $155 standard, $195 deluxe, $235 s/ villa low season; $185/ 215/295 high season). The rooms, which overhang the valley, are amazing, like something out of *The Hobbit.* Imagine natural stone, warm earth tones, huge hemispheric stone fireplaces, roughhewn four-poster king-size beds with canopy netting, tables hewn of diced timbers, TV and stereo, rocking chairs, hardwood floors and lofty ceilings, stone balconies with stone Jacuzzis and awesome views toward Poás. Lounges are lent color by Guatemalan fabrics. The mammoth skylit bathrooms resemble natural caverns and have natural stone Jacuzzi tubs and separate all-stone waterfall showers. Choose 650-square-foot Regular rooms or 800-square-foot deluxe rooms. The 1,200-square-foot Monarch Villa "honeymoon suite" is a two-story, two-bed/two-bath unit, with mezzanine bedrooms; the master bedroom is the ultimate in romantic indulgence, with a king-size wrought-iron and timber canopied bed a mile off the floor, and Jacuzzis even have their own fireplace and stained-glass window. Guests get to use all the facilities.

On the San Isidro Road: The modern and elegant **Hotel Buena Vista** (P.O. Box 760-4050, Alajuela, tel. 506/442-8585, fax 506/442-8701, bvista@racsa.co.cr, www.arweb.com/buenavista; in the U.S., tel. 800/506-2304; $55 s, $60 d standard, $65 s $70 d deluxe, $85 s/d junior suite, $105 s/d sundeck room low season; $65 s, $70 d standard, $80 s, $85 d deluxe, $105 s/d junior suite, $115 s/d sundeck high season), six km north of Alajuela at Las Pilas de San Isidro, has 25 clinically white, carpeted rooms, each with abundant tile work and hardwoods, two queen-size beds, cable TV, and telephone. Junior suites enjoy volcano views (five rooms have balconies). There's a pool, bar, and an elegant skylit restaurant. Rates include transfers.

The **Siempre Verde B&B** (tel. 506/449-5134, fax 506/449-5003, hotelsiempreverde @costaricense.com, $50 s/d), two km west of the Alajuela–San Isidro road, is a charming albeit simple bed-and-breakfast in an old wooden home set amid the coffee fields of the Doka Estate. The setting is sublime. It offers three upstairs rooms, plus a triple downstairs, all entirely of wood. They are drenched in sunlight and have modest but delightful decor, and deep tiled shower tubs. The larger of the upstairs rooms is beautiful, adorned in rich tropical colors. There's a large TV lounge, a huge airy patio, and a garden with macaws and toucans in cages, plus a bonsai *vivero* (plant farm). It has a café open to the public 1–6 P.M. Sat.–Sun. Rates include breakfast and tax.

I absolutely love  **Xandari** (Apdo. 1485, Alajuela 4050, tel. 506/443-2020, fax 506/442-4847, hotel@xandari.com, www.xandari.com; in the U.S., P.O. Box 1449, Summerland, CA 93067, tel. 805/684-7879 or 800/686-7879, fax 805/684-4295; $135–205 d low season; $175–255 d high season), a contempo stunner that is one of the finest hotels in the country. Xandari, perched amid the hotel's own coffee fields in the hills above Tacacori, five km north of Alajuela, is the masterful product of owner/architect Sherrill Brody's aesthetic vision and that of his artist wife, Charlene. The 17 villas are furnished with dark hardwoods and colorful fabrics, modern works of art and gallery pieces, soft-cushioned rattan chairs, sponge-washed walls, Guatemalan bedspreads and plump down pillows; rippling hardwood ceilings and voluptuously curving walls balanced by warm tropical pastels and stained-glass windows echo the theme in the public lounge. Each room has a kitchenette, its own expansive terrace with shady *ranchita,* and a voluminous bathroom with heaps of fluffy towels,

bathrobes, theater-dressing-room lighting, and a cavernous walk-in shower with a floor-to-ceiling window facing onto a private courtyard garden. Take your pick of king-size or two full-size beds. The restaurant serves superbly executed, reasonably priced, health-conscious meals (I enjoyed a stuffed red pepper, Caesar salad, and poached mahi mahi) supported by a full wine list. There are two lap pools with Jacuzzis; a handsome bar and lounge; a soundproofed TV lounge with VCR, well-stocked video library, and plump leather sofas; plus a crafts store, a studio for artists and yoga practitioners; a gym; and an electric car to transport guests to and from the full-service spa. A full range of treatments is offered at the **Xandari Spa Village** (tel. 506/443-2020, spa@xandari.com), from hot stone massage ($130 for 90 minutes) and holistic massage ($95 for 90 minutes) to facials ($65), body wraps ($65), pedicures, and even coffee and macadamia skin buff. The only noise is the birdsong and the swirling waters. Rates include airport transfers and breakfast. Single occupancy costs $20 less.

On the San Pedro Road: The following are in ascending order up the mountain.

Xandari resort and spa

© CHRISTOPHER P. BAKER

The Italian-owned **Hotel/Restaurant Las Fresas** (tel. 506/482-2620, fax 506/482-2587, www.lasfresas.com, $38 s/d cabins, $75 two-room cabins, $250 suite), between Sabana Redonda and Fraijanes, has six octagonal *cabinas* made of red volcanic stone, with hardwood interiors. Most are nicely but simply furnished and have cable TV, and clean tiled bathrooms with hot water. An all-hardwood suite in the main building is a stunner and boasts huge windows, an antique bed, polished hardwood furniture, a Jacuzzi, and a broad balcony with lounge chair and bamboo furniture from which to enjoy the magnificent view.

Nearby, **Jaulares Restaurant** (tel./fax 506/482-2155, restjaulares@racsa.co.cr, $20 s/d) rents five basic and rustic wooden *cabinas* overlooking a river accessible by trails; each features a fireplace. A larger cabin costs $70 for up to seven people.

At Poasito, the well-run and clean **Steak House El Churrasco** (tel. 506/482-2135, $25 s/d), has four rooms in a house next to the restaurant; all have private baths with hot water.

Above Poasito, **Lagunillas Lodge** (tel. 506/448-5506, $20 s, $25 d), two km below the park entrance, has eight simple cabins with shared bathroom and splendid views down the mountainside. They're lit by kerosene lamps, but the owners are planning to add electricity. There are trails for horseback rides, plus trout fishing, and a basic albeit homey Hansel-and-Gretel-type restaurant. Access is by four-wheel drive only, along a steep and rugged track.

Cabinas y Restaurante Mirador Quetzal (tel. 506/482-2090, $30 s, $35 d), midway between Poasito and the crater, has basic rooms with private bathrooms with hot water. It has a clean, modern restaurant with picture-postcard views.

Albergue Ecológico La Providencia (P.O. Box 319-1000, San José, cellular tel. 506/380-6315, $42 d, $53 quad), immediately below the park entrance, is a rustic jewel with six lonesome *cabañas* spread out among 50 hectares of forested hillside pasture on the upper flanks of Poás at 2,500 meters. You can hike or take a horse or a traditional cart to the huts. Views are fantastic. Each cabin has a small kitchenette with hot water

from a hydroelectric power plant. There's no heating, and it gets cold up here, so come prepared. Meals are cooked on a traditional stove in a rustic little restaurant. Horseback rides ($7 one hour, $25 per day) lead to sulfur springs and waterfalls. The property even has a small dairy for those who want to pull their own pints of warm milk. The staff do not speak English. It is accessed via a rugged dirt road (four-wheel drive recommended). Breakfasts cost $6; lunches and dinners are $10.

The **Orquídeas Inn** (Apdo. 394, Alajuela, tel. 506/433-9346, fax 506/433-9740, info @orquideasinn.com, www.orquideasinn.com,, $50–55 s, $60–65 d, $120 mini-suite, $130 geodesic dome), at Cruce de Grecia y Poas, has become a kind of home away from home for local expat gringos who pop in and out to sup and shoot the breeze at the hotel's famous Marilyn Monroe Bar. The hacienda-style home is set amid five acres of landscaped grounds and fruit orchards. The 12 a/c, tile-floored rooms have arched windows, arched doors hand-carved with orchid motifs, and matching arched headboards. A skylit geodesic dome with a kitchenette offers luxury perfect for lovers: a sunken tub and a spiral staircase to the king-size bed, and twin beds in the loft. Vases full of orchids and Guatemalan bedspreads and paintings add notes of bright color. An annex offers 14 large and airy a/c rooms with handsome light-blue sponge-washed walls and lively color schemes plus tile floors, patios, screened windows granting cross-ventilation, and private bathrooms. An open-air steak house grill was being added. There's a marvelous floodlit swimming pool with fountains and wooden sundeck (a second pool was to be added), and a souvenir store stocks fine national artisan work. Toucans, parrots, and a scarlet macaw are kept in cages.

Food

On the Vara Blanca Road: For German food, head to **Casa Bavaria** (tel. 506/483-0716, noon–10 P.M. Wed.–Sat., 11 A.M.–5 P.M. Sunday), a restaurant, café, and *biergarten* next to La Rana Holandesa.

The **Restaurant Vara Blanca** (tel. 506/482-2193), behind the gas station at Vara Blanca, is a rustic eatery of volcanic stone and timbers serving *comida típica*. Nearby, **Restaurante Colbert** (tel. 506/482-2776, jsuirres@racsa.co.cr, 6 A.M.–8 P.M.), at Vara Blanca, is a French-run bakery and café with an airy, well-lit hillside restaurant with magnificent views. It offers set breakfasts, plus croissants, crepes suzette, sandwiches, plus French-Tico fusion cuisine such as tilapia in tomato sauce ($4.50). It has espressos and cappuccinos, and offers Internet service.

La Paz Waterfall Gardens Nature Park & Wildlife Park has a magnificent buffet restaurant ($9) open 8 A.M.–4 P.M. daily.

On the San Pedro Road: I highly recommend **Ⓜ Restaurant Las Fresas** (tel. 506/482-2620, fax 506/482-2587, www.lasfresas.com), justifiably renowned for its Italian specialties and offering a tremendously elegant aesthetic, including a lounge with fireplace. I enjoyed superbly executed cuisine, including spinach and bacon salad, and sea bass with garlic cream sauce and mashed potatoes ($7.50). It's very popular with upscale Ticos and the expatriate crowd.

Further uphill, I also love the atmospheric and rustic **Ⓜ Jaulares Restaurant** (tel./fax 506/482-2155, restjaulares@racsa.co.cr, 8 A.M.–10 P.M.), serving meals cooked on an open wood-burning stove. Try the jalapeña steak ($9), or daily lunch special (*casado jaulares;* $4.75). It's favored by locals on Fri.–Sat. night, when it has live music, from bolero to rock.

At Poasito, the **Steak House El Churrasco** (9 A.M.–5 P.M. Tue.–Sun.) is a popular spot for tenderloins, *lengua en salsa,* and other meat dishes ($4 and up). Try the bean dip with tortillas and jalapeños, followed by tiramisu.

Getting There

Buses (tel. 506/449-5141) for Poasito depart Alajuela from Avenida Central, Calle 10 (three blocks west of the Mercado Central), Tues.–Fri. at 9 A.M., 1 P.M., 4:15 P.M., and 6:15 P.M. Return buses depart at 6 A.M., 10 A.M., 2 P.M., and 5 P.M. Buses operate hourly, 9 A.M.–5 P.M. weekends.

Ⓜ POÁS VOLCANO NATIONAL PARK

Few volcanoes allow you to drive all the way to the rim. Poás does—well, at least to within 300 meters, where a short stroll puts you at the very edge of one of the world's largest active craters (1.5 km wide). The viewing terrace gives a bird's-eye view not only 320 meters down into the hellish bowels of the volcano, with its greenish sulfuric pool, but also down over the northern lowlands.

> *Few volcanoes allow you to drive all the way to the rim. Poás does— The viewing terrace gives a bird's-eye view not only 320 meters down into the hellish bowels of the volcano, with its greenish sulfuric pool, but also down over the northern lowlands.*

Poás (2,708 meters) is a restless giant with a 40-year active cycle. It erupted moderately in the early 1950s and has been intermittently active ever since. The park is frequently closed to visitors because of sulfur gas emissions. Over the millennia it has vented its anger through three craters. Two now slumber under a blanket of vegetation; one even cradles a lake. But the main crater bubbles persistently with active fumaroles and a simmering lake. The sulfuric pool frequently changes hues and emits a geyser up to 200 meters into the steam-laden air. The water level of the lake has gone down about 15 meters during the past decade, one of several indications of a possible impending eruption. In the 1950s a small eruption pushed up a new cone on the crater floor; the cone is now 220 feet high and still puffing.

Oft as not it is foggy up here and mist floats like an apparition through the dwarf cloud forest draped with bromeliads and mosses. Clouds usually form midmorning. Plan an early-morning arrival to enhance your chances of a cloud-free visit. Temperatures vary widely. On a sunny day it can be 21°C (70°F). On a cloudy day, it is normally bitterly cold and windy at the crater rim. Dress accordingly.

Poás is popular on weekends with local Ticos who arrive by the busload with their blaring radios. Visit midweek if possible.

Trails

The **Botos Trail** just before the viewing platform leads to an extinct crater filled with a cold-water lake—Botos. This and the **Escalonia Trail,** which begins at the picnic area, provide for pleasant hikes. The park protects the headwaters of several important rivers, and the dense forests are home to emerald toucanets, coyotes, resplendent quetzals, sooty robins, hummingbirds, frogs, and the Poás squirrel, which is endemic to the volcano.

Information and Services

Poás National Park (tel./fax 506/482-2165, accvccr@racsa.co.cr, www.minae.go.cr/accvc, $7 adults, $1 students), is the most developed within the Costa Rican park system. It offers ample parking, toilets, and an exhibit hall and auditorium, where audiovisual presentations are given on Sunday. Upstairs is the **Heliconia Nature Store,** plus a café serving coffees, cappuccinos, and snacks such as muffins, sandwiches, and pizzas. There's wheelchair access to the exhibits and trails.

The park has no accommodations, and camping is not permitted.

The park is open 8 A.M.–3:30 P.M. daily May–Nov.; and 8 A.M.–5 P.M. Mon.–Thur. and 8 A.M.–4:30 P.M. Fri.–Sun. Dec.–April.

Getting There

TUASA (tel. 506/222-5325) bus no. 1241 departs San José daily at 8:30 A.M. from Avenida 2, Calles 12/14 ($3). You arrive at the volcano about 11 A.M. and depart at 2:30 P.M. Buses (tel. 506/441-0631) also leave from the plaza in Alajuela at 9 A.M. Buses fill quickly; get there early.

Most tour operators in San José offer day trips to Poás (average $35 half day, $55 full day). Many arrive fairly late in the morning, which reduces the chances of seeing anything before the clouds set in. Try to get a tour that arrives no later than 10 A.M.

There's a gas station at Poasito.

Alajuela to Zarcero via Sarchí

Hwy. 141 leads west from Alajuela, snaking through splendidly scenic coffee country and then climbing into an alpine setting—a marvelous drive!

GRECIA

Grecia, on Hwy. 141, some 18 km northwest of Alajuela, is an important market town famous for its rust-red, twin-spired **metal church** made of steel plates imported from Belgium in 1897. The church is an intriguing amalgam, with steps of pumice, a wooden interior, and an arched wooden ceiling with glass chandeliers, a beautiful tiled floor, stained-glass windows, and an all-marble altar that rises fancifully like one of Emperor Ludwig's fairy-tale castles. The church is fronted by a pretty park with tall palms, an obelisk erected to commemorate the foundation of Grecia in July 1864, fountains, and a domed music temple.

The **Museo de Cultura** (tel. 506/444-6767), on the park's northwest corner, houses a regional museum tracing the development of the area during the last 200 years.

World of Snakes

Just east of Grecia, on the main Sarchí road, the Austrian-run World of Snakes (tel./fax 506/494-3700, snakes@racsa.co.cr, 8 A.M.–4 P.M., $11 adults, $6 children and students) displays a collection of more than 300 live snakes from around the world, including many of Costa Rica's most beautiful critters. The facility breeds 50 different species for sale and for reintroduction to the wild. It educates visitors to dispel the negative

metal church, Grecia

© CHRISTOPHER P. BAKER

image with a clear message—don't harm snakes! For example, you'll learn how snakes are vital to helping keep rodent populations in check, thus preventing plagues. The critters live behind glass windows in re-creations of their natural habitats. You can handle non-venomous snakes.

Accommodations

Healthy Day Inn (tel./fax 506/444-5903, www.healthyday.com, $45 s/d), on the western edge of town, is described as a "naturistic health home." The 14 tastefully, albeit sparsely decorated rooms have parquet floors with throw rugs (carpets in upstairs rooms), hardwood ceilings, cable TVs, telephones, and private baths with hot water. The hotel offers therapeutic massage, reflexology, facials, sauna, hydrotherapy, and supervised macrobiotic diets. Amenities include a Jacuzzi, swimming pool, and lighted tennis court. The inn offers car rental ($20 daily) and tour guides. Rates include breakfast and airport transfers.

Posada Mimosa (Apdo. 135-4100 Grecia, tel./fax 506/494-5868, mimosa@mimosa.co.cr, www.mimosa.co.cr, $50 s, $60 d rooms, $70 daily, $300 weekly bedsit, $80 daily, $400 weekly guest house, $95 daily, $450 weekly family-size), in the hamlet of Rincón de Salas, is an exquisite bed-and-breakfast run by Canadians Tessa and Martin Borner. Set amid seven hectares of lush landscaped gardens and privately owned forest, the modern hillside home offers dramatic valley views, and the grounds are fantastic for birding. It has four no-frills rooms in the house, all with ceiling fans and private baths; a charming bedsit *casita* with fold-out bed; two guest house *casitas* with twin bed and fold-out bed, plus full kitchen; and a three-bedroom family-size *casita* with lounge and dining area plus kitchen. Traditional Costa Rican motifs adorn the walls, furnishings are modest, and well-lit bathrooms are graced with blue-and-white tiles. One room in the house is a huge family room with two double beds and a bunk. There's a small horizon swimming pool with views, a broad veranda with wicker sofas, and a poolside grill where breakfasts are served. Fairylights adorn the trees by night. The owners' own lounge (usually off-limits to guests) is festooned with artwork; they are tremendous conversationalists (many of their tales are regaled in Tessa's *Potholes to Paradise,* her story of running a hotel in the tropics). Martin is seriously into organic agriculture and works out in his kaftan on the Flintstone Exercise Trail. Rates include breakfast.

Services

There are two banks facing the main square. You can make international calls from the **ICE** (8 A.M.–3:30 P.M. Mon.–Fri.) office on the north side of the square.

Café Internet (tel. 506/444-0333, 2–9 P.M. Mon.–Sat, 9 A.M.–9 P.M. Sun.) is on the south side of the plaza.

Hospital San Francisco de Asis (tel. 506/444-5045) and the **Red Cross** (tel. 506/444-5292) provide medical care.

Getting There

Buses (tel. 506/258-2004) depart San José hourly from Calle 20, Avenida 5. The bus station in Grecia is at Avenida 2, Calles 4/6, two blocks west of the plaza.

Taxis congregate on the north side of the plaza.

SARCHÍ

Sarchí, 29 km northwest of Alajuela, is Costa Rica's crossroads of crafts, famous for the intricately detailed, hand-painted oxcarts that originated here in the middle of the 19th century (the town celebrates them on the first week of February with bull-riding, amusement rides, and, of course, a parade of oxcarts). Handcrafted souvenirs—from chess sets and salad bowls, leather sandals and rockers, to miniature oxcarts decorated in traditional geometric designs—are sold at shops all along the road of Sarchí Sur, which sits atop a steep hill about one km east of Sarchí Norte, the town center.

Sarchí Norte's **church,** done up in stuccoed motifs, is one of the most beautiful in the nation and has a vaulted hardwood ceiling and carvings—a gift of devotion from local artisans. Many whitewashed buildings are painted with the town's own floral motif trim. The name Sarchí, according to writer Carlos Gagini,

© CHRISTOPHER P. BAKER

Central Highlands

Sarchí Sur's main church

comes from the Aztec name Xalachi (under the volcano).

The town is surrounded by steep-sided valleys, with row upon row of coffee bushes cascading downhill like folds of green silk.

Sarchí is on most package-tour itineraries. Avoid weekends.

At **Fábrica de Carretas Joaquín Chaverrí** (Apdo. 19-4650 Sarchí, tel. 506/454-4411, fax 506/454-4494, oxcarts@racsa.co.cr, www.sarchicostarica.com), in Sarchí Sur, you can see souvenirs and oxcarts being painted in workshops at the rear. Joaquín's grandfather "invented" the 16-pie-wedge-piece wheel bound with a metal belt that has become the traditional oxcart wheel. The factory was founded in 1903 and now has 15 owner-partners, most of them Chaverrí family members.

Commercialized Sarchí Sur may strike you as kitschy, despite the quality of the crafts. For the real McCoy, check out **Taller Eloy Alfaro** (tel. 506/454-4131, 6 A.M.–5 P.M. Mon.–Thur., 6 A.M.–3 P.M. Friday), a traditional workshop in Sarchí Norte, where Señor Alfaro's family can be seen making yolks and oxcarts in traditional manner. In fact, this is the *only* place in the country still

Central Highlands

SARCHÍ

To Bosque de Paz

To Cabanas Paraiso Rio Verde,
Cabinas de Montaña Fantasia,
and Bosque de la Paz

To Grecia and
San José

LOS
RODRÍGUEZ

MUEBLERIA
EL ARTESANO

GUARDIA RURAL
(POLICE)

SOUVENIRS
EL SUEÑO

BUS STOP

RESTAURANT LAS
CARRETERAS

MUEBLERIA
EL FAMILIAR

SARCHÍ SUR

FÁBRICA DE CARRETAS
JOAQUIN CHAVERRI

PLAZA DE LA ARTESANIA

FÁBRICA DE MUEBLES
LA SARCHISEÑA

TALLER YENNY

CENTRO
TURISTICO
EL RIO

TAXIS

BANK

Río Trojas

CABINAS
MANDY

RESTAURANTE
SUPER MARISCOS

MUSMANNI

CALLE COLEGIO

TALLER
ELOY
ALFARO

HOTEL
CABINAS
ZAMORA

ICE

POST
OFFICE

BUS STOP

BANK

RED CROSS

GUARDIA
RURAL
(POLICE)

CEMETERY

SARCHÍ
NORTE

CALLE SAN RAFAEL

HOTEL VILLA
SARCHI LODGE

CALLE RODRIGUEZ

To Naranjo

SCALE NOT AVAILABLE

© AVALON TRAVEL PUBLISHING, INC.

making traditional working oxcarts. You can watch various family members making the carts of sturdy wood, with mahogany wheels, a body of cedar, coach pole of ironwood, and braces of lagarto, with the lathes and tools all still powered by an age-old waterwheel.

Shopping

There are dozens of places to choose from. The largest is **Fábrica de Carretas Joaquín Chaverrí** (see above). One hundred meters west is the **Plaza de la Artesanía,** a modern complex with 34 showrooms, souvenir stores, and restaurants.

You can order custom-made furniture from any of dozens of workshops *(talleres).*

Accommodations

In Sarchí Sur, **Hotel Cabinas Zamora** (tel. 506/454-4596, $25 s, $30 d) has seven simple, clean rooms with small cable TVs, fans, and private baths with hot water. A small single room with a/c costs $30 s. **Cabinas Mandy** (tel. 506/454-2397), 300 meters north and 100 meters west of the church, has simple cabins and secure parking.

Hotel Villa Sarchí (tel. 506/454-5000, hotelvilla@racsa.co.cr, $40 s, $45 d), one km northwest of Sarchí Norte, has eight simple, well-lit cabins with tile floors, cable TV, clean private baths with hot water, and hammocks and rockers on the porch with views toward Volcán Poás. There's a small swimming pool. Airport transfers are provided.

Cabinas Paraíso Río Verde (tel./fax 506/454-3003, paraisorioverde@racsa.co.cr, $20 s, $25 d budget rooms, $30 s, $40 d rooms, $40 s, $50 d cabins), about two km north of Sarchí Sur on the road to Bosque del Paz, is a somewhat basic German-run hostelry with two clean, simply furnished, four-person cabins with large and attractive bathrooms with hot water and him-and-her sinks. To the rear are three additional rooms (one with views), including two "budget" rooms with hardwood floors and ceiling fans. It has a no-frills dining room, where an all-you-can-eat breakfast is served. Its greatest advantage is its peaceful hillside setting, and the kidney-shaped pool and sundeck with spectacular views of four volcanos. Airport transfers are offered.

Cabinas de Montaña Fantasia (tel. 506/454-2007, $20 s/d), amid coffee fields two km further uphill, has nine simply furnished cabins with small TVs (local programming only), timber ceilings decorated with coffee sacks, kitchenettes, and small patios with awesome views. It has a restaurant (lunch and dinner only).

Food

For eats in Sarchí Norte try **Restaurante Super Mariscos** (tel. 506/454-4330), behind the Banco Nacional, for seafood. The circular and somewhat dark **Restaurante El Río** (tel. 506/454-4980, 10 A.M.–9 P.M.), beside the river between Sarchí Norte and Sarchí Sur, has a large menu running from ceviche and heart of palm cocktail to filet mignon in mushroom sauce ($7.50).

In Sarchí Sur there are several eateries in the Plaza de la Artesanía, including **La Troja del Abuelo** (tel. 506/454-4973), with a large menu of *típico* dishes (try the sea bass in mushroom sauce) and a large rear garden patio; and the small, homey **Restaurant Helechos** (tel. 506/454-4560, 10 A.M.–6 P.M., $6) which serves tacos, burgers, and such tantalizing dishes as tongue in salsa, garlic shrimp, and desserts, natural juices, and cappuccinos.

Restaurant Las Carrateras (tel. 506/454-1633, 9 A.M.–6 P.M., $5), adjoining Fábrica de Carretas Joaquín Chaverrí, has a shaded patio out back; it serves *típico* dishes plus chicken parmagiana, pastas, salads, and burgers.

Information and Services

There are **Banco Nacional** outlets in the Plaza de la Artesanía and one block west of the square in Sarchí Norte; both are open 8:30 A.M.–3 P.M. weekdays. The **post office** (7 A.M.–5 P.M. Mon.–Fri.) is 50 meters west of the square. The **police** (Guardia Rural) station is on the southwest corner of the soccer field in Sarchí Norte, as well as across from Fábrica de Carreta Joaquín Chaverrí.

Getting There and Around

An express bus departs San José from Calle 18,

Central Highlands

Avenida 3 every 30 minutes 5 A.M.–10 P.M. Another bus departs Calle 16, Avenidas 5, Mon.–Fri. at 12:15 P.M., 5:30 P.M. and 6 P.M.; returning at the same times. Tuan (tel. 506/441-3781) buses also depart Alajuela every 30 minutes, 5 A.M.–10 P.M., from Calle 8, Avenidas Central/1.

Taxis wait on the west side of the square in Sarchí Norte, or call **Sarchí Taxi Service** (tel. 506/454-4028).

ⓜ BOSQUE DE PAZ RAIN/CLOUD FOREST

From Sarchí, at a turnoff 100 meters east of the Río Trojas, a road climbs north up the mountain slopes via Luisa and Angeles to the saddle between Poás and Platanar Volcanoes—you are now high amid the cloud forest—before dropping sharply to **Bajos del Toro,** a tranquil Shangri-la hidden at the head of the valley of the Río Toro. The route is incredibly scenic, and at times daunting, as you weave along a road that clings precariously to the face of the often cloud-shrouded mountains. You can also reach Bajos del Toro via a dirt road from Zarcero.

The 400-hectare **Bosque de Paz Rain/Cloud Forest Biological Reserve,** accessed via a reclusive valley west of Bajos del Toro, boasts several hiking trails (two–six km) leading to waterfalls, a botanical garden, hummingbird gardens, and lookout points. The forests are replete with exotic wildlife, including howler, capuchin, and spider monkeys, cats, and—according to the owner—more bird species than anywhere else in the nation, not least quetzals, which hover near the lodge. Two streams tumble through the beautiful gardens.

About seven km north of Bajos del Toro is a 200-meter waterfall—**Catarata del Toro.** There are trails; the bottom of the falls is reached by a 500-step staircase! There's also a restaurant. Entrance costs $35, including lunch ($79 with transportation). Buses and jeep-taxis run from Sarchí. **Aventuras y Senderos** (tel. 506/463-3137, info@donbeto.com, www.donbeto.com), at Hotel Don Beto in Zarcero, offers a waterfall rappel of the Catarata del Toro.

Accommodations and Food

Bosque de Paz (Apdo. 130-1000, San José, tel. 506/234-6676, fax 506/225-0203, info @bosquedepaz.com, www.bosquedepaz.com, $94 pp) has a rustic stone and log lodge with a handsome restaurant serving *típico* food, plus two rooms with private baths and hot water, each for four people. A one-day excursion from San José for an additional fee includes lunch. Reservation required. Rates include three meals and taxes.

NARANJO TO CIUDAD QUESADA

Naranjo, five km west of Sarchí and three km north of the Pan-American Highway, is an important agricultural center with a pretty, twin-towered, cream-colored, red-roofed baroque church worth a stop. Thick limestone Corinthian columns support a fine ceiling. Notice the splendid religious paintings to the sides.

North of Naranjo, the main road leads to Ciudad Quesada and the northern lowlands. It is one of the most scenic drives in the country. Beyond **San Juanillo,** the scenery becomes distinctly alpine, with dairy cattle munching contentedly on the emerald mountain slopes. Higher up, beyond the hamlet of **Llano Bonito,** the road twists and coils as you ascend to **Zarcero,** a pleasant mountain town with an impressive setting beneath green mountains. Dominating the town is the whitewashed church fronted by a **topiary park.** The mark of the scissors is on every plant and bush. The work is that of Evangelisto Blanco, who has unleashed his wildest ideas in leafy splendor: a cat riding a motorcycle along the top of a hedge; an elephant with lightbulbs for eyes; corkscrews whose spiral foliage coils up and around the trunks like serpents around Eden's tree; even a bullring complete with matador, charging bull, and spectators. On virtually any day you can see Blanco snapping his pruning shears, evenly rounding off the rabbits and clipping straight the great cascading archway arbor that leads to the steps of the church.

At **Zapote,** eight km north of Zarcero, you reach the Continental Divide, with sweeping vistas of the northern lowlands far below. Zapote is gateway to **Juan Castro Blanco National Park** (tel. 506/460-7600 or 506/460-0055, achn@minae.go.cr). Part of the Arenal Conservation Area, the 14,453-hectare park protects forested slopes of the Cordillera de Tilarán extending from 700 meters elevation to 2,267 meters. At its heart is still-active Volcán Platanar (2,183 m). It is replete with wildlife, including Baird's tapir, and the resplendent quetzal at upper elevations. At last visit it had no tourist facilities.

Accommodations

Hotel Don Beto (tel. 506/463-3137, info @donbeto.com, www.donbeto.com, $25 d shared bath, $30 private bath), facing the north side of the church in Zarcero, is a handsome hostelry with eight clean, modestly furnished rooms with TVs and hot water. The veranda offers views over the topiary garden. It offers airport transfers ($20 each way) plus tours to Juan Castro Blanco National Park and Bosque de la Paz Rainforest Reserve.

Food

The **Restaurante El Mirador** (tel. 506/451-1959), near San Juanillo, has telescopes for better enjoying views over the valley and good *típico* food *a la leña* (grilled over coffee wood) that'll fill you up on a dime and that should be washed down with a refreshing fresh-fruit *refresco.*

The **Restaurante Hereford Grill BBQ Steak House** (tel. 506/454-4980, 11 A.M.–midnight), one km south of Zarcero, offers a delightful rustic ambience and such tempting fare as New York tenderloin strips ($7.50), grilled sea bass ($11), and ceviche. The restaurant, however, fails to take advantage of its hillside position; for the views, try next door at **Rancho Típico.**

Getting There

An express bus for Ciudad Quesada via Zarcero departs San José hourly 5 A.M.–7:30 P.M. from Atlántico Norte "terminal" (Calle 12, Avenida 9, tel. 506/255-4318); and from San Ramón at 5:45 A.M., 8:30 A.M., noon, 2:30 P.M., and 5 P.M. Buses for San Ramón depart from the southwest corner of the park in Zarcero at 7 A.M., 9:40 A.M., 1 P.M., 3:40 P.M., and 6:45 P.M. The bus stop for San José faces the church.

Central Highlands

© CHRISTOPHER P. BAKER

Zarcero

Alajuela to Atenas and San Ramón

LA GARITA

La Garita, spanning the Pan-American Highway (Hwy. 1) about 12 km west of Alajuela, is important for its location at the junction of Hwy. 3, which leads west for Atenas, Orotina, and Puntarenas (and east for Alajuela). The area boasts a salubrious climate, and La Garita is famed for ornamental-plant farms known as *viveros*. Group tours can be arranged to the nursery of **Orchid Alley** (tel. 506/487-7086, orchid@sol.racsa.co.cr), which grows more than 100,000 orchids on site. It sells blooms packaged in plastic boxes, plus live *guaria morada* orchids (the national flower) in sealed vials suitable for import into the United States.

⚔ Zoo Ave

This splendid zoo (tel. 506/433-8989, fax 506/433-9140, zooave@racsa.co.cr, www.zooave.org, 9 A.M.–5 P.M., $9 admission adults, $4 children), at Dulce Nombre, on Hwy. 3, about 3.5 km east of the Pan-American Highway, is a *must see*. It covers 59 hectares of landscaped grounds and is a wildlife rescue center for injured and confiscated wildlife. The fantastic bird collection (the largest in Central America) includes dozens of toucans, cranes, curassows, and parrots, and a veritable Pantone chart of more than 100 other Costa Rican bird species. Zoo Ave is one of only two zoos in the world to display resplendent quetzals. Macaws fly free. You'll also see crocodile, deer, turtles, ostrich, tapirs, peccaries, pumas, and all four species of indigenous monkeys in large enclosures. Noah would be proud: most creatures are in pairs or groups.

The goal is to breed national species for reintroduction into the wild. The zoo has successfully bred the scarlet macaw, green macaw, curassow, guan, and about 50 other native bird species with the help of a human-infant incubator. The breeding center is off-limits.

There's a small *soda* and bathrooms, and a visitors center that shows video presentations and offers educational events twice monthly.

To get to Zoo Ave., take either the Atenas or the La Garita bus from Alajuela. Both pass by the zoo.

Accommodations

Hotel La Rosa de América (tel./fax 506/433-2741, info@larosadeamerica.com, www.larosadeamerica.com, $47 s, $64 d low season, $53 s, $69 d high season),in Barrio San José de Alajuela, is a charming, midpriced, country-style option set back 100 meters south of La Mandarina on the main Alajuela–La Garita road amid exquisite gardens. The new American owners keep the place spic-and-span. Set amid a lushly landscaped garden, its 12 modestly appointed simple cabins have fans, cable TVs, tile floors, security boxes, and balconies with rocking chairs. Tropical breakfasts are served in a homey restaurant. There's a small swimming pool, plus a TV lounge with VCR/DVD player. Rates include breakfast and tax.

At the top end of the scale is the gracious **Hotel Martino Med-spa & Resort** (tel. 506/433-8382, fax 506/433-9052, martino@racsa.co.cr, www.hotelmartino.com, $130 s, $145 d low season, $140 s, $160 d high season), set amid six acres of lushly manicured grounds with classical statuary. The motif melds a classical Romanesque theme with abundant lacquered hardwoods, as in the majestic beamed, columned lounge boasting plump sofas with exquisite Italian fabrics. It has 34 a/c suites with hardwood ceilings, tile floors, double doors for sound-proofing, terraces (some facing a lake), spacious bathrooms with monogrammed towels, cable TVs, phones, minibars, and king-size beds with linens. A huge swimming pool is inset in a large terrace with a thatched grill. Facilities include an Italian restaurant (with live music nightly, plus dining until 3 A.M.), a bar, casino, tennis court, and a state-of-the-art gym and spa. Trails access a bird sanctuary.

Food

For a genuine local experience, I recommend

M Fiesta del Maíz (tel. 506/487-7057), on Hwy. 3, about one km west of the Pan-American Highway. This large, cafeteria-style restaurant is famous for its tasty corn meals: *chorreadas* (corn fritters), tamales (corn pudding), corn on the grill, tasty rice with corn and chicken, and other tempting morsels. Free tastings are offered. No plate costs more than $3.

The restaurant at **Hotel Martino Med-spa & Resort** serves Italian fare.

Services

Treat yourself to a skin or other health treatment at the **Cleopatra Spa** at Hotel Martino Med-spa & Resort (see above), with a replica of a Roman steam room and a Derma Clinic (for information, visit www.dermaclinic.com) offering treatments from liposculpture to skin transplants. Mud masks, massages, aromatherapy, and reflexology are offered, as are negative-ionized oxygen treatments.

Getting There

Buses for La Garita depart San José from the Coca-Cola bus terminal, and from Alajuela from Avenida Central, Calle 10.

ATENAS

Balmy Atenas, on Hwy. 3, five km west of La Garita, is an agricultural town renowned for its quality fruits and perpetually springlike climate (in 1994, *National Geographic* declared it the best climate in the world). Watch for the statue of the Virgin Mary on a hill one km east of town, which has a beautiful church surrounded by palms in the plaza, two blocks south of Hwy 3.

The old *camino de carretas* (oxcart trail) ran through Atenas, and during the peak of coffee harvest, trains of 800-plus carts would pass by, carrying beans to Puntarenas. In 2003, a massive iron monument to the *boyeros* (oxcart driver) was unveiled by Spanish blacksmith Manolo Torrecillas (tel. 506/446-8020), whose workshop is on the main road in Barrio Los Angeles.

The **Central American School of Animal Husbandry** (tel. 506/446-5050 or 506/446-5250), one km east of Atenas, welcomes visitors for a firsthand look at dairy operations, reforestry programs, iguana farming, and more on the 530-hectare property. Half-day ($40 with lunch at an old hacienda) and full-day tours ($60 including lunch and a horseback ride into the mountain forests) are offered; reservations must be made a week in advance. You can even milk cows!

Accommodations

Ana's Place B&B (Apdo. 66, Atenas, tel. 506/446-5019, fax 506/446-6579, davegray@yahoo.com, www.anasplace.com, from $25 s, $35 d), now under new owners, is a quiet home away from home on the east side of town. Italianate steps lead up to the house, with its spacious lounge and beautiful hardwood parquet floors. The 11 modestly furnished rooms vary markedly; some have shared baths. There are also two apartments with kitchenettes. The back lawn has an outside restaurant and a small swimming pool. (Turn left opposite the gas station as you enter Atenas from the east; follow the signs from here.) Rates include breakfast.

The Belgian-run **Hotel B&B Vista Atenas** (Apdo. 235-4013, Sabana Larga, Atenas, tel./fax 506/446-4272, vistaatenas@hotmail.com, www .vistaatenas.com, $35 s, $40 d room, $45 s/d cabin) is a pleasing modern property high in the hills about three km west of Atenas. The six rooms are airy and have heaps of light through floor-to-ceiling glass windows. Two cabins have kitchenettes and hammocks on verandas. All are clean and modestly furnished and have fans. There's a small pool and sundeck offering one of the most spectacular views in the country. The host is friendly, and the restaurant is a choice option.

Hotel Colinas del Sol (Apdo. 164, Atenas, tel. 506/446-4244, colinas@hotels.co.cr, $45 s/d), two km southeast of town, is a handsome upscale complex with eight red-tile-roofed bungalows and three smaller cabañas amid lush, beautifully landscaped grounds on a breezy hillside in the midst of the *campo*. The spacious units are well-lit and nicely appointed, with kitchenettes, attractive tiled bathrooms, and French doors opening to wide patios facing a large pool and sun deck. All have fans and hot water. An open-sided restaurant higher up has views toward Volcán Poás. Hiking trails, tennis, and horse rentals were to be added. The place is German-run, but the feel is contemporary Spanish.

Villas de la Colina (tel. 506/446-5015, fax 506/446-7858, kathryn@racsa.co.cr, $40 s/d), two km north of Hwy. 3, six km west of Atenas, has six simply furnished, all-wood hilltop cabins with lofty ceilings with fans, broad windows and terraces with hammocks with views, plus clean modern bathrooms with warm showers. There are arbors and a thatched restaurant, plus a pool. Horseback rides are offered.

Finca Huetares (P.O. Box 55-4013, Atenas, tel./fax 506/446-4147, brownie@racsa.co.cr, $30 s/d room, $45 apartment, $50 house low season; $40 room, $55 apartment, $65 house high season), two km east of Atenas and two km northeast via Barrio Los Angeles, is an eight-hectare fruit farm with fantastic vistas and trails. It's a peaceful place, named for an Indian tribe. Finca Huetares offers four rooms, four apartments, and two houses, all with cable TV and hot water. The modestly furnished apartments have a lounge and kitchen with microwave, plus fans and hot water. One is handicap-equipped. The place is pet friendly. Its well-named Restaurant Bella Vista features floor-to-ceiling windows with awesome views eastward, and sofas for enjoying them (open to the public noon–9 P.M. Sat.–Sun.). There's a large swimming pool and a kid's pool, and camping is permitted.

I highly recommend **El Cafetal Inn** (Apdo. 105, Atenas, tel. 506/446-5785, fax 506/446-7028, cafetal@cafetal.com.co.cr, www.cafetal.com, $79 s, $89 d standard, $89 s, $99 d with balcony, $105 s, $115 d Tower Room, $110 s, $120 d cottage), an elegant bed-and-breakfast on a small coffee and fruit *finca* in Santa Eulalia, about five km north of Atenas. Lee and Romy Rodríquez (he's Salvadoran, she's Colombian), the super-friendly owners, run their 10-bedroom hostelry like a true home away from home, earning praise from past guests ("a Garden of Eden," wrote one). The open-plan lounge has marble floors, a cascade, and plump leather sofas; light streams in through bay windows that proffer val-

ley and mountain vistas. The upstairs rooms (some quite small) are modestly appointed, but lively fabrics and bathrooms boasting wood vanities are nice touches. Lee and Romy have added a romantic Hansel-and-Gretel cottage with a king-size bed, sofa, cable TV, Persian rug on terra-cotta tile floor, kitchenette, and patio with volcano views. There's a large, clover-shaped swimming pool; a thatched coffee bar where hearty meals are served; and a pergola shaded by an arbor offering views over a canyon accessed by trails. Howler monkeys hang out in the trees nearby. Wedding packages and tours are offered. They also offer a two-bedroom house in Atenas with fireplace and Jacuzzi. Airport transfers cost $25 d ($2.50 extra persons). Deduct $10 in low season.

Food

La Trilla (tel. 506/446-5637, 9 A.M.–6 P.M. Mon.–Sat.), on the main road, offers bargain-priced *típico* dishes in a rustic ambience recalling the days when oxcarts laden with coffee stopped here en route to Puntarenas. For vegetarian dishes, head to **Café Internet** (tel. 506/446-6442), one block from the main plaza, a rainbow-hued Victorian home where fruit juices, herbal teas, and smoothies are also served. A great breakfast spot, **K-puchinos** (tel. 506/446-4184, 8 A.M.–10 P.M.), on the main plaza, is a popular Internet café and restaurant run by a Spanish couple who conjure up great Catalonian dishes, plus sandwiches and desserts.

The gaily colored, Mexican-run **Jalapeños** (tel. 506/446-6314, 11 A.M.–11 P.M.), four km west of town, offers authentic Mexican food, including *mole poblano,* a house specialty

I highly recommend **Ṃ Mirador del Cafetal,** (6 A.M.–6 P.M.) on the main highway about eight km west of Atenas. Owned by Lee and Romy (see El Cafetal Inn, above), it offers awesome vistas down through a coffee-clad valley toward the Pacific. This rustic delight has a 23-page menu (!) that includes granola, omelette, or *gallo pinto* breakfasts; soups and salads; creative lunches, from chicken fajitas ($5) to garlic sea bass with veggies and baked potato ($9), smoked chicken or fish cooked in banana leaves, and indigenous dishes; plus fruit smoothies ($2.50), ice cream and yogurt shakes ($3.50). A gift store sells Colombian pottery and artifacts; and there's a tree house for kids.

The modestly elegant restaurant at **Hotel B&B Vista Atenas** (tel./fax 506/446-4272, 6:30–10 P.M. Thur.–Sat.) serves French-Belgian cuisine, including pâté ($2.50) and smoked salmon ($7) appetizers, plus sea bass in salsa curry ($7) and filet mignon in pepper sauce ($7). A daily menu costs $10.

Services

There are two banks and a gas station in town. A post office stands one block west of the church. There's a local **Red Cross** (tel. 506/446-5161).

The **Balcón de Café** and **K-puchinos** both offer Internet services (see *Food,* above), as does **Planeta Rock Café Internet** (migueloliveros2001@yahoo.com).

Getting There

See *La Garita,* above, for bus schedules. The **taxi** stand is one block south and one block west of the plaza.

ROSARIO

This small mountain hamlet is hidden away just west of the Pan-American Highway, about eight km northwest of La Garita, eight km northeast of Atenas, and eight km southwest of Grecia. It's the gateway to the **Río Grande Canyon Nature Reserve,** a 3,700-acre nature reserve flanking a dramatic gorge. Access is via the Vista del Valle Plantation Inn; the exit is two km west of the Grecia turnoff from the Pan-American Highway. The valley is thickly forested with bamboo and has a series of waterfalls, one of which tumbles 100 meters.

Thrill seekers can leap off the 83-meter Puente Negro bridge over the Río Colorado, one km east of Rosario. **Tropical Bungee** (tel./fax 506/248-2212, bungee@bungee.co.cr, www .bungee.co.cr) offers bungee jumps under the guidance of "jump masters" using an 11-meter bungee. The company charges $45 for the first

jump, $70 for two jumps. Anyone with back, neck, or heart problems is advised not to jump. Jumps are offered 9 A.M.–3 P.M. Sat.–Sun., and weekdays by reservation in low season; and daily 9 A.M.–3 P.M. in high season. The San José–Puntarenas bus from Calle 12, Avenida 7, or the San José–Naranjo bus from Calle 16, Avenida 1, will drop you off at Salon Los Alfaro, a short walk north to the bridge.

Accommodations

M Vista del Valle Plantation Inn (Apdo. 185-4003, Alajuela, tel. 506/450-0800 or 888/535-8832, fax 506/451-1165, frontdesk@vistadelvalle .com, www.vistadelvalle.com, $90 s/d rooms, $135–160 s/d cottages), is a serene bed-and-breakfast on a working citrus and coffee *finca* on the edge of the Río Grande Canyon Preserve. Overlooking the river chasm, it has glorious views over the valley. Lush lawns fall away to meld into tall bamboo forest. The main lodge, which has one guestroom with private bathroom, is a Frank Lloyd Wright–style architectural marvel in wood; floor-to-ceiling plate-glass windows flood Vista del Valle with light. Seven cottages (including the two-bedroom Mango Manor, and three duplexes) are reached by stone trails; some have their own kitchens. All boast tasteful yet minimalist decor and furnishings—polished hardwood floors and four-poster beds with mosquito nets adding a romantic note—plus private balcony or wraparound veranda, and lavish Oriental-style bathrooms with granite tilework. The rustic but charming Mona Lisa cottage is suspended over the gorge, with stone floors in the bathroom and an outdoor shower and deck. Facilities include mountain bikes and a stable (lessons and trail rides are offered; $20 per hour). Gourmet lunches and candlelit dinners prepared by a professionally trained chef are served on an outdoor veranda cantilevered over the canyon. There's a beautiful pool and Jacuzzi fed by a water cascade. The amiable owners—Californians Johanna and Michael Bresnan—were planning to add a tennis court, gym, conference center, and private condominium units. Guests are offered three nights for the price of two May–June and Sep.–Oct. Rates include breakfast. Dinner costs $10.

PALMARES

Palmares, 1.5 km south from the Pan-American Highway, 10 km west of Naranjo, is renowned for its lively weeklong agricultural and civic fiesta held each mid-January. The impressive stone **church,** built in 1894, is attractive in its ornamental setting and is fronted by a peaceful plaza.

Wilson Arce Méndez (tel. 506/453-4210, wilsonarcem@hotmail.com) crafts gorgeous bowls and furniture from recycled trunks of hardwoods; you can visit his studio by appointment.

Ecotorunes Lodge (tel./fax 506/453-4300, 9 A.M.–6 P.M. Tue.–Thur. and Sunday, 9 A.M.–10 P.M. Friday, and 9 A.M.–midnight Saturday), a 10-hectare organic coffee farm at Candelaría, six km south of Palmares, is set amid landscaped hillside gardens with fabulous views. There are trails down to the canyon of the Río Grande, and locals flock on weekends to bathe in three large pools, one with a long waterslide. The thatched restaurant hosts live music on Saturday nights.

At Cocaleca, one km south of Palmares, is **Jardín de las Guarias** (tel. 506/452-0091, 7 A.M.–6 P.M., $3 admission), a private orchid collection. Owner Javier Solórzano Murillo has more than 180 orchid species on display, but it is Costa Rica's national flower, the violet *guaria morada* orchid, that blossoms most profusely—more than 40,000 of them. Javier planted his first orchid here in 1941. At least a dozen species are always in bloom. Best time, however, is February to April, when the place explodes into color. A small restaurant (open spring only) serves Costa Rican dishes, which you can enjoy beneath a shady amate tree.

Accommodations and Food

Hotel Rancho Mirador (tel./fax 506/451-1301, $50 s/d), on a coffee *finca* beside Hwy. 1, three km east of Palmares and four km west of Naranjo, is a soaring restaurant boasting stupendous views east along the length of the volcano-lined valley. It serves *comida típica* and is open 3 P.M.–midnight. It also has six rooms arrayed down the hillside perpendicular to the valley. They are clean, carpeted, and pleasingly

furnished, with TV, fan, and mini-refrigerator. Incredibly, the architect put the windows facing *west*—into the driveway. At least each room has a tiny balcony facing east. There's a small swimming pool. Rates include tax and breakfast.

Ecotorunes Lodge (see above, $37.50 up to four people) has five log cabins with tile floors and simple furnishes plus large walk-in showers with hot water. Windows do not offer views, alas, but there are small porches.

SAN RAMÓN

San Ramón, about 12 km due west of Naranjo, and one km north of Hwy. 1, is an agricultural and university town known for its Saturday *feria del agricultor* (farmer's market). The impressive **church** on the main square is built of steel manufactured by the Krups armament factory in Germany and has a beautiful colonial tile floor and stained-glass windows. The **San Ramón Museum** (1–5 P.M. Monday, Tuesday, Thursday, and Friday, 8 A.M.–5 P.M. Wednesday and Sat-

© CHRISTOPHER P. BAKER

monument of *boyeros* (oxcart drivers), San Ramón

urday, free admission) on the north side of the plaza, focuses on local history and has a motley collection; it features a re-created turn-of-the-century *campesino* home.

Accommodations and Food

La Posada Bed and Breakfast (P.O. Box 76-4250, San Ramón, tel. 506/445-7359, fax 506/447-2021, johotel@racsa.co.cr, www.posadahotel .com, $30 s, $40 d), 50 meters east of the hospital, is a beautiful conversion of a home furnished with antique reproductions, earth-tone decor, and polished hardwoods, albeit a bit gauche for some tastes. The 15 rooms in the original home surround a tiny courtyard and have hardwood walls and ceilings, 37-inch cable TVs (eight also have stereo systems), and huge bathrooms with hairdryers. Some downstairs rooms get little light; upstairs rooms are preferred and open to a balcony. Some have magnificent Louis XIV–style beds. Twelve carpeted rooms in a new annex across the street have lofty ceilings, similarly tasteful decor, including chaise lounges, but they are overly stuffed with furniture. It has a small gift store and laundry, plus Internet access and secure parking.

Catering to health-conscious travelers, **Hotel & Spa Casa Elena** (tel. 506/445-0004, casaelena @racsa.co.cr, www.costarelax.com) is set amid expansive grounds enjoying a magnificent view of the Pacific Ocean. It has 10 rooms (two singles) in the hotel. Alternately, choose the Casa Rosita guesthouse with two double rooms. A highlight is the 79-foot-long indoor pool, plus you can soak in the Jacuzzi or steam room. Yoga, meditation programs, and a wide range of therapy and beauty treatments, plus guided excursions, are offered. Gourmet vegetarian dishes are served. Contact the owner, Helene Wirt, for rates.

Restaurante Minor Arias (tel. 506/445-6305), on the southwest corner of the plaza, has a pleasant open patio as well as indoor dining, and serves native fare. And **Il Giardino** steakhouse and pizzeria is recommended (a huge châteaubriand with black pepper sauce for two costs about $14), with salad and garlic bread. **Musmanni,** one block north of the church, is a quality bakery.

Services

There are several banks.

If you want to stock up on cigars, check out **Don Pedro Cigars** (tel. 506/477-0093, cigar @costarricense.cr).

Getting There and Around

An express bus departs San José hourly from Calle 16, Avenidas 1/3, 5:15 A.M.–7:30 P.M. **Taxis** operate from the main plaza, or call Taxis San Ramón (tel. 506/445-5966 or 506/445-5110).

SAN RAMÓN TO LA TIGRA

San Ramón is a gateway to the northern lowlands via a mountain road that crests the cordillera, then begins a long sinuous descent to La Tigra. At **Angeles Norte,** about four km north of San Ramón, a road leads east nine km to the Los Angeles Cloud Forest Reserve.

About 18 km north of San Ramón, a dirt road leads west to the 7,800-hectare **Alberto Manuel Brenes Biological Reserve,** created in 1993 to protect watershed forest on the Atlantic slope of the Cordillera de Tilarán. It's administered by the University of Costa Rica. The terrain and vegetation resembles that of Los Angeles Cloud Forest Reserve. It has trails, plus cabins available by reservation (tel. 506/437-9904, cordinv @ns.so.ucr.ac.cr).

Tucked dramatically into the head of the valley, about 32 km north of San Ramón, is the **Valle Escondido Lodge,** reached via a steep and rugged dirt road that winds dramatically downhill through a working *finca* raising orchids and ornamental plants. All around are mountain cleaves clad in dark forest primeval. Guided horseback riding ($25, two hours) and hiking are offered on the 60-hectare plantation and 400 hectares of ranch land and primary forest. There's an artificial lake for fishing. Mountain bikes can be rented. Trails lead down to the Río La Balsa, a good spot for swimming.

Here, too, is the **San Lorenzo Canopy Tour,** with two options. The first features 13 platforms, eight cables, and two hanging bridges spanning two guided trails; or you can take the "Adventure Cable Tour" by zipline using six cables (the longest is 850 meters) in which you gain a speed of 80kph! The latter has two parallel cables, so you can race your best friend. Each costs $35 for 90 minutes, or $55 for both. There's also a "canyoning" option involving a waterfall rappel ($50).

Los Angeles Cloud Forest Reserve

This 800-hectare reserve provides the same experience as Monteverde Cloud Forest Preserve without the crowds or the quetzals. The reserve is part of the Villablanca *finca*, a cattle ranch owned by former president Rodrigo Carazón. It begins at 700 meters' elevation and tops out at 1,800 meters (when the clouds clear you can see Volcán Arenal). The hills are covered with thick cloud forest, with the calls of howler monkeys emanating from its shrouded interior. Bird species include bellbirds, trogons, and aricaris. Laureles trees have been planted to lure quetzals. Three species of monkeys abound, and other mammals such as ocelots, jaguars, and jaguarundis are present.

Two short trails (1.5 and two km) have wooden walkways with nonslip surfaces. A third, hard-hiking trail (plan on six to nine hours) descends past the waterfalls and natural swimming pools of the Ríos Balsa and Espino. Rain ponchos, flashlights, and umbrellas are provided. A **canopy tour** is offered using a 300-meter-long cable slung between seven treetop platforms ($38.50 per person).

No bags are allowed on the trail, as fanatical horticulturists have been stealing orchids. Guided hikes cost $20–24 pp depending on season ($12–15 self-guided). Horseback rides cost $12 per hour.

Accommodations and Food

The **Hotel Ecocolonia Resort** (tel./fax 506/222-2333, www.ecocolonia.com, $25–55) is an eco-lodge that stands amid 250 acres of rainforest, nine km by dirt road from the main road; the turn-off is 24 km northwest of San Ramón. Four-wheel drive is recommended. It has eight rooms

and two cabins, which vary widely. All have decks, and private, tiled bathrooms with hot water; some have outdoor Jacuzzis. There's a restaurant, plus bar and games room. Trails lead into the forest, and there's a stable.

Hotel Villablanca (tel. 506/200-5137 or 506/228-4603, fax 506/233-6896, villablan @amnet.co.cr, www.villablanca-costarica.com, $68 s, $85 d low season; $79 s, $99 d high season in cottages), a reclusive hacienda, sits atop the Continental Divide on the edge of the reserve. Features include a restaurant, a lounge with TV, and a lecture room. The main lodge resembles a colonial farmhouse. A separate lodge, El Cohombro, has four rooms with bunk beds for 42 people, plus its own kitchen and ping-pong table. The 48 cozy chalets (sleeping two–six people) surround the hacienda and feature rocking chairs and other dainty decor; a small fireplace decorates one corner and swinging saloon-style doors open onto a colonial tiled bathroom. The buffet-style meals are tasty and filling. *Bocas* are served at the bar in the evening. A tiny chapel is open for view by request.

Valle Escondido Lodge (P.O. Box 137-4250, San Ramón de Alajuela, tel. 506/231-0906, fax 506/232-9591, info@valleescondido.com, www .valleescondido.com, $60 s, $80 d) has 33 elegant, spacious *cabinas* with handsome, hand-crafted hardwood furniture, plus a terrace for enjoying the magnificent setting and tallying the many bird species. Two rooms are handicap equipped. Two restaurants serves *típico* cuisine and Italian, respectively. Cool off in the swimming pool, warm up in the Jacuzzi, or linger at the cocktail bar, which features live musicians and draws a local crowd on weekends. Round-trip transfers from San José are offered ($25). You can also camp.

The roadside **Restaurant La Gran Vista** (7 A.M.–5 P.M.), 400 meters west of the entry to Valle Escondido, of which it's a part, offers views, plus sandwiches, *casados* (set meals, such as beef with onion; $4.50), entrées such as chicken breast with mushroom sauce ($5.75), plus desserts and coffees.

North of San José

HEREDIA

Heredia (pop. 32,000), 11 km north of San José, and colloquially known as La Ciudad de las Flores (City of the Flowers), is surrounded by coffee fields on the lower slopes of Volcán Barva. A pleasant, slow-paced, nostalgic atmosphere pervades the grid-patterned town despite its jostling traffic. The **National University**—famed for its veterinary courses—is here, on the east side of town.

Heredia is centered around a weathered colonial cathedral—the **Basílica de la Imaculada Concepción**—containing beautiful stained-glass windows as well as bells delivered from Cuzco, Peru. The church was built in 1797. It is squat and thick-walled and has withstood many earthquakes. The church faces west onto lively **Parque Central,** shaded by large mango trees.

© CHRISTOPHER P. BAKER

El Fortín tower, on Heredia's main plaza

El Fortín, a circular fortress tower, borders the north side of the plaza. The gun slits widen to the outside, a curious piece of military-textbook heresy; in a classic piece of military ineptitude, eccentric president Alfredo González Flores (1914–17) designed them so that they allow bullets in easily but made it difficult for defenders to shoot out.

The **Casa de la Cultura** (tel. 506/260-1619 or 506/261-4485), next to El Fortín, contains a small art gallery and historic exhibits. It was once the residence of president González Flores, who was exiled in 1917 after a coup d'état. He was later welcomed back and ran much of his presidency from his home, where he lived until his death in 1962. The refurbished house is today a National Historic Monument. Open 9 A.M.– 9 p.m. daily; free.

The **Mercado Central** (Central Market) is a must-visit, brimming with locally grown produce; but *beware pickpockets!*

Entertainment

Bars popular with students include **Bar/Restaurant Cowboy** (Calle 9, Avenida 5) and **Bulevar** (Calle 7, Avenida Central), where you can enjoy hanging out on the open-air upstairs balcony. **Champs** (tel. 506/369-3322), in Plaza Heredia, has two bars and discos; open Wed.–Sun. upstairs, and Thur.–Sat. downstairs (Friday is ladies night). **Speed,** adjacent, is similar and has a shaded deck; Thursday is ladies night.

For roller skating, check out **Sala de Patines** (Calle Central, Avenidas 4/6, tel. 506/441-3164).

Spanish-Language Courses

Heredia is known for its language schools, which include **Centro Panamericano de Idiomas** (tel. 506/265-6306, fax 506/265-6866, info@cpi-edu.com, www.cpi-edu.com; in the U.S., tel. 888/682-0054) and **Intercultura** (tel. 506/260-8480, fax 506/260-9243, info@intercultura-costarica.com, www.spanish-intercultura.com).

Shopping

La Casa de las Revistas (Calle Central, Avenidas

Central Highlands

Central Highlands

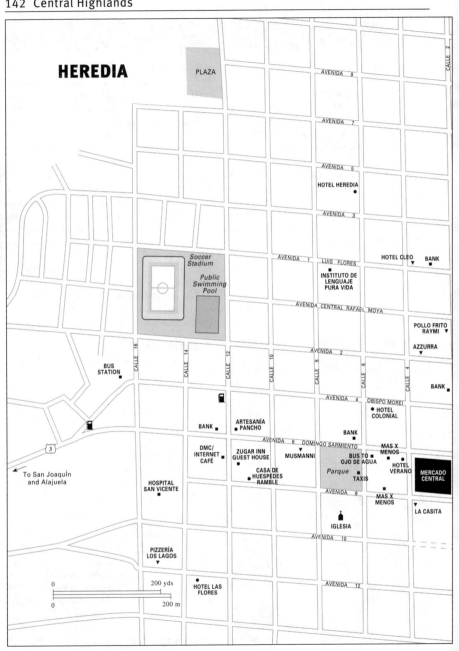

HEREDIA

PLAZA

AVENIDA 9

AVENIDA 7

AVENIDA 5

HOTEL HEREDIA

AVENIDA 3

Soccer Stadium

Public Swimming Pool

AVENIDA 1   LUIS FLORES   HOTEL CLEO   BANK

INSTITUTO DE LENGUAJE PURA VIDA

AVENIDA CENTRAL RAFAEL MOYA

POLLO FRITO RAYMI

AZZURRA

CALLE 16   CALLE 14   CALLE 12   CALLE 10   AVENIDA 2   CALLE 8   CALLE 6   CALLE 4

BUS STATION

BANK

AVENIDA 4   OBISPO MOREI   HOTEL COLONIAL

ARTESANÍA PANCHO

BANK

AVENIDA 6   DOMINGO SARMIENTO   MAS X MENOS

DMC/ INTERNET CAFÉ   ZUGAR INN GUEST HOUSE   MUSMANNI   BUS TO OJO DE AGUA   HOTEL VERANO   MERCADO CENTRAL

CASA DE HUESPEDES RAMBLE   Parque   TAXIS

To San Joaquín and Alajuela

HOSPITAL SAN VICENTE

AVENIDA 8   MAS X MENOS   LA CASITA

IGLESIA

AVENIDA 10

PIZZERÍA LOS LAGOS

0   200 yds
0   200 m

HOTEL LAS FLORES   AVENIDA 12

CALLE 2

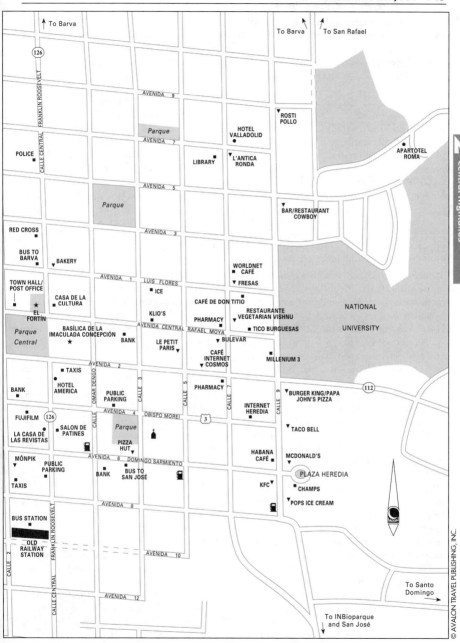

4/6) sells English-language magazines. **Fujifilm** (Avenida 4, Calles Central/2, tel. 506/237-8188) sells film.

The **Literate Cat** (tel./fax 506/262-5206, auster@racsa.co.cr, www.theliteratecat.com, 1–6:30 P.M. Monday, 10 a.m.–6:30 P.M. Tue.–Sat.), in Plaza Heredia, trades books and sells maps and souvenirs.

Kloi's Wild Vine (Avenida Central, Calles 3/5, tel. 506/262-4229) sells Asian batik and clothing, plus beachwear and crafts.

Accommodations

Under $25: The **Hotel Colonial** (Avenida 4, Calles 4/6, tel. 506/237-5258, $7 s, $10 d) has four clean and simply furnished rooms with hot water in shared bathrooms. A similar option, **Hotel Heredia** (Calle 6, Avenida 3/5, tel./fax 506/238-0880, heredia@hamerica.net, www .hamerica.net, $10 s, $15 d) is a charming old house with 10 alas shabby, sparely furnished rooms with private baths and hot water. It could be a gem with restoration. A better bargain is **Hotel Las Flores** (Avenida 12, Calles 12/14, tel. 506/261-8147, $12 s, $18 d), with 20 modern, tiled, spacious and well lit rooms with private bathrooms have hot water. It has secure parking.

$25–50: The best bet in this price range is **Zugar Inn Guest House** (Calle 12, Avenidas 6/8, tel./fax 506/261-1909, $25 s/d), a cozy little place with 10 dark, but clean rooms with fans and private baths with hot water. The **Casa de Huéspedes Ramble** (Avenida 8, Calles 10/12, tel. 506/238-3829, $15 s, $30 d), has 10 small but clean, well-kept wood-paneled rooms with minimal and feminine decor and tiny private baths with hot water. (Both the Zugar Inn and Ramble keep their entrance gates locked by an electronic lock—a potential safety hazard in a fire.)

The modern **Hotel América** (Calle Central, Avenidas 2/4, tel. 506/260-9292, fax 506/260-9293, info@hamerica.net, www.hamerica.net, $35 s, $45 d), 50 meters south of Parque Central, is a good bargain. It features 37 a/c rooms and four suites, all with telephones, and private baths with hot water. Decor (mauves, blues,

and creams) is pleasing. It has a steakhouse and offers 24-hour room service, plus cable TVs in public areas. The glassed-in rooftop provides city and mountain vistas. Tours of Heredia are offered. Rates include breakfast. The same owner has the **Hotel Ceos** (Avenida 1, Calles 2/4, tel. 506/262-2628, ceos@hamerica.net, $15 s, $25 d), a colonial home with 10 simply furnished, carpeted rooms with balconies. One large room has cable TV. The interior fails to live up to its splendid exterior, but it is perfectly adequate for budget travelers. It has a seafood restaurant.

Apart-Hotel Roma (tel. 506/260-0127, fax 506/262-1143, info@apart-hotelroma.com, www.apart-hotelroma.com, $35 s, $45 d), 150 meters east of the University Nacional, has small, individually decorated one- and two-bedroom suites with kitchenettes with microwave ovens, cable TVs, direct-dial telephones, and hot water. Some are cramped, others surprisingly elegant, and a suite has views. There's a restaurant and bar. Some readers report that a 5 percent discount has been offered to users of this guidebook—you might want to give it a try. Rates include tax.

$50–100: The class act in town is the **Hotel Valladolid** (Avenida 7, Calle 7, tel. 506/260-2905, fax 506/260-2912, valladol@racsa.co.cr, $49 s/d low season; $67 s, $77 d high season), with 11 a/c rooms featuring cable TVs, phones, and kitchenettes. The hotel has a sauna, Jacuzzi, rooftop solarium with great views, plus a bar and restaurant, as well as its own travel agency.

Food

First, head to **Le Petit Paris** (Calle 5, Avenidas Central/2, tel./fax 506/262-2524, 11 A.M.–10 p.m. Mon.–Sat.), an exquisite French restaurant with a patio. The menu features salads, sandwiches, soups, omelettes, pastas, and two dozen kinds of crepes ($2–5), plus special entreés such as chicken Normande and steak in pepper sauce ($4–5), and fondue Bourguignonne ($11). It has live jazz on Wednesday nights. The mood is enhanced by world music. Each month features a rotating art exhibition, plus slide shows.

Fresas (Calle 7, Avenida 1, tel. 506/262-5555), a clean, airy eatery, serves meals for less than $5, as well as all things strawberry, including ice creams, to be enjoyed on a veranda; open 8 A.M.–midnight daily.

Azzurra (tel. 506/260-9083, 7 A.M.–10 P.M.), formerly on the west side of the plaza, was slated to move 50 meters west on Avenida 2 at last visit. This café-*heladería* (ice creamery) is *the* hang out for local gringos and serves breakfasts (omelettes, pancakes, *gallo pinto*) as well as ice cream sundaes, including banana splits.

The clean, modestly elegant a/c **L'Antica Roma** (Avenida 7, Calle 7, tel. 506/262-8073), opposite the Hotel Valladolid, serves spaghettis and pizzas noon–midnight daily.

For vegetarian dishes, head to **Restaurante Vegetariano Vishnu** (Calle 7, Avenidas Central/1, tel. 506/237-2527, 8 a.m.–8 p.m. Sunday, 9 A.M.–6 P.M. Mon.–Sat.), serving sandwiches (from $1.50), veggie burgers ($1.50), *batidos* ($0.75 cents), etc., in several cubicle-like rooms. **Reyna's Kitchen** (tel. 506/268-3747) will deliver to your home. Typical dishes include spinach and tofu pie ($5), beef in orange sauce ($15), Salvadorian *pupusas* ($0.75 cents), and eggplant lasagne ($6.50).

For cappuccinos or espressos, head to **Café Don Tito** (Avenida 1, Calles 7/9, tel. 506/260-2212, 9 A.M.–6 P.M. Mon.–Fri., 9:30 A.M.–3 P.M. Saturday), a clean a/c coffee shop serving pastries and desserts. I also recommend **Espigas Repostería** (Avenida 2, Calle 2, tel. 506/237-3275, 7 a.m.–10 p.m.), a well-run café and bakery with a pleasing ambience. It serves pastries, patties, and a value-priced lunchtime buffet ($3.25).

I like **Spoon** (tel. 506/260-1333, 8 a.m.–7 p.m. Mon.–Fri., 9 a.m.–5 p.m. Sat.–Sun.), in Plaza Heredia; this clean, well-run a/c café serves a wide range of value-priced set meals, plus salads, pastries, and desserts.

You can buy baked goods at **Panadería Leandro** (Calle Central, Avenida 1) or at **Musmanni,** 50 meters south of the plaza.

Information

Hospital San Vicente (Calle 14, Avenida 8, tel. 506/237-1091) and **Red Cross** (Avenida 3, Calle

Central) provide medical service. There's a **pharmacy** at Avenida 2, Calle 7.

The police station is on Calle Central, Avenidas 5/7. Criminal investigation is handled by the OIJ (tel. 506/262-1011).

Services

There are more than half a dozen banks around town; see the map.

The post office is on the northwest corner of the plaza. You can make international calls from the **ICE** (Calle 3, Avenida 1) office.

Internet cafés are many. I recommend **Habana Café Internet** (Calle 9, Avenida 6, tel. 506/261-3303, 10 A.M.–11 p.m. Mon.–Fri., 10 A.M.–10 p.m. Sat.–Sun.); **Tico Burguesas Internet Café** (tel. 506/381-2839), open 24 hours year-round; **DMC Internet Café** (tel. 506/261-2774, 9 A.M.–6 p.m. Mon.–Sat.); **Café Internet Cosmos** (Avenida 2, Calle 5/7, tel. 506/262-4775); and **Worldnet Café** (tel. 506/262-6370, worldcaf@racsa.co.cr; 8 A.M.–10 p.m.).

Dirty laundry? Try **Lavandería La Margarita** (Avenida 6, Calles Central/2, tel. 506/237-0529).

The **library** (*biblioteca*) is on Avenida 7, Calle 7.

Getting There

Microbuses Rápido (tel. 506/238-8392 or 506/238-0506) offers bus service from San José every 10 minutes, 5 A.M.–midnight (and every 30 minutes, midnight–5 a.m.), from Calle 1, Avenidas 7/9, and from Calle 4, Avenidas 5/7. Bus no. 400A departs from Avenida 2, Calles 10/12, every 15 minutes, 6 A.M.–10 p.m.

Heredia has no central terminal. Buses depart for San José from both Avenida 6, Calles 1/3; to Barva every 30 minutes from Calle Central, Avenidas 1/3; to Ojo de Agua from Avenida 6, Calle 6; to Puerto Viejo de Sarapiquí at 6:30 A.M., noon, and 3 p.m. from the west side of Parque Central; to Sacramento (and Braulio Carrillo National Park) at 6:30 A.M., 11 a.m., and 4 P.M. from Avenida 8, Calles 2/4; and hourly to San José de la Montaña from Avenida 8, Calles 2/4.

Taxis wait on the south side of Parque Central,

or call Taxis Coopemargarita (tel. 506/238-3377 or 506/237-6163).

VICINITY OF HEREDIA

Barva

Barva, about two km north of Heredia amid coffee fields, is one of the oldest settlements in the country, with Barva and Poás Volcanoes behind creating a sublime setting. The **Basílica de Barva,** which dates back to 1767, features a grotto dedicated to the Virgin of Lourdes and faces onto a square surrounded by red-tiled colonial-era adobe houses. One of these—the former home of Cleto Gonzalez Víquez, twice president of Costa Rica— was declared a national landmark in 1985.

The **Museum of Popular Culture** (tel. 506/260-1619, 9 A.M.–4 p.m. Mon.–Fri., 10 A.M.– 5 p.m. Saturday and Sunday, $1.50), signed 1.5 km southeast of Barva, at Santa Lucía de Barva, presents a picture of rural life at the turn of the century. It is housed in a renovated, red-tile-roofed, mustard-colored home dating from 1885 and once owned by former president Alfredo González Flores; the house has been kept as it was when he died. Guided tours are offered for groups only, but individuals can explore at will.

A road leads northwest from Barva two km to **San Pedro de Barva,** home to the Instituto de Café (CICAFE, tel. 506/260-1874, 7 A.M.– 4 p.m. Mon.–Fri.) research laboratory and **Coffee Museum,** 400 meters north of the San Pedro church. The museum building is an adobe house dating from 1834. Inside are displays of antique coffee-making paraphernalia: pulp extractors, toasters, and grinders.

▼ Café Britt

Midway between Heredia and Barva is the *finca* and *beneficio* of Café Britt (Apdo. 528-3000, Heredia, tel. 506/260-2748, fax 506/238-1846, info@cafebritt.com, www.coffeetour.com; in the U.S., tel. 800/462-7488), where you can learn the story of Costa Rican coffee. The company, which roasts, packs, and exports to specialty stores around the world, welcomes visitors to its coffee fields and garden, which draws butterflies.

Five tours are offered. The standard is the "Coffee Tour," featuring a multimedia presentation including a live skit telling the history of coffee; daily at 9 A.M., 11 a.m., and 3 P.M. mid-December through April, and 11 A.M. only May through mid-December ($25 pp three hours, or $50 seven hours with lunch). Other tours combine the "Coffee Tour" with visits to the Butterfly Farm, La Paz Waterfall Garden, and the Rainforest Aerial Tram; one is timed to coincide with the coffee harvest (mid-November through February). All include an educational tour of the *finca* and roasting plant. There's a cinema for private events. You conclude in the tasting room, where you are shown how experts taste coffee. The factory store offers mail-order delivery to the United States. It has an elegant gourmet restaurant.

Santa Barbara de Heredia

This lively and compact town with colonial-era adobe houses is set amid colorful gardens in the heart of coffee country, about five km northwest of Heredia and three km west of Barva. **The Ark Herb Farm** (P.O. Box 46-3006, Barreal Heredia, tel. 506/239-2111, fax 506/239-2233, arkherb @racsa.co.cr; in the U.S., SJO 976, P.O. Box 025216, Miami, FL 33102; 9 A.M.–4 p.m. Mon.–Sat., or by appointment, $5 admission), 2.5 km above Santa Barbara de Heredia, covers 20 acres of tranquil gardens on the lower slopes of Barva. More than 400 varieties of medicinal herbs, shrubs, and trees from around the world are grown here under plastic roofs, mostly for export to North America, fresh cut. Another 600 species are grown in the garden. Extensive medicinal and culinary herb beds cover more than an acre. Owners "Tommy" and Patricia Thomas, who started the garden "as a hobby that got out of hand," offer fascinating one-hour tours that will leave you enthralled. Want to know which herb increases memory, or prevents flatulence? The garden also hosts volunteer workers in exchange for room and board.

Accommodations

La Casa Que Canta (tel. 506/771-4582, fax 506/771-8841, selvamar@racsa.co.cr, www .exploringcostarica.com/casaquecanta, from $43 to $30 s/d), is an American-run hostelry on five acres of lawns and orchards in Barrio Jesús, on the road from Santa Barbara to Barva. Loftily perched at 4,250 feet, it offers views over San José and the valley. It has two rooms in the main house, each with en-suite bathroom; one has a small office. A secluded riverside cottage has a kitchen and outdoor terrace. Three additional cottages each have a kitchen and dining room. All habitations have refrigerator, coffee maker, TV, telephone and internet access.

Imagine if Gaudí and Frank Lloyd Wright had combined their talents and visions; the result might be an architectural stunner as eclectic and electrifying as **Ν Finca Rosa Blanca Country Inn** (Apdo. 41, Santa Barbara de Heredia 3009, tel. 506/269-9392, fax 506/269-9555; in the U.S., SJO 3475, PO Box 025369, Miami, FL 33102-5216, tel. 800/327-9854; info@finca rosablanca.com, www.fincarosablanca.com, $155–240 s, $175–260 d). Inspired by Gaudí's architectonics and the Santa Fe style, the family-run Rosa Blanca is one of Costa Rica's preeminent boutique hotels. Its hillside position amid six hectares of coffee one km northeast of Santa Barbara de Heredia offers romantic vistas over coffee plants toward mountains almost mauve in the distance. Effusive tropical plants frame the snow-white house with its bridge-of-the–Starship *Enterprise* turret (actually, the honeymoon suite). The focal point is a circular atrium lounge with wraparound sofas and a open-hearth fireplace that resembles a mushroom. Flowers and creeping vines are everywhere, as is the dramatic artwork of Glenn Jampol, live-in owner, who has his art studio and wood workshop in the grounds. The whole is contrived by the genius of architect Francisco Rojas in a flurry of voluptuous curves and finely crafted hardwoods. The place is like a museum, with imaginative and tasteful statuettes, prints, and New Mexican artifacts in every delightful nook and cranny. It has six suites, a master suite, and two villas. Genuine hardwood antiques stand on rough stone floors. Walls are painted with trompe l'oeil landscapes. The stylish Blanco y Negro Room has a black-and-white checkerboard floor and a black bed made of coffeewood. The honeymoon suite has a bathroom with walls painted to resemble a tropical rainforest, with

water that tumbles down a rocky cascade into the fathoms-deep tub shaped liked a natural pool. A hardwood spiral staircase—each step shaped like a petal—twists up to the coup de grâce: a rotunda bedroom that caps the building's turret, with a canopied bed and wraparound windows. Bathrooms are graced by exquisite Mexican tiles. The ecologically sensitive hotel—it scored highest in the nation in recent sustainable tourism awards—has a horizon swimming pool fed by a cascade, plus a hot tub, a 800-meter trail, Internet access, a library, and a stable for guided rides ($18 per hour). Transfers are offered. Rates include full American breakfast. Extra persons cost $30, and a 10 percent discount is offered May–Nov.

Food

Ν Finca Rosa Blanca serves gourmet four-course dinners (using organic, estate-grown produce), with free-flowing wines poured in generous portions. Non-guests are welcome by reservation. Meals, prepared by local chef Pedro Alas (trained by Ray Bradley, formerly of New York's Bouley restaurant), are consistently of Michelin-rated quality, and a bargain to boot at $32 for a set meal served family-style around a stunning hardwood table at 7 P.M. If you arrive late, you won't be served.

Hotel Finca Rosa Blanca

Getting There

Buses depart Heredia for Barva from Calle Central, Avenidas 1/3. Buses drop off and depart from the south side of the plaza. A bus for Santa Barbara de Heredia departs Heredia from Avenida 1, Calles 1/3, every 15 minutes Mon.–Fri.

If driving from Heredia, Calles Central and 2 lead north to Barva, where you turn left at the plaza and head straight, westward, for Santa Barbara de Heredia.

THE SLOPES OF BARVA VOLCANO

San José de la Montaña

Half a kilometer north of Barva, the road forks. The left fork leads via the village of **Birrí** to Vara Blanca on the ridge of the Continental Divide. In Birrí, a road to the right at Restaurante Las Delicias leads east steeply uphill via the hamlet of Guacalillo to the hamlet of **Porrosatí** (also known as Paso Llano), a true alpine setting where the air is decidedly chilly.

The right fork at the Y-junction north of Barva also leads uphill to Porrosatí, five km above **San José de la Montaña** (1,550 meters), known for its pretty church and mountain resorts in the midst of pine forests.

At Porrosatí, a turnoff to the left from the Guardia Rural post leads via the hamlet of Sacramento to the **Braulio Carrillo National Park** ranger station (tel. 506/261-2619, 8 A.M.–4 p.m. Tues.–Sun., $6 admission) along a very steep, deeply rutted rock road; four-wheel drive is essential (and you'll be in first gear). You are only about three km from the summit of Volcán Barva (2,906 meters). The mountain's botanical treasures range from mosses to giant oaks, cypress, and cedar. A loop trail leads to the summit from Porrosatí (the trail is marked as BCNP Sector Barva) and circles back to the ranger station three km northeast of Sacramento (four or five hours of hiking, round-trip). The trail leads up through cloud forest—good for spotting resplendent quetzals—to the crater and a lookout point. Fog, however, is usually the order of the day.

You can also follow marked trails on a four-day hike from the summit all the way to Puerto Viejo de Sarapiquí, in the northern lowlands. There are huts en route. Take an Instituto Geográfica map and a compass, plus high-quality waterproof gear and warm clothing, and—of course—sufficient food and water. People have been lost for days in the park. You can camp beside the crater lake, behind the ranger station, or at two picnic areas with barbecue grills on the trail (no facilities).

Monte de la Cruz

Two km northeast of Heredia, and two east of Barva, lies **San Rafael,** on the lower slopes of Volcán Barva. A medieval stonemason would be proud of the town's recently restored, cream-colored Gothic church, with its buttresses and magnificent stained-glass windows. The church, completed only in 1962, is visible throughout the Meseta Central.

North of San Rafael, the road begins a progressive ascent, the temperatures begin to drop, and hints of the Swiss Tyrol begin to appear, with pine and cedar forests and emerald-green pastures grazed by dairy cattle. Expensive mansions line the road or lie hidden deep in the forest. Remnants of ancient oaks and other primary forests remain on the higher reaches

Ticos flock on weekends and holidays to a series of recreation areas, the largest and most popular being the upscale **Club Campestre El Castillo** (El Castillo Country Club, tel. 506/267-7111, $15 admission), with stunning views over the valley. It offers basketball, soccer, sauna, swimming pool, and the country's only ice rink. You need a passport.

At a Y-fork two km north of El Castillo, head right to **Monte de la Cruz Reserve** (Centro Turístico Monte de la Cruz, 8 A.M.–4 p.m. Mon.–Fri., 8 A.M.–5 p.m. weekends, $1 pp admission, $1 per vehicle), popular with weekend hikers from San José. This 15-hectare private forest reserve, eight km north of San Rafael, offers trails choked with ferns and wild orchids through pine forest and cloud forest great for bird-watching, including a chance to spot quetzals. It is often cloudy and usually exhilaratingly crisp, if not cold and wet; bring warm waterproof clothing.

The road—climbing steeply and deteriorating steadily—continues three km to the 170-acre **Cerro Dantas Wildlife Refuge** (Refugio de Vida Silvestre Cerro Dantas), part of Braulio Carrillo National Park, and known for its tapirs. Here, the Cerro Dantas Ecological Center offers environmental study and education programs.

The fork to the left north of El Castillo leads to the Parque Residencial del Monte, an exclusive residential area with the **Hotel Chalet Tirol** (see *Accommodations,* below) at 1,800 meters (5,900 feet) within a 15-hectare private cloud forest reserve. There's a "musique et lumiere" show. The hotel offers a full-day guided quetzal bird-watching trip into the **Tirol Cloud Forest** on the upper reaches of Barva ($75, including pickup in San José and lunch at the hotel). Horseback riding costs $65 with gourmet lunch.

Events

The **International Music Festival** is hosted at Hotel Chalet Tirol each July and August in the Salzburg Café Concert Dinner Theater, looking like a set for *The Sound of Music.* The classical concerts cost $14 each. The hotel also offers violin recitals and other musical and theatrical events throughout the year.

Accommodations

Birrí to Porrosatí: The **Hotel El Portico** (Apdo. 289, Heredia 3000, tel. 506/266-1000 or 506/237-6022, fax 506/260-6002, $45 s/d) is set in a six-hectare farm with forest trails. The atmospheric lodge has 18 rooms with rough-stone tiled floors and private bathrooms. There's a beautiful and spacious lounge with leather sofas, a large stone fireplace, and vast windows offering views down the mountainside. There's also a sauna and Jacuzzi, plus an atmospheric Swiss-style restaurant with bar. Beautiful artwork abounds. Landscaped grounds contain a small swimming pool and lake. It also has three exquisite cabins. Rates include tax.

Las Ardillas Spa Resort (Apdo. 44, Heredia 3009, tel./fax 506/260-2172, ardillas@racsa.co.cr, $60 s/d Mon.–Fri., $80 Sat.–Sun.) has eight rustic log-and-brick cabins, each with fireplace, kitchenette, and private bathroom. There's a

Central Highlands

© CHRISTOPHER P. BAKER

Hotel Chalet Tirol

game room, a bar and restaurant, children's play area, and simple spa with whirlpool and sauna and treatments from massage ($30 per hour) and mud wraps ($25) to hydrotherapy and aromatherapy. Hiking is offered. Meals are prepared on a wood-burning stove using organic, home-grown produce. Rates include breakfast and tax, plus spa treatment on weekends.

Associated with Las Ardillas, and further uphill, is **Cabañas La Montaña Milenas** ($60 s/d), a stone and timber lodge with 10 romantic albeit rustic log cabins in the woods to the rear; each has double and single bed, TV, and fireplace. The main lodge has sumptuous sofas in front of the hearth; upstairs is a Colorado-style bar with live music.

Cabañas Laudriana (tel. 506/219-4175 or 506/219-4050, $34 d, $56 quad, $66 six people), amid the pines at Porrosatí, has rustic A-frame wooden cabins with fireplaces, kitchens, and private bathrooms with hot water. There are beds downstairs and in a mezzanine. Two rustic restaurants are at hand.

San Rafael to Monte de la Cruz: The **Cerro Dantas Ecological Center** (tel. 506/276-4089 or 506/274-1997, fax 506/276-7217, pavoreal @racsa.co.cr, www.cerrodantas.co.cr, $50 pp) has simple dorm accommodations and a communal dining area. Rates include meals.

The Spanish-run **Hotel La Condesa Monte de la Cruz** (tel. 506/267-6000, fax 506/267-6200, ventas@lacondesahotel.com, www.hotel lacondesa.com, $115 s, $150 d standard, $156 s, $180 d suite), immediately above El Castillo Country Club at San Rafael de Heredia, is a classy option with a soaring skylit atrium lobby with dramatic cascade, plus classical stonework and terra-cotta tiles. It has 60 spacious, beautifully furnished rooms and 37 suites, the latter with king-size beds. All rooms have minibars, direct-dial telephones, cable TVs, and security boxes, plus hair dryers in the stylish marble bathrooms. Facilities include two restaurants, a heated indoor pool, children's pool, sauna, Jacuzzi, jogging track, squash court, gym, and free shuttles to San José. Rates include breakfast and dinner.

Hotel Chalet Tirol (Apdo. 7812-1000, San José, tel. 506/267-6222, fax 506/267-6229,

info@chalet-tirol.com, www.chalet-tirol.com, $80 s/d low season, $90 high season), is a delightful Tyrolean-style place with a superb French restaurant. Ten rustic yet charming twin-level alpine cabins—hand-painted in Swiss fashion—surround a small lawn. There are also 20 modern hotel rooms, each with a TV, fireplace, spacious bathroom, and furnishings from a Hansel-and-Gretel story. One suite has a spiral staircase to a mezzanine bedroom. There's a pool, sauna and massage/fitness room, plus two tennis courts. The lodge was owned by a former Costa Rican president, Alfredo González Flores (1914–17) and is worth a visit just to eat in the rough-hewn timbered dining room.

Hotel La Condesa Barbizon (tel. 506/267-6000, fax 506/267-6200, ventas@hotellacondesa .com, www.hotellacondesa.com, $80 s, $100 d standard, $115/150 junior suite, $150/180 villa) is a marvelous Spanish colonial-style lodge with views toward cloud-shrouded Barva. Roughhewn timbers re-create the feel of an English country inn. Tasteful art, expensive furnishings, and stained glass abound. It has 10 rooms, all with fireplaces and cable TV. The elegant dining room is centered on a mammoth open-hearth fireplace. It offers complimentary airport and San José transfers, plus horseback rides.

You can camp at **Campamento Shekirah,** 5.3 km above Guardia Rural on the road to Sacramento.

Food

The **Hotel Chalet Tirol** (tel. 506/267-6222, $7–16) serves superb French cuisine, such as rabbit marinated in prune sauce, sea bass with melted avocado, and shrimp in fennel-Pernod sauce. The dining room is graced by frilly curtains, window boxes, a blazing log fire in an old-world fireplace, brass chandeliers, and romantic candlelight. It has an upstairs snack bar serving sandwiches and the like. There's also a *biergarten.*

Hotel La Condesa Monte de la Cruz offers upscale dining in **La Florencia,** its signature Italian restaurant.

For a wonderful rustic mountain ambience, try **Las Ardillas** (see Accommodations, above, 8 A.M.10 p.m. Mon.–Thur., 8 A.M.–11 p.m.

Fri.–Sat., 8 A.M.–9 p.m. Sunday, $8), centered on a stone hearth and serving steak in red wine, filet mignon, almond sea bass, and the like.

I love **Baalbek** (tel. 506/267-6684, baalbek_bbq@racsa.co.cr, www.baalbekbarandgrill.com), 500 meters below Residencial El Castillo, at Los Angeles de San Rafael, an upscale Lebanese restaurant with elegant decor, sublime views, and splendid Mediterranean food. It has live music, from blues to Arabian (with belly-dancers!).

Getting There

Buses marked "Paso Llano" depart Heredia for San José de la Montaña, Porrosatí, and Sacramento from Avenida 8, Calles 2/4, Mon.–Sat. at 6:30 A.M., 11 A.M., and 4 P.M.; and Sundays 11 a.m. and 4 P.M. only. Hourly buses also go to San José de la Montaña. The last bus from Porrosatí departs for Heredia weekdays at 5 P.M.

Buses for San Rafael depart Heredia from the Mercado Central hourly 8 A.M.–8 p.m. Buses to El Castillo and Bosque de la Hoja depart Heredia from the Mercado Central hourly 8 A.M.–8 p.m. For Monte de la Cruz, take a bus departing 9 A.M., noon, or 4 P.M.

SANTO DOMINGO DE HEREDIA

Santa Domingo de Heredia, three km southeast of Heredia and three km north of San José, has two handsome historic churches plus many colonial houses restored to creamy grandeur.

Santo Domingo is home to **INBioparque** (tel. 506/244-4730, fax 506/244-4790, inbioparque @inbio.ac.cr, www.inbio.ac.cr, 7:30 A.M.–6:30 p.m., $12 admission adults, $10 students, $6 children), an educational park, about 400 m north and 250 m west of the Shell gas station, two km southwest of Santo Domingo. It's run by the Instituto Nacional de Biodiversidad, a nongovernmental organization devoted to cataloging Costa Rica's biodiversity. One exhibition hall focuses on the planet's biodiversity, including an interactive database for searching out information on virtually any living organism. The second hall lets you observe how Costa Rica was formed and inhabited, including man's degradation of the environment; it features a 3-D model of Costa Rica showing protected areas. However, there are few live exhibits, and many visitors come away disappointed. Interpretive trails lead through native habitats, with sheltered wildlife exhibits scattered along the trails. Botanists will have a field day, but don't expect to see much wildlife, except in the butterfly garden. Visitors can opt for guided tours (recommended; $3 for two hours), or a self-guided walk with booklet ($1.50). Last admission is 4 P.M. Transfers cost $10.

Accommodations

Debbie King's B&B (Apdo. 465, Heredia 3000, tel./fax 506/268-3084 or cell 506/380-8492, debbiecr@racsa.co.cr, www.ivaccommodations .com/debbiekingscountryinn.html; in the U.S., SJO 381, P.O. Box 025216, Miami, FL 33102-5216; $39 s, $49–69 d), in Concepcion de San Rafael de Heredia, is a small bed-and-breakfast on a coffee *finca* with great views over San José. Three large wood-paneled bedrooms have private baths. Upper rooms have wraparound balconies. Two cottages have kitchens and private baths and sleep four. And there's a rustic log cabin. The lounge in the main house offers delightful yesteryear decor, including chandelier. Dinners on request. The hotel's greatest asset is Debbie, an erstwhile Beverly Hills restaurateur, and her equally affable husband. It's 500 meters south *(sur)* of the *Pulpería El Trapiche* grocery and is hard to find. Rates include breakfast

The superbly run, Dutch-owned **Hotel Bougainvillea** (Apdo. 69, San José 2120, tel. 506/244-1414, fax 506/244-1313, bougain @racsa.co.cr, www.bougainvillea.co.cr, $67.50 s, $77.50 d), about 800 meters east of Santo Domingo, is a splendid option. This contemporary three-story hotel is set in vast landscaped grounds surrounded by a sea of coffee plants, with a beautiful view of the mountain ranges and San José. The 82 spacious rooms each have a/c, two double beds, TV, and balcony, plus luxurious bathrooms in newer rooms. Modern artwork decorates public areas. There's a gift shop, swimming pool, tennis court, and an elegant restaurant. A shuttle service runs into San José.

Food

The **Hotel Bougainvillea** is known for its excellent cuisine. It offers a *plato fuerte* (entrée, dessert, and coffee) for $10—a good value. On Sundays, it draws the local middle class for buffet brunch.

Northeast of San José

SAN JOSÉ TO BRAULIO CARRILLO

Northeast from San José, the Guápiles Highway (Hwy. 32) climbs up the saddle between Barva and Irazú Volcanoes, cuts through the Zurquí tunnel, and enters Braulio Carrillo National Park before descending to the Caribbean lowlands. Charming villages nestle on the lower slopes; the roads are a maze, however, and finding your way isn't easy.

At **San Jerónimo,** about 15 km northeast of San José and four km east of Hwy. 32, there begins a tortuous cobblestone road: the remains of the old **Carretera Carrillo** that still runs, in dilapidated condition, via Alto Palma to Bajo Hondura and the Alto Palma entrance to Braulio Carrillo National Park, 10 km northeast of San Jerónimo. The track was once used by oxcarts carrying coffee to the railway line that ran to Puerto Limón. (Turn left by the church on the small village green in San Jerónimo: the paved road eventually becomes the *carretera*.)

You can leave Hwy. 32 to visit **San Isidro** (not to be confused with San Isidro de Coronado), three km from the highway and eight km due east of Heredia. The town is known for its landmark white church, very Gothic with its pointed spires. The town is known for its **Easter procession.**

BRAULIO CARRILLO NATIONAL PARK

Rugged mountains, dormant volcanoes, deep canyons, swollen rivers, and seemingly interminable clouds, torrential rains, and persistent drizzle characterize Parque Nacional Braulio Carrillo, 20 km northeast of San José. The 47,699-hectare park (84 percent of which is primary forest) was established in 1978 and named in honor of the president who promoted the cultivation of coffee. It extends from 2,906 meters above sea level atop Volcán Barva down to 36 meters at La Selva, in Sarapiquí in the Caribbean lowlands. This represents the greatest altitudinal range of any Costa Rican park. Temperature and rainfall vary greatly and are extremely unpredictable. Annual rainfall is between 400 and 800 centimeters. Rains tend to diminish in March and April. With luck, you might even see the sun.

Encompassing five life zones ranging from tropical wet to cloud forest, Braulio Carrillo provides a home for 600 identified species of trees, more than 500 species of birds, and 135 species of mammals, including howler and capuchin monkeys, tapirs, jaguars, pumas, ocelots, deer, pacas, raccoons, peccaries, and the tepezcuintle, the park's mascot. The park provides excellent birding. Quetzals are common at higher elevations; the rare solitary eagle and umbrella bird live here; and toucans, parrots, and hummingbirds are ubiquitous.

The park protects several tree species fast disappearing elsewhere from overharvesting, among them, the palmito, valued for its heart. Those elephant-ear-size leaves common in Braulio Carrillo are *sombrilla del pobre* (poor man's umbrella).

The park is administered by the Central Volcanic Cordillera Conservation Area (tel. 506/290-8202, fax 506/290-4869).

Entrances

The main entrance, on Hwy. 32, is approximately 19 km northeast of San José, where there is a tollbooth (200 *colones*—$1.30). **Zurquí,** the main ranger station (tel. 506/233-4533, ext. 125, or 506/257-0922), is on the right two km north of the tunnel; drive slowly, as you come upon it suddenly on a downhill bend. The station sells basic maps in the information center. The **Puesto**

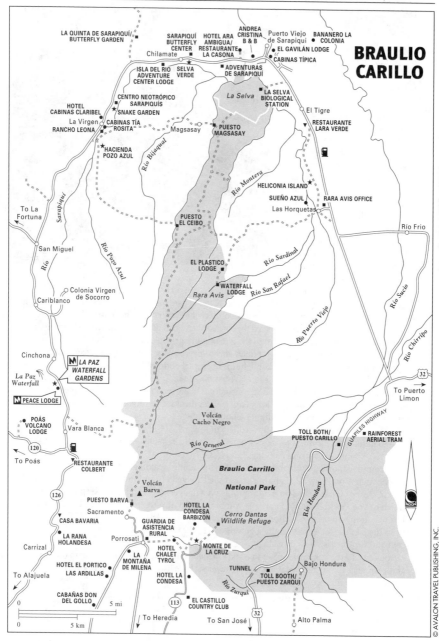

BRAULIO CARILLO

Central Highlands

THE RAINFOREST AERIAL TRAM

COURTESY RAINFOREST AERIAL TRAM

The Rainforest Aerial Tram, on a 354-hectare private nature reserve on the northeastern boundary of Braulio Carrillo National Park, is an unforgettable experience. Constructed at a cost of more than $2 million by Dr. Donald Perry, author of the fascinating book *Life Above the Jungle Floor,* the tram takes visitors on a guided 90-minute excursion through the rainforest canopy. The mysteries of the lush canopy unfold with each passing tree.

Your ride is preceded by an instructional video. Then it's a 1.3 km ride on any of 20 cable cars that travel 150 meters apart (each holds six people, including a guide armed with a walkie-talkie to communicate with other cars) in the manner of a ski-lift, giving you a new vantage on the "spectacular hanging gardens of the rainforest roof."

Perry hopes that by showing people the wonders of the rainforest, the tram will inspire people to help save the forests (he originated the concept after building the Automated Web near Rara Avis to support his research). "We liked the idea of putting people in cages, rather than animals," he says. There are short loop trails for hikes, including a trail for handicapped persons. Bird excursions are also offered (bring a flashlight for nocturnal outings).

Tram hours are 9 A.M.–4 P.M. Monday; 6 A.M.–4 P.M. Tue.–Sun. ($50 adults, half price children; no children under five). The fee includes as many tram rides as you wish. Expect a wait of up to one hour, as the lines are long (coffee, fruit drinks, and cookies are served). A restaurant serves breakfast, lunch, and dinner (about $7).

The office in San José (Apdo. 1959-1002 San José, tel. 506/257-5961, fax 506/257-6053, info@rainforesttram.com, www.rainforesttram.com, 6 A.M.–9 P.M. Mon.–Fri., 6 A.M.–6 P.M. Sat.–Sun.) is on the corner of Avenida 7 and Calle 7.

Accommodations are available: $80 s, $95 d for cabins, including three meals.

The tram is on Hwy. 32, eight km east of the Río Sucio (four km past the ranger station, 15 km west of Guápiles). The parking lot is on a dangerously fast bend. Keep your speed down or you could leave tire marks as you brake hard into the parking lot! The Guápiles bus will drop you off at Chichorronera la Reserva or "El Teleférico" ($1.50). You're driven from the parking lot 1.5 km along a gravel road to the visitor center (you must walk a brief trail and rope bridge over a river).

You can take the bus between San José and Guápiles, but be sure to tell the driver to drop you at the entrance to the tram. Many unfortunate guests have had to trek back uphill after the driver passed the entrance and kept going!

Carrillo (a.k.a. Quebrada González, tel. 506/233-4533, ext. 125, or 506/257-0922) ranger station, 22.5 km farther down the road, has a tollbooth in the center of the road for those entering the park from Limón.

Two other stations—**Puesto El Ceibo** and **Puesto Magsasay**—lie on the remote western fringes of the park, reached by rough trails from just south of La Virgen, on the main road to Puerto Viejo de Sarapiquí. You can also enter the Volcán Barva sector of the park via the **Puesto Barva** ranger station (tel. 506/261-2619), three km northeast of Sacramento, and via Alto Palma and Bajo Honduras, accessible from San José via San Vicente de Moravia or from the Guápiles Highway at a turnoff about three km south of the main park entrance. Entrance costs $6.

Trails and Facilities

Two short trails lead from Puesto Carrillo: **Los Botarramas** is approximately 1.6 km; **La Botella,** with waterfalls and views down the Patria Canyon, is 2.8 km. For additional exercise as you head down La Botella, turn left at a sign labeled Sendero. This path takes you 30 minutes deeper into the forest to the Río Sanguijuela. South of Puesto Carrillo is a parking area on the left (when heading north) with a lookout point and a trail to the Río Patria, where you can camp (no facilities). Another parking area beside the bridge over the Río Sucio ("Dirty River") has picnic tables and a short loop trail.

A one-km trail leads from south of the Zurquí Tunnel to a vista point. The entrance is steep, the rest easy. Another trail—the **Sendero Histórico**—followa the Río Hondura all the way from Bajo Honduras to the Guápiles Highway at a point near the Río Sucio. Check with a ranger.

A trail from Puesto Barva leads to the summit of Volcán Barva and loops around to Porrosatí (no ranger station). From the summit, you can continue all the way downhill to La Selva in the northern lowlands. It's a lengthy and arduous hike that may take several days, and is recommended only for experienced hikers with suitable equipment. There are no facilities. You can join this trail from Puesto El Ceibo and Puesto Magsasay; you can also drive in a short distance along a four-wheel-drive trail from Puesto Magsasay.

Bring sturdy raingear, and preferably hiking boots. The trails will most likely be muddy. Several hikers have been lost for days in the fog and torrential rains. If you intend to do serious hiking, let rangers know in advance, and check in with them when you return.

Safety Concerns: There have been armed robberies in the park. Hike with a park ranger if possible. Theft from cars parked near trailheads has also been a problem.

Getting There

Buses for Guápiles and Puerto Limón depart several times per hour from San José's Gran Terminal Caribe, at Calle Central, Avenidas 15/17; they drop off and pick up at the Zurquí and Puesto Carrillo ranger stations. For Alto Palma, take a bus from San José for San Jerónimo from Avenida 3, Calles 3/5. You can walk or take a taxi to Alto Palma from here (there also may be local bus service).

Most tour operators in San José can arrange half-day or full-day tours.

SAN ISIDRO DE CORONADO

San Isidro de Coronado is a somnolent country town six km northeast of the San José suburb of Guadalupe, and about four km east of Hwy. 32. The Gothic church is impressive. A **fiesta** is held here each 15 February.

The **Instituto Clodomiro Picado** (tel. 506/229-0344, fax 506/292-0485, www.icp.ucr.ac.cr), the "snake farm" of the University of Costa Rica, about one km southwest of Coronado, is dedicated to snake research. The institute was founded by Clodomiro Picado Twight, a Costa Rican genius born in 1887 and educated in Paris, where he later worked at the Pasteur Institute before returning home to work on immunizations, vaccinations, and serums. Evidence suggests he may have discovered penicillin before Alexander Fleming, the British scientist to whom its discovery is

Central Highlands

credited. Visitors are welcome (8 A.M.–noon and 1–4 P.M.). You'll see snakes of every kind, including the fearsome fer-de-lance, or *terciopelo*. A museum and serpentarium were being built at last visit.

A turn off from the Guadalupe–San Isidro road leads east, uphill to **Rancho Redondo,** scenically hoisted on the lower western flanks of Volcán Irazú, northwest of Cartago. The dramatic views are some of the best in the highlands, and very quickly you find yourself amid cattle and pasture.

Los Juncos Cloud Forest Reserve

From the church in San Isidro de Coronado, Calle Central leads uphill to **Los Nubes** and thence 14 km to Los Juncos, a 200-hectare reserve area of virgin cloud forest straddling the Continental Divide on the Caribbean slopes of Irazú Volcano, in the mist-shrouded mountains above San Isidro. A metal-walled farmhouse was once the home of Presidents Federico Tinoco and Mario Echandi. Trails through Los Juncos forest connect with Braulio Carrillo National Park. Guides lead hikes, followed by a home-cooked lunch served family style at the farmhouse (where overnight stays can be arranged). The trails have been left in a semi-natural state; rubber boots and raingear are provided. It's very misty up here, with everything covered in spongy moss and epiphytes. Quetzals are among the many bird species you may see.

Accommodations and Food

Hacienda San Miguel (Apdo. 135-1000, San José, tel. 506/229-5058, fax 506/229-1097, $28 s, $32 d standard, $42 s/ddeluxe) is a rustic yet modern and atmospheric stone-and-timber lodge on a working dairy farm 0.5 km east of Rancho Redondo. It has 15 simply furnished, carpeted rooms with stone and wood walls and stone bathrooms with spacious hot water showers; electric blankets are provided for chilly nights. Deluxe rooms are more spacious and have cable TV and king-size beds. The homey lounge boasts a fireplace, plump sofas, and a TV/VCR. There's also a Jacuzzi, and a game room with pool table, plus a restaurant serving creative dishes (open to the public 8 A.M.–10:30 P.M. Tue.–Sun., 8 A.M.–7 P.M. Fri.–Sat.). Horseback rides ($9 for two hours) and guided hikes lead through the pastures to forests and waterfalls, and you can visit the milking shed. Rates include breakfast.

The U.S.-run **Lone Star Grill** (tel. 506/229-7597), one km east of the church in San Isidro de Coronado, offers "A Taste of Texas"—including "the best fajitas south of the Río Grande"—with Texan-size margaritas. Choose from charbroiled meats, salads, burgers, soups, and "delectable desserts."

Getting There

Buses marked "Dulce Nombre de Coronado" depart for San Isidro de Coronado from Calle 3, Avenidas 5/7, in San José.

Cartago and Vicinity

East of San José, the Autopista Florencio del Castillo freeway passes through the suburb of Curridabat, climbs over the ridge known as Cerros de la Carpintera, then drops steeply to the colonial capital, Cartago, about 21 km southeast of San José.

CARTAGO

The city of Cartago (pop. 120,000) was founded in 1563 by Juan Vásquez de Coronado, the Spanish governor, as the nation's first city. Cartago—a Spanish word for Carthage, the ancient North African trading center—reigned as the colonial capital until losing its status to San José in the violent internecine squabbles of 1823. In 1841 and again in 1910 earthquakes toppled much of the city. Though the remains of the ruined cathedral testify to Mother Nature's destructive powers, many old buildings still stand. Volcán Irazú looms over Cartago and occasionally showers ash on the city.

Cartago's central landmark is the ruins of the **Iglesia de la Parroquia** (Avenida 2, Calle 2),

colloquially called "Las Ruinas," fronted by lawns and trees shading a statue of Melino Salazar Zunca, the "immortal tenor." Completed in 1575 to honor Saint James the Apostle, the church was destroyed by earthquakes and rebuilt a number of times before its final destruction in the earthquake of 1910. Today, only the walls remain.

If you're interested in churches, check out the modern **Iglesia Los Capuchinos** (Calles 4/6, Avenidas 3/5), with bougainvillea clambering up the bell tower; or the **Iglesia Bautista** (tel. 506/551-5075) on the northeast side of the motley **Plaza de la Independencia** (Avenida 2, Calle 13).

Other sites of tourist interest are few but include the **Elias Leiva Museum of Ethnography** (Museo Etnografío, Calle 3, Avenida 3/5, tel. 506/551-0895), in the San Luis Gonsaga school, which displays pre-Columbian and colonial artifacts (7 A.M.–2 p.m. Mon.–Fri.). The **Kirieti Indian History Museum** (tel. 506/573-7113), in Tobosi, about six km southwest of Cartago, traces

© JEAN MERCIER

Las Ruinas, Cartago

Central Highlands

the history of the indigenous people of the area. It displays mostly documents.

The community of **Aguacaliente,** about three km southeast of Cartago, is named for its *balneario* (swimming pool) fed by hot springs and surrounded by an exotic plant collection.

Be warned that Cartago is curiously devoid of accommodations, other than cheap and grungy refuges of last resort for those stranded.

Cathedral of Our Lady of the Angels

Cartago's gleaming blue-and-white, cupola-topped Basílica de Nuestra Señora de los Angeles

(Avenidas 2/4, Calles 14/16), 10 blocks east of the main plaza, is one of Costa Rica's most imposing structures. There's a unique beauty to the soaring, all-wood interior, with its marvelous stained-glass windows, its columns and walls painted in floral motifs, and its haze of smoke rising from votive candles to curl about the columns like an ethereal veil.

Cartago is the nation's religious center and home of Costa Rica's patron saint, La Negrita, or Virgen de los Angeles, and the goal of thousands of Costa Ricans during the annual *La Romería* pilgrimage. The eight-inch-high black

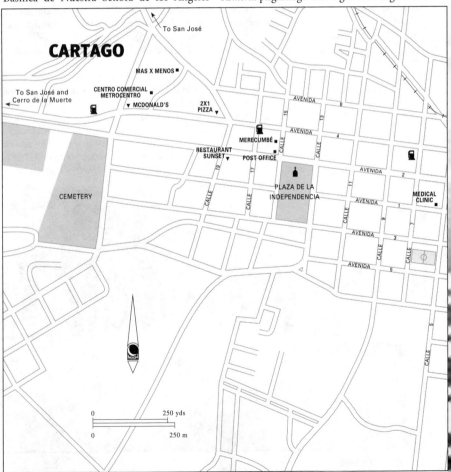

statue of La Negrita is embedded in a gold- and jewel-encrusted shrine above the main altar. According to the legend, in 1635 a mulatto peasant girl named Juana Pereira found a small stone statue of the Virgin holding the Christ child. Twice Juana took the statue home and placed it in a box, and twice it mysteriously reappeared at the spot where it was discovered. The cathedral is said to mark the spot (the first cathedral was toppled by an earthquake in 1926).

Beneath the basilica is the rock where Juana found La Negrita, plus a small room full of ex-votos or *promesas*: gold and silver charms, sports trophies, and other offerings for prayers answered, games won, and amorous conquests. Many are in the shape of various human parts, left by devotees seeking a cure for afflictions or in thanks for healing. Outside, a spring that flows beneath the basilica is said to have curative powers.

Food

Bar Restaurante La Parada, adjoining the bus station, is a pleasant *soda* serving local fare, including set lunches.

La Cabañita, facing the south side of the basilica, is a colorful little charmer that serves

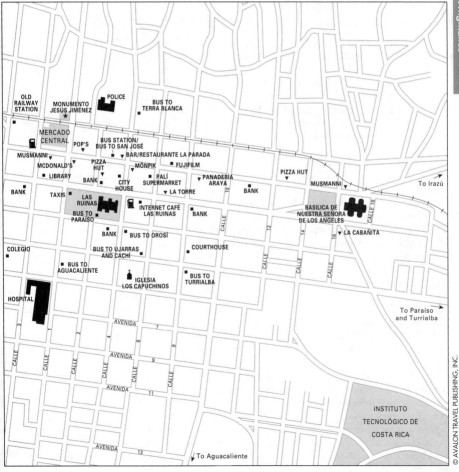

© AVALON TRAVEL PUBLISHING, INC.

THE LA NEGRITA PILGRIMAGE

Every 2 August, hundreds of Costa Ricans walk from towns far and wide to pay homage to the country's patron saint, La Negrita, at Cartago's Basílica de Nuestra Señora de la Concepción. The event attracts pilgrims from throughout Central America. Many *crawl* all the way from San José on their knees, starting at dawn! Others carry large wooden crosses. On any day, you can see the devout crawling down the aisle, muttering their invocations, repeating the sacred names, oblivious to the pain.

chicken dishes grilled over coffee wood. It has karaoke at night. The **Restaurant Sunset** (Calle 19, Avenida 2, tel. 506/551-0559) is the only modern restaurant in town and has pretensions toward elegance.

For breads and pastries, try **Panadería Araya** (Avenida 4, Calles 8/10), or **Musmanni,** on the north side of the basilica.

Information and Services

There's no shortage of banks downtown; see the map.

Medical clinics cluster around **Hospital Dr. Max Peralta** (Avenida 5, Calle 3/5, tel. 506/551-0611). There are more pharmacies, and dentists than you would care to count.

The police station is at Avenida 6, Calle 2. Criminal investigation is handled by the OIJ (tel. 506/550-0333).

Getting There

SACSA's (San José tel. 506/233-5350, Cartago tel. 506/551-0232) express bus departs San José from Calle 5, Avenidas 18/20, every 10 minutes, 5 A.M.–midnight, then hourly thereafter. Buses will drop you along Avenida 2, ending at the Basílica. Buses back to San José depart Cartago from Avenida 4, Calles 2/4, on a similar schedule.

In Cartago, buses depart for Turrialba from Avenida 3, Calles 8/10, every 30 minutes 6–10:30 A.M. and hourly thereafter until

10:30 P.M. Hourly buses also serve the following destinations, with departure points in parentheses: Aguacaliente (Calle 1, Avenida 3); Cachí (Calle 6, Avenidas 3); Lankester Gardens and Paraíso (Avenida 1, Calles 2/4); Orosi (Calle 4, Avenida 1); and Tierra Blanca (Calle 4, Avenida 6/8), on Volcán Irazú, at 7 A.M. and 9 A.M.

Taxis hang out on the north side of Las Ruinas. Otherwise, call Taxis El Carmen (tel. 506/551-4646). A *colectivo* (shared) taxi from San José costs about $2 from Avenida Central, Calles 11/13.

IRAZÚ VOLCANO NATIONAL PARK

The slopes north of Cartago rise gradually up the flanks of Volcán Irazú, a 21-km journey to the entrance to Volcán Irazú National Park (no telephone; contact MINAE in Cartago, tel. 506/551-9398, 8 A.M.–3:30 p.m., and Fri.–Sun. 8 A.M.–4:30 p.m. high season, $7 admission). The slopes are dotted with tidy farming villages with pastel houses. Dairy farming is an important industry, and communities are known for their cheese. The fertile fields around Cot are veritable salad bowls—carrots, onions, potatoes, and greens are grown intensively.

Volcán Irazú (3,432 m) derives its name from two tribal words: *ara* (point) and *tzu* (thunder). The volcano has been ephemerally active, most famously on 13 March 1963, the day that U.S. President John F. Kennedy landed in Costa Rica on an official visit: Irazú broke a 20-year silence and began disgorging great columns of smoke and ash. The eruption lasted two years. At one point, ash-filled vapor blasted up into overhanging clouds and triggered a storm that rained mud up to five inches thick over a wide area. No further activity was recorded until December 1994, when Irazú unexpectedly hiccuped gas, ash, and breccia.

The windswept 100-meter-deep Diego de la Haya crater contains a sometimes-pea-green, sometimes-rust-red, mineral-tinted lake. A larger crater is 300 meters deep. Two separate trails lead from the parking lot to the craters.

© JEAN MERCIER

main crater, Irazú Volcano

Follow those signed with blue-and-white symbols (*don't* follow other trails made by irresponsible folks whose feet destroy the fragile ecosystems). The crater rims are dangerously unstable. Keep your distance.

A sense of bleak desolation pervades the summit, like the surface of the moon. It is often foggy. Even on a sunny day expect a cold, dry, biting wind. Dress warmly. The average temperature is a chilly 7.3°C (45°F). Little vegetation lives at the summit, though stunted dwarf oaks, ferns, lichens, and other species are making a comeback. Best time to visit is March or April, the two driest months.

Don't be put off if the volcano is shrouded in fog. Often the clouds lie below the summit of the mountain—there's no way of telling until you drive up there—and you emerge into brilliant sunshine. On a clear day you can see both the Pacific and Atlantic oceans. The earlier in the morning you arrive, the better your chances of getting clear weather.

The **ranger booth** is two km below the summit. A mobile *soda* serves food and drinks on weekends, and the site has toilets and picnic benches. A visitor's center was planned at last

visit, with wheelchair access and information in braille.

Accommodations and Food

Hotel de Montaña (tel. 506/253-0827, fax 506/225-9647, gestoria@racsa.co.cr, $8 pp), in the former home of ex-president Ricardo Jiménez at San José de Chicua, has 20 basic wood-paneled rooms that will appeal only to the most hardy budget traveler. The pleasant restaurant, replete with fireplace, offers sandwiches and *platos especiales* ($3).

About one km further uphill is **Bar/Restaurante Linda Vista** (tel. 506/386-9097, $15 s, $21 d, $10 pp up to five people), which has a simple A-frame cabin for five people, with hot water and fabulous views. It claims to be the highest restaurant in Central America (2,693 meters). Take your business card to add to 30,000 others pinned on the walls. It serves *típico* dishes (average $6) and sandwiches; open 7 A.M.–6 p.m. daily.

The nicest place is **Restaurante 1910** (tel. 506/536-6063), a modern, clean Swiss-style eatery 400 meters above the Christ statue near Cot. It offers Costa Rican fare.

Getting There

A bus departs San José from Avenida 2, Calles 1/3, at 8 A.M. on weekends and holidays (and Wednesdays, Nov.–April), returning at 12:30 P.M. ($5). You can also hop aboard this bus in Cartago on Avenida 2, by Las Ruinas, at 8:45 A.M.

A taxi will cost upward of $20 from Cartago, $10 from Terra Blanca.

If you drive from Cartago, take the road leading northeast from the Basílica. At a Y-junction just below Cot, seven km northeast of Cartago, is a **statue of Jesus,** his arms outstretched as if to embrace the whole valley. The road to the right leads to Pacayas, Santa Cruz, and Guayabo National Monument. That to the left leads to Volcán Irazú National Park (turn right before Tierra Blanca; Irazú is signed). The paved road leads all the way to the mountaintop via Potrero Cerrado. (The most scenic route direct from San José is via the suburb of Guadalupe, then Vista de Mar, and Rancho Redondo, flanking the mountain.)

OROSI-CACHÍ VALLEY

Paraíso, a small town seven km east of Cartago on Hwy. 10, is gateway to the Orosi-Cachí Valley, to the southeast.

Finca Cristina (tel./fax 506/574-6426, organic@mail.ticonet.co.cr, www.cafecristina.com), a 12-hectare, environmentally sound organic coffee farm about two km east of Paraíso, at Birrisito de Paraíso, welcomes visitors by appointment only. There's no sign at the gate; look for a white arch, then take the next dirt road to the east. Guided tours cost $10.

South of Paraíso, Hwy. 224 drops steeply into the Orosi Valley, a self-contained world dedicated to raising coffee and centered on a huge manmade lake drained by the Río Reventazón. Hwy. 224 divides below Paraíso and loops around Lake Cachí: one way drops to Orosi, the other to Ujarrás; thus the valley makes a fine full-day circular tour.

Two km south of Paraíso, on the road to Orosi, is **Parque Doña Anacleto** (8 A.M.–3 p.m., $5 admission) an ICT park with lawns and picnic tables where you can stop to take in the fabulous

view of the valley from the **Mirador Orosi.** Steps lead up to a riot of shrubbery that, with the views, lures Ticos on weekends. Entrance is free. One hundred meters beyond, a dirt road on the right leads to the **Bar/Restaurant Mirador Sanchiri,** which has a **Butterfly Garden** where you can wander inside a netted garden.

Lankester Gardens

Covering 10.7 hectares of exuberant forest and gardens, Lankester Gardens (Apdo. 1031-7050, Cartago, tel. 506/552-3247, fax 506/552-3151, jbl@cariari.ucr.ac.cr, 8:30 A.M.–3:30 p.m., $3.50 admission), one km west of Paraíso, is one of the most valuable botanical centers in the Americas, with about 700 native and exotic orchid species, plus bromeliads, heliconias, bamboos, cacti, and palms, all laid out in gardens that span 27 acres. Species flower throughout the year, with peak blooming February through April. In all, the garden displays about 3,000 species, including 1,000 kinds of orchid.

The gardens, which attract a huge number of butterflies and birds, were conceived by an Englishman, Charles Lankester West, who arrived in Costa Rica in 1898 to work in coffee production. West was dedicated to the conservation of the local flora and the preservation of a representative collection of Central American species. He established the garden in 1917 as an adjunct to his coffee plantation called Las Cóncavas. After his death, the garden was donated to the University of Costa Rica in 1973. After an orientation, you're allowed to roam freely.

Buses depart Cartago for Paraíso from the southeast side of Las Ruinas on Avenida 1 every 30 minutes, 6 A.M.–10 p.m. Get off at the Camp Ayala electricity installation and walk approximately 600 meters to the south.

Orosi

The village of Orosi is the center of the coffee-growing region. Its main claim to fame is its charming **Church of San José de Orosi,** built by the Franciscans in 1735 of solid adobe with lime-covered walls, a rustic timbered roof, and terracotta tiled floor. The church is adorned with gilt icons. The recently restored church has withstood

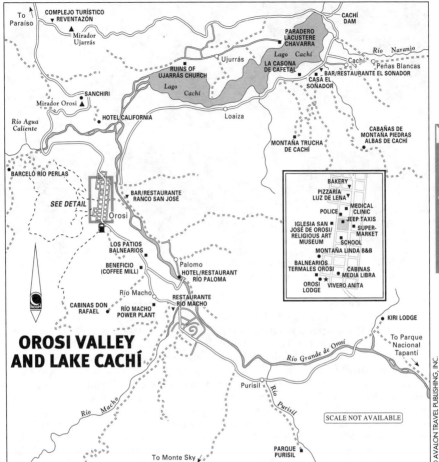

OROSI VALLEY AND LAKE CACHÍ

Map labels (clockwise from top):
To Paraíso · COMPLEJO TURÍSTICO REVENTAZÓN · Mirador Ujarrás · CACHÍ DAM · PARADERO LACUSTERE CHAVARRA · Río Naranjo · Lago Cachí · Ujurrás · RUINS OF UJARRÁS CHURCH · LA CASONA DE CAFETAL · Cachí · Peñas Blancas · BAR/RESTAURANTE EL SONADOR · CASA EL SOÑADOR · SANCHIRI · Lago Cachí · Mirador Orosi · HOTEL CALIFORNIA · Loaiza · Río Agua Caliente · MONTAÑA TRUCHA DE CACHÍ · CABAÑAS DE MONTAÑA PIEDRAS ALBAS DE CACHÍ · BARCELÓ RÍO PERLAS · BAR/RESTAURANTE RANCO SAN JOSÉ · SEE DETAIL · Orosi · LOS PATIOS BALNEARIOS · BENEFICIO (COFFEE MILL) · Palomo · HOTEL/RESTAURANT RÍO PALOMA · Río Macho · RESTAURANTE RÍO MACHO · CABINAS DON RAFAEL · RÍO MACHO POWER PLANT · KIRI LODGE · To Parque Nacional Tapantí · Río Grande de Orosi · Purisil · Río Purisil · Río Macho · SCALE NOT AVAILABLE · To Monte Sky · PARQUE PURISIL

Detail inset labels:
BAKERY · PIZZARIA LUZ DE LENA · MEDICAL CLINIC · POLICE · JEEP TAXIS · IGLESIA SAN JOSÉ DE OROSI/RELIGIOUS ART MUSEUM · SUPERMARKET · SCHOOL · MONTAÑA LINDA B&B · BALNEARIOS TERMALES OROSI · CABINAS MEDIA LIBRA · OROSI LODGE · VIVERO ANITA

© AVALON TRAVEL PUBLISHING, INC.

Central Highlands

earth tremors with barely a mark for almost three centuries. Note the old bell in the cracked church tower. The church adjoins a small **religious art museum** (tel. 506/533-3051, 1–5 P.M. Tue.–Sun., $1 admission) displaying furniture, paintings, icons, and even a monk's cell. Photography is not allowed without prior permission.

Balnearios Termales Orosi (tel. 506/533-2156, 7:30 a.m.–4 p.m. Wed.–Mon., $2 admission), two blocks west of the plaza, has thermal mineral pools (30°C), plus changing rooms and showers. It's clean and well-run. Another hot

springs, **Balnearios Los Patios** (tel. 506/533-3009, 8 A.M.–4 P.M., $2.50 admission), about one km south of Orosi, at Río Macho, has more simple pools, and a bar and restaurant.

Vivero Anita, next to Orosi Lodge, raises orchids and welcomes visitors ($0.75 cents).

South of town, the road divides at Río Macho: the main road crosses the river (a small toll is collected on Sunday) and turns north to continue around the lake's southern shore via the village of Cachí; a side road continues south nine km to Tapantí National Park.

© CHRISTOPHER P. BAKER

Children play soccer in front of the Church of San José de Orosi.

Río Grande Valley

South of Orosi, a dirt road leads to Tapantí via the Río Grande Valley past undulating rows of coffee plants. At **Purisil,** four km southeast of Orosi, a dirt road clambers uphill two km to **Parque de Purisil** (tel. 506/533-3333), gorgeously landscaped with lakes and cascades. It offers trout fishing ($4 per kg for what you catch, which the owners will prepare on-site); plus both a short and long trail, the latter a three-hour round-trip hike into the cloud forest. You can hire guides ($10 pp).

You'll pay $4 to fish for trout at **Kiri Lodge,** near the entrance to the national park; it has a three-km trail.

Around Lake Cachí

Lake Cachí (Lago Cachí) was created when the Instituto Costariccense de Electricidad built the Cachí Dam across the Río Reventazón to supply San José with hydroelectric power.

On the southern shore, just east of Cachí village, is **La Casona del Cafetal** (tel. 506/577-1414, 11 A.M.–6 p.m.), a coffee *finca* with bar and restaurant. It has horseback riding ($10).

A short distance east, **Casa El Soñador** (Dreamer's House, tel. 506/577-1186 or 506/577-1983, 9 A.M.–6 p.m. daily) is the unusual home of woodcarver Hermes Quesada, who carries on his father Macedonio's tradition of carving crude figurines from coffee plant roots. The house—with carved figures leaning over the windows (these, apparently, represent the town gossips)—is made entirely of rough-cut wood, with carvings adorning the outside walls. Upstairs is decorated with historical relics. Check out the *Last Supper* on one of the walls. Take time to read the newspaper clippings on the walls that tell about his life. Hermes also represents other local artists.

Paradero Lacustre Chavarra (tel. 506/574-7557, 8 A.M.–5 p.m., $1.75 entrance), one km east of Ujarrás, is an ICT recreational complex on the north shore of the lake. A basketball court, soccer field, and swimming pools are set amid landscaped grounds. It has a restaurant and bar. Cars costs $1.25 extra.

If you fancy fishing for trout, head to **Montaña Trucha de Cachí** (tel. 506/577-1457), 1.5 km south of Hwy. 224, near the village of Cachí; it's signed.

Ujarrás

Ujarrás, on the north shore of the lake, seven km southeast of Paraíso, is the site of the ruins of the **Church of Nuestra Señora de la Limpia Concepción,** built out of limestone between 1681 and 1693 to honor the Virgen del Rescate de Ujarrás. The church sits on the same site as a shrine built after an indigenous fisherman saw an apparition of the Virgin in a tree trunk. According to legend, when he attempted to carry the trunk to Ujarrás, it became so heavy that a team of men couldn't move it, a sign that the local priests interpreted as an indication from God to build a shrine.

The church, however, owes its existence to another miracle. In 1666, the pirates Mansfield and Morgan led a raiding party into the Turrialba Valley to sack the highland cities. They were routed after the defenders prayed at Ujarrás. The church was abandoned in 1833 after the region was flooded. The ruins—set in a beautiful walled garden and surrounded by coffee and banana plants—are open daily. Entrance is free.

Thousands of pilgrims from Paraíso make a pilgrimage to the church each Easter Sunday to honor the intercession of the Virgin Mary in the pirate attack. The procession begins at 7 A.M. (call tel. 506/574-7376 for information).

Sports and Recreation

Orosi Lodge offers excursions, including a "Coffee Mill & Private Hot Springs" tour that includes a visit to Valle Caliente Hotsprings, a stupendous private mountainside home with a landscaped horizon thermal pool ($45 full day). Orosi Lodge also rents mountain bikes ($3 per hour; $10 per day) and canoes ($25 per day, including transport to the lake).

Orosi Valle Verde Tours (tel. 506/533-3825), at Cabinas Media Libra, offers Jeep and horseback tours, plus a tour of Orosi.

Accommodations

Camping: You can camp for $2.50 pp ($3.50 if you rent a tent) at **Montaña Linda** (see below); and at **Paradero Lacustre Chavarra** (see above) for $3.

Church of Nuestra Señora de la Limpia Concepción, Ujarrás

Under $25: The **Montaña Linda** (Apdo. 83-7100 Paraíso, tel. 506/533-3640, international 506/533-2153, info@montanalinda.com, www .montanalinda.com, $5.50 pp dorm, $8 s, $12 d private room, $25 s/d bed-and-breakfast), one block north of Balnearios Termales, is a rustic yet homey and welcoming place run by a Dutch-Canadian couple. There are two dorms, eight private rooms with hot water, plus a bed-and-breakfast with three upstairs rooms (two with double beds, one with a double and a bunk). A hot tub was planned. Mountain bike rentals cost

Central Highlands

$4 daily. Meals are provided, but guests get kitchen privileges ($1).

Cabañas de Montaña Piedras Albas de Cachí (tel. 506/377-1462), about two km south of Cachí, has "fully equipped" cabinas with views, and trails into the surrounding primary forest.

The **Hotel California** (tel. 506/574-3026, $11 s, $19 d standard; $35 s/d suite) sits beside the Orosi River and is reached via a steep dirt road that begins about 400 meters south of Mirador Orosi. This Spanish colonial-style stone lodge has seven rooms, each distinct in shape, size, and character. Upstairs a vast lounge boasts soft-cushioned sofas and huge stone fireplace. There's a mediocre restaurant and bar. The place looked run-down at last visit.

$25–50: The **Sanchiri Mirador and Lodge** (P.O. Box 27-7100 Paraíso, tel. 506/574-5454, fax 506/574-8586, sanchiri@sol.racsa.co.cr, www.sanchiri.com, $25 s, $35 d low season; $30 s, $40 d high season), has 10 basic yet delightful hillside *cabinas* of various sizes made of rough-hewn logs and bamboo, with telephones and views over the valley. Bathrooms of natural stone have hot water. There's a larger cabin with three rooms and a kitchen for nine people. Ten more upscale bungalows were being added at last visit. It has a kid's playground. Rates include tax and breakfast.

I recommend the delightful **Orosi Lodge Cabinas y Cafetería** (P.O. Box 1122-7050 Orosi, tel./fax 506/533-3578, ccneck@racsa.co.cr, www.orosilodge.com, $35 s/d low season; $40 s/d high season), next to Balneario Martínez and run by Andy and Cornelia, a friendly German couple. Inspired by local architecture, with clay lamps and locally crafted hardwoods, it has six rooms in a charming two-story whitewashed structure. All have bamboo furnishings, firm mattresses, ceiling fans, tile or wooden (upstairs) floors, minibar and coffeemaker, colorful little bathrooms with hot water, plus balcony with views. It has a coffee shop; a '60s jukebox plays golden oldies.

One block east, the modern **Cabinas Media Libra** (P.O. Box 310-7050 Cartago, tel. 506/533-3838, fax 506/533-3737, cabmedia@racsa.co.cr,

$35 s/d) has seven clean, simply furnished rooms with black tile floors, flouncy bedspreads, color TVs, telephones, fans, and hot water. It has a restaurant. Rates include breakfast.

The riverside **Hotel Río Palomo** (Apdo. 220, Cartago 7050, tel. 506/533-3128, fax 506/551-2919, $12 s, $30 d) has 12 modest *cabinas* with private baths and hot water, some with kitchenettes. It's immediately east of a suspension bridge over the Río Macho, two km south of Orosi. The two cold-water swimming pools are open to non-guests.

Enjoying a superb mountainside setting, **Cabinas Don Rafael** (tel. 506/533-3445 or 506/574-7585, $26 up to four people), about two km south of Orosi and 1.5 km sharply uphill, offers five meagerly furnished cabins with balconies and kitchenettes. Two are of logs; three more modern units are of brick and feature tiles and clean bathrooms with hot water. One room sleeps up to 10 people in three bedrooms and has a lounge with TV, stereo, and sofas, plus kitchen ($50). It has secure parking and a small pool plus trails, a basketball court, and a grill.

$50–100: The most upscale place for miles is **Barceló Rancho Río Perlas Resort & Spa** (tel. 506/533-3341, fax 506/533-3085, ranchorioperlas @barcelocr.com, www.rancho-las-perlas-info.com, $101 s, $106 d standard, $106/111 superior, $116/121 junior suite, $126/131 suite low season; $125/130 standard, $130/135 superior, $140/145 junior suite, $150/155 suite high season), on the south side of the Rio Agua Caliente in a lush mountainside setting. Red-tiled villas stairstep the hillside and include six tastefully decorated standard rooms, 26 superiors, 15 junior suites, and two suites. All have cable TV, telephones, coffeemakers, mini-bar, security box, hair-dryers, and terraces. It has two restaurants, a swimming pool fed by thermal waters, ponds for fishing, and a spa offering a full range of treatments.

Food

Bar/Restaurant Mirador Sanchiri serves *comidas típica* ($6–10), enjoyed to stunning vistas through plate-glass windows.

In Orosi, the best place is **Orosi Lodge** (7 A.M.–7 p.m. daily) whose atmospheric café serves an excellent continental breakfast ($4), plus pizza ($3.50), sandwiches, croissants, bagels with salami and cheese, natural juices, and ice cream sundaes. It has a jukebox and table football, plus free newspapers. Nearby, the open-air, rustic **Restaurant Media Libra** (7 A.M.–9 p.m.) serves American breakfasts ($3.50), Greek salads, ceviche, sandwiches, curried chicken ($5.50), and beef Stroganoff with mashed potatoes ($6). Check your bill carefully.

Bar Restaurant El Nido, two blocks northeast of the soccer field, serves oven-roasted fare baked over coffee wood. Next door, **Pizzería Luz de Luna** (tel. 506/533-2309, 2–10 P.M. Mon.–Tue. and Thursday, 11:30 A.M.–10 P.M. Fri.–Sun.) serves oven-roasted pizzas.

Parque de Purisil (see above) has a splendidly rustic restaurant and agreeable setting. It serves salads, garlic trout ($7), and set lunches (from $2.50).

On the south side of the lake, **La Casona del Cafetal** (tel. 506/533-3280, 11 A.M.–6 P.M., $6) serves crepes, soups, salads, and dishes such as tilapia with mushrooms, garlic tilapia, trout, or jumbo shrimp, in pleasing surroundings. **Bar Restaurante El Sonador** (11 a.m.–midnight daily) is a local hangout with music videos on the TV. It serves inexpensive local fare, including ceviche, and you can fish for your own trout or tilapia.

The rustic **Restaurant El Cas,** 100 meters east of Ujarras ruins, serves local fare and snacks.

There's a bakery (tel. 506/533-3244, 4 A.M.–6 P.M. Mon.–Sat., 5 A.M.–noon Sunday) three blocks north of the soccer field in Orosi.

Information and Services

A **medical clinic** (tel. 506/533-3783, beeper 506/233-3333) is 50 meters northeast of the soccer field; that of Dr. Luis García Salazar (tel. 506/384-6842) is around the corner, to the northwest.

The **police station** is on the northwest corner of the soccer field.

Orosi Lodge (7 A.M.–7 p.m.) offers Internet access for $2 per hour.

Montaña Linda offers Spanish-language classes. Courses cost from $115 for 12 hours to $395 for 45 hours, including accommodation.

Getting There

Buses (tel. 506/574-6127) depart Cartago for Orosi from Calle 4, Avenida 1, every hour on the hour 8 A.M.–10 p.m. (25 cents). Return buses depart from the soccer field in Orosi 4:30 A.M.–10:30 p.m. Buses do not complete a circuit of Lake Cachí; you'll have to backtrack to Paraíso to visit Ujarrás and the Cachí dam by public bus. Buses depart Cartago for Cachí via Ujarrás from one block east and one block south of Las Ruinas.

Taxis El Rescate (tel. 506/574-4442) is in Paraíso. Jeep-taxis (tel. 506/533-3087) await custom on the north side of the soccer field in Orosi.

TAPANTÍ–MECIZO DE LA MUERTE

Parque Nacional Tapantí–Mecizo de la Muerte (7 A.M.–5 p.m., $6 admission), 27 km southeast of Cartago, sits astride the northern slopes of the Cordillera Talamanca, which boasts more rain and cloud cover than any other region in the country. Average rainfall for the Orosi region is 324 cm (128 inches); Tapantí gets much more—almost 800 cm (330 inches) of rain on the mid-elevation peaks. February through April are the driest months. Its many fast-flowing rivers and streams are excellent for fishing, permitted in designated areas April–Oct.

The 58,328-hectare park, at the headwaters of the Río Reventazón, climbs from 1,200 to 2,560 meters above sea level (it extends all the way up to Cerro de la Muerte) and forms a habitat for resplendent quetzals (often seen on the western slopes near the ranger station) and more than 260 other bird species, plus mammals such as river otters, tapirs, jaguars, ocelots, jaguarundis, howler monkeys, silky anteaters, and multitudinous snakes, frogs, and toads.

The park possesses several life zones, from lower montane rainforest to montane dwarf forest. Terrain is steep and rugged. Well-marked trails begin near the park entrance ranger station, which has a small nature display. The Oropendola Trail, which begins about 800 meters from the ranger station, leads to picnic shelters and a deep pool by the Río Macho where the hardy can swim in ice-cold waters. There's a vista point—a short trail leads from here to a waterfall viewpoint—about four km along. A trailhead opposite the beginning of the Oropendola Trail leads into the mountains. Other trails include the Fallen Trees Trail (Sendero Arboles Caidos), Sendero la Pava, and Sendero La Catarata, which leads to a waterfall.

The ranger station has a small exhibition.

Accommodations and Food

The ranger station (tel. 506/771-3297, fax 506/551-2970, acla-p@ns.minae.go.cr) has a *hospedaje* with a kitchen and bunk beds in clean, pleasant rooms ($4.50 per person with sleeping bag, $2.50 without). Rangers make meals ($1.25). **Kiri Lodge** (Apdo. 165-7100 Paraíso, tel. 506/533-2272, fax 506/591-2839, kirilodge@hotmail.com, $25 s, $35 d), at the base of the forested mountain 800 meters west of the park, has six cabins with handsome stone-walled showers. Some rooms have bunk beds. The restaurant specializes in trout culled from its own ponds; open 7 A.M.–8 p.m. Rates includes tax and breakfast.

Getting There

A bus departs Cartago at 6 A.M. and travels via Orosi as far as Purisil, five km from the park entrance (later buses go only as far as Río Macho, nine km from Tapantí). You can hike or take a jeep-taxi from Orosi or Purisil ($5 each way). If you befriend the park ranger before setting off to explore, he or she may call for a taxi to pick you up at a prearranged time.

CARTAGO TO CERRO DE LA MUERTE

South of Cartago, the Pan-American Highway (Hwy. 2) begins a daunting ascent over the Talamanca Mountains, cresting the range at Cerro de la Muerte ("Mountain of Death") at 3,491 meters before dropping down into the Valle de El General and the Pacific southwest. The vistas are staggering, and opportunities abound for hiking, trout fishing, and birding—notably for resplendent quetzals, which are common hereabouts, and toucanets, hummingbirds, orioles, and collared trogons are also commonly seen. The region is clad in native oak and cloud forest. The climate is brisk, so take a warm jacket if you want to go hiking or in the event of a breakdown.

Drive carefully! The road is often fog-bound (early to mid-morning are best, before the clouds roll in). It also zigzags with sudden hairpin turns; is washed out in places; and is used by buses and trailer rigs. Kilometer distance markers line the route.

Cartago to Cañon

At **Enpalme,** 30 km south of Cartago, a side road descends in a series of spectacular switchbacks to Santa María de Dota; while at **Vara de Roble** (two km north of Enpalme), another road leads west to San Cristóbal via La Lucha Sin Fin (see sidebar, *The Route of the Saints*). You can also reach Santa María de Dota from **Cañon,** five km south of Enpalme at Km 58 (where a yellow church perches over the roadside) via a dirt road that descends steeply to **Copey.** Copey is a small agricultural village at about 2,121 meters, eight km southwest of Cañon and five km east of Santa María de Dota. The area is famous as a center for trout fishing: you'll pass several trout farms along the road.

Cañon to Cerro de la Muerte

At Trinidad, five km south of Cañon, you pass through the **Tapantí–Mecizo de la Muerte National Park,** formerly Río Macho Forest Reserve. The **Cuenca Queberi Trail,** which begins at Km 61, leads into the reserve.

At Km 70, a side road leads to **Finca Eddie Serrano** (see Albergue Mirador de Quetzales in the *Accommodations* section, below, 8 A.M.–5 p.m., $7 admission), at 8,530 meters elevation, the perfect spot for viewing quetzals. (Up to 20 pairs of quetzals have been seen feeding in treetops near the *finca*. "We can almost guarantee that visitors will see quetzals," says owner Eddie Serrano.) Serrano and his wife and three children were pioneers, settling in this area more than 45 years ago. He and his family continue to work their 100-hectare dairy farm, cut decades ago from virgin forest, while collecting wild blackberries for sale in San José and raising trout for local hotels. Serrano leads guided quetzal hikes daily, 6:30 A.M.–4 p.m., and the Robledal Oak Forest Trail is open to self-guided hikes.

Farther south, at Km 71, is **Iyök Amí Cloudforest Reserve,** boasting equally good birdwatching and splendid 500-year-old trees accessed via six km of trails. At Km 76 you'll pass a refuge hut—**Casa Refugio de Ojo de Agua**—built for early pioneers who had to cross the mountains before a road existed to bring their produce to market in San José. The adobe hut is now a small museum displaying maps and historical information.

At Km 80, a turnoff—easy to miss—leads downhill (west) to the hamlet of San Gerardo de Dota, one of the best places in all Costa Rica for viewing quetzals.

Finally, at Km 89 you crest **Cerro de la Muerte.** The name derives not from the dozens who have lost their lives through auto accidents, but from the many poor *campesinos* who, often shoeless and in nothing more than shirt and pants, froze to death in days of yore while carrying sacks of produce to trade in San José. The summit is marked by a forest of radio antennae. A dirt road leads up to the antenna, from where you'll have miraculous views, weather permitting. At 3,000 meters the stunted vegetation is Andean *páramo,* complete with wind-sculpted shrubs, peat bogs, and marshy grasses. Be prepared for high winds.

Genesis II Cloud Forest Reserve

The Refugio Nacional de Vida Silvestre Fauna Genesis II (see *Accommodation,* below), three km east of Cañon, near the village of La Damita, at an elevation of about 2,360 meters, protects 38 hectares of primary forest bordering Tapantí National Park. It's a great spot for sighting resplendent quetzals, trogons, toucanets, and scores of

other bird species. You can even see quetzals right from the porch March–June. The well-maintained trail system covers 20 km. Bring a warm jacket and raingear.

You can take the **Talamanca Treescape canopy tour** using ziplines connecting three platforms that begin and end on the ground ($35 pp including park entrance, or $25 for overnight guests).

The owners, Englishman Steve Friedman and his Dutch-born wife, Paula, run a volunteer program for people willing to assist in trail building, reforestation, general maintenance, and research into flora and fauna. Month-long programs cost $600, including accommodations and meals. If requesting details by mail, enclose three international reply coupons, which you can obtain at any post office.

To get there from Hwy. 2, turn east at Cañon church and then right at the Y-fork by La Damita School. The trail is steep and very rough—you'll need a four-wheel drive. Day visits cost $10 (students $4), plus $10 for guided hikes.

Sports and Recreation

Trout can be caught in the rivers, as well as at about a dozen roadside trout farms with lakes. **Finca Los Prados,** 2.5 km west of the turnoff at Trinidad, has trout fishing ($3.50 per kg) plus a café. **Finca Madre Selva** (tel. 506/224-6388, $1 admission), two km east of the highway at Km 64, has seven lakes, plus barbecue pits, and trails into the forest. The owners will prepare your fish ($5.50 per kg).

Accommodations and Food

The following are arranged in rough order southward along the road.

Hotel Cerro Alto (tel. 506/571-1010, $16.50 Mon.–Fri., $33 Sat.–Sun., for up to four people), two km north of Enpalme, is a rustic log-and-bamboo lodge with views toward Irazú. It has eight A-frame chalets for four persons each, with heaters, kitchenettes, fireplaces, and private baths with hot water. There's a bar and restaurant, plus a tiny "swimming" pool and trails.

Ⓜ Genesis II (Apdo. 655, Cartago 7050, tel./fax 506/381-0739, info@genesis-two.com,

THE ROUTE OF THE SAINTS

S outh of San José lies a little-touristed region of hidden valleys perfect for a full-day drive along the scenic "Route of the Saints," so-called because most of the villages, which are hidden off the main road, are named after saints.

An alternate and popular approach to exploring these saintly villages is to drive south from Cartago along the Pan-American Highway—Hwy. 2—and to turn west at Enpalme or Canñon.

San José to San Ignacio De Acosta and San Gabriel

From San José's southern suburb of Desamparado, Hwy. 209 climbs into the Fila de Bustamante mountains via **Aserrí,** a pretty hillside town famed for its handsome church and for La Piedra de Aserrí—a massive boulder with, at its base, a cave once inhabited, apparently, by a witch. The gradient increases markedly to the crest of the mountains just north of **Tarbaca.** En route you gain a breathtaking view of Volcán Irazú.

Three km south of Tarbacia is a Y-junction. The road to the right (Hwy. 209) drops westward to **San Ignacio de Acosta,** a charming little town nestled on a hillside. You can see its whitewashed houses for miles around. The sun sets dramatically on its steep west-facing slopes. (For a wildly scenic drive, continue west from Acosta to the **Balneario Valle Cantado,** with swimming pools fed by hot springs (Fri.–Sun.). Beyond, the unpaved road switchbacks to **Tabarcia;** not to be confused with Tarbaca. Turn right in Tabarcia and you will climb to Hwy. 239, which

runs along the ridgecrest of the Cerros Escazú mountains; turn right to return to San José via Colón and Santa Ana.)

The road to the left (Hwy. 222) at the Y-junction south of Tarbaca leads to **San Gabriel,** gateway to the "Route of the Saints" proper.

San Gabriel to Santa María De Dota

Route 222 leads southeast from San Gabriel, dropping and rising through river valleys, via Frailes to **San Cristóbal Sur,** a market town better known to Ticos for **La Lucha Sin Fin** (The Endless Struggle), the *finca* of former president and national hero Don "Pepe" Figueres, who led the 1948 revolution from here, two km east of San Cristóbal. There's a **museum** in the high school; open weekends only (free). The only monument—the rusting remains of an engine, with a plaque bearing the words "Remember the fallen of both sides, 1948"—is hardly worth seeking out; if you insist, it's halfway downhill to the Colegio Técnico Profesional Industrial José Figueres Ferrer, one km west of La Lucha.

East of La Lucha, the road clambers precipitously through pine forests three km to the Pan-

view toward San Ignacio

American Highway. Instead, turn south from San Cristóbal and follow a scenic route via **San Pablo de León Cortes** to **San Marcos de Tarrazú,** dramatically situated over coffee fields and dominated by a handsome white church with a domed roof. You can visit the local coffee mill, **Beneficio Coopetarrazú** (tel./fax 506/546-6098, tarrazu@sol.racsa.co.cr), by prior arrangement.

From San Marcos, the main road climbs southeast to **Santa María de Dota,** a tranquil village whose main plaza has a small but dramatic granite monument honoring those who died in the 1948 revolution. The area has recently blossomed as a major coffee-producing area; Indians from as far away as Boca del Toro, in Panamá, provide the field labor. You can visit the **Beneficio Coopedota** (tel. 506/541-2828, fax 506/541-2827, coopdota@racsa.co.cr, www.dotacoffee.com, 9 A.M.–5 P.M. Mon.–Fri.), which handles the beans for 700 local producers and accepts visitors by reservation, in season; the visit includes a plantation tour, video, and tasting ($10). This modern facility produces 30,000 bags annually for Starbucks (30 percent of its total business); the bean husks fuel the driers.

The wonderful coffee of the region is available for purchase through **Down to Earth** (tel. 866/653-2784, reorder@godowntoearth.org, ww.godowntoearth.org).

From Santa María, the roads east snake steeply to the Pan-American Highway, with dramatic views en route.

Accommodations and Food

There are undistinguished budget hotels in San Marcos and Santa María.

Colinas Altavista Resort & Conference Center (tel. 506/230-4941, hotel@colinasaltavista.com, www.colinasaltavista.com, $48 s/d deluxe, $72 apartments, $132 master suite), outside Aserró, opened in 2003 with six deluxe rooms, 10 apartment units, and a three-bedroom master suite, all modestly furnished, with tile floors and broad verandas with gleaming hardwoods. The best thing are the magnificent views across the valley. It has a restaurant, and offers horseback riding.

Restaurant Chicharronera La Tranca, high on the mountain road north of Aserrí, has a breezy outdoor patio with stunning views down over San José and the far-off volcanoes. The rustic restaurant serves food prepared on an open-hearth grill.

The place to eat is **La Casona de Sara** (tel. 506/541-2258, open 6 A.M.), in Santa María (take the first left after the bridge into town when approaching from Enpalme). This clean family restaurant serves filling meals. Take a peek in the kitchen to choose from the simmering pots. A filling lunch costs about $3. It typically stays open until the last guest leaves.

If you're looking for entertainment, **Chicharroenera Cacique Asserí** (tel. 506/230-3088), in Aserrí, hosts marimba music and traditional dancing every Friday and Saturday.

Getting There

Buses from San José depart for Aserrí from Calle 2, Avenidas 6/8, and for San Ignacio from Calle 8, Avenidas 12/14, hourly 5:30 A.M.–10:30 P.M. There's bus service for San Ignacio from Aserrí.

Buses to San Marcos and Santa María depart San José from Avenida 16, Calles 19/21, at 7:15 A.M., 9 A.M., 11:30 A.M., 12:30 P.M., 3 P.M., 5 P.M., and 7:30 P.M. Return buses to San José depart Santa María at 4:30 A.M., 5:40 A.M., 7:15 A.M., 9:15 A.M., noon, 3 P.M., and 5 P.M.

www.genesis-two.com; in the U.S., SJO.2031, Unit C-101, P.O. Box 025216, 1601 NW 97th Ave., Miami, FL 33102-5216; $85 pp low season; $95 high season), has a covered wooden deck with space for four two-person tents ($3 pp with own tent; $5 with tent rental, plus $2 pp for use of platform). There's an "ecologically sensitive" outhouse, plus hot showers ($2 per day) and use of the kitchen ($1). Meals are served. And you can rent mattresses and extra blankets. It also offers five small, clean, carpeted bedrooms (one with double bed, the rest single) with quilted comforters, electric heaters and hot-water bottles (by request), and shared bathrooms with hot showers. Two rustic cabins in the lush gardens each sleep up to four people and share the bathrooms and toilets in the house. The cozy rough-hewn lodge has a cast-iron, wood-fired stove, a library, and a welcoming homey feel. The views through the forest are fabulous. Reader Yvonne Hodges reports the organic food is "excellent." The owners recommend a three-night minimum stay. Students get discounts. Rates includes all meals and guides.

The exquisite **El Toucanet Lodge** (tel./fax 506/541-1435, toucanet@racsa.co.cr, www .eltoucanet.com, $45 s, $58 d), on a 40-hectare fruit farm in the valley one km east of Copey, is perfect for birders—more than 170 species have been seen at the lodge; quetzals are virtually a daily occurrence. Made of stone and polished timbers, it has a wide veranda with valley views, a lounge with fireplace, and four rooms, plus a family cabin for six people with a fireplace, kitchenette, and hot water. Rooms are spacious and have hardwood floors and ceilings, simple furnishings, and clean tiled bathrooms with hot water. Two more rooms were to be added. It has a charming pinewood restaurant, plus a wood-fired, stone-lined hot tub. It offers hiking trails, plus horseback tours, a coffee tour, and a free quetzal tour for guests. Rates include breakfast.

Six km south of Cañon, at Km 61 at Macho Gaff, one km north of Trinidad, is **Tapantí Lodge** (Albergue de Montaña Tapantí, Apdo. 1818, San José 1002, tel./fax 506/232-0436,

$30 s, $50 d), a small, somewhat dowdy chalet-style hotel with 10 wooden, no-frills *cabinas* on a grassy ridge merging into cloud forest and Tapantí National Park. The rustic cabins sleep two, three, or five people, with worn furnishings, private bathroom with hot water, plus electric heater, living room, and balcony. A lounge has a TV, fireplace, bar, and cozy deep-cushioned chairs. The hotel has a small conference room, and a cozy bar-cum-restaurant serving Costa Rican meals and the lodge's specialty, Tapantí trout. There are trails for hiking and horseback riding, plus trout-fishing, quetzal hikes.

Nearby, at Km 70 on the Pan-American Highway, is **Ⓜ Albergue Mirador de Quetzales** (tel. 506/381-8456, $35 pp), at Finca Eddie Serano. This rustic yet cozy lodge is set amid cloud forest at 2,600 meters where quetzals congregate to nest. There are four rooms, plus 10 A-frame log cabins boasting marvelous views; all have one double and one single bed (some also have a bunk bed), and a private bath with hot water. You can camp for $5 pp under thatch with tables and barbecue grills (tent rental was planned at last visit). Rates include breakfast, dinner, and quetzal tour.

Iyök Amí Lodge (Apdo. 335-2100 San José, tel. 506/387-2238 or 770-9393, fax 506/771-2003, iyokbosque@yahoo.es, www.iyokami.com, $50 pp) has six carpeted bedrooms with electric blankets and hot water, plus a living room with TV and sound system. Volunteers pay $500 monthly to help maintain trails and teach English in local schools. Rates include meals.

All of the accommodations above serve food. In Copey, be sure to call in at **El Bus Varano** (6 A.M.–6 p.m.), an old U.S. school bus converted into a simple eatery where you can dine on simple fare such as tamales ($1), burgers ($1.25), and fried chicken, plus milkshakes (*batidos*).

Getting There

The San Isidro bus (see the *South Central Costa Rica* chapter) from San José departs Calle 16, Avenidas 1/3, and will drop you or pick you up anywhere along Hwy. 2. Most hotel owners will pick you up with advance notice.

Tour operators in San José offer tours with nights at one of the lodges.

The only gas station between Cartago and San Isidro de El General is at Enpalme.

SAN GERARDO DE DOTA

San Gerardo de Dota, nine km west and sharply downhill from the Pan-American Highway at Km 80, is an exquisite hamlet tucked at the base of a narrow wooded valley at 1,900 meters—a true Shangri-la cut-off from the rest of the world. It's a magnificent setting. The Río Savegre valley is a center for apples and peaches, and also attracts resplendent quetzals, especially during the April and May nesting season.

Albergue de Montaña Savegre hosts the **Quetzal Education Research Complex,** operated in association with the Southern Nazarene University of Oklahoma. The road (well-paved, but with a few tricky, washed-out sections) is snaking, steep, and breathtakingly beautiful (four-wheel drive recommended).

The valley has been slated as the course for a new highway linking Quepos to the Pan-American Highway.

Accommodations

Trogon Lodge (Grupo Mawamba, Apdo. 10980-1000 San José, tel. 506/293-8181, fax 506/239-7657, info@grupomawamba.com, www.grupomawamba.com, $43 s, $62 d) enjoys a beautiful and secluded setting at the head of the San Gerardo Valley, beside the burbling river

tumbling through exquisitely landscaped grounds. There are 10 simply appointed, two-bedroom hardwood cabins with tin roofs, tasteful fabrics, heater, bedside lamps, private bathroom with hot water, and veranda. Meals are served in a rustic lodge overlooking a trout pond. Fishing is available. Trails lead to waterfalls. Guided horseback tours ($10 per hour) and quetzal tours ($15) are offered, as is a canopy tour ($30) and mountain bike rentals ($15). Day visits cost $72 pp (four people minimum) including transport from San José, meals, and guided tour.

Hotel de Montaña Savegre (Apdo. 482, Cartago, tel. 506/771-1028, fax 506/740-1027, savegrehotel@racsa.co.cr, www.savegre.co.cr, $39 s, $49 d, or $72 pp, low season; $45 s, $59 d, or $78 pp, high season), in the midst of the tiny little community, has 20 rustic yet handsome all-wood cabins; basic but clean, with blankets, heaters, and private baths with hot water. There are also 10 newer, more spacious, wood-paneled cabins. It has conference facilities. There are trails (4–8 km), plus bird-watching trips ($55 half-day), cloud-forest hiking ($50 half-day), guided horseback riding ($12 per hour), and trout fishing ($50 half-day). Rates include all meals.

Rodolfo Chacón and his wife, Maribel, have four cabinas—**Cabinas El Quetzal** (tel. 506/771-2376, $25 pp), on the banks of the river. All have hot water. There's a children's playground. "We slept so well there with the woodstove going," reports one reader. Rates include three meals.

Turrialba and Vicinity

East of Cartago, Hwy. 230 snakes eastward through the valley of the Río Reventazón, falling gradually before a final steep descent to the regional center of Turrialba, at a considerably lower altitude than Cartago. The route leads via **Cervantes.** An alternate, less-traveled mountain route from Cartago leads via **Pacayas.** You can also reach Turrialba via Lake Cachí (from the north side of the dam), from where a badly potholed road winds east through the mountains.

TURRIALBA

Turrialba, a small town 65 km east of San José, was until recently an important stop on the old highway between San José and the Caribbean. The opening of the Guápiles Highway via Braulio Carrillo National Park two decades ago stole much of its thunder, and the town was further insulated when train service to the Caribbean was ended in 1991. The now-rusted tracks still dominate the town, which squats in a valley bottom

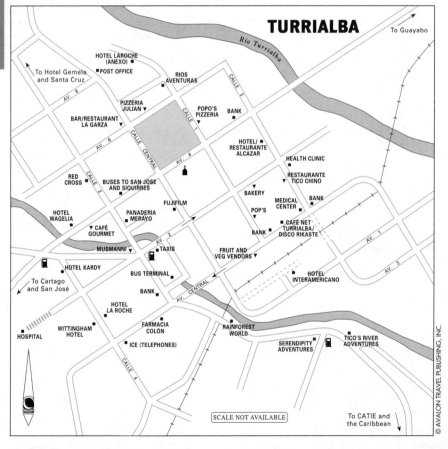

© AVALON TRAVEL PUBLISHING, INC.

on the banks of the Río Turrialba at 650 meters above sea level.

Turrialba is popular among kayakers and rafters as a base for whitewater adventures on the Ríos Reventazón and Pacuare. However, there's nothing to see in town, which is centered on the undistinguished **Parque la Dominica** with an equally obscure church on its southwest corner.

CATIE

The Center for Tropical Agriculture Investigation and Learning (Centro Agronómico Tropical de Investigación y Enseñanza, tel. 506/556-6431, ext. 2221, fax 506/556-8470), four km east of Turrialba, is one of the world's leading tropical agricultural research stations. It was established in the 1930s and today covers 880 hectares of landscaped grounds surrounding a lake full of waterfowl. CATIE is devoted to experimentation and research on livestock and tropical plants and crops, including more than 2,500 coffee varieties. CATIE also contains the largest library on tropical agriculture in the world.

Several trails provide superb bird-watching, and the laboratories, orchards, herbarium, and husbandry facilities are fascinating. Guided five-hour tours are given for groups only, but individual visitors can explore alone ($25) with three days' advance notice.

There's a modest 50-room hotel used by researchers but open to the public for $30 s, $38 d. You can also rent apartments with kitchens and beds for two people. It has a café.

Buses depart for CATIE from Avenida Central, Calle 2, in Turrialba. You can also catch the bus to Siquirres from Avenida 4, Calle 2, and ask to be dropped off.

Río Reventazón

About five km southeast of Turrialba and one km east of CATIE, you cross the Río Reventazón ("Exploding River"). The river, which begins its life at the Lake Cachí dam, was recently dammed about two km upstream of the bridge to create the 256-hectare (450,000-cubic-meter) **Lake Angostura.** The **Angostura Hydroelectric Project** (Proyecto Hidroelectrico

SAVE THE RÍOS PACUARE AND REVENTAZÓN

In 1985, the Costa Rican government recognized the Pacuare Gorge's scenic quality by making it a *zona protectorado,* the first designated Wild and Scenic river in the country. But the national electricity agency, ICE, already had plans to dam the gorge—which is one of the country's best potential sites for hydroelectric power generation. As ICE has pursued feasibility studies on its dam site, the Pacuare has become the focus of a classic development vs. preservation face-off.

The Guayabo-Siquirres Hydroelectric Project will inundate a 14-km stretch of river and 1,250 hectares of surrounding wilderness. The project will cost an estimated $1 billion, to be funded by the Inter-American Development Bank. The 180-meter-tall Siquirres Dam will be built at the scenic Dos Montañas ravine on the Río Pacuare and will flood 12.5 km of the best rapids. The 43.5-meter-tall Guayabo Dam, whose first phase was completed in 2003, is being built eight km northeast of Turrialba, on the Reventazón River. Four additional dams will be built on these rivers by 2010, two on the Reventazón (one of which is under construction), and two on the Pacuare. The Cabécar Indians of the Awari Indigenous Reserve face a loss of lands that they depend on for their livelihood.

If you're interested in helping save the Pacuare, contact **Fundación Ríos Tropicales** (Apdo. 472-1200 Pavas, San José, tel. 506/233-6455, fax 506/255-4354, info@riostropicales.com, www.riostropicales.com; in the U.S., SJO #130, P.O. Box 025240, Miami, FL 33102), or **Friends of the River/Fundación Ríos Tropicales** (128 J. St., Sacramento, CA 95814-2203, tel. 916/442-3155, www.friendsoftheriver.org).

Angostura), the largest hydroelectricity generating plant in the country, began humming in July 2000, producing a whopping 177 megawatts of electricity.

Below Lake Angostura, the river cascades down the eastern slopes of the Cordillera Central to the Caribbean plains. On a good day it serves up class III–IV rapids. Many companies offer one- to three-day trips on the Reventazón.

Sports and Recreation

Costa Rica Rios Aventuras (tel. 506/556-9617, www.costaricarios.com) offers guided hikes and rafting and rents kayaks. The U.S.-run **Serendipity Adventures** (tel. 734/995-0111 or 877/507-1358, fax 734/426-5026, info@serendipityadventures .com, www.serendipityadventures.com) offers hot-air ballooning, rafting, hiking, kayaking, and other adventures. Most are multi-day, multi-activity programs. **Rainforest World** (tel. 506/556-2678, rforestw@racsa.co.cr, www.rforestw.com; in the U.S., tel. 888/513-2808) offers whitewater trips.

Accommodations

Under $25: The U.S.-run **Hotel Interamericano** (P.O. Box 95-7150 Turrialba, tel. 506/556-0142, fax 506/556-7790, hotelint@racsa.co.cr, www.hotelinteramericano.com, $10 pp shared bath; $11 pp private bath), beloved of budget travelers, offers 22 clean rooms with cable TV and hot water. It offers Internet access and laundry, plus a small bar and a cafeteria serving breakfast. Kayakers and rafters congregate here.

The **Hotel La Roche** (Calle 4, Avenidas Central/1, no tel.), with a tidy restaurant and TV downstairs, has five basic rooms with shared bath with cold water for $6 s/d. The **Hotel La Roche Anexo** (tel. 506/556-7915), at the north end of Calle 3, is better, with 11 simple yet clean and spacious, albeit meagerly furnished rooms with private bath (no hot water) for $10 s/d. Noise from the bar/disco could be a serious problem, and at last visit river erosion was eating furiously at the nearby riverbank.

The **Wittingham Hotel** (tel. 506/556-8822, $7 s/d shared bath, $9 s/d private bath), opposite

La Roche, has seven clean rooms with TVs, fans, and hot water.

The **Hotel Alcazar** (Calle 3, Avenidas 2/4, tel. 506/556-7397, $12.50 pp) has seven small, simply furnished rooms with wooden floors, fans, cable TV, homey decor, plus tiny private bath and hot water. It has a colorful and noisy bar/restaurant to the rear.

The rambling **Hotel Kardy** (Calle 4, tel. 506/556-0050, hotelkardy@hotmail.com, $20 pp) offers two dorms plus 13 simply furnished, carpeted rooms with cable TV and fans. Rooms to the fore are airy and get heaps of light (as well as street noise); interior rooms are somewhat gloomy but have natural stone walls and are clean. No two rooms are the same. It has a pool table. Rates include breakfast.

$25–50: The pleasant **Hotel Wagelia** (Apdo. 99-1750 Turrialba, tel. 506/556-1566, fax 506/556-1596, hotelwagelia@racsa.co.cr, $41 s, $53 d), on Avenida 4, is the only class act in town. It has 18 well-lit, modestly decorated rooms with a/c, TVs, telephones, and private baths. They surround a lush courtyard. The hotel offers tours locally. The restaurant is one of Turrialba's best. Rates include breakfast and tax.

Outside town, the **Hotel Montaña Valle Verde** (tel. 506/556-4111, fax 506/557-2039, valleverdehotel@hotmail.com, $20 s, $25 d), on the mountainside two km west of Turrialba, offers 25 simply furnished rooms in a rustic log and stone lodge, each having stone floors, local TV, and stone showers with hot water. Local fare is served in the glass-enclosed restaurant with magnificent views. Rates include breakfast.

Food

Café Gourmet (tel. 506/556-9689, 6:30 A.M.–7 p.m. Mon.–Sat. and occasionally on Sundays), opposite the Hotel Wagelia, is a delightful option for pancakes ($1.50), *gallo pinto* breakfasts ($1.50), sandwiches, cheesecakes, and cappuccino, espresso, and teas.

Fancy pizza? Try **Popo's Pizza** (tel. 506/556-0064, 7 A.M.–11 p.m. Mon.–Sat., 11 A.M.–11 p.m. Sunday), on the east side of the plaza; or **Pizzería Julian** (tel. 506/556-1155), on the north side of the plaza.

There are several Chinese options. Try **Restaurante Tico Chino** (Calle 3, Avenidas Central/2, tel. 506/556-1793, 11 A.M.–11 p.m. Wed.–Mon.), a no-frills *soda* serving set lunches for below $2.

You can buy baked goods at **Musmanni,** at Calle 2, Avenida 2; or at **Panadería Merayo,** 50 meters north (5:30 A.M.–7 p.m. daily).

Information and Services

There are three banks on Avenida Central.

The **post office** is on Calle Central, Avenida 8. You can make international calls from the **ICE** office at the west end of Avenida Central.

The **Café Net Turrialba** (Avenida Central, Calles 1/3) charges $1.60 per hour for Internet access; 9 A.M.–10 p.m. Mon.–Fri., 9 A.M.–8 p.m. Saturday, and 10 A.M.–4 p.m. Sunday.

The **Hospital William Allen** (tel. 506/556-4343 or 506/556-1211) is on the west side of town. There's a **medical center** (tel. 506/556-0923) and clinical laboratory (tel. 506/556-1516) on Calle 3; open 7 A.M.–noon and 2–6 P.M.

Criminal investigation is handled by the OIJ (tel. 506/556-1573).

Getting There

Buses depart San José from Calle 13, Avenidas 6/8, hourly, 5 A.M.–10 p.m. via Cartago. Buses depart Cartago for Turrialba from Avenida 3, Calle 4. In Turrialba, buses (tel. 506/591-4145) for San José depart hourly from Avenida 4, Calle 2. Buses for Guayabo and Tuís leave from Calle 2, Avenidas 2/4.

Taxis congregate around the square.

⊠ GUAYABO NATIONAL MONUMENT

Monumento Nacional Guayabo (public phone, tel. 506/559-0099, 8 A.M.–3:30 p.m., $6 admission), on the southern flank of Volcán Turrialba, 19 km north of Turrialba, is the nation's only archaeological site of any significance. Don't expect anything of the scale or scope of the Mayan and Aztec ruins of Guatemala, Honduras,

© CHRISTOPHER P. BAKER

Pre-Columbian settlement, Guayabo National Monument

Mexico, or Belize. The society that lived here between 1000 B.C. AND a.d. 1400, when the town was mysteriously abandoned, was far less culturally advanced than its northern neighbors. No record exists of the Spanish having known of Guayabo. In fact, the site lay uncharted until re-discovered in the late 19th century. Systematic ex-cavations—still under way—were begun in 1968.

The 218-hectare monument encompasses a significant area of tropical wet forest on valley slopes surrounding the archaeological site. Trails lead to a lookout point, where you can surmise the layout of the pre-Columbian village, built between two rivers. To the south, a wide cob-bled pavement—most of it still hidden in the jungle—leads past ancient stone entrance gates and up a slight gradient to the village center, which at its peak housed an estimated 1,000 people. The cobbled pavement *(calzada)*, which is lined with impatiens, is in perfect alignment with the cone of Volcán Turrialba. It is being re-laid in its original form.

Conical bamboo living structures were built on large circular stone mounds *(montúculos)*, with paved pathways between them leading down to aqueducts—still working after 2,000 years—and a large water tank with an overflow so that the water was constantly replenished. About four hectares have been excavated and are open to the public via the Mound Viewing Trail. Note the monolithic rock carved with petroglyphs of an al-ligator and a jaguar.

The **ranger booth** sells maps and a self-guided pamphlet. Opposite the booth are the park ad-ministration office (tel./fax 506/556-9507, www.minae.go.cr/accvc), a picnic and camping area with shelters, an exhibition and projection hall, a miniature model of the site, plus a hut with pre-Columbian finds. Many of the artifacts unearthed here are on display at the National Museum in San José.

Accommodations and Food

The ranger station offers eight campsites with shelters ($2 pp), plus access to flush toilets, cold-water showers, and barbecue pits.

Albergue La Calzada (Apdo. 260, Turrialba 7150, tel. 506/559-0023, $10 s, $13 d), a Swiss-style lodge about 500 meters below the park en-trance, has four rooms, each with a table and twin beds. Private bathrooms were to be added. The lodge hints of the Alps and is surrounded by trickling water. Its rustic roadside restaurant serves *típico* meals, plus salads, and omelettes, and trout freshly caught from the on-site lake. The friendly owner, José Miguel, offers tours. José will meet the bus if you call ahead. Reserva-tions are required.

Getting There

Buses depart Turrialba for Guayabo village from Avenida 4, Calle 2 (from 100 meters south of the main bus terminal), Mon.–Sat. at 11 A.M. and 5:15 P.M. and Sunday at 9 A.M. Return buses depart Guayabo Mon.–Sat. at 12:30 and 5:30 P.M. and return at 4 P.M. (5 p.m. on Sun-day). You'll need to overnight if you take the 5:15 P.M. bus from Turrialba. A taxi from Turri-alba will cost about $30 round-trip.

The paved road from Turrialba deteriorates to a rough dirt and rock path about four km below Guayabo. You can approach Guayabo from the northwest, via Santa Cruz (see below); it's about 10 km by rough dirt road and is signed.

TURRIALBA VOLCANO NATIONAL PARK

Volcán Turrialba (3,329 meters), the country's most easterly volcano, was very active during the 19th century but has slumbered peacefully since. In 2001, it showed signs of activity after 135 years of dormancy. It can be very cold and rainy up here—bring sweaters and raingear.

A rough road for four-wheel drive vehicles only—first gear in places—winds north from **Santa Cruz,** about 12 km north of the town of Turrialba, to Bar Canada (three km), where a sign next to the bar marks the beginning of the trail. It's a scenically beautiful, hour-long ascent that deteriorates all the way and is brutal for the last three km.

You can also hike from the hamlet of **Santa Teresa,** reached by direct bus or car from Cartago via Pacayas, on the southwestern slope (this route is far easier than that from Santa

Cruz). The trail climbs through cloud forest to the summit, which features three craters, a *mirador* (lookout point), and guard house topped by an antenna. A trail at the summit leads to the crater floor; another circumnavigates the crater (there are active fumaroles on the western side).

Accommodations and Food

Volcán Turrialba Lodge (Apdo. 1632, San José 2050, tel. 506/273-4335, fax 506/273-0703, info@volcanturrialbalodge.com, www.volcanturrialbalodge.com, $45 pp) is set magnificently in the saddle between Irazú and Turrialba Volcanoes at 2,800 meters elevation, about three km north of Esperanza and eight km northwest of Santa Cruz. The rustic lodge—built from an old milking shed on a working farm—has 18 no-frills rooms with private baths. Meals are cooked over a wood fire and served in a cozy lounge heated by a woodstove. Guided hikes and horseback rides are offered, or you can choose a mountain bike or ox-drawn cart for exploration. Rates include all meals and taxes.

Guayabo Lodge (tel. 506/556-1628 or 506/538-8492, reservaciones@guayabolodge.com, www.guayabolodge.com, $50 s, $60 d), 400 meters west of Santa Cruz on the grounds of Finca Blanco y Negro, enjoys a hillside setting overlooking the valley toward the Talamancas. This modern two-story structure has 12 uniquely decorated rooms with parquet floors and delightful decor that includes wrought-iron beds. When not exploring the 80-hectare *finca,* settle yourself in a hammock on the patio and enjoy the superb views down across to the Cordillera Talamanca. The *finca* has its own dairy and cheese factory.

There's a basic campsite at the summit: **Cabañas Bajo Volcán Turrialba** (tel. 506/538-8513 or 506/360-1043) is at 2,350 m, accessed by four-wheel drive from the east side of Santa Cruz; it's 20 km to the cabins. Not reviewed.

Restaurante Las Tucanes (tel. 506/538-8872), 100 meters west of Guayabo Lodge, is a rustic yet appealing wayside stop with valley views. It serves *típico* dishes and has kids' swings.

Getting There

Buses depart Cartago for Pacayas and Santa Cruz from south of Las Ruinas, and from the bus center at Calle 2, Avenidas 2/4, in Turrialba. You can take a jeep-taxi from Santa Cruz or Pacayas.

TURRIALTICO TO SIQUIRRES

East of Turrialba, Hwy. 10 continues past CATIE two km to a Y-junction: the main highway descends to Siquirres and the Caribbean after switchbacking steeply uphill to tiny **Turrialtico,** eight km east of Turrialba. There's nothing of note here, but the views toward Volcán Turrialba and the Talamancas are superb.

Parque Viborana (tel. 506/538-1510, 8 A.M.–5 p.m. daily, $5 admission) is a serpentarium near Pavones, beyond Turrialtico. About 100 snakes are displayed in cages. You can even enter the large boa pit. It's quite safe (boas are nonvenomous), but be warned: the females won't take kindly to it, and their kettle-like hiss can be very frightening. Your visit begins in the open-air lecture room. Trails laced with plastic snakes lead into the forest. The admission includes an introductory lesson and a photo op with snakes.

Hernán García (tel. 506/384-6608) has a private institution at **Chitaria** where he breeds toucans, macaws, and other endangered birds under MINAE license. You can arrange visits through Turrialtico Lodge, by appointment.

Accommodations and Food

Turrialtico Mountain Lodge & Restaurant (Apdo. 121-7150, Turrialba, tel. 506/538-1111, fax 506/538-1575, info@turrialtico.com, www.turrialtico.com, $40 s, $45 d low season; $45 s, $50 d high season) is a pleasant option amid landscaped grounds with views over the Reventazón Valley. The 14 rustic and basically furnished rooms are atmospheric (but have "yucky" beds, according to one reader) and have private baths with hot water. The rustic yet handsome restaurant with large-screen TV offers seafood (like sea bass in garlic, $11), tenderloin ($8.50), and local fare, enjoyed at tables made from Sarchí oxcart wheels; open 7 A.M.–10 p.m. daily. Rates include breakfast and taxes.

Central Highlands

Another kilometer brings you to the **Pochotel Hotel/Restaurant** (P.O. Box 333-7150 Turrialba, tel. 506/538-1010, fax 506/538-1212, pochotel@hotmail.com, $31 s/d). A dirt road climbs steeply one km to a rustic restaurant with wide-open vistas and a second, plainer restaurant that compensates with a *mirador* from which to admire the magnificent views. The 11 cabins, each of a different size, have private baths with hot water. A reader describes them as "freezing" and "very drafty." Two newer cabins—#5 and #6—have splendid views through picture windows. The restaurant is open 7 A.M.–10 p.m. daily.

Getting There
Buses for Siquirres depart Turrialba from Avenida 4, Calle 2; ask to be let off at Turrialtico.

TURRIALBA TO CHIRRIPÓ INDIAN RESERVE
The branch road off Hwy. 10 two km east of CATIE leads to the valleys of the Río Atirro and Río Tuis.

Hacienda Atirro dominates the flatlands of the Reventazón and Atirro Rivers south of Turrialba. It is planted in sugarcane, macadamia nuts, and coffee, and is home to the acclaimed **Hotel Casa Turire,** where you can join tours and dine even if you aren't an overnight guest. A plantation tour ($20) includes a visit to the coffee mill, sugar mill (in season), and macadamia processing plant; choose either car or horseback. Much of the plantation has been flooded by the Proyecto Hidroelectrico Angostura to form Lake Angostura. Watersports are available, although the lake has become choked with water hyacinth.

Continuing east through the valley of the Río Tuis via the tiny communities of Tuis, Bajo Pacuare, and Hacienda Grano de Oro, you find yourself in an alpine plateau not unlike parts of Colorado—fabulous! You'll need four-wheel drive. A few km beyond, about 30 km east of Hwy. 10, the dirt road passes through the off-the-beaten-track hamlet of **Moravia del Chirripó** and peters out at **Hacienda Moravia,** from where trails filter into the foothills of the Cordillera Ta-

lamanca. Moravia is the gateway to the **Reserva Indígena Chirripó,** a remote Indian reserve that receives few visitors. The drive to Moravia is fabulously scenic. The Indian presence is strong, in local faces and in bright traditional garb.

You may be able to hire guides in Moravia for excursions into the Talamancas and **La Amistad International Peace Park** (see the *South Central Costa Rica* chapter). Evangelicals are particularly strong in this part of the world and even have a camp, **Campamento La Honduras** (tel. 506/556-0701), hidden deep in the valley of the Río Pacuare, 20 km along a dirt and rock road (the turnoff is 0.5 km east of Tuis).

Río Pacuare
Bajo Pacuare is a traditional starting point for whitewater rafting trips on the Río Pacuare, a thrilling river that plunges through remote canyons and rates as a classic whitewater run. Trips typically cost about $95 (one day) to $250 (two days) and $305 (three days).

Sports and Recreation
Lago Tours (tel. 506/556-4477), on the north side of Lago Angostura, offers boat trips ($12.50 for up to six people), banana boat rides ($3.50 for 20 minutes), aquabikes ($3.50 per hour), jet-ski ($45 per hour), kayaks ($3.50 per hour), and horseback rides ($5). Personally I find the notion of jet-skis appalling in such a peaceful setting! It has a pleasant, breeze-swept restaurant serving Colombian specialties (such as tongue in salsa) plus burgers and sandwiches; open 9 A.M.–6 p.m. Sun.–Tue., 9 A.M.–10 p.m. Wed.–Sat.

Nearby, **Paradero Turístico San Buenaventura,** a lakeside entertainment facility, has go-karts and basketball; 9 A.M.–5 p.m. daily.

Accommodations and Food
Rancho Naturalista (Apdo. 364, San José 1002, tel. 506/297-4134, fax 506/297-4135, johnerb @racsa.co.cr, www.ranchonaturalista.com; in the U.S., SJO 1425, P.O. Box 025316, Miami, FL 33102, tel. 888/246-8513; $135 pp), one km beyond Tuís and also known as Albergue de Montaña, is a rustically elegant hilltop hacienda-lodge owned by American evangelists Kathleen

and John Erb. It sits on a 50-hectare ranch surrounded by premontane rainforest at 900 meters' elevation at the end of a steep dirt-and-rock road. The mountain retreat is popular with nature and bird-watching groups (more than 410 bird species have been recorded by guests). Six spacious rooms have heaps of light (three have private baths). Upstairs rooms open through French doors onto a veranda with sweeping views. One room has a canopy bed and a bathroom large enough to wash a Boeing 747. The upstairs also has a lounge with library. Outside are six newer cabins with hammocks on the verandas, plus a two-bedroom *casa* with a lounge with plump sofas and massive walk-in shower with hot water, plus full kitchen. Down comforters are provided. Decor is of hardwoods, with beamed ceilings. Horseback riding is included. The ranch has an extensive trail system. Rates include three meals, guided hikes, and horseback riding.

Aventuras Naturales (tel. 506/225-3939 or 800/514-0411, avenat@racsa.co.cr, www.adventure costarica.com); **Costa Rica Expeditions** (tel. 506/257-0766, fax 506/257-1665, costaric @expeditions.co.cr, www.costaricaexpeditions .com); and **Ríos Tropicales Lodge** (tel. 506/233-6455, fax 506/255-4354, info@riostropicales .com, www.riostropicales.com) each maintain lodges in the Pacuare Canyon. You have to be a participant on the companies' river trips to stay here.

Albergue Hacienda Moravia (tel. 506/383-5868 or 506/257-4214, cabecar@racsa.co.cr) is a rustic Colorado-style log lodge in a Shangri-la of a setting. From its hilltop advantage, it boasts fantastic views across a green vale. It has 10 dorm-style rooms: six downstairs rooms have private baths; four upstairs rooms share baths with hot water. All rooms have roughhewn bunks with blankets. Local Indians put on traditional shows for groups. The hacienda is a working cattle farm. Call for rates.

The most outstanding hotel for miles is **Hotel Casa Turire** (P.O. Box 303-7150 Turrialba, tel. 506/531-1111, fax 506/531-1075, turire@racsa.co.cr, www.hotelcasaturire.com, $120 s/d standard, $140 junior superior, $150 junior suite, $220 master suite low season; $136/ 157/170/250 high season), on the south shore of Lake Angostura, about 15 km southeast of Turrialba. Quiet, relaxing, and romantic, this classical-style hotel is justifiably a member of the Small

Central Highlands

Hotel Casa Turire

Distinctive Hotels of Costa Rica. *Hideaways Reports* agreed: it has named Casa Turire a "Country House Hotel of the Year" worldwide. A wide wraparound veranda supported by eucalyptus columns opens onto manicured lawns and a small figure-eight pool and sunning deck. You sense the sublime the moment you arrive via a long palm-lined driveway and enter the atrium lobby of the modern plantation home, with its colonial-tiled floors, Roman pillars, and sumptuous leather sofas and chairs. The 12 spacious, lofty-ceilinged rooms have TVs and direct-dial telephones, comfortable mattresses, and sleek tiled bathrooms. Four suites have French doors opening onto private verandas, and the master suite has a Jacuzzi. The dining room proffers artistic food,

while an intimate bar has Edwardian hints. A gift store sells quality jewelry and artifacts. Mountain bikes and watercraft are available, and tours and excursions are offered. At last visit it had acquired new owners with plans to add a spa, plus bungalows, an eco-farm, mini-golf, and a stable. This is also the place to treat yourself to a meal: Culinary treats include fresh homemade bread, spicy *gallo pinto,* grilled sandwiches, and sublime coffee from the estate, plus exquisite desserts such as strawberry chantilly. The prices are fair, and the setting is handsome.

Getting There

Buses for Tuís depart from the bus center at Calle 2, Avenida 2/4, in Turrialba.

The Caribbean Coast

Costa Rica's Caribbean coast extends some 200 km south—from Nicaragua to Panamá. The zone—wholly within Limón Province—is divided into two distinct regions.

North of Puerto Limón, the port city midway down the coast, is a long, straight coastal strip backed by a broad alluvial plain cut through by the Tortuguero Canals, an inland waterway that parallels the coast all the way to the Nicaraguan border. Crocodiles, caimans, monkeys, sloths, and exotic birds can be seen from the tour boats that carry passengers through the jungle-lined canals and freshwater lagoons culminating in Tortuguero National Park and Barra del Colorado National Wildlife Refuge. A few roads have penetrated to the northern frontier

Must-Sees

M Tortuguero National Park: Wildlife galore awaits in this watery world where everyone gets around by boat. The beach is a prime nesting site for marine turtles; the national park is absolute tops for birding and animal viewing; and the village is a funky charmer (page 202).

M Barra del Colorado National Wildlife Refuge: The big one that didn't get away awaits you at this prime sportfishing spot near the Nicaraguan border. Several sportfishing lodges cater to anglers keen to tackle prize tarpon and snook (page 211).

M Aviarios del Caribe Sloth Refuge: Sloths are the prime draw, but this small refuge also has nature trails, plus canoe trips into an estuary abounding with wildlife (page 214).

M Cahuita: Popular with the offbeat crowd, this small village has heaps of character. Several eateries serve spicy local cuisine, and Cahuita National Park offers great beaches, diverse wildlife, and a small coral reef (page 217).

© CHRISTOPHER P. BAKER

Puerto Viejo

M Puerto Viejo: Drawing surfers and latter-day hippies, this somnolent village has tremendous budget accommodations. Activities include horseback riding and hikes to indigenous villages, and beautiful beaches ease south for miles (page 227).

M Gandoca-Manzanillo Refuge: This reserve spans several ecosystems teeming with animal life, from crocodiles to monkeys and manatees. Turtles also come ashore to lay eggs (page 243).

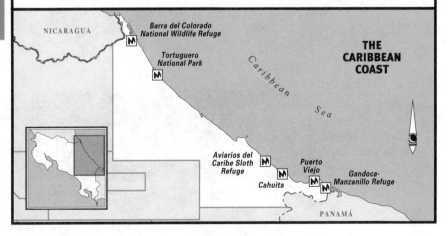

far inland of the coast, but they are often impassable except for brief periods in the dry season. For locals, motorized canoes *(cayucos* or *canoas)* and outpost traders resembling the *African Queen* are the main means of getting about the swampy waterways that meander through the dense, mostly uninhabited jungles.

South of Puerto Limón is the Talamanca coast, a narrow coastal plain broken by occasional headlands and coral reefs and backed by the looming Cordillera Talamanca (a Miskito word meaning "place of blood," referring to the seasonal slaughter of turtles). A succession of sandy shores leads the eye toward Panamá. The beaches are popular with surfers and offbeat adventurers.

The coast is sparsely settled, with tiny villages spaced far apart. Except for the coastal town of Puerto Limón, what few villages lie along the coast are ramshackle, browbeaten by tropical storms and the curse of an ailing economy recently given a boost by the tourism boom. Life along the Caribbean coast of Costa Rica is fundamentally different than in the rest of the country—it's perceived as altogether too melancholy to take seriously. Life is lived at an easy pace. It may take you a few days to get in the groove. Don't expect things to happen at the snap of your fingers.

The black *costeños* (coast dwellers), who form approximately one-third of Limón Province's population of 220,000, have little in common with the *sponyamon*—the "Spaniard man," or highland mestizo, who represents the conservative Latin American culture. More than anywhere else in Costa Rica, the peoples of the Caribbean coast reflect a mingling of races and cultures. There are Creoles of mixed African and European descent; black Caribs, whose ancestors were African and Caribbean Indian; mestizos, of mixed Spanish and Amerindian blood; more Chinese than one might expect in Limón; and, living in the foothills of the Talamancas, approximately 5,000 Bribrí and Cabecar indigenous peoples. In the north, Tortuguero and Barra del Colorado have many mixed-blooded people of Nicaraguan descent.

The early settlers of the coast were British pirates, smugglers, logcutters, and their slaves who brought their own Caribbean dialects with words that are still used today. During the late 19th century, increasing numbers of English-speaking Afro-Caribbean families—predominantly from Jamaica—came to build and work the Atlantic Railroad and banana plantations, eventually settling and infusing the local dialect with lilting parochial patois phrases familiar to travelers in the West Indies. Afro-Caribbean influences are also notable in the regional cuisine.

Until recently, most of the people lived a subsistence life of farming and fishing as past generations had done. Before the growth of tourism, 95 percent of the area's income was derived from farming and fishing. A few farmers still grow cacao; the coconut palm, too, is the "tree of life." Sweet and juicy citrus fruits fill the gardens, lobsters are plentiful, and large, tasty shrimp live in the rivers that rush down from the mountains.

West Indian life might be typified by the Rastafarians—specialists in coolness, composure, and witty repartee—one meets in Cahuita and Puerto Viejo. Where most Costa Ricans are reticent, many among the young males here are sullen, lackadaisical, even antagonistic (some young black men seem to harbor a resentment of white tourists). But most of the population have hearts of gold, and there's a strong, mutually supportive community that tourists may not easily see: when a local has a need, such as medical care, locals often club together to pay the bills. (Paula Palmer's *What Happen: A Folk History of Costa Rica's Talamanca Coast* and *Wa'apin Man* provide insight into the traditional Creole culture of the area.)

The Caribbean coast is generally hot and exceedingly wet (averaging 300–500 cm annually). Fortunately, light breezes blow consistently year-round. The region has no real dry season, and endures a "wet season" in which the rainfall can exceed 100 cm per month. Rains peak May–Aug. and again Dec.–Jan., when sudden storms blow in, bowing down the coconut palms and deluging the Talamancas. Puerto Limón's two distinct dry periods (Feb.–March and Sept.–Oct.) are shorter than those farther north, where the dry seasons can last into May and November. Whereas Tortuguero has shorter rainy seasons, it receives considerably more rain during the rainiest months: an average of 61 cm in January and 97 cm in July (by contrast, Puerto Limón's peak month is December, which averages 46 cm).

Although hurricanes may form in the Caribbean during late summer and fall, only one hurricane—Martha, which rushed ashore on 21 November 1969—has hit this coast during the last 100 years.

PLANNING YOUR TIME

Many are the visitors who arrive with no schedule, intend on kicking it until the money runs out or they otherwise get an urge to move on. This is particularly so of the funky, laid-back hamlets of **Cahuita** and **Puerto Viejo,** budget havens popular with surfers, the tie-dyed backpack set, and those seeking immersion in Creole culture. Most people stay at least a week to get in the groove and make the most of the southern Caribbean zone's many offbeat offerings, including **Cahuita National Park,** protecting a rainforest full of monkeys, as well as one of Costa Rica's few coral reefs. Surfers head to Puerto Viejo and the beaches that run south in a paternoster to the hamlet of **Manzanillo** and **Gandoca-Manzanillo Wildlife Refuge.**

You'll want to take horseback rides along the beach and/or a "dolphin safari" into Gandoca-Manzanillo, while experienced surfers might want to check out the Hawaiian-size waves two miles off Punta Cocles. I highly recommend a call at **Aviarios del Caribe Sloth & Wildlife Refuge.** And if you don't mind roughing it, consider an excursion into the Talamancas for overnight at **Reserva Indígena Yorku.**

Further north, most travelers head to **Tortuguero** for one to three days of viewing wildlife by rented canoe or on guided boat tours offered by nature lodges. Tortuguero is famous as the most important nesting site in the western Caribbean for the Pacific green turtle, one of four species that come ashore predictably at numerous beaches up and down this shore. Anglers favor **Barra del Colorado,** acknowledged for the best tarpon and snook fishing in the

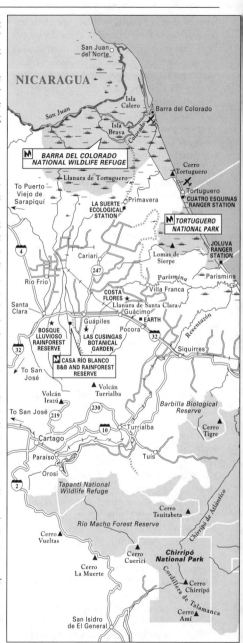

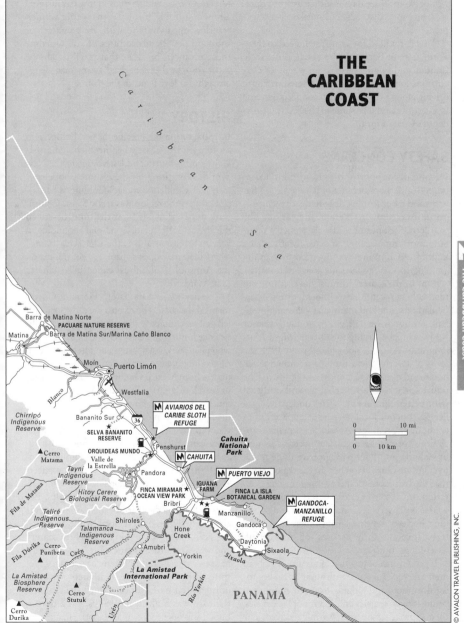

THE
**CARIBBEAN
COAST**

Caribbean

Sea

Barra de Matina Norte
PACUARE NATURE RESERVE
Matina   Barra de Matina Sur/Marina Caño Blanco

Moín   Puerto Limón

Westfalia

Blanco

Chirripó
Indigenous
Reserve   Bananito Sur

★ **SELVA BANANITO
RESERVE**

ORQUIDEAS MUNDO
Valle de   Penshurst
▲ Cerro   la Estrella
Matama   Pandora
Tayní
Indigenous
Reserve
Hitoy Cerere
Biological Reserve   **FINCA MIRAMAR
OCEAN VIEW PARK** ★
Teliré   Bribrí
Indigenous
Reserve   Shiroles
Talamanca
Fila de Matama   Indigenous
Reserve
▲ Cerro   Hone
Fila Dúrika   Punibeta   Creek
Coén   Amubri   ★ Yorkin
▲ Cerro
La Amistad   Stutuk   Río Yorkin
Biosphere
Reserve
▲
Cerro
Durika   Utén

🅼 *AVIARIOS DEL
CARIBE SLOTH
REFUGE*

**Cahuita
National
Park**

🅼 *CAHUITA*

🅼 *PUERTO VIEJO*

**IGUANA
FARM**

**FINCA LA ISLA
BOTANICAL GARDEN**

★★   🅼 *GANDOCA-
MANZANILLO
REFUGE*

Manzanillo

Gandoca

Daytonia

Sixaola

Sixaola

**La Amistad
International Park**

PANAMÁ

0 _____ 10 mi
0 _____ 10 km

The Caribbean Coast

© AVALON TRAVEL PUBLISHING, INC.

world; two or three days is sufficient. Tour operators and specialist lodges can make all arrangements.

There's no need for a car. You'll need to fly to Tortuguero or Barra, or take a boat. Buses serve Cahuita and Puerto Viejo, from where tour excursions to sites of interest are offered. If you're driving along Hwy. 32, which connects San José to Puerto Limón, take time to check out the gardens at **Costa Flora.**

SAFETY CONCERNS

Despite new opportunities from the tourism boom (or perhaps because of it), the region has witnessed a burgeoning drug trade, drawing opportunists from elsewhere in the nation. The southern Caribbean has also developed a reputation for crime against tourists. (Many young males from Limón have migrated to Cahuita and Puerto Viejo to take advantage of tourists.)

On both scores, things have improved markedly in recent years, although drugs—particularly cocaine and marijuana—are still prevalent. (You may be pestered by young Rastas or Rasta-wannabes trying to sell you drugs.) Most long-term residents don't like this; in 1998 the folks of Puerto Viejo torched a known crack house and chased the culprits out of town. The police force has been beefed up and outfitted with better equipment. Many undercover policemen operate locally—part of a new effort to eradicate the scourge. And local residents' associations formed by expatriate business owners in Cahuita and Puerto Viejo have done much to eradicate crime. Hoteliers in the region claim that the bad reputation is all a sad misrepresentation, but I keep getting letters from readers who've been victims. Don't let this put you off visiting, however—the negativity is more than counterbalanced by the scores of wonderful, welcoming souls.

It's also worth noting that local Afro-Caribbean men are very forward with their advances toward women, and judging from the number of young foreign females on the arms of local males, their approaches are often warmly received. The "rent-a-Rasta" syndrome engendered by these foreign women with gigolos in tow has inspired a reputation for "free love" that other women travelers must contend with. Be prepared for subtle to persistent overtures. If you welcome these advances, be aware that you'll usually be expected to be the moneybags. Many men charge outright for love beneath the palms.

HISTORY

In 1502, Columbus became the first European to set foot on this coast when he anchored at Isla Uvita on his fourth and last voyage to the New World. Navigating off these shores, hopelessly lost, half a millennium ago, Columbus had assumed that the region was really Siam. Columbus's son Ferdinand, 14 at the time, described the area as "lofty, full of rivers, and abounding in very tall trees, as also is the islet [Uva Island] where they grew thick as basil. . . . For this reason the Admiral [Columbus] called it La Huerta [The Garden]."

Twenty-two years later, Hernán Cortés mapped the coast. The records the early Spaniards left tell of contact with indigenous tribes: subsistence hunters and farmers, and skilled seamen who plied the coastal waters and interior rivers in carved longboats (Cortés even mentioned Aztec traders from Mexico visiting northern Costa Rica in search of gold). The indigenous culture was quickly decimated, however, for this was part of the Spanish Main of the conquistadors. Later it was also the haunt of rumrunners, gunrunners, mahogany cutters, and pirates, mostly British, attracted by the vast riches flowing through colonial Central America. Between raids, buccaneers anchored along the wild shorelines, where they allied themselves with local native peoples. Because of them, the Caribbean coast was never effectively settled or developed by the Spanish.

Cacao was grown here in the late 17th century and was Costa Rica's first export, an activity financed by well-to-do citizens of Cartago. Despite this, the region remained virtually uninhabited by Europeans until the Atlantic Railroad was built in the 1880s and a port at Limón was opened for coffee export. Jamaican laborers were brought in in significant numbers.

In 1882, the government began to offer land grants to encourage migration and cultivation of bananas. Plantations evolved and prospered until the 1930s, when they were hit by disease. With the demise of the banana industry, the region went into decline. During the 1960s, plantations were revived using more advanced technologies, and the industry now dominates the region's economy again. The government has assisted these efforts with new infrastructure and services, resulting in a rapid population increase.

Today, the port of Puerto Limón, along with its sister port of Moín, is the chief driving force of the urban economy. Beyond the city's hinterland, most people make their living from farming or as plantation laborers, and there are few and only small industries: sawmills, potteries, cabinetmakers, bakeries. Small-scale fishermen eke out a living from the sea, and families cling to a precarious living growing cacao (in 1979 the *Monilia* fungus wiped out most of the commercial crop), whose plump, bobbinlike pods are everywhere in the region. Increasingly, however, locals are being drawn into the tourism industry as guides and hotel workers.

Attempts to license exploration for petroleum off the Caribbean coast initiated by the ángel Rodríguez administration foundered in 2000 following concerted opposition from the locals.

Highway 32 to Puerto Limón

Highway 32 (the Guápiles Highway) connects San José with the Caribbean and runs east-west 104 km from the foot of the Cordillera Central to Puerto Limón. Drive carefully: the heavily trafficked Hwy. 32 coils steeply down the mountains and is often fog-bound, landslides are frequent, and Costa Rican drivers can be exceedingly reckless—all of which makes for a white-knuckle drive. Early morning is best, before the cloud and rains develop in earnest.

The road spills onto the northern lowlands at **Santa Clara,** where there's a gas station at the junction with Hwy. 4 and the northern lowlands. Hwy. 32 continues east along the base of the Cordillera Central and Talamanca Mountains. Afro-Caribbean people begin to appear with greater frequency, letting you know you are now in the Caribbean proper.

There are dozens of eateries along the highway; most close on Mondays.

GUÁPILES

The town of Guápiles, 14 km east of Santa Clara, is a center for the Río Frío banana region that spreads for miles to the north. There is no reason to visit.

The **Tropical Magic Forest** (tel. 506/392-2088, gmtours@racsa.co.cr, 9 A.M.–4 P.M.) offers a canopy tour using rappelling gear. The turnoff from Hwy. 32 is at the Restaurante Río Dante (see *Food,* below); 4WD is recommended for the 3.5-km dirt road.

To learn about poison-arrow frogs, check out the **Tropical Frog Garden** (tel. 506/710-8347), next to Roberto's Restaurant, about four km east of the Rainforest Aerial Tram. The **Río Danta Private Reserve,** a 24-acre reserve five km west of Guápiles, is another good place to spot poison-arrow frogs.

Artist Patricia Erickson (tel./fax 506/710-2264, brieri99@yahoo.com) welcomes visitors to her studio and gallery in her home on the banks of the Río Blanco, six km west of town. Her vibrant paintings dance with brilliant Caribbean colors, may of them portraying her trademark faceless Limonense women of color with floating limbs. Her husband, Brian, makes bamboo furniture and has a tropical garden.

Las Cusingas Botanical Garden (Las Cusingas Jardín Botánico, tel. 506/382-5805 or 506/710-0114, $5 admission), two km east of Guápiles and four km south by dirt road (the turn is at Soda Buenos Aires; 4WD recommended), undertakes research and raises ornamentals, medicinal plants, and fruit trees, and serves to educate visitors about tropical ecology and environmental awareness. Trails lead into tropical forest. Horseback rides are offered. Birding is excellent. Guided two-hour tours ($5) are given.

La Suerte Biological Field Station Lodge

This privately owned research and educational center (tel. 506/710-8005, info@lasuerte.org, www.lasuerte.org), at La Primavera, on the banks of the Río Suerte, near the southwestern border of Barra del Colorado and 20 km inland from Tortuguero National Park, has 10 km of rainforest trails open to ecotourists ($8 pp day visit, including lunch). It teaches workshops in tropical ecology, from primate behavior to herpetology. It has rustic accommodations with screened windows and bathrooms with hot water ($5 pp bunk, $10 pp private rooms). Meals are served family style. A bus leaves Cariari, 15 km north of Guápiles, daily at 6:30 A.M. and 10:30 A.M.

Accommodations and Food

West of Guápiles, the new **Hotel y Cabinas Lomas del Toro** (tel./fax 506/710-2934, $9 s/d cold water, from $12 s/d with a/c), overlooking the Río Toro Amarillo, about two km west of Guápiles, has 48 rooms with private bath. Twenty-two have cold water only and are sparsely furnished albeit clean. Air-conditioned rooms contain modest furnishings. All rooms have fan and cable TV. There's a swimming pool and restaurant.

BANANAS . . . TURNING GREEN OR NOT?

In 1967, banana plantations covered some 10,000 hectares of Costa Rica. Today, almost 50,000 hectares are given to bananas. Production has fallen in recent years (2.5 million tons in 1998 to 2.14 million tons in 2002, one-third below Ecuador, the world's largest banana exporter).

Banana production is a monoculture that causes ecological damage. Banana plants deplete ground nutrients quickly, requiring heavy doses of fertilizer to maintain productivity. Eventually, the land is rendered useless for other agricultural activities. Fertilizers washed down by streams have been blamed for the profuse growth of water hyacinth and reed grasses that now clog the canals and wildfowl habitats, such as the estuary of the Río Estrella. And silt washing down from the plantations is acknowledged as the principal cause of the death of the coral reef within Cahuita National Park and, more recently, of Gandoca-Manzanillo.

insecticide bags, near Cahuita

© CHRISTOPHER P. BAKER

Bananas are also prone to disease and insect assault. Pesticides such as the nematocide DBCP (banned in the U.S. but widely used in Costa Rica) are blamed for poisoning and sterilizing plantation workers, and for major fish kills in the Tortuguero canals. Even marine turtles are threatened. Plastic bags are wrapped around the fruit stems and filled with insecticides and fungicides, which kill the fungus responsible for the black marks on skins. (Once the stems were cut, the banana companies traditionally dumped the plastic bags in streams—a few years ago you could see

I highly recommend ◼ **Casa Río Blanco B&B and Rainforest Reserve** (Apdo. 241-7210, Guápiles, tel./fax 710-4124, casarioblanca@yahoo.com, $40 s, $50 d), on the banks of the Río Blanco about two km east of the Río Costa Rica (turn right and follow the dirt road 1.5 km) and only 12 km from the Rainforest Aerial Tram. It has two pleasant rooms in the main lodge, plus four "Cabañas in the Clouds," all with private baths with hot water. The charming all-hardwood cabins perch atop the river canyon and each have one entire screened wall open to a spacious porch so that you can look directly into the rainforest canopy and see the river, bubbling away below. They're warmly decorated with Guatemalan bedspreads and pre-Colombian pot-tery, and have educational materials on local wildlife. Solar lamps mark pathways at night. The delightful owners, Donna ("Miss D") and George Hinzman, lead birding and nature hikes. It's popular with birders: motmots, aracaria, and kingfishers are common. Sloths hang about on the property. A marvelous curiosity is the collection of pickled insects, snakes, and creepy miscellany—part of what Donna calls her "Rain Forest Education Center." A Jacuzzi was planned overlooking the waterfall behind the lodge. It's a great place to relax and view wildlife. Rates include breakfast.

David and Dalia Vaughan offer four-day, three-night rainforest adventures at **La Danta Salvaje** (tel./fax 506/750-0012, ladanta@racsa.co.cr), a

them washed up at flood levels on tree branches throughout the lowlands—to be washed out to sea, where turtles mistook them for jellyfish, ate them, and suffocated.)

Campaigns by local pressure groups and the threat of international boycotts have sparked a new awareness among the banana companies. The plastic bags are now recycled (for every ton of bananas, 2.14 tons of waste is produced). A project called Banana Amigo recommends management guidelines. Companies that follow the guidelines are awarded an Eco-OK seal of approval to help them export bananas; companies continuing to clear forests are not. The Eco-OK program is a joint project of the Costa Rican environmental group Fundación Ambio and the international Rainforest Alliance. The government-backed National Banana Corporation (CORBANA) has mounted a campaign to prove that it is cleaning up its act. The banana industry, it claims, is turning green.

Green or not, massive tracts of virgin forest continue to be put to the blade to meet the expansion of banana plantations. Banana producers assert that the industry provides badly needed jobs. Environmentalists claim that devastating environmental effects are not worth the trade-off for a product for which demand is so fickle. The multinational corporations, too, are hardly known for philanthropy. Workers' unions, for example, have historically been pushed out of the banana fields. Some banana companies have been accused of operating plantations under virtual slave-labor conditions. The Limón government and environmentalists have also denounced British company Geest's clearcutting of forests separating Barra del Colorado and Tortuguero National Parks. The fragile region was supposedly protected by a management plan, but the Calderón administration sided with the *bananeros,* and the Ministry of Natural Resources issued permits to Geest anyway, despite pleas from the local government of Limón—which derives its greatest source of income from bananas—to stop banana companies from clearcutting the forests of the Caribbean zone.

In 1999, the banana companies began scaling back due to overcapacity, and the first people to lose out have been the independent small-scale producers, many of them poor *campesinos,* who had been induced to clear their forests and raise bananas for sale to the big banana companies, who are no longer buying.

410-hectare private reserve bordering Braulio Carrillo. Accommodations are in a rustic yet cozy wooden lodge. It's a tough slog by 4WD, then a stiff hike to the mountainside property (helicopter transfers are also offered). It charges $210 including lodging, meals, and guided hikes.

In Guápiles, the lively **Hotel & Country Club Suerre** (P.O. Box 89-7210 Guápiles, tel. 506/710-7551, fax 506/710-6376, suerre@racsa .co.cr, www.suerre.com, $60 s, $75 d, $150 s/d junior suite), at the east end of town, is an elegant, modern hacienda-style property with 55 spacious a/c rooms appointed with hardwoods. Each has satellite TV. The hotel features an Olympic-size pool with a waterslide; tennis, basketball, and volleyball courts; a restaurant, two bars and a disco; a Jacuzzi and sauna; and a poolside café. It's popular with Tico families. Day guests can use the facilities for $2.50.

East of Guápiles, the **Jardín Botánico Las Cusingas** (see above, $30 up to four people) has a rustic two-bedroom cabin complete with a lounge, kitchen, bathroom with hot water, woodstove, and "the best cotton sheets we saw the whole trip," reports one reader (who was also "fed very inexpensively and deliciously").

The handsome **Restaurante Río Danta** (tel. 506/223-7490 or 506/223-2421, fax 506/222-5463, 11 A.M.–1 P.M.), five km west of Guápiles, serves *típico* lunches and has short trails leading into the adjacent forest (good for spotting poison-arrow frogs).

Bar Restaurant Selva Tropical, about 600 meters east of the turnoff for Guápiles, is a pleasant wayside eatery and has a butterfly garden; open daily

Getting There

Buses (tel. 506/222-0610) from San José depart the Gran Terminal del Caribe on Calle Central, Avenidas 13/15, every 30 minutes between 5 A.M. and 9 P.M. ($2.50). Buses from Puerto Limón depart hourly from Calle 2, Avenidas 1/2 ($1.50).

Buses depart Guápiles for Río Frío and Puerto Viejo de Sarapiquí daily at 4:30 A.M., 7:30 A.M., and 2 P.M.; and from Puerto Viejo de Sarapiquí

to Guápiles at 5:30 A.M., 7 A.M., noon, 1:15 P.M., 4 P.M., and 6 P.M.

GUÁCIMO

Guácimo is a small town and important truck stop about 12 km east of Guápiles and about 400 meters north of Hwy. 32. The town is about one km north of the highway; there are turnoffs two km apart, leading to the western and eastern end of town, with gas stations near each junction.

Signs point the way north to **Costa Flores** (tel. 506/716-7645, fax 506/716-6439, costaflo @sol.racsa.co.cr), a tropical flower farm said to be the largest in the world, with more than 600 varieties of plants blossoming gloriously across 120 blazingly colorful hectares. Day visitors are welcome. A restaurant sits amid beautifully laid-out pathways.

EARTH (Escuela de Agricultura de la Región Tropical Húmeda, tel. 506/713-0000, ext. 2700, www.earth.ac.cr), one km east of town, is a university that teaches agricultural techniques to students from Latin America. It specializes in researching ecologically sound, or sustainable, agriculture. EARTH has its own banana plantation and 400-hectare forest reserve with nature trails. Visitors are welcome. Costa Rica Expeditions (P.O. Box 6941-1000, San José, tel. 506/257-0766, fax 506/257-1665, costaric@expeditions .co.cr, www.costaricaexpeditions.com) offers a full-day tour.

Accommodations and Food

The nicest place is **Hotel and Restaurant Las Palmas** (P.O. Box 6944-1000 San José, tel. 506/760-0330 or 506/760-0305, fax 506/760-0296, riopalma@racsa.co.cr, $30 s, $35 d low season; $35 s, $40 d high season, $5 extra with a/c), 400 meters east of EARTH. It sits amid lush gardens shaded by tall trees on the banks of the Río Dos Novillos. The American-run hotel has 28 rustic yet cozy rooms with TVs, private baths, and hot water. There's a laundry, plus a figure-eight swimming pool. Trails lead into the nearby 200-hectare reserve, a good place to spot poison-arrow frogs.

Restaurant Las Palmas is open 6 A.M.–10:30 P.M.

Getting There

Buses for Guácimo leave San José from Gran Terminal del Caribe on Calle Central, Avenida 15/17 ($2.75), at 5:30 A.M., 7 A.M., 8:30 A.M., 10 A.M., 10:30 A.M., 11:30 A.M., 1:30 P.M., 3 P.M., and 6 P.M.

SIQUIRRES

Siquirres, 25 km east of Guácimo and 49 km west of Limón, is also a major railroad junction, echoing to the clanging of locomotives working freight for the banana companies. The tumbledown town has a **monument** to Mártires del Codo del Diablo in honor of those who lost their lives in the revolution of 1948. Otherwise, as one reader states, "Yuck! Don't bother" (with Siquirres).

The town is two km east of the Río Reventazón and one km west of the Río Pacuare. White-water rafters traditionally take out at Siquirres.

You can drive to the edge of Tortuguero (45 km) from Siquirres; the roads are signed from town.

About five km east of Siquirres, about 100 m west of the Río Pacuarito, a dirt road leads south 16 km to the remote and little-visited, 12,000-hectare **Barbilla National Park** (Parque Nacional Barbilla), on the northeast flank of the Talamanca Mountains and forming part of La Amistad Biosphere Reserve. Its creation in the face of heavy logging is a testament to the efforts of the Fundación Nairi, which has a small field station: Estación Biológica Barbilla. The park is administered by SINAC's Amistad Caribe Conservation Area office in Siquerres (tel. 506/768-5341, fax 506/768-8603, aclac@minae.go.cr, $6 admission). The ranger station at Las Brisas del Pacuarito (10 km from the highway) has restrooms and potable water.

Accommodations and Food

The **Hotel Akema** (tel. 506/768-6004, $5 pp shared bath, $15 s/d private bath), two blocks north and two east of the plaza, has 23 small and simply furnished but clean rooms with fans and shared bath with cold water. Six newer cabins to the rear have TV and private bath. There's a TV lounge and a small restaurant.

The **Complejo Turístico Pacuare** (tel. 506/768-6482, $15 s, $20 d, or $30 with a/c), east of town, has 30 clean, modern cabinas with fans and cable TVs. It has a restaurant and karaoke bar, plus a pool table.

Siquirres has plenty of basic *sodas,* including in the colorful Mercado Central.

Getting There

Buses for Siquirres leave San José from Gran Terminal del Caribe on Calle Central, Avenida 15/17, at 6:30 A.M., then hourly 8:30 A.M.–6 P.M. ($2.75). Buses from Siquirres depart hourly for Guápiles, Puerto Limón, and San José from the bus terminal on the main street, 50 meters north of the plaza. Return buses depart Siquirres for San José at the same times.

Puerto Limón and Vicinity

PUERTO LIMÓN

Puerto Limón (pop. 65,000) is an important maritime port, the only large town on the Caribbean coast and gateway to all other points. The harbor handles most of the sea trade for Costa Rica. Trucks hauling containers rumble along the main road day and night. And a new cruise port draws cruise ships. However, except for Carnival, when it gets in the groove, Puerto Limón is merely a jumping-off point for most travelers; tourist facilities are limited and there is little of interest to see.

Puerto Limón—usually referred to simply as "Limón"—has been described as a town of "sleazy charms." Until a few years ago it had more sleaze than charm. The earthquake of 22 April 1991 dealt Puerto Limón a serious blow—buckling pavements, toppling houses, and generally adding to the city's gone-to-seed appearance. But the city has come a long way since I first visited in 1992, as reflected in the razing of decrepit buildings and a sense of new-found prosperity.

Craggy Isla Uvita lies one km offshore. Columbus supposedly landed on the islet in 1502; it is now a national landmark park.

The city has a bad reputation among Ticos and is often referred to as Piedropolis (Crack City). It's true that you should beware of pickpockets by day and muggings at night, but reports of Limón's evils have been greatly inflated.

Orientation

Hwy. 32 from San José enters town from the west and becomes Avenida 1, paralleling the railway track that runs to the cruise port. The *avenidas* (east-west) are aligned north of Avenida 1 in sequential order. The *calles* (north-south) are numbered sequentially and run westward from the waterfront. The streets signs are not to be trusted. And few locals know the streets by numbers; instead they refer to landmarks and call the streets by colloquial names such as "Market Street" (Avenida 2). Most addresses and directions are given in direction and distance from the market or Parque Vargas. Most streets are one-way.

The road leading south from the junction of Avenida 1 and Calle 9 leads to Cahuita and Puerto Viejo. Avenida 6 leads out of town to Moín and the JAPDEVA dock, where boats can be hired for the trip to Tortuguero.

Sights

There's not much to hold you in town, although the **Mercado Central** (Avenidas Central/2, Calles 3/4), at the heart of town, is worth a browse. The new **Catholic church** at Calle 6, three blocks west of the *mercado,* was still in construction at last visit; it makes use of the campanile of the old cathedral, which was otherwise demolished.

Parque Vargas, at the east end of Avenidas 1 and 2, is literally an urban jungle, with palm promenades, looming hardwoods, and a tangle of vines and bromeliads centered on a crumbling bandstand. On the north side, a fading mural shows life in Limón since pre-Columbian days. A bronze bust of Christopher Columbus and his son Ferdinand, erected in 1990 for the 500th anniversary of their landing, faces the sea. On the west side of the park is the cream-colored stucco **Town Hall** (Alcadía), a fine example of tropical architecture, with open arcades, balconies, and louvered windows.

The **Museo Ethnográfico de Puerto Limón** (Museum of Ethnography, Calle 4, Avenidas 1/2, tel. 506/758-2130 or 506/758-3903, 9 A.M.–noon and 1–4 P.M. Mon.–Fri., free admission) displays artifacts, photography, and exhibits tracing the culture and history of the region. The **cemetery** spanning the road west of town contains La Colonia China, a Chinese quarter.

The **Limoncito Wildlife Refuge** extends south of town inland of the airport. There are no tourist facilities or tour options.

Entertainment and Events

The **Black Culture Festival** is hosted in September, with domino and oratory contests, music, and art. Contact the Black Star Line.

Each 12 October, Puerto Limón explodes in a bacchanal. The annual Columbus Day **Carnival** is celebrated with a fervor akin to the bump-and-grind style of Trinidad, with street bands, floats, and every ounce of Mardi Gras passion, though in a more makeshift fashion. The weeklong event attracts people from all over the country, and getting a hotel room is virtually impossible. Limonians paint their bodies from head to toe. Everything but insecticide is fermented to make napalm-strength liquor. And everyone gets down to reggae, salsa, and calypso. The celebrations include a Dance Festival—a rare opportunity to see dances from indigenous tribes, Afro-Caribbeans, and the Chinese communities—plus bands from throughout the Caribbean and Latin America, as well as beauty contests, craft stalls, fireworks, theater, and calypso contests. The seductive tempos lure you to dance, and life is reduced to a simple, joyful response to the most irresistible beat in the world. It is like the plague: you can only flee or succumb.

Most bars—of which there's no shortage—have a decidedly raffish quality, and an aura of impending violence pervades many by night. Women travelers should avoid **Bar Washington** (Calle 1, Avenida 2) and similar places for losers and boozers.

The weekend **Disco Acuario** in the Hotel Acón is jam-packed and sweaty, with a pulsing Latin beat (admission $3, including a beer; free to hotel guests). For calypso and reggae check out **Springfield,** on the road to Moín (the disco is unseen, at the back of the restaurant).

Accommodations

"I recognized it as a hotel by its tottering stairs, its unshaded bulbs, its moth-eaten furniture, its fusty smell." Thus, Paul Theroux (in *The Old Patagonian Express*) summed up Puerto Limón's hotel scene. Many among the town's several dozen budget hostelries—many Chinese-owned—are very basic (often, as Theroux says, little more than "nests of foul bedclothes"); some cater to prostitutes, and solo women travelers might be wise to avoid these places. Still, there are some reasonable options in town, plus resort hotels a few kilometers north of town

on the road to Moín (see *Portrete and Playa Bonita,* below).

At weekends, holidays, and Carnival week there are not enough rooms to go around, and you should book far ahead.

Safety Concerns: It's not safe to park outside anywhere in Puerto Limón at night; your car will probably be broken into. The Hotel Acón, Hotel Park, and Hotel International have secure garage parking at no extra charge.

Under $25: The **Hotel Palace** (Calle 2, Avenida 3, tel./fax 506/798-2604, $12 s, $14 d), with plant-festooned balconies, has clean albeit basic rooms with modern beds and private baths. The **Hotel Wilson** (Avenida 3, Calles 4/5, tel. 506/758-5028, $9 s/d shared bath, $18 s/d private bath) has clean but fairly dingy rooms with cold water only (some with shared bathroom; others with a/c, TV, and private bathroom), but the owner otherwise runs a tight ship. And the **Hotel Ng** (Calle 4, Avenida 5, tel. 506/758-2134, $3 s, $5 d shared bath, $7.50 s, $12 d private bath) has 15 clean rooms with fans, basic furnishings, lively tropical color schemes, and cold water only. It has a small grocery.

One of the best places, **Hotel Continental** (Avenida 5, Calles 2/3, tel. 506/798-0532, $7 s, $11 d) has 24 simple but spacious rooms with fans and private baths with hot water. It's spotlessly clean and offers secure parking. The same owners run the **Nuevo Hotel Internacional** (tel. 506/758-0434, $7 s, $11 d with fans; $9 s, $14 d with a/c) across the road; it has 22 tiled rooms of a similar standard to the Continental.

Likewise, the new **Hotel Costa del Sol** (Avenida 5, Calle 5, tel. 506/798-0808, grupodelso @racsa.co.cr, $8 s, $15 d), offers clean rooms with modest, modern furnishings, fans, and private baths with hot water. It has secure parking.

Also consider **Hotel Tete** (Avenida 3, Calles 4/5, tel. 506/758-1122, fax 506/758-0707, $10 s, $18 d with fan, $12/21 with a/c), with 14 simply furnished but adequate rooms featuring private bathrooms with hot water, and balconies with chairs.

$25–50: The best bet in town is the **Hotel Park** (Avenida 3, Calle 1, tel. 506/758-3476 or

506/798-0555, fax 506/758-4364, $35 s, $45 d standard; $37/48 ocean view with balcony), with 32 a/c rooms featuring TVs and private baths and overlooking the ocean. Prices vary according to room standard and view (more expensive ocean-view rooms catch the breeze and have balconies), though all have private bath with hot water. It has a nice restaurant, plus secure parking.

Slightly less appealing is the four-story **Hotel Acón** (Avenida 3, Calle 2/3, tel. 506/758-1010, fax 506/758-2924, $24 s, $32 d). Its 39 rooms have a/c and are clean and spacious, though dowdy. The hotel has a reasonable restaurant. Take a top-floor room away from the noise of the second-floor disco that reverberates Thurs.–Sun.

Food

You can sample local Caribbean dishes at the open-air *sodas* in and around the Mercado Central, where filling *casados* (set lunch meals) are offered for about $2. The open **Soda Mares** (Avenida 2, Calles 3/5, tel. 506/758-1347, 8 A.M.–8 P.M.), on the market's south side, is popular for watching the street buzz: *gallo pinto* (rice and beans) here costs about $2, and you can have a shrimp dish and beer for $5.

The most atmospheric place is **Restaurant La Salamander** (Avenida 3, Calle 2, no tel., 7:30 A.M.–6:30 P.M. Mon.–Fri., 8 A.M.–6 P.M. Saturday), in a colonial structure with aged tile floors and sponge-washed walls. It serves breakfasts such as *gallo pinto* ($2.50, including coffee), sandwiches and *casados* (set lunches; $3) plus pastries, desserts, and coffees. I also recommend the modestly upscale a/c **Restaurante Brisas del Caribe** (Avenida 2, tel. 506/758-0138, 7 A.M.–midnight), on the north side of Park Vargas, serving an excellent, bargain-priced set buffet of *típico* dishes ($1.50).

The ground-floor restaurant in the **Hotel Acón** (6:30 A.M.–10:30 P.M. Mon.–Sat., 7 A.M.–3 P.M. Sunday, $5) offers reasonably priced meals, including basic American breakfasts. The clean, a/c 24-hour restaurant in the **Hotel Park** is also recommended; it serves soups, salads, shrimp cocktail ($6), lobster ($14.50), sea bass in garlic ($6), pastas, and cheesecake.

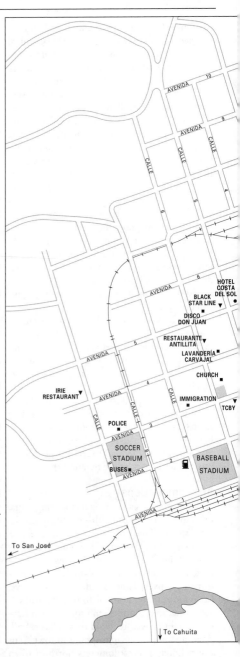

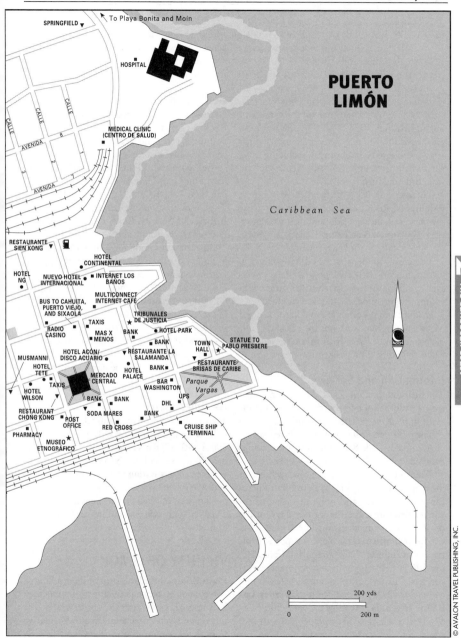

PUERTO
LIMÓN

Caribbean Sea

The Caribbean Coast

To Playa Bonita and Moín

SPRINGFIELD

HOSPITAL

CALLE
CALLE
CALLE
CALLE

AVENIDA

AVENIDA 8

AVENIDA

MEDICAL CLINIC
(CENTRO DE SALUD)

RESTAURANTE
SIEN KONG

HOTEL
NG

HOTEL
CONTINENTAL

NUEVO HOTEL
INTERNACIONAL

INTERNET LOS
BAÑOS

MULTICONNECT
INTERNET CAFÉ

BUS TO CAHUITA,
PUERTO VIEJO,
AND SIXAOLA

TRIBUNALES
DE JUSTICIA

RADIO
CASINO

TAXIS

MAS X
MENOS

BANK

HOTEL PARK

BANK

HOTEL ACÓN/
DISCO ACUARIO

MUSMANNI

HOTEL
TETE

TAXIS

MERCADO
CENTRAL

RESTAURANTE LA
SALAMANDA

HOTEL
PALACE

BANK

TOWN
HALL

STATUE TO
PABLO PRESBERE

RESTAURANTE
BRISAS DE CARIBE

HOTEL
WILSON

BANK

BANK

BAR
WASHINGTON

UPS

Parque
Vargas

RESTAURANT
CHONG KONG

POST
OFFICE

SODA MARES

DHL

BANK

PHARMACY

MUSEO
ETNOGRÁFICO

RED CROSS

CRUISE SHIP
TERMINAL

0   200 yds

0   200 m

For Caribbean dishes, head to the **Black Star Line** (Calle 5, Avenida 5, tel. 506/383-5491, 11 A.M.–10 P.M.), in an old wooden structure where locals gather to play dominoes and socialize; or the simple **Irie Restaurant** (Calle 9, Avenidas 4/5, tel. 506/758-3668), serving I-tal (Rastafarian) health foods and Jamaican fare, with seating on a small balcony. **Restaurant Springfield** (tel. 506/758-1203), one km north on the road to Moín, is favored by locals; it has zesty Caribbean dishes from $4, including garlic shrimp and fish in curry sauce (*please* refrain from ordering turtle meat).

There's no shortage of inexpensive Chinese restaurants. **Restaurant Chong Kong,** facing the market on the west side, and the modestly elegant **Restaurant Sien Kong** (Calle 3, Avenida 6, tel. 506/758-0254) are recommended.

The clean, modern, a/c **TGBY** (Avenida 3, Calle 5, tel. 506/758-0044, 6 A.M.–10 P.M.) offers salads, submarine sandwiches ($2), rice with shrimp, yogurt sundaes, and iced cappuccinos.

Produce and groceries are sold at the Central Market, and at **Mas X Menos** supermarket (Calle 3, Avenida 3). A lively **fruit market**(Avenida 4 Calles 4/7) is held on weekends.

Information and Services

The **hospital** (tel. 506/758-2222; for emergencies, tel. 506/758-0580) is at the north end of the seafront *malecón,* reached via Avenida 6.

The **police station** is on the northwest corner of Avenida 3, Calle 8. Criminal investigation is handled by the OIJ (tel. 506/799-1437).

There are three banks in the town center; see the map. There's only one bank south of Puerto Limón (at Bribrí), and none to the north; if you're spending more than a few days on the coast, change as much as you'll need here.

The **post office** is at Calle 4, Avenida 2. **Multiconnect Internet Café** (Avenida 4, Calles 2/3, tel. 506/758-1141, multiconnect@racsa.co.cr) charges $1 per hour; open 9 A.M.–10 P.M. Mon.–Fri., 1–9 P.M. Sat.–Sun.; **Internet Los Baños** (Avenida 5, Calles 2/3, tel. 506/828-6757) also charges $1; open 9 A.M.–10 P.M. Mon.–Sat., 9 A.M.–6 P.M. Sunday.

Lavandería Carvajal (Avenida 4, Calles 5/6,

tel. 506/792-4228) charges $7.50 per basket *(canasta)* for laundry; open 8 A.M.–6 P.M. Mon.–Fri., 8 A.M.–3 P.M. Saturday.

Immigration (Dirección de Migración y Extranjerá) is on Avenida 3, Calles 6/7.

Getting There

Nature Air and **SANSA** offer irregular service to the airport two km south of Limón. At last visit there were plans to extend the airport to receive international flights.

Transportes MEPE (tel. 506/257-8129) buses depart the Gran Terminal del Caribe, in San José, daily at 6 A.M., 10 A.M., 1:30 P.M., and 3:30 P.M. The buses continue to Cahuita, Puerto Viejo, Bribrí, and Sixaola. Buses to San José depart Puerto Limón from Calle 2, Avenida 2 ($2).

Buses depart Limón for Cahuita ($1), Puerto Viejo ($1.50), and Sixaola ($3) from opposite Radio Casino on Avenida 4 daily at 5 A.M., 7 A.M., 8 A.M., 10 A.M., noon, 1 P.M., 4 P.M., and 6 P.M. Buses depart Limón for Manzanillo ($2) at 6 A.M., 2:30 P.M., and 6 P.M. Buy tickets in advance at the *soda* beside the bus stop, as buses get crowded. Buses also serve Penshurst and the Valle de Estrella regularly from Calle 2. Around the corner on Calle 4 to the north is the bus stop for Playa Bonita and Moín.

Getting Around

Taxis await custom on the south side of the market.

Internet Los Baños (Avenida 5, Calles 2/3, tel. 506/828-6757) rents beach cruiser bicycles ("bananas") for $2 per hour, $15 per day.

There are **gas stations** on the corner of Calle 3 and Avenida 6, at Calle 7 and Avenida 2, and one km west of town on the Guápiles Highway. There are only two gas stations south of Puerto Limón.

VICINITY OF LIMÓN

Playa Bonita, four km north of Puerto Limón, boasts a golden beach popular with Limonenses. Swimming is safe only at the northern end. The surf is good, but unreliable. **Parque Recreativo Cariari,** to the north, is an untended public park, beyond which lies **Portrete,** an unsightly bay interesting only for the flocks of vultures that gather to feed on lobster scraps left by the local fishermen. The cove is said to have good right points for surfers at its southern end.

The port of **Moín,** six km north of Puerto Limón, is where Costa Rica's crude oil is received for processing (RECOPE has its main refinery here) and bananas are loaded for shipment to Europe and North America.

The only reason to visit Moín is to catch a boat to Tortuguero from the dock north of the railway tracks (after crossing the track, follow the road to the left).

Accommodations and Food

Cabinas Roca Mar (tel. 506/396-2211, $12 s, $20 d), on a breeze-swept hillock 100 meters inland of Playa Bonita, was under construction at last visit. It has 10 attractive, cross-ventilated cabins with tile floors, simple pine furnishings, fans, and private baths with cold water (hot water was planned). A restaurant was planned. Rates include tax.

Cabinas Oasis del Caribe (tel. 506/795-0024, moyso@racsa.co.cr, $18 s, $23 d) offers 15 oc-

tagonal cabins with cable TV and fans, in a lush hillside garden full of palms. There's a swimming pool and an open-sided restaurant. Two km farther north, overlooking Playa Bonita, is **Hotel Cocori** (tel. 506/798-1670, fax 506/758-2930, $35 s, $45 d), a modern clifftop complex with a pleasing ocean-view terrace restaurant—Bar/Restaurante Tía María—open to the breezes. It fills with Ticos on weekends, when the disco pumps out tunes loud enough to wake the dead. It has 25 simple but pleasing a/c rooms with cable TV, and private bathrooms with hot water. Rates include breakfast.

Hotel Mar y Luna (Apdo. 483, Moín, tel. 506/795-1132, fax 506/795-4828, $19 pp), formerly Hotel Moín Caribe, sits atop the hill above the dock to Tortuguero. It has 14 modestly appointed a/c rooms with TV and hot water. There's secure parking and a clean restaurant that has karaoke.

The **Hotel Matama** (Apdo. 606-7300 Puerto Limón, tel. 506/758-1123, fax 506/795-3399, info@matama.com, www.matama.com, $29 s, $38 d), two km farther north, has 16 spacious albeit dowdy a/c rooms and

The Caribbean Coast

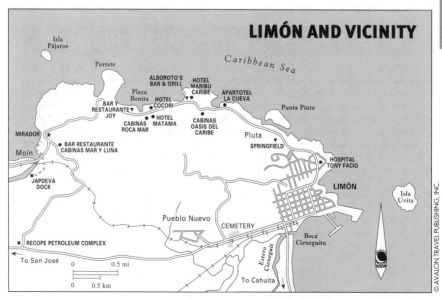

LIMÓN AND VICINITY

four-person and six-person villas with loft bedrooms, set in 22 hectares of landscaped gardens and forest with trails. Rooms have wicker furniture, cable TV, telephones, and large showers with olarium gardens. Some have lofts. The restaurant overlooks the gardens and swimming pool (with swim-up bar). Live music is hosted on weekends. Rates include breakfast and tax.

Hotel Maribu Caribe (Apdo. 1306-2050 San Pedro, tel. 506/795-2543, fax 506/795-3541, maribucaribe@hotmail.com, $66 s, $78 d standard, $112 family suite), at the south end of Playa Bonita, has a scenic setting above the ocean. The simple, uninspired resort, which caters mostly to Ticos, is centered on a swimming pool, with steps leading up to a restaurant for alfresco dining. A second, more romantic, open-air restaurant overlooks the ocean and catches the breeze. The hotel offers 17 round, thatched, African-style bungalows and 50 rooms, each with a/c, telephone, and private bath. Rooms have narrow beds and unappealing decor. Roomy showers make amends with piping hot water. The Maribu can arrange sportfishing and scuba diving trips, plus tours. Hotel Maribu Caribe and Hotel Matama both have reasonably good restaurants.

Restaurant Joy (tel. 506/795-0879, 9 A.M.–6 P.M. Mon.–Fri., 9 A.M.–8 P.M. Sat.–Sun.), at Playa Bonita, is run by a friendly and garrulous character, Johnny Dixon. His breezy bar and restaurant is a good place to hang and watch the surf pump ashore while savoring a shrimp cocktail ($9), ceviche ($6), snapper ($9), or rice and beans Caribbean style ($6).

Getting There

From Puerto Limón, the bus to Playa Bonita, Portrete, and Moín operates hourly from Calle 4, Avenida 4, opposite Radio Casino.

PUERTO LIMÓN TO TORTUGUERO

Lagoons and swamps dominate the coastal plains north of Limón. Many rivers meander through this region, carrying silt that the coastal tides conjure into long, straight, brown-sand beaches.

The only community along the canals between Limón and Tortuguero is **Parismina**, at the mouth of the Río Parismina, 45 km north of Moín. It is popular year-round with anglers. The spring tarpon season runs mid-January

COSTA RICA'S AQUATIC COASTAL HIGHWAY

During the Trejos administration (1966–70) four canals were dug from solid ground to link the natural channels and lagoons of the coastal swamplands stretching north of Moín to Tortuguero and the Río Colorado. Today these canals form a connected "highway"—virtually the only means of getting around along the coast. One can now travel from Siquirres eastward along the Río Pacuare to Moín, then northward to Tortuguero, and from there to the Río Colorado, which in turn connects with the Río San Juan, which will take you westward to Puerto Viejo de Sarapiquí.

The three-hour journey from Moín (or Parismina) to Tortuguero is a superb experience. All along the riverbanks are the ramshackle shacks of settlers who come and go with the river level, subsisting on corn and the canal's swarming fish, such as tarpon and gar.

The easygoing waterway is lined with rainforest vegetation in a thousand shades of green. The deep verdure of the foliage, the many brilliant flowers, the graceful festoons of vines and mosses intertwining themselves make for an endlessly fascinating journey. Noisy flocks of parrots speed by doing barrel rolls in tight formation. Several species of kingfishers patrol the banks; the largest, the Amazon kingfisher, is almost 30 cm long. In places the canopy arches over the canal, and howler monkeys sounding like rowdy teenagers may protest your passing. Keep a sharp eye out, too, for mud turtles and caimans absorbing the sun's rays on logs.

through May. Mid-August through November is the peak time for giant snook. Tuna, wahoo, king mackerel, snapper, and other game fish await offshore.

Sea turtles come ashore to nest all along the shore, notably at **Barra de Matina,** midway between Moín and Parismina (see the website www.costaricaturtles.com). Here, the **Pacuare Nature Reserve** exists primarily to protect the eggs of leatherback turtles from poachers during the nesting season. The reserve is run in conjunction with Rainforest Concern (in the U.K., 27 Landsdowne Crescent, London W11 2NS, tel. 020/7229-2093, fax 020/7221-4094, info @rainforestconcern.org, www.rainforestconcern.org) and is open to visitors March 25–Aug. 15. Volunteers are needed to join biologists and hired guards to patrol the beach, tag and measure turtles, and relocate nests (See the sidebar *Volunteer Programs to Save Turtles,* in the *Know Costa Rica* section). One-week minimum stay. Conselvatur (tel./fax 506/253-8118, conselva@sol .racsa.co.cr, www.conselvatur.com) offers an eight-day "Sea Turtle Research & Rainforest Exploration" that features Reserva Pacuare.

The reserves can be accessed by road via **Matina,** a banana town on the banks of the Río Matina four km north of Hwy. 32 (the turnoff is at Bristol, about 28 km east of Siquirres). **Caño Blanco Marina,** in the heart of a Geest banana processing plant near **Barra de Matina Sur,** about eight km northeast of Matina, is the main embarkation point for boat service to/from Tortuguero (see *Tortuguero Village and Laguna de Tortuguero,* below).

Accommodations and Food

In the village, budget hounds might try **La Rosa Espinoza** (tel. 506/710-1479, elizabetpark@hotmail.com, $10 pp), opposite the church, and set in a landscaped garden. It's run by Elizabeth Parker, who has four clean simple rooms with fans, porch, and private bath. She does laundry, arranges tours, and offers meals.

Nearby, and similar, **Iguana Verde** (no tel.) has three clean rooms with private bath. It has a café and grocery.

Also in the village, **Cariblanco Lodge** (tel. 506/393-5481, $18 s/d) has 10 clean rooms with fans, and private baths (some have hot water). It has an open-air restaurant serving Caribbean fare, and a bar draws locals for karaoke and dancing.

Sportfishing enthusiasts are catered to at three dedicated sportfishing lodges at Parismina:

© CHRISTOPHER P. BAKER

ships at banana-loading dock, Moín, near Puerto Limón

Caribbean Expedition Lodge (tel./fax 506/232-8118, lodge@costaricasportfishing.com, www.costaricasportfishing.com); **Río Parismina Lodge** (tel. 506/229-7597, fax 506/292-1207, fish@riop.com, www.riop.com; in the U.S., c/o Fishing Tours International, P.O. Box 460009, San Antonio, TX 78280, tel. 210/824-4442 or 800/338-5688, fax 210/824-0151); and **Jungle Tarpon Lodge** (in the U.S., 800/544-2261, greatalaska@greatalaska.com, www.greatalaska.com/costarica). All offer fishing packages and take in guests on an ad-hoc basis.

Chito's Lodge (tel. 506/768-8636, about $75 s, $100 d), two km north of Parismina, offers modest accommodations in a twin-story waterfront structure; six of the nine rooms share bathrooms. Owner Chito Sheddan likes to break out the banjo. He rents kayaks and offers fishing. Rates include meals.

Tortuguero and Barra del Colorado

ⓜ TORTUGUERO NATIONAL PARK

Parque Nacional Tortuguero extends north along the coast for 22 km from Jaloba, six km north of Parismina, to Tortuguero village. The 19,000-hectare park is a mosaic of deltas on an alluvial plain nestled between the Caribbean coast on the east and the low-lying volcanic hills of Coronel, Caño Moreno, and 300-meter-high Las Lomas de Sierpe—the Sierpe Peaks—on the west. The park protects the nesting beach of the green turtle, the offshore waters to a distance of 30 km, and the wetland forests extending inland for about 15 kilometers.

The park—one of the most varied within the park system—has 11 ecological habitats, from high rainforest to herbaceous marsh communities. Fronting the sea is the seemingly endless expanse of beach. Behind that is a narrow lagoon, connected to the sea at one end and fed by a river at the other; it parallels the beach for its full 35-km length. Back of the lagoon is a coastal rainforest and swamp com-

Tortuguero Canal

© JEAN MERCIER

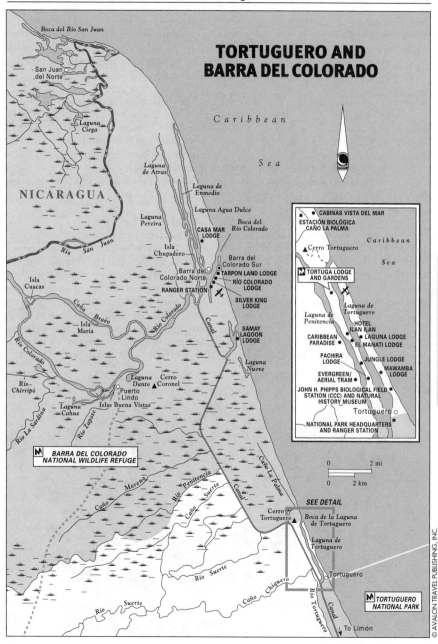

TORTUGUERO AND
BARRA DEL COLORADO

Boca del Río San Juan

San Juan
del Norte

Laguna
Ciega

Caribbean

Sea

NICARAGUA

Laguna
de Atras

Laguna de
Enmedio

Laguna
Pereira

Laguna Agua Dulce

CASA MAR
LODGE

Boca del
Río Colorado

Río San Juan

Isla
Chupadero

Barra del
Colorado Norte

Barra del
Colorado Sur

TARPON LAND LODGE

Isla
Cuacas

RÍO COLORADO
LODGE

RANGER STATION

Caño Bravo

Río Colorado

Isla
María

SILVER KING
LODGE

Río Colorado

Canal

SAMAY
LAGOON
LODGE

Río
Chirripó

Laguna
Nueve

Laguna
Cahue

Laguna
Danto

Cerro
Coronel

Puerto
Lindo

Islas Buena Vistas

Río La Sardina

Río Zapote

BARRA DEL COLORADO
NATIONAL WILDLIFE REFUGE

Caño Moreno

Río Penitencia

Caño Suerte

Canal

Caño La Palma

SEE DETAIL

Cerro
Tortuguero

Boca de la Laguna
de Tortuguero

Laguna de
Tortuguero

Río Suerte

Río Suerte

Caño Chiquero

Río Tortuguero

Canal

Tortuguero

TORTUGUERO
NATIONAL PARK

To Limón

Detail inset:

CABINAS VISTA DEL MAR

ESTACIÓN BIOLÓGICA
CAÑO LA PALMA

Cerro Tortuguero

Caribbean

Sea

TORTUGA LODGE
AND GARDENS

Laguna de
Tortuguero

Laguna de
Penitencia

HOTEL
ILAN ILAN

LAGUNA LODGE

CARIBBEAN
PARADISE

EL MANATI LODGE

PACHIRA
LODGE

JUNGLE LODGE

EVERGREEN/
AERIAL TRAM

MAWAMBA
LODGE

JOHN H. PHIPPS BIOLOGICAL FIELD
STATION (CCC) AND NATURAL
HISTORY MUSEUM

Tortuguero

NATIONAL PARK HEADQUARTERS
AND RANGER STATION

0   2 mi

0   2 km

The Caribbean Coast

© AVALON TRAVEL PUBLISHING, INC.

plex threaded by an infinite maze of serpentine channels and streams.

Tortuguero shelters more than 300 bird species, among them toucans, aricaris, oropendolas, herons, kingfishers, anhingas, jacanas, and the great green macaw; 57 species of amphibians and 111 of reptiles, including three species of marine turtles; and 60 mammal species, including 13 of Costa Rica's 16 endangered species, among them jaguars, tapirs, ocelots, cougars, river otters, and manatees.

Tortuguero's fragile manatee population was thought to be extinct until a population was found in remote lagoons. Traditionally they have been hunted for their flesh, reputedly tender and delicious, and for their very tough hides, but the greatest threat of late has been chemicals and sediments washing into the waterways from banana plantations. A decade ago a scientific study indicated that about 100 manatees inhabited the area. The population seems to be growing. They are rarely seen, although in 2003 one appeared in Tortuguero's main canal for the first time.

The wide-open canals are superb for spotting crocodiles, giant iguanas, and basilisk lizards basking atop the branches, and caimans luxuriating on the fallen raffia palm branches at the side of the river. One of my favorite pastimes is to watch bulldog bats skimming through the mist that rises from the water and scooping up a fish right on cue. Amazing!

The western half of the park is under great stress from logging and hunting, which have increased in recent years as roads intrude. The local community and hotel and tour operators are battling a proposed highway sponsored by banana and logging interests.

Rubbish disposal is a serious problem at Tortuguero: leave no trash.

Turtles

The park protects a vital nesting ground for green sea turtles, which find their way onto the brown-sand beaches every year from June through October (the greatest numbers arrive in September). Mid-February through July, giant leatherback turtles arrive to lay their eggs (with greatest frequency April–May), followed, in July, by female hawksbill turtles. Tortuguero is the most important green-turtle hatchery in the western Caribbean; annually as many as 30,000 greens

zipping along the Tortuguero Canal

© CHRISTOPHER P. BAKER

swim from their feeding grounds as far away as the Gulf of Mexico and Venezuela (most Tortuguero greens apparently arrive from the Miskito Bank feeding area of Nicaragua) to lay their eggs at the eons-old nesting site on the oceanside stretch of beach. Each female arrives two to six times, at 10- to 14-day intervals, and waits two or three years before nesting again.

During the 1950s, the Tortuguero nesting colony came to the attention of biologist-writer Archie Carr, a lifelong student of sea turtles. Carr enlisted sympathy through his eloquent writing, particularly *The Windward Road* (Gainesville: University of Florida Press, 1955). His lobby—originally called the Brotherhood of the Green Turtle—worked with the Costa Rican government to establish Tortuguero as a sanctuary where the endangered turtles could nest unmolested. The sanctuary was established in 1963 and the area was named a national park in 1970.

Local guides escort **Turtle Walks** at 8–10 P.M. and 10 P.M.–midnight each evening in turtle-nesting season ($10, including guide, who alone can buy tickets to access the beach at night). *No one is allowed on the 22-mile nesting sector without a guide after 6 P.M.* Only 400 people are allowed on the beach per night, apportioned by sector; 200 maximum every two hours. No cameras or flashlights are permitted. Keep quiet, as the slightest noise can send the turtle hurrying back to sea; and keep a discreet distance. You are asked to report any guide who digs up turtle hatchlings to show you—this is absolutely prohibited. Despite legislation, poachers from Barra and Limón still steal turtle eggs on the beaches, and cull turtles from the sea. Turtles are endangered; respect them.

When to Go

Rain falls year-round. The three wettest months are January, June, and July. The three driest are February, April, and November. Monsoon-type

The wide-open canals are superb for spotting crocodiles, giant iguanas, and basilisk lizards basking atop the branches, and caimans luxuriating on the fallen raffia palm branches at the side of the river. Bulldog bats skim through the mist and scoop up fish right on cue.

storms can lash the region at any time; rain invariably falls more heavily in the late afternoon and at night. The interior of the park is hot, humid (very humid on sunny days), and windless. Bring good raingear; a heavy-duty poncho is ideal (the lodges provide these for guests). It can be cool enough for a windbreaker or sweater while speeding upriver under cloudy weather.

Take insect repellent—the mosquitoes and no-see-ums (you'll need Avon's Skin-So-Soft for these) can be fierce.

Exploring Tortuguero

You can walk the entire length of the beach. Trails into the forests—frequently waterlogged—also begin at the park stations at both ends of the park. The 2-km-long El Gavilán Trail leads south from the Cuatro Esquinas ranger station south of Tortuguero village and takes in both beach and rainforest. A trail (in terrible condition at last visit) that begins north of Tortuga Lodge leads to **Cerro Tortuguero** (119 meters), two km north of Tortuga Lodge; from here—the highest point for miles around—you have a superb perspective over the swamps and coastline from the rusting lookout tower at the top.

You can hire dugout canoes (*cayucas* or *botes*) in Tortuguero village ($6 pp the first hour, $3 each additional hour, without a guide). Give the canoe a good inspection before shaking hands on the deal: paddle around until you feel comfortable and have ascertained that there are no leaks and that the canoe is stable. It's also a good idea to check on local currents and directions, as the former can be quite strong and it's easy to lose your bearings amid the maze of waterways. Skippered *pangas* (flat-bottomed boats with outboard motors) and *lanchas* (with inboard motor) can also be rented; try to rent one with a non-polluting four-stroke motor. And don't forget to pay your park entrance fee before entering Tortuguero National Park.

If you want to see wildlife you *absolutely* need

The Caribbean Coast

VOLUNTEERS FOR CONSERVATION

The Caribbean Conservation Corps (CCC, tel. 506/224-9215 or 506/238-8069, fax 506/225-7516, baulas@racsa.co.cr; in the U.S., 4424 NW 13th St. Suite #A1, Gainesville, FL 32609, tel. 352/373-6441 or 800/678-7853; ccc@cccturtle.org, www.cccturtle.org) needs volunteers to assist in research, including during its twice-yearly turtle tagging and monitoring programs. You should be willing to patrol up to five miles of beach nightly for 8–15 nights Accommodations are offered in the CCC dormitory at the John H. Phipps Biological Field Station (private a/c rooms in the scientists' residence are sometimes available for an additional fee). One- to three-week programs cost $1,360–$2,075. Rates include airfare, meals, and lodging.

The CCC also invites volunteers to join its fall and spring bird-research projects at Tortuguero. It involves mist-netting, identifying, banding, and studying resident and migrant birds during their ancient treks north and south (Tortuguero is along a prime migration flyway). No experience is needed. The fieldwork is complemented by guided hikes, boat tours, and other activities.

a guide, as otherwise you'll not see 10 percent of the wildlife you'll see in their company. The local guides—there are about 40 trained guides organized into a local cooperative—have binocular eyes: in even the darkest shadows, they can spot caimans, birds, crocodiles, and other animals you will most likely miss. You can hire local guides in the village for about $5 pp per hour. The best guides are employed by the local lodges.

The guide will lead you deep into the narrow *caños* and chug up the side streams where the vegetation narrows down to a murky closeness and he or she is forced to cut the motor and pole to make headway. Some creatures you'll see virtually at arm's reach. Exploring at night is not permitted.

You can also book guided trips at any of the lodges or through tour companies in San José.

Costa Rica Expeditions (P.O. Box 6941-1000, San José, tel. 506/257-0766, fax 506/257-1665, costaric@expeditions.co.cr, www.costaricaexpeditions.com) provides the best operation. **Rios Tropicales** (tel. 506/233-6455, fax 506/255-4354, info@riostropicales.com, www.riostropicales.com) offers a jungle kayaking package (from one to three nights) from Mawamba Lodge.

Tortuguero Safaris, in Tortuguero village, also has trips (see *Sports and Recreation*, in the *Tortuguero Village* section, below).

Information

Entrance costs $7 (or $10 for a three-day pass), and also includes access to Barra del Colorado Wildlife Refuge. The fee is payable at the **Cuatro Esquinas** ranger station (tel./fax 506/711-0756 or 506/710-7673), at the southern end of Tortuguero village, or at **Estación Jalova,** at the park's southern end (45 minutes by boat from Tortuguero village). No fee applies if you're in transit.

You can camp at Jalova, with outside showers and toilets.

The park administration (tel. 506/710-2929, acto@ns.minae.go.cr) is in Guápiles.

The **Caribbean Conservation Corps** (CCC, tel. 506/224-9215 or 506/238-8069, fax 506/225-7516, baulas@racsa.co.cr; in the U.S., 4424 NW 13th St. Suite #A1, Gainesville, FL 32609, tel. 352/373-6441 or 800/678-7853; ccc@cccturtle.org, www.cccturtle.org) maintains the John H. Phipps Biological Station and a Natural History Visitors Center (locals still call it by its old name, Casa Verde), five minutes' walk north of the village. You can **adopt a turtle** for $25.

TORTUGUERO VILLAGE

Somnolent, funky Tortuguero village (pop. 550), on the northern boundary of Tortuguero National Park, sprawls over a thin strip of land at the northern end of the **Canal de Tortuguero** and the southern end of **Laguna del Tortuguero,** at the junction with **Laguna Penitencia,** a pencil-thin canal that leads to Barra del Colorado. Laguna del Tortuguero extends north six km to the ocean, where the tannin-stained freshwater pours into the Caribbean. It is lined with nature lodges, spaced well apart.

It's an 80-km, three-hour journey along the Canal de Tortuguero from Moín; by small plane from San José, it's a 30-minute flight that sets you down on a thin strip of land with the ocean crashing on one side and the lagoon and the jungle on the other (the ocean here is not safe for swimming because of rip currents and the large number of sharks; barracudas—silvery assassins, terrifyingly dentured—also abound in the warm, shallow waters)

A lumber mill (now a rusting hulk of saw blades and metal framework) between the 1940s and 1972 provided steady work to the villagers, who supplemented their meager income selling turtle meat and shells, as had their forebears (many of whom came from San Andreas, Colombia). When the mill closed, the population began drifting away. Now tourism is booming and so is the local population.

The higgledy-piggledy village comprises a warren of narrow sandy trails (there are no roads) lined by rickety wooden houses and, increasingly, more substantial buildings spawned by the tourism boom. The south end

of the village is a rough place where drug trading is said to be common; it's best avoided after dark.

The **John H. Phipps Biological Field Station** (tel. 506/711-0680), about 500 meters north of the village, can be accessed by boat or via a trail behind the beach. It features a must-see **Natural History Visitor's Center** (10 A.M.–noon and 2–5:30 P.M. Mon.–Sat., 2–5:30 P.M. Sunday, $1 admission) with turtle exhibits and educational presentations on rainforest ecology, including a video about turtle ecology and a life-size model of turtles hatching, and another of a turtle laying her eggs. Its gift store is stocked with natural history books.

The **Joshua B. Powers Information Kiosk** *(kiosko de información),* on the north side of the soccer field, provides an educational take on local ecology and the history of Tortuguero.

There's small **butterfly garden** at Jungle Lodge, on Laguna del Tortuguero.

Entertainment and Events

Vida Caribeña, in the village center, hosts a Caribbean cultural show Mon.–Sat. at 3:30 P.M. ($15 including dinner).

Bar La Culebra is a funky rough-hewn bar

the village wharf, from Laguna Tortuguero

hanging over the water, where local men hang out sipping one too many beers while the womenfolk are tending home. It's a rough, colorful spot—when the *guaro* takes effect, your neighbor may decide to dive into the lagoon for the hell of it. There's dancing nightly at **Disco El Bochinche** in the Salon Brisas del Mar, 100 meters north of Cabinas Sabina.

Sports and Recreation

Tortuguero Safaris (tel. 506/711-0673, fax 506/711-0681, safari@racsa.co.cr; in the U.S., SJO 1882, P.O. Box 025216, Miami, FL 33102) offers guided trips. Trips are run by Daryl Loth, a multilingual Canadian naturalist, who offers canal trips ($15 pp for up to three hours), turtle-watching trips ($10), rainforest hikes ($15 two hours), and kayak rental ($10).

A multilingual German biologist and guide, Barbara Hartung, runs **Tinamon Tours** (tel. 506/842-6561, tinamon@racsa.co.cr, www .tinamontours.de), offering canoe tours, turtle-watching, and medicinal plant tours.

Emilio Williams runs **Caribeño Fishing Tours** (tel. 506/383-0200) for $30 per hour; his house is opposite Abastacedor La Riveriana.

Eddy Brown Sportfishing (P.O. Box 12854-1000 San José, tel. 506/834-2221 and 506/383-6097, fax 506/382-3350) operates from Tortuga Lodge using 26- and 28-foot boats with Bimini tops. Rates: $320–395 per fishing day, including lodging, all meals, and open bar. He also offers fishing by the hour ($50). The **Jungle Shop** also arranges fishing trips.

Aerial Trails Canopy Tour (tel. 506/824-5758), at Evergreen, has eight platforms and three suspension bridges and offers zipline tours at 6 A.M., 11 A.M., and 2 P.M. ($25, including transfers). You need to reserve 24 hours ahead.

You can rent hydrabikes (floating pedal-bikes) at Tortuga Lodge and Paraíso Tropical ($9 per hour; see below). You can rent kayaks at Manatí Lodge ($7.50 for two hours).

Accommodations in the Village

Tortuguero sometimes fills up; if you arrive without reservations, make it a priority to secure accommodations immediately. Most properties

now have telephones; for those that don't, you can reserve by calling Olger Rivera at Super Morpho, tel. 506/710-6716 (you'll need to provide a return telephone number so that hotel owners can confirm your reservation).

Camping: You can camp at the **Cuatro Esquinas ranger station** at the southern end of the village. The ground is often waterlogged, and snakes abound at night.

Under $25: Several properties are sub-par, including Cabinas Sabina.

The **John H. Phipps Biological Field Station** has dormitory accommodations for up to 24 people, with communal kitchen and bathroom, but for researchers, students, and volunteers only.

I recommend **Miss Junie's** (tel. 506/711-0683, $17 pp), at the north end of the village, with 12 clean and simply, albeit nicely, furnished rooms in a two-story unit, each with tiled floor, ceiling fan, screened windows, and large private bathroom with hot water. Rates include breakfast.

Cabinas Merycar (tel. 506/711-0671 and 506/811-0949) has 23 clean yet tiny bare-bones rooms with fans and shared for $5 pp. Cabins with hot water are slightly better for $7 pp. **Cabinas Tortuguero** (beeper tel. 506/223-3030 or 506/839-1200), toward the southern end of the village, is run by friendly Italians Pepe and Morena. It has 10 simple rooms, each with three single beds, ceiling fan, and private bath and hot water.

Cabinas Miriam (beeper tel. 506/223-3030, code 5757, $8 s, $15 d, or $10 pp in the annex), on the north side of the soccer field, has six simple rooms with fans and private bathroom with cold water. You should stay here for Miss Miriam's restaurant. A modern two-story annex 200 meters south has the nicer rooms.

$25–50: The nicest place by far is **Casa Marbella B&B** (tel. 506/711-0673, fax 506/711-0681, safari@racsa.co.cr, http://casamarbella .tripod.com/b_and_b; or c/o Daryl Loth, SJO 1882, PO Box 025216, Miami FL 33102-5216; $25 s, $35 d), a bed-and-breakfast with five airy, clean, delightfully simple bedrooms with terracotta floors, high ceilings with fans, and clinically clean and spacious bathrooms with tiled showers and solar-heated water. You can settle down in a common room to watch TV or enjoy games when rain strikes, plus there's Internet, a communal kitchen, and a dock with hammocks. Daryl, a Canadian, offers tours. Rates include a hearty Costa Rican breakfast.

Accommodations Outside the Village

Most nature lodges offer multi-day packages including transfers and tours.

The **Canadian Organization for Tropical Education and Rainforest Conservation** (COTERC, P.O. Box 335, Pickering, Ont. L1V 2R6, tel. 416/683-2116, info@coterc.org, www.coterc.org, $40 pp) has a research field station, Estación Biológica at Caño Palma, a dead-end channel about eight km north of Tortuguero. A dorm has bunk beds. You may also camp or sleep in hammocks. Rates include all meals and a guided walk on trails into the rainforest and swamps.

Turtle Beach Lodge (tel. 506/383-1652, info@turtlebeachlodge.com, www.turtlebeachlodge.com, from $200 s, $310 d low season; $230 s, $350 d high season for two-day/one night packages), also at Caño Palma, has 25 cabins raised on stilts, with fans, hot showers, and porches. Meals are served in an airy thatched restaurant, and you can relax in the hammock hut or take a cooling dip in the turtle-shaped pool.

Mawamba Lodge (P.O. Box 10980-1000 San José, tel. 506/223-7490, fax 506/222-5463, mawamba@racsa.co.cr, www.grupomawamba.com, $75 s/d), about 800 meters north of Tortuguero on the east side of Laguna del Tortuguero, has 52 attractive all-wood rooms with fans, screened windows, handsome private baths with large walk-in showers, and rocking chairs reached by canopied walkways. There's an airy family-style restaurant and bar, a swimming pool and sun deck, plus a Jacuzzi, game room, and nature trail; natural history presentations are given each evening.

Nearby, and almost identical to Mawamba, the **Laguna Lodge** (tel. 506/225-3740, fax 506/283-8031, laguna@sol.racsa.co.cr, www.lagunatortuguero.com, $45 s, $60 d), lies between the village and airstrip amid spacious landscaped grounds. The 52 modestly elegant, simply furnished rooms, in eight hardwood bungalows,

have heaps of light, ceiling fans, and spacious private baths, plus verandas. It has a swimming pool, boats for nature trips, a hip riverside *ranchito* restaurant and bar, and a dramatic reception lounge shaped like a caracol.

Set in lush grounds, **Pachira Lodge** (Apdo. 1818-1002 San José, tel. 506/256-7080, fax 506/223-1119, www.pachiralodge.com, from $229 s, $376 d for a two-day, one-night package), facing Mawamba on the west side of Laguna del Tortuguero, has 34 thatched cabins connected by thatched walkways; all have polished hardwood floors, lively fabrics on bamboo beds, plus fans, attractive private tiled bathrooms, and verandas. A handsome dining room serves buffet meals, and there's a gift store, bar, and heart-shaped pool. Guests get free use of canoes. Trails lead into adjacent forest. Rates include transfers.

Pachira Lodge has an annex—**Evergreen** (formerly Hollywood)—on the west bank of Laguna Penitencia. It has 16 small albeit handsome, nicely appointed A-frame cabins on stilts, some in a riverside clearing and others in the forest. There's a pool in a raised sun deck, plus a nice restaurant, and the Aerial Trails Canopy Tour.

The **Jungle Lodge** (tel. 506/233-0133, fax 506/258-9546, ventas@grupopapagayo.com, www.grupopapagayo.com, $65 pp), about 400 meters north of Pachira Lodge, is owned and operated by Grupo Papagayo, which promotes its three-day/two-night package featuring guided tours aboard the *Miss Caribe* and *Miss Amazonas* tour boats. Accommodations are in 43 rustic yet handsome, cross-ventilated *cabinas,* all with a double and a single bed, fans, large private bathrooms; they're linked by covered walkways. There's a small gift store, a game room, and a nice bar and restaurant. You can hire canoes, and it has hiking and fishing. Trails lead into the forest. Rates include meals and transfers.

The more basic **El Manatí Lodge** (tel./fax 506/383-0330, $20 pp), three km north of the village on the west side of Laguna de Tortuguero, has eight simply furnished rooms with floor fans and small private bathrooms with hot water, including two-room suites with bunks. It also has two-bedroom cabins. There's a charmingly rustic bar with ping-pong, where friendly owner Fernando plays host. You can rent canoes and kayaks ($5). Rates include breakfast.

Half a kilometer along Laguna Penitencia is **Samoa Lodge** (P.O. Box 15-1225, San José, tel. 506/233-2174, fax 506/248-2509, hotel caribbean @racsa.co.cr, or c/o Ecole Travel in San José, tel. 506/223-2240, $35 s, $45 d), formerly Caribbean Paradise Eco-Lodge. It features 16 spacious, thatch-roofed, modestly furnished cabins amid gardens with trails lined by bougainvillea. Each has three beds, ceiling fan, veranda, and a clean tiled bathroom with hot water. There's a rustic lounge with TV/VCR, plus a pool and sundeck, and kayaks ($10 per day). Tours are offered. It was remodeling at last visit, and adding eight new cabins. Rates include breakfast.

By far the most appealing place is **M Tortuga Lodge and Gardens** (P.O. Box 6941-1000, San José, tel. 506/257-0766, fax 506/257-1665, costaric@expeditions.co.cr, www.costaricaexpeditions.com, $83 s, $100 d low season; $96 s, $115 d high season), owned and operated by Costa Rica Expeditions. The eco-sensitive lodge, facing the airstrip four km north of town, includes guided tours in its room rates. It has 24 spacious and comfortable standard and deluxe riverfront rooms (each with ceiling fans plus fully equipped bathrooms) made of hardwoods and fronted by wide verandas with leather rocking chairs. Each has queen beds, huge screened windows, ceiling fans, and modern bathrooms with plenty of hot water. A restaurant serves excellent meals family-style. A stone-lined, gradual-entry swimming pool shines beside the river; there's a sun deck with lounge chairs. It's set amid 20 hectares of landscaped grounds and forest; a short (albeit muddy) nature trail offers good sightings of poison-arrow frogs and other wildlife. Service is exemplary. Tortuga is also the only fishing lodge in Tortuguero. The lodge offers hikes, turtle walks, and boat transfers, plus multi-day packages. Rates include taxes.

Food

Not to be missed is a meal at **M Miss Junie's,** whose mother, Sibella, used to feed the famed turtle conservationist Archie Carr (in a grim irony, his favorite dish was green turtle soup). Today, $5 will buy you a platter of fish, chicken, or steak, with rice and beans simmered in coconut milk, plus fruit juice and dessert. Reservations are needed. **Miss Miriam's** (7 A.M.–9:30 P.M.) on the north side of the soccer field, offers a similar experience and cuisine.

The colorful, thatched **Caoba** (9 A.M.–9 P.M.), riverside in the village center, serves French-Span-

Tortuga Lodge, Tortuguero

Roberto Brown Silva holds a tarpon at Tortuga Lodge.

ish cuisine, including crepes, plus pizza, brownies, cappuccinos, and shakes.

Evelyn, in the clean, open-air **Restaurant La Caribeña** (6 A.M.–9 P.M.) 20 meters east of Super Morpho, proffers *típico* dishes including *casados* (set meals, $3), burgers, and sandwiches, plus *batidos* and juices (50 cents–$1).

La Casona (tel. 506/399-4623, 9 A.M.–10 P.M.), on the north side of the soccer field, serves pancakes with bananas, plus omelettes, lasagne, and *casados.*

You can buy groceries at **Abastacedor La Riveriana.**

Information and Services

Daryl Loth mans the **Tortuguero Information Center** (see Casa Marbella, above) and is by far the best source of information.

Jungle Shop (tel. 506/823-3741, jungle @racsa.co.cr), in the village center, and **Paraíso Tropical** (tel. 506/710-0323), 50 meters farther north by the main dock, offer tourist information services. Both stock souvenirs, T-shirts, swimwear, posters, jewelry, and hammocks.

The medical clinic, facing the dock, is open Tuesday and Wednesday, 8 A.M.–4 P.M.

Super Morpho (tel. 506/710-6716) has one of the community telephones; Miss Junie (tel. 506/710-0523) has the other. The post office and police station are in the village center.

Getting There

Both **Nature Air** and **SANSA** operate scheduled daily flights between San Jose and the landing strip four km north of Tortuguero village.

Costa Rica Expeditions (see above) and other tour operators with lodges in Tortuguero operate private charter service; tour members get priority, but you may be able to get a spare seat (about $60 one-way). You can arrange charter flights for about $280 per plane, one-way.

Boats serve Tortuguero from Caño Blanco Marina (the office is in Edificio Las Arcadas, on Avenida 2, Calle 1, San José; tel./fax 506/259-8217), near Barra de Matina Sur (see *Barra de Matina,* above). A private *lancha* (boat) charter to Tortuguero costs about $120 one-way, $150 round-trip (boats vary in size from eight- to 20-

passenger vessels; most are canopied). A public boat leaves the wharf for Tortuguero at 1:30 P.M. ($10) and for Parismina at 5 P.M. ($1.25). Call ahead to confirm boat connections. To get to the marina from San José, take a 9 A.M. bus from San José's Gran Caribe bus terminal and get off at Siquirres, from where buses depart for Caño Blanco Marina Mon.–Fri. at 4:30 A.M. and 1 P.M. and Sat.–Sun. at 7 A.M. and 3 P.M. (return buses depart Caño Blanco Mon.–Fri. at 6 A.M. and 3:30 P.M.).

Caño Blanco Marina has two simple cabins with fans ($15 s/d), plus a restaurant and public toilets.

Public *lanchas* leave from La Geest Casa Verde at 1:30 P.M. and 3:30 P.M. ($20 pp round-trip); to get there, take a bus from San José's Gran Caribe bus terminal (6:30 A.M., 9 A.M., 10:30 A.M., and 1 P.M.) and get off at Cariari, 15 km northeast of Guápiles, from where a bus to La Geest leaves at noon and 2 P.M.

Boats also serve Tortuguero from the dock in Moín (tel. 506/795-1460). Expect to pay $50 pp for four people round-trip ($100 if you're alone; $150 for two people), returning the same day or any other day. No reservations are needed.

Tours operators in San José arrange individual bus-and-canal transfers to Tortuguero. I recommend **Costa Rica Expeditions** (see above).

Come prepared for rain. It can get cold zipping along in the rain. Some (but not all boats) provide rain ponchos.

BARRA DEL COLORADO NATIONAL WILDLIFE REFUGE

Refugio Nacional De Vida Silvestre Barra Del Colorado (91,200 hectares) protects the vast rainforests and wetlands extending north from the estuary of Lagunas del Tortuguero to the Río San Juan, the international border with Nicaragua. About 30 km from the sea, the Río San Juan divides, with the San Juan flowing northeast and the main branch—the Río Colorado—flowing southeast to the sea through the center of the reserve. Dozens of tributaries form a labyrinth of permanent sloughs and ephemeral

The Caribbean Coast

waterways that have made the region inaccessible to all but boat traffic.

The waterways are lined with ancient raffia palms. In the early winter, the tree-lined lagoons north of Barra are ablaze with the blossoms of bright yellow allamandas.

In many ways Barra Del Colorado is a replica of Tortuguero National Park—to which it is linked by canal—on a larger scale, and it protects a similar panoply of wildlife. Great green macaws wing screeching over the canopy, mixed flocks of antbirds follow advancing columns of army ants, and jabiru storks with two-meter wingspans circle above, flying so high that they are no more than motes in the sun. Large crocodiles inhabit the rivers and can be seen basking on mudbanks. Conservationists are struggling to protect the wildlife refuge from illegal logging.

Unexciting and ramshackle Barra del Colorado village sits astride the mouth of the 600-meter-wide Río Colorado. **Barra del Norte,** on the north side of the river, has no roads (just dirt paths littered with trash and a broken concrete walkway down its center between cabins made of corrugated tin and wooden crates). The slightly more salubrious **Barra del Sur** has the airstrip and most of the hamlet's few services. The locals are wary of strangers.

The village once prospered as a lumber center but went into decline during two decades of Nicaraguan conflict, when the village became a haven for Nicaraguan refugees. Locals mainly rely on fishing or serve as guides for the half-dozen sportfishing lodges, but drug trafficking is also entrenched.

Despite the end to the conflicts, tensions with Nicaragua run high, because Nicaragua disputes Costa Rica's territorial rights to land north of the Río Colorado and because the Río San Juan is entirely Nicaraguan territory (when you are on the water you are inside Nicaragua). Costa Ricans have right of use. Nicaraguan authorities charge foreigners for use of the Río San Juan ($5 pp, plus $7 per boat); you must carry your passport on the river.

There's a **ranger station** 400 meters west of Silver King Lodge. Entrance costs 75 cents (200 *colones*) payable at the ranger station, or at the

Cuatro Esquinas ranger station in Tortuguero village. For information, contact the park administration (tel. 506/710-2929 or 506/710-2939, fax 506/710-7673, acto@ns.minae.go.cr) in Guápiles.

Sportfishing

The rivers hereabouts are famous for their game fishing; all of the lodges specialize in sportfishing. Local tarpon are so abundant and feisty that a two-meter whopper might well jump into your boat. Gar—one of the oldest fish on earth, with an ancestry dating back 90 million years—is also common; growing up to two meters long, these bony-scaled fish have long, narrow, crocodile-like snouts full of vicious teeth.

Accommodations and Food

The sportfishing lodges hereabouts rely on group business. When there are no groups in, they can be lonely places. All offer multi-day packages.

Hardy budget travelers might try **Tarponland Lodge** (tel. 506/710-2141, $15 pp), in Barra del Sur. It offers 12 dingy *cabinas* with fans, and clean tiled bathrooms, some with hot water. There's a basic restaurant that occasionally doubles as a disco with flashing lights.

The German-run **Samay Lagoon Lodge** (tel. 506/384-7047, fax 506/383-6370, info@samay .com, www.samay.com; in the U.S., tel./fax 707/202-3644, $75 pp), on the south shore of Laguna Samay, six km south of Barra del Colorado, faces onto the Caribbean waterfront. It has 23 modestly furnished rooms with ceiling fans, mosquito nets, and tiled bathrooms with hot water. There's a handsome albeit rustic restaurant. It offers canoe tours, and you can rent fiberglass canoes. Fishing can be arranged. Rates include all meals and canoe use.

Casa Mar Fishing Lodge (Apdo. 825, San José, tel. 506/381-1380, fax 506/710-6592, info@casamarlodge.com, www.casamarlodge .com; or, in the U.S., Bob Marriott's Travel Center, 2634 W. Orangethorpe #6, Fullerton, CA 92833, tel. 714/578-1881 or 800/543-0282, fax 800/367-2299; $450 pp, packages from $1,325 pp for three nights), on Laguna Agua Dulce, about two km north of Barra, and now under new owners and management, has been totally refurbished. It offers

12 rustic, comfortable, and spacious thatched duplex cabins set in attractive landscaped grounds. Each has shining hardwoods, screened windows, fans, clean bathrooms, and wooden canoes that serve as planters. There's a tackle shop, a handsome restaurant, and a bar with leather Sarchí rockers, a dartboard, and large-screen TV/VCR.

The venerable **Río Colorado Lodge** (Apdo. 5094, San José 1000, tel. 506/710-6879 or 506/232-4063, fax 506/231-5987, tarpon4u @mindspring.com, www.riocoloradolodge.com; in the U.S., 12301 N. Oregon Ave., Tampa, FL 33612, tel. 813/931-4849 or 800/243-9777, fax 813/933-3280; $400 per person, all-inclusive, $120 for nonfishing guests), at Barra del Sur, has 18 comfortable a/c rooms open to the breeze; all have private baths, hot showers, electric fans; daily laundry service is free. The rooms and public areas are connected by covered walkways perched on stilts (when the river rises, the lodge extends only a few inches above the water). The lodge features an open-air riverfront restaurant, a TV and VCR room, an open bar, a game room, Jacuzzi, tackle shop, plus a large fleet of 5.5-meter boats with two fighting chairs. And there's a zoo featuring toucans, macaws (which it breeds for release), plus spider and capuchin monkeys ("Baby," the lodge's tapir, was shot and eaten by locals after it escaped). The lodge offers five-, six-, and seven-night packages.

Silver King Lodge (tel. 506/381-1403 or 800/309-8125, fax 506/381-0849, silverkinglodge@racsa.co.cr, www.silverkinglodge.com; in the U.S., Interlink 399, P.O. Box 025635, Miami, FL 33102, tel. 800/847-3474, fax 209/526-3007; $130 pp), 300 meters upriver, offers 10 spacious, modestly furnished duplexes linked by covered catwalks. All have queen-size beds with orthopedic mattresses, ceiling fans, coffeemakers, plus private baths with their own water heaters and large showers. Other features include a small swimming pool and sun deck with hammocks, a masseuse, a huge colonial-tiled indoor Jacuzzi, tackle shop, a restaurant serving all-you-can-eat buffets, and a bar with wide-screen TV and VCR. Free beer, rum, and soft drinks are included. Fishing is from 10 six-meter Carolina skiffs and eight-meter V-hulls,

plus five-meter aluminum canoes for nature trips ($30). A heavy-duty offshore craft permits deep-sea fishing. The lodge closes mid-June through August and in December. Rates include meals. Package prices—from $2,195 s, $1,810 pp d for three days fishing, to $3,164 s, $2,517 pp d for five days—include round-trip airfare from San José, alcoholic drinks, meals, transfers, and laundry service. Extra fishing days cost $485 s, $420 pp d.

A deluxe 20-meter a/c houseboat, the **Rain Goddess** (c/o Blue Wing International, tel. 506/231-4299, fax 506/231-3816, info@bluwing .com, www.bluwing.com; in the U.S., tel. 866/593-3168), offers fishing on the San Juan, Colorado, and adjacent Nicaraguan rivers. Six cabins each have a queen-size and single bed, sink, and vanity. Three shared bathrooms have hot water and showers. It has an observation deck and dining room, plus TV and VCR. Two outboards are towed for fishing otherwise inaccessible areas. Package rates were $1,750 per person ($850 non-anglers) for five days, with three days fishing; additional fishing days $350 per person ($110 non-anglers); including all meals plus air transportation from San José.

Food is available at any of the lodges above. In Barra del Sur, **Abastecedor Los Almendros** is a small grocery and bar.

Services

Diana's Souvenirs (tel. 506/710-6592), run by a Canadian, Diana Graves, offers fax and photocopying services and acts as the post office, public telephone, tourist information service, and Nature Air ticket rep.

There's another public telephone (tel. 506/710-2141) in the bar of the Tarponland Lodge. The tiny **police station** is wharfside at the end of the airstrip.

Getting There

Both SANSA and Nature Air fly daily from San José if they get two or more passengers. You can also charter a light plane from San José.

You can hire private boats from Tortuguero, Moín, Los Chiles, and Puerto Viejo de Sarapiquí.

A rough road leads from Puerto Viejo de Sarapiquí to Pavas (at the juncture of the Ríos Toro and Sarapiquí), where you can also charter a boat. *Do not attempt to reach Barra by boat without a guide, as there are several braided channels to negotiate and it is easy to get dangerously lost.*

A Copetrac (tel. 506/767-6139) bus departs Gran Terminal Caribe (Calle Central, Avenida 13), in San José, for Cariari, from where it's a 200-meter walk to connect with a noon or 2 P.M.

bus to Puerto Lindo on the Río Colorado, or a 2:30 P.M. bus to La Pavona. A *lancha* (water taxi) runs from here ($6 pp); or lodge boats will pick you up by prior arrangement. Buses also depart Guápiles to Cariari (21 km north).

Morpho Travel (tel. 506/711-0674), in Tortuguero, has boat service from Tortuguero to Pavones at 6 A.M. and 11:30 A.M., and from Pavones to Tortuguero at 8:30 A.M. and 1:30 P.M.

South of Puerto Limón

PUERTO LIMÓN TO CAHUITA

South of Puerto Limón, the shore is lined by brown-sand beach fringed by palms. The road makes brief forays inland to cross the Río Banano and, about 30 km south of Limón, the Río Estrella a few km north of the village of **Penshurst,** where a branch road leads into the Valle del Río Estrella. Near the coast, the Río Estrella gives rise to a dense network of channels and lagoons that shelter birds, including great flocks of snow-white cattle egrets, which roost at dusk on the riverbanks.

At last visit, the local banana company had built a dyke on the Río Estrella without an environmental study, resulting in flooding of neighboring sites, including Aviarios del Caribe. A court found against the company.

There are plans for a marina to be built at either Cahuita or Puerto Viejo.

Springtime is crab season, and the roads hereabouts are often smothered in crabs.

Aviarios del Caribe Sloth Refuge

This privately owned 75-hectare wildlife sanctuary (P.O. Box 569-7300 Puerto Limón, tel./fax 506/382-1335, aviarios@costarica.net, www .ogphoto.com/aviarios, free admission), one km north of the Río Estrella, protects a tropical humid forest and marshland ecosystem of freshwater lagoons threatened by the effects of fertilizers washing down from nearby banana plantations (the fertilizers have caused the marsh grasses to bloom prodigiously). The lagoons are a haven for

caimans, river otters, and river turtles, as well as more than 300 bird species, plus monkeys and sloths; jungle trails lead to a lookout blind.

You don't even need to head off into the sloughs, however, to spot wildlife—the owners have a veritable menagerie on-site, including Pink Cheeks the boa constrictor, Coco the croc-

Judy Arroyo and a two-toed sloth, Aviarios del Caribe

odile, a couple of tame toucans, dozens of poison-arrow frogs spawned in the hatchery, and about 40 sloths (not least the world-famous Buttercup, who arrived as the first sloth orphan when only three months old in 1992).

Aviarios del Caribe is the only sloth refuge and rehabilitation center in the world, and is an important center for research into this little-understood creature. It has the long-term goal of rehabilitating as many sloths as possible. Babies are raised and prepared for rehabilitation into the wild (they're fed on a goat milk formula; the milk study is funded by the Costa Rican dairy company, Don Pinos). Request to see the 20-minute video shot for TV.

It offers environmental education for local schools, and offers an "Adopt a Sloth" program. Volunteers are needed to help care for the sloths.

Guided canoe trips up the Río Estrella for up to five people cost $30 pp (3.5 hours).

Selva Bananito Reserve

This 950-hectare private reserve (Conselvatur P.O. Box 2333-2050 San José, tel. 506/253-8118, fax 506/280-0820, conselva@racsa.co.cr, www.selvabananito.com; in the U.S., 850 Juniper Ave., Kellogg, IA 50135-8677, tel./fax 515/236-3894), 15 km inland from Bananito (five km inland from the coast road), protects primary rainforest on the slopes of the Talamancas. Two-thirds is rainforest; the rest is devoted to low-impact agriculture and cattle management. Hiking (from $10) and horse-back riding (from $20) options are offered, as are tree-climbing using rope-and-saddle ($20–50), mountain biking (from $20), overnight camping ($60), bird-watching ($30), and other excursions. You can rent also bikes ($3 per hour; $12 per day). A trip to a Dole banana packing plant is offered.

The reserve is tough to get to; a high-clearance 4WD is absolutely essential for the muddy track churned into an assault course by logging trucks. There are no signs. Ask in the village of Bananito, where you cross the railway lines and keep going straight; take the right fork at the Y-junction. Eventually you'll get to a metal gate with a sign reading "No entrance. Private Prop-

erty." You've arrived. There are two more barbed wire gates to pass through, then you have to drive along a riverbed to cross to the lodge (or you can park at the farm facing the lodge).

Accommodations and Food

Hotel Colón Caribe (tel. 506/710-8103 or 506/256-5520, coloncaribe@colon.co.cr, www.coloncaribe.com, $55 pp low season, $75 pp high season), 22 km south of Puerto Limón and 200 meters from a lonesome beach that seems to stretch to eternity, is an attractive all-inclusive resort. The lobby provides a touch of Tahiti with its soaring *palenque* roof and attractive bamboo furnishings in bright floral prints. The restaurant is similar. Choose from 32 a/c *cabinas* or 11 standard rooms set amid shade trees and boasting cable TVs, and private bathrooms with hot water. There's a swimming pool, plus tennis court and volleyball. It also offers all-inclusive options ($112 pp low season, $126 pp high season) with meals, well drinks, and entertainment. Rates include tax.

Aviarios del Caribe (see above, $75 s/d standard, $85 s/d junior suites, $95 suite, $105 *cabaña*) offers one of the best bargains on the Caribbean coast. The modern all-wood nature lodge has seven spacious, modestly furnished rooms featuring tiled floors, and private bathrooms with hot water; most have king beds. One room (with queen bed) has gracious Prussian-blue tiles and coordinated fabrics. One family room for six people has two doubles and a bunk; a suite has a king-size bed, cool tiles underfoot, a small lounge with delightful sofa and furnishings, and a handsome bathroom. A delightful garden *cabaña* has a king-size bed in the loft accessed by spiral staircase, plus two twins. There's a small gym, laundry service, a TV and video room with library, and a screened upstairs restaurant with beautiful hardwood floors. The owners, Luis and Judy Arroyo, are keen conservationists and the place primarily appeals to nature lovers. Rates include breakfast.

Selva Bananito Lodge, (see above; cellular tel. 506/384-4278, $120 s, $200 d) has 11 elegant wooden cabins (built from salvaged timber, with roofs of recycled plastic) on stilts on a ridge. Each has a queen- and full-size bed, reading lamps, tiled bathroom and solar-heated water (there's no electricity), and deck with hammocks for enjoying the splendid mountain and valley views. More spacious cabins have terra-cotta floors, fold-away doors opening to verandas with hammocks, plus colonial-tile bathrooms with high-tech fittings and picture windows. Dining is family style (although I've received complains about food quality). A guided tour is included for stays of two nights or more, and mountain biking, overnight camping, and tree climbing are offered. Spanish-language courses are offered. Rates include taxes.

Getting There

The San José–Sixaola bus passes through Estrella (see *Getting There*, in the *Cahuita* section, below). Local buses depart Puerto Limón, Calles 3/4, Avenida 4, for the Valle de Estrella and Pandora every two hours 5 A.M.–6 P.M.

VALLE DEL RÍO ESTRELLA

The Valle del Río Estrella, inland of Penshurst, is a wide basin blanketed by banana plantations of the Dole Standard Fruit Company—you'll gain no idea of the vastness of these plantations driving along Hwy. 36. The Río Estrella is spawned in the foothills of the steep-sided, heavily forested Talamanca massif, where it collects the runoff of some 700 cm of rainfall and irrigates the banana plantations as it crosses the broad plains in search of the Caribbean.

Hitoy-Cerere Biological Reserve

Undeveloped and distinctly off the beaten track, the 9,050-hectare Reserva Biológica Hitoy-Cerere (tel. 506/798-3170, 8 A.M.–5 P.M., $6 admission), part of the Parque Internacional La Amistad, is one of the nation's least-visited parks. It is surrounded by three indigenous reservations—Talamanca, Telire, and Estrella. Dense evergreen forests are watered by innumerable rivers.

Take your pick of arduous trails or moderately easy walks from the ranger station along the deep valley of the Río Hitoy-Cirere to waterfalls with natural swimming holes. The park is a

starting point for trans-Talamanca journeys to the Pacific via a trail that leads south to the village of San José Cabecar and up the valley of the Río Coén and across the saddle between Cerro Betsú (2,500 meters) and Cerro Arbolado (2,626 meters) to Ujarrás, in the Valle de El General. Large sections of the park's western and southern flanks have not been explored, and trails into the interior are overgrown, unmarked, and challenging (indigenous guides are available for local hikes).

Rainfall is prodigious: seven meters a year is not unknown. When the sun shines, the park is spectacular. However, there is no defined dry season (March, September, and October are usually the driest months; July–Aug. and Nov.–Dec. are marked by torrential rains and storms). The result: one of the best specimens of wet tropical forest in the country. Large cats are found throughout the reserve, as well as margays, tapirs, peccaries, agoutis, pacas, otters, and monkeys. The park is one of the last remaining strongholds of the harpy eagle.

For information, contact the National Parks Service in San José (SINAC, Calle 25, Avenidas 8/10, San José, tel. 506/283-8004, fax 506/223-6963, aclac@nc.minae.go.cr, www.sinac.go.cr).

You can reserve basic lodging at the ranger station; researchers get priority. Camping is permitted, but there are no facilities.

Getting There

A local bus departs every two hours 5 A.M.–6 P.M. from Puerto Limón (Calles 3/4, Avenida 4) to the Estrella Valley Standard Fruit Co. banana plantation, 10 km from the park entrance. Taxis from Finca 6 in the Estrella Valley cost about $5.

A fascinating way to get close to the locals is to ride on the local "Banana Train" passenger service—not to be confused with the famous but defunct "Banana Train" that once operated from San José to Limón—that operates daily at 4 A.M. and 2:30 P.M. from Puerto Limón ($1.20 each way; tel. 506/758-3314). The round-trip journey takes about five hours. Don't expect comfort. Seats are of the old-school-bus variety, bolted to the floors. Your companions will be local plantation workers. The weary iron horse lurches to a stop at Finca 6 and Finca 8 before jerking along past Penshurst and winding west down the valley of the Río Estrella. The train returns for Limón at 6 A.M. and 4:30 P.M. If you want to take it one way only and continue to Cahuita or Puerto Viejo, get off at Bonifacio, 38 km south of Limón; from here, it's a 10-minute walk to the coastal highway, where you can hail any passing bus.

From Puerto Limón, turn right at Penshurst and follow the unpaved road via Pandora. The road to Hitoy-Cerere is usually passable even in rainy season, though a 4WD is needed. Jeep taxis from Cahuita cost about $30 each way (you will need to arrange your return pickup in advance if you stay overnight in the park).

Cahuita and Vicinity

⋈ CAHUITA

This offbeat village (pop. 3,000), 45 km south of Puerto Limón and one km east of Hwy. 36, is an in-vogue destination for the young backpacking crowd and others for whom an escapist vacation means back to basics. Cahuita (a combination of the Miskito words *cawi*—a small tree with red wood that flourishes in coastal lowlands and is used to make dugouts—and *ta,* which means point of land; hence, "mahogany point") is totally laidback and definitely not for those seeking luxuries. The village is no more than two parallel dirt streets crossed by four rutted streets overgrown with grass, with ramshackle houses spread apart.

What you get is golden and "black" sand beaches backed by coconut palms, an offshore coral reef (now severely depleted; see the sidebar *The Destruction of Cahuita's Coral Reefs*), and an immersion in Creole culture. One of the most endearing aspects of life on the southern Caribbean coast is the large number of Rastafarians, with their broad smiles, dreadlocks, and a lifestyle that revolves around reggae, rasta, and—discreetly-reefer. Bob Marley is God in Cahuita. Even the postmaster has dreads.

Cahuita has struggled to recover from a lingering negative perception fed by a brief series of robberies and a murder in 1994 at Estrella, compounded in March 2000 when two U.S. female students were brutally murdered nearby (the murderers hailed from San José). The bad publicity stuck; for several years, tourists and Ticos shunned Cahuita. The police force has been beefed up and is now an effective force (there's even a military police checkpoint on the main road north of Cahuita; every vehicle is searched). At last visit, Cahuita had regained its popularity, although it still draws predatory elements. The locals run a committee to police the community, keep the beaches clean, and generally foster improvements. And ever so slowly, Cahuita's dirt roads are being laid with interlocking-brick paving. "Soon come!"

North of Cahuita village is a black-sand beach (Playa Negra) that runs for several miles. Cahuita's more famous beach (Playa Blanca) is a two-km-long scimitar of golden sand that stretches south from the village along the shore of the national park. The two main beaches first won Bandera Azul (Blue Flag) awards for environmental quality in 1996. Beware riptides at the northern end of this

Cahuita

© CHRISTOPHER P. BAKER

The Caribbean Coast

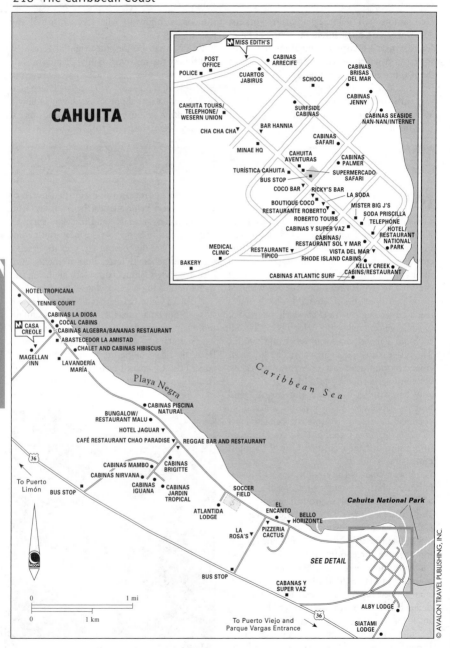

CAHUITA

Detail inset:

MISS EDITH'S
POST OFFICE
POLICE
CUARTOS JABIRUS
CABINAS ARRECIFE
SCHOOL
CABINAS BRISAS DEL MAR
CABINAS JENNY
CAHUITA TOURS/ TELEPHONE/ WESERN UNION
SURFSIDE CABINAS
CABINAS SEASIDE NAN-NAN/INTERNET
CHA CHA CHA
BAR HANNIA
CABINAS SAFARI
MINAE HQ
CAHUITA AVENTURAS
CABINAS PALMER
TURÍSTICA CAHUITA
SUPERMERCADO SAFARI
BUS STOP
COCO BAR
RICKY'S BAR
LA SODA
BOUTIQUE COCO
MISTER BIG J'S
RESTAURANTE ROBERTO
SODA PRISCILLA
ROBERTO TOURS
TELEPHONE
CABINAS Y SUPER VAZ
HOTEL/ RESTAURANT NATIONAL PARK
CABINAS/ RESTAURANT SOL Y MAR
MEDICAL CLINIC
RESTAURANTE TÍPICO
VISTA DEL MAR
RHODE ISLAND CABINS
BAKERY
KELLY CREEK CABINS/RESTAURANT
CABINAS ATLANTIC SURF

Main map:

HOTEL TROPICANA
TENNIS COURT
CABINAS LA DIOSA
COCAL CABINS
CASA CREOLE
CABINAS ALGEBRA/BANANAS RESTAURANT
ABASTECEDOR LA AMISTAD
CHALET AND CABINAS HIBISCUS
MAGELLAN INN
LAVANDERÍA MARÍA
Playa Negra
Caribbean Sea
CABINAS PISCINA NATURAL
BUNGALOW/ RESTAURANT MALU
HOTEL JAGUAR
CAFÉ RESTAURANT CHAO PARADISE
REGGAE BAR AND RESTAURANT
36
To Puerto Limón
BUS STOP
CABINAS MAMBO
CABINAS BRIGITTE
CABINAS NIRVANA
CABINAS IGUANA
CABINAS JARDIN TROPICAL
ATLANTIDA LODGE
SOCCER FIELD
EL ENCANTO
BELLO HORIZONTE
Cahuita National Park
LA ROSA'S
PIZZERIA CACTUS
SEE DETAIL
0   1 mi
0   1 km
BUS STOP
CABANAS Y SUPER VAZ
36
ALBY LODGE
To Puerto Viejo and Parque Vargas Entrance
SIATAMI LODGE

© AVALON TRAVEL PUBLISHING, INC.

beach. A second pale-sand beach lies farther along, beyond the rocky headland of Punta Cahuita; it is protected by an offshore coral reef and provides safer swimming in calmer waters.

Theft is a problem on the beach, Do not leave possessions unattended. Nude bathing is not allowed.

At last visit, Topo, of Magellan Inn, was planning a **Herpetarium,** with snakes and poison-dart frogs, intended to be a breeding center.

Finca Miramar Ocean View Park

This private 30-acre nature park (tel. 506/750-0238), about four km south of Cahuita, midway between Cahuita and Hone Creek, offers magnificent views up and down the coast from a hilltop mirador amid forest; it's a stiff hike up-hill. Day guests get use of a small swimming pool and sun deck; an oversize chess game under a shade canopy; and hiking trails that lead into the forest. A small *soda* serves snacks. It's accessed by a steep grade; 4WD is recommended. If you reserve two cabins, the place can be exclusively yours (see *Accommodations,* below). It has a shuttle service. Entrance is free.

Entertainment and Events

Cahuita hosts a five-day mini-Carnival—

THE DESTRUCTION OF CAHUITA'S CORAL REEFS

The most complex and variable community of organisms in the marine world is the coral reef. Corals are animals that secrete calcium carbonate (better known as limestone). Each individual soft-bodied coral polyp resembles a small sea anemone and is surrounded by an intricately structured calyx of calcium carbonate, an external skeleton that is built upon and multiplied over thousands of generations to form fabulous and massive reef structures.

The secret to coral growth is the symbiotic relationship with single-celled algae—zooxanthellae—that grow inside the cells of coral polyps and photosynthetically produce oxygen and nutrients, which are released as a kind of rent directly into the coral tissues. Zooxanthellae must have sustained exposure to sunlight to photosynthesize. Hence, coral flourishes close to the surface in clear, well-circulated tropical seawater warmed to a temperature that varies between 21° and 27°C (70° and 80°F).

The reef is a result of the balance between the production of calcium carbonate and a host of destructive forces. Though stinging cells protect it against some predators, coral is perennially gnawed away by certain snails and fish, surviving by its ability to repair itself and at the same time providing both habitat and food for other fauna.

Twenty years ago, Cahuita had a superb fringing reef—an aquatic version of the Hanging Gardens of Babylon. Today, much of it is dead following uplift during the 1991 earthquake and silt washing down from mainland rivers. Coral growth is hampered by freshwater runoff and by turbidity from land-generated sediments, which clog their pores so that zooxanthellae can no longer breathe. Along almost the entire Talamanca coast and the interior, trees are being logged, exposing the topsoil to the gnawing effects of tropical rains. The rivers bring agricultural runoff, too: poisonous pesticides used in the banana plantations and fertilizers that are ideal for the proliferation of seabed grasses and algae that starve coral of vital oxygen. It is only a matter of time before the reef is completely gone.

Prospects for the reef at Gandoca-Manzanillo are equally grim. The region's isolation is already a thing of the past. Ronal Umana, a marine biologist with the conservation group ANAI, fears that sedimentation and pollution could devastate the reef and tarpon and lobster nurseries.

Coral is a very resilient creature: a coral reef will grow back again if left alone. The Costa Rican government must move more quickly than it has to date if it is to save what little coral remains.

Carnavalitos Cahuita—in early December, when theater comes to town, the calypso and reggae is cranked up, and locals and tourists let their hair down. At other times, there's plenty of night action in Cahuita, though it's an almost exclusively male affair (as far as locals go).

The best place by far is **Ricky's Bar** (tel. 506/755-0228 or 755-0185), with a Jimmy Buffett's Margaritaville kinda feel. Run by Jenny, an affable Englishwoman, this tastefully decorated, hassle-free log and palm-thatch bar serves more than 30 killer cocktails ($2.50) and has happy hour nightly 8 –9 P.M., plus live music on Wednesday (party night) and Saturday (Caribbean Night). A beer garden was being added.

Coco's Bar, across the street, is another lively spot. This laid-back reggae bar has colorful Rastafarian decor and draws dreadlocked Rastas; it has a plank-floored disco complete with flashing lights to the rear and a terrace to the front with chess boards. The bar has a TV, and the cocktails are powerful ($2.50). Thursday is cocktail night, Friday it has live calypso, Saturday is party night, and Sunday is ladies night. Alas, it attracts a few drug dealers and leeches who hit clientele up for drinks.

More sedate bars include **Bar Hannia** and **Jardín Tropical,** which has pool tables.

Sports and Recreation

Turística Cahuita (tel. 506/755-0071, fax 506/755-0069, dltacb@racsa.co.cr) and **Cahuita Tours** (tel. 506/755-0232, fax 506/755-0082), in the village center, offer a panoply of tours and activities, including snorkeling trips ($15); birdwatching; fishing ($35); dolphin watching ($35); horseback rides (from $30); whitewater trips on the Pacuare ($85); plus trips to KeköLdi ($35) and even Boca del Toro, in Panamá ($130, three days). Open daily 9 A.M.–7 P.M. Cahuita Tours also offers scuba diving.

Mister Big J (tel. 506/755-0328) offers fishing and horseback rides.

Cabinas Brigitte offers guided horseback rides into the mountains ($40) or along the beach ($30).

You can rent boogie boards ($5) and beach chairs ($2) at Hotel Jaguar.

Accommodations

Cahuita offers lots of options; most are in the budget category. Choose carefully, as there is great variety in standards. Check that windows

riders at Playa Negra, Cahuita

© CHRISTOPHER P. BAKER

are secure. And bring your own soap, shampoo, and toiletries.

Camping: You can camp at **Cabinas Seaside** on the shore beneath palms for $2.50 pp, including use of showers and toilets. Don't pitch your tent too close to the beach; the no-see-ums there are vicious.

Under $25: *Playa Negra:* On the shorefront road about three km north of the village is **Cabinas Algebra** (tel./fax 506/755-0057, $10 cabins, $30 four-person unit low season; $15/40 high season), run by a German named Alfred and his charming wife, Andrea; they offer three double cabins with hot water, and a four-person unit with kitchen. I enjoyed a tasty, wholesome meal in the offbeat restaurant.

Nearby is **Cocal Cabinas** with small hardwood cabins plus a larger two-bedroom cabin with loft bedroom. All have fans and simple bathrooms with hot water. There's an aged, rustic communal kitchen. Its neighbor, **La Dios** (tel. 506/755-0178, goddess@racsa.co.cr), formerly Cabinas Ruby, has 10 cabins, including five with Jacuzzi tubs. It doubles as a meditation and yoga center, and has a rancho bar of natural stone and polished tree trunks.

Some 300 meters further south is **Cabinas Piscina Natural** (no tel., $18 s/d) run by a friendly chap called Walter and named for the natural seawater coral cove with sandy bottom, good for swimming. It has five small cabins (each has a double bed and bunk) with private baths and hot water, plus patios. There's a shady veranda over the pool in landscaped grounds with secure parking.

Farther south, a dirt road leads inland 50 meters to **Centro Turístico Brigitte** (tel. 506/755-0053 or 506/352-3053, brigittecahuita@hotmail .com, www.brigittecahuita.com, $20 s, $25 d without kitchen, $25 s, $35 d with kitchen), run by Swiss-born Brigitte. She has two simple cabins with hot water. Meals are served in a charming little restaurant, and Brigitte offers horseback tours ($19, half-day). She was planning to add two cheap rooms for $10 s, $15 d. Opposite Brigitte's is **Cabinas Mambo** ($25 s/d low season, $30 high season) a handsome two-story hardwood structure with four large rooms, each with mos-

quito nets, fan, hot water, and spacious veranda. Fishing and horseback rides are offered. You can get information on Cabinas Mambo at **Cabinas Jardín Tropical** (tel./fax 506/755-0033, jardintropical@racsa.co.cr, $30 cabin, $35–50 house), 20 meters inland and offering two charming and homey albeit rustic *cabinas* plus a two-bedroom house with a big kitchen. The cabins each have a kitchenette, hot water, and hammocks. There's a laundry, and poison-arrow frogs in the garden.

Nearby is **Cabinas Nirvana** (tel. 506/755-0110, nirvana99@racsa.co.cr, $30 shared bath, $45 d private bath and kitchen), a handsome, simple two-story hardwood structure with six cabins (four with private bath) with hot water. Breakfast is served on a terra-cotta patio. There's secure parking. Rates include breakfast. And the **Reggae Bar Restaurante,** 50 meters south, has three cabins with fans and private bath with cold water for $15 s/d.

Cahuita Village: A good option is the **Hotel National Park** (tel. 506/755-0245, $12 s, $20 d low season, $15 s, $25 d high season), directly in front of the park entrance. The 20 rooms are pleasant: clean and bright, with private baths and hot water. Oceanview rooms have larger beds and more facilities.

Cabinas Vaz (tel. 506/755-0218, fax 506/755-0283, $7 pp budget rooms year-round, $15 s, $20 d standard, $40 s, $50 d suite low season; $20 s, $25 d standard, $50 s, $60 d suite high season) has 18 clean but basically furnished cabinas with tiled floors, fans, and cold water. Two larger suites have king-size beds, fans, refrigerator, TV, and hot water. A pool and thatched bar with TV was to be added. It has secure parking.

Next door, and of similar quality, is **Cabinas Sol y Mar** (tel./fax 506/755-0237, $10 s, $14 d low season; $12 s, $16 d high season), with 11 simple rooms for four–six people, with pleasing private bathrooms with hot water. Rooms upstairs catch the breeze.

Past Cabinas Sol y Mar, the side road leads to a choice of half a dozen modest options.

On the east side of the village are several reasonable options beginning with **Cabinas Arrecife** (tel./fax 506/755-0081, $15 s, $20 d), whose 10 rooms have breezy verandas and are clean and roomy, if gloomy. Bathrooms have hot water. There's a delightful open-air dining area.

Cabinas Jenny (tel. 506/755-0256, jennys @racsa.co.cr, $15 downstairs, $20 upstairs low season; $20/30 high season), run by friendly young Rastas, has nine basic rooms on two levels, all with comfy mattresses, mosquito nets, and fans plus private bathrooms with hot water. Upstairs rooms have balconies. Nearby, **Cabinas Seaside Nan-Nan,** alias "Spencer Seaside Lodging," cannot be recommended.

Also on the shore is **Cabinas Brisas del Mar** (tel. 506/755-0011, $18 s/d), with clean, basic *cabinas* with fans and tiny private baths with hot water, plus patios with hammocks.

Surfside Cabinas (tel./fax 506/755-0246, $10 s, $15 d low season; $15 s, $20 d high season), has 14 modern, clean, basic rooms, each with refrigerator, louvered windows, fan, and private bath with hot water. It also has two two-bedroom units, plus a communal kitchen and laundry.

One block toward the beach is **Cabinas Palmer** (Apdo. 123, Puerto Limón, tel./fax 506/755-0243, kainerene@hotmail.com, $10 s, $15 d low season; $15 s, $20 d high season), which has 20 rooms (13 with hot water), mainly small but clean rooms with fans, plus three larger four-person rooms with refrigerator and kitchenette. The friendly owner Rene accepts credit cards. There's parking, and a sunny garden out back.

Near Parque Vargas: About 3.5 km south of Cahuita, on the road to Puerto Viejo, 200 meters north of the Parque Vargas park entrance, is **Cabinas Costa Azul** (tel./fax 506/755-0431, $15 s, $18 d), with eight simple rooms with TVs, fridges, fans, and private bath with hot water.

$25–50: *Playa Negra:* The Swiss-run **Bungalow Malu** (P.O. Box 23, Cahuita, tel./fax 506/755-0114, bungalowmalu@hotmail.com, $30 s, $35 d standard, $50 s, $55 d with kitchen, $40 s, $45 d with a/c) offers five exquisite, thatched, hardwood octagonal cabins enclosed in landscaped grounds. They're spacious and have

refrigerator, fans, Guatemalan bedspreads, and quaint stone-floored bathrooms with hot water, plus stone balconies. One unit has a kitchen. The restaurant offers fine Italian fare.

Cabinas Iguana (Apdo. 1049, Limón, tel. 506/755-0005, fax 506/755-0054, iguanas@racsa .co.cr, www.cabinas-iguana.com), farther south, is run by a Swiss couple. They offer a large wooden house sleeping six people for $50 low season; $65 high-season. A smaller house for three people costs $35/40, and there's a bungalow (without kitchen) with bunks and a double bed for $30/35. All have hot water, plus verandas with hammocks. It offers laundry service and a book exchange. There's a small, attractive pool and sun deck with cascade, and trails lead through the expansive grounds.

I recommend **El Encanto** (Apdo. 7302, Cahuita, tel./fax 506/755-0113, $35 s, $45 d low season; $45 s, $55 d high season), a splendid and fully equipped two-story hardwood home-turned-bed-and-breakfast run by French-Canadians. They offer three rooms in the main building, with queen-size orthopedic mattresses and Guatemalan bed covers, oriental carvings, tile floors, ceiling fans, and pleasant bathrooms. They also have cabins in the well-maintained garden, plus a small but exquisite patio restaurant and secure parking. It has a yoga center, and oozes peace and tranquility. Rates include breakfast (and taxes in low season).

Hotel Tropicana (tel./fax 506/755-0059, borgato@racsa.co.cr, $30 s, $35 d) is an Italian-run hardwood two-story structure with five large, clinically clean rooms with king-size beds, and private baths with large showers and hot water. They're set amid lawns and landscaped grounds. Breakfast is served on an upstairs veranda. Guests have Internet access. Dogs swarm at your heels.

Cahuita Village: The most charming option is **Kelly Creek Cabins & Restaurant** (tel. 506/755-0007, kellycr@racsa.co.cr, $35 s $40 d low season; $40 s, $45 d high season), behind a white picket fence immediately overlooking the park entrance. Run by a pleasant Spanish couple, it has four large rooms with private bath and hot water in a single, handsome, all-hardwood Thai-style structure with heaps of light pouring in through tall louvered windows. Elegant bed linens add a bright note, and there are mosquito net drapes. A restaurant serves Spanish cuisine overlooking the beach.

Another romantic gem is the private and peaceful Austrian-run **Alby Lodge** (tel./fax 506/755-0031, $35 s/d low season; $40 s/d high season), with four beautiful, thatched, Thai-style cabins sitting on stilts and widely spread apart amid lawns and bougainvillea. All have tons of character, with high-pitched roofs, screened and louvered windows, hardwood floors, bamboo furnishings, mosquito-net pendants on the ceiling, nice bathrooms with hot water, and private patios with hammocks and marvelous tables hewn from logs. There's a common kitchen. Rates include tax.

Nearby, **Sia Tami Lodge** (also known as Hotel Villas Exótica, tel. 506/755-0374 or 506/396-7618, $35 s/d low season, $40 s/d high season), a 10-minute walk inland, mostly caters to Spanish tour groups. Its 10 handsome *casitas* sit in their own gardens with hedges and lawns. Each has sponge-washed walls in earth tones, cool limestone floors, spacious kitchens, modest rattan and hardwood furnishings, mosquito nets over the beds, and large patios supported by tree trunks with hammocks. It has neither a restaurant nor pool. The setting is marvelous, although the bungalows disappoint.

$50–100: *Playa Negra:* The **Chalet & Cabinas Hibiscus** (Apdo. 943, Puerto Limón, tel. 506/755-0021, fax 506/755-0015, hibiscus @racsa.co.cr, www.hotels.co.cr/hibiscus.html, from $35 s/d low season, $45 s/d high season, $80 chalets low season, $100 high season) is one of the best places in Cahuita, with five pleasing *cabinas* plus four chalets for up to six people. There's no restaurant, but the units have kitchens, plus ceiling fans and hot water. Chalets have a spiral staircase up to the second floor, where rockers and hammocks allow a balcony siesta. There's a swimming pool, volleyball court, and game room.

The **Hotel Jaguar** looked very run-down at last visit and can no longer be recommended.

The French-Canadian-run **Atlantida Lodge** (tel. 506/755-0115, fax 506/755-0213, atlantic @racsa.co.cr, www.atlantida.co.cr, $30 s, $40 d low season; $45 s, $55 d high season) has 30 pleasing bamboo-roofed duplex cabins amid lush landscaped grounds with a little arched bridge spanning a pool filled with carp. Each has tile floors, a private terrace, fan, and private bathroom with hot water. There's a thatch restaurant with hammocks, plus a simple bar, small gym with Jacuzzi, a "boutique" and book exchange, a small exercise room, email service, and secure parking. Tours are offered.

The most charming place is the romantic **Magellan Inn** (Apdo. 1132, Puerto Limón, tel./fax 506/755-0035, magellaninn@racsa.co.cr, http://magellaninn.toposrealestate.com, $59 s/d standard, $79 s/d with a/c low season; $69 s/d standard, $89 s/d with a/c high season), set in lush landscaped grounds. Six spacious, modestly furnished and carpeted rooms are done up in mauves, with plentiful hardwoods in counterpoint. The bathrooms provide piping hot water. French doors open onto private patios with bamboo and soft-cushioned seats. Some rooms have a/c. The lounge, with its Oriental rugs and sofas, is an atmospheric place to relax, with jazz and classical music adding just the right notes. Its superb Casa Creole restaurant offers candlelit elegance. A sunken swimming pool is cut into a coral reef. Live-in owner Elizabeth Newton and daughter Teri and husband Topo are friendly souls and together speak English, German, French, and Spanish. Rates include continental breakfast.

Food

There's excellent eating in Cahuita, but the scene is ever-changing. Some places are only open in season (Dec.–May).

In Playa Negra, **Bananas Restaurant,** at Cabinas Algebra, is recommended for breakfasts, and at lunch and dinner serves salads, burgers, and a choice of fish, chicken, or steak with rice and beans and coconut sauce (from $5). **Belo Horizonte** (tel. 506/755-0206, 7:30 A.M.–5 P.M.), about 600 meters north of the village, is a simple bakery selling American and *típico* breakfasts ($2.50), plus awesome brownies, cakes, pastries, and fruit shakes *(batidos).* Also good for breakfasts is **Soda Priscilla** (7 A.M.–3 P.M. Mon.–Sat.), near Kelly Creek, where you can also fill up on *casados* (set meals) for $3.

The renowned ⓜ **Miss Edith's** (tel. 506/755-0248, 8 A.M.–10 P.M. Mon.–Sat., 6–10 P.M. Sunday, $6–10), one block north of the police station, is a homey place that offers inexpensive, spicy, aromatic Caribbean specialties such as "Rundown" (a spiced stew of fish, meat, and vegetables simmered in coconut milk), or lobster with curry and coconut milk ($14.50). Miss Edith brews herbal teas and offers a vegetarian menu, plus homemade ice cream on weekends. Breakfasts start at about $3.

Restaurante Roberto, with thatch and a sand floor, offers Caribbean dishes, such as squid in coconut sauce ($10). **Café Restaurant Chao Paradise** serves Caribbean cuisine, but several locals told me that it has a bad reputation and is best avoided. Instead, check out **Reggae Bar Restaurante,** a colorful hangout for local Rastas with a good selection of basic Italian and local dishes, enjoyed to the accompaniment of reggae music.

Pizzeria Cactus, on Playa Negra, serves pizza and spaghetti for $4–6. **Bungalow Restaurante Malu's** ($4–10) Italian open-air restaurant serves pastas and seafood.

The Spanish-run **La Rosa's** (tel. 506/755-0263, 6 A.M.–11 A.M. and noon–midnight), inland of Playa Negra, is a simple open-air eatery festooned with oropendola nests and serving European breakfasts, plus Spanish tapas, burgers, and entrées such as lobster in coconut sauce ($7.50) and steak in white sauce.

Some of the most creative cuisine is at ⓜ **Casa Creole** (6–9 P.M.) at the Magellan Inn, with such zesty fare as a garlic papaya appetizer, spiced shrimp Martinique in creole spice ($8), lobster with corn and ginger vanilla sauce ($8), and punch coco casa creole ($7). Be sure to start out with the pâté maison ($4) and, to end, profiteroles to fatten a pig. Try the killer cocktails, such as Rasta's Revenge. It serves dinner only.

On a par is **Cha Cha Cha** (tel. 506/394-4153, noon–10 P.M., $5–12), in Cahuita village. It serves superb "cuisine of the world" with such

CARIBBEAN SPICY

O ne of the pleasures of the Caribbean coast is the uniquely spicy local cuisine, which owes much to the populace's Jamaican heritage. The seductive flavors are lent predominantly by coconut, ginger, chiles, and black pepper. Breadfruit, used throughout the Caribbean isles but relatively unknown elsewhere in Costa Rica, is a staple, as are various tropical roots.

You'll even find ackee and saltfish (one of my favorite breakfasts), made of ackee fruit and resembling scrambled eggs in texture and color. It is often served with Johnny cakes, fried sponge dumplings that make great fillers to accompany escovietched fish, or Rundown, mackerel cooked in coconut milk. You must try highly spiced jerk chicken, fish, or pork, smoked at open-air grills and lent added flavor by tongue-searing pepper marinade.

Look, too, for patties, spicy meat and/or vegetable fold-over pies. Desserts include ginger cakes, pudin', *pan bon* (a kind of bread laced with caramelized sugar and, sometimes, a very sharp yellow cheese), banana brownies, and ice cream flavored with fresh fruits.

appetizers as humus ($2.50) and spicy coconut honey wings ($2.50), grilled Cajun chicken salad or grilled squid salad, and such entrées as fish pasta in white wine cream sauce with onion and garlic, or orange chicken breast, or corvina with shrimp and basil sauce. The rustic decor is romantic by candlelight, while world music adds just the right note.

The **Kelly Creek Cabins & Restaurant** (6:30 A.M.–10 P.M. Thur.–Tue.) is a winner with its salad, garlic shrimp, beer, and refresco special for $8. It also has paella and sangría, to be enjoyed on an open deck facing the beach.

Fancy Chinese? Try **Vista del Mar** (11 A.M.–10 P.M., $3–$11), serving dishes such as crab soup, fish fillet with garlic, and lobster in tomato sauce.

The pleasing, thatched **Restaurante Mariscos**, roadside, 100 meters west of the Parque Vargas park entrance, 3.5 km south of Cahuita, has a swimming pool.

Ricky's Bar was planning on adding an upstairs restaurant serving Tex-Mex, with a salad bar.

You can buy groceries at the well-stocked **Supermercado Safari** or **Super Vaz.**

Information and Services

Cahuita Tours acts as an informal tourist information office (see *Sports and Recreation,* above). **Boutique Coco,** two blocks east of Cahuita plaza, is a good spot to select a sensual batik wrap, bikini, or T-shirt. It also has jewelry and souvenirs. **Super Vaz,** opposite, has a boutique to the side. And **Mister Big J's,** by Boutique Coco, sells books, film, and cigars.

MINAE (tel. 506/755-0060, 8 A.M.– 4 P.M. Mon.–Fri.) has a National Parks Service office in the village.

There's a medical center at the entrance to town, on the main road from Hwy. 36.

The police station (Guardia Rural, tel. 506/755-0217 or 911) is next to the post office, at the north end of the village.

The nearest bank is in Bribrí, about 20 km farther south. Cahuita Tours can change dollars, as will most hotels. You can pay almost everywhere with dollars.

The post office (tel. 506/755-0096, 8 A.M.– noon and 1:30–5 P.M. Mon.–Fri.) is three blocks north of the plaza. There are public phones throughout the community.

Cabinas Brigitte has Internet service for $1.25 per 30 minutes, 7 A.M.–6 P.M. daily.

Mister Big J's (tel. 506/755-0328, 9 A.M.– noon and 1–6 P.M.) does laundry and charges $4 for a full basket, with three-hour turnaround. **Lavandería María** (tel. 506/755-0470), at the north end of Playa Negra, charges from $1.25. **Cabinas Brigitte** also offers laundry service ($3.50 a basket).

Getting There

Transportes MEPE (tel. 506/257-8129) buses depart the Gran Terminal del Caribe, in San José, daily at 6 A.M., 10 A.M., 1:30 P.M., and 3:30 P.M. The buses continue to Puerto Viejo, Bribrí, and Sixaola.

Buses depart Puerto Limón from Avenida 4, Calles 3/4, daily at 5 A.M., 7 A.M., 8 A.M., 10 A.M., noon, 1 P.M., 4 P.M., and 6 P.M. (one hour).

Buses depart Cahuita for San José at 7:30 A.M., 9:30 A.M., 11:30 A.M., and 4:30 P.M.; and for Limón at 6:15 A.M., 7 A.M., 9:15 A.M., 10:15 A.M., 11:15 A.M., 12:15 P.M., 1:15 P.M., 2:15 P.M., 3:15 P.M., 4:15 P.M., 5:15 P.M., and 6:45 P.M. Buses for Puerto Viejo depart at 5:45 A.M., 7:45 A.M., 8:45 A.M., 10:45 A.M., 1:45 P.M., 4:45 P.M., and 6:45 P.M.; and for Manzanillo ($1) at 6:50 A.M., 3:30 P.M., and 5 P.M. Buses for Bribrí and Sixaola depart at 5:45 A.M., 7:45 A.M., 8:45 A.M., 10:45 A.M., 12:45 P.M., 3:45 P.M., 5 P.M., and 7 P.M.

The nearest gas stations are at Penshurst and about 15 km southeast of Bribrí. Several locals sell gas (petrol) from jerry cans.

Getting Around

Cabinas Palmas and Cahuita Tours operate taxis that should be booked in advance.

There are no car rental agencies.

Cahuita Aventuras, in the village center, rents bicycles ($1 per hour, $7.50 daily) and mopeds ($4 hourly, $19 daily). **Turística Cahuita** rents bikes for $35 per day. **Cahuita Tours** has bicycles for $1.25 per hour or $6 a day.

CAHUITA NATIONAL PARK

Cahuita's 14 km of beaches are shaded by palm trees, lush forests, marshlands, and mangroves. Together they make up Cahuita National Park (1,067 hectares), created in 1970 to protect the 240 hectares of offshore coral reef that distinguish this park from its siblings. Animal life abounds in the diverse habitats behind the beach—an ideal place to catch a glimpse of tamanduas, pacas, coatis, raccoons, sloths, agoutis, armadillos, iguanas, and troops of howler and capuchin monkeys; and to focus your binoculars on ibis, rufous kingfisher, toucans, and parrots (and even, Dec.–Feb., macaws). Cahuita's freshwater rivers and estuaries are also good places to spot caimans. Snakes are commonly seen along the trail. Red land crabs and bright blue fiddler crabs—the latter with oversized claws—inhabit the shores.

The offshore reef lies between Puerto Vargas and Punta Cahuita and protects the northern stretch of the beautiful scimitar beach to the south. Smooth water here provides good swimming; it's possible to wade out to the edge of the coral with the water only at knee level. At the southern end of the park, beyond the reef, huge waves lunge onto the beach—a nesting site for three species of turtles—where tide pools form at low tide. Check with rangers about currents and where you can walk or snorkel safely.

Snorkelers can try their luck near Punta Cahuita or Punta Vargas (you must enter the water from the beach on the Punta Vargas side and swim out to the reef); you can also hire a local resident to take you out farther by boat. On the sea floor are massive brain corals and delicate, branching sea fans and feathers; nearer the surface are elkhorn corals, frondlike gorgonians spreading their fingers upward toward the light, lacy outcrops of tubipora—like delicately woven Spanish mantillas—and soft flowering corals swaying to the rhythms of the ocean currents.

Up to 500 species of fish gambol among the exquisite reefs. Here, amid sprawling thickets of bright blue staghorn, great rosettes of pale mauve brain coral, and dazzling yellow tubastras almost luminescent in the bright sunlight, a multicolored extravaganza of polka-dotted, piebald-dappled, zebra-striped fish protect their diminutive plots of liquid real estate among the reef's crowded underwater condominiums.

Besides what remains of the beautiful coral, there are two old shipwrecks about seven meters below the surface, both with visible ballast and cannons; one wreck has two cannons, and the second, a more exposed site, has 13. The average depth is six meters. The best time for diving and snorkeling is during the dry season, Feb.–April; water clarity during the rest of year is not good because of silt brought by rivers emptying from the Talamanca mountains.

Warning: Gangs of capuchin monkeys sometimes descend to the beach to greet you and beg for tidbits, often aggressively. Many folks report having been bitten. Feeding wild monkeys with human foodstuffs alters their habits and can adversely affect their health. *Don't feed the monkeys!* And guard your belongings. The monkeys aren't above taking off with your backpack.

Camping

You can stay at a camping area with picnic tables, water, pit latrines, and showers at the **administrative center** beside the beach, one km north of the Puerto Vargas Ranger Station ($2 pp per day). You can drive or hike in. Don't leave your gear unattended, as theft is a problem.

Information and Services

A footbridge leads into the park from the **Kelly Creek Ranger Station** (tel. 506/755-0461 or 506/755-0060) at the southern end of Cahuita village. Kelly Creek is shallow and easily waded. A shady seven-km nature trail leads from the Kelly Creek Ranger Station to the **Puerto Vargas Ranger Station** (tel. 506/755-0302), three km south of Cahuita midway along the park; the trail takes about two hours with time to stop for a swim. You must wade the Perozoso ("Sloth") River—its waters stained dark brown by tannins—just west of Punta Cahuita.

The main park entrance is about 400 meters west of Hwy. 36, about three km south of Cahuita (the Sixaola-bound bus will drop you off near the entrance). You can drive to the Puerto Vargas administrative center from here via dirt road; the entrance gate is locked after hours.

The Kelly Creek entrance station is open 6 A.M.–5 P.M. daily; the Puerto Vargas station is open 7 A.M.–4 P.M. daily Entrance costs $6 at Parque Vargas, and by donation at Kelly Creek.

Puerto Viejo and Vicinity

☒ PUERTO VIEJO

About 13 km south of Cahuita, the road forks just after Home Creek (also spelled Hone Creek). The main road turns east toward Bribrí; a spur leads three km to Playa Negra, a black-sand beach that curls east to Puerto Viejo, enclosing a small bay with a capsized barge in its center. The tiny headland of Punta Pirikiki at its eastern end separates Puerto Viejo from the sweep of beaches—Playa Pirikiki, Playa Chiquita, and others—that run all the way to Manzanillo and Panamá. You can walk along the beach from Cahuita at low tide.

Puerto Viejo is one of the most happenin' spots in Costa Rica. The discos are hopping, and, on peak weekends, you can't find a room to save your soul. Nonetheless, it is low-key and funky (vultures hop around lethargically on the streets, taking reluctant flight only when you approach within a meter or two).

The surfer, backpacker, and counterculture crowds (mostly Europeans and young North Americans) have firmly rooted here. Indeed, they dominate the scene, having settled and established bistros and restaurants alongside the locals. Telegraph poles and high wires today import the power of the 21st century (the supply is still not reliable; bring a flashlight), telephones arrived in 1997, and the sudden influx of tourists—including Ticos, who have recently wised up to the Caribbean's attractions—threatens to sweep away the last of the old ways. Not least, the scourge of crack and cocaine have come to town.

The overpriced **Caribe Butterfly Garden** (8 A.M.–4 P.M., $5 admission), at Cabinas Calalú east of town, has a netted garden with about 20 species of butterflies.

© CHRISTOPHER P. BAKER

Puerto Viejo

Finca la Isla Botanical Garden

This five-hectare botanical garden and farm (tel. 506/750-0046, jardbot@racsa.co.cr, 10 A.M.–4 P.M. Fri.–Mon., $2.50 admission, $8 with guided tour), one km west of town, is a treat for anyone interested in nature. Here, Lindy and Peter Kring grow spices, exotic fruits, and ornamental plants for sale. The couple have acres of native and introduced fruit trees. You can sample the fruits and even learn about chocolate production. There's also a rainforest loop trail, and a self-guided booklet for the garden. Toucans, sloths, and other animals are commonly seen, and poison-arrow and harlequin frogs make their homes in the bromeliads grown for sale. The *finca* is 400 meters from the road (200 meters west of El Pizote Lodge) and is signed. Lunches are offered by arrangement.

Keköldi Indigenous Reserve

The 3,547-hectare Keköldi reserve, in the hills immediately west of Puerto Viejo, extends south to the borders of the Gandoca-Manzanillo refuge. It is home to some 200 Bribrís and Cabecar people, who have formed the Talamanca Association for Ecotourism and Conservation (or ATEC;

PUERTO VIEJO DE TALAMANCA

see the sidebar *"ATEC: Grassroots Ecotourism"*). Reforestation and other conservation projects are ongoing. Gloria Mayorga, coauthor of *Taking Care of Sibö's Gift,* educates tourists on indigenous history and ways. Gloria and Juana Sánchez run the **Iguana Farm** (admission $1.50), an experimental project to raise green iguanas; the turnoff is 400 meters south of Hone Creek, beside Abastacedor El Cruce, then 200 meters along the dirt road to a short path that leads uphill to the Iguana Farm.

ATEC arranges visits ($17 half-day; $27 full-day) to Keköldi, with Gloria and her brother

Lucas as guides (Spanish only). Hiking and horseback trips into Keköldi are offered by Mauricio Salazar from Beach Cottages Chimúri (seven hours, $25 pp, including box lunch and a contribution to the Indian Association). Three-day trips cost $140, including overnight stays with the locals.

Entertainment and Events

The annual **South Caribbean Music Festival** (tel. 506/750-0062, fax 506/750-0408, festival @playarchiquitalodge.com) runs late February and early March, with performers spanning the spectrum from classical to calypso and reggae.

Puerto Viejo is known for its lively bars and discos (which rotate duty nightly off-season), and folks travel from as far afield as Limón to bop. The prize contenders are **Stanford's**—reggae! reggae! reggae!—and **Johnny's Place,** where the action spills onto the beach. Stanford's also has live music; Wednesday is Caribbean Night.

Neptuno Disco Bar has live music jams Wednesdays at 9 A.M., and two-for-ones on caipirinhas and piña coladas 9–11 P.M. **Café Musical,** above Calor Caribe, has live music Thur.–Sun. from 6 P.M., including calypso on Fridays and jazz on Sundays.

El Dorado (tel. 506/750-0604), next to Centro Comercial Mane, has a bar, pool table, board games, and movies on a TV. Every night is Ladies Nite. Open 8 A.M.–midnight. And the pleasant **Bar Maritza** in the Hotel Maritza has a TV, plus live calypso on Sunday evenings.

Bob Marley also rules at **Kaya's Place,** roadside 200 meters west of town, a cool spot to groove with the Rastas.

Hiking and Nature Tours

The local community organization **ATEC** offers hiking and nature excursions.

Mauricio Salazar at Beach Cottages Chimúri offers hikes to the Keköldi Indigenous Reserve, plus night walks (three hours; $10).

Puerto Viejo Tours (tel. 506/750-0411, fax 506/755-0082, puertoviejo@yahoo.com), offers local jungle hikes ($20), hiking ($35) at Cahuita,

CAMPING LAS OLAS
RESTAURANTE SALSA BRAVA
ANIMODO
LIZARD KING
STANFORD'S RESTAURANT CARIBE
LOTUS GARDEN
To Manzanillo
NEPTUNO BAR
BAR CARLOS
SODA IRMA
TAMANDUA LODGE
EL CAFÉ RICO / LAUNDRY
CABINAS CASA VERDE
SEE DETAIL
CABINAS TROPICAL
SODA MISS SAM'S
SODA Y CAMPING MISS ELENA'S
SCHOOL
COCO LOCO
CASHEW HILL JUNGLE LODGE
To Kiskadee
Caribbean Sea

0   200 yds
0   200 m

The Caribbean Coast

ATEC: GRASSROOTS ECOTOURISM

The grassroots Asociación Talamanca de Ecoturismo y Conservación (Talamanca Association of Ecotourism and Conservation, ATEC, tel./fax 506/750-0191 atecmail@racsa.co.cr, www.greencoast.com/atec.htm), in Puerto Viejo, trains locals as approved guides and sponsors environmental and cultural tours of the Talamanca coast ($15 half-day, $25 full-day) in an effort to promote ecologically sound tourism and assist small-scale, locally owned businesses. A portion of the cost is donated to community welfare projects. Options include "African-Caribbean Culture and Nature Walks," trips to the Keköldi Indigenous Reserve and Iguana Farm, rainforest hikes, snorkeling and fishing, bird and night walks, and overnight "Adventure Treks" into the Gandoca-Manzanillo reserve. Trips to the remote Talamanca indigenous reserves require one week's notice (groups only). Trips are limited to six people.

and white-water rafting tours ($75–85), plus trips to Gandoca-Manzanillo, Tortuguero (from $55), Keköldi ($60), and Boca del Toro in Panamá.

Terraventuras (tel. 506/750-0426, www.terraventuras.com, 8 A.M.–1 P.M. and 3:30–5:30 P.M. Mon.–Sat.) offers trips to Tortuguero ($50), the Indian reserves ($35), plus dolphin watching ($35), snorkeling ($35), and a rappeling canopy tour.

Rolf, of **Bushmaster Expeditions** (tel./fax 506/750-0283), offers nature tours to Gandoca ($40). ATV tours are offered by **Quad Adventours** (tel. 506/750-0632).

Surfing

Puerto Viejo is legendary among the surfing crowd. November through April, especially, the village is crowded with surfers, who come for a killer six-meter storm-generated wave called La Salsa Brava; November and December are supposedly the best months, though I've seen it cookin' in March. Beach Break, at Playa Cocles,

about three km south of Puerto Viejo, is good for novices and intermediates. The safest beach for swimming is Playa Negra and the small beach near the bus stop in town.

Kurt, at Hotel Puerto Viejo, rents boards and gives lessons, as does **Cabinas Grant** (tel. 506/750-0013).

Other Water Sports

Reef Runner Divers (tel./fax 506/750-0480, arrecifes55@hotmail.com), next to Pulpería Manuel León, offers guided dive tours ($40 one-tank, $60 two-tank, $50 night dive), PADI certification ($225), and dolphin and snorkeling tours. **Puerto Viejo Tours** also offers snorkeling. **Ocean Adventures** rents kayaks, boogies, and snorkeling and surfing gear, as does **Juppy & Tino Adventures** (tel. 506/750-0621), next door; the latter has kayak tours to Gandoca ($60). Also see *Playa Cocles to Punta Uva,* below.

The El Pizote Lodge offers fishing trips.

Horseback Riding

You can rent horses and take guided tours at **Don Antonio's** (tel. 506/750-0342), 600 meters south of town ($5 per hour). **Seahorse Stables** (tel. 506/750-0468, edwinsalem@yahoo.es), near Punta Cocles (see *Punta Cocles,* below), has tours by reservation only.

Shopping

Color Caribe (9 A.M.–8 P.M.) stocks a great selection of clothing, jewelry, and souvenirs, including hand-painted and silk-screened clothing, plus hammocks and colorful wind chimes.

Cabinas Casa Verde has a small but upscale boutique selling batiks, Panama hats, Panamian *molas,* and the like. Nearby, **LuluBelu** (tel. 506/750-0394, 1–9 P.M. Wed.–Mon.) is a colorful place selling an original range of ceramics, jewelry, and miscellany.

Accommodations and Camping

Demand is high; make your reservation in advance or secure a room as soon as you arrive. Beware touts who await your custom as the bus arrives and try to entice you to specific lodgings—they're known to tell lies to dissuade you

batik cloths, Puerto Viejo

from any specific place you may already have in mind.

The following are the best of dozens of options. Also see *Playa Cocles to Punta Uva,* below, for more accommodations.

The **Cabinas Casa Verde** charges $10–15 for camping in its secure gardens with exquisitely tiled toilets and showers.

Camping Las Olas (tel. 506/750-0424, $3.75 pp low season, $6.25 high season) is well-run and has large tents under metal shade platforms. It has basic toilets and showers. Discounts are offered if you bring your own tent.

The place to be is **Rocking J's** (tel. 506/ 750-0665, korchmaros@hotmail.com, www .rockingjs.com, $7 pp dorm, $20 s/d private room), a splendidly conceived and run backpackers' haven landscaped with ceramics and rough-hewn seats hewn from tree trunks; there's even a Tree House high atop a lopped-off trunk. The cheapest option is one of the sheltered camp sites beneath shade eaves; you can pitch your tent ($4; tent rental is $2 with mattress and sheets). You can also sleep outside at the "hammock hotel," with hammocks under shade canopies ($5), a little like a cross between an In-

dian tribal hut and a military camp. It also has two dorm rooms, plus private rooms in varying configurations with lofty bunks and desks below. Rooms share two solar-heated showers and five cold-water showers. Guests can use a community kitchen, plus there's laundry ($6), grill, and secure parking. It rents kayaks ($15 daily) and bicycles ($3 daily).

Soda y Camping Miss Elena (tel. 506/750-0580, $5 pp low season, $10 high season), on the southwest side of the village, charges $7 s/d including tent and cushion rental ($5 with your own tent). Miss Elena is a charmer and offers storage, baths, hammocks, parking, and real American breakfasts.

Under $25: Promising a great bargain, **Tamandua Lodge** (Apdo. 1728-3000 Heredia, tel./fax 506/750-0479, tamandualodge@racsa .co.cr) is run by Gustavo, a chatty, savvy owner who offers three small but exquisite rooms with tile floors, colorful decor, and metal four-poster beds with mosquito nets, plus fans, throw rugs, and stone-tiled bathrooms with cold water only. Louvered French doors open to a courtyard, with parking. Gustavo was adding a one-bed dorm room with kitchenette and shared bathroom, plus an upstairs apartment. He offers free laundry and coffee. Expect prices to rise.

I like **Cashew Hill Jungle Lodge** (tel. 506/750-0256, www.cashewhilllodge.com), on a hill on the southeast side of the soccer field. It has six simple *cabinas*. At last visit, new owners were upgrading.

Hotel Maritza (P.O. Box 8-7304 Puerto Viejo, tel. 506/750-0015, fax 506/750-0313, $10 s/d rooms; $20 d *cabinas*.), on the beachfront, has 14 clean rooms with ceiling fans, double and single beds, and private bath with hot water. On weekends, the bar and disco downstairs make the walls throb. There's parking in a well-groomed courtyard. Rates:

In the village, among the cheapest options and popular with surfers is the all-hardwood **Hotel Puerto Viejo** (no tel., from $5 pp shared bath, $8 pp private bath low season; $6.50/10 high season). It has 50 small and spartan rooms with fans, mosquito nets, and shared, tiled bathrooms (upstairs rooms are preferable). There are also more appealing cabins sleeping up to five at the rear. A remodeling and upgrade was under way at last visit. It is run by a friendly American, Kurt. It has security cameras throughout.

I love **Cabinas Jacaranda** (tel./fax 506/750-0069, $10–20 s, $14–25 d), with four cabins set in a pretty landscaped garden; three with shared bathroom with cold water only. The fourth cabin with fully equipped kitchen is for four people, has hot water, and rents weekly or monthly. It also has four simple wooden rooms. Furnishings are basic but delightful, with subdued tropical walls and colorful mosaic floors throughout. Japanese paper lanterns, mats, Guatemalan bedspreads, hammocks, and mosquito nets are nice touches.

The Swiss-run **Hotel Pura Vida** (tel. 506/750-0002, fax 506/750-0296, $12 s, $16 d shared bath low season; $15/19 high season; $22 s/d private bath low season; $25 high season) is nice: well-kept, with 10 large, pleasing rooms. An airy albeit soulless outside lounge has hammocks and easy chairs. Rates include taxes.

Café Rico (tel. 506/750-0510, $15 s/d year-round) has three simple hardwood cabins with lofty bamboo ceilings, clean bathrooms, bal-

conies; each sleeps three. One room upstairs has hot water and a wrap-around veranda with hammock. The two downstairs rooms have private bath.

Several choices are within one km of Puerto Viejo along the road that leads to Manzanillo. **Calalú Cabinas** (tel. 506/750-0042, $15 s, $20 d standard, $20 s, $25 d with kitchen low season; $5 extra high season) has five handsome little A-frame thatch huts in a compact garden, each cross-ventilated through screened louvered windows, with large walk-in showers, and porches with hammocks. Three units have kitchens; all have fans and hot water. It has a small butterfly garden; a pool was to be added.

Its neighbor, **Monte Sol** (tel./fax 506/750-0098, montesol@racsa.co.cr, www.montesol.net, $15 s/d low season, $20 s/d high season), is a bargain. It has six rooms with heaps of light and a tasteful offbeat motif (colored ceramic tiles and sponge-washed walls like swirled ice cream). Screened windows, mosquito nets, fans, and hot water are standard. The conscientious German owners also have an eight-person house that rents weekly or monthly. There's a handsome tree-shaded bar and dining terrace with fountain and pool-garden. It offers Internet services, plus tours by Mercedes Jeep.

I recommend **Kaya's Place** (tel. 506/750-0690, mariaanna7s@yahoo.se, www.kayasplace .com, $13 s, $15 d shared bath, $18 s, $20 d private bath low season; $15/20 shared bath, $20/30 private bath high season), a two-story stone-and-timber lodge supported by tree trunks washed up from the beach—the inspired creation of friendly young Rastas. It was still under construction at last visit, but looks to be a winner. It has 23 rooms, all charmingly albeit simply furnished with hardwood beds and furniture, screened windows, and walls in Caribbean pastels. Ten dorms have huge double bunks (some have share bathrooms; others have private baths, all tiled in pleasing sky blue). The structure has huge verandas with hammocks and beach views. To the rear are larger rooms with huge walk-in showers; some have loft bedrooms with king-size beds. The handsome restaurant will serve Caribbean cuisine. It has an Internet café.

$25–50: I like **Beach Cottages Chimúri** (tel./fax 506/750-0119, chimuribeach@racsa.co.cr, www.chimuribeach.com), west of town, with three nice log-and-thatch cabins set in pleasant grounds. Each is a different size; one, in Caribbean style, has a colorful gingerbread motif and a loft bedroom plus kitchenette and hot water ($25 low season, $35 high season; longer rentals are preferred: $225 weekly). A second three-person unit also has a loft bedroom ($45 high season; $290 weekly); a third, for four people, rents for $50 high season, $350 weekly. Both the latter have kitchens. Owner Mauricio Salazar, a generous, genteel host, offers guided day-trips into the KeköLdi Indigenous Reserve. Low-season rates are variable. Mauricio planned to reopen his Cabinas Chimurí, nearby; it was closed at last visit pending resolution of a legal issue.

In the village, the Italian-run **Cabinas Guarana** (tel. 506/750-0244, www.hotelguarana.com, $16 s, $20 d low season; $20 s, $25 d high season) is entered by a charming lobby with bar. It has 12 simple but clean and tastefully decorated rooms with colorful sponge-washed walls, fans, tile floors, mosquito nets, and private bath with hot water. Larger cabins have louvered windows, and cabins with hammocks. They're set in a lush garden with a tree house. Guests get use of a kitchen, and there's a laundry plus secure parking.

One of the nicest options, and a veritable bargain, is the clinically clean, Swiss-run **☒ Cabinas Casa Verde** (P.O. Box 37-7304 Puerto Viejo, tel. 506/750-0015, fax 506/750-0047, cabinascasaverde@ hotmail.com, www.cabinascasaverde.com, from $22 s, $24 d shared bathroom, from $34 s, $38 d private bath low season; from $26 s, $28 d shared, $45 s, $52 d high season). It has six cabins, five double rooms, and two single rooms, each with ceiling fans, mosquito nets, and lots of light, plus hot water in spotlessly clean showers and bathrooms. Wide balconies have hammocks. There's also a small bungalow, romantic as all get out, and nice for a family or small group. Owner Renée mixes his time between lazing in a hammock and fussing over running his place. Features include a gift store, café for guests, a laundry, secure parking, and a book exchange,

plus a tour booth (you can arrange horseback rides), small café for breakfast, and gift store. The lush garden includes exquisite showers and a poison-frog garden.

The German-run **Cabinas Tropical** (tel./fax 506/750-0283, rblancke@racsa.co.cr, www .cabinas-tropical.com, $20 s, $25 d low season; $25 s, $30 d high season), one block to the rear, has eight pleasing rooms: clean and airy, with ceiling fans, huge showers with hot water, mosquito nets, and wide French doors onto little verandas. Smaller single rooms are dingier; three newer rooms are larger and have refrigerators and balconies. It's quiet and secure. There's also parking. The friendly owner, Rolf, is a biologist and offers rainforest tours.

Cabinas Los Almendros (tel./ fax 510/750-0246, flchwg@racsa.co.cr, $15 s, $30 d rooms, $30 up to three people for cabins, $50 up to six people for apartments) is a modern structure with 10 rooms, four cabins, and three apartments around a courtyard with secure parking. The clean, spacious rooms are cross-ventilated, have both front and back entrances, double and single beds, ceiling fans, tile floors, and private bathrooms with hot water.

A favorite place is **Coco Loco** (tel./fax 506/750-0281, cocolocobb@puertoviejo.com or cocoloco@racsa.co.cr, www.cocolocolodge.de, $20 s, $25 d low season; $25 s, $30 d high season) on the southern point of the town, with five handsome Polynesian-style *cabinas* raised on stilts and reclusively nestled amid lawns. The log-and-thatch huts are simply furnished but crafted with exquisite care. They have mosquito nets over the beds, and hammocks on the porches. Simple breakfasts are served on a raised deck. A two-room bungalow with kitchen is also available. The charming owners, who are Austrian and live on-site, offer tours to Gandoca-Manzanillo ($35) and to the Los Cocles waterfall ($23). Rates are $15 more with kitchen.

El Pizote Lodge (Apdo. 1371-1000 San José, tel. 506/750-0227, fax 506/750-0226, pizotelg @hotmail.com, $49 s/d low season, $57 high season standard; $60/71 bungalows; $83/99 two-bedroom a/c bungalows; from $71/85 for cabañas; from $62/75 for a house), inland of

Playa Negra, is set in nicely landscaped grounds complete with giant hardwoods and sweeping lawns—a fine setting for eight small but clean and atmospheric rooms with four shared bathrooms with huge screened windows. There are also six bungalows and two houses. Units have overhead fans and bedside lamps. Four luxury bungalows have a/c, refrigerators, and hot water. The lodge even has a volleyball court, plus a pool table. The breeze-swept restaurant gets good reviews. It has a swimming pool.

Lizard King (tel. 506/250-0614, $35 up to four people), on the east side of town, is a sturdy two-story hardwood structure with 16 rooms, all with double and single bed, screened windows offering cross-ventilation, and large, clean modern bathrooms with hot water. Upstairs rooms have tall ceilings. It has a swimming pool, restaurant, and a disco in high season.

About 400 meters east of town, I like the Italian-run **Escape Caribeño** (tel./fax 506/750-0103, escapec@racsa.co.cr, www.escapecaribeno.com, $35 s, $40 d cabins low season, $45 s, $50 high season, $10 extra person; bungalows $65 for up to four people, $90 for up to seven people in high season), with 11 attractive hardwood cabins with double beds (some also have bunks) with mosquito nets, plus clean bathrooms with hot water, minibars, fans, and hammocks on the porch. They're widely spaced amid landscaped gardens and reached by raised wooden walkways. The brick-and-stucco bungalows across the road are also attractive, with raised ceilings, tile floors, and kitchenettes. There's also a wood-paneled house at the end of the garden for four people ($65 per day, one-week minimum). Gloria and Mauro are delightful hosts and were planning on adding two deluxe cabins. There's a large library.

$50–100: The **La Perla Negra** (tel. 506/750-0111, fax 506/750-0114, hotel@perlanegra-beachresort.com, www.perlanegra-beachresort.com, $40 s, $45 d low season; $80 s, $100 d peak season; $120 suites year-round), on Playa Negra, has 24 spacious rooms in a two-story all-hardwood structure cross-ventilated with glassless screened windows, charming albeit minimally appointed bathrooms with large walk-in showers,

and bare-bones furnishings. Some rooms have a separate mezzanine bedroom. Six luxury two-bedroom suites are spacious and have large balconies and handsome bathrooms. The place is owned by a friendly Polish couple, Marlena and Julian Grae, who run the place like a home. Horseback rides and jungle tours are offered, as are banana-boat rides. There's a lap pool, sun deck and bar, plus tennis court and basketball. Rates include breakfasts and tax.

Magin Moon (tel. 506/750-0115), next to La Perla Negra, is a handsome, self-contained beach bungalow for rent.

$100–150: Samasati Nature Retreat (Apdo. 203-2070, San José, tel. 506/224-1870, fax 506/224-5032, samasati@samasati.com, www .samasati.com; in the U.S., 721 Mountain View Ave., Petaluma, CA 94952, tel. 800/563-9643; $82 s, $124 d guesthouse; $148 s, $196 d bungalows) is a holistic retreat hidden amid 100 hectares of private rainforest nudging the mountainside one km inland of Hone Creek. It specializes in classes in yoga, shiatsu, reflexology, and other meditative practices, and offers daily, weekly, and monthly workshops and sessions, plus hikes, horseback rides, and excursions. You don't have to take yoga to stay here; anyone is welcome. Accommodations are in 10 handsome yet ascetically furnished Japanese-style log cabins with ocean and jungle vistas through glassless, floor-to-ceiling screened windows, all with verandas, loft bedrooms, and tiled walk-in showers. Larger units have mezzanine bedrooms with wrap-around windows. There are also five simpler rooms in a guesthouse with shared bathrooms, plus three two-bedroom *casas* with living rooms and kitchens. Vegetarian meals (and seafood by request) are served buffet-style in a handsome lodge perched on the mountainside and open to the elements to one side offering magnificent views over Puerto Viejo. It has a Jacuzzi. You'll need a 4WD for the rugged climb up the mountain. Rates include all meals and taxes.

Food

Puerto Viejo is blessed with a cosmopolitan range of eateries, even gourmet cuisine; also see *Playa Cocles to Punta Uva,* below.

For breakfast, I recommend **Café Rico** (tel. 506/750-0510, 6 A.M.– 2 P.M. Fri.– Wed.) a delightfully laid-back place serving on a shaded, palm-fringed veranda surrounded by lush bougainvillea; Roger, the English leasee, serves huevos rancheros ($4), omelettes ($4), granola with yogurt and fruit ($3.50), pancakes, plus sandwiches. I recommend the Annarosa special: fried potatos with cheddar cheese, fried eggs, and bacon.

Alternately, consider **Soda Tamara** (tel. 506/750-0148, 2–10 P.M. low season, 7 A.M.– 9 P.M. high season), with a shaded patio and full breakfasts (including granola with yogurt). The menu also runs to burgers and *típico* dishes such as fried fish with *patacones* (plantain), plus great *batidos* (milkshakes);

Restaurante Grant (Thur.– Tue. 7 A.M.– 10 P.M., $7), above Cabinas Grant, gets the breezes and offers breakfasts, plus fish fillet in white wine sauce, tenderloin steak in red wine and onion sauce, and pastas.

I like the palm-thatched, open-air, offbeat, Spanish-run **Salsa Brava** (tel. 506/750-0241, noon–4 P.M. and 6–10 P.M. Tue.–Sun., $4–10), with rainbow-hued furniture. The menu includes tuna ceviche salad, Caesar salad with chicken teriyaki, grilled garlic fish, plus sangría, and ice creams. Portions are huge and the fare surprisingly good.

El Dorado (tel. 506/750-0604), next to Centro Comercial Mane, is a popular pizza bar with TV and entertainment. The **Pizza Coral** (tel. 506/750-0051, 7 A.M.–noon and 5:30–9:30 P.M. Tue.–Sun.) serves good Italian fare ($6 and up for dinners), including pizzas (from $4) in a raised, open-air hardwood structure; as does **Café Viejo** (tel. 506/750-0817, 6–10 P.M.), the snazziest place in town, with pizzas (from $3), pastas ($5), and other Italian fare, including a large dessert and cocktail menu. The Italian-run **Animodo** (tel. 506/750-0257, 6–10:30 P.M. Mon.–Wed. low season; noon–4 P.M. and 6–10:30 P.M. Mon.–Wed. high season; and noon–10:30 P.M. Sat.–Sun. year-round, $5–12), overlooking the beach east of town, is a shaded open-air eatery recommended for Italian fare, such as corvina (sea bass) in chianti sauce, and gnocchi.

For Thai food, check out **Chile Rojo** (no tel., noon–10 P.M. Wed.–Mon., $2–7), a simple, charming, open-air space offering veggie samosas, Thai fish soup, Thai curries, etc. The open-air, candlelit **Lotus Garden** (tel. 506/750-0232, noon–11 P.M.) also serves Thai and Japanese food, including all-you-can-eat sushi (of average quality) from 3–11 P.M.

Oozing charm, **E-Z Times** (tel. 506/750-0673, 6:30 A.M.–11 P.M., $3–10) is a hip bar-restaurant in an old home with open-air patio. It serves ceviche, gnocci and salad, plus tapas and lamb, duck, and even quail entrées.

Miss Sam bakes tarts and bread and offers meals at **Soda Miss Sam's;** while Miss Daisy is renowned for her *pan bon,* ginger cakes, and meat-filled patties.

Well-stocked groceries include **Abastacedor Manuel León** (a.k.a. "Chino's") and **Super El Buen Precio,** at the entrance to town. For fresh baked goods head to **Pan Pay Panadería** (tel. 506/750-0081, 7 A.M.–6 P.M. Thur.–Tue.), which serves breakfast ($2.50) and has fruit salads ($2) and fruit-filled pastries, croissants, breads, tortillas, and coffees; or **Panadería Elizabeth** (6 A.M.–9 P.M.).

You can buy fresh produce and meats at **Carne Cuca.**

Information and Services

ATEC is the informal node of local activity and acts as a tourist information bureau. It's open 8 A.M.–9 P.M. Mon.–Tue. and Thur.–Sat.; 8 A.M.–8 P.M. Sunday; and 8 A.M.–noon and 2–9 P.M. Wednesday. **Soda Tamara,** opposite ATEC, has a bulletin board with tourist information. Two good online resources are www.puertoviejo.net and www.greencoast.com.

There's a **medical clinic** (tel. 506/750-0758 or cellular 506/841-9171; open 10 A.M.–7 P.M. Mon.–Fri. and weekends for emergencies) and a **dental clinic** (tel. 506/750-0303, or 506/750-0389 for emergencies) 50 meters inland from the bus stop. **Internet Ipromer** also has 24-hour medical services.

The **police station** (tel. 506/750-0230) is next to Johnny's Place.

Puerto Viejo has no bank—the nearest is in

The Caribbean Coast

Bribrí—but you can cash traveler's checks and change dollars for *colones* at Pulpería Manuel León (the owner charges 1 percent commission).

The **post office** (tel. 506/750-0404, 7:30 A.M.–5:30 P.M. Mon.–Fri.), in Centro Comercial Mane.

There are public telephones at Pulpería Manuel León (tel. 506/750-0452, 7 A.M.–7 P.M.); and outside the ATEC office (tel. 506/750-0188), which also has a fax service.

ATEC offers Internet access at 15 colones per minute ($2.25 per hour). The a/c **Video Mundo** (tel. 506/750-0651, 8 A.M.–10 P.M.), nearby, charges $1.15 per 30 minutes for Internet access. **Internet Ipromer** (tel. 506/750-0633, 9 A.M.–9 P.M.) charges $1.25 per hour.

The **laundry** (8 A.M.–7 P.M.) in Centro Comercial Mane charges $3 per load (it closes during sunny afternoons following rains). **Café Paris** charges $3.75 per load.

Getting There

See *Getting There* in the *Cahuita* section, above. The bus fare from San José to Puerto Viejo is $6.50. Return buses depart Puerto Viejo for San José at 7 A.M., 9 A.M., 11 A.M., and 4 P.M.; and for Limón at 5:30 A.M., 6 A.M., 9 A.M., 11:45 A.M., 1:45 P.M., 4 P.M., 5 P.M., and 5:30 P.M. The Puerto Limón–Puerto Viejo buses are usually crowded; get to the station early. You can buy tickets for Transport MEPE buses (tel. 506/750-0023), opposite the bus stop.

You can buy gas from Tony, at the green house 30 meters west of Neptuno Bar.

Getting Around

ATEC can arrange taxis. You can rent mountain bikes from **Casa Verde** and **Cabinas Grant** ($2.50 per day).

Ocean Adventures rents scooters ($12 for two hours, $28 full day).

PLAYA COCLES TO PUNTA UVA

South of Puerto Viejo, the paved road runs via Punta Cocles and Punta Uva to Manzanillo, a fishing village at the end of the road, 13 km southeast of Puerto Viejo. The beaches are marvelous: long and breathtakingly beautiful in a South Pacific kind of way. Coral-colored **Playa Cocles** runs southeast for four km from Puerto Viejo to the rocky point of Punta Cocles. Another stun-

surfers at Playa Cocles

© CHRISTOPHER P. BAKER

ning beach—**Playa Chiquita**—runs south four km to Punta Uva, where caimans can be seen in the swampy estuary of the Río Uva. From here, a five-km-long gray-sand beach curls gently southeast to Manzanillo, with dramatic ridgeback mountains in the distance. Coral reefs lie offshore, offering good snorkeling and diving.

Gandoca-Manzanillo Wildlife Refuge awaits beyond the end of the road.

There are no settlements (except the tiny hamlet of Punta Uva), just a string of cabinas along the dirt road. The majority are run by Europeans drawn to a life of idyll as laid-back hoteliers.

The colorful butterflies flitting down the road might draw you to the **Mariposario** (8 A.M.–5 P.M., $6 admission), a netted butterfly garden in the hills above Playa Chiquita. About 20 butterfly species fly free, and monkeys and other animals are easily seen on trails into the surrounding forest. There's a gift store.

Sports and Recreation

I recommend **Seahorse Stables** (tel. 506/750-0468, edwinsalem@yahoo.es), near Punta Cocles, offering horseback rides by reservation, including a beach tour ($40), jungle and "swim with horses" beach tour ($60), and to Manzanillo ($70). Edwin Salem, the charming and erudite Argentinian owner, arranges occasional polo matches on the beach. He also offers sailing lessons on his 18-foot Hobi-Cat, as well as overnight turtle-watching tours ($150 including lodging), plus surfing trips. Edwin was a semi-pro surfer and will take *experienced surfers only* to a breaking reef three km offshore with 40-foot "face" waves that break up to 20 feet!

You can rent kayaks and bicycles at **Bar Restaurant El Ranchito.**

Treat yourself to an open-air massage by Argentinian Marí Pérez (tel. 506/750-0216) at her rustic roadside home, about 500 meters east of Hotel Cariblue ($40).

Accommodations

Under $25: At **Cabinas El Tesoro** (tel. 506/750-0128, fax 506/750-0507, cabinaseltesoro @puertoviejo.net, $9 pp dorm; $11 pp cabinas; $35 s/d with fan, $55 s/d in newer a/c rooms year-round) about one km from Puerto Viejo, 11 simply furnished rooms have orthopedic mattresses, screened windows, fans, and private baths with hot water, plus hammocks on patios. There's also a his-and-hers surf dorm at the back, with a communal kitchen and his-and-hers toilets and showers. Three newer, more upscale rooms have earth-tone stucco, cross-ventilation, cable TV, refrigerators, and large walk-in showers; two have a/c. It's well-run by a friendly in-the-know American, Charlie Shannon. There's the Internet, unlimited free coffee, and parking.

The Canadian-run **Sloth Club** (tel. 506/750-0358, $15 s/d shared bath, $20 private bath) appeals for its peaceful and secluded beachfront setting rather than for its facilities. This old wooden home has five simple cabins with cross-ventilation, and porches with hammocks. They vary, some being barebones and appealing only to hardy budget travelers. One has a kitchenette.

$25–50: The **La Isla Inn** (tel./fax 506/750-0109, islainn@racsa.co.cr, www.puertoviejo.com/laisla.htm, $20 s, $30 d low season; $25 s, $40 d high season; $10 extra person; $50 for a big room sleeping four), just 50 meters from Playa Cocles, is a two-story all-hardwood structure with five rooms (three upstairs, two downstairs). The wide, upper-story veranda replete with hammocks grants views over the ocean. Rooms are large, with lots of light pouring in through screened windows, plus fans and nets to keep mosquitoes at bay, orthopedic mattresses, and private bathrooms with hot water. Six cabins were to be added.

La Costa de Papito (tel./fax 506/750-0080, costapapito@yahoo.com, www.greencoast.com/papito, $26–43 d low season; $34–52 high season), one km south, is run by Eddie Ryan, a New York hotelier who has conjured 10 simple yet tastefully decorated bungalows at the jungle edge in a lush five-acre garden. Each has ceiling fan, leopard-skin sheets (!), exquisite tiled bathrooms, and shady porches with hammocks under thatch. Four newer, smaller cabins have polished hardwoods and outside "rainforest" bathrooms with mosaic floors and sinks. There's a laundry, massage, and bicycle, surfboard, boogie board, and snorkel rentals. Rental and free transfers are offered. Hearty breakfasts are served on your porch. Rates include taxes.

The German-run **La Caracola** (tel. 506/750-0135, fax 506/750-0248, $40 s/d, $50 with kitchen), between Punta Cocles and Punta Uva, has 14 colorfully painted cabins with screened windows and private bath with hot water. They're raised on stilts with parking beneath. It has a simple beachside café plus a garden salon for relaxing in hammocks and lounge chairs.

I recommend **Aguas Claras** (tel. 506/750-0131, fax 506/750-0368, aguasclaras@racsa.co.cr, www.aguasclaras.net, $47 s/d, $84 three or four people, $160 up to six people), nearby, with five hardwood *casas* in well-groomed grounds. Each is a different size, accommodating two to six people. Of a delightful Victorian style, they have gingerbread trim, bright tropical color schemes, ceiling fans, modern tiled bathrooms with hot water, large full kitchens, and shady verandas with rattan furnishings.

The **Jardín Miraflores Lodge** (Apdo 6499, San José 1000, tel./fax 506/750-0038, in the U.S., SJO 2385, P.O. Box 025216, Miami, FL 33102-5216; miraflorereservation@mac.com, www.mirafloreslodge.com, from $25 s/d to $60 s/d), at Punta Cocles, is a true nature lover's paradise. Choose from double rooms with shared bathroom or private bathroom and balcony with hammock, and suites with king-size beds, private bathrooms, and living areas. Downstairs rooms have kitchenettes and king-size beds plus two sofa beds. Mosquito nets hang above the beds. It also has a basic six-bed dormitory with outside bathrooms for groups only ($10 per person). The charming hotel—a combination of indigenous Bribrí and Caribbean architecture of wood and bamboo—is adorned with Latin American fabrics, masks and art, and bamboo vases full of fresh tropical blooms. Upstairs, cool breezes bearing hummingbirds flow through the rooms. Health-conscious meals are served in a tiny, rustic, charming Indian-style rancho. You can also arrange boating and rent bikes; tours are offered. Rates include a hearty breakfast. Seventh day free.

Playa Chiquita Lodge (tel. 506/750-0062, fax 506/750-0408, info@playachiquita.com, www

.playachiquitalodge.com, $30 s, $39 d low season; $40 s, $49 d high season), three km south of Punta Cocles, is appealing for its jungle ambience. Eleven spacious "bungalows" offer murals, sunken bathrooms (no hot water), fans, and leather rocking chairs on a wide veranda. It also rents a one-bedroom apartment for $35/50 low/high season; and three budget rooms with cold water for $20. You can dine alfresco under thatch in the restaurant. The lodge arranges diving and snorkeling trips, boat trips to Punta Mona, plus bike and horse rentals. Public facilities were shabby at last visit, suggesting that upkeep may be an issue.

The Treehouse (www.costaricatreehouse.com, from $45 s/d low season, $55 s/d high season), at Punta Uva, is a rustic all-wood two-story structure with a fabulous Middle-Earth feel. It is built in and around a huge tree, with separate elements connected by a steel suspension bridge. Two bedrooms share a bathroom; a spiral staircase leads to a loft bedroom with king-size bed. There's also a beach house.

The Italian-run **Pachamama B&B** (tel. 506/759-9196, pachamamacaribe@yahoo.com, $35 s/d low season, $45 high season, including breakfast and tax; $80 s/d per day) enjoys a marvelous riverside forest setting amid trees festooned with epiphytes. It has two bungalows featuring pastel color schemes including sponge-washed floors, simple no-frills furnishings, mosquito nets, pleasing tiled bathrooms with hot water, plus hardwood decks. A spacious five-person *casa* has a raised floor with sofabed and lively color scheme. The *casa* is also available for $300 per week.

I recommend the Dutch-run **Playa Punta Uva Cabinas** (tel. 506/750-0431, crchichi @yahoo.com, $40 s/d; $45 studio), 500 meters south, hidden away behind the beach amid a tropical garden. It has two airy, lofty-ceilinged wooden gingerbread-trimmed cabinas that share a wide porch and a pleasantly tiled bathroom with warm water. They're simple and homey but adorable, and reached by a bougainvillea arbor. A spacious studio sleeps four people and has a fridge and private bathroom. Simple meals are served at a small rancho bar. You can rent kayaks. Monique, the charming owner, speaks Dutch,

French, English, Spanish, and German, and says she "wants only friendly people."

The new, French-run **Colibri Lodge** (tel. 506/759-9036, fax 506/759-9037, elcolibrilodge @racsa.co.cr, www.elcolibrilodge.4t.com, $30 s, $40 d), south of Punta Uva, has a lush jungly setting. Its 10 concrete cabins lack ventilation and get hot (the glass windows need replacing with screens), but they boast nice hardwood floors and color schemes, and modern bathrooms with hot water. It has a gourmet restaurant, and trails lead to the beach. Monkeys hang out in the trees overhead, and an adjacent lagoon harbors caiman. The owners are a delight. Rates include breakfast.

$50–100: I like **Cariblue Bungalows** (tel./fax 506/750-0057, cariblue@racsa.co.cr, www.cariblue.com, $60 s/d standard, $70 s/d bungalows low season; $70 s/d standard, $80 s/d bungalows high season), one km south of Puerto Viejo, with 15 handsome, spacious hardwood *cabinas* of varying sizes amid lawns with shade trees. Some have king-size beds. All have colorful sponge-washed decor, bamboo ceilings with fans, private bathrooms with mosaic tiles and hot water, plus sliding doors opening to delightful porches with hammock. There's a book exchange; boogie board and bike rentals; and a gift shop and TV lounge, and a freeform pool with Jacuzzi and wet bar were being added at last visit, as was a gym and jogging trail. An Italian seafood restaurant serves meals under thatch. A two-room house is also available. Rates include tax and buffet breakfast.

Also recommended, **Azánia Bungalows** (P.O. Box 86-7304 Puerto Viejo, tel. 506/750-0540, fax 506/750-0371, ifno@azania-costarica.com, www.azania-costarica.com, $45 s, $55 d low season, $55/65 high season), next to Cariblue, is another beautiful property in lush grounds. Eight thatched, hardwood cottages with large decks with hammocks are delightfully simple and have batik blinds on all-around screened windows, queen beds plus singles in a loft, and handsome bathrooms with colorful tiles, drop-down walk-in showers with sauna seating, and huge windows. Dogs are allowed. It rents bikes. A restaurant was being planned at last visit.

Casa Camarona (Apdo. 2070-1002, San José, tel. 506/750-0151, fax 506/222-6184, camarona @ticonet.co.cr, www.casacamarona.com, $36 s, $55 d; $48 s, $67 d a/c) is well-run by a Tico couple and offers 18 modestly furnished wooden rooms with tile floors and hot water. It has an intimate breeze-swept restaurant, La Palapa, decorated in Jamaican style. There's also a gift store, beach bar, laundry, safe parking, plus bicycle and kayak rental, and tours. The facilities are wheelchair accessible. At last visit, the owners were planning to add a/c and handicapped facilities. Rates include water sports.

Almost at Punta Cocles is the relatively upscale **Villas del Caribe** (Apdo. 8080, San José 1000, tel. 506/750-0202, fax 506/221-2801, info@villascaribe.net, www.villascaribe.net, $69 s/d low season, $79 high season, $89 peak season), with a superb location in the cusp of the bay. It has 12 attractive rooms in a two-story complex in landscaped gardens 50 meters from the beach. Fully equipped kitchen, hot water, and fans are standard. It has a restaurant and bar. The hotel is eco-conscious—even the soaps and toiletries are biodegradable. Rates include breakfast and tax.

The relatively upscale **Hotel Punta Cocles** (Apdo. 11020, San José 1000, tel. 506/750-0337, fax 506/750-0336, gandoca@racsa.co.cr, www.hotelpuntacocles.com, $55 s/d standard low season, $70 s/d high season, $95 up to six people with kitchenette low season, $100 high season), an oasis of tranquility about four km south of Puerto Viejo. Set 500 meters back from the beach, it sprawls over gently rising gardens covering 10 hectares, all but 2.4 of them still forested. Beach access is via a path that leads past towering tropical trees; nature trails lead into the private reserve. The hotel's 60 modern a/c cabins (five with kitchenettes) are placed wide apart. They're spacious, with hot water, ceiling fans, large closets, and comfortable—but noisy—beds. Wide porches are good for armchair bird-watching. Facilities include an open-air restaurant overlooking a swimming pool and sun deck for alfresco dining, a Jacuzzi, game room, and TV lounge. Guided tours are offered.

Hotel Kashá (P.O. Box 1991, Puerto Viejo, tel./fax 506/750-0205, reservations@costarica-hotelkasha.com, www.costarica-hotelkasha.com, $56 s, $64 d), an attractive place with 14 bungalows set back from the road amid the forest. The handsome hardwood units are spacious, with plenty of light, screened windows, ceiling fans, two double beds, and pleasant bathrooms with heated water and beautiful Italian ceramics. Some units are for two people; others are for four people. The hotel boasts a small *ranchito* restaurant and bar, plus a small but handsome pool with water cascade. It offers all-inclusive packages. Rates include tax and breakfast.

I love the French-owned ▼ **Shawandha Lodge** (tel. 506/750-0018, fax 506/750-0037, shawandha@racsa.co.cr, www.shawandhalodge .com, $75 s/d low season, $90 high season standard), one km farther south. It has 12 spacious, thatched, hardwood cabins hidden amid tall ceibas and merging seamlessly into the jungle. Each is marvelously furnished, with lofty wood-and-thatch ceilings and simple yet beautiful modern decor, including four-poster beds, screened windows, and large verandas with hammocks. The bathrooms are splendid, boasting large walk-in showers with exquisite tile work. A restaurant serves breakfast and dinner, and there's a splendid open-air lounge with contempo decor and plump bamboo-framed sofas. Rates include American breakfast.

The **Almonds & Corals Lodge Tent Camp** (tel. 506/759-9057 or 506/272-2024, fax 506/ 759-9056 or 506/272-2220, www.almondsandcorals .com, $60 s/d low season; $70 high season), is three km north of Manzanillo, with a lonesome setting a few leisurely steps from the beach. Each of 24 tent-huts is raised on a stilt platform, is protected by a roof, and features two singles or one double bed, a locker, night lamps, table and chairs, plus mosquito nets and deck with hammock—a touch of Kenya come to the Caribbean. Very atmospheric! Each cabin has its own shower and toilet in separate washhouses. Trees tower over the tent-huts. Raised walkways lead to the beach, pool, snack bar, and restaurant serving Costa Rican food. You can

rent kayaks, bicycles, and snorkeling gear. Tours are offered.

I recommend **La Casita,** a delightful cottage; for information, call Charlie at El Tesoro (tel. 506/750-0128).

Food
The following spots are listed from Puerto Viejo eastward.

Restaurante La Palapa (noon–10 P.M. Wed.–Mon., $6–12), a stone's throw away at Casa Camarona, is recommended for its Italian and seafood dishes with a nouvelle twist; it also serves burgers and sandwiches, and doubles as a disco after 10 P.M. And the **El Rinconcito** (no tel.), nearby, is a simple thatched eatery serving Peruvian seafood, including ceviche.

The finest cuisine east of San José is to be savored south of Punta Cocles at ▼ **La Pecora Nera** (tel. 506/750-0490, 11:30 A.M.–midnight high season only Tue.–Sun., $5 –12), a piece of "civilization" tucked off the main road and a genuine fine-dining experience in unpretentious surrounds at fair prices. Ilario Giannono and Andrea Blancardi, the young Italian owners, offer delicious bruschetta, spaghetti, pizzas, calzones, a large selection of daily specials, all exquisitely executed. I recommend the mixed starters plate, a meal in itself. No credit cards.

Also recommended is **El Duende Felíz** (tel. 506/750-0356, 5 –10:30 P.M. Thur.–Mon., $3 –$10), a cool and shady Italian restaurant in a beautiful wooden home and serving salads and pastas, and a house specialty of *lomito* (steak) mediteraneo, served on the deck overlooking a tropical garden.

Nearby, the no-frills **Restaurante Elena Brown's** (tel. 506/750-0265) offers simple yet tasty and filling Caribbean dishes. It draws a regular crowd of rough-and-ready expats and locals; it has a pool table, plus TV at the bar.

At Punta Uva, I love the **Bar Restaurant El Ranchito** (10 A.M.–4 P.M., closed Tue.–Thur. low season), a hidden gem accessed via the beach and 100 meters of dirt road. Set amid manicured gardens, with thatched dining areas, it serves sandwiches ($3.50) and simple rice and fish dishes ($9), plus ice creams and cocktails.

The **Colibri Lodge** (11 A.M.–6 P.M., $5) proffers French cuisine such as ham crepes, liver with garlic, and salads and sandwiches.

Services

Café Internet Río Negro (tel. 506/750-0801, 8 A.M.–8 P.M. Mon.–Sat.) charges 15 colones per minute and serves fruit shakes, sandwiches, and Argentinian *empañadas*. **Internet Café Negra** (tel. 506/750-0343) is two km east.

Manzanillo and Vicinity

MANZANILLO

This lonesome hamlet sits at the end of the road, 13 km south of Puerto Viejo. The populace has lived for generations in what is now the wildlife refuge, living off the sea and using the land to farm cacao until 1979, when the *Monilia* fungus wiped out the crop. Electricity arrived in Manzanillo for Christmas 1989, four years after the first dirt road linked it to the rest of the world. The hamlet has become a darling of the offbeat, alternative-travel set.

From Manzanillo, a five-km coastal trail leads to the fishing hamlet of **Punta Mona** (Monkey Point) and the heart of Gandoca-Manzanillo National Park. According to local legend,

Christopher Columbus himself named Monkey Point for the population of howler monkeys that still inhabits the swampy area, and Manzanillo for a great old manzanillo tree that once towered over the coast. The tree died in the 1940s and finally toppled into the sea in 1957.

Sports and Recreation

A local cooperative, **MANT Guides** (tel. 506/759-0643, grenald60@hotmail.com), offers birding, fishing, hiking, horseback riding, and snorkeling excursions, including full-day tarpon fishing in the Sixaola ($150 for two people).

Aquamore (tel. 506/759-9012, aquamor @racsa.co.cr, 6:30 A.M.–8 P.M.) is a full-service

The Caribbean Coast

© CHRISTOPHER P. BAKER

Playa Negra, Manzanillo

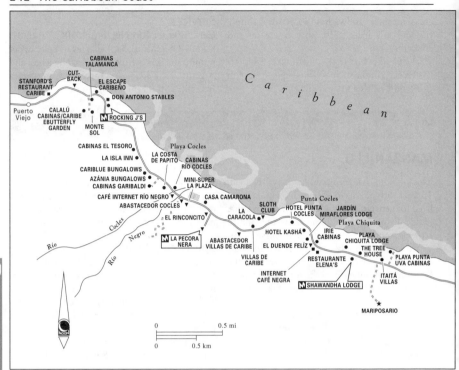

STANFORD'S
RESTAURANT
CARIBE

CABINAS
TALAMANCA

CUT-
BACK

EL ESCAPE
CARIBEÑO

DON ANTONIO STABLES

Puerto
Viejo

CALALÚ
CABINAS/CARIBE
EBUTTERFLY
GARDEN

MONTE
SOL

ROCKING J'S

CABINAS EL TESORO

LA ISLA INN

LA COSTA
DE PAPITO

Playa Cocles

CABINAS
RÍO COCLES

CARIBLUE BUNGALOWS

AZÁNIA BUNGALOWS
CABINAS GARIBALDI

MINI-SUPER
LA PLAZA

CAFÉ INTERNET RÍO NEGRO

CASA CAMARONA

ABASTACEDOR COCLES

EL RINCONCITO

LA
CARACOLA

SLOTH
CLUB

HOTEL PUNTA
COCLES

Punta Cocles

JARDÍN
MIRAFLORES LODGE

Playa Chiquita

LA PECORA
NERA

ABASTACEDOR
VILLAS DE CARIBE

HOTEL KASHÁ

EL DUENDE FELÍZ

IRIE
CABINAS

PLAYA
CHIQUITA LODGE

THE TREE
HOUSE

PLAYA PUNTA
UVA CABINAS

VILLAS DE
CARIBE

RESTAURANTE
ELENA'S

ITAITÁ
VILLAS

INTERNET
CAFÉ NEGRA

SHAWANDHA LODGE

Río

Cocles

Río

Negro

C a r i b b e a n

MARIPOSARIO

0   0.5 mi

0   0.5 km

dive shop offering dives ($30–40), PADI certification course ($375), and snorkeling ($12–35). It rents scuba and snorkel equipment ($3 per hour), plus kayaks ($6 per hour). It also offers kayak trips (from $15) and runs a Dolphin Observation Safari ($44).

Edwin Salem offers an overnight turtle-watching tour from Punta Cocles ($150, with accommodation, plus meals and snorkeling); see Seahorse Stables, above.

Accommodations and Food

Pangaea (tel. 506/759-9204, beeper tel. 506/244-9100, pangaea@racsa.co.cr, $25 s, $35 d), 100 meters inland of the beach, has two simple yet pleasing well-lit rooms with tin roofs, screened windows, fans, mosquito nets, hammocks on porches, and private bathrooms with hot water. It also has a beach house with kitchen for four people ($60). Rates include breakfast.

For your own house rental, I recommend the all-wood, beachfront **Dolphin Lodge** and **Coral Reef House** (tel. 506/586-5084, www.vrbo.com/18442, from $175 for Dolphin Lodge; from $1,000 weekly for Coral Reef), east of the river outside Manzanillo and inside the reserve. The former is a two-story, three-bedroom (each with two kings or four singles), three-bathroom beachhouse with kitchen; the latter has two stories with three bedrooms and two bathrooms, plus TV and VCR. No smokers. A caretaker and his family tend to guests full time and prepare meals.

Cabinas Maxi ($25 s/d or $32.50 s/d with refrigerator), adjoining Restaurant/Bar Maxi, has six modern, clean, simple concrete cabinas with TV, fans, bamboo furnishings, and private bathrooms.

Restaurant/Bar Maxi (tel. 506/759-9061, $4–9) serves *típico* dishes and seafood,

PUERTO VIEJO TO MANZANILLO

S e a

Punta Uva

BAR/RESTAURANTE
EL RANCHITO

Playa
Punta Uva

DELPHIN
GUEST HOUSE

RESTAURANT/
BAR MAXI

PARK HQ
Manzanillo

PACHAMAMA
B&B

ABASTACEDOR
PUNTA UVA

COLIBRI
LODGE

ALMONDS & CORALS
LODGE TENT CAMP

AQUAMORE

SODA

PANGEA

To Sixaola

© AVALON TRAVEL PUBLISHING, INC.

such as *pargo rojo* (red snapper) and lobster. Bar Maxi is one of the liveliest spots on the Caribbean. The gloomy disco-bar downstairs is enlivened by the slap of dominoes and the blast of Jimmy Cliff and Bob Marley, and the dancing spills out onto the sandy road. The upstairs bar (decorated with carved wooden motifs and wind chimes) has a breezy terrace and gets packed to the gills on weekends and holidays, even in the middle of the day. The restaurant is open 10 A.M.–10 P.M.; the bar is open until 2 A.M.

Several local ladies will cook meals with advance notice.

Getting There

Buses depart Puerto Limón for Manzanillo (two hours) via Puerto Viejo at 6 A.M., 2:30 P.M., and 6 P.M.; and from Puerto Viejo (45 minutes) for Manzanillo at 7:20 A.M., 4 P.M., and 7:15 P.M.

Return buses depart Manzanillo for Puerto Limón at 5 A.M., 8:30 A.M., and 5 P.M.

GANDOCA-MANZANILLO REFUGE

One of Costa Rica's best-kept secrets, 9,446-hectare Refugio Nacional de Vida Silvestre Gandoca-Manzanillo protects a spectacularly beautiful, brown-sand, palm-fringed, nine-km-long, crescent-shaped beach (littered with logs washed ashore) where four species of turtles—most abundantly, leatherback turtles—come ashore to lay their eggs (Jan.–April is best). Some 4,436 hectares of the park extends out to sea, protecting the shore breeding grounds for turtles. The ocean has riptides and is not safe for swimming.

The reserve—which is 65 percent tropical rainforest—also protects rare swamp habitats, including the only mangrove forest on Costa

Rica's Caribbean shores, two holillo palm swamps (important habitat for tapirs), a 300-hectare cativo forest, and a live coral reef 200 meters offshore.

The large freshwater **Gandoca Lagoon,** one km south of Gandoca village, runs up to 50 meters deep and has two openings into the sea. The estuary, full of red mangrove trees, is a complex world braided by small brackish streams and snakelike creeks, which sometimes interconnect, sometimes peter out in narrow cul-de-sacs, and sometimes open suddenly into broad lagoons that all look alike. The mangroves shelter both a giant oysterbed and a nursery for lobster and the swift and powerful tarpon. Manatees swim and breed here, as do crocodiles and caimans. The park is a seasonal or permanent home to at least 358 species of birds (including toucans, red-lored Amazon parakeets, and hawk-eagles) as well as margays, ocelots, pacas, and sloths. And a rare estuarine dolpin—the *tucuxí*—was recently discovered in the lagoons (see sidebar *The Tucuxí*).

The hamlets of Punta Uva, Manzanillo, Punta Mona, and Gandoca form part of the refuge. Because local communities live within the park, it is a mixed-management reserve; the locals' needs are integrated into park-management policies. For example, **Punta Mona Center for Sustainable Living and Education** (tel. 506/614-5735 or 506/391-2116; in the U.S., tel. 305/895-5782 or 800/551-7887, fax 305/892-1469; info@costaricanadventures.com, www.costaricanadventures.com) is an organic farm and environmental center on 12 hectares of abandoned cocao plantations. It teaches traditional and sustainable farming techniques and other environmentally sound practices. It accepts volunteers, and internships are available.

ASACODE (Asociación Sanmigueleña de Conservación y Desarrollo, tel. 506/751-2261 or 506/835-6819, www.asacode.or.cr) is a *campesino* organization that operates a private reserve-within-the-reserve at the hamlet of **San Miguel,** deep in the forest on the southern edge of Gandoca-Manzanillo. ASACODE shares an office and works in association with ANAI (Asociación Nacional de Asuntos Indígenas, tel.

506/750-0020 or 506/224-6090, fax 506/253-7524 in San José, anaicr@racsa.co.cr or volunteers @racsa.co.cr, www.anaicr.org) to protect the forest and to evolve a sustainable livelihood through reforestation and other earth-friendly methods.

Turtle Patrol

Volunteers are needed for the **Marine Turtle Conservation Project,** which conducts research and protects the turtles from predators and poachers (see sidebar *Volunteer Programs to Save the Turtles,* in the *Background* chapter). The tour of duty is one week. You patrol the beach at night, measuring and tagging turtles, camouflaging their nests, and discouraging egg-bandits. Contact **ANAI** (see above) or **ATEC** (see sidebar).

Exploring the Park

The park is easily explored simply by walking the beaches; trails also wind through the flat, lowland rainforest fringing the coast. A coastal track that skirts the swamps leads south from the east side of Manzanillo village to Gandoca village (two hours), where you can walk the beach one km south to Gandoca Lagoon. Beyond the lagoon, a trail winds through the jungle—teeming with monkeys, parrots, sloths, and snakes—ending at the Río Sixaola and the Panamá border. A guide is recommended.

You can hire a guide and boat in Sixaola to take you downriver to the mangrove swamps at the rivermouth (dangerous currents and reefs prevent access from the ocean). If you pilot yourself, stay away from the Panamanian side of the river, as the Panamanian border police are said to be touchy.

Entrance costs $6.

The **Manzanillo ranger station** (tel. 506/754-2133), is 200 meters south of the village.

Accommodations and Food

Camping is permitted in the park, but there are no facilities.

The sturdy two-story **MINAE Headquarters** (no tel.), at Gandoca, 0.5 km inland from the beach and park entrance, has four cross-venti-

THE TUCUXÍ DOLPHIN

The *tucuxí* dolphin (*Sotalia fluviatilis*) is a rare species whose existence hereabouts, though known to local fishermen for generations, only recently filtered out from the swamps of Manzanillo to the broader world. It is not a true riverine dolphin (such as the Amazonian and Ganges dolphins). The little-known species is found in freshwater rivers, estuaries, and adjacent coastal areas of South America and has recently been found as far north as Laguna Leimus, in Nicaragua.

Studies have shown that pods of *tucuxí* (pronounced "too koo shee") interact with pods of bottle-nosed dolphins, and interspecies mating has been observed.

Tours have sprung up to fulfill humankind's fascination with Flipper, although human incursion into the waterways threatens the dolphin's ecology.

The **Talamanca Dolphin Foundation** (tel. 506/759-9115 or 506/759-0612, aquamore@racsa.co.cr; in the U.S., 3150 Graf St. #8, Bozeman, MT 59715, tel./fax 406/586-5084; info@dolphinlink.org, www.dolphinlink.org), at Aquamor in Manzanillo, is a non-profit organization that conducts research into the dolphins, offers guided boating tours, and publishes human-dolphin regulations. Visitors, for example, may only take trips or swim with dolphins in the company of trained guides drawn from the local community.

lated rooms, each with two bunks, with shared bathrooms and toilets with cold water only. It serves meals.

Nearby, the basic **Albergue Ecoturismo El Yolillal,** 200 meters past the soccer field, has bunks for 12 people. It also makes meals. And **Cabinas Navely,** 100 meters inland of the beach, has four basic rooms with shared outside bathrooms with cold water for $15 pp. Simple meals are served.

By far the preferred option is the breezeswept **Cabinas Orquideas** (tel. 506/754-2392 or 506/262-7597, cellular 506/837-4079), run by a friendly elderly couple. They have 18 rooms. Four upstairs rooms have bunks and shared bath with cold water only for $10 pp ($18 with meals). Others have private bathrooms ($20 pp, or $25 with meals). There are hammocks under palms.

ASACODE Lodge is a rustic *albergue* at San Miguel run by the local farmers' association. The simple lodge sleeps up to 29 people with shared rooms and bathrooms, and solar-powered electricity. Contact the organization for rates, which depend on various factors.

Getting There

You can drive to Gandoca village via a 15-km dirt road that leads north from the Bribrí-Sixaola road; the turnoff is about three km west of Sixaola. Keep left at the crossroads 1.5 km down the road.

The Caribbean Coast

The Southwest

BRIBRÍ AND VICINITY

From Hone Creek, Hwy. 36 winds uphill through the foothills of the Talamancas and descends to Bribrí, a small town 60 km south of Puerto Limón, and the administrative center for the local banana industry and nearby Indian reserves. It is surrounded by bright green banana plantations spread out in a flat valley backed by tiers of far-off mountain. The indigenous influence is noticeable.

The paved road ends in **Bribrí,** but a dirt road leads south to Sixaola; others lead west through the gorge of the Río Sixaola and the village of **Bratsi,** where the vistas open up across the wide, wide Valle de Talamanca surrounded by soaring mountains—a region known as **Alta Talamanca.** The United Fruit Company once reigned supreme in the valley, and the history of the region is a sad tale of false promises (many of the tribes who opposed destruction of their forests at the turn of the century were hunted and jailed).

Talamanca Adventures (tel. 506/224-3570, fax 506/253-7524, info@talamanca-adventures .com, www.talamanca-adventures.com) offers eco-cultural tours of the region; it's affiliated with ANAI (see above).

Talamanca Indigenous Reserves

The **Reserva Indígena Talamanca-Bribrí** and **Reserva Indígena Talamanca-Cabecar** are incorporated into La Amistad International Peace Park, on the slopes of the Talamanca mountains. The parks were established to protect the traditional lifestyle of the indigenous people, though the communities and their land remain under constant threat from loggers and squatters (the tragically farcical story of the creation of the reserves is told in Anachristina Rossi's novel *La Loca de Gandoca*).

The native peoples have no villages of any substance, as they prefer to live apart. Though the people speak Spanish and wear Western clothing, their philosophy that all living things

are the work of Sibo, their god of creation (the BriBrí believe that Sibo created the BriBrí from corn kernels), and therefore sacred, has traditionally pitted the native peoples against pioneers. Government proposals to build a trans-Talamanca highway and a hydroelectric dam are being fought by the local tribes. The communities supplement their income by selling baskets and other crafts, and organically grown cacao.

The "capital" of the Talamanca-Bribrí reserve is the hamlet of **Shiroles.** You can walk 15 minutes uphill to **La Finca Educativa Indígena** (tel. 506/373-4181), an administrative center for the Bribrí people.

The Cabecar remain cautious of any tourist influx. **Amubri,** eight km west of Bratsi, is the "capital" and gateway to the reserve. If you go, enter with a sense of humility and respect. Do not attempt to treat the community members as a tourist oddity: you have as much to learn from the indigenous communities as to share.

The **Reserva Indígena Yorku** welcomes tourists. Guides offer mountain hikes to hot springs and mud baths. Artisans display their traditional crafts. The reserve is accessed by canoe up the Río Yorku from Bambú. The two-day, one-night trip includes lodging, transport, and meals ($50 pp, $25 extra day). Contact the **Estibrawpa Women's Group** (tel. 506/375-3372, or ANAI, tel. 506/750-0020, or ATEC, tel. 506/750-0188).

Accommodations and Food

In Shiroles, **La Finca Educativa Indígena** ($10 pp) has a 44-bed dorm and cafeteria. Breakfasts cost $4, lunches and dinners cost $6.50.

ACODEFO (Asociación de Conservación y Desarrollo Forestal de Talamanca, tel. 506/750-0582, acodefo@hotmail.com, $40 pp) has a two-story A-frame wooden lodge with six rooms and solar-generated power. Rates include three meals and guided excursion to the reserves.

Reserva Indígena Yorku has a lodge for 15 people.

Information and Services

Banco Nacional (10 A.M.–noon and 1–3:45 P.M.) in Bribrí has a $100 limit. It gets crowded and can take half a day to get money changed.

The post office faces the bank, as does the medical clinic. There's also a **Red Cross** (tel. 506/758-0125) evacuation center for emergencies

The **police station** (tel. 506/758-1865) faces the bank in Bribrí.

Getting There

The San José-Sixaola bus (see *Getting There*, in the *Cahuita* section, above) passes through Bribrí. Buses depart Puerto Viejo for Bribrí (30 minutes) and Sixaola at 6:15 A.M., 8:15 A.M., 9:15 A.M., 11:30 A.M., 12:30 P.M., 5:15 P.M., and 7:15 P.M. Buses depart Limón from Radio Casino for Bribrí and Sixaola at 5 A.M., 8 A.M., 10 A.M., 1 P.M., 4 P.M., and 6 P.M.

Buses depart Bribrí for San José at 6 A.M., 8:30 A.M., 10:30 A.M., and 3:30 P.M.; and for Limón at 6:15 A.M., 9 A.M., 11:15 A.M., 12:30 P.M., 2:15 P.M., and 4:15 P.M.

Buses depart Bribrí for Shiroles at 8 A.M., noon, and 5:30 P.M. It's a bumpy ride along an unpaved road.

SIXAOLA: CROSSING INTO PANAMÁ

Sixaola, 34 km southeast of Bribrí, is on the north bank of the 200-meter-wide, fast-flowing Río Sixaola. The only visitors to this dour border town are typically crossing the river into Panamá, and unless you want to visit Boca del Toro, there's little reason to enter Panamá here, as links with the rest of the country are tenuous. But you can walk or drive across the border at the bridge in Sixaola. Remember to advance your watches by one hour as you enter Panamá.

The Costa Rican Immigration (tel. 506/754-2044) and Customs (tel. 506/754-2837) posts face each other atop the railway embankment on the west side of the bridge. Both are open daily 7 A.M.–5 P.M.

The **Hotel el Imperio** (tel. 506/754-2289), is on the left as you come into Sixaola. Its sole room costs $8. There are a few other grim cabins, and a fistful of uninspired eateries. If you want to go to Guabito (or Changuinola, farther down the line) to shop, you can do so without getting exit stamps from Costa Rica (the bus from the Panamanian side of the border to Changuinola costs $1). You will have to leave your bags at Panamanian customs after walking across the bridge. There are no hotels in Guabito.

Buses depart Sixaola for San José at 5 A.M., 7:30 A.M., 9:30 A.M., and 2:30 P.M.; and for Limón at 5 A.M., 8 A.M., 10 A.M., 1 P.M., 3 P.M., and 5 P.M.

There's a Texaco **gas station** about 10 km east of Bribrí. You'll be stopped and possibly searched at the *comando* (military checkpoint) as you enter and depart Sixoala.

The Northern Zone

With all the hyperbole about Costa Rica's magnificent beaches and mountains, the Northern Zone has until recently gotten short shrift from tourists. During the colonial period, the region was a no-man's-land marked only by murky rivers cutting through the vast forested plains that sweep across most of Costa Rica, forming a huge triangle-shaped plain as green and as flat as a billiard table. Today, tourists are flocking, thanks to new roads, preeminent lowland rainforest, and the singular popularity of Arenal Volcano. The volcano has been the catalyst for a burgeoning adventure industry based in Fortuna, which is well-served by lodges and easily accessed from San José.

The northern lowlands constitute a 40,000-square-kilometer watershed drained by the Ríos Frío, San Carlos, and Sarapiquí and their tributaries, which flow north to the Río San Juan, forming the border with southern Nicaragua, where fighting took place during the 1980s. The rivers meander like restless snakes and commonly flood in the wet season, when much of the landscape is transformed into swampy marshlands. The region is made up of two separate plains *(llanuras):* in the west, the **Llanura de los Guatusos,** and farther east the **Llanura de San Carlos.**

Any ho-hum first impression is not a fair one. Skirting the foothills of the cordillera, the vistas southward are as grandiose as any in the country.

Must-Sees

Look for **M** to find the sights and activities you can't miss and **ℕ** for the best dining and lodging.

M Caño Negro Refuge: This croc-infested swamp and forest ecosystem is a birder's and wildlife lover's dream, and a nirvana for anglers come to hook tarpon, garfish, and snook (page 261).

M Tabacón Hot Springs: Here you can bathe in steaming waters that tumble from the bowels of Arenal Volcano to cascade through a landscaped garden (page 271).

M Arenal Volcano National Park: With a symmetrical volcano at its heart, this national park has hiking trails over still-warm lava flows, and the open spaces offer prime wildlife viewing (page 273).

M Arenal Rainforest Reserve: The aerial tram at this private reserve promises high-mountain rides and staggering vistas. Nature trails and canopy tours provide close-up encounters with wildlife (page 276).

M Arenal Botanical Gardens: No amount of rain can dampen this splendid garden, with fabulous birding to boot (page 279).

M Centro Neotrópico Sarapiquís: This educational center offers a triptych featuring a museum of indigenous culture, an archaeological park, and

Arenal Volcano

nature trails through the Tirimbina Rainforest Reserve (page 289).

M Selva Verde: Enfolded by rainforest, this dedicated nature lodge offers instant access to wildlife-rich terrain. Options include guided hikes by day and night, plus canoeing on the Río Sarapiquí (page 290).

M Heliconia Island: Naturalist Tim Ryan will guide you on a tour of his beautifully landscaped **Sarapiquí Botanical Garden** near Horquetas. In addition to heliconias, it also displays hundreds of species of ginger, palms, orchids, bamboo, and other tropical flora (page 295).

M The Northern Zone

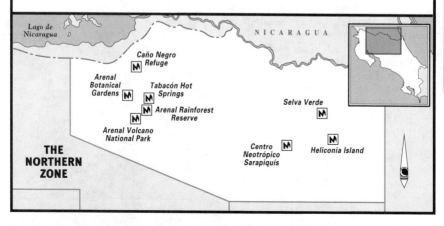

From below, Costa Rica's ethereal volcanic landscapes remind me of Bali. Pastures tumble down the mountainsides like folds of green silk. The plains are thick with chartreuse wands of rice. And the colors are like a painting by Matisse: emerald greens flowing into burning golds, soft pastels, and warm ochers relieved periodically by brilliant tropical colors, houses as blue as the morning sky and flower petals and rich soils as red as ripe tomatoes.

These plains were once rampant with tropical forest. During recent decades the lowlands have been transformed into a geometrical patchwork of farmland. Yet, there *is* still plenty of rainforest—much of it protected as private reserves—extending for miles across the plains and clambering up the north-facing slopes of the *cordilleras* whose scarp face hems the lowlands. The entire border zone with Nicaragua is also an agrarian front in the battle to establish the Si-a-Paz trans-national park.

Today, the region is a breadbasket for the nation, and most of the working population is employed in agriculture. The southern uplands of San Carlos, centered on the regional capital of Ciudad Quesada, devotes almost 70 percent of its territory to cattle and produces the best-quality milk in the nation. In the lowlands proper, dairy cattle give way to beef cattle and plantations of *pejibaye* palm and pineapples, bananas (in the east), and citrus (to the north). Nicaraguans have traditionally moved freely across the border by plying their watercraft up-river; today, they help sustain agriculture as cheap labor.

The climate has much in common with the Caribbean coast: warm, humid, and consistently wet. Temperatures hover at 25–27°C year-round. The climatic periods are not as well defined as those of other parts of the nation, and rarely does a week pass without a prolonged and heavy rain shower (it rains a little less from February to the beginning of May). Annual rainfall can exceed 450 cm in some parts. Precipitation tends to diminish and the dry season grows more pronounced northward and westward.

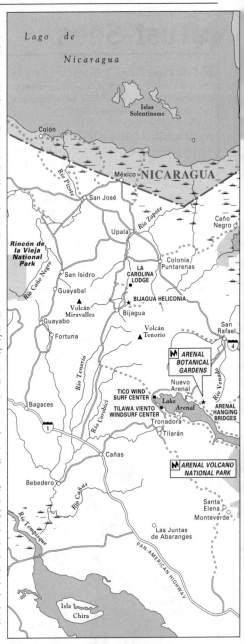

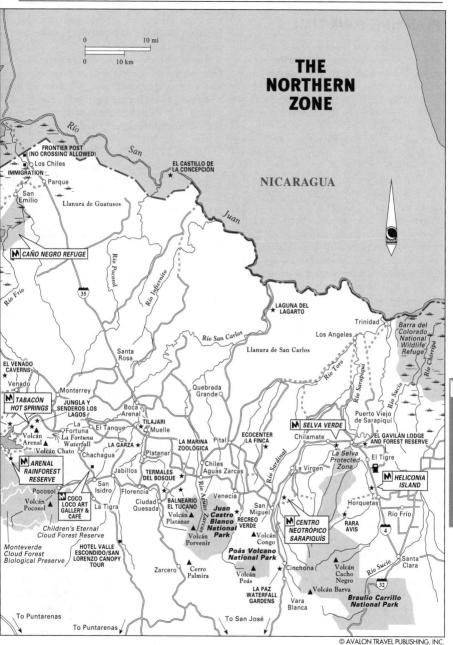

THE
NORTHERN
ZONE

0   10 mi

0   10 km

Río San

FRONTIER POST
(NO CROSSING ALLOWED)
Los Chiles
IMMIGRATION
Parque
San
Emilio
Llanura de Guatusos

EL CASTILLO DE
LA CONCEPCIÓN

NICARAGUA

Juan

M CAÑO NEGRO REFUGE

Río Pocosol

Río Frío

35

Río Infiernito

LAGUNA DEL
LAGARTO

Trinidad

Barra del
Colorado
National
Wildlife
Refuge

Río San Carlos

Los Angeles

Llanura de San Carlos

Río Toro

Río Chirripó

Río Sarapiquí

Río Sucio

Santa
Rosa

EL VENADO
CAVERNS

Venado

Monterrey

Quebrada
Grande

M TABACÓN
HOT SPRINGS

JUNGLA Y
SENDEROS LOS
LAGOS

Boca
Arenal

TILAJARI
Muelle

Puerto Viejo
de Sarapiquí

M SELVA VERDE

La
Fortuna
La Fortuna
Waterfall

El Tanque

Volcán
Arenal
Volcán Chato

LA GARZA

Platanar

LA MARINA
ZOOLÓGICA

Pital

ECOCENTER
LA FINCA

Chilamate

EL GAVILÁN LODGE
AND FOREST RESERVE

La Selva
Protected
Zone

El Tigre

M HELICONIA
ISLAND

M ARENAL
RAINFOREST
RESERVE

Chachagua

Jabillos

Chiles
Aguas Zarcas

La Virgen

Río Sardinal

Pocosol

Volcán
Pocosol

M COCO
LOCO ART
GALLERY &
CAFÉ

San
Isidro

La Tigra

Florencia

TERMALES
DEL BOSQUE

Río Aguas Zarcas

Venecia

San
Miguel

Hórquetas

Río Frío

4

Ciudad
Quesada

BALNEARIO
EL TUCANO

Volcán
Platanar

Juan
Castro
Blanco
National
Park

RECREO
VERDE

M CENTRO
NEOTRÓPICO
SARAPIQUÍS

RARA
AVIS

Río Sucio

Santa
Clara

Children's Eternal
Cloud Forest Reserve

HOTEL VALLE
ESCONDIDO/SAN
LORENZO CANOPY
TOUR

Volcán
Porvenir

Volcán
Congo

Poás Volcano
National Park

Monteverde
Cloud Forest
Biological Preserve

Zarcero

Cerro
Palmira

Volcán
Poás

Cinchona

Volcán
Cacho
Negro

32

To Puntarenas

LA PAZ
WATERFALL
GARDENS

Vara
Blanca

Volcán Barva

Braulio Carrillo
National Park

To Puntarenas

To San José

© AVALON TRAVEL PUBLISHING, INC.

The Northern Zone

PLANNING YOUR TIME

The region is a vast triangle, broad to the east and narrowing to the west. Much of the region is accessible only along rough dirt roads that turn to muddy quagmires in wet season; a 4WD is essential. You can descend from the central highlands via any of half a dozen routes that drop sharply down the steep north-facing slopes of the *cordilleras* and onto the plains. Choose your route according to your desired destination in the lowlands.

Most sites of interest congregate close to the base of the mountains, with the main draws concentrated near the towns of **La Fortuna** and **Puerto Viejo de Sarapiquí.** For the naturalist there are opportunities galore for birding and wildlife viewing, particularly around Puerto Viejo de Sarapiquí, where the lower slopes of Braulio Carrillo National Park provide easy immersion in wildlife-rich rainforest from half a dozen or so acclaimed nature lodges, such as **Selva Verde** and **Rara Avis.** Boat trips along the Río Sarapiquí are also recommended for spotting monkeys, crocodiles, green macaws, and other wildlife; and **Heliconia Island/Sarapiquí Botanical Garden** is a paradise for birders and botanists.

To the far west, the slopes of Tenorio and Miravalles Volcanoes are less developed, although a few rustic lodges offer trails. To the north, the town of Los Chiles is a gateway to **Caño Negro National Wildlife Refuge,** one of the nation's prime birding sites, but also drawing anglers to its sportfishing lodges.

The main center is La Fortuna, which is served by dozens of accommodations. Its situation at the foot of Arenal Volcano makes it a great base for exploring; three days here is about right. Numerous tour companies cater to active travelers with horseback riding, river trips, bicycle, and other adventure excursions, including to **Venado Caverns.** You'll want to spend time hiking **Arenal Volcano National Park,** perhaps from the **Arenal Observatory Lodge** and/or via a ride on the **Arenal Aerial Tram.** The volcano regularly hiccups clouds of ash into the air and spews red-hot lava down its steep flanks; the more time you linger, the greater your chance of seeing an eruption. Despite its appeals, **Tabacón Hot Springs** gets crowded with tour groups and its location is inherently dangerous.

Arenal Volcano looms magnificently over **Lake Arenal,** whose magnificent alpine setting makes for a stupendous drive. Windsurfing is a popular activity. Several top-notch accommodations and a splendid restaurant dot the lake, and the **Arenal Botanical Gardens** are worth checking out.

You should allocate no less than three days, and up to a week if you want to fully explore around La Fortuna and Puerto Viejo.

HISTORY

Corobicí people settled the western lowland region several thousand years ago and were divided into at least 12 distinct tribes. This indigenous population was decimated by internecine warfare with Nicaraguan tribes in the early Spanish colonial period.

The Spanish first descended from the central highlands on a foray into the lowland foothills in 1640. They called the region San Jerónimo de los Votos. But almost 200 years were to pass before the foothills were settled. Nonetheless, Spanish vessels navigated the Río San Juan all the way from the Caribbean to Lake Nicaragua, a journey of 195 kilometers. Pirates also periodically sailed up the river to loot and burn the lakeside settlements. One of the very few colonial remains in the region is El Castillo de la Concepción, a fort erected by the Spanish in 1675 to keep English pirates from progressing upstream (see *Along the Ríos Saripiquí and San Juan,* below). The ruins are in Nicaragua, three km west of where the Costa Rican border moves south of the river.

This early exploration was limited to the broad river channels, and colonization of most of the region has only occurred within this century. Only between 1815 and 1820 was the first road link with the Río Sarapiquí made, via a mud-and-dirt trail that went from Heredia via Vara Blanca. The river, which descends from Barva Volcano, in the early heyday of coffee became the most traveled route for getting to the Caribbean from the central highlands.

THE RÍO SAN JUAN CANAL

W ere it not for volcanoes, the Panamá Canal would probably have been built along the Río San Juan, the broad, easygoing river that forms the international boundary between Costa Rica and Nicaragua. Its gaping mouth and ample flow quickened the pulse of early European explorers seeking a short route between the Atlantic and Pacific Oceans, for its source is Lake Nicaragua—at 72 km wide and more than 160 km long, the largest body of fresh water between Lake Michigan and Lake Titicaca. Lake Nicaragua is so immense that it almost links the two oceans, and although its waters drain into the Caribbean, it is separated from the Pacific only by a narrow 17 km strip of land.

By 1551, the Spanish, Dutch, and Portuguese were all surveying this fortuitous piece of real estate for a direct route from sea to sea. For the next four centuries, engineers debated the feasibility of the Río San Juan Canal.

In 1850, at the height of the California gold rush, Gordon's Passenger Line opened the first commercial passenger service on the river. Gordon's transported eager fortune-seekers from New York to Nicaragua, then ferried them up the Río San Juan and across the lake. A mule then carried the argonauts to the Pacific coast, where a San Francisco–bound ship waited.

Transport magnate Cornelius Vanderbilt opened a rival ferry service in 1851 with a grander vision in mind: a canal across the isthmus. Events forestalled his dream, however. The Nicaraguans levied transit fees for use of the river. Vanderbilt called in the U.S. Navy to "protect American interests." The Navy reduced to rubble the unfortunate rivermouth town of San Juan del Norte (then called Greytown) and ushered in a century of strife for Nicaragua. On 1 May 1858, President Juanito Mora of Costa Rica and General Martínes of Nicaragua signed an agreement for the construction of the canal, to be financed with European capital. Unfortunately, the U.S. had a fit of jealous pique and used strong-arm tactics to ensure that the project was aborted.

U.S. interests in the Río San Juan canal were aroused again in the late 19th century, when the idea gained influential backing in Congress. Teams of engineers and tons of equipment were shipped to Greytown, railroad and machine shops were built, dredges brought in, and some 1,000 meters of canal were dug. But the U.S. got cold feet again in 1902, when Mount Pelée erupted in Martinique, killing 30,000 people (an enterprising promoter of the Panamá route sent each member of Congress a Nicaraguan stamp bearing the picture of a volcano as a reminder that a Río San Juan canal would forever be menaced by geological catastrophe).

In November 1903, Teddy Roosevelt's administration engineered a coup and swiftly signed an agreement that recognized Panamá's independence from Colombia. The treaty granted the U.S. the sole right to dig a canal (completed in 1914) across the Panamanian isthmus.

Even this fait accompli did not deter the dreamers. The fickle Americans tried twice to revive the project: in 1916, when the U.S. paid $3 million to Nicaragua for the right to build a canal and establish a naval base in the Gulf of Fonseca (Nicaragua's neighbors protested and the U.S. backed down); and during the post-WWII "Atoms for Peace" craze, when the U.S. Army Corps of Engineers proposed using nuclear bombs to open up the San Juan waterway!

The Northern Zone

The first pioneers—the Quesada family from San Ramón—formed a village, then known as La Uniá and today called Ciudad Quesada. Beginning in the 1950s the government helped finance small cattle farmers as part of its policy to promote new settlements outside the Meseta Central, and settlement began to edge slowly north. Meanwhile, construction by banana companies of new feeder railways in the eastern lowlands opened up virgin land for production, although places such as Upala and Los Chiles continued to use rivers for transportation to Limón until the late 1970s, when the construction of paved highways and bridges granted access to the rest of the country.

Ciudad Quesada and Vicinity

CIUDAD QUESADA

Ciudad Quesada (pop. 30,000), known locally as **San Carlos,** hovers above the plains at 650 meters elevation on the north-facing slope of the Cordillera de Tilarán, with the northern lowlands spread out at its feet. Despite its mountainside position, the bustling market town and transportation node is the hierarchical center of (and gateway to) the entire northern region. It is surrounded by lush pasture—some of the richest and most developed in the country—grazed by prize-specimen dairy cattle.

The tree-shaded **main plaza** is a good place to sit on a bench and watch the bustling activity.

North of Ciudad Quesada, the switchback road deposits you on the flat at the small town of **Florencia.** Here, turn right (north) at the stop sign for Muelle and Los Chiles; turn left for La Fortuna and Arenal.

Entertainment and Events

There's a small **casino** in the Hotel La Central. Disco **Titanic** (Avenida 4, Calles Central/2) has karaoke most nights. The annual **Cattle Fair** (Feria del Ganado) in April is one of the largest in the country, with a horse parade *(tope)* and general merriment.

Accommodations

Under $25: There's no shortage of budget accommodations in town, most offering a choice of shared or private bathrooms for around $5 per person. Try **Hotel Cristal** (Calle 2, Avenidas Central/1, tel. 506/460-0541), opposite the bus station; **Hotel del Norte** (Calle 1, Avenidas 1/3, tel. 506/460-1959); or **Hotel Ambiente** (Calle 2, Avenidas 2/4, tel. 506/460-0773).

Hotel El Parqueo (Avenida 7, Calles Central/2, tel. 506/460-2573, $12.50 s, $17.50 d) has 10 clean rooms in a converted home. All have modern tiles and small bathrooms; some have refrigerator and cable TV.

Hotel Don Goyo (Calle 2, Avenida 4, tel. 506/460-1780, fax 506/460-6383, $13 s, $23 d) offers 21 clean, modern rooms that stairstep down a hillside. Each has cable TV and private bath, hot water; most have heaps of light. The lackluster **Hotel Conquistador** (tel. 506/460-0546, fax 506/460-6311, $12 s, $21 d), half a kilometer south of the plaza, has a restaurant, secure parking, and 46 sparely furnished rooms with fans, cable TV, and clean private baths and hot water.

$25–50: The **Hotel y Casino La Central** (Calle 2, Avenidas Central/2, tel. 506/460-0301, fax 506/460-0391, hcentral@racsa.co.cr, $16 s, $26 d), on the west side of the plaza, has 48 clean, meagerly furnished rooms (some with balconies), with fans, TVs, and hot-water showers. There's a small casino and restaurant.

The best place around is **Hotel Loma Verde** (tel. 506/460-1976 or 506/384-4290, $17.50 s, $25 d with fan, $25 s, $30 d with a/c), about two km north of the town center and set in a pretty garden atop the scarp face overlooking the lowland plains. This well-kept, clinically clean, peaceful modern facility has whitewashed walls. The 18 rooms vary in size, but all have nice fabrics, cable TV, and private bathrooms with hot

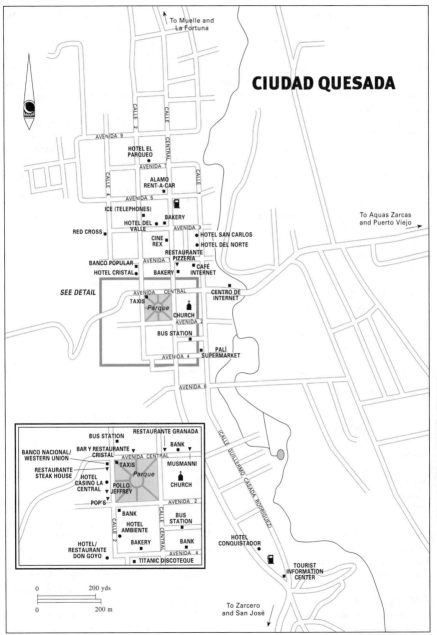

CIUDAD QUESADA

To Muelle and
La Fortuna

CALLE 2

CALLE CENTRAL

AVENIDA 9

HOTEL EL
PARQUEO

AVENIDA 7

ALAMO
RENT-A-CAR

CALLE 4

CALLE 1

AVENIDA 5

ICE (TELEPHONES)

BAKERY

HOTEL DEL
VALLE

AVENIDA 3

HOTEL SAN CARLOS

RED CROSS

CINE
REX

HOTEL DEL NORTE

RESTAURANTE
PIZZERIA

BANCO POPULAR

AVENIDA 1

CAFÉ
INTERNET

HOTEL CRISTAL

BAKERY

SEE DETAIL

AVENIDA   CENTRAL

CENTRO DE
INTERNET

TAXIS

Parque

CHURCH

AVENIDA 2

BUS STATION

PALÍ
SUPERMARKET

AVENIDA 4

AVENIDA 6

To Aquas Zarcas
and Puerto Viejo

The Northern Zone

BUS STATION

RESTAURANTE GRANADA

BANCO NACIONAL/
WESTERN UNION

BAR Y RESTAURANTE
CRISTAL

BANK

RESTAURANTE
STEAK HOUSE

AVENIDA CENTRAL

TAXIS

MUSMANNI

HOTEL
CASINO LA
CENTRAL

Parque

POLLO
JEFFREY

CHURCH

POP'S

AVENIDA 2

BANK

CALLE 2

BUS
STATION

HOTEL
AMBIENTE

CALLE CENTRAL

BANK

HOTEL/
RESTAURANTE
DON GOYO

BAKERY

AVENIDA 4

TITANIC DISCOTEQUE

CALLE GUILLERMO CASADA RODRIGUEZ

HOTEL
CONQUISTADOR

TOURIST
INFORMATION
CENTER

To Zarcero
and San José

0   200 yds

0   200 m

© AVALON TRAVEL PUBLISHING, INC.

water. Some rooms offer views. There's an open-air TV lounge with pool table under a plastic roof, plus parking. Rates include breakfast.

Food

The clean and modern **Restaurante Steak House** (tel. 506/460-3208, 11 A.M.–11 P.M.), on the west side of the plaza, specializes in *lomitos* (steaks) from $5.

Restaurante Don Goyo (7 A.M.–10 P.M., $5) is a clean, well-lit diner serving burgers, ceviche, garlic sea bass, steaks, etc. For pizzas, try **Restaurante Pizzería** (Calle Central, Avenidas 1/Central), an atmospheric restaurant with both indoor and outdoor dining.

Also on the west side of the plaza are **Pop's,** for ice creams, and **Pollo Jeffrey,** for fried chicken.

You can buy fresh bread and pastries at **Musmanni** (Avenida Central, Calles Central/1), and groceries at **Palí** (Avenida 4, Calle 1).

Information and Services

CATUZON, the Cámara de Turismo de la Zona Norte (Northern Zone Chamber of Tourism, tel. 506/479-9106, fax 506/479-9408, catuzon@racsa.co.cr, 8:30–11:30 A.M. and 1:30–5 P.M. Mon.–Sat.) has a tourist bureau at the Y-junction two blocks south of the main square.

The **Hospital Clínica Monte Sinai** (tel. 506/460-1080, hospitalmontesinai@medicos .sa.cr) is on Calle Central, about two km north of the plaza. The **Red Cross** is at Avenida 3, Calle 4. There are private doctors' offices and pharmacies opposite the hospital.

There are five banks in the center of town; see the map. **Western Union** (8 A.M.–5 P.M. Mon.–Fri.) has an office beside the Banco Nacional.

You can check and send email at **Café Internet** (Avenida 1, Calle Central/1, 9 A.M.–8:30 P.M. Mon.–Sat., 3–8 P.M. Sunday); and **Centro de Internet,** 200 meters east of the plaza, on the road to Aguas Zarcas.

Getting There

Express buses (Autotransportes, tel. 506/255-4318) depart San José from Calle 12, Avenidas 7/9, hourly 5 A.M.–7:30 P.M. (three hours via

Zarcero, $1.75). Buses to San José depart Ciudad Quesada hourly 5 A.M.–6:15 P.M.

In Ciudad Quesada, the two bus terminals are on the blocks immediately northwest and southeast of the plaza. Buses serve Arenal and Tilarán (via La Fortuna) at 6 A.M. and 3 P.M.; to La Fortuna at 5 A.M., 9:30 A.M., 1 P.M., 3 P.M., and 10 P.M.; to Los Chiles every two hours, 5 A.M.–5 P.M.; and to Puerto Viejo daily at 6 A.M., 10 A.M., and 3 P.M.

You can rent cars from **Alamo Rent-a-Car** (Avenida 5, Calle Central, tel. 506/460-0650).

AGUAS ZARCAS

Aguas Zarcas (Blue Waters), an important agricultural town at the foot of the cordillera, 15 km east of Ciudad Quesada, gets its name for the mineral hot springs that erupt from the base of the mountain. Parque Nacional Juan Castro Blanco flanks the slopes (see the *Central Highlands* chapter).

Termales del Bosque (tel. 506/460-4740, fax 506/460-1356, termales@racsa.co.cr), about five km east of Ciudad Quesada, is billed as an "ecological park" with hiking trails through botanical gardens, plus horseback rides ($15–45) and bathing in thermal mineral springs. It offers aromatic and mud applications, plus massage. The Canopy Challenge Tour treetop expedition (operated by The Original Canopy Tour company) whisks you through the forest canopy using suspension bridges, nets, and gliding cables ($45). Entrance costs $8 adults, $5 children.

From Aguas Zarcas, a paved road runs northwest 22 km to Muelle. The road from Ciudad Quesada continues east via **Venecia** (seven km east of Aguas Zarcas) to a T-junction at **San Miguel,** 24 km east of Aguas Zarcas. The road to the right leads south to Alajuela via Vara Blanca, nestled in the saddle of Poás and Barva Volcanoes (see the *Central Highlands* chapter); the road to the left leads to Puerto Viejo de Sarapiquí.

Two km east of Venecia, a road leads two km south to **Recreo Verde,** a splendid *centro turístico* tucked riverside, deep in the thickly forested valley of the Río Toro Amarillo—a magnificent setting! Three thermal pools (and two cold-water pools) hemmed by natural stone limn the river, a raging torrent to beware. There are lush lawns with volleyball, and you can explore the "Cave of Death" with a guide, marveling at the dripstone formations. Trails lead into the forest. Entrance costs $3.75.

La Marina Zoológica

This private zoo (tel. 506/474-2100 or 506/474-2202, lamarinazoo@latinmail.com, 8 A.M.–4 P.M., $3 admission adults, $1.50 children), opposite the gas station three km west of Aguas Zarcas, houses jaguars, tapirs, agoutis, peccaries, badgers, monkeys, and other mammal species, as well as birds from around the world. The Alfaro family has been taking in orphaned animals for three decades, and the zoo now has more than 450 species of animals and birds, many confiscated by the government from owners who lacked permits to keep them. The zoo even has two lions and successfully breeds tapirs. The zoo, on a working cattle *finca* spread throughout five hectares, is nonprofit; donations are appreciated.

Accommodations and Food

Recreo Verde (see above, $9 pp) has seven spacious log cabins with bunks and kitchens above the bank of the Río Toro Amarillo.

In Venecia, **Hotel Torre Fuerte** (tel. 506/472-2424, $18 s, $25 d) has 12 modern, clinically clean, spacious rooms in a two-story structure. Each has furnishings of thick bamboo, ceiling fan, local TV, tile floors, and modern private bathrooms and hot water. It has a pleasant restaurant serving salads, soups, pastas, and entrées such as garlic sea bass ($3.50), and filet mignon in mushroom sauce ($3.50); open 5:30 A.M.–10 P.M. daily.

Termales del Bosque (tel. 506/460-1356, fax 506/460-0311, $35 s, $45 d), has 29 attractive albeit small modern cabins with private bathrooms with hot water, and balconies amid landscaped grounds. Rates include breakfast.

Albergue San Juan Ecolodge (tel./fax 506/286-4203, cooprena@racsa.co.cr, www.agroecoturismo.net, $35 s, $45 d), at La Gloria de Aguas

Zarcas, is a rustic lodge with six two-bedroom units—each room sleeps up to four people—with private bath and hot water. This is a great place if you want to learn something and even become immersed in rural life. Rates include breakfast.

The **Hotel Occidental El Tucano** (tel. 506/460-6000, fax 506/460-1692, tucano @racsa.co.cr, www.occidentaltucano.com, $75 s/d standard, $83 deluxe, $90 master suite), eight km east of Ciudad Quesada, promises healing for those dipping their toes into the thermomineral waters (hot springs) that hiccup out of clefts in the rocks on which the hotel is built. The riverside hotel—built around a courtyard patio and large open-air swimming pool—is styled loosely as a Swiss chalet complex, with wrought-iron lanterns and window boxes full of flame-red flowers. The 87 guest rooms boast exquisite contemporary decor, including beautiful hardwoods and king-size beds. It has a restaurant known for its Italian cuisine, a casino, full-service spa, forest trails, gym, plus tennis, miniature golf, and horseback riding. Tours are available.

Getting There

Buses between Ciudad Quesada and San Miguel and Puerto Viejo stop along the route; or take the 3.5-hour bus ride from San José ($2.50).

PITAL

Pital, about six km northeast of Aguas Zarcas (turn right just north of Chiles) is an agricultural town.

A road leads due north from Pital to **Laguna Del Lagarto** (see below for contact information), a private reserve about 40 km north of Pital via the hamlet of Boca Topada (seven km southwest of Laguna del Lagarto). 4WD is recommended. The reserve protects 500 hectares of virgin rainforest and bayou swamps harboring crocodiles, caimans, turtles, poison-arrow frogs, as well as ocelots, sloths, and all kinds of colorful bird species, including the rare green macaw. There's a **butterfly garden,** plus forest trails for hiking and horseback rides ($20 two hours).

Three-hour boat trips on the San Carlos and San Juan Rivers cost $25 pp (minimum four people).

Accommodations

Hotel La Casona (tel. 506/473-3069, $12 s/d), on the south side of Pital, has nine modestly furnished rooms with fans, cable TV, and small, modern bathrooms with hot water. No meals are served.

The **Laguna del Lagarto Lodge** (tel. 506/ 289-8163, fax 506/289-5295, info@lagarto-lodge-costa-rica.com, http://adventure-costa-rica.com/laguna-del-lagarto, $32 s, $42 d shared bath, $38 s, $51 d private bath low season; $40 s, $57 d shared, $52 s, $58 d private high season) offers 20 rustic yet comfortable rooms in two buildings (18 with private baths, two with shared bath; all with hot water) on a hillock overlooking the lagoon. Each has a large terrace with a view overlooking the San Carlos River and forest. A natural lake surrounds the lodge, which has two large decks where you can relax and sip cocktails. A restaurant serves hearty Costa Rican buffet meals and arranges transfers.

Getting There

Buses (tel. 506/258-8914) for Pital depart San José from Calle 12, Avenidas 7/9, at 7:40 A.M., 12:30 P.M., 3 P.M., and 7:30 P.M. Buses depart Ciudad Quesada for Pital, where buses run twice daily to Boca Tapada. A taxi from Pital costs about $25 one-way.

MUELLE

This important crossroads village is 21 km north of Ciudad Quesada, at the junction of Hwy. 4 (running east-west between Upala and Puerto Viejo de Sarapiquí) and Hwy. 35 (north-south between Ciudad Quesada and Los Chiles). There's a gas station. The hamlet of Muelle ("dock") is one km to the north.

River trips down the Ríos Peñas Blancas are popular. I took a half-day kayaking safari float ($55) arranged by **Tilajari Resort Hotel and Country Club** (see *Accommodation,* below) and saw howler monkeys and crocodiles almost in reaching distance. Tilajari also has a **butterfly garden,** and hotel guests may walk inside the netted garden to learn about lepidopteran lore (7 A.M.–4 P.M.). The resort offers horseback riding and jungle walks through owner Jim Hamilton's 240-hectare cattle ranch and a contiguous 400-hectare rainforest reserve.

The **Reserva Biológica La Garza** (see Hotel La Garza, below), at Platanar, protects wildlife on a 600-hectare working cattle and stud farm that also has forest trails. Horseback rides (from $10 for 90 minutes) and hikes are offered. Day visitors are welcome to use the pool and facilities, which also include a basketball court and a tennis court.

Aqua-Ski Park, near Garza, five km north of Muelle, is a man-made lake offering water-skiing.

Accommodations

The **La Quinta Inn** (tel./fax 506/475-5260, www.laquintalodge.com, $10 pp *cabinas,* $35 up to four people in triple rooms), at Platanar, four km south of the Muelle crossroads, is a pleasant if modestly furnished hotel run by English-speaking Ticos, Jeanette and Bill Ugalde. Accommodations include two *cabinas* with hostel-style bunks for 10 people, and shared toilets and hot-water showers; a spacious triple room with attractive wood paneling and a roomy shower; and, upstairs, two triples with private baths, hot water, and lounges. The Ugaldes also rent a two-room apartment with a double bed and four bunks in the house, with a large upstairs balcony with hammocks ($32 up to three people, $60 up to six people). Meals are served in an open-air restaurant overlooking a swimming pool. There's a sauna and basketball and volleyball courts. Fishing trips are arranged.

Hotel La Garza (tel. 506/475-5222, fax 506/475-5015, information@hotellagarza.com, www.hotel-lagarza-arenal.com, $35 s, $48 d low season; $40 s, $55 d high season), also at Platanar, and reached by a suspension bridge over the river, has 12 beautifully kept a/c cabins with polished wood floors, ceiling fans, telephones, Guatemalan fabrics and bamboo furnishings, heaps of potted plants, and verandas with tables and chairs overlooking the Río Platanar. There's a pool with

CATTLE RANCHING IN COSTA RICA

"There was so much jungle 20 years ago, individual farmers had no concept of the cumulative damage," Jim Hamilton told me over a beer at the Tilajari Resort Hotel, which he owns. Though an American, Jim was once typical of the small-scale farmers who have turned the lowlands from jungle into Costa Rica's breadbasket in all of 30 years. Contrary to a popular perception, the story is not one of cattle barons and rapacious greed.

Jim was an atypical American, a poor gringo who started with nothing. He came to Costa Rica with the Peace Corps in 1969 and carried out the first census in Upala Province. After his work was finished he decided to clear a few acres and farm, "for the unique experience." He cleared his own land, milked his own cows, cooked his eggs on hot rocks, and learned his cattle skills from the locals.

Back then, the region was served only by horse trails and an airstrip often inoperable for days on end because of weather. It used to take Jim three days by river and horseback to travel between his two plots of land; in 1992, I made the same journey

Zebu cattle

by road in two hours. "Cattle was the only type of product that could be got to market. Cattle can walk," Jim explained. "There was no other way of making money." Hence, the land was cleared by hundreds of impoverished squatters and homesteaders, many of them government-sponsored settlers, who each raised a few head and grew corn to feed pigs, which could also be walked to market.

Cattle brought in cash but condemned the rainforests. "Poor farmers can't make a living by holding their land in jungle," Jim said ruefully. The initial ranchers were forced to sell their lumber to pay for the cost of their land and loans. (Interest rates for cattle farmers 20 years ago were subsidized by the World Bank, as agricultural economists saw the most hopeful future for Central American economies in beef.)

Once the area was developed, the government eventually brought in roads and electricity. Suddenly, other alternatives were possible. Since cattle farming is the least remunerative agribusiness (the return per hectare from cattle farms is only about one-quarter that from growing produce), very little land has been cleared for cattle within the last decade. Tropical fruits began to oust the hooved locusts. Alas, citrus fruits and bananas, which take up the best agricultural land in the lowlands, have pushed up land values enormously, and land is increasingly passing out of the hands of small-scale farmers and into those of the large fruit companies.

The Northern Zone

sundeck and a three-km hiking/jogging trail. The hotel is part of a 600-hectare working cattle and horse farm where you can hop in the saddle. Meals are served in a charming old farmhouse restaurant. Delightful! Rates include breakfast.

I recommend **Tilajari Resort Hotel and Country Club** (Apdo. 81, Ciudad Quesada, San Carlos, tel. 506/469-9091, fax 506/469-9095, info @tilajari.com, www.tilajari.com, $65 s/d standard, $75 junior suite, $85 family suite low season; $79 s, $89 d standard, $99 junior suite, $109 family suite high season), one km west from the Muelle crossroads. Crocodiles sun themselves on the banks of the Río San Carlos in plain view of guests; iguanas roost in the treetops; and hummingbirds feed at the trumpet vines and hibiscus that emblazon the 16 hectares of gardens. Tilajari has 76 spacious, modestly furnished a/c rooms (including four family suites), with tile floors, hardwood features, and private terraces overlooking the river. Some have king beds. It offers three tennis courts, a swimming pool, a children's pool, two racquetball courts, a sauna, a hot tub, and a Jacuzzi. There's an open-air bar and lounge with satellite TV, an open-sided riverside restaurant, the Jacaré Discotheque, and conference facilities. Ticos flock on weekends (Sunday is "tennis day"), when the place draws lots of kids.

Getting There

Buses to/from Los Chiles and San Rafael can drop you in Muelle (see Los Chiles, below).

Los Chiles and Vicinity

LOS CHILES

Los Chiles is a small frontier town on the Río Frío, about 100 km north of Ciudad Quesada and four km south of the Nicaraguan border. This was a sensitive region during the Nicaraguan conflicts of the 1980s—the Río Frío was a contra supply line, and for a while Los Chiles was a boomtown flush with CIA dollars.

The ruler-straight drive north from Muelle is modestly scenic, with the land rolling endlessly in a sea of lime-green pastures and waves of citrus—those of the TicoFrut company, whose *fincas* stretch all the way to the Nicaraguan border. The colors are marvelous, the intense greens made more so by soils as red as bright lipstick. There's a civil guard checkpoint a few kilometers south of town, and another about 20 km south of Los Chiles.

The Costa Rican Crocodile Research Association runs **La Rambla Experimental Station** (tel. 506/548-0037 or 506/378-3192, lpiedra@una.ac.cr) hereabouts.

Crossing into Nicaragua

Foreigners can cross into Nicaragua here by *colectivos* (shared water-taxis) that depart Los Chiles for San Carlos de Nicaragua daily 10 A.M.–3 P.M. ($8 pp). A private boat costs $100 (for up to 10 passengers); call **Los Petates** (tel. 506/471-1297) or **Osprey Tours** (tel. 506/471-2096).

The **immigration office** (tel. 506/471-1133, 8 A.M.–4 P.M.) is by the riverside wharf. No crossing is permitted by road; you'll be turned back at the frontier post (**Puesto Fronterizo de Tablillas**) six km north of Los Chiles at the end of a muddy (*very* muddy in rainy season) road.

Accommodations and Food

There are numerous *cabinas,* most of them dour and not worth recommending. An exception is **Cabinas Jabirú** (tel./fax 506/471-1496, $8 s, $10 d), with 12 simply furnished but clean and modern rooms with single and double beds; 10 rooms have private bath with hot water.

The nicest place is **Rancho Eco Directa** (tel./fax 506/471-1414, www.ecodirecta.com, $20 s, $25 d), opposite the Immigration office, 50 meters from the dock. This modern hotel is clean and features a pleasant, country-style bar and restaurant that is also the nicest in town. The eight spacious, simply furnished a/c rooms have private baths with hot water. There's secure parking, plus a laundry.

Centro Turístico El Gaspar (tel. 506/471-1422, fax 506/471-1033, ranchogaspar@hotmail

.com, $20 s/d fan, $22.50 s/d with a/c), outside town, has 10 simply furnished rooms with lofty ceilings and cool tile floors, but cold water only. Four rooms have a/c; seven have TV (local). The thatched restaurant is open 9 A.M.–11 P.M. daily and hosts karaoke on Thursday nights and live music on Saturday.

Information and Services

No Frills Sportfishing (tel. 506/471-1410), at the well-named Hotel No Frills, one km south of Los Chiles, offers fishing trips.

There's a hospital 500 meters south of town, and a clinic on the west side of the plaza.

The police station (tel. 506/471-1103) is on the main road as you enter town, and there's another by the wharf.

Servitur, at Cabinas Jabirú (see above), has information and offers a wide range of local tours.

There's a bank on the northeast side of the soccer field.

Getting There

You can charter flights to the small airstrip.

Express buses (tel. 506/222-3854) depart San José from Calle 12, Avenidas 7/9, at 5:30 A.M. and 3:30 P.M. (return buses depart at 5 A.M. and 3 P.M.). Buses run between Ciudad Quesada and Los Chiles throughout the day.

There's a gas station one km south of town, and another 22 km south of Los Chiles at Pavón.

◪ CAÑO NEGRO REFUGE

Caño Negro National Wildlife Refuge (Caño Negro Refugio Nacional de Vida Silvestre Fauna) is a remote tropical everglade teeming with wildlife. The 9,969-hectare reserve protects a lush lowland basin of soft, knee-deep watery sloughs and marshes centered on **Lago Caño Negro,** a seasonal lake fed by the fresh waters of the Río Frío, which makes an ideal waterway for guided boat tours from Los Chiles.

The region floods in wet season. In February, the dry season sets in (it generally lasts through April), Caño Negro dries out, and the area is reduced to shrunken lagoons; caiman gnash and slosh out pools in the muck, and wildlife congregate along the watercourses.

The crocodile colony of Caño Negro is perhaps the best-protected in Costa Rica, though caimans are far more numerous and easily seen. And looking down into waters as black as Costa Rican coffee, you may see the dim forms of big snook, silver-gold tarpon, and garish garfish.

Caño Negro is a birdwatcher's paradise. The reserve protects the largest colony of neotropic cormorants in Costa Rica and the only permanent colony of Nicaraguan grackle. Cattle egrets, wood storks, anhingas, roseate spoonbills, and other waterfowl gather in the thousands. The bright pink roseate spoonbill is one of Caño Negro's most spectacular wading birds. It is named for its spatulate bill, some 15–19 cm long, which it swings from side to side as it munches insects or small shellfish. Another of my favorites is the anhinga, a bird as adept underwater as in the air (it goes by three aliases: snakebird, for its serpentine neck; American darter, for its jerky movements; and water turkey, for the way its tail spreads in flight). You can see it solo or by the dozen, preening way up in the cypress trees.

The reserve is remarkable, too, for its population of endangered mammal species, including jaguars, cougars, tapirs, ocelots, and tayras. There are always sure to be plenty of monkeys playacting. The crocodile colony of Caño Negro is perhaps the best-protected in Costa Rica, though caimans are far more numerous and easily seen. And looking down into waters as black as Costa Rican coffee, you may see the dim forms of big snook, silver-gold tarpon, and garish garfish.

The mosquitoes—though tiny—eye your arrival greedily. Bring plenty of repellent.

The hamlet of **Caño Negro,** 23 km southwest of Los Chiles, nestles on the northwest shore of Lago Caño Negro. Locals make their living from fishing and guiding.

The **ranger station** (tel. 506/661-8464) is 400 meters inland from the dock. The regional

M The Northern Zone

office is in Los Chiles (tel. 506/460-6484, fax 506/460-5615, arayad@ns.minae.go.cr).

Sports and Recreation

Caño Negro's waters almost boil with tarpon, snook, drum, guapote, machaca, and mojarra. Fishing season is July–March (no fishing is allowed April–June); licenses ($30) are required, obtainable from the ranger station in the village, or through the various fishing lodges.

Hotel Caño Negro Fishing Club charges $30–40 per hour, including guide for fishing. It also offers lagoon tours ($15 per hour) and horseback tours ($8 per hour), and you can rent kayaks ($10 s, $15 d per hour) and bicycles. **Natural Lodge Caño Negro** also offers fishing, including three- to six-day fishing packages, plus birding and ecological excursions. See *Accommodations and Food,* below.

Local guides will take you fishing from Los Chiles or Caño Negro village.

Accommodations and Food

Albergue Caño Negro ($2 pp campsite; $8 pp cabin), as you enter the hamlet of Caño Negro, permits camping on lawns beneath fruit trees. There are tables and barbecue pits. Owner Alvaro Arguillas also has two rustic, bare-bones, two-story cabins on stilts, with screened windows, electricity, porches, and shared toilets and bathrooms beneath. Each unit has two bedrooms with a double and two single beds.

You can stay overnight in the Caño Negro ranger station if space is available ($6 pp). You'll need a sleeping bag and, ideally, a mosquito net. It has cold showers. Meals cost $5.

The Swiss-run **Hotel Caño Negro Fishing Club** (tel. 506/656-0071, fax 506/656-0260, info@canonegro.com, www.canonegro.com, $55 s/d), north of Caño Negro village, stands lakeside amid landscaped grounds with a citrus orchard. Eight handsome modern, cross-ventilated, a/c cabins sleep four people apiece, and have terra-cotta floors, lofty wooden ceilings with fans, and large modern bathrooms with hot water. There's a bar and restaurant, gift store, and tackle shop.

About 500 meters south, **Natural Lodge Caño Negro** (tel. 506/265-6370, fax 506/265-4561, info@canonegrolodge.com, www.canonegrolodge .com, $59 s, $69 d low season; $76 s, $86 d high season) has 10 spacious and comfortable bungalows with rich ochre color schemes, polished hardwoods, plus ceiling fan, security box, and handsome modern bathrooms with hot water (cable TV and a/c were to be added). The restaurant, open to all sides, has a rustic elegance. There's a swimming pool (unsightly at last visit) with Jacuzzi and swim-up bar. It has 16-foot skiffs for fishing, plus mini-golf, volleyball, and indoor games.

A similar option is **Caño Negro Villas** (tel. 506/471-1017, fax 506/487-5349, www.canonegrovillas.com, $35 s/d/t, $55 q for a two bedroom unit), on a 35-hectare finca (eight ha are protected forest) three km west of the village. Run by a friendly Spanish host, it has eight attractive cabins with terra-cotta floors, lofty wooden ceilings with fans, large kitchens, and handsome modern bathrooms with hot water. There's a thatch-and-bamboo bar and restaurant. Horseback rides, fishing trips, and a crocodile safari are offered.

The **Bar y Restaurante Las Vegas,** beside the bridge at San Emilio (see *Getting There,* below), is a most unlikely find. Says Jerry Ruhlow: "[It's] sort of a drive-in for boats, where you can get a cold beer or soda pop and plate of *gallo pinto.*"

Getting There

A road from El Parque, 10 km south of Los Chiles, runs 10 km west to a bridge at San Emilio, from where you can reach Caño Negro village via a dirt road that continues south to Colonia Puntarenas, on the main La Fortuna-Upala road (Hwy. 4). 4WD is recommended Storms and flooding in wet season occasionally put the bridge out of commission, and a watertaxi must ferry passengers.

A bus runs daily from Upala to Caño Negro village via Colonia Puntarenas when conditions allow.

You can rent a boat at the dock in Los Chiles for $60 for two people, or $15 pp for six people or more.

Tour operators in San José, Los Chiles, and throughout the lowlands offer guided day trips to Caño Negro.

Arenal and Vicinity

LA FORTUNA

La Fortuna is a picturesque little town and the main gateway to perfectly conical Volcán Arenal, which looms six km to the southwest. A decade ago, La Fortuna was a dusty little agricultural town with potholed dirt streets. Today it is thriving on the tourist traffic, and offers a broad choice of accommodations and activities.

In town there's nothing whatsoever to see except the church on the west side of the landscaped plaza, anchored by a sculpture of a volcano. **Cocodrilus Valle,** on the west side of town, is a crocodile farm and museum in development at last visit.

The La Catarata Ecolodge (see *Accommodation,* below), run by the local farmers' cooperative, Asociación Proambiente y Desarrollo de Zefa Trece (ASPROADES), has a **butterfly garden** and **Zoo Tepescuintle,** where tepescuintles (charming dog-sized rodents) are raised for release into the wild. Entrance by donation. It's open 7 A.M.–4 P.M. daily.

Ecocentro Danaus Butterfly Farm and Tropical Garden

This ecocenter (P.O. Box 12-4400 La Fortuna, tel. 506/460-8005, fax 506/479-8048, danaus @racsa.co.cr, 8 A.M.–3:30 P.M., $5 admission with tour), about 600 meters up a dirt road, three km east of town, is a marvelous place to learn about local flora and fauna. Trails lead to a netted butterfly garden, where around 30 species flit about on sunny days. A separate garden features red-eyed tree frogs and poison-dart frogs in re-creations of their natural environments; there are also eyelash vipers in cages. A small lake has caimans, turtles, and waterfowl. Tours take about one hour. Night tours are offered by Jacamar tours. A self-guided booklet costs $5.

Catarata La Fortuna

The La Fortuna Waterfall (8 A.M.–5 P.M., closed during heavy rains, $6 admission), about four km south of town, is in the care of a local community development group—the Asociación de Desarollo de La Fortuna (tel. 506/479-8078). The turnoff for the falls is two km southeast of town, where a rocky road leads uphill 2.5 km to the entrance. From here you have to negotiate a slippery and precipitous trail (20 minutes' walk) that leads down a steep ravine to the base of the cascade; there are steps and handrails for the steepest sections. You can swim, but it's not advised, particularly after heavy rains, when the river swells and any sudden surge in the cascade could prove deadly.

A *soda* serves burgers, sandwiches, shakes, and juices.

Entertainment

Music Bar Vagabondo, to the rear of Pizzería Vagabondo, has music nightly; and **Fruto del Mar,** on the west side of town, offers karaoke Wed.–Sat. nights.

The **Volcán Look Disco** (tel. 506/479-9690, 7 P.M.–12:30 A.M. Wed.–Sat.), four km west of town, specializes in karaoke and has a restaurant, pool tables, and ping-pong. It has happy hour 9 –11 P.M.

Casino Volcano is a no-frills casino, with an uninspired bar downstairs.

Lava Rock Café shows videos of the volcano upstairs nightly at 6 P.M. ($3).

Sports and Recreation

There are more than a dozen tour agencies; some offer their own tours, others feed into each other or into programs offered by larger operators. Most tour agencies offer a similar menu that includes fishing at Lake Arenal (typically $150 half-day); trips to Arenal Volcano and Tabacón (check that the entrance fee is included in the tour price), Catarata La Fortuna ($25), Caño Negro ($45), and Venado Caves ($35); mountain biking ($45); hiking to Cerro Chato ($65); horseback trips ($25), including to Monteverde ($45 one-way); a safari float on the Río Peñas Blancas ($35), and whitewater trips.

LA FORTUNA

To El Tanque

To Arenal

To La Cascada, Chachagua, and Arenal Country Inn

BIKE ARENAL

MEDICAL CLINIC

BANK

SCHOOL

LUNA TICA/PHARMACY

LA POSADA INN

GRINGO PETE'S

AVENTURAS ARENAL

LAUNDRY

ATV TOURS

CABINAS GUACAMAYA

CABINAS SISSY (OFFICE)

HOTEL/RESTAURANTE LA FORTUNA

MUSMANNI

POLICE

ARTESANÍA CHOROTEGA

AL TRAVEL

RESTAURANTE EL JARDIN

HELADERÍA ACUARIO

HOTEL SAN BOSCO

DENTAL CLINIC

INTERNET

BANK

EDIFICIO VITAL/BANK

PHARMACY

CANOPY TOUR

HOTEL LAS COLINAS

INSIDERS TRAVEL SHOP & INFO POINT/ARENAL RAINFOREST RESERVE OFFICE

SUNSET TOURS

SUNSET TOURS

LA CASCADA

HELADERÍA CONO ARENAL

TAXIS

PURA VIDA TOURS

BUS STOP (SAN JOSÉ, CIUDAD QUESADA)

SODA/INTERNET LA PARADA

ARTESANÍA GALERÍA ARENAL

SUPERMARKET

SODA VEGETARIANO/MACROBIÓTICA EL ANGEL AZUL

DESAFÍO

CHURCH

HOTEL PARAISO TROPICAL

CABINAS MANUEL

CABINAS CARMELA

BAKERY

LAVA ROCK CAFÉ/INTERBUS/JACAMAR TOURS

POST OFFICE

DON MANUEL INN/SUNSET TOURS

CABINAS EL BOSQUE

ALAMO RENT-A-CAR

CHOZA DEL LAUREL

HOTEL ARENAL JIREH

CABINAS HERVI

CABINAS LA AMISTAD

CABINAS LAS PALMAS

HORSE RENTAL (ALBERTO SERRANO)

LUIGI'S LODGE

RESTAURANTE LUIGI

CASINO VOLCANO

CALI RENT-A-BIKE

RESTAURANTE PURA VIDA

BULLRING

Burío

Río

SCALE NOT AVAILABLE

© AVALON TRAVEL PUBLISHING, INC.

LA FORTUNA TOUR COMPANIES

The following tour operators and wholesalers offer an eclectic menu.

Aguas Bravas (tel. 506/479-9025, fax 506/229-4837, info@aguas-bravas.co.cr, www.aguas-bravas.co.cr) specializes in whitewater rafting.

Aventuras Arenal (Apdo. 13-4417 La Fortuna, tel. 506/479-9133, fax 506/479-9295, avarenal@racsa.co.cr, www.arenalaventuras.com), two blocks east of the plaza, specializes in trips to the Northern Zone.

Desafío Adventure Center (tel. 506/479-9464, fax 506/479-9465, desafio@racsa.co.cr, www.desafiocostarica.com), on the north side of the plaza, specializes in rafting but offers a full range of tours and is recommended.

Jacamar Naturalist Tours (tel. 506/479-9767, fax 506/479-9456, jacamar@racsa.co.cr, www.arenaltours.com), at the Lava Rock Café, has ICT-licensed guides and wholesales tours.

Paraíso Tropical (tel. 506/479-9222, fax 506/479-9722, paraisotropical@racsa.co.cr) is run by a Scot named Zoltan Deutsch.

Pura Vida Tours (tel. 506/479-9045, info@puravidatrips.com, www.puravidatrips.com).

Sunset Tours (tel. 506/479-9101, fax 506/479-9415, sunsettours@racsa.co.cr, www.sunset-tours.com) acts as a full-service travel agency, in addition to offering the usual menu of tours.

You may be approached on the street by so-called guides. The local chamber of commerce warns tourists "not to take tours or information off the street." Instead, it urges you to use tourist offices or hotel services.

The best all-round company is **Desafio Adventure Center** (tel. 506/479-9816, fax 506/479-9052).

The **Costa Rica Arenal Canopy Tour** (tel. 506/479-9769, fax 506/479-8137, crcanopy@sracsa.co.cr, www.crarenalcanopy.com), 50 meters east of the soccer field, offers a package that begins with a 40-minute horseback ride, followed by a 10-minute walk through primary forest; you'll then whiz between five tree platforms

using rappelling equipment. Trips are offered at 8 A.M., 11 A.M., and 1 P.M. It costs $45.

Also see *La Fortuna to Lake Arenal,* below.

Horseback rides are extremely popular (typically $15 for four hours). A popular trip is to/from Monteverde, often as a one-way transfer—attractively billed as "the shortest and most convenient route"—between Fortuna and Monteverde. Keen competition among tour operators for these popular tours has driven down prices, forcing some operators to utilize elderly horses that can be bought cheap and worked to death as short-term investments on the muddy, arduous trail over the mountains. There are reports of these overtaxed, underfed beasts dying of exhaustion on the trail. Be sure to avoid any tour that uses the "Mirador" route (see *Monteverde,* in the *Guanacaste* chapter). Desafio (see above) is recommended, as is **La Fortuna Horseback Riding Center** (tel./fax 506/479-9197).

You can take quad-bike tours with **Fourtrax ATV Tours** (tel. 506/479-8444). **Canoa Aventuras** (tel/fax 506/479-8200, canoaaventuras@racas.co.cr), at Cabinas Mary, offers canoe trips on various rivers and at Caño Negro, plus an early-morning birding tour on the Río Fortuna ($45).

Shopping

Souvenir stores are a dime a dozen. **Artesanía Chorotega** (tel. 506/479-9738), one block east of the plaza, sells pre-Columbian-style ceramics and other crafts. **Artesanía Galería Arenal,** on the southeast side of the plaza, has a good selection of art and crafts. **Lunatica** (tel./fax 506/479-8255), on the drag opposite the school, sells quality art and clothing.

For hammocks, check out **Neptune's House of Hammocks,** about 800 meters west of town.

Accommodations

Fortuna is one of the most popular destinations in the country, and there are too many accommodations to list in full; their omission here does not necessarily indicate that they are not to be considered. More hotels come on line every year, and older properties continue to upgrade.

Nonetheless, space is at a premium in high season, when it pays to book ahead.

Also see *La Fortuna to Lake Arenal,* below.

Camping: You can camp at **Cabinas Sissy,** tel. 506/479-9256, on the southwest side of town, for $4.50, including use of the kitchen and bathrooms. **Hotel Flores** also permits camping.

Under $25: Backpackers should head to ⋈ **Gringo Pete's** (tel. 506/479-8521, $3 to $3.50 pp dorms, $4 pp private room), a rambling home-turned-hostel in lively color schemes (including stained glass), with an open-air dorm with eight bunk beds. A second dorm has seven bunks and en-suite shower. Three private rooms share bathrooms. There's a lounge with sofas and a communal kitchen, plus lockers, and hammocks and a barbecue grill outside. Tours are offered. The rates are unbeatable, a solid bargain.

La Posada Inn (tel. 506/479-9793, laposadainn @yahoo.com, $5 pp), on the main street opposite the school, is about as budget as La Fortuna gets; four basic wooden rooms with fans share a bathroom with hot water. It has Internet and a book exchange.

Don Manuel Inn (tel. 506/479-9069, sunsettours@racsa.co.cr, www.sunsettourscr.com, $5 pp rooms, $8 pp cabins), on the southwest side of the church, recently remodeled and has four simple rooms with shared bath, plus four cabins with large modern private bath. Rates include breakfast.

The **Cabinas Hervi** (tel. 506/479-9430, fax 506/479-9100, $15 s/d low season, $20 high season), 50 meters southwest of the church, has eight clean, simply appointed rooms in a modern two-story unit, all with cable TV, fans, and spacious showers with hot water. It also has two-bedroom apartments with kitchens for $25 (up to five people).

The **Hotel Las Colinas** (tel. 506/479-9305, fax 506/479-9160, hcolinas@racsa.co.cr, $6 pp, or $12 s, $25 d low season; $15 pp high season), 50 meters southeast of the soccer field, has 17 clean rooms with basic furniture, and private baths with hot water. Four rooms have bunks and a shared bath. It has Internet access, and rents binoculars ($10). Rates include breakfast.

Cabinas Carmela (tel. 506/479-9010, cabinascarmela@racsa.co.cr, $10 pp), on the southwest corner of the soccer field, has 13 clean rooms with hardwood walls, orthopedic mattresses, patios with hammocks and Sarchí rockers, plus private skylit bathrooms with hot water. Ten have cable TVs and refrigerators. There's secure parking. Rates include taxes. Rooms with TV and fridge cost $5 extra.

$25–50: About 400 meters east of town, **Villa Fortuna** (tel./fax 506/479-9139, $35 s/d low season, $40 high season) has 11 clinically clean, modestly furnished modern rooms with refrigerators, fans, tile floors, and private baths with hot water. Seven rooms have a/c and TVs. The landscaped grounds include a small swimming pool and caged toucans.

Cabinas Guacamaya (tel. 506/479-9393, fax 506/479-9087, info@cabinasguacamaya.com, www.cabinasguacamaya.com, $30 s, $35 d), 20 meters southwest of the school, is a modern house with nine clean, spacious a/c rooms with refrigerators, private baths with hot water, and patios with rockers. Rooms sleep three people. It has secure parking.

Hotel Paraíso Tropical (tel./fax 506/479-9222, paraisotropicalf@racsa.co.cr, $25 s, $35 d standard low season, $35/50 high season; $39 s, $46 d deluxe low season, $46/53 high season), on the south side of the church, has 11 spacious, modestly elegant a/c rooms with sponge-washed walls, fans, cable TV, microwave, coffeemaker, private bath, and hot water. Three rooms have king-size beds; four have refrigerators. Upstairs rooms are larger and have balconies with views. There's secure parking, a restaurant, and a tour office.

Cabinas La Amistad (tel. 506/479-9390 or 506/479-9364, fax 506/479-9342, laamistad @odilie.com, www.odilie.com, $10 pp low season, $15 high season; $35 s/d apartment low season, $50 s/d high season), had been entirely remodeled at last visit and now offers 13 rooms and four upstairs apartments, all with ceiling fans, cable TV, and private bath with hot water. The simply furnished downstairs rooms are a bit gloomy and open to the parking lot.

The well-run **Hotel Arenal Jireh** (tel. 506/479-9236, fax 506/479-9004, arenaljireh

@racsa.co.cr, www.arenaljireh.com, $25 s, $40 d low season; $30/45 high season), one block west of the church, offers pleasant and spacious a/c rooms with refrigerator, cable TV, tile floors, single and double bed, and hot water. Take an upper-story room in the three-story block for volcano views. There's a small swimming pool, laundry, gift store, and tour desk, plus it offers email and secure parking.

Hotel San Bosco (tel. 506/479-9050, fax 506/479-9109, fortuna@racsa.co.cr, www.arenal-volcano.com, $30 s, $35 d standard, $35/40 d with a/c and cable TV low season; $35 s, $40 d standard, $45/50 with a/c and cable TV high season), 200 meters north of the plaza, has 34 a/c rooms (11 are cabins) with private baths and hot water, plus two fully equipped homes for eight ($80/100 low/high season) and 14 people ($100/120). Some of the rooms are small and overpriced. It has a souvenir shop, plus swimming pool and Jacuzzi. Rates include tax and breakfast.

The well-run **Hotel Arenal Rossi** (tel. 506/479-9023, fax 506/479-9414, contactus @hotelarenalrossi, www.hotelarenalrossi.com, $36 s, $42–52 d low season; $40 s, $47–57 d high season), about two km west of Fortuna, offers 25 simple but pretty *cabinas* with refrigerators, TVs, and private baths with hot water. One has a full kitchen and skylit bathroom. Twelve have a/c. Rooms vary in size. "Immaculate and comfortable," reports a reader, but walls are thin. There's a steakhouse, plus a kids' pool and swings, and a gift store. Rates include tax and breakfast.

I also like **Hotel Bar Pizzeria Vagabondo** (tel. 506/479-9565, vagabond@racsa.co.cr, $20 s/d low season, $30 high season), 200 meters further west, with four attractive, modestly furnished rooms in a charming garden setting. None have views, alas, but they come with fan and cable TV, and private bath with hot water.

Cerro Chato Lodge B&B (tel. 506/479-9494, fax 506/479-9404, cerrochato@racsa.co.cr, www.geocities.com/cerrochatocr, $15 pp shared bath, $20 s, $35 d cabins), 1.5 km west and 1.5 km south of town, offers four rooms: two are in the owner's home, of which one has private bathroom and the other shares a bathroom with the family. Two cabins in the garden have clean private bathrooms with large walk-in showers. Rates include full breakfast.

Nearby, **La Catarata Ecolodge** (P.O. Box 6939-1000 San José, tel. 506/479-9522, fax 506/479-9168, catarata@racsa.co.cr, www.arenalfortuna.com, $25 s, $42 d) has nine attractive hardwood cabins with dainty decor, fans, verandas, and private baths and hot water. There's a small restaurant, butterfly garden, an orchid garden, and small zoo. It's run by a local cooperative. Rates include breakfast and tax.

Several reasonable options are available on the road between Fortuna and El Tanque. They offer no advantages in location, however, being further away from the volcano. One of my favorites is **Hotel Coloso Arenal** (tel. 506/479-8335, fax 506/479-8336, www.hotelcolosoarenal.com, $40 s, $45 d standard, $70/75 deluxe, $50/55 junior suite low season; $60 s, $65 d standard, $90/95 deluxe, $70/75 junior suite high season), run by a friendly young couple, with a charming rusticity to its 12 wood-lined a/c rooms and blue-tiled bathrooms with TV and mini-fridge; some, termed junior suites, are larger, and a suite has a king-size bed and huge Jacuzzi tub and walk-in shower. One room is handicap-equipped with ramps and wide doors. Rooms have security boxes. A swimming pool was to be added. The couple offer horseback and biking tours.

$50–100: The **Arenal Country Inn** (tel. 506/479-9670, fax 506/479-9433, info @arenalcountryinn.com, www.arenalcountryinn.com, $62 s, $68 d, $81 low season; $72/78/91 high season), 600 meters southeast of town, is a former *ganadería* (cattle farm) with 20 a/c cabins set amid seven hectares of lawns and tranquil landscaped gardens with a grandstand volcano view. Each has polished parquet floors, orthopedic mattress, a safety box, handsome modern bathrooms with huge walk-in showers, and a porch with volcano views. However, ceilings fans would be preferred, and trees block all views of the volcano. The former cattle corral has become a rather ascetic but intriguing restaurant and bar with pool table and TV, plus there's a handsome swimming pool and sun deck. Reception closes at

8 P.M., after which you're on your own! Rates include breakfast.

Luigi's Lodge (tel. 506/479-9636, fax 506/479-9898, info@luigislodge.com, www.luigislodge.com, $48 s/d low season, $60 s/d high season), at the west end of town, is a handsome two-story wooden lodge in quasi-Cretan style, with 20 simply furnished but comfortable a/c rooms on a salmon-pink theme. Each has a ceiling fan and tiled bathroom, and opens to a veranda offering volcano views. There's a restaurant, pool, Jacuzzi, Internet, gym, casino and bar, and daily shuttle service to La Fortuna. Rates include full breakfast.

Some 2.5 km west of town is **Hotel Restaurant La Pradera** (tel. 506/479-9597, fax 506/479-9167, $25 s, $30 d standard, $45 s/d deluxe low season; $30 s, $40 d standard, $55 s/d deluxe high season), with 16 standard a/c rooms and four deluxe rooms with Jacuzzis and king-size beds. Cabinas face the volcano amid pleasant grounds. It has an attractive steak restaurant and offers horseback riding, mountain biking, and jungle trails.

I like the reclusive **Lomas del Volcán** (P.O. Box 4-4417, La Fortuna, tel. 506/479-9000, fax 506/479-9770, info@lomasdelvolcan.com, www.lomasdelvolcan.com, $60 s, $70 d low season; $70 s, $80 d high season), set amid dairy pasture about one km off the main road and four km west of town. It has 13 spacious wooden cabins raised on stilts, with king-size and double beds, fans, refrigerator, beautiful modern bathrooms with hot water and handsome stained-glass shower doors, and volcano views from glass-enclosed porches. Nature trails lead from the property into nearby montane forest. Horses can be rented.

The **Las Cabañitas Resort** (Apdo. 5, San Carlos 4417, tel. 506/479-9400, fax 506/479-9408, cabanita@racsa.co.cr, www.cabanita.com, $64 s, $69 d low season, $80 s, $95 d high season), about one km east of town, is an appealing hotel with 39 cozy and comfortable wooden *cabinas* surrounded by lawns with trim borders. Each bungalow has two double beds or one queen-size bed, fan, telephone, private bathroom with hot water, and private porch with volcano vista. Six have a/c and cable TV. There's a swimming pool, tennis court, laundry service, and bar and restaurant.

Food

Vegetarians should head to **Soda Vegetariano** (tel. 506/479-9329, 8 A.M.–10 P.M. low season, 10 A.M.–10 P.M. high season), on the north side of the plaza, serving garlic bread ($1), salads ($2), veggie cheeseburgers ($2), wholewheat pastas, and caffeine-free maize coffee. And how about a breakfast of oatmeal with soy milk, and a soy milkshake?

The simple, clean **Soda La Parada** (tel. 506/479-9547), on the south side of the plaza, serves around the clock and offers lunchtime *casados* for $2. **Restaurant El Jardín** (tel. 506/479-9360, 7 A.M.–11 P.M.), 50 meters southeast of the plaza, is clean and airy and has *casados* for $2.50.

For real local fare, head to **Choza de Laurel** (tel. 506/479-9231, 6 A.M.–10 P.M.), a rustic Tican country inn with cloves of garlic hanging from the roof and an excellent *plato especial*—mixed plate of Costa Rican dishes ($4). Grilled chicken ($2–6) and *casados* ($3) are other good bets, but specials are expensive.

The thatch-roofed **Rancho La Cascada Restaurant** (tel. 506/479-9145, 6 A.M.–11 P.M.), on the north side of the soccer field, serves *típico* dishes, plus pastas ($3) and burgers ($2), and filling breakfasts. A reader reports ordering a fresh orange juice but receiving Tang.

The clean, modern, open-air **Lava Rock Café** (7 A.M.–10 P.M., $1.25–4), on the south side of the church, serves omelettes, filling *casados,* burgers, sandwiches, steaks and seafoods, plus tiramisu, cappuccinos, espressos, and *batidos* (milkshakes).

For elegance, head to **Ⓜ Restaurante Luigi** two blocks west of the plaza. Now enlarged, this airy upscale option lists a large pasta and pizza menu, plus the likes of bruschetta ($4.50), cream of mushroom soup ($3.50), beef Stroganoff ($10), and sea bass with shrimp ($15). It specializes in flambées, and has a large cocktail list.

For pizza, try open-air **Pizzería Vagabondo** (tel. 506/479-9565), breezeswept and serving pizzas *a la leña* (from the wood oven), plus pastas and salads.

For Chinese there's the modern a/c **Restaurante Pura Vida** (11 A.M.–11 P.M.), on the west side of town.

Craving steak? Make a beeline to **Steak House Arenal** (tel. 506/479-9023, 6 A.M.–10 P.M.), 800 meters west of town. This charming place is festooned with hanging plants and has traditional hardwood decor.

For ice cream, head to **Heladería Acuario** (11 A.M.–7 P.M.), 50 meters southeast of the plaza; or **Heladería Cono Arenal** (8 A.M.–11 P.M.), on the north side of the park.

Musmanni, two blocks east of the soccer field, sells baked goods. You can stock up on groceries at the **supermarket** 50 meters southwest of the soccer field.

Information and Services

Insiders Travel Shop & Info Point (tel./fax 506/479-9338, lafortuna@costarica-insiders .com), on the drag 20 meters southeast of the plaza, is a good resource; open 8 A.M.–9 P.M. Mon.–Sat., 8 A.M.–2 P.M. Sunday.

The **Clínica La Fortuna** (tel. 506/479-9142) is two blocks northeast of the gas station; open 7 A.M.–5 P.M. weekdays, 7 A.M.–noon Saturday. There's a **dental clinic** (tel. 506/479-9590) across the street. **Farmácia Dr. Max** is in the shopping center on the main street facing the school.

The **police station** (tel. 506/479-9689) is on the main drag, one block east of the plaza. For the traffic police *(tránsitos)* call tel. 506/479-9994.

There are three banks in town.

There are public phones around the plaza.

Insiders (see above) charges $1.50 per hour for Internet access; see above. **Desafío Expeditions** has email service: $1.50 for 10 minutes, and $0.20 per minute extra. The office of **Arenal Rain Forest Reserve** (tel. 506/479-8014) charges $2 per hour; open 7 A.M.–8 P.M. daily. **Sunset Tours** and **Arenal Evergreen Internet Café** also offer Internet access, as does **Internet La Parada** (tel. 506/479-9632).

The **laundry** (tel. 506/479-9737, 8 A.M.–9 P.M. Mon.–Sat.) on the main street, opposite the school, has one-hour service for $5.75 per load.

Getting There

Buses (tel. 506/255-4318) leave San José from Calle 12, Avenidas 7/9, daily at 6:15 A.M., 8:40 A.M., and 11:30 A.M. Return buses depart La Fortuna from the south side of the soccer field at noon and 2 P.M. Buses depart Ciudad Quesada for La Fortuna at 6 A.M. and 10:30 A.M. (via Chachagua; returning at 8 A.M. and 12:15 P.M.), and 1 P.M., 3:30 P.M., 5:15 P.M., and 6 P.M. Buses depart Tilarán for La Fortuna at 7 A.M. and 12:30 P.M. (four hours, $1.75), returning at 6 A.M. and 5:30 P.M.

The **"Arenal Express"** (tel. 506/479-9222, fax 506/479-9792, paraisotropical@racsa.co.cr) operates a bus service to San José (8 A.M. and 2 P.M.), Monteverde, (8 A.M.), Flamingo (8:15 A.M.), and to Tamarindo, Playas del Coco, and Liberia (8 A.M.).

Interbus (tel. 506/283-5573, www.interbusonline.com) and **Fantasy Bus** (tel. 506/232-3681) offer daily shuttles between San José and La Fortuna for $25.

Alamo (tel./fax 506/479-9090, fax 506/479-8215, www.alamocostarica.com) has an office at the west end of town.

Getting Around

Internet La Parada rents bicycles for $2 hourly, $10 daily. **Bike Rental Arenal** (tel. 506/479-9545, www.bikearenal.com) rents Cannondale mountain bikes ($12 half-day, $18 full-day) and has guided rides.

LA FORTUNA TO FLORENCIA

The road southeast from La Fortuna leads to Florencia via **Chachagua,** 10 km southeast of La Fortuna. About one km east of Chachagua, a dirt road leads west and dead-ends at the **Chachagua Rainforest Lodge,** a 130-hectare private forest reserve and cattle ranch nestled at the foot of the Tilarán mountain range. It has a small and inconsequential butterfly garden and orchid garden. The hacienda produces yucca, banana, papaya, and pineapple, and has an experimental fish farm (the fish—tilapia, an East African species much favored for its delicate flavor—find their way onto guests' dinner plates).

La Tigra, 12 km southeast of Chachagua, is a gateway to the Bosque Eterno de los Niños (Children's Eternal Forest) and Monteverde Cloud Forest Biological Reserve; you'll see a sign about 800 meters south of La Tigra and an information office one km north of town. See *Cordillera de Tilarán* in the *Guanacaste* chapter for details.

Accommodation and Food

Chachagua Rainforest Lodge (Apdo. 476-4005 San José, tel. 506/239-6464, fax 506/290-6506, www.chachaguarainforesthotel.com, $50 s, $55 d low season, $76 s, $84 d high season), at Chachagua, is a tranquil getaway with a gurgling brook cascading down through the property. The 22 spacious, simply appointed wooden cabins each have two double beds and a deck with a picnic table and benches for enjoying the natural surrounds. Showers feature two-way mirrored windows. Six cabins were to be added. The atmospheric natural-log restaurant looks out upon a corral where *sabaneros* offer rodeo shows. There's a swimming pool, plus horseback riding, and nature and bird-watching hikes.

You *must* visit **M Coco Loco Art Gallery & Café** (tel. 506/468-0990, kwetonal@netscape.net, 8 A.M.–5 P.M.), five km east of Chachagua. This exquisite, German-run roadside bistro serves Mediterranean salad ($4.50), Lebanese salad ($5), sub sandwiches, including BLT (from $3), plus tacos, smoothies, and coffees and teas. The fabulous decor is delightfully colorful.

Coco Loco's Art Gallery has various art galleries displaying the very finest Costa Rican crafts, including hammocks, exquisite marble carvings, ceramics, and exotic indigenous masks. It offers free shipping on purchases over $250.

LA FORTUNA TO LAKE ARENAL

West from La Fortuna, the road begins a gradual, winding ascent to Lake Arenal around the northern flank of Arenal volcano. It's a stupendously scenic drive.

Baldi Termae Spa (tel. 506/479-9652, 10 A.M.–10 P.M., $10 admission), some five km west of La Fortuna, has been expanded and beautifully landscaped as a competitor to the crowded Balneario Tabacón. It features nine hot mineral pools (69–95°F) lined with natural stone, with cascades and foliage. One pool has its own restaurant, plus there's a small snack bar and lockers.

A new facility, **Arenal Springs,** was due to open in 2005 with an extensive heliconia collection, hot springs, and infinity pools, plus 120 rooms and villas.

Arenal Hanging Bridges

This new attraction (tel. 506/253-5080, info @puentescolganes.com,www.hangingbridges.com , 7 A.M.–4 P.M., $20 admission, $30 with guided tour) opened in 2003 within a 250-hectare (618-acre) forest reserve about 20 km west of La Fortuna. Although offering only occasional glimpses of the volcano, the self-guided hike provides a marvelous entrée to forest ecology as you follow a three-km interpretive trail with 14 sturdy bridges (some up to 100 meters long) suspended across ravines and treetops. A guided night walk is offered at 7:30 P.M. There's a hilltop café-restaurant and gift store. A night tour costs $40; an early-morning birding tour costs $45.

Los Lagos Jungle and Trails

This quasi-theme park (tel. 506/479-8000, fax 506/479-8009, loslagos@racsa.co.cr, www.hotel-loslagos.com, $7 admission), six km west of La Fortuna, has 400 hectares of primary forest with trails, one of which leads to a mirador. (Until recently you could get close enough to Arenal's summit to see and hear rocks crashing down the lava flow that passes through the property. Two people were killed on the Congo Trail during an eruption in summer 2000, however, and the government ordered all but two km of trails closed.) Three water slides whorl down to hot- and cold-water swimming pools. There are ponds with turtles and waterfowl. And a crocodile farm raises these antediluvian critters for release into the wild as adults. Guided horseback rides ($25, three hours) are offered. A *soda* serves food on weekends. It also has accommodations.

ⓜ Tabacón Hot Springs

Balneario Tabacón (tel. 506/460-2020, fax 506/460-6229, info@tabacon.com, www.tabacon .com, 10 A.M.–10 P.M., $17 admission, $13 after 6 P.M., children $7), at the base of Arenal Volcano, on the edge of Arenal Volcano National Park, 13 km west of La Fortuna and six km east of Lake Arenal, is where the steaming waters of the Río Tabacón tumble from the lava fields and cascade alongside the road. A dip here is supposedly good for treating skin problems, arthritis, and muscular pains.

This Spanish colonial-style *balneario* (bathing resort) features five natural mineral pools and natural hot springs set in exotic gardens. The main stream (hot) and a side stream (cool) have been diverted through the grounds in a series of descending pools of varying temperatures between 27–39°C (80–102°F). Steam rises moodily amid beautifully landscaped vegetation. Even adults laugh as they whiz down the water slide. You can sit beneath a 20-meter-wide waterfall—like taking a hot shower—and lean back inside, where it feels like a sauna. The complex also has an indoor hot tub, plus a restaurant and three bars, including a swim-up bar in the main pool. Towels, lockers, and showers are available for a small deposit. Massages ($40 for 45 minutes), mud packs ($20), and other healing treatments complete the picture. You'll fall in love with Tabacón by night, too, when a dip becomes a romantic indulgence (and a jaw-dropping experience if the volcano is erupting). It's a staple with tour groups and gets very crowded.

The resort features a separate section—**La Fuentes Termales** ($6 admission)—100 meters further downhill. It has five steaming pools in landscaped grounds in a valley (lacking volcano views) below the hotel, from which you can glide, Rambo-like, by rappel on a **canopy tour** ($40 low season, $45 high season). It has toilets, changing rooms, and towels.

Previous concerns about theft from lockers and the car park seem to have been addressed.

Safety Concerns: Tabacón is a "high-risk zone" and lies directly in the path of the volcano's eruptive path (the former community of Tabacón was decimated in 1968 by an erup-

tion that killed 78 people; and in June 1975, an eruptive avalanche passed over the site of today's Balneario). A potentially deadly avalanche occurs within the zone once every two or three years, often without warning, and it is unlikely that anyone in its path could get out of the way in time.

Sports and Recreation

You can take a short canopy ride using rappelling gear at Tabacón.

Miradas Arenal Canopy Tour, at Miradas Arenal Hotel, features ziplines between 12 platforms and takes two hours to traverse the circuit in harness ($45). And **Arenal Paraíso Canopy Tour,** at the Arenal Paraíso Hotel, has two-hour tours at 8 A.M., 11 A.M., and 2:30 P.M.

Helicopter tours depart Hotel Montaña Fuego; $26 for 10 minutes, $86 for 30 minutes.

Lavas Trails Tacotal (tel./fax 506/460-9998, reservations@hoteltacotal.com, www.hoteltacotal .com), about eight km west of town, charges $5 for access to its trails; it has horseback rides.

Accommodations

If you want your own reclusive spot, check into **Posada Colonial** (tel. 506/460-5955, posadacol @yahoo.com), a bed-and-breakfast about nine km west of La Fortuna. This exquisite property sits amid beautifully tended grounds over a valley with volcano vistas. A pleasingly furnished, self-contained unit has a garage below and living quarters above, with a large sliding glass door onto a deck ($45 s/d, including breakfast). The Canadian owner, Grant, occasionally rents a room for four people in his sparely furnished wooden home ($45); the room, upstairs, has a private bath and wrap-around deck, and is perfect for families or two couples.

Opposite is **Miradas Arenal** (tel./fax 506/460-5828, $30 s, $40 d low season, $40/50 high season), with fine views. It has three attractive wooden cabins amid broad lawns. Each has tile floor, refrigerator, coffeemaker, bathrooms with views from tub/shower and hot water, and French doors that open to verandas.

Jungla y Senderos Los Lagos (tel. 506/479-8000, fax 506/479-8009, loslagos@racsa.co.cr, www.hotelloslagos.com, $51 s, $71 d standard, $64 s, $81 d superior low season; $69 s, $86 d standard, $79 s, $96 d superior high season) has 32 attractive a/c cabins with wooden ceilings, cable TV, phones, safety boxes, minibars, refrigerators, and private baths and hot water. All offer up-close volcano views. It also has two-bedroom villas with kitchens for the same price as superiors. Rates include taxes.

Volcano Lodge (tel. 506/460-6080, fax 506/460-6020, info@volcanolodgecostarica.com, www.volcanolodgecostarica.com, $65 d low season, $83 high season), about six km west of town, offers 20 beautifully appointed two-bedroom cottages with large picture windows, and porches with rockers for enjoying the volcano views beyond the swimming pool and lush gardens. Each a/c room has two double beds, safety box, and hot water. Facilities include a pool and Jacuzzi, plus free email and laundry service. The restaurant is one of the finest around (see *Food*, below).

Arenal Paraíso Resort & Spa (P.O. Box 84-4417 La Fortuna, tel. 506/460-5333, fax 506/460-5343, arenalparaiso@racsa.co.cr, www.arenalparaiso.com, $60 s/d standard, $90 s/d superior low season; $65 standard, $95 superior high season), about seven km west of town, has 21 pretty all-hardwood *cabinas* with fans, refrigerators, hot water, and porches offering volcano vistas. Fifty-five superior rooms also have a/c, cable TV, and telephone, while suites have Jacuzzis. There's a small restaurant and gift store, plus a spa with sauna, a gym, and lush gardens with trails plus five natural water pools and eight pools with thermal waters. It has a canopy tour.

Half a kilometer farther, and also amid lush grounds, is **Montaña de Fuego Resort & Spa** (tel. 506/460-1220, fax 506/460-1455, monfuego @racsa.co.cr, www.montanafuego.com, $95 s/d standard, $121 s/d deluxe), where 50 handsome hardwood a/c *cabinas* sit on a hillock with splendid views of the volcano from a veranda enclosed in glass (many rooms, however, face away from the volcano). Some are bungalow suites; others are more rustic. All have fans, cable TV, telephones, and private bathrooms with hot water,

and terraces. It has a glass-enclosed restaurant, plus a swimming pool and spa. Horseback trips and helicopter tours are offered. Rates include breakfast and tax.

A short distance farther brings you to **Hotel Restaurante Lavas Tacotal** (tel./fax 506/460-9998, reservations@hoteltacotal.com, www.hoteltacotal.com, $45 s, $74 d standard, $80 s, $95 d junior suite). The 13 spacious, stone-walled a/c rooms and two junior suites (with king-size beds and Jacuzzi tubs) have cable TV and private bath with hot water. They're supposedly aligned toward the volcano. Alas, the layout is off by a few degrees, as the volcano views are virtually obscured from the picture windows. The grounds contain a lake and swimming pool, plus the pleasant roadside *ranchito* restaurant with a floor of tree trunk slices in lieu of paving.

Tabacón Lodge (tel. 506/256-1500, fax 506/221-3075, sales@tabacon.com, www.tabacon.com, $139 s/d standard, $164 superior, $189 junior suite, $224 suite low season; $159/184/229/264 high season), 200 meters east and uphill of Balneario Tabacón, is set amid well-maintained verdant gardens. The property has 73 a/c rooms, each with two double beds, hardwood furniture, TV, phones, minibars, coffeemakers, patio affording a volcano view, large bathrooms, and upscale decor—exquisite hardwood furnishings, silent a/c, and intriguing artwork. Nine rooms are junior suites, refurbished in elegant style, with private garden Jacuzzis, minibars, and cotton bathrobes. Some are in bungalows, others are in a three-story property. There's a small gym, plus gourmet restaurant, a bar, a swim-up bar in a thermal pool, and the Iskandria spa. Rates include breakfast and unlimited access to the *balneario*.

Nearby, **Erupciones B&B** (tel./fax 506/460-8000, $45 s, $55 d) is a delightful little place with three cabins in a meadow on a cattle farm. Gaily colored in tropical colors, they're spacious, cross-lit and ventilated through louvered glass windows, and have tile floors, fans, clean modern bathrooms with hot water, and patios with table and chairs. Rates include breakfast.

Food

There's no entrance fee to eat at the **Restaurante Balneario Tabacón** (noon–9:30 P.M.), which serves splendid Tico and creative continental fare, such as French onion soup ($3), and sea bass in apple and chile pepper ($10). It also has salads and pastas ($3–5). The surroundings are unbeatable, and the service professional.

The elegant **Restaurante Arenal** (7 A.M.–10 P.M., $7) at the Volcano Lodge, combines intriguing decor with nouvelle Costa Rican cuisine, such as grilled corvina with passion fruit sauce and cassava croquettes, and grilled chicken breast and orange sauce with pickled fruits.

I recommend **Restaurante Mirador Arenal Steak House** (tel. 506/460-8353, 10 A.M.–10 P.M., $3.50–$11), a clean, modern restaurant featuring onion soup, gazpacho, tenderloin in jalapeño sauce, and tilapia in pimento sauce. The breezeswept **Restaurante Tacotal,** across the road, offer an identical menu in more elegant surrounds.

◪ ARENAL VOLCANO NATIONAL PARK

The 12,016-hectare Parque Nacional Volcán Arenal (8 A.M.–4 P.M., $6 admission) lies within the 204,000-hectare Arenal Conservation Area, a polyglot assemblage protecting 16 reserves in the region between the Guanacaste and Tilarán mountain ranges, and including Lake Arenal. The park has two volcanoes: Chato, whose collapsed crater contains an emerald lagoon surrounded by forest, and the perfectly conical Arenal.

The volcano (1,633 meters) is a picture-perfect cone. It's also Costa Rica's most active volcano and a must-see on any tourist's itinerary. Note, however, that it is most often covered in clouds and getting to *see* an eruption is a matter of luck (the dawn hours are best, before the clouds roll in; seasonally, you stand a reasonable chance in dry season, and less than favorable odds in rainy season). Arenal was sacred to pre-Columbian tribes

trailhead, Arenal Volcano National Park

ARENAL VOLCANO NATIONAL PARK

To Nuevo Arenal and Tilarán

ARENAL HANGING BRIDGES

ARENAL LODGE

Río Arenal

Río Tabacón

Río Chachagua

To El Tanque

LAS CABAÑITAS RESORT

VILLA FORTUNA

La Fortuna

CABIÑAS MARY/CANOA AVENTURA

ARENAL COUNTRY INN

NEPTUNO HOUSE

Río Burío

Fortuna

To Chachagua

GALERÍA AGUAS VERDES

ALBERGUE ECOTURÍSTICO LA CATARATA

CERRO CHATO LODGE

CANOPY TOUR

HOTEL RESTAURANTE LA PRADERA

LOMAS DEL VOLCÁN

HOTEL & STEAKHOUSE ROSSI

HOTEL FLORES

HOTEL/PIZZERÍA VAGABONDO

CATARATAS LA FORTUNA

Quebrada Guillermina

VOLCANO LODGE/ RESTAURANTE ARENAL

MIRADAS ARENAL/ CANOPY TOUR

POSADA COLONIAL

JUNGLA Y SENDEROS LOS LAGOS

BALDI TERMAE

VOLCANO LOOK DISCO

Quebrada Palmo

Volcán Chato

Laguna Volcán Chato

ARENAL PARAÍSO RESORT & SPA

HOTEL ERUPCIONES B&B

HOTEL TOCOTAL

Quebrada Tabacón

Volcán Arenal

Sendero Los Tucanes

ARENAL OBSERVATORY LODGE

HOTEL MONTAÑA FUEGO N RESORT & SPA

MIRADOR ARENAL STEAK HOUSE

TABACÓN LODGE

LAVA TRAILS

TABACÓN HOT SPRINGS

EL SILENCIO

RANGER STATION

Sendero Los Heliconias

ARENAL RAINFOREST RESERVE

Río Agua Caliente

POLICE

CAMPING

RANGER STATION & PARK ENTRANCE

Sendero Colada 92

PARK HQ

Río Piedras Negras

LINDA VISTA DEL NORTE

HOTEL CABIÑAS EL CASTILLO DORADO

EL CATILLO DE INSECTOS

Sendero Los Miradores

PRESA SANGREGADO (ICE)

Pueblo Nuevo

El Castillo

ARENAL VISTA LODGE

ALBERGUE DE ÁLVARO ARIAS OBREGÓN

Río Piedras Blancas

Lake Arenal

0   2 mi

0   2 km

© AVALON TRAVEL PUBLISHING, INC.

(it is easy to imagine sacrifices tossed into the inferno), but it slumbered peacefully throughout the colonial era. On 29 July 1968, it was awakened from its long sleep by a fateful earthquake. The massive explosion that resulted wiped out the villages of Tabacón and Pueblo Nuevo, whose entire populations perished. The blast was felt as far away as Boulder, Colorado.

It is regarded as one of the world's most active volcanoes. Its lava flows and eruptions have been constant, and on virtually any day you can see smoking cinder blocks tumbling down the steep slope from the horseshoe-shaped crater that opens to the west—or at night, watch a fiery cascade of lava spewing from the 140-meter-deep crater. Some days the volcano blows several times in an hour, spewing house-size rocks, sulfur dioxide and chloride gases, and red-hot lava. The volcano's active vent is on the western side, and the normal easterly wind blows most of the effluvia westward. Explosions and eruptions, however, occur on all sides.

MINAE's Comisión Nacional de Emergencías recently set up four "safety zones" around the volcano and is now regulating commercial development. It's a highly arbitrary zoning, however, and any cataclysmic eruption would devastate the entire area.

The turnoff to the entrance is 3.5 km east of Lake Arenal dam and 2.5 km west of Tabacón. The dirt access road leads 1.5 km to the **ranger station** (no tel.), which sells a small guide ($1) and has restrooms. A dirt road leads north from here 1.5 km to a parking lot and hiking trails.

The park headquarters (tel. 506/461-8499) is about 800 meters further west. A long-touted interpretive center was no closer to having materialized at last visit. Meanwhile, the Arenal Observatory Lodge (see *Accommodation,* below) has a small but interesting **Museum of Vulcanicity.**

For further information, contact the Arenal Conservation Headquarters (tel. 506/695-5180, fax 506/695-5982) in Tilarán.

Trails

The one-km **Las Heliconias Trail** leads from the ranger station past an area where vegetation is recolonizing the 1968 lava flow. The trail

intersects the **Look-Out Point Trail,** which leads 1.3 km from the ranger station to a *mirador*—a viewing area—from which you can watch active lava flowing. **Las Coladas Trail** begins at the intersection and leads 2.8 km to a lava flow from 1993.

The **Los Miradores Trail** begins at park headquarters and leads southwest 1.2 km to Lake Arenal. It is good for spotting wildlife. Farther east, beyond the Ríos Agua Caliente and La Danta, is the trailhead for **Los Tucanes Trail,** which leads to the southernmost lava flows (one hour).

You can also hike various trails at the **Arenal Observatory Lodge** (see below), where trails lead to the lava fields and to Cerro Chato's lagoon-filled extinct crater; $3 access. A guided hike is offered daily at 8:30 A.M. (complimentary to guests). The four-km-long Lava Trail (a tough climb back to the lodge; don't believe your guide if he/she says it is "easy") offers "howler monkeys, good birdwatching, dangerous lava" and is free; it takes about three hours round-trip. The Chato Trail (four hours) is longer and more difficult.

Hotels and tour companies in La Fortuna offer volcano tours and can arrange guides. A reader recommends **Geovani Solano** (tel. 506/479-9081, cell. 506/364-7926, www.geocities.com /geovaniprivatetours/), who leads a tough hike up Cerro Chato, including a canoe crossing of the crater lake.

Warning: Hiking too close to the volcano is not advisable. Heed warning signs. This isn't Disneyland! The volcano is totally unpredictable, and there is a strong possibility of losing your life if you venture into restricted zones. In 1988, a U.S. tourist was killed when hiking to the rim, and in August 2000, a guide and child died when Arenal erupted while they were hiking up its flanks. You also risk the lives of Red Cross personnel who must look for your body.

Accommodations and Food

No camping is allowed in the park. However, Jim Hamilton permits camping on his land adjacent to the ranger station ($2.50 pp), with basic toilets and showers. A small *soda* serves simple meals.

The Northern Zone

Enjoying an enviable setting, the ⓜ **Arenal Observatory Lodge** (Apdo. 321-1007, San José, tel. 506/692-2070 or 290-7011, fax 506/290-8427, info@arenal-observatory.co.cr, www.arenal-observatory.co.cr, $45 s, $59 d economy, $62/84 standard, $91/112 d Smithsonian, $122/125 junior suite low season; $52/67 economy, $73/95 standard, $102/128 Smithsonian, $146 s/d junior suite high season) is a ridgetop property on a 347-hectare reserve offering immaculate views over the lake and volcano, which looms only two km to the north and separated by a deep vale. The facility, built in 1987 as an observatory for the Smithsonian Institution and the University of Costa Rica, is acclaimed for its eco-sensitivity. It has 30 rooms of three types and continues to upgrade and improve. Wood-paneled standard rooms, adjacent to the lodge, have a double and bunk bed, though they're small and lack views. Four observatory rooms have nicer furnishings, terra-cotta floors, and volcano views through vast picture windows, as do nine modestly appointed but spacious superior rooms in the Smithsonian block, reached via a suspension bridge. Five new luxury Smithsonian rooms have two double beds, lofty ceilings with fans, gracious bathrooms, and floor-to-ceiling picture windows and glass doors permitting you to lie in bed and watch the eruptions. Five rooms are handicap-equipped and easily accessible. A converted farmhouse—**La Casona**—accommodates 14 more people in four rooms with shared bathrooms; three have volcano view ($35 s, $45 d; $325 whole house, including breakfast and dinner). And there's a lodge—**White Hawk Villa**—for 10 people, with views ($350; minimum two nights). The lodge offers horseback rides ($7 per hour), hikes (see above); a morning Lava Flow tour is free to guests, and canoeing on Lake Chato (free). And there's a splendid walk-in horizon-edge swimming pool, plus Jacuzzi, kid's pool, and wet bar. The lodge is closed one week in April and July each year for scientific monitoring. 4WD is recommended. Minibus transfers from San José cost $100 one-way (split between passengers). The lodge has earned four feathers in the Certificate of Sustainable Tourism program.

The **Arenal Observatory Lodge** restaurant is open to nonguests and serves breakfast 7–8:30 A.M., lunch 10 A.M.–5 P.M., and dinner 6–8:30 P.M. It's worth it for its magnificent vantage. I've enjoyed a cream of asparagus soup, chicken in curry sauce, and splendid tilapia dishes.

EL CASTILLO

The dirt road to Arenal Observatory Lodge splits about four km east of the ranger station, with one branch leading south along the southern edge of Lake Arenal via the tiny communities of El Castillo and Pueblo Nuevo, beyond which it deteriorates rapidly and requires a 4WD. The arduous route eventually connects with Tronadora (see *Lake Arenal*, below). There are several rivers to cross, and in wet season it's often impassible.

The **Jardín de Mariposas/Castillo de Insectos** (tel. 506/479-8014 or 506/358-6773, 8 A.M.–4 P.M., $8 admission adults, $5 students and children under 12), about one km above El Castillo, is a butterfly garden and insect museum with live scorpions, rhinoceros beetles, lizards, etc. About 45 species of butterflies flit beneath seven netted arenas. Snakes were to be added. It also has a botanical garden with medicinal plants.

ⓜ Arenal Rainforest Reserve

This newly created private reserve (tel. 506/479-9944, fax 506/479-8014, info@skytrek.com, www.arenalreserve.com, $40 admission including the tram and Sky Walk, $60 all-inclusive), near El Castillo, on the north-facing slopes of the Cordillera de Tilarán, was in construction at last visit and promises to be a winner. It offers phenomenal volcano views, to be enjoyed from an aerial tram that will eventually span 1,300 meters and an elevation of 236 meters, taking visitors up to *miradors* (look-out points) and trails. A Sky Trek zipline circuit and Sky Walk with suspension bridges are also to be built (see *Monteverde*, in the *Guanacaste* chapter, for information on Sky Trek and Sky Walk). There's a restaurant.

Accommodations

Alvaro Arias Obregón (tel. 506/828-6512 or 506/224-2400, $10) rents a basic room in El

Castillo. It's barebones, but clean and has a toilet and shower with cold water. He also offers horseback tours to Monteverde ($35) and to local waterfalls ($13). He and his wife are a delight. They live a simple *campesino* family life.

Nearby, **Hotel Cabinitas El Castillo Dorado** (tel./fax 506/383-7196, $15 pp), above El Castillo, has 10 cabinas, each with wooden ceilings, ceiling fan, TV, coffeemaker, and hot water. They're quaint, clean, and have large picture windows to three sides. There's a cozy restaurant with sweeping vistas. It arranges fishing and tours, including horseback rides to Monteverde ($40, four hours). Rates include breakfast.

Hotel Linda Vista Del Norte (tel. 506/692-2090, fax 506/692-2091, info@hlvn.com, www.hlvn.com; in the U.S., SJO 667, P.O. Box 025240, Miami, FL 33102; $50 s, $60 d standard, $80 s, $90 d junior suite low season; $60 s, $70 d standard, $90 s, $100 d junior suite high season), east of El Castillo, enjoys a splendid hilltop position with views of both lake and volcano. It adjoins a 210-hectare private forest reserve with trails. It has modestly furnished yet attractive cabins with ceiling fans, patios, and large walk-in showers with hot water. The 11 standard rooms have two full-size beds and a bunk bed. Two junior suites have two queen beds, a/c, and mini-refrigerator. A suite was being added at last visit. The restaurant has views. There's a laundry. Guided horseback tours are offered. Rates include taxes and breakfast.

The **Arenal Vista Lodge** (tel. 506/692-2079 or 506/221-0965, fax 506/221-6230, arenalvi @racsa.co.cr, www.arenalvistalodge.com, $70 s, $82 d low season; $76 s, $87 d high season), immediately west at the small community of Pueblo Nuevo, perches on a landscaped terraced hill with a private forest reserve behind. Twenty-eight handsome, Swedish-inspired cabins squat on the slopes and feature vast picture windows with window boxes and small balconies with lake views. Each has a private bath with hot water. A dining room and terrace offer panoramas. It has a swimming pool and sundeck, and offers tours.

LAKE ARENAL

This picture-perfect lake might have been transplanted from the English Lake District, surrounded as it is by emerald-green mountains. The looming mass of Volcán Arenal rises over

dairy cattle graze near Lake Arenal

© CHRISTOPHER P. BAKER

The Northern Zone

LAKE ARENAL

To San Rafael de Guastuso

To San Rafael de Guastuso

Río Cote

143

Río Piedra

To Cañas

Lake Coter

LAKE COTER ECOLODGE

HOTEL EL CIELO

VILLAS ALPINO

ROCK RIVER LODGE

ARENAL SPRINGS B&B

HOTEL ALTURAS DEL ARENAL

TICO WIND WINDSURF CENTER

TILAWA VIENTO SURF CENTER

HOTEL TILAWA

CONCRETE JUNGLE

Quebrada Azul

PLANTAS EOLICAS

FULL MOON DISCO

MYSTICA LODGE

RESTAURANTE WILLY'S CABALLO NEGRO

ESTABLO ARENAL/LUCKY DOG GALLERY

THE BIRD HOUSE B&B

CHALET NICHOLAS

Nuevo Arenal

HOTEL Y RESTAURANTE LA RANA DE ARENAL

BLUE BAY RESORT

CABINAS CARACOL

ARENAL COUNTRY CLUB

Lake Arenal

VILLA DECARY

GALLERY Y RESTAURANTE LAJAS

ARENAL BOTANICAL GARDENS

BUTTERFLY GARDEN

LA CEIBA TREE LODGE

Río Chiquito

HOTEL LA MANSION INN

MARINA Y CLUB LOS HEROES

TOAD HALL

142

142

Tilaran

142

Río Negro

To Monteverde

145

Chiripa

Río Chiquito

To La Fortuna

Venado

VENADO CAVERNS

4

Río Arenal

142

ARENAL LODGE

SEE "ARENAL VOLCANO NATIONAL PARK" MAP

ARENAL VOLCANO NATIONAL PARK

Volcán Arenal

ARENAL OBSERVATORY LODGE

Río Agua Caliente

TABACÓN HOT SPRINGS

ARENAL RAINFOREST RESERVE

El Castillo

Río Piedras Negras

Río Caño Negro

Pueblo Nuevo

ARENAL VISTA LODGE

2.5 mi

2.5 km

0

0

NUEVO ARENAL

SCHOOL

BANK

POST OFFICE/ POLICE

INTERNET CAFÉ

BAKERY LA SABROSA

RESTAURANTE CONCHA DEL MAR

BAR

SPORT CLUB DISCO

BAR RESTAURANTE TIPICO ARENAL

TOM'S PAN

ARENAL ADVENTURE TOURS

TRAMONTI

© AVALON TRAVEL PUBLISHING, INC.

the lake to the east. About 2–3 million years ago, tectonic movements created a depression that filled with a small lagoon. In 1973, the Costa Rican Institute of Electricity (ICE) built an 88-meter-long, 56-meter-tall dam at the eastern end of the valley, raising the level of the lagoon and creating a narrow 32-km-long reservoir covering 12,400 hectares. Satellite photos have identified several ancient settlements at the bottom of the lake; archaeological studies suggest they may be 2,000 years old.

In the morning the lake can look like a mirror, but the calm is short-lived. More normal are nearly constant 30- to 80-kph winds, which whip up whitecaps and turn the lake into one of the world's top windsurfing spots. The climate shifts eastward and the northeastern shores are backed by thick primary forest.

The only town along the entire perimeter is **Nuevo Arenal.** This small town on the north-central shore, 32 km northeast of Tilarán, immediately west of the Guanacaste-Alajuela provincial boundary, was created in 1973 when the manmade lake flooded the original settlement.

> *In the morning the lake can look like a mirror, but the calm is short-lived. More normal are nearly constant 30- to 80-kph winds, which whip up whitecaps and turn the lake into one of the world's top windsurfing spots.*

The lake is easily reached from La Fortuna in the northern lowlands, or from the Pan-American Highway via Tilarán. The road swings around the north and west side of the lake, linking the two towns. East of Nuevo Arenal, huge sections of the paved road had been washed out at last visit. Landslides are a frequent occurrence and often closes the road for days at a time.

A dirt road that begins just west of Toad Hall leads over the cordillera to Venado Caverns (see the *Northern Zone* chapter); another traverses the mountains, linking Lake Coter (a small lake, five km northwest of Nuevo Arenal) with San Rafael de Guatuso via the valley of the Río Quequer.

On the south side, a road is paved as far as the community of **Tronadora,** beyond which it turns to dirt and leads to El Catillo and Arenal Volcano National Park. Access is highly tenuous in wet season. The hamlet of **Río Chiquito** is an access point for passage between La Fortuna and Monteverde: see the sidebar *Between La Fortuna and Monteverde.*

Arenal Botanical Gardens

The marvelous Jardín Botánico de Arenal (tel. 506/695-4273, fax 506/694-4086, exoticseeds @hotmail.com, www.exoticseeds.com, 9 A.M.–5 P.M., $4 admission), four km east of town, blooms on the Continental Divide and harbors 2,500 rare tropical species, including a panoply of Costa Rican plants: anthuriums, bromeliads, ferns, even roses, plus orchids galore, and all six species of gorguras, all drawing birds in abundance. There's even an Asian garden with waterfalls. The collection of heliconias and ginger is particularly splendid. Visitors are limited to 20 per hour. A booklet corresponds to the numbered displays. The owner, Michael LeMay, like any true Englishman, can be seen coddling his plants with solicitude in even the rainiest weather. It also has a hummingbird "sanctuary" and a large butterfly garden. It's closed October.

Entertainment

The **Full Moon Disco** could be the wildest disco south of Acapulco on Saturday nights. This multi-tiered open-air hot spot has stone terraces and log-and-thatch eaves. It gets jam-packed with revelers dancing under the moonlight. Even the howler monkeys get in the groove from the branches overhead—true! Entrance is free. Shots—*tragos*—cost $1; beers cost $1.50. Owner Fernando Calderón sometimes has informal **horseraces** on a country-style track near the lodge.

The **Sport Club Disco,** next to the Aurora Inn, in Nuevo Arenal, cranks it up on Saturday nights. Entry is free ($2 when live bands play).

Hotel Tilawa has a microbrewery.

© CHRISTOPHER P. BAKER

windsurfers at Lake Arenal

Windsurfing and Water Sports

Lake Arenal is promoted as "a rival to Oregon's Columbia Gorge," though avid windsurfers tell me that's a bit of a stretch. Water temperatures remain at 18–21°C (65–70°F) year-round. Swells can top one meter. Says local windsurfing aficionado Jean Paul Cazedessus: "None of this '*Last* week it was ripping!' to be heard at Lake Arenal. It's every day, all day. Twenty-five mph is the *average* winter day's wind speed." Adds local surf expert Norman List, "Out here I've seen people get 30 feet of air. Speed is boring. We're out trying to do loops, jumps, jibes, and acrobatics!" November through January are the best, and June and October the worst months for windsurfing.

The **Tilawa Viento Surf Center** (tel. 506/695-5050, fax 506/695-5766, http://windsurf-costarica.com), on the southwest shore, has a rental fleet of ready-rigged boards. **Tico Wind Surf Center** (fax 506/695-5387; in the U.S., tel. 800/433-2423; info@ticowind.com, www.ticowind.com), on the western shore, is open December–April 9 A.M.–6 P.M.

Fishing

The lake is stocked with game fish—guapote, machaca, and (for lighter tackle enthusiasts) mojarra. Guapote (rainbow bass indigenous to Central America) is the most fierce fighter among the freshwater fish; a four-kg catch would be a trophy. The machaca (Central America's answer to American shad) is a relative of the piranha, whose voracious temperament it apparently shares. They weigh up to three kg and are said to be difficult to hook. *Mojarra*—described by angler Chet Young as "Costa Rica's bluegill with teeth!"—are also tricky to hook but are tasty. Most of the hotels hereabouts offer fishing tours.

Other Recreation

There's a **canopy tour** ($45) at the Eco-Lodge, which offers guided hiking ($15), horseback ($20) and mountain-bike rides, canoeing ($20) and kayaking ($20), fishing ($75), and water sports, plus tours throughout the region.

The **Establo Arenal** (tel. 506/694-4092), about three km west of Nuevo Arenal, rents horses ($30 half-day). **Xiloe Lodge** offers guided horseback rides for $6 per hour.

Skateboarders should head to **Concrete Jungle** (www.concretejungleskateparks.com), adjacent to Hotel Tilawa, where an international standard skateboard park was being built at last visit.

Shopping

The **Lucky Bug Gallery** (tel. 506/694-4515, www.luckybuggallery.com) sells a fabulous array of quality custom crafts, from metal insects and naked fairy lamps to masks, exquisite hammered tin pieces, and ceramics. It ships via UPS.

Accommodations

Hotels are listed in clockwise order from Tilarán; there are many more to choose from.

Camping: You can camp at Mirador Los Lagos (see below) for $5; and for $4 pp at an unnamed hillside campsite (tel. 506/296-0234 or 506/296-2520) at the extreme northeast side of the lake, west of Arenal Lodge.

$25–50: In Nuevo Arenal, **Tom's Pan** (tel./fax 506/694-4547, www.toms-pan.com), rents a simply furnished room with waterbed, cross-lit and ventilated through large windows.

At Tronadora, the German-run **Cabinas Caracol** (tel.506/693-1073, $25 s/d), one km further east, enjoys a hillside setting in well-maintained landscaped grounds. Three spacious cabinas have cool tile floors, pleasant fabrics, kitchenettes, TVs (on request), bathrooms with hot water, and patios.

Nearby, **Hotel Bahía Azul Lake Resort** (Apdo. 2-5710 Tilarán, tel. 506/695-5750, fax 506/695-8578, $35 up to four people), in a sheltered cove, has 19 rooms, all with private baths, roomy showers, and hot water, on sloping landscaped grounds. Basic and somewhat dated rooms are modestly furnished and have cable TVs, plus verandas with lake views, and the owner is friendly and conscientious. It has a small restaurant. It arranges seaplane transfers.

I recommend the hillside **Mystica Resort** (P.O. Box 29-5710 Tilarán, tel. 506/692-1001, fax 506/692-1002, mystica@racsa.co.cr, www.mysticalodge.com, $40 s, $60 d), on the west

shore, run by an Italian couple, Barbara Moglia and Francesco Carullo. It has a beautiful ambience and offers six large, simply furnished rooms and equally spacious bathrooms in lovely pastel earth tones. Each has desks, open closets, and odd, delightful touches. You can sit on your veranda festooned by an arbor and admire the landscaped grounds cascading to the lake below and the volcano in the distance. Barbara cooks wholesome breakfasts, served in the kitchen, while gourmet dinners are served in a cozy, high-ceilinged restaurant complete with fireplace and tasteful music. Rates include breakfast.

I also like **Rock River Lodge** (tel./fax 506/692-1180, rokriver@racsa.co.cr, http://rockriverlodge.com, $45 s/d standard, $65 bungalows), which has six romantic Santa Fe–style cabins and nine bungalows with private baths and hot water. A beautiful open-air restaurant has a magnificent stone fireplace in a Western-style lounge, with hardwood tables and chairs overlooking the lake. A large bar features an open-stove barbecue pit. The lodge offers mountain bike tours ($40 daily) and windsurfing at the Tico Wind windsurf center.

Villas Alpino (tel./fax 506/692-2010, $35 for up to four people), one of the best bargains around, has five rustic yet spacious self-contained Swiss-style cabins perched loftily on the hillside above sweeping lawns. Each has abundant hardwood decor, a double bed and bunk with tasteful Guatemalan fabrics, plentiful light, free beer in the fridge, and a veranda for enjoying the views. Each also has a carport. Dutch owner Ernesto de Le Ones operates to high standards. It was for sale at last visit.

The U.S.-run **Hotel El Cielo** (Apdo. 8, Arenal, tel./fax 506/694-4290, $20 s/d) is set amid 10 acres—much of it forested—two km west of Nuevo Arenal. It has seven *cabinas* with private rock-walled baths with murals and hot water, and verandas with chairs for enjoying the views. The lofty open-air restaurant with fireplace serves freshly caught seafood. Tours are offered. A backpacker special is $10 pp.

Hotel Alturas del Arenal (Apdo. 166, San José 1007, tel. 506/694-4039, fax 506/694-4670, alturasarenal@hotmail.com, $20 s, $35 d) is a modest place that offers 10 small, simply furnished rooms with private baths, plus a simple restaurant (breakfast only) with terra-cotta tiles and log supports reaching to the roof. The small lounge has a large TV. The lodge overlooks landscaped gardens with a Jacuzzi and a freshwater pool fed by natural springs. It offers fishing, boat, and horse trips, plus windsurfing; has a pool table; and offers Internet access. Rates include breakfast.

Hotel y Restaurante La Rana de Arenal (P.O. Box 5117, Arenal, tel./fax 506/694-4031, $25 s, $40 d) is a modern, German-owned place with seven rustic cabins and an apartment on landscaped grounds with lake views. All have private baths and hot water. The pleasant restaurant leans toward the Teutonic (schnitzel Vienna style, $7), but also has spaghetti and *típico* dishes. It has a tennis court and ping-pong. Rates include breakfast.

$50–100: The **Hotel Tilawa** (Apdo. 92, Tilarán 5710, tel. 506/695-5050, fax 506/695-5766, tilawa@racsa.co.cr, www.tilawa.com, $38 s, $48 d standard, $75 with kitchenette) is inspired by the Palace of Knossos on Crete: thick bulbous columns, walls painted with flowers and dolphins, and ocher pastels play on the Cretan theme. It has 24 spacious albeit simply furnished rooms and four junior suites with magnificent views over the lake: they have hardwood ceilings; two queen-size beds with orthopedic mattresses and bedspreads from Guatemala; direct-dial telephones; and skylit private bathrooms with hot water. Junior suites have kitchenettes, couches, and TVs. Alas, in inclement weather the place is blasted by wind and rains and, hence, drafty and damp. At last visit, six rooms were being converted into far more appealing apartments with thick columns and gorgeous bathrooms, in Cretan style; sliding glass doors will open to columned terraces with superb views. A bar and restaurant are somewhat shielded from the winds by floor-to-ceiling windows. The Delfin bar offers drinks and snacks beside a swimming pool. The hotel specializes in windsurfing, and offers a tennis court, mountain biking, horseback rides, plus fishing and tours. Apartments cost $125 per night, $800 per week (a minimum three nights is required).

Groups gravitate toward **Lake Coter Eco-Lodge** (Apdo. 85570-1000 San José, tel. 560/440-6768, fax 506/440-6725, ecolodge@racsa.co.cr, www.ecolodgecostarica.com, $45 s, $53 d standard, $50 s, $68 d cabins), an elegant hardwood and brick structure in landscaped grounds on the hills west of Lake Coter. A cozy lounge with deep-cushioned sofas is centered on a large open-hearth fireplace. The 23 standard rooms with hardwood walls are fairly small and modest, each with double bed and bunk, and private bath with hot water. A better bet are the 14 four-person duplex cabins atop the hill, with heaps of windows and patios offering great views. The lodge has a game room, a lounge bar, and a pleasing restaurant, and offers all manner of activities. About 29 km of trails lead through the forest.

Two friendly Great Danes welcome guests to the American-run **M Chalet Nicholas** (Apdo. 72-5710 Tilarán, tel./fax 506/694-4041, nicholas @racsa.co.cr, www.chaletnicholas.com, $39 s, $59 d), a splendid three-bedroom Colorado-style guesthouse reached up a bougainvillea-lined driveway two km west of Nuevo Arenal (at road marker Km 48). It exudes charm and all the comforts of home—including private bathrooms with fluffy towels. Two bedrooms are downstairs. A spiral staircase winds up to a larger "semi-private" loft bedroom with cozy sitting room boasting a deck good for bird-watching. All rooms have volcano views, orthopedic mattresses, and intriguing wall-hangings. The inn proffers a TV lounge with video library, a fruit orchard and orchid house, plus hiking and horseback riding ($20, three hours) along trails into an adjacent forest reserve. The organic meals get rave reviews. Americans owners John and Catherine Nicholas top it all with fine hospitality. No smokers. A splendid bargain. Rates include breakfast.

The charming **Villa Decary** (Nuevo Arenal 5717, Tilarán, cellular tel. 506/383-3012, fax 506/694-4330, info@villadecary.com, www .villadecary.com, $69 s, $79 d rooms; $99–119 *casitas*) is a small country inn on a former fruit and coffee *finca* on three hilly hectares between Nuevo Arenal and the botanical gardens. The contemporary two-story structure glows with light pouring in through French doors and windows. Hardwood furniture gleams. Five large bedrooms each have bright Guatemalan covers, plus a private bath and a balcony with a handy rail that serves as bench and table. Three new cabinas are perched farther up the hill. The gardens and surrounding forest are great for birding. A deck offers views. The U.S.-run hotel is gay-friendly. No credit cards. Rates include full breakfast.

La Ceiba Tree Lodge (Apdo. 9, Tilarán, tel./fax 506/692-8050, cellular tel. 506/814-4004, ceibaldg@racsa.co.cr, $29 s, $49 d standard, $64 suite low season; $39 s, $64 d standard, $79 suite high season), about six km east of town, is a small German-run bed-and-breakfast amid a 16-hectare farm that swathes the hillside and is shaded by a mammoth ceiba tree. It's reached via a steep, narrow lane lined with tropical flowers. Five large rooms have plenty of light, orthopedic mattresses, plus private baths with hot water. There's also a suite, plus a small apartment with kitchen. Breakfast is served on the patio of the owner's fabulous A-frame contemporary house with fine lake views. Trails lead into a private forest reserve. You can rent a sailboat. Rates include breakfast.

The Swiss-owned **Hotel & Restaurant Los Héroes** (tel. 506/692-8012, fax 506/692-8014, heroes@racsa.co.cr, www.hotellosheroes.com, $55 s/d standard, $65 s/d mini-suite) is a chalet-style hotel with hints of the Alps at every turn. Twelve nicely appointed rooms feature brass beds and balconies. Upper-story rooms are larger. International cuisine is served in the Tyrolean restaurant. Highlights include a pool and Jacuzzi, plus stables for horseback rides, a boat for dinner and sunset cruises, and even a Swiss train that runs one km uphill to a mirador! Owner Hans Ulrich maintains the place to Swiss standards. Credit cards are not accepted. Two fully furnished, two-bedroom apartments are available ($115 for up to six people). Rates include continental breakfast.

Arenal Lodge (Apdo. 1195-1250 Escazú, tel. 506/253-5080 or 506/460-1881, fax 506/253-5016 or 506/460-6119, reservations@arenallodge.com, www.arenallodge.com, $58 s, $65 d standard, $86/91 junior suite, $91/103 chalet low season; $64 s, $71 d standard, $114/119 junior suite, $117/125 chalet high season), at the extreme northeast of the lake, is a Spanish colonial-style lodge with an inviting atmosphere. New owners had completely remodeled the property at last visit. The 34 spacious and attractive wooden rooms—some with volcano view—include six economy rooms, 16 junior suites, 10 chalets, and two suites, all with wall-to-wall louvered windows, with king-size rattan beds and rattan furnishings, microwave, refrigerator, private baths and hot showers, plus balconies with rockers. There's a library, a lounge bar, cable TV, and a full-size pool table, plus a beautiful restaurant with view. The lodge specializes in fishing ($150 for two people, five hours), and offers ATV tours and excursions, plus a butterfly garden. It has Internet service. You reach the lodge via a steep, two-km-long road.

The **Arenal Country Club** (tel. 506/693-1001, fax 506/693-1002, info@arenalcountryclub.com, www.arenalcountryclub.com, $40 pp low season, $50 pp peak season), at Tronadora, on the south shore, is a health-oriented facility boasting a mammoth thatched rancho covering one of three tennis courts. A swimming pool is enclosed within an atrium, with whirlpools under a clear plastic roof. And there's a small gym, an aerobics room, a sauna, plus steam bath. The five apartments are above, in two-story, three-bedroom, three-bathroom, fully equipped townhouses built into the hillside, with views. They're spacious and beautiful, light pours in through wall-to-wall picture windows, and each has kitchen, washing machine, dryer, iron, and modern conveniences. Its elegant restaurant has a soaring *ranchita* roof. A game room offers pool and darts, and there's a TV lounge. That said, the place was looking run-down at last visit.

$150–250: I highly recommend the **⋈ Hotel La Mansion Inn** (Apdo. 31, La Fortuna, tel. 506/692-8018, fax 506/692-8019, info@lamansionarenal.com, www.lamansionarenal.com, $175 s/d deluxe, $225 s/d suite low season; $200 deluxe, $250 suite high season), eight km east of Nuevo Arenal, and the most beautiful place for miles. Its stunning meadowy hillside setting is complemented by bougainvillea clambering over bamboo rails and 14 *cabinas* with views over the lake. Each beautifully decorated unit has a timbered ceiling, elegant antiques and wrought-iron furniture, and a mezzanine bedroom with king-size bed, with a small lounge below. Radio and CD players are standard (no TVs). French doors open onto a veranda with Sarchí rockers. Two exquisite suites boast polished stone floors with throw rugs, open fireplaces, soaring wooden ceilings, minibars, cable TV, phones, office desks, colonial-tiled bathrooms, and kitchenettes with wooden fridges. Five luxury rooms take the decor to new heights. Each unit has its own sheltered carport. The open-air bar (shaped like a ship's prow) and restaurant are decorated with nautical motifs. There's a spring-fed, horizon-edge swimming pool. Guests get use of horses, canoes, and rowboats, and tours are offered. Rates include breakfast and horseback riding.

For a unique perspective, consider the *Rain Goddess* (tel. 506/231-4299 or 866/593-3168, fax 506/231-3816, info@bluwing.com, www.bluwing.com; in the U.S., 7801 NW 37st. Miami FL 33166), a deluxe 65-foot cruise vessel that was due to relocate to Lake Arenal in early 2004. It has two double and four triple wood-paneled cabins. Gourmet meals are served.

Food

For breakfast, I head to **Ⱦ Tom's Pan** (tel./fax 506/694-4547, www.toms-pan.com), in Nuevo Arenal. This delightfully rustic outdoor café is splendid for enjoying American breakfasts, sandwiches, beef stew with veggies, lasagne, dumplings with bacon, sauerkraut, and Tom's pastries and other splendid baked goods.

Most hotels have restaurants. Check out **Los Heroes** (7 A.M.–3 P.M. and 6–8 P.M. Monday and Wednesday, 7 A.M.–9 P.M. other days, $1.50 –$5) where the French-Swiss menu includes beef bouillon, smoked pork cutlet, and fondue, washed down with kirsch.

The charming restaurant at **Mystica Lake Lodge** (noon–9 P.M., $5) has a splendid Italian menu: pasta al pomodoro, 16 types of pizza, and a large Italian wine list. In Nuevo Arenal, I also like the delightful **Tramonti** (tel. 506/695-5266, ext. 282, $3–5), for highly praised pizzas baked in a wood-burning oven, and tasty fettucine served on an outdoor patio.

The drive along the north shore is worth it merely to dine at the colorful **Ⱦ Restaurante Willy's Caballo Negro** (tel. 506/694-4515, 8 A.M.–5 P.M. and for dinner by reservation, $5 –$8), adjoining the Lucky Bug Gallery two km west of Nuevo Arenal. It has an eclectic menu ranging from schnitzel and chicken cordon bleu to eggplant parmesan, plus cappuccinos. You dine overlooking a delightful garden and lake.

Likewise, near La Mansion, **Toad Hall** (tel./fax 506/479-9178, info@toadhall-gallery.com, www.toadhall-gallery.com), equal parts deli, café, gallery, book shop, and general store, is a gem. It was for sale at last visit.

Gallery y Restaurante Lajas (tel. 506/694-4385, 8 A.M.–5 P.M.), 300 meters east of Villa Decary, is a pleasing, modern café-cum-restaurant serving espressos and cappuccinos, sandwiches, salads, soups, plus seafood dishes and tenderloin in mushroom sauce ($7.50) on an open-air veranda.

The restaurant at **Tilawa** ($5–10) serves an eclectic international menu that includes fajitas, fish Kiev, sea bass in beer, with pasta with mushroom and asparagus sauce, and pizzas. It's a pleasant dining experience in clear weather; otherwise take a sweater and windbreaker, and you could be the only diner.

Information and Services

There's a bank and gas station in Nuevo Arenal.

Lucky Bug Gallery (see *Shopping*, above) offers Internet access and massage. **Tom's Pan** also has Internet access.

Getting There

You can fly by seaplane from San José's Pavas airport.

Buses (Garaje Barquero, tel. 506/232-5660) depart San José for Nuevo Arenal from Calle 16, Avenidas 1/3, at 6:15 A.M., 8:40 A.M., and 11:30 A.M. Additional buses depart Ciudad Quesada (San Carlos) for Tabacón and Nuevo Arenal daily at 6 A.M. and 3 P.M. and continue on to Tilarán. Buses depart Cañas for Tilarán and Nuevo Arenal at 7:30 A.M., 9 A.M., 11 A.M., and 3 P.M. (50 cents).

An express bus departs Nuevo Arenal for San José via Ciudad Quesada at 2:45 P.M.; additional buses depart for Ciudad Quesada at 8 A.M. and 2 P.M. A bus marked "Guatuso" also departs Are-nal at 1:30 P.M. for San Rafael, Caño Negro, and Upala in the northern lowlands.

Getting Around
You can take a 40-minute boat transfer from the **Tilawa Surf Center** to the dam, where a bus takes you to Fortuna; the catamaran leaves at 2–3 P.M. ($30 with six people minimum).

La Fortuna to Upala

Relatively few tourists drive the route between La Fortuna (or, more correctly, Tanque, five km east of La Fortuna) and Upala, in the extreme north-west of the Northern Zone. Hwy. 4 connects the two. The few travelers who venture this way are mostly heading for Caño Negro National Park.

EL VENADO CAVERNS
At **Jicarito,** about 25 km northwest of Tanque and 15 km southeast of San Rafael de Guatuso, a paved road leads south seven km to the mountain hamlet of **Venado,** nestled in a valley bottom and famous for the **Venado Caverns,** two km farther west. The limestone chambers, which ex-tend 2,700 meters and are replete with stalac-tites, stalagmites, and underground streams, weren't discovered until 1945, when the owner of the farm fell into the hole. The cavern is on the farm of Wilbert Solis (tel. 506/384-9616 or 506/479-9101). You park at the farm, where a guide will lead you on a two-hour exploration of the caverns. The $10 admission includes a flash-light, safety helmet, and rubber boots. Bats and tiny, colorless frogs and fish inhabit the caves, which also contain seashell fossils and a "shrine" that glows luminously. Expect to get soaked and covered with ooze. The farm has a rustic *soda,* a swimming pool, and changing rooms.

You can also reach Venado via a rough dirt road from the north shore of Lake Arenal.

Tour operators in La Fortuna offer tours to Venado for about $35 (see *La Fortuna* section).

Accommodations and Food
Hospedaje Las Brisas (public tel. 506/460-1954, $7 s, $10 d), in the hamlet of Venado, has six basic albeit clean and appealing rooms, with pastel wooden walls and shared bathrooms with cold water. It is run by a delightful old lady, María Nuñoz, whom you may join on rockers on the patio.

Getting There
A bus departs Ciudad Quesada for Venado daily at 2 P.M.

SAN RAFAEL DE GUATUSO
San Rafael de Guatuso is a mundane agricul-tural town on the Río Frío, 40 km northwest of Tanque. There is little of interest in San Rafael (often called Guatuso), the center of the local canton, which subsists largely on cattle ranch-ing and rice farming. Still, you can rent boats and guides here for trips down the Río Frío to Caño Negro National Wildlife Refuge.

At **Colonia Puntarenas,** 25 km northwest of San Rafael and 12 km southeast of Upala, a dirt road leads north to Caño Negro.

Accommodations and Food
There are several basic hostelries in town. The best is **Cabinas Tío Henry** (tel. 506/464-0344, $6 pp with shared bath; $12 s, $15 d with a/c, cable TV, and private bath), two blocks southwest of the soccer field in the cen-ter of town, a no-frills 10-room hotel; each room has a double bed or two single beds and a balcony.

Bar y Restaurante El Rodeo (tel. 506/470-8057), about five km west of Colonia Puntarenas,

THE GUATUSO CULTURE

"**W**e were 12 communities until the Nicaraguans searching for rubber came to our land and fought with us," Eliécer Velas Alvarez, a member of the El Sol tribe of the Guatuso clans of Corobicí, told reporter Wendy Schmidt.

Only three of the tribal communities—El Sol, La Margarita, and Tongibe—survived the withering encroachments of the last few centuries. Today, about 400 of the natives survive on the Tongibe reservation *(palenque)* on the plains at the foot of Volcán Tenorio, near San Rafael de Guatuso, on land ceded to them by the government in the 1960s. Today, they are mostly farmers who grow corn and a type of root called *tiquisqui.*

Until a few generations ago, Guatusos strolled through San Rafael wearing clothes made of cured tree bark, called *tana.* And these lowlands once rang with the sound of women pounding away at soggy *tana* bark, like metal-beaters hammering gold.

"When I was a little girl, we used *tana* cloth and nothing else," recalls Rebecca Lizondo Lizondo, a full Tongibe, who learned the art from her mother (who, in turn, had learned from *her* mother). "This is how my grandmother would have made *tana,*" Rebecca explains, as she reaches for a slender strip of moist bark, lays it across a small wooden block, and raises a heavy mallet to beat the bark into thin tissue. Stripped of its outer casing, the bark is first soaked in a stream to render it soft and malleable. "The strips are then hammered to any degree of thinness desired," says Rebecca, striking quickly with a resounding rat-a-tat-tat. When the bark felt like soft corduroy, it was ready to be spread out to bleach and dry in the strong sun, then stitched together like leather.

Of course, no one wears *tana* these days. But the Guatusos take great pride in their heritage. Many continue to speak their native dialect, Maleku. Radio Sistema Cultural Maleku (tel. 506/225-9036) airs programs and announcements in Maleku, and Eliécer Velas Alvarez instructs the youngsters in Maleku at the elementary school in Tongibe. Alvarez, reports Wendy Schmidt, "has to buy chalk and books and erasers from his own pocket," and when it rains the schoolroom floods.

The Guatusos developed jade ornaments and carvings, bowls of terra-cotta, and bows and arrows of *pejibaye,* a tree of the palm family. The San Rafael area has many ancient tombs, and jade arrowheads and other age-old artifacts are constantly being dug up.

is the nicest place to eat between Guatuso and Upala.

Information and Services

There's a gas station four blocks south of the main road; plus two banks, a medical clinic, and a well-stocked pharmacy.

Getting There

Buses depart Tilarán and Ciudad Quesada every two hours for San Rafael de Guatuso.

UPALA

Upala, 40 km northwest of San Rafael de Guatuso, is an agricultural town only 10 km south of the Nicaraguan border. Dirt roads lead north to Lake Nicaragua, but foreigners are not allowed to enter Nicaragua here.

The paved road between San Rafael and Upala is in relatively good condition. Northwest of Upala, the road (unpaved) leads to Brasilia via Santa Cecilia and, from there, by paved road to La Cruz, on the Pan-American Highway in the extreme northwest of Costa Rica.

From Upala a paved road leads south via the saddle between Tenorio and Miravalles Volcanoes before descending to the Pan-American Highway in Guanacaste. The only town is **Bijagua,** a center for cheese-making 38 km north of Cañas, on the northwest flank of Volcán Tenorio, a steep-faced, archetypically conical cone.

Accommodations

In Upala, the best bet is **Hotel Upala** (tel. 506/470-0169, $7.50 s, $11 d), on the south side of the soccer field. It has 18 clean, modern rooms with fans, louvered windows, cable TV, and private baths (some with cold water only).

Information and Services

There's a **hospital** (tel. 506/470-0058).

There's a bank five blocks north of the bridge in Upala. The **police station** (Guardia Rural, tel. 506/470-0134) is 100 meters north and west of the bridge. There's a 24-hour gas station on the northwest side of Upala, and another just west of Santa Cecilia.

Getting There

Buses for Upala depart San José from Calle 12, Avenidas 7/9, at 3:45 A.M. and 3:15 P.M. Return buses depart Upala at 5 A.M. and 9 A.M. Local buses also link Upala with San José via San Rafael and Ciudad Quesada (departs Ciudad Quesada at 3:30 P.M.; returns from Upala at 9 A.M.); and from Cañas. Buses also run daily to Caño Negro Wildlife Refuge when conditions permit.

There's an **airstrip** east of town. You can charter an air taxi from San José.

TENORIO VOLCANO NATIONAL PARK

Volcán Tenorio (1,916 meters), rising southeast of Upala, is blanketed in cloud forest and montane rainforest and protected within the little-visited Parque Nacional Volcán Tenorio ($6 admission, $1 if entered via the private reserves below). Local hiking is superb (albeit often hard going on higher slopes). Cougars and jaguars tread the forests, where sloths, howler and white-faced monkeys, agoutis, ocelots, toucans, tanagers, and many other fabulous birds and beasts abound.

A dirt road that begins five km north of Bijagua, on the west side of Tenorio, leads about 11 km to the main park entrance, with a **ranger station** (tel. 506/695-5180, fax 506/695-5982). The park headquarters (tel. 506/466-8610) is at Bijagua. A trail leads to the summit via the Río Celeste and thermal springs.

Several private reserves abut the park and grant access via trials. For example, about 200 meters north of the park access road, another dirt road leads to the U.S.-owned **La Carolina Lodge,** a ranch and stables with trails into the park, including to **Los Chorros** thermal springs, with fumaroles and boiling mud-pools nearby. Horseback rides are offered.

Another dirt road leads east from Bijagua two km to **Heliconia Ecolodge,** an ecotourist lodge and biological station run by a local cooperative. The lodge sits at 700 meters elevation abutting the park. Three trails lead into prime rainforest and cloud forest; it's a 90-minute walk by well-maintained trail to the summit, where an arduous and slippery trail leads to **Lago Las Dantas** (Tapir Lake), where it is common to see tapirs drinking at dusk in the waters that fill the volcanic crater. Heliconia Ecolodge even has a children's trail. Guided hikes are offered. The station has a small butterfly and insect exhibit, plus horseback riding.

From the San Rafael-Upala road, you can follow a road west from the hamlet of Río Celeste to **Finca de Alvarado Duran** (tel. 506/464-0393), from where trails lead up Tenorio to the **Rio Celeste Waterfall** (also known as the La Paz Waterfall) plunging 50 meters into the teal-blue lagoon, whose waters are "dyed" a jewel-like turquoise by volcanic minerals. Be prepared for an exhilarating though daunting hike. En route, you pass the towering **El Arbol de la Paz** ("Peace Tree"), one of the oldest and largest trees in the nation, dedicated by former President Oscar Arias Sánchez in 1989 as a symbol of peace.

Alvarado Duran offers horseback rides from Río Celeste ($25 including lunch), and guided hikes ($20 including breakfast or lunch).

Accommodations

Cabinas Bijagua and **Cabinas Zamora,** both on the main road in Bijagua, offer simple rooms.

Heliconia Ecolodge (tel. 506/248-2538, fax 506/248-1659, cooprena@racsa.co.cr, www .turismoruralcr.com, $30 s, $35 d low season, $35/40 high season) has six basic but well-kept rooms (two have a double bed and a bunk; four have two bunks) in a simple wooden structure with small bathrooms and hot showers, plus a bar/restaurant serving three meals (lunch and dinner $5). The biological station has its own cabin with kitchen and propane stove. The setting is splendid, with views of Miravalles volcano and as far north as Lake Nicaragua. Rates include breakfast.

Andre LeFranc manages **La Carolina Lodge** (tel. 506/380-1656, info@lacarolinalodge.com, www.lacarolinalodge.com, $75 pp), a rustic farmstead on the north flank of Tenorio. There's a seven-bed dorm and three double rooms with solar-powered electricity and shared bathrooms with hot water. A wooden deck hangs over a natural river-fed pool good for swimming, and a porch has rockers and hammocks. It's about six km from the highway (turn east at Bar Mirador) along a rugged dirt road. Rates include meals, guided hikes, and horseback riding.

Getting There

Buses run between Cañas and Upala several times daily. You can call the lodge from the phone box in Bijagua to request transport to the lodge.

Taxis from San Rafael de Guatuso to Río Celeste cost $10 each way

Puerto Viejo de Sarapiquí and Vicinity

The Llanura de San Carlos comprises the easternmost part of the northern lowlands. The Ríos San Carlos, Sarapiquí, and other rivers snake across the landscape, vast sections of which are waterlogged for much of the year. The region today is dependent on the banana industry that extends eastward almost the whole way to the Caribbean in a gridwork maze of dirt roads and rail tracks linking towns named Finca UCR, Finca Paulina, Finca Agua, Finca Zona Siete, and Fincas 1, 2, 3, and so on.

Fortunately, swaths of rainforest still stretch north to the Río San Juan, linking Braulio Carrillo National Park with the rainforests of the Nicaraguan lowlands, much of which is protected within private reserves. Fishing is good, and there are crocodiles and river turtles, plus sloths, monkeys, and superb birdlife to see while traveling on the rivers. Even manatees have been seen in the lagoons between the Río San Carlos and Río Sarapiquí.

Grassroots environmental activism is well-rooted. Foremost among these groups is the **Asociación para el Bienestar Ambiental de Sarapiquí** (ABAS, tel./fax 506/766-6732 or 506/235-5394). The area is one of the last refuges for the endangered green macaw, which is threatened by loss of habitat. ABAS, one of 18 local independent environmental organizations under MINAE, works to purchase lots along the rivers to secure nesting areas and, specifically, to protect individual trees upon which the bird depends for food and nests.

Routes to Puerto Viejo

There are two scenic routes to Puerto Viejo from San José, forming a loop ringing Braulio Carrillo National Park (see the Braulio Carrillo map, in the *Central Highlands* chapter.)

The less trafficked and less challenging western route is via Vara Blanca, between the saddle of Poás and Barva Volcanoes, then dropping down to San Miguel, La Virgen, and Chilamate. (See the *Central Highlands* chapter for a description of the route from Vara Blanca to San Miguel.)

The easterly route traverses the saddle between Barva and Irazú Volcanoes via Hwy. 32 (Guápiles Highway), dropping down through Braulio Carrillo National Park then north via Las Horquetas.

Buses from San José to Puerto Viejo complete the circle in both directions.

SAN MIGUEL TO PUERTO VIEJO DE SARAPIQUÍ

From San Miguel, where the road that drops down from Vara Blanca (see the *Central Highlands* chapter) meets that for La Fortuna, the road falls northward through the valley of the Río Sarapiquí, which offers kayaking and whitewater rafting. About 10 km north of San Miguel, you drop onto the plains at the hamlet of **La**

SHARKS IN THE RÍO SAN JUAN

If you see a shark fin slicing the surface of the Río San Juan, you will be forgiven for thinking you've come down with heat stroke. In fact, there *are* sharks in the freshwater river! The creatures, along with other species normally associated with salt water—tarpon and sawfish, for example—migrate between the Atlantic Ocean and the murky waters of Lake Nicaragua, navigating 169 km of river and rapids en route. All three fish are classified as euryhaline species—they can cross from salt water to fresh and back again with no ill effects.

For centuries, scientists were confounded by the sharks' presence in Lake Nicaragua. The lake is separated from the Pacific by a 17-km chunk of land, and, since rapids on the Río San Juan seemingly prevent large fish from passing easily from the Caribbean, surely, the thinking went, the lake must have once been connected to one or the other ocean. Uplift of the Central American isthmus must have trapped the sharks in the lake.

Studies in the early 1960s, however, showed that there were no marine sediments on the lake bottom. Thus, the lake was never part of the Atlantic or the Pacific. (It was actually formed when a huge block of land dropped between two fault lines; the depression then filled with water.)

Then, ichthyologists decided to tag sharks with electronic tracking devices. It wasn't long before sharks tagged in the Caribbean turned up in Lake Nicaragua, and vice versa. Incredibly, the sharks—and presumably the tarpon and sawfish—are indeed able to negotiate the rapids and move back and forth between lake and sea.

Virgen. Call in at **Rancho Leona** to visit the Internet Café and stained-glass studio where Ken Upcraft conjures fabulous windows and other master-quality glasswork using the copper foil technique. Ken, an aficionado of Star Craft and War Craft computer strategy games, has more than 500 video games on CD and invites call-ins to play on the computer network. Ken also maintains a private forest reserve on the edge of Braulio Carrillo National Park, 14 km east of La Virgen. You have to hike in (one-hour minimum) from Comunidad de San Ramón.

The **Snake Garden** (tel. 506/761-1059, fax 506/761-1060, crotalosp@costarricense.cr, 9 A.M.–5:30 P.M., $5 admission adults, $3 children), immediately north of La Virgen, exhibits some 70 species of snakes, plus iguanas, turtles, and other reptiles. It features most of the major endemic snake species plus a variety of foreign snakes, including a 15-foot-long albino Burmese python.

Hacienda Pozo Azul (tel. 506/761-1360, fax 506/761-1448, info@haciendapozoazul.com, www.haciendapozoazul.com), at La Virgén, raises Holstein cattle and offer horseback rides (from one hour to one day) into the forest, with a swim in the Río Sarapiquí. It also has whitewater trips.

You can ride horses and milk cows at **Ecocenter La Finca** (tel. 506/710-8344, fax 506/476-0224, lafinca@racsa.co.cr, $1.75 admission adults, $1 children), at Los Angeles de Río Cuarto, four km west of La Virgen, a farm and wildlife shelter that raises tapirs, peccaries, white-tailed deer, monkeys, green macaws, and other animal and bird species for introduction to the wild. You can even ride a tame buffalo.

Centro Neotrópico Sarapiquís

This facility (P.O. Box 86-3009 La Virgen de Sarapiqui, tel. 506/761-1004, fax 506/761-1415, magistra@racsa.co.cr, www.sarapiquis.org, $12 admission, $14 with guide), on the banks of Río Sarapiquí about one km north of La Virgen, is sponsored by the Belgian nonprofit Landscape Foundation and serves as a scientific research and educational center.

The **National Museum of Indigenous Culture,** with more than 400 pre-Columbian artifacts and a 60-seat movie theater, is a centerpiece of the center. There's an archaeological dig—**Alma Alta Archaeological Park**—of four indigenous tombs dating from 800–155 A.D., plus a reconstruction of an Indian village. A farm

The Northern Zone

EXPLORING THE RÍOS SARAPIQUÍ AND SAN JUAN

Long narrow boats ply the rivers and will take you all the way to Barra del Colorado and Tortuguero. The nature viewing is fantastic, with birds galore, monkeys and sloths in the trees along the riverbank, and crocodiles and caimans poking their nostrils and eyes above the muddy waters.

You may even visit **El Castillo de la Inmaculada Concepción,** built by the Spanish in 1675 on a hill dominating the river and intended to repel pirates and English invaders. In 1789, Capt. Horatio Nelson (of Battle of Trafalgar fame) captured the small fortress. The ruins are in Nicaragua, three km west of where the Costa Rican border moves south of the river. This entire river strip is now protected within **Indio-Maíz Biological Reserve,** spanning the Costa Rican and Nicaraguan borders.

The hamlet of **La Trinidad** lies on the east bank of the Río Sarapiquí at its junction with the Río San Juan; the hamlet of **Los Angeles** sits on the west bank. Rough dirt roads push north from Puerto Viejo to both communities.

You can explore the rainforest canopy at the **Sarapiquí Canopy Tour** (tel. 506/290-6015, www.crfunadventures.com), which has 15 platforms, a suspension bridge, and one km of zipline. A regular water-taxi departs the dock in Puerto

Viejo at 11 A.M. for Trinidad and the Río San Juan ($2). Water-taxis are also for hire, from slender motorized canoes to canopied tour boats for 8–20 passengers. Trips cost about $20 per hour for up to five people; shorter journeys cost about $6 per hour. A full-day trip to the Río San Juan and back costs about $125 per boat. Expect to pay $200–300 for a charter boat all the way down the Río San Juan to Barra del Colorado and Tortuguero National Parks.

Oasis Nature Tours (P.O. Box 21-3069 Puerto Viejo de Sarapiquí, tel. 506/766-6108, info@oasisnaturetours.com, www.oasisnaturetours.com) offers half-day boat tours on the river, plus trips to Tortuguero. **Grupo Mawamba** (tel. 506/293-8181, fax 506/239-7657, info@grupomawamba .com, www.grupomawamba.com) offers a one-day tour with lunch at a thatched riverside restaurant ($79 adult, $40 child). Other tour operators in San José also offer trips on the Río Sarapiquí, as do all the local lodges.

Transportes Cocodrilo (based at the Hotel Bambú) operates a water-taxi to Barra del Colorado from Puerto Viejo on Tuesday and Friday at 9 A.M. ($35), continuing to Tortuguero at 12:30 P.M. ($20). The boat departs Tortuguero 9 A.M. Thursday and Sunday for Barra del Colorado, continuing to Puerto Viejo at 10:30 A.M.

---

grows fruits and vegetables based on ecological farming practices. And there's an astronomical observatory, and a formal botanical garden with about 500 native species. Facilities include a splendid hotel, and a conference center for educational forums and workshops.

A 250-meter-long canopied bridge leads across the deep river gorge and into the **Tirimbina Rainforest Reserve** (tel. 506/761-1579, fax 506/761-1576, tirimbin@racsa.co.cr, www .tirimbina.org, $3), which has eight km of trails, with suspension bridges and a 360-foot canopy walkway. A museum portrays life in the forest. Nature walks cost $12–20 ($6 for children); walks along a canopy trail cost $14; and a three-hour "World of Bats" night walk is offered with 24-hour reservation. It runs research and special topic workshops.

La Quinta de Sarapiquí

This hacienda-style property (P.O. Box 43-3-69 Puerto Viejo de Sarapiqui, tel. 506/761-1052 or 506/761-1300, fax 506/761-1395, quinta@racsa .co.cr, www.quintasarapiqui.com), on the banks of the Río Sardinal, at Bajo de Chilamate, about three km north of La Virgen and 10 km west of Puerto Viejo, features separate butterfly and frog gardens, a tree house for kids, and a botanical garden full of *baston de emperador* and ginger. A trail leads along the riverside, where poison-dart frogs are easily seen by day. Horseback trips and guided hikes are offered.

Selva Verde

Selva Verde (tel. 506/766-6800, fax 506/766-6011, selvaver@racsa.co.cr, www.selvaverde.com, 7 A.M.–3 P.M., $5 admission with guide, free to

Ken Upcraft makes a stained glass piece at Rancho Leona.

hotel guests), on the banks of the Río Sarapiquí, about one km east of Chilamate and eight km west of Puerto Viejo, is a private reserve protecting some 192 hectares of primary rainforest adjacent to Braulio Carrillo National Park. At its heart is an internationally acclaimed nature lodge and the **Sarapiquí Conservation Learning Center** (Centro de Enseñanza), with a lecture room and library. The reserve is renowned for its birdlife, including oropendolas, motmots, parrots, jacamars, sunbitterns, and other exotic lowland tropical birds. Poison-arrow frogs are easily spotted. Walking trails lead through the forests: trail maps are provided, and the lodge has a fine staff of naturalist guides. Guided hiking cost $8 (2.5 hours). Selva Verde also offers trips up the river by canopied boat ($8), guided canoe trips ($45 half-day), and horseback trips ($12 pp, three hours). Mountain bikes are also available ($25 half-day).

It has a small butterfly garden—the **Sarapiquí Butterfly Center**—accessed independently, roadside, 200 meters downhill from the lodge entrance.

Accommodations

Under $25: The **Hotel Cabinas Claribel** (tel. 506/761-1190, $17 s/d), at the north end of La Virgen, has 12 basically furnished cabins with fans, private bath and cold water.

Rancho Leona (tel. 506/841-5341, kayak @rancholeona.com, www.rancholeona.com, $9 pp), is recommended for its family coziness and delightfully funky ambience. The seven rooms, in a rambling wooden lodge, are rustic but appealing, with fans, stained-glass skylights, and solar-heated showers. Some rooms have bunks. Ken Upcraft runs the place like an offbeat clubhouse. Ken is also a kayaker and offers full-day kayaking trips. When you return, hop into the stone and timber riverside sweat lodge ("big enough for 16 people") or the cooling tub. Ken invites guests to play computer strategy games on the computer network.

Cabinas Tia Rosita (tel. 506/761-1032, $9 s, $15 d), next door, is a clean, modern place with four rooms and four cabins attached to a restaurant. The spacious, well-lit cabins have lofty ceilings, tile floors, TVs, and fans.

Islas del Río Adventure Center Lodge (tel./fax 506/766-6524, $6 pp), at Bajos de Chilamate, sits on seven hectares of forested property on the banks of the Río Sarapiquí. It offers five simple hardwood rooms in a lodge, each with fans and private bath with hot water. There's an open-air restaurant with a riverside patio. IYH members receive discounts. Tico meals are served in the open-air dining room. The Sarapiquí Aguas Bravas rafting company is based here. Guided hikes and horseback trips are offered.

$50–100: At **La Quinta de Sarapiquí Lodge** (see above, $50 s, $60 d), 15 widely spaced, clinically clean, well-lit cabins have contemporary furnishings, ceiling fans, and private baths with hot water (the units were being upgraded and enlarged at last visit). A swimming pool and deck are suspended over the river. An open dining room and bar, a well-stocked gift store, plus a riverside trail for hikes and mountain bikes or horseback rides complete the picture. Bird-watching is particularly good, and past guests speak well of the food and "congenial atmosphere."

Perfect for naturalists, **M Selva Verde** (see above, $54 s, $90 d) has a 45-room lodge—divided into the River Lodge and the Creek Lodge—set in 20 acres of forest on the banks of the Río Sarapiquí. Thatched walkways lead between the spacious and airy hardwood cabins, which are raised on stilts. Choose between cabins with private baths at the River Lodge and rooms with shared baths at the Creek Lodge; all units are simply furnished in pleasing pastels and have ceiling fans, two single beds, screened windows, large bathrooms with piping hot water, and verandas slung with hammocks and rockers. Highlights include a large library and game room, and a conference room with scheduled lectures. Meals are served buffet-style in a new dining room with bar. The lodge offers laundry service and provides rubber boots and oversized umbrellas. Selva Verde is popular with academic and tour groups (particularly with Elderhostel groups), so book well in advance.

Centro Neotrópico SarapiquíS (see above, $70 s/d standard, $77 deluxe low season; $82 s/d standard, $90 deluxe high season), built loosely to resemble an indigenous village, is a marvelous upscale option centered on a thatched, all-log eco-lodge, with four circular structures held aloft by timbers; contemporary counterpoints include a color scheme of pleasing ochre yellow and sienna red. Each of three units has eight rooms shaped like pie slices arrayed in a circle around an atrium. All feature ochre walls, lively fabrics, simple handmade furniture, natural stone floors, fans, large walk-in showers, and telephone with Internet access. They're delightful but, alas, lack windows. In each, a glass door opens to a wraparound veranda overlooking the gardens or river. The main lodge features the lobby, bar, gift shop, and a splendid restaurant (see *Food,* below). Paths lit by wrought-iron lamps lead through the grounds.

Food

Rancho Leona provides meals by reservation only and has eclectic offbeat decor that includes stained-glass windows, homemade Tiffany lamps, oropendola nests hanging from the roof, and cushioned tree stumps for stools.

The restaurant at **Selva Verde** is open to nonguests, so pop in for filling and tasty homestyle Costa Rican cooking.

The elegant café-style **José Castro Zeledón Restaurant,** at Centro Neotrópico SarapiquíS, offers á la carte meals in low season and a buffet in high season; breakfast costs $5, lunch and dinner each cost $10. An adjacent bar provides a quiet spot for sipping a cocktail while absorbing the forest views across the river canyon.

Getting There

The Río Frío bus departs San José from Calle 12, Avenidas 7/9, at 6:30 A.M., noon, and 3 P.M.

PUERTO VIEJO DE SARAPIQUÍ

This small landlocked town (not to be confused with Puerto Viejo de Talamanca, on the

WHITE WATER ON THE RÍO SARAPIQUÍ

This section of the Río Sarapiquí offers a prime whitewater challenge, notably for kayaks. The most popular put-in point is at La Virgen, with Class II and III rapids below. A second put-in point is Chilamate, offering more gentle floats: Class I and II.

Several companies offer tours. **Kayak Jungle Tours** (tel. 506/841-5341, kayak@rancholeona.com, www.rancholeona.com) offers five-day kayaking trips on the Sarapiquí River, and through Caño Negro National Wildlife Refuge.

Aguas Bravas (tel. 506/296-2072, info@aguas-bravas.co.cr, www.aguas-bravas.co.cr), at Islas del Río, and **Aventuras del Sarapiquí** (tel./fax 506/766-6768, www.sarapiqui.com), in Puerto Viejo, offer Class III/V whitewater rafting trips, as do **Costa Rica Expeditions** (P.O. Box 6941-1000, San José, tel. 506/257-0766, fax 506/257-1665, costaric@expeditions.co.cr, www.costaricaexpeditions.com) and **Ríos Tropicales** (tel. 506/233-6455, fax 506/255-4354, info@riostropicales.com, www.riostropicales.com) in San José.

Caribbean coast), 34 km north of Hwy. 32, at the confluence of the Ríos Puerto Viejo and Sarapiquí was in colonial times Costa Rica's main shipping port. Prior to the arrival of rail and road, boats laden with produce and passengers plied the Sarapiquí northbound to the Río San Juan, then turned east for the sea. Today the local economy is dominated by banana plantations: you can take a tour of **Bananero La Colonia** (tel. 506/768-8683), five km southeast of Puerto Viejo, by appointment.

Puerto Viejo is the base for waterborne nature viewing or fishing trips on the Río Saripiquí.

Sports and Recreation

Aguas Bravas (www.aguas-bravas.co.cr), opposite the Banco Nacional at the east end of town, has tourist information, rents kayaks, and offers birding, boating, and other trips.

Costa Rica Fun Adventures, two km north of town, offers tours, horseback riding, and river trips. It's reached via the road that leads north from the Banco Nacional.

Accommodations

Under $25: Immediately west of the soccer field is the modern **Mi Lindo Sarapiquí** (tel. 506/766-6281, fax 506/766-6074, lindo @sarapiquirainforest.com, $12 s, $20 d), with 14 clean rooms with TVs, fans, and private baths and hot water. It has a pleasing open-air restaurant.

Hotel Ara Ambigua (tel. 506/766-7101, fax 506/766-6401, www.hotelaraambigua.com, $15 s, $25 d), sitting on a hillside 400 meters north of La Guáira, about one km west of Puerto Viejo, is a rustic but adorable farmhouse property in traditional Costa Rican style. It's named for the scientific name of the green parrot, which can sometimes be seen on the property. It has 13 simply furnished Hansel and Gretel–style *cabinas,* some with natural stone floors; all have hot water. It has a delightful restaurant, plus swimming pool. A small lake has geese and other waterfowl, plus crocodiles and caimans; and there's a frog garden *(ranario)* with poison-arrow frogs. Hiking trails lead into the forest.

The attractive **Hotel & Club Campestre Los Cuajipales** (tel. 506/283-9797, loscuajipales @consorciosci.com, $15 up to four people), about three km northeast of town, is set amid landscaped grounds, drawing locals to its lively bar with pool tables under thatch. It offers three stone-and-timber cabins with private bathrooms with cold water. You can rent tents for camping ($2.50 per person). It has a dock with boats and offers volleyball, tilapia fishing, and trails.

$25–50: The **Hotel Bambú** (Apdo. 1518, Guadalupe 2100, tel. 506/766-6005, fax 506/ 766-6132, info@elbambu.com, www.elbambu .com, $45 s, $55 d), facing the soccer field, has nine clean, modern rooms with ceiling fans,

TVs, and private baths with hot water. It also has two self-sufficient apartments for six people, plus a large modern restaurant. Rates include breakfast.

My preferred choice, and highly recommended, is **Ⓜ Andrea Cristina Bed & Breakfast** (P.O. Box 14, Puerto Viejo de Sarapiquí, tel./fax 506/766-6265, alex@andreacristina.com, www .andreacristina.com, $20 s, $30 d year-round bungalow; $25 s year-round, $35 d low season, $40 high season cabin) half a kilometer west of town in the community of La Guáira. This pleasing place has four rooms with various combinations of beds, lofty wooden ceilings, tile floors, and private baths with hot water. Two additional, simple yet appealing A-frame

bungalows at the bottom of the garden share a bathroom. There's a restaurant with patio in the garden, which attracts sloths and kinkajous. It's run by friendly owners, Alexander and Floribell Martínez. English-speaking Alex is a leading local conservationist and a trove of information for anyone serious about nature studies. Readers have raved about the breakfasts and organic dinners. Rates include breakfast.

Food

The restaurant at **Mi Lindo Sarapiquí** has an extensive menu. The skylit restaurant at **Hotel Bambú** has also been recommended.

For marvelous ambience, head to Hotel Ara

THE BINATIONAL PARK

The idea for a transboundary park along the northern border with Nicaragua germinated in 1974. Little progress was made, however, until 1985, when Nicaraguan President Daniel Ortega seized on the idea as a way to demilitarize the area, which was then being used by anti-Sandinista rebels. Ortega proposed the region be declared an international park for peace and gave it the name Si-a-Paz—Yes to Peace. Efforts by the Arias administration to kick the rebels out of Costa Rica's northern zone led to demilitarization of the area, but lack of funding and political difficulties prevented the two countries from making much progress on the Si-a-Paz project. Since 1990, improved relations between the countries and the end of the Nicaraguan war have allowed the governments to dedicate more money to the project, which presents a last chance to save Central America's largest and wettest tract of rainforest. Natural resources once made inaccessible by guerrilla warfare are now being plundered by loggers. In the wake of peace in Nicaragua, thousands of people displaced by the war have drifted back to the area, chasing dreams of a better life.

The idea is to enable people to make a living in one place, to involve them in conservation efforts and provide them with ecologically sustainable livelihoods so that they won't have to keep eating away at the forest's receding edge. The park design requires a full evaluation of existing human and natural resources, social and cultural considerations, demographics, and development potential. Si-a-Paz planners want to wrap buffer zones of low-impact agriculture and agroforestry around core habitats, with whole communities integrated into the park design.

By 2003, the efforts had led to formalization of the boundaries of a new national park, the 30,000-hectare Maquenque National Park, a massive swath to encompass heavily logged and denuded terrain between the Sarapiquí and San Carlos Rivers and extending northward from Braulio Carrillo National Park to the Indio Maíz Biological Reserve, which protects nearly half a million hectares of rainforest—one of the largest areas of undisturbed wilderness in Central America—in the southeast corner of Nicaragua. However, relocation of and compensation to expropriated farmers, to the tune of $25 million, are major hurdles. If and when it's completed, Maquenque will link the El Castillo–San Juan Biological Corridor with the San Juan–La Selva Biological Corridor, covering 340,000 hectares and 29 protected areas, including Tortuguero National Park and Barra del Colorado Wildlife Refuge.

Ambigua, where the rustic farmhouse **Restaurant La Casona** is adorned with saddles and farm implements hanging from the dark, wood-beamed ceiling; it serves *típico* dishes.

Information and Services

Alexander Martinez, at the **Andrea Cristina Bed & Breakfast,** is an invaluable resource. He arranges nature and bird-watching tours, plus tours to Nicaragua.

Souvenirs Río Sarapiquí (tel. 506/766-6727) offers tour information and sells crafts.

MINAE (the ministry in charge of national parks) has an office next to the police station, but it is *not* a tourist information office.

There are two banks near the soccer field. Both have ATM machines that accept credit cards.

The post office is at the west end of town. **Cafenet de Sarapiquí** (tel. 506/766-6223 or 506/393-9034, 8 A.M.–10 P.M.), at the west end of town, offers Internet access.

The **Red Cross** (tel. 506/710-6901, ext. 212) is at the west end of town.

The police (Guardia Rural) station is opposite the post office, 100 meters east of the soccer field.

Getting There

Buses (tel. 506/257-6858) depart San José from Calle Central, Avenida 13, daily at 6:30 A.M., 8 A.M., 10 A.M., 11:30 A.M., 1:30 P.M., 2:30 P.M., 3:30 P.M., 4:30 P.M., and 6 P.M., via the Guápiles Highway and Horquetas (four hours, $2). You can also take a bus from the same bus stop via Heredia and Vara Blanca at 6:30 A.M., noon, and 3:30 P.M. Buses depart Ciudad Quesada for Puerto Viejo at 5 A.M., 6 A.M., 10 A.M., 3 P.M., and 5:30 P.M. ($1.10).

Buses depart Puerto Viejo for San José at 5:30 A.M., 7 A.M., 8 A.M., 11 A.M., 1:30 P.M., 3 P.M., 4:30 P.M., and 5:30 P.M. via Horquetas; and 7:45 A.M., 11:30 A.M., and 4:15 P.M. via Vara Blanca. Buses for Ciudad Quesada depart at 5:45 A.M., 8:45 A.M., 12:15 P.M., 2 P.M., and 3:30 P.M.

Taxis wait on the north side of the soccer field, next to the bus stop.

There's a gas station at the southern entrance to town.

SOUTH OF PUERTO VIEJO

Highway 4 runs due south from Puerto Viejo for 34 km and connects with Hwy. 32, the main highway between San José and the Caribbean lowlands. The forested slopes of Braulio Carrillo rise to the west. The flatlands to the east are carpeted with banana plantations. Rutted dirt roads and rail tracks crisscross the land, connecting plantation settlements and processing plants with the regional center of **Río Frío,** about eight km east of Hwy. 4.

The only other community of note is the hamlet of **Las Horquetas,** 17 km north of the Guápiles Highway and 17 km south of Puerto Viejo.

El Gavilán Lodge and Forest Reserve (Apdo. 445-2010, San José 2010, tel. 506/766-6743 or 506/234-9507, fax 506/253-6556, gavilan@racsa .co.cr, www.gavilanlodge.com), a 180-hectare private forest reserve on the east bank of the Río Sarapiquí, is splendid for bird-watching. It offers horseback rides ($15 pp), guided hikes, and fishing trips. If driving, it is accessed by a dirt road about two km south of town and one km north of La Selva; the lodge is about two km north from the junction.

Heliconia Island

Isla Las Heliconias (tel. 506/762-0520 or 506/397-3948, fax 506/766-6247, timryan @heliconiaisland.com, www.heliconiaisland.com, $12 admission, including drink and tour, $25 with lunch), about five km north of Horquetas, is indeed an island-turned-heliconia garden created with an artist's eye and lovingly tended by naturalist Tim Ryan. Exquisite! The garden was started in 1992 and today boasts about 80 species of heliconia, plus ginger and other plants, shaded by almendro trees in which green macaws nest. Tim gives a fascinating spiel; among the esoteric lore Tim imparts is why we owe chocolate to heliconias and the fact that the essence for Chanel No. 5 perfume is synthesized from the Illan Illan species. The garden also includes palms, orchids, and bamboo from around the world. Needless to say, birds—more than 200 species at last count—abound (the BBC filmed *Hummingbird Hotel* here). You can swim in the Puerto Viejo river.

There's a small Japanese-style lodge with restaurant serving salads, chayote soup, gazpacho, etc. Tim was adding an art gallery at last visit. A torchlit nighttime tour costs $35. A combo offers a tour and jungle float.

La Selva Biological Station

La Selva (tel. 506/766-6565, fax 506/766-6535, laselva@sloth.ots.ac.cr, www.ots.ac.cr), four km south of Puerto Viejo, is a biological research station run by the Organization of Tropical Studies (OTS). The station, which includes laboratories, teaching facilities, and experimental plots, is centered on a 1,500-hectare biological reserve—mostly premontane rainforest but with varied habitats—linked to the northern extension of Braulio Carrillo National Park.

More than 420 bird species have been identified here, as have more than 500 species of butterflies, 120 species of mammals, and 55 species of snakes. The arboretum displays more than 1,000 tree species.

Almost 60 km of trails snake through the reserve. Many are no more than dirt trails, which deteriorate to muddy quagmires after heavy rain. Annual precipitation is over 400 cm; even the driest months (February and March) receive almost 20 cm of rain. Rubber boots or waterproof hiking boots are essential, as is raingear (an umbrella is extremely useful for photographers wishing to protect their cameras). Some trails have boardwalks. The gift shop sells *Walking La Selva* (R. Whittall and B. Farnsworth), a handy guide to the trails. Keep a wary eye out for snakes. Guided nature walks are offered daily at 8 A.M. and 1:30 P.M. ($26 adults; $15.50 children 5–12 half-day; $36/20 full-day). You may not explore alone.

Visitors are welcome with notice: impromptu appearances are not welcome. Only 65 people at a time are allowed in the reserve, including scientists. It is often booked solid months in advance. Reservations are essential, even for day visits.

The OTS operates a shuttle van from San José on Monday ($10), space permitting (researchers and students have priority); and between La Selva and Puerto Viejo, Monday through Saturday. Buses from San José will drop you off at the entrance to La Selva. You'll need to walk from the road to La Selva (two km). There are no bellhops: pack light.

Rara Avis

This 1,280-hectare rainforest reserve (P.O. Box 8105-1000, San José, tel. 506/764-3131 or 506/253-0844, fax 506/764-4187 or 506/257-4876, raraavis@racsa.co.cr, www.rara-avis .com), abutting Braulio Carrillo National Park, 15 km west of Las Horquetas, contains two lodges, a biological research station, and a host of novel projects designed to show that a rainforest can be *economically* viable if left intact, not cut down. Projects include producing exportable orchids and ornamental air plants, seedlings of popular timber trees for reforestation projects, macadamias, philodendrons for wicker, *pacas* for meat, and ecotourism. And there's a butterfly farm and orchid garden. Founder Amos Bien is demonstrating to the surrounding communities that a cottage industry can be borne by the forest, so that they see the forest not "as something they must cut down in order to earn a living, but rather as the source of that living."

More than 360 bird species—including snowcap hummingbirds, great green macaws, toucans, blue-and-gold tanagers, and umbrella birds—inhabit the reserve. There are jaguars, tapirs, monkeys, anteaters, coatimundis, butterflies galore, and a zillion other wildlife species.

Rara Avis gets up to a phenomenal 5.5 meters of rain a year; it has no dry months.

Visitors can view the canopy from two platforms ($35, including two-hour guided hike), including one at the foot of a spectacular double waterfall. A trained instructor will teach you how to use rappelling gear. You can swim at the waterfalls, but be aware that flash floods can pour over the break unannounced. When this happened in the spring of 1992, three Canadians were swept to their deaths.

The miles of hiking trails range from easy to difficult. Rubber boots are recommended (the lodge has boots to lend for those with U.S. shoe sizes of 12 or smaller). You can explore alone or on guided hikes.

Rara Avis is not a place for a day visit. Plan on at least one overnight.

Some people I've spoken to consider the experience of getting to Rara Davis part of the fun, others have stated that no reward is worth hours of bumping about on the back of a canopied trailer.

Buses from San José depart Calle 12, Avenidas 7/9, daily at 7 A.M. via the Guápiles Highway (do *not* take the bus via Heredia). Buses also run later, but you'll need the 7 A.M. bus to meet the transfer to Rara Avis from Las Horquetas at 9 A.M. Get off at El Cruce para Horquetas, where a taxi—arranged through Rara Avis's San José office—will take you to Las Horquetas. If driving, you can leave your car in a parking lot at the Rara Avis office in Las Horquetas (you should be at Las Horquetas by 8:30 A.M.). The transfer from Las Horquetas to Rara Avis takes two hours. Later arrivals can rent horses ($10), but not after noon. The vehicle leaves Rara Avis for Las Horquetas at 2 P.M., arriving in time for the 6 P.M. bus to San José. Buses for San José also leave Las Horquetas throughout the day.

Accommodations

Camping: You can camp at **Isla Las Heliconias** (see above) for $15, but you must supply your own tent.

$25–50: Across the river, east of Puerto Viejo, is the peaceful no-frills **El Gavilán Lodge** (see above, $45 s, $50 d). Four rooms in the main two-story structure have hardwood verandas and rockers, plus bungalows with 13 simply appointed rooms with private bathrooms and hot water. Simple meals are served in an open-air restaurant beneath a bamboo roof (no alcohol; bring your own). It has an open-air Jacuzzi and kid's playground. Boating, hiking, and excursions are offered. You can take a boat to El Gavilán from the wharf in Puerto Viejo. Rates include breakfast.

$50–100: La Selva (see above, $78 s, $125 d, $56 extra person, $21 children) has comfortable dormitory-style accommodations with four bunks per room and communal bathrooms, some fitted to accommodate visitors with wheelchairs. It has private rooms, but researchers and students get priority. Tourists are allowed to stay here only on a space-available basis. Rates include a guided hike. Meals are served bang on time and latecomers get the crumbs; no alcohol is served. Laundry service is offered. *Reservations are essential.* Rates include all meals.

Rara Avis (see above, $75 s, $130 d Waterfall Lodge, $85 s, $150 d River Edge low season; $80s, $140 d Waterfall Lodge, $90 s, $160 d River Edge high season) has two lodges at about 600 meters elevation, plus you can stay in Dr. Perry's Tree-Top Cabin 30 meters up in the crown of a tree; or in the two-room River Edge Cabin, ideal for bird-watchers and honeymooners, replete with hammocks on a balcony, solar lighting, and private bath with hot water (at the Tree-Top Cabin, water is hauled up in a bucket; you relieve yourself in a Port-A-Potti). Waterfall Lodge, three km farther into the forest at the end of the dirt road, features eight corner rooms, each with private bathtub and hot water, and a wraparound balcony with great views. A two-night minimum stay is required. Reservations are essential. Rates are for two nights and include meals.

The **Hotel Sueño Azul** (P.O. Box 3630-1000, San José, tel. 506/764-4244, fax 506/764-3129, info@suenoazulresort.com, $70 s, $86 d, $110 junior suite) is an upscale hotel near Horquetas. It melds rustic log features (including four-poster beds) with modern tiles, plus private bathrooms with hot water. A pleasant *rancho* restaurant overlooks a freeform pool. There's a lagoon and trails into adjacent forest ($7 entrance; $17 guided trip to waterfalls), and horseback riding is offered ($10 per hour).

The Northern Zone

Guanacaste and the Northwest

Guanacaste has been called Costa Rica's "Wild West." Travelers who emerge from the verdant central highlands or southern Pacific are greeted with an entirely different and dramatic scenic climate, culture, and landscape. The name Guanacaste derives from *quahnacaztlan,* a native word (place near the ear trees) for the tall and broad *guanacaste* (free ear or ear pod) tree—the national tree—which spreads its gnarled branches long and low to the ground; in the heat of summer, all that walks, crawls, or flies gathers in its cool shade in the heat of midday.

The region is clearly divided into lowland and highland. The lowlands, to the west, comprise a vast alluvial plain of seasonally parched rolling hills broadening to the north and dominated by giant cattle ranches interspersed with smaller pockets of cultivation. To the east rises a mountain meniscus—the Cordillera de Guanacaste and Cordillera de Tilarán—that separate northward into symmetrical volcanic cones spiced with bubbling mud pits and steaming vents. These mountains are lushly forested on their higher slopes. Rivers cascade down the flanks, slow to a

Must-Sees

Look for **M** to find the sights and activities you can't miss and **M** for the best dining and lodging.

M Monteverde, Cerro Plano, and Santa Elena: These popular mountain communities known for their cloud forest reserve have no end of attractions, not least stupendous opportunities for wildlife viewing (page 313).

M Selvatura: This new attraction in Santa Elena includes the **Jewels of the Rainforest Bio-Art Exhibition,** one of the nation's preeminent nature displays (page 318).

M Monteverde Cloud Forest: The *sine qua non* of a visit to Monteverde, this world-famous biological reserve is laced by nature trails fabulous for viewing wildlife (page 328).

M Las Pumas Cat Zoo: You're guaranteed eyeball-to-eyeball encounters with all the big cats you're not likely to see in the wild (page 334).

M Río Corobicí: A float trip on this relatively calm river is fun for all the family (page 335).

M Palo Verde National Park: Birding *par excellence* is the name of the game at this watery world best explored by boat (page 340).

© CHRISTOPHER P. BAKER

Visitors set out on a tour from Hacienda Los Inocentes.

M Rincón de la Vieja: Magnificent scenery, bubbling mudpools, and trails to the volcano summit are highlights at this national park (page 348).

M Santa Rosa National Park: The finest of the dry-forest reserves offers unrivaled wildlife viewing and top-notch surfing (page 354).

M Hacienda Los Inocentes Wildlife Center: Enjoying a fabulous location at the base of Orosi volcano, this wildlife reserve specializes in horseback rides from a centenarian lodge (page 362).

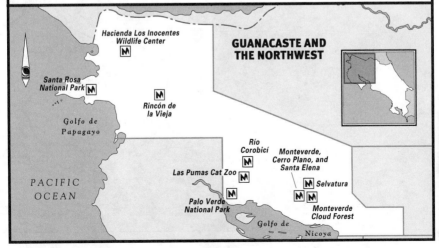

Hacienda Los Inocentes
Wildlife Center
M

GUANACASTE AND THE NORTHWEST

Santa Rosa
National Park M

Rincón de
la Vieja
M

Golfo de
Papagayo

Río
Corobicí

Monteverde,
Cerro Plano, and
Santa Elena

PACIFIC
OCEAN

Las Pumas Cat Zoo
M

M Selvatura

M M

Palo Verde
National Park
M

Monteverde
Cloud Forest

Golfo de
Nicoya

Guanacaste

GUANACASTE AND THE NORTHWEST

Peñas Blancas

Cárdenas

La Virgen

Isla Bolaños National Wildlife Refuge

La Cruz

HACIENDA LOS INOCENTES WILDLIFE CENTER

Santa Cecilia

Golfo de

Santa Elena

Bahía Salinas

PLANET WINDSURFING CENTER

PUREWIND PRO-CENTER

Guanacaste

Volcán Orosí

Brasili

Cordillera de Guanacaste

Bahía Junquillal National Wildlife Refuge

Volcán Cacao

National

Peninsula de Santa Elena

Santa Rosa National Park (Murciélago Sector)

Park

Quebrada Grande

Volcán Rincón de la Vieja

BUENA VISTA LODGE & ADVENTURE CENTER

SANTA ROSA NATIONAL PARK

LA CASONA

Potrerillos

HOTEL BORINQUEN MOUNTAIN RESORT THERMAE & SPA

Santa Rosa National Park (Santa Rosa Sector)

Cañas Dulce

Golfo de

Bahía Naranjo

Río Tempisquito

Curubandé

Río Colorado

Río Liberia

Papagayo

DANIEL ODUBER INTERNATIONAL AIRPORT

Liberia

P A C I F I C

Bahía Culebra

21

Comunidad

Playas del Coco

Lomas Barbudal Biological Reserve

Filadelfia

Río Tempisque

O C E A N

PALO VERDE NATIONAL PARK

Bahía Tamarindo

Río Cañas

Puerto Humo

Tamarindo

160

Santa Cruz

Guaitíl

Río Diriá

Nicoya

Junquillal

0   10 mi

0   10 km

Hojancha

Río Nosara

Nosara

Bahía Garza

Sámara

Río Ora

MOON

Guanacaste

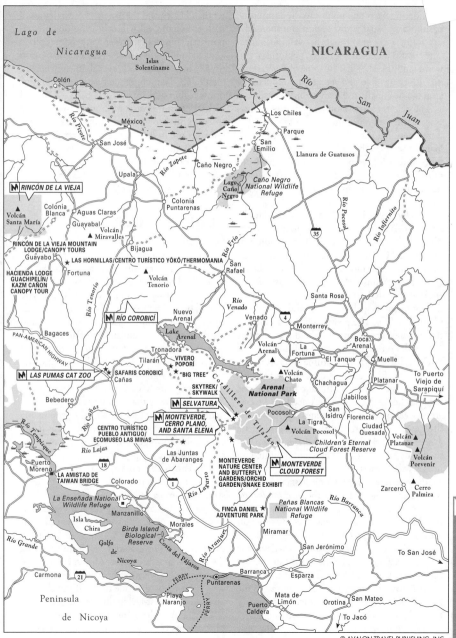

Lago de Nicaragua

Islas Solentiname

NICARAGUA

Río San Juan

Colón

México

San José

Los Chiles

Parque

San Emilio

Río Zapote

Caño Negro

Llanura de Guatusos

Upala

Colonia Puntarenas

Lago Caño Negro

Caño Negro National Wildlife Refuge

Río Pocosol

Río Infiernito

Ⓜ RINCÓN DE LA VIEJA

▲ Volcán Santa María

Colonia Blanca

Aguas Claras

Guayabal

▲ Volcán Miravalles

35

RINCÓN DE LA VIEJA MOUNTAIN LODGE/CANOPY TOURS

Guayabo

HACIENDA LODGE GUACHIPELÍN/ KAZM CAÑON CANOPY TOUR

Fortuna

Bijagua

★ **LAS HORNILLAS/CENTRO TURÍSTICO YÖKÖ/THERMOMANIA**

▲ Volcán Tenorio

San Rafael

Río Frío

Río Venado

Santa Rosa

Ⓜ RÍO COROBICÍ

Bagaces

Nuevo Arenal

Tronadora

Lake Arenal

Venado

Monterrey

4

Boca Arenal

PAN-AMERICAN HIGHWAY

Tilarán

VIVERO POPORÍ

★

Volcán Arenal ▲

La Fortuna

El Tanque

Muelle

Ⓜ LAS PUMAS CAT ZOO

SAFARIS COROBICÍ ★

★ **"BIG TREE"**

Cañas

▼ Volcán Chato

Chachagua

Jabillos

Platanar

To Puerto Viejo de Sarapiquí

Bebedero

SKYTREK/ SKYWALK

Cordillera de Tilarán

Arenal National Park

Pocosol

San Isidro

Florencia

Ciudad Quesada

▲ Volcán Platanar

Ⓜ SELVATURA

Ⓜ MONTEVERDE, CERRO PLANO, AND SANTA ELENA

La Tigra

▲ Volcán Pocosol

Río Tempisque

Río Cañas

CENTRO TURÍSTICO PUEBLO ANTIGUO/ ECOMUSEO LAS MINAS

Children's Eternal Cloud Forest Reserve

▲ Volcán Porvenir

Zarcero

Río Lajas

Las Juntas de Abaranges

MONTEVERDE NATURE CENTER AND BUTTERFLY GARDENS/ORCHID GARDEN/SNAKE EXHIBIT

Ⓜ MONTEVERDE CLOUD FOREST

▲ Cerro Palmira

Puerto Moreno

18

LA AMISTAD DE TAIWAN BRIDGE

Colorado

1

Río Lagarto

La Enseñada National Wildlife Refuge

Manzanillo

Isla Chira

Morales

Río Aranjuez

FINCA DANIEL ADVENTURE PARK ★

Peñas Blancas National Wildlife Refuge

Río Barranca

Birds Island Biological Reserve

Miramar

San Jerónimo

To San José

Río Grande

Golfo de Nicoya

Costa del Pájaros

Carmona

21

Barranca

Esparza

Orotina

San Mateo

Peninsula de Nicoya

FERRY

Puntarenas

Mata de Limón

FERRY

Playa Naranjo

Puerto Caldera

To Jacó

Ⓜ Guanacaste

meandering pace, and pour into the Tempisque basin, an unusually arid region smothered by dry forest and cut through by watery sloughs. The coast is indented with bays, peninsulas, and warm sandy beaches that are some of the least visited, least accessible, and yet most beautiful in the country. Sea turtles use many as nurseries.

The country's first national park, Santa Rosa, was established here, the first of more than a dozen national parks, wildlife refuges, and biological reserves in the region. The array of ecosystems and wildlife in the region ranges from pristine shores to volcanic heights, encompassing just about every imaginable ecosystem within Costa Rica.

Equally, no region of Costa Rica displays its cultural heritage as overtly as Guanacaste, whose distinct flavor owes much to the blending of Spanish and Chorotega Indian cultures (although the culture went into rapid decline with the arrival of the Spanish, the Chorotega weren't entirely decimated, and today one can still see deeply bronzed wide-set faces and pockets of Chorotega life). The people who today inhabit the province are tied to old bloodlines and live and work on the cusp between cultures.

Costa Rica's national costume and music emanate from this region, as does the *punto guanacasteco,* the country's official dance. And the regional heritage can still be traced in the creation of clay pottery and figurines. The *campesino* life here revolves around the horse and cattle ranch, and dark-skinned *sabaneros* (cowboys) shaded by wide-brimmed hats and mounted on horses with lassoes and machetes at their sides are the preeminent sight. Come fiesta time, nothing rouses so much cheer as the *corridas de toros* (bullfights) and *topes,* the region's colorful horse parades in which the Guanacastecans show off their meticulously groomed horses and the horses' fancy footwork. Guanacastecans love a fiesta: the biggest occurs each 25 July, when Guanacaste celebrates its independence from Nicaragua.

Guanacaste's climate is in total contrast to the rest of the country. The province averages less than 162 cm (65 inches) of rain a year, though regional variation is extreme. For half the year (Nov.–April) the plains receive no rain, it is hot-

ter than Hades, and the sun beats down hard as a nail, although cool winds bearing down from northern latitudes can lower temperatures pleasantly along the coast Dec.–Feb. The dry season usually lingers slightly longer than elsewhere in Costa Rica. The Tempisque Basin is the country's driest region and receives less than 45 cm (18 inches) of rain in years of drought, mostly in a few torrential downpours during the six-month rainy season. In the wet season, everything turns green and the air is freshly scented. The mountain slopes receive much more rain, noticeably so on the eastern slopes, which are cloud-draped and deluged for much of the year.

PLANNING YOUR TIME

Guanacaste is a large region; its numerous attractions are spread out and getting between any two major regions can eat up the better part of a day. The region is diverse enough to justify exploring in its entirety, for which you should budget no less than a week. Monteverde alone requires a minimum of two days, and ideally four to take advantage of all that it offers. Nor would you wish to rush exploring Rincón de la Vieja National Park, requiring two or three nights.

Recent years have seen a boost in regional tourism following the opening of the new international airport at Liberia, which serves mainly charters. The airport is well-served by car rental companies, so you can head out with your own wheels without any palaver.

The Pan-American Highway (Hwy. 1) cuts through the heart of lowland Guanacaste, ruler-straight almost all the way between the Nicaraguan border in the north and Puntarenas in the south. Juggernaut trucks frequent the fast-paced and potholed road, which is one lane in either direction. Drive cautiously! North of Liberia the route is superbly scenic. Almost every site of importance lies within a short reach of the highway, accessed by dirt side roads. If traveling by bus, sit on the east-facing side for the best views.

Central American Tours (tel. 506/667-0085, cat@catours.co.cr, www.catours.co.cr) specializes in tours of Guanacaste.

A PALETTE IN BLOOM

In the midst of dry-season drought, Guanacaste explodes in Monet colors—not wildflowers, but a Technicolor blossoming of trees as fervent flowers burst open on bare branches. In November, the saffron-bright flowering of the guachipelín sets in motion a chain reaction that lasts for six months. Individual trees of a particular genus are somehow keyed to explode in unison, often in a climax lasting as little as a day. Two or three bouquets of a single species may occur in a season. The colors are never static. In January, it's the turn of pink *poui* (savannah oak) and yellow *poui* (black bark tree). By February, canary-bright *Corteza amarillo* and the trumpet-shaped yellow blossoms of *Tabebuia chrysanta* dot the landscape. In March delicate pink curao appears. As the curao wanes, *Tabebuia rosea* bursts forth in subtle pinks, whites, and lilacs. The *malinche*—royal poinciana or flame tree—closes out the six-month parade of blossoming trees with a dramatic display as red as bright lipstick.

Touristy it might be, but **Monteverde,** the big draw, delivers in heaps. Its numerous attractions include canopy tours; horseback riding; art galleries; orchid, snake, frog, and butterfly exhibits; and, at Selvatura, the one-of-a-kind **Jewels of the Rainforest Bio-Art Exhibition** is worth the arduous uphill journey to Monteverde in its own right. Most visitors come to hike in the **Monteverde Cloud Forest Biological Reserve,** the most famous of several similar reserves that make up the Arenal-Monteverde Protection Zone. Monteverde appeals to every budget, age group, and interest, and boasts scores of accommodations to suite every taste.

Back in the lowlands, the town of **Cañas** offers **Las Pumas Cat Zoo** and the **Río Corobicí,** the former a refuge for big-cat species; the latter good for relatively calm whitewater trips. To the north, few visitors bother with **Miravalles Volcano,** which is your gain: several recreational facilities take advantage of thermal waters that also feed bubbling mudpots and geysers. A sidetrip to **Palo Verde National Park,** with more than a dozen distinct habitats, is recommended for birders. Nearby, **Liberia** is worth a stop for its well-preserved colonial homesteads. The city is gateway to both the Nicoya peninsula and **Rincón de la Vieja National Park,** popular for hikes (overnight if you wish) to the summit and for horseback rides and canopy tours from nature lodges outside the park.

Santa Rosa National Park is more easily accessed from the Pan-American Highway and is popular for nature trails offering easy viewing of a dizzying array of animals and birds. It also has splendid beaches, great surfing, and La Casona, a historic building considered a national shrine. Equestrians in particular will enjoy a day or two at **Hacienda Los Inocentes Wildlife Conservation and Recreation Center,** one of the nation's preeminent wildlife-viewing sites.

Visit **Puntarenas,** the main town, solely to access the ferry to southern Nicoya, or perhaps for a cruise-excursion to **Isla Tortuga.**

HISTORY

The Guanacaste-Nicoya region was the center of a vibrant pre-Columbian culture—the Chorotegas, who celebrated the Fiesta del Maíz (Festival of Corn) and worshiped the sun with the public sacrifice of young virgins and ritual cannibalism. Descended from the Olmecs of Mexico, they arrived in the area around the 8th century and soon established themselves as the most advanced group in the region. Their culture was centered on *milpas,* or cornfields. Many of the stone metates (small stool-like tables for grinding corn) on display in the National Museum in San José are from the region. Some of the most beautiful pieces were delicately shaped into anthropomorphic axe-gods and two-headed crocodiles—totems derived from the Olmec culture.

The Chorotegas were particularly skilled at carving jade and achieved their zenith in craftsmanship between the last century B.C. and the 5th century A.D. Blue jade was considered the most precious of objects. Archaeologists, however, aren't sure where the blue jade came from. There are no known jade deposits in Costa Rica, and the nearest known source of green jade was more than 800 km north in Guatemala.

The region was colonized early by Spaniards, who established the cattle industry that dominates to this day. Between 1570 and 1821, Guanacaste (including Nicoya) was an independent province within the Captaincy General of Guatemala, a federation of Spanish provinces in Central America. The province was delivered to Nicaragua in 1787, and to Costa Rica in 1812. In 1821, when the Captaincy General was dissolved and autonomy granted to the Central American nations, Guanacaste had to choose between Nicaragua and Costa Rica. Rancor between Liberians—cattle ranchers with strong Nicaraguan ties—and Nicoyans who favored union with Costa Rica lingered until a plebiscite in 1824. Guanacaste officially became part of Costa Rica by treaty in 1858.

The Southern Plains

The Pan-American Highway (Hwy. 1) descends from the central highlands to the Pacific plains via **Esparza,** at the foot of the mountains about 15 km east of Puntarenas.

PUNTARENAS

Five km long but only five blocks wide at its widest, this sultry port town, 120 km west of San José, is built on a long narrow spit—Puntarenas means "Sandy Point"—-running west from the suburb of **Cocal** and backed to the north by a mangrove estuary; to the south are the Gulf of Nicoya and a beach cluttered with driftwood.

Puntarenas has long been favored by Josefinos seeking R and R. The old wharves on the estuary side feature decrepit fishing boats leaning against ramshackle piers popular with pelicans. Ernest Hemingway, you sense, would have loved the local color—the old women rocking under shade eaves, the men lolling about in shorts and flip-flops, the bar-girls beckoning from balconies at the occasional drunk staggering home.

The peninsula was colonized by the Spaniards as early as 1522. The early port grew to prominence and was declared a free port in 1847, a year after completion of an oxcart road from the Meseta Central. Oxcarts laden with coffee made the lumbering descent to Puntarenas in convoys; the beans were shipped from here via Cape Horn to Europe, launching Puntarenas to relative prosperity. At its height Puntarenas had streetcars like those of San Francisco. It remained the country's main port until the Atlantic Railroad to Limón, on the Caribbean coast, was completed in 1890 (the railroad between San José and Puntarenas would not be completed for another 20 years). Earlier this century, Puntarenas also developed a large conch-pearl fleet. Some 80 percent of Porteños, as the inhabitants of Puntarenas are called, still make their livings from the sea, often going out for days at a time to haul in corvina, wahoo, dorado, shrimp, lobster, and tuna.

Puntarenas even enjoyed favor as a *balneario*— a place for Josefinos to sun and bathe on weekends. Alas, when international tourists began to arrive in numbers in the 1970s, and resorts sprang up elsewhere to lure them, Puntarenas was left behind in the tourism sweepstakes. In 1993, the city fathers initiated efforts to boost Puntarenas' fortunes by giving it a facelift. The kilometers-long beach has been transformed from a dump to a pleasant stretch of sand. Trees have been planted and a fountain installed near the newly opened Casa de Cultura. An artisans' market lines the tourist boardwalk.

The town's main usefulness is as the departure point for day cruises to islands in the Gulf of Nicoya and for the ferries to Playa Naranjo and Paquera, on the Nicoya Peninsula.

Sights

The **church** (Avenida Central, Calles 5/7), built in 1902 of flagstones, abuts the recently renovated **Antigua Comandancia de la Plaza,** a mock-fortress-style building complete with tiny battlements and bars on its windows. It once served as a barracks and city jail; today it houses the **Casa de la Cultura y Museo de Historia Maritimo** (tel. 506/661-1394 or 506/661-5036, 9:45 A.M.–noon and 1–5:15 P.M. Tue.–Sun.), with a library, art gallery, and marine history museum featuring well-done displays of the life of fishermen, model boats, pirates, etc., plus exhibits on city life from the pre-Columbian and coffee era. It hosts plays and concerts. Craft stores adds color.

The **Municipal Market** is also worth a look for its vitality and color.

Everything of import seems to happen along the **Paseo de las Turistas,** a boulevard paralleling the Gulf of Nicoya and abuzz with vendors, beachcombers, and locals flirting and trying to keep cool in the waters. The beach widens and improves to the east, notably so at **Playa San Isidro,** about eight km east of the town at the far eastern end of the peninsula. On the north side of the peninsula, the sheltered gulf shore—the estuary—is lined with fishing vessels in various states of decrepitude. Roseate spoonbills, storks, and other birds pick among the shallows.

Ernest Hemingway, you sense, would have loved the local color of Puntarenas—the old women rocking under shade eaves, the men lolling about in shorts and flip-flops, the bar-girls beckoning from balconies at the occasional drunk staggering home.

Entertainment and Events

Every mid-July the city honors Carmen, Virgin of the Sea, in the annual **Sea Festival.** Religious processions are accompanied by carnival rides, boat and bicycle races, dancing, and a boating regatta with nearly every boat in the area decorated in colorful flags and banners. The local Chinese community contributes with its dragon boats.

In summer, concerts and plays are put on at the Casa de la Cultura.

A series of bars along Paseo de las Turistas cater to the locals. **Caribbean Breeze** (Calle 23) has karaoke on Fri.–Sat. nights, and "nostalgia" music on Wednesdays at its colorful bar with

TV. **Kimbo's** (Calles 7/9), also known as Bar Passport, has karaoke on Thursdays, plus a large-screen TV. The a/c **Bakan Bar** (Calle 15), above Pizzería Valetta, is a modestly elegant option for cocktails. Otherwise, the local bars are overwhelmingly raffish (guard against pickpockets).

There's a small, unsophisticated **Playa de Oro Casino** (Paseo, Calle 15). A better option is the casino in the Fiesta Caribbean Village resort.

Cine Millenium (Paseo de las Turistas, Calles 15/17, tel. 506/661-4759) shows movies at 7 P.M. ($1.25).

Sports and Recreation

Pacific Ocean Winds, at Fiesta Caribbean Village, operates a high-tech catamaran offering two-hour cruises Wed.–Sat. at 11 A.M., 1:30 P.M., and 4 P.M.

Accommodations

Puntarenas is a muggy place, so check that ventilation is efficient (this is one place in Costa Rica where you'll be glad for a/c). If possible, take a hotel on the gulf side to catch the breezes. Many of the low-end hotels downtown are volatile refuges of drunks and cheap hookers who may beckon males from the upstairs windows. Things improve west of downtown.

Under $25: One of the better budget bargains is the well-run **Hotel Río** (Calle Central, Avenida 3, tel. 506/661-0331, fax 506/661-0938, $5 s, $7.50 d shared bath; $7.50 s, $11 d private bath), with 90 clean, basic rooms with fans and cold water, and handy for the *lancha* dock to Paquera.

Hotel y Restaurant Cayuga (Calle 4, Avenidas Central/1, tel. 506/661-0344, fax 506/661-1280, $14 s, $20 d, or $25 s, $35 d with TV and telephone) is simple, clean, and well kept, a bargain popular with gringos. The 31 rooms have a/c and private baths with cold water. There's a restaurant and secure parking.

The rambling, ramshackle, rickety **Gran Hotel Imperial** (Paseo de las Turistas, Calle Central, tel./fax 506/661-0579, $12 s, $22 d), next to

Guanacaste

PUNTARENAS

El Estero

SEE DETAIL

PUNTARENAS

FERRY TERMINAL
(PAQUERA AND
PLAYA NARANJA)

BAR MAR/
MARINA
RESTAURANTE

RED
CROSS

HOTEL
LA PUNTA

TICKET
OFFICE

CALLE 11

CALLE 7

CALLE 5

CALLE 3

CALLE 1

AVENIDA CENTRAL

CALLE CENTRAL

CALLE 2

CALLE 4

CALLE 6

C. 8

CALLE 37

C. 37

CALLE 35

CALLE 33

CALLE 31

CALLE 29

CALLE 27

CALLE 25

CALLE 23

CALLE 21

CALLE 19

CALLE 17

CALLE 15

CALLE 13

CALLE 9

AVENIDA 2

AVENIDA 4

HOTEL
YADRAN

POLICE

CABANAS MIREY

PASEO DE LOS TURISTAS

PASEO LEÓN CORTES

CARIBBEAN BREEZE

MILLENIUM CYBER CAFÉ

LA CARAVELLE

PLAYA DE ORO
CASINO

HELADERÍA

HOTEL
TIOGA

STEAK HOUSE
LA YUNTA

RESTAURANTE
ALOHA

Golfo de Nicoya

PACIFIC OCEAN

Estero Vueltas

Estero Ciruelas

Estero Chacarita

CALLE 86

CALLE 86

CALLE 84

CALLE 84

HOTEL
PORTOBELLO

COSTA RICA
YACHT CLUB

ANGOSTURA

POCHOTE

**SEE ABOVE FOR
CONTINUATION**

Playa Pochote

Playa Angostura

Playa

Golfo de Nicoya

PACIFIC OCEAN

| 0 | 500 yds |
| 0 | 500 m |

MOON

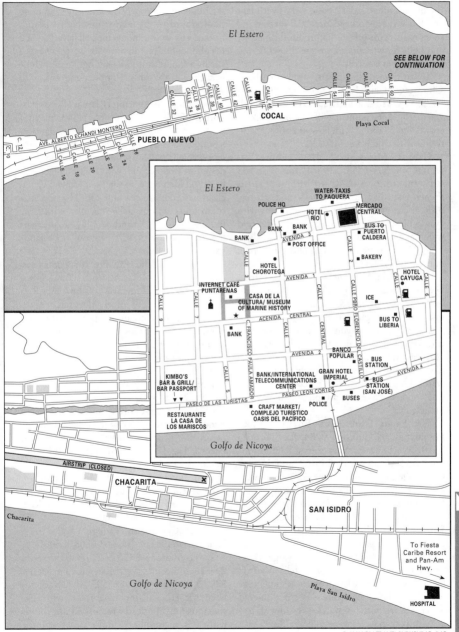

El Estero

SEE BELOW FOR
CONTINUATION

COCAL

Playa Cocal

PUEBLO NUEVO

AVE. ALBERTO ECHANDI MONTERO

CALLE 32
CALLE 34
CALLE 36
CALLE 38
CALLE 40
CALLE 42
CALLE 44
CALLE 46
CALLE 16
CALLE 18
CALLE 20
CALLE 22
CALLE 24
CALLE 26
CALLE 54
CALLE 56
CALLE 58
CALLE 60
C. 12
C. 10

El Estero

WATER-TAXIS
TO PAQUERA

POLICE HQ

MERCADO
CENTRAL

HOTEL
RIO

BANK

BANK

BANK

AVENIDA 3

POST OFFICE

BUS TO
PUERTO
CALDERA

BAKERY

HOTEL
CHOROTEGA

AVENIDA

HOTEL
CAYUGA

INTERNET CAFÉ
PUNTARENAS

CASA DE LA
CULTURA/ MUSEUM
OF MARINE HISTORY

ACENIDA
CENTRAL

ICE

BUS TO
LIBERIA

BANK

AVENIDA 2

BANCO
POPULAR

BUS
STATION

KIMBO'S
BAR & GRILL/
BAR PASSPORT

BANK/INTERNATIONAL
TELECOMMUNICATIONS
CENTER

GRAN HOTEL
IMPERIAL

PASEO LEON CORTES

BUS
STATION
(SAN JOSÉ)

AVENIDA 4

PASEO DE LAS TURISTAS

CRAFT MARKET/
COMPLEJO TURÍSTICO
OASIS DEL PACÍFICO

POLICE

BUSES

RESTAURANTE
LA CASA DE
LOS MARISCOS

Golfo de Nicoya

C. FRANCISCO PAULA AMADOR
CALLE 9
CALLE 7
CALLE 5
CALLE 3
CALLE 1
CALLE CENTRAL
CALLE 2
CALLE PBRO FLORENCIO DEL CASTILLO
CALLE 4
CALLE 6

AIRSTRIP (CLOSED)

CHACARITA

SAN ISIDRO

Chacarita

To Fiesta
Caribe Resort
and Pan-Am
Hwy.

Golfo de Nicoya

Playa San Isidro

HOSPITAL

N

Guanacaste

© AVALON TRAVEL PUBLISHING, INC.

the bus terminal, has 12 basic rooms with fans and hot water; two have local TV. Take an upstairs room with private bathroom for balcony and light (downstairs rooms are dingy). It was remodeling at last visit.

To the west, the clean, well-run **Hotel Chorotega** (Calle 1, Avenida 3, tel. 506/661-0998, $9 s, $15 d shared bath; $15 s, $25 d private bath), once popular with the backpacking crowd, has 38 rooms with fans and private bathrooms with cold water only.

Cabinas Mirey (Calle 15, Avenidas 2/4, tel./fax 506/661-1553, $20 s/d Mon.–Fri.; $33 s/d standard, or $42.40 s/d with kitchen) is French-Canadian run and has 15 modestly furnished, clean, somewhat dark a/c rooms with fans, cable TV, and private bathrooms with cold water. Some have kitchens and/or mini-fridges. There's laundry, secure parking, plus a small pool in the rear courtyards.

$25–50: The American-run **Hotel La Punta**, (Avenida 1, Calles 35/37, tel./fax 506/661-0696, $20 s, $30 d with fan, $30 s, $35 d with a/c), is one of the better places in this price bracket and a good place to rest your head if you want to catch the early-morning ferry to Nicoya. The 12 pleasant if spartan rooms have fans (some have a/c) and spacious private baths with hot water. Upper rooms have balconies. It has a small pool and a restaurant, plus parking. Rates include tax.

The **Yacht Club** (P.O. Box 151-5400, Puntarenas, tel. 506/661-0784, fax 506/661-2518, cryacht@racsa.co.cr, $26 s, $38 d economy, $32/45 standard, $45/62 superior), at Cocal, offers accommodations in 25 rooms with private baths with hot water. Economy rooms have fans, standards have a/c, and superiors have a/c, TV, and mini-fridge. It also has villas ($70, or $90 with a/c). There's an open-air restaurant-cum-bar, plus a pool.

$50–100: The venerable **Hotel Tioga** (Paseo de las Turistas, Avenidas 15/17, tel. 506/661-0271, fax 506/661-0127, costarica@hoteltioga.com, www.hoteltioga.com, $41 s/d with cold water, $59 s/d with hot water, $76 s/d with balcony and ocean view low season; $59/82/99 high season) has 46 a/c rooms surrounding a pleas-

ing but compact courtyard with tiny swimming pool graced by its own palm-shaded island. Rooms vary in size and quality; all have TVs and telephones but not all have hot water. There's a small casino, plus secure parking. Rates include breakfast in the fourth-floor restaurant, with views over the gulf.

Next door, the **Apartotel Alamar** (Paseo de las Turistas, Calle 32, tel. 506/661-4343, fax 506/661-2726, info@alamarcr.com, www.alamarcr.com, $60 one-bedroom, $80 two-bedroom) offers spacious two-story units in contemporary design in lively colors, with wall murals. Each has a full kitchen, cool tile floor, cable TV, and clean bathroom in sea-blue tile. The one-bedroom units are especially spacious, with large lounges. It has laundry, plus a pleasant breezeswept courtyard with pool, rock landscaping, and a Jacuzzi.

Hotel Porto Bello (P.O. Box 108, Puntarenas, tel. 506/661-1322, fax 506/661-0036, $40 s, $50 d), a stone's throw west of the Costa Rica Yacht Club, has 36 nicely decorated high-ceilinged rooms with a/c and private baths with hot water. Private patios and balconies open onto lush grounds with a nice pool beneath shade trees. A pleasing restaurant serves grilled meats and seafood.

Hotel Yadran (P.O. Box 14, Puntarenas 5400, Avenida 2, Calles 31/33, tel. 506/661-2662, fax 506/661-1944, yadran@ticonet.co.cr, $76 s/d standard, $88 sea view), at the breezy tip of the peninsula, provides views across the bay to Nicoya. The 42 rooms have private baths, hot water, a/c, cable TVs, and balconies or verandas. The hotel has two small pools, a whirlpool, a discotheque, and an upstairs restaurant with bay vistas serving Spanish cuisine. Overpriced! Rates include tax, year-round.

Fiesta Caribbean Village (Apdo. 171, Puntarenas 5400, tel. 506/663-0808 or 506/220-2412, fax 506/663-0856 or 220-3409, reservas @fiestaresort.com, www.fiestaresort.com, $160 s, $200 d low season; $185 s, $230 d high season) is an attractive all-inclusive resort with 230 spacious and modestly furnished a/c rooms with TVs, including 87 junior suites, and the opulent presidential suite. Facilities include two restaurants, a seafood bar, an a/c gym, an immense and beautiful free-form swimming pool with island bar, plus two other sizeable pools (one with Jacuzzi jets). The expansive grounds contain volleyball and tennis courts. Lady Luck beckons in the casino (gamblers get free drinks), after which you can hit the disco; and nightly skits are offered in the theater. Sea kayaking, windsurfing, scuba diving, and personal watercraft are offered. The resort is popular with mass-market package-tour groups, Tico families (there are children's activities throughout the day), and young Ticos who know a good thing when they see it. Rates are all-inclusive.

Food

Cheap *sodas* abound near the Central Market and along the Paseo de las Turistas, between Calles Central and 3.

The best restaurant in town is the Belgian-run **La Caravelle** (Calles 21/23, tel. 506/661-2262, 6–11 P.M. Tue.–Thur., noon–12:30 A.M. and 6–11 P.M. Fri.–Sun., $4–10), an elegant, even romantic wood-paneled a/c restaurant serving French cuisine. Typical dishes include cream of lobster soup, and a superb seabass with white wine and palmito purée. The delightful decor plays on a French theme.

The Cuban-American run **Caribbean Breeze** (Paseo de las Turistas, Calle 23, tel. 506/661-2034, 11 A.M.–midnight, $2.25–8), next to La Caravelle, is well-named and serves ceviche, *bocas* such as stuffed jalapeños with plantain, garlic octopus, and Caribbean dishes. It has entertainment by night.

There are plenty of other options along Paseo, including the charming **La Casa de los Mariscos** (Calles 7/9), serving good seafood; and the rustically elegant **Steak House La Yunta** (Calle 21, tel. 506/661-3216), in a historic two-story seafront house.

Chinese restaurants concentrate at the junction of Calle Central and Avenida Central.

Bar Mar-Marina Restaurant (Avenida 3, Calle 33, tel. 506/661-3064, 6 A.M.–8 P.M.) adjoins the ferry terminal and is handy for a meal if you're catching the ferry.

Musmanni (Avenida Central, Calles Central/1) sells baked goods. The central market (Avenida 3, Calle Central) sells produce.

Information and Services

The **Monseñor Sanabria Hospital** (tel. 506/663-0033) is eight km east of town, at the west end of San Isidro. There's a branch hospital at Paseo de las Turistas and Calle 9. You'll find plenty of pharmacies in town.

The **police** (tel. 506/661-0740) is at Paseo and Calle Central. Criminal investigation is handled by the OIJ (tel. 506/630-0377).

There are several banks downtown; see the map.

The **post office** is on Avenida 3, Calle Central/1. You can make calls from the **International Telecommunications Center** (Paseo de las Turistas, Calle Central/1).

Internet Café Puntarenas (tel. 506/661-4044, 9 A.M.–9 P.M.), tucked behind the Casa de la Cultura, charges $1 per hour. **Coonatramar** (Avenida 3, Calles 33/35, tel. 506/661-1069 or 661-9011, www.coonatramar.com, 8 A.M.–5 P.M. daily) has Internet service, as does **Millenium Cyber Café** (Paseo, Calle 17, tel. 506/661-4759, 8 A.M.–10 P.M. daily).

Getting There

Empresarios Unidos (in San José tel. 506/222-0064, in Puntarenas tel. 506/661-2158), buses depart San José from Calle 16, Avenidas 10/12, daily every 40 minutes, 6 A.M.–7 P.M. ($3).

Return buses depart Puntarenas for San José from the bus station (Calle 2, Paseo de las Turistas, tel. 506/661-2158) every 30 minutes, 5:30 A.M.–7 P.M. ($2.50). Buses also depart Puntarenas for Cañas and Tilarán at 11:30 A.M. and 4:15 P.M.; Monteverde at 2 P.M.; Jacó and Quepos at 5 A.M., 11 A.M., and 2:30 P.M.; and Liberia at 5 A.M., 7 A.M., 9:30 A.M., 11 A.M., 12:30 P.M., and 3 P.M.

Car-and-passenger ferries for the Nicoya Peninsula leave the Coonatramar ferry terminal (Avenida 3, Calles 33/35, tel. 506/661-9011, fax 506/661-2197, www.coonatramar.com); the office is open Mon.–Sat. 8 A.M.–5 P.M. Passenger only water-taxis also operated. For details see the

Guanacaste

sidebar, *Ferries to and from Nicoya* in the *Nicoya Peninsula* chapter. Buses marked "Ferry" operate along Avenida Central to the ferry terminal ($2).

The **Costa Rica Yacht Club and Marina** (tel. 506/661-0784, fax 506/661-2518, cryacht@racsa .co.cr) offers a safe anchorage and has a lift and dry dock, electricity, compressor, gas and diesel, fax and telephone, and accommodations.

Getting Around
Buses ply up and down Avenidas Central and 2. Coopepuntarenas (tel. 506/663-0053 or 506/663-1635) offers taxi service.

You can rent bicycles at Cabinas Mirey (tel. 506/661-4505).

PEÑAS BLANCAS WILDLIFE REFUGE
Eleven km north of Esparza on Hwy. 1, a side road winds east to the village of **Miramar,** on the western slopes of the Cordillera Tilarán. Gold has been mined hereabouts since 1815; you can still visit **Las Minas de Montes de Oro,** where guests are taken inside the tunnels and shown the old-fashioned manner of sifting for gold (the modern operation is now high-tech). It has a functioning waterwheel. (In 2001, Wheaton River Minerals of Canada announced plans to establish an open-pit gold mine. Locals are opposed, not least because the mine would produce an estimated 15 million tons of cyanide-contaminated waste.)

The sole concession to visit the mine is owned by **Finca Daniel Adventure Park** (see Vista Golfo de Nicoya Lodge, in the *Accommodations and Food* section, below), a 27-hectare ranch and fruit farm in the hills four km north of Miramar at Tajo Alto. There are trails, and horseback rides to waterfalls ($29), to the nearby gold mines ($30, including mine entrance; four hours), and into the cloud forest ($44), where monkeys and quetzals are frequently seen. It offers a canopy tour with 11 cables for various skill levels (the longest is 700 meters long), including a beginners' line that runs in front of the restaurant, permitting dad to wave to the kids as he passes ($25); a

second, more elaborate, zipline system with 25 cables was being added at last visit. Day visitors are welcome ($4 to use the swimming pool, including towels; no charge if you eat at the restaurant).

Eighteen km northeast of Miramar, in an area known as Tajo Alto, is **Zapotal,** gateway to the **La Mancuerna Private Ecological Reserve** (tel. 506/661-8241), at 1,500 meters elevation and protecting the Alberto Manuel Brénas Cloud Forest. It has horseback riding and hiking in cloud forests good for spotting quetzals, toucans, and a panoply of other wildlife. Zapotal is also gateway to Peñas Blancas Wildlife Refuge.

The 2,400-hectare **Refugio Silvestre de Peñas Blancas,** 33 km northeast of Puntarenas, protects the watersheds of the Ríos Barranca and Ciruelas, on the forested southern slopes of the Cordillera de Tilarán. The mountain slopes rise steeply from rolling plains carved with deep canyons to 1,400 meters atop Zapotal peak. Vegetation ranges from tropical dry forest in the southerly lower elevation to moist deciduous and premontane moist forest higher up. The region has been extensively deforested, but there remains plenty of wildlife, including howler and white-faced monkeys, red brocket deer, kinkajous, and any of 70-plus species of birds, including toucans and quetzals at the highest elevations.

Peñas Blancas refers to the white cliffs that lend the park its name. The sedimentary rocks originated from the skeletal remains of subaqueous creatures.

Steep trails follow the Río Jabonal. Camping is permitted. There are no visitor facilities—and very few visitors.

Accommodations and Food
Vista Golfo de Nicoya Lodge (P.O. Box 02-5550, Miramar, tel. 506/639-8303, fax 506/639-8130, vistago@racsa.co.cr, www.vistadelgolfo.com, $30 s/d shared bath year-round, $41 s, $48 d private bath low season, $55 s, $58 d high season, $48–58 family room low season, $58–68 high season) is an atmospheric modern hotel at Finca Daniel Adventure Park, boasting great views over the Gulf of Nicoya. It has rooms and apartments for two to eight people (one has a kitchenette)

with modest but pleasant decor and balconies. There's a swimming pool fed by spring water and a hot tub in a small garden. It features the **Bar y Restaurant El Túcano,** where you can dine beneath the shade of a huge spreading tree.

The German-run **Finca El Mirador B&B** (tel./fax 506/639 8774, heckmann@racsa.co.cr, www.finca-mirador.com, $38 s/d) is a delightful-looking, red-tile-roofed mountainside home with three cabins with warm ocher decor and hot water showers. There's a swimming pool. It's two km along a dirt road that begins about 600 meters before Finca Daniel.

Getting There

Buses depart San José for Miramar at 5:30 A.M., 7:30 A.M., and 12:30 P.M., returning at 7 A.M., 12:30 P.M., and 4:45 P.M. Direct buses depart Puntarenas for Miramar at 9:30 A.M. (Sundays at 10:30 A.M.); return buses depart Miramar at 4:30 P.M. (Sundays at 5:45 P.M.).

COSTA DE PÁJAROS

At San Gerardo, on the Pan-American Highway, 40 km north of Puntarenas, a paved road leads west to Punta Morales and the Golfo de Nicoya. There's fabulous bird-watching among the mangroves that line the shore—known as the Costa de Pájaros—stretching north to **Manzanillo,** the estuary of the Río Abangaritos, and, beyond, to the estuary of the Río Tempisque. The mangroves are home to ibis, herons, pelicans, parrots, egrets, and caimans. You can follow this coast through cattle country via a road north from four km east of Punta Morales (a dead-end) to Hwy. 18, five km east of the Tempisque bridge.

(The turnoff for the bridge from the Pan-American Highway is at Km 168, four km north of the turnoff for Las Juntas and 20 km south of Cañas.)

La Enseñada National Wildlife Refuge (La Enseñada Refugio Nacional de Vida Silvestre) is near Abangaritos, two km north of Manzanillo, 17 km from the Pan-American Highway. The 380-hectare wildlife refuge is part of a family-run cattle *finca* and salt farm (papayas and watermelons are also grown), with nature trails and a lake—Laguna Agua Dulce—replete with waterfowl and crocodiles. The lodge offers boat trips to Palo Verde ($46), a tractor tour of the *finca* ($15), plus horseback tours ($15), including to Monteverde and Arenal. A mangrove tour costs $23 pp.

The **Birds Island Biological Reserve** (Isla Pájaros Reserva Biológica) is about 600 meters offshore from Punta Morales. The 3.8-hectare reserve protects a colony of brown pelicans and other seabirds that live on this scrub-covered rocky islet rising 45 meters above the Gulf of Nicoya. Access is restricted to biological researchers.

Accommodations

The Italian-owned **La Enseñada Lodge** (Apdo. 318-1250, Escazú, tel. 506/289-6655, fax 506/289-5281, laensenada@yahoo.com, www.laensenada.net, $26 s, $43 d low season; $31 s, $50 d high season) enjoys a breezy location at the heart of La Enseñada Wildlife Refuge, with tremendous views down the bougainvillea-splashed lawns to the mangrove-lined gulf. It has 22 rustic yet spacious, comfortable wooden *cabinas,* cross-ventilated by screened windows, with two double beds, private baths with solar hot water and verandas with hammocks. Meals are served in a thatched restaurant. It has a tennis court and swimming pool.

LAS JUNTAS DE ABANGARES

Las Juntas, at the base of the Cordillera Tilarán about 50 km north of Esparza and six km east of Hwy. 1 (the turnoff is at Km 164, about 12 km north of the Río Lagarto and the turnoff for Monteverde), is splashed with colorful flowers and trim pastel-painted houses. A tree-lined main boulevard and streets paved with interlocking stones add to the orderliness. Small it may be but Las Juntas figures big in the region's history. When gold was discovered in the nearby mountains in 1884, it sparked a gold rush. Hungry prospectors came from all over the world to sift the earth for nuggets. Las Juntas was a Wild West town. Inflated gold prices have lured many *oreros*

M

Guanacaste

(miners) back to the old mines and streams (about 40 kilos of gold a week are recovered).

That pint-size **locomotive**—the *María Cristina*—that sits in the town plaza once hauled ore for the Abangares Gold Fields Company and dates from 1904. Railroad pioneer Minor Keith was the major shareholder, and the train is named for his wife. The *oreros* are honored with a fine bronze **statue** in a triangular plaza on the other side of an arched bridge at the northeast corner of town (turn left about 100 meters beyond the park).

The road northeast from the triangular plaza leads into the Cordillera Tilarán via **Candelaria** and then (to the right) Monteverde or (to the left) Tilarán; it is relatively untraveled, and 4WD is recommended. In places the views are fantastic. Three km from Las Juntas, a side road leads to the hamlet of **La Sierra,** then drops sharply into the valley of the Río Aguas Claras and the **Centro Turístico Pueblo Antiguo** (tel. 506/662-1913 or 506/255-1233, fax 506/233-2685, goldmine @desacarga.co.cr, 10 A.M.–9 P.M., $4 admisson), with a tremendous setting amid 60 forested hectares. This "touristic complex" has two hot thermal pools and a cold-water pool, plus a cavern-style stone-lined steam room and two Jacuzzis. It has changing rooms, three bars, and a restaurant with forest views, plus a lake stocked with trout and tilapia (you can catch your own). Nature tours are offered, as is a "Gold Mine Adventure" down the dank candlelit tunnels (helmets and flashlights are provided). Live music was to be introduced, as was a canopy tour with rappeling and suspension bridges ($25).

Further downhill, and belonging to the Centro, is the **Ecomuseo Las Minas,** displaying mining equipment and the ruins of a turn-of-the-century mining center.

Mina Tours (tel. 506/662-0753), in Las Juntas, also offers tours of a miners' cooperative.

Accommodations and Food

Cabinas El Elcanto (tel. 506/662-0677, $7 s,

monument of gold miners, Las Juntas de Abaranges

$12 d fans, $8 s, $15 d a/c), 100 meters northeast of the triangular plaza, has 14 clean, simple, modern rooms with fans, private baths, and cold water. Five additional rooms have a/c and hot water. All have cable TV.

Finca Rincos B&B (tel./fax 506/662-1403, www.pke.net/costarica, $30 s, $50 d), marvelously situated beside the Río San Juan, six km southeast of Las Juntas, is run by a delightful Swiss couple. This stone-and-timber property has two small, simply furnished rooms with clean modern bathrooms. Guests can use the Internet. Meals are prepared on request. It has a wood-fired oven for pizzas, and a grill. The farm has horses. And there are waterfalls and hot springs nearby, plus a pond stocked with tilapia, and wildlife abounds. Rates include breakfast.

Centro Turístico Pueblo Antiguo (see above, $45 up to four people) had three spacious wooden cabins at last visit, and 15 more—including two-story "luxury" bungalows—were to be added. Each has tile floor, fans, rattan sofas and chairs, two queen beds, basic kitchens with microwave, clean modern private bathroom with hot water, and veranda with rockers. TVs were to be added.

The **Cantina Caballo Blanco** facing the triangular plaza is a colorful place with pool tables painted in lively motifs, and walls festooned with paraphernalia of the *oreros'* life.

Getting There
Buses (tel. 506/222-1867) depart San José for Las Juntas from Calle 12, Avenida 9, daily at 11 A.M. and 5 P.M.; and from Cañas at 9:30 A.M. and 2:50 P.M. Return buses to San José depart Las Juntas at 6:30 A.M. and 12:30 P.M.

Buses depart Liberia for Juntas at 3:50 P.M.

Monteverde and Vicinity

MONTEVERDE, CERRO PLANO, AND SANTA ELENA

Monteverde, 35 km north from the Pan-American Highway, means "Green Mountain," an appropriate name for one of the most idyllic pastoral settings in Costa Rica. Cows munch contentedly, and horse-drawn wagons loaded with milk cans still make the rounds in this world-famous community atop a secluded 1,400-meter-high plateau in the Cordillera de Tilarán. Monteverde is actually a sprawling agricultural community; the Monteverde Cloud Forest Biological Reserve (see *Arenal-Monteverde Protection Zone,* below), which is what most visitors come to see, is a few kilometers southeast and higher up. A growing number of attractions (including canopy tours) are found north of Santa Elena, which has its own cloud forest reserve.

Monteverde is populated by North American Quakers and their Tico-born offspring. There is no concentrated village to speak of; most of the homes are hidden from view in the forest, accessible by foot trail and scattered along the dirt road that leads to Monteverde Cloud Forest Biological Reserve from the village of **Santa Elena,** a community of Tico families that is distinct from Monteverde and is the center of things hereabouts: the bank, stores, bars (these being absent, of course, in a Quaker community), and other services are here. Separating the communities of Santa Elena and Monteverde is the region of **Cerro Plano,** where most accommodations concentrate.

The three communities are effectively one. However, residents of Monteverde are upset that residents of Santa Elena poach their business. For example, a sign immediately after the toll booth at the entrance to Santa Elena reads "Welcome to Monteverde."

The fame of the preserve has spawned an ever-increasing influx of tourists. Dozens of cabinas and lodges cater to visitors. Community members are divided about the issue of tourism growth, and there is vociferous opposition to plans to pave the road from the Pan-American Highway.

Cheese Factory
La Lechería (tel. 506/645-5436, 7:30 A.M.–5 P.M.

To Tilaran

To Santa Elena Cloud
Forest Reserve, Selvatura, Skytrek,
Skywalk, and Aventura Canopy Tour

UNICORNO DISCO

MONTEVERDE CLOUD
FOREST LODGE/
CANOPY TOUR

BULLRING

CLOUD FOREST
SCHOOL FOUNDATION

SEE DETAIL

SANTA
ELENA

RESTAURANTE
SAPO DORADO

CLARO DE
LUNA

MEDICAL CENTER/
POST OFFICE

LAUNDRY LA AMISTAD
MONTEVERDE ORCHID GARDEN
JOHNNY'S PIZZERIA

HOTEL/RESTAURANTE
EL ATARDECER

SUPER CERRO PLANO

CABINAS SOL Y LUNA

RANARIO

HOTEL
POCO A
POCO

HISTORIAS INTERNET CAFÉ/
GREEN TRAILS

CABINAS/RESTAURANT
LAS PALMERAS

HOTEL HELICONIA

EL RODEO STABLES

MONTEVERDE LODGE

BULLRING

FLOR DE VIDA

CERRO PLANO

TOLL BOOTH

HOTEL/RESTAURANTE
DE LUCÍA INN

RESTAURANTE
EL DORADO

STABLES

BAR ORQUIDEAS

AERIAL
ADVENTURES

HOTEL EL
ESTABLO

SKYWALK/SKY
TREK OFFICE

CENTRO
PANAMERICANO
DE IDIOMAS

NIDIA LODGE

PENSIÓN MANAKIN

CABAÑAS
LOS PINOS

HOTEL DE MONTAÑA
MONTEVERDE

ECOLOFICAL FARM
WILDLIFE REFUGE

MONTEVERDE
CONSERVATION
LEAGUE/VISITORS CENTER

HOTEL BELLBIRD INN

MONTEVERDE NATURE CENTER
AND BUTTERFLY GARDENS

GALERÍA
EXTASIS

Quebrada Sucia

LA ESTRELLA
STABLE

HOTEL EL BOSQUE/
RESTAURANTE Y PIZZERÍA TRAMONTI

LOS
LLANOS

Quebrada Maquina

CAFÉ MONTEVERDE/SUPERMARKET
CASEM GALLERY

BAJO DEL TIGRE
TRAIL

To Lagarto and
Pan-American Hwy.

0   200 yds

0   200 m

Quebrada Cuecha

To San Luis

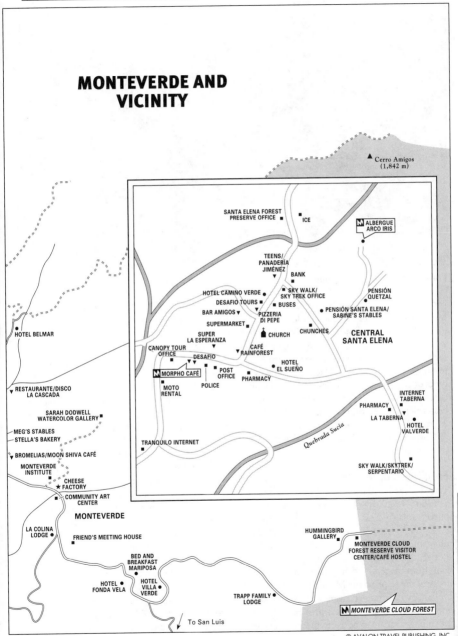

MONTEVERDE AND VICINITY

▲ Cerro Amigos (1,842 m)

SANTA ELENA FOREST PRESERVE OFFICE
ICE
ALBERGUE ARCO IRIS

TEENS/ PANADERIA JIMÉNEZ
BANK
HOTEL CAMINO VERDE
SKY WALK/ SKY TREK OFFICE
PENSIÓN QUETZAL
DESAFIO TOURS
BUSES
BAR AMIGOS
PIZZERIA DI PEPE
PENSIÓN SANTA ELENA/ SABINE'S STABLES
SUPERMARKET
SUPER LA ESPERANZA
CHURCH
CHUNCHES
CENTRAL SANTA ELENA

CANOPY TOUR OFFICE
CAFÉ RAINFOREST
DESAFIO
HOTEL EL SUEÑO
MORPHO CAFÉ
POST OFFICE
PHARMACY
MOTO RENTAL
POLICE

INTERNET TABERNA
PHARMACY
LA TABERNA
HOTEL VALVERDE

HOTEL BELMAR

RESTAURANTE/DISCO LA CASCADA

SARAH DODWELL WATERCOLOR GALLERY

MEG'S STABLES
STELLA'S BAKERY

BROMELIAS/MOON SHIVA CAFÉ
MONTEVERDE INSTITUTE
CHEESE FACTORY
COMMUNITY ART CENTER

MONTEVERDE

TRANQUILO INTERNET

Quebrada Sucia

SKY WALK/SKYTREK/ SERPENTARIO

LA COLINA LODGE
FRIEND'S MEETING HOUSE

HUMMINGBIRD GALLERY
MONTEVERDE CLOUD FOREST RESERVE VISITOR CENTER/CAFÉ HOSTEL

BED AND BREAKFAST MARIPOSA

HOTEL FONDA VELA
HOTEL VILLA VERDE

TRAPP FAMILY LODGE

MONTEVERDE CLOUD FOREST

To San Luis

Guanacaste

© AVALON TRAVEL PUBLISHING, INC.

Cowboys watch a soccer game in Santa Elena.

Mon.–Sat., 7:30 A.M.–12:30 P.M. Sunday), in Monteverde, is famous throughout Costa Rica for its quality cheeses. Production began in 1953 when the original Quaker settlers bought 50 Jersey cattle and began producing pasteurized Monteverde Gouda cheese. The factory produces 14 types of cheese—from parmesan and Emmantel to Danish-style dambo and Monte Rico, the best-seller. Guided tours are offered (9 A.M. and 2 P.M., $8 pp, $5 students).

Costa Rica Study Tours (tel. 506/645-5436) offers tours.

Frog Pond of Monteverde

The impressive Ranario de Monteverde (tel. 506/645-6320, fax 506/645-6318, ranariomv@racsa.co.cr, www.monteverdetours.com, 9 A.M.–8:30 P.M., $8 admission adults, $5 children/students), 300 meters north of Monteverde Lodge, displays 20 species of frogs and amphibians, from the red-eyed-tree frog and transparent frogs to the elephantine Marine toad, all housed in large, well-arranged display cases. It also has salamanders, a few snakes, plus termites and other bugs that are to be fed to the frogs. Evening is best, when the frogs become more active.

Monteverde Butterfly Gardens

Founded by North American biologist Jim Wolfe and his wife, Marta Salazar, the educational Jardín de las Mariposas (Apdo. 40, Sante Elena de Monteverde, tel. 506/777-0973, fax 506/645-5512, info@butterflygardens.co.cr, www .butterflygardens.co.cr, 9:30 A.M.–4 P.M., $15 admission adults, $8 children/students, including one-hour guided tour) features a nature center and three distinct habitats: a 450-square-meter netted butterfly flyway and two greenhouses (one representing lowland forest habitat, the second set up as a mid-elevation forest understory, darker and more moist than the first). Together, they are filled with native plant species and hundreds of tropical butterflies representing more than 40 species (the Monteverde region has some 550 species).

Guided tours begin in the visitors center, where scores of butterflies and other bugs are mounted for view and rhinoceros beetles, stick insects, and tarantulas and the wasps that prey on them crawl around inside display cases. There's a library and a computer station with butterfly interactive software, plus an auditorium where videos are shown throughout the day.

© CHRISTOPHER P. BAKER

Guanacaste

COSTA RICA'S QUAKER VILLAGE

Monteverde was founded in 1951 by a group of 44 North American Quakers—most from Fairhope, Alabama—who as a matter of conscience had refused to register for the draft. Led by John Campbell and Wilford "Wolf" Guindon, they chose Costa Rica for a new home because it had done away with its army. With the help of their Costa Rican neighbors, the Quakers began developing the community that exists today. They built roads and cleared much of the virgin forest for dairy farming. They decided to make cheese because it was the only product that could be stored and moved to market (without spoiling) along a muddy oxcart trail. Cheese is still a mainstay of the local economy, and the Quaker organization is still active in Monteverde (it meets every Wednesday morning at the Friends' Meeting House; visitors are welcome).

The area had been heavily deforested when Guindon and company arrived. Monteverde's founders, however, were environmentally conscious and set aside a heavily timbered region near the headwaters of the Río Guacimal to be held undisturbed and in common to safeguard the water source for their small hydroelectric plant. The area attracted scientists, especially after a small brilliantly colored frog—the golden toad—was discovered in 1964. In 1972, under threat of homesteading in the surrounding cloud forest, visiting scientists George and Harriet Powell joined forces with longtime resident Wilford Guindon and, overcoming local resistance, established a 328-hectare wildlife sanctuary. In 1975, the 554-hectare community watershed reserve was annexed with the aid of a $40,000 grant from the World Wildlife Fund. Together they formed the initial core of the Monteverde Cloud Forest Biological Reserve.

Don't expect to find the Quakers walking down the road dressed like the chap off the oatmeal box. *Cuaquerismo* (Quakerism) in Monteverde is a low-key affair.

The unique highlight is the three-camera "bug cam" that shows macro-detail, real-time insect life, including inside the leaf-cutter ant nest.

Volunteers are sought for two-month-long assignments as docents.

Mid-morning is the best time to visit, when the butterflies become active (and most tourists are in the reserve).

Monteverde Orchid Garden

It took five years of arduous work to collate this collection, but now you can admire the results of the Monteverde Orchid Investigation Project, an ongoing effort to document and research local orchids. Short paths wind through the compact Orquídeas de Monteverde, (tel. 506/645-5510, 8 A.M.–5 P.M., $5 admission), displaying almost 500 species native to the region and arranged in 22 groups ("sub-tribes"), each marked with an educational placard. Miniatures are preponderant, including the world's smallest flower, *Platystele jungermanniodes,* about the size of a pinhead

(fortunately, you are handed a magnifying glass upon arrival).

Private Reserves

The private 30-hectare **Bajo del Tigre** (Jaguar Canyon, 7:30 A.M.–5:30 P.M., $5 admission), contiguous with the Monteverde Cloud Forest Biological Reserve and administered by the Monteverde Conservation League (see *Information,* below), is at a lower elevation than the Cloud Forest Preserve and thus offers a different variety of plant and animal life. Quetzals are more easily seen here, for example, than higher up in the wetter, mistier cloud forest. The same is true for the three-wattled bellbird and long-tailed manikin. Access is off the main road, just above the CASEM Gallery. Facilities include a Children's Nature Center, a self-guided interpretative trail, an arboretum, and a visitor's center and library. Guided tours are offered Mon.–Wed. at 7:30 A.M. and 1 P.M., plus guided night tours Thurs.–Sun. at 7 P.M.

Ecological Farm Wildlife Refuge (Finca Ecológico; Apdo. 92-5655, Monteverde, tel. 506/645-5554, fax 506/645-5363, 7 A.M.–5 P.M., $7 admission adults, $5 students), on the same road as the Butterfly Garden, is at a lower elevation than the Monteverde Cloud Forest Biological Reserve. It receives less rain and clouds. The vegetation is also less dense and you have an excellent chance of seeing coatimundis, sloths, agoutis, porcupines, and white-faced monkeys, as well as butterflies and birds. Four signed trails lead through the 17-hectare property. It offers a twilight tour at 5:30 P.M. ($14 pp).

Selvatura

The new Selvatura (tel. 506/645-5929, info@selvatura.com, www.selvatura.com), two km north of Sky Walk, offers canopy exploration along treetop walkways with 800 meters of bridges ($15 adults, $12 students, $10 children), and/or via a 20-platform zipline canopy tour ($35 adults, $30 students, $25 children). It also has a hummingbird garden ($3), a vast domed butterfly garden ($10), and a climbing wall. Guided nature hikes are offered ($35).

The unique, not-to-be-missed highlight is the **Jewels of the Rainforest Bio-Art Exhibition,** featuring the stupendous Whitten insect collection. It was in preparation at last visit. Exhibits will include a "Biodiversity Bank" with dozens of spectacular and informative displays. Of course, there'll be a wall of Neotropical Butterflies, and a World of Beetles, from Tutankhamen scarabs to the giants of the beetle word. A Silk Room will display elegant moths. The Victorian Room will feature decorative and patterned exhibits, and the Jewel Room will be all black and will feature gold and silver beetles. Other special themes include paleontology and medical entomology; a *Phasmid* (stick insects and family) room; a room dedicated to the indigenous peoples and their decorative use of insects; and Grandpa's marine collection, displaying crabs, lobsters, and other exhibits collated by Richard's dad, Horace Whitten. It will have a 3,000-square-foot auditorium. And a laboratory will have real-time video permitting you to watch Dr. Whitten and Margaret at work.

"Stunning, educational, and fun!" says Smithsonian entomologist David Roubik.

Serpentario

This den of snakes (tel. 506/645-6002, www.snaketour.com, 9 A.M.–8 P.M., $7 admission, including guide.), on the eastern fringe of Santa Elena village, lets you get up close and personal with a repertoire of coiled constrictors and venomous vipers and kin, as well as their prey: frogs, chameleons, and the like. The dreaded fer-de-lance is here, along with 25 or so other species separated from you by thick panes of glass. Labels are in Spanish only.

Entertainment and Events

The **Monteverde Music Festival** is hosted each January through April by the Monteverde Institute (P.O. Box 69-5655 Monteverde, tel. 506/645-5053 or 506/645-5219, grusso@mvinstitute.org, www.mvinstitute.org/music, 5 P.M. Thurs.–Sat., $9 tickets) and features leading exponents of classical, jazz, and Latin forms. A shuttle bus departs Santa Elena at about 4 P.M. and runs between the hotels. Dress warmly and bring a flashlight.

El Sol Retreat & Spa (tel. 506/645-5838, fax 506/645-5042) hosts more intimate performances by Music Festival artists by reservation only ($25), including glass of wine and a sauna.

A **slide show,** *Natural History of Cloud Forest Animals,* is offered daily at 11 A.M. at the Hummingbird Gallery ($3; reservations required: tel. 506/645-5122); groups of four people or more can arrange an afternoon viewing. A **multimedia show**—*Sounds and Scenes of the Cloud Forest*—is also offered nightly at 6:15 P.M. at the Monteverde Lodge ($5). And the Hotel Belmar has a slide show Sat.–Thurs. at 8 P.M. ($5).

Moon Shiva Café (tel. 506/645-6270), at Bromelias art gallery, in Monteverde, has live music and cultural events, such as cooking lessons and guitar lessons. Its "New Moon" parties feature fire dancing!

For a taste of local color, wet your whistle at **Bar Amigos,** in Santa Elena, and **Unicorno Disco,** facing the soccer field north of the village. Both have pool tables.

JEWELS OF THE RAINFOREST

The Whitten Entomological Collection (tel. 506/645-5929 or 506/661-8254, insect@racsa.co.cr, www.rainforestjewels.co.cr) of more than 50,000 insects—truly "Jewels of the Rainforest"—from around the world displays a small fraction of Richard Whitten's more than 50 years of collecting: the largest collection of big, bizarre, and beautiful butterflies, beetles, and other bugs in the world. It surely is the most colorful—a veritable calliope of shimmering greens, neon blues, startling reds, silvers, and golds. Whitten began collecting "bugs" at a tender age; today his 1,900 boxes include more than one million specimens, much of them collected in Costa Rica.

The major part of the permanent collection is housed in the "Jewels of the Rainforest Exhibit," at Selvatura, in Monteverde. Exhibits at other locations are planned.

The stunning, dynamic displays combine art, science, music, and video to entertain and educate about insect mimicry, protective coloration and other camouflage, prey-predator relationships, and more. The creativity is sheer choreography. Exhibits glitter against a background of opera and classical music, the climactic highs of the arias and ponderous lows of the cellos seemingly rising and falling to the drama of the displays, many of them re-creations of natural habitats under domed glass, the brilliant conception of Richard's wife, Margaret. Part of the exhibit is dedicated to a collection of every species in the country. Other exhibits include shimmering beetles displayed against black velvet, like opal jewelry, and boxes of bugs majestically turned into caskets of gems. Some beetles are bigger than your fist; some moths outsize a salad plate. An unexpected treat may be an impromptu performance by Whitten (a former professional concert performer) displaying his talents on the glockenspiel, accordion, piano, or organ.

© CHRISTOPHER P. BAKER

Margaret and Richard Whitten with Jewels of the Rainforest exhibits

The happening dance spot at last visit was **Taberna** (tel. 506/645-5883), on the east side of Santa Elena, with a nightly disco (free entry); Mondays, Tuesdays, and Thursdays are the best nights. **La Cascada** (tel. 506/645-5186), in Cerro Plano, is favored for Fri.–Sat. nights.

Sports and Recreation
The **Cámara de Empresarios Turísticas y Afinas de Monteverde** (CETAM) and **Asociación de Tour Operadores de Monteverde** are umbrella groups of tour operators and related businesses that oversee tourist development and guard against the problem of "freelancers" and tour

agencies that manipulate information so that they can maximize their commissions. Most tour agencies sell into the same programs.

An intriguing way to explore the Santa Elena Cloud Forest Reserve (see *Arenal-Monteverde Protection Zone,* below) is by ascending into the forest canopy on a **Sky Walk** (Apdo. 57-5655, Monteverde, tel. 506/645-5238, fax 506/645-5796, info@skywalk.co.cr, www.skywalk.co.cr), which offers a monkey's-eye view of things. You walk along five suspension bridges and platforms and 1,000 meters of pathways permitting viewing from ground level to the treetops, where you are right in there with the epiphytes. Open

Guanacaste

7 A.M.–4 P.M. daily. The two-hour walk costs $15 ($25 with guide), students $12 ($22 with guide), $6 children under 12, including boots and poncho; it's $10 extra for a guided tour offered 8 A.M. and 1:30 P.M. A jeep-taxi leaves the bank in Santa Elena village for Sky Walk at 7:15 A.M., 9 A.M., 11:15 A.M., and 1:15 P.M. ($1 pp). The office is open 6 A.M.–9 P.M. daily.

The same company offers a two-hour **Sky Trek** (fax 506/645-5796, Info@skytrek.com, www .skytrek.com) for the more adventurous. You'll whiz through the canopy in a harness attached to a zipline that runs between three treetop canopies, spanning two kilometers! Don't expect to see much; you're too busy hanging on as you speed down the lines. Tours are offered at 7:30 A.M., 9:30 A.M., 10:30 A.M., 11:30 A.M., 1:30 P.M., 2 P.M., 2:30 P.M., and 3 P.M. ($40 adults, $32 students).

The **Aventura Canopy Tour** (tel. 506/645-6959, fax 506/645-6901, mauaventura@hotmail.com, 6 A.M.–6 P.M.), on the road to the Sky Walk, has 16 zipline cables plus rappeling.

A less adrenaline-charged option is **Aerial Adventures** (tel. 506/645-5960, wmvargas@racsa .co.cr), in Cerro Plano, an elevated electrically propelled tramway that whisks you through the treetops in open carriages that operate like ski-lift chairs. The metal rails extend for 1.5 km through forest and pasture. The ride takes about 75 minutes ($15). Night tours are also offered.

The following have stables and rent horses (usually about $7–10 per hour) and offer guided tours: **Meg's Stables** (tel. 506/645-5052); **La Estrella** (tel. 506/645-5075); **Sabine's Smiling Horses** (tel. 506/645-5051, www.horseback-riding-tour.com); and **Terra Viva** (tel. 506/645-5553). **Pensión Santa Elena** offers a six-hour horseback tour to the San Luís waterfalls ($35), including two hours hiking, and **Desafio** (tel. 506/645-5874, fax 506/645-5904, www.monteverdetours.com) is among the companies offering horseback trips to La Fortuna ($65); see sidebar, *Between Monteverde and La Fortuna,* regarding the "mirador trail."

The **Las Delicias Campesinas** (tel. 506/645-7032) rents ATVs for $30 first hour, $25 each additional hour.

For tours of the local community, try **Costa Rica Study Tours** (tel. 506/645-5436, crstudy @racsa.co.cr, www.crstudytours.com), which offers tours of the Finca Cielo Verde) coffee farm and *beneficio* (processing factory) at 8 A.M. and 1 P.M.; $15 including transport.

Shopping

The **Artisans' Cooperative of Santa Elena and Monteverde** (CASEM, tel. 506/645-5190, fax 506/645-5898, casemcr@yahoo.com, 8 A.M.– 5 P.M. Mon.–Sat.) features the handmade wares of 140 local artisans. Sales directly benefit the artists. Next door is the coffee roaster of **Café Monteverde** (tel. 506/645-5006, fax 506/645-5623, 7:30 A.M.–6 P.M. Mon.–Sat., 9 A.M.–4 P.M. Sunday) where you can taste and buy locally produced coffee ($2 per half-pound).

Galería Extasis (tel./fax 506/645-5548, www.galeriaxtasis.com, 9 A.M.–6 P.M.) sells exquisite paintings, hardwood sculptures, jewelry, bowls, and other creative art by gifted artist Marco Tulio Brenes.

A path just west of La Lechería leads 400 meters uphill to the **Sarah Dodwell Watercolor Gallery** (tel. 506/645-5047), where the local artist displays her distinctive watercolors, which decorate the walls of many local hotels.

Nearby, **Bromelia's** (tel. 506/645-6272, wainmayn@racsa.co.cr) is a delightful space selling books and quality batiks, jewelry, and carvings.

The **Hummingbird Gallery** (tel. 506/645-5030), 100 meters below the entrance to the Monteverde Cloud Forest Biological Reserve, is well stocked with souvenirs. Also check out the **Monteverde Studios of the Arts** and the **Centro Cerámica,** both selling works by local artists.

In Santa Elena, **Chunches** (tel./fax 506/645-5147, standley@racsa.co.cr, 8 A.M.–6 P.M.) sells U.S. and English magazines and newspapers, plus a large selection of books—especially on natural history—in English and Spanish, as wells as maps and laminated *Costa Rican Field Guides.*

For unique clothing, try **Sumag Artesanía,** also selling handmade rugs.

Accommodations

Monteverde is a popular destination, and the

choice is wide and varied. Accommodations, however, may be difficult to obtain in dry season, when tour companies block space. Book well ahead if possible, especially for Christmas and Easter. Unless otherwise noted, mail all correspondence to the generic Monteverde postal box number (P.O. Box 10165-1000, San José).

There are many more accommodations to choose from than presented here.

Camping: You can camp at **Albergue Arco Iris** ($3 pp) in Santa Elena. The campers' bathroom is magnificent, stone inlaid with blue mosaic tile. In Cerro Plano, **Camping Charlie,** next to La Cascada restaurant, charges $3 for riverside camping. **Hotel Fonda Vela** has a shady camping area, as does **Cabinas La Colina.**

Under $25 Santa Elena: A popular offering among budget travelers is the **Pensión Santa Elena** (tel. 506/645-5051, fax 506/645-6060, info@monteverdeinfo.com, www.monteverde-info.com, $5 pp dorm with shared bathroom, $7 single room with shared bath, $15 d with private bath, $25 d suite), owned by a super-friendly French Canadian. It has 20 clean though basic rooms of varying sizes (some dark), including two "honeymoon suites." Some have private baths, others share, with separate baths for men and women, but hot water is never guaranteed. Very colorful decor. The hotel provides free use of kitchen services, plus laundry service ($2), Internet access, and travel information. It also offers horseback riding.

Hotel Camino Verde (tel. 506/645-6296, fax 506/645-5916, www.monteverdeinfocenter.com, $5 pp shared bath, $8–10 pp private bath), across the street, has 22 clean but dark (many are windowless) and basically furnished rooms with hot water. Some share bathrooms. It has laundry service and Internet. Meals are provided ($3 breakfast, $4 dinner), but guests can use the kitchen.

Under $25 Cerro Plano/Monteverde: The **Pensión Manakin** (tel. 506/645-5080, manakin@racsa.co.cr, $10 pp shared bath, $15 pp rooms with double bed and bunk plus private bath), is a basic bed-and-breakfast with nine rooms with bunk beds and hot water. It also has three cabins with private bath for six people; five

more cabins were to be added. Breakfast is served in the stone-and-timber lounge. Land Rover tours are offered for groups, and it offers Internet access plus a laundry.

The family-run **Hotel Bellbird Inn** (tel./fax 506/645-5026 or 506/645-5518, $8 pp with shared bath; $10 pp with private bath) primarily acts as a hotel for students of the Monteverde Institute, but takes guests when not full. This small wooden alpine lodge has nine minimally furnished rooms with hot water (some with clean, tiled shared bathrooms; three have private baths). Some have bunks; others have a single and double bed. There's a simple restaurant. Groups of students are charged $23 pp including three meals.

$25–50 Santa Elena: The **Hotel El Sueño** (tel. 506/645-5021 or 506/645-6695, $15 s, $25 d) has 18 double rooms with private baths with hot water. Some are dark and uninviting and have cold water only; newer, all-wood rooms are spacious and well-lit, with clean modern bathrooms. There's a TV lounge, small restaurant, and Internet service. Rates include breakfast.

The German-run **Sunset Hotel** (tel. 506/645-5048, fax 506/645-5228, $20 s, $28 d low season; $25 s, $36 d high season), one km northeast of Santa Elena, has 10 attractive, brightly lit, wood-trimmed rooms with private baths with hot water. You have panoramic views from your veranda and the restaurant. The owner is friendly. Rates include tax and breakfast.

Hotel Poco a Poco (tel. 506/645-6000, fax 506/645-6264, pocoapoco@racsa.co.cr, $30 s, $40 d), about 500 meters outside the village center, has five spacious and attractive *cabinas* of natural stone and timber, lofty ceilings, with tile floors, double beds, local TV, and clean modern bathrooms with hot water, but neither fans nor a/c. Two cabins and a two-story unit with four rooms were to be added. It has a restaurant.

Cabinas Sol y Luna (tel./fax 506/645-5629, $10 pp low season, $15 s, $26 d high season), on the west side of Santa Elena, has 10 wooden cabins with tile floors, patios, and clean, modern private bath and hot water. One larger, carpeted unit is a "honeymoon" suite with sofa and bright fabrics.

Nearby, the **Hotel Atardecer** (tel. 506/645-5685, fax 506/645-5462, cjimenez5239@hotmail.com, $10 pp shared bath, $15 pp private bath) is a two-story wooden structure with 11 well-lit, carpeted rooms in differing configurations, all with private bathrooms with hot water in spacious walk-in showers. It has a clean, pleasant restaurant, plus laundry. Rates include tax.

One of the more exciting hotels is **Hotel Claro de Luna** (tel./fax 506/645-5269, reservations@hotelclarodeluna.com, www.hotelclarodeluna.com, $41 s, $48 d standard, $45 s, $53 d deluxe), to the southwest of Santa Elena, a uniquely attractive place with romantic appeal. It resembles a Swiss cottage with cantilevered eaves and gingerbread trim. Its nine rooms draw heaps of light and have sponge-washed walls, polished hardwood floors and ceilings, intriguing contemporary touches, and beautiful bathrooms with colonial tile. Two rooms, plus a pool and a Jacuzzi, were to be added. Breakfast is served in a gracious dining room, with a broad terrace overlooking the landscaped garden.

$25–50 Cerro Plano/Monteverde: The **La Colina Lodge** (P.O. Box 24, Monteverde, tel. 506/645-5009, fax 506/645-5580, lacolina@hotmail.com, www.lacolina.com; in the U.S., tel. 970/352-4767; $15 s, $22 d shared bath, $22/29 private bath low season; $25/35 shared bath, $30/45 private bath high season) has three rooms with private baths (one with double bed, one with two bunks, a third with double and bunk), plus nine rooms with shared bath with hot water. The rooms boast handcrafted furnishings and Guatemalan spreads. Some rooms are dark. There's a laundry, a TV room, book exchange, and a charming simple alpine restaurant. It also has a carriage house for $35 s/d low season, $50 high season.

The family-run **Bed and Breakfast Mariposa** (Apdo. 72-5655 Monteverde, tel. 506/645-5013, vmfamilia@costarricense.cr, $25 s, $35 d small, $30/40 large), only 1.5 km below the reserve, has three simple cabins, each with a double and a single bed and a private bath with hot water. Three newer, larger cabins have verandas, plus there's a *casa* with kitchen, sleeping nine people. Rates include breakfast.

Cabañas Los Pinos (Apdo. 70, San José, tel. 506/645-5252, fax 506/645-5005, jovino @lospino.net, www.lospinos.net, $40 s/d one-bedroom, $45 s/d two-bedroom, $50 three-bedroom low season; $75 two-room, $85 three-bedroom high season), has 12 *cabinas* in an alpine setting with lots of cedars. Four are larger units with a double and sofabed. All but one unit has a kitchenette and a private bath with hot water. Varying sizes sleep up to six people. Rates include tax.

Hotel Villa Verde (Apdo. 16 C.P., Monteverde 5655, tel. 506/645-5025, fax 506/645-5115, estefany@racsa.co.cr, $49 s, $65 d rooms, $80 s/d villas), has 20 compact, rustic *cabinas,* plus new apartment rooms with hardwood floors, roomy kitchenettes, a small lounge with fireplace, and large bedrooms, each with four beds (one double, three singles). Villa suites have fireplaces and tubs. Voluminous tiled bathrooms have hot water. The stone-and-timber lodge and restaurant offer a homey atmosphere. Two new blocks feature 18 rooms, plus an atrium restaurant and bar. And separate homes sleep up to seven people. It has a game room and offers horseback tours. Rates include breakfast.

$50–100 Santa Elena: I adore **M El Sol Retreat & Spa** (tel. 506/645-5838, fax 506/645-5042, imoinoc@racsa.co.cr, www.elsolnuestro.com, $60 s/d, or $80 s/d for larger cabin), five km before you arrive at Santa Elena. This unique and calming holistic retreat, run by a delightful and erudite German-Spanish couple, Elizabeth and Ignacio, has a forest setting that enjoys a warmer climate than the Monteverde area uphill. Its two charming Tom Sawyer–style log cabins boast awesome views down the valley toward the plains of Guanacaste. Each features bright fabrics and tub-shower, and comes equipped with king-size bed, kitchenette with microwave, toaster, and fridge, plus roughhewn furniture and hammocks on decks. A third, larger cabin with parquet floors hangs on the hill and has a mezzanine bedroom and a lounge with deep-cushion sofabed. A Finnish sauna sits beside a fantastic landscaped springwater horizon swimming pool edged by a wooden sundeck. Wholesome homemade health meals (cooked on an outdoor wood-fired stove) are served in an exquisite wooden home; breakfasts are delivered to your cabins. Musicians from the Music Festival often perform here for guests. Elizabeth gives "energy" treatments and offers bread-making classes; Ignacio gives cooking classes. Guided horseback rides are offered ($10). Trails lead into the forest full of monkeys. Parrots and toucans abound.

In Santa Elena proper, the splendid, German-owned **N Albergue Arco Iris** (Apdo. 003-5655, Santa Elena de Monteverde, tel. 506/645-5067, fax 506/645-5022, arcoiris@racsa.co.cr, www.arcoirislodge.com, $18 s, $27 d with bunks, $40 s, $45 d standard low season; $18 s, $30 d with bunks, $45 s, $50 d standard high season) is run with Teutonic efficiency. It has 12 handsome stone-and-hardwood *cabinas* amid a spacious garden with deck chairs on a hillside backed by a two-hectare forest reserve. They feature terracotta tile floors and orthopedic mattresses with Guatemalan spreads. All have clean, private baths and hot water. And some have bunks; one is family-sized with two bedrooms. The airy restaurant offers breakfast only. Horses can be rented ($25, two hours for a guided tour), and there's a library, laundry, and safety-deposit box. The owner speaks English, Dutch, German, Italian, and Spanish.

The recently upgraded **Monteverde Cloud Forest Lodge** (P.O. Box 531-1000 San José, tel. 506/645-5058, fax 506/645-5168, info@cloudforestlodge.com, www.cloudforestlodge.com, $60 s, $70 d), also northeast of Santa Elena, earns raves from readers. It is surrounded by gardens set on a 25-hectare private forest reserve. The 18 wood-and-stone *cabinas* are clean and spacious, with large clerestory windows, peaked ceilings, and large bathrooms. There's a large-screen TV and VCR. It has lawns, a duck pond, and five km of trails into the nearby forests. There are views of Nicoya from the deck. You can climb the huge figs out back, and a daunting circular staircase leads to the entrance of the Sky Walk, at Santa Elena Cloud Forest Reserve; the Canopy Tour runs through the reserve. No smokers.

Vista Verde Lodge (tel. 506/380-1517, vistaverde@racsa.co.cr, www.vistaverdelodge.com, $55 s, $65 d), four km north of the Sky Walk, in the community of San Gerardo, on a steep and eroded dirt road that leads off the road to the Santa Elena Reserve, offers fabulous views of Arenal Volcano and Lake Arenal enjoyed through picture windows in the 10 spacious all-wood rooms with private bathrooms and hot water. It has a restaurant, and hikes and horseback rides are offered. It gets cool and cloudy up here. Rates include breakfast.

One km further, and also offering fantastic views towards Arenal Volcano, is **Mirador Lodge San Gerardo** (P.O. Box 19-5655, tel. 506/645-5087, fax 506/645-5354, miradorq@racsa.co.cr, www.monteverdesangerardolodge.com, $20 pp in dorms, $35 s, $45 d in cabins), a rustic no-frills lodge with seven rooms with wood-burning stoves, and basic but clean bathrooms with hot water. Two rooms are bunk-style with shared baths. Home-cooked meals are provided, as are horseback rides to Lake Arenal ($65 four hours).

$50–100 Cerro Plano/Monteverde: The **Hotel Finca Valverde** (Apdo. 2-5655, Monteverde, tel. 506/645-5157, fax 506/645-5216, info@monteverde.co.cr, $35 s, $58 d low season; $45 s, $64 d high season), amid a setting of forest and pasture on the east side of Santa Elena, and reached by a suspension bridge, has 10 rooms, plus 10 cozy if somewhat spartan double-unit wooden cabins with single beds in lofts and spacious bathrooms with bathtubs marvelous for soaking after a crisp hike. Its atmospheric alpine-style restaurant has plate-glass windows, and you can rent horses ($7 per hour). Rates include breakfast and tax.

Nearby, I like the stone-and-timber **Nidia Lodge** (P.O. Box 99-5655 Monteverde, tel. 506/645-6082, fax 506/645-6105, www.flormonteverde.com, $35 s, $50 d standard, $45 s, $60 d "semi-suite"), with a two-story unit with four standards with tile floors, and private bathrooms with hot water. Upstairs "semi-suites" have balconies, refrigerators, and tub showers. It has a charmingly rustic restaurant serving local fare and seafood.

Anyone familiar with the old **El Establo Hotel, Restaurant & Stable** (Apdo. 549-2050 San Pedro, tel. 506/645-5033 or 506/645-5110, fax 506/645-5041, establo@racsa.co.cr,

N
Guanacaste

www.hotelelestablo.com, $57 s, $71 standard, $92 s, $128 d junior suite; $121 s, $171 d suite) may be surprised by the recent upgrade, now offering rooms in four types including suites. The original two-story wood-and-stone structure contains 20 carpeted standard rooms with cinderblock walls; those on the ground floor open onto a wood-floored gallery lounge with deep-cushioned sofas and an open fireplace. Each room has a double and a single bed, plus a pleasing bathroom with hot water, and heaps of light from the wraparound windows. A newer block on the hillside has a striking contemporary aesthetic and offers 18 junior suites with polished stone floors and exotic tiles, plus 12 upper-story, carpeted suites with king-size beds in lofts (plus double beds downstairs), oversize rattan furniture, and rockers on balconies. There's a TV lounge, and El Establo has its own horse stable, plus a swimming pool and trails.

Sapo Dorado (Apdo. 9, Monteverde 5655, tel. 506/645-5010 or 800/788-7857, fax 506/645-5180, elsapo@racsa.co.cr, www.sapodorado.com, $52 s, $63 d "classic," $63/75 "sunset" low season; $70/80 "classic," $80/90 "sunset" high season), run by descendants of the original Quakers, has 30 large rooms in 10 handsome stone-and-timber duplex cabins spread apart on the hillside, with great views. There are two types—"classic suite" (older, with fireplaces) and "sunset suite"—each with private bath, two queen beds, orthopedic mattresses, fireplace, and private balcony. Honeymooners should note that hotel rules prohibit the "moving of furniture or gymnastics after 9 P.M." Chalets are spread through landscaped, hilly grounds. The acclaimed restaurant with open-air terrace and views out across the gulf is famous for its natural-food meals. Trails lead through pastures and forest. It offers professional massage.

Hotel Heliconia (Apdo. 10921-1000 San José, tel. 506/645-5109, fax 506/645-5007, roxanab@heliconia.com, www.hotelheliconia.com, $74 s, $78 d), in landscaped grounds at the foot of the private, 284-hectare Heliconia Cloud Forest Reserve, is an appealing Swiss-style chalet of lacquered cedar with lots of light. Home-style comforts include deep-cushioned sofas in the lobby, hand-painted curtains, and orthopedic mattresses in the 33 bedrooms (21 standards, 10 junior suites, two family suites), which have rocking chairs on the veranda. Older units are simply furnished. Newer spa cabins in a two-story stone-and-hardwood structure offer a little more sophistication. Family suites are carpeted and have two king beds (one in a loft), solarium lounges (which get hot), and huge bathrooms. It has an elegant restaurant, horse rides, a Jacuzzi, and spa treatments.

Hotel de Montaña Monteverde (Apdo. 2070-1002 San José, tel. 506/645-5046, fax 506/645-5320, info@monteverdemountainhotel.com, www.monteverdemountainhotel.com, $58 s/d standard, $76 superior, $94 deluxe and honeymoon suite) is set in expansive grounds, which include a lake and 15-hectare private reserve. Spacious rooms—30 doubles and suites, each with private bath with hot water—have hardwood floors and verandas with rockers and are otherwise sparsely furnished. Rooms in the newer block are slightly more elegant. Suites get higher marks for their fireplaces and king-size beds; one has its own Jacuzzi. The hotel has a whirlpool and a sauna, plus a large restaurant, a bar, a lounge with TV, and veranda offering views over the gulf.

Hotel Belmar (Apdo. 17-5655, Monteverde, tel. 506/645-5201, fax 506/645-5135, belmar@centralamerica.com, www.hotelbelmar.com, $70 s, $80 d rooms; $60 s, $70 d chalet) is a beautiful, ivy-clad, Swiss-style hotel with two chalets featuring 28 clean, comfortable, recently remodeled rooms that are the prettiest in Monteverde, including charming older chalets. Four are family rooms. French doors in most rooms and lounges open onto balconies with grand views; a west-facing glass wall catches the sunset. Spacious, modestly elegant, wood-paneled rooms in a new addition offer large bathrooms. All have private bath with marble highlights, and hot water. The large restaurant serves hearty meals and also has views. The lounge in the older building is a quiet spot for reading and games and for slide shows on Fridays. A trail leads up to the mountain crest. Facilities include a Jacuzzi, volleyball court, pool table, kid's playground, art exhibitions, and Internet. The hotel offers tours, and will prepare box lunches for hikers. It has three feathers in the Certificate of Sustainable Tourism ratings. Rates include tax.

In similar vein, the alpine-style **Hotel Fonda Vela** (P.O. Box 70060-1000 San José, tel. 506/645-5125 or 506/257-1413, fax 506/645-5119 or 506/257-1416, info@fondavela.com, www.fondavela.com, $76 s, $85 d standard, $85 s, $94 d junior suites) has 20 standard rooms and 20 junior suites in nine buildings. Rich decor and abundant hardwoods add to the appeal. Some rooms have hardwood floors; others have flagstone floors. All are wheelchair accessible and have a choice of two queens or a king bed. Most have views over the Gulf of Nicoya. A glass-fronted restaurant with an open-air balcony overlooks forested grounds, through which a narrow trail leads to a Swiss-style chalet. There's also a bar and TV room, and a tiny gym.

The **Trapp Family Lodge** (P.O. Box 70-5655 Monteverde, tel. 506/645-5858, fax 506/645-5990, trappfam@racsa.co.cr, www.trappfam.com, $60 s, $70 d), enjoys the distinct advantage of being the hotel closest to the Monteverde Cloud Forest Biological Reserve, just one km away. It has 20 spacious albeit modestly furnished rooms in a two-story all-wood structure enjoying a beautiful forested locale. All have two double beds, venetian windows, wide balconies, and private bath with hot water. There's a large restaurant serving Italian meals, and a cozy TV lounge.

$100–150 Cerro Plano/Monteverde: The modern **M̄ Monteverde Lodge** (c/o Costa Rica Expeditions, P.O. Box 6941-1000, San José, tel. 506/257-0766, fax 506/257-1665, costaric @expeditions.co.cr, www.costaricaexpeditions .com, $83 s, $100 d low season, $96/115 high season) is easily the most outstanding hotel and also a good bargain. A cavernous entrance foyer leads up to a spacious and elegant open-plan dining room with a soaring beamed ceiling, and a cozy bar with leather chairs around an open hearth. Chessboards and backgammon are at hand. The bar looks down on a large Jacuzzi (open 24 hours) enclosed by a glass atrium. Wraparound windows offer wonderful views over the landscaped grounds and forested valley.

Rooms are spacious and elegant, with large windows, two double beds, and well-lit bathrooms stocked with fluffy towels. The lodge, set amid beautifully landscaped gardens, is operated by Costa Rica Expeditions and is popular with bird-watching and nature groups. Cuisine is superb. Rates include taxes.

Food

For breakfast, try **Chunches,** in Santa Elena, selling pastries, espressos, cappuccinos, teas, and juices. **Stella's Bakery** (tel. 506/645-5560 www.stellasbakery.com, 7 A.M.–5 P.M.), in Monteverde, sells granola with homemade yogurt ($2), pancakes, omelettes, plus homemade bread, cookies, granola, sticky buns, doughnuts, sandwiches, and killer milkshakes ($3).

The hip in-spot at last visit was **M̄ Morpho Café** (tel. 506/645-5607, 11 A.M.–10 P.M., $3–8), in Santa Elena. It serves coffees, ice creams, and *batidos* (milkshakes). It has tremendous decor, with roughhewn furniture, natural stone and sponge-washed walls, and cool music. The menu ranges from salads, sandwiches, killer burgers, pastas, and *casados* (set meals for $3), to sweet-and-sour pork chops and seabass Dijon.

For elegant dining, **Monteverde Lodge** (6–8:20 A.M., noon–2 P.M., and 6–8:30 A.M., breakfast $6.50, lunch and dinner $11) offers excellent, inexpensive cuisine to all-comers. A typical dinner might include cream of tomato soup, and seabass. It has a large wine list, starting at $12. The **M̄ Restaurante Sapo Dorado** (noon –3 P.M. and 5:30–9:30 P.M., $5 –16) is recommended for vegetarian dishes, including whole-grain pizza, banana bread, and tofu with vegetarian primavera; plus baked orange chicken with peppercorn, shrimp in sambuca mushroom sauce, and killer desserts, such as chocolate espresso mousse.

Restaurante Mediteraneo (6 A.M.–10 P.M., $4 –10), at Hotel Heliconia, is a modestly elegant option for such treats as Caesar salad, shrimp cocktail, vegetarian fusilli, and baked squid with shrimp.

For Tex-Mex, head to **Restaurante El Dorado** (tel. 506/645-7017, 10 A.M.–10 P.M., $5–10), modestly elegant and serving the usual

Mexican fare, including fajitas, and beef in jalapeño sauce.

Moon Shiva Café (tel. 506/645-6270, 10 A.M.–10 P.M.), at Bromelias art gallery in Monteverde, has a delightful ambiance, with world music. Its simple "international fusion" menu includes mixed salad, crepes, nachos, burgers, etc.

A reader reports that the **Pizzeria Di Pepe** (tel. 506/645-5153, 10 A.M.–11 P.M., $5–10), in Santa Elena, "has the *best vegetarian pizza* in all Costa Rica." **Restaurante y Pizzería Tramonti** (tel. 506/645-6190, 6–9 A.M., 11:30 A.M.–3 P.M., and 5:30–9:30 P.M., $7) offers good ambience along with carpaccio, lasagna, fried squid, pizzas, etc. **Johnny's Pizzería** (tel. 506/645-5066, 11:30 A.M.–9:30 P.M.) is classy, with a wide-ranging pizza menu ($3.50–10, small–large), plus pastas and daily specials such as smoked salmon and capers. **Restaurant Las Palmeras** (tel. 506/645-5450, 11 A.M.–9 P.M. daily) also has pizzas plus steaks and chicken dishes; its neighbor, the **Restaurant de Lucía** (tel. 506/645-5337, 11 A.M.–9 P.M.), is genuinely Italian, with cappuccinos, lasagnas, and vegetarian dishes.

Vegetarians are served by **Flor de Vida** (tel. 506/645-6081, 7 A.M.–10 P.M. Mon.–Sat., $1.50–3), a classy little place offering veggie burgers, veggie lasagne, veggie chili with salad, and the like.

Teens, in Santa Elena, is a clean, modern eatery and ice cream store above **Panadería Jiménez** (5 A.M.–6:30 P.M. Mon.–Sat., 5 A.M.–10:30 A.M. Sunday), which sells sandwiches, breads, and pastries. **Café Rainforest** (7 A.M.–7 P.M. Mon.–Sat., 8 A.M.–7 P.M. Sunday), in Santa Elena, is a nice place to relax over cappuccino, natural juices, or shakes. And **Café Monteverde** (tel. 506/645-5006, 7:30 A.M.–6 P.M. Mon.–Sat., 9 A.M.–4 P.M. Sunday) serves cappuccinos, espressos, etc.

For groceries, head to the well-stocked **Super La Esperanza** in Santa Elena, or the smaller **Super Cerro Plano,** one km east. You can buy baked goods at **Musmanni,** next to La Esperanza.

Educational Courses

The **Centro Panamericano de Idiomas** (P.O. Box 68, Monteverde, tel./fax 506/645-5448, info@cpi-edu.com, www.cpi-edu.com), offers Spanish-language courses at its impressive facility.

The **Monteverde Institute** (Apdo. 69-5655, Monteverde, tel. 506/645-5053, fax 506/645-5219, mvi@mvinstitute.org, www.mvinstitute.org) hosts one-week arts workshops at the Monteverde Studios of the Arts (June–Aug.), plus courses in biology, ecology, agriculture, and natural history.

Ritmo Latino Monteverde (tel. 506/645-5565) offers dance classes, from swing to salsa.

Volunteering

The **Cloud Forest School Foundation** (Centro de Educación Creativa, Apdo. 23-5655, Monteverde, tel. 506/645-5161, fax 506/645-5480, info@cloudforestschool.org, www.cloudforestschool.org) educates local children with an environmentally based bilingual curriculum. Volunteer teachers are needed, as are international couriers bringing school supplies; and donations for land purchase are welcomed.

Information

Desafio Tours (tel. 506/645-5874), opposite the bus stop in Santa Elena, and **Tour Information & Reservations** (tel. 506/645-7090), 300 meters east of Monteverde Lodge, book tours and offer tourist advice; as does **Green Trails** (tel. 506/645-6916, greentrailsgf@yahoo.com), in Cerro Plano (open 8 A.M.–6 P.M. Mon.–Fri., 8 A.M.–1 P.M. Saturday).

The **Monteverde Conservation League** (tel. 506/645-5003, fax 506/645-5104, acmmcl@racsa.co.cr, www.acmonteverde.com, 8 A.M.–5 P.M. Mon.–Fri., 8 A.M.–noon Saturday), opposite the Butterfly Garden, is a marvelous resource for information on ecological projects and the reserves.

A good Web resource is www.monteverde-info.com.

The **Centro Médico Monteverde** (tel. 506/645-7080) is on the east side of Santa Elena. And the **Red Cross** (tel. 128 or 506/645-6128) is on the north side of Santa Elena.

The **police** (Guardia Rural, tel. 117 or 506/645-5127) faces Super La Esperanza, in Santa Elena.

BETWEEN MONTEVERDE AND LA FORTUNA

For many travelers in Monteverde, the next destination of choice is La Fortuna (or vice versa). There are several ways of getting between them.

Tour operators offer a four-hour horseback ride from Monteverde to Río Chiquito, where you take a one-hour boat ride across Lake Arenal, then a 30-minute jeep ride to La Fortuna. The trip leaves at 7:30 A.M. ($65; check at Pensión Santa Elena, in Monteverde).

Several tour operators have been accused of working their horses to death—literally—on the arduous old El Castillo–Monteverde mountain trail, on which the poorly fed horses exhaust themselves thigh deep in mud on the steep hills during wet season. Be sure to book a trip that goes via Río Chiquito, and not El Castillo. And check to see that the horses are not used both ways on the same day.

Alternately, you can take a 90-minute jeep ride to Río Chiquito, where you take a one-hour boat ride across Lake Arenal, then a 30-minute jeep ride to La Fortuna: the trip ($25) leaves Monteverde daily at 8 A.M.

Services

The **Banco Nacional** (tel. 506/645-5027), in Santa Elena, is open 8:30 A.M.–3:30 P.M. weekdays. Super La Esperanza has a cash-advance ATM.

The post office is in the center of Santa Elena.

In Cerro Plano, **Las Delicias Campesinas** (tel. 506/645-7032, 11 A.M.–8 P.M.) has Internet service for $3 per hour, as do **Historia Internet Café** (tel. 506/645-6914, 8 A.M.–9 P.M.); **Tranquilo Internet** (tel. 506/645-6782, 9 A.M.–9 P.M.), on the southwest side of Santa Elena; **Desafío** (tel. 506/645-5874, 8 A.M.–8 P.M.); **Internet Taberna** (tel. 506/645-5825, 11 A.M.–7 P.M.); and the **Monteverde Orchid Garden** (8 A.M.–9 P.M.), which has an Internet café charging $2.75 per hour.

Chunches offers same-day wash and dry for $5. **Las Delicias Campesinas** (tel. 506/645-7032), in Cerro Plano, has self-service laundry ($6 per load); nearby **Laundry La Amistad** (tel. 506/645-5504) is open 6 A.M.–8 P.M.

Getting There

Beware touts who intercept arriving buses, cars, and taxis in an attempt to direct you to their properties or businesses at which they'll receive commissions. It's a growing hassle!

Transmonteverde (tel. 506/645-5159, fax 506/645-5644, in San José tel. 506/222-3854) operates bus service; the office in Santa Elena is open 5:45 A.M.–11 A.M. daily, and also 1:30–5 P.M. Mon.–Fri. and 1:30–3 P.M. Sat.–Sun. Buy your return bus ticket from the Trans-Monteverde ticket office as soon as you arrive in Santa Elena; otherwise you might be out of luck.

Buses (four hours; $4.50) depart San José from Calle 12, Avenidas 7/9, daily at 6:30 A.M. and 2:30 P.M.; the return bus departs from Santa Elena at 6:30 A.M. and 2:30 P.M. Buses also depart Calles 2 and 4 in Puntarenas at 6 A.M. and 2:15 P.M. (you can pick it up at the Río Lagarto turnoff for Monteverde on the Pan-American Highway). A bus departs Tilarán for Monteverde at 12:30 P.M.

Interbus (tel. 506/282-5573 or 800/748-8853, www.interbusonline.com) and **Fantasy Bus** (tel. 506/232-3681) each operate minibus shuttles between San José and Monteverde ($30).

The **"Arenal Express"** (tel. 506/479-9222, fax 506/479-9792, paraisotropical@racsa.co.cr) operates a bus service to La Fortuna (8 A.M.) and Tamarindo (8:30 A.M.). **Flor y Fauna Monteverde Tours** offers a Jeep transfer to La Fortuna ($25).

There are two turnoffs for Monteverde from Hwy. 1. The first is via Sardinal (the turnoff is at Rancho Grande, about 10 km south of San Gerardo). The second is about seven km north of San Gerardo (100 meters before the bridge over the Río Lagarto), 37 km north of Esparza. The roads lead 35 km uphill, a gut-jolting, vertiginous dirt road that is almost as famous as the place it leads to. The drive takes 1.5 –2 hours. Take it slowly and enjoy the spectacular mountain scenery. A tollbooth just below Santa Elena collects a 50-*colones* toll.

Also see *Monteverde to Tilarán,* below.

Drive slowly through Santa Elena and Monteverde. Speed limit in the area is 20 kph.

Evelio Fonseca Mata (tel. 506/645-0958) runs a private **minibus** service to and from San José for four people for $200 round-trip.

Getting Around

There is no local bus service.

Moto/Bike Rental (tel. 506/381-5518), in front of Santa Elena supermarket, rents mountain bicycles ($7 first hour, $20 per day) and small motorcycles, plus 250cc ATVs ($30 per day).

ARENAL-MONTEVERDE PROTECTION ZONE

Created in 1991, this "protection zone" encompasses more than 30,000 hectares, most of which is within the Monteverde Cloud Forest Biological Reserve and the adjoining Children's Eternal Cloud Forest. It protects land extending down both the Caribbean and Pacific slopes of the Cordillera de Tilarán and encompasses eight distinct ecological zones. Temperature and humidity change dramatically over relatively short distances, producing a great diversity of forest types with little change in elevation (which begins at 660 meters on the Caribbean side and attains 1,859 meters atop Cerro Sin Nombre). Wind-battered elfin woods on exposed ridges are spectacularly dwarfed, whereas more protected areas have majestically tall trees festooned with orchids, bromeliads, ferns, and vines. Poorly drained areas support swamp forests, huge philodendrons, tall bamboo, and giant tree ferns from the age of the dinosaurs. Humid trade winds blowing in off the sea shroud the forest in a veil of mist. Clouds sift through the forest primeval.

Temperatures range 13–24°C (55–75°F). Average annual rainfall is 242 cm (97 inches), falling mostly between June and November. A drier climate prevails from December to April, though windswept mists remain common and driving rain a possibility. February through May, quetzals are in the cloud forest. Later, they migrate downhill, where they can be seen around the hotels of Monteverde. Just after dawn is a good time to spot quetzals, which are particularly active in the early morning, especially in the mating season (April and May).

Early morning and late afternoon are the best times to see birds. Midmorning peak hours are to be avoided.

M Monteverde Cloud Forest

The 14,200-hectare Reserva Biológica Bosque Nuboso Monteverde (tel. 506/645-5122, fax 506/645-5034, montever@racsa.co.cr, www.cct.or.cr, 7 A.M.–4 P.M., $12 admission adults, $6 students with student card, $3.50 residents, free for children under six), six km east of Santa Elena, is acclaimed as one of the most outstanding wildlife sanctuaries in the New World tropics. The preserve, which is owned and administered by the Tropical Science Center of Costa Rica, protects more than 100 species of mammals, more than 400 species of birds, and more than 1,200 species of amphibians and reptiles. It is one of the few remaining habitats of all five species of the cat family: jaguar, ocelot, puma, margay, and jaguarundi. Bird species embrace black guan, emerald toucanet, the three-wattled bellbird (an endangered species whose metallic "BONK!" call carries for almost two miles), and 30 local hummingbird species. Hundreds of visitors come to Costa Rica to visit Monteverde in hopes of seeing a resplendent quetzal (approximately 100 pairs nest in the reserve).

The reserve has kilometers of trails, sections of which are not for the weak-hearted. Parts ooze with mud; other sections have been covered with raised wooden walkways. Knowledgeable locals wear rubber boots. A maximum of 120 people are allowed on the trails at any one time. Shorter nature trails are concentrated in an area called "The Triangle."

Longer trails lead down the Pacific slopes. **Sendero Valle** leads to La Cascada, a triple

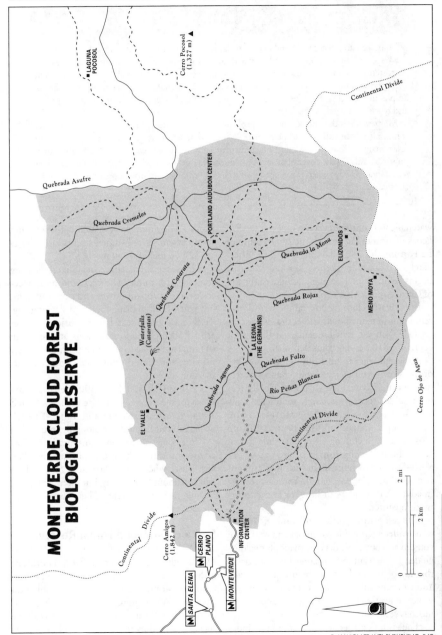

MONTEVERDE CLOUD FOREST BIOLOGICAL RESERVE

LAGUNA POCOSOL

Cerro Pocosol (1,327 m)

Continental Divide

Quebrada Asufre

Quebrada Cremelos

PORTLAND AUDUBON CENTER

Quebrada la Mona

ELIZONDOS

Quebrada Catarata

Quebrada Rojas

MENO MOYA

Waterfalls (Cataratas)

LA LEONA (THE GERMANS)

Quebrada Falto

Quebrada Lagona

Río Peñas Blancas

Cerro Ojo de Agua

EL VALLE

Continental Divide

2 mi

2 km

Continental Divide

Cerro Amigos (1,842 m)

CERRO PLANO

MONTEVERDE

INFORMATION CENTER

SANTA ELENA

© AVALON TRAVEL PUBLISHING, INC.

Guanacaste

THE DISAPPEARANCE OF THE GOLDEN TOAD

One of Monteverde's several claims to fame is the inch-long golden toad, an endemic species that is supposedly both deaf and dumb. In fact, the montane rainforest reserve owes its existence in part to the discovery of this brilliant, neon orange arboreal toad—discovered in 1964 and so stunning that one biologist harbored "a suspicion that someone had dipped the examples in enamel paint." The males are the orange ones; females, which are larger, are yellow and black with patches of scarlet.

Monteverde is the only known home of this fabulous creature. But don't expect to see one. It may already be extinct. Although in 1986 it could be seen in large quantities, by 1988 very few remained. To my knowledge, no confirmed sightings have been made since 1996. It may now exist only on the cover of tourist brochures. No one is sure whether or not the demise of *sapo dorado (Bufo periglenes)* is related to the global diminution of frog populations during the last decade.

waterfall, and continues via the valley of the Río Peñas Blancas to Pocosol, about 20 km south of La Fortuna. It's a full-day hike (20 km). Alternately, you can follow a three-km-long trail that begins behind Hotel Belmar and hike to the top of Cerro Amigos (1,842 meters).

Bring warm clothing and raingear. You may rent boots in many hotels and at the visitor center ($1). You can rent binoculars at the visitor center for $10 per day (plus deposit).

Although you can hike through the preserve on your own, you increase your chances of seeing wildlife if you hike with a guide. Three-hour guided tours *(caminatas)* are offered daily at 7:30 A.M., 8 A.M., and 1 P.M. (minimum three people, maximum nine people; $15 pp plus entrance, including 40-minute slide show). A five-hour birding tour is offered at 6 A.M. ($40–50). A two-hour night hike by flashlight is offered at 7:15 P.M. ($13). You can reserve in advance through your hotel or at the information center.

The reservations office and store at the entrance offer a self-guide pamphlet and trail map; you can also buy more detailed maps plus wildlife guides. If you want to hike alone, buy your ticket the day before and set out before the crowds. You can rent rubber boots at the store. A café serves omelettes ($1.75), burgers, sandwiches, mochas ($1), etc.

The visitor's center and field station includes dormitory-style lodging and kitchens for up to 39 people. The dorms have shared baths with hot water. Scientists and students get priority. Rates are $27 pp including all meals.

The reserve has three basic backpacking shelters with bunks, showers, and hydroelectricity, plus propane stoves and pots and pans, but you'll need to bring food and sleeping bag. Trail crews and researchers get priority. Rates are $3.50 nightly. Reservations are essential; the huts are locked (you pick up the key after making your reservation; see contact information, above)

x A bus (tel. 506/645-5390) departs Santa Elena for the reserve Mon.–Sat. at 6:35 A.M. and 1 P.M., returning at noon and 3 P.M. ($1 each way). You can flag it down along the route.

Most hotels can arrange transportation. Otherwise you can walk up the hill: muddy when wet, dusty when dry. A taxi from Santa Elena will cost about $5 one-way, but there are reports of gouging in recent years. There's parking near the entrance.

Santa Elena Cloud Forest Reserve
This 600-hectare cloud forest reserve (7 A.M.–4 P.M., $9 adults, $5 students) is five km northeast of Santa Elena, at a slightly higher elevation than the Monteverde Cloud Forest Biological Reserve (4WD required). The reserve is owned by the Santa Elena community. It boasts all the species claimed by its eastern neighbor—quetzals, deer, sloths, ocelots, and howler and ca-

puchin monkeys—plus spider monkeys, which are absent from the Monteverde reserve. It receives far fewer visitors. It has four one-way trails (from 1.4 to 4.8 km) and a lookout point and observation tower with views toward Volcán Arenal. At a higher elevation than Monteverde, it tends to be cloudier and wetter.

The reserve is the site of the **Monteverde Cloud Forest Ecological Center** (tel. 506/645-5390), a forest farm started in March 1992 to educate youngsters and local farmers on forest ecology and conservation. There's also a visitor/information center. Guides are available, as are dormitory accommodations for students, with a laboratory, library, and kitchen. The accommodations may eventually be available to tourists. Volunteers of any age are welcome as teachers, researchers, and for maintenance work.

The foundation offers three-hour guided hikes at 7:30 A.M. and 11:30 A.M. plus a night tour at 7 P.M. ($15 for the guide). You can buy trail maps and a self-guided trail booklet—and rent rubber boots ($1)—at the information center.

The Santa Elena Cloud Forest Reserve office is in Santa Elena (P.O. Box 90-5655, Monteverde, tel. 506/645-5693, fax 506/645-5390, rbnctpse @racsa.co.cr, www.monteverdeinfo.com/reserve.htm).

Shuttles for ticket-holders leave Santa Elena at 6:45 A.M., 11 A.M., and 2:30 P.M. A collective taxi leaves Santa Elena village at 6:45 A.M., 8 A.M., 10:30 A.M., 12:30 P.M., and 2 P.M., but you must book the day before ($2 per person, tel. 506/645-5051). A regular taxi costs about $7 each way.

Children's Eternal Cloud Forest

Abutting the Monteverde Cloud Forest Biological Reserve to the north and east, the Bosque Eterno De Los Niños is the largest private reserve in Central America. It is administered by the Monteverde Conservation League (Apdo. 10165, San José 1000, tel. 506/645-5003, fax 506/645-5104, acmmcl@racsa.co.cr, www .acmonteverde.com).

The dream of a rainforest saved by children began in 1987 at a small primary school in rural Sweden. A study of tropical forests

prompted nine-year-old Roland Teinsuu to ask what he could do to keep the rainforest and the animals that live in it safe from destruction. Young Roland's question launched a group campaign to raise money to help the League buy and save threatened rainforest in Costa Rica. Roland and his classmates raised enough money to buy six hectares of rainforest at a cost of $250 per hectare, including surveying, title search, and legal fees connected with purchase. Out of this initial success a group of children dedicated to saving the tropical rainforest formed Barnens Regnskog ("Children's Rain Forest"). The vision took hold, sweeping the globe, with contributions flocking in from the far corners.

The original six-hectare preserve, established near Monteverde in 1988, has grown to more than 22,000 hectares and counting.

There are rustic cabins with fully equipped kitchens and showers, and three meals are served daily. Guides are available by request. There are two field stations: at Poco Sol, on the lower eastern slopes, with eight rooms (six with private bath) for 26 people and 10 km of hiking trails;

Guanacaste

and San Gerardo, at 1,220 meters elevation, a 3.5-km walk from the Santa Elena Cloud Forest Reserve, with accommodations for 26 people and six km of trails.

Ecolodge San Luís

This ecolodge (Apdo. 36, Santa Elena de Monteverde, tel. 506/645-8049, fax 506/645-8050, www.ecolodgesanluis.com) is affiliated with the University of Georgia and doubles as an integrated tourism, research, and education project on a 70-hectare working farm at San Luís eight km southeast of Monteverde (the turnoff to San Luís is immediately east of Hotel Fonda Vela on the road to the Monteverde reserve). Resident biologists work with members of the San Luís community to develop a model for sustainable development. There are fruit trees, vegetable gardens, coffee fields, and large stands of wildlife-rich forest, including cloud forest.

The station offers a wide range of activities: from hiking, horseback rides, bird-watching, cloud-forest hiking, and night walks to hands-on laboratory study (there's even a computer lab). All the while you get to intermingle with scientists, students, and community members. Open-air classes are given, including an intensive seven-day tropical biology course. And you can even help farm or participate in scientific research. It's one of the best models I know for getting to experience and appreciate Costa Rica's *campesino* culture.

As for accommodations, there's a cozy wood-paneled bunkhouse—a former milking shed—with 30 bunks and shared baths, and four rooms with 2–12 beds. It also has a four-room, 16-bed bungalow with private baths and verandas, plus 12 *cabinas* for three or four people each. Tico fare is cooked over a woodstove and served family-style in the book-lined dining room; wash it down with coffee grown on the farm. Rates are $55 s bunkhouse, $80 s, $90 d cabin, $60 s, $70 d bungalow low season; $5 more in high season, including meals and activities.

Tilarán and Vicinity

MONTEVERDE TO TILARÁN

If traveling to Lake Arenal, you can avoid the long descent to the Pan-American Highway and the 67-km journey to the lake via Cañas to Tilarán by following the rough dirt road west from Santa Elena via Cabeceras and Quebrada Grande. There are lots of junctions, and the roads are unsigned. It's beautiful scenery all the way.

Cataratas de Viento Fresco (tel. 506/661-8193, 8 A.M.–5 P.M.), 11 km east of Tilarán and 25 km west of Monteverde, has 120-foot waterfalls, a waterslide, trails, and horseback riding.

Accommodations

Ecoverde Lodge los Olivos (c/o tel. 506/248-2538, fax 506/248-1659, cooprena@racsa.co.cr, www.turismoruralcr.com, $30 s, $35 d low season; $35/40 high season), in the hamlet of Monte los Olivos, near Las Nubes, seven km north of Santa Elena, is run by the local community. The rustic yet enchanting lodge, which sits on stilts above a lake and is surrounded by forest, boasts four cabins with private baths and hot water plus five rooms in the biological station with shared bath and hot water. There's a restaurant with panoramic views, and trails lead into the forest; guided hikes and horseback trips are offered. A *mirador* offers views of Arenal Volcano. Guided horseback and hiking trips are offered. Rates include breakfast.

TILARÁN

Tilarán, about 23 km east of Cañas and the Pan-American Highway, is a spruce little highland town with a pretty square and a park with cedars and pines in front of the church. At this elevation (550 meters), the air is crisp and stirred by breezes working their way over the crest of the Cordillera de Tilarán from Lake Arenal, five km to the northeast. The countryside hereabouts is reminiscent of the rolling hill country of England—the Mendips or Downs.

Local attractions include the **Vivero Poporí** (tel. 506/695-5047, 7:30 A.M.–6 P.M., \$2 admission), otherwise known as Teresa's Orchid Garden, run by an erudite and friendly Cuban woman who knows her tropical orchids. The garden, about two km south of town, also has a small **butterfly garden** with about 22 species.

The **"Big Tree,"** behind a small farm called Finca Palo Grande, about three km south of town, is billed as "the largest tree in Costa Rica." This ceiba has an astounding 10-meter base, incredibly flanged, and was a sapling when Columbus landed! Trails lead into a forest full of monkeys. The turnoff down a dirt road to the left is unmarked; after about 800 meters you'll see a sign; turn left into the farm.

The last weekend in April (and again in mid-June) Tilarán plays host to a rodeo and a livestock show, and the town fills up.

Sports and Recreation

Ferens Lajas (tel. 506/695-8306) operates a tour information booth in **Super Guayo,** two blocks north and one block east of the plaza.

Tilatur (tel. 506/695-8671), next to the bus stop, one block northwest of the plaza, offers fishing trips and sells fishing tackle.

Shopping

La Carreta is one of the best-stocked stores outside San José, with high-quality jewelry and crafts.

Accommodations

Cabinas Hotel y Restaurante Mary (tel. 506/695-5479, \$5 pp basic, \$11 s, \$20 d for TV and private bath), on the southeast side of the park, has 18 rooms with TV and private baths with hot water. It has a bar and restaurant adjoining.

A recommended bargain is **Hotel El Sueño** (tel. 506/695-5347, \$15 s, \$25 d standard, \$20 s, \$30 d deluxe), one block north of the plaza, and one of the best hotels for its price in the country. Sixteen rooms, all with TVs, fans, and private baths with hot water, surround a sunlit second-floor courtyard with a fountain. Four newer, more deluxe rooms have refrigerators and

somewhat more ostentatious furnishings. Herman and Sonia Vargas, the friendly owners, provide fruit and toiletry baskets. Secure parking. Downstairs is the hotel's Restaurant El Parque, with good seafood dishes.

The **Hotel Guadalupe** (tel./fax 506/695-5943, \$16 s, \$28 d), on the north side of the plaza, is also modern and attractive, with 24 modestly furnished rooms with fans and private bathrooms with hot water. Some rooms have cable TV, and there's a TV lounge. Rates include breakfast. **Hotel Naralit** (tel. 506/695-5393, fax 506/695-6767, \$15 s, \$20 d), on the south side of the church, has 26 pleasing rooms with glass-enclosed porches and private baths. It's small but ultraclean and well-run and offers secure parking. Some cabins have cable TV.

La Carreta Boutique Hotel (tel. 506/695-6593, fax 506/695-6593, lacarret@racsa.co.cr, \$60 s/d standard, \$100 suite), one block east of the church, is a charming bed-and-breakfast whose four rooms (several skylit) are each distinct. Some have beautiful wrought-iron beds and furnishings and exquisite bedspreads, plus colonial tiles, lofty ceilings, and niches with pottery. Cable TVs, ceiling fans, and private bathrooms with hot water are standard. Room 1 has a Chinese motif. A suite is fabulous and features a ceramic beehive fireplace. Two triples in a wooden extension to the rear are less appealing, despite gorgeous bathrooms. The rear garden has a patio and hot tub.

Food

La Carreta (noon–9 P.M., \$7), once among the region's finest restaurants, isn't quite what it was since the original owners sold, and it no longer serves breakfast. However, it still manages creative meals such as an excellent tilapia with almonds and herbs, Creole chicken, plus pastas and pizzas.

For breakfast, head to **Mi Cocina** (tel. 506/695-8610, 6 A.M.–7:30 P.M.), a little mom-and-pop place on the west side of the plaza. It serves excellent *gallo pinto*, plus enchiladas, chalupas, ceviche, and Tex-Mex fare, and coffees.

Musmanni, next to Mi Cocina, sells baked goods.

Information and Services

The headquarters of the **Area Conservación de Arenal-Tempisque** (tel. 506/695-5908, fax 506/695-5982) is one block northwest of the plaza.

There are three banks around the town square, which has public telephones.

Café Internet is one block north of the plaza; it has a coffee shop. **Cicsa** (tel. 506/695-6619, 7:30 A.M.–10 P.M. Mon.–Sat. and 1–10 P.M. Sunday), below the Hotel El Sueño, offers Internet service.

The **Red Cross** (tel. 506/695-5256) is one block east of the church.

The **police station** adjoins the bus station.

Getting There and Around

The Tilarán bus station is 50 meters west of the plaza. Buses (tel. 506/222-3854) depart San José for Tilarán from Calle 12, Avenidas 7/9 daily at 7:30 A.M., 9:30 A.M., 12:45 P.M., 3:45 P.M., and

6:30 P.M. (four hours via Cañas, $1.40). The bus continues to Nuevo Arenal. Local buses depart Cañas for Tilarán at 7:30 A.M., 9 A.M., 11 A.M., and 3 P.M. Buses (tel. 506/460-0326, four hours) depart Ciudad Quesada (San Carlos) for Tilarán via La Fortuna, Tabacón, and Nuevo Arenal daily at 6 A.M. and 3 P.M. From Monteverde, a bus for Tilarán departs Santa Elena daily at 7 A.M.; returning at 1 P.M. (three hours).

Buses depart Tilarán for San José at 5 A.M., 7 A.M., 7:45 A.M., 2 P.M., and 4:45 P.M.; for Cañas at 5 A.M., 7:30 A.M., 10 A.M., 12:30 P.M., and 3:30 P.M.; for Ciudad Quesada at 7 A.M. and 12:30 P.M.; for Monteverde at 12:30 P.M.; for Nuevo Arenal at 10 A.M., 4 P.M., and 10 P.M.; and for Puntarenas at 6 A.M. and 1 P.M.

There's a **gas station** two blocks northeast of the plaza.

For taxis call **Unidos Tilarán** (tel. 506/695-5324), or hail one on the west side of the plaza.

Cañas to Liberia

The first impression as you continue northwest along Hwy. 1 from Cañas is of a vast barren plain, burning hot in dry season, with palms rising like tattered umbrellas over the scrubby landscape, flanked to the east by the steep-sided volcanoes of the Cordillera de Guanacaste, from which rivers feed the marshy wetlands of the Tempisque Basin. Away from the main highway, the villages of whitewashed houses are as welcoming as any in the country. For the traveler interested in history or architecture, there are some intriguing sites. And the area is charged with scenic beauty. Looking at this austere plain, shimmering and phantasmagorical in its infinity, conjures images of the wanderings of the demented Don Quixote across stark La Mancha. And, just as the old knight errant found in that spare landscape, the far northwest of Costa Rica is rich with opportunities for "adventures elbow-deep."

CAÑAS

Cañas is a modest-sized town and a pivotal point for exploring Palo Verde National Park (west) or

Lake Arenal (east), and for rafting trips on the Río Coribicí. Named for the white-flowered wild cane that still grows in patches hereabouts, Cañas is also known as Ciudad de la Amistad (City of Friendship). It is indisputably a cowboy town, as the many tanned *sabaneros* riding horses and shaded by wide-brimmed hats attest.

A paved road runs west from Cañas 14 km to the village of **Bebedero,** a gateway to Palo Verde National Park and a stone's throw away on the west bank of the Río Tenorio. There's no road access to the park from here. However, boats will take you across the wide Río Tenorio.

Seven km north of Cañas (and one km north of the Río Corobicí), a well-paved road (Hwy. 6) leads northeast 58 km to Upala in the northern lowlands via the low-lying saddle of Tenorio and Miravalles Volcanoes.

ⓜ Las Pumas Cat Zoo

Las Pumas (tel. 506/669-6044), five km north of Cañas, was founded by the late Lily Bodmer de Hagnauer, a Swiss-born environmentalist whose passion was saving and raising big cats: ocelots,

© CHRISTOPHER P. BAKER

Tenorio Volcano

a jaguar, cougars, margays, jaguarundis, and "tiger" cats. All six species are housed in large chain-link cages, but beware: there are no guardrails (nor guards) and the temptation to reach out to stroke a cat through the mesh is tempting but stupid. These are not house cats! Most of the animals were either injured or orphaned and have been reared by Lily or her family, who still run the zoo.

Other species include deer, fox, monkeys, peccaries, macaws, toucans, and dozens of parrots and other birds all getting along in the large cages. It also raises hundreds of Australian budgerigars and rabbits for sale. By selling only nonnative species, it hopes to help change the pet-keeping habits of Ticos.

The zoo needs donations (each jaguar costs $1,200 a year to feed).

Open daily 8 A.M.–4 P.M. No fee, but donations are requested. The zoo is tucked behind Safari Corobicí. Follow the dirt road 100 meters.

Río Corobicí

Six km north of Cañas, the Pan-American Highway crosses the Río Corobicí. The 40-km-long river is fed by controlled runoff from Lake Arenal,

providing water year-round, good for rafting. The trip is a relatively calm Class II run described as a "nature float." Though it cuts through cattle country and rice paddies, the river is lined with a riparian forest of mahogany, ceiba, and palms. Motmots, herons, crested caracaras, egrets, and toucans are common, as are howler monkeys, caimans, and iguanas basking on the riverbanks. With luck, you might even spot a crocodile. Pools provide excellent swimming.

Safaris Corobicí (P.O. Box 99-5700 Corobicí, Cañas, tel./fax 506/669-6091 or 506/669-6191, safaris@racsa.co.cr, www.nicoya.com) has an office beside Hwy. 1, about 400 meters south of the river. Two-hour guided trips cost $37. It has a three-hour bird-watching float ($45), plus a half-day float including lunch ($60).

Accommodations

Camping: You can camp at **Hotel Bed and Breakfast Capazauri** (see below) for $4 pp, $6 with breakfast. It has showers and toilets.

The **Hotel y Restaurante Corral** (tel. 506/669-0622, $18 s, $35 d), at the junction of Avenida 3 and the Pan-American Highway, has 28 clean and spacious rooms with a/c and

Guanacaste

To Liberia

PAN-AMERICAN HIGHWAY

BUS
TERMINAL

TAXIS

AVENIDA 11

AVENIDA 9

MINAE HQ

AVENIDA 7

CALLE 3

AVENIDA 5

FUJIFLIM

*Soccer
Stadium*

CALLE 2

CALLE CENTRAL

*Plaza de Toros
(Bullring)*

TELECOMMUNICACIONES
INTERNACIONALES

SISTEC
INTERNET

CALLE 1

AVENIDA 3

CIBERC@ÑAS

PALI
SUPERMARKET

HOTEL
CAÑAS

J&E LATINA
INTERNET

NUEVO
HOTEL
CAÑAS

BANK

BANK

PHARMACY

PHARMACY/DHL

POST OFFICE

HOTEL/
RESTAURANTE
CORRAL

RESTAURANTE
LEI TU

MUSMANNI

CEMETERY

CALLE 4

PHARMACY

HOTEL
PARQUE

AVENIDA 2

RESTAURANTE
MEY-JO

BANK

ICE (TELEPHONES)

To Bebedero

0   200 yds

0   200 m

BUS TO
SAN JOSÉ

PAN-AMERICAN HIGHWAY

To Puntarenas
and San José

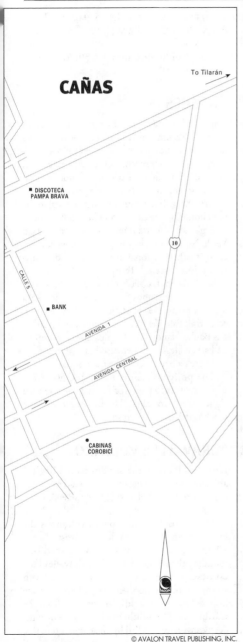

CAÑAS

To Tilarán

■ DISCOTECA PAMPA BRAVA

10

CALLE 5

■ BANK

AVENIDA 1

AVENIDA CENTRAL

● CABINAS COROBICÍ

© AVALON TRAVEL PUBLISHING, INC.

private baths with cold water; many rooms have TVs. Traffic noise may be a concern.

Cabinas Corobicí (tel. 506/669-0241, $10 pp) has 13 small and basic but well-kept *cabinas* with fans and private baths with cold water. Take the two *cabinas* on the left: they're larger. It has secure parking.

The **Hotel Cañas** (tel. 506/669-0039, fax 506/669-1319, $13 s, $19 d no TV; $17 s, $20 with TV; $18 s, $29 d with a/c and TV) has 45 simple no-frills rooms with fans, some with cable TV. Its restaurant is the best in town.

The best place in town is the modern **Nuevo Hotel Cañas** (Calle 2, Avenida 3, tel. 506/669-1294, fax 506/669-1319, $27 s, $43 d), one block west. It's popular with Tico families, who flock to the swimming pool and Jacuzzi. It has 26 a/c rooms with telephones, cable TV, and private baths with hot water. Rates include tax.

Hotel Bed and Breakfast Capazuri (tel. 506/669-6280, fax 506/669-6080, capazuri @racsa.co.cr, $20 s, $36 d with fan, $25 s, $41 d with a/c), is two km north of town, on the east side of Hwy. 1. The live-in owners have 16 rooms in two modern blocks on a small *finca* and orchards, plus 10 new cabinas set amid lawns. Rooms vary in size, but all are clean and meagerly furnished, with fans and private baths (11 have hot water). Six rooms have a/c.

Food

The nicest place to eat is the modern a/c restaurant in the **Hotel Cañas,** which features cowboy paraphernalia on the walls.

There's half a dozen or so Chinese restaurants to choose from in Cañas; there's a concentration on Avenida 1 around Calles 2/4.

Hotel Hacienda La Pacífica (tel. 506/669-6050, fax 506/669-0555, pacifica@racsa.co.cr, 7 A.M.–9 P.M., $3–15), on the Pan-American Highway one km north of town, is a private country club, though its colonial-style restaurant is open to the public. The menu includes cream of tomato soup, pastas, tenderloin pepper steak, and jumbo shrimp skewer.

Guanacaste

Restaurante Corobicí (tel. 506/669-6262, rincon@racsa.co.cr, 8 A.M.–8 P.M.), beside the Pan-American Highway, is a pleasant place to eat, with good seafood dishes and a porch over the river where you can watch rafters go by. It is popular with tour groups. I enjoyed a sea bass in garlic ($6) washed down with superb lemonade. A nature trail follows the river.

Information and Services

Farmacia Cañas (tel. 506/669-0748) is on Avenida 1, two blocks east of the plaza.

Criminal investigation is handled by the OIJ (tel. 506/669-3444).

There are three banks in the town center; see the map.

The post office is on Avenida 3, 30 meters west of Calle 4. You can make international calls from **Telecommunicaciones Internacionales** (Calle 2, Avenida 5) and the **ICE** office, on Calle Central, one block south of the square.

Internet Ciberc@ñas (Avenida 3, Calles 1/3, tel. 506/669-5232) is open 8:15 A.M.–9 P.M. Mon.–Sat., 2–9 P.M. Sundays; **Sistec Internet** (Calle 1, Avenidas 3/5, tel. 506/669-3090) and **J&R Internet** (Calle Central, Avenida 1/3) also have service.

Getting There

Buses (tel. 506/222-3006) depart San José for Cañas from Calle 16, Avenidas 3/5, daily at 8:30 A.M., 10:20 A.M., 11:50 A.M., 1:40 P.M., and 3 P.M.; plus Friday and Sunday at 6:15 P.M. (three hours; $3). An express bus (tel. 506/666-0138) departs Puntarenas for Liberia via Cañas at 5:30 P.M. (Empresa Arata).

Buses depart Cañas for San José from Calle 1, Avenidas 9/11, at 6 A.M., 9:15 A.M., 12:30 P.M., and 2:15 P.M. (plus Friday and Sunday at 3 P.M. and 5:15 P.M.). Buses depart Cañas for destinations throughout Guanacaste from Calle 1, Avenidas 9/11, including to Arenal and Tilarán (6 A.M., 9 A.M., 10:30 A.M., noon, 1:45 P.M., 3:30 P.M., and 5:30 P.M.); Bebedero (5 A.M., 9 A.M., 11 A.M., 1 P.M., 3 P.M., and 5 P.M.); Las Juntas (9 A.M. and 2:50 P.M.); Liberia (5:45 A.M., 7 A.M., 7:30 A.M., 9 A.M., 11:30 A.M., 3 P.M., and 5 P.M.); Puntarenas (6 A.M., 6:40 A.M., 9:30 A.M., 11 A.M.,

12:30 P.M., 1:30 P.M., and 4:15 P.M.); and Upala (6 A.M., 8:40 A.M., 11 A.M., 1 P.M., 3:30 P.M., and 5:15 P.M.).

Taxis Unidos de Cañas (tel. 506/669-0898) has taxis on call.

BAGACES

The small, nondescript town of Bagaces is on Hwy. 1, 22 km north of Cañas. Many of the houses are quite ancient, and several adobe-brick houses date back several centuries. Otherwise, even the most diligent search will not turn up anything more interesting than a bust of ex-president General Tomás Guardia on a pedestal in the park honoring the city's most illustrious child.

Bagaces is important only as a gateway to Palo Verde National Park (west) and Miravalles volcano (east). A regional office of **Area de Conservación Arenal-Tempisque** (ACT, tel. 506/671-1455, fax 506/671-1062, 8 A.M.–4 P.M. Mon.–Fri.), is opposite the junction for Palo Verde, next to the gas station on Hwy. 1. ACT comprises Palo Verde, Barra Honda, and Marino Las Baulas National Parks, plus Lomas Barbudal and several lesser-known reserves.

There's a bank facing the main square.

The **police** (Guardia Rural, tel. 506/671-1173) is 50 meters east of Hwy. 1, on the road signed for Miravalles. The bus station is one block north of the main square.

MIRAVALLES VOLCANO

Hwy. 164 leads northeast from central Bagaces and climbs steadily north up the western shoulder of Miravalles Volcano (2,028 meters). It is a fabulously scenic drive.

The almost perfectly conical volcano is the highest in the Cordillera de Guanacaste. Some 10,850 hectares of important watershed surrounding the volcano forms the **Miravalles Forest Reserve.** The western slopes are covered with savanna scrub; the northern and eastern slopes are lush, fed by moist clouds that sweep in from the Caribbean. The southern slopes are cut with deep canyons and licked by ancient lava tongues, with fumaroles spouting and hissing like mini

Don't get too close to Miravalles Volcano's boiling mudpools!

Old Faithfuls. The Miravalles forests, replete with wildlife (monkeys, cats, coatimundis, tapirs on the higher slopes, and a huge array of bird species), are easily accessed from the road.

Hwy. 164 runs via the village of **Guayabo,** 21 km north of Bagaces. It is paved as far as **Guayabal,** seven km north of Guayabo, then gives way to a hellishly potholed road as you descend five km to **Aguas Claras** and, beyond, the hamlet of San José in the northern lowlands.

A loop road from Hwy. 164 leads east via the community of **Fortuna** and the Las Hornillas fumaroles.

Las Hornillas

Most of the geothermal activity is concentrated on the southwest flank at Las Hornillas (Little Ovens), an area of intense bubbling mudpots and fumaroles expelling foul gases and steam. Here the Costa Rican Institute of Electricity (ICE) harnesses geothermal energy for electric power, with two plants that tap the superheated

vapor deep within the volcano's bowels. You can visit the main **geothermal plant** (tel. 506/673-1111, ext. 232), about two km north of Fortuna, by appointment.

Centro Turístico Yökö (tel. 506/673-0410, fax 506/673-0770, $4 admission), is a recreation park amid lawns one km west of Las Hornillas, with five clean thermal pools (ranging from 30°C to 50°C) and plunge pools set amid 13 hectares. A waterslide plunges into a thermal pool, plus there's a kid's pool and a manmade cave that serves as a sauna room. A lake stocked with tilapia was being added for fishing. A trail with interpretive signs leads into the nearby forest. It also has a whirlpool spa, wet bar in one of the pools, a bar and restaurant, plus showers, lockers, and changing rooms. Massage is offered, as are horseback rides ($15, four hours). Yökö is an Indian word for "hot."

Nearby, **Centro Turístico Termomanía** (tel. 506/673-0268 or 822-2602, $4 admission) is a similar offering with seven thermal pools, a waterslide, mud masks and sauna, plus a small zoo with deer. It even has go-kart racing. The highlight is the *hornillas*—bubbling mudpools and fumaroles—immediately adjacent to the property. You can wander around freely. It's totally unguarded and very dangerous—*keep your distance!*

Accommodations and Food

I recommend **Centro Turístico Yökö** (see above, $30 s, $50 d), which has 12 spacious cabins with tile floors, raised roofs, verandas with volcano views, plus ceiling fans, and large private bath and walk-in showers with thermal water. It has a restaurant with large-screen TV. Rates include breakfast and use of facilities.

A lesser option is **Miravalles Volcano Lodge** (tel. 506/673-0823, fax 506/673-0350, mvolvano @racsa.co.cr, $25 s, $35 d with fan; $45 s, 55 d with a/c), four km north of Guayabo and squatting amid cattle pasture at the base of the looming volcano. The lodge has eight spacious, modestly furnished rooms with lofty wooden ceilings, and private baths with hot water. There's a restaurant and a lounge with cable TV. No rooms have volcano views. Trails lead into a private 212-hectare forest reserve

Guanacaste

that includes wetlands fed by thermal waters, sulfur springs, and waterfalls. Horseback rides are offered.

Budget-hounds might consider **Santa María Volcano Lodge** (tel. 506/381-5290 or 506/235-0642, fax 506/666-2313 or 506/272-6236, $5 pp), one km west of Colonia Blanca, on the northeast slope of Rincón de la Vieja and reached from Aguas Claras. The basic wooden lodge has rough-hewn furniture and torn leather seats but is otherwise clean, and has six clean, rooms with modern private bathrooms and hot water (two have shared bath). Better are the two small rustic cabins—like something from *Goldilocks and the Three Bears*—with tree trunks for stools, a double bed, a bunk and two single beds, stone-lined bathrooms, and porches looking over the banana and citrus groves. It is part of a cattle *finca*. Tepezcuintles are raised here for release into the wild. Horseback rides and hiking tours are offered.

⊠ PALO VERDE NATIONAL PARK

Palo Verde National Park, 28 km south of Bagaces, protects 13,058 hectares of floodplain, marshes, limestone ridges, and seasonal pools in the heart of the driest region of Costa Rica—the Tempisque basin, at the mouth of the Río Tempisque in the Gulf of Nicoya. The park, which derives its name from the *palo verde* (green tree) or horsebean shrub that retains a bright green coloration year-round, is contiguous to the north with the remote 7,354-hectare **Dr. Rafael Lucas Rodríguez Caballero Wildlife Refuge** and, beyond that, the **Lomas Barbudal Biological Reserve.** The three, together with Barra Honda National Park and adjacent areas, form the Tempisque Megapark and have a similar variety of habitats, not least patches of dry forest that once extended along the entire Pacific coast of Mesoamerica.

Dry forest was even more vast than the rainforest, but also more vulnerable to encroaching civilization. For half the year, from November to March, no rain relieves the heat of the Tempisque basin, leaving plants and trees parched and withered. Fires started by local farmers eviscerate

the tinder-dry forests, opening holes quickly filled by ecological opportunists such as African jaraguá, an exotic grass brought to Costa Rica in the late 19th century to grow pastures. Jaraguá rebounds quickly from fire and grazing pressures, reaching four-meter-high combustible stands. Rolling, rocky terrain spared Lomas Barbudal, in particular, from the changes wrought on the rest of Guanacaste Province by plows and cows. Here, the dry forest remains largely intact and several endangered tree species thrive: mahogany, Panamá redwood, gonzalo alves, rosewood, sandbox (popular with scarlet macaws), and the cannonball tree *(balas de cañón)*. A relative of the Brazil nut tree, the cannonball tree produces a pungent, nonedible fruit that grows to the size of a bowling ball and dangles from a long stem. Several evergreen tree species also line the banks of the waterways, creating riparian corridors inhabited by species not usually found in dry forests.

Unlike Costa Rica's moist forests, the tropical dry forests undergo a dramatic seasonal transformation. In the midst of drought, vibrant yellow and pink flowers synchronically burst onto bare branches, earning the moniker "big bang reproducers." Myriad bees—at least 250 species—moths, bats, and wasps pollinate the flowers. And moist fruits ripen throughout the dry season, feeding monkeys, squirrels, peccaries, and other mammalian frugivores.

In all, there are 15 different habitats (including several types of swamp and marshland) and a corresponding diversity of fauna. Plump crocodiles wallow on the muddy riverbanks, salivating, no doubt, at the sight of coatis, white-tailed deer, and other mammals come down to the water to ⚫ drink. Birds abound, including such endangered species as the great curassow, yellow-naped parrot, and king vulture.

The banks of the Tempisque, which is tidal, are also lined with archaeological sites.

The corridors of swamp forest linking Palo Verde and Dr. Rafael Lucas Rodríguez Caballero with Lomas Barbudal continue to shrink; local farmers have invested in permits to clear the swamp forest and plant crops, increasing the isolation of both reserves. To save the mangroves, the

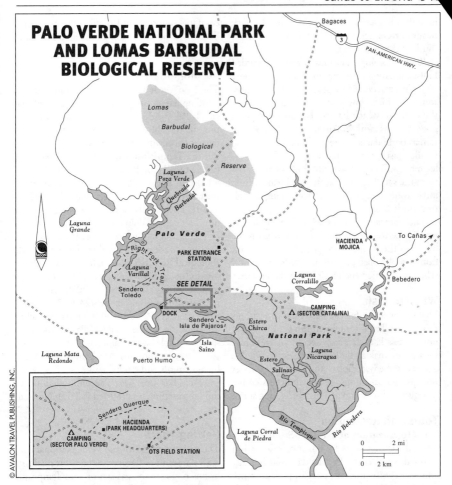

PALO VERDE NATIONAL PARK AND LOMAS BARBUDAL BIOLOGICAL RESERVE

Bagaces

PAN-AMERICAN HWY.

Lomas

Barbudal

Biological

Reserve

Laguna Poza Verde

Quebrada Barbudal

Laguna Grande

Palo Verde

Right Fork Trail

PARK ENTRANCE STATION

HACIENDA MOJICA

To Cañas

Laguna Varillal

SEE DETAIL

Laguna Corralillo

Bebedero

Sendero Toledo

DOCK

Sendero Isla de Pajaros

Estero Chirca

CAMPING (SECTOR CATALINA)

National Park

Isla Saino

Estero Salinas

Laguna Nicaragua

Laguna Mata Redondo

Puerto Humo

© AVALON TRAVEL PUBLISHING, INC.

Sendero Querque

HACIENDA (PARK HEADQUARTERS)

CAMPING (SECTOR PALO VERDE)

OTS FIELD STATION

Laguna Corral de Piedra

Río Tempisque

Río Bebedera

0   2 mi

0   2 km

Cipancí National Wildlife Refuge was proclaimed in 2001 along 3,500 square km of riverside bordering the Tempisque and Bebedero Rivers.

Palo Verde National Park (Parque Nacional Palo Verde, $6 admission) is best known as a bird-watchers' paradise. More than 300 bird species have been recorded, not least great curassows and the only permanent colony of scarlet macaws in the dry tropics. At least a quarter of a million wading birds and waterfowl flock here in fall and winter, when much of the arid alluvial plain swells into a lake. **Isla de Pájaros,** in the middle of the Río Tempisque, is replete with waterbirds, including white ibis, roseate spoonbills, anhingas, and wood storks; jabiru storks, the largest storks in the world; and the nation's largest colony of black-crowned night herons.

Three well-maintained trails lead through deciduous tropical forest and marshland to lookout points over the lagoons. Others lead to limestone caves and large waterholes such as Laguna Bocana, which are gathering places for a diversity of birds and animals. Limestone cliffs rise be-

Guanacaste

ld Hacienda Palo Verde, now the **park quarters** (tel./fax 506/200-0125), eight km south of the park entrance.

Reserva Biológica Lomas Barbudal (Bearded Hills, admission by donation) is a 2,279-hectare biological reserve fed by protected river systems, some of which flow year-round, among them the Cabuya, which has sandy-bottomed pools good for swimming. Along with Palo Verde, Lomas Barbudal is also one of the few remaining Pacific coast forests that attracts the colorful scarlet macaw. The macaws are fond of the seeds from the sandbox tree's segmented fruit, whose inner tissue contains a caustic latex strong enough to corrode flesh.

The Lomas Barbudal **park office** and **information center** (Casa de Patrimonio) is on the banks of the Río Cabuyo. Trails span the park from here. It's open on a 10-days-on/four-days-off schedule. Picnic benches sit under shade trees.

When to Visit

Dry season is by far the best time to visit, although the Tempisque basin can get dizzyingly hot. Access is easier, and deciduous trees lose their leaves, making bird-watching easier. Wildlife gathers by the waterholes. And there are far fewer mosquitoes and bugs. When the rains come, mosquitoes burst into action—bring bug spray.

Tours and Recreation

The **Organization of Tropical Studies** offers natural history visits by advance reservation (guided walks cost $15 half-day, $30 full day adults, $10/20 children, plus $6 park entrance fee). The park rangers will take you out on their boat for $10 pp. Or you can hire boats in Puerto Humo or Bebedero (see *Getting There,* below).

Most tour companies in San José also offer river tours in Palo Verde. **Costa Rica Fun Adventures** (P.O. Box 100-1260 Escazú, tel. 506/290-6015, fax 506/296-0533, funadven@racsa.co.cr) offers boat trips, as does **Tempisque Eco-Adventures & Canopy Tour** (tel. 506/687-1212, info@tempisqueecoadventures.com), just north of the highway immediately west of the Tempisque bridge. **Cocodrilo Safari** (tel. 506/654-4123, ext. 8913, elco-

cosafari@yahoo.es), at Paradisus Playa Conchal Beach & Golf Resort, in Conchal, offers Land Rover safaris.

Accommodations

The Palo Verde National Park administration building has a campsite ($2) beside the old Hacienda Palo Verde. Water, showers, and barbecue pits are available. You may be able to stay with rangers ($10) with advance notice: for information call the **Tempisque Conservation Area** office (tel. 506/671-1062, fax 506/671-1290, 8 A.M.–4 P.M.), in Bagaces. Spanish-speakers might try the ranger station radio telephone (tel. 506/233-4160). There is also a campsite seven km east near Laguna Coralillo (no facilities).

Visitors can stay in a dormitory for 30 people at the Organization of Tropical Studies' **Palo Verde Biological Research Station,** (tel. 506/676-2050, pverde@ots.ac.cr, www.ots.duke.edu/en/paloverde; for reservations, P.O. Box 676-2050, San Pedro, tel. 506/240-6696, fax 506/240-6783, reservas@ots.ac.cr, $55 s, $100 d adults, $20 children), at the northern end of Palo Verde, on a space-available basis. It also has four rooms with two private bathrooms. Meals are served. Rates include meals and guided walk.

Lomas Barbudal has no accommodations, although camping is permitted ($2.50). No facilities.

Getting There

The main entrance to Palo Verde National Park is 28 km south of Bagaces, along a dirt road that begins opposite the gas station and Tempisque Conservation Area office on Hwy. 1. The route is well signed; follow the power lines past the turnoff for Lomas Barbudal. No buses travel this route. A jeep-taxi from Bagaces costs about $15 one-way.

Coming from the Nicoya peninsula, a bus operates from the town of Nicoya to Puerto Humo (see the *Nicoya* chapter), where you can hire a boat to take you three km upriver to the Chamorro dock, the trailhead to park headquarters (it's a two-km walk). Note that boats are not allowed within more than 50 meters of Isla de Pájaros. Alternately, you can drive from Filadelfia or Santa

Cruz to Hacienda El Viejo: the park is four km east from El Viejo, and the Río Tempisque two km farther. A local boatman will ferry you downriver to the park dock; the park headquarters is then an hour's walk east along a rough track that is muddy and swampy in wet season.

You can also hire a boat at Puerto Moreno, on the west bank of the Tempisque, two km south of the bridge.

The unpaved access road for Lomas Barbudal Biological Reserve is off Hwy. 1, at the Km 221 marker near Pijijes, about 10 km north of Bagaces. A dirt road—4WD recommended—leads six km to a lookout point with views over a valley whose hillsides are clad w[...] The road descends steeply from he[...] entrance (you can't drive across the riv[...] the park, but you can parallel the river to[...] and even, it is said, circumnavigate the reserve). If conditions are particularly muddy you may park at the lookout point and hike to the ranger station rather than face not being able to return via the dauntingly steep ascent from the ranger station in your car. A jeep-taxi from Bagaces will cost about $25 round-trip.

Palo Verde and Lomas Barbudal are also linked by a rough dirt road that connects to the Palo Verde park entrance station.

Liberia and Vicinity

LIBERIA

Liberia, 26 km north of Bagaces, is the provincial capital and a social, economic, and transportation hub of Guanacaste. It is also one of the country's most intriguing historic cities, with charming aged structures made of blinding white ignimbrite, for which it is called the "White City." There's a rich simplicity, a purity to the surrounding landscape, to the craggy, penurious hills and the cubist houses sheathed in white light like a sort of celestial glow. Many old adobe homes still stand to the south of the landscaped central plaza, with high-ceilinged interiors and kitchens opening onto classical courtyards. Old corner houses have doors—*puertas del sol*—that open on two sides to catch both morning and afternoon sun.

Many of the houses along **Calle Real** (Calle Central, between Avenidas Central/8) have been restored. This could well be the most historic street in the nation.

The leafy plaza hosts a modern white church—**Iglesia Imaculada Concepción de María**—and older town hall flying the Guanacastecan flag, the only provincial flag in the country.

The **Museo de Sabanero** (tel. 506/666-1606, 8 A.M.–noon and 1–4 P.M. Mon.–Sat., $0.50 admission), housed in the **Casa de Cultura,** three blocks south of the plaza on Calle 1, honors the local cowboy tradition with saddles and other *sabanero* memorabilia. The Casa de Cultura is a pretty colonial-era building that is a perfect example of a structure with doors on each corner. A **statue** also honors the *sabaneros* in the central median along Avenida Central at Calle 10. At the far end of Avenida Central, also known as Avenida 25 Julio, is **La Agonía Church,** with a stuccoed adobe exterior, simple adornments, and a small **Religious Art Museum.** Behind the church is **Parque Rodolfo Salazar,** surrounded by old cottages. Finally, just one block east of the central plaza, is the old city jail, still in use, with barred windows and towers at each corner.

North of Liberia, the scenery is magnificent, with volcanoes—one, two, three—marching in a row to the east, convex, like the volcanoes of childhood vision.

Entertainment and Events

The best time to visit is 25 July, **Día de Guanacaste,** when the whole town bursts into life to celebrate Guanacaste's secession from Nicaragua in 1812. Rodeos, a cattle show, bullfights, parades, mariachi and marimba music, firecrackers, and stalls selling local specialty dishes should keep you entertained. A similar passion is stirred each first week of September for the Semana Cultural.

Guanacaste

Both the Best Western Hotel & Casino El Sitio and Best Western Hotel Las Espuelas host live music. The former also has a small **casino,** open nightly 4 P.M.–5 A.M. (closed Sunday). The **Disco Kurú** (tel. 506/666-0769, $3 admission), across the street, pulses Thur.–Sat. and has karaoke Mon.–Wed.

Accommodations

Under $25: A reasonable choice is **Hotel Liberia** (Calle Central, Avenida 2, tel./fax 506/666-0161, hotelliberia@hotmail.com, $5 pp with shared bathroom, $9 pp with private bathroom), in an old building with 13 small, basic, clean rooms with fans and basic bathrooms with cold water. New rooms to the rear have bunks and terracotta floors. It has secure parking, a laundry, Internet service, backpacker information center, a TV in the pleasant sky-lit lounge, and transfers to Santa Rosa and Rincón de la Vieja national parks. It serves all-you-can-eat breakfasts.

La Posada del Tope (Calle Central, Avenidas 2/4, tel. 506/666-1313, fax 506/666-2136, $5 pp) is a pleasing and well-kept colonial-era home with six basic rooms with fans; they share one bathroom. Guests get use of the kitchen. In similar vein, **Hospedaje La Casona** (Calle Central, Avenidas 4/6, tel./fax 506/666-2971, $5 pp) is a cute rose-pink wooden home with 10 basic rooms with shared bathrooms. It has a TV lounge and tour office.

$25–50: The **Hotel Guanacaste** (P.O. Box 251-5000 Liberia, tel. 506/666-0085, fax 506/666-2287, htlguana@racsa.co.cr, www.hicr.org, $17 s, $30 d, or $10 pp with IYH card) is part of the Costa Rican Youth Hostel chain and thereby affiliated with IYH. This popular option has 25 simple rooms with fans, some with private baths with cold water. Most are dorms with bunk beds, a favorite of truckers using the Pan-American Highway. Some at the back have a lounge, kitchen, and large communal bathroom. There's table tennis, plus a restaurant, TV lounge, and secure parking. Camping is available; $4 pp. The hotel offers its own tours as well as twice-daily transfers to Rincón de la Vieja.

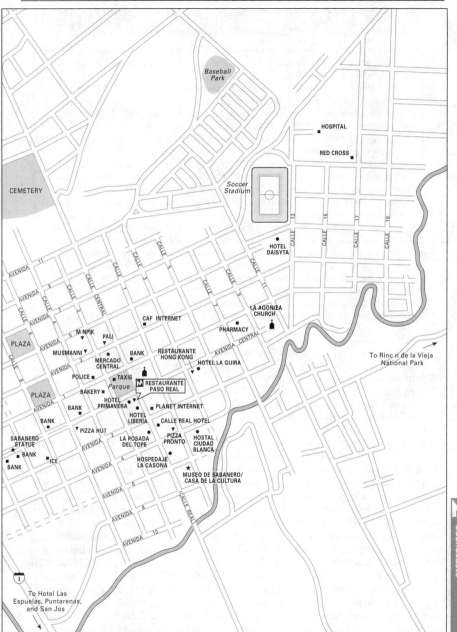

CEMETERY

Baseball Park

HOSPITAL

RED CROSS

Soccer Stadium

CALLE 13

CALLE 15

CALLE 17

CALLE 19

HOTEL DAISYTA

CALLE 11

AVENIDA 11

AVENIDA 9

CALLE CENTRAL

CALLE 7

CALLE 5

CALLE 3

CALLE 1

CAFÉ INTERNET

LA AGONÍA CHURCH

PHARMACY

AVENIDA CENTRAL

To Rincón de la Vieja National Park

PLAZA

M NPIK

PALI

MUSMANNI

MERCADO CENTRAL

BANK

RESTAURANTE HONG KONG

HOTEL LA GUIRA

POLICE

TAXIS

Parque

RESTAURANTE PASO REAL

BAKERY

HOTEL PRIMAVERA

HOTEL LIBERÍA

PLANET INTERNET

CALLE REAL HOTEL

BANK

PIZZA HUT

LA POSADA DEL TOPE

PIZZA PRONTO

HOSTAL CIUDAD BLANCA

PLAZA

BANK

SABANERO STATUE

BANK

ICE

BANK

HOSPEDAJE LA CASONA

MUSEO DE SABANERO/ CASA DE LA CULTURA

CALLE REAL

AVENIDA 6

AVENIDA 8

AVENIDA 10

To Hotel Las Espuelas, Puntarenas, and San José

Guanacaste

© AVALON TRAVEL PUBLISHING, INC.

COSTA RICAN RODEO

Cowboys are a common sight on the big cattle ranches (and the streets) of Guanacaste, Costa Rica's grassy Wild West. And they have been since Spanish colonial days, when a *sabanero* (cowboy) culture evolved.

At roundup time, the cowboys of various ranches would get together to gather in the cattle. The roundup usually closed with a wild party and cowboy competitions. Breaking wild broncos, of course, was part of the *sabanero's* daily work. By the turn of the 19th century, bull riding had developed as a way for *sabaneros* to prove who was the toughest of the hard-drinking, fist-fighting breed. Fortified with *guaro,* they hopped onto wild bulls to pit their wits and courage against the bucking fury.

The tradition evolved into the *festejos populares,* folk festivals. These festivals, held throughout Guanacaste, keep alive a deep-rooted tradition of Costa Rican culture: *recorridos de toros* (bull riding), bronco riding, homestyle Tico bullfighting, and demonstrations of the Costa Rican saddle horse. Today's festivals—more commonly called *topes* or *fiestas cívicas*—usually raise revenue to finance community projects.

The bulls are enraged before being released into the ring, where *vaqueteros* are on hand to distract the wild and dangerous animals if a rider is thrown or injured. (Their title comes from *vaqueta,* a piece of leather originally used by cowboys on haciendas to make stubborn bulls move in the direction desired, much as the red cape is used by Spanish matadors.)

Over time, bull riding has become a professional sport and evolved into its modern form. Cowboys ride bareback and hang onto angry, jumping, twisting, 680-kg bulls with only one hand (or "freestyle"—with *no* hands), while the *vaqueta* has given way to red cloth (called a *capote* or *muleta*) or even the occasional clown. The *recorridos* also feature "best bull" competitions and incredible displays of skill—such as *sabanareos* who lasso bulls with their backs turned to the animals.

The events are a grand excuse for inebriation. As more and more beer is consumed, it fuels bravado, and scores of Ticos pour into the ring. A general melée ensues as Ticos try to prove their manhood by running past the bull, which is kept enraged with an occasional prod from an electric fork or a sharp instrument. The bull is never killed, but it's a pathetic sight nonetheless.

A recommended alternative is **Hotel Primavera** (tel. 506/666-0464, fax 506/666-3069, $25 s, $37 d with fans, $30 s, $49 d with a/c), facing the plaza on Avenida Central. This modern, colonial-style structure has secure parking in a courtyard, plus 36 clean, modestly furnished rooms with cable TV and small private bathrooms with, alas, cold water only.

Hotel Daisyta (Avenida 3, Calle 13, tel. 506/666-0197 or 506/666-0877, $20 s, $30 d) has 25 simple a/c rooms with cable TV, coffeemaker, pleasing tropical color schemes with wall murals and dark-stained wooden hints, and private baths (some have cold water only). Amenities include a small swimming pool, bar and restaurant, plus secure parking and a laundry.

The venerable and popular **Hotel Bramadero** (Apdo. 193-5000 Liberia, tel. 506/666-0371, fax 506/666-0203, $23 s, $32 d low season; $37 s, $45 d high season), beside Hwy. 1 at Avenida 1, is a motel-style hotel with 25 a/c rooms with simple, uninspired furniture, cable TV, terraces, and clean private bathrooms with hot water. Rooms around the pool are particularly appealing. There's an atmospheric roadside restaurant.

The *posada*-style **Hostal Ciudad Blanca** (Avenida 4, Calles 1/3, tel. 506/666-3962, fax 506/666-4382, $30 s, $50 d) is an atmospheric old wooden house with fleur-de-lys grillwork and colonial tile floors, a charming patio, and 12 modestly decorated, albeit gloomy rooms with pretty bedspreads, a/c, cable TVs, phones, and private bath with hot water. The bar and restaurant is a popular spot. Alas, it's overpriced.

The Spanish-style **Hotel Boyeros** (Apdo. 85-5000 Liberia, tel. 506/666-0995, fax 506/666-2529, $37 s, $45 d), next to Hwy. 1 at Avenida 2, has 70 a/c rooms with cable TV, telephones, and private baths with hot water surrounding a large pool and a *palenque* bar in landscaped grounds. All rooms have a private patio or balcony and are pleasantly furnished. Next door is a 24-hour restaurant and bar that can get very noisy on weekends; noise from Hwy. 1 may be an issue as well. Take a room to the rear.

The new **Hotel La Guira** (Avenida Central, Calles 3/5, tel. 506/666-0000, fax 506/666-4444, $25 s, $37.50 d with fan, $29 s, $49 d with a/c) is a two-story structure around a courtyard offering secure parking. The 55 smallish, cool rooms have lemon-colored walls and frumpy decor, plus small albeit clean bathrooms. Some have a/c and cable TV. Only three have hot water.

$50–100: The **Best Western Hotel & Casino El Sitio** (Apdo. 134-5000, Liberia, tel. 506/666-1211, fax 506/666-2059, htlsitio@guanacaste .co.cr, www.bestwestern.co.cr, $50 s, $60 d low season; $55/65 high season), 150 meters west of Hwy. 1 on the road to Nicoya, is a modern motel-type lodging with 52 spacious rooms with private baths. Rooms are modestly furnished and have either a/c or fan, plus satellite TV, direct-dial telephone, and security box. The hotel has atmospheric Guanacastecan trimmings: red-tiled roofs, local landscape paintings, and wagon-wheel chandelier. There's a large swimming pool and sun deck, plus gift store and tour desk.

In similar vein, the **Best Western Hotel Las Espuelas** (tel. 506/666-0144, fax 506/666-2441, espuelas@racsa.co.cr, $58 s, $70 d low season; $64 s, $76 d high season) is a modest hotel set amid tropical gardens facing Hwy. 1, two km south of Liberia. The 44 spacious, modestly furnished rooms have a/c, telephones, cable TVs, and modern private baths with hot water. A country-style, beam-ceilinged restaurant serves expensive seafood and bread fresh from the oven. The hotel has a pleasant lounge with sofas and lots of potted plants, plus a large pool, hammocks under trees, and a poolside with folkloric entertainment (for gr bicycles and offers tours.

Food

A tremendous breakfast option is **Ñ Café Europa** (tel. 506/668-1081, 6 A.M.–6 P.M., $7.50), a German bakery two km west of the airport. Here, Hans, the owner, grinds his own flour to conjure succulent croissants, Danish pastries, pumpernickel breads, and other delights, including burgers, breaded pork cutlets, and pork and beef in red wine sauce. He serves cappuccinos, etc.

An outstanding eatery is **Ñ Restaurante Paso Real,** (tel. 506/666-3455, 11 A.M.–10 P.M., $5–10), on the south side of the plaza. This clean, modern, modestly elegant upstairs seafood restaurant has options for indoor a/c or patio dining with views over the plaza. It offers salads, soups, pastas, ceviche, and entrées such as fish with brandy sauce, shrimp and parmesan, squid and octopus with seafood sauce, and Mexican-style shrimp jalapeños, plus *casados.*

The atmospheric **Pizza Pronto** (Calle 1, Avenida 4, tel. 506/666-2098, noon–3 P.M. and 6–11 P.M.) serves 24 types of wood-fired pizzas in a charmingly rustic colonial home with art gallery.

The best of several Chinese restaurants in town is **Restaurante Hong Kong** (Avenida Central, Calle 3).

You can stock up at the **Palí** (Avenida 3, Calle Central) supermarket. For baked goods, head to **Musmanni** (Avenida 3, Calle 2).

Information and Services

The helpful **Liberia Chamber of Commerce Tourist Information Center** (tel. 506/666-1306, 8 A.M.–noon and 1:30–5 P.M. Mon.–Sat.) is three blocks south of the plaza in the Casa de Cultura.

Hospital Dr. Enrique Baltodano Briceño (tel. 506/666-0011) is at Avenida 4, Calles Central/2. The **Red Cross** is on the southeast corner of the hospital. There are plenty of **pharmacies.**

The **police station** is on Avenida 1, one block west of the plaza. Criminal investigation is handled by the OIJ (tel. 506/690-2901).

There are numerous banks along Avenida Central. Most have 24-hour ATMs.

The **post office** (Calle 8, Avenida 3) is open 7:30 A.M.–8 P.M. The **ICE telecommunications office** is on Calle 8 and Avenidas Central/2. There are **public telephones** in the plaza.

Planet Internet (Calle Central, Avenida Central/2, cellular tel. 506/378-9292, 8 A.M.–10 P.M. Mon.–Thur., 8 A.M.–11 P.M. Fri.–Sat.) charges $0.75 per hour. **Café Internet @ngelo** (Avenida 3, Calle1, tel. 506/665-1669) is open 9 A.M.–11 P.M. daily.

There's a **laundry** at Avenida Central, Calle 9.

Swiss Travel (tel. 506/667-0100) has a full-service travel and tour agency west of the airport.

Getting There

SANSA and NatureAir offer scheduled service between San José and **Daniel Oduber International Airport** (tel. 506/668-1032), 12 km west of town. Lacsa did not serve Liberia at last visit, but the following airlines did serve the airport: Skyservice (from Toronto, Monday, Thursday, Friday); American Trans-Air (from Orlando, Monday); ATA (from Orlando, Friday); Atlantic Air (from Nicaragua, daily); Delta (from Atlanta, Wednesday, Saturday, Sunday); Northwest (from Minneapolis, Saturday); and USA300 (from Baltimore, Detroit, Newark, and Philadelphia, Wednesday). The airport has a snack bar, toilets, and public telephones, plus a bank; and immigration (tel. 506/668-1014) and customs (tel. 506/668-1068).

Buses (tel. 506/256-9552) depart San José for Liberia from Calle 14, Avenidas 1/3, daily at 6 A.M., 7 A.M., 9 A.M., 10 A.M., 11 A.M., noon, 1 P.M., 3 P.M., 5 P.M., 6 P.M., and 8 P.M. (four hours, $4.50). A bus (tel. 506/666-0138) departs Puntarenas for Liberia daily at 12:30 P.M. (2.5 hours, $1.75), returning at 8:30 A.M. Buses from Nicoya and Santa Cruz depart for Liberia hourly, 5 A.M.–8 P.M.

Buses for Nicaragua leave Liberia at 7 A.M. (Sirca), and 8 A.M. and noon (Transnica).

Return buses depart Liberia for San José from the bus terminal at Avenida 7 and Calle 12 at 6 A.M., 6:30 A.M., 9 A.M., 12:15 P.M., and 5 P.M. Pulmitan buses depart from Avenida 9 and Calle 12 at hourly 4–8 A.M., plus 10 A.M., noon, and every two hours, 2–8 P.M.

Buses depart Liberia for Bagaces and Cañas (5;45 A.M., 7:30 A.M., 10:25 A.M., 1:30 P.M., 4:15 P.M., and 5:30 P.M.); Santa Cruz (5:30 A.M.–7:30 P.M.); Nicoya (5 A.M.–7 P.M.); Playa Panamá/Hermosa (5:15 A.M., 7:15 A.M., 11:30 A.M., 1 P.M., 3:30 P.M., 5:30 P.M., and 7 P.M.); and La Cruz (5:30 A.M.,. 8:30 A.M., 9 A.M., 11 A.M., noon, 2 P.M., 3 P.M., 4:30 P.M., 5:30 P.M., and 8 P.M.) The express bus from San José departs Liberia for Peñas Blancas at 5:30 A.M., 8:30 A.M., 11 A.M., 2 P.M., and 6 P.M.

There are three gas stations at the junction of Hwy. 1 and Avenida Central.

Getting Around

For car rental, I recommend **Europcar** (tel. 506/668-1023, fax 506/668-1145), with an outlet near the airport. **Avis** has an outlet 100 meters west of Hwy. 1 on the road to Nicoya; **Toyota Rent-a-Car** has an office on Avenida Central, Calle 10; and **Sol Rent-a-Car** (tel. 506/666-2222, fax 506/666-2898, solcar@racsa.co.cr) has an office next to Hotel Bramadero. **National Car Rental** has an office in the Best Western Hotel & Casino El Sitio. There are several other car rental agencies near the airport.

Taxis gather at the northwest corner of the plaza and by the bus station.

Ⓜ RINCÓN DE LA VIEJA

Rincón de la Vieja (1,895 meters), an active volcano in a period of relative calm, is the largest of five volcanoes that make up the Cordillera de Guanacaste. The volcano is composed of nine separate but contiguous craters, with dormant **Santa María** (1,916 meters) the tallest and most easterly. Its crater harbors a forest-rimmed lake popular with quetzals, linnets, and tapirs. The main crater—**Von Seebach**—still steams. Icy Lake Los Jilgueros lies between the two craters. The last serious eruption was in 1983. Rincón, however, spewed lava and acid gases on 8 May 1991, causing destructive *lahores* (ash-mud flows). The slopes still bear reminders of the destructive force of the acid cloud that burnt

en route to Rincón de la Vieja National Park

away much of the vegetation on the southeastern slope.

The 14,083-hectare Parque Nacional Volcán Rincón de la Vieja extends from 650 to 1,965 meters in elevation on both the Caribbean and Pacific flanks of the *cordillera*. The Pacific side has a distinct dry season (if you want to climb to the craters, Feb.–April is best); by contrast, the Caribbean side is lush and wet year-round, with as much as 500 cm of rainfall annually on higher slopes. The park is known for its profusion of orchid species. More than 300 species of birds include quetzals, toucanets, the elegant trogon, eagles, three-wattled bellbirds, and the curassow. Mammals include cougars; howler, spider, and white-faced monkeys; and kinkajous, sloths, tapirs, tayras, and even jaguars.

The lower slopes can be explored along relatively easy trails that begin at the park headquarters. The **Sendero Encantado** leads through cloud forest full of *guaria morada* orchids (the national flower) and links with a 12-km trail that continues to **Las Pailas** (Cauldrons), 50 hectares of bubbling mud volcanoes, boiling thermal waters, vapor geysers, and the so-called Hornillas (Ovens) geyser of sulfur dioxide and hydrogen sulfide. Be careful when walking around: it is possible to step through the crust and scald yourself, or worse. This trail continues to the summit.

Between the cloud forest and Las Pailas, a side trail (marked Aguas Thermales) leads to soothing hot-sulfur springs called **Los Azufrales** (Sulfurs). The thermal waters (42°C) form small pools where you may bathe and take advantage of their curative properties. Use the cold-water stream nearby for cooling off after a good soak in the thermal springs. **Las Hornillas** are sulfurous fumaroles on the devastated southern slope of the volcano. Another trail leads to the **Hidden Waterfalls**, four continuous falls (three of which exceed 70 meters) in the Agria Ravine. You'll find a perfect bathing hole at the base of one of the falls.

You must hike one trail at a time, and report to the ranger station before setting out on each subsequent trail. If you don't report, rangers set out to find you after a specified time.

the Summit

elatively straightforward. You can do
ip to the summit and back in a day,
two days from park headquarters. The trail begins at the Santa María Ranger Station, leads
past Las Hornillas and the Las Pailas Ranger
Station, and snakes up the steep, scrubby mountainside through elephant grass and dense groves
of twisted, stunted copel clusia, a perfumed tree
species common near mountain summits. En
route, you cross a bleak expanse of purple lava
fossilized by the blitz of the sun. Trails are
marked by cairns, though it is easy to get lost if
the clouds set in; consider hiring a local guide.
The upper slopes are of loose scree. Be particularly careful on your descent.

It can be cool up here, but the powerful view
and the hard, windy silence make for a pro-
found experience. From on high, you have a
splendid view of the wide Guanacaste plain
shimmering in the heat like a dreamworld between hallucination and reality, and, beyond,
the mountains of Nicoya glistening like hammered gold from the sunlight slanting in from
the south. On a clear day, you can see Lake
Nicaragua. Magical! You have only the sighing of
the wind for company.

It will probably be cloudy, however, in which
case you may need to camp near the top to ascend the summit the next morning before the
clouds set in (there's a campsite about five km
from Las Pailas; it's about two hours to the summit of Von Seebach from there). The beach of
Linnet Bird Lagoon—a whale-shaped lagoon
filled with very cold water, southeast of the active
volcano—is recommended for camping. Bring a
waterproof tent and clothing, plus mosquito repellent. The grasses harbor ticks and other biting
critters: consider long pants.

Fill up with water at the ranger station before
your hike.

Camping

You can camp at the **ranger stations** ($2 pp).
Bring a sleeping bag and mosquito netting. Make
reservations by calling the park headquarters in
Santa Rosa. A shady campsite next to an old
sugarcane-processing plant, 500 meters from

the Santa María ranger station, has a bathroom.
There's another campsite on the banks of the
Río Colorado, near the Las Pailas Ranger Station,
with showers, toilets, and water. Camp here if
hiking to the summit. Otherwise you may camp
where you like; however, there are lots of ticks. It
can get cold at night; come prepared.

There are several nature lodges on the edge
of the park.

Information and Services

The park headquarters is at **Hacienda Santa
María,** about 27 km northeast of Liberia (a sign
on Hwy. 1 on the south side of Liberia points the
way to the "Sector Santa María"). The 19th-cen-
tury farmstead was once owned by former U.S.
president Lyndon B. Johnson, who sold it to the
park service. It contains an exhibition room and
is linked by a six-km trail to the **Las Pailas
Ranger Station** (tel. 506/661-8189), on the
southwestern flank of the volcano. Las Pailas is
reached via a road from Curubandé (see *Rincón
de la Vieja Vicinity,* below). Admission costs $6.

The park is administered from the Guanacaste
Conservation Area office in Santa Rosa National
Park (tel. 506/666-5051, fax 506/666-5020,
www.acguanacaste.ac.cr); see *Santa Rosa National Park,* below.

Getting There

The road to the Santa María Ranger Station begins from the Barrio Victoria suburb of Liberia,
where Avenida 6 leads east 25 km via Colonia La
Libertad (a side road leads to San Jorge—see *Accommodations,* below—which can also be reached
by a rough dirt road from Guayabo, north of
Bagaces). The road is deeply rutted (and muddy
in wet season); 4WD is recommended. Lodges
arrange transfers, and the Hotel Guanacaste in
Liberia has transfers daily at 7 A.M. and 4 P.M.
($7 pp each way, three people minimum). A taxi
from Liberia will cost about $30–40 each way.
Park rangers may take you if they're heading to or
from town.

The Santa María and Las Pailas ranger stations are linked by trails, or you can reach Las
Pailas from Hwy. 1 via a turnoff about six km
north of Liberia: the dirt road leads past the vil-

lage of Curubandé (10 km) to the gates of Hacienda Lodge Guachipelín (see below). The gates are open during daylight hours. Ostensibly you pay a $2.50 fee for the right to use the private road. The dirt road leads three km to Hacienda Lodge Guachipelín (the toll is reimbursed if you stay here) and, beyond, to Rincón de la Vieja Lodge (no refund) and Las Pailas Ranger Station. A bus departs Liberia for Curubandé at 2 P.M. on Monday, Wednesday, and Friday.

Take your sunglasses: the roads are blinding white. The rock is ignimbrite, the white volcanic rock used to build the houses of Liberia.

VICINITY OF RINCÓN DE LA VIEJA

There are several haciendas and nature lodges on the lower slopes of Rincón de la Vieja. Together they offer a panoply of activities. All accept day visitors as well as offering accommodations.

Via Curubandé

Hacienda Lodge Guachipelín (P.O. Box 636-4050 Alajuela, tel. 506/666-8075, fax 506/442-1910, info@guachipelin.com, www.guachipelin .com), a centenarian working cattle ranch east of Curubandé, 18 km from Hwy. 1 and eight km south of the Santa María Ranger Station, offers more than 1,000 hectares of terrain from dry forest to open savanna, plus a 1,200-hectare tree-reforestation project. It offers guided horseback rides ($10–22) and even gives riding lessons, and has an eight-day horseback-riding tour around Rincón de la Vieja; horses are not allowed within the park. It also has volcano hikes and nature excursions. You can rent mountain bikes ($10).

The hacienda also has the **Kazm Cañon canopy tour,** operated by the Original Canopy Tour, where you can whiz across a canyon and between treetops from 10 platforms. It costs $45 ($35 students, $25 children).

Rincón de la Vieja Lodge (P.O. Box 160-5000 Liberia, tel./fax 506/661-8198, info@ricon delaviejalodge.com, www.rincondelavie jalodge.com), five km beyond Hacienda Lodge Guachipelín and only one km below the park

© CHRISTOPHER P. BAKER

Hacienda Guachipelín

near Las Pailas, is a superb base for exploring the park, with six types of tropical forest on its 900-acre private reserve. It, too, offers a zipline **canopy tour.** You're at one with the monkeys as you glide between any of 21 treetop canopy platforms elevated up to 170 feet. The "trail" lasts 2.5 hours ($50, or $82 by night, or $108 including overnight in the canopy). It offers horse tours ($30–45), mountain biking ($5 per hour), and nature tours. The property also includes a roofed corral and a dairy farm. You can hire guides for hikes ($15 pp).

Via Cañas Dulces

Beyond **Cañas Dulces,** four km east of Hwy. 1 (the turnoff is 11 km north of Liberia; don't mistake this for Cañas, further south on Hwy. 1), the road turns to dirt and climbs uphill 13 km to **Buena Vista Mountain Lodge & Adventure Center** (P.O. Box 373-5000, Liberia, tel./fax 506/661-8158, information@buenavistalodge .com, www.buenavistacr.com), a 1,600-hectare

Guanacaste

ranch nestling high on the northwest flank of the mountain. The lodge offers a variety of guided hikes ($20) and horseback trips ($35–35). It has a **canopy tour,** which uses rappelling equipment on 960 meters of cable slung between trees ($30–35); there's also an 850-meter-long trail with 17 hanging bridges ($20). The highlight is a 420-meter **water slide**—like a toboggan run—ending with a plunge into a pool ($20); you descend on an inner tube while wearing a helmet. Mud treatments and thermal saunas are also offered. And rodeos and "bullfights" are sometimes hosted in a corral.

One km below Buena Vista Lodge, a side road leads three km to **Hotel Borinquen Mountain Resort Thermae & Spa** (P.O. Box 108-5000 Liberia, tel. 506/666-0363 or 666-5098, fax 506/666-2931, borinquenresort@aol.com, www .borinquenresort.com), an upscale mountain resort built around bubbling *pilas* (mud ponds) where steam rises sibilantly amid the trees, drawing you to the rustic steam room built over a bubbling hot spring that feeds the whirlpool spas. It specializes in thermal treatments, including full-body mineral mud masks. When it dries, you stand beneath an outdoor shower and—hey presto!—you're like new ($10). It has plunge pools (one hot, one tepid, one cold) and a beautiful landscaped swimming pool with Jacuzzi. Borinquen also offers guided hiking ($10), horseback riding ($25, three hours), waterfall ride ($28), plus an all-terrain *cuadrociclo* (ATV) safari ($30, two hours). You can also rent the ATVs for $30 hourly. It is surrounded by primary forest accessed by trails; monkeys abound. Day visits cost $10; or $26 for a package including lunch and use of the thermal spa.

Buses depart Liberia for Cañas Dulces at 5:30 A.M., noon, and 5:30 P.M.

Accommodations and Food

Near Santa María, (see *Getting There,* in the *Rincón de la Vieja National Park* section, above), the **Rinconcito Lodge** (tel. 506/666-2764 or

Hotel Borinquen's swimming pool

506/380-8193, rinconcito@racsa.co.cr, $10 pp shared bath, $16s, $20 d private bath) is a working farm offering five rudimentary rooms in a cement-block house with warm water (two rooms have shared bathrooms). There are lots of flying insects, so a mosquito net is a good idea, and the electricity shuts off at 10 P.M. Horses and guides are available, and simple *típico* meals are served. The friendly owners—Gerardo and María Inés Badilla—offer transfers from Liberia ($35 round-trip for up to six people). Breakfast costs $3, lunch and dinner cost $5 each.

Near Curubandé, the **Quinta Splendida** (tel./fax 506/666-8289) about 10 km along the road, on the southern edge of Currubandé village, is a rustic farm run by a German couple with children. They offer camping ($5 with own tent, or $8 s/d with tent rental), but rental tents are small. It has a toilet and sink, but no shower. Breakfasts cost $2.50.

I love the ⚑ **Posada el Encuentro Inn** (P.O. Box 367-5000 Liberia, tel./fax 506/382-0815, $35 s, $40 d *casitas,* $40/50 suites low season; $55 s, $65 d *casitas,* $70/80 suites high season), an off-the-beaten-track surprise about five km east of the turnoff for Rincón via Currubandé, and owned by delightful sibling duo Gilmar and Wilma Angulo Ménez, who speak English, German, and Spanish. This exquisite private home built of stone sits on a breeze-swept hilltop with marvelous volcano views. It has two *casitas* with two large bedrooms, private baths with beautiful colonial tiles and huge walk-in showers, and private terraces; and seven graciously appointed rooms and junior suites in the main residence. They're done up in whitewashed stone with mauve and canary yellow counterpoints and have lofty wooden ceilings with fans, plus spacious bathrooms. It has a swimming pool in a concrete sun deck with shade umbrellas and lounge chairs, plus billiards and bicycles. It also offers horseback rides. The restaurant is open to the public 6 A.M.–11 P.M. daily. Rates include tax and breakfast.

Hacienda Lodge Guachipelín (see above, $36 s, $52 d) has metamorphosed from a rustic no-frills option to a more sophisticated treat. The hardwood lodge, on a working cattle ranch, now boasts a gracious lobby with exquisite wrought-iron sofas, Internet, and a bar overlooking a kidney-shaped pool under shade trees. It has 34 small and simply appointed bedrooms, all with fans and wide verandas. There's a cozy lounge with deep-cushioned sofas and a TV, plus verandas with rockers. Four rooms in the old *casona* overlook the corral, where you can watch cattle and horses being worked. The stone and timber bar-restaurant at the entrance to the hacienda is open to the public and offers rustic elegance, plus buffet dinners to the accompaniment of marimba players; open 6 A.M.–10 P.M. daily. It boasts views of the volcano. A transfer from Liberia costs $25 (or $35 from the airport).

I also like **Rincón de la Vieja Mountain Lodge** (see above, $15 pp hostel year-round, $47 s/d standard, $57 s/d bungalow low season; $58 standard, $70 bungalow high season), a rustic and charming all-hardwood lodge converted from a family hacienda. The lodge offers nine dorm rooms with bunks; 22 pleasing though dark standard rooms with private bathrooms with cold water; plus 11 Colorado-style log bungalows for six to eight people. All have verandas and shared bath. There are two small pools in the lush gardens and, beyond that, forest. Electricity is generated by a stream. The lodge is 500 meters beyond the Río Colorado, which you can safely cross by 4WD. It's 1.5 km to the right from the fork for the park. Meals average $10 for breakfast, $12 dinner. Students receive discounts. Rates include taxes.

Near Cañas Dulces, the **Buena Vista Mountain Lodge & Adventure Center** (see above, $15 pp dorms for six; $35 s, $35 d private room low season; $35 s, $47 d high season) has 77 rooms including dorms with two double beds and a bunk, and 11 double rooms with private baths with hot water. The rustic and delightful cabins are hewn of stone and rough timbers, with pewter-washed floors and verandas looking down over lush lawns and a lake. Locally crafted rockers add to the atmosphere. You can admire the setting while soaking in a natural steam bath ringed by volcanic stone, and there's a bamboo sauna. Transfers from Cañas Dulces

⚑ **Guanacaste**

cost $15 round-trip. A rustic restaurant serves buffet meals. You can camp for $10.

The beautiful **Hotel Borinquen Mountain Resort Thermae & Spa** (see above, $100 s, $135 d low season; $125 s, $150 d high season), in colonial hacienda style, has a classically aged feel. It offers 33 capacious rooms in single and duplex red-tile-roofed bungalows spaced apart on the grassy hills; they're well-lit and have ceramic floors, lofty wooden ceilings, two double beds, a/c, fans, cable TVs, orthopedic mattresses, rockers, and French doors opening to verandas. Handmade furnishings include wrought-iron candelabras and rustic country antiques (take your pick of decor: pre-Columbian or Spanish colonial). Guests move around on electric golf carts. Facilities include a tennis court, beauty salon, gym, spa, and a swimming pool with swim-up bar. There are trails for hiking and horseback rides.

The Far North

QUEBRADA GRANDE

The village of **Quebrada Grande,** eight km east of Hwy. 1—the turnoff is at **Potrerillos,** 23 km north of Liberia (there's a Guardia Rural checkpoint at the junction)—sits on the lower saddle between Volcán Rincón de la Vieja to the southeast and Volcán Cacao (see *Guanacaste National Park,* below) to the northeast. It is surrounded by grasslands ranged by cattle. Several *haciendas* welcome visitors for horseback trail rides, including **Santa Clara Lodge** and **Nueva Zelandia Lodge** (see *Accommodations,* below). The latter is a 500-hectare *finca* that includes a 200-hectare dairy farm and 250 hectares of tropical dry and humid forest abounding with wildlife. It has trails and guided volcano tours, and a working dairy farm where you can also learn how cheese and homemade sour cream are processed.

Accommodations

Santa Clara Lodge (Apdo. 17-5000, Liberia, tel. 506/691-8062 or 506/361-2805, $10 pp with shared bath, $22 s/d with private bath), four km east of Quebrada Grande by rocky road, is a very rustic cattle ranch with eight simple rooms, some with shared bath. Two rooms have bunk beds. Though crudely furnished, the well-kept rooms have pretty decor plus louvered windows. Home-style meals are served alfresco on a veranda. A thatched bar overlooks a small duck pond. A mineral spring feeds a soaking pool, said to be therapeutic. It is surrounded by 118 hectares of savanna and forest. Horseback riding is available.

Nueva Zelandia Lodge (tel./fax 506/691-8177, bricha@racsa.co.cr, www.costarica.tourism.co.cr/hotels/nzelandia/index.html, $50 pp low season, $55 high season), about 13 km east of Quebrada Honda on the road to Upala, is on the southeast side of Volcán Cacao, in the saddle between Rincón de la Vieja. It is surrounded by primary forest and is sufficiently high to enjoy views of the Gulf of Papagayo and Lake Nicaragua. The rustic but cozy lodge has a TV lounge and capacity for 15 people in simply appointed but perfectly adequate and pleasing accommodations. It also has **camping.** Credit cards are accepted. Rates include tax, plus meals and tours.

Getting There

A bus runs from Liberia to Quebrada Grande at 3 P.M.; a second bus departs Quebrada Grande at 4 P.M. for Nueva Zelandia. Group transfers from Daniel Oduber Airport cost $20 pp. The road turns to dirt about five km east of Quebrada Grande.

◼ SANTA ROSA NATIONAL PARK

Santa Rosa was founded in 1972 as the country's first national park. The 49,515-hectare park, which covers much of the Santa Elena peninsula, is part of a mosaic of ecologically interdependent parks and reserves—the 110,000-hectare

Guanacaste Conservation Area (GCA)—that incorporates Santa Rosa National Park, Rincón de la Vieja National Park, Bolaños Island Wildlife Refuge, the Junquillal Bay National Wildlife Refuge, and the Horizontes Experimental Station, abutting Santa Rosa to the south.

Parque Nacional Santa Rosa is most famous for Hacienda Santa Rosa—better known as La Casona—the nation's most cherished historic monument. It was here in 1856 that the mercenary army of American adventurer William Walker was defeated by a ragamuffin army of Costa Rican volunteers. The old hacienda-turned-museum alone is well worth the visit.

The park is a mosaic of 10 distinct habitats, including mangrove swamp, savanna, and oak forest, which attract more than 250 bird species and 115 mammal species (half of them bats, including two vampire species), among them relatively easily seen animals such as white-tailed deer; coatimundis; howler, spider, and white-faced monkeys; and anteaters. In the wet season the land is as green as emeralds, and wildlife disperses. In dry season, however, wildlife congregates at watering holes and is easily spotted. Jaguars, margays, ocelots, pumas, and jaguarundis

are here, but are seldom seen. Santa Rosa is a vitally important nesting site for ridleys and other turtle species.

The park is divided into two sections: the more important and accessible Santa Rosa Sector to the south (the entrance is at Km 269 on Hwy. 1, 37 km north of Liberia) and the Murciélago Sector (the turnoff from Hwy. 1 is 10 km farther north, via Cuajiniquil), separated by a swathe of privately owned land.

Santa Rosa Sector

On the right, one km past the entrance gate, a rough dirt road leads to a rusting armored personnel carrier beside a memorial cross commemorating the Battle of 1955, when Somoza, the Nicaraguan strongman, made an ill-fated foray into Costa Rica.

Six km farther on the paved road is **La Casona,** a magnificent colonial homestead (actually, it's a replica, rebuilt in 2001 after arsonists burned the original down) with a beautiful setting atop a slight rise overlooking a stone corral where the battle with William Walker was fought. Alas, the fire destroyed the antique furnishings and collection of photos, illustrations, carbines, and

La Casona, Santa Rosa National Park

Guanacaste

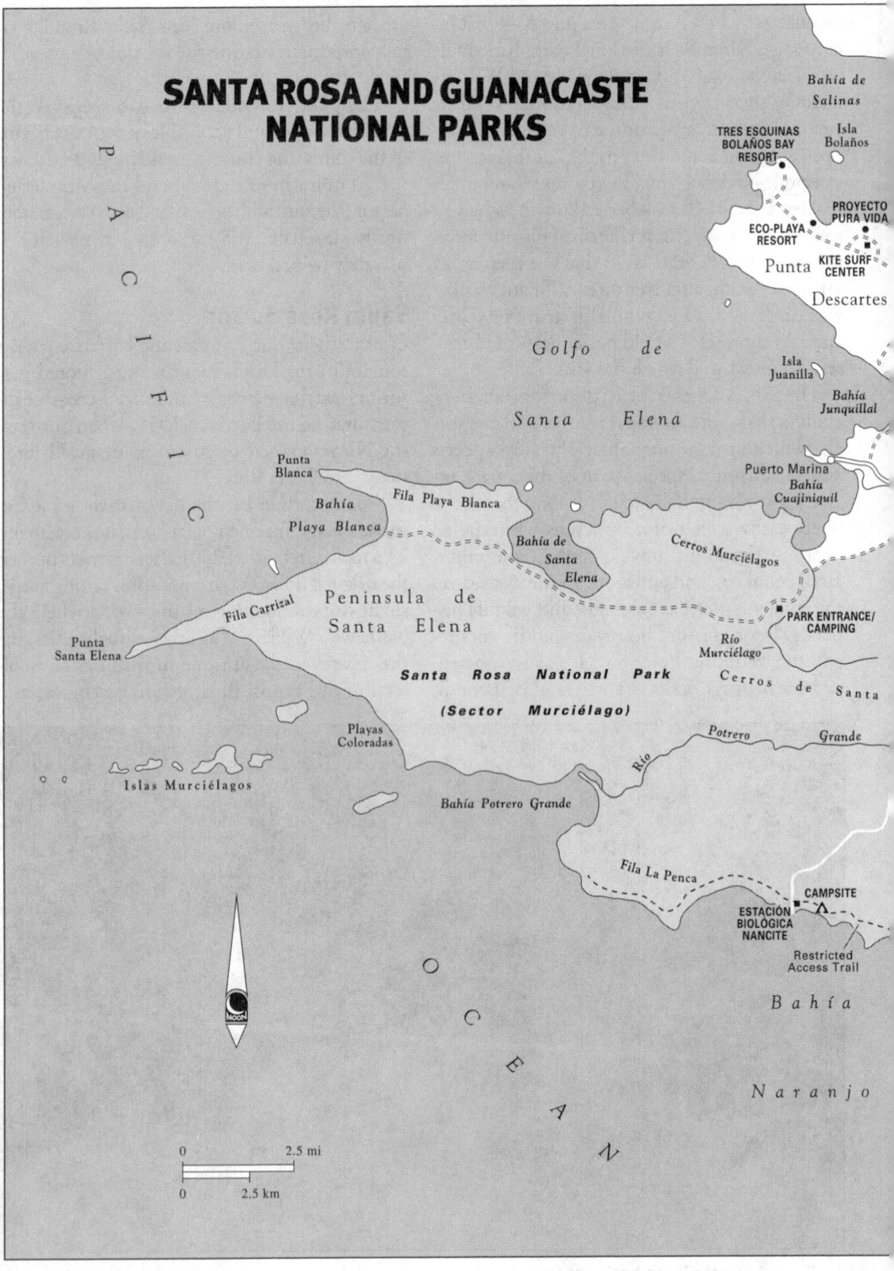

SANTA ROSA AND GUANACASTE NATIONAL PARKS

P A C I F I C

Bahía de Salinas

TRES ESQUINAS
BOLAÑOS BAY
RESORT

Isla Bolaños

PROYECTO PURA VIDA

ECO-PLAYA RESORT

KITE SURF CENTER

Punta

Descartes

Golfo   de

Isla Juanilla

Bahía Junquillal

Santa   Elena

Punta Blanca

Fila Playa Blanca

Bahía Playa Blanca

Puerto Marina
Bahía Cuajiniquil

Bahía de Santa Elena

Cerros Murciélagos

Peninsula   de
Santa   Elena

Fila Carrizal

PARK ENTRANCE/
CAMPING

Punta Santa Elena

Río Murciélago

Santa   Rosa   National   Park

Cerros   de   Santa

(Sector   Murciélago)

Playas Coloradas

Potrero

Grande

Islas Murciélagos

Río

Bahía Potrero Grande

Fila La Penca

CAMPSITE

ESTACIÓN BIOLÓGICA NANCITE

Restricted Access Trail

O

C

E

A

N

Bahía

Naranjo

| 0 | 2.5 mi |
| 0 | 2.5 km |

MOON

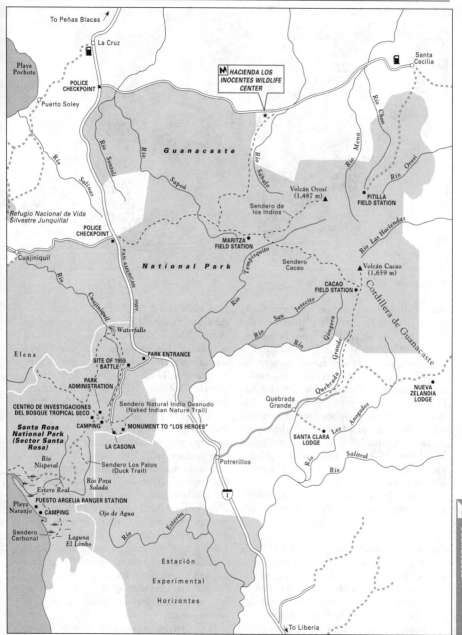

To Peñas Blacas

La Cruz

Playa
Pochote

POLICE
CHECKPOINT

Puerto Soley

Río Salitras

Santa
Cecilia

**HACIENDA LOS
INOCENTES WILDLIFE
CENTER**

Guanacaste

Río Sapoá

Río Sábalo

Río Mena

Río Chan

Río Orosí

Volcán Orosí
(1,487 m)

Sendero de
los Indios

PITILLA
FIELD STATION

*Refugio Nacional de Vida
Silvestre Junquillal*

POLICE
CHECKPOINT

MARITZA
FIELD STATION

Río Las Haciendas

Cuajiniquil

National Park

Río Cuajiniquil

PAN-AMERICAN HWY.

Río Tempisquito

Sendero
Cacao

Volcán Cacao
(1,659 m)

CACAO
FIELD STATION

Río San Josecito

Río Góngora

Cordillera de Guanacaste

Waterfalls

Elena

SITE OF 1955
BATTLE

PARK ENTRANCE

PARK
ADMINISTRATION

CENTRO DE INVESTIGACIONES
DEL BOSQUE TROPICAL SECO

Sendero Natural Indio Desnudo
(Naked Indian Nature Trail)

CAMPING

MONUMENT TO "LOS HEROES"

*Santa Rosa
National Park
(Sector Santa
Rosa)*

LA CASONA

Río Nisperal

Sendero Los Patos
(Duck Trail)

*Río Poza
Salada*

Potrerillos

Río Grande

Quebrada
Grande

Quebrada Grande

Río Los Anogados

NUEVA
ZELANDIA
LODGE

SANTA CLARA
LODGE

Estero Real

PUESTO ARGELIA RANGER STATION

Playa
Naranjo

CAMPING

Ojo de Agua

Río Esterón

Río Salitral

Sendero
Carbonal

Laguna
El Limbo

*Estación
Experimental
Horizontes*

To Liberia

© AVALON TRAVEL PUBLISHING, INC.

Guanacaste

lizard at Santa Rosa National Park

other military paraphernalia commemorating the battle of 20 March 1856. Battles were also fought here during the 1919 Sapoá Revolution and in 1955. Harmless bats fly in and out. The garden contains rocks with Indian petroglyphs.

Trails are marked in detail on the map sold at the park entrance. The **Naked Indian** loop trail (1.5 km) begins just before the house and leads through dry-forest woodlands with streams and waterfalls and gumbo-limbo trees whose peeling red bark earned them the nickname "naked Indian trees." The **Los Patos** trail, which has several watering holes during dry season, is one of the best trails for spotting mammals.

The paved road ends just beyond the administration area. From here, a dirt road drops steeply to the beaches—Playa Naranjo and Playa Nancite, 13 km from La Casona. Negotiating this road takes good driving skills; A 4WD with high ground clearance is essential, but passage is never guaranteed, not least because the Río Nisperal can be impassable in wet season. Park officials sometimes close the road and will charge you a fee if you have to be hauled out.

The deserted white-sand **Playa Nancite** (about a one-hour hike over a headland from Estero Real, at the end of the dirt road) is renowned as the site for the annual *arribadas,* the mass nestings of olive ridley turtles which occur only here and at Ostional, farther south. More than 75,000 turtles will gather out to sea and come ashore over the space of a few days, with the possibility of up to 10,000 reptiles on the beach at any one time in September and October. Although the exact trigger is unknown, *arribadas* seem to coincide with falling barometric pressure in autumn and are apparently associated with a waxing three-quarter moon. You can usually see solitary turtles at other times August through December. Stephen E. Cornelius's illustrated book *The Sea Turtles of Santa Rosa National Park* (Costa Rica: National Park Foundation, 1986) provides an insight into the life of the ridley turtle. Latest data suggests that the turtle population at Nancite is declining. Playa Nancite is a research site; access is restricted and permits are needed, though anyone can get one from the ranger station, or at Programa de Ecoturismo, c/o Centro de los Investigaciones (see below). There's a limit of 30 people per day.

Playa Naranjo is a beautiful, kilometers-long, pale gray sand beach that is legendary in surfing lore for its steep, powerful tubular waves and for **Witches Rock** rising like a sentinel out of the water. The beach is bounded by craggy headlands and frequently visited by monkeys, iguanas, and other wildlife. Crocodiles lurk in the mangrove swamps at the southern end of the beach. At night, plankton light up with a brilliant phosphorescence as you walk the drying sand in the wake of high tide.

Playa Potrero Grande, north of Nancite, and other beaches on the central Santa Elena peninsula offer some of the best "machine-like" surf in the country, with double overhead waves rolling in one after the other. The makers of *Endless Summer II,* the sequel to the classic surfing movie, caught the Potrero Grande break perfectly. You can hire a boat at Jobo or any of the fishing villages in the Golfo Santa Elena to take you to Potrero Grande or **Islas Murciélagos** (Bat Islands), slung in a chain beneath Cabo Santa Elena, the westernmost point of the peninsula. The Bat Islands are a renowned scuba diving site for advanced divers; sharks (bull, tiger, and black-tip) are there in numbers, along with whale sharks.

Murciélago Sector

The entrance to the Murciélago Sector of Santa Rosa National Park is 15 km west of Hwy. 1, 10 km north of the Santa Rosa Sector park entrance (there's a police checkpoint at the turnoff; have your passport ready for inspection). The road winds downhill to a coastal valley through spectacularly hilly countryside to the hamlet of **Cuajiniquíl,** tucked half a kilometer south of the road, which continues northwest to Bahía Cuajiniquíl.

You arrive at a Y-fork in Cuajiniquíl: the road to Murciélago (eight km) is to the left. There are three rivers to ford en route. You'll pass the old CIA training camp for the Nicaraguan contras on your right. The place—Murciélago Hacienda—was owned by the Nicaraguan dictator Somoza's family before being expropriated in 1979, when the Murciélago Sector was incorporated into Santa Rosa National Park. It's now a training camp for the Costa Rican police force. Armed guards may stop you for an ID check as you pass.

A few hundred meters farther, the road runs alongside the "secret" airstrip (hidden behind tall grass to your left) that Oliver North had built to supply the contras. The park entrance is 0.5 km beyond the airstrip.

It's another 16 km to **Playa Blanca,** a beautiful horseshoe-shaped white-sand beach—one of the most isolated in the country—about five km wide and enjoyed only by pelicans and frigate birds. The road ends here. Waterfalls are surrounded by ferns and palms in **Cuajiniquil Canyon,** which has its own moist microclimate. The **Poza El General** watering hole attracts waterfowl and other animals year-round and is reached along a rough trail.

Here you'll find Ollie's Point, named after Oliver North. "What Ollie probably never knew," says surfer Peter Brennan, "is that just off the coast there's a hot right point."

Information

The park entrance station (tel. 506/666-5051, ext. 219, 8 A.M.–4 P.M., $7 admission), at the Santa Rosa Sector sells maps showing trails and campgrounds. The **park administration office** (Apdo 169-5000, Liberia, tel. 506/666-5051, fax 506/666-5020, acg@acguanacaste.ac.cr, www .acguanacaste.ac.cr) can provide additional information.

The **Dry Tropical Forest Investigation Center** (Centro de los Investigaciones, Apdo. 169-5000 Liberia, tel. 506/666-5051, ext. 233), next to the administrative center near La Casona, undertakes biological research. It is not open to visitors.

Accommodations

The Santa Rosa Sector has three **campsites.** La Casona campsite, 400 meters west of the administrative center near La Casona, is shaded by guanacaste trees and has barbecue pits, picnic tables, and bathrooms ($2 pp). It can get muddy here in the wet season. The shady Argelia campsite at Playa Naranjo has sites with fire pits and picnic tables and benches. There are shared showers, sinks, and outhouse toilets, and water from a well (it is not potable, so boil it or bring bottled water). The campsite at the north end of Playa

Guanacaste

Nancite is for use by permit only (see above). Take lots of water.

Dry Tropical Forest Investigation Center accommodates guests on a space-available basis. Reservations are recommended. Rates are $15 pp, $10 scientists, $6 students and assistants.

In the Murciélago Sector, you can camp at the ranger station, where there's a bathroom, showers, water, and picnic tables ($2 pp). There are also cabins for researchers only.

In Cuanjiniquíl, **Cabinas Santa Elena,** has two rooms with shared bath and cold water; call the local pulpería (tel. 506/679-9112) and leave a message.

Raccoons abound, and will stop at nothing to get at your food. Do *not* leave food in your tent. Fires are a serious hazard (the Parks Service issues a pamphlet, *Preventing Forest Fires*).

Food

The park administration area has a small *cocina* (kitchen) serving meals by reservation only at 6:30–7:30 A.M., 11:30 A.M.–12:30 P.M., and 5–6 P.M.

Getting There

Buses (tel. 506/256-9072) depart San José for La Cruz and Peñas Blancas from Calle 14, Avenidas 3/5, daily at 5 A.M., 7 A.M., 7:45 A.M., 1:20 P.M., and 4:10 P.M., passing the park entrance—35 km north of Liberia—en route to the Nicaraguan border (six hours). Buses depart Liberia for Santa Rosa and La Cruz from Avenida 5, Calle 14, at 5:30 A.M., 8:30 A.M., 11 A.M., 2 P.M., and 6 P.M. You'll have to walk or hitchhike from the park entrance (seven km to La Casona and the park headquarters, another 13 km to Playa Naranjo).

Buses from La Cruz and Peñas Blancas pass the park en route to San José at 6:25 A.M., 8:15 A.M., 10:10 A.M., 1:30 P.M., 4:20 P.M., and 6 P.M.; and en route to Liberia at 12:30 P.M., 3:40 P.M., and 5:15 P.M.

Buses to Murciélago Sector depart La Cruz for Cuajiniquil at 5 A.M. and noon, and from Liberia for Cuajiniquil at 5:45 A.M. and 3:30 P.M. (returning at 7 A.M. and 4:45 P.M.). You can catch the Liberia–Cuajiniquil–La Cruz bus from the Santa Rosa entrance at 4 P.M. From Cuajiniquil

you may have to walk the eight km to the park entrance.

GUANACASTE NATIONAL PARK

The mammoth Parque Nacional Guanacaste ($6 admission), one of the least visited and least developed parks in the nation, protects more than 84,000 hectares of savanna, dry forest, rainforest, and cloud forests extending east from Hwy. 1 to 1,659 meters atop Volcán Cacao. The park is contiguous with Santa Rosa National Park (to the west) and protects the migratory routes of myriad creatures, many of which move seasonally between the lowlands and the steep slopes of Volcán Cacao and the dramatically conical Volcán Orosi (1,487 meters), whose wind-battered and rain-drenched eastern slopes contrast sharply with the flora and fauna on the dry plains. Orosi long since ceased activity and shows no signs of a crater.

The park includes significant areas of cattle pasture, which are carefully managed to permit natural reforestation. It is one of the most closely monitored parks scientifically, with three permanent biological stations. The **Pitilla Biological Station** is at 600 meters elevation on the northeast side of Cacao amid the lush, rain-soaked forest. It is reached via a rough dirt road from Santa Cecilia, 28 km east of Hwy. 1 beyond Hacienda Los Inocentes (see below). A 4WD is essential. It's a nine-km drive via Esperanza. Ask locals for the correct route. **Cacao Field Station** (also called Mengo) sits at the edge of a cloud forest at 1,100 meters on the southwestern slope of Volcán Cacao. You can get there by hiking or taking a horse 10 km along a rough dirt trail from Quebrada Grande (see *Quebrada Grande,* above); the turnoff from Hwy. 1 is at Potrerillos, nine km south of the Santa Rosa National Park turnoff. You'll see a sign for the station 500 meters beyond Dos Ríos (11 km beyond Quebrada Grande). The road—paved for the first four km—deteriorates gradually. Four-wheel-drive vehicles can make it to within 300 meters of the station in dry season, with permission; in wet season you'll

Orosi Volcano, as seen from Hacienda los Inocentes

probably need to park at Gongora, about five km before Cacao, and proceed on foot or horseback.

Maritza Field Station is farther north, at about 650 meters on the western side of the saddle between Cacao and Orosi Volcanoes. You get there from Hwy. 1 via a dirt road to the right at the Cuajiniquil crossroads. It's 15 km. There are barbed-wire gates: simply close them behind you. Four-wheel drive is essential in wet season. The station has a research laboratory. From here you can hike to Cacao Biological Station. Another trail leads to El Pedregal.

At **El Pedregal,** on the Llano de los Indios (a plain on the western slope of Orosi), almost 100 petroglyphs representing a pantheon of chiseled supernatural beings lie half-buried in the luxurious undergrowth that cloaks the mountain's hide.

The park is administered from the Guanacaste Regional Conservation Area Headquarters at Santa Rosa.

Accommodations

You can camp at any of the ranger stations ($1.50 per day).

The biological stations provide spartan dormitory accommodations on a space-available basis; for reservations, contact the park headquarters in Santa Rosa National Park, which can also arrange transportation. **Cacao Field Station** has a lodge with five rustic dormitories for up to 30 people. It has water, but no towels or electricity. Bring camping gear for cooking. It offers staggering views. **Maritza Field Station** is less rustic and has beds for 32 people, with shared bath, water, electricity, and a dining hall. The **Pitilla Biological Station** has accommodations for 20 people, with electricity, water, CB radio, and basic meals. Students and researchers get priority. Rates are $15 pp, $10 scientists, $6 students and assistants.

BAHÍA JUNQUILLAL REFUGE

The 505-hectare Refugio Nacional de Vida Silvestre Bahía Junquillal, north of Murciélago, is part of the Guanacaste Conservation Area. The calm bay is backed by tropical dry forest and is a refuge for pelicans, frigate birds, and other seabirds, as well as marine turtles, which come

RESTORING THE DRY FOREST

Guanacaste National Park includes large expanses of eroded pasture that once were covered with native dry forest, which at the time of the Spaniards' colonization carpeted a greater area of Mesoamerica than did rainforests. It was also more vulnerable to encroaching civilization. After 400 years of burning, only 2 percent of Central America's dry forest remains. (Fires, used to clear pasture, often become free-running blazes that sweep across the landscape. If the fires can be quelled, trees can take root again.)

In Costa Rica, American biologist Daniel Janzen has for two decades led an attempt to restore the vanished dry forest to nearly 60,000 hectares of ranchland around a remnant 10,000-acre nucleus. Janzen, a professor of ecology at the University of Pennsylvania, has spent six months of every year for more than 30 years studying the intricate relationships between animals and plants in Guanacaste Province. He helped establish the Costa Rican National Institute for Biodiversity.

A key is to nurture a conservation ethic among the surrounding communities. Education for grade-school children is viewed as part of the ongoing management of the park; all fourth-, fifth-, and sixth-grade children in the region get an intense course in basic biology. And many of the farmers who formerly ranched land are being retrained as park guards, research assistants, and guides.

Another 2,400-hectare project is centered on Lomas Barbudal Biological Reserve in southern Guanacaste. Lomas Barbudal is one of the few remaining Pacific coast forests favored by the endangered scarlet macaw, which has a penchant for the seeds of the sandbox tree (the Spanish found the seed's hard casing perfect for storing sand, which was sprinkled on documents to absorb wet ink; hence its name).

ashore to lay their eggs on the beautiful, two-km-wide, half-moon, gray-sand beach. The beach is popular with Ticos, who descend on weekends and holidays.

The recreation area is reached via the road to Cuajiniquil and the Murciélago sector of Santa Rosa National Park. Continue on the main road past Cuajiniquil for two km, where a deeply rutted dirt road leads north to the recreation area. You can continue around Bahía Junquillal to Bahía Salinas but you'll need a 4WD with high ground clearance in wet season.

There's a **ranger station** (tel. 506/679-9692, $1.75 admission foreigners, 75 cents nationals). Rangers offer guided tours. Trees shade the well-organized camping area, which includes latrines, barbecue pits, tables, and showers ($2 pp). Water is rationed to one hour daily.

LA CRUZ

La Cruz—gateway to Nicaragua (19 km north)—is dramatically situated atop the edge of an es-

carpment that rises east of Bahía de Salinas. A good time to visit is May, when it hosts its annual and lively **Fiesta Cívica.**

There's a police checkpoint on Hwy. 1 three km south of La Cruz, at the junction of Hwy. 4, which runs east to Upala in the northern lowlands. Following Hwy. 4, you begin to feel the influence of the moister Caribbean: vegetation and microclimates change dramatically within a few kilometers, dry deciduous forest giving way to evergreen forest cloaked in epiphytes, and flatlands give way to rolling hills covered with citrus plantations. At **Santa Cecilia,** 27 km east of Hwy. 1, a dirt road leads north seven km to the hamlet of **La Virgen,** where you have stupendous vistas down over Lake Nicaragua, with classically conical volcanoes in the distance.

Hacienda Los Inocentes Wildlife Center

This 1,000-hectare ranch (Apdo. 228-3000 Heredia, tel. 506/79-9190 or 506/265-5484, fax

Visitors set out on a tour from Hacienda Los Inocentes.

506/679-9224 or 506/265-4385, info@losinocentes lodge.com, www.losinocenteslodge.com), on Hwy. 4 about 16 km east of Hwy. 1, lies on the northern edge of Guanacaste National Park, on the lower northern slopes of Volcán Orosi. Until recently, it was a ranch with 8,000 head of cattle (the estate belonged to the Inocentes family, which owned almost one-third of Guanacaste). The former pasture is being returned to native forest. It now operates as an ecotourist and biological research center and boasts one of the most stunning settings in Costa Rica, with the great ascendant bulk of Orosi looming ominously to the south. The hacienda has a stable of 160 horses and specializes in horseback nature rides ($35, two hours with guide; $70, six hours to Orosi; $100 to Nicaragua). It's one of Costa Rica's finest bird-watching sites: toucans, oropendolas, and collared aracaris are especially prolific. Garrulous parrots and scarlet and great green macaws fly free in the hacienda grounds. There are hiking trails, and tractor-trailer tours ($35 for three hours, or $40 full-day with lunch). Meals cost $11. A taxi from La Cruz costs about $15 one-way.

Accommodations and Food

Hotel Bella Vista (tel. 506/679-8060, hotelbv @yahoo.de, $5 dorms, $10 pp rooms), one block west of the plaza in La Cruz, is run by a savvy Dutchman and has 30 simply furnished rooms in a two-story structure that opens to an attractive sundeck and pool. They have wood-lined walls, fans, orthopedic mattresses, and private bathrooms (some with hot water). Some have kingsize beds; others have a double and bunk. Backpackers' dorms were being constructed at last visit. The Bella Vista's open-air bar and restaurant are the happening scene. Options include *casados* (set meals, $2.50), shrimp and garlic ($7.50), steak with salad, etc.

The modern **Hostal de Julia** (tel. 506/679-9084), one block north and east of the plaza, has 12 rooms in a courtyard. It has a pleasant feel, with colonial hints, but was not open when I called by.

My favorite hostelry in town is **Amalia Inn** (tel./fax 506/679-9618), 100 meters south of the plaza. This charming place is operated by a friendly Tica, Amalia Bounds, and boasts a fabulous clifftop perch with views over Bahía Salinas and north along the Nicaraguan coast. Its eight rooms are large and cool, with tile floors, leather sofas, and striking paintings by Amalia's late husband, Lester. All have private bathrooms. A pool is handy for cooling off, though the inn's setting is breezy enough. Amalia will make breakfast, and you can prepare picnics in the kitchen. Trails lead down the forested escarpment. It makes a good base for exploring Nicaragua; you can leave your rental car here and take a bus or taxi to the border. Rates: $30 low season, $45 high season up to six people, including tax.

Ⓝ Hacienda Los Inocentes (see above, $20 pp room only; $46 pp year-round including three meals and tax) is centered on a beautiful vintage lodge built in 1890 of gleaming teak by the grandfather of Violeta de Chamorro, ex-president of Nicaragua. The main lodge has 11 modest but pleasant rooms surrounded by a wide veranda with wicker rockers and hammocks for relaxing and savoring the views and sunsets: two suites have private bathrooms upstairs; the other rooms have private bathrooms downstairs. There are also 12 cabins down the hill. Older cabins each have a double and two single beds; newer log cabins (sleeping six people) have one double and two bunks, plus modern bathrooms with forceful hot water. The restaurant serves pleasing meals (a treat is to have a toucan hop onto your breakfast table), and there's a small bar, an exquisite kidney-shaped pool with swim-up wet bar and a Jacuzzi, plus beach volleyball, basketball, and soccer field.

Information and Services

There's a bank opposite the gas station on Hwy. 1 as you enter La Cruz. The **police** station (tel. 506/679-9197) and medical clinic are here, too.

There's an **Internet café** one block north of the plaza.

Getting There

See *Santa Rosa National Park,* above, for bus schedules. Slower buses also operate from Liberia. Buses for San José depart La Cruz at about 7:15 A.M., 10:30 A.M., 3:30 P.M., and 6 P.M., though these originate at the Nicaraguan border and are often full by the time they pull into La Cruz. You can buy tickets from the *pulpería* (tel. 506/679-9108), next to the bus station.

A bus departs La Cruz for Santa Cecilia daily at 5 A.M., 10:30 A.M., 1:30 P.M., 7 P.M., and 7:30 P.M.

BAHÍA SALINAS

Immediately west of the plaza in La Cruz, a paved road drops to the flask-shaped Bahía Salinas, ringed by beaches backed by penurious coastal plains—this pocket of northwest Guanacaste is one of the driest in the country, with less than 150 cm of annual rainfall—lined with salt pans and mangroves that attract wading birds and crocodiles. The beaches are of white sand fading to brown-gray along the shore of **Punta Descartes,** separating the bay from Bahía Junquillal to the south. High winds blow almost nonstop Dec.–April, making this a prime spot for windsurfing (as well as for pelicans and frigate birds, wheeling and sliding magnificently).

The road, unpaved, leads past the hamlet of **Puerto Soley,** where the road splits. The left fork leads to Bahía Junquillal; 4WD is essential in wet season. The right fork leads via **Playa Copal** to **Jobo,** a fishing village inland from Bahía Jobo at the tip of Punta Descartes; and—taking another fork to the left—to **Manzanillo,** where colorful fishing boats and views across the Golfo de Santa Elena make up for the pebbly beach. Turn right in Jobo and then left at a Y-junction for the exquisite beach at **Playa Rajada;** turn right for **Playa Jobo** and **Playa La Coyotera.**

Bolaños Island National Wildlife Refuge

Bolaños Island is a rugged, oval-shaped rocky crag, 25 hectares in area, about half a kilometer east of Punta Descartes. The island rises dramatically to a height of 81 meters. It is grown over with drought-resistant shrubs that serve as nesting sites for island birds.

Refugio Nacional de Vida Silvestre Isla Bolaños is a wildlife refuge protecting one of only four nesting sites in Costa Rica for the brown pelican, and the only known nesting site for the American oystercatcher. As many as 200 frigate birds also nest here during the Jan.–March mating season, predominantly on the southwestern cliffs to take advantage of strong winds that give lift to their large wingspans. (Because they have small bodies and tiny feet, but very wide wings and extremely long tails, they cannot run to take off but need a high ledge from which to launch themselves into flight.)

Visitors are not allowed to set foot on the island, but you can hire a boat and guide in Puerto Soley or Jobo to take you within 50 meters.

Accommodations and Food

Proyecto Pura-Vida (cellular tel. 506/389-6784, velrey@racsa.co.cr; in Italy, Via Valverde 52, 37122 Verona, tel. 348/4454626, fax 045/592950; http://sartorige@o45.it, $30–45 rooms up to four people, $50–100 villas up to seven people) has eight private villas plus seven smaller units in the "Residencial Pura Vida." The villas, which vary in size, have gorgeous hardwood floors and ceilings and lots of stonework, plus dramatic views from their hillside setting. Some are simpler units with loft bedrooms. Cabins in the *residencial* are badly designed and almost monastic, and construction standards are wanting. Your hosts are a delightful Italian couple.

The Dutch-owned **Eco-Playa Resort** (tel. 506/679-9380 or 506/289-8920, fax 506/289-4536, ecohotel@racsa.co.cr, www.ecoplaya.com, $71 s/d studios, $90 s/d junior suite, $110–164 suite low season; $82/110/159-197 high season) is an attractive modern all-suite complex on Playa La Coyotera, on the western shore of the bay, with landscaped lawns leading onto a thin and unappealing beach. Squat, red-tile-roofed bungalows are aligned zig-zag-style in two rows obliquely facing the beach. The 36 large rooms feature open-plan lounges with terra-cotta floors, a/c, ceiling fans, TVs, telephones, kitchenettes, and upscale, motel-style decor. The soaring *palenque* restaurant opens to a crescent-shaped pool—one of three pools—and sun deck. It also has an all-inclusive plan.

Tours and Activities

Tico-Wind (info@ticowind.com, www.ticowind.com) at Eco-Playa Resort, and the **Kite Surf Center** (tel. 506/672-0218 or 396-4653, www.suntoursandfun.com/kitesurfing.htm), at Playa Copal, rent boards and offers classes and courses in windsurfing.

Getting There

Buses depart La Cruz daily at 5:30 A.M., 10:30 A.M., and 1 P.M. for Puerto Soley and Jobo. Return buses depart Jobo 90 minutes later. A taxi will cost about $3 one-way to Puerto Soley, $8 to Jobo.

PEÑAS BLANCAS: CROSSING INTO NICARAGUA

Peñas Blancas, 19 km north of La Cruz, is the border post for Nicaragua. Be careful driving the Pan-American Highway, which hereabouts is dangerously potholed and chock-a-block with articulated trucks hurtling along.

The bus terminal building contains the **Oficina de Migración** (immigration office, tel. 506/679-9025), a bank, restaurant, and **Costa Rican Tourism Institute** (ICT, tel. 506/677-0138). Change money before crossing into Nicaragua (you get a better exchange rate on the Costa Rican side). See *Getting There* in the *Santa Rosa National Park* section, above, for bus schedules to Peñas Blancas. Buses depart Peñas Blancas for San José at 5 A.M., 7:15 A.M., 10:30 A.M., 10:40 A.M., 1:30 P.M., 2:45 P.M., and 3:30 P.M.

Guanacaste

Nicoya Peninsula

Known for its magnificent beaches and a long dry season with sizzling sunshine, the Nicoya Peninsula is a broad, hooked protuberance—130 km long and averaging 50 km wide—separated from the Guanacaste plains by the Río Tempisque and Gulf of Nicoya. Most tourist activity is along the dramatically sculpted Pacific shoreline. Away from the coast, Nicoya is mostly mountainous, cut by deep valleys whose bottoms are much denuded for pasture.

More than 70 percent of Costa Rica's coastal resort infrastructure is in Nicoya. Much is con-

centrated in some half a dozen resort communities in northern Nicoya, where the Gulf of Papagayo Project plans on turning the Bahía de Culebra region into a massive resort complex. Several deluxe hotels and a golf course are already in place, with more to follow, tilting the demographics away from eco-conscious travelers toward a more package-tourist crowd. The opening of the Daniel Oduber International Airport at Liberia in 1996 has significantly boosted package tourist arrivals. Elsewhere along the coast, residential condo complexes are sprouting like

![M] ust-Sees

Look for to find the sights and activities you can't miss and for the best dining and lodging.

M Guaitíl: Ancient pottery traditions are kept alive at this charming village, where you can witness ceramics being crafted in age-old fashion (page 379).

M The Murciélagos: Experienced scuba divers can swim among large pelagics in warm waters around these offshore islands. Whale sharks and manta rays are commonly sighted (page 394).

M Playa Conchal: The country's only truly white-sand beach is popular for watersports, including snorkeling in warm turquoise waters. It can get crowded, but the pros outnumber the cons (page 400).

M Playa Grande: Here, surfers can enjoy consistent action while nature lovers can kayak or take boat trips in search of crocodiles, birds, and other wildlife protected by **Playa Grande Marine Turtle National Park.** The highlight in season is a chance to witness giant leatherback turtles laying eggs (page 403).

M Ostional National Wildlife Refuge: Site of a unique mass turtle nesting, this remote reserve has

few services, but the experience of witnessing an *arribada* will sear your memory for the rest of your life (page 422).

M Nosara: Beautiful beaches, cracking surf, plentiful wildlife, and a broad choice of accommodations combine to make Nosara a choice destination (page 427).

M Isla Tortuga: Stunning beaches, nature trails, warm turquoise waters, and plenty of watersports await passengers on day cruises to this gorgeous little isle off southeast Nicoya (page 447).

M Cabo Blanco Absolute Wildlife Reserve: This remote reserve is unrivaled locally for wildlife viewing, with all the main critters on show (page 456).

M Malpaís: This burgeoning yet offbeat community is the gateway to **Playa Santa Teresa,** the perfect spot to bag some rays, ride the waves, and chill. Accommodations range from budget to super-deluxe (page 457).

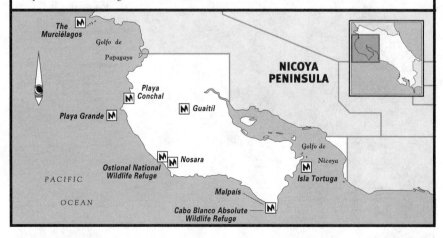

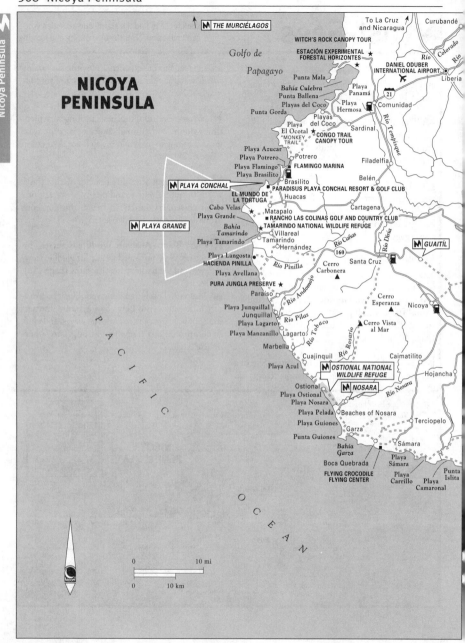

NICOYA PENINSULA

Golfo de Papagayo

THE MURCIÉLAGOS

To La Cruz and Nicaragua • Curubandé

WITCH'S ROCK CANOPY TOUR

ESTACIÓN EXPERIMENTAL FORESTAL HORIZONTES

DANIEL ODUBER INTERNATIONAL AIRPORT

Río Colorado
Río
Liberia

Punta Mala
Bahía Culebra
Punta Ballena
Playas del Coco
Punta Gorda

Playa Panamá
Playa Hermosa
Comunidad

Playas del Coco
Playa El Ocotal "MONKEY TRAIL"
Sardinal

Río Tempisque

CONGO TRAIL CANOPY TOUR

Playa Azucar
Playa Potrero   Potrero
Playa Flamingo   FLAMINGO MARINA
Playa Brasilito

Filadelfia
Belén

PLAYA CONCHAL
Brasilito
PARADISUS PLAYA CONCHAL RESORT & GOLF CLUB
EL MUNDO DE LA TORTUGA   Huacas

Cabo Velas
Playa Grande   Matapalo
PLAYA GRANDE
RANCHO LAS COLINAS GOLF AND COUNTRY CLUB
TAMARINDO NATIONAL WILDLIFE REFUGE

Cartagena

Bahía Tamarindo   Villareal
Playa Tamarindo   Tamarindo
Hernández
Río Cañas

GUAITÍL

Río Diría

160

Playa Langosta
HACIENDA PINILLA
Playa Avellana
PURA JUNGLA PRESERVE
Paraíso

Río Pinilla
Cerro Carbonera   Santa Cruz

Río Andamojo

Cerro Esperanza   Nicoya

Playa Junquillal
Junquillal
Playa Lagarto
Playa Manzanillo   Lagarto
Marbella

Río Pilas
Río Tabaco

Río Rosario
Cerro Vista al Mar

Caimatilito

Cuajinquil
Playa Azul

OSTIONAL NATIONAL WILDLIFE REFUGE
Hojancha

Ostional
Playa Ostional
Playa Nosara
Playa Pelada   Beaches of Nosara
Playa Guiones
Punta Guiones
Bahía Garza
Boca Quebrada
FLYING CROCODILE FLYING CENTER

NOSARA
Río Nosara

Garza   Terciopelo

Sámara
Playa Sámara
Playa Carrillo   Playa Camaronal
Punta Islita

P A C I F I C   O C E A N

0   10 mi
0   10 km

To Upala
Bijagua
Guayabo
Fortuna
Liberia
▲ Volcán Tenorio
San Rafael
Santa Rosa
35
Río Tenorio
Río Corobicí
Nuevo Arenal
Venado
Monterrey
Río Venado
4
Bagaces
PAN-AMERICAN HIGHWAY
Lake Arenal
La Fortuna
El Tanque
Lomas Barbudal Biological Reserve
Tronadora
Tilarán
▲ Volcán Arenal
▲ Volcán Chato
Chachagua
Cañas
Monteverde Cloud Forest Biological Preserve
Cordillera de Tilarán
Arenal National Park
Jabillos
Palo Verde National Park
Bebedero
Pocosol
San Isidro
Río Cañas
Santa Elena
Monteverde
▲ Volcán Pocosol
La Tigra
Puerto Humo
Las Juntas de Abaranges
Río Tempisque
Río Lajas
Children's Eternal Cloud Forest Reserve
Barra Honda N.P.
Puerto Moreno
18
Colorado
1
Río Lagarto
Peñas Blancas National Wildlife Refuge
Nacaome
Quebrada Honda
LA AMISTAD DE TAIWAN BRIDGE
LA ENSEÑADA NATIONAL WILDLIFE REFUGE
San Gerardo
Golfo de Nicoya
Manzanillo
Morales
Miramar
To San José
La Mansión
Isla Chira
Birds Island Biological Reserve
Costa del Pájaros
Río Aranjuez
San Jerónimo
Río Grande
Zapotal
Carmona
21
Isla Venado
Isla Bejuco
Isla Caballo
Barranca
Esparaza
San Mateo
▲ Cerro Azul
Jicaral
Playa Naranjo
FERRY
Isla San Lucas
Puntarenas
Congrejal (Soledad)
Peninsula de Nicoya
Gigante
Puerto Caldera
Mata de Limón
Orotina
Río Ora
Bejuco Islita
Jabillo
Quebrada Grande
Cerro Buenavista
Río Guarial
Punta Coral
Islas Guayabo and Negritos Biological Reserves
Playa Bejuco
Pueblo Nuevo
Zapote
PROFELIS ★
Paquera
FERRY
Punta Coyote
San Francisco de Coyote
▲ Cerro Frío
BARCELÓ LOS DELFINES GOLF & COUNTRY CLUB
★ CURÚ NATIONAL WILDLIFE REFUGE
Playa Coyote
Río Frío
Pochote
M ISLA TORTUGA
Playa San Miguel
Playa Caletas
Playa Bongo
Bajos de Arío
Tambor
Punta Tambor
Río Bongo
Río Arío
NATURE LODGE FINCA LOS CABALLOS
Bahía Ballena
Playa Tambor
Playa Manzanillo
Cóbano
Punta Piedra Amarilla
VIVERO SOLERA
Playa Cocalito
Montezuma
Santa Teresa
Playa Cocal
NICOLAS WEISSENBURG ABSOLUTE RESERVE
Playa Santa Teresa
Playa Montezuma
M MALPAÍS
Cabuya
Cabo Blanco
M CABO BLANCO ABSOLUTE WILDLIFE RESERVE
Isla Cabo Blanco

mushrooms on a damp log, additionally changing the face of the region.

Though each beach community has its own distinct appeal, most remain barefoot and button-down, appealing to laid-back travelers who can hang with the locals and appreciate the wildlife that comes down to the shore. This is particularly so of the southern beaches. Waves pump ashore along much of the coastline, and many beaches have been discovered by surfers, who are opening up heretofore hidden sections of jungle-lined shore. Newly cut roads are linking the last pockets of the erstwhile inaccessible Pacific coast, though negotiating the dirt highways that link coastal communities is always tricky—which is part of the fun.

Predominantly dry to the north and progressively moist to the south, the peninsula offers a variety of ecosystems, with no shortage of opportunities for nature viewing; monkeys, coatis, sloths, and other wildlife species inhabit the forests along the shore. Two of the premier nesting sites for marine turtles are here. The offshore waters are beloved of scuba divers and for sportfishing. And watersports are well-developed.

The best time to visit is December through April, when rain is virtually unheard of (average annual rainfall is less than 150 cm in some areas). The rainy season generally arrives in May and lasts until November, turning dirt roads into muddy (and often impassable) quagmires sure to test your driving skills to the max. September and October are the wettest months. The so-called Papagayo winds—heavy northerlies *(nortes)*—blow strongly from January (sometimes earlier) through March, and are felt mostly in northern Nicoya. Gusts of 100 kph are not uncommon. Surfers rave about the rainy season (May–Oct.), when swells are consistent and waves—fast and tubular—can be 1.5 meters or more.

PLANNING YOUR TIME

Many visitors choose to spend a majority of their time within Costa Rica at Nicoya's beaches, which would require perhaps a month to sample in earnest. One week to 10 days should be sufficient to sample two or three of the best beaches. In the north, Tamarindo makes a good base for exploring further afield, but the poor state of coast roads is not conducive to round-trip travel. It's perhaps best to keep moving on, north or south.

There's no shortage of options for accommodations for any budget, although reservations

Traditional ox-carts are a common sight in Nicoya.

are highly recommended for holiday periods, when Ticos flock.

Few beaches are of the powdered-sugar variety. If white-sand floats your boat, head to **Playa Flamingo** or nearby **Playa Conchal,** which is backed by the country's largest resort hotel, complete with golf course and watersports. **Montezuma,** a charming little community on the southern tip of Nicoya, also has a superb white-sand beach.

The most complete services and range of accommodations are found at **Tamarindo,** a surfing center with a wide range of other activities, plus several fine restaurants. **Playas del Coco** and adjacent beach resorts of Ocotal and Hermosa, while less attractive than other beaches, are bases for sportfishing and scuba diving. Surfers can choose from dozens of beaches: the best begin at Playa Grande and extend south to **Malpaís and Playa Santa Teresa;** many are remote and have few, if any, facilities. **Playa Carrillo to Manzanillo,** with several of the most superb and lonesome beaches—almost all favored by marine turtles for nesting—is a fabulous adventure by 4WD, like an Indiana Jones adventure come alive.

Two nature experiences stand out: a visit to **Playa Grande Marine Turtle National Park** to see the leatherback turtles laying eggs, and the **Ostional National Wildlife Refuge** during its unique mass invasions of olive ridley turtles. These are, for me, the most momentous guaranteed wildlife encounters in Costa Rica. **Curú National Wildlife Refuge** and **Cabo Blanco Wildlife Refuge** offer their own nature highlights, as does **Nosara,** another prime surf destination.

Don't leave Nicoya without calling in at the village of **Guaitíl,** where Chorotega women have kept the spark of a nearly dead culture alive by making pottery in the same fashion their ancestors did one thousand years ago. Nearby, **Barra Honda National Park** is the nation's preeminent spelunking site.

Getting to the Coast

Driving from San José to the coast resorts takes a minimum of four or five hours. A single highway (Hwy. 21) runs north-south along the eastern plains of Nicoya, linking Liberia with the towns of Filadelfia, Santa Cruz, and Nicoya, then south (deteriorating all the while) to Playa Naranjo, Paquera, Tambor, and Montezuma. Spur roads snake west over the mountains, connecting beach communities to civilization. Excepting a short section south of Sámara, no paved highway links the various beach resorts, which are connected by a network of dirt roads roughly paralleling the coast; at times you will need to head inland to connect with another access road. Plan accordingly, and allow much more time than may be obvious by looking at a map. Several sections require river fordings—no easy task in wet season, when many such rivers are impassable (the section between Sámara and Malpaís is one of the most daunting and adventurous of wet season drives in the country).

A 4WD is essential. It's wise to fill up wherever you find gas available (often it will be poured from a can—and cost about double what it would at a true gas station). The roads are blanketed with fine choking dust in dry season; car interiors can get so dirty after one or two weeks that rental companies may charge a cleaning fee (a/c and sealed windows will keep the dust out).

The Pan-American Highway (Hwy. 1) **via Liberia** gives relatively quick access to the beaches of northern Nicoya via Hwy. 21, which runs west for 20 km to Comunidad, gateway to Bahía de Culebra, the Playas de Coco region, and Tamarindo.

The main access to central Nicoya from Hwy. 1 (the Pan-American Highway) is via the **Puente de Amistad con Taiwan** (Friendship with Taiwan Bridge), which opened in 2003 to replace the erstwhile Tempisque ferry. The bridge trims 96 km from the journey between San José and Nicoya. The bridge, on Hwy. 18, is about 27 km west of Hwy. 1 (the turnoff from Hwy. 1 is two km north of Limonal). Hwy. 18 connects with Hwy. 21.

Daily car and passenger **ferries** cross from Puntarenas to Naranjo and Paquera, giving access to southern Nicoya. See sidebar *Ferries to and from Nicoya* for details.

Highway 2: Tempisque Bridge to Filadelfia

The community of **Puerto Moreno** sits on the western bank of the Río Tempisque, about two km south of the Tempisque Bridge, or **Puente de Amistad con Taiwan,** a suspension bridge whose construction was a gift from the Taiwanese government. The ferry, which served Nicoya for 26 years, has been retired.

Hwy. 18 continues west 15 km to a T-junction with Hwy. 21. The town of Nicoya, the regional capital, is 15 km north of the T-junction (Hwy. 21 loops north via Santa Cruz and Filadelfia to reconnect with Hwy. 1 at Liberia).

Tempisque Eco-Adventures & Canopy Tour (tel. 506/687-1212, info@tempisqueecoadventures .com), just north of the highway immediately west of the bridge, has a canopy tour and offers boat trips to Palo Verde National Park.

BARRA HONDA NATIONAL PARK

The 2,295-hectare Parque Nacional Barra Honda (8 A.M.–4 P.M., $6 admission), accessed via Hwy. 18 and 13 km west of the Río Tempisque, is known for its limestone caverns dating back 70 million years (42 have been discovered to date). Skeletons, utensils, and ornaments dating back to 300 B.C. have been discovered inside the Nicoya Cave.

The deepest cavern thus far explored is the 240-meter-deep Santa Ana Cave, known for its Hall of Pearls, full of stalactites and stalagmites. Terciopelo Cave is named for the eponymous snake found dead at the bottom of the cave during the first exploration; it is reached via an exciting 30-meter vertical descent to a sloping plane that leads to the bottom, 63 meters down.

Mushroom Hall is named for the shape of its calcareous formations. The Hall of the Caverns has large Medusa-like formations, including a figure resembling a lion's head. And columns in Hall Number Five, and "The Organ" in Terciopelo, produce musical tones when struck. Some of the caverns are frequented by bats, in-cluding the Pozo Hediondo (Fetid Pit) Cave, which is named for the quantity of excrement accumulated by its abundant bat population. Blind salamanders and endemic fish species have also evolved in the caves.

The caves are not easily accessible and are risky for those not duly equipped.

Above ground, the hilly dry forest terrain is a refuge for howler monkeys, deer, agoutis, peccaries, kinkajous, anteaters, and many bird species, including scarlet macaws. The park tops out at Mount Barra Honda (442 meters), which has intriguing rock formations and provides an excellent view of the Gulf of Nicoya. Las Cascadas are strange limestone formations formed by calcareous sedimentation along a riverbed.

In March 1997, 5 percent of the park was destroyed in a devastating fire, so no fooling around with matches. The **Los Laureles ranger station** has basic trail maps.

Accommodations

There's a campsite ($2 pp) close to the Terciopelo Cavern, about 400 meters from the ranger station. It has basic showers and toilets plus picnic tables and water. **Hawkview Mountain,** another campsite, is beside the main road near the turnoff for Barra Honda.

Proyecto Nacaome (tel. 506/685-5580. $6 pp), a local cooperative just outside the park entrance, offers three basic cabins, each with two double beds and a bunk plus showers with cold water. Guide services are offered and meals ($3) cooked on a *leña* (woodstove) are provided. You can also camp for $2 pp.

Guides and Tours

You must be accompanied by a guide from the **Asociación de Guías Ecologistas de Barra Honda.** For reservations, contact the National Parks office in Nicoya (tel. 506/686-6760, jicaro @minae.go.cr), in Santa Cruz (tel. 506/680-1920), or the regional headquarters in Bagaces (506/671-1455, fax 506/671-1062).

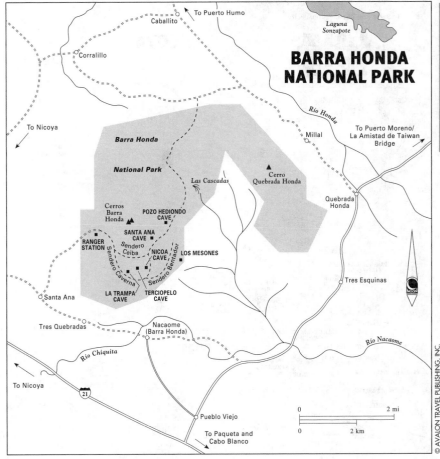

Cave descents are allowed during dry season only (although, reportedly, not during Holy Week).

Getting There

The turnoff for the Nacaome (Barra Honda) ranger station is 1.5 km east of Hwy. 21 and 15 km west of the Tempisque Bridge. From here, an all-weather gravel road leads four km to Nacaome, from where it climbs steeply in places, all the while deteriorating (4WD recommended); signs point the way to the entrance, about six km farther via Santa Ana. A bus departs Nicoya for Santa Ana and Nacaome daily at noon; you can walk from either to the park entrance. You can also enter the park from the east via a road from Quebrada Honda (tough going and not recommended) and from Hwy. 21 immediately east of Nicoya township.

NICOYA

Nicoya, about 78 km south of Liberia, is Costa Rica's oldest colonial city. Today it bustles as the agricultural and administrative heart of the region. The town is named for the Chorotega chief

Nicoya Peninsula

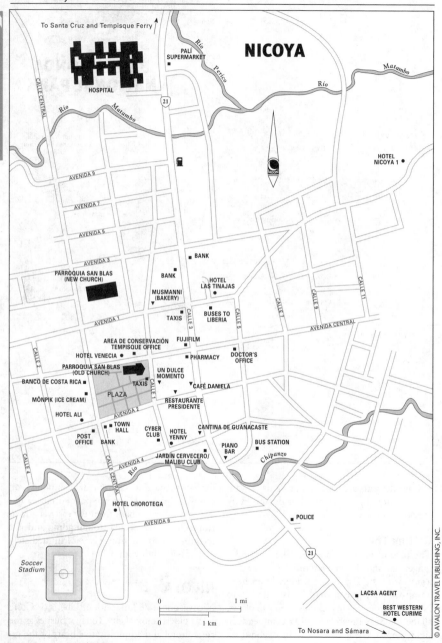

To Santa Cruz and Tempisque Ferry

PALI SUPERMARKET

NICOYA

Río Perico

Río Matambo

Río

HOSPITAL

Río Matambo

21

HOTEL NICOYA 1

AVENIDA 9

AVENIDA 7

AVENIDA 5

AVENIDA 3

BANK

PARROQUIA SAN BLAS (NEW CHURCH)

BANK

HOTEL LAS TINAJAS

MUSMANNI (BAKERY)

CALLE 3

CALLE 5

CALLE 7

CALLE 9

CALLE 11

AVENIDA 1

TAXIS

BUSES TO LIBERIA

AVENIDA CENTRAL

CALLE 2

AREA DE CONSERVACIÓN TEMPISQUE OFFICE

FUJIFILM

PHARMACY

DOCTOR'S OFFICE

HOTEL VENECIA

PARROQUIA SAN BLAS (OLD CHURCH)

UN DULCE MOMENTO

BANCO DE COSTA RICA

TAXIS

CALLE 1

CAFÉ DANIELA

PLAZA

MÒNPIK (ICE CREAM)

RESTAURANTE PRESIDENTE

HOTEL ALI

AVENIDA 2

TOWN HALL

CYBER CLUB

HOTEL YENNY

CANTINA DE GUANACASTE

POST OFFICE

BANK

PIANO BAR

BUS STATION

CALLE 4

AVENIDA 4

JARDÍN CERVECERO/ MALIBU CLUB

Río

Chipanzo

HOTEL CHOROTEGA

CALLE CENTRAL

AVENIDA 6

POLICE

21

Soccer Stadium

0   1 mi

0   1 km

LACSA AGENT

BEST WESTERN HOTEL CURIME

To Nosara and Sámara

© AVALON TRAVEL PUBLISHING, INC.

who presented Spanish conquistador and *arriviste* Gil González Dávila with gold. The native heritage is still apparent in the facial features of area residents.

The only site of interest is the **Parroquia San Blas** (8 A.M.–noon and 2–6 P.M.; closed Wednesday and Sunday). church built in the 16th century, gleaming anew following a restoration and decorating the town's peaceful plaza. It contains a museum of pre-Columbian silver, bronze, and copper icons, and other objects.

A road leads northeast 27 km from Nicoya via Corralillo to **Puerto Humo,** a settlement on the west bank of the Río Tempisque due north of Barra Honda. The bird-watching hereabouts is splendid. Puerto Humo is a gateway to Palo Verde National Park, which begins on the other side of the river. Boats can be hired. If driving the unpaved road, a 4WD is recommended, especially in rainy season. A bus serves Puerto Humo twice daily, departing Nicoya township at 10:30 A.M. and 2:45 P.M. Return buses depart Puerto Humo at 6 A.M. and 12:30 P.M.

FESTIVAL OF LA VIRGEN DE GUADALUPE

Try to visit Nicoya on 12 December, when villagers carry a dark-skinned image of La Virgen de Guadalupe through the streets accompanied by flutes, drums, and dancers. The festival combines the Catholic celebration of the Virgin of Guadalupe with the traditions of the Chorotega legend of La Yequita (Little Mare), a mare that interceded to prevent twin brothers from fighting to the death for the love of a princess.

The religious ceremony is a good excuse for bullfights, explosive fireworks *(bombas)*, concerts, and general merriment. Many locals get sozzled on *chicha*, a heady brew made from fermented corn and sugar and drunk from hollow gourds. Ancient native music is played, and it is easy to imagine a time when Nicoya was the center of the Chorotega culture.

Accommodations

Under $25: At Puerto Humo, you can camp for $2 pp near the Aventuras Arenal office on the riverside near the dock.

In Nicoya, the **Hotel Venecia** (tel. 506/685-5325, $4 pp basic, $9 s, $11 d), on the north side of the plaza, has 37 clean but basic rooms with fans (some with private baths). It has newer, much nicer units in a two-story unit at the back. It has secure parking.

The best budget bet in town is the **Hotel Chorotega** (Calle Central, Avenida 6, tel. 506/685-5245, $4 pp shared bath, $7 s, $10 d private bath, $12 s, $16 d with hot water and TV), with 24 spic-and-span rooms with fans and cold water only. And **Hotel Yenny** (Calle 1, Avenida 4, tel. 506/685-5050, $12 s, $20 d) offers good value. It has 32 budget a/c rooms with TV and private baths with cold water only.

The **Hotel Las Tinajas** (Avenida 1, Calle 5, tel./fax 506/685-5081 or 506/685-5777, $10 s, $13 d standard, $15 s, $20 d with a/c) has 28 spacious, light, and clean rooms with fans and private baths with cold water. Family rooms can sleep seven people. Students with ID get $5 discount.

$25–50: The **Best Western Hotel Curime** (P.O. Box 51-5200 Nicoya, tel. 506/685-5238, fax 506/685-5530, $22 s, $30 d room, $30 s, $38 d cabin low season; $26 s, $35 d room, $40 s, $50 d cabin high season), 400 meters south of town on the road to Playa Sámara, has 20 a/c *cabinas* and six rooms with private baths with hot water in landscaped grounds. It has a swimming pool and children's pool, plus a restaurant, but it is far below the normal Best Western standards.

Hotel Nicoya I (tel. 506/686-6331, $25 s, $30 d) has eight a/c rooms with fan and private bathrooms with hot water. The same owner has **Hotel Nicoya II** (tel. 506/389-9745, $20 s, $25 d) on Hwy. 21, 500 meters north of the hospital, with eight clean, wood-lined a/c rooms with tile floors, TVs, and modern bathrooms with cold water only. It has secure parking.

The nicest place is **Hotel Río Tempisque De Lujo** (tel. 506/686-6650, $38 s, $41 d), on Hwy. 21, 800 meters north of the junction for Nicoya township, with 30 well-lit, spacious a/c cabins in groomed gardens set back from the road for peace and quiet. They display handsome use of cement block. Each has tile floor, beautiful raised hardwood ceiling, two double beds, cable TV, refrigerator, coffeemaker, microwave, and pleasing bathrooms with hairdryer and hot water. There's a swimming pool and Jacuzzi in lush gardens.

Food

There are simple *sodas* on three corners of the plaza. My favorite is **Un Dulce Momento** (tel. 506/686-4584, 10 A.M.–10 P.M.), an Italian-run café and pizzería with shaded outdoor seating.

For Chinese fare head to **Restaurante Presidente** (Avenida 2, Calles 1/3, tel. 506/685-5291, 10 A.M.–11 P.M.). I also like **Bar y Restaurante Nicoya** (Calle 3, Avenidas Central/2) for its quasi-Chinese ambience; I enjoyed a fish fillet Hawaiian style with pineapple ($4.75). Next door, the open-air **Café Daniela** (tel. 506/686-6148, 7 A.M.–9:45 P.M. Mon.–Sat., 5–9:45 P.M. Sunday) serves salads, pizzas, fresh-baked breads and cookies, and has *casados* (set meals, $2).

The **Cantina El Guanacaste** (Avenida 4, Calle 3) is a working-class bar with fantastic decor: deer hides and antlers on the walls, which are painted with cowboy scenes. It serves basic local fare, and *bocas* with drinks.

You can stock up on groceries at the **Palí** supermarket, opposite the hospital. There's a **Musmanni** bakery at Calle 1, Avenida 1. **Mönpik,** on the west side of the plaza, sells ice cream.

Information and Services

MINAE (tel. 506/686-6760, fax 506/685-5667, 8 A.M.–4 P.M. Mon.–Fri.), on the north side of the plaza, administers the Tempisque Conservation Area.

The **hospital** (tel. 506/685-5066) is on the north side of town. There are several pharmacies on Calles 1 and 3.

The police station is about 500 meters south of the town center, on Calle 3.

There are three banks in the town center; see the map.

The **post office** (Avenida 2, Calle Central) is open 7:30 A.M.–5:30 P.M.

The **Cyber Club Internet Café** (Calle 1, Avenidas 2/4, tel. 506/686-7143, 8 A.M.–8:30 P.M. Mon.–Sat., 1–9 P.M. Sunday) is above the liquor store.

Fujifilm has an outlet at Calle 3, Avenida Central.

Getting There

The **Taca** agent (tel. 506/686-6840) is 100 meters north of Hotel Curime.

Buses (Tracopa Alfaro, tel. 506/222-2666 or 506/222-2750, tracopa@racsa.co.cr) depart San José for Nicoya from Calle 14, Avenidas 3/5, at 6:30 A.M., 8 A.M., 10 A.M., 12:30 P.M., 1:30 P.M., 2 P.M., 3 P.M., and 5 P.M. ($5; six hours). Buses also serve Nicoya from Liberia hourly, 5 A.M.–7 P.M.

Return buses depart Nicoya for San José from Avenida 4, Calle 3, at 4:45 A.M., 5 A.M., 7:30 A.M., 9:30 A.M., noon, 2:30 P.M., and 4:30 P.M. and for Santa Cruz hourly, 6 A.M.–9 P.M.; for Liberia hourly, 5 A.M.–7 P.M.; for Playa Naranjo at 5:15 A.M. and 1 P.M.; for Sámara at 6 A.M., 7:45 A.M., 10 A.M. (to Carillo), noon (to Carillo), 3 P.M. (to Carillo), 4:20 P.M., and 5 P.M.; and for Nosara at 1 P.M. Buses also serve other towns throughout the peninsula.

SANTA CRUZ

This small town, 20 km north of Nicoya, is the "National Folklore City" and a gateway to Playas Tamarindo and Junquillal, 30 km to the west. Santa Cruz is renowned for its traditional music, food, and dance, which can be sampled during *fiestas cívicas* each 15 January and 25 July.

The ruin of an old church (toppled by an earthquake in 1950) stands next to its modern replacement with a star-shaped roof. The gracious plaza boasts a Mayan-style cupola, lampshades with Mayan motifs, and monuments on each corner.

Directions in the city are normally given from the **Plaza de los Mangos,** a grassy square four blocks north of the church. The two plazas are separated by a quarter of old wooden homes. Alas, a ruinous fire swept through the historic center in March 1993, claiming many fine buildings.

FERRIES TO AND FROM NICOYA

Two car-and-passenger ferries cross the Río Tempisque and Gulf of Nicoya, shortening the driving distance to or from the Nicoya Peninsula. In high season and on weekends, lines can get long, and you should get there at least an hour before departure time (even further ahead of time during holiday periods). Departure times change frequently. Always call ahead to confirm.

Puntarenas to Paquera

Two companies operate ferries to Paquera, at the southeastern tip of the Nicoya Peninsula. Both depart from Avenida 3, Calles 33, in Puntarenas.

Naviera Tambor (tel. 506/661-2084) operates an air-conditioned car-and-passenger ferry to Paquera. It holds 45 vehicles and 225 passengers and departs Puntarenas at 4 A.M., 8 A.M., noon, 4 P.M., and 8 P.M. Return ferries depart Paquera at 6 A.M., 10 A.M., 2 P.M., 6 P.M., and 9:30 P.M. ($1.60 adults, $1 children, $11.30 cars, $3.40 motorbikes).

The **Ferry Peninsular** (tel. 506/641-0515, ferrypeninsular@racsa.co.cr), or La Paquereña ferry, departs Puntarenas daily at 8:45 A.M., 2 P.M., and 8:15 P.M. Return ferries depart Paquera at 6 A.M., 11:15 A.M., and 6 P.M. ($1.50 pedestrians; $9 car and passengers).

A passengers-only **lancha** (water-taxi, tel. 506/661-0515) also departs for Paquera, in Nicoya, at 6:15 A.M., 11 A.M., and 3 P.M. from a dock adjacent to the market on Avenida 3, Calles 2/Central. Rates: $1.25 adults, $1 for bicycles and children. The return lanchas depart Paquera at 8 A.M., 1 P.M., and 4:45 P.M. Buses meet this ferry and offer service Cóbano, Montezuma, and Malpaís.

Puntarenas to Naranjo

Playa Naranjo is two-thirds down the Nicoya Peninsula, and makes a perfect landing stage if you're heading to Sámara or Nosara.

The **Coonatramar Ferry** (tel. 506/661-1069 or 506/661-9011, www.coonatramar.com) holds 50 vehicles and 500 passengers and departs Puntarenas from Avenida 3, Calles 33/35, at 6 A.M., 10 A.M., 2:20 P.M., and 7 P.M. ($1.60 adult, 75 cents child, $3.25 car). The return ferry departs Playa Naranjo at 7:30 A.M., 12:30 P.M., 5 P.M., and 9 P.M. Buy your ticket from a booth to the left of the gates at Naranjo, but be sure to park in line first.

Buses meet the ferry for Jicaral, Coyote, Bejuco, Carmona, and Nicoya. Hotel representatives will pick you up with notice.

Accommodations

Pensión Isabel (tel. 506/680-0173, $5 pp), 150 meters east of the main plaza, has eight rooms with fans and shared bath with cold water.

A good deal is the motel-style **Hotel La Estancia** (tel./fax 506/680-0476, $13 s, $20 d with fans, $18 s, $27 with a/c), which has 15 pleasing modern units with fans, TVs, and private baths with hot water. Spacious family rooms have four beds. Some rooms are dark. Secure parking. Laundry service.

The motel-style **Hotel Diría** (Apdo. 58, Santa Cruz, tel. 506/680-0080, fax 506/680-0442, hoteldiria@hotmail.com, from $35 s, $40 d), at the junction of Hwy. 21 and the main street into town, is centered on a pool and grounds full of palms. The 50 recently refurbished a/c rooms (some have fans only) have clean airy bathrooms.

The El Bambú restaurant was being remodeled at last visit.

Outshining all contenders is the **Hotel La Calle de Alcalá** (Apdo. 14-5150, Santa Cruz, tel. 506/680-0000, fax 506/680-1633, $20 s, $40 d, $60 junior suite, $70 suite with Jacuzzi), one block south of Plaza de los Mangos. This Spanish-run hotel boasts a lively contempo decor and pleasing aesthetic. It has 29 a/c rooms with cable TVs, cool white or charcoal-gray tile floors, bamboo furnishings, and pastels. They're set around an attractive swimming pool with swim-up *ranchito* bar. It has secure parking.

Food

For rustic ambience, try **Pipo's Mariscos**, facing Parque Ramos, in an old farmhouse-style building decorated in farm implements and open

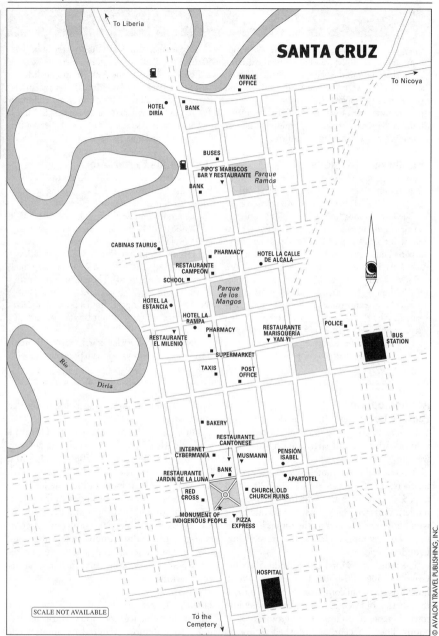

To Liberia

SANTA CRUZ

To Nicoya

MINAE
OFFICE

HOTEL
DIRÍA

BANK

BUSES

PIPO'S MARISCOS
BAR Y RESTAURANTE

Parque
Ramos

BANK

CABINAS TAURUS

PHARMACY

HOTEL LA CALLE
DE ALCALÁ

RESTAURANTE
CAMPEÓN

SCHOOL

Parque
de los
Mangos

HOTEL LA
ESTANCIA

HOTEL LA
RAMPA

PHARMACY

RESTAURANTE
MARISQUERÍA
YAN YI

POLICE

RESTAURANTE
EL MILENIO

SUPERMARKET

BUS
STATION

TAXIS

POST
OFFICE

Río
Diría

BAKERY

RESTAURANTE
CANTONESE

INTERNET
CYBERMANIA

MUSMANNI

PENSIÓN
ISABEL

RESTAURANTE
JARDÍN DE LA LUNA

BANK

RED
CROSS

APARTOTEL

CHURCH, OLD
CHURCH RUINS

MONUMENT OF
INDIGENOUS PEOPLE

PIZZA
EXPRESS

SCALE NOT AVAILABLE

HOSPITAL

To the
Cemetery

© AVALON TRAVEL PUBLISHING, INC.

to the plaza through metal *rejas*. It serves shrimp, lobster, octopus, and other seafood.

The most elegant restaurant in town is at **Hotel La Calle de Alcalá,** serving *típico* dishes and seafood such as octopus in garlic ($6) plus filet mignon ($8). Alternately, try **Restaurante El Milenio** (tel. 506/680-3237, 10 A.M.–midnight Sun.–Thur., 10 A.M.–1 P.M. Fri.–Sat.), one block west of Parque de los Mangos. This clean, modern a/c eatery has a large-screen TV and offers seafoods with a Chinese touch, all below $6.

There are lots of Chinese restaurants, **Restaurante Cantonese,** 50 meters north of the plaza, being the best.

For pizza, try **Sabro Pizza Express** (tel. 506/680-1090), on the south side of the main plaza.

For baked goods, try **Musmanni,** 50 meters north of the main plaza.

Information and Services

MINAE (tel./fax 506/680-1820 or 506/680-1930, 8 A.M.–4 P.M. Mon.–Fri.) has a regional sub-office on the highway. However, it is not set up to assist tourists and has minimal information.

There are banks on Hwy. 21 at the entrance to town and on the north side of the main plaza.

The post office is two blocks northeast of the main plaza.

Cybermania (tel. 506/680-4520, 8:30 A.M.–9:30 P.M. Mon.–Sat., 9 A.M.–8:30 P.M. Sunday), one block north of the main plaza, charges $0.50 cents per 15 minutes for Internet access.

There are several clinics and pharmacies in the town center. The Red Cross is on the west side of the plaza.

The **police station** (tel. 506/680-0136) is on the northwest side of the bus station.

Getting There

Tralapa buses (tel. 506/221-7202, in Santa Cruz tel. 506/680-0392) depart San José for Santa Cruz from Calle 20, Avenidas 1/3, at 7 A.M., 9 A.M., 10 A.M., 11 A.M., noon, 1 P.M., 2 P.M., 4 P.M., and 6 P.M. Buses for Santa Cruz depart Liberia hourly, 5:30 A.M.–7:30 P.M. (returning at the same time); from Nicoya hourly, 6 A.M.–

9 P.M. (returning at the same time); and from Puntarenas at 6 A.M. and 4 P.M.

Buses depart Santa Cruz for San José at 3 A.M., 4:30 A.M., 5 A.M., 6:30 A.M., 8:30 A.M., 10:15 A.M., 11:30 A.M., 1:30 P.M., and 5 P.M.; for Puntarenas at 6:05 A.M. and 3:20 P.M.; and for Playa Junquillal at 4:45 A.M.; and Playa Flamingo at 9 A.M. and 2 P.M. **Trampsa** buses depart Santa Cruz for Tamarindo and Matapalo at 4:20 A.M., 5:30 A.M., 8:30 A.M., 10:30 A.M., 1:30 P.M. and 3:30 P.M. A direct bus departs Santa Cruz for Tamarindo at 12:30 P.M., returning at 8:30 A.M. Return buses depart Tamarindo at 6 A.M., 7:15 A.M., 9 A.M., 12 P.M., 2:30 P.M., 4:15 P.M., and 10 P.M.

The **gas station** is one block west of the Hotel Diría.

N GUAITÍL

I highly recommend a trip to Guaitíl, 12 km east of Santa Cruz, to see ethnic pottery being made (the turnoff from the main highway is two km east of Santa Cruz). Guaitíl is a tranquil little village where many of the inhabitants—descendants of Chorotegas—have been making their unique pottery of red or black or ocher using the same methods for generations, turning the pots on wheels beneath shady trees and displaying them on roadside racks and tables. A renaissance of cultural pride has emerged, fostered by tourist interest.

There are several artists' cooperatives. You're welcome to watch villagers such as Marita Ruíz or Marielos Briseño and her mother, Flora, or Cristhina Briceño and her mother, Higinia Chavarría (every cooperative seems to be attended by the family matriarch: women run the businesses and sustain families and village structures) molding ceramics by hand with clay dug from the hills above the hamlet. They use the same process as did their ancestors, including polishing the pottery with small jadelike grinding stones taken from nearby archaeological sites and said by the local women to have been made by shamans.

The women happily take you to the back of the house to see the large open-hearth kilns where

© CHRISTOPHER P. BAKER

A Chorotega woman fires pots in a traditional oven in Guaitíl.

the pots are fired. Everyone has a slightly different style. A children's cooperative offers surprisingly high-quality work handcrafted by youngsters.

The paved road ends at Guaitíl. The dirt road continues southeast to **San Vicente,** which also makes pottery, then slices through the Valle del Río Viejo to Nicoya.

Getting There

Buses depart Santa Cruz for Guaitil every two hours 7 A.M.–5 P.M. Hotels and tour companies throughout Nicoya also offer tours, as do some tour companies in San José.

FILADELFIA

Filadelfia, 18 km north of Santa Cruz and 31 km southwest of Liberia, is the regional center for northern Nicoya, and the main gateway to Playa Flamingo and Tamarindo via **Belén,** six km south of Filadelfia.

About 10 km north of Filadelia, midway between Daniel Oduber International Airport, is the hamlet of **Comunidad** and the turnoff for Playa del Coco.

Proyecto Ecoturístico Loma Larga (tel. 506/651-8152, lomalarga@latinmail.com), at the village of Ortega, about 10 km southeast of Filadelfia, is run by a local cooperative. The villagers preserve local sites of indigenous architectural interest, have various projects to revitalize traditional culture, and offer wildlife trips along the Río Tempisque and into Palo Verde National Park.

Buses pass through Filadelfia en route between Nicoya, Santa Cruz, and Liberia. There are two **gas stations** on Hwy. 21 near Filadelfia, and at Comunidad (at the intersection for Cocos)

Playas del Coco and Vicinity

BAHÍA CULEBRA

Nicoya's most northerly beaches ring the massive horseshoe-shaped Bahía Culebra (Snake Bay), enclosed to the north by the Nacascolo Peninsula, tipped by Punta Mala and, to the south, by the headland of Punta Ballena. The huge bay (so deep that U.S. submarines apparently used it during World War II) is a natural amphitheater rimmed by scarp cliffs cut with lonesome coves sheltering gray- and white-sand beaches and small mangrove swamps good for bird-watching. There are remains of a pre-Columbian native settlement on the western shore of the bay at Nacascolo.

The north and south sides are approached separately by a pincer movement. The south side, where resorts have been opening thick and fast at Playa Panamá, is reached via the road from Comunidad to Playa del Coco (the road divides two km east of Playas del Coco and four km west of Sardinal: a turnoff leads three km north to Playa Hermosa and, beyond Punta Ballena, to Playa Panamá).

VICINITY OF PLAYAS DEL COCO

FOUR SEASONS
RESORT COSTA RICA

Bahía de Culebra

Playa
Arenilla

FIESTA PREMIER PAPAGAYO

GIARDINI
DI PAPAGAYO

PACIFIC

OCEAN

Bahía
Panama

Playa
Buena

OCCIDENTAL COSTA
SMERALDA HOTEL

VILLAS DEL
PESCADOR

Punta Ballena

COSTA BLANCA
DEL PACIFICO

Playa Panama

EL NAKUTI RESORT
HOTEL & VILLAS

RESTAURANTE COSTA
CANGREJOS

RESTAURANTE/
VILLAS DEL PESCADOR

Bahía Playa
Hermosa

SEE DETAIL

RESTAURANTE
RUSSO

PANAMA

HERMOSA

HOTEL
PLAYA HERMOSA

Playa Hermosa

Playa Pedregosa

THE MONKEY BAR

Punta
Cacique

VILLA
HERMOSA

HOTEL
FINISTERRE

VILLA CELINA

VILLA DEL
SUEÑO

CACIQUE
DEL MAR

VILLA KOKOMO

MONTE PARAÍSO

Bahía el Coco

HOTEL
VISTA MAR

VILLA
DEL SOL

CABINAS CHALE

Playa del Coco

PLAYA
DEL COCO

To Playa
El Ocotal

SEE "PLAYA
DEL COCO" MAP

HOTEL FLOR
DE ITABO

RESORT DIVERS

RANCHO ARMADILLO

VILLAS NACASCOL

HERMOSA DETAIL

BAR Y
RESTAURANTE
PUESTA SOL

CONDOVAC
LA COSTA

HOTEL
EL VELERO

SOL PLAYA
HERMOSA

CABINAS
LAS CASONA

BOCA BAR

VILLA ACACIA

IGUANA
INN

DIVING SAFARIS/
PURA VIDA ADVENTURES

VILLAS
HUETARES

HERMOSA

ECOTEL

RESTAURANTE Y
SUPERMARKET AQUA
SPORT/BATHROOMS

PLAYA
HERMOSA INN

0   0.5 mi

0   0.5 km

MOON

© AVALON TRAVEL PUBLISHING, INC.

The north shore is reached from two km north of Comunidad via a road immediately west of the Río Tempisque at Guardia. This road is a fast, sweeping, well-paved, lonesome beauty of a drive that dead-ends after 15 km or so in an arterial network of dirt roads that lead down to a dozen beaches awaiting the bulldozer's maw. En route you pass **Witch's Rock Canopy Tour** (tel. 506/666-7546, fax 506/666-1624, witchsrock-canoytour@hotmail.com, 8 A.M.–4 P.M.), 18 km from Guardia. It has 23 platforms over a 2.5-km course with four hanging bridges and even a tunnel ($40).

Accommodations

The **Hotel Occidental Allegro Papagayo** (tel. 506/690-9900, fax 506/690-9910, reservas.hap @oh-es.com, www.occidental-hoteles.com; in North America, tel. 800/858-2258) overlooks Playa Manzanillo from a superb breeze-swept hillside perch. This four-star, all-inclusive resort has 308 graciously appointed a/c rooms in three-story edifices stair-stepping the hillside. Rooms feature terra-cotta floors, contemporary furnishings, ceiling fans, security box, elegant bathrooms, mini-fridges, and balconies. Action centers on the huge pool with swim-up bar. A theater hosts shows, and there's a disco and sports bar, plus watersports and scuba. Alas, the paltry gray-sand beach holds little attraction, though the Spanish colonial-style resort is handsome indeed. There's a mangrove estuary adjacent. A

THE GULF OF PAPAGAYO PROJECT

In 1993, the Costa Rican Tourism Institute (ICT) began to push roads into the hitherto inaccessible Nacascolo Peninsula. The government also leased 2,000 hectares surrounding the bay as part of the long-troubled Gulf of Papagayo Tourism Project of the ICT, begun in 1974 but left to languish until a few years ago, when development suddenly took off exponentially with the enthusiastic backing of the Rafael Calderón administration. The mini-Cancún that began to emerge was intended to push Costa Rica into the big leagues of resort tourism.

Grupo Papagayo, a conglomerate of independent companies headed by Mexico's Grupo Situr, planned to build as many as 15,000 hotel rooms on its 911-hectare, 88-km-long coastal concession (almost the entire Nacascolo Peninsula) in a 15-year development. Plans called for more than a dozen major hotels, along with at least two golf courses, a 300-yacht marina, an equestrian center and tennis center, time-share condominiums, private villas, and other amenities. The project gathered steam, multiplied, and ground was broken.

Developers and environmentalists squared off over the project, which featured prominently in the presidential election debate in 1994. An independent review panel created by the victorious Figueres administration expressed particular concern about illegal activities, unlawful exemptions, and environmental degradation, including sedimentation in the bay caused by poorly managed movement of topsoil. In March 1995, the former tourism minister and 12 other senior ICT officials were indicted as charges of corruption began to fly.

The Figueres administration created a permanent Environmental Monitoring Plan to oversee the project and declared Bahía Culebra a "coastal marine zone for special management." The Nacascolo Peninsula is an area of archaeological importance with many pre-Columbian sites. When it was discovered that the bulldozers were plowing heedlessly, the government issued an executive decree to declare the peninsula a place of historic importance. To improve its image, the grupo changed the name of the project to "Ecodesarollo Papagayo," or Papagayo Eco-Development. Then the company went bankrupt, bursting the Papagayo bubble. The bulldozers remained idle.

In 1999, North American investors took over and development is ongoing, marked by the opening in early 2004 of the Four Seasons Resort.

bus service runs a circuit around the resort. Call for rates.

The super-deluxe **Four Seasons Resort Costa Rica at Peninsula Papagayo** (tel. 506/696-0000, fax 506/696-0010, www.fourseasons.com/costarica/index.html), at the tip of Punta Mala, promises to bring a whole new panache to the region, with 153 spacious guest rooms, including 25 suites, plus facilities that include a massive full-service spa and a championship 18-hole golf course.

PLAYA HERMOSA

Playa Hermosa, separated from Playa del Coco to the south by Punta Cacique and from Bahía Culebra to the north by Punta Ballena, is a pleasant two-km-wide, curving gray-sand beach with good tide pools at its northern end. The southern end of the beach (reached by the first turnoff to the left from the main road) is like a piece of rural Mexico: funky red-tile-roofed shacks, old fishing boats drawn up like beached whales, nets hung out to dry, cockerels scurrying around, pigs lazing beneath the shade trees.

Accommodations

Under $25: Budget travelers might try the **Ecotel** (tel. 506/672-0488), next to Playa Hermosa Inn, with basic rooms for $10–15 pp, plus a beach house for $30–50. The German-owned **Cabinas Las Casona** (tel. 506/672-0025, $20 s/d low season, $30 s/d high season) is an old wooden home and offers eight simple but clean rooms with fans, small kitchenettes, and private baths with cold water.

$25–50: The U.S-run **Villa Kokomo B&B** (P.O. Box 214-5000 Playa Hermosa, tel. 506/672-0105, kokomo@racsa.co.cr, www.villaokokomo.com, $25 s, $35 d low season; $35 s, $49 d high season) is a modern two-story home on a steep hillside on the approach road to Playa Hermosa, with views of the bay and inland forest. The four rooms each have a distinct and lively color scheme, plus ceramic floors, ceiling fan, modest yet pleasant furnishings, veranda, and large walk-in showers. Meals are served on a patio deck that has a small plunge pool. Rates include full breakfast.

Hotel Playa Hermosa (tel./fax 506/672-0046, $25 s/d, $40 s/d), at the southern end of the beach,

© CHRISTOPHER P. BAKER

Playa Hermosa, southeast Nicoya

has 20 simple, pink, cement-block *cabinas,* a bit dour but clean and fine if you don't care about aesthetics. They have private bathrooms with hot water, and two have a/c. An Italian restaurant is in an old home facing the beach.

$50–100: The charming **Villa Acacia** (tel. 506/672-1000, fax 506/672-0272, www.villacacia .com, $65 s/d low season, $90 s/d high season), 250 meters west, offers eight handsome, octagonal, red-tile-roofed a/c bungalows with cable TV, raised ceilings, security boxes, and kitchens. Eight additional a/c rooms are in two-story units. There's a pool, sundeck, restaurant, and Internet café.

The U.S.-run **Playa Hermosa Inn** (tel. 506/ 672-0050, fax 506/672-0060, samaci@racsa .co.cr, www.costarica-beach-hotel.com, $30 s, $40 d with fan, $40 s, $50 d with a/c) has eight modestly furnished but pleasant rooms and two *cabinas* (plus an a/c apartment) in palm-shaded grounds. All have fans, private baths with hot water, and wide, shady terraces with wicker seats. It was looking a bit shabby at last visit. The apartment costs $80 low season, $100 high season. Rates include breakfast and tax.

A better bet is **Hotel El Velero** (Apdo. 49-5019 Playa del Coco, tel. 506/672-1015, fax 506/672-0016, elvelerocr@yahoo.com, www .costaricahotel.net, $59 s/d low season; $72 high season), an intimate Spanish colonial-style hostelry with 22 modestly appointed a/c rooms (some also have fans). The hotel was recently upgraded and has both upstairs and downstairs restaurants open to the breezes, plus a boutique and a small pool surrounded by shady palms. The hotel offers tours, as well as boat trips and scuba diving. It hosts a barbecue twice weekly.

Undisputably the best place in town is the splendid Canadian-run **Villas del Sueño** (tel. 506/248-0098, fax 506/258-6363, delsueno @racsa.co.cr, www.villadelsueno.com, $54 s/d standard, $69 superior low season; $74 s/d standard rooms, $89 superior high season), an exquisite Spanish colonial-style building offering "hotel service with a home ambience." The charming owners—Claude and Sylvia—offer six a/c rooms in the main house and eight rooms in two two-story, whitewashed stone buildings surrounding a lushly landscaped courtyard with

Martha Herbst and friend with parrot, Playa Hermosa

a swimming pool. The rooms boast terra-cotta tiled floors, lofty hardwood ceilings with fans, large picture windows, contemporary artwork, beautiful batik fabrics, bamboo furniture, soft pastels, and private bathrooms. You can dine alfresco on the best cuisine in town, and it hosts live music. It has a quality gift store. Three-night low-season packages include a fourth night free.

The other sure-fire winner is the Canadian-owned **Hotel La Finisterra** (tel. 506/670-0293, fax 506/672-0227, finisterra@hotmail.com, www.finisterra.net, $59 s/d low season, $69 s/d high season), atop the breezy headland at the south end of the beach. What views! La Finisterra is a handsome contemporary structure. The 10 simply furnished rooms boast fans, attractive bamboo furniture, and wide, screened windows; some have forest (not beach) views, and a/c was planned at last visit. The open-sided restaurant looks over a charming irregular-shaped swimming pool. The owners have a 38-foot sailboat ($60 full-day tour); sportfishing tours are arranged. Rates include tax and full breakfast.

Villas Huetares (P.O. Box 068-4400 Guanacaste, tel./fax 506/672-0052, 506/672-0051, $60 low season, $90 high season for up to six people) is an apartment-style complex of 15 two-bedroom bungalows in lush grounds. They're spacious, with modestly furnished lounges, safes, and well-stocked kitchens. The places get hot, though, despite the a/c. And the bathrooms are poorly designed. Still, the whole is pleasant enough, with a pool, sun deck, and small bar. It's popular with Tico families. Rates include tax.

$100–150: The **Condovac La Costa** (tel. 506/672-0150, reservaciones@condovac.com, www.condovac.com, $62, $80 d) commands the hill at the northern end of the beach. The modern and attractive large-scale complex enjoys a marvelous breezy setting with superb ocean views. It offers 101 a/c villas stair-stepping down to the beach amid lawns and bougainvillea. Each complex has its own pool and adjacent *palenque* bar. There's a selection of bars and restaurants. The hotel offers a full complement of tours, sportfishing, and scuba diving.

For large-resort elegance, there's **Sol Playa Hermosa** (tel. 670-0405 or 800-336-3542, fax 506/670-0349, www.solmelia.com), next to Condovac La Costa, with 54 deluxe hotel rooms, all with satellite TVs, telephones, two double beds, and oceanview balconies. It also has 106 attractive villas, 24 with private pools. There's a swimming pool, three restaurants, and a disco, and tours and fishing are offered. Call for rates.

Self-catering options include **Villa Hermosa** (tel. 506/665-0420, fax 506/672-0039); **Villas Colina** (506/672-0246); or the deluxe **Monte Paraíso** (c/o Remax, tel. 506/672-0255, www.remax-tresaamigoscr.com), a three-bedroom, three-bathroom oceanview spot with pool. The best bet is **Villas el Oasis** (contact Villas del Sueño), handsome studio apartments and villas that share a courtyard pool and Jacuzzi beautifully lit at night by fiber-optic lights. Each villa has a one-bedroom apartment downstairs ($111 daily, $715 weekly low season; $169/999 high season) and two efficiencies upstairs ($85 daily, $535 weekly low season; $119/699 high season).

Food

The best food for miles is served at **Villas del Sueño,** where the rotating daily menu may include scalopini parmesan; tenderloin with brandy and three-pepper sauce; mahi mahi with shrimp and cream sauce ($15.50); and profiteroles ($5–13). Elegant place settings, low lighting, and mellow music enhance the atmosphere. It does special dinners, such as for Valentines' Day. It has live music 7 A.M.–10:30 P.M. Nov.–April.

Similarly, the **Hotel Finisterra's** (2–10 P.M. Wed.–Mon.) restaurant is open to the public, with a creative French chef conjuring Caesar salad ($3.50), filet mignon with peppercorn sauce ($10), and daily pastas. Friday is sushi night. It earns rave reviews and draws diners from afar.

The a/c roadside restaurant at **Villa Acacia** (6 A.M.–10 P.M., $5) serves American breakfasts, *casados* (set lunches), sandwiches, shakes, and coffee.

Locals rave about **Puesta Sol,** a beachside eatery good for lunch. It's said to have excellent local and international fare, plus live music.

Restaurante Aqua Sport (6:30 A.M.–9 P.M.) has a pleasing thatched beachfront restaurant with crepes, ceviche, salads, and a wide-ranging seafood menu.

Entertainment

The Monkey Bar (tel. 506/672-0267, 5 P.M.–midnight) is an atmospheric, all-log stilt hut with a soaring thatched roof. It features Monday night football and music videos on TV; there's also a pool table, and live bands sometimes perform. And free shots are occasionally handed out. The parking lot has the most amazing strangler fig you'll ever see! Check it out!

Villas del Sueño has live bands three nights weekly in high season, plus guest appearances in low season.

Tours and Activities

Diving Safaris (tel. 506/672-0012) claims to be the largest land-based dive operator in Costa Rica. It has daily two-tank dive trips ($65), night and Nitrox dives, and courses. Snorkelers can accompany dive boats ($30).

John Leckie, a friendly Scot, owns **Dive Hermosa** and offers custom scuba dives and PADI certification ($375). Ask for him at the Monkey Bar (tel. 506/672-1055).

Aqua Sport (tel. 506/670-0050, fax 506/672-0060, samaci@racsa.co.cr) offers kayaks ($4 per hour), sailboards ($15), aqua bikes ($5), canoes ($4), plus banana-boat rides ($2.50 pp), snorkeling ($20) and boat tours ($33 per hour, eight people), and fishing (from $40 per hour to $400 full day).

Spanish Dancer (tel. 506/672-0012, cellular tel. 506/395-6090) is a 36-foot catamaran that sails daily at 10 A.M. on a five-hour fun cruise ($50 including hotel pickup, lunch, and beverages), and again for sunset cruises.

Pura Vida Adventures (tel. 506/670-1090 or 506/387-2359) offers sportfishing, surfing, and snorkeling.

Kitesurfing School (tel. 506/396-4653, fax 506/672-0218, bertoldi@racsa.co.cr, www.suntoursandfun.com/kitesurfing.htm) offers eight-hour tuition for $160, with accommodation at a studio apartment.

Gaviota Tours (tel. 506/672-0143, gaviotalouise@hotmail.com) offers excursions.

Services

Aqua Sport has a public telephone, souvenir shop, and general store (open daily 6 A.M.–9 P.M.). Villa Acacia has an Internet café. Iguana Inn has a laundry.

Getting There

A bus departs San José for Playa Hermosa from Calle 12, Avenidas 5/7, daily at 3:20 P.M. (five hours). A bus departs Liberia for Playa Hermosa daily at 7:30 A.M., 11:30 A.M., 3:30 P.M., 5:30 P.M., and 7 P.M. Both buses continue to Playa Panamá. Buses depart Hermosa for San José at 5 A.M., and for Liberia at 5 A.M., 6 A.M., 10 A.M., 4 P.M. and 5 P.M.

A taxi from Coco will run about $5 one-way; from Liberia about $15.

PLAYA PANAMÁ

The road continues one km to Playa Panamá, a narrow, two-km-wide gray-sand beach in a cove encusped by low, scrub-covered hills—a bay within a bay. The beach is popular with Ticos who camp along the beach. Weekends and holidays get crowded.

The road dead-ends atop the headland overlooking **Playa Arenilla** and Bahía Culebra. One km south of Playa Panamá, a branch road leads west to **Playa Buena.**

Accommodations

$100–150: I like the **El Nakuti Resort Hotel & Villas** (tel. 506/672-0121 or 506/233-0133, fax 506/672-0120 or 506/256-9546, ventas@grupopapagayo.com, www.grupopapagayo.com, $50 s/d standard, $58 s/d superior, $68 s/d junior suite), a handsome modern property with 19 thatched chalets arrayed in the style of an indigenous village in landscaped grounds. Sponge-washed walls in warm ochers enhance the mood. Each well-designed a/c bungalow has a separate living room with kitchen; king-or double-beds with vibrant fabrics in mezzanine bedroom; satellite TV, direct-dial telephone, hairdryer, safety deposit box, floor to ceiling glass sliding doors, and bathrooms with huge walk-in showers. There's a large pool and kids' pool. It has sea kayaks, snorkeling, water-skiing, sunset cruises, plus mountain bike and ATV rentals. Rates include tax.

Giardini di Papagayo (tel./fax 506/672-0067 or 233-0133, fax 506/672-9546 or 256-9546, info @grupopapagayo.com,www.grupopapagayo .com, $42 s/d standard, $60 s/d superior, $70 s/d junior suite), a condo-villa resort complex with a superb setting on the headland between Playa Hermosa and Playa Buena, offers grand vistas. The theme is a contemporary take on Spanish colonial. It has 25 two- and four-bedroom villas with king-size beds and contemporary furnishings.

The **Costa Blanca del Pacífico** (tel. 506/672-0096, fax 506/672-0239, costabl@racsa.co.cr, www.costablancadelpacifico.com, $70 low season, $150 high season up to eight people), on the tip of Punta Ballena, offers 28 contemporary-colonial a/c "villas" (actually, one- and two-bedroom suites) with ceramic floors, tasteful fabrics, plus cable TV, fans, refrigerators, balconies with wrought-iron balustrades, spacious bathrooms, and a kitchen and lounge. A clifftop restaurant in *rancho* style opens to a vast sun deck, and there's a swim-up bar by the pool. It lacked guests at last visit.

At Playa Buena, the beautiful and expansive all-inclusive **Occidental Costa Smeralda** (Apdo. 434-1150 San José, tel. 506/672-0193 or 506/ 866/809-9330, fax 506/672-0041, www .occidental-hoteles.com) draws a mostly Tico clientele. The airy lobby sets the tone for the contemporary Spanish-colonial resort, with its terra-cotta tile floor and elegant wicker furniture. The 114 beautiful a/c bungalows stair-step grassy lawns, with sweeping views across the bay. Hardwoods and terra-cotta tiles abound. Closet space is plentiful, and good lighting and huge mirrors adorn the bathrooms. Plate-glass walls and doors proffer priceless vistas. Suites have mezzanine bedrooms and king-size beds, plus deep sea-green marble in the bathrooms, which have Jacuzzis. It has two restaurant, and a large pool set like a jewel on the slopes. There's a ten-

nis court and shops, plus scuba diving and tours. Call for rates.

$150–200: The marvelously situated **Fiesta Premier Papagayo Resort** (tel. 506/296-6263, fax 506/220-3409, ventas@enjoygroup.net, www .fiestapremier.com), formerly the Blue Bay Resort, is a sprawling all-inclusive property with 160 Spanish colonial-style duplex bungalows nestled amid bougainvillea, shade trees, and palms on the scarp face overlooking the brown-sand Playa Arenilla, immediately north of Playa Panamá. At last visit it was being entirely remodeled under the new Fiesta ownership.

Food

For unique atmosphere, try **Restaurante El Pescador** (11 A.M.–8 P.M.) next to El Nakuti, with deep-cushion sofas, rattan chairs, and a tremendous swimming pool with alcoved shade areas. It serves ceviche, burgers and fries ($2.50), sandwiches, shakes, etc.

The simple, hilltop **Restaurante Russo** (tel. 506/672-1045, 10 A.M.–midnight) serves genuine Russian food from the hands of Sergio. The menu runs from Georgian salad, and meat soup with pickles and olives, to borscht ($5), and smoked fish with cabbage roll.

PLAYAS DEL COCO

Playas del Coco, 35 km west of Liberia, is one of the most accessible beach resorts in Guanacaste. The place can be crowded during busy weekends and holidays, when Josefinos flock here. A two-km-wide gray-sand beach (it is referred to in the plural—Playas del Coco) lines the horseshoe-shaped bay. There's plenty of local color, not least because Coco is still an active fishing village; the touristy area is to the east; the laid-back fishing village is to the west, with fishing boats in the bay making perfect perches for pelicans.

Alas, the ocelots, birds, and monkeys that were common north of Coco have been scared away in recent years by dynamiting and wholesale clear-cutting by the developers of the failed Cacique del Mar residential resort project (now abandoned).

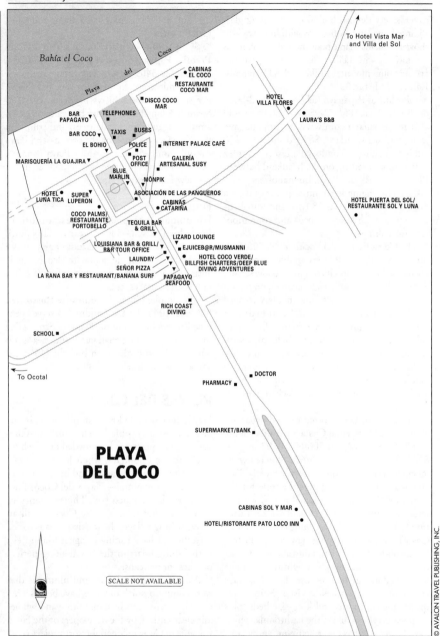

Bahía el Coco

To Hotel Vista Mar
and Villa del Sol

Coco

del

Playa

CABINAS
EL COCO

RESTAURANTE
COCO MAR

DISCO COCO
MAR

HOTEL
VILLA FLORES

LAURA'S B&B

BAR
PAPAGAYO

TELEPHONES

BAR COCO

TAXIS

BUSES

EL BOHIO

POLICE

INTERNET PALACE CAFÉ

MARISQUERÍA LA GUAJIRA

POST
OFFICE

GALERÍA
ARTESANAL SUSY

BLUE
MARLIN

MONPIK

HOTEL
LUNA TICA

SUPER
LUPERON

ASOCIACIÓN DE LAS PANGUEROS

CABINAS
CATARINA

HOTEL PUERTA DEL SOL/
RESTAURANTE SOL Y LUNA

COCO PALMS/
RESTAURANTE
PORTOBELLO

TEQUILA BAR
& GRILL

LIZARD LOUNGE

LOUISIANA BAR & GRILL/
R&R TOUR OFFICE

EJUICEB@R/MUSMANNI

LAUNDRY

HOTEL COCO VERDE/
BILLFISH CHARTERS/DEEP BLUE
DIVING ADVENTURES

SEÑOR PIZZA

LA RANA BAR Y RESTAURANT/BANANA SURF

PAPAGAYO
SEAFOOD

RICH COAST
DIVING

SCHOOL

To Ocotal

DOCTOR

PHARMACY

SUPERMARKET/BANK

PLAYA
DEL COCO

CABINAS SOL Y MAR

HOTEL/RISTORANTE PATO LOCO INN

SCALE NOT AVAILABLE

MOON

© AVALON TRAVEL PUBLISHING, INC.

Accommodations

Under $25: A reader warns against **Cabinas Arrecife.**

The beachfront **Cabinas El Coco** (Apdo. 2-5059 Playa del Coco, tel. 506/670-0110, fax 506/670-0167, cocomar@racsa.co.cr, $10 s, $15 d with fan, $25 s, $30 d with a/c and TV) has 76 small and basic but clean rooms with hot water. The beachfront rooms are nicer than the more basic rooms to the rear, which are noisier and get no breezes. All have private baths and fans. It has a restaurant and a disco.

Hotel Luna Tica (Apdo. 67-5059 Playa del Coco, tel. 506/670-0127, fax 506/670-0434, $10 pp) has 21 rooms with fans and private baths with cold water only. The older *cabinas* on the beach are dark and stuffy. Newer rooms in the annex across the street are nicer and the same price. It has rental car service and offers fishing and boating tours.

Laura's House B&B (tel. 506/670-0751, casalauracr@yahoo.com, $15 s, $25 with fan, $25 s, $35 d with a/c) is run by a delightful young Tica and offers seven rooms in a two-story house, all with clean albeit small private bathrooms with cold water only. Downstairs rooms are pleasingly cool; some have bunks. There's a pool in the courtyard with hammocks under shade trees.

$25–50: The **Cabinas Sol y Mar** (tel. 506/670-1111, fax 506/670-0808, $30 s/d low season, $41 s/d high season) is a nice spot with six spacious, modern, a/c *cabinas* for eight people with cable TVs, kitchenettes and lounge, plus fans and private baths with cold water. It has a pool in a handsome courtyard.

Similarly, **Coco Palms** (tel. 506/670-0367, fax 506/670-0117, hotelcocopalms@hotmail.com, $20 s, $35 d), on the west side of the soccer field, offers 20 spacious, adequately furnished rooms arrayed along an atrium corridor with fans and roomy private bathrooms with hot water. There's also a lap pool and the delightful Restaurante Portobello.

The pleasing, Italian-run **Hotel Pato Loco Inn** (Apdo. 87, Playas del Coco, tel./fax 506/670-0145, patoloco@racsa.co.cr, $35 s/d with fan, $45 with a/c low season; $40/50 high season) has attractive rooms—three triples, one double, and two fully equipped apartments—with orthopedic mattresses, central a/c, and modest furnishings with hardwood accents. There's a small but quality Italian restaurant. The owners also rent an a/c apartment for $150 weekly, or $500–600 per month.

The nicest motel-style property around is the **Best Western Hotel Coco Verde** (Apdo. 61-5059 Playas del Coco, tel. 506/670-0112, fax 506/670-0555, cocoverd@racsa.co.cr, www.cocoverde.com, $50 s, $65 d low season; $65 s, $80 d high season), in the heart of town, with 33 spacious rooms with modest decor and silent, remote-control a/c in a modern two-story complex with a lap pool. There's a restaurant with lively decor serving *típico* dishes.

Also appealing is the U.S.-run **Hotel Villa Flores** (tel. 506/670-0269, fax 506/670-0787, villafloresbb@yahoo.com, www.hotel-villa-flores.com, $45 s/d standard, $55 s/d "deluxe" low season; $60/70 high season), inland of the beach about 200 meters north of town, a handsome Spanish colonial-style hostelry run to high standards. Ceramics abound. Its 10 modestly furnished yet charming rooms (recently refurbished under new owners) have lots of light and bright color schemes, plus cable TV. Larger "deluxe" upstairs rooms have a/c and open to a wraparound veranda; one has a huge mosaic-lined tub. A restaurant overlooks lawns with hammocks slung beneath the palms. There's a gym, and an attractive pool with *ranchito* bar.

Further east, the **Villa del Sol** (tel./fax 506/670-0085, villasol@racsa.co.cr, www.villadelsol.com, $25 s, $30 d shared bathroom, $35 s, $45 d private bathroom low season; $30 s, $35 d shared bathroom, $45 s, $55 d private bathroom high season; $50 low season, $60 high season apartments), set amid lawns, is a homey Canadian-run bed-and-breakfast with an open atrium lounge. Seven rooms vary considerably, though all have ceiling fans, tile floors, and simple decor blessed with lively colors. Five a/c rooms have private bathrooms and balconies plus king-size bed; one has a triangular shower. It also offers six new studio apartments with kitchenettes, tiled floors, modestly elegant furnishings, small

TVs, telephones, and full kitchens. There's a swimming pool and Jacuzzi plus barbecue on the sun deck, where simple lunches and French-inspired dinners are served. It has secure parking. The delightful owners—Jocelyne and Serge Boucher—also rent upscale villas for $350–1,000 weekly; plus you can rent the entire house for $2,000 low season, $2,500 high season. Rates include continental breakfast.

$50–100: If you don't mind being out of town, **Villas Nacazcol** (tel./fax 506/670-1179, rhnacazcol@hotmail.com, $60 up to four people, $85 up to eight people low season; $80/100 high season), about 400 meters east of the turnoff for Playa Hermosa, on the approach road east of Coco, has 75 comfortable and pleasing a/c *cabinas* with cable TV, refrigerators, microwave, wrought-iron bedsteads, and large kitchenettes; some are handsome neo-colonial style. They open to lush lawns and a beautiful pool. It also has a tennis court, pool, billiards, and a video room, plus a disco with karaoke.

I adore the **Hotel Puerta del Sol** (Apdo. 43-5019 Playas del Coco, tel. 506/670-0195, fax 506/670-0650, hotelsol@racsa.co.cr, www .lapuertadelsol.com, $40 s, $60 d standard, $80 suites low season; $50 s, $80 d standard, $100 suites high season), an intimate canary-yellow hotel with an Italian aesthetic. The 10 white-washed rooms (with tropical pastels in counterpoint) are made exquisite by soft-contoured "walls" enveloping king-sized beds and melding into wraparound sofas built into the walls (even the sofas have orthopedic mattresses), and wrought-iron fittings in the bathrooms. All have a/c, TVs, phones, safes, and patios. Two are suites with refrigerators. *Casitas* were being added. A small airy lounge has games and a TV, and there's a garden with a charming lap pool and gym. The restaurant is the best in town. Free scuba lessons are offered in the pool. Rates include breakfast.

Hotel Flor de Itabo (Apdo. 32-5059 Playas del Coco, tel. 506/670-0011, fax 506/670-0003, info@flordeitabo.com, www.flordeitabo.com, $45 s, $70 d standard, $65 s, $90 d deluxe, $120 four-person apartment), about one km before Coco, is under German-Italian management and is big on sportfishing. The 10 spacious standard rooms have lofty hardwood ceilings, a/c, satellite TVs, refrigerators, coffeemakers, and Guatemalan bedspreads, plus large tiled bathrooms with hot water. Seven "deluxe" rooms have Jacuzzis. Eight bungalow apartments have kitchens and fans but no a/c. The Sailfish Restaurant opens onto a pool in landscaped grounds full of bougainvillea, palms, and birdlife, including parrots and macaws, many of which were rescued from various traumas and arrived with ruffled feathers. (There are caged peccaries, too.) There's also a casino. The hotel specializes in fishing trips and also offers scuba diving. Day guests are charged $2.

Hotel Vista Mar (tel./fax 506/670-0753, hvistamar@racsa.co.cr, www.beach-hotels-in-costa-rica.com, $35 s, $45 d low season; $45 s, $55 d high season) is a handsome hacienda-style hotel with nine a/c rooms facing a grassy courtyard with palm-shaded swimming pool and red-tile-roofed bar with wood-fired oven. The lounge—replete with terra-cotta tile floors, Oriental throw rugs, and deep-cushioned sofas—opens to a breezy breakfast terrace with wicker rockers facing onto lawns facing the beach. Room 9 has a voluminous bathroom with step-down shower. Rates include breakfast and tax.

For peaceful reclusivity, I recommend **Rancho Armadillo** (P.O. Box 15-5019 Playas del Coco, tel. 506/670-0108, fax 506/670-0441, info @ranchoarmadillo.com, www.ranchoarmadillo .com, $65 s, $75 d standard, $106 two-bedroom suite low season; $80 s, $90 d standard, $127 suite high season). This home-away-from-home is a beautiful Spanish-colonial-style hacienda on a 10-hectare hillside *finca* 1.5 km from the beach. The six spacious bungalows include a two-bedroom suite. All have a/c, fans, magnificent hardwood furniture, wrought-iron balustrades, lofty wooden ceilings, hardwood floors, screened doors, colorful Guatemalan bedspreads, stained-glass windows, "rainforest" showers, and coffeemakers, plus refrigerators and cable TVs. The voluminous bathrooms are adorned with exquisite tile work and stained glass. Halogen bulbs in the ceiling provide great light for reading. The honeymoon suite is huge. There's also a house for families or groups, plus a fabulous self-serve, open-air kitchen beside the swimming pool, a gym, an open-air *mirador* lounge with hammocks and rockers, and a library. Ceramic, stone, and wood miniatures of namesake armadillos pop up all over the house. The owners, Rick and Debbie, plan to add a putting green, and will offer tours. Meals are offered by request. The estate is available for exclusive rental during peak season, with Rick, the owner, as chef (he was for years a professional chef). Rates include breakfast.

Food

The **Best Western Coco Verde** offers a buffet breakfast 7–10 A.M. ($4).

Budget hounds might try the breezy **Restaurante Coco Mar,** which offers inexpensive seafood and *típico* dishes and is a good place to check out the action on the beach. **Papagayo Seafood** (tel. 506/670-0298, noon–10 P.M.) is a clean U.S.-run eatery that is open-air downstairs and air-conditioned upstairs. The menu includes sashimi ($7), and blackened Cajun-style catch of the day ($7.50). It also sells fresh fish at a streetside outlet. **La Rana** (4 P.M.–midnight Tue.–Sun., $4–$9) adjoining, is good for inexpensive dishes such as *churrasco*, roast chicken, and burritos and tacos Next door, **Banana Surf** has a simple open-air pizzería.

The modern a/c **Louisiana Bar & Grill** (no tel., 11 A.M.–10 P.M. Fri.–Wed.), opposite Best Western Coco Verde, serves creole shrimp ($10), squid with onion and chile ($7), ceviche, and the like.

Restaurante Portobello (tel. 506/670-0153, 7 A.M.–3 P.M. and 4–10 P.M. Tue.–Sun.), on the west side of the soccer field, is a modestly elegant, Mediterranean-style eatery with a creative menu featuring sautéed black tip shark ($6), curry shrimp stir fry ($8), plus quesadillas, tacos, and a large salad and sandwich selection, plus desserts.

For prize Italian fare, head to **Restaurante Sol y Luna** at Hotel Puerta del Sol; it serves pastas ($5), cannelloni ($7.50), lasagne ($8), stuffed crÊpes, tiramisu, and daily specials, enjoyed amid exquisite Romanesque decor. It also serves cappuccinos and espressos, plus a large wine list and 15 types of beer. Open Wed.–Mon. 5–10 P.M.

Sailfish Restaurant in the Hotel Flor de Itabo specializes in seafood, plus T-bone and New York steaks.

You can stock up at the **supermarket** on the southeast corner of the soccer field, or **Super Luperon,** on the west side.

Entertainment and Events

Coco hosts a five-day fiesta cívica in late January, with bullfights, rodeos, folkloric dancing, female beauty contests, etc.

Bar Coco and **Bohio Bar & Yacht Club,** next door, are popular with local expats; the latter sometimes has karaoke; the "happy hour" 4–7 P.M. features free *bocas.*

The **Lizard Lounge,** 150 meters south of the plaza, has a pool table, plus a happy hour daily 5–7 P.M. Wednesday is Italian night; Thursday is Ladies Night with sexy male dancers; and you're offered $2 shots Fri.–Sat. The simple open-air **Tequila Bar & Grill,** nearby, is a good place for shots; it also serves seafoods and Tex-Mex.

The **Disco Coco Mar** is a no-frills disco on Saturday, and karaoke other nights.

Gamblers can can try their hand with Lady Luck at the small **casinos** in Hotel Flor de Itabo (open daily 8 P.M.–2 A.M.) and **Best Western Coco Verde.**

Tours and Activities

The **Asociación de las Pangueros** (tel. 506/670-0228 or 387-9166, rocasurf@hotmail.com), the local fishermen's association, offers boats and guide services; it's represented at **Pura Vida Adventures** (tel. 506/670-1090). **Billfisher Sportfishing Charters** (tel. 506/670-0112, coverd@racsa.co.cr, www.billfishersportfishing .com), based at Coco Verde Hotel charges $700 full-day.

Papagayo Sportfishing, tel. 670-0354, fax 670-0446, offers surfing trips, plus snorkeling and sportfishing, as does **Resort Divers de Costa Rica,** on the approach road into Playas del Cocos; the latter also offers sunset cruises ($45) and PADI certification ($375). And **Rich Coast Diving**

© CHRISTOPHER P. BAKER

fishing boat, Playas del Coco

(tel./fax 506/670-0176, dive@richcoastdiving .com, www.richcoastdiving.com; in North America, tel. 800/434-8464) has a full-service dive center, plus a 35-foot trimaran for charter.

Information and Services

R&R Tours (tel. 506/670-0573) is a tour information and booking center run by Evelyn, from Guam.

The post office (8 A.M.–noon and 2–5:30 P.M. Mon.–Fri.) faces the plaza. There are public telephones at the plaza.

The off-beat **ejuiceb@r** (tel. 506/670-0563) charges $1.25 per hour for Internet use; daily 8 A.M.–8 P.M. Other options include the overly a/c **Internet Leslie** (tel. 506/670-0156), at Cabinas Catarina (8 A.M.–10 P.M. Mon.–Sat., 2–10 P.M. Sunday), and nicer **Internet Palace Café** (tel. 506/670-0450, 8 A.M.–8 P.M. Sun.–Mon., 10 A.M.–10 P.M. Fri.–Sat.), near the southeast corner of the plaza

There's a doctor's office on the approach road into town, and a pharmacy opposite. The **Red Cross** (tel. 506/670-0190) is in Sardinal, eight km east of Coco.

The **police station** (tel. 506/670-0258) faces the plaza.

There's a **laundry** (8:30 A.M.–6 P.M. Mon.–Sat.) next to Banana Surf, 200 meters south of the plaza.

Craft and souvenir stalls line the east side of the soccer field. *Don't buy coral—this only encourages destruction of the tiny offshore coral reef.*

Getting There

Buses (tel. 506/222-1650), buses depart San José from Calles 14, Avenidas 1/3 daily at 4 A.M., 8 A.M. and 2 P.M. ($3; five hours), returning at 8 A.M., 2 P.M., and 4 P.M. Buses depart Liberia (Arata, tel. 666-0138), for Coco at 5:30 A.M., 7 A.M., 9:30 A.M., 11 A.M., 12:30 P.M., 2:30 P.M., 4:30 P.M., and 6:30 P.M., returning at 5:30 A.M., 7 A.M., 9 A.M., 11 A.M., 3 P.M., 5 P.M., and 6 P.M.

There's a gas station in Sardinal.

PLAYA EL OCOTAL

This secluded gray-sand beach is three km southwest of Playa del Coco within the cusp of steep cliffs. It's smaller and more reclusive than Coco, but gets the overflow on busy weekends. The rocky headlands at each end have tide pools. Ocotal is a base for sportfishing and scuba diving. At Las Corridas, a dive spot only a kilometer from Ocotal, divers are sure of coming face-to-face with massive jewfish, which make this rock reef their home. Divers have even seen black marlin cruising gracefully in the area.

Accommodations

Camping is not permitted.

The pleasant Spanish-run **Ocotal Inn B&B** (tel. 506/670-0835, fax 506/570-0526, www.ocotalinn.com, $25 s, $40 d low season; $30 s, $55 d high season), mid-way to Ocotal, has simply furnished no-smoking rooms with raised wooden ceilings. It has a small plunge pool.

The bay is dominated by **El Ocotal Beach Resort & Marina** (Apdo. 1013-1002, San José, tel. 506/670-0083, fax 506/670-0321, elocotal @racsa.co.cr, www.ocotalresort.com, $85 s, $110 d standard, $160–180 bungalows, $195 suite low season; $110 s, $125 d standard, $180–200 bungalows, $235 suite high season), a gleaming whitewashed structure that stair-steps up the cliffs at the southern end of the beach. It has 71 attractive rooms, all with a/c, fans, freezers, two queen-size beds each, satellite TVs, direct-dial telephones, and ocean views. The original 12 rooms are in six duplex bungalows; newer rooms have their own Jacuzzi, sunning area, and pool. The lobby and restaurant sit atop a knoll with views along the coast. Three small pools each have *ranchitos* for shade, and there're tennis courts and horseback riding, plus a fully equipped dive shop, sportfishing boats, and car rental.

Among boutique hotels, **Hotel Villa Casa Blanca** (tel. 506/670-0518, fax 506/670-0448, vcblanca@racsa.co.cr, $55 s/d standard, $75 s/d suite, $95 condo low season; $75 s/d standard, $100 s/d suite, $115 condo high season) sets a standard for beachside bed and breakfasts. A stay here is like being a guest in a personal home. The upscale Spanish-style villa is set in a lush landscaped garden full of yuccas and bougainvillea. The small swimming pool has a swim-up bar and a sun deck with lounge chairs. Inside, the

fishing boats at Ocotal

© CHRISTOPHER P. BAKER

hotel epitomizes subdued elegance with its intimate and romantic allure: sponge-washed walls, four-poster beds (six rooms), stenciled murals, and massive bathrooms with deep tubs and wall-to-wall mirrors. The 14 rooms include four suites with more elegant furnishings, two designated as honeymoon suites. You can relax I a whirlpool, and there's a patio restaurant and grill. It also has a condominium with kitchen. The prices are a bargain.

Bahía Pez Vela ($350 nightly, $2400 weekly low season; $375/2500 high season) an erstwhile sportfishing resort had metamorphosed at last visit into new three-bedroom townhouses with a beautiful pool and bar at the center.

Food

The rustic and offbeat beachfront **Father Rooster Restaurant** (11 A.M.–11 P.M.) run by Steve, a friendly Floridian, is the cool, hip happening place to be. It serves seafood dishes, quesadillas, burgers, caesar salads, etc., plus huge margaritas ($4.50). It has a sand volleyball court, plus pool table, darts, and dancing on Saturdays.

If you're feeling flush, try the cuisine at **El Ocotal,** which one reader raves about. There's indoor or outdoor dining on a raised deck.

◪ THE MURCIÉLAGOS

Lying south of Cabo Santa Elena, some 35 km northwest of Playas del Coco, the Isla Murciélagos archipelago of tiny islands rise from the sea like witch's fingers. Encompassed within Santa Rosa National Park (see the Santa Rosa National Park section, in the Guanacaste chap-

ter), the surrounding waters are renowned among divers, luring scuba enthusiasts for the thrill of swimming among giant grouper, eagle rays, and great bull sharks. Dive operators based at El Ocotal offer trips. **El Ocotal Diving Safaris**(www.ocotaldiving.com) offers a free introductory dive daily and rents equipment. It charges from $64 for two-tank dives; night dives cost $49. Snorkeling costs from $25, full-day. Deep-sea fishing costs $425/645 half-/full-day (up to four people). Sportsfishing excursions are also offered.

Playa Flamingo and Vicinity

Playa Flamingo is the central community serving a series of contiguous beaches accessed by paved road via the communities of **Portegolpe** and **Huacas** (reached from Hwy 21 via Belén, eight km south of Filadelfia; from Playa del Coco, you have to return inland to Filadelfia, then Huacas). The **Monkey Park** (tel. 506/653-8060, fax 506/653-8127, esmerajm@racsa.co.cr), at Portegolpe, is an animal rescue center that takes in injured and confiscated monkeys that cannot survive in the wild. It has a breeding program and accepts visitors for a one-hour guided tour.

At Huacas, you turn right for Playas Brasilito, Flamingo, Potrero, Penca, and Azucar, where the road ends. If you don't turn right, the road keeps straight for **Matapalo,** where you turn right for Playa Conchal, and left for Playa Grande (see *Tamarindo and Vicinity* section).

A more direct route is via a dirt road—the "Monkey Trail"—that begins three km east of Playa del Coco and one km west of Sardinal and leads to Playas Azúcar, Potrero, and Flamingo. It can be rough going in wet season and includes a river fording that can be tricky after heavy rains. It leads past the hidden beaches of Playa Danta and Playa Zapotal, site of a proposed 400-hectare tourist project. About nine km southwest from Sardinal is the **Congo Trail Canopy Tour** (tel. 506/666-4422, congotrail@racsa.co.cr, 8 A.M.– 5 P.M.), where for $35 you can whiz between treetop platforms on a steel cable (you're attached by harness), granting a monkey's-eye view with

the howler (congo) monkeys. It also has a **butterfly farm** and restaurant.

The **Jardín Botánico Cuatro Mangoes** (tel. 506/697-0087), opposite the canopy tour has guided horseback tours ($10 per hour), and ornamental gardens in the midst of the forest. Folkloric dances are hosted on a stage.

The following beaches are listed in north to south order, assuming access via the "Monkey Trail."

PLAYAS POTRERO AND AZÚCAR

The "Monkey Trail" emerges at Playa Potrero, about 16 km southwest of Sardinal and immediately northeast of Playa Flamingo, from which it is separated by Bahía Potrero. The gray-sand beach curls southward for about three km from the rustic and charming fishing hamlet of **Potrero** and is popular with campers during holidays. The calm sheltered waters are safe for swimming. A large community of expats lives south of Potrero village and inland of the beach in widespaced houses connected by a gridlike maze of dirt roads.

North of Potrero, a dirt road leads to **Playa Penca,** a beautiful almost-white-sand beach backed by a protected mangrove estuary—that of the Río Salinas—and rare saltwater forest replete with monkeys, coatis, and plentiful birdlife, including parrots, roseate spoonbills, and egrets.

oxcart in Potrero

From Penca, the dirt road coils north three km to **Playa Azúcar** (Sugar Beach), a narrow, 400-meter-wide spit of sun-drenched coral-colored sand that just might have you dreaming of retiring here. It is separated from an even more lonesome beach—Playa Danta—by steep cliffs to the north. There's good snorkeling offshore.

There's no bus service.

The community has a website: www.potrerobeach.com.

Accommodations

Camping: You can camp along Playa Potrero (no facilities). **Mayra's Camping and Cabins** (tel. 506/654-4273, $2 campsites; $12.50 cabins) has showers and toilets. There are also simple cabins with private bathrooms.

$25–50: At **Cabinas Cristina** (tel. 506/654-4006, fax 506/654-4128, danielbo@racsa.co.cr, $30 s/d with fan, $35 with kitchen, $40 s/d with a/c and TV, $50 with a/c and kitchen) you have the benefit of a small pool. The six simple all-wood *cabinas* are set in shady albeit unkempt gardens and each sleeps four people, with private bathrooms and hot water.

The Italian-run **Cabinas Isolina** (tel. 506/654-4333, fax 506/654-4313, www.isolinabeach.com, $35 s, $40 d standard, $45 s, $50 d with kitchenette, $70 villa), one km south of Potrero, has 11 attractive if simple and somewhat dark a/c cabins with cable TVs, double and single beds with beautiful spreads (two have kitchenettes), and private bathrooms with hot water. It also has three villas, plus a pool and restaurant in lush gardens.

Bahía Esmeralda Hotel and Restaurant (tel./fax 506/654-4480, www.hotelbahiaesmeralda .com, $30 s, $38 d rooms with fans, $38 s, $52 d with a/c, $72 four-person apartments, $90 six-person villa) is a modern, Italian-run hotel 200 meters on the southern edge of Potrero hamlet. The four simply furnished rooms, four houses, and eight apartments, feature red-tile roofs and have all cable TV, lofty hardwood ceilings, double beds and bunks and modern conveniences. Italian fare is served in an open-sided restaurant, and there's a swimming pool in lush gardens. Horseback tours and bike rental are available, as is a boat for turtle tours and fishing.

The best bargain around is **Casa Sunset Bed & Breakfast** (tel. 506/654-4265, c/o sfranklin

@racsa.co.cr, "attention Martha," $20 s, $40 d), on the hill behind Playa Penca. It's the slightly off-beat home of Martha (and Martin), ably assisted by their cats, parrot, dogs, and horses. Where else are you invited to pull a beer from the ice chest and flop on the couch in front of a TV? Maybe I got special treatment. Still, it seems there are always friends and neighbors popping in to shoot the breeze. The house sits midway up the hill above a *ranchito* bar that serves *bocas*. Seven simple yet attractive cabins cascade down the hill. One has a kitchen. Each has a double (or two singles) and bunk, plus ceiling and floor fans, and large bathrooms with hot water. Verandas have rockers. Four rooms in the main house are also offered. There's a pool and sun deck. Horseback rides and fishing trips are offered. Rates include breakfast.

Villagio Flor de Pacífico (tel. 506/654-4664, fax 506/654-4663, info@hotelflordepacifico.com, www.hotelflordepacifico.com), on the "Monkey Trail" 400 meters inland of Potrero village and a 15-minute walk from the beach, is a modern Italian-run resort amid lush expansive gardens. Its 50 modestly furnished one- and two-bedroom villas get hot, but have a/c, fans, lofty wooden ceilings, and cool tile floors, plus kitchens. Facilities include two pools, tennis, and an Italian restaurant. Call for rates.

The class act in Potrero is the **Monte Carlo Beach Resort** (tel./fax 506/654-5048, mcbeach @racsa.co.cr, www.monte-carlo-beach-resort.com, $50 s/d low season, $70 high season) with five one- and two-bedroom a/c villas (more were being added) graced by a beautiful aesthetic enhanced by bright colors, antique reproduction furnishings, ceiling fans, cable TV, large tiled bathrooms, kitchenettes, and patios. The rooms get hot, alas! There's a landscaped pool and elegant restaurant in lush grounds that flow onto the beach. It offers sportfishing.

The **Bahía Potrero Beach & Fishing Resort,** in landscaped grounds at the north end of Playa Potrero, was closed at last visit and being entirely remodeled.

I recommend, **Hotel Sugar Beach** (Apdo. 90-5051, Santa Cruz, tel. 506/654-4242, fax 506/654-4239, sugarb@racsa.co.cr, www.sugar-beach.com; in the U.S., tel. 800/958-4735, $80 s/d standard, $100 s/d deluxe, $120–140 suites low season, $110/138/165–high season), offering the privacy of a secluded setting on a beach-front rise amid 10 hectares of lawns and forest full of wildlife. Choose from 16 new rooms in eight handsome Spanish colonial-style duplexes, or 10 older units connected by stone pathways; all recently refurbished under new owners with rich color schemes, attractive stained hardwoods, and a gracious feel. Each spacious room has two queen-size beds, verandas, a/c, fans, satellite TVs, and tiled floors. Also available are a three-bedroom beach house and an apartment suite. A large open-air restaurant looks over the beach, there's a small pool, and horseback rides and tours. Costa Rica Outriggers is based here.

Food

I recommend **Monte Carlo Beach Resort** (6 A.M.–9:30 P.M. Thur.–Tue., $6–10) for its gourmet continental fare, such as crêpes with mushroom and ham, sea bass with cream of chili sauce, and pork in basil sauce.

A favorite of locals, **El Grillo,** 300 meters inland of the beach, is an open-air bar and grill serving light fare and French gourmet cuisine. It has music on Fridays, including classic oldies and R&B. It's run by friendly and conscientious Canadian couple, who spotlight the palms by night.

The **Surfside Super** (tel. 506/654-4291), on the main road between Potrero and Flamingo, specializes in imported and gourmet foodstuffs.

Information and Services

Lina at **Bienestar Laundry** (tel. 506/654-4662) offers same-day laundry service, except Sunday.

Martin Harvey, at Casa Sunset, offers fishing trips (from $250 half-day for two people).

PLAYA FLAMINGO

Playa Flamingo, immediately south of Potrero and facing it from the west side of the bay, is also called **Playa Blanca** (the name preferred by developers). The two-km-wide scimitar of white sand—one of the most magnificent beaches in

© JEAN MERCIER

Playa Flamingo

Costa Rica—lines the north end of Bahía Flamingo (there are no flamingos). Nonetheless, there's only a smattering of hotels, and little nightlife.

The area is favored by wealthy Ticos and gringos (North Americans now own most of the land hereabouts), and expensive villas sit atop the headlands north and south of the beach, many with their own little coves as private as one's innermost thoughts.

The marina hosts a large sportfishing fleet (the annual **International Sportfishing Tournament** is held here each May and June).

Entertainment and Events

The **Monkey Bar** at the Flamingo Marina Resort has a happy hour daily at 5:30 P.M. It has live music on Friday, barbecue on Saturdays, ESPN with pizza on Sunday, and Monday night football (in season).

The always lively bar at the **Mariner Inn** (6 A.M.–10 P.M.) features cable TV and has happy hour daily 5–6:30 P.M.

Disco Amberes, on the hill, has a spacious lounge bar, a lively disco, and a small casino that opens at 8 P.M. Live bands occasionally play from 9:30 P.M. Video slots and card tables are offered at **Flamingo Bay Resort & Casino.**

Sports and Recreation

The *Shannon,* a 52-foot cutter, runs day and sunset cruises ($45–150 pp) plus multi-day cruises as far afield as Isla Cocos; contact Flamingo Marina (see Flamingo Marina, below). Excursions are also offered aboard the *Papagayo,* a Hardin 45 Ketch that sails a sunset cruise ($40 with dinner on board) and can be chartered for customized cruises; call Capt. Dick Neal or Peter Neal (tel. 506/654-4063 or 654-4062).

The Edge (tel./fax 506/654-4946, theedge @costaricaexotic.com, www.costaricaexotic.com), on the Potrero side of the bridge, 100 meters east of the marina, offers diving ($50/75 one-/two-tank dives), including to the Murciélagos ($135). **Costa Rica Diving** (tel./fax 506/654-4148, coridive@racsa.co.cr, www.costarica-diving.com) offers dives ($75 two tanks) and snorkeling ($35).

Several companies offer sportfishing. **Costa Rica VIP Sportfishing** (tel. 506/654-4049 or 800/346-2629, fax 506/654-4968, twocan@racsa.co.cr, www.vipsportfishing.com) uses the 90-foot *Two-Can* mother ship with deluxe staterooms for sportfishing (May–Oct.).

The Edge has a 47-foot sportfishing boat for charter ($800/1,200 half-/full-day for up to eight people).

The Edge has kayak-snorkeling trips ($35) and surf trips to Witch's Rock, and rents boogie boards ($5 two hours).

EcoTrans (tel. 506/654-4852, fax 506/654-4961, ecotrans@racsa.co.cr, www.ecotranscostarica.com), in Flamingo Marina Resort, offers tours to Palo Verde National Park ($75), Guaitil ($35), and Arenal ($110).

You can also rent a **Hydro-disc** (tel. 506/654-4263) beside the bank; and **Costa Rica Diving** offers ATV tours.

Costa Rican Outriggers (tel. 506/654-4576 or 383-3013, outriggers_guanacaste@yahoo.com) offers half-day kayak and outrigger trips, including snorkeling.

Accommodations

$50–100: The **Mariner Inn** (tel. 506/654-4081, fax 506/654-4024, marinerinn@racsa.co.cr, $34 s/d standard, $45 with a/c and fridge, $68 suite year-round), a 12-room Spanish colonial-style hotel down by the marina, is popular with mariners. Dark hardwoods fill the a/c rooms that feature color TVs, blue-and-white tile work, and terra-cotta tile floors. A suite has a minibar and kitchenette. A pool and sun deck sit next to a moody, elegant bar of dark hardwoods. The restaurant specializes in seafood.

The three-story, haphazardly arranged **Flamingo Marina Resort** (Apdo. 321-1002, San José, tel. 506/654-4141, fax 506/654-4035, tickledpink@flamingomarina.com,www.flamingomarina.com; in the U.S., tel. 800/276-7501, $65 s/d standard, $115 suite, $140–210 apartments low season, $85 s.d standard, $145 suite, $180–280 high season), on the hill overlooking the marina, has pleasing rooms with grand views towards Playa Potrero. It offers three types of accommodations in 123 spacious a/c rooms with lively contempo decor, tile floors, ceiling fans, a/c, refrigerators, TVs, and telephones. Suites have king-size beds, plus whirlpools on private terraces. And there are larger, beachfront, one- to three-bedroom apartments and bungalows. The pleasant terrace restaurant opens onto a circular swimming pool with the thatched swim-up Monkey Bar (you can barter a toy monkey for a drink). There're also a long lap-pool and two other pools, plus whirlpool, tennis court, gift shop, tour office, and full-service dive shop. Sportfishing, surfing, and golf packages are offered. Rates include breakfast and tax.

The hotel also offers **Flamingo All Suites** for rent, with one to three bedrooms, immediately uphill from the hotel and with full access to the latter's facilities.

$100–150: The only place down by the beach is the **Flamingo Beach Resort** (Apdo. 7082-1000, San José, tel. 506/654-4010, fax 506/654-4060, flamingo_beach@racsa.co.cr, www.resortflamingobeach.com, from $85 s/d standard, $160 s/d suite low season; from $120 s/d standard, $225 s/d suite high season), a large-scale complex centered on a voluminous pool with a swim-up bar. It has 91 spacious rooms, including eight surfside suites, five ocean-view suites, and 23 luxury two-bedroom apartments. All have a/c, fans, telephones, satellite TVs, minibars, hair dryers, and private balconies. One- and two-bedroom suites feature sitting rooms, dining areas, kitchenettes, king beds, and whirlpool tubs. There are three bars, a shaded open-air snack bar and two restaurants, plus tennis courts, large gym, Turkish bath, game room, beauty salon, souvenir shop, rental car agency, and sportfishing office, and a casino operates in high season. A reader complains about theft here, and unresponsive management.

The Flamingo Beach Resort also offers **Best Western Presidential Suites,** on a bluff facing south above the Banco de Costa Rica.

The **Hotel Flamingo Towers** (tel. 506/654-4175 or 233-2711, $65 s/d), atop the peninsula, has five deluxe modern penthouse suites in a clifftop tower with views north through plate-glass doors that open to breeze-swept balconies. The a/c suites gleam in snowy whites, with tile floors and rattan and deep-red hardwood furnishings. All have kitchenettes, nice, well-lit bathrooms, but inappropriately small beds for such large rooms.

Food

My favorite place is **Ṃ Marie's Restaurant** (tel. 506/654-4136, 6:30 A.M.–9:30 P.M.), opposite the entrance to the Flamingo Beach Resort, and run by an English woman who offers fish and chips ($6), calamari ($4), burritos, chicken from the wood oven, and a large selection of sandwiches, ice cream sundaes, plus cappuccinos, lattes, mochas, and espressos ($1–2). A nice touch is the burlwood tables with fish motifs.

For unpretentious dining I also like the thatched, breezeswept **Soda Restaurante Pleamar** (tel. 506/654-4521, 7 A.M.–4 P.M. Mondays, 7 A.M.–9 P.M. Tue.–Sun., $–$15), with a splendid beachfront site in the cusp of Bahía Potrero, 400 meters east of the marina. It serves ceviche, burgers, lobster, and garlic fish.

The upstairs bar at the **Mariners' Inn** features spaghetti with meatballs ($8), and grilled chicken breast with heart of palm salad.

Supermercado Flamingo is a well-stocked general store at Plaza Que Pasa.

Information and Services

There's a bank on the hill above the marina. Flamingo Marina has public telephones.

Costa Rica Diving has an Internet Café.

There's a doctor's office on the second floor of the Presidential Suites, above the bank. If you need the **Red Cross,** call 506/680-0522, ext. 168.

Gay Clarke at **Century 21** (tel. 506/654-4004, joleneclarke@hotmail.com) acts as a tour information and reservation agent.

Centro Panamericano de Idiomas (tel. 506/654-5002, fax 506/654-5001, cpi2000 @racsa.co.cr, www.cpi-edu.com), 100 meters east of the marina, offers Spanish language courses.

Getting There

Century 21 acts as the SANSA agent.

Buses (tel. 506/221-7202) depart San José from Calle 20, Avenida 3, daily at 8 A.M., 11 A.M., and 3 P.M. ($3; six hours). The buses travel via Matapalo and Playa Brasilito and continue to Playa Potrero. Buses (tel. 506/680-0392) depart Santa Cruz for Playas Brasilito, Flamingo, and Potrero at 6:30 A.M. and 3 P.M.

Fantasy Bus (tel. 506/232-3681) has daily bus shuttle ($30) between Flamingo/Tamarindo and San José and between Flamingo/Tamarindo and La Fortuna, Jacó, Manuel Antonio, and Monteverde. **Interbus** (tel. 506/283-5573, www.interbusonline.com) operates a similar shuttle between Flamingo/Tamarindo and San José ($25), and between Flamingo and La Fortuna ($25) and Monteverde ($38).

Buses depart Flamingo for San José at 9 A.M. and 2 P.M., and for Santa Cruz at 9 A.M. and 5 P.M.

To get to Flamingo from Playas Coco, Hermosa, or Panamá, take a bus to Comunidad, where you can catch a southbound bus for Santa Cruz or Nicoya; get off at Belén, and catch a bus for Flamingo (buses from San José pass by around 10:30 A.M. and 2:30 P.M.).

The marina (tel. 506/654-4203, fax 506/654-4536, marflam@marflam.com, www.marflam.com, office 6:30 A.M.–noon and 1–3 P.M. Mon.–Fri., and 7:30–11:30 A.M. Saturday) has dock space for 80 yachts up to 24 meters long, with diesel, gasoline, and 120-volt and 220-volt electricity and fresh water ($8 per foot per month). The marina also has a floating dry dock for maintenance and a 20-ton crane. You can call the **dockmaster** on channels 16, 86 or 87.

Boats arriving from international waters must clear customs and immigration at Playa del Coco (if you arrange it ahead, the C&I people will come to you in Flamingo). There's a bonding service ($100) if you wish to leave your yacht for extended periods. You'll need four copies of your passport plus the Certificate of Entry (Certificado de Entrada) obtained from immigration in Playa del Coco.

Economy Rent-a-Car has an office above the chamber of commerce. There's a gas station on the road from Brasilito.

PLAYA CONCHAL

The hamlet of **Brasilito,** about four km south of Flamingo and three km north of Huacas, is a popular tourist spot drawing an incongruous mix of offbeat budget travelers and the packaged all-inclusive resort set, drawn to the massive Paradisus Playa Conchal Beach & Golf Resort (formerly the Melía Conchal Resort), owned by Spain's Sol Meliá corporation.

The light-gray sand beach at Brasilito melds westward into the more mesmerizing **Playa Conchal,** one of Costa Rica's finest beaches. The beach lies in the cusp of a scalloped bay with turquoise waters, a rarity in Costa Rica. The beach is composed, uniquely, of zillions of tiny seashells that move with soft rustling sounds as you walk; the waters are of crystalline Caribbean quality perfect for snorkeling. It's illegal to remove shells. Please leave them for future generations to enjoy.

The land behind the beach comprises the Paradisus resort, whose guests spill onto the beach, which has water sports concessions. You can buy day (8 A.M.–5 P.M.) and/or night (6 P.M.–1 A.M.) passes ($65) that permit nonguests to use the resort facilities. Its highlight is an 18-hole golf course designed by the king of designers, Robert Trent Jones, Jr. (Locals claim that the company twisted elbows to have Brasilito's delightfully funky beachfront homes and restaurants bulldozed so as to grant it exclusive beach access. When bulldozers and a squad of police showed up to demolish one such *cantina,* the local community arrived en masse to occupy the restaurant and save it from demolition.)

Conchal can also be accessed by road from the west via the hamlet of **Matapalo,** three km west of Huacas, where a rough dirt road leads from the northwest corner of the soccer field to the west end of Playa Conchal (four km). A side road on the Matapalo-Conchal road leads west to **Playa Real,** a stunning little beauty of a beach nestled in a sculpted bay with a tiny tombolo leading to a

> *The beach is composed, uniquely, of zillions of tiny seashells that move with soft rustling sounds as you walk; the waters are of crystalline Caribbean quality perfect for snorkeling.*

rocky island. Venerable fishing boats make good resting spots for pelicans. It's the only place in Costa Rica where I can recall exclaiming, "Aah! This is where I want to build my home!"

Sports and Recreation

Brasilito Excursiones (tel. 506/654-4237, fax 506/654-4247, www.brasilito.com or www.ridingcostarica.com) offers horseback riding on the beach ($30 two hours) and at Finca Montejicar, two km south of Brasilito. It also rents kayaks ($15/20 half-/full-day) and 250cc Yamaha dirt bikes ($30/40 half-/full-day). And it offers scuba diving ($70 two tanks), sailing ($30 sunset cruise, $75 full-day cruise), boogie board and snorkel rental ($5/10 half-/full-day), and snorkeling trips ($35).

Costa Rica Temptations (tel. 506/654-4585, fax 506/654-4130, guanacaste@costarica4u.com, 8 A.M.–6 P.M. Mon.–Fri. and 8 A.M.–2 P.M. Sat.–Sun.), 100 meters south of the soccer field, offers tours throughout Nicoya and Guanacaste. It also acts as an agent for Nacional Rent-a-Car and SANSA, and offers transfers to Tamarindo and beyond.

Brasilito Sport Adventure (tel. 506/654-4087), opposite Hotel Conchal, offers ATV (all-terrain vehicle) tours by quadricycle.

At Paradisus Playa Conchal Beach & Golf Resort, **Tio Sports** offers water sports plus scuba diving ($72 two tanks), and **Cocodrilo Safari** (tel. 506/654-4123, ext. 8913, elcocosafari @yahoo.es) offers Land Rover safaris to Palo Verde National Park.

Maratonga **Sailing Trips** (tel. 506/653-8341) offers sailing half-day ($60), full-day ($85), and sunset trips ($45).

Greens fees at the Paradisus Playa Conchal Beach & Golf Resort golf course cost $80 including cart.

Accommodations

Camping: You can camp under shade trees ($2 pp low season, $3 high season) behind the beach at **Brasilito Lodge** (tel./fax 506/654-4452, www.brasilito-conchal.com), an otherwise un-kempt, German-run place that also has seven motley cabins not worth recommending.

Under $25: A Swiss couple runs **Cabinas Ojos Azules** (tel./fax 506/654-4336, from $5 pp.), 100 meters south of the soccer field, with 14 clean and neatly furnished yet basic cabins for up to eight people. Some have hot water; many have mirrored headboards. There's a laundry, a small plunge pool, and a *rancho* with hammocks. Fresh home-baked bread accompanies the filling breakfast.

$25–50: The **Hotel Conchal** (tel. 506/654-4257, $20 s/d low season; $30 high season), 200 meters south of the soccer field, has nine pretty, ocher-colored Spanish colonial-style cabins with fans and private baths and cold water in a land-scaped garden full of bougainvillea. It offers horse and bike rentals.

Cabinas La Gloria (tel./fax 506/654-4878, $25 s, $35 d), behind Pizzería Il Forno, has four spacious and cool, well-lit cabins with terra-cotta floors, fans, small cable TVs, refrigerators, clean bathrooms with hot water, plus patios; two rooms have a/c. Rates include tax.

Apartotel & Restaurant Nany (tel. 506/654-4320, cabnany@racsa.co.cr, $30 s/d with fan, $30 s, $40 d with a/c low season; $40 s/d with fan, $40 s, $50 d with a/c high season) continues to mature and how has 11 uniquely designed, spacious modern, two-bedroom a/c "apartments" with kitchenettes and tall half-moon windows, ceilings fans, cable TVs, security box, and pri-vate baths with hot water. It has an open-air restaurant and a plunge pool.

A German couple, Josef Compes and Manuela Klasen, run **Hotel Brasilito** (tel. 506/654-4237, fax 506/654-4247, hotel@brasilito.com, www .brasilito.com, $15 s, $20 d low season; $25 s, $30 d high season, $10 more with beach view), 50 meters from both the beach and soccer field. This well-run hotel has 15 simple rooms with fans and private baths with hot water, in a daffodil-yellow wooden home adorned with flowerboxes. It has an atmospheric restaurant. Rates include tax.

The U.S.-run **Condor Lodge and Beach Re-sort** (tel. 506/654-4050, fax 506/654-4044,

condorlodge@cs.com, www.condorlodge.com, $60 s/d standard, $110 s/d suite low season; $80/150 high season) sits atop the hill, 600 me-ters inland and south of the beach. The 30 com-fortable and a/c rooms were recently refurbished in a ho-hum homely style. All have fans, cable TVs and VCRs, telephones, refrigerators, and private bathrooms with hot water (some have king-size beds). There are also two- and three-bedroom houses with kitchens (one-week mini-mum). The open-terrace dining room—offering spectacular views—is topped by a lofty lounge bar and casino, with a disco on weekends. There's also a TV lounge and small library. A swimming pool with cascade is set on the lofty sun deck. A beach club also has a pool plus bar-and-grill and volleyball.

Playa Real is the setting for the Italian-run **Bahía de Las Piratas Resort** (tel. 506/654-4651, fax 506/654-4654, info@bahiadelospiratas .com, www.bahiadelospiratas.com, $77 s/d suites, $95–148 villas low season; $87 s/d suites, $115–188 villas high season). This complex of 15 Spanish colonial-style condos and villas (with 40 rooms total) stairsteps the hill amid land-scaped grounds with a small swimming pool and thatched bar. All have tile floors, lofty hard-wood ceilings, a/c and fans, small TVs, CD players, and verandas with splendid coastal views. Horseback riding, scuba diving, and sportfishing are offered.

The **Paradisus Playa Conchal Beach & Golf Resort** (P.O. Box 499-4005 San Antonio de Belén, tel. 506/654-4123, fax 506/654-4181, info@meliaplayaconchal.com, www.solmelia.es, $224 s, $358 d junior suite, $336 s, $538 d suite low season; $254 s, $418 d junior suite, $381 s, $628 d suite high season), spans 285 hectares—the largest resort in the country—and is surrounded by rippling fairways. The re-sort has 308 open-plan junior suites and two master suites in 37 two-story units amid land-scaped grounds behind the beach. They are beau-tiful, with exquisite marble bathrooms, mezzanine bedrooms supported by columns, and lounges with soft-cushioned sofas. Each has a satellite TV, a hair dryer, telephone, mini-bar, safety box, and a/c. The massive free-form swimming pool is a setting for noisy aerobics and games. It has three restaurants, two bars, a disco, a theater with nightly shows, tennis courts, plus the luxurious golf course. There's a pro golf shop, plus tour offices and car rental; hiking, horseback riding, and bicycle tours are offered. Canopied buses whisk you around. If you like a canned group experience, this is as good as it gets in Costa Rica. Readers have complained that meals are mediocre and outrageously priced. Anyone can partake of the Paradisus Resort's bars, disco, and theater by purchasing a night pass ($65).

Food

For breakfasts, head to the Hotel Brasilito's breezy, bougainvillea-festooned **Las Playas Restaurant** (tel. 506/654-4596, 7:30 A.M.–10 P.M. Tue.–Sun.), serving grilled croissants ($2.50–3), eggs ranchero ($3), and more. The wide-ranging lunch menu includes a club sandwich with avocado, while Teutonic fare includes apfelstrudel. Steaks and seafood highlight the dinner menu ($8–12).

The **Bar y Restaurante Camaron Dorado** (tel. 506/654-4028), 100 meters north of the soccer field, is the best of a dozen or so similar eateries in the village. Try the filling specials or Camaron Dorado Salad ($8, for which you get lobster, shrimp, calamari, cheese, and ham heaped in with the greens).

The **Restaurante El Galeón** (7 A.M.–11 P.M.) at the Hotel Las Piratas, is a handsome rustic spot with great vistas; it serves Italian fare, including pizzas (from $6), antipasto with ceviche ($6), and specialty pastas.

For views, head to the **Condor Lodge and Beach Resort**, ($4–$8) serving seafoods, chicken dishes, etc.

The **Pizzeria Il Forno** (tel. 506/654-4125, $4–$12) offers pleasant outdoor dining under thatch. In addition to pizzas, it has smoked salmon salad, garlic shrimp, and calzones and pastas.

The **Faisanda** Italian restaurant, at Paradisus Playa Conchal Beach & Golf Resort, offers elegant dining at exorbitant prices.

You can buy groceries at **Super Lopez** (tel. 506/654-4374).

Information and Services

There's an international telephone and tourist information center at Bar y Restaurante Camaron Dorado.

Hotel Brasilito offers Internet access for $3 per half-hour.

The **police station** (tel. 506/654-4425) is on the main road, facing the soccer field.

Getting There

Brasilito Excursiones has airport transfers between Brasilito and San José ($25).

The Flamingo-bound buses from San José and Santa Cruz stop in Matapalo and Brasilito. Buses depart Matapalo for Santa Cruz at 5 A.M., 8 A.M., and 4:30 P.M.; and for Santa Rosa and Tamarindo at 12:30 P.M.

You can call a taxi (tel. 506/836-1739).

A **gas station** is one km north of Brasilito.

Tamarindo and Vicinity

Tamarindo, a former fishing village that is burgeoning into Guanacaste's most developed resort, offers prime wildlife viewing, a scintillating beach, surfing action, and a choice of accommodations spanning shoestring to sophisticated.

A great site to visit for online information is www.tamarindo.com.

Safety Concerns: Recent years have seen a growth in robberies against tourists. Rental car break-ins are common, particularly at the informal parking lot at Playa Grande National Park's entrance gates and in the parking lot of the Hotel Las Tortugas, which has no security. There are police hereabouts, but still you need to ensure that you don't leave any valuables in your car. Drugs have also encroached, and hustlers can be a nuisance.

◪ PLAYA GRANDE

Costa Rican beaches don't come more beautiful than **Playa Grande,** a seemingly endless curve of sand (varying from coral-white to gray) with water as blue as the summer sky. A beach trail to the north leads along the cape through dry forest and deposits you at **Playa Ventanas,** a pristine scalloped swath of white sand, with tide pools for snorkeling and bathing. Surf pumps ashore at high tide; Playa Grande is renowned among surfers for its consistency and good mix of lefts and rights. Surfing expert Mark Kelly rates it as "maybe the best overall spot in the country."

The entire shoreline is protected within the 445-hectare **Playa Grande Marine Turtle National Park** (Parque Nacional Marino Las Baulas), which guards the prime nesting site of the leatherback turtle on the Pacific coast, including 22,000 hectares out to sea. The beach was incorporated into the national park system in May 1990 after a 15-year battle between developers and conservationists. At issue is the fate of the leatherback turtle—and the amazing fact that humankind stands on the brink of terminating forever a miracle that has played itself out

annually at Playa Grande for the past several million years.

The park is the result of efforts by Louis Wilson, owner of Hotel Las Tortugas, and his former wife, Marianel Pastor. In the 1970s, a cookie company was harvesting the turtles' eggs. The beach was subdivided among 30 or so egg poachers, who sold Louis and Marianel "rights" to take tourists on to their sections of sand. Once the tourists left, the *hueveros* would steal the eggs. In the 1980s, Asian fleets began harvesting eggs here. The government agreed to support the couple's conservation efforts only if they could show that the site was economically viable as a tourist destination. Much of the land backing the beach was owned by developers, who had until recently been prevented from constructing homes and hotels. Things have come full circle. The locals have taken over all guiding (each guide is certified through an accredited course), and Las Baulas is now a model for similar experiments worldwide.

The beach sweeps south to the mouth of the Río Matapalo, which forms a 400-hectare mangrove estuary behind the beach. The ecosystem is protected within **Tamarindo National Wildlife Refuge** (Refugio Nacional de Vida Silvestre Tamarindo, tel. 506/296-7074) and features crocodiles, anteaters, and monkeys. Waterbirds and raptors gather, especially in dry season. The wildlife population is increasing; deer and even ocelots and other cats are seen with greater frequency. The **ranger station** is about 500 meters upriver from the estuary.

Hiking is allowed on the north side of the estuary and along the beach. Trails are not marked.

The hamlet of **Comunidad Playa Grande** is on the main approach road, 600 meters inland from the beach.

Visiting the Turtles of Playa Grande

Turtles call at Playa Grande year-round. The nesting season for the giant leatherback is Oct.–March, when females come ashore every night at high tide. Sometimes as many as 100 turtles

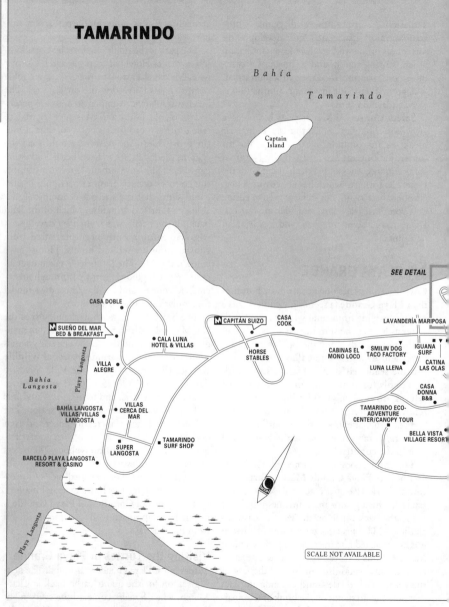

TAMARINDO

Bahía Tamarindo

Captain Island

SEE DETAIL

CASA DOBLE

SUEÑO DEL MAR
BED & BREAKFAST

CALA LUNA
HOTEL & VILLAS

CAPITÁN SUIZO

CASA
COOK

LAVANDERÍA MARIPOSA

Playa Langosta

VILLA
ALEGRE

HORSE
STABLES

CABINAS EL
MONO LOCO

SMILIN DOG
TACO FACTORY

IGUANA
SURF

LUNA LLENA

CATINA
LAS OLAS

*Bahía
Langosta*

CASA
DONNA
B&B

BAHÍA LANGOSTA
VILLAS/VILLAS
LANGOSTA

VILLAS
CERCA DEL
MAR

TAMARINDO ECO-
ADVENTURE
CENTER/CANOPY TOUR

SUPER
LANGOSTA

TAMARINDO
SURF SHOP

BELLA VISTA
VILLAGE RESORT

BARCELÓ PLAYA LANGOSTA
RESORT & CASINO

Playa Langosta

SCALE NOT AVAILABLE

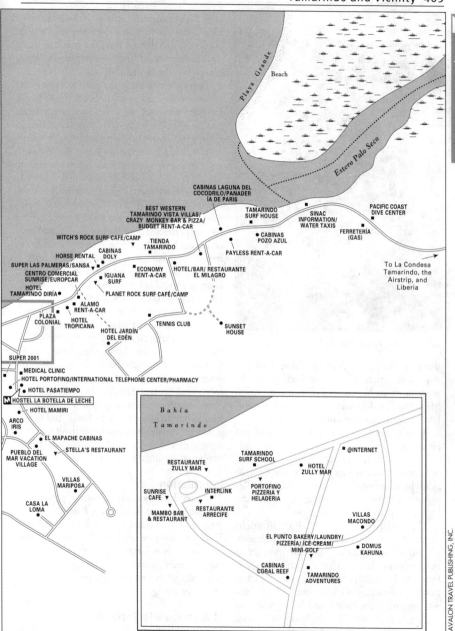

Playa Grande

Beach

Estero Palo Seco

CABINAS LAGUNA DEL
COCODRILO/PANADER
IA DE PARIS

TAMARINDO
SURF HOUSE

SINAC
INFORMATION/
WATER TAXIS

PACIFIC COAST
DIVE CENTER

BEST WESTERN
TAMARINDO VISTA VILLAS/
CRAZY MONKEY BAR & PIZZA/
BUDGET RENT-A-CAR

FERRETERÍA
(GAS)

WITCH'S ROCK SURF CAFÉ/CAMP

TIENDA
TAMARINDO

CABINAS
POZO AZUL

CABINAS
DOLY

PAYLESS RENT-A-CAR

HORSE RENTAL

SUPER LAS PALMERAS/SANSA

ECONOMY
RENT-A-CAR

HOTEL/BAR/ RESTAURANTE
EL MILAGRO

To La Condesa
Tamarindo, the
Airstrip, and
Liberia

CENTRO COMERCIAL
SUNRISE/EUROPCAR

IGUANA
SURF

HOTEL
TAMARINDO DIRÍA

PLANET ROCK SURF CAFÉ/CAMP

ALAMO
RENT-A-CAR

PLAZA
COLONIAL

HOTEL
TROPICANA

TENNIS CLUB

SUNSET
HOUSE

HOTEL JARDÍN
DEL EDÉN

SUPER 2001

MEDICAL CLINIC

HOTEL PORTOFINO/INTERNATIONAL TELEPHONE CENTER/PHARMACY

HOTEL PASATIEMPO

HOSTEL LA BOTELLA DE LECHE

HOTEL MAMIRI

ARCO
IRIS

EL MAPACHE CABINAS

STELLA'S RESTAURANT

PUEBLO DEL
MAR VACATION
VILLAGE

VILLAS
MARIPOSA

CASA LA
LOMA

Bahía
Tamarindo

@INTERNET

TAMARINDO
SURF SCHOOL

HOTEL
ZULLY MAR

RESTAURANTE
ZULLY MAR

PORTOFINO
PIZZERIA Y
HELADERIA

SUNRISE
CAFÉ

INTERLINK

MAMBO BAR
& RESTAURANT

RESTAURANTE
ARRECIFE

VILLAS
MACONDO

EL PUNTO BAKERY/LAUNDRY/
PIZZERÍA/ ICE-CREAM/
MINI-GOLF

DOMUS
KAHUNA

CABINAS
CORAL REEF

TAMARINDO
ADVENTURES

turtle tracks, Playa Grande

© CHRISTOPHER P. BAKER

might be seen in a single night. (Olive ridley turtles can sometimes also be seen here, as may the more rarely seen, smaller Pacific green turtles, May–Aug.) Mid-October through mid-November is best for avoiding hordes of tourists.

A visit here is a humbling, reverential experience.

Each female leatherback will nest as many as 12 times a season, every 10 days or so (usually at night to avoid dehydration). Most turtles prefer the center of the beach, just above the high-tide mark.

The beach is open to visitors at night (6 P.M.–6 A.M.) October 15 through February 15, and off-limits the rest of the year (there are no restrictions on daytime visits); it is open at night February 15 through March 15 solely for environmental education. Guides from the local community roam the beach and lead groups to nesting turtles, guided by other guides who spot for turtles and call in the location via walkie-talkies. Visitors are not allowed to walk the beach

after dusk unescorted; *guides—$7—are mandatory.* Groups cannot exceed 15 people, and only 60 people are allowed onto the beach at night at each entry point (four groups per gate; eight groups maximum nightly).

There are two entrance gates to the beach: one where the road meets the beach by the Hotel Las Tortugas, and the second at the southern end, by Villas Baulas. You buy your tickets ($6) at either gate. *Reservations are mandatory,* although entry without a reservation is possible if there's space in a group (don't count on it, as demand usually exceeds supply). You can make reservations up to eight days in advance, or between 8 A.M.–5 P.M. for a same-day visit. At certain times the waiting time can be two hours before you are permitted onto the beach. (**Safety Concerns:** car break-ins are an everyday occurrence near the park entrances, including in and around the car park of the Hotel Tortuga, with thieves hanging around in broad daylight! Why Louis of Hotel Tortuga doesn't hire security guards or put lights in his pitch-black parking lot is beyond me. Don't leave *anything* in your vehicle.)

Resist the temptation to follow the example of the many thoughtless visitors who get too close to the turtles, try to touch them, ride their backs, or otherwise display a lack of common sense and respect. Flashlights and camera flashes are *not* permitted (professional photographers can apply in advance for permission to use a flash). And watch your step. Newborn turtles are difficult to see at night as they scurry down to the sea. Many are inadvertently crushed by tourists' feet.

Information

The **park headquarters** (Centro Operaciones Parque Nacional Marina las Baulas, tel./fax 506/653-0470) is 100 meters east of Hotel Las Tortugas, whose owner, Louis Wilson, is still the best source of information on the area. It features an auditorium on turtle ecology. *Viewing the film is obligatory for all people intending to witness the turtles nesting.*

El Mundo de la Tortuga

The World of the Turtle museum (tel./fax 506/653-0471, 4 P.M.–6 A.M., $5 admission) is

THE LEATHERBACK TURTLE

The leatherback turtle *(Dermochelys coriacea)* is the world's largest reptile and a true relic from the age of the dinosaurs; fossils date back 100 million years. The average adult weighs about 455 kg (1,000 pounds) and is two meters (six feet) in length, though males have been known to attain a staggering 2,000 pounds! It is found in all the world's oceans except the Arctic.

Though it nests on the warm beaches of Costa Rica, the *baula* (as it is locally known) has evolved as a deep-diving cold water critter: its great, near-cylindrical bulk retains body heat in cold waters (it can maintain a body temperature of 18°C in near-frigid water). The leatherback travels great distances feeding in the open ocean and often crossing between continents, as far afield as subarctic waters, where its black body helps absorb the sun's warming rays. Like seals, the leatherback has a thick oily layer of fat for insulation. Its preferred food is jellyfish (the leatherback has scissor-like jaws for cutting its rubbery prey, and long backward-pointing spines line its throat to prevent squishy prey from escaping), which are most numerous in temperate latitudes.

The females—which reach reproductive age between 15 and 50 years—prefer to nest on steep beaches that have a deepwater approach, thus avoiding long-distance crawls. Nesting occurs during the middle hours of the night—the coolest hours. Leather-back eggs take longer to hatch—70 days on average—than those of other sea turtles (35–75 percent of eggs hatch).

Whereas in other turtle species, the boney exterior carapace is formed by flattened, widened ribs that are fused and covered with corneous tissues resembling the human fingernail, the leatherback has an interior skeleton of narrow ribs linked by tiny bony plates all encased by a thick "shell" of leathery, cartilaginous skin. The leatherback's tapered body is streamlined for hydrodynamic efficiency, with seven longitudinal ridges that act like a boat's keel, and long, powerful flippers for maximum propulsion. Leatherbacks have been

COURTESY WILDLAND ADVENTURES

A female leatherback turtle lays her eggs at Playa Grande.

shown to dive deeper than 1,300 meters (4,000 feet), where their small lungs, flexible frames, squishy bodies, and other specialist adaptations permit the animal to withstand well over 1,500 pounds of pressure per square inch.

The species is close to extinction. Only 117 nesters arrived at Las Baulas in 2000, less than 10 percent the number only a decade prior.

Contributions to help save leatherback turtles can be sent marked Programa de Tortugas Marinas to Karen and Scott Eckert, **Hubbs Sea World Research Institute** (2595 Ingraham St., San Diego, CA 92109, tel. 619/226-3870, fax 619/226-3944, www.hswri.org), or to the **Leatherback Trust** (161 Merion Av., Haddonfield, NJ 08033, tel. 215/895-2627, www.leatherback.org).

200 meters from the main entrance gate and a must-visit before watching the turtles. Self-guided audio tours (20 minutes) are offered in four languages. The displays are splendid and highly educational. Did you know that the brain of a 1,000-pound leatherback weighs only one-quarter ounce? Or that the turtles eat mostly jellyfish? Or that they're found in all of the world's oceans as far north as the Arctic? The museum is open by night, and you can sit in the outside patio and await your turn to visit the turtles. It has a splendid gift shop. *Fantastic!* Free educational programs are given to locals. It's open Oct.–May, when the turtles are present; it is sometimes open other months. A guided tour costs $25, including beach walk.

Sports and Recreation

Most hotels and tour companies in Tamarindo and Flamingo offer turtle-watching tours (about $25) and a "Jungle Boat Safari," aboard a 20-passenger, environmentally sound pontoon boat that takes you into the mangrove-rich Tamarindo Wildlife Refuge ($20).

Cooperativa Portoturbo (tel. 506/653-0225) offers boat trips into the refuge ($26 including park entrance).

Hotel Tortuga rents longboards (from $10 one hour, $20 per day) and boogie boards ($5 one hour, $7 per day).

The Hotel y Restaurant Bula Bula has a **beach club** at the south end of the beach, with funball ($10), volleyball ($5), ocean kayaks ($5), boogie boards ($3), and boules ($1).

Pura Vida Café (tel. 506/653-0835, www.puravidatours.com) has Internet service, and offers surf lessons ($50). **Pura Vida Realty,** next door, rents surfboards ($8 one hour, $30 per day), boogie boards ($8 half-day, $15 per day), snorkel gear ($10), and beach chairs and umbrellas.

Accommodations

Camping: Camping is not allowed on the beach. You can camp at **Centro Vacacional Playa Grande,** at Comunidad Playa Grande; it has showers and toilets ($2 pp).

Under $25: The **Centro Vacacional Playa Grande** (tel./fax 506/653-0834, $8 pp) has 11 two-bedroom a/c *cabinas* (eight with kitchenettes) with kitchens, refrigerators, and fans, and private bathrooms with cold water only. There are shade trees on the lawn, plus an outdoor restaurant, pool, free laundry, and taxi service.

$25–50: I recommend **Jammin Surf Camp** (tel. 506/653-0469, $13 pp dorm, $22.50 pp cabins). It has three small but delightful A-frame wood-and-thatch cabins on stilts, including a dorm with screened windows. Air-conditioning was to be added. A courtyard has a pool and thatched shade areas with hammocks. It has a simple roadside *soda.*

$50–100: A talkative Brit named James runs **Hotel & Restaurante El Bucanero** (tel./fax 506/653-0480, jandrews@elbucanero.com, www.elbucanero.com, $35 s/d low season, $45 high season), 200 meters south of Hotel Las Tortugas. It has eight modern rooms with fans (most have a/c) and private baths with hot water. It has a breezy upstairs restaurant with beach views and a TV.

Nearby is the **Playa Grande Inn** (tel./fax 506/653-0719, www.playagrandeinn.com), formerly Bulldog Surf Camp, a handsome surf camp with eight *cabinas.* Alas, the employee in charge during my visit refused to let me look around or to give me information.

I usually stay at **Hotel Las Tortugas** (Apdo. 164-5150, Santa Cruz, tel. 506/653-0423, fax 506/653-0458, surfegg@cool.co.cr, www.tamarindo.com, $40 s/d economy, $50 s/d standard, $75 suite low season; $50 economy, $70 standard, $100 suite high season), a comfortable ecolodge. The 11 rooms vary markedly, though all have a/c, pewter-colored stone floors, orthopedic mattresses, plus private baths with hot water. The hotel, described as "a mirthful combination of colonial and modern architecture," has a turtle-shaped swimming pool with sun deck, plus a large Jacuzzi. (Since newborn turtles are attracted to light and adults can be disoriented by it, there are no ocean views to the south, where the nesting beach is.) The restaurant is a highlight, with an outdoor patio and great food (see *Food,* below). "We have a stoked staff and the food is ripping!" says owner Louis.

The hotel rents surfboards and canoes for trips into the estuary ($30 half-day), and has horseback riding ($25) and a mangrove boat tour ($25). "We're an ol' Hemingway kind of place," says Louis.

Louis also rents six apartments and four houses.

I adore the **Hotel Bula Bula** (formerly Hotel Cantarana, tel. 506/653-0975, fax 653-0491, tel. 877/658-2880 in North America, www.hotel-bulabula.com, $40 s, $60 d low season; US$60 s, US$80 d high season), in lush gardens adjoining the mangrove estuary, two km south of Las Tortugas. This attractive place is now in the hands of two vivacious U.S. entrepreneurs, one a professional restaurateur ("Bula Bula" means "happy happy"). The 10 newly refurbished a/c rooms are fabulous, with rich color schemes, king-size beds with orthopedic mattresses, batik wall hangings, and fresh flowers, plus fans, screened windows, and a shady balcony. The rooms surround a pool in a landscaped garden. It has an excellent restaurant and bar, popular with locals.

The classiest act is **Hotelito Si Si Si** (tel. 506/ 653-0715, fax 506/653-0982, www.hotelitosisisi .com, $85 s/d), a gorgeous contemporary villa in Miami style, with a freeform pool and Jacuzzi in a lush garden with sundeck. It has four rooms with cool limestone floors, beautiful hardwood fittings, silent a/c, ceiling fans (resembling airplane propellers) made of brushed steel, plentiful closets, and gorgeous modern bathrooms with marble. It offers a TV lounge, sand volleyball, a mini tennis court, and hammocks. Rates include breakfast. Otherwise, no food is served.

Casa y Cabinas Linda Vista (tel./fax 506/653-0474, helentvl@jps.net, www.tamarindo.com/kai, $60–90 one-bedroom units, $130 two-story house), 400 meters inland of the north end of the beach, is a neatly kept, expansive hilltop retreat with panoramic views. The U.S. owners offer two nice little one-bedroom *casitas* (one with kitchen, the other with kitchenette) under shade trees with hammocks. They have windows to all sides, and receive heaps of light; plus tile floors. A two-story house for up to seven people is made of hardwoods and volcanic rock and has a full kitchen.

Beach villas can be rented through **Costa Rica Conexion** (tel./fax 506/683-0498).

Villa Baula Beach Resort, at the southern end of the beach, does not receive good reviews.

Food

Centro Vacacional Playa Grande has an inexpensive *soda* selling *típico* dishes. **Pizzería Horno de Leña,** 100 meters north, offers plenty of ambience, the better to enjoy pizzas fired in a traditional outdoor oven.

My favorite place to dine is **Hotel Las Tortugas,** where you can take your pick of burgers, sandwiches, tenderloin, shrimp, and chicken in wine or garlic sauce. Try the apple pie with ice cream.

The elegant restaurant at **Hotel y Restaurant Bula Bula** serves international cuisine, including quesadillas, chicken wings, shrimp and crabcakes, Long Island duckling with merlot and raspberry reduction ($17), and blackened tuna ($9). Wednesday is rib night.

Hotel & Restaurante El Bucanero (7 A.M.–10 P.M.) has a more down-to-earth upstairs eatery serving *gallo pinto* ($2.50), sandwiches, fish fillet ($10), and jumbo shrimp ($12.50).

You can stock up at **Super Pura Vida,** in Comunidad Playa Grande.

Getting There

The Flamingo-bound buses from San José and Santa Cruz stop in Matapalo, where you can walk or catch a taxi.

From Flamingo, road access is via Matapalo, six km east of Playa Grande (turn left at the soccer field in Matapolo). A rough dirt road also links Tamarindo and Playa Grande via Villareal, but the route isn't always obvious.

A water-taxi runs between Tamarindo, docking on the estuary near the Hotel Bula Bula. It departs for Tamarindo at 7:30 A.M. Mon.–Sat., then every two hours ($1).

TAMARINDO

Playa Tamarindo, eight km south of Huacas, is Nicoya's most developed beach resort and is especially popular with backpacking surfers. It gets full in high season.

The gray-sand beach is about two km wide, and very deep when the tide goes out—perfect for strolling and watching pelicans dive for fish. It has rocky outcrops, good for tide-pooling. It's backed by tamarind trees, which give the beach its name. No-see-ums—tiny sand flies that pack a jumbo-size bite—are a problem around dusk. There's a smaller beach south of the main beach, with tidepools and relatively fewer people. Riptides are common, so ask locals in the know for the safest places to swim.

The Río Matapalo washes onto the beach at its northern end, giving direct access to the Tamarindo Wildlife Refuge via the Estero Palo Seco (a boatman will ferry you for $0.50); you can wade across at low tide, although crocodiles are sometimes present, as they are in the mangroves at the eastern end of Playa Tamarindo.

To the south, separated by a headland from Playa Tamarindo, is **Playa Langosta,** a beautiful white-sand beach that stretches beyond the wide estuary of the Río Tamarindo for several kilometers (see *Playa Langosta,* below).

The following website is a good resource: www.tamarindobeach.org.

Entertainment and Events

Costa Rica's annual **International Music Festival** is hosted in July and August at Hotel Cala Luna and Villa Alegre B&B.

The **Best Western Tamarindo Vista Villas** has a disco, and live music on Sundays nights. The same hotel's **Monkey Bar** has Monday night football, with free shots at touchdowns; Wednesday is ladies' night, with free cocktails for the gals; Thursday is all-you-can-eat pasta; Friday is tequila shooters night. It shows Sunday football on a big-screen TV.

The nightlife scene is fluid, but at last visit the **Mambo Bar and Restaurant,** in the village center, was the happening spot. The no-frills open-air bar has a pool table, cheap drinks, and music. **Planet Rock** has a bar, pool table, pinball machines, and large-screen TV, and hosts rock music Tuesdays, Thursdays, and Saturdays, salsa on Fridays, and reggae on Sundays. Wednesday is ladies' night.

The **Crazy Monkey Bar** has ladies' night on Friday, and two-for-one pizza on Saturday. And **Bar Restaurante Pasatiempo** has an open mike on Tuesday nights.

The **Witch's Rock Surf Camp** (tel. 506/653-0078) is a surfers' hangout with a pool table, hammocks, and a café/bar.

There are **casinos** at the Barceló Playa Langosta (8 P.M.–3 A.M.) and Tamarindo Diría, in Plaza Colonial (6–11 P.M.).

Sports and Recreation

The **Tamarindo Ecoaventure Center** (tel. 506/653-0507, fax 653-0926, info@tamarindoecoadventurecenter.com, www.tamarindoecoadventurecenter.com), on the south side of Tamarindo, has a canopy tour ($35).

Harding Fishing (tel./fax 506/653-0623) has sunset cruises ($45) and day cruises, including snorkeling trips aboard the 45-foot ketch *Lemuria.*

The **Pacific Coast Dive Center** (tel. 506/653-0267, pacificcoastdivecenter@hotmail.com) has snorkeling trips ($35) and scuba trips ($65 two tanks).

Fishing outfitters include **Tamarindo Sportfishing** (tel./fax 506/653-0092, www.tamarindosportfishing.com); **Lone Star Sportfishing** (tel. 506/653-0101, lonestar@racsa.co.cr); and **Papagayo Excursions** (tel. 506/653-0254, fax 506/653-0227, papagayo@racsa.co.cr), in Plaza Colonial.

A dozen or so outlets cater to surfers. **Iguana Surf** (tel. 506/653-0148, www.iguanasurf.net, 8 A.M.–6 P.M.), with outlets at Hotel Pueblo Dorado and 100 meters east of Hotel Tamarindo Diría, rents surfboards (from $15 per day), offers surf-taxi service to out-of-the-way surfing spots, and has surf lessons ($35).

The **Costa Rican Surf Camp** (www.costaricansurfcamp.com), at Tamarindo Vista Villas, offers tuition for $2,250 one week, $4,000 two weeks. **Witch's Rock Surf Camp** (tel. 506/653-0078, www.witchsrocksurfcamp.com) offers weeklong and nine-day surf packages. **Tamarindo Surf School** (tel. 506/653-0923, www.tamaraindosurfschool.com) charges $25 for two-hour classes. And Doug Ortiz offers private lessons and excursions at **Catch a Wave** (tel. 506/653-0312).

Iguana Surf rents kayaks ($7.50 hourly, $35 per day) and has ATV quad trips ($45 driver, $15 passenger), snorkeling tours ($30), and kayak trips into the estuary ($30).

Papagayo Excursions runs surf tours ($125), ATV tours ($90), horseback trips ($30), kayak trips ($35), boat tours ($26), and banana-boat rides ($8). It also has windsurfing and scuba diving, and excursions.

Tamarindo Adventures (tel. 506/653-0108, tamquad@racsa.co.cr, www.tamarindoadventures .com), upstairs in the Tamarindo Shopping Center, offers a medley of tours and specializes in tours by ATV quads ($49 daily). It also rents kayaks (from $25), snorkeling gear (from $4), surfboards (from $6), and boogie boards (from $6). It offers kayak tours ($35) and surf lessons (from $29).

The **Nahault Outdoor Center** (tel./fax 506/825-1307, nahaultoutdoor@hotmail.comm) rents kayaks ($25 half-day) and offers kayak trips (from $45).

You can rent horses for beach rides ($10 per hour) on the beach.

Shopping

Matiz Tropical and **Souvenirs Guanacaste** have large selections of quality souvenirs, including pottery from Guaitil.

Tienda la Tortuga, in Plaza Colonial, sells Cuban cigars, plus souvenirs and magazines. **Tienda Tamarindo** has more conventional souvenirs, plus magazines, swimwear, and the like.

Accommodations

Tamarindo has dozens of options; those listed here are recommended in their price bracket.

Under $25: Few budget properties come up to par. The notable exception is **M Hostel La Botella de Leche** (tel. 506/653-0944, labotelladeleche@racsa.co.cr, www.labotelladeleche.com, $12 pp low season, $15 pp high season), one of the nicest backpackers' spots in the country. Run to high standards by a delightful Argentinian woman, Mariana Nogaro, this classy surfers' hostel has contempo decor, a large-screen TV in the lounge, a clean open kitchen, plus two private rooms and 10 his-and-hers dorms, all with a/c, fans, lockers, and clean modern bathrooms. It has surfboard rental, Internet, and lockers.

The **Hotel Mono Loco** (tel./fax 506/653-0238, $10 pp dorm, $15 pp private room), on the road to Playa Langosta, has a backpackers' dorm with shared bath, plus eight rooms (recently refurbished with Indian fabrics and handsome roughhewn pieces by new owners) with tile floors, ceiling fans, and private baths and hot water. It caters primarily to Ticos, and rooms are crammed with multiple beds. The rooms face into a garden with pool. There's a shared kitchen; you dine under shade at bench tables.

$25–50: The **Cabinas Pozo Azul** (tel. 506/653-0280, $12.50 pp, or $39 s/d with a/c), at the entrance to town, has 27 spacious and clean rooms with fans and private baths with cold water; some have a/c and kitchenettes. Ask for a room with covered parking. There's a pool.

Villas Macondo (tel. 653-0812, info@villas macondo.com, www.villasmacondo.com, $20 s, $25 d room low season, $26 s, $32 d high season, $60 one-bedroom, $75 two-bedroom low season; $80 one-bedroom, $100 two-bedroom high season), run by a German couple, is a delightful spot with five double rooms, each with ceiling fan, alarm-clock radio, safety box, and solar-heated bathrooms. Four larger rooms have a/c. Or, choose spacious, fully equipped, two-story one- or two-bedroom apartments with cool tile floors and hardwood furnishings plus cable TVs. There's a community kitchen, and you can cool off in a kidney-shaped pool or relax in your hammock on the patio.

Across the street, **Domus Kahuna** (tel. 506/653-0648, reservations@domuskahuma .com, www.domuskahuna.com, $40 two-bedroom, $60 three-bedroom low season; $70 two-bedroom, $90 three-bedroom high season) has three simply furnished one-bedroom and three two-bedroom apartments in a landscaped garden. Roughhewn timbers add a nice note to the earthtone structures, with classic Central American architectural hints.

Sitting atop a hill on the southeast edge of town is the German-run **Casa La Loma** (tel. 506/653-0339, ruudodette@racsa.co.cr, $25 s/d low season, $45 s/d high season), which has four a/c rooms in a two-story structure. All have terracotta tile floors, ceiling fans, screened windows, rattan double beds, kitchenette with refrigerator, clean bathrooms with hot water, and patios with hammocks.

Nearby, **Casa Donna B&B** (tel. 506/653-0132, casadonna@racsa.co.cr, www.casadonna.net, $40 s/d rooms, $50 s/d cabins low season, $60 s/d rooms, $70 cabins high season) is a three-story Italianate villa with four rooms and two cabinas, all with a/c and private bathrooms, batiks, earth-tile floors, and wooden ceilings with fans. Guests get kitchen privileges. There's a pool. The entire villa rents as a single unit Sep.–Dec. (from $2,700 per week). Rates include breakfast.

The French-run **Cabinas La Laguna del Cocodrilo** (tel. 506/653-0065, lalagunadelcoco-drilo.com, $35 s/d with fan, $40 s/d with a/c low season; $40 s, $50 d with a/c high season) has a unique location: the natural back garden merges into the adjacent lagoon with crocodiles. It has 10 rooms (six with a/c) with fans, terracotta tile floors, minimalist but charming decor including batik wall hangings, ceiling fans, and beautiful glazed bathrooms with hot water. Some rooms have stone terraces facing the beach. It has a bakery.

In the center, the **Hotel Zully Mar** (Apdo. 68, Santa Cruz, tel. 506/653-0140, fax 506/653-0028, zullymar@racsa.co.cr, www.tr506.com/zullymar, $27 s, $35 d basic cabin, $32/43 with fan, $42/50 with a/c low season; $40 s/d basic cabin, $52 with fan, $58 with a/c high season) has raised itself from shoestring status and is now a well-run property with 27 clean rooms (eight with a/c, refrigerator, and safe) with private baths, though most still have cold water. The old wing is still popular with backpackers (despite being overpriced), though a newer wing has metamorphosed Zully Mar into a simple albeit stylish hotel with a pool.

The Italian-run two-story **Hotel Mamiri** (tel./fax 506/653-0079, $15 s, $25 d low season; $25 s, $35 d high season), southeast of the center,

has nine attractively furnished rooms with sponge-washed ocher walls, Guatemalan throw rugs, private baths and hot water. The bar and restaurant is a classy little place, plus there's a communal kitchen in the garden. It also has apartments for $35 low season; $45 high season.

Another offbeat winner is **Cabinas Arco Iris** (tel. 506/653-0330, fax 506/653-0943, cabinasarcoiris@yaoo.it, www.hotelarcoiris.com, $25–45 s/d low season; $35–55 d high season), Italian run but resembling more a piece of Haight-Ashbury, with wind chimes, New Age music, batiks hanging from the ceiling, and a rainbow color scheme. It has six *cabinas* of differing layouts and sizes, all with private baths and hot water, and some two-bedroom units with kitchens. Each has a striking and endearing decor. All have gaily painted exteriors and black or dark-colored floors. It has turned its simple kitchen and restaurant into a suite, but guests in simpler units get use of a communal kitchen in the garden. It has a dojo where the owner teaches karate and yoga. Tribal tattoo and massage are available.

$50–100: The hillside, all-suite **Best Western Tamarindo Vista Villas** (tel. 506/653-0114 or 800/522-3241, fax 506/653-0115, tamvv@racsa.co.cr, www.tamarindovistavillas.com, $84 s/d standard, $104 s/d oceanview, $124–204 suites low season; $89 standard, $119 oceanview, $139–219 suites high season) offers 32 oceanview one- to three-bedroom suites handsomely appointed with a/c, fans, telephone, TV and VCR, full kitchens, and spacious verandas and balconies. The property is centered on a twin-turreted lounge area and offers an oceanview swimming pool with waterfall, swim-up bar, open-air poolside restaurant, and a video store and disco.

Hotel Pasatiempo (tel. 506/653-0096, fax 506/653-0275, passtime@racsa.co.cr, www .hotelpasatiempo.com, $39 s, $49 d, $69 suites low season; $49/59/79 high season) has 11 attractive, spacious, well-lit thatched cabins around a pool in pretty grounds full of bougainvillea, bananas, and palms. Each unit has a/c, ceiling fan, and patio with hammock. Note the beautiful hand-carved doors and hand-painted murals in each room. It has a book exchange, pool table, and table soccer, and you can rent snorkeling gear. The Yucca Bar hosts live music.

Across the road, the two-story, Italian-run **Hotel Portofino** (tel. 506/653-0578, fax 506/656-0576, portofino@sol.racsa.co.cr, www.portofino.itgo.com, $49 s/d, $64–94 three to six people low season; $64 s/d, $89–129 three to six people high season) has eight modestly decorated, spacious, two-bedroom a/c apartments with tile floors, cable TVs, phone, fully-equipped kitchens, and appealing bathrooms. It has a pool, secure parking, and a romantic restaurant (see *Food*).

Next door, the attractive **Hotel/Bar/Restaurante El Milagro** (P.O. Box 145-5150, Santa Cruz, tel. 506/653-0042, fax 506/653-0050, flokiro@racsa.co.cr, www.elmilagro.com, $50 s, $55 d with fan, $60 s, $65 d with a/c low season; $70 s, $75 d with fan, $80 s, $85 d with a/c high season) has charm. The 32 modern conical cabinas—set in soothing, breezy, landscaped grounds with a swimming pool—have a/c or fans, and private baths with hot water. A restaurant serves seafood under the watchful guidance of European management. There's also a kids' pool. Rates include breakfast.

A pleasing option nearby is the classy **Pueblo del Mar Vacation Village** (tel. 506/653-0200, pueblodelmar@costarica.net, www.costarica.net/pueblomar, $65–90 low season; $80–105 high season), a Mediterranean-style village with nine one-bedroom and 20 two-bedroom townhouse condos arrayed in an oval around a pool complex. They have elegant modern decor of ochers and orange, hardwood accents, and tasteful furnishings; most have a/c.

Villas Mariposa, immediately east of Pueblo Dorado, is almost identical and can be rented through the Century 21 office.

Nearby, looking like a South African kraal, is the **Bella Vista Village Resort,** Apdo. 143, Santa Cruz 5150, tel./fax 506/653-0036, belvista@racsa.co.cr, www.tamarindo.com/bella/, $50 s, $55 d low season; $55 s, $90 d high season), featuring six hilltop, thatched, four-person bungalows with fully furnished kitchens, living rooms, dining areas, and loft bedrooms. They're fabulous within—the soaring roofs supported by graceful beams, the fabrics rich, the simple decor highlighted by an individual motif. A pool is set in lush landscaped grounds. The "kraal" commands marvelous views over the treetops to the ocean.

About two km before town, directly opposite the airstrip, is **La Condesa Tamarindo** (tel. 506/653-0861, fax 506/693-0807, reservations @hotellacondesa.com, www.hotellacondesa.com, $70 s, $110 d low season; $88 s, $144 d high season), formerly Tamarindo Costa Real Resort. This impressive property has 29 modestly furnished bungalows (nine are apartments) with ocher-washed walls and Tyrolean roofs. Each has a/c, ceiling fan, cable TV, telephone, minibar, safety box, plus terra-cotta tile floors and rough white plaster walls. They look down over a massive freeform swimming pool. There's a restaurant and café-cum-bar, plus tennis courts (lit at night) and a sand volleyball court. Rates include breakfast and tax.

The exquisite, Italian-run, canary-yellow **Luna Llena** (tel. 506/653-0082, fax 506/653-0120, lunalle@racsa.co.cr, www.lunallena.com, $45 s, $55 d rooms, $55/65 bungalows low season; $55 s, $65 d rooms, $75/85 bungalows high season) has bungalows around an alluring swimming pool with swim-up bar and a raised wooden sun deck with a Jacuzzi. Stone pathways run through the stylish property, whose sponge-washed conical bungalows are done up in lively Caribbean colors and have tasteful decor, including terra-cotta floors; a spiral staircase leads to a loft bedroom, and the semicircular bathrooms are marvelous. All have fans, refrigerators, and private baths with hot water. Eight new rooms have a/c, wrought-iron pieces, French doors onto balconies, and huge bathrooms with large walk-in showers and beautiful tile. There's a small restaurant and a laundry. Rates include tax and breakfast (the seventh day is free).

Nearby, I love the 🅜 **Sueño del Mar Bed and Breakfast** (tel. 506/653-0284, innkeeper @sueno-del-mar.com, www.sueno-del-mar.com; in the U.S., 4 Mountview Center, Burlington, VT 05401, tel. 802/658-8041; moneyn@aol.com, $75 s/d, $95 s/d casita low season; $95 s/d, $160 s/d casita high season), a truly exquisite Spanish colonial house with rooms cascading down a shaded alcove to a small landscaped garden that opens onto the beach. Each is cool and shaded, with rough-hewn timbers, white-washed stone walls, terra-cotta tile floors, security boxes, screened arched windows with shutters, and tasteful fabrics. Most have exquisite rainforest showers. The huge upstairs suite is a true gem, with all-around screened windows, timber floor and raised ceiling, mosquito net on the four-poster bed made of logs, and a Goldilocks'-cottage feel to the bathroom with rainforest shower with gorgeous tilework. It also has a *casita* for four people. The property briefly went downhill a few years ago, but has been revitalized and at last visit management had clearly reenergized its interest in guests' welfare. The property is now a delight, with a sensuous serenity to the place. A small landscaped pool and wooden sundeck has been added, along with thatched shade area with hammock, perfect for enjoying cocktails and *bocas*. Complimentary snorkel gear, boogie boards, and bikes are available. Rates include full breakfast.

$100–150: Down by the shores, **Hotel Tamarindo Diría** (Apdo. 21, Santa Cruz, tel. 506/653-0032, fax 506/653-0208, reservaciones @eldiria.com, www.eldiria.co.cr, $100 s/d gardenview, $121 s/d oceanview, $142 s/d deluxe low season; $137 s/d gardenview, $152 oceanview, $180 s/d deluxe high season) ranks in the top tier with its quasi-Balinese motif and rich color scheme. The lobby boasting Guanacastecan pieces and elegant rolled-arm chaise longues opens to an exquisite horizon pool with fountains, with lawns and ocean beyond. It has 113 a/c rooms (including 47 deluxe and 28 premium) with terra-cotta tile floors, ceiling fans, pleasing furnishings, cable TVs, phones, minibars, and safes. Some have a Jacuzzi and many are wheelchair accessible. A large and airy restaurant with a beautiful hardwood ceiling opens onto an expansive bar and outside cocktail terrace. It has a kids' pool, tennis courts, a small casino, golf driving range, plus a boutique, sportfishing and tours.

Hotel Tamarindo Diría also offers new, one- and two-bedroom **Tamarindo Diría Beach Resort Condominiums,** on the hillside across the street.

One of my recommended favorites is the Mediterranean-style **Hotel Jardín del Edén** (tel. 506/653-0137, fax 506/653-0111, frontdesk @jardindeleden.com, www.jardindeleden.com, $60 s small, $70 s large, $80 d, $100 apartment low season; $80/105/120/130 high season), on a bluff overlooking Tamarindo. Truly a hillside "garden of Eden," it is managed by a youthful new owner and earns laurels for its amorous tenor. It offers five salmon-pink Spanish-style villas with 19 rooms, plus two fully equipped apartments, all with lively tropical colors, exquisite murals, wicker furniture, cable TVs, telephones, phones, safes, hairdryers, and spacious terrace-porches offering ocean views. The two-bedroom apartments have terra-cotta floors and beautiful kitchens with colonial tiles. A stunning pool with swim-up bar and magnificent Jacuzzi and a large sun deck with shady *ranchitos* are set in lush gardens floodlit at night, creating a colorful quasi-*son et lumière*. The restaurant is one of the best in town (see *Food*). There's a small open-air gym, and tours use the hotel's own 29-foot boat. Rates include buffet breakfast.

Another great bet is **Cala Luna Hotel and Villas** (tel. 506/653-0214, fax 506/653-0213, reservations@calaluna.com, www.calaluna.com, $139 s/d deluxe, $249 garden villa, $311 master suite low season; $167 s/d deluxe, $334 garden villa, $418 master suite high season), one km south of the village center, with sponge-washed walls in gold-ocher and flame orange. Spanish tile and rough-hewn timbers add to the cozy New Mexico–Central American style. The 20 hotel rooms, 16 garden villas, and five master villas surround a pool in a small landscaped garden. Each villa also has its own pool. Comfort is the keynote: king-size beds are standard, as are ceiling fans and abundant hardwoods, minibars, and safes, and all villas have TVs and CD players. There's a boutique and tour desk, pool bar, plus an evocative candlelit restaurant. Tours, horseback rides, and fishing trips are offered.

Thomas Douglas, owner of Hotel Santo Tomás in San José, rents **Tamarindo Surf House,** tel. 506/255-0448, fax 506/222-3950, info @surfhouse.com, www.thesurfhouse.com, from $95 low season, from $120 high season), at the entrance to Tamarindo. The two-story, three-bedroom, two-bathroom beachhouse sleeps eight people. It has a CD player, hammocks and barbecue pit on the lawns.

Casa Cook (tel. 506/653-0125, fax 506/653-0753, casacook@racsa.co.cr, www.tamarindo .com/cook, from $125 to $205 without a/c, $135 to $215 with a/c), about one km west of town, has three one-bedroom *casitas,* a pool and patio, and two large bedrooms with private baths in the main house. One of the *casitas* has its own pool. All sleep four and have cable TV and kitchens.

Enjoying a perfect beachfront location at Playa Langosta, **Casa Doble** (tel. 506/653-0312, fax 506/653-0192, townley@racsa.co.cr, www.casadoble .coom, $75 s/d room, $95 s/d cabin, $115 s/d suite low season, $100/125/150 high season) has six individually themed a/c rooms plus a *casa* and *cabinas.* All have heaps of light, raised ceilings with fans, South American spreads and rugs; some have TVs, and one has an ocean terrace. A two-bedroom family unit with ocean views shares a bathroom. Cabins are especially gracious and have mezzanine bedrooms and kitchenettes. A huge TV lounge with raised wooden ceiling has plentiful sofas. Guests get kitchen privileges, although a full buffet breakfast is served. There's a horizon pool and sundeck with lounge chairs. You can rent the entire house (for up to 18 people).

I also love **Villa Alegre** (tel. 506/653-0270, fax 506/653-0287, vialegre@racsa.co.cr, www .villaalegrecostarica.com, $85–95 d room, $135 suite low season; $100–115 d room, $155 suite mid-season; $110–125 d room, $175 suite high season), a contemporary beachfront bed-and-breakfast run by gracious hosts Barry and Suzye Lawson from California, who specialize in wedding and honeymoon packages. The main house has lofty ceilings, tile floors, lots of hardwood hints, a magnificent lounge with library, and four a/c bedrooms with French doors opening onto a private patio. Two *casitas*—one sleeping four people—each have a

living room, bedroom, and small but fully equipped kitchen; two other rooms can be combined into a mini-suite (one has an outside shower in its own patio garden). The rooms are individually decorated with the globe-trotting couple's collection of art, rugs, and miscellany; each room boasts the decor of a particular country, from Guatemala to Japan. The Mexico and Russia rooms are wheelchair-accessible. Book "Caribe" or "Russia," designated for honeymooners. A vast veranda overlooks a swimming pool, with a thatched bar serving *bocas*. Shuffleboard, volleyball, pool volleyball, and videos are on hand, and golf packages are offered. Rates include breakfast on the veranda, there's an honor bar, and guests get use of the kitchen.

The expansive and handsome **Barceló Playa Langosta Resort & Casino** (tel. 506/653-0363, fax 506/653-0415, playalangosta@barcelocr.com, www.barcelo.com, from $87 s, $144 d low season; from $173 s, $216 d high season), is Tamarindo's first megaresort. It sits above the river estuary (a source of controversy due to destruction of protected mangroves during construction). It has 140 rooms in three categories in nine two- and three-story blocks arrayed around a freeform pool, with a whirlpool for 30, set in lush landscaped grounds. It has a casino, boutique, tour desk, and tours. Rates include tax.

Bahía Langosta Condominiums ($125 one-bedroom, $185 two-bedroom, $200 three-bedroom low season; $150/185/245 high season) has 23 condos. Guests get free access to Barceló resort next door. **Villa Langosta,** next door, also has tasteful condominiums at similar rates.

My preferred place to rest my head is the Swiss-run **Capitán Suizo** (tel. 506/653-0075, fax 506/653-0292, capsuizo@racsa.co.cr, www .hotelcapitansuizo.com, $85 s/d standard, $115 with a/c, $135 bungalow, $300 apartment low season; $110/130/150/325 high season), a deserving member of the Small Distinctive Hotels of Costa Rica. Beach-loving cognoscenti will appreciate the resort's casual sophistication. Even the local howler monkeys have decided this is the place to be! Pathways coil sinuously through a botanical rush hour of heliconias, bougainvillea, palms, and shade trees to a wide sundeck and large amoeba-shaped pool with a faux beach shelving gently into the water. A serene, simple beauty pervades the 22 rooms and eight bungalows with natural gray-stone floors and deep-red hardwoods. Halogen lamps inset in the ceiling provide super lighting; soft-lit lanterns provide a more romantic note. Each spacious bungalow features a mezzanine bedroom with king-size bed and huge glass sliding doors. Bathrooms are the size of some other hotel rooms (bungalows have tubs plus "rainforest" showers), and feature huge wicker-mesh closets. The bar and restaurant are among Tamarindo's finset. Capitán Suizo has its own horse stable ($20 first hour, $10 each extra hour), plus kayaks, boogie boards, and a game room. Rates includeg breakfast.

$250 and up: The hard-to-reach yet electrifying **Sunset House** (tel./fax 506/653-0098, pacific @racsa.co.cr, www.tamarindo.com/sunset; in the U.S., Lexie Paulk-Hutton-SJO 3111, 1601 NW 97th Ave., Unit C-101, PO Box 025216, Miami, FL 33102-5216; $550 daily) is an exquisite 3,500-square-foot villa designed by an award-winning American architect. It exudes charm and boasts Spanish tiled floors, plus murals, cushioned concrete sofas, and tropical hardwood furniture in the cozy lounge with CD stereo. It has four spacious a/c bedrooms, including one with king-sized bed and another with a queen plus bunk bed. All have ocean views, and one of two bathrooms is a rock-walled outdoor shower. There's a freeform horizon pool, and sun deck with lounge chairs, barbecue, and wet bar. Catering can be arranged.

Food

Tamarindo is blessed with some of the most creative restaurateurs in the country.

For breakfasts, try the beachfront **Nogui Bar/Sunrise Café**, a popular place for gringo breakfasts. **Sueño del Mar** serves breakfasts to walk-in guests off the beach.

The French **Panadería La Laguna del Cocodrilo** (tel. 506/653-0065, 6 A.M.–7 P.M.), formerly Johan's Bakery, has an all-you-can-eat buffet breakfast in the garden ($5). It also sells delicious croissants, chocolate eclairs, fruit tarts, baquettes, and bread, pus enchiladas and *empañadas* (sandwiches) at lunch.

For inexpensive meals, the **Iguana Grill,** at Iguana Surf, is an atmospheric spot of hewn logs topped by thatch. It sells cheap *casados* (set meals), plus smoothies ($2), espressos, mochas, and cappuccinos ($1–1.50).

Choose from any of a dozen open-air seafood eateries by the traffic circle. **Zully Mar** enjoys a great beachfront location and serves seafoods such as shrimp ceviche ($5.50), breaded calamari ($6).

Stella's Fine Dining (tel. 506/653-0127) offers gourmet dining under a pretty *palenque*. It has tempting vegetarian and seafood dishes (including sushi) such as breaded calamari with tzatziki, Thai fish curry, and wood-roasted tenderloin soaked in garlic and red wine, plus pizzas ($1–6) fired in an earth oven. Choose from a 50-label wine list. Free shuttles are offered.

The splendid **El Jardín del Edén,** at the hotel of that name, serves Mediterranean-inspired seafood dishes such as jumbo shrimp in whiskey, lobster in lemon sauce, or peppered tenderloin. The thatched eatery has heavy-duty hardwood tables inlaid with beautiful Spanish tiles. Pop in at breakfast for a fresh croissant from the patisserie.

For the best nouvelle dining in town, head to **N Capitán Suizo** (tel. 506/653-0075, 7 A.M.–9:15 P.M.), where German chef Roland merges European influences into a tropical setting. The creative menu runs from a perfect tomato soup to tilapia with olives, fresh tomato sauce, and macadamia vegetables. I've also enjoyed a curried chicken ($6), corvina in mango sauce ($8), and tilapia in caper sauce ($10). The dinner menu changes daily.

Smilin Dog Taco Factory sells tacos ($1.75), burritos ($3), veggie burritos, quesadillas, plus soft drinks (no alcohol).

For baked goods, try the French-run **El Punto** (tel. 506/653-0410, 7:30 A.M.–11 P.M.), a simple roadside café that also serves ice creams and a full French menu that includes pâté ($5.50) and salmon in white wine sauce ($8).

For groceries, head to **Supermercado Tamarindo** (9 A.M.–5 P.M.) or **Super Las Palmeras,** 100 meters east of Hotel Tamarindo Diriá.

Information and Services

For tourist information, head to the U.S.-run **Costa Rica Paradise Tour Information** (7 A.M.–6 P.M.), in Plaza Colonial, a full booking agency run by a savvy father-and-son team.

Dr. Quijada has a **medical clinic** (tel. 506/653-0544, 3–8 P.M. Mon.–Fri., 9 A.M.–noon Saturday) next to Hostel La Botella de Leche. The main pharmacy (tel. 506/653-0210, or 506/821-9605 for 24-hour emergencies) is next to Hotel Portofino.

The bank in Plaza Colonial is open 8:30 A.M.–3:45 P.M. Mon.–Fri.

The **International Telephone Center,** in the Apartotel Portofino, is open 8 A.M.–10 P.M.

@Internet (tel. 506/653-1025, 9 A.M.–9 P.M.), 50 meters west of Plaza Colonial, charges $5 per hour and has prepaid cards plus international telephone and fax service. **Interlink** (tel. 506/653-0605, 9 A.M.–10:30 P.M.), next to Hotel Zully Mar, charges $0.75 for 10 minutes and also offers international calling. **Internet Surf** (tel. 506/653-0881, andreatamarindo@hotmail .com, 9 A.M.–9 P.M. Mon.–Sat.) charges $2.50 per hour.

Lavandería Mariposa (8 A.M.–noon and 4–7 P.M. Mon.–Sat.) offers laundry service. **Lavandería El Punto** (tel. 506/653-0870, 8 A.M.–5 P.M.) charges $1.25 per kilo.

Getting There

The airstrip (no tel.) is one km east of town. **SANSA** (tel. 506/840-1803) and **Nature Air** operate scheduled daily service between Tamarindo and San José. The SANSA office is on the main street.

A $3 departure tax is collected at the airport.

Buses (tel. 506/222-2750) depart San José from Calle 14, Avenidas 3/5, at 3:30 P.M.; and from Calle 20, Avenida 3 (Tralapa, tel. 506/221-7202), at 4 P.M. Return buses depart Tamarindo at 3:30 A.M. and 5:45 A.M. (Mon.–Sat.), plus 9 A.M. (Monday), and at 5:45 A.M., and 12:30 P.M. on Sunday.

Buses depart Santa Cruz daily at 4:30 A.M., 5:30 A.M., 8:30 A.M., 10:30 A.M., 1:30 P.M., 3:30 P.M., and 8 P.M.; return buses depart Tamarindo at 6 A.M., 9 A.M., noon, 2:30 P.M., and 4:15 P.M.

Buses depart Tamarindo for Liberia at 5:45 A.M., 7:30 A.M., 9 A.M., 1 P.M., 2 P.M., and 4:30 P.M.; for Santa Cruz at 6 A.M., 9 A.M., noon, 2:30 P.M., and 4:15 P.M.

Fantasy Bus and **Interbus** offer shuttles; see *Getting There and Away,* in the *Playa Flamingo* section, above, for information.

I recommend **Europcar** (tel. 506/653-0145), in Centro Comercial Sunrise. Alamo Rent-a-Car, Economy Rent-a-Car, and Payless Car Rental also have outlets; see the map.

There's no gas station, but the **Ferretería,** at the entrance to town, sells gas ($2.75 per gallon at last visit).

Getting Around

Tamarindo Adventures rents scooters ($39), motorcycles ($49), and mountain bikes ($20 per day).

Taxi service is sporadic. Hugo Retana (tel. 506/653-0080) is available 24 hours.

Tamarindo to Junquillal

PLAYAS LANGOSTA AND AVELLANAS

Langosta is in the throes of megaresort and condo development, despite its importance as a nesting site for turtles. This is a popular surf spot famed for its rocky left and reefy shore breaks. If swimming, beware of riptides.

From Tamarindo, you must backtrack to Villarreal to continue southward via Hernández (three km south of Villarreal). The coastal road is a lonesome, narrow dirt affair that becomes impassable in sections in the wet season, when you may have better luck approaching Playa Avellana and Lagartillo from the south via Paraíso, reached by paved road from Santa Cruz.

Most of Playa Langosta backs onto **Hacienda Pinilla** (tel. 506/680-3000, fax 506/680-3165, www.haciendapinilla.com), which stretches south for several kilometers and covers 1,800 hectares. At last visit this former cattle ranch was being developed as the most upscale residential resort community in the country, with a championship 18-hole golf course. Trails lead through a nature reserve with lagoons. There's a stable for horse rides ($15–35). Eventually it will have hundreds of villas and condos for rent, plus several top-flight hotels.

Playa Avellanas, 12 km south of Tamarindo, has been discovered by surfers. This beautiful coral-colored beach has lots of tidepools and is renowned for its barrel surf. You can rent surfboards for $15/25 half-/full-day, and go fishing ($50 per hour) on the *Manta Too* at Cabinas Las Olas (see below).

Theft and car break-ins are major problems at the beaches. Never leave items in your car!

Accommodations and Food

You can **camp** at **Bar y Restaurante Gregorio's,** a bar and restaurant under thatch ($2 pp). It also has three basic *cabinas* ($15 s, $20 d) with private baths and cold water. The rustic place has piglets underfoot.

Cabinas Iguana Verde. a pleasing structure of brick-and-roughhewn logs, 50 meters beyond Gregorio's, has cheap rooms with cold showers and shared outside toilets for $10 pp.

Swiss-run **Cabinas Las Olas** (P.O. Box 1404-1250, Escazú, tel. 506/658-8315 or 506/233-4455, fax 506/222-8685, www.cabinaslasolas.co.cr, $40 s, $50 d low season, $55 s, $65 d high season) is an "upscale" surfer's place with 10 bungalows widely spaced amid the dry forest. Each has private bathroom, bidet, and hot water. A raised wooden walkway leads 300 meters across mangroves to the beach. The video-bar and restaurant have an appealing ambience. It has ping-pong, rents kayaks ($15/25 half/full-day), boogie boards ($5/8) snorkeling gear ($5/8), and mountain bikes ($18/30), and surfboards were to be added.

At last visit, deluxe accommodations at **Hacienda Pinilla** were under construction, including the Posada del Sol Hotel; eight suites in the Casa de Golf; three more rustic Pequeña Finca Beach Houses; and two-, three-, and four-bedroom villas.

PLAYAS LAGARTILLO AND NEGRA

Playa Lagartillo, beyond Punta Pargos, just south of Playa Avellanas, is another gray-sand beach with tidepools. Lagartillo is separated by Punta Pargos from Playa Negra, centered on the community of **Los Pargos.** It, too, has been discovered by the surfing crowd.

About five km south of Los Pargos, the dirt road cuts inland about eight km to the tiny hamlet of **Paraíso,** where another dirt road leads back to the coast and dead-ends at Playa Junquillal. There's a gas station here. (In wet season, when driving between Los Pargos and Paraíso, stick to the main dirt road, not the secondary dirt road nearer the coast that runs past Pablo's Picasso, which can be a quagmire.)

Villa-condominium communities have gone up at Playa Negra, part of a tidal wave of similar projects mushrooming along this coast.

Pura Jungla Preserve (P.O. Box 12, Santa Cruz, tel. 506/658-8160, ray@lapurajungla.com, www.purajungla.com) is an eco-community in the hills one km north of Paraíso. The brainchild of environmentalist and philosopher Ray Beise, the 235-hectare nature preserve is designed to show that beautiful homes can be built in harmony with their natural surroundings. Ray has returned erstwhile cattle pasture to forest that now draws a plethora of wildlife, including monkeys and cats. There's an exotic fruit orchard, experimental tree farm, organic banana grove, and nature trails, one of which leads to an observation platform and another to waterfalls.

Accommodations

You can camp amid well-trimmed lawns at the U.S.-run **Aloha Amigos,** reached by a side road of the dirt coast road. This pleasing place has hammocks under shade trees, plus toilets and showers with cold water only. It also has cabinas with patios, and a bunk room with shared bathroom. Jerry, the Hawaiian owner, and his son Joey rent boards ($10 per day) and do board repair.

A delightful Peruvian couple run **Kontiki** (tel. 506/698-8117, kontikiplayanegra@yahoo.com, $10 s, $20 d, $25 quad) a rustic Robinson Crusoe-could-have-lived-here farmhouse with a wonderful offbeat ambience about three km north of Los Pargos, between Lagartillo and Negra. It has five thatched cabinas raised on stilts, with shared bath and cold water; one rates as a virtual treehouse and features two dorms with "Goldilocks and the Three Bears"-style bunks and a double bed (howler monkeys hangout in the treetops at eye level). The place abounds with pre-Columbian figurines. You're served Peruvian dishes cooked in an outdoor oven. Rates include breakfast.

You'll love the three-story, all-hardwood, windowless **ℕ Mono Congo Lodge** (P.O. Box 177-5150, Santa Cruz, tel. 506/658-8261, fax 506/658-8260, findedia@aol.com, www.monocongo lodge.com, $25 s, $30 d low season; $45 s, $50 d high season) a Colorado-style lodge—about one km north of Los Pargos—that has been described as "a mixture of Swiss Family Robinson

tree house and Australian outback bed-and-breakfast." It is run by new owners, Kim and Justin, from Virginia. The lodge, which is hand-built of stone and hardwoods, has six simply furnished rooms with magnificent high beds boasting orthopedic mattresses, mosquito nets, and Indian batik covers; plus screened windows, and exquisite tilework in the bathrooms (some have stone walls). A wraparound veranda has hammocks and leather lounge chairs. It's surrounded by fruit trees and dry forest. Horseback riding tours, boat charters, and massage can be arranged. A pool was to be added. Rates include breakfast.

Pablo's Picasso (tel. 506/658-8158, pabloscr @hotmail.com, $8.50 pp bunks, $15 pp *cabina* with fan, $45 s/d *cabina* with a/c and kitchen), at Playa Negra, 500 meters south of Los Pargos, is legendary among surfers. This rustic hostelry and surfers' gathering spot is run by a friendly Yank named Paul. He offers a huge loft with bunks, plus three-person *cabinas* with fans and private baths with cold water, and two a/c *cabinas* with kitchens. You can camp for $4 pp, including toilets and showers. Hammocks are slung beneath the rustic bar. You can enjoy movies on the VCR while sitting in oversized wooden seats that inspire a Goldilocks-in-Papa-Bear's-chair sensation.

The kraal-like **Hotel Playa Negra** (P.O. Box 31-5150 Santa Cruz, tel. 506/658-8034, fax 506/658-8035, www.playanegra.com, $40 s, $50 d low season; $50 s, $60 d high season), beachside 500 meters west of Los Pargos, enjoys a breezy locale. Its circular thatched *cabinas* are exquisitely, albeit simply decorated, with sponge-painted walls, sensuous curves, and soft pastels, Guatemalan print bedspreads, and mosaic-tiled bathrooms. Each has a lofty wooden ceiling and is cross-ventilated through screened, louvered windows. A French chef conjures tasty food that you can enjoy at the huge crook-shaped bar with TV. There's a pool table, small swimming pool, and boutique. It closes each October.

Rancho Playa Negra (www.ranchoplayanegra.com) is a residential community under construction at last visit. Condo-villa units will be available for rent.

Food

Mono Congo Lodge (7 A.M.–9 P.M.) serves omelettes, huevos rancheros, burgers, sandwiches, plus gourmet dishes such as spinach gorgonzola salad with cranberry ($6) and Jamaican jerk fish with pineapple mango salsa ($9.50).

I recommend **Café Playa Negra** (tel. 506/658-8143, www.cafeplayanegra.com, 7 A.M.–3 P.M. and 6–9 P.M.), in Los Pargos. Here, a Peruvian named Carlos conjures superb pancakes, French toast, quiches, sandwiches, ceviche, fettucines ($4), Thai chicken ($3), and lemon pie, plus killer *batidos* (shakes). The café also offers Internet connections ($2.50 per hour) and laundry service($7.50 per load).

Paul, at **Pablo's Picasso** (7 A.M.–10 P.M.), serves "burgers as big as your head," plus pancakes ($3), sandwiches, and pastas.

You can buy groceries at **Mini-Super Los Pargos,** opposite Café Playa Negra; and baked goods at **Secret Spot Bakery,** 100 meters south.

PLAYA JUNQUILLAL

Playa Junquillal, four km southwest of Paraíso and 31 km west of Santa Cruz, is an attractive four-km-long light-gray-sand beach with rock platforms and tidepools. Beware the high surf and strong riptides. The beachfront road dead-ends to the south at the wide and deep Río Andumolo, whose mangrove estuary is home to birds and crocodiles.

For some reason, most of the expats here are Germans.

Accommodations and Food

Camping Los Malinches (tel./fax 506/658-8429, $5 pp, $8 per day RVs), about 500 meters south of Hotel Iguanazul, has thatched camp spaces on the lawn, with clean bathrooms and showers and water. It has electrical hookups for RVs. It has hammocks beneath the malinche trees.

The **Iguanazul Beach Resort** (P.O. Box 130-5150, Santa Cruz, tel. 506/658-8124, fax 506/658-8123, info@iguanazul.com, www.iguanazul.com, $47 s, $55 d standard, $55/64 oceanview, $64/72 with a/c low season; $60/70 standard,

$70/80 oceanview, $80/90 with a/c high season), enjoys a breezy clifftop setting overlooking the beach. Its 24 rooms (six with a/c) are set around a pleasant pool surrounded by palm-shaded lawns. They're pleasing enough (albeit a bit short on light) and have security boxes, and colonial tile bathrooms with large walk-in showers. The resort had been spruced up at last visit but still rates as ho-hum. An elegant restaurant and bar open onto the pool, and there's a TV lounge, volleyball court, pool table, and small souvenir store.

Villa Roberta B&B (Apdo. 68-5150, Santa Cruz, tel. 506/658-8127, fax 506/658-8128, dietzcom@racsa.co.cr; in Germany, Noricus Tours GmbH, Rothenburger Str. 5, 90443 Nürnberg, tel. 11/92-96-960; $40–60 low season; $60–80 high season) is a modern hilltop home about 400 meters inland of the beach. It rents two spacious rooms in the garden. One is a very attractive double room with a black stone floor and king-size bed, and a beautiful bathroom with stone floor, sink, and shower. The second is an a/c apartment with lofty ceiling, small kitchen, and a tasteful bathroom with a bidet. Each has a pleasing motif with dark hardwood accents and sea-blue tiles. It has a deep kidney-shaped pool plus hammocks on verandas. Breakfast is served on an upstairs veranda.

About 100 meters south, a German-Tico couple run **El Castillo Divertido** (tel./fax 506/658-8428, castillodivertido@hotmail.com, $25 s, $32 d low season; $28 s, $39 d high season), a crenelated three-story structure with a breezy hillside setting 300 meters inland of the beach. It has seven simply furnished rooms with large louvered-glass windows, private bath (three have hot water and ocean view). There's a rooftop sun deck with bar and a small restaurant.

About 400 meters south is the Swiss-run **Guacamaya Lodge** (P.O. Box 6-5150, Santa Cruz, tel. 506/658-8431, fax 506/658-8164, www .guacamayalodge.com, $30 s, $35 d low season; $45 s, $50 d high season), with six clean, octagonal *cabinas* with private bath, hot water, and hammocks on the porch. The bar-cum-restaurant serving international fare has ocean views. There's a plunge pool and children's pool, beach volleyball, gift store, and horseback riding ($15 per hour). It also has two smaller rooms with shared bath ($15 s/d); plus a house with kitchen for four people ($90 per day low season, $120 high season). Rates include tax. **Paradise Riding** (tel. 506/658-8162), opposite Guacamaya Lodge, offers horseback rides ($59).

The **El Lugarcito Bed and Breakfast** (P.O. Box 214-5150, Santa Cruz, tel./fax 658-8436, $50 s/d) nearby is a splendid two-story home entered through lofty stable-like doors, with stone floors and lofty ceilings and tasteful decor enhanced by traditional pottery. The two simple but pleasant rooms have fans and halogen ceiling lights. It has a delightful half-moon bar in the garden patio with hammocks. Mieke, the Dutch owner, is a PADI-certified diving instructor; she puts on a weekly barbecue. Her hubbie, Maarten, leads hikes and offers tours far and wide.

Hotel Tatanka (tel. 506/658-8426, fax 506/658-8312, tatanka@racsa.co.cr, www.crica .com/tatanka, $34 s, $50 d low season; $44 s, $58 d high season), a stone's throw south, is an Italian inspiration with 10 rooms with ocher-washed walls, fans, simple furnishings, private bath and hot water, and verandas looking onto the lawns inset with a pool. An open-sided pizzeria is elegantly rustic and shows movies. It rents horses, kayaks, and motorcycles. Rates include breakfast and tax.

Within shouting distance is the **Hibiscus Hotel** (tel./fax 506/658-8437, $30 s, $40 d), set amid landscaped grounds full of palms and plantains and run by a German couple. All five rooms—genteel and spotless—have fans and private baths with hot water, plus hammocks on terraces. Quality seafood is served in a pretty little dining area.

In the center of the beach, the German-run **Villa Serena** (P.O. Box 17-5150, Santa Cruz, tel./fax 506/658-8430; in the USA, tel. 800/671-7757, $36 s, $45 d low season; $70 s/d with fan, $100 with a/c high season) has 10 modern bungalows. The spacious, light, and airy rooms—all with fans and private baths with hot water—are spread out among palms and surrounded by emerald-green grass and flowery gardens. The villa has a cozy lounge overlooking the beach, a library, and a swimming pool, and a hibiscus-encircled tennis court. Dinners are served on an elevated veranda overlooking the ocean. It offers spa treatments.

For an upscale condo option, check out **Las Brisas del Mar** (lavtica@yahoo.com, www. vacationaccommodations.net), an 18-unit condo complex in the hills.

El Castillo Divertido (8–10:30 A.M. and 7–10 P.M.) serves European dishes heavy on German fare and offers a *plato del día* for $8.

Getting There

A bus (tel. 506/221-7202) departs San José for Junquillal from Avenida 3, Calle 20, daily at 2 P.M. ($5; five hours). A bus departs Santa Cruz at 6:30 P.M. Return buses depart for Santa Cruz and San José at 5 A.M.

Junquillal to Nosara

PLAYA LAGARTO TO OSTIONAL

South of Junquillal, the dirt road—one of my favorite stretches of road in Costa Rica—leads along a lonesome stretch of coast to Nosara (35 km south of Junquillal). Fabulous beaches lie hidden along this route, albeit for most of the way out of sight of the shore. There are few hotels. Just forest, cattle pasture, lonesome rustic dwellings, and an occasional ramshackle fishing village.

If driving south from Tamarindo or west from Santa Cruz on the Santa Cruz–Junquillal road, you must turn south at Soda Las Lucas, four km east of Paraíso—the turnoff is signed for Marbella (16 km) and Nosara. (Another, much rougher, track begins from opposite a thatched *ranchito* called Pochotes Pamperos on the north side of the road, about two km west of Soda Las Lucas. A 4WD is recommended and essential in wet season—last time I tried this, the road was impassable, though bridges had been built over most of the little rivers that had to be forded just a few years ago.)

About six km south of the junction, the road briefly hits the shore at **Lagarto** before curling inland to **Marbella,** from where a side road runs down to **Playa Lagarcito.** Four km further you'll pass black-sand **Playa Azul.** About eight km farther south, a turnoff from the coast road leads to the fishing hamlet of **San Juanillo.** Ostional is five km further south.

Accommodations and Food

Casa Mango (tel. 506/682-8032, donjim@racsa .co.cr, $10 pp), on a hillside three km south of Marbella, has four handsome yet barebones wooden *cabinas* with fans, and shared bathrooms with cold water only; plus a thatched *casa* with kitchen ($60 up to six people). It has a restaurant and bar with pool table and veranda with rockers.

Upscale travelers might check into **The Sanctuary** (tel. 506/682-8111, fax 506/682-8113, www.thesanctuaryresort.com; in the U.S., c/o Holiday Systems, tel. 800/353-0774, fax 702/

260-8941, www.holidaysystems.com), a full-blown resort at Playa Azul. It was in the process of completion at last visit. It has condos in a gracious contemporary take on colonial plantation style. There's a spa, tennis, swimming pool, and water sports. Its Blue Dolphin Bar & Grill (tel. 506/682-8228, 7:30 A.M.–10 P.M., $10) offers gorgeous decor blending blue tiles and pillars, elegant place settings, and a menu featuring sandwiches, filet mignon, lobster, and fettuccines.

Here's a recommended winner! **Tree Tops B&B** (P.O. Box 42-5150, Santa Cruz, tel./fax 506/682-8298, jphunter@racsa.co.cr, $75 d) is a totally reclusive one-room bed-and-breakfast tucked above a cove at San Juanillo. This charming place is the home of former race-car champion Jack Hunter and his wife, Karen—delightful hosts who go out of their way to make you feel at home. You're the only guest. There's one simply furnished room with outdoor shower. You're here for the spectacular solitude and setting that includes a horseshoe reef with live coral that's great for snorkeling, and a private beach for an all-over tan. Monkeys cavort in the treetops. You can dine and relax in hammocks on a rustic thatched veranda on stilts. The couple offers turtle safaris to Ostional, plus a swim-with-turtle excursion ("I got to hold a turtle in my arms. What a wonderful experience!" gushed one guest), plus sportfishing tours ($280 half-day for up to three people); catch your own fish and Karen will prepare sushi. She also fixes up mean Thai pasta salads, Moroccan food, and cappuccino or espresso. The couple planned to add two rooms. Rates include a real English breakfast. Reservations essential.

OSTIONAL NATIONAL WILDLIFE REFUGE

The 248-hectare Refugio Nacional Silvestre Vida Ostional begins at Punta India, about two km south of San Juanillo, and extends along 15 km of shoreline to Punta Guiones, eight km south of the village of Nosara. It incorporates the beaches of Playa Ostional, Playa Nosara, and Playa Guiones.

The village of **Ostional** is midway along Playa Ostional, which has some of the tallest breaking waves in the country. The refuge, one of the world's most important sea turtle hatcheries, was created to protect one of two vitally important nesting sites in Costa Rica for the *lora*, or olive ridley turtle (the other is Playa Nancite, in Santa Rosa National Park). A significant proportion of the world's Pacific ridley turtle population nests at Ostional, invading the beach en masse for up to one week at a time July–Dec. (peak season is August and September), and singly or in small groups at other times during the year.

Time your arrival correctly and out beyond the breakers you may see a vast flotilla of turtles massed shoulder to shoulder, waiting their turn to swarm ashore, dig a hole in the sand, and drop in the seeds for tomorrow's turtles. The legions pour out of the surf in endless waves until they are so densely packed that, in the words of the great turtle expert Archie Carr, "one could have walked a mile without touching the earth—literally. You could have run a whole mile down the beach on the backs of turtles and never have set foot on the sand."

It's a stupendous sight, this *arribada* (arrival). Of the world's eight marine turtle species, only the females of the olive ridley and its Atlantic cousin, Kemp's ridley, stage *arribadas*. Synchronized mass nestings are known to occur at only nine beaches worldwide (in Mexico, Nicaragua, Honduras, Surinam, Orissa in India, and Costa Rica). Playa Ostional is the most important of these.

So tightly packed is the horde that the turtles feverishly clamber over one another in their efforts to find an unoccupied nesting site. As they dig, sweeping their flippers back and forth, the petulant females scatter sand over one another and the air is filled with the slapping of flippers on shells. By the time the *arribada* is over, more than 150,000 turtles may have stormed this prodigal place and 15 million eggs may lie buried in the sand.

Leatherback turtles also come ashore to nest in smaller numbers Oct.–Jan., with *arribadas* most

months starting with the last quarter of the moon. In 1997, for the first time, an *arribada* occurred at Playa Nosara, *south* of Ostional.

You can walk the entire length of the beach's 15-km shoreline, which is littered with broken eggshells. Although turtles can handle the strong currents, humans have a harder time: swimming is not advised. Howler monkeys, coatimundis, and kinkajous frequent the forest inland from the beach. The mangrove swamp at the mouth of the Río Nosara is a nesting site for many of the 190 bird species hereabouts (see *Nosara Biological Reserve,* below).

Wealthy foreigners have bought much of the land surrounding the refuge. Environmentalists fear that development, the influx of too many people in this sacred refuge, and the lights and human activity will discourage the turtles from nesting. The local community is hostile to tourism development, after the lesson of Nosara, its southerly neighbor, where foreign buyers have forced land values out of the reach of local residents. This unwanted development threatens to remove the community's control over its resources. Hotel developers are also pushing hard to get permits, but so far Ostional residents have had the courts on their side. The priority is the purchase of the land adjacent to Ostional to establish buffer zones and ensure the protection of the nesting grounds. Only then can the indigenous community be assured that it has taken command of a sustainable egg-harvesting program that meets the challenge of protecting the turtles while addressing the community's needs.

Turtle Viewing

You must check in with ADIO (see *Information,* below) before exploring the beach; a guide is compulsory ($7) any time of year. An entry fee of $6 is payable at the *puesto* (ranger station) at the southern end of the village, where you check in. You watch a video before entering the beach as a group.

All vehicles arriving at night are requested to turn off their headlights when approaching the beach. Flashlights are also forbidden, and no flash photography is permitted. Personal contact

RESPITE FOR THE RIDLEY

As the female ridley covers her nest with toeless flat feet and pounds back to the sea without ever looking back, does she know that she was herself hatched at Ostional 20 or more years ago? In those 20 years, the little boys who watched her mother come up to shore and then stole her eggs have grown up. A generation has passed, but the grown men who have not gone to the city to make it big will still take her eggs and sell them to cantinas to be drunk raw so that men might have strength in their loins. At dawn the whole village will descend on the beach. The men of Ostional will feel for the nests with their heels, then the women and girls will dig deep and remove the eggs and place them in rice sacks ready for shipment to bars.

Though guards were first placed at Ostional in 1979 to protect the endangered ridley, the egg harvest continues. But all is not what it seems. Elsewhere in Costa Rica, harvesting turtle eggs is illegal and usually occurs only in the dead of night. At Ostional it occurs legally and by daylight.

The seeming rape of the ridley—called *lora* locally—is the pith of a bold conservation program that aims to help the turtles by allowing the local community to commercially harvest eggs in a rational manner. "The main goal . . . is to achieve social growth of the community through controlled removal of eggs without compromising the reproduction and conservation of the species," says Claudette Mo, professor of biology at the National University of Costa Rica.

Dramatic declines in ridley populations are evident throughout Central America. During the late 1970s, massive commercial exploitation of ridleys developed in Ecuador, where a significant proportion of Costa Rica's nesting population spends the nonnesting season feeding on macroplankton. Up to 150,000 adult ridleys were being killed to make "shoes for Italian pimps," in the words of Archie Carr. Ecuador banned the practice in 1981, but "resource pirates" from Asia still fish for turtles off Ecuador—routinely violating the latter's territorial rights. Mexico continued the slaughter until 1990. And tens of thousands of ridleys are still caught by shrimp trawlers along the coasts of Central America.

Costa Rica outlawed the taking of turtle eggs nationwide in 1966. But egg poaching is a time-honored tradition. The coming of the first *arribada* to Ostional in 1961 was a bonanza to the people of Ostional. Their village became the major source of turtle eggs in Costa Rica. Coatis, coyotes, raccoons, and other egg-hungry marauders take a heavy toll on the tasty eggs, too. Ridley turtles have thus hit on a formula for outwitting their predators—or at least of surviving despite them: they deposit millions of eggs at a time (in any one season, 30 million eggs might be laid at Ostional). Since the *arribada* follows a strategy that assumes that only a fraction of eggs will incubate successfully, the turtle invasions vary in size and timing year by year.

Ironically, the most efficient scourge are the turtles themselves! Since Ostional beach is literally covered with thousands of turtles, the eggs laid during the first days of an *arribada* are often dug up by turtles arriving later. Often before they can hatch, a second *arribada* occurs. Again the beach is covered with crawling reptiles. As the newcomers dig, many inadvertently excavate and destroy the eggs laid by their predecessors and the beach becomes strewn with rotting embryos. Even without human interference, only one percent to eight percent of eggs in a given *arribada* will hatch.

By the early 1970s, destruction of the Nancite and Ostional hatcheries was far along. The turtle population seemed to be below the minimum required to maintain the species, and after a decade of study scientists concluded that uncontrolled poaching of eggs would ultimately exterminate the nesting colony. They also reasoned that a *controlled* harvest would actually rejuvenate the turtle population. Such a harvest during the first two nights of an *arribada* would *improve* hatch rates at Ostional by reducing the number of broken eggs and crowded conditions that together create a spawning ground for bacteria and fungi that prevent the development of embryos.

In 1987, the Costa Rican Congress finally approved a management plan that would legalize egg harvesting at Ostional. The statute that universally prohibited egg harvesting was reformed to permit the residents of Ostional to take and sell turtle eggs. The unique legal right to harvest eggs is vested in members of the Asociación Desarrollo Integral de Ostional (ADIO). The University of Costa Rica, which has maintained a biological research station at Ostional since 1980, is legally responsible for preparing an annual plan and review and for providing the scientific criteria to guide the community toward a sustainable cash-based use of their natural resource.

A quota is established for each *arribada*. Sometimes, no eggs are harvested; in the dry season (Dec.–May), as many as 35 percent of eggs may be taken; when the beach is hotter than Hades, the embryos become dehydrated, and the hatching rate falls below one percent. The idea is to save eggs that would be broken anyway or that otherwise have a low expectation of hatching.

The egg collectors are organized into work groups, each assigned to its own tract of beach. The men mark the nests with a tag. The women follow, extract the eggs, and place them in sacks to be washed in the sea. The eggs are then carted to the village packing center and placed into small plastic bags pre-stamped with the seal of ADIO. By law, eggs may be taken only during the first 36 hours of an *arribada*. After that, the villagers protect the nests from poachers and the hatchlings from ravenous beasts.

The project has seeded a conservationist ethic among community members. When, in 1972, scientists arrived to initiate the first studies, a field assistant was beaten, and the locals punctured the scientists' tires and interfered with their efforts to tag the turtles. Today, the villagers help biologists count and monitor the turtles. Even the mayor of Nicoya was taken to court by ADIO after villagers caught him with two bags of poached turtle eggs! The Guardia Rural (police) used to confiscate the poachers' eggs and sell them themselves. Then the police, became enthusiastic beneficiaries of the program—income from the sale of legally harvested eggs paid for construction of a Guardia Rural office at Ostional. (Corruption has gradually seeped back in, critics claim. Anny Chaves and Leslie du Toit, man-and-wife environmentalists who were instrumental in setting up the harvesting program and gaining protection for the turtle, were attacked and ousted in 1995 when the couple discovered corruption among the locals supervising the program.)

The eggs are dealt to distributors who sell on a smaller scale at a contract-fixed price to bakers (which favor turtle eggs over those of hens; turtle eggs give dough greater "lift") and bars, brothels, and street vendors who sell the eggs as *bocas*. The law stipulates that net revenues from the sale of eggs be divided between the community (80 percent) and the Ministry of Agriculture. ADIO distributes 70 percent of its share among association members as payment for their labors, and 30 percent to the Sea Turtle Project and communal projects. ADIO also pays the biologists' salaries. Profits have funded construction of a health center, a house for schoolteachers, the ADIO office, and a Sea Turtle Research Lab.

Scientists claim that the project also has the potential to stop the poaching of eggs on other beaches. It's a matter of economics: poachers have been undercut by cheaper eggs from Ostional. Studies also show that the turtle population has stabilized. Recent *arribadas* have increased in size. And hatch rates are up dramatically.

Alas, illegal fishing within the marine park boundaries kills hundreds of turtles each year.

with turtles is prohibited, as is disturbance of markers placed on the beach.

Accommodations and Food

Camping is allowed on the west side of the soccer field, next to the shore.

Pacha Mama (Apdo. 110, Boca de Nosara 5233, tel. 506/289-7081, fax 506/228-5173, pachamama@tyohar.org, www.pacha-mama.org, $50–70 bungalows, $18–30 family and "luxurious" bungalows weekly) is a "spiritual-ecological village," or commune, on a hilltop plateau near Limonal at the north end of Ostional, about three km inland. Camping is allowed ($175 camping first week, $140 subsequent weeks, including all meals) and tents, mattresses, etc., can be rented; and there are simple thatched cabins "from basic to luxury." Healings from acupuncture to Tibetan pulsing are offered. It has an Internet/juice bar, and earth foods are served. Children are welcome. Attendees are required to contribute some labor to chores.

Cabinas Ostional (tel. 506/682-0428), 50 meters south of the soccer field, has six clean, pleasing rooms sleeping three people, with fans and private baths with cold water only for $10 pp. Two newer cabins have lofty thatched ceilings. About 100 meters south, the **Pulpería y Hospedaje Las Guacamayas** (tel. 506/682-0430 $4 pp) has four small but clean rooms with two single beds, fans, and shared bathroom with cold water only.

At the north end of Ostional is the Hungarian-owned **Hotel Rancho Brovella** (tel. 506/380-5639 or fax 506/258-1732, webmaster@brovella.com, $35 s/d room, $80 apartment, $100 *casas*), a hilltop retreat with a splendid setting offering views. It has 12 a/c *cabinas,* each with fans, TV, and a private bath with hot water. It also has two two-bedroom *casas* and a two-bedroom apartment. There's a breezy terrace with a plunge pool and a sun deck, plus a large U-shaped bar and restaurant. Plans include tennis courts, horseback riding ($15 per hour), plus fishing ($20 per hour), and turtle tours ($20). Mountain bikes can be rented ($10 per day). Rates include breakfast.

An American couple, Darin and Kim, rent their **Finca Un Amor** (tel. 506/682-0619, darin@nosararealestate.com, www.fincaunamor.com, $25 s/d daily year-round, $650 per week low season; $800 high season), about four km south of Ostional and reached via a steep 4WD climb. The two-story, two-bedroom (one is a loft perfect for kids), open-plan log house has a tremendous ambience, plus large kitchen and a TV lounge, but only a funky outdoor bathroom with cold-water shower. The couple are also developing a Gaudí-meets-Fred Flintstone hilltop resort themed on a water garden with slides.

Restaurant Mirador Las Loras (tel. 506/682-0418, 7—10 P.M.), atop a hill at the south end of Ostional, is the preferred eatery. It sells burgers, spaghetti, seafood, and *casados* ($3–5).

Information and Services

The **ADIO** (Asociación Desarrollo Integral de Ostional, tel./fax 506/682-0470, adiotort@racsa.co.cr, http://ostionalcr.tripod.com) office is beside the road, on the northwest corner of the soccer field. Rodrigo Morera, the community leader, is helpful. The **toll and ranger booth,** run by ADIO, is 200 meters south of the soccer field, at the junction of the path to **Doug Robinson Marine Research Laboratory** (tel. 506/207-5966, cachi@biologia.vcr.ac.cr). The rustic hut houses research volunteers and scientists.

The *pulpería* at the northern end of the soccer field has a **public telephone.**

There's a **police station** (tel. 506/828-2892) here.

Getting There

A bus (tel. 506/221-7202) departs San José for Santa Cruz at 7 A.M., arriving at noon; from here, take the 12:30 P.M. bus to Ostional (three hours, returning at 5 A.M.); it may not run in wet season. Alternately, an Alfaro bus departs San José for Nosara at 6 A.M., arriving around noon. You can take a taxi (about $8) or walk to Ostional.

The dirt road between Ostional and Nosara requires you to ford the Río La Montaña (about five km south of Ostional), which can be impassable during wet season; sometimes a tractor will be there to pull you through for a fee. About one km further the road divides; that to the left (east) fords the Río Nosara just before entering the village of Nosara and is impassable in all but the most favorable conditions (the bridge has washed out); that to the right crosses the Río Nosara via a bridge and the community of **Santa Marta.**

Nosara to Sámara

NOSARA

Nosara boasts three of the best beaches in Nicoya, each with rocky tidepools where the seawater is heated by the sun—great for soaking. They are part of the Ostional Wildlife Refuge and are backed by hills smothered in moist tropical forest. **Playa Nosara** extends north from Punta Nosara and the river estuary to Ostional. It's backed by mangroves. An *arribada* occurred here for the first time in 1997. More are expected. Tiny **Playa Pelada** is tucked in a cove south of Punta Nosara, and has a blowhole at the south and a bat cave at the north end. **Playa Guiones,** separated from Playa Pelada by Punta Pelada, is a ruler-straight, five-km-long expanse of white sand washed by surf and, hence, popular with surfers. Swimmers need to beware of strong riptides.

The sleepy village of **Bocas de Nosara** is five km inland from the coast, five km south of Ostional, on the banks of the Río Nosara. It maintains a simple traditional Tico lifestyle, but otherwise offers little of appeal.

A large foreign community lives four km south of the village, where about 200 homes (almost all owned by foreign residents) are hidden amid the forest in the area known as the **Beaches of Nosara.** The roads are an intestinal labyrinth. Like any maze, it's easy to enter but getting out is sheer puzzlement, with dirt roads coiling and uncoiling like a snake. The **Nosara Civic Association** (tel. 506/682-0008, nosaracivicassociation@yahoo.com), the property owners' organization, keeps a tight rein on development.

The maritime zone fronting the beach is protected by the Forest Service, and wildlife abounds in the sprawling primary forest: coatimundis and howler monkeys are particularly common.

About 40 hectares are protected in the private **Reserva Biológica Nosara** (belonging to Lagarta Lodge) along the river, which harbors caimans and crocodiles.

For further information on Nosara, visit www.nosara.com or www.nosaratravel.com.

Entertainment and Events

In the village, the most atmospheric bars are **Bambú,** with live marimba on Saturdays; and **Disco Bar Tropicana,** with disco on Saturdays at 9 P.M. The **Gringo Grill** at Blew Dog Surf Club has an eight-ball tourney on Saturday at 2 P.M.; live music on Friday nights; and live tango on Monday nights.

Café de Paris has an open-air movie Fridays at 7 P.M. (free).

Sports and Recreation

Nosara Surf Shop (tel. 506/682-0186, fax 506/682-0451, www.safarisurfschool.com) is run by two Hawaiian brothers, who have a "Safari Surf School." It sells and rents boogie boards and surfboards.

Corky Carrol's Surf School, at Harbor Reef, offers lessons ($50 private; $30 pp group) and surfboard rental. Both Corky's and **Casa Río Nosara** offer jungle tours, kayak rental, plus horseback riding and boat trips. **Boca Nosara Tours** (tel. 506/682-0610, www.holidaynosa .com) offers horseback riding, fishing, plus canoeing and birding.

Iguana Expeditions, at the Gilded Iguana, offers sea-kayaking (from $35).

Black Marlin Sportfishing, also at Harbor Reef, and **Aventura Pelada Sportfishing** (tel. 506/682-0173) offer sportfishing.

Tuanis (see *Shopping*) rents snorkel gear ($5 daily) and offers guided turtle tours to Ostional ($10).

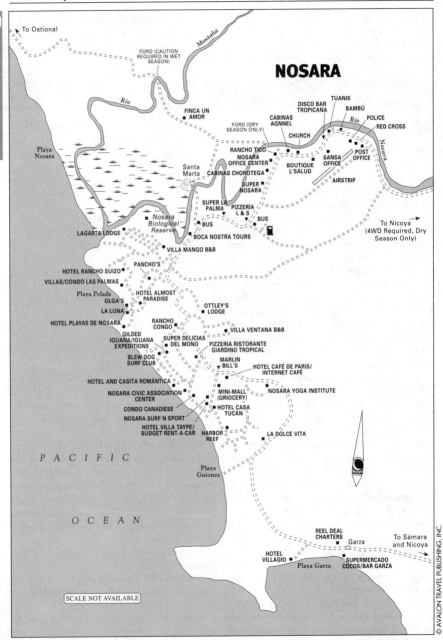

To Ostional

FORD (CAUTION REQUIRED IN WET SEASON)

Montaña

NOSARA

Río

FINCA UN AMOR

DISCO BAR TROPICANA

TUANIS

BAMBÚ

POLICE

RED CROSS

CABINAS AGNNEL

FORD (DRY SEASON ONLY)

CHURCH

Río

Playa Nosara

Santa Marta

RANCHO TICO

NOSARA OFFICE CENTER

CABINAS CHOROTEGA

BOUTIQUE L'SALUD

SANSA OFFICE

POST OFFICE

AIRSTRIP

Nosara

SUPER NOSARA

SUPER LA PALMA

PIZZERÍA L & S

BUS

To Nicoya (4WD Required, Dry Season Only)

Nosara Biological Reserve

BUS

BOCA NOSTRA TOURS

LAGARTA LODGE

VILLA MANGO B&B

PANCHO'S

HOTEL RANCHO SUIZO

VILLAS/CONDO LAS PALMAS

Playa Pelada

OLGA'S

LA LUNA

HOTEL PLAYAS DE NOSARA

HOTEL ALMOST PARADISE

OTTLEY'S LODGE

RANCHO CONGO

VILLA VENTANA B&B

GILDED IGUANA/IGUANA EXPEDITIONS

SUPER DELICIAS DEL MONO

PIZZERIA RISTORANTE GIARDINO TROPICAL

BLEW DOG SURF CLUB

MARLIN BILL'S

HOTEL CAFÉ DE PARIS/ INTERNET CAFÉ

HOTEL AND CASITA ROMÁNTICA

NOSARA CIVIC ASSOCIATION CENTER

MINI-MALL (GRIOCERY)

NOSARA YOGA INSTITUTE

CONDO CANADIESE

NOSARA SURF N SPORT

HOTEL CASA TUCÁN

HOTEL VILLA TAYPE/ BUDGET RENT-A-CAR

HARBOR REEF

LA DOLCE VITA

PACIFIC

Playa Guiones

OCEAN

REEL DEAL CHARTERS

Garza

To Sámara and Nicoya

HOTEL VILLAGIO

Playa Garza

SUPERMERCADO COCOS/BAR GARZA

SCALE NOT AVAILABLE

© AVALON TRAVEL PUBLISHING, INC.

NOSARA YOGA INSTITUTE

This nonresidential yoga education center (tel. 506/682-0071 or 866/439-4704, fax 506/682-0072, info@nosarayoga.com, www.nosarayoga.com) is dedicated to professional training and advanced career development for teachers and practitioners in the field of yoga and bodywork. A strong focus is given to health consciousness and spiritual renewal (its motif—a frog—symbolizes prosperity and abundance). Perched in the hills behind Playa Guiones, it's the perfect place to relax and recharge.

The insitute specializes in advanced techniques and offers intensive one- to four-week programs in yoga, meditation, Pranassage (private one-on-one yoga session, combining yoga assists and hand contact to support clients in deepening their yoga practice), plus nature and health programs.

My first visit to Costa Rica was as a participant in a holistic health retreat led by owner Amba Henderson, who runs the institute with husband Don Stapleton. Amba was program director (1977–83) of the renowned Kripalu Center for Yoga and Health in Massachusetts, of which Don was onetime CEO and for 20 years a monastic devotee. The couple continue to teach at Kripalu, and at the Omega Institute.

Accommodations

Camping: You can camp at Blew Dog Surf Camp (see below; $5).

Under $25: In the village, **Chorotega Bar y Cabinas** (tel. 506/682-0105) and **Cabinas Agnnel** (tel. 506/682-0142) offer simple rooms with private baths with cold water for about $5 pp.

$25–50: At Playa Guiones, **Rancho Congo** (tel./fax 506/682-0078, $25 s/d) has two large, cool cabins with raised thatched roofs, tile floors, fans, huge walk-in showers, and breezy verandas. The charming owner speaks fluent English, French, Spanish, and German. Rates include breakfast served on a porch. *A bargain!*

Café de Paris (see below) has a large dorm room with four beds for $29 s low season, $39 s high season ($10 each extra person);

Blew Dog Surf Camp (tel. 506/682-0080, info@blewdogs.com, www.blewdogs.com, $30 s/d) has nine octagonal cabins with tin roofs, screened openings, and hot water; they vary in size. Some have neat kitchenettes. Its Gringo Grill is a cool place with hammocks, pool table, and a floor entirely of diced tree trunks. It has a small pool with waterfall. It arranges surf trips to lonesome beach breaks.

The **Gilded Iguana** (tel. 506/680-0749, fax 506/682-0259, pattyedoe@racsa.co.cr, $25 s/d small, $35 s/d large, $45 s/d suite low season;

$40 s/d small, $50 large, $60 suite peak season) has four spacious, cross-ventilated rooms—two up, two down—with fans, refrigerators, coffeemakers, toasters, and large walk-in showers with hot water. There are also two two-bedroom suites. There's a pleasing bar-cum-restaurant with TV, and sea-kayaking is offered. Six a/c units were to be added.

Ottley's Lodge (tel. 506/682-0633, fax 506/682-0611, g_ottley@yahoo.com, www.lodge vistadelmar.com, $45 s/d), also known as Lodge Vista del Mar, astride a ridgetop high in the hills overlooking Beaches of Nosara, is recommended for its awesome vistas of both jungle and coast. This three-story modern structure has nine cross-ventilated rooms and one suite, all modestly furnished, with fans, cool limestone floors, and private bathroom with hot water. One has a/c. It has an Olympic-length lap pool, plus laundry, and a simple outdoor kitchen for guests. Rates include breakfast.

Casa Tucán (tel./fax 506/682-0113, info @casatucan.net, www.casatucan.net, $29 s/d small units, $39 s/d large units), opposite Hotel Villa Taype, is run by Richard Moffett, whose home sits amid lawns, with a pool and airy *ranchito* restaurant. Eight modestly furnished apartments for four people, with kitchen, are in a two-story adjunct.

Hotel Almost Paradise (P.O. Box 15, Nosara 5233, tel./fax 682-0173, AlmostParadise@iname .com, www.infoweb.co.cr/paradise, $30 s, $45 d) is another German-owned property that enjoys a hilltop setting 10 minutes from the beach. Its haphazardly charming construction (marred by some ugly tin roofs) is enhanced by creeping vines and flowers. Six rooms of different sizes all have private baths with hot water, plus access to a wide balcony with hammocks and splendid vistas. The restaurant serves mostly German and vegetarian fare. It has a pool. Rates include breakfast.

Readers continue to complain about the intrusive, never-ending construction, and other problems, at **Hotel Playas de Nosara** (P.O. Box 4-5257, Nosara, tel./fax 506/682-0121, vailas @racsa.co.cr, www.nosarabeachhotel.com), which squats atop Punta Guiones.

$50–100: If setting is foremost in mind, then check out **Lagarta Lodge** (P.O. Box 18-5233, Nosara, tel. 506/682-0035, fax 506/682-0135, lagarta@racsa.co.cr, www.lagarta.com, $45 s, $50 d low season; $60 s, $65 d high season), with a setting atop Punta Nosara offering stupendous vistas north along Ostional. Four rooms are in a two-story house (the upper story reached by a spiral staircase), and three are in a smaller unit with whitewashed stone walls. The latter, with one entire wall a screened window, have mezzanine bedrooms overlooking voluminous open showers and bathrooms. Some have king-size beds. The lodge has a swimming pool and trails leading down to the river and the Reserva Biológica Nosara; boats and canoes are rented ($10). Readers have raved about the meals. Rates include tax and breakfast.

At Playa Guiones, the Swiss-run **Rancho Suizo Lodge** (tel. 506/682-0057, fax 506/682-0055, rsuizo@infoweb.co.cr, www.nosara.ch, $28 s/d low season, $38 s/d high season) has 10 thatched *cabinas* with small but pleasant rooms and private baths with hot water. It has a restaurant and Jacuzzi. The lush grounds contain hammocks and a small aviary. Trails lead to the beach. It's run by René Spinnier and Ruth Léscher, who have created an agreeable ambience, despite a reputation for feistiness. A notice in the cabinas

reads "No opposite sex visitors" (two female German guests reported, "Sex is *verboten!*" I think they jest), and other readers have complained about prices and lackadaisical service. Rates include tax and buffet.

The German-run, beachfront **Hotel y Casita Romántica** (P.O. Box 45-5233, Nosara, tel./fax 506/682-0019 or 506/682-0272, casroma@racsa .co.cr, www.hotelcasaromantica.com, $45 s, $55 d low season; $55 s, $65 d high season) offers eight rooms in beautiful two-story houses with exquisitely patterned tile floors and gracious yellows and earth tones. Upper rooms are cross-ventilated two-bedroom apartments with kitchens, and wide shaded veranda with lounge chairs. The landscaped grounds contain a pool, *ranchito* with hammocks, and restaurant. It has a tennis court, and you can rent surf and boogie boards. Rates include breakfast.

The German-run **Hotel Villa Taype** (P.O. Box 8-5233, Nosara, tel. 506/682-0333, fax 506/682-0187, info@villataype.com, www .villataype.com, $35 s, $40 d with fan $45 s, $60 d with a/c, $90 bungalows low season; $40 s, $50 d with fan, $60/75 with a/c, $100 bungalows high season), within spitting distance of the beach, offers four small yet pleasingly furnished rooms with fans, 12 rooms and five bungalows, each with TV, refrigerator, and terrace, plus private baths and hot water (nine have a/c). The landscaped grounds boast shade trees, a swimming pool, a tennis court, plus a large bar and restaurant. There's a second restaurant and TV lounge. It rents surf and boogie boards. Rates include breakfast.

The attractive **Café de Paris** (P.O. Box 52-5253 Nosara, tel. 506/682-0087, fax 506/682-0089, info@cafedeparis.net, www.cafedeparis.net, $29 s, $39 d standard, $49 s, $59 d with kitchenette low season; $39 s, $49 d standard, $59 s, $69 d with kitchenette high season) is run by a young French couple who have 12 simply furnished a/c rooms with ceiling fans, a slanted wooden ceiling with egress for the heat, and private bath with hot water. Rooms vary in size, and include a two-bedroom "suite bungalow" with kitchen. There are also five bungalows plus two hilltop villas billed as "luxury," though moderate is more accurate: they offer fabulous views and each has a spiral staircase to two and three bedrooms, respectively, plus hardwood floors, simple furnishings, an open kitchen ($99 bungalow, $100 beach house, $120 villas year-round). The restaurant is beneath a soaring *ranchito*. Facilities include a souvenir store, the splendid café, a lap pool, pool table, massage, and Internet café. The owners also manage three two-bedroom beach houses (next to Gilded Iguana) with kitchens. It closes for October. Rates include breakfast.

Set in lush gardens, **Harbor Reef Lodge** (P.O. Box 27-5233 Bocas de Nosara, tel. 506/682-0059, fax 506/682-0060, reservaciones@racsa.co.cr, www.harborreef.com, $50 s, $58 d rooms, $70–85 suites, from $100 for houses low season; $69 s, $74 d rooms, $90–109 suites, from $125 for houses high season) has four handsomely appointed a/c suites with large sitting rooms and wet bars, hardwood ceilings and furnishings, louvered and screened windows, refrigerators, and balconies. Four Playa Guiones suites have kitchens, and it has six two-, three-, and four-bedroom *casas*. Facilities include a thatched restaurant, a raised deck with pool and wet bar, and a souvenir store. Sportfishing and a variety of tours are offered.

Pancho's (tel. 506/682-0591, panchoscr @racsa.co.cr, $50 s/d with fan, $60 s/d with a/c) offers great promise, though only half-complete at last visit, when it had three cross-ventilated cabins facing a magnificent circular pool lit by night. Each has ceiling fans, terra-cotta floors, raised ceilings, kitchens, and private bathrooms with hot water. Steve and his Mexican wife, Ofelia, were adding A-frames with lofts.

Prefer self-catering? **Condo Canadiense del Sol** (tel. 506/682-0350, rong@telusplanet.net, www.condocandiense.com, $70 s/d low season, $105 s/d high season) has four condo units with huge lounges, lots of white tilework, raised wooden ceilings with fans, and large walk-in showers. They're simply albeit nicely furnished and open to a lush garden with freeform pool, sundeck, and shade *rancho*.

Run by a delightful French-Portuguese couple, **Villa Mango B&B** (tel. 506/682-0130, villa-mango@racsa.co.cr, www.villamangocr.com, $59 s, $79 d) is a real bed-and-breakfast that enjoys views over Playa Guiones. At last visit it had two bedrooms; two additional rooms and three cabins were to be added. Highlights include parquet floors, raised wooden ceilings, and large picture windows, although the villa is modestly furnished. It has a kidney-shaped pool (monkeys come to drink!) and sundeck with bamboo rockers and hammocks. It is "lifestyle-friendly." Rates include breakfast and tax.

At the deluxe end of the scale, head two km uphill to **Villa La Ventana B&B** (tel. 506/682-0316, www.villalaventana.com, $100 s/d low season, $120 high season), the spectacular home of Jim and Linda Wall. This huge home boasts terra-cotta floors and gorgeous furnishings on an African wildlife theme—leopard-skin covers, zebra rugs, etc. It has three rooms, all with four-poster wrought-iron beds, rattan furnishings, ceiling fans, and private terraces; the master suite is a true stunner with all-around vistas tailor-made for *Condé Nast Traveler's* "Room with a View." The highlight is a columned terrace inset with horizon pool and stupendous views. It's bargain-priced.

Bibi and Arne Bendixen (tel. 540/297-8485, bandab@mindspring.com) rent apartments nearby. And Alexa Bolles runs **Nosara Beach Rentals** (www.nosarabeachrentals.com).

Food

The **Gringo Grill** (11:30 A.M.–midnight, $3–5) at Blew Dog Surf Camp, is favored by surfers. Its menu ranges from buffalo wings and grilled chicken sandwiches to sushi.

Marlin Bill's (tel. 506/682-0458, 11 A.M.–2 P.M., and 6 P.M.–midnight, $3.50–13) offers great dining on a lofty, breeze-swept terrace with views. Lunch might include blackened tuna salad or sandwich, French onion soup ($3.50), and brownie sundae or Key lime pie. Pork loin chops, New York strip steak, and eggplant parmesan typify the dinner menu. The bar has a TV.

Olga's, a rustic place fronting Playa Pelada, is recommended for seafood ($5 average). Tucked above the beach 50 meters to the south is **La Luna Bar and Grill** (11 A.M.–9 P.M., $5), an atmospheric place with cobblestone floor and bottle-green glass bricks, and a terrace for dining by sunset; it serves lentil soup, sushi rolls, carpaccio, etc., and plays world music from Dylan to reggae. **Café de Paris** (7 A.M.–11 P.M., $4–10) serves crepes, French toast, omelettes; sandwiches such as chicken curry or turkey; and entrées such as penne pasta with creamed pesto fish, and duck breast in green pepper sauce, plus 12 types of pizza.

The **Gilded Iguana** (tel. 506/682-0259, pattydoe@racsa.co.cr, $2.50–8) is a favorite with locals and serves super tacos, stuffed jalapeños, tuna salad, seafoods, and great shakes. It has live music Tuesday nights.

For Italian, check out **Giardino Tropicale** (tel. 506/682-0258, 6–10 P.M.), a rustic affair that offers 12 types of pizza, plus pastas. **Casa Tucán** (7 A.M.–11 P.M.) serves pizzas and gourmet Italian fare (owner Richard is a graduate of the California Culinary Academy). And the thatched restaurant at **Hotel y Casita Romántica** (6–9 P.M. Mon.–Sat.) serves international fare (from beef stroganoff to seafood) in a delightful poolside setting.

La Dolce Vita (tel. 506/682-0107), two km south on the road to Sámara, also serves nouvelle treats, such as penne fish, and grouper butter lemon ($6–8) in a rustic rough-hewn log-and-thatch restaurant that can get lively in season.

Pancho's (tel. 506/682-0591, noon–9:30 P.M. high season only) serves Mexican fare (all dishes under $5) and killer margaritas under thatch.

The **Harbor Reef General Store** and **Mini-Super Delicias del Mundo** in Beaches of Nosara sell groceries and deli items, as does **Super La Paloma,** in Boca de Nosara.

Information and Services

Tuanis (tel./fax 506/682-0249, tuanisart@racsa .co.cr) has a splendid selection of batiks, hammocks, and swimsuits; the shop also acts as a tourist information center and rents cruiser ("banana") bikes ($8 daily, $40 weekly).

Nosara Surf Shop rents ATVs (from $25 daily).

There's a **Red Cross** (tel. 506/682-0175), on the northeast side of the soccer field in Nosara; a clinic 600 meters east of the soccer field oper-

ates an ambulance and is open 7 A.M.–4 P.M. Mon.–Thurs., 7 A.M.–noon Friday. **Boutiq L'Salud** (tel. 506/682-0282), south of the soccer field, is the local pharmacy.

The **police station**, on the northeast side of the soccer field, has no telephone; call the public telephone (tel. 506/682-0088 or 506/682-0288) outside the station.

A bank was being built at last visit, next to Café de Paris.

The post office (7:30–11:30 A.M. and 1:30–5:30 P.M. Mon.–Fri.) is at the north end of the runway.

Café de Paris (7 A.M.–9 P.M.) has an Internet café with satellite connection ($10 per hour). **Nosara Office Center** (tel. 506/682-0181, newsfund@racsa.co.cr) offers email, fax, and photocopying services.

Café de Paris also has a **laundry,** as does **Mini-Super Delicias del Mundo** ($6 per bag).

Getting There

Sansa (tel. 506/257-9414, www.grupotaca.com) and **Nature Air** (tel. 506/220-3054, www.natureair.com) have twice-daily service between San José and Nosara.

A bus (tel. 506/222-2750) departs San José for Nosara from Calle 14, Avenidas 3/5, daily at 6 A.M.; the return bus departs from Bocas del Nosara at 12:45 P.M. A bus departs Nicoya for Nosara at 5 A.M., 10 A.M., noon, and 2:30 P.M., returning at 5 A.M., 7 A.M., noon, and 3 P.M.

Budget Rent-a-Car is represented at Hotel Villa Taype.

There is no longer a direct road link between Nosara and Nicoya. You must drive south 15 km to Barco Quebrado and turn inland; the dirt road meets the paved Nicoya-Sámara road at Terciopelo.

Clemente Matarrita sells gas at his little "Servicentro Nosara" in Bocas de Nosara.

BAHÍA GARZA TO SÁMARA

The dirt road from Nosara leads south to Playa Sámara (26 km) via the horseshoe-shaped **Bahía Garza** (8 km south of Nosara), rimmed by a pebbly white-sand beach. Beyond Garza the road—

4WD recommended—cuts inland from the coast, which remains out of view the rest of the way.

At **Barco Quebrado,** about 15 km south of Nosara and 11 km north of Sámara, a road heads north uphill to Terciopelo, on the paved Sámara–Nicoya road (en route, you ford the Río Frío). Continuing south from Barco Quebrado on the coast road, you reach **Esterones,** where a side road leads two km to **Playa Buena Vista,** in Bahía Montereyna, while the "main" road divides, north for Terciopelo and south for Sámara (the direct coast road to Sámara requires fording the Río Buena Vista, which isn't always possible; if impassable, take a one-km detour on the Terciopelo road then turn right for Sámara). There are crocodiles in the river estuary and adjacent lagoons.

Accommodations

The once pleasant **Hotel el Villaggio** has a splendid location at Playa Garza, but at last visit was looking extremely run-down and cannot be recommended.

Campers, backpackers, and offbeat travelers will appreciate **El Castillo Montereyna,** (tel. 506/824-2822, $12 pp dorms, $15 pp private rooms), at Playa Buena Vista, beside the mouth of the river. Friendly, English-speaking owner Don Claus, from Germany, has created a rambling freeform house of natural stone painted in lively tropical pastels, with glassless wrought-iron windows. This Moroccan-inspired oddity has two dorms, and eight rooms with private bathrooms; campers share toilets and showers in the garden. Simple barbecue dinners are served at a rainbow-hued beachfront bar with tin-roof and communal kitchen. It's used by the back-to-basics Green Tortoise tour company.

You'll fall in love with the German-run **Flying Crocodile Lodge** (tel./fax 506/656-0483, flycroco@racsa.co.cr, www.flying-crocodile.com, $30 s, $40 d standard, $45 s, $55 d larger unit low season; $40 s, $50 d standard, $60 s, $70 d larger unit high season), between Esterones and Playa Buena Vista. This marvelous spot is an artistic vision with eight thatched, exquisite cabins spaced well apart in beautifully maintained grounds. Each boasts walls splashed with lively murals, plus hardwood floors, curving concrete bench seats with cushions, a soothing melange of Caribbean colors, and endearing bathrooms boasting black stone floors. Some have futon beds; others have bamboo furniture with contempo fabrics. One has a loft bedroom and a magnificent all-stone bathroom with murals. Two smaller, wooden units are lofts in octagonal huts with conical roofs, screened windows, and beds draped with mosquito nets. The coup de grâce is the Oriental Apartment, with a uniquely creative Moorish motif: its white tile floor is inset with a star mosaic and melds into blue tile, sky-blue and mango-red walls inset with Moorish windows; plate-glass windows reach from floor to ceiling; and the imaginative skylit freeform bathroom is topped by a ceiling inset with stars of stained glass. It also has a/c bungalows with kitchen. A pool has a water swing and slide. It has horses and rents mountain bikes, motorcycles, and 4WD vehicles.

Alegría (tel. 506/390-9026, info@alegria-cr.de, www.alegria-cr.de, $20 s/d low season, $25 s/d high season), 400 meters toward the coast beyond Flying Crocodile, is a seminar center and yoga retreat. It offers eight cabin-tents made of bamboo, with woven palm floors, clear plastic A-frame roofs, and mosquito nets and mattresses. They're accessed by a steep trail. It has an open-air yoga platform (also used for Sunday salsa lessons) and an open-air kitchen-bar and terrace with tatami mats overhanging the hillside with astounding views over Playa Esterones. Guests cook for each other and share outdoor "rainforest" showers. The Belgian owner also rents a beautiful wooden home ($50 s/d nightly, $200 per week) with wrap-around veranda and huge, gorgeous bathroom with step-down shower of natural stone. Rates include breakfast and lunch.

Activities

Fancy a flight in an Ultra-light plane? Then head to **Flying Crocodile Flying Center** (see above), where Guido, a licensed commercial pilot, will take you up in one of his five Ultra-lights ($60 for 20 minutes). Licensed pilots can rent the planes ($70 per flying hour). And flying lessons are offered ($90).

Reel Deal Charters (tel. 506/396-9894), in Garza, offers sportfishing.

Playa Sámara to Carrillo

PLAYA SÁMARA

Playa Sámara, about 15 km south of Garza, is a popular budget destination for Ticos as well as surfers, and travelers in search of the offbeat. The lure is its relative accessibility and attractive horseshoe-shaped bay with a light-gray beach, about three km long.

Sámara can be reached directly from Nicoya by paved road (Hwy. 150) via Belén. The village is in the center of the beach. A cattle *finca* divides it from **Cangrejal,** a hamlet at the north end of the beach. They are connected by road, but you can drive along the beach. Playa Sámara extends south about two km to the small ramshackle fishing community of **Matapalo,** where the most enormous strangler fig tree you'll ever see grows in the sands!

Useful links include www.virtualsamara.com and www.samarabeach.com.

Entertainment

The **Tutti Frutti** is a low-key bar and disco at the Hotel Playa Sámara; it's a smoke-filled, sweat-box kinda place and produces a fair share of local drunks. The *real* disco scene happens at **Hotel Isla Chora** on Thursday, Friday, and Saturday nights, in high season only.

Sports and Recreation

Tropical Latitudes (tel./fax 506/656-0120, rocio@latitude10.com) is a U.S.-run tour-planning service that also represents **Bike Costa Rica,** which offers mountain bike tours.

Sámara Sub Sport Diving (tel. 506/656-0700, samarasub@hotmail.com) offers scuba diving and snorkeling.

Jesse's Surf School (tel. 506/656-0055, whiteagle@racsa.co.cr) rents surfboards and offers beginner's lessons.

Accommodations

Camping: I recommend **Camping Río Lagarto** (tel. 506/656-0028, $4 pp), with thatched campsites on lawns with a pleasant beachfront, riverside setting. It has a small restaurant. You can rent tents ($1).

Camping and Bar Olas (tel. 506/656-0187, olas@virtualsamara.com, www.virtualsamara.com, $30 s/d) is a simple Yankee-owned beachside bar and restaurant with shaded campsites with lockers for $3 per person. It also has palm-thatch A-frame huts. There's a pool table, and snorkel gear, surfboards, and bicycles can be rented.

Under $25: Several very basic places at Cangrejal cannot be recommended.

Budget travelers should skip the **Hotel/Restaurant Playa Sámara** (tel. 506/656-0190), popular with Ticos, and consider **Cabinas Arena** (tel. 506/656-0320, $6 pp low season; $8 pp high season), with 12 clean, simply furnished rooms in a modern two-story unit; each has a fan and private bath with cold water. Upstairs rooms have verandas.

Chalets Coquito (tel. 506/656-0122, $10 s, $15 d low season; $20/25 high season) has six simply furnished A-frame chalets with one-up, one-down units. Each has screened, louvered windows, fans, clean albeit small private bathrooms with hot water, and small patios.

Casa Naranja (tel./fax 506/656-0220, $12 pp year-round) is named for the color of this charming two-story home run by two French women. Rooms have fans and private bathrooms with hot water. Rates include breakfast.

The Italian-run **Cabinas Brasas** (tel./fax 506/656-0741, $26 s/d) has four clean, simply furnished rooms with king-size beds, fans, verandas, and private baths with hot water. There's also a large unit that accommodates four people. It rents snorkeling gear and mountain bikes, and has a simple open-air eatery.

At Matapalo, **Cabinas El Mango** (tel. 506/656-0355. $6.50 d low season; $10 high season) has five upstairs rooms with fans, and private bath but cold water only. It has a simple *soda* (simple restaurant) popular with local fishermen.

$25–50: A good bargain is the German-run **Hotel Belvedere** (tel./fax 506/656-0213, hotel-

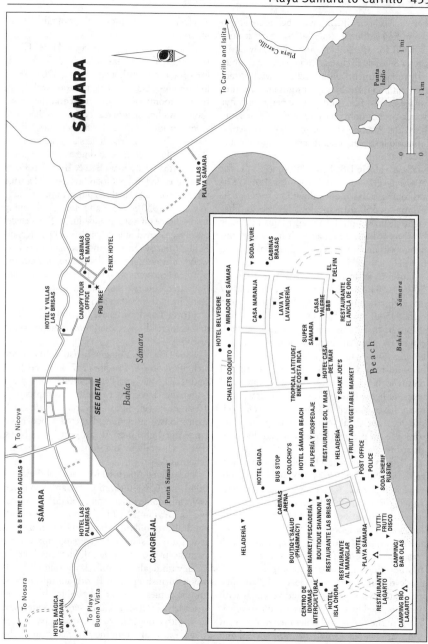

© AVALON TRAVEL PUBLISHING, INC.

belvedere@hotmail.com, www.belvederesamara
.com, $35 s/d low season, $42 s/d high season,
$55 s/d for apartments year-round), with 12
pretty Swiss-style chalets (ranging from doubles
to two apartments with kitchens) with attractive bamboo furnishings, mosquito nets, whitewashed walls, fans, and private baths with hot
water. Some rooms have king-size beds; some
have a/c. A stone-walled, mosaic-tiled Jacuzzi
sits amid lush gardens, and a pool. Rates include
breakfast and tax.

Casa Valerie B&B (tel. 506/656-0511, fax
506/656-0317, casavaleriaf@hotmail.com, $20
s/d rooms, $40 s/d bungalows low season; $30
s/d rooms, $50 s/d bungalows high season) has
eight clean, simply furnished rooms plus four
beachfront bungalows, all with hot water, and
hammocks under the palms. Valerie makes filling
health food breakfasts.

Hotel Casa del Mar (tel. 506/656-0264, fax
506/656-0129, casasama@racsa.co.cr, www
.casadelmarsamara.com, $20 s, $30 d shared
bath, $35/40 private bath low season; $34 s, 40 d
shared bath, $46/58 private bath high season),
run by French-Canadians, is one of several good
bargains in town. This relaxing and well-run
bed-and-breakfast has 17 modestly furnished
rooms with fans, private baths, hot water, and
heaps of light through louvered windows (two
rooms have a kitchenette). Attractive decor, good-
size beds, and a balcony overlooking the ocean
complete the picture. There's a Jacuzzi. Rates include breakfast and tax.

The Swiss-Italian-run **Hotel Mágica Cantar-
rana** (tel. 506/656-0071, fax 506/656-0260,
magica@racsa.co.cr, www.playasamara.com, $35 s,
$45 d rooms, $59 s/d one-bedroom apartment, $129 two-bedroom apartment low sea-
son; $45 s, $55 d rooms, $79 s/d one-bedroom
apartment, $139 two-bedroom apartment high
season), on the road to Playa Buena Vista, is
another modern, two-story complex with 10
modestly furnished rooms featuring fans, private baths with hot water, and verandas with
hammocks. Upstairs rooms are cross-ventilated by the doors and balconies to the front
and rear. There's a small swimming pool and
sun terrace, a shady open-sided restaurant, and

an open-air TV lounge with pool table. It offers tours.

Charm and character pervade **Hotel Giada**
(tel. 506/656-0132, fax 506/656-0131, htgiada
@racsa.co.cr, www.hotelgiada.net, $26 s, $38 d
low season; $29 s, $44 d high season), with 13 attractive rooms with faux terra-cotta tile floors,
sponge-washed ocher/cream decor, bamboo beds
(some are king-size), and wide balconies. There's
a pool, plus a pizzeria. It acts as a Sansa agent.
Rates include breakfast and tax.

A German couple run **Bed & Breakfast Entre
Dos Aguas** (tel./fax 506/656-0641, entredosaguas
@racsa.co.cr, $24 small, $29 medium, $42 large
low season; $30/35/45 high season), a charming
tropical take on a stone-and-timber Swiss chalet
set in a groomed hillside garden, 400 meters inland. It has seven pleasing rooms with rustic
wooden furnishings, tile floors, fans, and circular
private bathrooms with walls of riverstones plus
hot water. There's a stone bar and a shaded patio.
Rates include breakfast and tax.

Hotel Las Palmeras, betwixt the village
and Cangrejal, was closed for a total remake at
last visit.

$50–100: The **Villagio Turístico Isla Chora**
(tel. 506/656-0174 or 506/257-3032, fax 506/
656-0173, islachora@samarabeach.com, www
.samarabeach.com) is a handsome complex with
10 simple yet elegant rooms and four a/c apartments in two-story units that circle a pool amid
landscaped grounds. At last visit it was being
used exclusively by the Centro de Idiomas Intercultural.

The striking **Apartotel Mirador** (tel. 506/656-
0044, fax 656-0046, mdsamara@racsa.co.cr,
www.miradordesamara.com, $60 up to five peo-
ple low season, $110 high season) commands
the hill overlooking Sámara. German-owned,
it sets a high standard. Five large apartments
each sleep five and have full kitchens. They're
clean within, almost clinical, with simple hardwood furnishings and floors, mosquito nets,
and balconies. A beautiful pool fed by a water
cascade is inset in a multi-tiered wooden sun
deck with lounge chairs. Imagine the panoramic
views, especially from the tower containing the
open-walled restaurant—serving nouvelle cui-

sine from a French chef—and bar. This property has lots of steps.

Hotel Sámara Beach (tel. 506/656-0218, fax 506/656-0326, samara@racsa.co.cr, www.hotel samarabeach.com, $30 s, $45 d with fan, $40/55 with a/c low season; $55/65 with fan, $65/75 with a/c high season) is a two-story, 20-room complex with private baths and hot water. Rooms are spacious and bright and have king-size beds, and patios; some have a/c. The hotel has a small swimming pool, plus a bar-cum-restaurant under thatch. It offers tours and rents bicycles ($5 per hour). Rates include tax and breakfast.

Bill, a friendly fella from Washington state, runs the **Fenix Hotel** (P.O. Box 31-5235 Sámara, tel. 506/656-0158, fax 506/656-0162, confenix@racsa.co.cr, www.fenixhotel.com, $45 s/d low season, $65 high season), at Matapalo. It has six simple rooms pleasantly furnished with lively fabrics and bamboo, each with lofty ceiling with fan, mosquito nets on beds, a fully equipped kitchen, plus shower with hot water. They face onto a plunge pool. It has a laundry.

Genuinely upscale, **Hotel Las Brisas del Pacífico** (P.O. Box 14, Playa Sámara, tel. 506/656-0250, fax 506/656-0076, brisasdelpacifico@racsa .co.cr, www.lasbrisascostarica.com, $65 s, $70 d junior bungalow, $85 s, $95 d a/c sky room, $80–100 s, $85–105 bungalow low season; $80 s, $85 d junior bungalow, $100 s, $105 d a/c sky room, $100–120 s, $105–125 bungalow high season), about 600 meters south of Sámara, is a German-run hotel with 38 rooms with whitewashed stone walls, and private baths with hot water (some have a/c; others have fans) Facilities include an open-air restaurant facing the ocean, two swimming pools, two Jacuzzis, and a shady lounging area under palms. Separate bungalows sit on a hill, with ocean views.

If you prefer a "tourist village" feel, consider **Villas Playa Sámara** (tel. 506/656-0372, fax 506/656-0109, hotel@villasplayasamara.com, www.villasplayasamara.com), at the southern end of Playa Sámara, two km south of Matapalo. It operates as a timeshare for Costa Ricans, and can get lively on weekends.

Food

The open-air **Restaurante Sol** 506/656-0531) offers breakfasts *pinto* ($3), and burgers, sandwic...es, tortillas, and *casados* (set meals, $3–4), plus *batidos* ($1). Opposite is **Restaurante Las Brasas** (tel. 506/656-0546, noon–10 P.M.), an atmospheric open-air log structure serving gazpacho ($3.75), paella ($9), omelettes, and surf-and-turf.

The roadside **Pizzería & Pasta A Go Go** at Hotel Giada is an atmospheric Italian restaurant with pastas, and more than 20 types of pizzas; open 1–10 P.M. daily.

I like the creative menu at the thatched, beach-front **Restaurante El Ancla** (10 A.M.–10 P.M. Fri.–Wed., $5–10), serving beef stroganoff, garlic sea bass, and calamari.

Nearby, my favorite spot is the thatched **El Delfin** (tel. 506/656-0418, 9 A.M.–10 P.M., $2.50–9), an open-air beachfront restaurant run by a charming French family. It's romantically floodlit at night; jazz riffs add their own romantic note. The menu includes salade niçoise, fish in white wine sauce, pastas, thin-crust pizza, and scrumptious desserts such as banana splits.

The yang to El Delfin's yin is **Soda Sheriff Rustic** (7 A.M.–9 P.M. Tue.–Sun.), a perfectly no-frills roughhewn diner right on the sands. Even better is **Shake Joe's** (tel. 506/656-0717, 10 A.M.–10 P.M. Tue.–Sun., $2.50–8), an offbeat hangout with oversize sofas with Guatemalan fabrics, plus roughhewn tables and hammocks strewn around the gravel courtyard; it serves a French toast breakfast with tuna salad and eggs, plus smoked salmon, salade niçoise, and ravioli.

The **Casa Naranja** (6–10 P.M.) offers Afro-Caribbean-French fusion cuisine and has a *crepería* selling crepes; its menu includes *crema de asparagus, medaillons de boeuf* in green pepper sauce, and banana rum mousse.

The thatched, open-air, and colorful **Restaurante Colocho's** (tel. 506/656-0393, 11 A.M.–10 P.M.) also serves good, reasonably priced seafood, including paellas, and *casados* (set meals; $2.50).

You can buy groceries at **Super La Sámara.**

Information and Services

The post office and **police** (tel. 506/656-0436) are by the beach, near the soccer field. There's a public telephone here.

The **Boutiq L'Salud** (tel. 506/656-0727) is a small pharmacy next to Cabinas Arena; 8 A.M.–5 P.M. Mon.–Fri., 8 A.M.–noon Saturday.

Lava Ya Lavandería (tel. 506/656-0059) is open 8 A.M.–6 P.M. daily.

The **Centro de Idiomas Intercultural** (tel. 506/656-0127, www.interculturacostarica.com) offers language courses from $175 per week.

Getting There

Sansa (tel. 506/257-9414, www.grupotaca.com) and **Nature Air** (tel. 506/220-3054, www.natureair.com) fly daily to Playa Carillo (see *Playa Carrillo,* below).

Buses (Tracopa Alfaro, tel. 506/222-2666, tracopa@racsa.co.cr) depart San José for Sámara from Calles 14, Avenidas 3/5, daily at 12:30 P.M. and 6:15 P.M. ($7; five hours). Buses depart Nicoya (Empresa Rojas, tel. 506/685-5032; three blocks east of the park) for Sámara daily at 6 A.M., 7:45 A.M., 10 A.M. (to Carillo), noon (to Carillo), 3 P.M. (to Carillo), 4:20 P.M., and 5 P.M.$1.25).

Buses depart from behind Cabinas Arenas in Sámara for San José at 4:30 A.M. and 8:45 A.M.; and for Nicoya at 5:30 A.M., 6 A.M. (from Carrillo), 7 A.M., 8:45 A.M., 11:15 A.M. (from Carrillo), 1:15 P.M. (from Carrillo), 4:30 P.M., and 5:30 P.M. (from Carrillo).

PLAYA CARRILLO

South of Sámara, the paved road continues over **Punta Indio** and drops down to coral-colored Playa Carrillo (five km south of Sámara), one of the finest beaches in Costa Rica, fringed with palm trees and encusped by wooded cliffs. An offshore reef protects the bay. The fishing hamlet of Carrillo nestles around the estuary of the Río Sangrado at the southern end of the bay. Other beaches—Playa Laguna and Playa del Sur—are tucked into hidden coves further south.

Sports and Recreation

Rick Ruhlow (tel./fax 506/656-0091, kingfish@racsa.co.cr) also offers sportfishing, as does **Costa Rica VIP Sportfishing** (tel. 506/654-4049 or 800/346-2629, fax 506/654-4968, twocan@racsa.co.cr, www.vipsportfishing.com), which uses the *Two-Can* mother ship for sportfishing (Dec.–April.).

VIP Watersports (tel. 506/656-0606), on the hill below Guanamar, offers tour information and an Internet café.

Accommodations and Food

I like the U.S.-run **Punto Carrillo Sunset B&B** (tel. 506/656-0011, fax 506/656-0009, puertocarillosunset@yahoo.com, $60 s/d), a beautiful hilltop property with a marvelous wooden deck inset with pool, and an open, thatched bar and restaurant with views. It has eight a/c rooms with solar-heated hot water showers. Rates include breakfast.

A dirt road near the south end of the beach leads uphill to **Guesthouse Casa Pericos** (tel. 506/656-0061, $ 8 pp dorm, $12 pp rooms), run by a young German couple, Tom and Petra, who have three well-lit, cross-ventilated, simply furnished rooms with heaps of large screened windows. Guests can use the kitchen. The downstairs room has a beautiful sea-blue tile floor; two upstairs rooms have A-frame roofs, wooden floors, dorm-style beds (one has three singles; the other has two singles and a bunk), and simple bathroom with cold water. Hammocks are slung on a breezy veranda with views through the trees to the beach. Tom is a PADI instructor and offers diving and horseback tours.

A charmer is the **Hotel Esperanza** (tel./fax 506/656-0564, esperanz@racsa.co.cr, www.hotelesperanza.com, $30–40 s/d low season, $40–50 high season), a French-Canadian family-run bed-and-breakfast 100 meters north of Guanamar and set in a delightful garden with an arbor. It has seven rooms—some larger than others—arrayed along an arcade; each has attractive wooden furnishings, fans, quality linens, and bathrooms with murals, tile trim, and hot water. A restaurant for guests only specializes in seafood. The owners are fluent in English, French, Spanish, and German. Rates include full breakfast.

About three km south of Carrillo is a gem: **El Sueño Tropical** (tel. 506/656-0151, fax 506/656-0152, info@elsuenotropical.com, www .elsuenotropical.com, $37 s, $43 d room, $69/84 apartments low season; $47 s $54 d rooms, $85/94 apartments high season, $10 more for a/c), run by three gracious and charming brothers from Verona, Italy. The tropical motif is everywhere throughout this lushly landscaped setting. There are 12 clean, simple a/c bungalows with terra-cotta tiles, king-size bamboo beds, and direct-dial telephones. There are also three new apartments. The elegant hilltop restaurant has a soaring *palenque* roof. There's a pool and a kids' pool. Howler monkeys abound in the surrounding forest. It has a minibus for tours. Rates include breakfast.

Guanamar Beach and Sportfishing Resort (P.O. Box 7-1880, San José, tel. 506/656-0054, fax 506/656-0001, info@hotelguanamar.com, www.hotelguanamar.com, $45 s/d standard, $50 deluxe, $110 suite low season; $110 s/d standard, $120 deluxe, $180 suite high season), on the hillside at the southern end of the bay, is one of Costa Rica's premier sportfishing resorts. Forty a/c *cabinas*—connected by manicured walkways—cascade down the hillside. Each has ceiling fans, bright furniture in primary colors, satellite TV, phone, and private patio. The resort has a romantic rough wood-and-thatch restaurant, a small casino, and a small swimming pool. It has a private airstrip, plus watersports, horseback riding, and mountain bikes.

Vanni, the gifted Italian chef at **El Sueño Tropical,** produces such delights as fusilli, and ravioli de pescado ($5–8).

The handsome, open-air, thatched **Toucan Too/Bar El Yate** (tel. 506/656-0791), on the hill below Guanamar, serves ceviche and other seafood dishes.

Playa Carrillo to Manzanillo

The extreme southwest shore of Nicoya Peninsula is one of the most remote coastal strips in Costa Rica. Sections are still undiscovered. The beaches are beautiful and the coastal scenery at times sublime, though the driving is tricky.

South of Carrillo, the dirt road continues a few miles in good condition, then deteriorates to a mere trail in places. In the words of the old spiritual, there are many rivers to cross. The tricky route (there are several unmarked junctions) can thwart even the hardiest 4WD in wet season, or after prolonged rains in dry season. For those who thrill to adventure, it's a helluva lot of fun.

Don't attempt the section south of Carrillo by ordinary sedan or at night, and especially not in wet season unless it's unusually dry—many tourists have had to have their cars hauled out of rivers that proved impossible to ford.

PLAYA CAMARONAL TO PUNTA BEJUCO

Playa Camaronal, beyond Punta El Roble about five km south of Playa Carrillo, is a remote three-km-long gray-sand beach that is a popular nesting site for leatherback and Pacific ridley turtles (*loras*).

A dirt road leads south nine km from Camaronal to **Playa Islita,** a pebbly black-sand beach squeezed between soaring headlands that will have your 4WD wheezing in first gear. (You'll need to cross the wide Río Ora, which is negotiable at low tide but proved impassable when I attempted it in wet season in 2000, and in 2003, when I heard rumors that a bridge was to be built.) The turnoff is about two km west of the hamlet of Carmén. You may be forced to take the main, unpaved road inland over hill and dale via Carmén, the hamlet of San Martín and **Soledad** (also called Cangrejal), where you turn south for Islita. From Cangrejal, it's a scramble—4WD essential—over steep mountains then a drop into the valley of the Río Bejuco. *Phew!*

The community of **Islita** is enlivened by an **Open-Air Contemporary Art Museum** (Museo de Arte Contemporáneo al Aire Libre), with houses, tree trunks, and even sign posts decorated in bright paints and mosaics. The museum extends to an "artistically enhanced forest" and incorporates murals, carvings, and other works by local and leading contemporary Costa Rican artists.

South of the community of Islita, in the valley bottom, the road climbs over Punta Barranquilla before dropping to **Playa Corazalito.** The dirt road then cuts inland to the village of **Corazalito** (with an airstrip) and continues parallel to and about two km from the shore. The beach is backed by a large mangrove swamp replete with wildlife.

At the hamlet of **Quebrada Seca,** two km south of Corazalito, a side road leads two km to **Playa Bejuco,** a four-km-long gray-sand beach with a mangrove swamp at the southern end, within the meniscus of Punta Bejuco. The dirt road continues south from Quebrada Seca four km to **Pueblo Nuevo,** where the road from Cangrejal connects with Carmona and Hwy. 21; on the hill one km south of Pueblo Nuevo, a side road that begins at the hairpin bend leads to the funky fishing community of **Puerto Bejuco.**

Accommodations and Food

Villas Malinche (tel. 506/655-8044, $18 pp), in Quebrada Seca, has three nicely appointed, modern a/c cabinas with ceiling fans, cable TV, kitchenettes, spacious private bathrooms with hot water, and wide terraces. There's a restaurant and bar with pool table.

I highly recommend **M Hotel Hacienda Punta Islita** (Apdo. 6054-1000, San José, tel. 506/231-6122, fax 506/231-0715, info@hotel puntaislita.com,www.hotelpuntaislita.com; in North America, tel. 800/525-4800; $170 s/d rooms, $300 junior suite low season; $198/330 high season), commanding a hilltop above Playa Islita. A member of Small Luxury Hotels of the World, it embodies the essence of a luxurious in-vogue retreat. You enter via a grand lobby with a thatched roof held aloft by massive tree trunks and open to three sides, with a sunken bar and a wooden sundeck and horizon swimming pool seemingly melding into the endless blues of the Pacific. Rich color schemes are enhanced by terra-cotta tile floors and colorful tilework, and props from the movie *1492*—log canoes, old barrels, and huge wrought-iron candelabra. The colony includes 20 hillside bungalows in Santa Fe style, eight junior suites (each with whirlpool spa on an oceanview deck), and five two-bedroom *casitas.* All are luxuriously equipped with king-size beds (or two queens), spacious bathrooms (complete with hair dryers), ceiling fans and a/c, minibar, TV, and private terrace. There's also a three-bedroom casita sleeping six people, with its own swimming pool. A TV lounge and library boasts deep-cushioned sofas. And the elegant 1492 restaurant is acclaimed; the cuisine is top-notch and worth the drive in itself. A private forest reserve has trails for horseback rides and nature hikes, plus canopy tour; there's a gym, full-service spa, two tennis courts, and golf driving range, plus a beach club with watersports. 4WD vehicles can be rented.

Bar Barranquilla (tel. 506/368-2655, 11 A.M.–midnight low season, 8 A.M.–midnight high season), atop Punta Barranquilla, offers spectacular vistas from its half-moon deck. It serves *comida típica* and seafoods.

The German-run **Restaurante Azul Plata** (11 A.M.–10 P.M.), at Playa Bejuco, serves pizzas.

Getting There

Sansa (tel. 506/257-9414, www.grupotaca.com) and **Nature Air** (tel. 506/220-3054, www .natureair.com) fly daily to Islita from San José. Hotel Hacienda Punta Islita offers air transfers.

You can buy gas at the house of Ann Arias Chávez, on the southwest corner of the soccer field in Quebrada Seca.

PLAYA SAN MIGUEL TO PUNTA COYOTE

Crossing the Río Bejuco south of Pueblo Nuevo, you arrive at the hamlet of **San Miguel,** at the northern end of **Playa San Miguel,** reached by a side road. The silver-sand beach is a prime turtle-nesting site; there's a ranger station at the southern end of the beach, which is protected as part of the Tempisque Conservation Area.

The beach is backed by cattle pasture and runs south into **Playa Coyote,** a lonesome six-km-

© CHRISTOPHER P. BAKER

Playa San Miguel

long stunner backed by a large mangrove swamp and steep cliffs. The beaches, which are separated by a river estuary, are fantastically wide at low tide. The wide Río Jabillo pours into the sea at the south end of Playa Coyote, which, like Playa San Miguel, is reached by a side road that extends two km north and south along the shore. The surfing is superb.

The Río Jabillo and marshy foreshore force the coast road inland for six km to the village of **San Francisco de Coyote,** connected by road inland over the mountains with Hwy. 21. If you're continuing south for Malpaís, you must ford (*vano* in Spanish) the **Río Jabillo;** the main road shown on most maps (a right turn at the crossroads on the southwest side of the soccer field in San Francisco when heading south from Sámara) leads southwest five km to Punta Coyote, but it is usually flooded and rarely passable; *you run a serious risk of becoming stuck in mud or drowning the engine if you try this route!* Instead, follow the road leading due east from the soccer field (straight across the crossroads when driv-

ing south from Sámara); you'll cross the river after about 600 meters (in 2003 wet season this, too, was impassable).

See *Punta Coyote to Manzanillo,* below, for the route south of San Francisco.

Accommodations and Food

You can camp beneath shade trees at **Rancho Los Maderos,** a simple bar and restaurant at Playa San Miguel; $1 pp.

The Swiss-run **Chez Bruno B&B** (tel. 506/655-8157, fax 506/655-8156, $5 pp low season, $10 pp high season dorm; $25 pp room year-round), on the headland overlooking the north end of Playa San Miguel, has a basic dorm room with outside shower and toilet. It also has two modern, spacious, cross-lit apartments with louvered windows, terra-cotta floors, ceiling fans, and cold water only. Terraces have lounge chairs. A trail leads to the beach.

The U.S.-run **Blue Pelican** (tel. 506/655-8046, $15 s/d downstairs, $25 s/d upstairs), a three-story wooden house on Playa San Miguel, has six charming yet basic rooms with Goldilocks-and-the-Three-Bears roughhewn four-poster beds, ceiling fans, and shared bathrooms with murals but cold water only. A large room upstairs sleeps five people; smaller rooms are downstairs, including dorm room. There's a veranda with hammocks. The rustic bar/restaurant, for guests only, serves inviting seafoods such as Portuguese seafood stew ($9).

Hotel Arca de Noe (tel./fax 506/665-8065, arcanoe@racsa.co.cr, $10 pp bunk, $35 s/d with cold water, $40 s/d with hot water, $45 s/d with a/c low season; $45/50/55 high season), one km farther south on the main road inland of the shore, is an elegant, modern, Italian-run hacienda-style property with lush landscaped grounds and a large swimming pool lined by mosaic tiles. It has five basically furnished bunk rooms with fans and clean, ample bathrooms, plus 10 a/c *cabinas* with lofty wooden ceilings, fans, verandas, louvered windows, exquisite fabrics, and private baths with hot water. It also has five simple rooms with bunks and cold water only There's a lounge and a restaurant serving Italian fare, including pizzas, that's open to the public 8–10 A.M., noon–2 P.M., and 6–9 P.M. It rents bicycles ($5 daily) and horses ($7 per hour). Rates include breakfast.

Cabinas Rey (tel. 506/655-1055, $2 per tent, $5 pp room with shared bath, $12 *cabinas*), beside the soccer field in San Francisco de Coyote, has 12 *cabinas* with private baths and cold water (up to four people), and rooms with shared bath. It permits camping with outside toilets and showers. It has horses for rent, plus a simple restaurant.

Services

Coyote Online (tel. 506/655-1007, 2–6 P.M. Mon.–Tue. and Thur.–Fri.), behind Cabinas Rey, has Internet service.

PUNTA COYOTE TO MANZANILLO

Playa Caletas is reached by a spur road south of San Francisco de Coyote (the turnoff, by a *hacienda,* is incorrectly signed as "Playa Coyote"). This miles-long brown-sand beach has no settlements. Nothing. It's just you and the turtles that come ashore to lay eggs. Playa Caletas—a great surfing beach—extends southward into **Playa Bongo, Playa Arío,** and **Playa Manzanillo**—together forming a 12-km-long expanse of sand running ruler-straight and broken by the estuaries of the Río Bongo and Río Ario, inhabited by crocodiles (once while driving this road at night, I came around a bend to find a crocodile plodding across the road). Marshy shore flats force the coast road inland.

The route between Caletas and Manzanillo is a true adventure and 4WD is absolutely essential. In wet seasons, the route is often impassable. Heed the following southbound directions carefully.

South of Caletas, keep straight via the hamlet of **Quebrada Nando** until you reach a major Y-fork by a field. Turn right (if you miss the junction you'll know it, as you'll soon come to a 90-degree left turn, then run along a disused airstrip; this road continues north four km to the hamlet of Río Frío); in past years, a sign pointed to the right for the **Río Bongo.** The river crossing is tricky, often with dangerously deep channels (they change yearly with each rainy season); if the way across isn't clear, wait for a local to show you the way.

ALTERNATE SOUTHERN ROUTE IN WET SEASON

After unduly wet weather, the Jabillo, Caño Seco, Bongo, and Ario Rivers can all be impassable, forcing you to have to cross the mountainous Nicoya peninsula to Jicaral, on Hwy. 21, and from there make the long journey around the peninsula via Paquera and Tambor to reach Manzanillo, Malpaís, and/or Montezuma. This adds at least 120 km to your journey and will take a good five hours or so.

The sole alternative is to cut inland from either San Francisco de Coyote (if the Río Jabillo is impassable) or Quebrada Nando (if the Río Bongo is impassable) and attempt to reach Cóbano via the hamlet of **Río Frío.** To get there from San Francisco de Coyote, head inland eight km on Hwy. 132 to Jabillo; three km further, turn right. Río Frío is signed. Follow the valley of the Río Juan de León and Río Bongo (the former becomes the latter, which here is crossed via a bridge) and at Río Frío turn left (east). To get to Río Frío from Quebrada Nando, see *Punta Coyote to Manzanillo.*

East of Río Frío, the track begins to deteriorate markedly. You'll ford the Caño Seco. After a few km you'll ascend a very steep and *very* muddy hill that can be a serious challenge, both going up and descending on the other side. About one km beyond this challenge you'll reach the Río Ario, which must be forded. Even here the river proved impassable in the unduly wet summer of 2003 in a Toyota RAV-4, although I figure that a Toyota Four-Runner or equivalent would have had the ground clearance to cross.

If you get through, chalk it up on your resume!

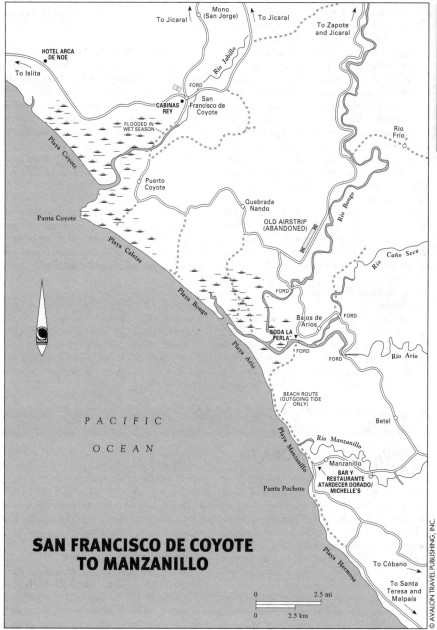

Nicoya Peninsula

To Jicaral

Mono
(San Jorge)

To Jicaral

To Zapote
and Jicaral

HOTEL ARCA
DE NOE

To Islita

Río Jabillo

FORD

CABINAS
REY

San
Francisco de
Coyote

FLOODED IN
WET SEASON

Playa Coyote

Río
Frío

Puerto
Coyote

Punta Coyote

Quebrada
Nando

OLD AIRSTRIP
(ABANDONED)

Río Bongo

Río
Caño Seco

Playa Caletas

Playa Bongo

FORD

Playa Ario

Bajos de
Arios

FORD

SODA LA
PERLA

FORD

Río Ario

FORD

PACIFIC

BEACH ROUTE
(OUTGOING TIDE
ONLY)

Betel

OCEAN

Playa Manzanillo

Río Manzanillo

Manzanillo

Punta Pochote

BAR Y
RESTAURANTE
ATARDECER DORADO/
MICHELLE'S

**SAN FRANCISCO DE COYOTE
TO MANZANILLO**

Playa Hermosa

To Cóbano

To Santa
Teresa and
Malpaís

0   2.5 mi

0   2.5 km

© AVALON TRAVEL PUBLISHING, INC.

Once across, it's about two km to **Soda La Perla** (a good place to check local conditions), where the dirt road veers left. About one km along you must ford the **Río Caño Seco,** another challenge that requires scouting before crossing. Shortly beyond, you reach the 30-meter-wide **Río Arío Negro.** The shallow crossing is oblique; the egress on the far bank is 50 yards to the left. *Many vehicles have tried to go straight across and have churned up the far bank into what looks like a road; believe me, it is a dead-end grave; if the sudden drop in the river here doesn't get you, the muddy cul-de-sac will.* Again, it's often best to wait for a local to arrive and show the way.

About five or so km further, turn right at the only junction, just beyond the hamlet of **Betel.** The descent will deposit you by the shore at **Manzanillo,** a small fishing hamlet. South of Manzanillo, the tenuous coast road (a devil in wet season) leads over **Punta Pochote** and alongside **Playa Hermosa** to Playa Santa Teresa and Malpaís.

Alternately, from Soda La Perla you can follow a minor dirt road that leads down to Playa Arío (you'll have to ford the Río Arío en route). You can then drive four km along the beach to Playa Manzanillo, where you meet the main road as it comes back to the coast. (**Safety Concerns:**

Do not attempt to drive along Playa Arío except on an outgoing tide.)

Accommodations and Food

In Manzanillo, several no-frills budget *cabinas* include **Bar y Restaurante Atardecer Dorado** (tel. 506/360-9377), with two basic rooms with bed only (and funky outhouse toilets) for $10 pp. The bar (with TV and jukebox) is a lively center for locals. It serves filling meals; try the *filete al ajillo* (garlic fish, $2).

The U.S.-owned **Michelle's** ($95 d) on a hill behind Bar y Restaurante Atardecer Dorado, is a Robinson Crusoe type of place with two no-frills A-frame thatched huts on stilts, with queen-size beds and nothing else except outside toilets and showers. It offers what it claims to be "five-course gourmet dinners." It has a beachfront *soda* selling burgers, hot dogs, pastries, and ice creams. It's vastly overpriced. Rates include breakfast and dinner.

Getting There

Reportedly, a bus departs San José daily at 3 P.M. from Calle 12, Avenidas 7/9, and travels via the Puntarenas–Playa Naranjo ferry and Jicaral to Coyote, Bejuco, and Islita (arriving around 11 P.M.). Return buses are said to depart Bejuco at 4 A.M., passing via San Francisco de Coyote at 5 A.M.

Southeast Nicoya

HIGHWAY 21: CARMONA TO PLAYA NARANJO

South from Barra Honda (16 km west of the Tempisque Bridge), Hwy. 21 winds along the southern shore of the Gulf of Nicoya via Jicaral to Playa Naranjo, beyond which it swings south around the Nicoya Peninsula bound for Paquera, Montezuma, and Malpaís. When I last drove it, the road was partially paved, with large sections worn to the bone. *Jarring!*

Playa Naranjo, 65 km south of Pueblo Viejo, is the terminal for the Puntarenas ferry. There's a gas station and supermarket here. **Seascape Kayak Tours** (tel. 506/747-1884 or 866/747-

1884, fax 506/641-8091, info@seasacapekayak tours.com, www.seascapekayaktours.com), at Hotel Oasis del Pacifico, offers kayaking.

Nonguests can use the facilities at Hotel Oasis del Pacífico ($5; see below) while waiting for the ferry. It arranges sportfishing ($30 per day) and has sea kayaks ($10 per hour).

Accommodations and Food

The nicest of several accommodations at Playa Naranjo is the modern **Hotel El Ancla** (tel. 506/641-8095, $10 s/d with fan, $15 s/d with a/c low season, $15/20, respectively, high season), just 200 meters from the ferry terminal, with nine brightly decorated a/c rooms fronted by a

PROFELIS

Profelis, or Center for Investigation And Conservation of Wildcats (Asociación Centro de Investigación Rescate y Rehabilitación de Gatos Salvajes, P.O. Box 47-5357, Paquera, Puntarenas, tel. 506/641-0644 or 641-0646 (or 222-6806 in San José), fax 506/641-0647 (or 257-9752 in San José), profelis@profelis.com, www.seibermarco.de/profelis) occupies a remote corner of Hacienda Matambú, a 3,500- hectare private wildlife reserve at San Rafael de Paquera, about five km west of Paquera. Created in 1992 by German biologists, Siegfried Weisel and Sabine Weber, Profelis promotes the conservation of small wildcats using captive felines that have been confiscated by the Costa Rican Ministry of Energy and Environment. The program includes the rescue and rehabilitation of the animals, and their eventual reintroduction to the wild.

Profelis has only the four "small" wildcat species that live in Costa Rica: ocelot (Leopardus pardalis), margay (Leopardus pardalis), oncilla or tiger cat (Leopardus tigrinus), and jaguarundi (Herpailurus yaguaroundi). At last visit, it had about 40 animals, mostly margays and ocelots. Most adult wild cats are loners, and ocelots and jaguarundis are kept singly; margays (which are willing to share their "territory" with a fellow of the opposite sex) are kept as pairs, resulting in successful breeding.

At last visit, visitors were prohibited from entering the large animal enclosures, which replicate natural surroundings and are connected by a tunnel system that permits minimal human presence. However, plans call for a separate area to be created for public education and will feature individual wildcats (including "Tafa," a semi-tame ocelot female) that have been excluded from the investigation and rehabilitation program.

Facilities include a veterinary clinic and a prey breeding area (the cats are fed quails and guinea pigs).

The project is financed by donations, and welcomes volunteers to assist (veterinary and biology students and animal keepers are particularly sought). Volunteer are housed free and are charged $30 weekly for "habitational costs."

---

wide porch with hammocks. The grounds include a pool and attractive thatched bar and restaurant.

Alternatives include **Hotel El Maquinay** (tel./fax 506/641-8011), an elegant hacienda-type property; **Hotel El Paso** (P.O. Box 232, San José 2120, tel./fax 506/641-8133), 600 meters northwest of the ferry; and **Hotel Oasis del Pacífico** (P.O. Box 200-5400, Puntarenas, tel. 506/641-8092, fax 506/641-8091, wilhow@racsa.co.cr; in the U.S., P.L. Wilhelm 1552, P.O. Box 025216, Miami, FL 33102-5216; $25 s, $36 d fans, $42 s, $55 d a/c low season; $30 s, $45 d fan, $45 s, $65 d a/c high season), 600 meters south of the ferry terminal. This last hotel has 36 comfortable chalet-type rooms with fans, double beds, and hot water, plus a swimming pool.

ISLA SAN LUCAS

Isla San Lucas (615 hectares), five km east of Naranjo, has been called the Island of Unspeakable Horrors, the Island of Silence, and Devil's Island. From afar, it seems a pleasant palm-fringed place—a place, perhaps, where you might actually *wish* to be washed ashore and languish for a few months or even years in splendid sun-washed isolation. Yet a visit to Isla San Lucas once amounted to an excursion to hell.

Until a few years ago, this was the site of the most dreaded prison in the Costa Rican penal system, with a legacy dating back 400 years. In the 16th century, the Spanish conquistador Gonzalo Fernandez Oviedo used San Lucas as a concentration camp for local Chara people, who were slaughtered on the site of their sacred burial grounds. The Costa Rican government turned it into a detention center for political prisoners in 1862. In 1991, it closed.

Should you visit the grim bastion, the ghosts of murderers, miscreants, and maltreated innocents will be your guides. A cobbled pathway leads to the main prison building (the prisoner who built it was promised his freedom once he completed his task; reportedly it took him 20 years). The chapel has become a bat grotto, and only graffiti remains to tell of the horror and hopelessness. There are still guards here, but today their role is to protect the island's resident wildlife from would-be poachers. The guards will escort you to the diminutive cells. There are no restrictions on visiting.

The Island of the Lonely Men, a biographical account written in 1971 by former prisoner José León Sánchez, tells of the betrayals, the madness, and the perpetual frustrations of attempts to escape this spine-chilling place.

To get to Isla San Lucas, you can rent motorboats through the Costa Rica Yacht Club (tel. 506/661-0784), in Puntarenas, or Oasis del Pacífico (tel. 506/641-8092) in Playa Naranjo.

PAQUERA AND VICINITY

The coast road turns south from Playa Naranjo to Paquera, where the climate begins to grow more humid and the vegetation begins to thicken. This unpaved section is very hilly, with tortuous switchbacks. It's a despairingly jolting ride (it improves south of Paquera). It's all part of the price for some marvelous views out over the Gulf of Nicoya—including toward Isla Guayabo, which comes into view about six km south of Playa Naranjo, where the road briefly meets the coast at **Gigante,** at the north end of **Bahía Luminosa** (also called Bahía Gigante).

Paquera, 24 km south of Playa Naranjo, is where the Paquera ferry arrives and departs to/from Puntarenas. The ferry berth is three km northeast of Paquera. A dirt track two km east of town on the south side of the ferry road leads to the tip, **Punta Corralillo,** where you have a good view of Islas Negritos.

Offshore, **Islas Guayabo and Negritos Biological Reserves** protect nesting sites of the brown booby, frigate bird, pelican, and other seabirds. In winter, 6.8-hectare Reservas Biológica Isla Guayabo (about three km northeast of Gigante) is also a nesting site for the peregrine falcon. They are off-limits to visitors.

Dolphins and whales are often sighted offshore (January is the best month for whales). The mountainous interior inland of Paquera was recently proclaimed a protected wilderness: the **Zona Protectora Península de Nicoya.**

Isla Gitana

This tiny island in the middle of Bahía Luminosa was once a burial site for local peoples (hence its other name, Isla Muertos—Island of the Dead—by which it is marked on maps). Superstitious Tico workers will not stay on the island at night. The undergrowth is wild, and cacti abound, so appropriate footwear is recommended. The isle, 400 meters offshore from Punta Gigante, has a palm-thatch beachside restaurant-cum-bar strewn with icons of a mariner's life. The place was run as a private island resort by late residents Carl and Loida Reugg, who ran the **Fantasy Island Yacht Club,** a once-popular hangout for sailors, who would unwind in a *palapa* bar that looked as if it washed up from the sea.

You can hire a boat on the mainland beach. You can also reach the island by sea kayak from Bahía Gigante, a 30-minute paddle journey.

Accommodations

The North American–run **Hotel Bahía el Gigante** (P.O. Box 1886, San José, tel./fax 506/661-8231, www.hotelbahiagigante.com), at Bahía el Gigante, was being totally remodeled by new owners at last visit. Previously it had four condos and 12 spacious rooms with fans and large bathrooms with hot water. It has a swimming pool and restaurant, and trails lead through primal forest.

Bahía Luminosa Resort (tel. 506/641-0386, fax 506/641-0387, tropics@racsa.co.cr, www .bahialuminosa.com; in the U.S., 730 Duncan Dr., Yreka, CA 96097, tel. 530/842-3322, fax 530/842-1539; $39 s/d fan, $50 s/d a/c), at Playa

Pánama, midway between Paquera and Playa Naranjo, is a run-down place that might serve as a refuge in stormy weather. Rates include continental breakfast.

Services

Paquera has banks, and a gas station, 400 meters northeast of town on the road to the ferry berth.

CURÚ NATIONAL WILDLIFE REFUGE

The Curú Refugio Nacional de Vida Silvestre (tel. 506/641-0590 or 506/661-2392, refugiocuru @yadoo.com) forms part of a 1,214-hectare *hacienda*, two-thirds of which is preserved as primary forest. It is tucked in the fold of Golfo Curú, four km south of Paquera, and is part privately owned. The 84-hectare reserve includes 4.5 km of coastline with a series of tiny coves and three beautiful white-sand beaches—Playas Curú, Colorada, and Quesera—nestled beneath green slopes. Olive ridley and hawksbill turtles nest on the crystalline beaches. Mangrove swamps extend inland along the Río Curú, backed by forested hills. It hosts at least 150 other species. Mammals include agoutis; ocelots; margays; pumas; howler, capuchin, and endangered spider monkeys; white-tailed deer; sloths; and anteaters.

Visitation is by prior arrangement only. Guided tours are offered (your tip is their pay). Trails are marked. The bus between Paquera and Cóbano passes the unmarked gate. Ask the driver to let you off.

ISLA TORTUGA

This stunningly beautiful, 320-hectare island lies three km offshore of Curú. Tortuga is as close to an idyllic tropical isle as you'll find in Costa Rica. The main attraction is a magnificent white-sand beach lined with tall coconut palms.

Indisputably Costa Rica's most exquisite isle, Tortuga is a favorite destination of excursion boats. Cruises depart Puntarenas and Los Sueños marina, at Playa Herradura, near Jacó. It's a 90-minute journey aboard any of a half-dozen cruise boats. Each of the cruise companies that put day-trippers ashore gets its own section of the beach. It can get a bit cramped on weekends, when three or four boats might disgorge their passengers at the same time. Still, it makes for a tremendous trip on a sunny day. You can snorkel, swim, play volleyball, hike, or simply snooze in the sun. There are oar and pedal boats and water-bicycles, kayaks, and Spyaks (glass-bottom boats). You can also hike into the forested hills, and take a treetop canopy tour using professional climbing gear to whiz you along steel cables slung between treetops.

Isla Tortuga is also accessible from Montezuma, although most day visits originate from Playa Herradura in Jacó, and to a lesser degree, Puntarenas. Several companies offer these scenic day cruises, passing the isles of Negritos, San Lucas, Gitana, and Guayabo. **Calypso Cruises** (tel. 506/256-2727, fax 506/256-6767, www.calypso-tours.com) is one of the best.

TAMBOR

Tambor, 18 km southwest of Paquera, is a small fishing village fronted by a gray-sand beach in **Bahía Ballena** (Whale Bay), a deep-pocket bay rimmed by **Playa Tambor** and backed by forested hills. The beach extends north to **Playa Pochote**. The fishing hamlet of **Pochote,** about six km northeast of Tambor, is surrounded by mangrove swamps that harbor waterfowl and caimans (mosquitoes and no-see-ums abound).

Sports and Recreation

You can play a round of golf or tennis ($5) at the nine-hole **Tango Mar Golf Club** (see *Accommodation,* below). Play is free for guests; others pay a $25 greens fee for a day of unlimited play. Tango Mar offers tours, sportfishing, and horseback riding.

Tropic World Diving Station (tel. 506/661-1915, fax 506/661-2069) offers diving programs out of the Playa Tambor Beach Resort.

Paraíso ATV Center (tel. 506/683-0383, www.paraisocostarica.net) offers jungle tours by all-terrain quads.

DAY TRIPPING TO ISLA TORTUGA

Day trips to **Isla Tortuga** are a popular item on any tourist menu. Boat cruises Los Sueños marina, at Playa Herradura, near Jacó (see the Central Pacific chapter), and trips are also available departing Puntarenas (see the Guanacaste chapter) and Montezuma (see the Montezuma section, this chapter). It's a 90-minute journey aboard any of a half-dozen cruise boats.

The cruise is superbly scenic, passing the isles of Negritos, San Lucas, Gitana, and Guayabo. En route you may spot manta rays or pilot whales in the warm waters. Even giant whale sharks have been seen basking off Isla Tortuga. You'll normally have about two hours on Isla Tortuga, with a buffet lunch served on the beach, plus options for hiking, sea kayaking, snorkeling, and other activities.

The following are offered:

Calypso Cruises (tel. 506/256-2727, fax 506/256-6767, www.calypsotours.com) began the trend in 1979 aboard the venerable *Calypso,* which faithfully operated daily until 1994, when it was replaced by a the space-age *Manta Raya,* a luxurious catamaran with soft leather seating, full bar, freshwater showers, and even an underwater viewing window. It carries up to 100 passengers and features a fishing platform and two whirlpools, and the ability to "drive" right up onto the beach. Transfers from San José are provided, with snacks served en route, washed down by *coco locos* (rum, coconut milk, and coconut liqueur, served in a coconut). Daily departures are offered during dry season (15 Dec.–15 April; $99, including transfer from San José); Wednesday, Friday, and Sunday in wet season ($89). Trips depart from Puntarenas.

The company also has cruises to **Punta Coral Private Reserve** (www.puntacoral.com), where snorkeling, sea kayaking, and other activities are offered. It offers "Paradise Weddings" in a South Seas setting.

Bay Island Cruises (tel. 506/258-3536, bayislan@racsa.co.cr) offers cruises year-round aboard the *Bay Princess,* an ultramodern 16-meter cruise yacht with room for 70 passengers. The ship has a sun deck and music, and cocktails and snacks are served during the cruise. Trips from Jacó cost $75 low season, $95 high season.

Sea Ventures (tel. 506/258-1694, fax 506/221-1548) also offers trips aboard its sleek 29-meter namesake vessel. A three-day "Sailing/Nature Adventure" combines two days sailing in the Gulf of Nicoya and one day at Cabo Blanco National Reserve, with overnights on board (the trip departs and returns to Playa Herradura, north of Jacó; $445).

Freedom Cruises (tel. 506/291-0191, fax 506/220-0910, freedomcruises@racsa.co.cr) offers cruises aboard the sleek new *Breeze,* which accommodates 125 people.

Accommodations

$10–25: Budget hounds might try **Cabinas y Restaurante Cristina** (tel. 506/683-0028, eduardon@racsa.co.cr, $12.50 s/d with shared bath, $17.50 s, $22.50 d private bath, $25 *casita*), with nine simply furnished but clean and adequate rooms with fans, large louvered windows, and cold water. It also has an a/c *casita* with kitchen, sleeping four people.

The popular and unpretentious gringo-run **Hotel Dos Lagartos** (tel. 506/683-0236, aulwes@costarica.net, $13 s, $17 d shared bath; $25 s/d private bath), next to Tambor Tropical,

has 22 rooms set amid lawns with palms. The owners, correctly, claim that it is "plain, simple, cheap and clean." Rooms are well lit but small, basically furnished, and have cold water only; five have private baths, and the rest have shared baths. There's a bar and restaurant downstairs.

$50–100: I like the flame-orange, *posada*-style **Costa Coral** (P.O. Box 83-Cóbano, tel. 506/683-0105, fax 506/683-0016, coscoral@racsa.co.cr, www.costacoral.com, $40 s/d with fan, $50 s/d with a/c and TV low season; $45/55 high season), a colorful little beauty of a hotel on the main road in Tambor. It has six a/c rooms in three two-story Spanish-colonial structures arrayed around an exquisite pool with whirlpool. The charming decor includes wrought iron, potted plants, climbing ivy, ceramic lamps, and a harmonious ocher-and-blue color scheme, terra-cotta floors, and balconies with tables. Each unit has a kitchenette-lounge, satellite TV, and safe. The upstairs restaurant offers ambience and good cuisine, and its gift store is splendidly stocked. It was adding two villas and a café at last visit.

$100–150: The architecturally dramatic **Tambor Tropical** (tel. 506/683-0011, fax 506/683-0013, info@tambortropical.com; www.tambortropical.com; in the U.S., 867 Liberty St. NE, Salem, OR 97301, tel. 530/365-2872 or 866/890-2537; $150 s/d lower, $175 s/d upper year-round) is a perfect place to laze in the shade of a swaying palm. Ten handcrafted two-story hexagonal *cabinas* (one unit upstairs, one unit down) face the beach amid lush landscaped grounds with an exquisite pool and Jacuzzi. The rooms are graced by voluminous bathrooms with deep-well showers, wraparound balconies, and fully equipped kitchens with captains' chairs. Everything is handmade of native hardwoods, all of it lacquered to a nautical shine. There's also a boutique, and a restaurant serving simple international cuisine. Snorkeling, horseback riding, and estuary boat trips are offered, and End of the Line Sportfishing (tel. 506/683-0453) is based here. Rates include breakfast.

$150–250: If all-inclusive package resorts are your thing, consider the controversial **Barceló Playa Tambor Resort & Casino** (tel. 506/683-0303, fax 506/683-0304, playatambor@barcelo.com, www.barcelo.com), the first megaresort in the nation (it created a political storm when accused of violating protective laws). Sprawling across a 2,400-hectare site, the all-inclusive planned resort has 402 rooms in two three-story blocks, each with terrace or balcony, a/c, refrigerator, cable TV, self-dial phone, and deep bathtub. The grounds are uninspired and the gray-sand beach is unimpressive, but the amenities make amends. The resort has its own airstrip and a helicopter landing strip. Call for rates.

The **Barceló Los Delfines Golf & Country Club** (tel. 506/683-0303, fax 506/683-0331, losdelfines@barcelo.com, www.barcelo.com), adjacent to the sibling Playa Tambor Resort & Casino, east of Tambor, comprises 64 Spanish-style, two-bedroom a/c villas arrayed in military camp fashion around a nine-hole golf course. Each has TV, telephone, refrigerator, and security box. The clubhouse has a swimming pool and restaurant, plus bar, disco, shops, and tennis courts. Guests have access to the Playa Tambor Resort & Casino. Call for rates.

My favorite hostelry hereabouts is the Dutch-run **Tango Mar** (P.O. Box 1-1260 Escazú, tel. 506/683-0001, fax 506/683-0003, info@tangomar.com, www.tangomar.com, $145 s/d oceanfront rooms and suites, $195 s/d Tiki Suites, $400–900 villas low season; $165/210/450–1,000, respectively, high season), five km southwest of Tambor. It enjoys a beautiful beachfront setting backed by hectares of beautifully tended grounds splashed with bougainvillea and hibiscus. It has 25 rooms in individually styled Polynesian thatched *cabañas*—Tiki Suites—raised on stilts, with tile floors, rattan furniture, refrigerator, TV, phone, coffeemaker, safe, silent a/c, whirlpool, four-poster bed with mosquito netting, and a golf cart. There are also a dozen spacious oceanfront rooms with large balconies, plus Tropical Suites, all in lively livery. You can also choose four- and five-person villas. It has two swimming pools, a nine-hole golf course, soccer field, stables, water sports, an Internet office, plus massage and yoga. It rents 4WD vehicles. Rates include American breakfast.

Food

Restaurant Cristina (8 A.M.–9 P.M.) proffers good seafoods and pastas on a shady patio for those on a budget, as does the small restaurant in Hotel Dos Lagartos.

The **Restaurante Arrecife** (11 A.M.–2 P.M. and 6–10 P.M. low season; 11A.M.–11 P.M. high season, $4–9), in the Costa Coral, is a charmer with its lofty wooden ceiling, rich, lively color scheme, and dishes such as ceviche, club sandwich, burgers, fettucine, chicken with orange sauce, and sea bass with heart-of-palm sauce. It has a large-screen TV and karaoke.

The elegant **Tango Mar** (6:30–10 A.M., 11:30 A.M.–3:30 P.M., and 6:30–10 P.M., $4.50–22) restaurant is open to the public and serves burgers and toasted sandwiches for lunch, plus appetizers such as avocado, tomato and mozzarella, and entrées like pastas, chicken macadamia, Jamaican-style prawns, and daily specials.

You can buy groceries at **Super Lapa,** next to Cabinas Cristina.

Services

The **Toucan Boutique,** in Hotel Costa Coral, has a tourist information service and one of the best-stocked souvenir stores beyond San José.

There are **public telephones** outside Super Lapa.

Getting There

Sansa (tel. 506/257-9414, www.grupotaca.com) and **Nature Air** (tel. 506/220-3054, www.natureair.com) fly daily to Tambor from San José, with connecting service to other resorts

For bus connections, see *Paquera.*

Panga Taxi (tel. 506/643-3780) offers water-taxi service to Isla Tortuga, Tambor, Montezuma, and Malpaís, in Nicoya ($35).

Southern Nicoya

CÓBANO

Cóbano, a crossroads village 25 km southwest of Paquera, is the gateway to Malpaís and to Montezuma (five km) and Cabo Blanco Absolute Nature Reserve. Buses for Malpaís (due west) and the Paquera ferry depart from here, and many budget travelers spend the night here to catch the early-morning buses.

The **Hotel y Restaurante Caoba** (tel. 506/642-0219, $7 pp shared bath, $8 private bath), at the junction by the bus stop, has nine modest but well-kept wood-paneled rooms: four with private baths, five with shared.

The **police station** (tel. 506/642-0708) and post office are 200 meters east of the bank.

There are public telephones in front of the bank in the center of town.

There's a **medical clinic** (tel. 506/642-0950 or 506/380-4125) 100 meters south of the bank.

Buses to Montezuma depart Cóbano from outside the Hotel Caoba at 9 A.M. and 6 P.M., and for Paquera at 5:30 A.M. and 2 P.M.

The gas station is one km east of town.

MONTEZUMA

Montezuma is a charming beachside retreat popular with budget-minded backpackers and coun-terculture travelers seeking an offbeat experience. It's blessed with budget accommodations and a marvelous beach. The fantastic beaches east of Montezuma are backed by forest-festooned cliffs from which streams tumble down to the sands. Monkeys frolic in the forests behind the beach. Strong currents are a problem; Playa Grande, about two km northeast of Montezuma, is reportedly the safest beach.

The **Nicolas Weissenburg Absolute Reserve** (Reserva Absoluta Nicolas Weissenburg) was created in 1998 to protect the shoreline and forested hills to the east of Montezuma. It's strictly off-limits, though you can go horseback riding and hiking along trails edging the reserve at **Nature Lodge Finca los Caballos** (see *Accommodation,* below).

Business owners are prone to shut up shop on a whim—sometimes for days at a time, or longer. No posted hours. No apologies!

Safety Conerns: The waterfall and swimming hole two km southwest of town, on the road to Cabo Blanco (the trail leads upstream from the Restaurante La Cascada) is dangerous. Do not climb or jump from the top of the fall. Several lives have been lost this way.

Entertainment and Events

The **Montezuma Music Festival** (tel. 506/642-0090) is held each July.

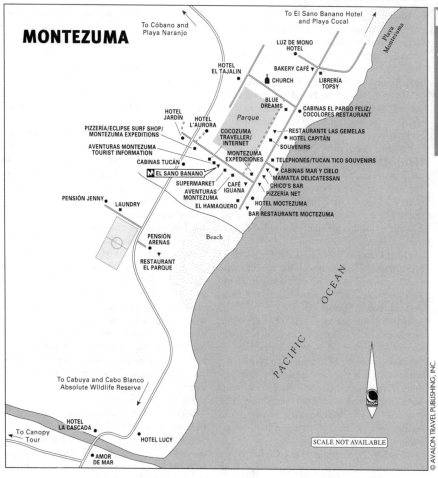

MONTEZUMA

El Sano Banano shows movies nightly at 7:30 P.M. (free with dinner or $5 minimum order). **Chico's** is the liveliest place to sup. **Luz de Mono** hosts shows from classical to jazz and rock at its atrium theater-bar.

Sports and Recreation

Aventuras Montezuma (tel./fax 506/642-0005) and **Montezuma Expeditions** (tel. 506/440-8078, fax 506/440-8006, info@montezuma expeditions.com, www.montezumaexpeditions .com) offer horseback rides, fishing, kayak-

ing, snorkeling, and biking, plus tours to Isla Tortuga and Cabo Blanco. Aventuras Montezuma also rents small motorcycles ($40 per day). **El Sano Banano** (7:30 A.M.–9:30 P.M.) has a tour desk offering similar options. You can take horseback rides at **Finca los Caballos** ($12 per hour).

Accommodations

Camping: You can camp for $2 pp at **Pensión Arenas** (tel. 506/642-0649), west of Montezuma. Don't leave things unattended.

Under $25: There's little to choose from between the various low-end properties, all with basic rooms with shared bathrooms with cold water for around $5 pp, such as **Hotel Lyz** (tel. 506/642-0568); **Pensión Arenas,** next door; **Pensión Jenny,** on the hill; **Cabinas Tucán** (tel. 506/642-0284); or the **Hotel el Capitán** (tel. 506/642-0069), which has 18 bare-bones rooms in a rickety old wooden home (three have private bathrooms).

The best bet in this price range is beachfront **Hotel Moctezuma** (tel./fax 506/642-0058, $5 pp shared bath, $7.50 pp private bath), with 28 spacious and clean rooms with fans; seven have shared baths, 15 have private baths with hot water. The annex across the road is less appealing. The main unit has a restaurant and bar directly over the beach.

Hotel Lucy (tel. 506/642-0273, $6 pp), about one km west of town, has 10 basic rooms with fans and shared bath with cold water in an old wooden house. There's a shady restaurant, and a veranda faces the ocean.

Hotel L'Aurora (tel./fax 506/642-0051, hotelaurora@racsa.co.cr, $12 s/d shared bathroom, $16–30 s, $15–35 d depending on room size), run by a German-Tico couple, is a whitewashed house surrounded by lush gardens. The nine basic rooms have fans. Some have shared bath with cold water only. Upstairs is an airy lounge with bamboo and leather sofas, a small library, and hammocks. Rooms downstairs are dark.

$25–50: The **Cabinas Mar y Cielo** (tel./fax 506/642-0261, $20 s/d low season; $35 high season), alias Chico's, has six rooms fronting the beach, all with fans and private baths. Rooms vary in size.

The German/Tica-run **Cabinas El Pargo Feliz** (tel. 506/642-0064, $20–25 s/d low season; $25–30 s/d high season) has eight spacious, clean, basically furnished modern *cabinas* with wooden floors, chipboard walls, fans, queen-size beds, tiled bathroom with cold water only, and hammocks on wide verandas. It has a rustic thatched restaurant.

The three-story **Hotel El Tajalin** (tel. 506/642-0061, fax 506/642-0527, tajalin@racsa.co.cr, $30 s/d with fan, $45 s/d with a/c low season; $50/70

high season) has 11 modestly decorated rooms with tile floors, fans, and private bath with hot water. Nine rooms have a/c and TV. Some rooms are dark.

Hotel La Cascada (tel./fax 506/642-0057, $10 pp low season, $30 s/d high season), west of town, has 14 modestly furnished rooms with fans and private baths with cold water. Downstairs rooms are dark.

Cabinas Playa Las Manchas (tel. 506/642-0415, casukri@hotmail.com, www.playalasmanchas .com, $13 s, $17 rooms, $25 and $50 cabins low season; $20 s, $30 d rooms, $50/100 cabins high season), nearby, has two attractive, simply furnished rooms and four wooden cabins with lots of large windows, a kitchen, and private bath and hot water. There's a disco.

I like **Hotel Las Rocas** (P.O. Box 14-5361 Cobano, tel./fax 506/642-0393, lasrocas@racsa .co.cr, $25 s/d home, $40–50 apartment low season; $30 home, $55–70 apartment high season), three km west of Montezuma, which has three simply furnished, cross-ventilated rooms with fans and shared bath upstairs in an old wooden home amid large boulders. A wide balcony has hammocks and deep sofas. Gisella, the Italian owner, also has two apartments in a two-story unit: one is for two people, the other for five; both have kitchens. Gisella cooks meals ($9 pp) in the small restaurant.

$50–100: By far the best place for miles is **M El Sano Banano Hotel** (tel. 506/642-0638, fax 506/642-0631, reservations@elbanano.com, www.elbanano.com, $72 s/d rooms, $83 suites, $89–132 bungalows low season; $83/95/99–143, respectively, high season), a 10-minute walk along the beach 800 meters east of the village. Owners Lenny and Patricia Iacono have created a totally delightful property spread across eight hectares of beachfront that is a lush fantasia of ginger, pandanus, and riotous greens. It has three three-story suites (for up to four people) with kitchens; a three-bedroom apartment; plus eight concrete-and-riverstone bungalows, all accessed by well-manicured paths lit at night. All have fans, private bath, fridge, coffeemaker, and Guatemalan bedspreads. French doors open to verandas within spitting distance of the ocean. The dome

© CHRISTOPHER P. BAKER

the swimming pool at El Sano Banano

bungalows have private outdoor showers, kitchens, and a double bed downstairs and a king bed in the loft. The coup de grâce is an exquisite freeform pool in a faux-natural setting of rocks with water cascading and foliage tumbling all around.

The same owners also offer a bed-and-breakfast ($50 s/d low season, $55 s/d high season) above the Sano Banano restaurant, in town. The a/c rooms are decorated in New Mexican style and have satellite TV and hot-water showers.

Hotel El Jardín (P.O. Box 17-5361 Montezuma, tel. 506/642-0548, fax 506/642-0074, jardin@racsa.co.cr, www.hoteleljardin.com, $40 d low season, $70 high season) offers 10 hillside *cabinas* with fans, hammocks on the veranda, refrigerators, and private baths (some with hot water). Each elegant *cabina* is individually styled in hardwoods and shaded by trees in landscaped grounds with pool and Jacuzzi. It also has two a/c *casitas* for $300 per week.

The relaxing **Hotel Amor de Mar** (tel./ fax 506/642-0262, shoebox@racsa.co.cr, www .amordemar.com, $25–65 low season; $35–75 d high season), 600 meters west of the village, enjoys a fabulous location on a sheltered headland,

with a private tidepool and views along the coast in both directions. The hotel is set in pleasant landscaped lawns, one km west of Montezuma, with hammocks beneath shady palms. They have 11 rooms (all but two have private baths, some with hot water), all unique in size and decor, made entirely of hardwoods, and opening onto a large veranda.

I love the German-run **Hotel Horizontes de Montezuma** (P.O. Box 77-5361, Cobano, tel./fax 506/642-0534, collina@racsa.co.cr, www .horizontes-montezuma.com, $25 s, $39 d small room, $35 s, $40 d larger room low season; $35/49 small, $45/59 large high season), midway between Cóbano and Montezuma. This Victorian-style home has seven rooms around a skylit atrium—saturating the hallway of black-and-white tile with magnesium light—and opening to a wraparound veranda with hammocks. The appealing rooms have whitewashed wooden ceilings with fans, terra-cotta floors, sky-blue fabrics, and bathrooms done up in dark-blue tiles. Nice! A shady and aesthetically pleasing restaurant opens to the small pool; full breakfasts are offered. Two classrooms are used for Spanish-language instruction.

Nature Lodge Finca los Caballos (P.O. Box 22, Cóbano, tel./fax 506/642-0124, naturelc @racsa.co.cr, www.naturelodge.net, $49 s, $57 d low season; $54 s, $62 d high season, including taxes), on a 16-hectare ranch abutting the Nicolas Weissenburg Absolute Reserve, midway between Cóbano and Montezuma, is beloved of birders and equestrians. It has eight small, uninspired rooms with sponge-washed ocher walls, orthopedic mattresses, fans, and private bathrooms with hot water. There's also a two-bedroom bungalow with kitchen. A fan-shaped horizon swimming pool is inset in a wooden deck offering views across forested hills to the ocean, reached via trails. Barbara MacGregor, the charming Canadian owner, is a champion rider—"I carried my dream of having a dude ranch to Costa Rica"—who competes (and wins) in local rodeos and offers horseback tours, including moonlight trips ($15 per hour). The meals are splendid, including a full breakfast. Massage is offered. The bungalow costs $75/80

nightly, $414/450 weekly low/high season, by reservation only.

An also-ran is the **Luz de Mono Hotel** (P.O. Box 76-5361, Cobano, tel. 506/642-0090, fax 506/642-0010, luzdmono@sol.racsa.co.cr, www .luzdemono.com, $75 d standard, $140 casita low season; $100 standard, $175 casita high season), centered on a lofty circular atrium with restaurant with conical roof and bamboo furnishings. It has 12 hotel rooms, plus eight uninspired solid stone and simply furnished *casitas* with bathrooms. The rooms—which rise above a moat and are accessed by ramps—have queen-size beds or two singles, refrigerator, coffeemaker, solar-heated water, tile floors, minibar, fans, security box, and modern art; the two single room and six twinroom houses have queen-size beds, kitchen, terrace, security box, and Jacuzzis. The Blue Congo Bar hosts stage shows. It offers horseback riding ($40, six hours). Readers complain of poor service. Rates include breakfast and tax.

Food

For breakfast, head to the **Bakery Café** (tel. 506/642-0458, 6 A.M.–4 P.M. Mon.–Sat., 6 A.M.–2:30 P.M. Sunday) for *gallo pinto,* banana bread, soyburgers, and tuna sandwiches served on a pleasant raised patio; or to  **El Sano Banano** (tel. 506/642-0638, 6 A.M.–10 P.M.), where I recommend the scrambled tofu breakfast. This popular natural-food restaurant serves garlic breads, pastas, yogurts, veggie curry, nightly dinner specials, plus fresh-fruit thirst quenchers and ice cream, and prepares lunches to go.

Café Iguana has waffles and muffins, plus cappuccinos, espressos, and natural juices.

Restaurante Moctezuma, upstairs at Hotel Moctezuma, is an atmospheric open-air eatery with rustic furniture and views over the ocean and beach. **Cocolores Restaurant,** at Cabinas el Pargo Feliz, has reasonably priced lobster ($12) and fish dishes (about $4). You can get tasty pastas and filling *casados* at **Restaurant El Parque,** on the village beach.

Pizza Net (tel. 506/642-0059, 10:30 A.M.– 10 P.M.) offers 50 varieties, from Hawaiian pizza to margarita pizza ($1.25 small to $11 for a large Hawaiian).

© CHRISTOPHER P. BAKER

lunch on the beach at Montezuma

Restaurant Congo Azul (7 A.M.–10 P.M., 11 A.M.–5 P.M., and 6–10 P.M.), at the Luz de Mono Hotel, claims to serve "gourmet" Latin-Italian fusion cuisine, but there wasn't a single staff member on hand at my last visit. It serves wine produced from its own vineyard!

You can buy groceries and baked goods at **Mamatea Delicatessan.**

Information and Services

The tour desk at **El Sano Banano** is the best resource.

There's no bank. **Pizza Net** (tel. 506/642-0059, pizzanet@racsa.co.cr) is an Internet *pizzería* charging $0.25 per minute, and $2 for each 30 minutes.

Getting There

A bus for Cóbano and Montezuma ($4) meets the Paquera ferry, departing Paquera at 6:15 A.M., 7:30 A.M., 10 A.M., 12:30 P.M., 2 P.M., 4:30 P.M., and 6:15 P.M. The bus for Paquera departs Montezuma at 5:30A.M., 8:05 A.M., 10 A.M., noon, 2:15 P.M., and 4 P.M.; and from Cóbano (from outside the Hotel Caoba) 15 minutes later.

A taxi to Montezuma from Tambor airport costs about $15.

Aventuras en Montezuma offers a water-taxi to Jacó (from $25 pp, depending on number of passengers), while **Montezuma Expeditions** offers daily transfers to Tamarindo, plus a daily minibus shuttle to/from San José ($35) and between other key destinations in the northwest.

CABUYA

The dirt road continues west from Montezuma to Cabuya, a tiny hamlet nine km southwest of Montezuma and two km northeast of Cabo Blanco reserve. A rough rock-and-dirt track leads north to Malpaís (seven km; 4WD essential—and even with 4WD passable only in dry season), climbing tenuously over the mountainous cape that forms Cabo Blanco; turn right at Mini-Super Cabuya, where the road to the left leads to the rocky shore. **Isla Cabuya,** about 200 meters offshore, has been used as a cemetery for the village of Cabuya. You can walk out to the island at low tide and see perhaps two dozen graves marked with crude crosses.

© CHRISTOPHER P. BAKER

Paquera ferry

Accommodations and Food

Restaurante y Cabinas El Ancla de Oro (tel. 506/642-0369, lamont@racsa.co.cr, $20 s/d low season, $30 high season) has camping for $5 per tent low season, $8 high season. It also has three delightful thatched hardwood A-framed cabins on tall stilts (one sleeps five). Mosquito nets are provided. The restaurant serves tasty treats such as fish curry with coconut milk ($5.50), shrimp curry ($8), and garlic herb bread. The owners, Alex Villaloboso and his English wife, Fiona, rent horses ($20), mountain bikes ($10), and kayaks, and also rent other cabins nearby.

Hotel Cabo Blanco (tel. 506/642-0332, caboblanco@crosswinds.net, www.crosswinds .net/~caboblanco, $25 with fans, $30 with a/c), 800 meters east of Cabuya, nestles amid palms and offers 10 rooms with cable TV and orthopedic beds. There's a freeform pool, a kids' pool, a gym, and rental kayaks. It is closed seasonally.

Nearby, the modest **Hotel Celaje** (tel./fax 506/642-0374, celaje@racsa.co.cr, www.celaje .com, $30 s, $35 d low season; $35 s, $45 d high season) has seven simple yet attractive thatched beachfront four-person *cabinas* with private baths and patios with hammocks. It has a nice pool with Jacuzzi, as well as a tempting *ranchito* restaurant serving continental food and real Belgian beer (day guests can use the pool if they eat). New Belgian owners were planning to upgrade at last visit. It offers bicycle and kayak rentals and arranges horseback riding and sportfishing.

Getting There

A bus departs Montezuma for Cabuya at 8:15 A.M., 10:15 A.M., 2:15 P.M., and 6:15 P.M. ($1 each way). See the next section for onward bus routes.

◤ CABO BLANCO ABSOLUTE WILDLIFE RESERVE

This jewel of nature at the very tip of the Nicoya Peninsula is where Costa Rica's quest to bank its natural resources for the future began. The 1,172-hectare Reserva Natural Absoluta Cabo Blanco (8 A.M.–4 P.M. Wed.–Sun., plus Monday and Tuesday during holidays, $8 admission)—the oldest protected area in the country—was created in October 1963 thanks to the tireless efforts of Nils Olof Wessberg, a Swedish immigrant commonly referred to as the father of Costa Rica's national park system (for a discussion of Wessberg's influence, see David Rains Wallace's excellent book *The Quetzal and the Macaw: The Story of Costa Rica's National Parks*). Olof and his wife, Karen, settled in the area in 1955, when this corner of the Nicoya Peninsula was still covered with a mix of evergreen and deciduous forest—an island in a sea of rapidly falling trees, rising settlements, and cattle ranches. They bought a rocky, mountainous plot of land and spent 10 years developing fruit orchards.

In 1960, when the first patch of cleared land appeared at Cabo Blanco, Olof launched an appeal to save the land. "Only in one spot is there today some of the wildlife that was formerly everywhere in the northwest," Olof wrote. "Here live the puma and the *manigordo* (ocelot), deer, peccary, tepiscuintle, pizote, kinkajou, chulumuco (tayra), kongo (howler monkey), carablanca (capuchin monkey), and miriki (spider monkey). The jaguar and tapir are already extinct . . . . When we settled here six years ago the mountain was always green. Today it has great brown patches, and in March and April it is shrouded in smoke, much of it on fire . . . Two years more, and the mountain will be dead. Who is going to save it? It can be had at the ridiculously low price of $10 an acre . . . But it has to be done immediately."

Although several international organizations responded with money, buying the land and protecting the area cost blood, sweat, and tears. Conservation had not yet entered national consciousness. The first warden killed the last 10 spider monkeys for their meat; the third warden felled trees to grow crops. When one of Olof's supporters suggested the need for a national parks service to the Costa Rican government, they responded enthusiastically.

Olof Wessberg was murdered in the Osa Peninsula in the summer of 1975 while campaigning to have that region declared a national park. A plaque near the Cabo Blanco ranger station stands in his honor.

The reserve is named after the vertical-walled island at its tip, which owes its name to the accumulation of guano deposited by seabirds, including Costa Rica's largest community of brown boobies (some 500 breeding pairs). The reserve was originally off-limits to visitors. Today, about one-third is accessible along hiking trails, some steep in parts. **Sendero Sueco** leads uphill and then down onto the totally unspoiled white-sand beaches of Playa Balsita and Playa Cabo Blanco, which are separated by a headland (you can walk around it at low tide). A coastal trail, **Sendero El Barco,** leads west from Playa Balsitas to the western boundary of the park. All have tidepools. Check tide tables with the park rangers before setting off—otherwise you could get stuck. Torrential downpours are common April–Dec.

Information

The ranger station (tel./fax 506/642-0093, cablanco@ns.minae.go.cr) sells a trail map. Camping is not allowed, even at the ranger station.

You cannot enter via the ranger station *(puesto)* at Malpaís, on the north side of the reserve.

Getting There

The Montezuma-Cabuya bus continues to Cabo Blanco (see *Cabuya,* above), conditions permitting. The Cabuya–Montezuma bus departs at 7 A.M., 9 A.M., 1 P.M., and 4:40 P.M.

Aventuras en Montezuma offers transfers to Cabo Blanco by reservation ($6 round-trip). Collective taxis depart Montezuma for Cabo at 7 and 9 A.M., returning at 3 and 4 P.M. ($1.50 pp). A private taxi costs about $12 one-way.

The dirt road deteriorates badly before Cabo Blanco and gets very muddy in the wet season.

Many people walk from Montezuma (11 km)—a hot and tiring walk.

MALPAÍS

The shoreline immediately north of Cabo Blanco is a lively surfers' paradise with some of the most splendid surfing beaches in the country. A road that leads west 10 km from Cóbano hits the shore at the hamlet of **Carmen,** known in the surfing realm as **Malpaís.** The tiny fishing hamlet of Malpaís is actually three km south of Carmen, but no matter; this dirt road deadends at the hamlet and turns inland briefly,

© CHRISTOPHER P. BAKER

Playa Santa Teresa

a surf sign at Malpaís

© CHRISTOPHER P. BAKER

Entertainment and Events

Malpaís Surf Camp has a lively bar that shows surf videos and has open mike and live music on Wednesday and Saturdays; there's ping-pong, table soccer, a pool table, and a mechanical bull.

La Lora is the in-vogue bar in Santa Teresa; it has a pool table and dancing.

Sports and Recreation

Canopy del Pacífico (tel. 506/640-0071, silmon @racsa.co.cr, www.malpais.net/canopy.htm) offers tours by zipline between the treetops.

Pacific Divers (tel. 506/640-0187, www.pacificdivers-costarica.com) offers scuba trips ($45, one tank; $75 two tank).

Malpaís Surf Camp offers surf instruction ($30 for 90 minutes) with a "stand up" guarantee. **Santa Teresa Surf Camp** (tel. 506/640-0106) rents boards and offers surf lessons.

Accommodations

Camping: Camping y Cabinas Zeneida is tucked amid shade trees (with hammocks) beside the beach in Santa Teresa. It charges $3 pp for camping, including toilets and showers. It also has two A-frame cabins with loft bedrooms and toilets and kitchenettes below, plus a thatched cabin ($5 pp). The owners will cook meals ($3 breakfast, $5 dinner).

Soda Roca Mar (tel. 506/640-0250, $2.50 pp low season, $4 high season), at the north end of Santa Teresa, has beachfront camping under palms, with outside toilets and showers. It has a *soda* and two basic cabins.

Under $25: One of the best bets is **Frank's Place** (tel./fax 506640-0096, frank5@racsa.co.cr, $10 pp shared bath, $22 d private bath, $40 with a/c, $47 with kitchen low season; $12 shared bath, $28 private bath, $45 with a/c, $58 with kitchen high season), at the junction for Cóbano, with 24 cabins, nine with shared bathrooms. Four have a/c and TV. It also has rooms with kitchenettes, plus two *casitas* with kitchens. Its restaurant is popular, and it has a pool plus Internet access, and tours and transfers.

The well-run **M Malpaís Surf Camp and Resort** (tel./fax 506/642-0061, surfcamp@racsa .co.cr, www.malpaissurfcamp.com, $10 pp camp

ending at the northern entrance gate to Cabo Blanco Absolute Wildlife Reserve (entry to the park is *not* allowed here). A rocky track that begins 800 meters north of the dead-end links Cabuya with Malpaís.

North from Carmen, the dirt road parallels **Playa Carmen** and **Playa Santa Teresa,** a seemingly endless beach with coral-colored sand, pumping surf, and dramatic rocky islets offshore. The community of **Santa Teresa** straggles along the road but is centered on a soccer field. The road continues to Manzanillo, where the going gets tougher.

The past few years have seen a phenomenal tourist development, propelling Santa Teresa from offbeat obscurity to popularity, aided in 2002 when the finest resort in the country opened here.

The following website is a good resource: www.malpais.net.

beds, $25 s/d cabins with shared bath, $65 d casita), 200 meters south of the junction, has a panoply of accommodations set in eight hectares of grounds. You can camp for $5 pp, with showers and toilets. A hillside oceanview *rancho* has "semi-private" camp beds beneath a tin roof with walls of palm leaves on three sides (the fourth is open to the ocean) and shared baths. There are also *cabinas* with shared bath with cold water, and poolside *casitas* with stone floors, tall louvered screened windows, and beautiful tile bathrooms with hot water. There's a pool, and you can rent horses ($15 per hour), and surfboards ($6 half-day, $10 full-day). It has a lively bar.

Ingo offers eight rooms at **Cabinas Playa Santa Teresa** (tel./fax 640-0137, $20 s/d, or $25 with kitchen low season; $30/35 high season), built around a massive strangler fig favored by howler monkeys. Three have kitchens; all have two double beds and private baths with cold water. It has hammocks under shade, plus parking.

Farther north, Jorge Soto has **Cabinas Capitán,** with three solidly constructed all-wood cabins with louvered windows for $600 monthly. Daily and weekly rentals are offered. He has sea-kayaks, too.

$25–50: I like **Ritmo Tropical** (tel. 506/640-0174, rtropical@racsa.co.cr, $30 s/d low season, $40 high season), 400 meters south of Frank's Place, with seven modern, cross-ventilated, well-lit cabins in a landscaped complex, each for four people and each with hardwood ceilings with fans, modest furnishings, and nice private bathroom with hot water. It has secure parking, plus an Italian restaurant (Thur.–Tue.).

Cabinas Rancho Itauna (tel./fax 640-0095, ranchositauna@yahoo.com, $35/40 without/with kitchen low season; $50/60 high season), in Santa Teresa, is run by a charming Austrian-Brazilian couple and offers four rooms in two octagonal two-story buildings linked by a patio span. Each room has a fan, refrigerator, double bed plus bunk, and private bathroom with hot water. Two rooms have a kitchen. It also rents a budget room for four people with kitchen and shared shower ($10 pp) up the road. The pleasing restaurant serves international cuisine. Rates include tax.

Casitas del Capitán (tel. 506/640-0064, $40 s/d smaller, $70 higher low season, $45/80 high season; $40 cabins low season, $45 high season; $65 room in house low season, $75 high season), toward the north end of Santa Teresa, has two spacious, albeit simply furnished concrete *cabinas* with small kitchens. The upper, two-bedroom unit is nicer.

The well-maintained, U.S.-run **Santa Teresa Surf Camp** offers wonderful *cabinas* with beautiful color schemes. It has one spacious cabin with sloping tin roof, ceiling fans, cement tile floors, and kitchenette with large fridge; large louvered windows open to a terrace. Four other cabins have clean, shared outside bathrooms with cold-water showers. And a beachfront, two-bedroom a/c house has cable TV, colorful walk-in showers, large kitchen, and wrap-around veranda.

$50–100: The **Star Mountain Eco-Resort** (tel. 506/640-0101 and 506/640-0102, starmountain @racsa.co.cr, www.starmountaineco.com, $65 s, $75 d rooms, $25 pp *casita*), two km northeast of Malpaís, on the track to Cabuya, is a gem tucked in the hills amid an 80-hectare private forest reserve, with trails (the turnoff is 400 meters north of the soccer field in Malpaís). The four charming *cabinas* are simple yet tastefully decorated with soft pastels and hardwood accents, cross-ventilated with louvered windows, with Sarchí rockers on the veranda. A casita bunkhouse sleeps up to nine people. Hammocks are slung between trees, there's a pool, and guided horseback rides are offered ($8 per hour). Grilled meats and fish are prepared in a huge open oven. It's run by a Belgian couple.

Sunset Reef (P.O. Box 100-5361, Cóbano, tel./fax 506/642-0012 or tel. 506/282-4160, fax 506/282-4162, info@altatravelplanners.com, $55 s, $65 d low season; $85 s/d high season) is built on a rocky headland at the end of the road. It's marvelously secluded. The 14 spacious, modestly furnished, all-hardwood rooms in a two-story block have two double beds, fans, wide windows, and skylit bathrooms. The simple restaurant has an equally simple menu. An exquisite little freeform swimming pool and Jacuzzi sit on the cliff face amid beautifully landscaped grounds. Also available are boat tours and diving, plus bicycle and kayak rentals for $10 per day.

Hotel Flor Blanca, Playa Santa Teresa

© CHRISTOPHER P. BAKER

The delightful **Trópico Látino Lodge** (tel. 506/640-0062, fax 506/640-0117, tropico @centralamerica.com, www.hoteltropicolatino .com, $45 s, $55 d standard, $55/65 oceanview low season; $55 s, $65 d standard, $65/75 oceanview high season), at Playa Santa Teresa, backs a rocky foreshore with hammocks under shade trees. There's a pool and Jacuzzi, and a breezy bar and restaurant (serving excellent cuisine) by the shore. It has 10 high-ceilinged, simply furnished wooden bungalows amid lawns; each has charcoal tile floors, wide shady verandas with hammocks, a king-size bed and a sofa bed, mosquito nets, fans, and a private bath with hot water. Two newer cabins have ocean views. It arranges fishing, horseback rides, and tours. Rates include tax.

$100 and Up: The French-owned **Hotel Restaurante Milarepa** (P.O. Box 49-5361, Cóbano, tel. 506/640-0023, fax 506/640-0168, milarepa@racsa.co.cr, www.milarepahotel.com, $100 s/d standard, $120 beachfront), at the north end of Playa Santa Teresa, exemplifies luxurious simplicity and is one of the nicest places. It has four cabins, spaced apart amid lawns inset with a lap pool. Two cabins are literally on the beach! They're made of bamboo and rise from a cement base: exquisite appointments include a

Japanese motif, and four-poster beds in the center of the room, with mosquito drapes, plus open-air bathroom-showers (with hot water) in their own patio gardens. One wall folds back entirely to offer ocean vistas, magnificent at sunset! It has a splendid restaurant, plus a pool inset in the lawn.

Stunning and serene are fitting descriptions for **M Hotel Flor Blanca** (tel. 506/640-0232, fax 506/640-0226, florblanca@expressmail.net, www.florblanca.com, $250 one-bedroom, $450 two-bedroom low season; $290 one-bedroom, $490 two-bedroom high season), the finest beach resort in the country. Since opening in 2002, this world-class stunner has taken Malpaís up a notch or five. The boutique hotel enjoys a uniquely advantageous position on seven acres of beachfront at the north end of Santa Teresa, with a fantastic stretch of beach with killer breakers. Imbued with a calming Asiatic influence (Tibetan prayer flags flutter over the entrance), it offers 10 luxury oceanside villas stairstepping down to the beach, with fragrant plumeria and namesake florblanca trees dropping petals at your feet as you walk stone pathways that curl down through an Asian garden, lit at night by soft-glowing lamps. The motif is Santa Fe–

meets–Bali in ochers, earth tones, soft creams, and yellows. The mammoth villas have brick-and-terra-cotta floors and super-high ceilings, and are furnished with wall lamps, silent a/c, large wall safes with security boxes, quality rattan furnishings, tasteful art pieces (African masks, hanging batiks, etc.), and exquisite furnishings, from lamps of tethered bamboo stalks to the hardwood side tables sitting on polished treetrunks and king-size beds on raised hardwood pedestals. Each has a kitchenette, a vast lounge opening to half-moon veranda with recliners, and stone-floored "rainforest" bathrooms with lush gardens, huge scalloped sinks, and separate showers and oversize tub. A sumptuous open-air lounge has a piano and large-screen TV/VCR with video library. There's a broad sundeck with shade umbrellas and a walk-in landscaped horizon pool fed by a waterfall with swim-up bar. The superb oceanfront restaurant is worth a visit in its own right. It offers tours, including horseback riding at the cattle roundup at Hacienda Ario ($60 three hours). It has a music room with big-screen TV and piano. Yoga, kickboxing, and dance classes are offered in a world-class dojo. The Kennedys have vacationed here. Rates include breakfast.

Food

Frank's Place (8 A.M.–9 P.M., $2–6) is the most popular gathering spot, and serves American breakfasts, omelettes, burgers, sandwiches, and seafood, and cheap *casados* (set meals) in an open, airy setting. **Malpaís Surf Camp** also serves American breakfasts (from $3) plus lunch and dinner.

Vegetarians are served by **Jungle Juice** (tel. 506/640-0279, $3.50), serving health foods like pancakes, veggie burgers, quesadillas, and fresh juices.

The restaurant at **Rancho Itauna** (7:30–9:30 A.M. and 6:30–9 P.M. high season only) specializes in Brazilian seafood dishes, but also manages schnitzel, spicy Thai curries, spaghetti, and burritos, and has a barbecue on Thursdays. It hosts live music on Tuesdays and is known for its full moon and New Year's bashes.

The open-air restaurant at the **Hotel Restaurante Milarepa** (8–9:30 A.M., 11:30 A.M.–1:30 P.M., and 7–10 P.M.) specializes in nouvelle Mediterranean cuisine, with a French chef at the helm.

I highly recommend the **Ṇ Nectar Bar & Restaurante** (6:30 A.M.–3 P.M. café only, 3–6 P.M. sushi only, 6–9 P.M. full menu) at Flor Blanca, where Canadian chef Damien Geneau conjures up fabulous Asian-Pacific-Latin fusion creations, including such appetizers as smoked trout, cream cheese, and scallion maki roll appetizers ($6.50), and salmon scallion and caviar jumbo roll ($7.50). Entrées include Chinese five-spice marinated duck breast with caramelized red onion latkes and butter-wilted spinach ($18). The raised hemispheric bar is a good place to enjoy sushi. It plays cool music, from jazz to classical.

The other surefire winner is the restaurant at **Trópico Látino Lodge** ($7) where the recherché menu lists the likes of fish in coconut sauce, chicken curry, and penne with vodka and bacon.

You can stock up on groceries at the **Mini-Super El Almendro** and at **Super Santa Teresa.**

Information and Services

You can buy gasoline at a *pulpería* 0.5 km north of the soccer field. There are public telephones outside Frank's Place, and at Pulpería El Mango facing the soccer field.

A 24-hour ambulance (tel. 506/642-0630 or 506/380-4125) serves Cóbano and the area.

Info Service (tel. 506/640-0229) has Internet service 9 A.M.–5 P.M. Mon.–Sat.

The **Santa Teresa Surf Camp** doubles as a Spanish-language school.

Getting There

Montezuma Expeditions (tel. 506/440-8078, fax 506/440-8006, info@montezumaexpeditions.com) has a daily minibus shuttle from San José ($35).

There's daily bus service between Cóbano and Malpaís.

Cabinas Marazul has a taxi service ($25 to Montezuma, $40 to Tambor, $45 to Paquera), plus a boat for rent.

Taíno Gas (tel. 506/640-0009), in Santa Teresa, is open 7 A.M.–6 P.M.

Central Pacific

The central Pacific region comprises a thin coastal plain narrowing to the southeast and backed by steep-sided mountains cloaked in dense forest. The coast is lined by long gray-sand beaches renowned for fantastic surf. It is distinguished from more northerly shores by its wetter climate: Carara National Park, in the north, marks the boundary between the tropical dry zone and the tropical wet to the south. The region grows gradually humid southward, with the vegetation growing ever more luxuriant. No surprise then that this region has some of the nation's prime national parks, where visitors are virtually guaranteed to see scarlet macaws

screeching overhead and rare spider monkeys swinging from treetop to treetop.

Rivers cascade down from the precipitous mountains, providing opportunities to hike to the base of spectacular waterfalls. The rivers slow to a crawl amid extensive mangrove swamps separated by miles-long sandy swathes interspersed with craggy headlands. Several of these estuarine systems are home to thriving populations of crocodiles, as easily seen here than anywhere in the nation. Indeed, despite the popularity of the surfers' party town of Jacó and more relaxed Manuel Antonio (the foremost attraction), the region retains a kind of wild quality. The Costanera

Sur highway to Manuel Antonio—once a journey akin to purgatory—has been leveled and graded, and the nearby gateway and sportfishing town of Quepos (as well as Jacó) are in the throes of rampant development. But for now the route further south is still an adventure, and parts of this region are still being opened up, luring offbeat travelers in search of tomorrow's find.

South of Jacó, vast groves of African palms smother the coastal plains. Interspersed among them are quaint workers' villages, with gaily painted plantation houses raised on stilts around a soccer field. Otherwise, places of cultural interest are few.

Hwy. 34 (the Costanera Sur) runs the length of the coast, linking the region with Puntarenas and Guanacaste to the north and Golfo Dulce and Osa southward. It is paved almost the entire way and at last visit was being widened and tarred with the intent that Hwy. 34 will become the new Pan-American Highway linking Nicaragua and Panamá (doing away with the need to head up over Cerro de la Muerte and shortening the route considerably). The traffic flow has increased markedly, for better or worse.

The region has distinct wet and dry seasons: May–Nov. and Dec.–April, respectively.

PLANNING YOUR TIME

The Central Pacific zone is almost wholeheartedly a beach destination, particularly favored by surfers: **Playa Hermosa** and **Dominical** are their favored haunts. The area is easily explored along the single coast highway, with dead-end side roads branching off to specific attractions as if from a tree. Sites of interest are relatively few, other than the national parks and nature reserves and, of course, the beaches. Allocate a week minimum to explore the entire region north to south, although three days is sufficient if you wish to concentrate on Manuel Antonio or Jacó or Dominical.

The most developed of the beach resorts is **Jacó,** long a staple of Canadian package charter groups but recently, having spruced itself up, an in-vogue destination for young and hip travelers. It's a favorite of surfers and of Tico youth. If you like an active nightlife, this is also for you, but I find the place overrated. If quality is your gig, move along, being sure to call in at **Villa Caletas,** perhaps the finest hotel in the country, where day visitors can dine and take advantage of the facilities: dress accordingly!

The best-known and most beautiful beaches are those of **Manuel Antonio National Park,** just south of the hip sportfishing town of **Quepos,** boasting between them a fine array of accommodations (Manuel Antonio is blessed with upscale options; Quepos caters to the budget end). Clear waters and a coral reef make Manuel Antonio a favorite of snorkelers, while a lush tropical forest with well-groomed nature trails and abundant wildlife makes this one of the most visited parks in the nation. **Carara National Park** also offers a feast of wildlife wonders and has the advantage of being accessed direct from the Costanera Sur. Wanna go croc-spotting? Sign up for a crocodile safari on the **Río Tárcoles,** a perfect complement to hiking in nearby Carara. Kayak trips in search of dolphins and whales are a popular option along the **Brunca Coast.** And a stay at **Finca Brian y Emilia,** in the hills of **Escaleras,** will satisfy any longings to get back to your earthy roots.

Manmade facilities worth a call include **Turu Ba-ri Parque Tropical,** offering a medley of attractions from a petting zoo to an aerial tramway; **Rainmaker Conservation Project** with its boardwalks in the sky; and **Savegre River Plantation,** which promises a thrilling water-themed recreational park and deluxe accommodations.

The months of Dec.–April anywhere along the central Pacific coast are particularly busy, when Costa Ricans take their "summer" holidays (the long school break is January and February). This is particularly true of beaches such as Playas Esterillos Oeste, Centro, and Este, which have thus far been eschewed by travelers although popular with Tico families with second homes.

Must-Sees

Look for **M** to find the sights and activities you
can't miss and **N** for the best dining and lodging.

M Tárcoles: You're sure to see crocs close up on this
river, with fabulous birding to boot (page 467).

M Carara National Park: This reserve at the
meeting point of moist and dry tropical ecosystems is easily accessed. Monkeys, sloths, and
macaws are virtually guaranteed (page 469).

M Villas Caletas: A destination in its own right, this
deluxe resort hotel perched atop a headland welcomes call-in visitors for meals and to enjoy music
concerts in its open-air ampitheater (page 470).

M Rainmaker Conservation Project: Boardwalks in the sky? Yes, elevated walkways lead you
through the forest canopy at this private reserve in
the mountains (page 484).

M Manuel Antonio National Park: Popular and
heavily visited, this small rainforest preserve offers diverse wildlife, good nature trails, beautiful
beaches, and a small coral reef ideal for snorkeling
(page 501).

M Savegre River Plantation: When completed,
this one-of-a-kind theme-park resort hotel will

Manual Antonio National Park

feature fabulous manmade lakes and activities
(page 505).

M Barú National Wildlife Refuge: Wildlife
abounds in this small reserve, which spans numerous ecosystems, from mangroves to montane rainforest (page 507).

M Escaleras: Here you can ride on horseback
through the rainforest, where rugged mountain
trails lead to stunning waterfalls. Stay at Bella Vista
Ranch Lodge or Finca Brian y Emilia, which offers
an option for overnighting with a *campesino* family
(page 510).

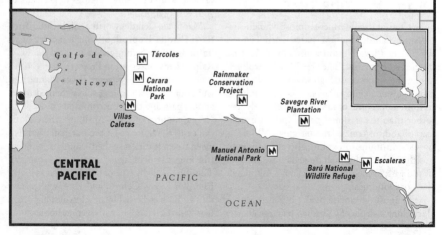

CENTRAL
PACIFIC

Golfo de

Nicoya

M Tárcoles

M Carara
National
Park

Rainmaker
Conservation
Project
M

Savegre River
Plantation
M

Villas
Caletas

Manuel Antonio **M**
National Park

Barú National
Wildlife Refuge **M**

M Escaleras

PACIFIC

OCEAN

CENTRAL PACIFIC

Puntarenas
Caldera
Punta Caldera
Tivives
Playa Guacalillo

CANOPY TOUR
MAHOGANY PARK
Mata de
Limón
Río Machuca
Cascajal

San Mateo
Orotina
239

San Pablo de
Turrubares

TURU-BARI
PARQUE TROPICAL

CARARA NATIONAL PARK

Río Pods

San José
2
Cartago

Alto
Cedral

Volcán
Irazú

Cordillera de Talamanca

Río Macho
Forest Reserve

Cerro
Cuericí

Cerro Urán

Cerro
Tsuitabeta

Chirripó
National
Park

Cerro
Chirripó Grande
Cerro
Chirripó

Cerro Ena

Cerro Amo
Cerro Ami

Cerro
Bolas

Palmar
Norte

Ciudad
Cortés

Río Grande de Térraba

34

Ojochal

Terra-Sierpe
International
Humid Forest
Reserve

Playa Piñuela
Tortuga
Abajo

Whale Marine
National Park

Playa Ballena
Punta Uvita
Playa Hermosa
Punta
Dominical

Uvita
ORO VERDE
Cerro
Uvita

Quebrada
Grande
Piñuela

Río Peñuela

San Isidro de
El General

Río General

2

Río Chirripó del Pacífico

Nauyaca
Waterfalls

BARÚ NATIONAL
WILDLIFE REFUGE
FINCA BRIAN Y EMILIA

BELLA VISTA RANCH LODGE/
Rancho Merced N.W.R.

Dominical

Barú
PARQUE
REPTILIANO

Barú

243

ESCALERAS

Cerro
San Juan
Río San Juan

Cerro Lira

Fila Zapotales

Río Savegre

SAVEGRE RIVER
PLANTATION

WILDLIFE RESCUE CENTER

Fila
San Bosco

Cerro
Camorra

Cerro
de la Muerta

Cerro Urán

Cerro
Vueltas

Cerro San Jeronimo

Fila de Bustamente

Cerro Caraigres

Cerro Turrubares

Santiago

Cerro Bijagualito

Carara

Río Candelaria

PAN-AMERICAN
HIGHWAY

RAINMAKER
CONSERVATION
PROJECT

RAFIKI SAFARI LODGE

Río Naranjo

Río Canas

Fila Chonta

Palo

Río Dumas

Río Tulín

Río Paquita

Parrita

Isla
Palo Seco

Isla
Dumas

Quepos

Manuel Antonio
Punta Quepos
Playa Manuel Antonio

MANUEL ANTONIO
NATIONAL PARK

Punta Catedral

Silencio
Londres

Savegre

Playa
Savegre

Portalón
Ecological
Wildlife Refuge

Matapalo
Playa
Matapalo

Playa Barú

Playa
Platanillo

PACIFIC OCEAN

Finca
la Palma

Estero los
Este

CREADO NATURALEZA
NATURE RESERVE

Cerro
Cangreja

RANCHO
MONTEREY

LA CATARATA
(MANANTIAL DE AGUA VIVA)

WATERFALL
CANOPY TOUR

Biagual

Bijagual

JARDIN PURA VIDA

Playa
de Jacó

Jacó

Playa
Herradura

Punta Leona

VILLAS CALETAS

34

Playa Hermosa

Esterillos Oeste
Punta Judas
Playa Esterillos Oeste
Playa Esterillos Este
Esterillos Este

Punta Conejo

Playa Tárcoles
Tárcoles

TÁRCOLES

LOS SUEÑOS MARRIOTT
BEACH & GOLF RESORT/
LOS SUEÑOS MARINA

27

PACIFIC OCEAN

0   10 mi

0   10 km

N

© AVALON TRAVEL PUBLISHING, INC.

North of Jacó

OROTINA

From the central highlands, Hwy. 3 descends to Orotina, gateway to the central Pacific. The road drops steeply, with hairpin bends, washed-out sections of road, slow-moving trucks, and Costa Ricans overtaking like suicidal maniacs. It's single-lane in each direction. *Drive cautiously!* A new, more direct highway linking the central highlands—via Santiago de Puriscal—with the Pacific at Parrita just 30 km north of Manuel Antonio was incomplete at press time. But you can also take a less-trafficked route west from San José via Santiago de Puriscal and San Pablo de Turrubares: the deteriorated paved road sidles magnificently downhill to Orotina, where it joins Hwy. 3.

Orotina is hidden 400 meters northwest of Hwy 3, which six km west of town merges with Hwy. 27 (for Puntarenas) and Hwy. 34 for Jacó and Manuel Antonio. The town is centered on an attractive plaza shaded by palms and has a railway track running down the main street.

The erstwhile **Iguana Park** has closed. However, **Waterland Jungle Park,** eight km outside Orotina, was in construction at last visit.

Canopy Tour Mahogany Park (c/o The Original Canopy Tour, tel. 506/257-5149 in San José, fax 506/256-7626, canopy@canopytour.com, www.canopytour.com/drake.html) is on a 120-hectare forest reserve. You'll ascend to the treetops and traverse from platform to platform using pulleys on horizontal cables.

Turu Ba-ri Parque Tropical

This adventure theme park (tel. 506/250-0705, fax 506/250-8643, info@turubari.com, www.turubari.com), at San Juan de Mata, four km south of Orotina, claims to be the biggest tropical theme park in Central America. Extending over 496 acres, it is accessed via an aerial tramway with enclosed gondolas that whisks you on a "sky ride tour" ($15) down from a plateau into the valley of the Río Tárcoles (land shuttles are also offered). Highlights include a 16-platform canopy tour via zipline ($20, two hours; offered at 9 A.M., 11:30 A.M., and 2 P.M.), plus guided horseback rides ($10–20), trails, a petting zoo, and vast tropical gardens with a butterfly garden and theme gardens dedicated to palms, orchids, bamboos, etc. (the full Tropical Park tour costs from $55). Kids can have fun in two mazes. And a Finca Campesina replicates life of yore on a typical country farm. It also has mountain bike rentals. It has two restaurants plus a bar and grill.

Accommodations

Seeking a bed-and-breakfast charmer? Head to the family-run **La Finca Que Ama** (tel. 506/419-0110, contactus@costaricafinca.com, www.costaricafinca.com, $129 s/d low season, $149 high season), outside San Pablo de Turrubares, about 10 km east of Orotina on the road to Santiago de Puriscal, and set in an eight-acre estate with trails. It has 10 modestly furnished duplex *casitas* (billed as "junior suites") with satellite TV, DVD player, mini-fridge, coffeemaker, telephone, terrace, and private bathrooms with hot water. Gourmet meals are served on a veranda with magnificent views. There's a lounge, game room, Internet access, bar, and infinity-edge swimming pool.

WEST OF OROTINA

West of Orotina, the land slopes gently toward the Gulf of Nicoya. Hwy. 27 connects Orotina with the port city of Puntarenas: the road leads through savanna land munched by hardy cattle and hits the coast at Mata de Limón, facing the Bahía de Caldera. The bay is shadowed by **Punta Corralillo,** a headland south of which mangrove swamps stretch along the shoreline for 20 km to the mouth of the Río Tárcoles.

Tivives has a pleasant and peaceful four-km-wide beach backed by 670 hectares of mangrove swamps at the mouth of the Río Jesús María. Crocodiles cool off in the mangroves. Good bird-watching, too. Howler and white-faced monkeys live here. And jaguarundis and ocelots have even been sighted on the beach.

Two km south of Tivives is **Playa Guacalillo,** site of Proyecto Vacacional Bajamar, centered on the hamlet of Bajamar. The unremarkable gray-sand beach is backed by a lagoon full of wading birds. **Grupo Mawamba** (tel. 506/293-8181, fax 506/239-7657, info@grupomawamba.com, www.grupomawamba.com) offers a "Tropical Mangrove River Adventure" by canopied boat.

Cruise ships berth a few kilometers south, at **Puerto Caldera.**

N TÁRCOLES

Twenty-five km south of Orotina, Hwy. 34 crosses the **Río Tárcoles.** The bridge over the river is the easiest place in the country for spotting crocodiles, which bask on the mudbanks below the bridge: (don't lean over too far). *Several tourists have been victims of armed robberies near the bridge. There is now a police post here, but caution is still required.*

Crocodiles gather in even greater numbers at the rivermouth, five km west, where the fishing village of Tárcoles is deriving new income offering croc-spotting trips. The estuary is also fantastic for bird-watching: more than 400 species

have been identified here. Gulls, terns, and herons congregate on the sandbars. Frigate birds wheel overhead, while cormorants and kingfishers fish in the lagoons. Roseate spoonbills add a splash of color. And scarlet macaws fly overhead on their way to and from roosts in the mangrove swamps that extend 15 km northward.

The turnoff for Tárcoles is signed five km south of the bridge; the dirt road leads north about two km to a Y-fork where you should go right for the river and safari departure point, and left for the beach and Tarcol Lodge.

At the turnoff for Tárcoles from Hwy. 34, a dirt road leads east and climbs steeply to the hamlet of **Bijagual.** About two km above the road is the **Villa Lapas Sky Walk** a canopy tour with bridges and ziplines and fantastic views down over the coast. You must buy tickets at the Villa Lapas Hotel.

Continuing uphill, about five km from Hwy. 34 you pass the **Catarata Manantial de Agua Viva** (tel./fax 506/661-8263, 8 A.M.–3 P.M., $10 admission), where a three-km trail drops steeply to this spectacular 183-meter-high waterfall. There are *miradors* and benches for wildlife viewing. Best time is rainy season, when the falls are

© CHRISTOPHER P. BAKER

boats on the Río Tárcoles

going full tilt. They don't cascade in one great plume but rather tumble down the rockface to natural pools good for swimming. There are scarlet macaw nesting sites, and poison-arrow frogs hop along the paths. The trail is a stiff 45-minute hike. Camping is permitted. A bus from Orotina to Bijagual (departs 11 A.M.; returns from Bijagual at 5:30 A.M.) will drop you at the front gate. You can buy snacks and drinks.

Another two km brings you to **Pura Vida Botanical Garden** (tel. 506/200-5040, pvgardens@racsa.co.cr, 8 A.M.–5 P.M.). Manicured gravel trails offer dramatic views over mountain ridges toward the Manantial de Agua Viva waterfall and the coast. A self-guided tour ($15) takes about one hour. It has a delightful restaurant and a gift store.

Accommodations and Food

Restaurante y Cabinas El Cocodrilo (tel. 506/661-8261, $22.50 s/d), on the north side of the bridge of the Río Tarcoles, has eight basic *cabinas* with fans and shared baths with cold water. There's a kids' playground, a souvenir store, and an atmospheric restaurant serving *típico* dishes and *casados* (set meals, $2.50).

In Tárcoles village, **Hotel Carara** (tel. 506/637-0178, $25 pp) has 30 simple rooms with shared or private bath and fan or a/c. There's a small bar and restaurant, and a small swimming pool, plus ping-pong and a pool table. Rates include breakfast and tax.

Hotel Villa Lapas (Apdo. 419-4005 San José, tel. 506/222-5191, fax 506/222-3450, hvlapas @racsa.co.cr, www.villalapas.com, $161–193 s, $210–278 d all-inclusive), on the road to Manatial waterfall, is an all-inclusive resort amid beautifully landscaped grounds on the edge of Carara Reserve. It has 55 comfortable a/c rooms aligned along the river with simple yet attractive decor, queen-size beds, terra-cotta floors, fan, and large bathrooms. Facilities include an elegant, hacienda-style restaurant/bar with a deck over the river, plus a swimming pool, two new whirlpools, mini-golf, volleyball, and nature trails that lead into a 280-hectare private reserve of secondary forest bordering Carara. There's a netted butterfly garden and small gym. Birding and nature walks are offered. A reader complains about mildew.

Tarcol Lodge, an old, run-down, two-story wooden house on the banks of the Río Tárcoles

a jungle tour boat on the Río Tárcoles

estuary, acclaims itself as a nature lodge but cannot be recommended.

Crocodile-Spotting Tours

Jungle Crocodile Safari (tel./fax 506/637-0338 or 506/241-1853, info@costaricanaturetour.com, www.costaricanaturetour.com) offers a two-hour croc-spotting trip upriver aboard a pontoon boat ($25). It has an office in the village. Also in the village, **Crocodile Man Tours** (tel./fax 506/637-0426, crocodilemancr@hotmail.com) offers similar tours, as does **J.D.'s Watersports** (tel. 506/257-3857, jdwatersports.com).

ⓜ CARARA NATIONAL PARK

Rainforest exploration doesn't come any easier than at Carara, 20 km south of Orotina and beginning immediately south of the Tárcoles bridge. Carara (the Huetar name for crocodile) is unique in that it lies at the apex of the Amazonian and Mesoamerican ecosystems—a climatological zone of transition from the dry of the Pacific north to the very humid southern coast—and is a meeting place for species from both. The 5,242-hectare park borders the Pan-American Highway, so you can literally step from your car and enter the last significant stand of primary forest of its kind on the Pacific coast.

Carara was once part of the huge Finca La Coyola, one of the biggest haciendas in Costa Rica. The Cervantes family protected the area for generations before the land passed to the National Parks Service. The land was expropriated in 1977 as part of an agrarian resettlement program for landless *campesinos;* in April 1979, 4,700 hectares were pared off to form a biological reserve, which was elevated to national park status in 2000.

Carara protects evergreen forest of great complexity and density. The diversity of trees is one of the highest in the world. The 10 rarest hardwoods in the country are here, as are some of the rarest and most spectacular animals of tropical America: American crocodiles, great anteaters, ocelots, spider monkeys, and poison-arrow frogs. Carara is also one of the best bird-watching localities in all Costa Rica. Fiery-billed aracari and

hikers at Carara National Park

toucan are common. Boat-billed herons, with their curious keel-shaped beaks, are common along the watercourses. And around dawn and dusk, scarlet macaws—there are at least 40 breeding pairs—can be seen in flight as they migrate daily between the wet forest interior and the coastal mangrove swamps. The bridge over the Río Tárcoles is a good place to spot them as they fly over. Carara also has numerous pre-Columbian archaeological sites dating back at least 2,000 years.

Driest months are March and April. Bring insect repellent, water, boots, and long pants.

Information

The **Visitors Center** (Centro de Visitantes, tel. 506/200-5023, 8 A.M.–4 P.M. low season, 7 A.M.–5 P.M. high season, $8 admission) and park headquarters (tel. 506/383-9953, raviles @ns.minae.go.cr) sit beside the coastal highway, three km south of the Río Tárcoles, and has exhibitions, an auditorium, and bathrooms. You'll find picnic tables here, plus Las Araceas Nature Trail, a one-km loop; and a handicapped-acces-

Central Pacific

sible trail that links to the Quebrada Bonita trail. The 4.5-km Laguna Meandrica Trail begins beside the highway and follows an old road paralleling the Río Tárcoles; the entrance gate, however, is usually locked. The rest of Carara is off-limits. Camping is not allowed.

Most tour operators in San José arrange tours to Carara. Even if you want to explore on your own, it pays to have a guide, which can be booked through Costa Rica Expeditions or other tour operators (see *Resources*, in the appendix).

Several armed robberies have occurred in the past. You should avoid parking by the Laguna Meandrica Trail. Park by the visitor center and ask rangers about current conditions. The rangers can arrange local guides ($15 pp up to four people). Bilingual ranger Christian Chavarría Villalobos (tel. 506/428-6022, christianc @yahoo.com) can be hired.

> *Fiery-billed aracari and toucan are common. And around dawn and dusk, scarlet macaws—there are at least 40 breeding pairs—can be seen in flight as they migrate daily between the wet forest interior and the coastal mangrove swamps.*

Getting There

All buses bound between San José or Puntarenas and Jacó and Quepos pass by the reserve. Buses may be full on the weekend.

PLAYA HERRADURA

A series of coves and beaches lines the coast south of Tárcoles, beginning with **Playa Malo,** a scenic bay fringed by a scalloped, 800-meter-wide, white-sand beach. Fishing boats bob at anchor and are roosts for pelicans. At the south end rises the headland of Punta Leona, smothered with forest protected in a 300-hectare private nature reserve—part of a self-contained resort called Punta Leona. The beaches have been off-limits to the public for years, despite court rulings ordering that public access be granted. The reception gate is roadside, three km south of Punta Malo.

About seven km from both Tárcoles and Jacó, just south of the Río Caña Blanca, is a turnoff for **Playa Herradura,** which gained attention a few years ago as a film set for the movie *1492,* starring

Gérard Depardieu as Columbus. The pebbly, gray-sand beach is swarmed by Ticos on weekends and holidays. For now—but surely not for long—marine turtles come ashore to lay their eggs July–Dec. Playa Herradura hit the big time in 1999 with the opening of the mammoth **Los Sueños Marriott Beach & Golf Resort** (see *Accommodation,* below), worth visiting to see the fallen 300-year-old ceiba tree toppled by a storm in 2001 and which has since been carved by Fabio Brenes Morales into the form of a sleeping woman guarded by an angel and giant iguana.

Villas Caletas

South of Punta Leona the road climbs steeply before dropping down to Playa Herradura. At the crest of the rise is the entrance to Villa Caletas, a fabulous resort hotel atop a 500-meter headland. You owe it to yourself to pay a visit to sip a cocktail, have lunch or dinner, and admire the staggering views (see *Accommodation and Food,* below). Centerpiece of this splendid oasis is the sensational horizon pool and wooden deck suspended miraculously as if in midair. A whimsical waterfall and patinated griffins and statues add fairy-tale notes, and an orchid garden is another treat. Two restaurants offer ambitious food. A boutique sells top-quality ceramics and gold jewelry. Aromatherapy, massage, and other treatments are offered in the hilltop Serenity Spa, and there's a glass-walled a/c gym. The coup de grâce is a cliff-face Greek amphitheater - a setting for jazz and classical concerts. The 160-hectare property swoops down through deep green forest to Playa Caletas, with a beach bar. It's a stiff hike, or you can take the six-times-daily beach shuttle.

Entertainment and Events

Villa Caletas has monthly music concerts, particularly jazz and New Age. Costa Rica's annual International Music Festival is hosted here each July and August.

Stellar's Casino, at Los Sueños, is open 2 P.M.–midnight Sun.–Wed., 2 P.M.–1 A.M. Thurs.–Sat.

Sports and Recreation

Freedom Cruises (tel. 506/291-0191, fax 506/220-0910, www.breezecruises.com) operates a small ship, the *Breezes*, on one-day trips to Isla Tortuga from Los Sueños marina. **Sail FX** (tel. 506/643-1017, www.lossuenossailing.com) offers sailing trips from Los Sueños marina.

Costa Rica Fishing Charters (tel. 506/643-2906, cellular tel. 506/364-2123, www.costaricafishingcharters.com; in the U.S., tel. 800/215-0276), based at Los Sueños Marina, charges half-day $700, full-day $1,000 using a 34-foot Custom Crusader. **Costa Rica Dreams** (tel. 506/643-3942, fax 506/643-2301, www.costaricadreams.com; in the U.S., tel. 732/901-8625) offers sportfishing from Los Sueños Marina.

A round of golf at **Los Sueños Marriott Beach & Golf Resort** (tel. 506/630-9092) costs $95 for guests, $140 nonguests, including cart. Club rental costs $35.

Accommodations

Camping on the beach is not permitted.

Steve N' Lisa's Paradise Cove (tel./fax 506/637-0168, $15 pp), on the roadside at Playa Malo, rents four two-story oceanside a/c *cabinas* with kitchens overlooking Playa Malo.

If you like planned resorts, consider **Punta Leona Beach Hotel** (Apdo. 8592-1000, San José, tel. 506/661-2414 or 506/231-3131, fax 506/232-0791, info@hotelpuntaleona.com, www.hotelpuntaleona.com, from $58 s, $66 d standard, $135 s/d junior suite, $165–225 s/d suites low season; $72/82 standard, $170 junior suite, $195–240 suite high season; $92–150 chalets year-round; $150 family apartments year-round). The 108 a/c bungalows and rooms are modern and spacious, with TV and large showers. It also has 35 one- and two-bedroom apartments, and 15 suites with full kitchens. There are three restaurants, plus three bars and grills, a large pool and sunning area, small discotheque, children's video arcade, and panoply of water sports. It's popular with Ticos.

The swank **Los Sueños Marriott Beach & Golf Resort** (tel. 506/643-3886 or 506/630-9000, fax 506/643-3895 or 506/630-9090, costaric@marriott.co.cr, www.lossuenosresort .com, $135–215 s/d rooms, $650 suites low season) mega-resort and residential complex is centered on a championship golf course cut into forested hills. At its heart is a four-story hotel in Spanish-colonial style—lots of red tile, natural stone, and wrought iron—but nonetheless with an anywhere-USA feel. Its 201 regally appointed a/c rooms feature tile floors, ceiling fans, king or double beds, satellite TV with pay-per-view movies, phones, safes, minibars, irons and ironing boards, hair dryers, plus Juliet balconies. Choose from six restaurants, a casino, and a wide range of sports, shopping, and services. Suspended walkways lead through the forest canopy, and there's a 300-slip marina. Long-term plans call for 800 condo units; most were complete at last visit, many will be available to rent.

To feel like royalty or a Hollywood star, head to the palatial **M Hotel Villa Caletas** (P.O. Box 12358-1000, San José, tel. 506/637-0606, fax 506/637-0404, reservations@villacaletas.com, www.hotelvillacaletas.com, $120–150 s/d standard, $210 junior suite, $230–310 suite, $160 villa low season; $140–170/235/270–350/180, respectively, high season), a member of the Small Distinctive Hotels of Costa Rica and the finest resort hotel in Costa Rica. Imagine a French colonial–style gingerbread villa—reached by a winding hillcrest driveway lined with Roman urns—and self-contained matching *casitas* overlooking the sea. Surround each with sensuous, tropical greenery, then add a Hellenic motif and sublime decor, stunning museum pieces, and an aquarium a zoo would be proud of. Spacious public lounges in black, grays, and whites boast black wicker furniture, hand-painted terra-cotta tilework, tasteful paintings, Renaissance antiques, giant clam shells, and Oriental rugs. You'll think you've entered the Louvre! It has 35 luxurious a/c accommodations in eight categories, including eight huge, high-ceilinged, individually styled bedrooms in the main house. Each is done up in warm tropical colors, with antique-style beds, Japanese-style lampshades, floor-to-ceiling silk

French curtains and bedspreads of Indian provenance, cable TVs, minibar, security boxes, and verandas opening onto stunning ocean vistas. Separate bungalows include junior suites, suites with outside spa, and self-contained master-suite villas in their own private gardens with their private parking and entrance, whirlpool tubs with wrap-around windows, terraces with hammocks, horizon swimming pools, and bedrooms mirrored wall to wall for the ultimate romantic experience. Some are a hefty hike up and down stone-walled pathways zigzagging through the lush grounds. Guests get golf privileges at the nearby Los Sueños resort. One English couple I spoke to thought it "OTT . . . over the top, dear!" But more typically, I overheard one guest say, "We're coming back, and we're bringing friends." Another exclaimed, "You can't help but be happy here; it's so wonderful!"

Food

Steve N' Lisa's Paradise Cove (tel. 506/637-0594, 7 A.M.–10 P.M., $2–12) offers breezy patio dining overlooking the beach, and has great burgers, grilled chicken and tuna melt sandwiches, lobster, fettuccine, and salads.

Ⅻ Villa Caletas (see above) offers a sublime setting in which to enjoy gourmet nouvelle cuisine ($10 breakfast, $22 lunch, $33 three-course dinner), such as an appetizer of mozarella, tomatoes, and basil, or beef tenderloin carpaccio; and for entrées, marlin with coconut milk and rum sauce, snook with asparagus sauce, or tenderloin with blackberry demiglaze. Breakfast on the mountaintop with New Age music playing softly is a sublime way to start the day. Each July–Aug. it hosts a Gastronomic Festival with a different national theme each week.

At **Los Sueños,** the six dining options include a *nuevo latino* specialty restaurant, a gourmet coffee shop, and, at the marina, El Galeón (tel. 506/643-2536), with creative international dishes and seafoods.

Getting There and Around

Los Sueños Marina (tel. 506/643-3886) has a state-of-the-art dock with 200 slips for boats up to 200 feet, with cable TV, Internet, and telephone hookups.

Panga Taxi (tel. 506/643-3780) offers water-taxi service to Isla Tortuga, Tambor, Montezuma, Malpaís, and Nicoya ($35).

Jacó and Vicinity

Jacó is the closest beach resort to San José and therefore popular with Josefinos as well as backpackers, surfers, and the young offbeat party crowd. It gets packed on holidays and on weekends in dry season. It was the country's first developed beach resort, when it was put on the map by wintering Canadian charter groups (you can still see Canadian flags flying in tribute to the power of the maple-leaf dollar). Jacó faded from the spotlight for a few years but has bounced back with vigor.

The snowbird scene has been diluted by Ticos (a mix of families and young adults on a fling) and, increasingly, Europeans—especially Italians—bringing a nascent sophistication. It has heaps of hotels, restaurants, and souvenir stores. However, businesses are fluid. Many places mentioned here are likely to have closed their doors or moved to new locations by the time you read this.

Highway 34 runs inland, parallel to Jacó, which lies 400 meters west of the highway and is linked by four access roads. The main strip in town—Avenida Pastro Díaz—runs south two km to the Río Quebrada Seca and the suburb of Garabito. Everything lines the single main street, which parallels the beach for its full length.

Frankly, I've never been enamored of Jacó. The three-km-long beach is not particularly appealing, and swimming is discouraged (signs warn of dangerous rip currents, and the river estuaries at each end of the beach are said to be polluted). If peace and quiet are your thing, give Jacó a wide berth.

Lighthouse Point (tel. 506/643-3284), formerly Jungle Park Wildlife Reserve, on Hwy. 34

© CHRISTOPHER P. BAKER

Playa Jacó seen from a tour boat

and the northerly junction into Jacó, has 11 acres of botanical gardens, with crocodiles and caimans. A butterfly farm was being added at last visit, when the **Pacific Rainforest Aerial Tram** (tel. 506/257-5961, fax 506/257-6053, www.rainforestram.com, 9 A.M.–4 P.M. Monday, 6 A.M.–4 P.M. Tue.–Sun.) was under construction nearby. When complete it will have 18 handicap-equipped gondolas (with canvas awnings and guides), which will ride through the treetops.

ENTERTAINMENT

Jacó has no shortage of bar action. At last visit, the real action was shared between three lively bar-discos: **Onyx,** a cool, hip, happening spot with pool tab les and a large-screen TV; **Filthy McNasty's,** which despite its name is a pleasant spot to tipple; and **Beatles Bar,** the most atmospheric place, with pool tables, darts, table football, TV, and classic music, although its clientele is predominantly males and working girls.

Cocodrilo's Disco, beside the beach, is replete with flashing lights and jet-roar techno music that lures dancers like lemmings on a mission ($3 cover). The other disco of choice is **Disco**

La Central (tel. 506/643-3076), at the south end of town, with a popular beachfront bar.

You can try your luck in the **casinos** of the Hotel Cocal (11 A.M.–3 A.M.); or the Hotel Amapola (open 7 P.M.–3 A.M.), where the casino is open nightly in high season but only on weekends in low season.

SPORTS AND RECREATION

Tour operators come and go here like spring blooms. Many are unlicensed and arrive in town to set up only for the Dec.–March season, then disappear. *Caveat emptor!*

Canopy Tours

The **Waterfall Canopy Tour** (tel. 506/643-3322, www.aterfallscanopy.com) has 14 platforms, a waterslide, suspension bridge, 80-foot rappel, and a Tarzan swing; tours are offered at 8 A.M., 11 A.M., and 2 P.M.

The **Canopy Adventure** (tel./fax 506/643-3271, caopyadventure@hotmail.com, 8 A.M.–4 P.M.) has 12 platforms and two km of cable, including an "X-cable" for "extreme adventure."

Surfing

A dozen or so outlets on the main street cater

Central Pacific

JACÓ

↑ To Puntarenas

34

VILLAS TUCÁN CALVO ●

JUNGLE PARK
WILDLIFE RESERVE ★

LIGHTHOUSE POINT
STEAK AND SEAFOOD HOUSE

Quebrada   Dona   Marta

Quebrada   Bonita

Quebrada

VILLA
MORALVA

HOTEL
POCHOTE
GRANDE ●

CAPTAIN BRIGH'S
BAR & GRILL ▶

CABINAS ANTONIO ●

HOTEL
EL JARDIN ●

PLAZA JACÓ
PIZZA HUT/BAR ZARPE/
BANK/BUDGET RENT-A-CAR
▶ FANTASY BUS STOP ■

BEST WESTERN JACÓ
BEACH RESORT

C. ANITA

C. BRIBRI

C. LAS
PALMERAS

VILLA CREOLE ●

■ CENTRO MEDICO BOLAÑOS

HOTEL COPACABANA ●

p l a y a   J a c ó

Central Pacific

to surfers. One of the largest is **Mother of Fear Surf Shop** (tel. 506/643-2001), which rents and repairs boards, offers surf lessons, and has more than 100 boards ($10–20 per day). A chap called Chuck does surfboard repair at **Chuck's Surboard Repair,** on Calle Anita. He also offers a surf report, board rentals, and lessons.

Horseback Riding

The **Jacó Equestrian Center** (tel. 506/643-1569) offers rides, as does **Diana's Trail Rides** (tel. 506/643-3808).@4:Tours

Several tour companies along the main strip offer a similar menu of canopy tours, kayaking, crocodile tours, and trips farther afield.

Costa Rica Outriggers (tel. 506/643-1233, www.kayakjaco.com) offers outrigger canoe and kayak trips.

The **Marlin del Rey** (tel. 506/643-2467, randu1@racsa.co.cr) catamaran offers three-hour tours to Isla Tortuga, plus sunset cruises.

Solutions Tourism & Services (tel. 506/643-3485, solutionsagency02@hotmail.com), in Multi-Centro Costa Brava, is a full-service travel agency.

SHOPPING

One of the largest selections is at **Lighthouse Point,** which also has a humidor stocked with Cuban cigars. There are a score of boutiques along the main drag. **Galeria Arte La Heliconia** is a trendy art gallery. **Books & Stuff** (tel. 506/643-2508), on the drag, sells magazines and used and new books.

ACCOMMODATIONS

Many hotels are overpriced. Look at standards as much as prices; ask about surfers' discounts, and consider wet ("green") season, when discounts are offered. There are many more hotels than can be recommended here.

Camping

Try **Camping Madrigal** (tel. 506/643-3230, $2 per campsite), at the extreme southern end of

the beach; this large campground has picnic tables beneath shade trees. It has toilets and showers.

Camping Charlies, in central Jacó, charges $2.50 pp for camping under shade trees. It has basic outdoor showers and toilets, and a very basic kitchen.

Under $25

At the north end, **Cabinas Antonio** (tel. 506/643-3043, $12.50 s, $20 d low season, $12.50 pp high season) is a popular bargain for budget travelers, with 13 rooms offering fans, and private baths with hot water.

Hotel Lido (tel. 506/643-3171, tochine@hotmail.com, $20 s/d with fan, $30 with a/c low seasonm, $30 s/d with fan, $40 with a/c high season) has nine dark but spacious, simply furnished rooms with cable TV, kitchenettes with refrigerators, and private baths with hot water. There's a small pool and laundry.

Further south, **Cabinas Alice** (tel. 506/643-3061, $20 budget, $35 newer rooms, up to four people) has 22 motel-style rooms. Older rooms are basic. Five newer rooms with kitchens and hot water are far more pleasant (by the week only). Large mango trees shade a popular, tiny open-air restaurant.

In Garabito try **Cabinas Naranjal** (tel./fax 506/643-3006, $10 pp with fan, $13 with a/c low season; $13.50 pp fan, $16 a/c high season), with 14 clean modern *cabinas* (six with TV) with fans and private baths and hot water.

$25–50

The **Hotel El Jardín** (tel. 506/643-3050, $20 s, $25 d low season; $30 s, $35 d high season) has 10 rather dark rooms with fans and private baths with hot water, including three a/c cabins with TV. Highlights include a pool in a small courtyard with palms. A second floor may be added with ocean views. It has parking and surfers' rates.

In the center, the two-story **Jacó Jungle Inn** (tel. 506/643-3193, fax 506/643-1664, $20 s, $25 d) has 15 rooms with fans, and five with a/c, TV, refrigerator, and security box. All have private baths with hot water. It has a small pool, a Jacuzzi, and secure parking.

The French/Swiss-owned **Hotel Poseidon** (tel. 506/643-1642 or 888/643-1242, info @hotel-poseidon.com, www.hotel-poseidon.com, $40 s/d with fan, $50–60 with a/c low season; $65/80–90 high season) boasts a stunning fronticepiece with carved wooden columns bearing Poseidon motifs, and Persian throw rugs on the faux-marble floor of the elegant, stone-walled, open-walled restaurant. There's a tiny pool with Jacuzzi and swim-up bar. The 15 large rooms are modestly furnished, with soft foam mattresses and see-through curtains. The bathrooms have large mosaic-tiled showers. Upstairs a/c rooms get the light; downstairs rooms (fans only) are a bit dingy.

The French-owned **Villas Estrellamar** (Apdo. 33, Playa Jacó, tel. 506/643-3102, fax 506/643-3453, brunot@racsa.co.cr, www.hotels.co.cr/estrellamar.html, $23 s/d fan rooms, $33 s/d a/c rooms, $43 bungalows low season; $41 s/d fan, $51 s/d a/c room $61 bungalows high season) has 10 standard a/c *cabinas* and 18 bungalows with kitchens set in landscaped grounds 50 meters east of the strip. Each has a refrigerator and a stove, plus a double and a single bed. There's a pool and a small bar.

The American-run **Cabinas Zabamar** (tel./fax 506/643-3174, $13 s, $20 d with fans, $26/33 with a/c low season; $56/67 high season for up to four people) is popular with surfers. Its 20 clean and modern cabins (10 with fans, 10 with a/c) have hammocks on the patios; some have refrigerators. There's a swimming pool and a small bar and restaurant under thatch.

I like **Villa Creole** (tel. 506/643-3298, fax 506/643-3882, info@villacreole.net, $35 s/d low season, $45 high season), a French-run place with nine elegant, well-lit a/c rooms around a large pool with water cascade and an orchid garden. The a/c rooms have large closets, fans, refrigerators, orthopedic mattresses, Guatemalan fabrics, kitchenettes, security boxes, patios, and stone-walled private baths with hot water. A minibus is on hand for tours, a *rancho* restaurant (open high season only) serves French Creole cuisine, and there's parking. New owners were upgrading at last visit. Rates include tax.

Hotel Kangaroo (tel./fax 506/643-3351, virgoo@racsa.co.cr, www.costaricanet.net/kangaroo, $10 s, $20 d low season; $20 s, $35 d high season), in Garabito, has 10 simply furnished rooms with fans and private baths with hot water. Take an upstairs room; downstairs rooms are dingy. Some have bunks. There's a small pool out back. The friendly Slovak owner rents mountain bikes and offers bicycle tours.

$50–100

The German-run **Hotel Pochote Grande** (Apdo. 42, Jacó, tel. 506/643-3236, pochote@racsa.co.cr, $45 s/d low season, $55 s/d high season), on the north bank of the river, has 24 attractive beachfront rooms in shaded grounds with a pool. The clean, modern, modestly furnished rooms have private baths with hot water; four have a/c. The restaurant specializes in international fare.

Villa Moralva (tel. 506/643-3069, $83 up to six people), nearby, has 10 two-bedroom cabins in a secure and well-maintained garden. Each has screened windows, kitchen, dining room, and clean, tiled, private bathroom with hot water. It has a pool and kid's pool.

Villas Tucán Calvo (tel./fax 506/643-3532, $400 per month) has five modern two-bedroom villa-apartments with kitchens and living rooms (each for five people) around a small swimming pool with sundeck on a breezy ridge one km northeast of town. It rents on a monthly basis only.

The beachside **Hotel Mango Mar** (tel./fax 506/643-3670, $27 s, $33 d low season; $38 s, $51 d high season), in neoclassical Spanish-colonial style, has two apartments and 12 a/c rooms with kitchenettes and nice furnishings. It offers a pool with Jacuzzi and red-brick sun terrace, plus private parking.

Next door, the U.S.-owned **Hotel Cocal and Casino** (tel. 506/643-1201, fax 506/643-3082, cocalcr@racsa.co.cr, www.hotelcocalandcasino.com, in the U.S., tel. 800/732-9266, $59 s/d standard, $69 oceanfront, $75 with a/c, $110 suite low season; $95/105/110/140 high season) is also elegant and appealing. The hacienda-style hotel is popular with charter groups. Arched porticos grace 43 spacious a/c rooms with security

Central Pacific

boxes surrounding a courtyard with two pools and a bar. An upstairs restaurant overlooking the beach serves international cuisine; there's a small casino. No children.

The contemporary, beachfront **Hotel Balcón del Mar** (tel. 506/643-2223, fax 506/643-3251, balcon@racsa.co.cr, www.hotelbalcondelmar.com, $50 s, $60 d low season, $60/75 high season) has 21 modestly furnished a/c rooms in a three-story unit, each with refrigerator, private bath and hot water, plus balcony. There's an elegant Mediterranean-style restaurant serving seafood, plus a small pool and Internet access.

I like **Hotel & Chalets Tangerí** (P.O. Box 622-4050, Alajuela, tel. 506/643-3001, fax 506/643-3636, tangeri@racsa.co.cr, www.hotel tangeri.com, $70 s/d rooms, $115 chalets, $100–143 villas low season; $82/144/128–172 high season) for its delightful decor in 14 small a/c rooms with cable TV, refrigerator, and private baths with hot water. It also has 10 villas with kitchens with kitchens; a three-bedroom "grand villa;" and two chalets. There's a bar and restaurant, plus a small swimming pool, kiddies' pool, and sand volleyball in the neatly manicured grounds.

The Dutch-run **Hotel Mar de Luz** (P.O. Box 143, Jacó, tel./fax 506/643-3259, mardeluz@racsa.co.cr, www.mardeluz.com, $40 s/d low season, $57.50 s/d high season), across the street, has modestly furnished a/c apartments with kitchenettes, cable TV, and security boxes, terraces, and private baths with hot water arrayed around a lush garden with a lap pool, kiddies' pool, and solar-heated Jacuzzi. Some units are lined appealingly with river stones and have orthopedic mattresses and mezzanine bedrooms. Junior suites in a two-story structure have tile floors, cable TV, safes, and nicer furnishings. There's a barbecue, plus laundry service, terraces with chess sets, ping-pong, and table soccer. The friendly owners are multilingual.

Canciones del Mar (tel. 506/643-3273, fax 506/643-3296, cancionesdelmar@sesteo.com, www.cancionesdelmar.com, $55 one-bedroom, $99 two-bedroom low season; $85/140 high season) is a condo-hotel with 10 a/c suite apartments enclosed within gardens with a pool

spanned by a river-stone bridge. Each has kitchen, terrace, and cable TV.

The beachfront **Hotel Copacabana** (tel./fax 506/643-3131, hotcopa@racsa.co.cr, www.copacabanahotel.com, $69 s/d studio, $109 s/d suites), which burned to the ground a few years ago, has rebuilt in contemporary style. It offers standards, studios, suites, and junior suites, all with a/c, ceiling fans, cable TV, coffeemaker, microwave, and minibar/fridge. It has a charming garden eatery and a sports bar, plus a swim-up bar in the pool in the rear garden.

The **Vista Guapa Surf Camp** (tel. 506/643-2380, fax 506/643-3242, www.vistaguapa.com, info@vistaguapa.com, $64 s, $68 d low season; $72 s, $79 d high season), owned by former Costa Rican surf champion Alvaro Solano, is a thoroughly modern surprise. Its raised-ceiling clubhouse has walls of glass, a spacious TV lounge and huge diced-log table and chairs where meals are served, plus a large wooden deck with hammocks. There's a small pool. It offers six a/c rooms on a ridgetop (a steep hike); all are spacious, with heaps of light, terra-cotta floors, security boxes, tall wooden Goldilocks-and-the-Three-Bears beds, modern tiled bathrooms, and glass French doors opening to wooden decks with hammocks. It offers a Beginners Packages and a Basic Surfers Package, including surfing, meals, and all transfers. Free shuttles between San José are offered on Saturdays.

An Italian runs **Hotel Piccolo Pueblo** (tel. 506/643-4062, $25 s, $30 with fan, $35 s, $40 d with a/c, $45 s, $52 d suite low season; $40 s/d with fan, $50 s/d with a/c, $70 s/d suite high season), a modern structure with 11 modestly furnished rooms and four suites (three with a/c) set around a pool and garden with thatched shade and hammocks. All have tile floors, refrigerators, and modern bathrooms with bidets and hot water.

$100–150

The **Hotel Club del Mar** (Apdo. 107-4023 Jacó, tel. 506/643-3194, fax 506/643-3550, hotelclub delmar@racsa.co.cr, www.clubdelmarcostarica .com, $100 s/d rooms, $150 one-bedroom condo, $220 two-bedroom condo low season;

$120 d rooms, $175 one-bedroom casita, $250 two-bedroom casita high season), nestled beneath the cliffs at the southern end of Jacó, was recently torn down and rebuilt from scratch in elegant contemporary vogue. It now has eight hotel rooms, 22 one- and two-bedroom condos, and a penthouse suite. The spacious, conservatively furnished condos have huge lounges with green tile floors with throw rugs, rich hardwoods, king-size beds, twin bathrooms, and full kitchens. The suite has a quasi-Asiatic motif. Three rooms are wheelchair-accessible. There's a pool and kid's pool in lush grounds, plus a sunken horseshoe-shaped tapas bar and a Serenity Spa. It rents kayaks and surfboards.

Lighthouse Point (see above, $100 low season, $150 high season) offers nine fully furnished two-bedroom *casas* with a/c, cable TVs, and stereos, plus fully equipped kitchens. Guests have access to all the park's facilities, including tennis and swimming pool, plus the fabulous restaurant and bar (see *Food,* below).

Best Western Jacó Beach Resort (tel. 506/643-1000 or 506/220-1772, fax 506/643-3246, bwjbreservas@grupomarta.com; in North America, tel. 800/528-1234; $101 s, $142 d rooms low season; $110 s, $170 d rooms high season), at the north end of the drag, offers 130 a/c rooms, all with pool or garden exposures, tile floors, phones, TVs, safes, and bright floral spreads. Superior rooms have TVs and refrigerators. A TV in the lobby pipes in 24-hour CNN. Amenities include El Muelle restaurant and bar, a discotheque, car rental, swimming pool, floodlit tennis court, volleyball court, plus moped, bicycle, sailboat, sea kayak, and surfboard rentals. Daily transportation to and from San José. It also rents out 28 deluxe villas, each sleeping five people and with dining and living rooms, terrace, and kitchenette. The villas, across the street, have a swimming pool.

The best self-catering complex in town is the new, Canadian-run **Apartotel Girasol** (tel./fax 506/643-1591, girasol@girasol.com, www.girasol.com, $69 s/d low season, $99 s/d high season), at the southern end of the beach, with 16 new, quality apartments in a nicely manicured garden setting with direct beach access. Each has a balcony or terrace, a/c, fans in wooden ceilings, wicker furniture, nice fabrics, and modern kitchen. There's a pool and secure parking.

The upscale **Barceló Amapola & Casino** (Apdo. 133, Jacó, tel. 506/643-2255, fax 506/643-3668, amapola@barcelo.com, www.barcelocostarica.com/amapola.htm, $96 s, $128 d low season; $131 s, $178 d high season) is an all-inclusive hotel with two-story condo-style units in beautifully landscaped grounds some distance from the beach. It has 44 standard rooms, six suites, and three fully equipped villas—all with a/c, cable TV, security box, modest furnishings, and hot water. Facilities include two swimming pools, a pool bar, and a Jacuzzi, plus a casino and a disco.

FOOD

The place for breakfast is the 24-hour **M** **Lighthouse Point Steak and Seafood House** (tel. 506/643-3083), serving wholesome American breakfasts from buttermilk pancakes to veggie omelettes. The far-reaching lunch and dinner menu runs from sushi, "monster subs," and burgers, to inexpensive *casados* (set lunches), Thai shrimp ($8), crocodile nuggets ($9), stir-fries, and a full Mexican menu. It also has smoothies and other frozen drinks ($2). It offers great music and ambience, with roughhewn polished furniture, and walls and ceilings festooned with surfboards and stuffed gamefish. Free transfers from Jacó are offered.

Good alternatives are **Sunrise Breakfast Place** (tel. 506/643-3361, 7 A.M.–noon), serving waffles, eggs Benedict ($3.50), omelettes, and more; and **Banana Café** (tel. 506/693-3206), a simple place serving pancakes, omelettes, burgers, sandwiches, etc.

I highly recommend **M** **Pacific Bistro** (tel. 506/643-3771, 6–10 P.M. Wed.–Mon.), where Californian chef Kent Green conjures up Pacific Rim dishes using fresh ingredients. The menu includes shitake mushroom–topped salmon with beure blanc ($8), filet mignon ($9), and spicy Indonesian shrimp noodles, served in large portions (half-portions are offered).

Another of my favorites is the elegant **Hotel Poseidon Restaurant** (7 A.M.–2 P.M. and 6–11 P.M.), with consistently good dishes such as marlin ceviche ($2), and jumbo prawn in spicy peanut sauce ($19.50). Breakfasts include biscuits with gravy ($3.50) and bagel and eggs ($5). The ambience is tremendous.

You can't go wrong at the elegant, open-air **Bar Restaurante Colonial** (tel. 506/643-3332, 10 A.M.–11 P.M. Mon.–Fri., 7 A.M.–midnight Sat.–Sun., $4.50–12), centered on an octagonal bar under a skylight. Its wide-ranging menu runs from burgers, onion rings, chowders, and ceviche to chicken in honey, and mussels in garlic and olive oil.

The small, intimate, Israeli-run **Mega Gem Restaurant** (noon–10 P.M.) offers delightful decor and serves omelettes, pastas, pizzas, and falafel.

For seafoods, head to **Marisquería el Hicaco,** one of the nicest places: modestly elegant, open-air, and facing the ocean, fittingly it serves seafood. It has a lobsterfest each Wednesday.

For surf-and-turf, try **La Hacienda** (tel. 506/643-3191, 9 A.M.–9 P.M. low season, 6:30 A.M.–11 P.M. high season), a popular *marisquería* serving steak and lobster. **Tangerí** ($10) has an elegant open-air eatery serving filet mignon and whole fried snapper. The elegant **Pancho Villa** (tel. 506/643-3571, $5–15), opposite Banco Popular, serves surf-and-turf, and seafood fettuccine, but also has Mexican fare, sushi, and such specialties as vinaigrette chicken with honey.

Bar Zarpe in Plaza Jacó is said to have the best burgers in town.

Craving Chinese? Try the U.S.-run **Hong Kong Fuey** (tel. 506/643-2145), a fan-cooled little charmer with real Chinese staff. For sushi, head to the small, clean, a/c **Tsunami** (tel. 506/368-7003, 5–11 P.M.), in Multi-Centro Costa Brava.

The **19th Hole,** upstairs in Centro Comercial Il Galeone, is a modern a/c coffee shop selling cappuccinos, espressos, etc. For ice cream, head to **Pop's,** nearby.

For baked goods, try **Panadería Tosso,** 100 meters east of Avenida Pastor Díaz; or **Musmanni,** on the main drag.

Super Frutástica has a fresh produce market, and meats, as does **Super Olas. Max X Menos,** 50 meters south of Banco Nacional, is the town's largest supermarket. You can buy health foods from **Miravalles Naturales,** 50 meters south of Centro Comercial El Paso. It also serves ice creams and fruit juices.

INFORMATION AND SERVICES

Local tour operators can provide tourist information.

The **Centro Médico Bolaños** (tel. 506/643-2323) is 400 meters east of the drag in the center of town. **Centro Médico Integral** (tel. 506/643-3205), 50 meters south of Banco Nacional, is open daily 8 A.M.–8 P.M. (it's above a **pharmacy;** tel. 506/643-1127). The **Red Cross** (tel. 506/643-3090) has ambulance service; as does **Emergencias 2000** (tel. 506/380-4125), on Hwy. 21 midway between Herradura and Jacó; and **CARE** (tel. 506/353-7456, beeper 506/296-2626), in the center of Jacó. **Farmacia Fischel** (tel. 506/643-2705), in Centro Comercial Il Galeone, is open 8 A.M.–10:30 P.M. daily.

There's a **police station** (tel. 506/643-3011) on the beach, next to Hotel Balcón del Mar, and another police station (same tel.) in Garabito. The OIJ (Costa Rica's equivalent of the FBI or CID, tel. 506/643-1723) is represented.

There are four banks, including **Banco San José,** upstairs in Centro Comercial II Galeone. **Western Union** is toward the north end of town.

International Central (tel. 506/643-2601), in Centro Comercial El Paso, is an international call center; open 7:30 A.M.–9 P.M. The post office is 50 meters east of the soccer field in Garabito.

Café Internet (tel. 504/643-3780) charges $1.50 per hour and is open 8 A.M.–10 P.M. daily. The **Internet Café** (tel. 506/643-2141), opposite Pancho Villa at the south end of town, is open 9 A.M.–7:30 P.M. daily.

Lavandería Puro Blanco (tel. 506/643-1025), on the drag at the south end of town, will deliver. **Aquamatic** is a coin-operated self-serve laundry 150 meters further south.

GETTING THERE AND AROUND

You can charter an air-taxi to the airstrip at the northern end of Jacó.

Buses (tel. 506/223-1109) depart San José from Calle 16, Avenidas 1/3, at 7:30 A.M., 10:30 A.M., 1 P.M., 3:30 P.M. and 6 P.M. (2.5 hours). Buses between San José and Quepos and Manuel Antonio also stop in Jacó.

Fantasy Bus (tel. 506/232-3681) has a daily bus shuttle between San José and Jacó ($21) at 3 P.M. (return departure at 8:30 A.M.); between Jacó and Flamingo ($30), Tamarindo, and Sámara ($25) at 8 A.M.; and between Jacó and La Fortuna ($25) and Monteverde ($38) at 8 A.M.

From Puntarenas, buses to Jacó and Quepos depart from near the train station at 6 A.M., 11 A.M., 2:30 P.M., and 4:30 P.M. Buses depart Quepos for Jacó at 4:30 A.M., 7:30 A.M., 10:30 A.M., and 3 P.M.; and Jacó for Quepos at 6 A.M., noon, 4 P.M., and 6 P.M.

Return buses depart Jacó for San José at 5 A.M., 11 A.M., and 3 P.M., and for Puntarenas at 6 A.M., 9 A.M., noon, and 4:30 P.M., from the Supermercado, picking up at the north end of town also.

Car rental companies in Jacó include **Budget Rent-a-Car** (tel. 506/643-100), in Plaza de Jacó; **Economy Rent-a-Car** (tel./fax 506/643-3280), toward the north end of town; and **National Car Rental,** on the drag toward the south end of town.

Kevin's Transfers (tel. 506/643-2604, cellular tel. 506/361-9218, comeeds@yahoo.com), run by an American, offers meet-and-greet airport transfers and rides nationwide using an a/c minivan (from $55).

Panga Express (tel. 506/643-3560) offers water-taxi service between Jacó and Malpaís, Tambor, and Isla Tortuga ($35).

Rent@Me (tel. 506/301-2780, rent_me3000@yahoo.com) charges $1 hourly, $10 per day, for bicycle rental; and $25 daily for scooters.

For taxis, call **Taxi Jacó** (tel. 506/643-3009).

PLAYA HERMOSA

Highway 34 south from Jacó crests a steep headland, beyond which Playa Hermosa comes into sight (there's a mirador for enjoyed the incredible view); the beach is 10 km long and arrow straight, with surf pummeling ashore along its whole length. Playa Hermosa is a favorite of surfers, and the setting for an international surfing championship each August.

The **Chiclets Tree-Tour** (tel. 506/643-1880, chicletstree@yahoo.com, www.jacobeach.co.cr), on Hwy. 21, is a canopy tour with 13 platforms.

Sports and Recreation

Discovery Horseback Stables (tel. 506/838-7550, horseback@racsa.co.cr) has guided tours.

Cabinas Las Olas offers tours and rents boogie boards, surfboards, snorkeling gear, and mountain bikes.

Accommodations

Under $25: Budget-minded surfers like the no-frills **Cabinas Rancho Grande** (tel. 506/643-3529, $10 pp), at the north end of the beach. This three-story, rough-hewn log and bamboo structure has seven basic rooms with private bathrooms. The top floor has a single A-frame room. There are fans, but no hot water. It's run by Floridians Rhonda and Brian, who offer guests use of the kitchen. It has a pool table.

An alternative is **Ola Bonita,** (tel. 506/643-3990, olabonita@usanet.co.cr, $10/15 pp low/high season), with seven fully equipped rooms with private bath and cold water. They're cross-ventilated, have kitchenettes, and walls of whitewashed stone, and are simply furnished with a double and bunk beds. Downstairs rooms are dark. It has a small pool.

My budget pick, beloved of surfers, is the offbeat **Cabinas Las Arenas** (tel. 506/643-3508, arnoldflather@hotmail.com, www.cabinaslasarenas.com, $15 pp year-round), well run by a Yorkshire-Canadian transplant. The seven rooms are in a two-story unit, each with refrigerator, fan, stove, and private bath and hot water. It has a rustic yet atmospheric bar-restaurant, and a riverstone courtyard over the beach.

$25–50: The Argentinian-run **Posada Playa Hermosa** (tel. 506/643-2640, gonzalezfischer@yahoo.com, $15 pp low season, $20 high season), 300 meters south of Terraza del Pacífico, has five simply furnished, ocher-painted, log-beamed cabins in a delightful Robinson Crusoe kinda place. Each has private bathroom with cold water only. Fischer Bros. surfboard rental and repair is here.

U.S. surfer dudes Jason and Jonathan run **Cabinas Las Olas** (P.O. Box 258, Jacó, tel./fax 643-3687, jonathanhonig@hotmail.com, www.cabinaslasolas.com, $20 pp cabin, $40–50 d room). This modern three-story structure has eight nicely kept rooms with kitchenettes and patios. There are also three cabins, each with two single beds below and a double in the loft. There's a pool and a restaurant beachside.

And U.S. surf dudes Tobik and Dennis have opened **Cabinas Brisa del Mar** (tel. 506/643-2078, brisadelmar@racsa.co.cr, $25 s, $30 d year-round) with four clean, modern a/c rooms with tile floors, cable TV, refrigerator, and private bathroom with hot water. It has a community kitchen, basketball court, and ping-pong.

Hotel Villas Hermosa (tel. 506/643-3373, fax 506/643-3506, taycole@racsa.co.cr, www.surf-hermosa.com, $40–65 s/d depending on size) has twelve spacious, fully furnished, a/c self-catering cabins, each complete with kitchen, one double and two single beds (some have two singles). There's a small pool, wet bar, and secure parking. Surfers' packages are offered.

Next door, and similar, is the U.S.-run **Hotel La Iguana Perezoza** (tel./fax 506/643-1042, lazylizard@lazyliz.com, $25 s, $35 d), with six *cabinas* in landscaped grounds with a tiny pool fed by a water cascade emanating from a Jacuzzi. Rooms are spacious, tiled, simply furnished, and have a/c, fans in wooden ceilings, and cold water only (hot water was planned). A shady restaurant offers meals.

The handsome, Italian-run **Costanera B&B** (tel. 506/643-1942, costanera@racsa.co.cr, www.costaneraplayahermosa.com, $20 s, $30 d standard, $30/40 with a/c), next to Casa Pura Vida, has four spacious a/c rooms with raised wooden ceilings with fans, tile floors, cross-ventilation, charming antique reproduction furnishings, private bath with cold water only, and expansive terraces over the beach. Sunlight pours in through large windows. One has two bedrooms and a kitchen.

$50–100: At the extreme north end of the beach is **Terraza del Pacífico** (Apdo. 168, Jacó, tel. 506/643-3222, fax 506/643-3424, terraza @racsa.co.cr or info@terraza-del-pacifico.com, www.terraza-del-pacifico.com, $92 s/d low season, $102 high season), a modern complex that caters to the more upscale surf crowd. This contemporary Spanish colonial–style property has a superb beachfront location. The 43 rooms, including three suites, have a/c, satellite TVs, telephones, security boxes, and sofa beds and double beds. The landscaped grounds boast a circular pool with a swim-up bar. There's a casino, and a restaurant and bar. Rates include breakfast and tax.

More intimate is the modern **Hotel Fuego del Sol** (P.O. Box 85570-1000 San José, tel. 506/643-3737, fax 506/643-3736, ventas @ecolodgecostarica.com, www.fuegodelsolhotel.com, $47 s, $57 d room, $93 junior suite, $119 master suite, $82 apartment low season, $57 s, $67 d room, $103 junior suite, $129 master suite high season), a handsome two-story colonial-style structure in landscaped grounds. It has 18 spacious a/c rooms and two suites, with cool tiles painted in tropical motifs, fans, TVs, minibars, and private baths with hot water, plus a pool with swim-up bar, gym, and beachfront restaurant. It has a one-week surf camp with tuition.

A North Carolina gal named Mellicent runs **Casa Pura Vida** (tel./fax 506/643-2039, millicent@casapuravida.com, $50 s/d), a pleasing two-story home-away-from-home in Spanish hacienda style. The three a/c apartments have terra-cotta floors, fans, and nice fabrics, but are otherwise simply furnished (and the construction standard is poor). Take an upstairs room; they get the breezes and have leather rockers on a veranda. There's a pool and a *rancho* with hammocks, plus a laundry, and massage is offered.

The **Backyard Oceanfront Rooms** (tel./fax 506/643-1311, backyard@racsa.co.cr, www.backyardhotel.net, $90 s/d room low season, $100 s/d high season, $145 suite year-round) has six spacious standard a/c rooms and 12 suites, all with contemporary furnishings, high ceilings, cable TV, refrigerators, and large sliding glass doors. Upstairs suites have huge verandas. It has a small pool.

Food

A surfer named Tom Ford runs the roadside **Jungle Surf Café**, which offers simple cabins for $7 pp and has cafe serving Tex-Mex, "killer omelettes," burgers, barbecued chicken, and filet mignon. Surf movies play on the TV at the bar.

The roughhewn, Rastafarian-themed **Jammin Café** (tel. 506/643-1853, 7 A.M.–9 P.M., $4), at Cabinas Las Arenas, serves pancakes, omelettes, etc., for breakfast, plus nachos, chicken quesadillas, ceviche, and vegetarian Rasta pasta in Caribbean sauce.

The restaurant at **Cabinas Las Olas** ($5) serves filling burritos, quarter-pound burgers, and seared ahi.

PLAYAS ESTERILLOS OESTE AND CENTRO

Playa Esterillos Oeste is south of Hermosa, with craggy Punta Judas between them, reached by a side road. It's another favorite with surfers and with littering Ticos on holidays and weekends. The seven-km-long beach has tidepools at its northern end, where a **sculpture of a mermaid** sits atop the rocks. Beware strong currents; you can swim safely at the northern end of the beach, where an ancient mosaic of mollusk fossils is embedded in the rock strata.

The sandy beachfront track runs south to an estuary, beyond which lies **Esterillos Centro,** accessed by a separate road signed off Hwy. 34 (you'll need to backtrack to the highway).

Rancho Monterey (tel. 506/778-8000, fax 506/778-8001, www.haciendamonterey.com) is a working cattle ranch with a huge stable offering horseback rides, wrangler programs, plus rodeo and other ranch activities. It has special kids' dude ranch weeks. Other facilities were being added at last visit, including an oceanfront amphitheater and an art pavilion.

Costa Rica Sky Riders offers Ultralight flights.

Accommodations and Food

You can **camp** beneath shade trees at the extreme north of the beach.

The dozen or so uninspired food and dining options include **Bar/Restaurante Shake** (tel. 506/778-8285, $37.50 low season, $50 high season up to five people), reached via a side road that leads north to Punta Judas. This elevated restaurant sits at the very north end of the beach and serves *típico* dishes. It has two large apartments with local TV and refrigerators.

At Esterillos Centro, the French-Canadian-run **La Felicidad Country Inn** (P.O. Box 73-6300, Parrita, tel./fax 506/780-8125, www.lafelicidad.com, $15 s, $25 d low season; $20 s, $32 d high season) is a simple wooden home with nine rooms (one with shared bath) of varying sizes, with cool tile floors, pleasant bathrooms, and hammocks under *ranchitas*. Three rooms upstairs have wooden floors, kitchenettes, and balconies. Two are adapted for travelers with disabilities. The bar and restaurant are popular with locals. There's a small swimming pool. Rates include breakfast.

The **Walt Paraíso Hotel** (tel. 506/778-8060, fax 506/778-8069, walterco@racsa.co.cr, $20 with fans, $25 with a/c up to five people), 300 meters inland, at the southern end of Esterillo Este, is a new project with eight rooms complete at last visit. Another 30 rooms were planned around the pool with waterfall and Jacuzzi. They're spacious, tiled, and have ceiling fans, huge closets, and large walk-in showers with hot water.

The **Hotel Monterey del Mar & Art Colony** (www.monterydelmar.com), was under construction at Rancho Monterey at last visit. It will have 27 deluxe rooms and suites, with king beds, cable TV, telephones, coffeemaker, and terraces.

The elegant **La Piazzetta** (tel. 506/778-8025, 11:30 A.M.–2:30 P.M. and 6:30–11 P.M.), at Rancho Monterrey, serves Italian fare. Its coffee shop is open 2:30–6:30 P.M.

PLAYAS ESTERILLOS ESTE, BEJUCO, AND PALMA

Playa Esterillos Este, separated by a river from Esterillos Centro, is identical to its northerly siblings: kilometers long, ruler-straight, with gray sand cleansed by high surf. There's a grass airstrip paralleling the beach at its northern end, accessed off Hwy. 34. The southern end of the beach is known as **Playa Bejuco,** reached via a separate access road.

Farther south, about four km north of Parrita, a dirt road leads west from the coast road—Costanera Sur—and zigzags through African palm plantations until you emerge at Playa Palma (also known as Playa Bandera), separated from Bejuco by yet another rivermouth.

Accommodations and Food

Exuding charming ambience, the **Home Spa** (tel. 506/778-8035, www.costaricahomespa.com; in the U.S., tel. 718/596-8668; $60 s/d low season, $75 high season), at Esterillos Este, is owned by the Coronado Academy but leased to a U.S. owner who at last visit was turning it into a "natural living retreat and spa." Incense wafts through the four cabins with king-size beds and batik covers, plus spiral staircase to a loft bedroom, and private bathrooms with hot water. It has a handsome lounge with warm fabrics, plus a beautiful pool, and hammocks under palms. A gourmet chef caters Asian-fusion cuisine. Rates include continental breakfast.

Auberge du Pélican (Apdo. 47, Parrita 6300, tel./fax 506/778-8105, aubergepelican@racsa .co.cr, $40 s/d), 200 meters further south, now under U.S. management, was remodeling at last visit. There are eight rooms (two are accessible for wheelchairs) in a two-story house, plus two rooms in a separate *casita*. Each has ceiling fan, hot water, and security box. Upper-story rooms have heaps of light and are breezy. One has an outside bathroom. There are hammocks beneath shady palms, plus a barbecue pit, a small pool, and a shuffleboard court. Rates include breakfast.

The **Fleur de Esterillos** (P.O. Box 41-6300 Parrita, tel./fax 506/778-8045, business@racsa .co.cr, $65 d, $300 per week), 200 meters farther south, has nine chalets, each different but all simply and attractively furnished, with terracotta tile floors, ceiling fans, small kitchen, and patio. There's a small pool and a small thatched restaurant.

The **Monterrey del Mar,** at the northern end of Esterillo Este, is a large all-inclusive development under the Rancho Monterrey umbrella.

The marvelous **Tulú Restaurant** (tel. 506/778-8493), opposite Auberge du Pélican, is a simple country-style eatery in lively tropical colors, serving seafood (including lobster) and local fare.

Tours and Activities

You can take an **Air Jungle Beach Safari** (tel. 506/778-8710, www.flycosta.org) by twin-engine, open-cockpit airplane ($69). The company also offers hang-gliding in tandem with a certified instructor ($69).

PARRITA

This small town, 45 km south of Jacó, is a center for the 1,700-hectare African oil palm ranch. Driving Hwy. 34 you'll pass oil-processing plants and plantation villages of gaily painted, two-story stilt houses set around a soccer field.

A dirt road immediately south of Parrita leads eight km to **Playa Palo Seco,** a gray-sand beach backed by the mangrove swamps and braided channels of the Palo Seco and Damas estuaries. The **Damas Estuary** mangrove forest is home to crocodiles, monkeys, pumas, coatimundis, and wading and water birds by the thousands. **Isla Damas** lies across the 400-meter-wide estuary and is reached by boat ($1.50 each way) from the dock one km southwest of **Damas,** 12 km south of Parrita on Hwy. 34. You can walk across the island to a beach, or visit the small **zoo.**

Cambute Tours (tel. 506/777-3229, fax 506/777-3064, cambutetour@terra.com) offers guided boat tours ($60 including transfers), as does **Jorge's Mangrove Tour** (tel./fax 506/777-1050), in Quepos.

The **Río Parrita** cascades from the Fila Bustamante mountain range, offering Class II/III whitewater rafting.

Rainmaker Conservation Project

Rainmaker (tel. 506/777-3565, fax 506/777-3563, rainmakerusa@hotmail.com, www .rainmakercostarica.com) is a 540-hectare private reserve on the forested slopes of the Fila Chonta mountains, near the village of Pocares (the turnoff is by a water tower), southeast of Parrita and seven km inland of Hwy. 21. The main draw is a treetop trail formed by six suspension bridges slung between trees to form a 250-meter aerial walkway through the rainforest canopy ($65 canopy walk, half-day, including hotel transfers). Far below, a wooden boardwalk and other bridges lead you through a river canyon, with cool pools for bathing. It's a stiff climb up several hundred steps to reach the first platform. A four-hour guided river walk costs $45 with hotel transfers; 8 A.M.–3 P.M.

Other trails lead into the reserve, which climbs through four distinct ecological zones—including cloud forest—up to 1,700 meters elevation. Horseback riding is offered to the Damas Caves, which have stalactites and stalagmites.

Reservations are needed to visit. Hotels and tour operators in Quepos and Manuel Antonio offer tour excursions. There's a restaurant and interpretive center. It is closed on Sunday.

Accommodations and Food

At Playa Palo Seco, the beachfront **Beso del Viento** (tel. 506/779-9674, fax 506/779-9615, bdviento@racsa.co.cr, $40 s, $45 d rooms, $60–100 apartments) offers six rooms in the main house and three apartments of varying sizes with kitchens. The new French owners arrange horse rides and were planning to add a restaurant and pool. An eight-meter sportfishing boat is available for charters and tours to Manuel Antonio and farther afield. Rates include breakfast.

Pueblo Real (P.O. Box 151-6350, Quepos, tel. 506/777-1403, fax 506/777-0827, lagunaka @racsa.co.cr, $80 s/d low season; $100 high season), near the dock one km southwest of Damas, spreads across 120 hectares on the banks of the river. It features 28 fully furnished Spanish-style condos with elegant rooms boasting modern furnishings, a/c, TVs, phones, and balconies. Facilities include two tennis courts, a pool, and marina.

Dockside, a floating restaurant called **La Tortuga** (tel. 506/777-3229 or cellular 506/382-6378, 11 A.M.–9 P.M. Tues.–Sun.) serves seafood and international dishes.

Getting There

Tour operators in Quepos offer guided excursions. A taxi from Quepos costs about $5.

Quepos and Manuel Antonio National Park

QUEPOS

Quepos (pop. 11,000) is known for sportfishing and is the gateway for travelers heading to Manuel Antonio National Park, seven km south. There's little of interest to see in town, except perhaps the dilapidated fishing village of **Boca Vieja,** with rickety plank walkways extending over a muddy beach; and the old residential compounds of the Standard Fruit Company, whose clapboard homes are hidden in the hills south of town.

In February 1563, the conquistador Juan Vásquez de Coronado arrived in the region. One of the first missions in Costa Rica was established here in 1570; you can still see the ruins up the **Río Naranjo** (see below).

Toward the end of the 19th century, agricultural colonies were established in the coastal plains, followed by banana plantations in the 1930s. Bananas came to dominate the economy, and Quepos rose to prominence as a banana-exporting port. The plantations were blighted by disease in the 1950s, and the bananas were replaced by African palms, which produce oil for food, cosmetics, and machine oil. The trees stretch in neatly ordered rows for miles north and south of Quepos.

The tourism boom has created sewage problems for Quepos and neighboring Manuel Antonio. The waters off Quepos's El Cocal beach are considered high-risk.

Río Naranjo

Three km east of Quepos, a dirt road leads

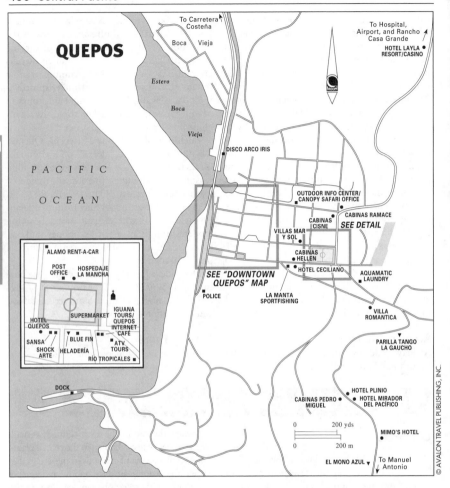

Central Pacific

northeast via the community of Londres to the Fila Nara mountain range. The area is popular with day excursions to **Rancho Los Tucanes** (tel. 506/779-1001), on the banks of the Río Naranjo. It offers ATV tours, and horseback rides to the 90-meter Los Tucanos waterfall. You'll pass through pepper and vanilla plantations en route to the highland rainforest, full of exotic birds and wildlife.

Villa Vanilla (tel. 506/779-1155, vanilla @racsa.co.cr, www.rainforestspices.com), at Londres, is an organic spice farm with three km of trails. It has cabins.

Buses run from Quepos to Londres daily at 4:30 A.M., 7 A.M., 9 A.M., noon, 4 P.M., and 6 P.M.

Entertainment and Events

Quepos's three-week **Carnivale** (mid-February to early March) offers plenty of entertainment.

The lively, unpretentious **El Banco Bar** (3 P.M.–1 A.M. Thur.–Tue.) is a Key West kind of place for aging hippies and has satellite TV, darts, and live rock bands. Another hit for live music and dancing is **El Gran Escape,** a lively spot run by a vivacious gringa named Marsha. It

© JEAN MERCIER

Playa Manuel Antonio

has ESPN on TV, and was playing '70s soul hits the last time I enjoyed a tequila-befuddled night here.

The moody **Mar y Blues** (10 A.M.–2 A.M.), opposite, is another popular spot that was playing blues music when I called in.

For disco, head to **Arco Iris,** on a barge north of the bridge into town ($2).

Hotel Layla has a nightclub, and a casino, as does the Hotel Kamuk.

Sports and Recreation

Lynch Tourist Service (tel. 506/777-1170, fax 506/777-1571, lyntur@racsa.co.cr, www .lynchtravel.com) and **Costa Rica Temptations** (tel. 506/777-5130, fax 506/777-5129, quepos @costarica4u.com, www.costarica4u.com) offer a full range of local tours.

The **Canopy Safari** (tel. 506/777-0100, fax 506/777-3623, canopysa@racsa.co.cr, www .canopysafari.com) features nine ziplines and three rappel lines. And the **Titi Canopy Tour** (tel. 506/777-1020, fax 506/777-1575, www .titicanopytours.com), at Hotel Rancho Casa Grande, has 16 platforms and 12 cables.

Gaia Link Tours (tel. 506/777-1219, adventures @gaialinktours.com) has a'Five-in-One tour that includes a visit to the Río Paraíso Biological Reserve, plus canopy tour, hiking, and horseback riding.

For guided mountain-bike tours, try **Estrella Tours** (tel./fax 506/777-1286, estrellatour @hotmail.com, www.puertoquepos.com), with beginner to advanced programs. **Finca Valmy Tours** (tel. 506/779-1118, fax 506/779-1269, fincavalmy@hotmail.com) offers guided horseback rides.

Both **Amigos Del Río** (tel. 506/777-0082, fax 506/777-2248, amigorio@racsa.co.cr, www .amigosdelrio.com) and **Iguana Tours** (tel. 506/777-1262, iguana@iguanatours.com, www .iguanatours.com) offer sea-kayaking trips to the mangrove lagoons of Damas ($65) and Manuel Antonio ($44), plus kayaking and river-rafting trips down the Ríos Naranjo and Parrita (Class II/III, $65–90).

Rios Tropicales (tel. 506/777-4092, fax 506/777-4094) has similar tours.

The Quepos region offers outstanding sportfishing for marlin and sailfish, December through

August. The inshore reefs are also home to large populations of snapper, amberjack, wahoo, and tuna. The biggest operator is **Costa Rican Dreams** (tel. 506/777-0593, fax 506/777-0592). Others include **La Manta Sportfishing** (tel. 506/777-4999), on the southeast side of the soccer field; **Sportfishing Quepos** (www.sportfishing quepos.com); **J.P. Sportfishing Tours** (tel./fax 506/777-0757); and **Bluefin Sportfishing** (Apdo. 223-6350, Quepos, tel. 506/777-4999, fax 506/777-0674, bluefin@racsa.co.cr, www .bluefinsportfishing.com). Its associate company, **Bluefin Tours,** offers rafting, horseback riding, and other trips.

Also see Hotel & Villas Karahe, in the *Quepos to Manuel Antonio* section, below.

Fancy tearing around on an ATV? **Fourtrax Adventures** (tel. 506/777-1825, www.fourtrax-adventure.com) offers tours.

Costa Rica Adventure Divers (tel. 506/777-0234, www.costaricadiving.com) offers scuba-diving trips, including certification; plus snorkeling, and dolphin encounters ($85).

Planet Dolpin (tel. 506/777-2137, fax 506/777-1647, dolphncr@racsa.co.cr, www.planet dolphin.com) has an Aquatic Discovery Adventure in search of whales and dolphins by canopied boat ($65, with snorkeling), plus a Catamaran Island Adventure to Manuel Antonio National Park by 55-foot cat ($65).

Sunset Sails Tours (tel. 506/777-1304, sun-setsailstours@hotmail.com) offers sailing excursions.

Accommodations

There are many more budget options than can be recommended here.

$10–25: In the budget category try **Hotel Mar y Luna** (tel. 506/777-0394, $7.50 pp shared bath, $16 s/d private bath), with 17 small, basic upper-floor rooms with fans and shared baths; ground-floor rooms have private baths with hot water but no windows. The owner is friendly and helpful and keeps his place spic-and-span. It has a tour office and laundry.

Hotel Quepos (tel. 506/777-0274), above the SANSA office on the southwest side of the soccer field; **Hotel Ramus** (tel. 506/777-0245);

and **Hotel Melissa** (tel. 506/777-0025), nearby, all have clean rooms with ceiling fans and private baths with cold water only for below $10 pp. The latter has secure parking and was planning hot water.

Hotel Malinche (tel. 506/777-0093, $10 s, $15 d older; $14 pp newer with fan, $20 with a/c) has 29 well-kept, attractive rooms divided between older (with fans and cold water) and newer wings (with hot water and, in some, a/c).

The Italian-run **Villas Mar y Sol Inn** (tel. 506/777-0307, $8 s, $15 d), two blocks east of the bus station, has eight simply furnished a/c cabins with fans, refrigerators, and private bathrooms. There's a communal kitchen and laundry in the rough garden with parking.

The family-run **Hotel Ceciliano** (tel./fax 506/777-0192, $10 s/d shared bath, $15 s/d private bath low season; $15 s/d shared bath, $20 s/d private bath high season) has 22 light and airy rooms—14 with private baths with hot water (shared baths have cold water only)—with immaculately clean tiled floors, a garden with caged birds, patio restaurant, and laundry service.

Hotel Pueblo (tel. 506/777-1003, $8 pp with fans; $30 s/d with a/c and TV), on the north side of the bus station, is a backpackers' favorite with eight simple but adequate rooms with private bath. Security may be an issue, as the restaurant is open 24 hours, and the joint is busy.

Slightly more pleasant, **Cabinas Hellen** (tel. 506/777-0504, $13 s/d low season, $17 s/d high season), 50 meters southwest of the soccer field, has five simple rooms with fans, refrigerators, and private baths and hot water.

$25–50: Cabinas Ramace (tel. 506/777-0590, $20 s/d with fans, $25 s/d with a/c low season; $25/30 high season), on the north side of town, has 10 cabins, each with a double and two single beds, fans (one per bed), refrigerator, plus private bath and hot water. Newer units have a/c and cable TV.

Nearby, the constantly improving **Cabinas El Cisne** (tel. 506/777-0719, $20 s, $30 d with fan, $30 s, $40 with a/c), also with secure parking, has 12 cabins with fans, private baths, and hot water; plus 12 newer, more spacious rooms in

MANUEL ANTONIO FOR GAYS AND LESBIANS

Manuel Antonio National Park is popular with a gay and lesbian clientele, drawn to the several hotels that cater to them. **La Playita** beach (also known as Playa Silvia), north of Espadilla, is a gay hangout and pickup spot. The following places accept a gay-lesbian clientele only:

Hotel Casa Blanca (Apdo 194-6350 Quepos, tel./fax 506/777-1316, cblanca@sracsa.co.cr, www.hotelcasablanca.com, $50 s/d rooms, $80 apartments, $120 suites low season; $80/120/180 high season) is run by Americans Don and Jack. It has four standard rooms, two two-bedroom suites, four apartments, and a home; all have fans and a/c, plus refrigerator, security boxes, and private bathroom, albeit uninspired furnishings. There are two pools set in tropical gardens, plus a bar.

Nearby, the sumptuously decorated **La Plantacion** (alias Big Rubys, tel. 506/777-1332, fax 506/777-0432, costarica@bigrubys.com, www.bigrubys.com, $75–115 s/d low season, $95–160 high season) enjoys a hillside setting surrounded by rainforest. It offers 24 a/c rooms, of which 12 are deluxe three- or four-bedroom units; all have ceiling fans, crafted furniture, king beds, cable TV/VCR, with kitchen, lounge, dining room, and patios. There's a pool and sun deck with hot tub, and secure parking. A restaurant serves French cuisine, and complimentary cocktails are served in the evening. Rates include full breakfast. It's closed in October.

Villa La Roca (Apdo. 143-6350 Quepos, tel./fax 506/777-1349, mantonio@villaroca.com, www.villaroca.com, $39–70 low season, $54–93 high season) offers six rooms and seven apartments, all with ceiling fans, refrigerators, private baths and hot-water showers, and private terraces offering fabulous views. Some have a/c and kitchens.

Cockatoo Bar (cockatoo@racsa.co.cr) is a gay and lesbian bar and has dancing. It also offers access to clothing-optional La Playita beach. It's open daily 4 P.M.–midnight.

Central Pacific

a three-story unit (some have a/c and refrigerator). Each has a double and single bed.

$50–100: I like **Hotel Sirena** (tel. 506/777-0528, fax 506/777-0165, $20 pp), with 14 double rooms (most with a/c) with fans and private baths and hot water. A central sun deck has a pool. The hotel specializes in horseback trips and offers rafting and fishing.

The aptly named and reclusive **Hotel Villa Romántica** (tel. 506/777-0037, fax 506/777-0604, villarom@racsa.co.cr, www.villaromantica .com, $39 s, $49 d low season, $55 s, $69 d high season), on the southeast edge of town, is a two-tiered Mediterranean-style building set in landscaped grounds. Sixteen simply but nicely appointed rooms have spacious bathrooms and heaps of light, plus fans (some have a/c), and balconies overlooking a swimming pool. It offers free email service for guests. Rates include breakfast.

The **Best Western Hotel Kamuk** (P.O Box 18-6350, Quepos, tel. 506/777-0871, fax 506/777-0258, info@kamuk.co.cr, $50 s/d stan-

dard, $70 s/d superior low season, $60/80 high season) is the class act in town. It has 28 spacious and elegant, nicely furnished a/c rooms (some with balconies; all with TVs and telephones), all beautifully decorated in light pastels. The Miraolas Bar and Restaurant on the third floor has vistas over El Cocal Beach and serves good international cuisine. There's a small boutique, a pool, plus a classy bar and small casino. Rates include continental breakfast.

One of the nicest places is **Hotel Layla** (tel. 506/777-3445, fax 506/777-3446, laylaresort @racsa.co.cr, $58 s/d), a contemporary style hotel on a hill about one km northeast of Quepos. Its 20 nicely appointed a/c rooms have coffee-makers, cable TV, tile floors, raised ceilings with fans, and private bathrooms with hot water. It has a handsome thatched restaurant, plus a pool and sundeck, and a casino and nightclub.

To be close to nature, consider **Hotel Rancho Casa Grande** (P.O. Box 618-2010 Zapote, San José, tel. 506/777-3130, fax 506/777-1575, hotel-rcg@racsa.co.cr, www.hotelcasagrande.com, $80 s/d rooms, $85 one-room bungalow, $110 two-room bungalow low season, $95/110/125 high season), about four km northeast from town on the road to the Quepos airport. Set in 73 hectares, it has 14 modestly furnished a/c rooms and 10 fully equipped bungalows (with king-size beds) amid sprawling lawns. All have TVs. Highlights include a pool, Jacuzzi, horseback riding, and nature trails into the surrounding forest.

Food

The place to start your day is **El Patio Café** (6 A.M.–6 P.M.), serving *gallo pinto,* granola with fruit and yoghurt ($3), plus ice cream sundaes, homemade baked goods, sandwiches, and raspberry iced mochas, lattes, espressos, etc. Next door, **Café Milagro** (tel. 506/777-1707, www.cafemilagro.com, 9 A.M.–5 P.M. Mon.–Sat.) roasts its coffee fresh, and sells iced coffee, espresso, and cappuccino ($1.75), etc.

My favorite spot is **M El Gran Escape Restaurante** (tel. 506/777-0395, info@elgranescapte .net, 7 A.M.–11 P.M., $5–9), serving salads, seafood, surf-and-turf, tuna melts, enchiladas, killer burgers, and coconut curry chicken, with large portions at bargain prices; upstairs is a sushi bar.

For Mexican fare, head to **Dos Locos** (tel. 506/777-1526, 7 A.M.–11 P.M. Mon.–Sat., 11 A.M.–8 P.M. Sunday, $4–8), offering breakfast omelettes, plus chimichangas, chili con carne; my *burrito gigante* was superb. The **El Banco Bar** is recommended for Tex-Mex enchiladas, deep-fried fish fingers ($5), and Chef Stephen's dinner specials, from tenderloin to catch-of-the-day.

Escalofrio (tel. 506/777-0833, 2:30 P.M.–10 P.M.) is an atmospheric Italian spot open to the street and serving spaghettis and pizza. You can also gorge on banana splits and shakes at this "Italian ice cream factory." Alternately, try the modestly elegant **Bar y Pizzeria Oasis** (tel. 506/777-0650, $3–6), with a large pasta menu, gnocchi, and pizzas.

The *Mercado Central* has numerous budget *sodas* serving local fare. The **Bar Restaurante Mira Olas** (tel. 506/777-0379, 3–11 P.M.), atop Hotel Kamuk, has an extensive seafood menu (try the octopus in garlic sauce, $4), including two-for-one sushi on Tuesdays.

I like **Parrilla Tango La Gaucha,** an Argentinian roadside grill on the road to Manuel Antonio. It serves meats.

You'll think you're in New York when you pop into **Gastronomia L'Angolo** (tel. 506/777-4129, 7 A.M.–8 P.M. Mon.–Sat.), a *real* Italian deli with hams, cheeses, etc.

For baked goods, head to **Musmanni,** one block north of the bus station, or the **bakery** opposite Hotel Sirena. You can stock up on groceries at **Super Mas,** opposite the bus station.

Information and Services

The various tour agencies above provide tourist information.

Quepolandia is a free tourist monthly distributed locally.

Hospital Dr. Max Teran V (tel. 506/777-0020) is three km south of town on the Costanera Sur. There's a medical clinic on Avenida 0. The Red Cross is one block east of the bus station. **Farmacia Quepos** (tel. 506/777-0038) is open 7 A.M.–9 P.M. There's a **dentist** (tel. 506/777-1228) next to Elegante Rent-a-Car.

The **police station** (tel. 506/777-2117) is 100 meters south of the plaza, on Avenida 0; the OIJ (tel. 506/777-0511, fax 506/777-1511) is two blocks northeast of the bus station.

There are three banks in town; see the map. **Western Union** has an office 20 meters north of Café Milagro.

The post office is on the north side of the soccer field. Public telephones face the ocean in front of the park.

Artenet (tel. 506/777-3447, artenet@racsa.co .cr) charges $1.50 per hour for Internet access; open Mon.–Sat. 8 A.M.–7 P.M. **Compunet** (tel. 506/777-2374, 10 A.M.–11 P.M. Mon.–Sat., and 5–11 P.M. Sunday) also charges $1.50 per hour.

Aqua-Matic Laundromat (tel. 506/777-0196) is 200 meters southeast of the soccer field. **Hotel Mar y Luna** (tel. 506/777-1484, 7 A.M.–midnight) has a laundry with two-hour service.

Boutique Mot Mot, an outlet for the Fundación Neotropical, and **Shock Arte** have the best array of souvenirs.

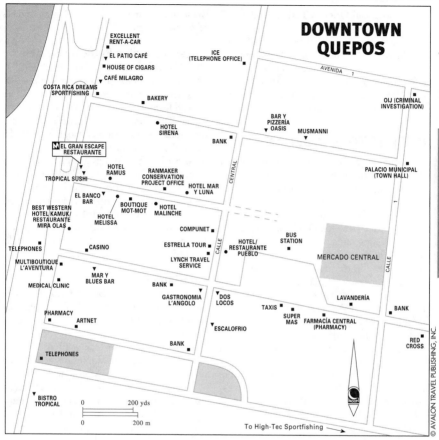

DOWNTOWN QUEPOS

EXCELLENT RENT-A-CAR
EL PATIO CAFÉ
HOUSE OF CIGARS
CAFÉ MILAGRO
COSTA RICA DREAMS SPORTFISHING
ICE (TELEPHONE OFFICE)
AVENIDA 1
OIJ (CRIMINAL INVESTIGATION)
BAKERY
HOTEL SIRENA
BAR Y PIZZERÍA OASIS
MUSMANNI
BANK
EL GRAN ESCAPE RESTAURANTE
HOTEL RAMUS
RANMAKER CONSERVATION PROJECT OFFICE
TROPICAL SUSHI
HOTEL MAR Y LUNA
PALACIO MUNICIPAL (TOWN HALL)
EL BANCO BAR
BOUTIQUE MOT-MOT
HOTEL MALINCHE
BEST WESTERN HOTEL KAMUK/ RESTAURANTE MIRA OLAS
HOTEL MELISSA
COMPUNET
TELEPHONES
CASINO
ESTRELLA TOUR
HOTEL/ RESTAURANTE PUEBLO
BUS STATION
MERCADO CENTRAL
MULTIBOUTIQUE L'AVENTURA
LYNCH TRAVEL SERVICE
MEDICAL CLINIC
MAR Y BLUES BAR
BANK
GASTRONOMIA L'ANGOLO
DOS LOCOS
LAVANDERÍA
PHARMACY
ARTNET
TAXIS
SUPER MAS
FARMACÍA CENTRAL (PHARMACY)
BANK
ESCALOFRIO
RED CROSS
BANK
TELEPHONES
BISTRO TROPICAL
0   200 yds
0   200 m
To High-Tec Sportfishing
CENTRAL
CALLE
CALLE

Central Pacific

© AVALON TRAVEL PUBLISHING, INC.

Getting There

Both **SANSA** (tel. 506/777-0676 in Quepos; open Mon.–Fri. 7 A.M.–5 P.M., Saturday 7 am.–12:30 P.M.) and **Nature Air** (tel. 506/220-3054, www.natureair.com) have scheduled daily service to Quepos. In Quepos, Lynch Travel Service (see *Sports and Recreation,* above) does air ticketing. SANSA offers hotel/airport transfers ($5 pp).

Direct buses (tel. 506/223-5567, in Manuel Antonio, tel. 506/777-0318) depart San José for Manuel Antonio via Quepos from Calle 16, Avenidas 1/3 at 6 A.M., noon, 6 P.M. and 6:30 P.M. (3.5 hours); return buses depart Quepos at 6 A.M., 9:30 A.M., noon, and 5 P.M. (Direct buses originate in Manuel Antonio and fill up fast.) Buses depart Puntarenas for Quepos daily at 5 A.M., 11 A.M., 2:30 P.M., and 4:30 P.M., returning at 4:30 A.M., 7:30 A.M., 10:30 A.M., and 3 P.M. Buses depart San Isidro for Quepos at 7 A.M. and 1:30 P.M. via Dominical; return buses depart Quepos at 5 A.M. and 1:30 P.M. Buy your ticket as far in advance as possible. The ticket office in Quepos is open 7–11 A.M. and 1–5 P.M. Mon.–Sat., 7 A.M.–2 P.M. Sunday.

Getting Around

Quepos received street signs in 2000, but since none of the locals ever use street names, the workers didn't know which way to point them, so the signs can't be trusted!

For taxis, call **Quepos Taxi** (tel. 506/777-0277).

Elegante Rent-a-Car (tel. 506/777-3052) has an office next to Café Milagro. **Economy** (tel. 506/777-5353) has an office opposite Restaurante Barba Roja, on the road to Manuel Antonio. **Alamo Rent-a-Car** has an office 50 meters northwest of the soccer field.

QUEPOS TO MANUEL ANTONIO

Southeast of Quepos, a road climbs sharply over the forested headland of Punta Quepos and snakes, dips, and rises south along a ridgecrest for seven km before dropping down to Manuel Antonio—one of the two most touted destinations in Costa Rica—fringed by **Playa Espadilla,** a two-km-long scimitar of gray sand arcing east to west. There are other beaches tucked into tiny coves reached by dirt trails from the main road. There are occasional tantalizing views down to the beaches, but for most of the way the roadside is thickly forested. An army of hotels and restaurants lines the road.

There are lifeguards *(guardavivas)* at Playa Espadilla during high season. Prior to their advent, the ocean claimed 5–10 lives a year. Beware of riptides when swimming. Crocodiles are said to inhabit the lagoon at the north end of Playa Espadilla, beyond which lies **Playita** (a.k.a. Playa Silvia), a small beach encusped by tall headlands and favored by gays.

There is no community at Manuel Antonio, which consists of a handful of hotels and restaurants catering to the visitors descending on Manuel Antonio National Park, immediately east.

The **Fairchild C-123 transport plane,** roadside opposite Casitas Eclipse, dates from 1954 and now serves as a bar. The plane was used by the CIA to run arms to the contras in Nicaragua and, according to the posted spiel, when shot down by the Sandinistas was responsible for "breaking open the 'contra affair' that exposed the story and the Reagan administration's illegal and secret scheme." Aboard was CIA operative Eugene Hasenfus, whose existence set in motion an "incredible chain of cover-ups and lies that would mushroom into one of the biggest scandals of American history."

Fincas Naturales Butterfly Garden

This 16-hectare nature refuge (tel. 506/777-0850, info@butterflygardens.co.cr, www.butterflygardens.co.cr) is a project of Hotel Si Como No and features multilevel trails and a butterfly garden. The forested reserve is excellent for sighting monkeys and other endangered wildlife. Uniquely, the trails have ultraviolet lighting to show off insect markings normally visible by night to other insects with ultraviolet vision! Five different tours are offered, as is a nocturnal "Sound'n'Image Presentation." Entrance costs $15 adults, $8 children. It has guided birding tours Mon.–Sat. at 4 P.M. and 6 P.M. high season only ($25); and guided nature walks Mon.–Sat. at 9 A.M. and 1 P.M. ($25).

Entertainment

I like the **La Cantina Bar & Grill,** a caboose on rails across from Costa Verde, for its sports bar with CNN and ESPN. It hosts live music six nights weekly.

Another intriguing bar is **El Avión** (tel. 506/777-3378, 2–10 P.M.), inside the Fairchild C-123. It has live music Mon.–Sat.

The **Bat Cave** (7 P.M.–midnight) at La Mansion Inn is a piece of Tolkein fantasy, not least because it is entered by a Lilliputian door. This limestone cave-turned-bar has fishtanks inset in the walls, and a stupendous polished hardwood bartop.

There's a small casino and cigar bar at the **Hotel Divisamar** (7 P.M.–2 A.M.) and a more sophisticated casino at **El Parador.**

Mar y Sombra doubles as a disco at night.

How about a movie in a surround-sound theater? Then head to **Si Como No,** showing top classics nightly at 8:30 P.M. ($5).

Sports and Recreation

Marlboro Stables (tel. 506/777-1108), 200 meters before Playa Espadilla, and **Quepos Trail Rides** (tel. 506/777-0566), next to Barba Roja Restaurant, offers guided horseback rides, as does **Equus Stables** (tel. 506/777-0001), midway between Quepos and the park.

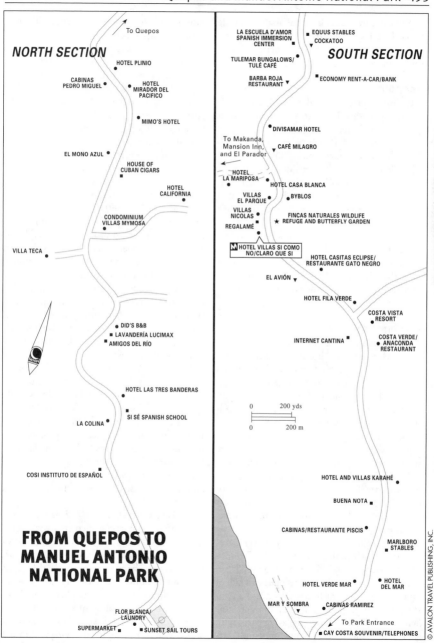

NORTH SECTION

To Quepos

HOTEL PLINIO

CABINAS
PEDRO MIGUEL

HOTEL
MIRADOR DEL
PACIFICO

MIMO'S HOTEL

EL MONO AZUL

HOUSE OF
CUBAN CIGARS

HOTEL
CALIFORNIA

CONDOMINIUM
VILLAS MYMOSA

VILLA TECA

DID'S B&B
LAVANDERÍA LUCIMAX
AMIGOS DEL RÍO

HOTEL LAS TRES BANDERAS

SI SÉ SPANISH SCHOOL

LA COLINA

COSI INSTITUTO DE ESPAÑOL

**FROM QUEPOS TO
MANUEL ANTONIO
NATIONAL PARK**

FLOR BLANCA/
LAUNDRY

SUPERMARKET   SUNSET SAIL TOURS

SOUTH SECTION

LA ESCUELA D'AMOR
SPANISH IMMERSION
CENTER

EQUUS STABLES
COCKATOO

TULEMAR BUNGALOWS/
TULÉ CAFÉ

BARBA ROJA
RESTAURANT

ECONOMY RENT-A-CAR/BANK

DIVISAMAR HOTEL

To Makanda,
Mansion Inn,
and El Parador

CAFÉ MILAGRO

HOTEL
LA MARIPOSA

HOTEL CASA BLANCA

VILLAS
EL PARQUE

BYBLOS

VILLAS
NICOLAS

FINCAS NATURALES WILDLIFE
REFUGE AND BUTTERFLY GARDEN

REGALAMÉ

HOTEL VILLAS SI COMO
NO/CLARO QUE SI

HOTEL CASITAS ECLIPSE/
RESTAURANTE GATO NEGRO

EL AVIÓN

HOTEL FILA VERDE

COSTA VISTA
RESORT

INTERNET CANTINA

COSTA VERDE/
ANACONDA
RESTAURANT

0   200 yds

0   200 m

HOTEL AND VILLAS KARAHÉ

BUENA NOTA

CABINAS/RESTAURANTE PISCIS

MARLBORO
STABLES

HOTEL VERDE MAR

HOTEL
DEL MAR

MAR Y SOMBRA   CABINAS RAMIREZ

To Park Entrance

CAY COSTA SOUVENIR/TELEPHONES

Central Pacific

© AVALON TRAVEL PUBLISHING, INC.

You can hire guides from the **Asociación de Guias Locales de Aguirre** (AGUILA), the local guide association that works to increased environmental awareness.

Shopping

Cay Costa Souvenirs, on the beachfront, sells T-shirts, film, postcards, and toiletries. Several stalls down by the beach hawk jewelry, hash pipes, and other trinkets. **Buena Nota** (tel. 506/777-1002, buennota@racsa.co.cr), 800 meters uphill from the beach, sells beachwear, handicrafts, postcards, maps, books, and international magazines. For quality art, head to **Regalame,** at Si Como No, or **Spheres Gallery,** at the Barba Roja restaurant.

The finest cigar I have smoked in my life comes from the hands of Coela, a delightful Cuban-born roller at **House of Cuban Cigars** (tel. 506/777-2341, 9 A.M.–7 P.M. Mon.–Sat.), which sells both premium Cuban cigars and others rolled on-site.

Accommodations

Budget hotels are mostly found down near the beach. More expensive hotels have loftier, breezy perches (some charge for location). Hilltop hotels may have steep steps; inquire. It can be a tough, hot walk back up the hill from the beach if you don't want to wait for the bus; check to see if your hotel offers van service.

Hotels in each price category are listed as they appear along the road south from Quepos. There are many more options than recommended here.

Camping: You can camp near the park entrance under shade trees on lawns at the back of the Hotel Manuel Antonio ($2 pp; showers cost 25 cents); it will supply tents ($6). **Cabinas Ramírez** charges $3 for camping.

Under $25: For a no-frills options, try **Cabinas Pedro Miguel** (tel./fax 506/777-0035, pmiguel@racsa.co.cr, $25 s, $35 d rooms, $65 s/d larger units), tucked off the road one km south of Quepos. It has 18 small, basic rooms in a two-story building, with cement floors and cinderblock walls, and fans and private baths with cold water. Four other spacious yet simply furnished units have kitchenettes, mezzanine bed-

rooms, and sleep up to five people. There's a small cooling-off pool.

Albergue Costa Linda (tel. 506/777-0304, manuelantonio-costalinda.com, $7.50 pp rooms, $35 s/d apartment), 200 meters inland of Playa Espadilla, is a hostel with 22 basic rooms with shared outside toilets and showers. It also has apartments with private baths. The handsome frontage belies the dour interior, though the restaurant is attractive.

$25–50: The venerable **Hotel Plinio** (Apdo. 71, Quepos, tel. 506/777-0055, fax 506/777-0558, plinio@racsa.co.cr, www.hotelplinio.com, $30 s, $35 d, $50–60 suites, $50 jungle house low season; $55 s, $60 d, $85/110 two-/three-story suites, $110 jungle house high season) has a *palenque* roof, hardwoods surrounded by banana groves, an open restaurant serving Asian-influenced cuisine, and bar resembling a rambling East African treehouse. Some of the 13 rooms have two beds; three have a/c. Rooms are dark but clean and have hot water. There's an attractive swimming pool. A nature trail leads uphill through 10 hectares of primary forest to the highest point around, where a wooden *mirador* proffers a 360-degree vista.

El Mono Azul (Apdo. 297, Quepos, tel. 506/777-1548, fax 506/777-1954, monoazul @racsa.co.cr, www.monoazul.com, $35 s, $40 d low season; $45/50 high season) has 20 clean and comfortable rooms in handsome condo-style units facing a small and pretty oval pool. Each has one double bed and bunk beds, ceiling fans, and hot shower. There's a small gym, Internet café, game room, art gallery (see *Shopping,* below), and movies are shown free in the highly rated restaurant.

Hotel La Colina (tel. 506/777-0231, fax 506/777-1553, lacolina@racsa.co.cr, www.lacolina .com, $39 s/d standard, $70 s/d suite, $50 s/d casita, $60 s/d casa low season; $49/80/65/75 high season), about two km south of Quepos, has simple rooms in a two-story *ranchito*-style house with black-and-white checkered floors. Rooms are dark but pleasant enough, and have a/c and cable TV. Six newer suites are more upscale, with lots of light, plus views from balconies. It also has two *casitas.* There's a small two-tier pool with cascade, and a nice *rancho* restaurant.

Cabinas/Restaurante Piscis (tel./fax 506/777-0046, vivpisc@racsa.co.cr, $10 s, $15 d shared bath, $30 s/d private bath, $35 s/d cabins, including tax), about one km north of Manuel Antonio, has 12 clean and spacious but basic *cabinas* with fans and private baths with cold water. There's a wide patio veranda plus atmospheric restaurant.

Hotel del Mar (tel./fax 506/777-0543, www.hoteldelmar-costarica.com, $40 with fan, $52 with a/c, $58 with king bed low season; $55/65/70 high season), at the bottom of the hill near the beach, has 12 adequate though relatively small rooms (eight have a/c) with rust-red cement floors (some have terra-cotta), balconies, fans, large windows, and private baths; four rooms have hot water.

Restaurante/Hotel Vela Bar (Apdo. 13, Quepos, tel. 506/777-0413, fax 506/777-1071, velabar@maqbeach.com, $30 d room, $35 with a/c year-round, $55 *casita* low season, $65 high season), near the park entrance, has 11 *cabinas* with fans and private baths with hot water, plus a house and two small apartments with kitchen. Some have a/c. It has a popular thatched restaurant and bar.

The delightful **Cabinas Espadilla** (tel. 506/777-2113, fax 506/777-0416, cabinas @espadilla.com, www.espadilla.com, $45 s/d low season, $68 s/d high season) has modestly furnished units a short stroll from the beach.

$50–100: If you want to be by the park entrance, consider **Hotel Manuel Antonio** (tel. 506/777-1237, fax 506/777-5172, $52 s, $58 d low season, $64 s, $69 d high season), which offers 26 spacious a/c rooms in a modern two-story unit in Spanish colonial style; each has ceiling fans, security boxes, and private bathrooms with hot water. There's a swimming pool and a simple restaurant.

The well-kept **Hotel Playa Espadilla** (Apdo. 195, Quepos, tel. 506/777-2135, fax 506/777-0903, hotel@espadilla.com, www.espadilla.com, from $79 s, $84 d room, $93/99 with kitchen low season; $93 s, $107 d room, $111/122 with kitchen high season), 100 meters inland, has 16 large units in two-story blocks set in attractive grounds with nine hectares of private reserve accessed by trails. All have a/c, refrigerators, fans, cable TV, security box, and large private bathroom with hot water (four have kitchenettes). There's a thatched restaurant, swimming pool, tennis court, bar, secure parking, and *pilas* (laundry sinks).

Nearby, the **Inn on the Park** (tel. 506/777-1515, fax 506/777-3468, www.innonthepark hotel.com, $70 s/d low season, $100 suite low season, $100/140 high season) is a modern three-story salmon-colored unit. The spacious rooms with tile floors feature king-size beds, plus sofabed, ceiling fans, cable TV, refrigerator, security box, beautiful hardwood furniture, large bathrooms, and glass French doors opening to verandas. A master suite has a large lounge with deep-cushion sofas. There's a small pool in the rear courtyard with deck. Rates include breakfast.

The German-run **Hotel Mirador del Pacífico** (Apdo. 164, Quepos, tel./fax 506/777-0119, mirador@racsa.co.cr, www.elmiradorcostarica .com, $40s, $60 d with fan, $60 s/d with a/c low season, $50 with fan, $80 with a/c high season) has 22 pretty rooms, with fans and private baths with hot water, lots of light, and private patios and verandas. Rooms are in rough-hewn wood structures raised on stilts amid lush tropical grounds. A plank walkway leads to the swimming pool. A funicular will carry you up the steep hill. Little Polynesian tikis peek from behind tropical plants. It also has three villa apartments. The Mirador Restaurant serves international fare. A villa with kitchenette costs $95.

Mimo's Apartotel (P.O. Box 228-6358, Manuel Antonio, tel. 506/777-0054, fax 506/777-2217, hminos@racsa.co.cr, www.hotelmimos .com, $35 standard, $55 junior suite low season, $55 standard, $85 junior suite high season) is a beautiful Spanish-style villa with 11 spacious and attractive units comprising four standards, six junior suites, and one six-person apartment-style suite with sofabed and kitchenette. All have a/c, cable TV, security box, private verandas, and hammock. Each room has a double bed and futon. There's a small swimming pool and a

Jacuzzi. The Italian owners pamper guests and make excellent Italian meals.

The French-Canadian-run **Condominium Villas Mymosa** (tel. 506/777-1254, fax 506/777-2454, mymosa@racsa.co.cr, www.villasmymosa .com, $45 s/d junior villa, $55 villa, $75 s/d deluxe low season; $75/85/100 high season), just beyond Bungalows Las Palmas, is a splendid option with 10 large villas in three types, including two-bedroom villas, each with a king-size and queen-size bed in one room divided by a half-height wall. All have a/c, terra-cotta floors, floor and ceiling fans, fully equipped kitchen, tasteful decor and furnishings, and exquisite bathrooms. The handsome units surround a pool, and there's a restaurant.

The newly remodeled **Hotel California** (tel. 506/777-1234, fax 506/777-1062, hotelcal@racsa .co.cr, www.hotel-california.com, $70 s/d standard, $80 s/d deluxe low season; $105 standard, $125 deluxe high season), farther up the side road, is now under French owners. The three-story hotel with the name you'll never forget has terra-cotta tile throughout, plus 22 graciously appointed rooms with raised ceilings, hardwood beds, cable TVs, minibars, telephones, security boxes, wide French doors, and marvelous views from the balconies overlooking a pool with wooden deck.

One of my favorite places is **Didi's B&B** (tel. 506/777-0069, fax 506/777-2863, www.didiscr .com, $30 s, $35 d with fan, $40 s, $45 with a/c low season; $40 s, $45 d with fan, $50 s, $55 d with a/c high season), run by a charming Italian couple. Raised above the road, this strawberry pink villa has a shaded, broad wooden terrace of polished hardwood, and a TV lounge with oversize deep-cushion bamboo sofa and seats. Mosquito coils are a thoughtful touch. It has three rooms with simple but charming furniture, ceiling fans, cable TV, wooden floors, and skylit bathrooms with attractive tiles and hot water. Organic meals are made for guests. There's a Jacuzzi.

I like **Villa Teca** (Apdo. 180-6350, Quepos, tel. 506/777-1117, fax 506/777-1578, hvteca @racsa.co.cr, www.hotelvillatecacr.com, $60 s, $73 d low season; $70 s, $82 d high season), an exquisite, aesthetically appealing modern property with daffodil-yellow, red-tile-roofed villas scattered throughout the lushly vegetated hillside. There are 40 rooms in 20 a/c bungalows, each with two twin beds (with beautiful tropical floral spreads), terrace, plus private bath with hot water. Other highlights include an attractive pool and sun deck plus thatched restaurant, and a free shuttle to and from the beach. Rates include tax.

I highly recommend **Hotel Las Tres Banderas** (Apdo. 258-6350, Quepos, tel. 506/777-1521 or 506/777-1284, fax 506/777-1478, banderas@racsa.co.cr, www.hotel-tres-banderas .com, from $35 s, $40–45 d standard, $75 suite low season; $55/$60–65/95 high season), a handsome two-story Spanish colonial–style property run by friendly Polish owner Andrzej Nowacki and his partner Christopher. Its 14 a/c rooms come in three types, including three suites abounding in hardwoods and Peruvian wall-hangings. They're roomy and pleasant, with lots of light, big balconies opening to both pool (front) and landscaped grounds and forest (rear), and exquisite bathrooms with pretty tiles. All have TVs. Suites have minibars and small refrigerators. Meals are prepared at an outside grill and served on the patio beside the pool (replete with cascade and mosaic tiles showing the U.S., Polish, and Tican flags—the eponymous three flags—plus a large Jacuzzi inset in stone); see *Food*, below. Trails lead into the forest. There's a game room, and a TV in the bar.

Divisamar Hotel (Apdo. 82-6350, Quepos, tel. 506/777-0371, fax 506/777-0525, info @divisimar.com, www.divisimar.com, $55 s/d standard, $70 superior low season; $75/85 high season) is a three-story unit with 12 modestly appealing a/c rooms and 12 superior rooms around a small pool in landscaped grounds. All have telephone and private bath with hot water (some have TVs, which can be requested for all rooms). The hotel has a whirlpool, souvenir shop, and open-air bar and restaurant with a pleasant outside dining terrace (buffet breakfast only). It also has a casino and cigar bar. Rates include continental breakfast.

The Canadian-run **Nature's Beachfront Aparthotel** (tel. 506/777-1473, fax 506/777-

1475, beaches@racsa.co.cr, www.maqbeach.com/
natures.html, $29 s, $34 d studios low season,
$34 s, $39 d high season; $59 luxury suites low
season, $69 high season) offers one of the world's
premier beachfront vistas, although you'll want
wheels for easy access (it sits beachside at the
bottom of a dirt road far from the main highway). It has four self-catering units, including
three studios and a backpackers' studio, all clinically white, with ceiling fans, kitchenettes, security boxes, and bathrooms with large walk-in
showers and hot water. An upstairs penthouse
sleeps eight people and has a wrap-around wall of
glass, cable TV, and huge terrace. According to
readers, however, standards are lacking and upkeep is questionable.

Villas El Parque (Apdo. 111, Quepos, tel. 506/
777-0096, fax 506/777-0538, vparque@racsa
.co.cr, www.hotelvillaselparque.com, $66 junior
suite, $83 deluxe junior suite, $93–102 suite,
$149 villa low season; $98/108/119-139/208
high season) has 17 standard rooms, 16 villas
(no kitchens), plus 18 suites with kitchens, in
handsome Mediterranean style, all with a/c, cable
TVs, phones, terra-cotta tile floors, ceiling fans,
and large balconies with hammocks and views
out over the park. Delightful decor includes lively
Guatemalan bedspreads. Suites can be combined
with standard rooms to form bi-level villas. One
suite is wheelchair-accessible. There's a restaurant plus triple-level swimming pool. Monkeys
visit the property every afternoon at "monkey
hour." It has sportfishing packages.

Villas Nicolas (Apdo. 236, Quepos, tel. 506/
777-0481, fax 506/777-0451, sales@villasnicolas
.com, www.villasnicolas.com, $55–90 d one-
bedroom, $135–145 two-bedroom low season;
$70–120 one-bedroom, $180–200 two-bedroom high season) has 12 privately owned, individually furnished one- and two-bedroom villa
suites (in six types), all with private ocean-view verandas overlooking lush grounds. Upper-story
verandas have concrete benches with soft-cushioned sofas. Rooms are large and pleasantly furnished, with fans and private baths with hot
water. Smaller bedrooms upstairs have no
kitchens. There's a narrow swimming pool and a
sun deck.

Hotel and Villas Karahé (Apdo. 100-6350,
Quepos, tel. 506/777-0170, fax 506/777-1075,
karahe@racsa.cr.cr, www.karahe.com, $75–100
s/d, $60–70 villas) has 32 a/c rooms, including 16
beachside rooms and nine *cabinas*. Terrace rooms
are reached by a miniature funicular or stairs.
They're large and well lit and boast marble floors,
nice bathrooms, good views, and beautiful
grounds. The rustic restaurant's house specialties include shish kebabs. A private trail leads to
the beach, where there's a pool and a snack bar.
The hotel rents boogie boards ($5 per day) and
has Karahe Sportfishing.

I like the **Hotel Verde Mar** (P.O. Box 348-
6350, Quepos, tel. 506/777-1805, fax 506/777-
1311, verdemar@racsa.co.cr; in Canada, tel.
604/925-4772; $45 s/d economy, $55 standard, $65 suite low season; $70/80/90 high
season), behind Playa Espadilla. It has 20 a/c
rooms in a two-story structure with balconies
supported on rough-hewn logs. Each room is
painted in soft pastels and has a queen bed,
ceiling fan, and kitchenette; plus eight suites
with two queens and a kitchen. Soothing pastels
and log timbers add calming notes. There's a
pool, and a raised walkway ("77 steps") leads
to the beach.

Hotel Villa Bosque (tel. 506/777-0463,
fax 506/777-0401, $58 s, $69 d low season;
$69 s, $81 d high season), set back from the
beach close to the park boundary, is a Spanish-
colonial remake with 17 pleasant, atmospheric
a/c rooms that each sleep three people; rooms
have fans, cable TV, security boxes, and private
baths with hot water, plus verandas/patios with
chairs. It has a restaurant serving surf-and-
turf, and a pool on the raised terrace. Potted
plants abound.

$100–150: The **Costa Vista Resort** (tel.
506/777-1221, fax 506/777-1497, info
@costavistaresort.com, www.costavistaresort.com,
$122 pp low season) is an attractive, three-story,
salmon-pink, thatched structure in quasi-
Mediterranean style. All 13 rooms (some with
a/c) have a terrace with lounge chairs for enjoying
the views. Each has a private bathroom, terra-
cotta tiles, coffeemaker, plus double bed and a
bunk. There's a pool and restaurant. At last visit

it was adding condominiums and planning to go all-inclusive under new owners.

The **Byblos** (Apdo. 112, Quepos, tel. 506/777-0411, fax 506/777-0009, byblos@racsa.co.cr or info@byblos.co.cr, $70 s/d bungalows, $80 junior suites, $90 suite low season; $105/110/120 high season) is a stylish quasi-Swiss lodge in lush landscaped grounds. A wonderful pool and sun deck are set in a hollow surrounded by jungle. Seven whitewashed stone bungalows are spaced widely apart and have private balconies overlooking banana groves and primary forest. Nine spacious junior suites in the main unit have individual color schemes, wicker furniture, refrigerators, cable TVs, telephones, coffeemakers, and large triangular bathrooms. Small windows do not take advantage of the lofty position. A breezy restaurant, pizza parlor, and sports bar overlook the grounds.

Hotel La Mariposa (Apdo. 4, Quepos, tel. 506/777-0355, fax 506/777-0050, mariposa@racsa.co.cr, www.hotelmariposa.com; in the U.S., tel. 800/416-2747; $115 d standard, $130 deluxe, $150 villa and junior suite, $215 master suite, $240 Penthouse low season; $155/175/215/310/375 high season) is dramatically perched on cliffs above the sea, with magnificent views over Manuel Antonio National Park. It has 60 a/c rooms. Eight vast standard rooms in the main house offer garden views from lower stories, and fabulous coastal views from upper rooms, enjoyed through picture windows and wraparound balconies; each has terra-cotta floors, hardwoods, and exquisite tilework in the bathrooms, but they are accessed by a frail metal spiral staircase that can induce vertigo in the weak-hearted! Ten split-level Mediterranean-style cottage-villas nestle on the hillcrest; each has a deck—with outside whirlpools in the junior suites—and a sky-lit bathroom, but the modest furnishings disappoint. Deluxe units have beam ceilings with fans, Guatemalan furniture, plus whirlpool bathtubs. At last visit, 15 premier suites were being added, including a penthouse with walls of glass; they have limestone floors and lively contemporary furnishings. The restaurant serves French-inspired fare. Facilities include two swimming pools with swim-up bars, a massage room, and gift store. A nature trail leads to the beach.

Hotel Casitas Eclipse (P.O. Box 11-6350, Quepos, tel./fax 506/777-0408 or 506/777-1738, eclipseh@racsa.co.cr, www.casitaseclipse

view over Manuel Antonio National Park, from Hotel La Mariposa

© JEAN MERCIER

.com, $58 s, $64 d standard, $90 d suite, $150 casita low season; $76 s, $80 d standard, $150 d suite, $375 casita high season) is an intimate property offering 30 rooms in nine beautiful, well-lit, brightly decorated, whitewashed Mediterranean-style, two-story, a/c villas set in a hollow around three swimming pools with sun terraces and bougainvillea cascading over white walls. You can rent the entire villa or one floor only. Some rooms have a refrigerator; others have fully equipped kitchens. French owned. The effect is marvelous, although one reader complains about upkeep. Rates include breakfast.

Costa Verde (Apdo. 6944-6350, Quepos, tel. 506/777-0584, fax 506/777-0560, reservations @costaverde.net, www.hotelcostaverde.com, $65 efficiency, $85 studio, $99 studio plus, $125 penthouse low season; $79/105/129/155 high season) is a three-story modern unit offering four types of spacious accommodations: efficiencies, studios, studio apartments, and a penthouse, all with heaps of light. Sliding doors backed by screen doors open onto verandas with rockers and views. Some rooms face away from the ocean. Reception is hidden behind a railroad caboose on rails, and another caboose across the road is now an Internet café, sports bar, and grill. The Anaconda Restaurant has views.

$150–250: The **Tulemar Bungalows** (Apdo. 225-6350 Quepos, tel. 506/777-0580, fax 506/ 777-1579, tulemar@racsa.co.cr, www.tulemar .com, $148 s/d standard, $246 premium low season; $249/412 high season; $339/558 peak season) claims its "own exclusive beach," reached by a road winding steeply through a 13-hectare private forest reserve. Tulemar's oceanview octagonal a/c bungalows are higher up, surrounded by trees and lawns, and offer 13 standard and seven premium rooms (the latter with their own common pool and bar). All have in-room safes, TVs and VCRs, telephones, fans, hairdryers, kitchenettes, and beautiful interiors highlighted by 180-degree windows and bulbous skylights. There's a small horizon swimming pool with a bar, plus a shop and snack bar. More deluxe bungalows and a condominium complex have multi-bedroom units on two levels accessed by a bridged walkway;

each has a whirlpool and a glass-paneled wall. Nature walks are offered.

My favorite place is **M Makanda by the Sea** (Apdo. 29-6350, Quepos, tel. 506/777-0442, fax 506/777-1032, makanda@racsa.co.cr, www .makanda.com, $175 studios, $265 villas low season; $230/350 high season), a beauty blessed by an enviable setting. Three elegant villas and three studios are lined by walkways weaving through a series of Japanese gardens designed into the hillside. Each is different, though all are of contemporary vogue, with king-size beds, vaulted ceilings, polished hardwoods, and handcrafted tile enhancing the minimalist decor that melds suave Milan with soothing Kyoto. The timber-beamed bedrooms have wall-to-wall French doors that open to wraparound verandas. The aesthetic vision extends to a pool suspended on the hillside, with a circular Jacuzzi inset like a jewel and, to one side, a tiny restaurant—the Sunsport Poolside Bar and Grill—shaded by medieval-style canopies. A complimentary breakfast is delivered to your door each morning.

The luxurious and somewhat pretentious **La Mansion Inn** (P.O. Box 380-6350, Quepos, tel. 506/777-3487, fax 506/777-0002, quepos@racsa .co.cr, www.lamansioninn.com, $125 s/d deluxe room, $275 s/d suite, $1250 Presidential Suite low season; $175/475/1500 high season) has a contemporary Spanish colonial theme, with not a hint of the tropics. It boasts original artwork and tremendous views. Each of the 11 perfumed a/c rooms and five suites comes with fruit basket and wine bottle, and features French drapes, hardwood pieces, handmade Italian furnishings (including gracious king-size wrought-iron beds), large walk-in showers, luxurious fittings, and safes. The huge one-, two-, and three-bedroom suites have plate-glass windows, marble bathrooms, en-suite Jacuzzis, and 24-carat gold faucets! A freeform pool complex is fed by a water cascade from a Jacuzzi. Six-course gourmet dinners are offered, with wine from the hotel's own label, and the bar is one of a kind (see *Entertainment,* below).

Hotel and Beach Club El Parador (Apdo. 284-6350, Quepos, tel. 506/777-1414, fax 506/777-1437, info@hotelparador.com,

Central Pacific

www.hotelparador.com, $130 s/d standard, $150 deluxe, $185 premium, $225 junior suite low season; $175/200/260/350 high season), near the tip of Punta Quepos, overlooks Playa Biesanz and Playa Espedilla. El Parador was conceived to be a flashback to the romantic *pousadas* of Spain, with antique farm implements, a suit of armor, and weaponry. The hub is the main hall-cum-dining room, with hefty oak beams, Spanish tiles, antique wrought-iron chandeliers, tapestries, Persian rugs, antiques and historic artifacts, and thick-timbered wooden doors and shuttered windows from Spanish castles. The 25 standard rooms, 20 deluxe rooms, and 15 suites (complete with Jacuzzi), however, are furnished in contemporary vogue. Most have a king-size or two queen beds, plus minibar. Premium rooms are larger and better furnished. Facilities include a huge terrace bar, stone-lined wine-tasting room-cum-casino, a *mirador ranchita* bar-cum-restaurant, mini-golf course, two swimming pools, daily cultural events, hair salon, health spa, business center, and a helicopter landing pad.

I love ⛰ **Hotel Villas Si Como No** (Apdo. 5-6350, Quepos, tel. 506/777-0777, fax 506/777-1093, sicomono@racsa.co.cr, www.sicomono.com, $140 standard, $160 superior, $175 deluxe low season; $210 deluxe suite, $160/180/195/225 high season), with its flamboyant peaked *mirador* entrance. The hotel has 58 spacious suites with terra-cotta floors, tropical prints, queen- or king-size beds of rustic teak, mosquito nets, halogen reading lamps, bathrooms with bench seats and glass-brick walls, and French doors opening to balconies with views. Apartment units also have living rooms, master bedrooms, dining rooms, and kitchens. I much prefer the 18 newer deluxe, wheelchair-accessible units, which have a classy contemporary aesthetic, plus king beds, oversize sofas, rheostat lighting, and fabulous bathrooms with huge walk-in showers and gracious stained-glass windows. Three honeymoon suites have garden Jacuzzis. The structures are supported by columns resembling palm trees, with leafy branches for eaves. The rails and fences resemble thick bamboo. The hotel is ecologically sensitive, with state-of-the-art recycling, sewage systems, solar lighting, and a/c systems, plus double-pane windows and doors. A pool and sun deck feature a water slide, cascades, whirlpool, and swim-up bar (by night it's like a *son et lumière*!) A second pool is adults only. It has two restaurants, including one of Manuel Antonio's finest. There's also a state-of-the-art movie theater, a conference center and an upscale spa.

Escape Villas (tel. 506/777-5258, fax 506/777-5265, info@villascostarica.com, www.vivalas villas.com; in the U.S., tel. 866/839-5526) is a villa rental agency.

At last visit, a super-deluxe condo project, **Arenas del Mar,** was under construction immediately behind the beach at Playa Silvia.

Food

The place for breakfast is **Café Milagro** (tel. 506/777-0794, 6 A.M.–6 P.M. low season, 6 A.M.–10 P.M. high season), opposite Hotel Casa Blanca, with a full array of coffee drinks, pastries, and sandwiches to be enjoyed on a tree-shaded patio.

Down by the beach, the open-air **Mar y Sombra** (tel. 506/777-0003) serves seafood dishes and local specialties for under $5. The simple but popular **Marlin Restaurante** (tel. 506/777-1134), 200 meters east, offers seafoods and steaks in a two-story structure with options for open-air dining. It serves killer margueritas and piña coladas, and has happy hour 4:30–6:30 P.M. Nearby, **Restaurante Atardecer** has a nice upstairs bar of roughhewn woods.

Barba Roja Restaurant (tel. 506/777-0331) is acclaimed for its delicious seafood and steaks (from $8), plus Mexican fare and daily specials, and ocean-view alfresco dining great for sunsets.

The elegant open-air ⛰ **Claro Que Si** (6:30 A.M.–9:30 P.M.) at Si Como No has a tremendous hip feel and a killer menu. I enjoyed fried squid ($6), roasted bell peppers, olives and avocado salad ($6), stuffed ravioli with seafood and spinach ($9), and chocolate ice cream pie.

My favorite place is the ⛰ **Sunspot Poolside Bar and Grill** (tel. 506/777-0442, 11 A.M.–11 P.M.), at Makanda, a classy spot serving *bocas* such as calamari, and mussels in Chardonnay broth ($7–9), as well as quesadillas, sandwiches, and huge salads for lunch. Dinner is a romantic, candlelit, gourmet affair; the menu includes gourmet pizzas, scallops with blackberry and balsamic reduction ($20), and divine foccacia with homemade herb butter. The extensive wine list includes many California reserves. Closed October.

I also love **Gato Negro** (tel. 506/777-1728, 6:30 A.M.–10 P.M.), at Hotel Eclipse, for its warm ambience, conscientious service, and superb Mediterranean cuisine, such as tagliatelle and salad niçoise, carpaccio, pastas, etc.

Many people rave about the elegant restaurant at **La Mariposa,** ($4–12), which has a creative menu: *paté de pollo* with green peppercorn, leek and shrimp soup, and breast of chicken in French wine and mustard are typical. I've found the food okay but undistinguished—but, oh, those views!

I also recommend a Polish-inspired meal at **Tres Banderas** (by reservation only). Try the *bigos* (Polish sauerkraut and meats), the house special of trout with tarragon and white wine sauce ($12), the superb ceviche, and the "Blue Tico" house cocktail.

Information and Services

Anita Myketuk runs a tourist-information bureau at **Buena Nota,** 800 meters uphill from the beach.

The **Internet Cantina,** across from Costa Verde, offers Internet access, as does **Regalame** (7:30 A.M.–10 P.M.), next to Hotel Si Como No.

Lavandería Lucimax (tel. 506/777-2164), opposite Didi's B&B, has a public laundry, as does Hotel Flor Blanca.

Centro de Idiomas del Pacífico (tel. 506/777-0805, info@cipacifico.com, www.cipacifico.com), at Cabinas Pedro Miguel, has personalized Spanish programs; as do **La Escuela de Idiomas D'Amore** (tel./fax 506/777-1143, damore@sol .racsa.co.cr, www.escueladamore.com), about three km south of Quepos; and **Si Sé Spanish School** (tel./fax 506/777-4642, www.sisespanishschool.com), south of Hotel Tres Banderas.

Getting There

Public buses depart Quepos for Manuel Antonio every 30 minutes, 7 A.M.–8 P.M. and will pick you up (and drop you off) along the road if you flag them down.

A private taxi from Quepos will cost about $4 to Manuel Antonio. A *colectivo* (shared) taxi costs 50 cents pp.

ⓝ MANUEL ANTONIO NATIONAL PARK

Tiny it may be, but this 682-hectare national park epitomizes everything tourists flock to Costa Rica to see: stunning beaches, a magnificent setting with islands offshore, lush rainforest laced with a network of welcoming trails, and wildlife galore—all within walking distance of your hotel.

Despite its diminutive size, Manuel Antonio is one of the country's most popular parks, with as many as 150,000 visitors annually in peak years. A few years ago the deluge of visitors threatened to spoil the very things they had come to see. In 1994, the Park Service began limiting the numbers of visitors to 600 per day (800 on Saturday and Sunday), and the park is now closed on Monday. Consider visiting in the "green" or wet season. Litter and pollution are additional problems. Pack out what you pack in.

Howler monkeys move languorously from branch to branch, iguanas shimmy up trunks, toucans and scarlet macaws flap by. About 350 squirrel monkeys live in the park, another 500 on its outer boundaries. And capuchin (white-faced) monkeys welcome you at treetop height on the beaches, where they will steal your belongings given half a chance. Some of them have become aggressive in recent years, and attacks on humans have been reported.

It is illegal to feed the monkeys. If you're caught, you may be ejected from the park. Studies have found an increase in heart disease and heart failure among the local monkey population attributed to human foods. Do not leave food lying around.

The park is too small to sustain a healthy and viable population of certain animals. Corridors that allow animals access to areas outside the park have been taken up by hotels, so that the park has, in recent years, become an island. As a result, the titi (squirrel monkey) population is

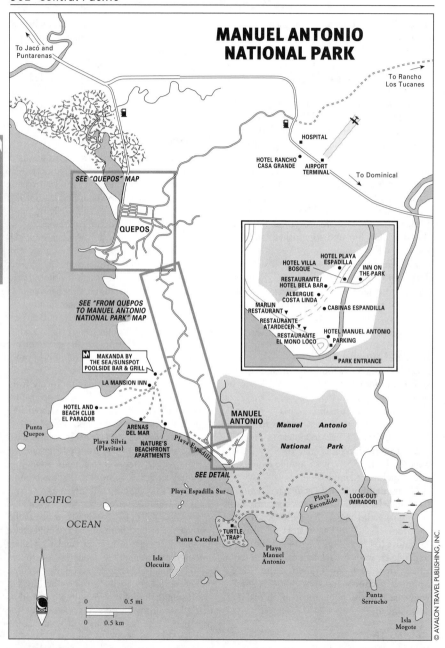

MANUEL ANTONIO
NATIONAL PARK

To Jacó and
Puntarenas

To Rancho
Los Tucanes

HOSPITAL

HOTEL RANCHO
CASA GRANDE   AIRPORT
TERMINAL

To Dominical

SEE "QUEPOS" MAP

QUEPOS

SEE "FROM QUEPOS
TO MANUEL ANTONIO
NATIONAL PARK" MAP

HOTEL PLAYA
ESPADILLA
HOTEL VILLA
BOSQUE   INN ON
THE PARK
RESTAURANTE/
HOTEL BELA BAR
ALBERGUE
COSTA LINDA
MARLIN   CABINAS ESPANDILLA
RESTAURANT
RESTAURANTE
ATARDECER   HOTEL MANUEL ANTONIO
RESTAURANTE   PARKING
EL MONO LOCO

PARK ENTRANCE

MAKANDA BY
THE SEA/SUNSPOT
POOLSIDE BAR & GRILL

LA MANSION INN

HOTEL AND
BEACH CLUB
EL PARADOR

MANUEL
ANTONIO   Manuel   Antonio

ARENAS
DEL MAR   National   Park
Punta
Quepos   Playa Silvia   NATURE'S
(Playitas)   BEACHFRONT
APARTMENTS

Playa Espadilla

SEE DETAIL

Playa Espadilla Sur

PACIFIC

OCEAN

Playa
Escondido   LOOK-OUT
(MIRADOR)

TURTLE
TRAP
Punta Catedral   Playa
Manuel
Antonio
Isla
Olocuita

Punta
Serrucho

0   0.5 mi

0   0.5 km

Isla
Mogote

Central Pacific

© CHRISTOPHER P. BAKER

monkey at Playa Manuel Antonio

declining. The local **Association of Women, Family, & Quepos Community** (tel. 506/777-2020) works to save the titi.

Beaches and Trails

The park has four lovely beaches: Espadilla Sur, Manuel Antonio, Escondido, and Playita. The prettiest is Playa Manuel Antonio, a small scimitar of coral-white sand with a small coral reef. It's separated from Playa Espadilla Sur by a *tombolo*—a natural land bridge formed over eons through the accumulation of sand—tipped by **Punta Catedral,** an erstwhile island now linked to the mainland. The hike to the top of Punta Catedral (100 meters) along a steep and sometimes muddy trail takes about an hour from Playa Espadilla Sur (also known as the Second Beach). Espadilla Sur and Manuel Antonio offer tidal pools brimming with minnows and crayfish, plus good snorkeling, especially during dry season when the water is generally clear.

At the far right on Playa Manuel Antonio, you can see ancient turtle traps dug out of the rocks by pre-Columbian Quepoas. Female sea turtles would swim over the rocks to the beach on the high tide. The tidal variation at this point is as much as three meters; the turtles would be caught in the carved-out traps on the return journey as the tide level dropped. The people also used female-turtle decoys made of balsa to attract male turtles over the rocks. Olive ridley and green turtles still occasionally come ashore at Playa Manuel Antonio.

Between bouts of beaching, you can explore the park's network of wide trails, which lead into a swatch of humid tropical forest. Manuel Antonio's treetop carnival is best experienced by following the **Perezoso Trail,** named after the sloths that favor the secondary growth along the trail. You might see marmosets, ocelots, river otters, pacas, and spectacled caimans in more remote riverine areas.

Hire a guide. A guide can show you other interesting tree species—among them, the *gaupinol negro,* an endemic species that is in danger of extinction; *cedro maria,* which produces a yellow resin used as a traditional medicine;

© CHRISTOPHER P. BAKER

Playa Espadilla

vaco lechoso, which exudes a thick white latex that also has medicinal properties, and the manchineel tree *(manzanillo),* or "beach apple"—common along the beaches. The manchineel is highly toxic and possesses a sap that irritates the skin. Its tempting apple-like fruits are also poisonous. Avoid touching any part of the tree. Also, don't use its wood for fires—the smoke will irritate your lungs.

Information

The park **entrance** is at the eastern end of Playa Espadilla, where you wade across the shallow Río Camaronera. Rowboats are on hand at high tide (30 cents), when you may otherwise be waist-deep.

The park is open 7 A.M.–4 P.M. Tue.–Sun. The $7 admission is payable at the **ranger station** (tel./fax 506/777-0654). There's a small open-air natural-history **museum** and information center on Playa Manuel Antonio.

Camping is not allowed in the park. There are no accommodations or snack bars.

Cautions

Theft is a major problem on the beaches, not least by the monkeys. Don't leave your things unguarded while you swim. There's parking by the creek near the park entrance ($2.50), but security is an issue. Don't leave anything in your vehicle.

There are riptides on Playa Espadilla.

Quepos to Dominical

South of Quepos, Hwy. 34 leads almost ruler-straight, 45 km southeast to Dominical. At last visit this bone-jarring skunk of a dirt road was being leveled and paved. The first few miles south of town pass a sea of African palms.

SAVEGRE

Twenty-five km southeast of Quepos, at the hamlet of **Savegre,** a dirt road leads inland six km up the valley of the Río Savegre to the community of **El Silencio,** at the base of the mountains. Here, the local farmer's cooperative operates the **Centro Eco-Turístico Comunitario de Silencio.** It's a great spot for lunch and has a butterfly garden, well-marked trails, plus horseback rides ($20, three hours) and rafting trips. There's a **Wildlife Rescue Center** nearby ($8 for guided tour).

The **Río Naranjo** and **Río Savegre** flow down from the rainforest-clad mountains and eventually fan out into an estuary in Manuel Antonio National Park. In wet season both offer Class II–V whitewater action. Tour operators in Quepos and San José offer trips.

Rafiki Safari Lodge (see *Accommodations,* below), 10 km beyond El Silencio and 19 km from Hwy. 21, has a wildlife reintroduction program, including tapir breeding. It offers a full-day whitewater special ($85 including breakfast and lunch). The thatched restaurant is a great spot to dine.

⊠ Savegre River Plantation

Named for the surrounding coconut plantation, this stunning resort-cum-recreational facility is fed by waters diverted from the river (and cleansed of silt). It features several recreational lakes (the largest 2.5 hectares) and 20 swimming pools with beaches and rocky shorelines. The lakes drop 35 feet in stages, with horizon edges; some 28 billion gallons of water will pass through each year. Each lake is themed, night-lit, and features a swim-up bar. One features a standing wave perfect for boogie-board-

ing and water-skiing; another has a variable wave with controllable left and right breaks for surfing. You can enjoy tubing on a lazy river, and there are jump-off spots into the deeper pools, which range up to 20 feet deep. There's beach volleyball, horseback trails, ziplines over the water, and a spa.

Accommodations and Food

Albergue El Silencio (Apdo. 65-6035, Quepos, tel./fax 506/779-9554, coopsilencio@racsa.co.cr, www.turismoruralcr.com, $30 s, $35 d low season, $35/40 high season) is a rustic lodge nestled on a breezy hill at the north end of Silencio village, with views down over a sea of palms. There are nine thatch-and-wood cabins (some with bunks) with lofts with two single beds, screened windows, and tiled private baths with cold water. Rates include breakfast.

You'll love ⊠ **Rafiki Safari Lodge** (tel. 506/777-2250, info@rafikisafari.com, www.rafikisafari.com, $130 s, $205 d low season, $131 s, $225 d high season), run by a hospitable South African family. It offers nine genuine luxury African-safari four-person tents on stilts, with roughhewn timber beds, gracious fabrics, and huge, graciously appointed skylit bathrooms with fire-heated hot water showers. They also have large wooden decks. Quality international dining at the thatched Lekker Bar includes meats from a South Africa "braai" (barbecue). It has a waterslide into a spring water pool, and offers float trips on the Río Savegre, plus kayaking, fishing, hiking, and birding trips. Dinners for nonguests are offered by reservation (7–9 P.M.).

Aiming at recreational-minded, monied clients, the **Savegre River Plantation** will have 16 deluxe tri-level lakeside villas, seven riverside villas, and a hillside hotel when complete in 2004/5. Each villa will have acrylic viewing areas in the floors, plus its own bamboo raft and sundeck pier, perfect for riding out to the fine dining Tom Sawyer's Restaurant. You even get your own Tarzan swing.

© CHRISTOPHER P. BAKER

African date palm fruits, near Savegre

PLAYA MATAPALO

Playa Matapalo, five km south of Savegre, is a beautiful gray-sand beach two km east of the coast road: the turnoff is in the hamlet of **Matapalo.** The beach is a surfer's paradise—it has two rivermouth breaks—albeit as yet not drawing surfers (be cautious when swimming, as there are strong riptides). Fishing from the beach is guaranteed to deliver a snapper, snook, or other champ species. A large number of Swiss and Germans have settled to live offbeat lifestyles.

South of Matapalo, habitation is sparse and the lonesome road is rutted all the way to Dominical, a few kilometers before which you cross the Río Hatillo Viejo; you can hike or take horseback rides up the valley to the **Terciopelo Waterfalls,** a three-tiered cascade tumbling 120 feet into pools good for swimming.

Accommodations and Food

At Playa Matapalo, *cabinas* are spread apart along a dirt road that extends north along the beach.

The nicest place is the Swiss-run **El Coquito del Pacífico** (tel./fax 506/384-7220, el-coquito @gmx.net, www.elcoquito.com, $31 s, $41 d

low season; $45/55 high season), with eight clean and pleasant *cabinas* amid shady palms with hammocks slung beneath. Each has large private bath, hot water, cool tile floors, and fans. There's a small restaurant serving a muesli breakfast, plus *típico* and continental lunches and dinners. An oval swimming pool highlights the landscaped grounds. Rates include tax.

A dirt road from the bridge in Matapalo leads two km inland to **Centro del Mundo** (tel. 506/777-1383, www.matapalo.com), a backpackers' haven with basic rooms for $15.

El Castillo B&B (tel. 506/836-8059 or cellular 506/392-3460, www.elcastillo.net, $30 s/d low season, $65 s/d high season), in the hills two km inland, is a beautiful two-story modern house with a huge, becolumned atrium TV lounge with half-moon sofa with views through the arcing doorway. It has four bedrooms modestly furnished in rattan, with raised, beamed ceilings and private bathrooms with large walk-in showers. They open to a wrap-around veranda. There's a spring-fed plunge pool. The turnoff is 0.5 km north of Matapalo; you'll need a 4WD. Rates include breakfast.

Getting There

A bus departs San José daily for Dominical and Uvita at 3 P.M. via Quepos (departing Quepos at 7 P.M.) and passing Matapalo at 8:30 A.M. Another bus departs weekends at 5 A.M. (departing Quepos at 9:15 A.M.) and passes Matapalo at 10:45 A.M. The northbound bus departs Uvita at 4:30 A.M. and Dominical at 6 A.M., passing Matapalo at 6:30 A.M. On weekends, a second bus departs Uvita at 12:30 P.M. and Dominical at 1:15 P.M., passing Matapalo at 2:30 P.M.

DOMINICAL

Dominical, 45 km southeast of Quepos, is a tiny, laid-back "resort" favored by surfers, backpackers, and the college-age crowd. Dressing up means putting on a tank top and pair of sandals.

The four-km-long beach is beautiful albeit pebbly, and the warm waters attract whales and dolphins close to shore. Río Barú supposedly empties polluted waters into the sea near the beach north of the village. At dusk check out the riverbank, where egrets roost en masse.

The beach extends south five km from Dominical to **Dominicalito,** a little fishing village in the lee of Punta Dominical, at the southern end of the bay.

Swimming is dangerous because of riptides—there were 20 drownings in 2001! If trouble strikes, call **Dominical Lifeguards** (tel. 506/787-0210).

Ⓜ Barú National Wildlife Refuge

This national wildlife refuge, one km north of Dominical, was created from a 330-hectare private preserve at Hacienda Barú (tel. 506/787-0003, fax 506/787-0004, hacbaru@racsa.co.cr, www.haciendabaru.com). It protects three km of beach plus mangrove swamp and at least 40 hectares of primary rainforest: a safe haven for anteaters, ocelots, kinkajous, tayras, capuchin monkeys, and jaguarundis. More than 310 bird species have been recorded: roseate spoonbills, magnificent frigate birds, boat-billed herons, kingfishers, curassows, falcons, cormorants, anhingas, and owls, among others. Olive ridley and hawksbill turtles come ashore to nest at Playa Barú. Trails ($3 pp access fee) lead through pas-

ture, fruit orchards, cacao plantations, and forest. More than a dozen petroglyphs carved onto large rocks are the most obvious remains of what may be an ancient ceremonial site.

There's a canopy tour observation platform suspended 100 feet up ($35), and guided tree-climbing is offered ($40 low season, $45 high season) in either a bosun's chair with a winch or using rappelling equipment ($70). You can rent horses (from $15, two hours). A series of guided hikes (from $20) include "A Night in the Jungle" that ends at a fully equipped jungle tent camp ($50 low season, $60 high season). Kayak tours of the mangroves cost $35.

Local children have a "Save the Ridley Turtle" program; a nursery raises turtle hatchlings.

Entertainment

San Clemente Bar & Grill has a pool table, table football, darts, ping-pong and a large TV showing videos and sports events.

Thrusters is a stone-and-thatch bar with pool tables, and a disco on weekend. The happening scene, however, is **Roca Verde,** one km south of Dominical; live music is offered on Sunday afternoon, and the bar has a TV.

Sports and Recreation

Southern Expeditions (tel. 506/787-0100, fax 506/787-0203, expedicionessur@racsa.co.cr) offers all manner of active excursions.

Kayak Joe Tours (tel. 506/787-0121, fax 506/787-0049), in Plaza Pacífica, offers kayak trips.

San Clemente Surf Shack rents surfboards ($10–15 per day) and boogie boards ($5), plus snorkel gear.

Tree of Life Tours (tel. 506/787-0184, info@treeoflifetours.com, www.treeoflifetours.com) offers guided hikes to the Diamante Verde waterfall, a pre-Columbian site where you can opt to overnight on camp beds. It also has rappelling and horseback trips.

Also see Hacienda Barú; and *Escaleras,* below.

Accommodations

The **Selva Mar Reservation Service** (tel. 506/771-4582, fax 506/771-8841, selvamar@racsa

.co.cr, www.exploringcostarica.com), in San Isidro, acts as a hotel and tour reservation agency for properties.

Camping: *Theft is a major problem, and tents on the beach are routinely burglarized here!* Stick to **Camping Antorchas** (tel. 506/787-0307, $4 pp camping, $8 pp dorm), with two-story shade platforms for tents and hammocks. It also has a dorm room, and three private rooms with double beds and shared bathrooms, plus a communal kitchen, laundry, parking, and cold-water showers. You can rent tents ($1 pp).

An alternative is **Dominical Backpackers Hostel,** with a female dorm, three mixed dorms, and two private rooms, all with shared bathrooms, Rates: $10 pp. Toward the south end of Dominical, **Piranys** (tel. 506/787-0196, piranys @hotmail.com, $2 pp camping, $10 private room) is an offbeat backpackers' hostel run by a Spanish hippie-surfer. You can pitch your tent upstairs on a deck with A-frame roof (you can rent a tent for $0.50 pp daily). Plus there are two private rooms with shared bath. There's a communal kitchen, and board rentals and repair.

Under $25: The **Posada Del Sol** (Apdo. 9-8156, Dominical, tel./fax 506/787-0085, posadadelsol@racsa.co.cr, $15 s, $25 d low season; $20/30 high season) has five rooms with private bathrooms with hot water. They're pleasant, with plenty of light, fans, patios, plus laundry service. An apartment upstairs costs $200 d weekly.

Surfers gravitate to **Tortilla Flats** (tel. 506/787-0033, $20 s/d with fan, $25 s/d with a/c, $40 s/d suite low season; $25/35/50 high season), with 19 clean albeit modest beachside cabins and rooms—some in a two-story unit—with fans, hammocks on patios, and private baths with hot water. There's an upstairs suite with balcony. Nice! There's also a restaurant.

Hotel Río Lindo (tel. 506/787-0028, fax 506/787-0078, riolindo@baslink.com, $30 s/d with fan, $40 s/d with a/c low season; $40/50 high season), at the northern entrance to Dominical, has five standard rooms with fans, and five deluxe a/c rooms downstairs. All have large double shower-bathtubs with hot water. Upstairs

rooms catch the breeze. It has a swimming pool with wet bar plus a whirlpool.

DiuWak Hotel (tel. 506/787-0087, fax 506/787-0089, diuwak@racsa.co.cr, www.diuwak.com, $30 d room, $50 suite, $60 bungalow low season; $40/60/70 high season) has 18 simple but tasteful, spacious rooms, plus four suites, amid a landscaped garden 50 meters from the beach. Each has a double and single bed, ceiling fan, and charming porch plus private bath with hot water. Four a/c suites have TV, kitchenettes and dining area, plus living room, bathroom, and bedroom with bamboo furniture. There's a Jacuzzi, restaurant, and souvenir shop.

Cabinas San Clemente (tel. 506/787-0026, fax 506/787-0055, snclemte@racsa.co.cr, from $20 with fan, $30 with a/c low season, from $30/35 high season), owned by Mike, of San Clemente Bar & Grill, offers 16 large airy rooms in a two-story beachfront unit with a bamboo roof, natural stone, and thatched veranda. All have hardwood floors and shuttered windows and fans, and private bathrooms with cold water; some have a/c and hot water. It also rents five fully furnished houses (prices vary). Rates are based on room size and number of people.

$50–100: The **Villas Río Mar Jungle & Beach Resort** (tel. 506/787-0052, fax 506/787-0054, info@villasriomar.com, www.villasriomar .com, $50 s, $55 d low season; $70 s/d high season) is secluded beside the Río Barú, 800 meters northeast of Dominical. Ten thatch-roofed bungalows house 40 recently refurbished junior suites with comfortable king-size beds, louvered windows, bamboo furnishings, lanterns, lacy mosquito-net curtains, and French doors, plus hair dryers, telephones, and spacious and elegant verandas with bamboo-framed sofas and a hammock. The hotel boasts a conference room, plus tennis courts and an attractive pool with swim-up bar and Jacuzzi. It provides a beach shuttle, has tubes for floats down the Río Barú, and rents mountain bikes.

I also like the hip U.S.-owned **Hotel Roca Verde** (tel. 506/787-0036, fax 506/787-0013, info@rocaverde.net, www.hotelrocaverde.com, $55 s/d low season, $75 high season), a colorful place offering 10 a/c rooms in a two-story unit.

Ochers predominate (including the sponge-washed cement floor with pebble inlay around the edges), hardwoods abound, and wall murals, glass brick, and tile mosaics highlight the bathrooms. Things revolve around a chic, breeze-swept bar; there's also a pool and sun deck.

Two km south of Dominical is **Costa Paraíso Lodge** (Apdo. 578-8000, San Isidro, tel./fax 506/787-0025, costapar@racsa.co.cr, www.dominical.net/costaparaiso, $90 s/d guesthouse, $75–85 casitas), with a fabulous location over a rocky inlet. This beautiful, reclusive property offers two attractive, fully furnished, cross-ventilated guesthouses with lofty wooden ceilings, kitchens, ceiling fans, and bamboo furniture. It also has four two-bedroom *casitas* (two with kitchenettes; two with kitchens). They're set in lush lawns falling down to the shore. It's reached via a steep trail that leads to a beautiful rocky shore.

Hotel Las Casitas de Puertocito (tel. 506/393-4327, fax 506/743-8150, pascasitas @pocketmail.com, www.lascasitashotel.com, $39 s/d small unit, $45 s/d larger unit low season; $45/55 high season), six km south of Dominical, was used as a backdrop in the movie *A Corner of Paradise* and is run by a charming Italian. Six split-level cabins have a queen-size bed on an open loft, plus a single bed on the ground floor, with bamboo furniture and Guatemalan prints, a bathroom with hot water, and a wide patio complete with tiny kitchenette. A tiny *ranchito* restaurant serves Italian dishes. You can arrange hiking, horseback rides, snorkeling, fishing, etc. Rates include breakfast.

A stone's throw south, the U.S.-run **Coconut Grove** (tel./fax 506/787-0130, cocogrov@pocket mail.com, www.coconutgrovecostarica.com, $50–75 low season, $65–100 high season) sits in a cove and is a hidden charmer. It has two houses and four bungalows (with kitchenettes), all with a/c, cool tile floors, wooden ceilings with fans, orthopedic mattresses, simple but pleasant furnishings, and verandas with rockers. The owners have lots of Great Danes. There's a small pool and bar with hammocks.

Hacienda Barú (see above, $40 s/d low season, $60 s/d high season) has a three-bedroom house for rent 400 meters from the beach, with hot water, fans, and kitchen. There are also six two-bedroom cabins in a grassy clearing backed by forest: each has two doubles and one single bed, fans, hot water, refrigerator, and cooking facilities, plus patio. Camping is allowed.

Looking for apartment suites? Try the modern, beautifully furnished **Plaza Suites** (tel. 506/787-0012, fax 506/787-0049, www.caracolicostarica.com), on the highway one km south of Dominical.

Food

For breakfast I gravitate to **Roca Verde,** serving excellent, filling *gallo pinto,* plus granola, fruit, and yoghurt; and for lunch or dinner to **San Clemente Bar & Grill** (tel. 506/787-0026, 7 A.M.–10 P.M., $2–8), with a shaded open-air bar serving hearty breakfasts (including a filling "Starving Surfers Special"), plus burgers, Tex-Mex and Cajun (nachos, blackened chicken sandwiches), and a killer tuna melt. And imagine grilled mahi mahi with honey, rosemary, and orange sauce served with fresh vegetables! Open daily

I like **El Rincón** (tel. 506/787-0048, noon–10 P.M.), a pleasant open-air café with deck over the ocean; it serves pizzas, burgers, sandwiches, and Argentinian and Italian fare. Nearby, **Sunshine Natural Foods** (7 A.M.–6 P.M. Mon.–Sat., 7 A.M.–4 P.M. Sunday) is a simple shack selling cinnamon rolls, brownies, etc., for breakfast.

The restaurant at **Villas Jungle & Beach Resort** hosts a steak dinner special on Friday night ($10), and lobster dinner special on Saturday nights ($12).

Local expatriates gather at **Monkey House** (tel. 506/787-0121, 6–9 P.M. Fri.–Mon., $7), in Plaza Pacifica, serving such creative dishes as coconut tempura prawns with sweet chili sauce, and rum and Coke–marinated chicken with baby potatoes. It has a large wine selection and specialty drinks.

You can buy groceries next to Diuwak Hotel (7 A.M.–10 P.M.).

Information and Services

Southern Expeditions (tel. 506/787-0100, fax

Central Pacific

506/787-0203, expedicionessur@racsa.co.cr) offers tourist information.

The **Dominical Information Center** at San Clemente Bar & Grill serves as a post office.

Internet access is offered by **Internet del Río** (tel. 506/787-0156, internetdelrio@hotmail.com, 8:30 A.M.–10 P.M.), in Plaza del Río; **Café Internet** (tel. 506/787-0133, 7 A.M.–8 P.M.), next to Diuwak Hotel; and **Colibri Internet Café** (tel. 506/787-0191, 8:30 A.M.–8 P.M.), above San Clemente Bar & Grill.

The **police station** (tel. 506/787-0011) is at the southern end of the village.

Lavandería Las Olas (tel. 506/787-0105) is open daily 7 A.M.–9 P.M. **Clemente Bar & Grill** also has a laundry ($2 per kg); open 7 A.M.–9 P.M.

Ecole Travel (tel. 506/787-0145) is in Plaza del Río.

Adventure Education Center (tel./fax 506/787-0023, www.adventuresspanishschool.com) offers Spanish-language tuition.

Getting There

Buses (tel. 506/771-2550) depart San Isidro de El General for Dominical at 8 A.M. and 6 P.M. Southbound buses from Quepos depart at 7 A.M., 7:15 A.M., 2:45 P.M., and 3:30 P.M. Buses depart Dominical for Quepos and San José at 5:45 A.M. and 1:45 P.M.; for Quepos at 8:20 A.M. and 3 P.M.; for San Isidro at 6 A.M. and 2 P.M.; and for Dominical and Uvita at 11 A.M.

The gas station is about one km north of Dominical.

N ESCALERAS

If you overdose on the sun, sand, and surf, head into the lush mountains inland of Dominicalito, where a series of dirt roads lead steeply uphill to **Escaleras** (Staircases), a forest-clad region fantastic for horseback rides at Bella Vista Ranch Lodge or hikes from Finca Brian y Emilia.

Finca Brian y Emilia

Whenever I research Costa Rica, I delight in visiting this rustic, remote, 10-hectare, economically sustainable fruit farm (Apdo. 2-8000, San Isidro de El General, cellular tel. 506/396-6206) run by

Lynetta Cornelius tastes durian at Finca Brian y Emilia in Escaleras.

Missouri transplant Brian, with his charming and artistic daughter, Emilia. Brian has about 100 species of fruit trees in production (many of them unusual species such as the mangosteen, rambutan, and the deliciously sweet but foul-smelling durian, the most important commercial fruit in Southeast Asia), as well as nuts and spices and a collection of local orchids. He will share his enlightened perspective and textbook knowledge on a fascinating tour of the mountainside orchard.

Brian sees his *finca* as a key to conservation with his unique method of soil improvement through subsistence agriculture. His 25 years of devotion have resulted in a serendipitous spiritual simplicity that is palpable even to the casual visitor. He is endeavoring to establish university affiliation to expand the farm's volunteer program in such projects as reforestation of near-extinct native trees. Investors are also needed to amplify the land area of the farm so as to perpetually conserve this unique spot as a protected sanctuary.

Brian guides day visitors on hikes, including a ridgetop trail that leads to a Yosemite-like setting

A PROTECTED GREEENWAY: PASEO DE LA DANTA

The **Asociación de los Amigos de la Naturaleza del Pacifico Central y Sur** (ASANA, Apdo. 215-8000 San Isidro de Pérez Zéledon, tel./fax 506/787-0254) is a nonprofit organization working to create a network of ecological corridors connecting Corcovado National Park with La Amistad International Peace Park via the Pacific coastal mountain range. The project—named Paseo de la Danta (Tapir Trail)—aims to coordinate community involvement as a prerequisite in creating the 96-km-long pathway of protected forests.

The threat of deforestation has increased since completion of the Costera Sur highway and a subsequent influx of tourism and commercial development. Lands that are not currently held by conscientious owners are being sold and parceled off due to the high price of land and the poor agricultural market. The key is educating local stakeholders on the necessity and long-term benefits of conservation and restoration of natural ecosystems. ASANA urgently needs donations.

Central Pacific

and connects with the Santo Cristo waterfall. Rubber boots are provided. The wildlife viewing and birding is fantastic. Even ocelots are regularly sighted. Rare chestnut-mandibled toucans and king vultures are common. A three-day minimum is required for the Santo Cristo trek, including an unforgettable overnight with the Alpizar family.

A day visit includes lunch, farm and forest tour, and a soak in a streamside rock-walled pool heated by a wood-fired oven ($25 adults, $10 for children under 12). Children will enjoy interacting with, and learning from, Emilia.

Volunteers are sought to assist with harvesting fruit and other farm tasks. Volunteers work 50 hours in a two-week minimum and pay a $60 fee upon arrival.

A 4WD is recommended for the steep 2.5-km climb from the school in Dominicalito.

Entertainment

"Movies in the Jungle" are offered alfresco at **Toby & Kim's Escaleras Cinema,** in the garden of Marina Vista on Fridays.

Accommodations

For a totally reclusive, totally rustic escape, head to **N Finca Brian y Emilia** (see above, $30 pp Birdhouse, $60 pp Ocelot House), where guests can find harmony with nature. Reports one reader: "We loved it so much! Their guest cabin was so incredibly ULTIMATE!" Your home away from home is a cozy albeit spartan cabin—"Ocelot House"—with private bath and a solar-heated shower. It sleeps three; a folding cot on the balcony could accommodate a fourth person. Farther up the mountain is a more basic hut—the "Birdhouse"—without plumbing. At night, after superb Costa Rican–style all-natural meals, you can soak by starlight in the rock-walled hot tub. Advance reservations are requested; a two-night minimum stay is required. Rates include meals, snacks, hot tub, and tour (children under 15 pay $15).

The **Bella Vista Ranch Lodge** (Apdo. 459-8000, San Isidro, tel. 506/388-0155; in North America, tel.800/909-4469, www.bellavistalodge .com, $35 s, $45 d room, $55 s, $65 d cabin low season; $45/55 room, $65/75 cabin high season) is a rustic Colorado-style ranch perched loftily on a plateau with sweeping coastal vistas as far as Nicoya, Osa, and Cerro de la Muerte. The converted farmhouse has four simple but comfortable and quaint rooms with shared bath and solar-heated water. There are also spacious two-bedroom cabins with all-around screened windows, tiled bathrooms, and verandas. The lodge has a restaurant and specializes in horseback tours (typically $35–40, two hours). One reader has raved about this tranquil, environmentally conscious getaway; another tells of the hosting Dyers' "warmth and hospitality."

Another marvelous option is **Villa Escaleras** (doug@villasescaleras.com, www.villas-escaleras .com; in North America, tel. 773/883-1047;

from $240), perched dramatically at 400 meters elevation, one km south of Bella Vista, with staggering views as far south as Osa. It offers four deluxe, vaulted-ceiling bedrooms boasting an exquisite aesthetic. Decor highlights include purpleheart floors and colorful Guatemalan fabrics, Peruvian wall hangings, and lots of sunlight. The 4,000-square-foot villa has a bar and library, and swimming pool and terrace. Tiled bathrooms feature pressurized hot water.

Equally exquisite is **The Necochea Inn** (c/o Selva Mar, tel. 506/771-4582, fax 506/771-8841, selvamar@racsa.co.cr, www.exploringcostarica .com, $65–100 low season, $75–125 high season), a luxuriously appointed hideaway with four rooms with individual and eclectic decor, including hardwood floors and private balconies. Two rooms (one with king-size bed) share a bathroom with Jacuzzi tub and double sinks. A master suite also has a king-size bed, Jacuzzi, glass shower, and wraparound deck with ocean views. The inn has a game room, library, and full bar, plus a pool with sun deck that stairsteps to natural springs. Rates include gourmet breakfast.

Pacific Edge (Apdo. 531-8000, San Isidro de El General, tel. 506/771-8841 or 381-4369, fax 506/771-4582, pacificedge@pocketmail.com, $50 s/d standard, $75 s/d bungalow), reached via its own steep dirt road half a kilometer south of the turnoff for Bella Vista, has four cabins stairstepping down the lower mountain slopes, with grand vistas northward. Walkways lead to the rustic yet comfortable cabins, which have all-around screened windows, fans, small refrigerators, and hammocks on their verandas. One is a two-bedroom bungalow with living room and kitchen. Each cabin has a "half-kitchenette." And there's an exquisite freeform pool and deck

with views. It's run by an amiable Californian, Susie, and her affable Limey husband, George Atkinson. Susie whips up mean cuisine spanning the globe in her bamboo restaurant. These former mariners arrange hikes, horseback trips, fishing, sailing, and more.

DOMINICAL TO SAN ISIDRO

A paved road leads east from Dominical to San Isidro, winding up through the valley of the Río Barú into the Fila Costanera mountains, where the climate cools and you may find yourself suddenly high amid swirling clouds.

Parque Reptilandia (tel. 506/308-8855, 5vistas @racsa.co.cr, 9 A.M.–5 P.M.), near Platanillo, about 10 km east of Dominical, is a reptile park with turtles, crocodiles, snakes, lizards, etc., from throughout Latin America. A self-guided tour costs $10.

Nauyaca Waterfalls

Near Platanillo, signs point the way east to these magnificent waterfalls, tumbling 70 meters in two cascades that plunge into deep pools good for swimming. They're surrounded by tropical moist forest full of wildlife accessed by trails. The falls, which are six km east of the road, also go by other names: Don Lulo's and Santo Cristo. You can reach them on horseback from Escaleras or from **Don Lulo's** (tel. 506/787-0198, fax 506/771-2003, ciprotur@racsa.co.cr, www .ecotourism.co.cr/nauyacawaterfalls), at Platanillo, where a trail leads via the hamlet of Libano. The guided horseback tour leaves at 8 A.M., returning at 3 P.M. ($35, reservations essential). Don Lulo also has a **mini-zoo** with macaws, toucans, and *tepezcuintles*. Tour companies in Dominical offer trips to the falls.

The Brunca Coast

This until-recently-undiscovered coast extends south from Dominical. The recently laid Costera Sur highway slices south along the forested coast past long beaches with pummeling surf and estuaries full of wildlife. The pencil-thin coastal plain is backed by steep mountains perfect for hiking and horseback trips. Only recently made accessible, tourist development is booming.

UVITA

South of Dominicalito, seemingly endless **Playa Hermosa** extends south to the headland of **Punta Uvita,** a tombolo (a narrow sandbar connecting an island to the mainland), jutting out west of the tiny hamlet of Uvita, 16 km south of Dominical. The Río Uvita, immediately south of the village, pours into the sea south of Punta Uvita at **Bahía,** the northern boundary of Ballena Marine National Park. Bahía, one km east of the Costanera Sur and one km south of Uvita, is a popular and lively holiday spot for Ticos, who flock to the river estuary and camp along the beach, turning it into a veritable squatter's camp–cum–garbage dump.

Tourism is booming along this coast.

Crocodiles abound in the lagoons and mangroves around Bahía. A great place to see them is **Rancho Merced National Wildlife Refuge** (cellular tel. 506/823-5858, or c/o Selva Mar), a 1,250-hectare biological reserve on a cattle ranch that includes mangrove wetlands. You can play "cowboy for a day" and learn to drive cattle and rope calves ($60 for three hours; 7 A.M.–2 P.M.). Rancho Merced also rents horses ($35 for three hours), offers hiking in the mountains, and arranges a boating tour to Ballena Marine National Park ($5–55 pp). Entry costs $10 for day visitors (free to guests in their *cabina*).

Backing the narrow coastal strip are the steep, lushly forested **Fila Tinomastes** mountains.

Oro Verde Biological Reserve

This rustic *finca* (tel./fax 506/743-8072 or 771-4582, www.costarica-birding-oroverde.com) in the valley of the Río Uvita, a little north and three km inland of Uvita, is owned by the gracious Duartes family. The property is fabulous for birding and boasts 300 hectares of primary forest with trails. You can even participate in the farming. A five-hour jungle tour costs $35 including lunch. Horseback rides cost $5 pp per hour, by reservation. 4WD is recommended.

Sports and Recreation

Skyline (tel. 506/743-8037, skyline@racsa.co.cr, www.flyultralight.com) offers flights by Ultralight planes.

Delfin Tour (tel. 506/743-8013) offers kayak, boat, and snorkel trips.

Accommodations

In Uvita, you can camp at **Toucan Hotel** for $2.50 pp (see below). You can also camp ($10 per tent) at **Oro Verde** ($12 pp), which has two basic yet comfortable two-bedroom bungalows; cabins were being added at last visit.

First choice for backpackers should be the clean, well-run **Toucan Hotel** (tel. 506/743-8140, tucanhotel@yahoo.com, www.tucanhotel.com; in the U.S., P.O. Box 783, Three Rivers, CA 93271; $7 pp dorm room, $8 s, $12 d "backpacker" room, $25 with a/c), operated by a friendly Yankee named Steven. Three rooms (each different) share a bathroom. A fourth room has a/c, kitchen, and private bathroom. Plus there's a wooden cabin. Guests have free Internet access; laundry; a Sony Playstation and TV/VCR and DVD player; and a gravel-lined outdoor communal kitchen and bar with hammocks and swing seats under shade. Steven offers a work-exchange program.

Cabina El Kurukuzungo ($20 s, $35 d, or $60 pp) at Rancho La Merced has two units (one for six people; one for 10) in the foothills on the road to Oro Verde. Each has a kitchen and a private bathroom with cold water only, and no electricity. Meals are cooked in a small *ranchito* restaurant. Rates include a tour and all meals.

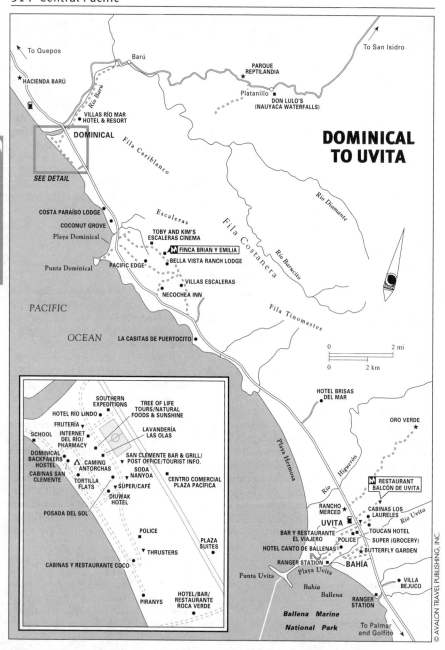

To Quepos

★ HACIENDA BARÚ

Barú

PARQUE
REPTILANDIA

To San Isidro

Río Barú

VILLAS RÍO MAR
HOTEL & RESORT

DOMINICAL

Platanillo

DON LULO'S
(NAUYACA WATERFALLS)

Fila Cariblanco

DOMINICAL
TO UVITA

SEE DETAIL

COSTA PARAÍSO LODGE

COCONUT GROVE

Playa Dominical

Punta Dominical

PACIFIC EDGE

Escaleras

TOBY AND KIM'S
ESCALERAS CINEMA

M FINCA BRIAN Y EMILIA

BELLA VISTA RANCH LODGE

VILLAS ESCALERAS

NECOCHEA INN

Fila Costanera

Río Diamante

Río Barucito

Fila Tinomastes

PACIFIC

OCEAN

LA CASITAS DE PUERTOCITO

0   2 mi
0   2 km

HOTEL BRISAS
DEL MAR

ORO VERDE ★

SOUTHERN
EXPEDITIONS

TREE OF LIFE
TOURS/NATURAL
FOODS & SUNSHINE

HOTEL RÍO LINDO

FRUTERÍA

SCHOOL

INTERNET
DEL RÍO/
PHARMACY

LAVANDERÍA
LAS OLAS

DOMINICAL
BACKPAKERS
HOSTEL

CAMING
ANTORCHAS

SAN CLEMENTE BAR & GRILL/
POST OFFICE/TOURIST INFO.

CABINAS SAN
CLEMENTE

TORTILLA
FLATS

SODA
NANYOA

SUPER/CAFÉ

CENTRO COMERCIAL
PLAZA PACÍFICA

DIUWAK
HOTEL

POSADA DEL SOL

POLICE

PLAZA
SUITES

THRUSTERS

CABINAS Y RESTAURANTE COCO

PIRANYS

HOTEL/BAR/
RESTAURANTE
ROCA VERDE

Playa Hermosa

Río Higuerón

Río Uvita

M RESTAURANT
BALCÓN DE UVITA

RANCHO
MERCED ★

CABINAS LOS
LAURELES

UVITA

BAR Y RESTAURANTE
EL VIAJERO

HOTEL CANTO DE BALLENAS

POLICE

TOUCAN HOTEL

SUPER (GROCERY)

★ BUTTERFLY GARDEN

RANGER STATION

Punta Uvita

Playa Uvita

BAHÍA

VILLA
BEJUCO ●

Bahía

Ballena

RANGER
STATION

Ballena Marine

National Park

To Palmar
and Golfito

© AVALON TRAVEL PUBLISHING, INC.

I like the rustic **Cabinas Los Laureles** (tel. 506/743-8008 or 506/743-8235, $15 s, $17.50 d), in Uvita, set amid a grove of laurel trees. Four rooms have private bath and cold water. There are also four twin-story, pitched-roofed *cabinas* with timbered beams and private baths, plus parking and porch. Congenial owner Victor Pérez offers horseback trips ($4 per hour), plus boat rides to Ballena Marine National Park. His wife serves tasty breakfasts.

There are several modest budget options in Bahía

The **Hotel Canto de Ballenas** (tel. 506/743-8083, cantodeballenas@racsa.co.cr, www.agroecoturismo.com, $30 s, $35 d low season; $35 s, $40 d high season), run by the rural cooperative Coopeuvita, at Bahía, has 12 spacious albeit rustic, cross-ventilated rooms in wooden huts, each with a double and single bed, screened windows, fans, tile floors, and private bathroom. Four are handicapped-equipped. A pool (also with handicapped access) was to be added. Rates include breakfast.

My favorite place hereabouts is **Balcón de Uvita** (Apdo. 964-8000 San Isidro, tel./fax 506/743-8034, info@balcondeuvita.com, www.balcondeuvita.com, $51 s/d low season; $61 high season), in the hills one km inland of Uvita. This charming old wooden home is run by a Dutch-Indonesian couple, Bart and Gabriela, and has three well-ventilated stone-walled cabins with screened windows, orthopedic mattresses, huge walk-in showers with solar-heated water, plus tiny balconies with vast views. There's an outdoor kitchenette, plus a marvelous restaurant (see below), and a guitar-shaped pool inset in the stone sundeck in grounds full of birdsong. A 4WD is required. Rates include tax.

Two km south of Uvita is **Villas Bejuco** (Apdo. 101-8000 San Isidro, tel./fax 506/771-0965, $35 s/d), with 10 clean, handsome, modern hillside cabins with double and single beds, private baths with cold water (hot water was to be added), and views of both mountain and beach. There's a restaurant, a swimming pool and sun deck, plus horseback riding and boat excursions.

Whales & Dolphins Ecolodge (tel./fax 506/770-3557, ecolodge@whalesanddolphins.net, www.whalesanddolphins.net, $85 s, $108 d standard, $117 s, $140 d suite low season; $117/140 standard, $147/170 suite high season), on a bluff overlooking Playa Hermosa, has five suites and 14 standard rooms (two handicap-equipped), all with a/c, TV, telephone, security box, hairdryer, minibar, pool, gym, and restaurant and bar.

Food

At Uvita, try the breezy modern **Bar y Restaurante El Viajero,** serving a *casado* of mixed seafood, chicken and rice, and salad ($2.50).

The best place for miles is 〽 **Restaurant Balcón de Uvita** (see above, 11 A.M.–9 P.M. Thur.–Sun.), serving gourmet Indonesian and Thai food that lures locals from far and wide. Dishes range from Thai curry ($6) to an Indonesian rijsttaffel (rice table; $9), and there's even profiteroles.

There are several lively *típico* restaurants in Bahía.

Information and Services

Toucan Hotel has Internet service 10 A.M.–8 P.M. Mon.–Sat.

There's a **police station** on the highway in Uvita; it has no telephone (call the grocery next door, tel. 506/743-8043).

Getting There

Buses for Uvita and Bahía depart San José from Avenida 3, Calle 18, Mon.–Fri. at 1:30 P.M. and 4 P.M. ($1.50); return buses depart at 5 A.M. and 1 P.M. Buses depart San Isidro from Calle 1, Avenidas 4/6, at 9 A.M. and 4 P.M.; return buses depart Bahía at 6 A.M. and 2 P.M. Buses also serve Uvita from Quepos ($3.50).

There's a gas station at Uvita.

WHALE MARINE NATIONAL PARK

Completion of the Costanera Sur Highway has opened up one of Costa Rica's most inaccessible regions: the lush, once untrammeled section of coastline south of Uvita. Its miles-long beaches have for eons been favored by female marine

THE GREAT WHALE PARADE

August through March, you can count on humpbacks playing up and down the Pacific coast of the Americas. Increasingly, they're showing up off the coast of Costa Rica.

Remarkably little is known about the ecology of whales. Until recently, for example, scientists believed that North Pacific humpbacks limited their breeding to the waters off Japan, Hawaii, and Mexico's Sea of Cortez. New findings, however, suggest that whales may get amorous off the coast of Costa Rica, too.

Individual whales are identified by the white markings on the underside of their flukes. These "fingerprints" have revealed that whales seen Dec.–March migrate from Californian waters, while those seen July–Oct. come from Antarctica. Thus two distinct populations of humpbacks exist here.

To learn more about humpback habits and activities, the Oceanic Society has an ongoing study to identify individual creatures and trace their migrations. The society needs volunteers on weeklong midwinter trips offered through Elderhostel. It's a marvelous opportunity for eyeball-to-eyeball encounters with the gentle giants of the deep.

For more information, contact **Cascadia Research Collective** (218 1/2 W. 4th Ave., Olympia, WA 98501, tel. 360/943-7325, www.cascadiaresearch.org).

turtles for nesting and are now finding favor with surfers.

Playa Tortuga, near the hamlet of **Tortuga Abajo,** sweeps south to the mouth of the Río Terraba and the vast wildlife-rich mangrove swamps of the Delta del Terraba, Costa Rica's largest such habitat (see *Terraba-Sierpe International Humid Forest Reserve,* in the *Sierpe* section, in the *Golfo Dulce and Peninsula de Osa* chapter); the estuary of the Río Terraba is awesome for fishing for snapper, catfish, and snook. One km south of Tortuga Abajo, a road leads inland two km to the community of **Ojochal.** French-Canadians dominate the expat scene hereabouts.

The Costanera Sur swings south to Palmar Norte, gateway to the Golfo Dulce and Osa region.

The **Parque Nacional Ballena Marina** was created in February 1990 to protect the shoreline of Bahía de Coronado plus 4,500 hectares of water surrounding Isla Ballena. The park extends south for 15 km from Uvita to Punta Piñuela, and about 15 km out to sea.

The park harbors within its relatively small area important mangroves and the largest coral reef on the Pacific coast of Central America. Green marine iguanas live on algae in the salt-water pools. They litter the golden-sand beaches like prehistoric jetsam, their bodies angled at 90 degrees to catch the sun's rays most directly. Once they reach 37°C, they pop down to the sea for a bite to eat. Olive ridley and hawksbill turtles come ashore May–Nov. to lay their eggs (September and October are the best months to visit). Common and bottle-nosed dolphins frolic offshore. And the bay is the southernmost mating site for the humpback whale, which migrates from Alaska, Baja California, and Hawaii (Dec.–April).

Snorkeling is good close to shore during low tides. There are caves worth exploring. Isla Ballena and the rocks known as Las Tres Hermanas (The Three Sisters) are havens for frigate birds and boobies as well as pelicans and even ibises.

Sedimentation resulting from construction of the coastal highway has killed off much of the coral reef.

Sports and Recreation

El Cocodrilo Technical Scubadive & Fishing Center (albacor@mac.com, www.crocodive.com) also offers dive trips locally and to Isla Caño, plus snorkeling, and fishing. **Mystic Dive Center** (fax 506/788-8351, mysticdive@yahoo.com, www.mysticdivecenter.com) at the Centro Comercial plaza at Ojochal; and **Crocodile Center** (tel. 506/393-7963), on the road to El Perozoso, offer snorkeling and scuba trips.

Villas Gaia also offers excursions and activities from sea-kayaking to sportfishing, and diving. And **Flying Dutchman River Tours,** at Hotel Posada del Tortuga, offers mangrove kayak tours ($25), river fishing (from $75 half-day), night tours in search of crocodiles, plus river transfers by air-boat from Palmar Sur airport ($25 pp).

Accommodations

Also see *Uvita,* above.

You can **camp** on the beach; the ranger stations have water. You can camp at **Rancho Soluna,** at Ojochal (see below); it has showers and bathrooms.

At **Playa Ballena,** budget-hounds might try the **Pensión Roca Paraíso** (tel. 506/383-5213 or 507/674-8180, $20 s/d), an offbeat *albergue* in an old wooden home nestled right up to Playa Ballena in the heart of the national park. It has three basic rooms with shared bathroom, semi-open to public view (there are screen windows, not walls) and shared kitchen. Meals are made by request.

I like the German-run **Finca Bavaria** (no tel., info@finca-bavaria.com, www.finca-bavaria.de, $35 s, $42 d small, $42/49 large low season; $45/52 small, $52/59 large high season), about five km south of Uvita and one km inland of Playa Ballena, not least for its tremendous hillside setting. It offers five bungalows with a beautiful aesthetic that includes louvered glass windows, raised wooden ceilings, bamboo and rattan furnishings, halogen lamps, mosquito nets over the beds, and hot water in clinically clean bathrooms with glass-brick showers. Trails that lead through the forested 15-hectare property prove splendid for birding and spotting wildlife. Filling and delicious meals are served, washed down with chilled German beer served in steins (dinners are offered for nonguests by reservation). There's a swimming pool in the landscaped garden with hammock gazebo.

At **Playa Tortuga,** I adore the 🅼 **Lookout at Turtle Beach** (cellular tel. 506/378-7473, info@hotelcostarica.com, www.hotelcostarica.com), two km south of Piñuela and inland of Playa Tortuga. New owners Carol and Steve Lipworth have imbued this hilltop hotel with a bold and beautiful contemporary aesthetic with harmonic and lively pastels. Paths weave through lush landscaped gardens to bungalows with delightfully bright color schemes (such as fresh lime, or turquoise and mint, with crisp white linens), cool tile floors, raised wooden ceilings with fans, huge louvered glass windows, and terraces with hammocks. A mirador offers fantastic views over both beach and jungle. Gourmet meals are prepared by a professional chef. At last visit, the hotel wasn't yet open to guests, and the owners were considering opening for groups only. Call for rates.

The delightful Dutch-owned **Villas Gaia** (Apdo. 809, San José, tel. 506/363-3928, fax 506/256-9996, info@villasgaia.com, www.villasgaia.com, $60 s/d room, $11 s/d casita), 200 meters south of Paraíso, is another good option. The 12 colorful wooden *cabinas* dot the forested hillside: they feature muted pastel decor and minimalist furnishings, a double and single bed with orthopedic mattresses, and solar hot water. One cabin is equipped for handicapped guests. A sun deck and open-sided thatched bar overhanging the pool boast views down over the forest and mangroves. The restaurant is recommended, and boat tours, snorkeling and fishing, hiking, bird-watching, horseback riding, diving, and excursions are offered.

The French-Canadian **Villa del Bosque** (tel. 506/383-2112, fax 506/786-6358, villaselbosque @yahoo.com, www.villaselbosque.com; international fax 801/218-7936, $30 d cabins, $45 d in the room), immediately south of Villas Gaia, enjoys a breeze-swept clifftop locale. It has two spacious, modestly furnished cabins with tile floors, fans, full kitchen, and hot water. There're also three rooms in the main lodge, plus a pool, a raised wooden deck with hammocks, and lots of orchids. It also rents houses.

"Gringo Mike" and his wife, Karen, are great hosts at **Hotel Playa Tortuga** (tel. 506/384-5489, fax 506/294-3747, ptortuga@racsa.co.cr, www.hotel-posada.com, $65 s/d standard, $75–95 new rooms), a two-story hacienda-style building that sits atop a breeze-swept point about

200 meters south of Villas Gaia. It features a long shady terrace with antique rockers, and offers 10 spacious and cool a/c rooms with timber ceilings, fans, antique reproduction furniture, and large bathrooms with hot water. Alas, rooms were much in need of repair at last visit, when a new wing with more upscale, modern, handicapped-equipped units with central a/c and king-size beds was being added (along with a honeymoon suite). There's a TV lounge with VCR. Gringo Mike (real name Armando) cooks up a storm at Armando's Kitchen. Backpackers are catered to nearby at Turtle Cottage, with six rooms. Rates include breakfast.

At **Ojochal,** several options for budget travelers include **Rancho Soluna** (tel./fax 506/788-8210, solunacr@yahoo.com, $20 s, $25 d low season; $25/30 high season), which has two simple rooms and two cabins with private bathrooms. It has a restaurant and bar with pool table, plus a small pool in the garden.

The English-run, vine-entwined **Hotel El Perezoso** (tel./fax 506/786-6358, elpoerosozocr @yahoo.com, www.elperozoso.net, $30 s, $38 d standard, $35 s, $45 d tower low season; $35 s, $45 d standard, $42 s, $52 d tower high season), in the hills above Ojochal, offers seven modestly furnished yet pleasing rooms, each individually styled, but all with hardwood ceilings with fans, batik wall hangings, balconies accessed by French doors, and large walk-in showers (four share bathrooms with hot water). One room is a penthouse atop a tower, with a deck. It has a pool inset in lawns and offers magnificent views. The owner is a professional chef.

Sitting in beautiful gardens, the French-Canadian **Hacienda de los Sueños** (tel. 506/678-9720, hacienda_suenos@hotmail.com, $40 s/d) has two rooms in a two-story house, with bamboo and plastic furnishings, ceiling fans, a simple kitchen. There's a pool, and trails lead into the forest.

A recommended eco-lodge, although not reviewed, is **La Cusinga Lodge** (tel./fax 506/771-2465, lacusinga@yahoo.com, www.lacusingalodge .com), at Finca Tres Hermanas, a farm involved in reforestation and sustainable agriculture. There are trails extending into the hills

Food

I highly recommend the **Villas Gaia's** (7 A.M.–9 P.M., $6) elegant roadside restaurant, which serves excellent and filling breakfasts, plus creative sandwiches, excellent *casados* (set meals), and international fare such as superb Thai curry and macadamia-crusted fish fillet.

The other surefire winner is the open-air Ⅿ **Exótica Café** (tel. 506/369-9261, resto_exotica @hotmail.com, 11 A.M.–9 P.M. Mon.–Sat., $2.25–9), a hole-in-the-wall with world-class cuisine, at Ojochal. You dine by candlelight at tables hewn of diced treetrunks. I enjoyed a green salad with raspberry vinaigrette, Tahitian fish carpaccio, fish filet with banana curry sauce, and shrimps with Ricard and garlic sauce. It boasts an extensive international wine list.

Gringo Mike competes with gourmet pizzas and Italian fare at **Armando's Kitchen,** which has its own bakery. In Ojochal, **Dos Gringos Pizzería** also makes superb pizzas (Thur.–Sun. only).

Bar Restaurante Boca Coronado, at Posada Playa Tortuga, sits over the river estuary and offers unpretentious seafoods and local fare. Nearby, the ***Manglar Sur*** floating restaurant offers a romantic ambience and serves *bocas*. It has a mangrove tour on Sundays at 10 A.M.($20).

Panadería Francesca and, nearby, **Dulce Lucy,** behind Exótica Café, in Ojochal, sell baked goods.

Information and Services

The ranger station (tel./fax 506/743-8236) is in Uvita; the park headquarters (tel. 506/786-7161) is at Bahía, three km south of Uvita. There are other ranger stations at La Colonia and Playa Ballena, at the southern end of the park. Entrance costs $1 at Uvita, and $6 at Playa Ballena.

The **Ojochal Internet Café** (tel. info@ojochal-internet-cafe.com, 8 A.M.–noon and 2–5 P.M. Mon.–Fri.; 8 A.M.–1 P.M. Saturday) is a *real* Internet café serving cappuccinos, espressos, etc. It charges $1 for 10 minutes, and $0.60 per 10 minutes thereafter.

Vicky's Laundry is behind Exótica Café, in Ojochal.

There's a gas station at the Centro Comercial plaza at Ojochal.

Getting There

You can hire a **boat** and guide at any of the fishing hamlets between Palmar and the park, or in Dominical or Uvita, to take you to the reef or Isla Ballena (about $30 per hour, $45 two hours).

The *Manglar Sur* (tel. 506/788-8351, manglarsur@hotmail.com, www.manglarsur.com), a twin-tier riverboat, offers tours of the mangroves for $10 per person; or $55 adult, $35 child with dinner.

Golfo Dulce and Peninsula de Osa

Costa Rica's southwesternmost region is a distinct oblong landmass, framed on its east by the Fila Costeña mountain chain and indented in the center by a vast gulf called Golfo Dulce. Curling around the gulf to the north is the mountainous, hook-shaped Peninsula de Osa and, to the south, the pendulous Peninsula de Burica. North and south of the gulf are two broad fertile plains smothered by banana plantations—the Valle de Diquis, to the northwest, separating the region from the central Pacific by a large mangrove ecosystem fed by the Río Grande de Terraba, and the Valle de Coto Colorado, extending south to the border with Panamá.

Nature lovers with a taste for the remote and rugged will find themselves in their element. A seamless expanse of rainforest enfolds the few towns and scattered settlements, many of them small beach com-

munities beloved of diehard surfers. Star billing goes to the Osa Peninsula, smothered in a vast wilderness of thick jungle filled with the stentorian roar of howler monkeys, the screeches of scarlet macaws, and the constant dripping of water. Much of the jungle—a repository for some of the nation's greatest wildlife treasures—is protected within a series of contiguous parks and reserves served by remote jungle lodges.

The region is the largest gold source in the country, as it has been since pre-Columbian times. In the early 1980s, gold

Must-Sees

M Terraba–Sierpe Reserve: This vast mangrove ecosystem teeming with wildlife can be explored by boat from Sierpe and Ojochal (page 527).

M Drake Bay: A dramatic setting close to Corcovado and Caño Island add to the appeal of this hidden corner, where nature lodges specialize in sportfishing and diving. It's now accessible by an improved road, but you'll still need to ford a river (page 531).

M Corcovado National Park: Jaguars, tapirs, crocodiles, colorful snakes, and monkeys and scarlet macaws galore are among the easily seen wildlife in this rugged rainforest reserve. Numerous lodges and tent-camps nearby grant access (page 544).

M Playa Zancudo: A magnificent beach and dramatic setting combine with low-key accommodations to provide a lazy, laid-back retreat where all you need is a hammock and swimwear (page 555).

© CHRISTOPHER P. BAKER

Pavones

M Pavones: This surfers' paradise has it all: great waves, stupendous palm-shaded beaches, and plenty of budget options for eats and places to rest your head. Tiskita Lodge is a rustic delight for nature lovers (page 558).

M Coco Island National Park: This remote isle is off-limits to all but experienced scuba divers come to commune with pelagics, including whale sharks, rays, and hammerhead sharks (page 565).

M Golfo Dulce

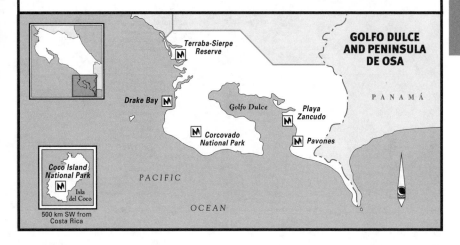

GOLFO DULCE
AND PENINSULA
DE OSA

Terraba-Sierpe
Reserve **M**

Drake Bay **M**

Golfo Dulce

Playa
Zancudo **M**

PANAMÁ

M Corcovado
National Park

M Pavones

Coco Island
National Park
M Isla
del Coco

PACIFIC

OCEAN

500 km SW from
Costa Rica

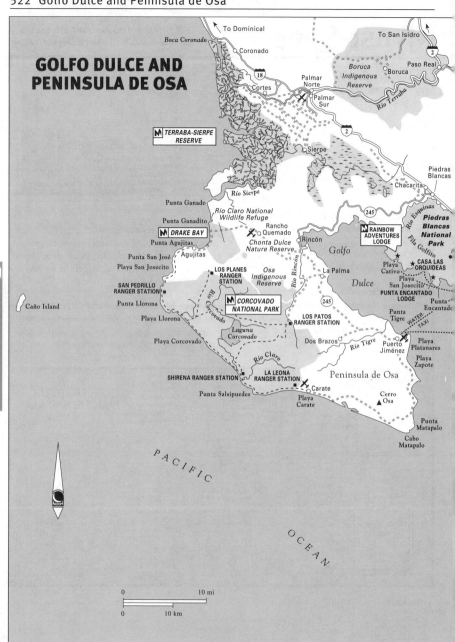

GOLFO DULCE AND PENINSULA DE OSA

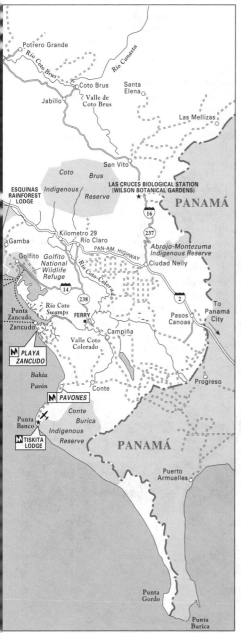

fever destroyed thousands of hectares of the Osa forests: the physical devastation was a deciding factor in the creation of Corcovado National Park. Rivers such as the Tigre and Claro still produce sizeable nuggets, and ex-gold miners have turned to eco-tourism and today lead visitors on gold-mining forays.

The waters of the Golfo Dulce are rich in game fish, and the area is popular with sportfishers. Whales occasionally call in, and three species of dolphin—bottle-nosed, black spotted, and spinner—frolic in the gulf, which after sunset is charged by luminescent microbes. Though the gulf is protected and relatively calm, surfers flock for the ripping waves that wash the southeast tip of the Osa Peninsula and push nose-first onto the beaches of the Peninsula de Burica, where indigenous communities exist in isolation within the mountains of the extreme south of Costa Rica. Far, far out in the briny, some 300 km offshore to the southwest, is Cocos Island, a craggy, relatively desolate isle jutting up from the sea.

This is one of Costa Rica's wettest regions. Trade winds from the southeast discharge their rains on the Fila Costeña mountains year-round; be prepared for rain and a lingering wet season: the area receives 4–8 meters of rain annually! Violent thunderstorms move in Oct.–Dec.

PLANNING YOUR TIME

Many visitors fly in to Corcovado—the main draw—and/or Drake Bay, and fly out after a brief two-day stay. You'll short-change yourself with such a strict regimen, however, if you really want to savor the Osa. Allow at least a couple of extra days to chill.

Scheduled air service is offered to Palmar, Ciudad Neily, and Puerto Jiménez, and Jeep-taxis and local tour operators offer connecting service to almost anywhere you may then wish to journey. If you're driving yourself, a 4WD is virtually mandatory to negotiate the at-times-appalling dirt roads of the Osa and Burica peninsulas. In wet season, the road to Corcovado can prove impassable to all but the larger 4WDs.

Golfo Dulce

Even in dry season (Nov.–May) it's wise to plan on some rain.

Accommodations tend to cater to nature lovers: take your pick from safari-style tent-camps to unpretentious yet truly deluxe eco-lodges. Dozens of nature lodges limn the western shores of the Osa Peninsula and the contiguous Piedras Blancas, while beach resorts that primarily draw surfers and the student crowd tend toward the budget spectrum.

Hwy. 2 (the Pan-American Highway) cuts a more or less ruler-straight line along the base of the Fila Costeña mountains, connecting the towns of Palmar (to the north) with Ciudad Neily and Paso Canoas (to the south), on the border with Panamá. The towns offer no interest to travelers, other than as way-stops in time of need.

Sierpe, a port hamlet in the midst of banana plantations, is starting point for boat forays into the **Terraba-Sierpe International Humid Forest Reserve.** These trips from Sierpe provide intriguing options for wildlife viewing. Boats from Sierpe have traditionally been the normal means of accessing **Drake Bay,** the only community on the western side of the Osa peninsula. Drake Bay has some splendid accommodations for every budget and particularly caters to sportfishers and divers. If you're planning on visiting **Caño Island,** you'll typically do so from here. A coast trail grants access to **Corcovado National Park,** which offers some of the finest wildlife viewing in Costa Rica. Tapirs are relatively easily seen, and jaguar sightings are as likely here as anywhere else in the country. As a minimum, two days are required to adequately explore Corcovado; add two days if you plan on hiking the coast trail from one end to the other.

The main gateway to Corcovado is **Puerto Jiménez,** until recently catering exclusively to the surfing and backpacking crowd, but broadening its appeal with the addition of a sportfishing lodge and aesthetically delightful accommodations at nearby **Playa Platanares.** This beach has an enviable setting adjacent to a mangrove ecosystem harboring crocodiles and all manner of wildlife. Centrally located Puerto Jiménez makes an ideal base for exploring the region; water-taxis connect with the laid-back surfers's beach communities of **Zancudo** and especially **Pavones,** and the otherwise hard-to-reach beaches of Golfo Dulce.

pre-Columbian *bolo,* Sierpe

© CHRISTOPHER P. BAKER

Though it is pulling itself up by its bootstraps, **Golfito,** the only town of any size, can be given a wide berth; this unsavory port town holds little attraction except as a gateway to the little-visited **Golfito National Wildlife Refuge** (there are better places to spot wildlife) and as a base for sportfishing forays and journeys by dive-boat to **Cocos Island,** famous as a world-class dive site.

A good resource is *The Southern Costa Rica Guide,* by Alex del Sol. Also visit the following website: www.costaricasur.com.

HISTORY

The indigenous peoples, as distinct from their northerly neighbors, had historical links with South America, and the region was already a center of gold production when Europeans arrived in the early 1500s. Pre-Columbian goldsmiths pounded out decorative ornaments and used a lost-wax technique to make representations of important symbols, including crocodiles, scorpions, jaguars, and eagles.

Spaniards searched in vain for the legendary gold of Veragua and forsook the inhospitable region for the more temperate terrain and climate of Guanacaste and the central highlands. Perhaps for this reason, the archaeological background of the region is less complete than for the rest of the country, despite the ubiquity of perfectly spherical granite balls (*bolas* or *esferas de piedra*) unique to the Osa. The spheres range from a few centimeters to three meters across and weigh as much as 16 tons. They litter the forest floors in no perceptible order, but have been found in groups of as many as 25. No one is certain when they were carved or how, or for what purpose, although it is probable that they had religious or ceremonial significance. The spheres and gold ornaments dating back to A.D. 400–1400 provide the only physical legacy of the indigenous Diquis culture.

Most towns in the region were born late this century, spawned by the demand for bananas. The United Fruit Company established banana plantations here in 1938 and dominated the regional economy and polity until it pulled out in 1985.

Valle de Diquis

PALMAR

Palmar sits at the foot of the canyon of the Río Grande de Terraba, at the head of the Valle de Diquis, 125 km southeast of San Isidro and 81 km northwest of Golfito. The small town is a service center for the banana plantations of the Valle de Diquis and a major crossroads at the junction of the highways to/from Dominical and the central Pacific coast (north), Golfito and the Osa Peninsula (south), and San Isidro and Valle de El General (east).

The town is divided into Palmar Norte and Palmar Sur by the Río Terraba. **Palmar Norte** is the main center, but there is nothing here of touristic appeal. The Chinese presence is strong. **Palmar Sur,** southwest of the bridge over the river, displays pre-Columbian granite spheres in the plaza alongside a venerable steam locomotive that once hauled bananas.

Ciudad Cortés, seven km north of Palmar, lies west of the highway and is a base for exploring the Delta de Terraba (see *Sierpe,* below). **Coopemangle** (c/o Cooperena, tel. 506/248-2538, fax 506/248-1659, cooprena@racsa.co.cr, www.turismoruralcr.com), a local cooperative at Coronado, five km north of Cortés, offers lodging and guided boat trips

Accommodations

There are several no-frills budget accommodations.

Cabinas Ticos Alemán (tel. 506/786-6232, $11 s/d, $17.50 pp with a/c and TV), on the Pan-American Highway, has 25 basic but well-lit motel-style rooms with private bath; some with a/c, TV, and hot water (others have cold water only). It has secure parking.

Hotel y Cabinas Casa Amarilla (tel. 506/786-6251, $3 pp shared bath, $10 s, $15 d private bath) has 19 clean but basic rooms in an old wooden home, with shared bath and cold water only. The 16 slightly better rooms in a modern motel-style unit to the rear have private bath with cold water only. There's a TV in the lounge.

I recommend **Hotel y Cabinas Osa** ($5–10 s/d rooms, $12.50 s, $15 d cabins), in Palmar Norte center, with 10 spacious barebones, wood-paneled rooms with lots of light, fans, and shared bathrooms with cold water. Four wooden cabins in the rear courtyard are far better, and have cable TVs and hot water. There's secure parking. Reception is in the clothes store next door.

Information and Services

There's a bank, post office, and police station. The regional hospital is in Cortés.

Café Internet B&F (tel. 506/787-6167), in Palmar Norte, charges $2 per hour; open 8 A.M.–8 P.M. Mon.–Sat.

Getting There

SANSA (tel. 506/257-9414, www.grupotaca .com) and **Nature Air** (tel. 506/220-3054, www.natureair.com) both fly daily to Palmar.

Buses (tel. 506/222-2666) depart San José for Palmar from Calle 14, Avenidas 3/5, at 5 A.M., 7 A.M., 8:30 A.M., 10 A.M., 1 P.M., 2:30 P.M., and 6 P.M. (five hours, $4.25). Return buses depart Palmar Norte at 5:25 A.M., 6:15 A.M., 8:15 A.M., 10 A.M., 1 P.M., 2:30 P.M., and 4:45 P.M.

Buses for Sierpe leave from Supermercado Térraba in Palmar five times daily (50 cents).

There's a gas station immediately north of the bridge.

SIERPE

The end-of-the-road village of Sierpe, 15 km due south of Palmar, is a funky little hamlet on the banks of the Río Sierpe, trapped forlornly between banana plantations and swamp (the first three km is paved, then it's about seven more potholed km of harrowing abuse). If driving north along the Pan-American Highway, you can bypass Palmar: turn west 400 meters south of the Río Culebra and follow a dirt road eight km through cattle pasture and forest until you reach Eco-Manglares Lodge, where a rickety suspension bridge (just wide enough for a Toyota RAV-4 to squeeze by with millimeters to spare) over

boat on Río Sierpe

© CHRISTOPHER P. BAKER

the Río Estero Azul deposits you two km northeast of Sierpe.

Sierpe serves as departure point for boats to Drake Bay and for exploring the Delta de Terraba.

N Terraba-Sierpe Reserve

The 22,000-hectare Reserva Forestal del Humedad Internacional Terraba-Sierpe is a vast network of mangrove swamps fed by the waters of the Ríos Terraba (to the north) and Sierpe (to the south), which near the sea form an intricate lacework of channels and tidal *esteros* punctuated by islets anchored by *manglares* (mangroves). The delta, which extends along 40 km of shoreline, is a home to crocodiles, caimans, and myriad wading and water birds.

You can hire dugouts and *"especiales"* (motorboats) for guided tours from Sierpe, Palmar, or Cortés ($125 full day, up to six people).

Accommodations and Food

Cabinas Las Gaviota de Osa (tel. 506/786-7591, fax 506/786-7579) has six *cabinas* with fans and private bath with cold water only for $8.50 pp.

The two-story, motel-style, German-run **Oleaje Sereno Hotel** (tel. 506/786-7580, fax 506/786-7111, $25 s, $35 d, $10 extra person), 50 meters from the dock, has 10 nicely furnished rooms with a/c, ceiling fans, double and single beds, and private baths with hot water. A veranda and restaurant overlook the river. Excursions are offered.

The secluded **Eco-Manglares Lodge** (tel. 506/786-7414, fax 506/786-7441, ciprotur@racsa .co.cr, www.ecotourism.co.cr/ecomanglares, $35 s, $45 d), on the east bank of the Río Estero Azul (accessed by a narrow suspension bridge), two km northeast of Sierpe, has rustic, all-wood, thatched *cabinas* set on stilts amid lawns and fruit trees. Each has rough-hewn bedframes, Sarchí rockers, large screened windows, private bath with hot-water shower, plus a patio. It even has a pizzería offering Italian fare. Tours are offered. Rates include breakfast.

The best place for miles—a real charmer—is the Italian-run **N Veragua River Lodge** (tel./fax 506/788-8111 or tel. 506/296-3896, fax 506/231-7089, $35 s/d), on the east bank of the Río Estero Azul. The artist owner, Benedicto, has turned this old two-story, thatched riverside house into a splendid *albergue*. Inside is like a piece of Sienna transplanted, simply yet tastefully furnished with sponge-washed walls, old wicker and antiques, aging sofas, and Oriental throw rugs on the terra-cotta floors. There's a pool table in the parlor. The upper floor has a library-lounge. Three rooms in the house share a Victorian-style bathroom with clawfoot tub, louvered windows, and a rocker. One of the rooms is in the loft, with dormer windows and a honeymoon feel. Four cabins in the garden are more simple yet still romantic; some have iron-frame beds. Guests share the kitchen and outside rotisserie oven in a stone courtyard. Benedicto offers tours. Ten cabins were to be added. The lodge is reached by the rickety suspension bridge, beyond which Veragua is 800 meters further east along the dirt road; or you can take a canoe ride across the river. Rates include breakfast. The beach house costs $100 for up to five people.

Eco-lodges upriver from Sierpe and accessed solely by boat include **Río Sierpe Lodge** (P.O.Box 85-8150 Palmar Norte, tel. 506/384-5595, info@riosierpelodge.com, www .riosierpelodge.com), 25 km downriver from Sierpe near the rivermouth. It specializes in fishing and diving excursions. The 11 wood-paneled rooms are rustic but large, and each has a private bathroom with solar-heated water. Six additional rooms have lofts. There's a large dining and recreational area with a library. The lodge also has trails into the nearby rainforests, and offers hiking, horseback trips, kayaking, and excursions. It specializes in multi-day packages. Contact the hotel for rates.

A good alternative is **Sabalo Lodge** (tel. 506/770-1457, fax 506/771-5586, info@ sabalolodge.com, www.sabalolodge.com), a family-run ecolodge midway between Sierpe and Drake Bay. It offers elegant rusticity and close-up access to the mangroves and rainforest. Rooms and cabins are solar-powered and modestly but charmingly appointed. Home-cooked meals are served, and tours and fishing trips are offered. It specializes in multi-day packages. Contact the hotel for rates.

Tours and Activities

Vittatus (tel./fax 506/786-7647, vittatustour-operator@yahoo.com), by the waterfront, has kayaking, dolphin and whale trips, plus tours to Corcovado and Indian reservations. Nearby, **Tour**

Gaviotas de Osa has mangrove and crocodile tours by day and night.

Getting There

Buses and taxis (about $12) operate from Palmar Norte. Cabinas La Gaviota de Osa has water-taxi service to Drake Bay ($70–85 up to five people; $130–140 for 6–11 people; $185–200 12–18 people), and to Corcovado and Caño Island ($175/250/400). **Oleana Sereno** charges $15 pp to Caño Island or to Corcovado.

The Osa Peninsula

Access to the Osa Peninsula is via a single road that runs along the east coast to Puerto Jiménez (the only town of significance) and Cabo Matapalo (the southeastern naze of Osa), before curling west to dead-end midway along the southern coast at Carate, on the border with Corcovado National Park. The turnoff from the Pan-American Highway (Hwy. 2) is at **Chacarita,** about 32 km southeast of Palmar and 26 km northwest of Río Claro (the turnoff for Golfito). There's a gas station at the junction.

The road to Puerto Jiménez is paved as far as **Rincón,** 42 km south of Chacarita (beyond Rincón the road is badly potholed and either hellaciously muddy or dusty, depending on the weather). Here you begin to get your first sense of the cathedral-like immensity of the rainforests of the Osa Peninsula.

At **La Palma,** a hamlet 11 km south of Rincón, turn left for Puerto Jiménez. To the right, the gravel and mud road leads 12 km up the **Valle del Río Rincón** to the **Estación Los Patos** ranger station, easternmost entry point to Corcovado National Park. It's a great hike through virgin jungle from here to the Sirena ranger station on the coast (but you'll want to get going at sunup). En route to Los Patos, you'll pass the **Reserva Indígena Guyamí,** with a primary rainforest reserve. **CoopeUnioro** (c/o Cooprena, tel. 506/248-2538, fax 506/248-1659, cooprena@racsa.co.cr, www.turismorulcr.com), on a hillside about four km before Los Patos, is a local cooperative of ex-gold miners who offer guided tours.

Sports and Recreation

Safari Osa Tours has a multisport center at Jardín de las Aves Lodge; guided horseback tours are a specialty ($8 per hour with lunch). Guided boat excursions cost $250/$375 half/full day.

Accommodations and Food

The **Cabinas Golfo Dulce** (tel. 506/775-0244, $15 s, $20 d), in Rincón, has seven basically furnished rooms with verandas in a two-story lodge. Five rooms have shared bath; the rest have private bath but cold water only. It offers boat tours.

The **Osa Palma Lodge** (tel. 506/823-6241 or 506/380-5291, $7 pp bunk rooms, $50 s, $76 d cabins, $50 s/d "Lookout Room"), 1.5 km southwest of La Palma, sits atop a ridge with views across the Golfo Dulce. At last visit, 10 cabins were under construction; simple units have twin bunks and shared bathrooms, while more spacious thatched units have two double beds and spacious bathrooms with walk-in showers (hot water was to be added). You can also rent the "Lookout Room," above the modern open-air restaurant; it has a king-size bed, screened windows on all sides, but cold water only. Guided hikes are offered. Rates include meals.

Outside the Guyamí reserve, one km from Los Patos, is **Cabinas Corcovado** (tel. 506/775-0433 for messages, fax 506/775-0033, $5 per tent, $5 pp shared bath, $6 pp private bath), which has two basic rooms with shared bathrooms; four rooms with private baths and cold

Gulfe Dulce from near Rincón, Osa Peninsula

water; plus a platform where campers can tether their tarps or tents. The owner, ex-miner Luis Angulo, is a trained guide ($8 hourly) who offers camping trips; horses can also be rented ($6 hourly). Meals cost $10 daily.

An alternative, about 10 km farther, beyond the Los Patos trailhead, is the rustic **Albergue Ecoturístico Cerro de Oro** (tel./fax 506/259-3605, cooprena@racsa.co.cr, www.turismoruralcr.com, $30 s, $35 d low season, $35/40 high season), run by a local cooperative. Rooms have shared baths with cold water and solar electricity. There are also three houses available. The cooks conjure tasty meals, served in a rancho-style dining room. The lodge offers guided hikes and horseback trips. Rates include breakfast.

I recommend the Swiss-Tico-run **Suital Lodge** (P.O. Box 40-8250, Ciudad Neily, tel./fax 506/826-0342, suitalcr@hotmail.com, $18 s, $30 d rooms, $26 s, $40 d cabin low season, $20 s, $36 room, $30 s, $45 d cabin high season), between Chacarita and Rincón. This simple but pleasing wooden lodge has hillside vistas down over the gulf, plus two rustic rooms in the charming, breezeswept lodge; each has ceiling fan and louvered windows, although they share a bathroom with cold water (hot water was to be added). Three spacious, cross-ventilated and cross-lit wooden cabins sit on stilts and have ceiling fans, mosquito nets over beds, small terraces with rockers, and hot-water showers. Meals are served, and box lunches are prepared. There are four km of trails, including to the beach.

The rustic **Jardín de Aves Lodge** (tel. 506/735-5676, johnreid@safariosa.com, www.safariosa.com, $35 s, $45 d), between La Palma and Puerto Jiménez, is the home of American John Reid, who runs a working farm, forest reclamation project, and wildlife refuge: Refugio Río Terrones. It has four hardwood cabins. The Bobo Cabin sits on stilts over a creek, and has an outdoor bathroom. All have screened walls, and decks; some have hot water. John also rents a two-story cabin sleeping eight people. There's a barbecue pit, communal kitchen, and outside dining area. John has horseback and other tours, plus scuba and snorkeling, and fishing in ponds stocked with tilapia and guapote. He was adding a tent site, and introducing a volunteer program at last visit. Scarlet macaws and monkeys hang out in the trees. Rates include breakfast.

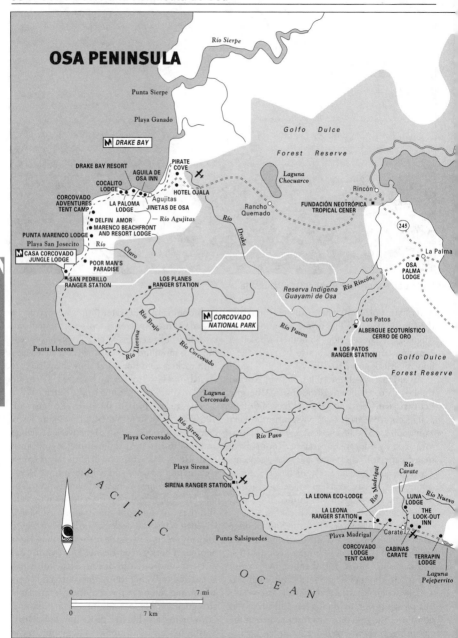

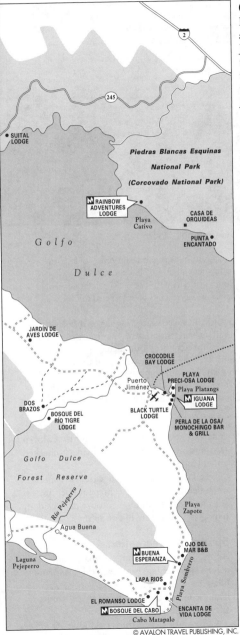

© AVALON TRAVEL PUBLISHING, INC.

Getting There

Buses operate four times daily between La Palma and Puerto Jiménez. The earliest departs Puerto Jiménez at 5:30 A.M. (You must hike or hitch the 12-km dirt-and-mud road to the park entrance at Los Patos.) The last bus from La Palma to Puerto Jiménez is at 2 P.M. The San José–Puerto Jiménez bus can drop you off here.

DRAKE BAY

A dirt road that begins about one km south of Rincón leads via the community of **Rancho Quemado** to Bahía Drake (pronounced "DRA-cay" locally), a large sweeping bay on northwest Osa. **Laguna Chocuarco**, near Rancho Quemado, is good for spotting crocodiles and tapirs (the Corcovado Agroecotourism Association, on the western side of Rancho Quemado, offers canoe trips).

Drake Bay extends southward below the mouth of the Río Sierpe, which provides the main access. A small village—**Agujitas**—lies at the southern end of the two-km-wide crescent bay, which is good for forays into Río Claro National Wildlife Refuge (eight km) and Corcovado National Park (13 km south), or to Caño Island, which dominates the view out to sea. The indigenous heritage is strong: the village is famous as one of only two places in Central America that make reverse-appliqué stitched *molas* (the other place is the San Blas islands in Panamá, where the work is far more ornate). Otherwise, it has changed little since the day in March 1579 when Sir Francis Drake sailed past Caño Island and anchored the *Golden Hind* in the tranquil bay that now bears his name.

The wilderness surrounding Drake Bay is replete with wildlife, including scarlet macaws. Humpbacks and other whale species pass by close to shore. There's good snorkeling at the southern end of the bay, where a coastal trail leads to the mouth of the Río Agujitas, good for swimming and jungle exploration by canoe. You can follow a trail up the river canyon, which you cross by a suspension

ABUSING THE OSA

The Osa region has had a tormented history in recent decades at the hands of gold miners, hunters, and loggers (half of the land that now forms Corcovado National Park, for example, was obtained in a land trade from the Osa Productos Forestales logging company). A logging permit allows felling if done in a "sustainable" way, but the laws go unenforced.

Most logging occurs in buffer zones adjacent to Corcovado National Park. The opening of a road linking Rincón with Bahía Drake in 1997 resulted in a cutting frenzy

signs of deforestation

© CHRISTOPHER P. BAKER

within the forest reserves (it is claimed that the road was put in against the wishes of local inhabitants following lobbying by the loggers). In November 1997, a special commission found serious violations by loggers and "technical errors" by ministry officials in favor of logging interests. That month a moratorium *(veda)* on logging in Osa was issued following a grassroots campaign by local residents.

The loggers are accused of being a *mafiosi* who pay locals to allow illegal logging on their land, while people who speak out against them often end up being intimidated into silence or even killed. Even the people of Guaymís reservation succumbed to the profit interest and sold out to loggers. Fortunately, the environmental ministry has been split into two distinct units, separating officials who grant permits from those who oversee compliance.

Meanwhile, the United Fruit Company is accused of a history of hiring professional poachers to systematically hunt out native animal and bird species that might adversely affect their food

bridge, to **Playa Cocalito** (immediately south) and **Playa Caletas** (four km), where there's a **Blue Morphis Butterfly Farm** (part of Corcovado Lodge Tent Camp). A paternoster of golden sand beaches lie farther south, ending at **Playa Josecito** on the edge of Corcovado National Park.

Río Claro National Wildlife Refuge

This 500-hectare nature reserve sits above and behind Playa Caletas and Punta Marenco. The reserve forms a buffer zone for Corcovado National Park and is home to all four monkey species and other wildlife species common to Corcovado. The area's 400-plus bird species include the scarlet macaw, great curassow, tou-

can, and several species of brightly colored tanagers, not least the endemic black-cheeked ant-tanager.

The Punta Marenco Lodge (see *Accommodations,* below) serves as a center for scientific research and welcomes ecotourists. Resident biologists lead nature hikes ($35).

Sports and Recreation

All the lodges can arrange scuba diving, snorkeling, sportfishing, horseback rides, and jungle hikes into Corcovado National Park or Caño Island. Scuba divers must bring their own buoyancy compensators and regulators.

Corcovado Expeditions (tel. 506/396-7774, corcovadoexpeditions@hotmail.com), in Aguji-

crops. Although those days are over, hunting by Ticos of tapir, jaguars, peccaries, and other big mammals continues under the nose—and even in collusion with—park staff. *Oreros* occasionally show up in Puerto Jiménez with ocelot skins and other poached animals for sale. Scarlet macaw nests are routinely poached. The turtle population continues to be devastated by the local populace, who poach the nests simply because there is nobody to stop them. Poison is being used to harvest fish from coastal breeding lagoons such as Peje Perro and Peje Perrito. And the system of issuing wildlife permits is routinely abused by people who obtain a permit for "rescuing" a specific animal, then use the permit to trade other animals. It's a lucrative trade. Local expats claim that some of the money finds its way to park rangers who routinely turn a blind eye (one conscientious ranger was fired for reporting his superiors after catching them eating endangered tepezcuintles). In any event, the rangers are not equipped to fight fire with fire. "They're ticket sellers!" says a prominent expat.

The Osa Peninsula was even slated to get Central America's largest woodchip mill, courtesy of Ston Forestal, a Costa Rican subsidiary of the paper giant Stone Container Corporation of Chicago. The chip mill would have dramatically increased truck traffic, and caused excessive pollution that would have threatened marine life of the Golfo Dulce (the gulf is an anoxic (lacking oxygen) body because of its limited water circulation, and weak dispersion makes the gulf especially susceptible to a buildup of chemical pollution and sediment runoff). Community efforts to fight the project forced Ston Forestal to shelve its project.

COVIRENA (tel. 506/283-4746, fax 506/283-5148), a branch of the park service, exists to combat logging and poaching. The moving force behind efforts is the local expat community. To resolve the politically charged issue, there's even talk of privatizing Corcovado. Stay tuned.

Fundación Corcovado (tel. 506/281-0656, www.corcovadofoundation.org or www.fundacioncorcovado.org; in the U.S., Interlink #665, P.O. Box 02-5635, Miami, FL 33102) works to save Corcovado's wildlife.

For a history of the problem, including violence associated with creation of Corcovado National Park, see David Rains Wallace's *The Quetzal and the Macaw: The Story of Costa Rica's National Parks*.

tas, offers tours to Corcovado ($50), Isla Caño ($55), and the Terraba mangroves ($70), as well as dolphin-spotting tours ($75), poison frog tours ($20), and birding ($20).

The **Original Canopy Tour** (tel. 506/257-5149 in San José, www.canopytour.com/drake.html) lets you explore the rainforest canopy from seven platforms, a suspended walkway, and four traverse cables that permit you to soar between treetops suspended in a harness; $45 adults, $35 students, $25 children.

Accommodations

All the lodges offer multi-day packages and arrange boat transfers.

Camping: You can camp on the lawn behind **Corcovado Expeditions** in Agujitas ($5 pp); it has toilets and a cold-water shower.

Under $25: At Rancho Quemado, the **Soda Café** (c/o public tel. 506/735-5145, $2.50 pp), a charming wooden café with white picket fence, has three simple rooms with bunks and shared bath with cold water. It's run by Enrique Ojando and Consuelo Torres, charming hosts who offer meals 6 A.M.–9 P.M.

$50–100: I like the simple charm of the no-frills **Hotel Ojalá** (tel. 506/380-4763, $50 pp), one km north of Agujitas. This two-story wooden structure has three rooms downstairs, with lofty ceilings, tile floors, fans, and private bathrooms with hot water. It specializes in sportfishing, and has a restaurant. Rates include all meals.

© CHRISTOPHER P. BAKER

Drake Bay

The charmingly rustic **Drake Bay Mirador Lodge** (P.O. Box 14, Palmar Norte, tel. 506/735-5440 or cellular 506/387-9138, info@mirador .co.cr, www.mirador.co.cr, $35 pp), atop a hill on the north side of Agujitas, offers great views. It has three simple but pleasing rooms in a wooden stilt unit with bamboo walls. Each has private baths and cold water. There's a deck, and meals are served using veggies from the organic garden; hot meals are cooked in the wood-burning oven. Rates include meals.

Enjoying a splendid waterfront setting, **Jinetes de Osa** (tel. 506/236-5637 or 506/371-1598, crventur@costaricadiving.com, www.costarica diving.com, $45 pp low season, $60 high season), at the southern edge of Agujitas, is a dedicated dive resort with nine rooms, each sleeping three people, with fans, cool tile floors, screened glassless windows, Guatemalan spreads, and spacious bathrooms with hot water. Rates include meals.

Also specializing in diving, **Pirate Cove** (tel. 506/234-6154 or 506/393-9449, erlane@racsa .co.cr, www.piratecovecostarica.com), overlooking the mouth of the Río Drake, north of Agujitas, has a delightful ambience. The lodge has

eight elegant wooden cabins set amid landscaped grounds and connected by wooden walkways. Each has two beds with orthopedic mattresses, mosquito netting, and deck with hammock, and there's solar-powered electricity. Dining is family style—predominantly Italian fare—on a shaded deck. Pirate Cove is fully equipped for dives, including two custom dive boats. Contact the lodge for rates.

At Playa Cocalita, **Cocalito Lodge** (Apdo. 63, Palmar Norte, tel./fax 506/786-6335, berrybend@aol.com; in Canada tel. 519/782-3978; $39 s, $50 d low season; $50 s, $65 d high season) sits between forest and beach amid orchid-filled gardens. The rustic lodge, a model ecological project on the edge of a 14-hectare property, has nine simple but clean and handsomely appointed cabins with private tiled baths with solar-heated water. The lodge boasts a large library. Hikes, horseback rides, and scuba diving packages are available. Rates include meals.

$100–150: Despite its marvelous shorefront location on the south side of the Río Agujitas rivermouth, **Drake Bay Resort** (Apdo. 98-8150, Palmar Norte, Osa, tel./fax 506/770-8012, or

SWIM WITH DOLPHINS

Drake Bay draws hundreds of dolphins, which are commonly seen cavorting close to shore. Species include pantropic spotted dolphins, spinner dolphins, bottle-nosed dolphins, rough-toothed dolphins, and common dolphins. The pantropic dolphins are aerial acrobats, and are often seen leaping and cavorting, drawing you into the water with their inimitable smiles. Humpback whales, orcas, pilot whales, sperm whales, sei whales, and pseudorcas (false killer whales) are also found in the area.

The **Delfin Amor Marine Education Center and Drake Bay Cetacean Foundation** (tel. 506/394-2632 or 866/527-5558, sierra@divinedolphin.com, www.divinedolphin.com), founded by marine biologist Sierra Goodman, monitors the dolphin population, which it works to protect, while educating locals and tourists on dolphin ecology.

Sierra offers dolphin encounters where you swim with the dolphins ($95, including lunch). When considered safe, and when the dolphins are willing, visitors can get into the water with them, although this is never guaranteed; otherwise you'll watch as they play-act. A nine-day program is also offered, with visits further afield (from $1,200). The animals are much more approachable with snorkels than with noisy scuba gear.

Despite their cheery smiles, dolphins are wild creatures and thereby unpredictable. Some precautions are in order:

Remain passive if a dolphin approaches.

Don't swim after dolphins or touch them unless so instructed, as they may see your behavior as threatening. A dolphin's bite can do severe damage!

If a dolphin shows aggressive behavior, exit the water.

Golfo Dulce

tel. 506/382-0147, emichaud@drakebay.com, www.drakebay.com, $85 pp standard, $125 suite low season; $95 pp standard, $135 suite high season) has a ho-hum aesthetic to its 20 two- and four-person *cabinas* with ceiling fans, tile floors, oceanview patios, and modern bathrooms with solar-heated showers. Four rooms are more upscale; one is misleading named a "honeymoon suite." There's a rustic dining room, open-air bar, saltwater pool, and free laundry. The resort specializes in diving expeditions, and offers horseback riding, whale-watching trips, rainforests trips, etc.

At Playa San Josecito, a Tico named Pincho Amaya and his gringa wife, Jenny, run **Poor Man's Paradise** (tel. 506/771-4582 or 506/383-4209, www.mypoormansparadise.com; in the U.S., tel. 877/352-1200; $40 pp tent-cabin, $46 pp shared bath, $60 pp cabin). They have two rooms, plus 12 tent-cabins, all with shared baths. You can also camp ($8, meals cost extra). Meals are served in an airy *rancho*. Electricity shuts off at 9 P.M. Pincho offers sportfishing. Rates include meals.

Two tent camps at Playa Caletas compete. The **Corcovado Adventures Tent Camp** (tel. 506/384-1679, info@corcovado.com, www.corcovado.com, $50 pp low season, $60 pp high season) has two-person tents pitched on wooden platforms, protected by thatched tarps. Each has a closet, wooden beds made up with cotton sheets, plus two armchairs. It has communal washrooms, and hearty meals are served in a rancho-style dining room. There's a butterfly garden. Guided hikes and horseback rides are offered, and you can rent sea kayaks. Rates include meals. Nearby, the U.S.-run **Delfin Amor Eco Lodge** (tel. 506/394-2632, reservations @divinedolphin.com, www.divinedolphin.com; in the U.S., tel. 831/345-8484; $85 pp) offers 10 simply furnished safari tent-cabins with two double beds and comfy mattresses. There's no electricity, but guests get fluorescent lights. It specializes in dolphin encounters (see above), and offers scuba, sportfishing, and horseback riding. Rates include all meals.

Marenco Beach & Rainforest Lodge (Apdo. 4025-1000, San José, tel. 506/258-1919, fax

506/255-1346, info@marencolodge.com, www
.marencolodge.com; in the U.S., tel. 800/278-6223;
$50–65 rooms, $75 s/d bungalows) features a
hilltop lodge set in beautiful gardens, and accommodates up to 40 people in 17 rustic
thatched bamboo-and-wood cabins, each with
raised palm-thatched roofs, simple yet pleasing
decor, a private bathroom with tiled showers,
and a terrace offering panoramic ocean views.
Meals are served family style in a large dining
hall overlooking a rocky shore. Transfers are
arranged.

$150–250: The beautiful **Punta Marenco
Lodge** (P.O. Box 462-2120, San José, tel. 506/
222-3305, fax 506/222-5852, info@puntamarenco
.com, www.puntamarenco.com, $120 s, $150
d) has rustic hilltop *cabinas* with private bathroom with cold water, plus terraces with fabulous
views. Family-style meals are served.

The class-act in Aguitas is the U.S.-run **Aguila
de Osa Inn** (Apdo. 10486-1000, San José,
tel. 506/296-2190, fax 506/232-7722, info
@aguiladeosa.com, www.aguiladeosainn.com,
$186 s, $290 d low season; $198 s, $308 d high
season), on the north bank at the mouth of the
Río Agujitas. It specializes in diving and sportfishing. The 14 stone-faced rooms are spacious
and have cathedral ceilings with fans, screened
glassless windows, bamboo beds with Guatemalan
spreads, plus exquisite bathrooms with huge
walk-in showers with piping hot water. Junior
suites further up the hill have magnificent views
and wraparound verandas with hammocks. The
focal point is the circular open-air restaurant
with high-pitched thatched roof and beautiful
hardwood floors. The inn offers scuba diving,
plus whale-watching, and there are Garrett 31s
for sportfishing. Rates include meals.

A delightful, serenely landscaped alternative
is **La Paloma Lodge** (Adpo. 97-4005, San Antonio del Belén, tel. 506/239-2801, fax 506/239-
0954, info@lapalomalodge.com, www.lapaloma
lodge.com, $100 pp standard, $120 deluxe low
season, $120/145 high season), which perches
atop a cliff overlooking Playa Cocalito and offers
a superb view of Caño Island. Five spacious
thatched ranchos—simply furnished with hammocks on the balcony—and five more attrac-

tively furnished comfortable cabins perched on
stilts have ceiling fans, orthopedic mattresses,
private baths with solar-heated water, and balconies. The thatched clubhouse is a perfect spot
for family-style dining. There's a small pool with
bar. Hikes and horseback rides are offered, as are
boats trips to Caño Island, plus sportfishing and
light-tackle fishing, and there's a fully stocked
dive shop. Rates include meals.

For exquisite decor, choose the deluxe **M Casa
Corcovado Jungle Lodge** (Apdo. 1482-1250,
Escazú, tel. 506/256-3181, fax 506/256-7409,
corcovado@racsa.co.cr, www.casacorcovado.com;
in the U.S., Interlink #253, P.O. Box 526770,
Miami, FL 3125-6770, tel. 888/896-6097), run
by Chicago expat Steven Lill, who has conjured
a wonderful hilltop resort from a defunct cacao
plantation. There are 14 thatched, conical *cabinas* (including two "honeymoon" units) with
hardwood four-poster beds and mosquito nets,
ceiling fans, twin-level ceilings, and huge showers with hot water and designer fixtures. The
rooms have ceramic tile floors, doors have
stained-glass windows, and walls are enlivened by
sponge-washing in blue pastels. There's also a
lounge and library, plus a *mirador* bar. Trails lace
the 120-hectare property. A small spring-fed pool
provides cooling dips. It has several boats, and
guided hikes, sea kayaking, scuba diving, and
tours are offered. The restaurant serves gourmet
cuisine, family-style. Multi-day packages begin at
$715 s, $1,230 d for a two-night minimum, including transportation, hikes, meals, etc.

Nearby, and not visited by the author, is the recently opened **Paradise Bay Rainforest Lodge**
(www.paradisebaylodge.com), with four standard rooms and two junior suites.

Food

Most accommodations provide meals: the two
recommended stand-outs in Aguitas are **Jinetes
de Osa,** with a rustic but attractive open-air
bar that serves Costa Rican cuisine as well as
great burgers and hot dogs; and **Aguila de
Osa Inn** (see above), where meals include treats
such as sashimi with ginger and horseradish
sauce (a nice touch is the free wine offered
with dinner).

Pirate Drake (tel. 506/351-5240, 9 A.M.–10 P.M.), on a hilltop north of Agujitas, serves seafoods and local fare.

Information and Services

In Agujitas, the *pulpería* (el. 506/771-2336) has the only public telephone; everyone else in town communicates via radio. The **Hospital Clínica Biblica** is by the beach in Agujitas.

Drake Bay Tourist Information Office (tel. 506/387-9138) is in Agujitas.

Getting There

Both **Sansa** (tel. 506/257-9414, www.grupotaca.com) and **Nature Air** (tel. 506/220-3054, www.natureair.com) provide scheduled air service to Agujitas. You can charter a small plane to Drake Bay. **Alfa Romeo** charges $245 for up to four passengers.

The dirt road from Rincón via Rancho Quemado (there's bus service from Rincón) is sometimes impassable in wet season—the main stumbling block is the Río Drake, which must be forded.

Boats travel downriver to Drake Bay from Sierpe. The trip takes two hours down the jungle-draped Río Sierpe ($15 pp). Lodges arrange transfers for guests. **Corcovado Expeditions** (see above) offers boat transfers to Sierpe ($15 pp) and to Corcovado ($150 boat charter).

Puerto Jiménez and Vicinity

Golfo Dulce

DOS BRAZOS DE RÍO TIGRE

About 25 km southeast of La Palma, four km before Puerto Jiménez, a turnoff to the right follows the Río Tigre 14 km west to Dos Brazos, the old center of gold mining, at the easternmost entrance to Corcovado National Park.

Pre-Columbian peoples sifted gold from the streams of the Osa millennia ago. But it wasn't until the 1980s that gold fever struck. After gold panners—*oreros*—found some major nuggets, prospectors poured into the region. At the boom's heyday, at least 3,000 miners were entrenched in Corcovado National Park. Because of the devastation they wrought—dynamiting riverbeds, polluting rivers, and felling trees—the Park Service and Civil Guard ousted the miners in 1986. The *oreros* were promised indemnity for their lost income, but it went unpaid for over a year. In a dramatic protest, they camped out in the parks of San José until the government came up with the money. Most *oreros* have turned to other ventures—not least ecotourism—but it is not unusual to bump into a lucky (or luckless) *orero* celebrating (or commiserating) over a beer in a bar.

Dos Brazos is one km from the border of Corcovado National Park.

Accommodations and Food

The **Bosque del Río Tigre Sanctuary & Lodge** (tel. 506/775-1422, fax 506/735-5045, losminerosdeltigre@yahoo.com, $75 pp) is an "ecotourist shelter" with six rooms (the largest sleeps six people) with murals, bamboo furnishings, and private baths, plus electricity in the evening. A restaurant looks out over the river. The lodge is run by the Asociación de Productores Villa Nueva: gold-panning trips, horseback rides, and Corcovado excursions are offered. Turn left at the bridge as you enter Dos Brazos; the lodge is one-quarter mile up the valley, surrounded by forest. You need to ford the river, which can be impassable in wet season. Rates include meals.

Getting There and Away

Buses service Dos Brazos from Puerto Jiménez. A *colectivo* taxi departs Super 96 daily at 11 A.M. and 4 P.M. (return trips depart Dos Brazos at 7 A.M. and 1:30 P.M.).

PUERTO JIMÉNEZ

This small, laid-back town is popular with the backpacking crowd and surfers. Locals have colorful tales to tell of gambling and general debauchery during the gold-boom days in the 1980s, when the town briefly flourished, prostitutes

PUERTO JIMÉNEZ

Golfo Dulce

To Rincón

CABINAS PUERTO JIMÉNEZ

CABINAS IGUANA IGUANA

PIZZA ROCK

OSA NATURAL

CABINAS THOMPSON

POST OFFICE

ICE (TELEPHONES)

EL RANCHITO

BUS STATION

RED CROSS

MEDICAL CLINIC

POLICE

BAKERY

COLECTIVO BUS

SUPER 96

CAFENET EL SOL

JUANITAS MEXICAN BAR AND GRILL

CABINAS/RESTAURANTE CAROLINA/ESCONDIDO TREX

CICLO DEPORTIVO

CABINAS/ RESTAURANTE ORO VERDE

CABINAS SODA KATIE

ARTISANS STORE

HELADERÍA

HORSE RENTALS

LAUNDRY

CABINAS MARCELINA

TABOGA AQUATIC TOURS

BANK

NATUREAIR

To Corcovado

SWIMMING POOL (PROJECTED)

CABINAS EYLIN

CABINAS AGUA LUNA

RESTAURANTE AGUA LUNA

PUERTO JIMÉNEZ YACHT CLUB (CAMPING)

PARROT BAY VILLAGE

Estero and Mangroves

CORCOVADO NATIONAL PARK HEADQUARTERS, VISITORS' CENTER

GIFT SHOP

LAPA RÍOS

ALFA ROMEO AERO TAXI

AIRSTRIP

To Playa Platanares and Crocodile Bay Lodge

0   100 yds
0   100 m

© AVALON TRAVEL PUBLISHING, INC.

Golfo Dulce

charged by the ounce, and miners bought bottles of whiskey just to throw at the walls.

A mangrove estuary lies to the northeast of town beyond a pleasant brown-sand beach. The wetlands are fed by the **Río Platanares.** You stand a superb chance of seeing caimans, white-faced monkeys, freshwater turtles, rays, even river otters and crocodile, and scarlet macaws can be seen and heard squawking in the treetops and flying overhead. The mangroves extend east to **Playa Platanares** (a.k.a. Playa Preciosa), a gorgeous miles-long swath of sand about three km east of town. A reef lies offshore in jade-colored waters, the forest behind the beach abounds with monkeys and other wildlife (even a jaguar has

been sighted on the beach), and the views across the gulf are fantastic. Five species of marine turtles come ashore to lay eggs on the beach, notably May–Dec. There's a **turtle *vivero*** (hatchery) in front of Playa Preciosa Lodge; the population coming ashore continues to decline dramatically. Nocturnal turtle tours can be arranged (no flashlights are permitted).

There's a small **butterfly garden** at Crocodile Bay Lodge; see *Accommodations,* below ($10).

Sports and Recreation

Escondido Trex (Apdo. 9, Puerto Jiménez, tel./fax 506/735-5210, osatrex@racsa.co.cr, www .escondidotrex.com) offers active adventures, from fishing, snorkeling, and sea kayaking to waterfall rappelling, and gold-mining trips, plus a sunset dolphin watch ($35).

CafeNet Tours has mangrove kayaking ($35), dolphin-watching ($35), and rainforest hiking ($40). Mike Boston of **Osa Aventura** (tel. 506/735-5670, info@osaaventura.com, www .osaaventura.com) offers expeditions to Corcovado, Laguna Pejeperrito (see below), and Caño Island. And **Sportfishing La Raya** (stephentidswell345 @hotmail.com) charges $200 half-day, $380 full-day for fishing.

At last visit, a **public swimming pool** was being planned one block west of the gas station.

Accommodations

Camping: You can camp on breezy oceanfront lawns at the Puerto Jiménez Yacht Club, northeast of town (see below); it has basic facilities. You can rent tents from **Soda Corcovado** (tel. 506/735-5539).

Under $25: There's no shortage of no-frills budget cabinas, most of a similar standard. Those to be recommended include **Cabinas Iguana Iguana** (tel. 506/735-5158, 2iguana@racsa.co.cr, $7.50 pp), at the entrance to town and which has 10 basic but comfortable rooms with fans plus private baths and cold water. There's a lively little bar and restaurant, plus a swimming pool.

Cabinas Puerto Jiménez (tel. 506/755-5090, $10 s, $20 d), 100 meters east, has 10 modern, simple and clean *cabinas* with fans and private bathrooms with cold water only in palm-shaded grounds. Some get lots of light; others are dark.

Cabinas Marcelina (tel. 506/735-5007, fax 506/735-5045, cabmarce@hotmail.com, $7 s, $12 d), 200 meters south of the soccer field, has six clean, simply furnished rooms with private baths and fans. It can arrange fishing trips, horseback rides, and even gold-panning expeditions.

Cabinas Carolina (tel. 506/735-5185, $12 s/d with fan, $20 s/d with a/c), in the heart of town, is associated with the popular restaurant. They're spacious and have private baths.

Cabinas Eylin (tel. 506/735-5011, $15 pp large front rooms, $10 per room smaller rooms),

400 yards west of the gas station en route to Cabo Matapalo, has three rooms. The spacious front rooms sleep four people each and are handsomely appointed, with cathedral ceilings, hardwood furniture, TVs, lounge chairs, and tiled floors and bath. A smaller room for two is to the rear.

$25–50: One of the best places in town is **Cabinas Oro Verde** (tel. 506/735-5241, elbago @hotmail.com, $7 pp), a two-story building run by Kyle (an American) and his Tica wife, Emelia. It has 10 clean, simple, but adequate rooms with lots of light. Some are large. The bakery and restaurant downstairs are recommended.

On the beachfront, the modern **Agua Luna Restaurant and Cabinas** (tel./fax 506/735-5393, agualu@racsa.co.cr, $25 s, $45 d) is one of the nicer places and has clean, simply furnished a/c rooms with large windows, TVs, and private baths; six rooms have hot water.

$100–150: The nicest place in town is **Parrot Bay Village** (Apdo. 91, Puerto Jiménez, tel. 506/735-5180, www.parrotbayvillage.com, $70 s, $80 d low season, $90 s, $110 d high season), formerly Doña Leta's Bungalows, on the ocean-front northeast of the airstrip. Newly renovated, it has three two-story cabins, plus four octagonal wood-and-thatch cabins, all attractively furnished, with wooden ceilings, fans, kitchenettes, plus private baths and hot water. There's beach volleyball, and a handsome open-air restaurant and bar. Tours are offered, and guests have free use of kayaks.

The **Crocodile Bay Lodge** (info@crocodilebay .com, www.crocodilebay.com; in the U.S., 100 Landing Ct., Suite A, Novato, CA 94945, tel. 415/209-9976 or 800/733-1115, fax 415/209-6177; $125 pp), about one km east of town, specializes in sportfishing, with 20 spacious, graciously furnished a/c rooms in two-story fourplex units; 12 rooms have Jacuzzis, and all have tile floors, wooden ceilings, polished hardwoods, and French doors opening to spacious verandas. It has an ascetic a/c bar and charmless restaurant, plus beautiful freeform pool fed by a water cascade, and a butterfly garden. It has its own pier and offers inshore and offshore fishing, plus kayaking. Rates include meals and drinks.

At Playa Platanares, I love the beachfront **N** **Iguana Lodge** (Apdo. 8, Puerto Jiménez, tel./fax 506/735-5205, www.iguanalodge.com, $85 pp standard, $95 pp deluxe high season), which boasts a breezy setting and a grand, luxuriously rustic aesthetic. The lodge, which is named for the "iggies" hanging out in nearby trees, has a Gaudíesque feel in its curvaceous layout. There are four hardwood cabins raised on stilts, with louvered windows on all sides and broad verandas. Shared showers and bathrooms (candlelit at night) are located nearby. Newer, more luxurious cabins have private bathrooms. It's run by two friendly former lawyers—Loran and Toby Cleaver—from Colorado who gave it all up to live in harmony with nature. Gourmet meals are served family-style on a wide veranda. There's a frog garden, and trails lead into the adjacent forest. Local excursions are offered. Rates include meals.

Loran and Toby also own the dramatic and appealing **Pearl of the Osa** ($40 s, $55 d standard, $275 villa low season; $55 s, $75 d standard, $325 villa high season), next door. This lime-green wooden lodge has eight upstairs rooms, with walls washed in soft pastels, plus ceiling fans, cross-ventilation through screened windows, simple rattan furniture, and private bathrooms with cold water only. It has a magnificent bar and grill below. And a simply furnished three-bedroom house—**Villa Villa Kula**—includes master suite with its own wraparound veranda.

The **Black Turtle Lodge** (btlodge@racsa.co.cr, www.blackturtlelodge.com, $70 s, $100 d cabin, $80 s, $130 d treehouse low season; $90/140 cabin, $110/170 treehouse high season), opened in 2002 adjacent to Iguana Lodge as a carbon copy run by American transplants Mary and Geoff Botosan (a former professional chef). They have two treehouse *cabinas* (raised on treetrunk logs) and two cabins amid the jungle and hidden from the ocean, just steps away. Each unit has slanted roofs of clear recycled plastic, all-around screened glassless windows, a balcony, and shared outside bathrooms with stone-floor showers. You're lulled to sleep by the sound of chirping tree-frogs from the frog pond. There's a yoga platform. Family dining is offered by candlelight (the cuisine is superb). The couple were planning to add a *casa* and tent-cabins, and they'll rent their own three-story wooden home with two bedrooms and third loft bedroom, and bamboo and rattan furniture. Rates including meals.

Food

Restaurante Carolina (tel./fax 506/735-5185, 7 A.M.–10 P.M.) is popular with local expats for its large, inexpensive menu, including *típico* dishes and chicken cordon bleu and fettucine alfredo.

Agua Luna, on the northeast side of town, catches the breezes and has good seafood and Chinese dishes; try the wonton soup, or *pescado al ajillo* (fish with garlic) for about $3.

N **Juanitas Mexican Bar & Grill** (tel. 506/735-5056, 10 A.M.–midnight), run by a real Mexican lady, is the real McCoy, serving excellent Mexican fare in atmospheric surrounds (it offers a 20 percent discount 11 A.M.–3 P.M. Mon.–Fri., and has happy hour 4–6 P.M.). It has crab races on Thursday and live music some Fridays.

When in town, I head to the **Monochingo Bar & Grill,** at Pearl of the Osa, at Playa Platanares, for its magnificent aesthetic, with a beautiful hardwood bar and spacious shaded patio with hammocks. It serves chicken fingers, nachos, burritos, burgers, tuna melt, and *casados* (set meals).

There's a bakery (*panadería*) 50 meters south of the soccer field.

Information and Services

Escondido Trex (see *Sports and Recreation,* above), **Osa Natural,** and **Cafenet el Sol** offer tourist information service.

The **Osa Conservation Area headquarters** (tel. 506/735-5036 or 506/735-5580, fax 506/735-5276, corcovado@minae.go.cr, 7:30 A.M.–noon and 1–5 P.M. Mon.–Fri.), beside the airstrip, has a tourist information office. You must register here if you plan on visiting Corcovado on your own.

There's a **clinic** (tel. 506/735-5029) and a **Red Cross** (tel. 506/735-5109) for emergencies.

The **police station** (tel. 506/735-5114) is 50 meters south of the soccer field.

Banco Nacional (tel. 506/735-5155) accepts only Visa (not MasterCard), as is the case for every business in town.

The post office is on the west side of the soccer field. You can make international calls from **Osa Natural** (tel. 506/735-5440, 8 A.M.–9 P.M.), on the west side of the soccer field, which charges $3 per hour online time; and **Cafenet el Sol** (tel. 506/735-5717, pdcollar@racsa.co.cr, 7 A.M.–10 P.M.), which charges $6 per hour of Internet time.

Getting There and Around

Sansa (tel. 506/257-9414, www.grupotaca.com) and **Nature Air** (tel. 506/220-3054, www.natureair.com) have scheduled daily flights. **Alfa Romeo Aero Taxi** (tel. 506/775-1512, fax 506/735-5178) has an office at the airstrip.

Buses (tel. 506/257-4141; in Puerto Jiménez, 506/771-2550) depart San José for Puerto Jiménez from Calle 14, Avenidas 9/11, daily at 6 A.M. and noon (10 hours; $5); and from San Isidro de El General at 5:30 A.M. and noon (five hours; $4.50). Buses depart Ciudad Neily for Puerto Jiménez at 9:30 A.M. and 7 P.M. ($2.50); and from Golfito for Puerto Jiménez from the municipal dock daily at 11 A.M.

Buses for San Isidro and San José depart Puerto Jiménez at 5 A.M. and 11 A.M.; and to Ciudad Neily at 4:30 A.M. and 10:30 A.M.

A water-taxi (*lancha*) runs daily from the Muelle Bananero in Golfito at 11:30 A.M., and returns at 6 A.M. (tel. 506/775-0472; $2.50; 90-minute journey). **Ciclo Deportivo** (tel. 506/735-5297) rents bicycles for $1.25 hourly, $15 per day.

PUERTO JIMÉNEZ TO CARATE

The southeast shores of Osa are lined with hidden beaches—**Playa Tamales, Playa Sombrero**—in the lee of craggy headlands, notably **Cabo Matapalo** at the southeast tip of the Osa peninsula about 18 km south of Puerto Jiménez. This section of coast is popular with the long-board surf set, who come for the powerful six-foot waves, especially in late July through August. At Matapalo, a side road leads through an arched

"gate" and winds three km to the beach at Cabo Matapalo; it is lined with private homes tucked in the forest.

The rough dirt road peters out at **Carate,** 43 km from Puerto Jiménez, consisting of an airstrip and a small *pulpería* (grocery); beyond the *pulpería,* the dirt track heads uphill to Luna Lodge (see *Accommodations,* below). The road to Carate takes about two hours under good conditions. It gets gradually narrower and bumpier and muddier. There are a few rivers to ford. A 4WD is essential.

The La Leona Ranger Station, at the entrance to Corcovado National Park, is about two km along the beach.

About three km east of Carate, you pass **Laguna Pejeperrito,** good for spotting crocodiles, caimans, and waterfowl.

Accommodations

Camping: At Carate, you can camp at **Cabinas Carate,** which has showers with cold water and charges $5 per tent; and in front of the *pulpería,* which has bathrooms, showers, and water faucet.

Under $25: The **Cabinas Carate,** beside the airstrip, has five basic *cabinas* without fans, and with cold water only in private bathrooms for $10 pp.

$25–50: The **Terrapin Lodge** (tel. 506/735-5211 or 506/735-5049, www.terrapinlodge.com, $65 s, $120 d), about 400 meters inland of the beach one km east of Carate, offers five simply appointed all-wood cabins in the forest; all have private bathrooms with cold water only. Meals are served in a charming skylit restaurant on stilts, with hammocks. It has a pool. Rates include all meals.

$25–50: Seeking a safari-style experience? **La Leona Eco-Lodge** (tel. 506/735-5705, laleona @racsa.co.cr, $20 s, $30 d), just 200 meters from the La Leona ranger station, is a simple tent-camp with 12 tent-cabins on wooden platforms; each with two small mattress-beds. They share a bathhouse with four bathrooms and showers. Meal prices are outrageous, however.

At Carbonera, I like the offbeat, German-run **Ojo del Mar B&B** (tel. 506/735-5062, ojodelmar @yahoo.com, $25 pp tent cabin, $35 pp cabin), enjoying a reclusive forest setting and with two open-sided bamboo cabins with "rainforest" showers, plus two double beds with batiks and mosquito nets (one cabin has a loft bedroom). They share a clean outdoor bathroom. There's also a simple tent cabin at the rivermouth, by the beach. Meals are served in a charming Robinson Crusoe–style dining area. It has no electricity. Rates include breakfast.

Nearby, I also like the eclectic **Buena Esperanza** (fax 506/735-5773, martinatica@hotmail.com, $25 pp) for its colorful Moroccan-style decor and unique arrangement: its windowless, open-sided "cabinas" have low cement walls with wrap-around sofas (of soft-edged cement) with batiks and Army-fatigue cushions, sponge-washed concrete floors, and roughhewn beds with mosquito nets. Shared outdoor showers and toilets have cold water only. Its offbeat bar-restaurant is a popular hang-out. Rates include breakfast.

$150–250: The **Encanta la Vida** (tel./fax 506/735-5678 or 735-3209; in the U.S., tel. 805/969-4270, fax 805/969-0238; $75 pp suite, $85 pp honeymoon suite), in the gated community of Matapalo, is a three-story wooden lodge, handsomely decorated and fringed by wide verandas with hammocks and rockers with views over both ocean and jungle. It has two beautiful suites plus a honeymoon suite, all with mosquito nets over four-poster roughhewn beds, heaps of closet space, and huge walk-in showers. A reader reports loving a stay here and found the staff "very accommodating." It requires a two-day minimum stay. Rates include meals.

The Spanish-run **El Remanso Lodge** (tel./fax 506/735-5569, elremanso@racsa.co.cr, www.elremanso.com, $85 pp standard, $110 pp deluxe), atop Cabo Matapalo, offers five spacious and airy cabins painted in lively pastels, with sponge-washed concrete floors and a gorgeous, simple aesthetic that includes soft-contoured concrete bed bases, batik covers, hammocks, and wall-to-wall louvered windows to three sides. French doors open to broad verandas. It also has a two-story group cabin for four people. Trails lead to a magnificent two-story cabin with four-poster bed, polished hardwood floor,

and huge walk-in shower. It has a beautiful restaurant for guests only; a deck with plunge pool; plus a zipline (it specializes in waterfall rappelling). Rates include all meals.

Nearby, Tim Cowman rents his **Casa Tortuga de Oro** (tel. 506/735-5062, www.costarica.com/tortuga; in the U.S.A., tel. 415/457-0341; $30 pp), a two-story, two-bath house featuring rare hardwoods. It sleeps up to six people. Two-day minimum.

A deluxe gem is **🅼 Bosque del Cabo** (tel./fax 506/735-5206, fax 506/381-4847, boscabo@racsa.co.cr, www.bosquedelcabo.com; in the U.S., Interlink 528, P.O. Box 025635, Miami, FL 33102; $150 s, $230 d standard, $155/250 d deluxe low season; $165 s, $250 d standard, $175/270 deluxe high season), atop the 180-meter cliff of Cabo Matapalo and part of a 140-hectare forest reserve. Set in landscaped grounds are seven thatched clifftop *cabinas* with superb ocean views over Playa Matapalo. There are lanterns, but no electricity; screened open-air showers have their own little gardens; verandas have hammocks. Three splendid deluxe cabins each have terra-cotta floors, king-size bed with mosquito net, chic decor, and lofty rough-hewn stable doors that open to a wraparound veranda with sublime ocean vistas. Then there's the Casa Blanca and Casa Miramar, exquisitely decorated two-bedroom villas with open-plan kitchens, bedrooms with bamboo-framed king-size beds, CD players, and wraparound verandas with hammocks and rockers. Lanterns light the place at night. There's a cooling-off pool fed by spring waters, plus sundeck, and a yoga platform. Meals are eaten family style under thatch. It offers hikes and horseback rides, and there's a zipline canopy tour. It's a stiff 150-meter clamber to the beach.

The **Lookout Inn** (tel./fax 506/735-5431, terryconroy@yahoo.com, www.lookout-inn.com, $68-99 pp) sits on the hillside one km east of Carate. Terry and Wendy, from New Mexico, are live-in owners of this three-story house with seven tall-ceilinged, tastefully decorated bedrooms. Sponge-washed walls merge with bamboo furnishings and tropical hardwood accents, not least bed frames made from tree trunks. Solar electricity heats the water delivered in large showers. A lounge has a small library. A spiral staircase opens onto a *mirador* with hammocks, a telescope, and fabulous vistas along the coast. Monkeys come down to the forested property, which extends uphill to the ridge; and macaws screech by like jet fighters. A swimming pool and deck are inset in the garden below, and a pond draws poison-arrow frogs. Guests get free use of kayaks, canoes, mountain bikes, and boogie boards. Rates include meals.

I love the calming **Luna Lodge** (tel./fax 506/735-5431, cellular 506/380-5036, information @lunalodge.com, www.lunalodge.com; in the U.S., SJO63, P.O. Box 025216, Miami, FL 33102, tel. 888/409-8448; $50 pp tent, $90 pp cabin low season; $65/125 high season), nestling in the hills above Carate amid primary rainforest and centered on a massive thatched rancho reception lounge/restaurant with deck offering fabulous views. Eight circular, simply yet delightfully

view from Luna Lodge

furnished bungalows stairstep the hill, reached via paths of black slate. Each has a balcony; exquisite "rainforest" bathrooms have shower-tubs enclosed by a stone wall with garden. There are also seven safari-style budget tents reached by a stiff uphill climb. The bar and restaurant offers international cuisine, and a wellness center offers yoga, tai chi, massage, etc. Hikes, sea kayaking, and horseback trips are offered, as are beach transfers ($4). A pool was to be added. To get there, you have to crisscross the Río Carate several times, a demanding task after heavy rains; the river is often impassable and vehicles frequently have to be towed out! Fortunately, once across, the steep hill is paved. Rates include taxes, meals, and tour.

For a marvelous jungly experience, I recommend **Corcovado Lodge Tent Camp** (c/o Costa Rica Expeditions, P.O. Box 6941-1000, San José, tel. 506/257-0766, fax 506/257-1665, costaric @expeditions.co.cr, www.costaricaexpeditions .com, $57 s, $97 d), a civilized safari-style tent camp fronted by palms immediately behind the beach and 1.5 km west of Carate, a short hike from Corcovado National Park. It's the perfect base for exploring the park. The beachfront facility has 20 roomy and comfortable walk-in tents on pedestals. Guests sleep on sturdy bamboo cots raised off the floor. Ablutions are in two shared bathhouses (cold water only). Electricity is supplied by a small generator and is limited to certain hours in the dining area and bathhouse. Meals are served family-style in a thatched restaurant, and there's an atmospheric bar. An inflatable pontoon vessel provides transfers to Corcovado National Park. Those with loftier pretensions can try sleeping in a tree-house tent suspended on a platform 30 meters in the air ($125). Rates include breakfast and dinner.

$250 and up: Who can resist ℕ **Lapa Ríos** (Apdo. 100, Puerto Jiménez, tel. 506/735-5130, fax 506/735-5179, info@laparios.com, www .laparios.com, $254 s, $354 d low season; $328 s, $428 d high season), an exquisite resort with a great location atop a ridge overlooking Cabo Matapalo? Fourteen romantic, luxuriously appointed bungalows reached by wooden walkways come with two queen-size beds, gleaming hardwood floors, screened windows, a patio garden complete with outdoor shower (you also have a tiled indoor shower), and louvered French doors opening to a private terrace. The thatched lodge has a spiral staircase augering up from the restaurant to a *mirador* (lookout platform). There's a small pool with sun deck and bar. The property is backed by a 400-hectare private reserve. Walks in the rainforest (including a night tour with the "Bug Lady"), kayaking, horseback rides, plus a full-day Corcovado tour with air transfers to/from Sirena are offered. The owners are active environmentalists and savvy marketers, thanks to which their resort attracts the rich and famous. Rates include taxes and meals.

Fiery-billed aracari and toucan are common. And around dawn and dusk, scarlet macaws—there are at least 40 breeding pairs—can be seen in flight as they migrate daily between the wet forest interior and the coastal mangrove swamps.

Food

The ◪ **Buena Esperanza** (10 A.M.– Mon.– Sat., brunch only Sundays) draws surfers for its tremendous offbeat ambience and international cuisine (Thai, Mexican, etc.) at budget rates.

The tasteful **El Eclipse Restaurant** (7 A.M.– 7 P.M.) at Luna Lodge serves native and continental fare. And **Lapa Ríos** offers splendid continental dishes in its *mirador* restaurant.

Getting There

SAETA (tel. 506/232-9514) flies to Carate from San José ($400 per planeload) and Puerto Jiménez ($215 up to four passengers). **Aeronaves de Costa Rica** (tel. 506/775-0278) offers charter flights from Golfito to Carate. Air charters may not be in operation during "wet" season, from May to December.

A *colectivo* truck runs daily from Puerto Jiménez at 6 A.M. and 1:30 P.M., departing Carate for Puerto Jiménez at 8:30 A.M. and 4 P.M. ($6). It stops at Matapalo ($3).

You can rent a jeep-taxi ($60 per carload).

Water-taxis run to Playas Tamales and Sombrero.

◪ CORCOVADO NATIONAL PARK

Parque Nacional Corcovado—the Amazon of Costa Rica—is the largest stronghold of Pacific coastline primary forest, which has been all but destroyed from Mexico to South America. Its 41,788 hectares encompass eight habitats, from mangrove swamp and jolillo palm grove to montane forest. The park protects more than 400 species of birds (20 are endemic), 116 of amphibians and reptiles, and 139 of mammals—representing 10 percent of the mammals in the Americas—on only 0.000101777 percent of the landmass. Its healthy population of scarlet macaws (about 1,200 birds) is the largest concentration in Central America. You can expect to see large flocks of macaws in flight or feeding on almond trees by the shoreline.

Corcovado is a good place to spot the red-eyed tree frog (listen for his single-note mating "cluck"), the glass frog with its transparent skin, and enamel-bright poison-arrow frogs. And you can watch fishing bats doing just that over rivers at night. You can even try your own hand for snook inside the mouths of the coastal rivers on incoming tides.

Corcovado is one of only two places in the country that harbor squirrel monkeys (the other is Manuel Antonio). It's also one of the last stands in the world for the harpy eagle. Four species of sea turtles—green, Pacific ridley, hawksbill, and leatherback—nest on the park's beaches. And the park supports a healthy population of tapirs and of big cats, which like to hang around the periphery of the Corcovado Lagoon. Jaguar paw prints are commonly seen in the mud trails, and the cats are often sighted. (The park's mammal population—notably peccaries—is under intense pressure from illegal hunters.)

The Osa Peninsula bears the brunt of torrential rains from April to December. It receives up to 400 cm per year. The driest months, Jan.–April, are the best times to visit.

Recreation and tours can be arranged in Puerto Jiménez. Most tour operators in San José can also arrange tours.

Information

The park has three entry points: **La Leona,** on the southeast corner near Carate; **Los Patos,** on the northern perimeter; and **San Pedrillo,** at the northwest corner, 18 km south of Drake Bay. You can hike or fly into the park headquarters at **Sirena,** midway between La Leona and San Pedrillo. There's also a remote ranger station at **Los Planes,** on the northern border midway between San Pedrillo and Los Patos. All are linked by trails. Entrance costs $8 and is good for the duration of your stay.

The park is administered through the Osa Conservation Area headquarters in Puerto Jiménez (tel. 506/735-5036 or 506/735-5580, fax 506/735-5276, corcovado@minae.go.cr).

Accommodations

A basic bunkhouse with foam mattresses (but no sleeping bags or linens), plus attic rooms, are available at Sirena for $5 pp; reservations are essential (contact the Corcovado park headquarters in Puerto Jiménez as far ahead as possible). Other ranger stations may be able to squeeze you into one of their basic rooms; San Pedrillo, La Leona, and Los Patos each have room for 12 people, plus showers and water. The rangers will cook meals by prior arrangement ($5 breakfast, $7 lunch and dinner), but you have to supply your own food.

Camping is allowed only at ranger stations ($2). Rangers can radio ahead to the various stations within the park and book you in for dinner and a tent spot. No-see-ums (pesky microscopic flies you'll not forget in a hurry) infest the beaches and come out to find you at dusk. Take a watertight tent, a mosquito net, and plenty of insect repellent. There are occasional shelters in addition to the ranger stations. You can rent tents and stoves in Puerto Jiménez from Escondido Trex; Mini Mercado El Tigre (tel. 506/735-5075); and Cabinas Iguana Iguana ($7 per day).

Hiking Trails

Corcovado has a well-developed trail system, though the trails are primitive. Several short trails (two to six hours) make for rewarding half- or full-day hikes. Longer trails grant an in-depth backpacking experience in the rainforest. Allow about three days to hike from one end of the park to the other. It can be hot and sweaty. Horseflies and mosquitoes can be a pain in the butt. And spiderwebs span the trails, which are in places badly eroded, poorly maintained, and poorly marked. Buy the relevant Instituto Geográfico 1:50,000 scale map if you plan on serious hiking.

From La Leona, it's 15 km to Sirena, following the beach for most of the way. Allow up to eight hours. Beyond Salsipuedes Point, the trail cuts inland through the rainforest. Don't try this at high or waning tide: you must cross some rocky points that are cut off by high tide. Don't trust the ranger's statements: consult a tide table before you arrive. The hike from La Leona to the Magrigal waterfall is particularly recommended, but few local guides will take you.

From Sirena, a trail leads northeast to Los Patos via Corcovado Lagoon. Another trail—only possible at low tide (not least because sharks, mostly hammerheads, like to come up the rivermouths in the hours immediately before and after high tide)—leads to the San Pedrillo Ranger Station (23 km). There are three rivers to wade. The trick is to reach the Río Sirena and slightly shallower Ríos Llorona before the water is thigh-deep. Here, watch for the crocodiles upstream. Don't let me put you off; dozens of hikers follow the trail each week. Halfway, the trail winds steeply into the rainforest and is often slippery—good shoes are essential. The last three kilometers are along the beach. The full-day hike takes you past La Llorona, a 30-meter-high waterfall that cascades spectacularly onto the beach. From San Pedrillo, you can continue another 10 km to Drake Bay and Marenco Beachfront and Resort Lodge. Tapirs are said to come down to the beach around sunrise, but you must remain silent at all times, as the animals are timid and may never return once scared away.

Golfo Dulce

From Los Patos, the trail south climbs steeply for six km before flattening out for the final 14 km to the Sirena Research Station. The trail is well marked but narrow, overgrown in parts, and has several river crossings where it is easy to lose the trail on the other side. You must wade. Be especially careful in rainy season, when you may find yourself hip-deep. There are three small shelters en route. A side trail will take you to Corcovado Lagoon. Allow up to eight hours. Another trail leads from Los Patos to Los Planes.

Safety Concerns: Beware riptides: swim only where rangers advise it may be safe. Sharks reportedly cruise the inshore waters, though there are no recorded incidents of unprovoked attacks here. And crocodiles inhabit the estuaries of the Río Claro and Río Sirena; if crossing either river, do so as far upriver as possible. Corovado also has a large population of peccaries, a massive-necked razor-backed hog that grows to the size of a large hound.

Getting There

You can charter an air-taxi to fly you to Sirena from Puerto Jiménez with **Alfa Romeo Aero Taxi** ($110). Also see *Puerto Jiménez to Carate,* above.

Boats from Marenco and Drake Bay will take you to either San Pedrillo or Sirena.

CAÑO ISLAND BIOLOGICAL RESERVE

Caño Island ($8 admission) is 17 km off the western tip of the Osa Peninsula, directly west of Drake Bay. It is of interest primarily for its importance as a pre-Columbian cemetery. Many tombs and artifacts—pestles, corn-grinding tables, and granite spheres *(bolas)*—are gathering moss in the rainforest undergrowth. The 300-hectare island is ringed with secluded white-sand beaches that attract olive ridley turtles. Among its residents are boa constrictors (the only poiso-

nous snakes here are sea snakes), giant frogs, a variety of hummingbirds, and three mammal species: a marsupial, the paca (which was introduced), and a bat. Surprisingly, only 13 terrestrial bird species are found here. Snorkelers can see brilliant tropical fish and moray eels among the coral beds. Offshore waters teem with common and bottle-nosed dolphins, and sperm, pilot, and humpback whales.

Caño Island gets struck by lightning more often than any other part of Central America, and for that reason was considered sacred by pre-Columbian peoples, who used it as a burial ground.

In 1973, Caño was leased to a Spanish developer with plans to build a megaresort. The island, however, was heroically saved by an outburst of popular displeasure and was named Reserva Biológica Isla Caño. It is administered as part of Corcovado National Park.

A wide and well-maintained trail leads steeply uphill from the **ranger station.** Pre-Columbian tombs are scattered along the trail. Call the Osa Conservation Area headquarters for information (see *Puerto Jiménez*).

It is forbidden to overnight.

Volunteers

The **Oceanic Society** (Fort Mason Center, Bldg. E, San Francisco, CA 94123, tel. 415/441-1106 or 800/326-7491, fax 415/474-3395, www .oceanic-society.org) offers a whale research trip as part of its marine science research project. No research experience is necessary.

Getting There

Most lodges in the region offer trips, as do several tour operators in San José and Golfito, and you can hire a boat from Golfito or Drake Bay.

The Oceanic Society also offers an 11-day "Natural History & Whale-Watching Tour" that combines a visit to Caño with Corcovado and Monteverde.

Golfito and Golfo Dulce

The Golfo Dulce region fringes the huge bay of the same name, framed by the Osa Peninsula to the west and the Fila Costeña mountains to the north. The region is centered on the town of Golfito, which lies on the north shore of the gulf. The bay is rimmed by swamplands, lonesome beaches (several with nature and/or fishing lodges at which to rest your head), and remote tracts of rainforest accessible only by boat.

Humpback whales and dolphins are frequently seen in the bay.

Río Claro, about 15 km west of Ciudad Neily and 64 km southeast of Palmar, is a major junction at the turnoff for Golfito from Hwy. 2. It's about 23 km to Golfito from here. Río Claro has a plethora of restaurants and *sodas,* plus a gas station and taxi service.

PIEDRAS BLANCAS NATIONAL PARK

In 1991, a tract of the Esquinas Forest north of Golfito and centered on the village of **La Gamba** was named Piedras Blancas and incorporated into Corcovado National Park. In 1999, it was split off and named a national park in its own right. It has been a troubled park, as land within its bounds is still in private ownership, and logging permits issued before 1991 apparently remain valid.

The Austrian government underwrites local efforts to save the forest. A cooperative provides income for local families whose members are employed at Esquinas Rainforest Lodge and on fruit farms and a botanical garden; it also has a tepezcuintle breeding program. Guides ($15) can be hired for hiking. The "Rainforest of the Austrians" also operates **La Gamba Biological Station** in conjunction with the University of Vienna.

The turnoff from the Pan-American Highway is at Km 37, midway between Piedras Blancas and Río Claro (Gamba is six km from the highway; 4WD not required). You can also get there via a very rough dirt road that leads north from Golfito (4WD required).

Beaches

The following beaches (and their lodges) can only be accessed by boat, but are popular day trips from Golfito.

Playa San Josecito, about 10 km northwest and a 25-minute boat ride from Golfito, is a wide, lonesome, shingly brown-sand beach, popular for day trips from town. The jungle sweeps right down to the shore, as it does a few km north at **Playa Cativo.** Dolphins swim thick as sardines close to shore.

Casa de Orquídeas (tel. 506/775-0353, $5 admission, with guided tour) is a private botanical garden at the northwest end of Playa San Josecito. This labor of love culminates the 20-odd-year efforts of Ron and Trudy MacAllister. Ornamental plants, not least of them 100 species of orchids, attract zillions of birds. Two-hour guided tours are offered at 8:15 A.M. Sun.–Thurs. Tour operators throughout Golfo Dulce offer tours to the garden; otherwise take a water-taxi from Golfito or any of the local lodges.

Accommodations

La Gamba Biological Station (c/o Esquinas Rainforest Lodge, $6 pp) accommodates eight people in a small, self-contained farmhouse.

The splendidly reclusive **Esquinas Rainforest Lodge** (tel./fax 506/775-0901, esquinas@racsa.co.cr, www.esquinaslodge.com, $110 s, $160 d low season; $125 s, $190 d high season) is built of natural stone and timbers. Its five duplex cabins are connected by a covered walkway to the main lodge, which features an open-walled lounge offering views of the forest. Each of the 10 rooms has rattan furniture and lively decor, ceiling fan, terra-cotta floors, screened glassless windows, porches with rockers and hammocks, plus modern bathrooms with hot water. Facilities include a bar, gift shop, library, and thatched dining room plus naturally filtered swimming pool. No more than 25 people at a time are allowed, to minimize impact on wildlife. Excursions are offered. Rates include three meals and taxes.

Golfo Dulce

caiman at Esquinas Rainforest Lodge

Anglers are catered to at **Golfito Sailfish Rancho** (5700 Memorial Hwy., Suite 107, Tampa, FL 33615, tel. 813/249-9908 or 800/450-9908, fax 813/889-9189, advmkt1@juno.com, www .golfitosailfish.com, $100 pp), at Punta Encantado, 15 minutes by boat from Golfito. This modern sportfishing lodge offers 10 spacious, pleasingly decorated rooms with ceiling fans, two double beds, safe, and walk-in showers with hot water. Dining is in a handsome open-air restaurant, and there's an open bar, plus a plunge pool fed by a waterfall. Most folks come in to fish on multi-day packages; contact the resort for rates.

The Swiss-run **Golfo Dulce Lodge** (Apdo. 137-8201, Golfito, tel. 506/821-5398 or 506/232-0400, fax 506/775-0573 or 506/232-0363, info@golfodulcelodge.com, www.golfodulcelodge .com, $105 s, $170 d room, $115/180 bungalow low season; $115 s, $190 d room, $130/210 bungalow high season), surrounded by 275 hectares of forest at Playa San Josecito, has five handsome wooden bungalows plus a brick cabin

with bamboo furnishings, large veranda with hammocks and rockers, and tiled bathrooms. There are also three rooms with verandas. There's a small swimming pool and a *rancho*-style restaurant and bar. Sea kayaking, horseback riding, hikes, and excursions are offered. Electricity is supplied by a Pelton wheel; water is recycled; and sewage is treated in septic tanks. Rates include boat transfers, all meals, and taxes.

Nearby, **Casa de Orquídeas** (see above, $125 d five nights, $150 weekly) has a lone two-room cabin for four people, with kitchenette, private bathroom, and solar electricity. Bring your own food. Rates include transfers.

Rainbow Adventures Lodge (tel. 506/735-5062, info@rainbowcostarica.com, www.rainbowcostarica.com; in the U.S., 8504 SW 43rd Ave., Portland, OR 97219, tel. 503/380-6532 or 800/565-0722; $235–275 s, $355–395 d) is on a private nature reserve at Playa Cativo. The sturdily handsome three-story lodge—run by Virginian John Lovell—is constructed of hardwoods and set in a lush, landscaped garden. Antiques and beautiful rugs adorn the walls, and vases are full of fresh-cut flowers. Three double rooms with private baths open onto ocean-view verandas. There's a penthouse suite on the third level with 360-degree vistas, plus two exquisite, two-bedroom handcrafted *cabinas* (with two bedrooms and private bathrooms) on the grounds. Solar heating provides warm water. There's an open-air dining terrace, and the lodge offers snorkeling gear, boat rentals, and guided tours. There's no dock, and you may need to hike in over sandy tidal flats after jumping into thigh-deep water. Children under four free. Rates include all meals and transportation from Golfito

GOLFITO

Golfito, the most important town in the Pacific southwest, is for travelers who love forlorn ports, this one a muggy, funky, semi-down-at-the-heels place that you may recognize as a setting from the movie *Chico Mendes,* the true story of the Brazilian rubber-trapper murdered for his efforts to protect the rainforest.

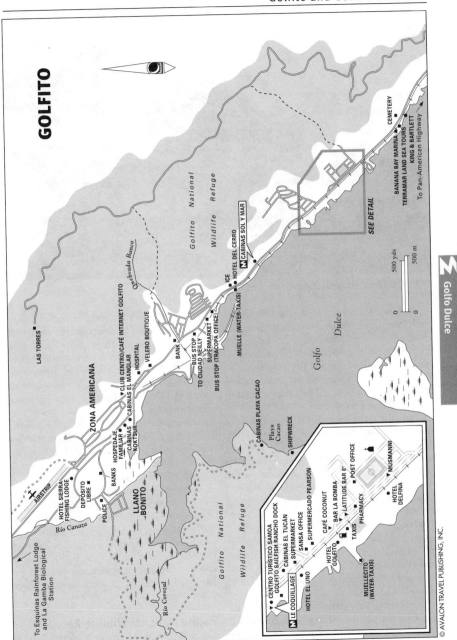

GOLFITO

Golfo Dulce

To Esquinas Rainforest Lodge and La Gamba Biological Station

LAS TORRES

AIRSTRIP

ZONA AMERICANA

Rio Canaza

Hotel Sierra Fishing Lodge

DEPÓSITO LIBRE

BANKS

POLICE

LLANO BONITO

HOSPEDAJE FAMILIAR

CABINAS KOKTSUR

CLUB CENTRO/CAFÉ INTERNET GOLFITO

CABINAS EL MANGLAR

HOSPITAL

VELERO BOUTIQUE

BANK

BUS STOP TO CIUDAD NEILLY

SUPERMARKET

BUS STOP (TRACOPA OFFICE)

Quebrada Banco

Golfito National Wildlife Refuge

ICE

HOTEL DEL CERRO

CABINAS SOL Y MAR

MUELLE (WATER-TAXIS)

CABINAS PLAYA CACAO

Playa Cacao

SHIPWRECK

Golfo Dulce

Golfito National Wildlife Refuge

Rio Corozal

SEE DETAIL

CEMETERY

BANANA BAY MARINA

TERRAMAR LAND SEA TOURS

KING & BARTLETT

To Pan-American Highway

0   500 yds
0   500 m

Detail:

CENTRO TURÍSTICO SAMOA

GOLFITO SAILFISH RANCHO DOCK

LE COQUILLAGE

HOTEL EL UNO

CABINAS EL TUCAN

SUPERMARKET

SANSA OFFICE

SUPERMERCADO PEARSON

CAFÉ COCONUT

BAR LA BOMBA

HOTEL GOLFITO

LATITUDE BAR 8°

TAXIS

PHARMACY

POST OFFICE

MUSMANNI

HOTEL DELFINA

MUELLECITO (WATER-TAXIS)

© AVALON TRAVEL PUBLISHING, INC.

© CHRISTOPHER P. BAKER

old United Fruit housing, Zona Americana, Golfito

The town was born in 1938, when the United Fruit Company moved its headquarters here after shutting down operations on the Caribbean coast. By 1955, more than 90 percent of the nation's banana exports were shipped from Golfito. The United Fruit Company closed its doors and pulled out of Golfito in 1985 after a series of crippling labor strikes.

The town sprawls for several kilometers along a single road on the estuary of the Río Golfito. Forested mountains form a backdrop a few hundred meters inland. There are two distinct parts of town. First entered, to the southeast, is the **Pueblo Civil,** the run-down working-class section full of tumbledown houses (many hanging on stilts over the water). The Pueblo Civil extends northwest to the compact town center, a quarter of cheap bar life, with an uninspired plaza featuring an antique **locomotive.** Nearby, the Hotel Centro Turístico Samoa has a small **Museo Marino** displaying a large collection of seashells and coral.

About two km farther is the **Muelle de Golfito,** the banana-loading dock (also called Muelle Bananero) at the southern end of the **Zona Americana,** a more tranquil and orderly quarter where the administrative staff of United Fruit used to live. The distinct architectural style of the Zona is reminiscent of the British Raj, with brightly painted, two-story wooden houses raised on stilts set in manicured gardens shaded by tall trees hung with epiphytes and lianas. Here, too, is the **Depósito Libre,** a duty-free shopping compound (enclosed by high walls) that lures Ticos in droves on weekends, when the town's dozens of cheap *cabinas* fill up. (Golfito was declared a duty-free port in 1990—an attempt to offset the economic decline that followed United Fruit's strategic retreat.)

The town is popular as a sportfishing center. The bay is not recommended for swimming.

Warning: Golfito attracts its fair share of tropical vagabonds, broken-hearted misfits, and roughneck military-type expatriates, many of them on the lam from the law. In 2002, a U.S. university student on an exchange program was murdered in Golfito. Be cautious with whom you interact.

Golfito National Wildlife Refuge

The 1,309-hectare Refugio Nacional de Vida Silvestre Golfito, created to protect the city's watershed, is formed of primary rainforest covering the steep mountains inland. Trails lead through the reserve, which connects northward with Piedras Blancas National Park. All four species of Costa Rican monkeys live in the refuge, as do scarlet macaws, anteaters, agouti, margay, raccoon, jaguarundi, and a menagerie of other wildlife.

A sign across from the Plaza Deportes soccer field in the Pueblo Civil about two km south of the town center points the way along a dirt road that leads about five km uphill to Las Torres radio station. Alternately, you can also take a steep trail from opposite Hotel Centro Turístico Samoa. A third option is the road that parallels the airstrip; it leads past the Hotel Sierra and, deteriorating all the while, deposits you three km farther at a sign for "Senderos Naturales" (nature trails). Lastly, you can take the dirt road beyond the Depósito Libre that leads through the reserve to Esquinas. Local tour operators and guides lead tours.

The administrative office (tel. 506/789-9092, fax 506/789-9292, rioclaro@minae.go.cr) is in Chacarita.

Playa Cacao

The vision of Golfito improves dramatically from across the bay at Playa Cacao, literally at the end of the road, five km southwest of Golfito. Popeye the Sailor would have felt at home here. Funky charm was never funkier or more charming. The road from Golfito winds around the shore, with great views, and spills steeply down to the shingly, brown-sand beach (the rough, narrow dirt can be a harpy in wet season, when the mud gets thigh-deep).

About 200 meters to the east is a beached 19-meter-long trawler, virtually derelict and looking like the place Popeye might actually live. A one-legged sailor, Thomas Clairmont (alias Captain Tom), turned his wreck into a "hotel" when he washed ashore in 1954 after his boat capsized. Tom died in 1993, and the infamous bar and "hotel" where Tom told his tales is no longer operating. John Wayne anchored here in 1966 and left his signature in the guestbook.

Entertainment

The liveliest place in town is **Centro Turística Samoa,** near the plaza, which has a dart board (a darts club meets on Monday nights), table soccer, and a pool table, plus music at the bar that is shaped like a sailing ship with a busty mermaid prow; at last visit it was awaiting a 24-hour license. The **Bar La Bomba,** upstairs opposite the gas station, is another lively, colorful bar. Expatriate gringos gravitate toward the **Latitude Bar 8°,** opposite Hotel Costa Surf.

The **Club Centro** (tel. 506/775-0119), in Zona Americana, has a skittles alley, and a volleyball court upstairs.

King & Bartlett (tel. 506/775-1624) has an upscale bar with a pool table.

Sports and Recreation

Many sportfishing vessels are berthed here. Prime season for sailfish is Dec.–May; for marlin, June–Sep.; and for snook, May–Sep.

Banana Bay Marina and **King & Bartlett** hotel offer sportfishing packages and charters,

Bobby McGinnis cleans fish at Banana Bay Marina in Golfito.

Golfo Dulce

as does **Sportfishing Unlimited** (tel./fax 506/776-0036, john@sportfishing.co.cr, www .sportfishing.co.cr).

Also see Golfito Sailfish Rancho, under *Accommodations* in the *Piedras Blancas National Park* section.

Land-Sea Tours (see *Information*, below) offers tours to the Golfito Wildlife Refuge, the Río Coto swamps, and horseback riding.

Accommodations

Under $25: The town is awash in budget—and often grim—accommodations not worth recommending. Some are quasi-brothels.

The **La Purruja Lodge** (tel. 506/775-1054, w.rosenberg@gmx.net, www.purruja.com, $15 s, $25 d), four km east of Golfito, is a great bargain. It has five attractive modern *cabinas* with lots of windows, and is set amid landscaped lawns on a hill overlooking a forested valley. It has a pool table and darts, plus Internet. Swiss owner Walter Rosenberg offers hiking tours to Corcovado. Trails lead into the nearby forest and botanical garden. Rates include breakfast. There's a camping area ($2.50 per tent).

In the center, **Cabinas El Tucán** (tel. 506/775-0553, $5 pp cold water, $25 s/d with a/c), opposite Centro Turístico Samoa, has 16 small, simple rooms with fans and private bathrooms with cold water only. Twelve new rooms have a/c, TVs, refrigerators, and hot water. And **Hotel Golfito** (tel. 506/775-0047, $10 s/d with fans, $16 with a/c), next to the gas station, has 16 basic but clean rooms with private bathrooms and fans (six with a/c and hot water).

The most atmospheric places are at the north end of town and include **Cabinas Koktsur** (tel. 506/775-1191, $10 s/d), with eight simple, clean rooms in a well-kept old wooden home. Each has a fan plus a private bath with cold water. The hostess is friendly and serves simple meals. Next door, **Cabinas El Manglar** (tel. 506/775-0510); **Cabinas Caña Blanca** (tel. 506/775-0124, canablan@racsa.co.cr); and **Hospedaje Familiar** (tel. 506/775-0217) are of a similar standard and price.

$25–50: The **Hotel y Restaurante el Gran Ceibo** (tel./fax 506/775-0403, $25 s/d with fan;

$35 with a/c), where the road meets the shore at the entrance to Golfito, has 27 clean, well-lit rooms in modern two-story and one-story units. All have cool tile floors, TV, and clean bathrooms; 10 have a/c and hot water; the others have fans and cold water. There's a ho-hum open-air restaurant and a nice poolside breakfast area, plus a swimming pool and kids' pool.

Nearby, **Las Gaviotas** (Apdo. 12-8201, Golfito, tel. 506/775-0062, fax 506/775-0544, lasgaviotas@hotmail.com, www.ecotourism.co.cr /lasgaviotas, $42 s/d with fan, $54 with a/c and kitchenette, $84 a/c bungalows) has 21 modest albeit recently renovated rooms with cable TV, refrigerators, private porches, and spacious tiled bathrooms with large showers. The outdoor restaurant overlooks the gulf and serves excellent seafoods. There's a pool, a sun deck, and a souvenir shop.

Your best bet in this price range is **Hotel Centro Turístico Samoa** (tel. 506/775-0233, fax 506/775-0573, samoadelsur@racsa.co.cr, $37–40 up to four people low season, $50 high season), on the waterfront in the center of Golfito. It has 14 well-kept *cabinas* with fans, TVs, and private baths with hot water. There's an excellent restaurant and the liveliest bar in town. It also accepts RV campers for $15 per vehicle in a guarded parking lot with gleaming showers and toilets. It rents bicycles. A pool was being added.

I also like the **Hotel Sierra Fishing Lodge** (Apdo. 37, Golfito, tel. 506/775-0666, fax 506/775-0506, hotelsierra@racsa.co.cr, www .hotelsierra.com, $40 s/d), between the airport and the duty-free zone, with 72 well-lit, modestly furnished a/c rooms with jade-tile floors, TVs, private baths, telephones, and room service. There's a pool with wet bar, a children's pool, plus a pleasant restaurant, bar, and disco. Despite its name, it's not a fishing lodge.

$50–100: A recommended option at Playa Cacao, **Cabinas Playa Cacao** (c/o tel. 506/221-1169, fax 506/256-4850, info@kapsplace.com or isabel@racsa.co.cr, www.kapsplace.com/EN/ other/, $40 s/d low season, $50 s/d high season), alias "Isabel's Place," is an eccentric charmer with six African-style thatch-roofed, tile-floored cottages, each with two beds, fan, refrigerator, and private bathroom with hot water. Three have kitchens. There's also a log cabin that is occasionally available. It has a small restaurant, laundry, and swimming pool fed by a multi-tiered cascade falling from a whirlpool set in the hillside. Isabel offers horseback rides and deep-sea fishing (it has its own dock). You can rent canoes. It can be tough to get to by road in wet season, but you can take a water-taxi right to Isabel's pier. It's most appropriate for self-sufficient folks.

The class act in town is the thoroughly contemporary **Banana Bay Marina** (tel. 506/775-0838, bbmarina@racsa.co.cr, www.bananabaymarina .com, $75 s/d rooms, $125 s/d suite), with three standard a/c rooms and a gorgeous master suite, all with gracious mint and sea-green decor, terra-cotta floors, ceiling fans, and large bathrooms with walk-in hot-water showers. The master suite has its own computer, cable TV, and sofa set. It has a lively and colorful bar and restaurant, plus Internet café, and the best sportfishing marina in town.

Next door, another new sportfishing lodge, this one in more traditional style, is **King & Bartlett** (tel. 506/775-1624, kingandbartlettsi @yahoo.com, http://kingandbartlettsportfish-ing.com; in the U.S., tel. 954/288-6366) has also opened. It has six large a/c rooms with satellite TV and lots of polished hardwoods. There's a large bar and seafood restaurant, plus a 24-slip marina. It specializes in sportfishing packages. Call for rates.

Food

The small and charming **Coconut Café** (tel. 506/775-0518, coconut@sol.racsa.co.cr, 6:30 A.M.–10 P.M. Mon.–Sat.) is a hub of gringo activity. It serves burgers, tostadas, sandwiches, veggie burritos ($3.50), and the best American breakfasts in town, including a fruit plate with yogurt and granola ($2.75), and omelettes ($3–4). It also sells cappuccinos and espressos.

Latitude Bar 8° (tel. 506/775-0235), opposite Hotel Costa Surf, is another meeting spot for expats eager to start their day with omelettes, pancakes, and other hearty breakfasts.

For elegance and variety, head to **Banana Bay Marina** (6 A.M.–10 P.M., $2.50–8), where the menu includes spicy Louisana gumbo, and pork loin with mushroom pasta and veggies. **King & Bartlett** is a worthy alternative.

Banana Bay Marina, Golfito

© CHRISTOPHER P. BAKER

For seafoods, I recommend the open-air, squeaky-clean **M Le Coquillage** (7 A.M.–midnight) at Centro Turística Samoa, which also offers a wide menu from burgers ($2) and pizzas to paella. Portions are filling, and my *corvina al ajillo* (garlic sea bass; $5) was splendid.

Musmanni, 200 meters south of the gas station, sells baked goods.

Information and Services

Land-Sea Tours (Apdo. 113, Golfito, tel./fax 506/775-1614, landsea@racsa.co.cr, 7:30 A.M.–5 P.M. Mon.–Fri., and 7:30 A.M.–noon Saturday), on the waterfront at Km 2, is run by Katie Duncan, a friendly, helpful gringa who knows the local scene like the back of her hand. Land-Sea is a one-stop, full-service tourist center. It acts as the local SANSA airline agent, and as a tour and hotel reservation center. There's storage.

Café Coconut has a bulletin board and is a good place to meet budget travelers.

The **Hospital de Golfito** (tel. 506/775-0011) is in the Zona Americana.

The police station post is in front of the Depósito Libre.

There are three banks in the Depósito Libre, and a Banco Nacional on the main road in the Zona Americana.

The post office is on the northwest side of the soccer field, in Pueblo Civil. There are telephones along the main boulevard and around the central plaza, and you can make international calls from Land-Sea Tours.

Café Coconut offers Internet service, as do Land-Sea Tours and Banana Bay Marina. The **Club Centro** (1:30–8:30 P.M. Tues.–Sun.), in the Zona Americana, charges $1.50 per hour for Internet access (30 minutes minimum).

Land-Sea Tours has laundry service.

Getting There

Both **Sansa**(tel. 506/257-9414, www.grupotaca.com) and **Nature Air** (tel. 506/220-3054, www.natureair.com) operate scheduled flights to Golfito.

Buses (tel. 506/222-2666) depart San José from Calle 14, Avenidas 3/5, daily at 7 A.M. and 3 P.M. (eight hours, $5). The return bus departs Golfito at 5 A.M. and 1 P.M.

Buses depart for Ciudad Neily hourly from Club Latino; buses to Zancudo depart the Muellecito (the little dock immediately north of the gas station in the center of Golfito) at 1:30 P.M.; and for Puerto Jiménez from the Muelle at 11 A.M.

The **Association ABOCOP** (tel. 506/775-0712), opposite the ICE, operates **water-taxis** *(lanchas)* to Playa Cacao, Punta Encanto, Zancudo, and Puerto Jiménez ($5 pp each way), to Playa Cacao ($1 pp each way), Playa Zancudo ($5 pp each way), and other beaches.

Golfito is a popular port-of-call for yachters. The **Banana Bay Marina** (tel. 506/775-0838, bbmarina@racsa.co.cr, www.bananabaymarina.com) and **King & Bartlett** (tel. 506/775-1624, kingandbartlettsi@yahoo.com, http://kingand bartlettsportfishing.com) are the best of several private marinas.

The **immigration office** (tel. 506/775-0487, 7–11 A.M. and 12:30–4 P.M. Mon.–Fri.) is beside the Muelle.

There's no car rental in Golfito. Land-Sea Tours can arrange a chauffeured car.

Getting Around

Buses run between the two ends of town. *Colectivos* (shared taxis) also cruise up and down and will run you anywhere in town for 75 cents, picking up and dropping off passengers along the way.

You can call for a taxi (tel. 506/775-2242).

The Burica Peninsula and Valle de Coto Colorado

The rugged Peninsula de Burica, on the east side of Golfo Dulce, forms the southernmost tip of Costa Rica. Its dramatically beautiful coast is washed by surf. To the northeast, the Valle de Coto Colorado is planted with banana trees stretching to the border with Panamá

▶ PLAYA ZANCUDO

Playa Zancudo, strung below the estuary of the Río Coto Colorado, is one of my favorite spots, exuding a South Seas feel. Absolutely ultimate! The ruler-straight gray-sand beach (littered with coconuts) stretches about six km along a slender spit backed by the eerie mangroves of the **Río Coto Swamps,** fed by the estuarine waters of the Río Coto Colorado. Waterfowl are plentiful. And with luck you may see monkeys and river otters, and crocodiles and caimans basking on the riverbanks, motionless as logs.

The fishing is good in the fresh water (there are several docks on the estuary side) and in the surf at the wide rivermouth. The wavers are good for windsurfing and, when the waves are up, surfing, when it offers a perfect beach break, lessening to the north. Avoid the beach at dusk, and during the full moon, when the no-see-ums are voracious.

The hamlet of **Zancudo** is near the rivermouth at the north end of the spit, reached along a sandy roller-coaster of a track along which a few dozen North American and European residents have chosen to live a laid-back life beneath the palms.

Zancudo is only 10 km from Golfito as the crow flies, but driving there is another thing. The village is 44 km from the Pan-American Highway.

Entertainment

The bar at **Cabinas Sol y Mar** is a local meeting spot and hosts karaoke, plus a volleyball game on Saturday and horseshoes on Sunday. The bar at **Zancudo Beach Club** shows movies on Tues-

palm on Zancudo beach

day nights. **Estero Mar,** in the village, host occasional dances favored by locals.

Sports and Recreation

Golfito Sportfishing (tel. 506/776-0007, fax 506/775-0373, info@costaricasportfishing.com, www.costaricafishing.com) has 25-foot center consoles for charter. It also has multiday packages, as does **Sportfishing Unlimited** (tel./fax 506/776-0036), just south of the Zancudo Lodge; and **Arena Alta Adventures & Sportfishing** (tel. 506/776-0115, arenaalta@aol.com, www.costaricasailfish.com), at Cabinas Arena Alta, which also offers inshore and river fishing, plus water-skiing, parasailing, jungle tours, horseback riding, and trips to Pavones ($20 pp).

Zancudo Boat Tours at Cabinas Los Cocos rents surfboards, paddleboats, and snorkeling equipment, plus kayak trips up the Río Coto, and trips to the Casa de Orquídeas botanical gardens.

© CHRISTOPHER P. BAKER

▶ Golfo Dulce

THE MARCH OF THE SOLDIER CRABS

If you think you see the beach moving, it's not the heat waves nor last night's excess of *guaro* messing with your mind. Daily, whole columns of seashells—little whelks and conchs of green and blue and russet—come marching down from the roots of the mangroves onto the sand. Scavengers only an inch long, soldier crabs are born and grow up without protective shells. For self-preservation they move—"lock, stock, and abdomen," says one writer—into empty seashells they find cast up on the beach. Although they grow, their seashell houses do not; thus whole battalions of crabs continually seek newer and larger quarters. When threatened, a soldier crab pulls back into its shell, totally blocking the entrance with one big claw.

Accommodations

You can camp at **Cabinas Sol y Mar** (see below) for $2 pp.

For budget digs, your best bet is the basic, Tico-run **Restaurante y Cabinas Tranquilo** (tel. 506/776-0131, fax 506/776-0143, $7 pp), near the southern end and offering four rustic rooms of handsome hardwoods above the restaurant, with a double and single bed, and hammocks on the veranda. Two larger rooms are in a separate building. All share bathrooms and showers downstairs, with cold water only. There's a laundry.

About two km farther brings you to the hamlet, where **Cabinas Los Loritos** (tel./fax 506/776-0073, $24 up to four people) has two large two-story thatched cabins, each with four beds in loft bedrooms and private bathroom with tiled showers. One has hot water.

I like **Coloso del Mar** (tel. 506/776-0050, info@coloso-del-mar.com, www.coloso-del-mar.com, $20 s/d low season; $25 s, $45 d high season), 200 meters north of Tranquilo, for its four rustic, simply furnished, yet lovely palm-shaded wooden cabins with ceiling fans, firm mattresses, screened windows, porches, safes, and hot-water showers. It has a quaint wooden restaurant, plus

a gift shop and Internet café. Boat trips and water-taxi service are offered.

About two km further, and a node of local action, is **Cabinas Sol y Mar** (Apdo. 87, Golfito, tel. 506/776-0014, fax 506/776-0015, solymar @zancudo.com, www.zancudo.com, $25 s/d economy cabin, $35 s/d duplex, $39 non-duplex cabin), with a pleasant casual ambience and landscaped grounds. The five simple *cabinas* (two are geodesic domes) and larger rooms are tastefully furnished with canvas sofas, Guatemalan bedspreads, ceiling fans, and private skylit bathrooms with hot water and pebble-and-tile floors. It also has two a/c rooms with TVs (but cold water only) above the restaurant and bar popular with locals. There's volleyball and other games. It's run by North Americans, Rick and Lori, who have a gift store. The couple also has a three-story oceanfront cottage for four people for up to $625 monthly.

Zancudo Beach Club (tel. 506/776-0087, fax 506/776-0052, zbc@costarica.net, www .zancudobeachclub.com, $40 cabins, $55 "villa" low season; $60/75 high season), run by Yankee transplants Gary and Debbie Walsh, is a laid-back place popular with surfers. It has three cabins of varnished hardwoods on stilts spread across 250 meters of beachfront; each has fans, hammocks, and well-lit private bathroom. All have orthopedic mattresses, microwaves, coffeemakers, screened porches, and solar-heated water. A new two-story house has an upstairs "villa" (with terra-cotta floors, a white-and-turquoise color scheme, mini-fridge, and spacious modern bathroom) and simpler downstairs unit. It has a restaurant and DVD movies, plus its own stables with sunrise and sunset rides. Rates include tax.

Cabinas Los Cocos (tel./fax 506/776-0012, loscocos@racsa.co.cr, $40–45 s/d low season, $50–55 s/d high season), about 600 meters north of Sol y Mar, has four attractive, self-catering oceanfront units tucked amid landscaped grounds and linked by walkways lined with shells. One is a thatched, hardwood unit with a double bed downstairs and another in the loft; two others are venerable refurbished banana-company properties shipped from Palmar. Each has a kitchenette, mosquito nets, both inside and outside showers, and a veranda with hammocks. The place is run by a delightful couple: Susan (a gringa) and Andrew (a Brit) Robertson.

Cabinas Arena Alta (tel. 506/776-0115, arenaalta@aol.com, www.costaricasailfish.com, $20 s/d low season, $65 s/d high season) sits beside the estuary at the north end of the village. Four modern albeit dark and uninspired a/c cabins face into the garden and have mirrored windows (to reflect sun), private bathrooms with hot water, and broad terraces with wooden swing seats. It specializes in sportfishing, and rents kayaks.

Roy's Zancudo Lodge (Apdo. 41, Golfito, tel. 506/776-0008 or 877/528-6980, fax 506/776-0011, fishroys@racsa.co.cr, www.royszancudo lodge.com, $110 pp), at the far north end of Zancudo, is a sportfishing lodge with eight *cabinas* and 12 hotel rooms in a two-story unit set around lawns with palms and a swimming pool. The two-tone-green a/c units have beautiful hardwood floors, simple furnishings, fans, telephones, private baths with hot water, and verandas. Larger units have a lounge and attractive fabrics. There's also a restaurant and bar with pool table. The lodge—which closes each October—uses 25-foot center console boats and holds 50 world records. Three-day packages start at $2,525 s, $4,300 d, including one night in San José, round-trip airfare from San José to Golfito, and boat transfer to Zancudo, plus meals, drinks, and accommodations. Rates include meals.

Food

For breakfast, head to **N Cabinas Sol y Mar,** where the menu includes real omelettes, French toast, home fries, home-baked breads and muffins, and coffee from a real espresso machine. The lunch and dinner menu includes "Western-style" food with an Italian and California twist. The nightly special when I visited was tuna with capers, rice, choyote squash, and green beans with roasted pepper sauce ($6). In high season, a French gourmet chef resides.

Zancudo Beach Club has a full menu ranging from Chinese to French, including choice porterhouse steaks served in the breezy upstairs restaurant overlooking the beach. It serves pizzas on Saturday nights, and chicken and ribs on Sunday.

Coloso del Mar (10 A.M.–10 P.M.) has a small roadside restaurant specializing in international fare slanted toward German.

I like the Italian-run, open-air **Restaurante Puerta Negra,** serving jumbo shrimp, homemade ravioli and pastas, and Italian wine. If it's closed, try **Restaurante Iguana Verde,** 200 meters north, and serving pizzas on Tuesday and Saturday.

Mini-Super Tres Amigos, opposite Zancudo Beach Club, and **Abastacedor Buen Precio,** at the south end of the village, sell groceries. There's a bakery just north of Roy's Zancudo Lodge.

Information and Services

There are public telephones along the main drag.

Cabinas Arena Alta (8 A.M.–4 P.M.) has an Internet café.

The police station (tel. 506/776-0166) is on the north side of Zancudo village.

Getting There

A bus departs from the municipal dock in Golfito for Zancudo daily at 2 P.M. Another departs Ciudad Neily for Zancudo at 1:30 P.M.

The paved road to Zancudo begins about eight km south of the Pan-American Highway, midway along the road to Golfito; the turn is signed at El Rodeo Salon, in únion. An aging two-car ferry will transport you across the Río Coto, 18 km beyond El Rodeo; the ferry operates daily 5 A.M.–8 P.M. ($1 per car, 20 cents pedestrians). On the south bank, the intermittently paved road runs five km to a Y-junction (La Cruce) at Pueblo Nuevo; turn right for Zancudo and Pavones and continue about 10 km to a T-junction at Conte. Turn right here: Zancudo (18 km) and Pavones (22 km) are signed. This road divides two km along; take the right-hand fork for Zancudo, and the left for Pavones.

The **Mini-Super Tres Amigos,** 100 meters north of Zancudo Beach Club, sells gas.

A *lancha* (water-taxi) departs Golfito's *muellecito* (dock) for Zancudo daily at between 11:30 A.M. to noon, returning from Zancudo at 6 A.M. ($2).

Golfo Dulce

Rio Coto ferry, near Zancudo

© CHRISTOPHER P. BAKER

The *Arena Alta Happy Hour* departs the pier at Samoa, in Golfito, at 8:30 A.M.

Zancudo Boat Tours at Cabinas Los Cocos also offers service ($20).

Getting Around

You can walk everywhere, but Zancudo is stretched out over several kilometers. Rent a bike from Los Cocos or Macondo. Locals get around on golf carts.

PAVONES

From Conte, a bumpy potholed road clambers over the hills south of Zancudo and drops to Punta Pilón and Pavones, a legend in the surfing world for possessing one of the longest waves in the world—more than a kilometer on a good day. The waves are at their best April through October, during rainy season, when surfers flock for the legendary very-fast-and-very-hollow tubular left. Riptides are common and swimmers should beware.

The fishing hamlet of **Pavones,** which is backed by hills clad in rainforest, was served by a single telephone at last visit; it's in the *pulpería*

next to the soccer field. The fishing for tarpon and snook is good right from shore.

The coast hereabouts is as beautiful as any in the country. South from Pavones, the dirt road crosses the Río Claro and follows the dramatically scenic and rocky coast about five km to the tiny beach community of **Punta Banco,** at the easternmost edge of Golfo Dulce. About two km south of Punta Banco you reach the end of the road. From here, the Peninsula de Burica sweeps southeast 50 km to Punta Burica along a lonesome stretch of coast within the **Reserva Indígena Guaymí,** protecting the mountainous lands of the Guaymí people.

In the late 1990s, the region went through a period of land disputes that resulted in the area getting negative press. That's all over now, thank goodness. In any event, tourists are not affected.

Tiskita Lodge

Farm. Nature lodge. Exotic-fruit station. Biological reserve. Seaside retreat. **Tiskita Lodge** (c/o Costa Rica Sun Tours, tel. 506/296-8125, fax 506/296-8133, tiskita@racsa.co.cr, www.tiskita-lodge .co.cr) is all these and more. Overlooking Punta

© CHRISTOPHER P. BAKER

bus to Pavones

Banco, one km north of the village, Tiskita—the Guaymí name for "fish eagle"—offers sweeping panoramas of the Pacific and the Osa Peninsula. The rustic old lodge is surrounded by 150 hectares of privately owned virgin rainforest, with pools for swimming and a Minotaur's maze of trails perfect for nature lovers; one leads to the beach (most follow the ridges, in old native fashion); another leads sharply uphill to a series of cascades and pools. Guided birding hikes are offered: a booklet helps bird-watchers identify scarlet-rumped and blue-gray tanagers, toucans, laughing falcons, blue parrots, macaws, etc. Horse rides cost $30 half-day.

Owner Peter Aspinall's pride and joy is his tropical-fruit farm, which contains the most extensive collection of tropical fruits in Costa Rica. Peter, who was raised locally and farmsteaded the property in the 1970s and has reforested vast acres of former pasture, is also involved in a scarlet macaw release program.

Tiskita Sea Turtle Restoration Project
Endangered ridley turtles (plus hawksbill and green turtles in lesser numbers) lay their eggs along these shores, predominantly in Aug.–Dec.

The locals have long considered them a resource to be harvested for eggs and meat, and the majority of female turtles have had their nests poached. In 1996, the Earth Island Institute began a program to instill a conservation ethic in the local community. It initiated a program to collect and hatch turtle eggs. Locals are now paid with groceries to bring in turtle eggs in good condition. Eggs are placed in a nursery to be incubated and the hatchlings then released directly into the ocean, dramatically increasing their chance of survival. Poaching of nests has been reduced from 100 percent of nests in 1995 to less than 20 percent, and the hatcheries now achieve a better than 80 percent hatching rate for translocated eggs.

Fundación Tiskita operates a small arts and crafts store (open 3–5 P.M. Tuesday, Friday, and Sunday) in Punta Banco.

Accommodations
Under $25: At Punta Banco, the impecunious might try **Pulpería Raquel,** with six simple upstairs rooms and outside bathrooms with cold water for $2.50 pp; or **Pulpería La Cuevita,** with similar rooms and prices.

In Pavones, the Italian-run **Soda/Restaurant La Piña,** (c_biasi@yahoo.com, $5 pp room, $10 pp cabin, $15 pp duplex), 400 meters north of the soccer field, permits camping, has one basic room above the restaurant with private bathroom, plus a more substantial cabin with wooden ceiling and tiled private bathroom. There's also a two-story duplex of timber and riverstone. The restaurant serves Italian dishes, including wood-oven pizza (a reader raves about the wholesome food), and the owners rent surfboards and offer horseback riding to the Guaymi reserve.

Cabinas Maureen ($10 pp with fan, $15 pp with a/c), facing the soccer field in the heart of Pavones, has six small albeit high-ceilinged, hardwood rooms in a two-story unit (each sleeps four people); they share four bathrooms. Rates: $6 pp. A stone's throw east is **Cabinas Willy Willy,** with four modern cabins: two with a/c and fan, and two with fan only. All have private bath with cold water.

I like the Italian-run **Cabinas y Pizzería Alerí** ($10 pp) nearby, with four spacious, simply furnished rooms and a pizza (and pasta) parlor amid

landscaped grounds. The rooms have stucco walls, fans, orthopedic mattresses, tiled private bathrooms, and French doors opening to views.

There are half a dozen other budget accommodations of a similar standard within shouting distance.

Cabinas La Ponderosa (Apdo. 109-8201 Golfito, tel. 506/824-4145, www.cabinaslaponderosa.com; in the U.S., 5281 N.W. 19th Ave., Fort Lauderdale, FL 33308, tel. 954/771-9166; $25 pp with fan, $36 pp with a/c, $75 house), about 400 meters south, is a surfers' lodge run by U.S. surfer dudes. It's set in lush gardens and offers five well-made, handsome two-story cabins with varnished hardwoods, fans, large screened windows, and private baths with hot water; three have a/c. A dining room serves everything from burgers and tuna melts to seafood. It has a lounge with bar, TV/VCR, ping-pong, and sand volleyball court. It also rents a two-bedroom house with king-size bed and kitchen. It has meal plans.

The U.S.-run **Cabinas Mira Olas** (Apdo. 32, Golfito, cellular tel. 506/393-7742, $25 s/d small unit, $30 s/d large unit; $120/160 weekly) has two beautifully decorated albeit rustic log *cabinas* with fans, kitchenettes, and outdoor showers with warm water. They're set amid lush lawns.

I adore the gorgeous  **Casa Siempre Domingo Bed and Breakfast** (tel./fax 506/820-4709, heidi@casa-domingo.com, www.casa-domingo.com, $50 s/d), a deluxe, breeze-brushed Colorado-style lodge nestled on the hillside 400 meters inland, 1.5 km south of the Río Claro. Owned and run by East Coasters Greg and Heidi, this beautiful lodge is set amid hibiscus-tinged lawns surrounded by 15 acres of jungle-clad slopes (trails leads into the rainforest). A mammoth cathedral ceiling soars over the lounge and dining room done up in evocative tropical style, with plentiful bamboo and jungly prints. The four rooms have two doubles or a double and single, ceramic tile floors, plus walk-in closets. The restaurant serves hearty fare. There's a laundry. And you'll enjoy dramatic ocean vistas from the sprawling deck. Rates include breakfast.

I also like the U.S.-run **Sotavento Plantanal,** tel. 506/391-3468, hilario@sotaventoplantanal

© CHRISTOPHER P. BAKER

Pavones palms

Golfo Dulce

© CHRISTOPHER P. BAKER

Guaymi Indian girl on horseback at Pavones

.com, www.sotaventoplantanal.com, $60 Casa Poinsietta, $80 Casa Vista Grande) offers two simple hillside wooden houses with tremendous views. The first, in a two-story unit with TV lounge and kitchen, has two bedrooms with wooden shutters, mosquito nets, old wooden trunks for seats, and a large walk-in shower. The second, also two stories and higher up the slope, has two bedrooms and a massive dining table in the open kitchen. You can rent horses and surfboards, and boogie boards and fishing poles come free.

I recommend **Tiskita Lodge** (see above, $135 s, $220 d low season, $145/240 high season), centered on a charming old farmhouse that serves as lounge and dining room. There are 16 spacious rooms in nine rustic, sparsely furnished, but huge and comfortable wooden cabins accommodating up to 28 people in a combination of double, twin, and bunk beds (with rather soft mattresses). Each cabin has screened windows, beamed ceiling, wide veranda with hammock and Adirondack chair, plus a stone-lined outdoor bathroom with shower and solar-heated water. At last visit, rooms were being upgraded. A water-powered Pelton wheel and solar panels

provide electricity. "Country-style" meals are served family-style at set times (don't be late), and packed lunches are provided for hikers. It has a small swimming pool and a rustic bar. It closes mid-Sept.–mid-Oct. Two- to seven-day packages are offered. Rates include meals plus guided walks.

Food

The best place is **Café de la Suerte** (7:30 A.M.– 5:30 P.M., $3) on the plaza in Pavones. This simple open-air eatery serves granola with yogurt and fruit, plus sandwiches, hummus, omelettes, cappuccinos, and fruit shakes. Next door, **Restaurante Surfer** (6 A.M.–10 P.M.), at Cabinas Maureen, has a TV and serves *típico* dishes. Nearby, the beachfront **Esquina del Mar** is the center of social life hereabouts and has ping-pong, a dart board, and dominoes.

The **La Manta Club,** in Pavones, sells falafel, hummus, shish kebab, and ice creams, iced teas, and iced coffee drinks, enjoyed in a splendid thatched bar with hammocks. Movies are shown on a big screen at 6 P.M.

There's a grocery—**Abastecedor Willy Willy**— next to Café de la Suerte.

surfers at Pavones

At Punta Banco, I like the simple, open-air **Rancho Marea Alta,** serving seafoods and local fare. You can buy groceries at **Mini-Super Punta Banco.**

Information and Services
The public telephone (tel. 506/770-8221) is at Soda La Plaza, beside the soccer field in Pavones.

Waves Arte Nativo (tel./fax 506/383-6939, nativo@racsa.co.cr, 1–5 P.M. Mon.–Sat.), in Pavones, is a gift store that also offers telephone, fax, and Internet service.

There's a police station four km north of Pavones.

La Manta Club (see above) has a laundry.

Getting There
A private airstrip allows direct access to Tiskita by chartered plane (55 minutes from San José).

A bus departs Golfito for Pavones and Punta Banco at 10:30 A.M. and 3 P.M., returning at 5 A.M. and noon.

See *Zancudo,* above, for a description of the route by car. Note that the coast road that leads south from Pavones ends at the mouth of the Río Claro, one km south of the village. To cross it and continue to Punta Banco, back up and turn inland at Escuela Las Gemelas, then right at Super Mares; you'll cross a bridge, then drop back down to the coast. Tiskita is one km farther south. A 4WD taxi will cost you about $50 from Golfito.

You can drive by 4WD between Zancudo and Pavones along the beach, *but only at low tide.* Don't attempt this without trustworthy local advice, otherwise the sea will take your car.

A private water-taxi charter from Golfito will cost about $65 one-way.

Dr. Bob Bacher (tel. 305/931-0918, chentaijiinternational@yahoo.com, http://chentaiji international.com) offers personalized tai chi vacation packages to Pavones.

Ciudad Neily and Vicinity

CIUDAD NEILY

Ciudad Neily squats at the base of the Fila Costeña mountains, beside the Pan-American Highway, 18 km northwest of Panamá and 15 km east of Río Claro and the turnoff for Golfito. The town is surrounded by banana plantations and functions as the node for plantation operations. There is nothing to hold your interest, though you are likely to see indigenous women in colorful traditional dress, usually sitting on the sidewalk with their children, begging for a meager living.

North from Ciudad Neily, a road switchbacks steeply 1,000 meters to San Vito (31 km). It has many hairpin bends and offers views. South from town, a road leads through a sea of African palm plantations (owned by Palma Tica) to the airstrip at **Coto 47**. Highway 2 continues southeast to the Panamanian border. The valley of the Río Corredores has one of the nation's largest **caverns**, full of stalagmites and stalactites; blind fish swim in the river flowing within the stygian gloom.

Accommodations

There's no shortage of budget hotels in the $5–15 range. Hot water is a luxury. One of the best bets is **Cabinas Heileen** (tel. 506/783-3080, $5 pp with fans, $8 pp with TVs), in a nicely kept home festooned with epiphytes. Its 10 simple but clean rooms have fans and private baths with cold water (one room has hot water). Five rooms have TVs.

To catch an early bus, check into **Hotel Cabinas El Rancho** (tel. 506/783-3060, $7 s, $12 d with fan; $15 s, $22 d with a/c and TV), next to the bus station. It has handsome albeit simple cabins with a/c, cable TV, and telephones; plus more basic cubicle-type rooms with private baths in a large courtyard, with a bar and restaurant.

The nicest place in town is **Hotel Andrea** (tel./fax 506/783-3784, $19 s/d with fans, $24 s/d with a/c), with 35 rooms in a handsome two-story colonial-style property festooned with hanging plants, 50 meters west of the bus station. Rooms are clean, with tile floors and modest furnishings. All have TV and hot water, and 14 have a/c. It has secure parking, and an appealing open-air restaurant and bar. A bargain!

Food

Hotel Andrea (6 A.M.–12:30 A.M., $1.50–5) has the most elegant eatery in town. The menu includes pancakes and honey, huevos rancheros, omelettes, plus onion soup, shrimp salad, pastas, and filet mignon.

The clean, modern **Restaurante La Moderna** (tel. 506/783-3097), on the main street, one block east of the plaza, has an eclectic menu ranging from burgers and pizza to ceviche and *típico* dishes; I enjoyed a superb garlic sea bass in a special house sauce *(salsa especial)*. The best of several Chinese options is **Restaurante Hua Guen,** on Hwy. 2.

You can stock up on groceries at the **Palí** supermarket, opposite the bus station; and baked goods at **Deli Pan del Sur.**

Information and Services

The hospital is 1.5 km southeast of town on Hwy. 2. There are doctors' offices immediately north of the plaza, and several pharmacies around town. The **Red Cross** (tel. 506/783-3757) is on the northeast side of town, opposite the **police station** (no tel.; call the public phone outside, tel. 506/783-4066).

There are three banks in the center.

The post office is on the northeast side of town. **Internet** (tel. 506/783-4492), at the north end of town, charges $4 per hour before 4 P.M., $1.75 per hour 4–10 P.M.

Getting There

The airport is four km south of town, at Coto 47; it is hidden away from the road (the turnoff is beside the public telephone booth at the roadside, half a kilometer before the paving gives out). **Sansa** (tel. 506/257-9414, www.grupotaca.com)

Golfo Dulce

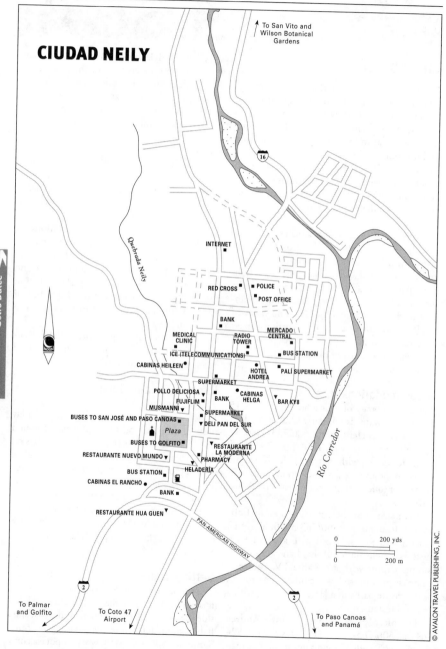

CIUDAD NEILY

To San Vito and
Wilson Botanical
Gardens

16

INTERNET

RED CROSS ■ POLICE
■ POST OFFICE

BANK ■

MEDICAL   RADIO   MERCADO
CLINIC   TOWER   CENTRAL
■ ICE (TELECOMMUNICATIONS)■   ■ BUS STATION

CABINAS HEILEEN ●   HOTEL   PALÍ SUPERMARKET
                                     ANDREA ■
                         SUPERMARKET ■
POLLO DELICIOSA ▼   ■ CABINAS
          FUJIFLIM ▼   BANK ■ HELGA ▼ BAR KY8
     MUSMANNI ▼
BUSES TO SAN JOSÉ AND PASO CANOAS ■ ▼ SUPERMARKET
                         ▼ DELI PAN DEL SUR
                    Plaza
     BUSES TO GOLFITO ■   ▼ RESTAURANTE
                               LA MODERNA
RESTAURANTE NUEVO MUNDO ▼ ▼ PHARMACY
     BUS STATION ■   ▼ HELADERÍA
CABINAS EL RANCHO ●
          BANK ■

RESTAURANTE HUA GUEN ▼
          PAN-AMERICAN HIGHWAY

Quebrada Neily

MOON

Río Corredor

0   200 yds
0   200 m

© AVALON TRAVEL PUBLISHING, INC.

Golfo Dulce

2
To Palmar
and Golfito

To Coto 47
Airport

2
To Paso Canoas
and Panamá

and **Nature Air** (tel. 506/220-3054, www .natureair.com) both have scheduled service to Coto 47.

Buses (tel. 506/222-2666) depart San José for Ciudad Neily from Calle 14, Avenidas 3/5, at 5 A.M., 7:30 A.M., 11 A.M., 1 P.M., 4:30 P.M., and 6 P.M. (eight hours). Buses for San José depart Ciudad Neily at 4:10 A.M., 5:30 A.M., 9 A.M., and 3 P.M.; and for Golfito hourly 6 A.M.–7 P.M.; for Paso Canoas (on the Panamá border) hourly 6 A.M.–6 P.M.; for Puerto Jiménez at 7 A.M. and 2 P.M.; for San Vito at 6 A.M., 11 A.M., 1 P.M., and 3 P.M.; and for Cortes at 4:45 A.M., 6 A.M., 9:15 A.M., noon, 2:30 P.M., 4:30 P.M., and 5:45 P.M.

For taxis call **Taxi Ciudad Neily** (tel. 506/783-3374).

PASO CANOAS: CROSSING INTO PANAMÁ

There's absolutely no reason to visit ugly, stinky Paso Canoas unless you intend to cross into Panamá (see the sidebar *Crossing into Nicaragua and Panamá,* in the *Know Costa Rica* section). Endless stalls and shops selling duty-free goods are strung out along the road paralleling the border. Avoid Easter week and the months before Christmas, when Paso Canoas is a zoo.

In past years, cars departing town were searched at the Customs checkpoint on the Pan-American Highway, at the entrance to town, even if you hadn't crossed into Panamá. At last visit this was no longer true.

Accommodations and Food

There are lots of accommodation choices, though all have only cold water unless noted. Few are worth recommending.

One of the best options is the modern, motel-style **Cabinas Alpina** (tel. 506/732-2018, $4 pp for basic rooms, $14 s/d for nicer a/c rooms upstairs), two blocks south of the bus terminal, offering rooms away from the bustle with tiled floors, TVs, and private baths. It also has secure parking and a laundry. Opposite, the salmon-pink **Hotel Azteca** (tel. 506/732-2217, $6 pp with fan, $10 with a/c), another of the nicer

properties, has 49 rooms with private bath but cold water only; four have a/c and TV. It has a pleasant restaurant.

Even nicer is the modern **Hotel Real Victoria** (tel. 506/732-2586, fax 506/732-2762, $12 s/d with fan, $20 s/d with a/c and TV), one block east, with 33 modest but adequate rooms with fans, and private baths with cold water only. It has a small swimming pool, small restaurant, and secure parking.

The best eatery is **Restaurante Brunca Steak House,** opposite the bus terminal and popular with truckers. Several *sodas* near the border post sell cheap *casados* (set luncheons).

Information and Services

There's a bank 100 meters west of the border post. The police station, (tel. 506/732-2106) is 100 meters west of the border post. **Customs** and **immigration** (tel. 506/732-2150) are next to the bus terminal.

Getting There

Buses (tel. 506/222-2666) depart San José for Paso Canoas from Calle 14, Avenidas 3/5, daily at 5 A.M., 7:30 A.M., 11 A.M., 1 P.M., 4:30 P.M., and 6 P.M. (eight hours, approximately $6.50). Buses leave Paso Canoas for San José at 4:10 A.M., 7:30 A.M., 9 A.M., and 3 P.M. Buses also run frequently from Ciudad Neily to the border (about 25 cents), and from Golfito almost hourly, 5:30 A.M.–6:15 A.M. Weekend buses to and from Paso Canoas fill up early; reservations are recommended. Local buses depart for Neily every hour.

See the chart *Buses from San José,* in the *San José* chapter, for bus service to Panamá.

There's a gas station just west of town.

Taxis wait in front of the border crossing (about $10 to Ciudad Neily).

▼ COCO ISLAND NATIONAL PARK

The only true oceanic island off Central America, Isla Cocos—500 km southwest of Costa Rica—is a 52-square-km mountainous chunk of land that rises to 634 meters at Iglesias Peak.

Golfo Dulce

Declared a UNESCO World Heritage Site in 1997, the island is the northernmost and oldest of a chain of volcanoes, mostly submarine, stretching south along the Cocos Ridge to the equator, where several come to the surface as the Galápagos Islands. These islands were formed by a hot spot, which pushes up volcanic material from beneath the earth's crust. The hot spot remains stationary while the sea floor moves across it. Over time, the volcanic cone is transported away from the hot spot and a new volcano arises in the same place.

Cliffs reach higher than 100 meters around almost the entire island and dramatic waterfalls cascade onto the beach.

The island was discovered in 1526 by Juan Cabezas and first appeared on a map in 1542. Prisoners lived here in watery solitude in the late 1800s, and occasional settlers have tried to eke a living. Today it is inhabited only by national park guards who patrol the park equipped with small Zodiacs. The only safe anchorage for entry is at Chatham Bay, on the northeast corner, where scores of rocks are etched with the names and dates of ships dating back to the 17th century.

PIRATES' GOLD ON COCO ISLAND

Cocos' forested hills supposedly harbor gold doubloons. More than 500 expeditions have sought in vain to find the Lima Booty—gold and silver ingots that mysteriously disappeared while en route to Spain under the care of Captain James Thompson. The pirate William Davies supposedly hid his treasure here in 1684, as did Portuguese buccaneer Benito "Bloody Sword" Bonito in 1889. The government has placed a "virtual moratorium" on treasure hunts, although the Ministry of Natural Resources sanctioned a hunt in January 1992 by North American computer company owner John Hodges—for a rights fee of $100,000. Christopher Weston's book *Cocos Island—Old Pirate's Haven* (San José: Imprenta y Litografia Trejos, 1990) tells the island's tale.

There are no native mammals. The surrounding waters, however, are home to four unique species of marine mollusks. One endemic plant is christened Franklin Roosevelt, after the U.S. president who made several visits to the island. The island has one butterfly and two lizard species to call its own. And three species of birds are endemic: the Cocos Island finch, Cocos Island cuckoo, and the Ridgeway or Cocos flycatcher (the Cocos Island finch is a subspecies of the famous Galápagos finches, which inspired Darwin's revolutionary theory of evolution). Three species of boobies—red-footed, masked, and brown—live here, too. Cocos is also a popular spot for frigate birds to roost and mate. The white tern, which may hover above your head, is the *espíritu santu,* or Holy Spirit bird. Feral pigs, introduced in the 18th century by passing sailors, today number about 5,000 and have caused substantial erosion. The island's isolation attracts poachers seeking black coral, seashells, and lobster, and fishermen who violate the no-fishing zone to net sharks for fins, which are treasured in Asia.

Access to the island is restricted.

Friends of Cocos Island (FAICO, tel. 240-9383, www.cocosisland.org) works to protect the area from illegal fishing.

Diving

The island is one of the world's best diving spots, famous for its massive schools of white-tipped and hammerhead sharks and eerie manta rays, pilot whales, whale sharks, and sailfish. *Cocos is for experienced divers only:* drop-offs are deep, currents are continually changing, and beginning divers would freak at the huge shark populations (in fact, converging ocean currents stir up such a wealth of nutrients that the sharks have a surfeit of fish to feed on, and taking a chunk out of divers is probably the last thing on their minds). Snorkelers swimming closer to the surface can revel in moray eels and colorful reef fish.

Four vessels are used for diving at Cocos Island, usually operating 10-day itineraries out of Los Sueños Marina. The *Okeanos Aggressor* (P.O. Box 330-1000, San José, tel. 506/257-0191, ext. 196, fax 506/256-8095, sales@okeanoscocosisland

.com, www.okeanoscocosisland.com; in the U.S., tel. 866/653-2667) is a 34-meter, fully a/c, 10-stateroom ship with complete facilities for 21 divers, including an E-2 film processing lab and helicopter landing pad. It offers eight-, nine-, and 10-day trips from $3,095 pp all-inclusive (the $35 per day park fee is extra).

The *Undersea Hunter* (tel. 506/228-6613, fax 506/289 -7334, info@underseahunter.com, www.underseahunter.com; in the U.S., P.O. Box 025216, Dept. 314, Miami, FL 33102-5216) is a 27-meter steel-hull ship with two compressors and 50 tanks, seven cabins, and a capacity for 14 divers. Its larger sister ship, the *Sea Hunter,* is a 38-meter steel vessel that accommodates 18 divers in eight cabins, all with private bath. There's a film processing lab and two eight-meter dive boats, plus a helicopter landing pad and movie theater.

Cabo Blanco Divers (tel. 506/825-2918, fax 506/642-0467, caboblancodivers@yahoo.com, www.caboblancodivers.com) offers trips.

Information

For information, contact the National Parks Service (tel. 506/283-0022 or tel./fax 506/258-7350, islacoco@ns.minae.co.cr), or the **ranger station** (satellite tel. 0087-468712-0010). There are no accommodations, and camping is not allowed.

Golfo Dulce

South-Central Costa Rica

The south-central region is the Cinderella of Costa Rican tourism. A larger proportion of the region is protected as national park or forest reserve than in any other part of the country. Much—in fact the majority—remains inaccessible and unexplored. Herein lies the beauty: huge regions such as Chirripó National Park and La Amistad International Peace Park, of which Chirripó is part, harbor incredibly diverse populations of Central American flora and fauna.

The region is dominated to the east by the massive and daunting Talamanca massif. Slanting southeast and paralleling the Talamancas to the west is a range of lower-elevation mountains called the Fila Costeña. Between the two lies the 100-km-long by 30-km-wide Valle de El General, extending into the Valle de Coto Brus to the south. The valley is a center of agriculture, with pineapples covering the flatlands of the Río General, and coffee smothering the slopes of Coto Brus. The rivers that drain the valley merge to form the Río Grande de Terraba, which slices through the Fila Costeña to reach the sea.

The region is home to the nation's largest concentration of indigenous people. In the remote highland reaches, and occasionally in towns, you'll see indigenous Guaymis and Borucas women dressed in traditional colorful garb, often walking barefoot, their small frames laden with

babies or bulging bags. Like native people worldwide, they are caught in a vicious cycle of poverty. But, says Gail Hewson, director of Finca Cantaros, "These people are not at all preoccupied by the fact that they are poor. In fact [they] are extravagantly rich in spirit and cheerfulness."

The regional climate varies with topography. The saturated clouds moving in from the Pacific dump most of their rain on the western slopes of the Fila Costeña, and the Valle de El General sits in a rain shadow. To the east, the Talamanca massif is rain-drenched and fog bound for much of the year; rainfall increases southward. Temperatures drop as elevation climbs and atop the Talamancas approach freezing.

PLANNING YOUR TIME

The region is linked to San José by the Pan-American Highway (Hwy. 2), which runs south from Cartago, climbs over the Cerro de la Muerte, and descends to San Isidro (also known as Pérez Zeledón) in the Valle de El General. South of Buenos Aires, the Pan-Am exits the valley via the gorge of the Río Grande de Terraba, linking it with the Golfo Dulce region. Another road transcends the Fila Costeña and links San Isidro de El General with Dominical on the central Pacific coast. The daunting and dangerous drive over Cerro de la Muerte should not be underrated. If you're a timid driver, consider taking the alternate and much longer route via the Costanera Sur highway, which grants access to South Central region via Dominical. Otherwise, the drive is to be enjoyed as one of the nation's most scenic.

The main regional centers of **San Isidro** (in the north) and **San Vito** (in the south) make logical bases for exploring further afield.

Most travelers pass the region by in their haste to and from the Golfo Dulce region. True, tourist facilities might appear at first glance to be relatively undeveloped. But travelers seeking virtually unexplored terrain find nirvana in the remote **Talamancas,** where rugged hiking trails grant access to lightly populated areas teeming with wildlife. A less challenging option is the popular trek up Chirripó, the nation's highest mountain, enshrined within **Chirripó National Park.** Even for non-trekkers, the **Río Chirripó Valley** is a delightful Shangri-la good for birding, and invigorating for its crisp alpine setting; it makes a great excursion from San Isidro. Some of the best birding is at **Los Cusingos Neotropical Bird Sanctuary;** and at **Las Cruces Biological Station,** with well-maintained trails, rivaling anywhere in the country for wildlife viewing. Las Cruces' **Wilson Botanical Garden** is a superlative among tropical gardens, a tonic for your spirits in even the rainiest weather. And **Avalon Reserve and Biological Station,** between Cerro de la Muerte and San Isidro, is recommended for its sublime setting and for hiking in cloud forest where quetzals are commonly seen.

Much of the mountain fastness is incorporated within indigenous reserves, such as **Boruca Indian Reserve,** which welcomes visitors. Tourist facilities are minimal.

As yet, the region lacks a canopy tour. And other organized activities are minimal, with the exception of **whitewater rafting** on the Ríos Chirripó and General.

Selva Mar (tel. 506/771-4582, fax 506/771-8841, selvamar@racsa.co.cr, www.exploring costarica.com) acts as a tour information center and reservation service for lodging and tours throughout the region. Also visit www.costaric-asur.com for regional information.

Must-Sees

M **Avalon Biological Station:** This high-mountain cloud-forest reserve has nature trails and is a great place to spot quetzals. Accommodations are rustic, but charming for it (page 572).

M **Los Cusingos Bird Sanctuary:** Birders should make haste to this fabulous birding site, where visitors can commune with one of the prime neotropical ornithologists (page 573).

M **Río Chirripó Valley:** Tucked into a fold of the Talamanca mountains, this splendidly scenic valley is home to **Chirripó National Park.** Its fabulous opportunities for birding and hiking culminate in the two-day hike to the summit of Chirripó (page 576).

M **Las Cruces Biological Station:** This reserve and research station has miles of nature trails through humid montane ecosystems, offering magnificent wildlife viewing. The highlight is the **Wilson Botanical Garden,** a jewel among tropical botanical gardens (page 589).

Río Chirripó

© CHRISTOPHER P. BAKER

South-Central

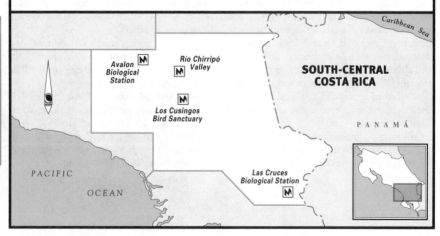

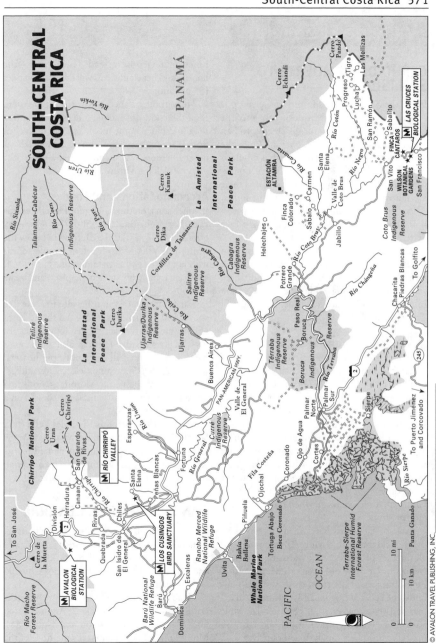

South-Central

© AVALON TRAVEL PUBLISHING, INC.

Valle de El General

CERRO DE LA MUERTE TO SAN ISIDRO

From the 3,491-meter summit of Cerro de la Muerte, about 100 km south of San José, the Pan-American Highway drops steeply to San Isidro, in the Valle de El General. When the clouds part, you are rewarded with a fabulous vista, the whole Valle de El General spread out before you. The route is often fog-bound and there are many large trucks—some without lights. There are frequent landslides, fathoms-deep potholes, and too many accidents for comfort. Take extreme care. Avoid this road at night!

A statue of Christ balances precariously on the cliff face above the highway two km north of **San Rafael** (Km 104). A small, traditional *trapiche* (ox-driven sugar mill) is still in operation immediately below at a roadside *soda* called **El Trapiche de Nayo.**

🅜 Avalon Biological Station

This 150-hectare private reserve and biological research station (Apdo 846, San Isidro de El General, tel. 506/380-2107 or tel./fax 506/771-2264, glenmom@racsa.co.cr), at 2,800 meters elevation, high atop a ridge of the Talamancas known as the Fila Zapotales, is named for the mythical kingdom of Arthurian legend where a priestess magically lifts the mists on the far side of the holy lake. Appropriately, the lodge sits in the midst of cloud forest, with spectacular views down over the Valle de El General. Time your soak for 8 P.M. or so, when the clouds religiously part.

Most of the guests here are volunteers, who come to do trail maintenance, landscaping, and all manner of chores. Bird-watching is superb (with similar flora and fauna to Monteverde), including lots of quetzals, three-wattled bellbirds, the collared trogon, and toucanets. An expert bird-watching guide costs $60 per day, while a two-hour Cloud-Forest Birding hike costs $3 pp. Hikes include a tough three-hour river walk ($6), and a five-hour slog to waterfalls ($8) with

lunch in a Tico farmstead. Gwenavyer—the horse—and her equine pals will take you on rides ($5 per hour).

The turnoff is signed at Km 107, at División. It's a three-km drive along a deeply rutted dirt road (4WD recommended). You can take a bus from Coca-Cola to San Isidro de El General; get off at División, where you can get a taxi at the *pulpería* (ask for Arturo).

Accommodations and Food

If you're stuck on the mountain, **Hotel/Restaurant Las Georgina** (tel. 506/770-8043, fax 506/279-9511, $7.50–18 d), five km below the summit at Villa Mills, has four simple rooms with hot water: two have bunks; one has a TV. It also has a cabin with kitchen, fireplace, and views for $60.

You can camp at **Avalon Private Reserve** (see above, $10 pp in bunks, $25–30 d shared bath, $50 private bath), which also has four rustic cabins with private baths. There are also some rooms with shared bath. All have portable heaters, woolen blankets, hot water, electricity, and astounding views best enjoyed from a wood-fired hot tub. Simple yet tasty meals are cooked on a wood-fired stove.

At Km 119 is **Mirador Vista del Valle** (tel./fax 506/384-4685, ciprotur@racsa.co.cr, www.ecotourism.co.cr), a restaurant named for its stunning view. It has a simple wooden *cabina,* and bird-watching and fishing are offered.

SAN ISIDRO DE EL GENERAL

San Isidro, regional capital of the Valle de El General, is an agricultural market town; gateway to Chirripó National Park and Dominical; and a base for rafting trips on the Ríos Chirripó and General.

There is little to see in town. The small **Southern Regional Museum** (Calle 2, Avenida 1, tel. 506/771-5273, 8 A.M.–noon and 1–4:30 P.M. Mon.–Fri., free admission) tells the story of the local indigenous peoples.

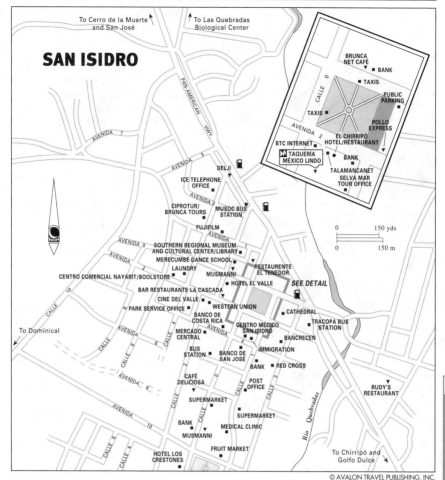

© AVALON TRAVEL PUBLISHING, INC.

Attesting to San Isidro's lack of classical lineage (the town was founded in 1897, though most of it is post-WWII) is the concrete carbuncle—ahem, I mean **cathedral**—on the east side of the plaza, looking like a massive Nazi fortification transplanted from Normandy.

Los Cusingos Bird Sanctuary

This 142-hectare bird sanctuary, in Quizarrá de Pérez Zeledón, on the lower slopes of Chirripó, near the small community of Santa Elena, 15 km southeast of San Isidro, is owned by Dr.

Alexander Skutch (co-author with Gary Stiles of *Birds of Costa Rica*) and run by the Tropical Science Center. The reserve is surrounded by primary forest, home to more than 300 bird species. Visits are allowed by appointment only. Admission is limited to researchers, students, naturalists, and bird-watchers.

You get there via General Viejo (five km east of San Isidro from the San Gerardo de Rivas road, then south for Peñas Blanca) or from the Hwy. 2 via Peñas Blancas (then north for General Viejo). Turn east for Quizarra-Santa Elena. After three

statue of Christ off the Pan-American Highway near San Isidro

km go straight at the crossroads for Santa Elena. At the cemetery, go downhill for Los Cusingos.

For information, contact the Tropical Science Center (P.O. Box 8-3870-1000, San José, tel. 506/253-3276, fax 506/253-4963, cusingos@cct .or.cr, www.cct.or.cr/cusin_in.htm).

Entertainment and Events

The town comes alive late January and early February for its **Fiesta Cívica,** when agricultural fairs, bullfights, and general festivities occur. The best time to visit, however, is 15 May, for the **Día del Boyero** (Day of the Oxcart Driver), featuring a colorful oxcart parade.

The upstairs, open-air **Bar Restaurante La Cascada** is the local gathering spot of choice. For dancing, try **Tai Kee Disco,** just north of Hotel del Sur Country Club, which has a casino (7 P.M.–4 A.M. nightly) or **Winds Disco** (tel. 506/771-6462, open Tue.–Sun.), 3.5 km north of town, at Mirador La Torre.

Accommodations

Most options for budget travelers are grim and can't be recommended.

Try the **Hotel/Restaurante El Chirripó** (tel. 506/771-0529, fax 506/771-0410, $5 s, $9 d shared bath; $9 s, $15 d private bath and TV), on the southwest side of the square and offering 41 rooms with hot water, plus a pleasing outdoor restaurant. The **Hotel El Valle** (Calle 2, Avenida 0, tel. 506/771-0246, $7 pp shared bath; $10 s, $16 d private bath and TV) has 18 well-lit rooms with fans, balconies, and hot water.

A better bet is the modern **Hotel y Restaurante San Isidro** (tel. 506/770-3444, fax 506/770-3673, $11 s, $20 d), two km south of town. Centered on a two-story atrium, it has 40 smallish a/c rooms modestly furnished with contemporary decor, fans, cable TV, and clean bathrooms with hot water. It has an Internet café and secure parking.

The class act in town is **Hotel Los Crestones** (tel. 506/770-1200, fax 506/771-6012, hcrestones @racsa.co.cr, $35 s, $40 d with fan, $40 s, $45 d with a/c), a tranquil three-story property done up in a complimentary cream-and-green color scheme, and tasteful rattan furniture. It has 16 rooms (some with a/c) with ceiling fans, cable TV, balconies festooned with climbing plants, and modern bathrooms. It has a small but elegant café-restaurant, plus secure parking.

The **Hotel del Sur Country Club & Casino** (Apdo. 4-8000, San Isidro, tel. 506/771-3033, fax 506/771-0527, $45 s, $48 d standard; $65 s, $68 d superior), six km south of San Isidro, is popular with businessfolk. However, the 27 a/c standard rooms with satellite TV are dowdy and overpriced. It also has 20 newly renovated suites plus 10 self-sufficient *cabinas* with separate living and dining room. Some rooms are handicapped-equipped. A restaurant and bar opens onto a heavily chlorinated swimming pool and landscaped grounds with volleyball and tennis courts. There's a casino.

Food

The **Restaurant Chirripó** (7 A.M.–10 P.M.), facing the plaza, is recommended for an early breakfast. It also serves *casados* (set meals). **Rudy's**

Restaurant (tel. 506/771-7393), an American diner off the main highway, south of town, also has a large breakfast menu, and later in the day serves tuna salad, nachos, and charbroiled or Cajun chicken.

The nicest place in town is **Bar Restaurante La Cascada** (Avenida 2, Calle 2), with potted plants, an open-air terrace, and a reasonably priced international menu. Another clean and appealing option is **Delji** (tel. 506/773-5747), a U.S.-style diner serving roast chicken, burgers, and sandwiches. It also has an outlet off Hwy. 2 at Calle 4.

I always gravitate to the nicely decorated **N Taquería México Lindo** (tel. 506/771-8222, 9:30 A.M.–8 P.M. Mon.–Sat., $1–5), on the west side of the plaza, where a Mexican cook produces the real enchilada, plus burritos and other dishes. Be sure to try the coconut and vanilla flans.

For baked goods, cappuccinos, espressos, etc., I prefer **Café Deliciosa,** (Avenida 8, Calles 0/2), where you can dine outside on the patio; **Musmanni** has outlets three blocks southwest of the plaza, and at Avenida 0, Calles 0/2.

You can eat cheaply at *sodas* at the **Mercado Central,** adjoining the bus station.

Information and Services

The regional promotion board, **CIPROTUR** (tel. 506/770-9393, ciprotur@racsa.co.cr), has a tourist information office at Calle 4, Avenidas 1/3. **Selva Mar** (Calle 1, Avenidas 2/4, tel. 506/771-4582, fax 506/771-8841, selvamar @racsa.co.cr, www.exploringcostarica.com) offers complete tourist information and acts as a reservation service.

The regional **Parks Service office** (Calle 2, Avenidas 4/6, tel. 506/771-3155 or 506/771-4836, fax 506/771-3297, aclap@ms.minae.go.cr, 8 A.M.–noon and 1–4 P.M. Mon.–Fri.) administers La Amistad International Peace Park.

The **hospital** (tel. 506/771-3122) is on the southwest side of town. Medical centers include **Centro Médico San Isidro** (Avenida 4, Calles Central/1, tel. 506/771-4467). There are several pharmacies.

There are several banks in the town center; see the maps. **BanCrecen,** two blocks west of the plaza on Avenida 2, represents **Western Union** (tel. 506/771-8535, 9 A.M.–9 P.M. Mon.–Fri., 9 A.M.–2 P.M. Saturday).

The **post office** (tel. 506/770-1669) is three blocks south of the plaza, on Calle 1. There are plenty of telephones throughout town.

You can send and receive email at **Brunca Net Café** (tel. 506/771-3235, brunc@netcafe.com), on the northeast side of the plaza; and at **BTC Internet** (8:30 A.M.–9 P.M. Mon.–Fri., 8 A.M.–8 P.M. Saturday, and 10 A.M.–4 P.M. Sunday), on the plaza's south side.

There's a laundry on Calle 4, Avenidas 0/2.

Fujicolor (Avenida 1, Calles 2/4, tel. 506/771-4563) sells film.

The library (Calle 2, Avenida 1, 7 A.M.–noon and 1:30–5:30 P.M. Mon.–Fri.) is above the museum.

Getting There

Buses (tel. 506/222-2422) depart Calle Central, Avenida 22, in San José at 5:30 A.M. 6:30 A.M., 7:30 A.M., 8:30 A.M., 9:30 A.M., 10:30 A.M., 11:30 A.M., 12:30 P.M., 1:30 P.M., 2:30 P.M., 3:30 P.M., 4:30 P.M., 5 P.M., and 5:30 P.M. Return buses (in San Isidro, tel. 506/771-0414) depart from Hwy. 2 at the junction of Avenida 0 in San Isidro at 5 A.M., 5:30 A.M., 6:30 A.M., 7 A.M., 7:30 A.M., 8:30 A.M., 9:30 A.M., 10:30 A.M., 11:30 A.M., 12:30 P.M., 1:30 P.M., 2:30 P.M., 3:30 P.M., 4:30 P.M., and 5:30 A.M.

The regional bus station in San Isidro is at Calle Central and Avenidas 4/6. Transportes Blanco (tel. 506/771-2550) operates buses from Quepos via Dominical at 5 A.M. and 1:30 P.M., returning from San Isidro at 5 A.M. and 1:30 P.M.; and from Uvita via Dominical at 6 A.M. and 2 P.M., returning at 6 A.M. and 3 P.M. You can also catch Tracopa buses to Buenos Aires, Ciudad Neily, David in Panamá, Golfito, Palmar, Puerto Jiménez, and San Vito. Buses depart for San Gerardo at 2 P.M.; Quebrada at 9:15 A.M., 11:15 A.M., 12:15 P.M., 3:15 P.M., and 5:15 P.M.; for Palmares at 9:30 A.M., noon, and 4:30 P.M.; and Buenos Aires at 5:15 A.M., 7:30 A.M., 10 A.M., 12:15 P.M., 3 P.M., and 5 P.M.

There are gas stations on Hwy. 2.

South-Central

Chirripó and Vicinity

ⓜ RÍO CHIRRIPÓ VALLEY

The Valle del Río Chirripó cuts deeply into the Talamancas northeast of San Isidro, fed by waters cascading down from Cerro Chirripó (3,819 meters), Costa Rica's highest mountain. The river is favored for trout fishing, while the warm valley microclimate is kind to fruit trees: orchards of peaches and apples cover the lower slopes. The drive offers spectacular scenery.

Rivas, a little village six km east of San Isidro, is famous for the **"Rock of the Indian,"** a giant rock carved with pre-Columbian Indian motifs, enclosed by a wire fence (but nonetheless defaced by vandals' graffiti) at the base of a tree 100 meters north of **Rancho La Botija** (tel. /fax 506/770-2146, labotija@racsa.co.cr, www.ecotourism.co.cr/docs/labotija, 9 A.M.–5 P.M. Tues.–Sun., $5 admission adults, $1.50 children). This coffee and fruit *finca* has a 150-year-old *trapiche,* or sugar mill, trails, a lake with tilapia, an atmospheric café, a swimming pool with changing rooms and security boxes, plus horse rentals ($4 per hour), and children's playground amid lawns.

Passing through the hamlet of **Canáan,** 18 km northeast of San Isidro, you arrive at **San Gerardo de Rivas,** where the Río Blanco flows into the Río Chirripó. This quaint village, on the southwest flank of Chirripó at 1,300 meters, is the gateway to Chirripó National Park. The setting is temptingly alpine, the air crisp. The scent of pines and the burbling of rushing streams fill the air. Mountain flanks rise sheer from the valleys. And the locale is perfect for hiking and bird-watching.

The ranger station for Chirripó National Park is on the south side of the Río Blanco, as you enter San Gerardo, which straggles uphill for about one km and is centered on a soccer field. About 800 km above the soccer field, the dirt road divides: that to the right clambers steeply for about one km to the trailhead to Chirripó National Park. It continues in deteriorating condition 1.5 km to **Chirripó Cloudbridge Reserve**

house with spectacular garden at Herradura, Río Chirripó Valley

(www.cloudbridge.org), a private reserve and reforestation project with trails.

A dirt road to the left at a Y-fork follows the Río Blanco upstream three km to the hamlet of **Herradura** and thence, growing steeper and more tenuous, to the tinier hamlet of **Río Blanco,** where you can hike to Cerro Chirripó and Cerro Urán.

Museo el Pelicano

This small "museum" on a coffee *finca* between Canáan and San Gerardo displays the eclectic and unique works of local artist Rafael Elizondo Basulta. Crafted from stones and natural timbers, the exhibits include a five-meter snake hewn from a branch. My favorite is a half-scale motorbike made from 1,000 twigs and other pieces of wood. Many of Rafael's stone sculptures are displayed in the beautifully landscaped garden. With luck you may be invited into his charming

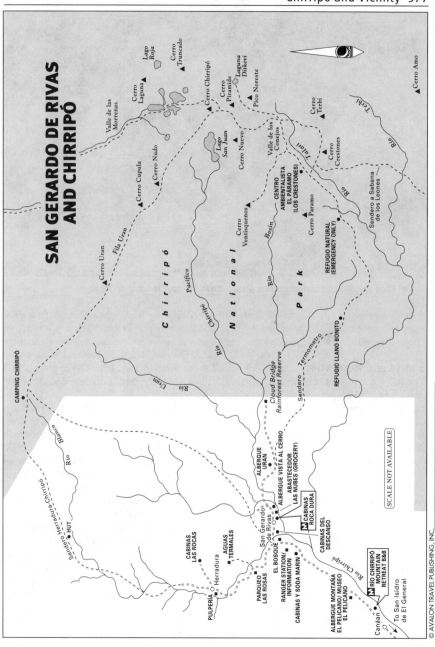

SAN GERARDO DE RIVAS
AND CHIRRIPÓ

Lago
Roja

Cerro
Truncado

Cerro
Laguna

Valle de las
Morrenas

Cerro Chirripó

Laguna
Ditkevi

Cerro
Piramide

Pico Noreste

Cerro Amo

Cerro Cupula

Cerro Nudo

Lago
San Juan

Cerro Nuevo

Valle de los
Conejos

Cerro
Terbi

Cerro Uran

Fila Uran

Cerro
Ventisquenos

Basin

Río Talari

Cerro
Crestones

Río Tebri

Chirripó

Río Pacifico

Río Chirripó

National

Río

CENTRO
AMBIENTALISTA
EL PÁRAMO
(LOS CRESTONES)

Cerro Paramo

Park

Sendero a Sabana
de los Leones

REFUGIO NATURAL
(EMERGENCY ONLY)

Sendero Termometro

REFUGIO LLANO BONITO

CAMPING CHIRRIPÓ

Río Uran

Río Blanco

Cloud Bridge
Rainforest Reserve

ALBERGUE
URAN

ABASTECEDOR
LAS NUBES (GROCERY)

ALBERGUE VISTA AL CERRO

San Gerardo
de Rivas

CABINAS
ROCA DURA

CABINAS DEL
DESCANSO

Sendero Herradura-Chirripó

HUT

Herradura

CABINAS
LAS ROCAS

AGUAS
TERMALES

PULPERIA

PARQUEO
LAS ROSAS

EL BOSQUE

RANGER STATION/
INFORMATION

CABINAS Y SODA MARIN

ALBERGUE MONTAÑA
EL PELICANO/ MUSEO
EL PELICANO

RÍO CHIRRIPÓ
MOUNTAIN
RETREAT B&B

Río Chirripó

Cañáan

To San Isidro
de El General

SCALE NOT AVAILABLE

© AVALON TRAVEL PUBLISHING, INC.

South-Central

© CHRISTOPHER P. BAKER

Rafael Elizondo Basulta and sculpture, Museo de Pelicano, Río Chirripó Valley

house to see the tree trunks hewn magically into a storage cupboard and even a wooden fridge. Entrance is free.

Sports and Recreation

The Río Chirripó and the larger Río General, which it feeds, are popular for kayaking and rafting, with enormous volumes of water creating Class III and IV rapids with gigantic waves. See *Recreation and Tours* section, in the *Know Costa Rica* section, for rafting companies.

Chirripó Horse Tours (www.cloudbridge.org), at Cabinas El Descanso, offers horseback rides.

Accommodations and Food

Midway between San Isidro and San Gerardo is **Auberge de Montagne Talari** (Apdo. 517-8000, San Isidro, tel./fax 506/771-0341, talaripz@racsa .co.cr, $32 s, $48 d low season; $36 s, $52 d high season), a small resort nestled over the Río Chirripó on an eight-hectare property partially reforested with secondary forest good for birdwatching. There are tables and chairs under shade trees. The setting is remarkably like that of the foothills of the California Sierras in the U.S. Much of the balance is made up of orchards. It's

very calming. The eight soulless but adequate rooms have private baths and hot water; four have minibars and terraces proffering grand vistas. There's a swimming pool and a little restaurant where Jan, the Dutch owner, plays jazz on the piano. Horseback rides can be arranged, and hikes are offered.

Also below San Gerardo, **Rancho la Botija** (see above, $52 s/d) has four simple yet beautiful little cabins with wooden walls, bamboo ceilings, and romantic charm, plus private bathrooms with hot water. Eight newer cabins are more spacious. There's a garden with a handsome swimming pool, and the rustic and charming Café Trapiche full of antique paraphernalia. Rates include breakfast.

An outstanding and unique recommendation is **Río Chirripó Mountain Retreat B&B** (tel. 506/771-4582, www.riochirripo.com; in the U.S., tel. 707/937-3775; $35 s/d downstairs, $40 s/d upstairs cabins, $50 s/d *casa*), one km above Canáan. Enjoying an exquisite setting in a ravine beneath huge granite boulders, this Italian-run charmer is one of the most appealing mountain lodges in Costa Rica, not least thanks to its Santa Fe aesthetic. Its heart is a huge lounge in a circular *ranchito* with soaring *palenque* roof, ocher stucco, Aztec motifs, New Mexican throw rugs, Guatemalan clothes for wall hangings, sofa seats with batik cushions arcing around a raised brick fireplace, and open walls with views toward the mountains. A delightful dining area adjoining is swarmed by bougainvillea. It has eight rustic wooden cabins hanging over the river. They boast gorgeous decor with soothing earth-tone color schemes (including red-painted cement floors), wooden beds with Guatemalan bedspreads, cross-ventilation, balconies, and walk-in showers with hot water. A separate (and meagerly furnished) riverside *casa* has a wooden floor, raised ceiling with bamboo beams, and exquisite ceramics. Trails lead down to a swimming pool and wooden sundeck.

Albergue Montaña El Pelicano (Apdo. 942-8000, San Gerardo de Rivas, tel. 506/390-4194, fax 506/770-3526, elizondomartinez@yahoo .com, www.hotelelpelicano.com, $8 pp low season; $10 high season, $20 s/d cabin), 800 meters above Canáan, is another splendid option on the mountainside coffee *finca* of Rafael Elizondo. Focal point is a large alpine-style wooden lodge with 10 skylit and bare-bones hostel-type upstairs rooms sharing four spic-and-span toilets and tiled showers with hot water. Walls do not reach the ceiling, so no romantic antics please. There's also a charming cabin. Trails lead into the forest. It has a restaurant full of intriguing art hewn from driftwood, plus a swimming pool.

In San Gerardo, the **Cabinas y Soda Marín** (cellular tel. 506/308-6735, www.cabinasmarin .com, $6 pp shared bath, $12 pp private bath), next to the ranger station below San Gerardo, has eight simple but clean cabins with hot water. It has a basic restaurant and *pulpería* (general store) where you can buy food for the hike up Chirripó. Similarly, **Bar/Restaurant El Bosque** (c/o tel. 506/771-4129, $5 pp shared bath, $7 pp private bath), 100 meters uphill, has eight clean but small bare-bones cabins, each with two bunks and hot water. It has a charming patio restaurant overhanging the cascades. It permits camping for $3.50 pp.

Cabinas del Descanso (tel. 506/771-7962 or cellular 506/309-0067, $2.50 pp camping, $7 pp in dorms, $10 pp in *cabinas*), 200 meters uphill from the ranger station, has a tiny dorm with bunks and shared baths, plus nine newer, more spacious and relatively salubrious *cabinas* with double beds and hot water (two rooms have private baths). It also permits camping (there are cold-water showers). There's a rustic yet charming restaurant serving filling *típico* meals. The Elizondo family welcomes you warmly; leads treks (including birding); offers trout fishing; and will drive you to the park entrance.

Lovers of the offbeat and hip should try **Ⓜ Cabinas Roca Dura** (c/o tel. 506/771-1866, $5 pp with shared bathrooms, $8–10 pp with private bath), facing the soccer field, a rambling wooden house favored by trekkers. It has nine basic, drafty rooms, most with bunks, hippie-era murals, and all with hot water (two rooms have private bath), plus choice views over the river. Downstairs rooms are built onto the rock face with granite boulders for walls and ceiling. The rustic wooden bar/restaurant above serves pizzas and *típico* dishes. It offers guided horseback rides ($21), and has a funky "hot tub" comprising a bathtub in a riverstone hut. The friendly owner, Luis Hernandez, permits camping and rents camping equipment; he also rents a very simple mountainside house above the village ($50 weekly).

About the village, **Albergue Vista al Cerro** (tel. 506/373-3365, $7 pp bunk rooms, $11 s/d private room) features a skylit corridor onto which open four rooms with stained cement floors, wood walls, and two bunks and a single bed. They share clean, tiled showers and toilets. A fifth room has a double bed and private bathroom.

Albergue Urán (tel. 506/771-1669 or 506/388-2333, $8 pp small room, $30 s/d larger room), 100 meters below the Chirripó trailhead, enjoys a pleasant hillside setting gaily planted with ornamentals, and offers 10 simple but well-kept rooms barrack-style in a modern wooden two-story structure with tin roof and shared bathrooms with hot water. Upper-story rooms get more light. It has a *pulpería* (grocery), and clean, airy restaurant. A larger room has four beds and a private bathroom.

In Herradura, the *pulpería* (public tel. 506/771-1199), on the east side of the river, has camping space for $3 pp (you can rent camping equipment) and offers rooms at **Casa de Vijita Mora,** nearby. **Cabinas Las Rocas,** 1.5 km above Herradura, also rent rooms.

Services
It's worth noting that **Pulpería La Nubes** (tel. 506/771-1866) has the only public phone in San Gerardo de Rivas.

Getting There
Buses depart San Isidro for San Gerardo de Rivas at 5:30 A.M. and 2 P.M., returning at 7 A.M. and 4 P.M. A 10:30 A.M. bus from San José (Calle 16, Avenidas 1/3; $1 each way) to San Isidro will get you there in time for the 2 P.M. bus. There's another San Gerardo nearby, so be sure to specify San Gerardo de Rivas.

If driving, the turnoff for Rivas and San Gerardo is opposite Pollo Brasilita, one km south of San Isidro. A 4WD taxi from San Isidro will cost about $8.

CHIRRIPÓ NATIONAL PARK

Chirripó Parque Nacional ($10 admission, $15 two days) protects 50,150 hectares of high-elevation terrain surrounding Cerro Chirripó (3,819 meters), Central America's highest peak. The park is contiguous with La Amistad International Peace Park to the south; together they form the Amistad-Talamanca Regional Conservation Unit. Flora and fauna thrive here relatively unmolested by humans. One remote section of the park is called Savannah of the Lions, after its large population of pumas. Tapirs and jaguars are both common, though rarely seen. And the mountain forests protect several hundred bird species.

Cloud forest, above 2,500 meters, covers almost half the park, which features three distinct life zones; the park is topped off by subalpine rainy *páramo,* marked by contorted dwarf trees and marshy grasses that dry out on the Pacific

© CHRISTOPHER P. BAKER

Río Chirripó

slopes Jan.–May (presenting perfect conditions for raging fires fanned by high winds; much of this area still bears the scars of a huge fire that raged across 2,000 hectares in April 1992).

Cerro Chirripó was held sacred by pre-Columbian peoples. Tribal leaders and shamans performed rituals atop the lofty shrine; lesser mortals who ventured up Chirripó were killed. Magnetic fields are said to swing wildly at the top, particularly near Los Crestones, huge boulders thought to have been the most sacred of indigenous sites.

Just as Sir Edmund Hillary climbed Everest "because it was there," so Chirripó lures the intrepid who seek the satisfaction of reaching the summit (the first recorded climb was made by a priest, Father Agustín Blessing, in 1904). Many Ticos choose to hike the mountain during the week preceding Easter, when the weather is usually dry. Avoid holidays, when the huts may be full. The hike is no Sunday picnic but requires no technical expertise. The trails are well marked.

CLIMBING CHIRRIPÓ

You can do the 16-km hike to the summit in a day, but it normally takes two days (three days roundtrip). You should call the National Parks Service three days in advance to register; pay your fee at the ranger station upon arrival at San Gerardo. There are distance markers every two kilometers. *Pack out all your trash, and bury human waste.* Take only photographs, leave only footprints.

Day 1

Today is 14 km, mostly steeply uphill. Less fit hikers should begin not long after dawn, as it can take 12 hours or even longer in bad conditions (fitter hikers should be able to hike this section in six or seven hours). You can hire local porters to carry your packs to base camp.

From the soccer field in San Gerardo, walk uphill about 600 meters to the Y-fork; turn right, cross the bridge, and follow the rocky track one km uphill. The trailhead is well-signed on the right, 100 meters above Albergue Urán (you can drive up to this point with a 4WD; several homesteads advertise parking for a small fee). There's a stream one-half kilometer beyond Refugio Llano Bonito, beyond which you begin a grueling uphill stretch called La Cuesta del Agua. Allow at least two hours for this section of the hike. The climb crests at Monte Sin Fé (Faithless Mountain). You'll see a rudimentary wooden shelter at the halfway point, beyond which you pass into dwarf cloud forest adorned with old man's beard. Expect to see plentiful toucanets, trogons, monkeys, and more lower down.

About six km below the summit is a cave large enough to sleep five or six people if rains dictate. From here a two-km final climb—La Cuesta de los Arrepentidos (Repentants' Hill)—takes you to Centro Ambientalista El Paraíso, beside the Río Talari beneath an intriguing rock formation called Los Crestones. The lodge has heating, but be prepared for a cold night anyway.

Day 2

Today, up and onto the trail by dawn to make the summit before the fog rolls in. It's about a 90-minute hike from the hut via the Valle de los Conejos (Rabbits' Valley). On clear days the view is awesome! With luck, you'll be able to see both the Pacific and the Caribbean. Take time, too, if you can stand the cold, for a dip in Lago San Juan (if it's sunny, you'll quickly dry off and warm up on the rocks). You'll pass waterfalls en route to the top, giving you an understanding of why the Talamancan Indians called it Chirripó—"Place of Enchanted Waters."

You can head back to San Gerardo the same day, or contemplate a roundtrip hike to Cerro Ventisqueros, the second-highest mountain in Costa Rica: the trail begins below the Valle de los Conejos. You can spend your second night at another hut in the Valle de las Morenas, on the northern side of Chirripó (reportedly you need to obtain the key from the ranger in San Gerardo). With a local guide, you could also follow the Camino de los Indios, a trail that passes over Cerro Urán and the far northern Talamancas. Do not try to follow this or any other trails without an experienced guide!

Only 40 visitors are allowed within the park at any one time (you may be told there's a waiting list; experienced hikers recommend showing up anyway, as there are usually lots of no-shows). Nobody is allowed to hike without a guide. The park service is pushing the lesser-known Herradura Trail (minimum three days/two nights), via Paso de los Indios, with the first night atop Cerro Urán.

Weather

The weather is unpredictable—dress accordingly. The hike to the summit from San Gerardo ascends 2,500 meters. When the bitterly cold wind kicks in, the humidity and windchill factor can drop temperatures to -5°C. Rain is always a possibility, even in "dry season," and a short downpour usually occurs midafternoon. Fog is almost a daily occurrence at higher elevations, often forming in midmorning. And temperatures can fall below freezing at night. February and March are the driest months.

Information

The **ranger station** (no tel., 6:30 A.M.–4:30 P.M.) is in San Gerardo de Rivas. It has toilets and a conference room. It sells a *Visitors Guide* (75 cents) and map (75 cents) showing trails to the summit; the station does not sell the 1:50,000 topographical survey (sections 3444 II San Isidro and 3544 III Durika; if you plan on hiking to nearby peaks, you may also need sections 3544 IV Fila Norte and 3444 I Cuerici), available from the Instituto Geográfico Nacional in San José.

The park is administered from the **La Amistad Biosphere Reserve** office in San Isidro (tel. 506/771-3155 or 506/771-4836, fax 506/771-3297, aclap@ms.minae.go.cr); see the sidebar *La Amistad International Friendship Park,* and the regional sections later this chapter.

Chirripó Trek (Calle 1, Avenidas 2/4, tel. 506/771-4582, fax 506/771-8841, trekking @chirripo.com, www.chirripo.com), in San Isidro, offers guided treks.

What to Take

- Warm clothes—preferably layered clothing for varying temperatures and humidity. A polypropylene jacket remains warm when wet.
- Raingear. A poncho is best.
- Good hiking boots. The path is wet and slippery.
- Warm sleeping bag—good to 0°C.
- Flashlight with spare batteries.
- A compass and map.
- Water. There is no water supply for the first half of the hike.
- Food, including snacks. Dried bananas and peanuts are good energy boosters.
- Bag for litter/garbage.
- Wind/sun protection.

Accommodations

There's a cave refuge halfway up the mountain, and an open-air hut—**Refugio Llano Bonito**—with a one-night limit ($5). The **Centro Ambientalista El Páramo,** 14 km from the trailhead, can sleep 40 persons, with two bunks to each room, and shared bathrooms with lukewarm showers, a communal kitchen, and solar-powered electricity 6–8 P.M. You can rent sleeping bags, blankets, and stoves, which are permitted only within the *albergue.* Rates: $10 pp per night.

Camping is *not* permitted except at **Camping Chirripó,** 10 km from the trailhead on the Herradura trail.

Guides and Equipment

The communities of San Gerardo and Herradura run an association of guides and porters *(arrieros).* Prices are fixed at $30 per day, with a 35-pound limit per porter. The porters are selected democratically from a rotating list. If you want to attempt the Herradura Trail, check with José Mora at the *pulpería* (tel. 506/771-1199), in Herradura.

You can rent stoves, gas canisters, sleeping bags, and more at **Roca Dura.**

Buenos Aires and Vicinity

BUENOS AIRES

About 40 km south of San Isidro the air becomes redolent of sweet-smelling pineapples, the economic mainstay of the Valle de El General, which is centered on Buenos Aires, a small agricultural town in the midst of an endless seagreen ocean of spiky *piñas*. The nondescript town, 63 km south of San Isidro de El General, is three km northeast of Hwy. 2, near the base of the Talamanca mountains. It makes a good base for exploring La Amistad International Peace Park.

Southeast from Buenos Aires, the Pan-American Highway follows the Río General 25 km to its confluence with the Río Coto Brus at Paso Real.

Accommodations and Food

I recommend **Cabinas Fabi** (tel. 506/730-1110

FIESTA DE LOS DIABLITOS

Every year on 30 December a conch shell sounds at midnight across the dark hills of the Fila Sinancra. Men disguised as devils burst from the hills into Boruca and go from house to house, performing skits and receiving rewards of tamales and *chicha*, the traditional corn liquor. This is the Fiesta de los Diablitos. Drums and flutes play while villagers, dressed in burlap sacks and traditional balsa-wood masks, energize a pantheon of chiseled supernatural beings. Another dresses as a bull. Plied with *chicha*, the man becomes the animal and the animal the man, just as in the Roman Catholic tradition the sacrament becomes the body of the Lord. The *diablitos* chase, prod, and taunt the bull. Three days of celebrations and performances end with the symbolic killing of the bull, which is then reduced to ashes on a pyre. The festival reenacts the battles between native forebears and Spanish conquistadors with a dramatic twist: the Indians win.

or 506/828-1763, $9 s, $11 d), 50 meters west of the bus station. It has six spacious, modern cabins with tiled floors, ceiling fans, TVs (local), and private bath with cold water. There's secure parking.

There's a **Musmanni** bakery on the east side of the bus station.

Information and Services

There are two banks on the plaza. The **police station** (tel. 117 or 506/730-0103) is one block northeast of the plaza; there's a medical clinic on the southeast corner of the plaza, and a **Red Cross** (tel. 506/730-0078) when entering town.

Getting There

The Zona Sur bus (tel. 506/221-4214) to Ciudad Neily and Panamá departs San José from Avenida 18, Calle 4, and will drop you at Buenos Aires. The bus station in Buenos Aires is one block west of the plaza.

See *San Isidro de El General,* above, for bus schedules from San Isidro.

LA AMISTAD FRIENDSHIP PARK—NORTH

Buenos Aires is a gateway to La Amistad International Friendship Park, which provides unparalleled opportunities for wildlife viewing, particularly of animals such as pumas and jaguars. The mountains around Buenos Aires are home to several indigenous tribes.

A dirt road that begins in Buenos Aires leads north 10 km to the hamlet of **Ujarrás,** beyond which the boulder-strewn dirt road continues four km to **Balneario de Aguas Termales** (a.k.a. Rocas Calientes), where thermal waters pour forth amid a rock landscape; you have to cross a rickety suspension bridge the width of your outstretched arms. (From Buenos Aires, follow the "Ujarrás" signs to the high school; turn right, then left and follow the dirt road to a water storage tank, on the right, in the midst of

South-Central

pineapple fields; about 50 meters beyond the tank, turn left, then turn left at the Y-fork at Rancho Cabecar restaurant.)

Ujarrás is gateway to the **Durika Indigenous Reserve** (Reserva Indígena Durika) and La Amistad International Friendship Park. A trail from Ujarrás crosses the Talamancas via Cerro Abolado and the valley of the Río Taparí, ending in the Hitoy-Cerere Biological Reserve on the Caribbean side. It's a strenuous, 54-km, three-or four-day hike. *Do not attempt this hike without an indigenous guide.* Register in advance at the CONAI (Indigenous Affairs) office at Ujarrás.

Another dirt road that begins at the gas station at **Brujo,** 10 km southeast of Buenos Aires, leads north to the **Cabagra Indigenous Reserve** (Reserva Indígena Cabagra).

Durika Biological Reserve

Founded in 1989 as Finca Anael, this 700-hectare farm reserve (Asociación Durika, Apdo. 9, Buenos Aires, tel. 506/730-0082, fax 506/730-0003, durikas@gema.com, or c/o Annie McCormick, tel.506/ 240-2320, fax 506/223-0341) is the outgrowth of a self-sufficient agricultural community of 100 or so members who work on behalf of conservation. The community welcomes ecotourists. A guide is assigned to you. Besides the opportunity to milk the goats, feed the goats, make yogurt and cheese, try your hand at carpentry, and participate in organic farming, you can attend classes in martial arts, meditation, and art. Guided hikes include one to an indigenous village, plus a five-day camping trip to the summit of Cerro Durika.

LA AMISTAD INTERNATIONAL FRIENDSHIP PARK

The 193,929-hectare International Friendship Park is shared with neighboring Panamá. Together with the adjacent Chirripó National Park, the Hitoy-Cerere Biological Reserve, Tapantí National Park, Las Tablas and Barbilla Protective Zones, Las Cruces Biological Station, and a handful of Indian reservations, it forms the 600,000-hectare Amistad Biosphere Reserve, a UNESCO World Heritage Site also known as the Amistad-Talamanca Regional Conservation Unit—the largest biological reserve in the Central American isthmus, protecting both the Caribbean and Pacific slopes of the Talamancas.

The park transcends the Cordillera Talamanca ranges, rising from 150 meters above sea level on the Caribbean side to 3,819 meters atop Cerro Chirripó. The Talamancas are made up of separate mountain chains with only a limited history of volcanic activity; none of the mountains is considered a volcano. La Amistad's eight life zones form habitats for flora and fauna representing at least 60 percent of the nation's various species, including no fewer than 450 bird species (not least the country's largest population of resplendent quetzals and 49 endemic species), as well as the country's largest density of tapirs, jaguars, harpy eagles, ocelots, and many other endangered species. The park protects important watersheds harboring the largest stands of tropical rainforests and moist forests in the isthmus. Cloud forests extend to 2,800 meters, with alpine *páramo* vegetation in the upper reaches.

The indigenous heritage is particularly strong here, and this is one of the few areas in Costa Rica where you are likely to see indigenous people dressed in traditional, brightly colored ethnic clothing.

Information and Trails

Much of this massive park remains unexplored. It has no facilities, and those few trails that exist are unmarked and often barely discernible. Unless you're an experienced trekker, don't even think about hiking into the park without a guide. Weather is extremely fickle. And you are most likely too many kilometers from human contact in case of an emergency.

The park is administered from San Isidro (tel. 506/771-3155 or 506/771-4836, fax 506/771-3297, aclap@ms.minae.go.cr) and has five official entry points, accessed via Buenos Aires, Helechales, Altamira, and San Vito. Admission costs $6.

To get there, follow the "Ujarrás" signs to Rancho Cabecar restaurant (see above), then take the right at the Y-fork and continue uphill 15 km until you see the entrance for the farm.

Accommodations and Food
Albergue de Montaña Angeles de Paraíso (tel. 506/730-0034 or 506/730-1715, $2 pp camping, $2.50 dorm), on the southern edge of Ujarrás, is a delightful spot with a basic backpackers' dorm with shared outside toilets. Three small swimming pools were a bit grungy at last visit. Set amid a fruit orchard, it has a soccer pitch, thatched shade areas with hammocks, a lagoon stocked with tilapia, and a rustic restaurant serving local fare. Two cabins were to be added.

Finca Anael (see above, $10 pp dorm, $40 s, $70 d cabins) has a basic dorm hut, but you'll need to bring your own sleeping bag. It also has three simple, candlelit cabins with fantastic views: one has two beds and a private bathroom; the others each have four beds and share a bathroom. Rates include meals and transfers.

Rancho Cabecar serves local fare and has a pool table and live music.

Getting There
Buses depart Buenos Aires for Potrero Grande at 6:30 A.M. and noon; you can get a jeep-taxi from here. Buses also serve Ujarrás from Buenos Aires.

RÍO GRANDE DE TERRABA VALLEY
Southwest of Buenos Aires, at **Paso Real** (there is no community as such), the Pan-American Highway and Río Grande de Terraba swing west and run through a ravine in the Fila Costeña mountains (the valley is slated to be dammed to create the nation's largest hydroelectricity project, the mammoth 1,500-megawatt Boruca Project, to go on line in 2010 yet opposed by local indigenous groups), connecting the Valle de El General to Palmar and the Golfo Dulce region.

About 10 km south of Paso Real, a dirt road leads sharply uphill and runs along a ridgetop (offering fantastic views) to **Boruca,** a slow-paced

Marina Lázaro weaves in the traditional manner in Boruca.

hamlet set in a verdant valley in the heart of the **Boruca Indian Reserve.** The Reserva Indígena Boruca, in the Fila Sinancra, comprises a series of Indian villages and tiny *fincas* scattered throughout the mountains.

There's a tiny **Museo Comunitario Boruca** honoring the local culture. It's funded by the sale of beautiful carved balsa-wood masks, weavings, and other crafts. Some 35 local artisans have a cooperative centered on the home of Marina Lazaro Morales, fronting the plaza.

Accommodations
The **Bar, Soda y Cabinas Boruca** (no tel.), in Boruca, has five basic rooms with private bathrooms with cold water for $7.50 s/d. You can also stay with local families by prior arrangement; call the public administrator for information (tel. 506/730-1673).

Getting There
A bus departs Buenos Aires for Boruca at 11:30 A.M. and 3:30 P.M. (two hours). The return bus departs Boruca at 6:30 A.M. and 1 P.M.

South-Central

Valle de Coto Brus

This large valley is drained by the Río Coto Brus and its tributaries, which flow west to meet the Río General at Paso Real, where the rivers turn south as the Río Terraba. Coffee is the principal crop in the valley, with dark-green bushes flanking the steep slopes of the lower Talamancas to the north and, to the south, the various ridges that make up the Fila Costeña. The summits of Cerro Kamuk (3,549 meters) and Cerro Fabrega (3,336 meters) loom massively overhead.

The Río Terraba is spanned by a bridge one km south of Paso Real. From here, Hwy. 237 leads to San Vito, the regional capital on a ridgetop at the head of the valley. It's one of the most scenic drives in the country, with magnificent views across the valley toward the bulk of the Talamancas.

LA AMISTAD FRIENDSHIP PARK—CENTRAL

Three km southeast of the bridge over the Río Terraba, a dirt road off Hwy. 237 leads north five km to **Potrero Grande** and thence 12 km to **Helechales** and the **Estación Tres Colinas** ranger station for La Amistad International Peace Park; 4WD required.

Another rough dirt road begins at Guácimo (also known as Las Tablas) on Hwy. 237 about three km north of Jabillo and about 18 km southeast of the Terraba River; it leads 21 km via the communities of **El Carmén** and **Altamira** to the La Amistad International Friendship Park headquarters at **Estación Altamira** (tel./fax 506/730-0846), on the edge of the cloud forest. Neither the road nor Altamira are marked on most road maps (turn left about three km above El Carmén; it's easy going to Altamira, beyond which it's a steep two-km 4WD climb).

The Altamira ranger station has a small ecology museum. Trails include Sendero Valle del Silencio, a six-hour, 20-km hike into the cloud forest good for spotting quetzals. There's a basic three-room dorm; reservation required.

TRACOPA buses (tel. 506/771-3297) between Buenos Aires and San Vito will drop you at Las Tablas, where you can take a jeep-taxi to Altamira.

Dayquis Indian children near Progreso, La Amistad Friendship Park

Accommodations

Estación Atlamira has a camping area with toilets and showers, drinking water, and a picnic area for $2 pp (you'll need to bring stoves and gas containers). There's even a TV lounge with sofas. Meals cost $1.

Adjoining the ranger station is **Senderos Alturas** ($7.50 pp), a private and very rustic bar and restaurant with spectacular views. It rents two basic dorm rooms, each with eight bunks and corrugated tin roof and outside shower and toilet.

In El Carmén, Marialeno Garbanzo Camacho is the gracious owner of **Soda y Cabinas La Amistad** (tel. 506/743-1080, $5 pp), next to the police station. She has eight simple, clean rooms with fans and shared outside bathrooms with hot water. The *soda* (simple restaurant) is open 6 A.M.–9 P.M.

SAN VITO

San Vito is a pleasant hill town that nestles on the east-facing flank of the Fila Costeña, overlooking the Valle de Coto Brus, at 990 meters above sea level. The town was founded by Italian immigrants in the early 1850s. The tiny park at the top of the hill as you enter town from Buenos Aires or Ciudad Neily has a life-size statue of two children under an umbrella dedicated to "La Fraternidad Italo-Costarricense."

Finca Cántaros

This 9.5-hectare reserve (tel. 506/773-3760, fax 506/773-4214, 8 A.M.–4 P.M. Sat.–Sun. high season, by request low season, $0.75 cents admission), surrounding a one-hectare lake, at Linda Vista, three km southeast of San Vito, is centered on a beautifully restored farmhouse converted into a fine arts and crafts gallery, with a children's library and education center that teaches local ecology and culture. Trails lead to **Laguna Julia,** which attracts grebes, gallinules, herons, and cormorants. The gallery sells exquisite ceramics, jewelry, Ecuadorian blankets, and hand-painted wooden statues.

Accommodations

Cabinas Nelly (tel. 506/773-3741), on the west side of town, has six rooms with private baths and hot water (but only one with fan) for $5 pp. The **Hotel Rino** (tel. 506/773-3071, fax 506/773-4214, $9.50 s, $17 d with fan, $12 pp with cable TV, $17.50/$26 with bathtub), on the main street, has 13 simple but adequate rooms with private bathrooms and hot-water showers.

Also try **Cabinas Las Huacas** (tel. 506/773-3115, $7 s, $12 d), with 21 simply furnished rooms with cable TV, plus private baths and hot water, in a dour compound on the west side of town. Four rooms have fans. There's a bar.

The nicest place in town is **Hotel El Ceibo** (tel. 506/773-3025, fax 506/773-5025, $16 s, $27 d), with 38 modern a/c rooms with fans and private baths with hot water, a large restaurant, a lounge with TV, plus a small bar.

Of similar quality, **Cabinas La Riviera** (tel. 506/773-3295, $13 pp), cater-corner to the plaza, is a modern hotel with eight carpeted, no-frills rooms, but heaps of light through huge windows, cable TV, and large bathrooms with hot water. It has a fast-food restaurant.

Food

The **Hotel El Ceibo** restaurant serves cannelloni, lemon scalloppini, and fresh tuna spaghetti. **Pizzeria Lilliana,** 50 meters west of the plaza, is recommended for Italian fare; I had a tasty pizza (from $3) served on the patio.

Soda Tatiana is a clinically clean café recommended for fast food and local fare.

You can stock up on groceries at **Supermercado BM,** near the gas station west of town. There's a bakery one block south of the bus station.

Information and Services

The **hospital** (tel. 506/773-3103) is two km south of town, on the road to Ciudad Neily. **Centro Médico Saralú** (tel. 506/773-3206, 10 A.M.–noon and 2–6 P.M.), on the west side of town, has a pharmacy adjoining. The **Red Cross** (tel. 506/773-3196) is on the northwest side of town.

There are two banks on the main street.

Neurotec Internet (tel. 506/773-3521, 8 A.M.–noon and 1–8 P.M. Mon.–Sat.), 60 meters west of the gas station, charges $1 per hour.

South-Central

South-Central

SAN VITO

To Santa Elena

POST OFFICE ■

POLICE ■

■ BUS TERMINAL (TRACOPA)

RED CROSS ■

BUS STATION (CEPUL) ■

SODA TATIANA ▼

NEUROTEC
INTERNET ■

CABINAS NELLY ■

▼ PANADERÍA

PHARMACY ▼

HOTEL RINO ●

HELADERÍA ▼

■ SUPERMARKET

MONUMENTO A LA
FRATERNIDAD
★

● HOTEL EL CEIBO

JEEP (MONUMENT)
★

■ TOWN HALL

● HOTEL LA RIVIERA

BANK ■

PIZZERIA
LILLIANA ▼

PLAZA

TAXIS

ICE
(TELEPHONE
OFFICE) ■

BANK ■

BUS TO CIUDAD NEILY/
CAÑAS GORDAS/SABALITO/
LAS MELLIZAS

BANK ■

DOCTOR ■

RESTAURANTE JIMAR ▼

CABINAS
LA HUACAS ●

RESTAURANTE NELLY ▼

CENTRO MÉDICO
SABALÚ ■

SUPERMARKET ■

To San Isidro

To Wilson Botanical Gardens
and Ciudad Neily

To Las Tablas, San Vito Aerodrome,
and La Amistad International Friendship Park

0   200 yds

0   200 m

The post office and police station (tel. 506/773-3225) adjoin each other, 200 meters up the hill north of the main bus station.

Getting There

You can charter an air-taxi to San Vito. Buses (tel. 506/222-2666) depart San José from Calle 14, Avenida 5, at 5:45 A.M., 8:15 A.M., 11:30 A.M., and 2:45 P.M. Buses depart the main bus terminal on the main street in San Vito for San José at 5 A.M., 7:30 A.M., 10 A.M., and 3 P.M. Buy tickets in advance. Buses from San Isidro depart at 5:30 A.M. and 2 P.M., returning at 6:45 A.M. and 1:30 P.M.

Buses depart Terminal Cepul for Ciudad Neily at 5:30 A.M., 7 A.M., 7:30 A.M., 9 A.M., 11 A.M., noon, 2 P.M., and 5 P.M. ($1.50); and to Las Mellizas at 9:30 A.M., 2 P.M., and 5 P.M. Buses from Ciudad Neily depart at 6 A.M., 11 A.M., 1 P.M., and 3 P.M. Buses for Las Tablas depart at 10:30 A.M. and 3 P.M.

ⓜ LAS CRUCES BIOLOGICAL STATION

This biological research station (tel. 506/773-4004, fax 506/773-3665, lcruces@hortus.ots .ac.cr), six km south of San Vito, is a botanist's delight. The center, in the midst of a 266-hectare forest reserve, is run by the Organization of Tropical Studies (P.O. Box 676-2050 San Pedro, tel. 506/240-6696, fax 506/240-6783, reservas@ots .ac.cr; in the U.S., OTS, Duke University, P.O. Box 90630, Durham, NC 27708-0630, tel. 919/684-5774, fax 919/684-5661) and acts as a center for research and scientific training by staff and students of the 50 or so universities that make up OTS, as well as for public education (there's a research library and laboratory, plus lecture room with audiovisual equipment). New plants are propagated for horticulture, and species threatened with habitat loss and extinction are maintained for future reforestation efforts.

The reserve is in mid-elevation tropical rain-forest along a ridge of the Fila Zapote. During the wet season, heavy fog and afternoon clouds spill over the ridge, nourishing a rich epiphytic flora of orchids, bromeliads, ferns, and aeroids. The forest is a vital habitat for pacas, anteaters, opossums, kinkajous, porcupines, armadillos, sloths, tayras, monkeys, deer, small cats, and more than 35 species of bats. Bird-watching at Las Cruces is especially rewarding: more than 330 species have been recorded.

Maintaining the reserve—proclaimed part of La Amistad Biosphere Reserve—is the cornerstone of a larger effort to save the watershed of the Río Java. Visitation only accounts for about 30 percent of funds required to support the station, which seeks donors, or "amigos." You can subscribe to the *Amigos Newsletter*.

A gift store sells T-shirts, the beautiful OTS calendar, souvenirs, and a wide array of booklets on ecology.

Wilson Botanical Gardens

The spectacular highlight of the Las Cruces station is the 10 hectares of cultivated gardens (8 A.M.–4 P.M., closed Monday, $10 admission adult, $8 children half-day, $25 adult, $10 children full day) established in 1963 by Robert and Catherine Wilson, former owners of Fantastic Gardens in Miami. The garden was inspired by the famous Brazilian gardener Roberto Burle-Marx, a friend of Wilson's, who designed much of the garden following his vision of parterres as a palette. Wilson and his wife are buried in a humble grave on the grounds. There's a picnic area and benches where you may sit and absorb the beauty. Approximately 10 km of well-maintained, gently sloping trails (and many more in the forest reserve) meander through the Fern Grove, Orchid Grotto, the largest palm collection in the world (with about 700 of the world's 2,600 or so species), agave and lily beds, and heliconia groves containing more than 7,000 plant species.

The garden is a repository for the Begonia Society and Heliconia Society, and also has many cacti species that are already extinct in their native habitats. There are also greenhouses with large collections of anthuriums, ferns (a specialty of Luis Diego Gómez, the Las Cruces director), elkhorns, and more.

Annual rainfall is a whopping 380 cm, but the gardens will enliven your spirit in even the rainiest weather.

Rates include guided walk (by reservation). Students receive discounts.

Accommodations

Las Cruces ($70 s, $125 d) will accept drop-by overnighters on a space-available basis. It's advisable to reserve c/o OTS (see above). It has 12 spacious, modestly elegant twin rooms with picture windows opening to prow-shaped verandas with views. Hardwoods abound, and private bathrooms have hot water. Dining is family-style. There's a laundry. Special discount rates apply for researchers and students with accredited projects. Rates include meals and taxes.

Getting There

Local buses stop at the gardens and operate from San Vito at 7 A.M., 11 A.M., 1:30 P.M., and 4 P.M.; and from the garden gate to San Vito at 6:30 A.M., 7:30 A.M., 1:45 P.M., and 4 P.M. Buses depart Ciudad Neily for the gardens at 7 A.M. and 1 P.M.

A **taxi** from San Vito costs about $3.

LA AMISTAD FRIENDSHIP PARK—SOUTH

Northeast of San Vito, the Talamancas are protected within La Amistad, which extends south of the Panamanian border and provides splendid options for spotting quetzals, pumas, and other rare wildlife.

The **Estación Pittier** (tel./fax 506/773-4060), at Progreso, about 30 km northeast of San Vito, has an exhibition room and a *mirador,* plus basic facilities. It is reached via the road through Sabalito, Unión, and Río Negro: at Sabalito, six km east of San Vito, turn left at the gas station, and left again at Centro Social El Nicoyano, at La Trucha. There are no signs, so ask. You can also continue straight past Centro Social El Nicoyano until you reach the police station at Las Mellizas; here, turn left for **La Amistad Lodge,** on a 1,215-hectare farm within Las Tablas Protective Zone, a private wildlife reserve adjoining La Amistad International Friendship Park. Horseback rides and guided hiking are offered along 60 km of trails. La Amistad Lodge is 3.5 km along a rocky skunk of a road. 4WD required

From La Amistad Lodge, a trail leads to the remote **Estación Las Tablas.** It's a rugged 10-km hike or drive via 4WD (conditions permitting); continue uphill from the lodge and take the right fork beyond the gates.

You can also enter La Amistad International Friendship Park via the equally remote **Estación La Escuadra** ranger station, at Agua Caliente, in the Cotón valley some 30 km northeast of San Vito and reached via the communities of Juntas, Poma, and Santa Elena; 4WD required.

Accommodations

You can camp at **Estación Las Tablas,** which has no facilities; $2 pp.

The three-story, Swiss-style, all-wood **La Amistad Lodge** (P.O. Box 774-1000, San José, tel. 506/289-7667, fax 506/289-7858, amistad @racsa.co.cr, $45 pp low season, $65 pp high season) has seven simple yet adequate rooms with large tiled bathrooms. The lodge boasts a stone fireplace, lathe-turned balustrades, a third-floor balcony, and a restaurant where meals are served family-style. There are also three *cabinas,* which have verandas with rockers. Rates include meals.

La Amistad Lodge also has two high-mountain camps: one (at 1,600 meters) with a dining room and bathroom but no electricity; the other at 1,800 meters with basic facilities. It's a rugged four-hour drive in wet season from the lodge. Rates ($65) include meals.

Getting There

Buses depart San Vito for Cotón at 3 P.M., for Progreso and Las Mellizas at 9:30 A.M. and 2 P.M., for Las Tablas at 10:30 A.M. and 3 P.M., and for Santa Elena at 10 A.M. and 4 P.M. **Jeep-taxis** will run you there in dry season from San Vito (about $50 round-trip).

Know
Costa Rica

The Land

Travelers moving south overland through Central America gradually have their choice of routes whittled away until they finally reach the end of the road in the swamps and forests of Darien, in Panamá, where the tenuous land bridge separating the two great American continents is almost pinched out and the Pacific Ocean and the Caribbean Sea almost meet. Costa Rica lies at the northern point of this apex—a pivotal region separating two oceans and two continents vastly different in character.

The region is a crucible. There are few places in the world where the forces of nature so actively interplay. Distinct climatic patterns clash and merge; the great landmasses and their offshore cousins, the Cocos and Caribbean plates, jostle and shove one another, triggering earthquakes and spawning sometimes cataclysmic volcanic eruptions; and the flora and fauna of the North and South American realms—as well as those of the Caribbean and the Pacific—come together and play Russian roulette with the forces of evolution. The result is an incredible diversity of terrain, biota, and weather concentrated in a country barely bigger than the state of New Hampshire.

GEOGRAPHY

At 50,895 square kilometers, Costa Rica is the second-smallest Central American nation after El Salvador. At its narrowest point, in the south, only 119 km (75 miles) separate the Caribbean from the Pacific. At its broadest point, Costa Rica is a mere 280 km (175 miles) wide. On the ruler-straight eastern seaboard, barely 160 km (100 miles) separate the Nicaraguan and Panamanian borders. And while the Pacific coast is longer, it is still only 480 km (300 miles) from the northernmost tip to the Panamanian border as the crow flies.

Lying between 8 and 11 degrees north of the equator, Costa Rica sits wholly within the tropics, a fact quickly confirmed in the middle of a rainy afternoon in the middle of the rainy season in the middle of the sodden Caribbean lowlands or the Talamanca mountains. Elevation and extremes of relief, however, temper the stereotypical tropical climate. In fact, the nation boasts more than a dozen distinct climatic zones. Atop the highest mountains in cooler months, even ice and snow aren't unknown.

A Backbone of Mountains

Costa Rica sits astride a jagged series of volcanoes and mountains, part of the great Andean–Sierra Madre chain that runs the length of the western littoral of the Americas. From the Pacific coast of Costa Rica, great cones and domes dominate the landscape, and you're usually in sight of volcanoes in the northern part of the country.

The mountains rise in the nation's northwestern corner as a low, narrow band of hills. They grow steeper and broader and ever more rugged until they gird Costa Rica coast to coast at the Panamanian border, where they separate the Caribbean and Pacific from one another as surely as if these were the towering Himalayas.

Volcanic activity has fractured this mountainous backbone into distinct cordilleras. In the northwest, the Cordillera de Guanacaste rises in a leapfrogging series of volcanoes, including Rincón de la Vieja and Miravalles, whose steaming vents have been harnessed to provide geothermal energy. To the southeast is the Cordillera de Tilarán, dominated by Arenal, one of the world's most active volcanoes. To the east and rising even higher is the Cordillera Central, with four great volcanoes—Poás, Barva, Irazú and Turrialba—that gird the central highlands and within whose cusp lies the Meseta Central, an elevated plateau ranging in height from 900 to 1,787 meters. To the south of the valley rises the Cordillera Talamanca, an uplifted mountain region that tops out at the summit of Cerro Chirripó (3,819 meters), Costa Rica's highest peak.

Meseta Central

The Meseta Central, the heart and heartbeat of the nation, comprises a rich agricultural valley cradled by the flanks of the Cordillera Talamanca to the south, and by the fickle volcanoes of the Cordillera Central to the north and east. San José, the capital, lies at its center. At an elevation of 1,150 meters, San José enjoys year-round temperatures above 21°C (70°F), reliable rainfall, and rich volcanic soils—major reasons why almost two-thirds of the nation's population lives in the valley.

The Meseta Central measures about 40 km north to south and 80 km east to west and is divided from a smaller valley by the low-lying Cerros de la Carpintera that rise a few miles east of San José. Beyond lies the somewhat smaller Cartago Valley, at a slightly higher elevation. To the east the turbulent Reventazón—a favorite of white-water enthusiasts—tumbles to the Caribbean lowlands. The Río Virilla exits more leisurely, draining the San José Valley to the west.

Northern Zone and Caribbean Coast

The broad, pancake-flat, wedge-shaped northern lowlands are cut off from the more densely populated highlands by a languorous drape of hardwood forest. The low-lying plains or *llanuras,* which make up one-fifth of the nation's land area, extend along the entire length of the Río San Juan, whose course demarcates the Nicaraguan border. Farther south the plains narrow to a funnel along the Caribbean coast.

Westward, cattle ranches and banana and citrus plantations give way to pleats of green velveteen jungle ascending the steep eastern slopes of the central mountains, which run along a northwest-southeast axis, forming the third side of the wedge. Numerous rivers drop quickly from the mountains to the plains, where they snake along sluggishly. Beautiful beaches, many of gray or black sand, line the Caribbean coast, which sidles gently south.

Pacific Coast

Beaches are a major calling card of Costa Rica's Pacific coast, which is deeply indented with bays and inlets and two large gulfs—the Golfo de Nicoya (in the north) and Golfo Dulce (in the south), enfolded by the hilly, hook-nosed peninsulas of Nicoya and Osa, respectively. Mountains tilt precipitously toward the Pacific, coming closer to the ocean here than on the Caribbean side, and the slender coastal plain is only a few kilometers wide. North of the Golfo de Nicoya, the coastal strip widens to form a broad lowland belt of savanna—the Tempisque Basin. The basin is drained by the Río Tempisque, and narrows northward until hemmed in near the Nicaraguan border by the juncture of the Cordillera de Guanacaste and rolling, often steep, coastal hills that follow the arc of the Nicoya Peninsula.

A narrow, 64-km-long intermontane basin known as the Valle de El General runs parallel to and nestles comfortably between the Cordillera Talamanca and the coastal mountains—*Fila Costeña*—of the Pacific southwest. The Ríos General and Coto Brus and their many tributaries have carved a deep, steep-sided trough.

An Unstable Land

Costa Rica lies at the boundary where the Pacific's Cocos Plate—a piece of the earth's crust some 510 km wide—meets the crustal plate underlying the Caribbean. The two are converging as the Cocos Plate moves east at a rate of about 10 cm a year. It is a classic subduction zone in which the Caribbean Plate is forced under the Cocos—one of the most dynamic junctures on earth. Central America has been an isthmus, a peninsula, and even an archipelago in the not-so-distant geological past. It has therefore been both a corridor for and a barrier to landward movements, and it has been an area in which migrants have flourished, new life forms have emerged, and new ways of life have evolved. The Central America we know today became recognizable only in recent geological history. In fact, Costa Rica has one of the youngest surface areas in the Americas—only three million years old—for the volatile region has only recently been thrust from beneath the sea.

PLATE TECTONICS

Until the 1960s, when the theory of plate tectonics revolutionized the earth sciences, geologists trying to explain the distribution of earthquakes and volcanoes were at a loss. When earthquakes and volcanoes were plotted on a map, geologists realized that the planet is a puzzle—literally. The pieces of the terrestrial jigsaw are some 25 tectonic plates, interconnected pieces of the earth's crust (the lithosphere), 40–95 miles thick. Seven major plates carry the continents and ocean basins on their backs.

These plates are in continual motion, ponderously inching along on endless journeys across the surface of the earth, powered by forces originating deep within the earth. They ride on a viscous layer called the aesthenosphere, with a molten component welling up to the earth's surface on great convection currents fueled by heat from the core of our planet.

As the plates move, they pull apart or collide, unleashing titanic geological forces. When two plates slide past each other or converge—as off the Pacific coast of Central America—the geological forces generally drive one plate beneath the other, causing earthquakes. The friction created by one plate grinding beneath another melts part of both crusts, forming magma—molten rock—which wells up under pressure, erupting to form a chain of volcanoes.

In its travels eastward, the Cocos Plate gradually broke into seven fragments, which today move forward at varying depths and angles. This fracturing and competitive movement causes the frequent earthquakes with which Costa Ricans contend. The forces that thrust the Cocos and Caribbean Plates together continue to build inexorably.

From insignificant tremors to catastrophic blockbusters, most earthquakes are caused by the slippage of masses of rock along earth fractures or faults. Rocks possess elastic properties, and in time this elasticity allows rocks to accumulate strain energy as tectonic plates or their component sections jostle each other. Friction can contain the strain and hold the rocks in place for years. But eventually, as with a rubber band stretched beyond its breaking point, strain overcomes frictional lock and the fault ruptures at its weakest point.

Suddenly, the pent-up energy is released in the form of an earthquake—seismic waves that radiate in all directions from the point of rupture, the "focus." This seismic activity can last for a fraction of a second to, for a major earthquake, several minutes. Pressure waves traveling at five miles per second race from the quake's epicenter through the bedrock, compressing and extending the ground like an accordion. Following in their wake come waves that thrust the earth up and down, whipping along at three miles per second.

The most devastating earthquakes generally occur in subduction zones, when one tectonic plate plunges beneath another. Ocean trench quakes off the coast of Costa Rica have been recorded at 8.9 on the Richter scale and are among history's most awesome, heaving the sea floor sometimes scores of feet. These ruptures often propagate upward, touching off other, lower-magnitude tremors. This is what happened when the powerful 7.4 quake struck Costa Rica on 22 April 1991. That massive quake, which originated near the Caribbean town of Pandora (112 km southeast of San José), left at least 27 people dead, more than 400 injured, 13,000 homeless, and more than 3,260 buildings destroyed in Limón Province. The earthquake caused the Atlantic coastline to rise permanently—in parts by as much as 1.5 meters, thrusting coral reefs above the ocean surface and reducing them to bleached calcareous skeletons.

Volcanoes

Costa Rica lies at the heart of one of the most active volcanic regions on earth. The beauty of the

Costa Rican landscape has been enhanced by volcanic cones—part of the Pacific Rim of Fire—that march the length of Central America. Costa Rica is home to seven of the isthmus' 42 active volcanoes, plus 60 dormant or extinct ones. Some have the look classically associated with volcanoes—a graceful, symmetrical cone rising to a single crater. Others are sprawling, weathered mountains whose once-noble summits have collapsed into huge depressions called calderas (from the Portuguese word for "cauldron"). Still others, such as on Cocos Island, have smooth, shield-shaped outlines with rounded tops pocked by tiny craters.

Visitors seeking to peer into the bowels of a rumbling volcano can do so easily. Atop Poás's crater rim, for example, you can gape down into the great well-like vent and see pools of molten lava bubbling menacingly, giving off diabolical, gut-wrenching fumes of chlorine and sulfur—and emitting explosive cracks, like the sound of distant artillery.

Several national parks have been created around active volcanoes. An excellent descriptive guide is Guillermo Alvarado's *Costa Rica; Land of Volcanoes,* which offers scientific explanations in layperson's terms.

In 1963, Irazú (3,412 meters) broke a 20-year silence, disgorging great clouds of smoke and ash. The eruptions triggered a bizarre storm that showered San José with 13 cm of muddy ash, snuffing out the 1964 coffee crop but enriching the Meseta Central for years to come. The binge lasted for two years, then abruptly ceased (although it began rumbling again in 1996). Poás (2,692 meters) has been particularly violent during the past 30 years. In the 1950s, the restless four-mile-wide giant awoke with a roar after a 60-year snooze, and it has been huffing and puffing ever since. Eruptions then kicked up a new cone about 100 meters tall. Two of Poás's craters now slumber under blankets of vegetation (one even cradles a lake), but the third crater belches and bubbles persistently. Volcanologists monitor the volcano constantly for impending eruptions.

Arenal (1,624 meters) gives a more spectacular light-and-sound show. After a four-century-long Rip van Winkle–like dormancy, this 4,000-year-young juvenile began spouting in 1968, when it laid waste to a four-square-mile area. Arenal's activity, sometimes minor and sometimes not, continues unabated; it erupted spectacularly in August 2000, killing two people and forcing the evacuation of Tabacón. Though more placid, Miravalles, Turrialba, and Rincón de la Vieja, among Costa Rica's coterie of coquettish volcanoes, also occasionally fling fiery fountains of lava and breccia into the air. Rincón blew in 1995, doing damage in Upala.

The type of magma that fuels most Central American volcanoes is thick, viscous, and so filled with gases that the erupting magma often blasts violently into the air. If it erupts in great quantity, it may leave a void within the volcano's interior, into which the top of the mountain crumbles to form a caldera. Irazú is a classic example. Its top fell in eons ago. Since then, however, small eruptions have built up three new volcanic cones within the ancient caldera.

CLIMATE

When talk turns to Costa Rica's climate, hyperbole flows as thick and as fast as the waterfalls that cascade in ribbons of quicksilver down through the forest-clad mountains. English 19th-century novelist Anthony Trollope was among the first to wax lyrical: "No climate can, I imagine, be more favorable to fertility and to man's comfort at the same time than that of the interior of Costa Rica."

The country lies wholly within the tropics, yet boasts at least a dozen climatic zones and is markedly diverse in local microclimates, which make generalizations on temperature and rainfall misleading.

Most regions have a rainy season (May–Nov.) and a dry season (Dec.–April). Rainfall almost everywhere follows a predictable schedule. In general, highland ridges are wet, and windward sides always are the wettest.

The terms "summer" *(verano)* and "winter" *(invierno)* are used by Ticans to designate their dry and wet seasons, respectively. Since the Tican "summer"—which in broad terms lasts December through April—occurs in what are winter months elsewhere in the Northern Hemisphere (and vice versa), it can be confusing.

Temperatures

Temperatures, dictated more by elevation and location than by season, range from tropical on the coastal plains to temperate in the interior highlands. Mean temperatures average 27°C (82°F) at sea level on the Caribbean coast and 32°C (89°F) on the Pacific lowlands. In the highlands, the weather is refreshingly clear and invigorating. San José's daily temperatures are in the 70s almost year-round, with little monthly variation; the average annual temperature is 20°C (68°F), and there's never a need for air-conditioning. A heat wave is when the mercury reaches the 80s; if it falls below 65°F, it's considered cold. The record high for San José is only 92°F; record low is 49°F. It has never snowed in San José. Nights are usually in the 60s year-round, so bring a sweater.

Temperatures fall steadily as elevation climbs (about one degree for every 100-meter gain). They rarely exceed a mean of 10°C (48°F) atop Chirripó (at 3,819 m, the highest mountain), where frost is frequent and enveloping clouds drift dark and ominous among the mountain passes. You'll definitely need a warm sweater or jacket for the mountains, where the difference between daytime highs and nighttime lows is greatest.

The length of daylight varies only slightly throughout the year. Sunrise is around 6 A.M. and sunset about 6 P.M., and the sun's path is never far from overhead, so seasonal variations in temperatures rarely exceed five degrees in any given location.

Everywhere, March to May are the hottest months, with September and October not far behind. Cool winds bearing down from northern latitudes lower temperatures during December, January, and February, particularly on the northern Pacific coast, where certain days during summer (dry season) months can be surprisingly cool. The most extreme daily fluctuations occur during the dry season, when

clear skies at night allow maximum heat loss through radiation. In the wet season, nights are generally warmer, as the heat built up during the day is trapped by clouds.

Rainfall

Rain is a fact of life in Costa Rica. Annual precipitation averages 250 cm (100 inches) nationwide. Depending on the region, the majority of this may fall in relatively few days—sometimes fewer than 15 per year. In drier years, the Tempisque Basin in Guanacaste, for example, receives as little as 48 cm (18 inches), mostly in a few torrential downpours. The mountains, by contrast, often exceed 385 cm (150 inches) per year, sometimes as much as 7.6 meters (25 feet) on the more exposed easterly facing slopes. And don't expect to stay dry in the montane rainforests; even on the sunniest days, the humid forests produce their own internal rain as water vapor condenses on the cool leaves and falls.

Generally, rains occur in the early afternoons in the highlands, midafternoons in the Pacific lowlands, and late afternoons (and commonly during the night) in the Atlantic lowlands. Sometimes it falls in sudden torrents called *aguaceros,* sometimes it falls hard and steady, and sometimes it sheets down without letup for several days and nights.

Dry season on the Meseta Central and throughout the western regions is December through April. In Guanacaste, the dry season usually lingers slightly longer; the northwest coast (the driest part of the country) often has few rainy days even during wet season. On the Atlantic coast, the so-called dry season starts in January and runs through April.

Even in the rainy season, days often start out warm and sunny, although *temporales* (morning rains) are not uncommon. In the highlands, rain generally falls in midafternoon and evening, and long rainy days are uncommon. Be prepared: 23 hours of a given day may be dry and pleasant; during the 24th, the rain can come down with the force of a waterfall. The sudden onset of a relatively dry period, called *veranillo* (little summer), sometimes occurs in July and August or August and September, particularly along the Pacific coast.

Seasonal patterns can vary, especially in years when the occasional weather phenomenon known as El Niño sets in, as it did with devastating force in 1997. The freak weather it produces is caused by an abnormal warming of ocean waters off the Pacific coast, resulting in volatile changes in air masses.

Rarely do **hurricanes** strike Costa Rica, although Hurricane Cesár came ashore on 27 July 1996, killing 41 people and trashing the Pacific southwest.

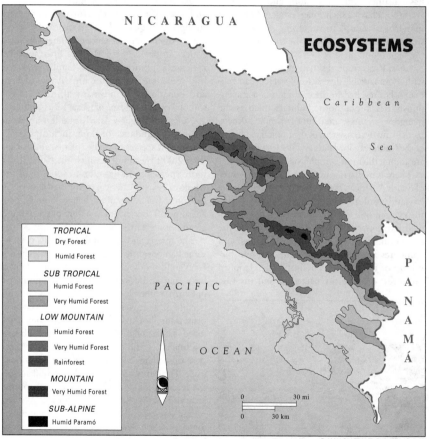

ECOSYSTEMS

NICARAGUA

Caribbean

Sea

PACIFIC

OCEAN

PANAMÁ

TROPICAL
  Dry Forest
  Humid Forest

SUB TROPICAL
  Humid Forest
  Very Humid Forest

LOW MOUNTAIN
  Humid Forest
  Very Humid Forest
  Rainforest

MOUNTAIN
  Very Humid Forest

SUB-ALPINE
  Humid Paramó

0   30 mi
0   30 km

© AVALON TRAVEL PUBLISHING, INC.

Flora

In 1947, biologist L. H. Holdridge introduced a system of classifying vegetation types or "zones" according to a matrix based on combinations of temperature, rainfall, and seasonality. Each zone has a distinct natural vegetation and ecosystem. Costa Rica has 12 such zones, ranging from tidal mangrove swamps to subalpine *paramó* with stunted dwarf plants above the timberline atop the high mountains.

Costa Rica's tropical situation, in combination with its remarkable diversity of local relief and climates, has resulted in the evolution of a stupendously rich biota. Some habitats, such as the mangrove swamps, are relatively simple. Others, particularly the ecosystem of the tropical rainforests of the Caribbean lowlands and the Osa Peninsula, are among the most complex on the planet.

There is no barrier in Costa Rica to the entry of South American species of flora; as a result, the lowland rainforests have strong affinities with the *selva* (jungle) of South America and form a distinctive assemblage of species in which the large number of palms, tree ferns, lianas, and epiphytes attest to the constant heat and humidity of the region. The impressive tropical rainforest of eastern Costa Rica and the Osa

Sombrilla de Pobre ("Poor Man's Umbrella")

Peninsula gives way on the central Pacific to a dry evergreen forest at lower elevations and dry deciduous forest farther north. These, too, are of essentially South American composition. Above about 1,000 meters, the species are fewer and the affinities with North America are stronger. In the Cordillera Talamanca, conifers of South American provenance are joined by North American oaks. Above the tree line (approximately 3,000 meters), hikers familiar with the mid-elevation flora of the high Andes of Peru and Ecuador will find many affinities in the shrubby open landscape of Costa Rica's cordillera.

Not surprisingly, Costa Rica offers an extraordinary abundance of flora, including more than 9,000 species of higher plants, and no less than 2,000 species of bromeliads. It has many more species of ferns—about 800—than the whole of North America, including Mexico. Of heliconias (members of the banana family) there are some 30 species. It is a nation of green upon green upon green.

The forests and grasslands flare with color—some flamboyantly so, as plants advertise the delights and rewards they offer, including the ultimate bribe, nectar. Begonias, anthuriums, and blood of Christ, named for the red splotches on the underside of its leaves, are common. My favorite plant is the "hot lips" *(labios ardientes)*, sometimes called "hooker's lips" *(labios de puta)*, whose bright red bracts remind me of Mick Jagger's famous pout or, perhaps more appropriately, Madonna's smile. The vermilion *poró* tree (the bright flame-of-the-forest), pink-and-white meadow oak, purple jacaranda, and the almost fluorescent-yellow *corteza amarilla* all add their seasonal bouquets to the landscape. And the morning glory spreads its thick lavender carpets across lowland pastures, joined by carnal red passion-flowers (their unromantically foul smell is a crafty device to enlist the help of flies in pollination).

Many plants play out the game of love and reproduction in the heat of the tropical night, when they emit fragrances designed to attract

tropical flowers

specific insect species. Other flowering species employ markings on their petals to indicate the exact placing of the rewards insects seek. Many orchid species, for example, are marked with lines and spots like an airfield, to show the insect where to land and in which direction to taxi. Others display colors invisible to the human eye, yet clearly perceptible by insects whose eyesight spans the ultraviolet spectrum. And a remarkable holly species *(Ocotea tenera)* occasionally changes sex, being male one year and female the next, to increase its chance of pollination.

The most abundant flora in rainforest environments are ferns, light-gap pioneers found from sea level to the highest elevations. The big tree ferns—sometimes called *rabo de mico* (monkey-tail) ferns, an allusion to the uncurling young fronds—are relics from the age of the dinosaurs, sometimes four meters tall, with fiddleheads large enough to grace a cello. Others are epiphytes (plants that take root on plants but that are not parasitic), arboreal "nesters," or climbers whose long leaves can grapple upward for 20 meters or more.

The epiphytic environment is extremely poor in mineral nutrients. The bromeliads—brilliantly flowering, spiky-leafed "air" plants up to 120 cm across—have developed tanks or cisterns that hold great quantities of rainwater and decaying detritus in the whorled bases of their tightly overlapping stiff leaves. The plants gain nourishment from dissolved nutrients in the cisterns (it's a symbiotic relationship: often the host tree will put roots down into the epiphyte to absorb its nutrients). Known as tank epiphytes, they provide trysting places and homes for tiny aquatic animals high above the ground.

All plants depend on light to power the chemical process by which they synthesize their body substances from simple elements. Height is therefore of utmost importance. When an old tree falls, the strong, unaccustomed light triggers seeds that have lain dormant, and banana palms and ginger plants, heliconias and cecropias—all plants that live in the sunshine on riverbanks or in forest clearings—burst into life and put out big broad leaves to soak up the sun, to flower and to fruit. Another prominent plant is the poor man's umbrella *(sombrilla de pobre),* whose name you'll remember if you get caught in a downpour while in the rainforest; its giant leaves make excellent impromptu shelters.

TROPICAL RAINFOREST

Once upon a time, about 140 million years ago, near the beginning of the Cretaceous period in the age of dinosaurs, before the freezing embraces of the Ice Ages, thick evergreen forests blanketed much of the world's warm, humid surface. Today's tropical rainforests—the densest and richest proliferation of plants ever known—are the survivors of these primeval jungles of ages past.

These forests, the largest of which is Brazil's Amazonian jungle, are found in a narrow belt that girdles the earth at the equator. In the tropics, constant sunlight, endless rains, and high temperatures year-round spell life. The steamy atmosphere and fast nutrient turnover have pro-

heliconias

moted favorable growth conditions and intense competition, allowing the forest flora to evolve into an extraordinary multitude of different species, exploiting to the full every conceivable niche. Nowhere else on earth is biological productivity and diversity so evident: tropical rainforests contain more than half of all living things known to man (the number of insect species in a hectare of rainforest is so great that no successful count has been made).

Only superficially does the rainforest resemble the fictional jungles of Tarzan. Yes, the foliage can indeed be so dense that you cannot move without a machete. But since only about 10 percent of the total sunlight manages to penetrate through the forest canopy, the undergrowth is generally correspondingly sparse, and the forest floor surprisingly open and relatively easy to move about in. Within the shadowed jungle the dark subaqueous greens are lit here and there by beams of sunlight pouring down from above. (The plants array their leaves to avoid leaf shade; others are shaded purple underneath to help reflect back the light passing through the leaf; and the "walking palm" literally walks across the forest floor in search of light on its stiltlike roots.)

The stagnant air is loaded with moisture. There is supposedly even a fungus that flourishes inside binoculars and cameras and eats away the protective coating of lenses. To a visitor, the tropical rainforest seems always the same: uniform heat and stifling 90 percent humidity. But this is true only near the ground. High in the tops of the trees, where the sun comes and goes, breezes blow, and moisture has a chance to be carried away, the swings in temperature between day and night are as much as 15 degrees, and the humidity may drop from 95 percent, its fairly constant nighttime level, to as low as 60 percent as the sun rises and warms the forest. Thus, within 30 vertical meters, two distinctly different climates prevail.

Botanists have distinguished among 30 or so different types of rainforest, whose species content is determined by temperature and rainfall. Tropical evergreen rainforest exists in areas of high rainfall (at least 200 cm) and regular high temperatures averaging no less than 25°C (77°F).

© CHRISTOPHER P. BAKER

the tropical rainforest of Braulio Carrillo National Park

In Costa Rica, the lush tropical evergreen rainforest of the Caribbean lowlands gives way on the Pacific side to a seasonally dry evergreen forest in the well-watered south.

Costa Rica's tropical rainforests are places of peace and renewal, like a vast vaulted cathedral, mysterious, strangely silent, and of majestic proportions. As one writer says: "a fourteenth-century stonemason would have felt at home [in the rainforest], with its buttressed, moss-columned, towering trees and dark recesses."

Plunging deep into the forest, visitors are soon struck by how much variety there is. While in temperate forests distinct species of flora congregate neatly into distinctive plant "neighborhoods" with few other species interspersed, in the rainforest you may pass one example of a particular tree species, then not see another for half a mile. In between, however, are hundreds of other species. In the rainforest, too, life is piled upon life—literally. The firm and unyielding forest floor is a "dark factory of decomposition," where bacteria, mold, and insects work unceasingly, degrading the constant rain of leaf litter and dislodged fruits into nutrient molecules.

Strange-shaped umbrellas, curtains, and globes of fungi proliferate, too. They are key to providing the nourishment vital to the jungle's life cycle. While a fallen leaf from a North American oak may take a year to decompose, a leaf in the tropical rainforest will fully decay within a month. If these precious nutrients and minerals thus released are not to be washed away by the daily drenching of rain, they must be reclaimed quickly and returned to the canopy to restart the cycle of life. The trees suck up the minerals and nutrients through a thick mat of rootlets that grow close to the surface of the inordinately thin soil. To counteract their inherent instability, many species grow side buttresses: wafer-thin flanges that radiate in a ring around the base of the tree like the tail fins of rockets.

The dark nave of the rainforest cathedral is rich with ferns, saplings, and herbaceous plants, seeping in moisture. For every tree in the jungle, there is a clinging vine fighting for a glimpse of the sun. Instead of using up valuable time and energy in building their own supports, these clutching vines and lianas rely on the straight, limbless trunks typical of rainforest tree species to provide a support in their quest for sunlight. They ride piggyback to the canopy, where they continue to snake through the treetops, sometimes reaching lengths of 300 meters. One species spirals around its host like a corkscrew; another cements itself to a tree with three-pronged tendrils.

The bully of the forest, however, is the strangler fig, which isn't content to merely coexist. While most lianas and vines take root in the ground and grow upward, the strangler figs do the opposite. After sprouting in the forest canopy from seeds dropped by birds and bats, the strangler fig sends roots to the ground, where they dig into the soil and provide a boost of sustenance.

Slowly but surely—it may take a full century—the roots grow and envelop the host tree, choking it until it dies and rots away, leaving a hollow, trellised, freestanding cylinder.

The vigorous competition for light and space has promoted the evolution of long, slender, branchless trunks, many well over 35 meters tall, and flat-topped crowns with foliage so dense that rainwater from driving tropical downpours often may not reach the ground for 10 minutes. This

ORCHIDS

It's appropriate that the orchid is the national flower of Costa Rica: the country has more than 1,400 identified species, the richest orchid flora in Central America. And countless others probably await discovery. At any time of year you're sure to find dozens of species in bloom, from sea level to the highest, subfreezing reaches of Chirripó. There is no best time for viewing orchids, although the beginning of both the dry season (especially in the wettest rainforest regions) and the wet season are said to be particularly favorable. Orchid lovers should head for the cloud forests; there the greatest diversity exists in humid mid-elevation environments where they are abundant as tropical epiphytes (constituting 88 percent of orchid species).

Orchids are not only the largest family of flowering plants, they're also the most diverse—poke around with magnifying glass in hand and you'll come across species with flowers less than one millimeter across. Others, like the native *Phragmipedium caudatum,* have pendulant petals that can reach more than half a meter. Some flower for only one day; others last several weeks.

While not all orchids lead epiphytic lives—the Spanish called them *parasitos*—those that do are the most exotic of epiphytes, classics of their kind, so heartachingly beautiful that collectors can't resist their siren call and threaten their existence.

Orchids have evolved a remarkable array of ingenious pollination techniques. Some species self-pollinate. Others attract insects by sexual impersonation. One species, for example, produces a flower that closely resembles the form of a female wasp—complete with eyes, antennae, and wings. It even gives off the odor of a female wasp in mating condition. Male wasps, deceived, attempt to copulate with it. In their vigor, they deposit pollen within the orchid flower and immediately afterward receive a fresh batch to carry to the next false female. Male bees and other insects are known to use the pollen of orchids as a perfume to attract females.

Guile seems to be the forte of orchids. One species drugs its visitors. Bees clamber into its throat and sip a nectar so intoxicating that after the merest taste they become so inebriated they lose their footing and slip into a small bucket of liquid. Escape is offered up a spout—the proverbial light at the end of the tunnel. As the drunken insect totters up, it has to wriggle beneath an overhanging rod, which showers its back with pollen.

Pollination techniques have become so species-specific that hybridization of different orchid species is avoided by each having developed its own morphological configuration to attach its pollen, and receive it in return, to a specific part of the insect's body.

An annual orchid show is held each March at Instituto Nacional de Biodiversidad (INBio), near San José.

Orquídeas del Bosque (tel. 506/232-1466, fax 506/296-6349, www.costaricanorchids.com) sells orchids for export.

great vaulted canopy—the clerestory of the rainforest cathedral—is the jungle's powerhouse, where more than 90 percent of photosynthesis takes place. Above this dense carpet of greenery rise a few scattered giants towering to heights of 70 meters or more.

The scaffolding of massive boughs is colonized at all levels by a riot of bromeliads, ferns, and other epiphytes. Tiny spores sprout on the bark, gain a foothold, and spread like luxuriant carpets. As they die and decay, they form compost on the branch capable of supporting larger plants that feed on the leaf mold and draw moisture by dangling their roots into the humid air. Soon every available surface is a great hanging gallery of giant elkhorns and ferns, often reaching such weights that whole tree limbs are torn away and crash down to join the decaying litter on the forest floor.

The Babylonian gardens of the jungle ceiling—naturalist William Beebe called it an "undiscovered continent"—also host a staggeringly complex, unseen world of wildlife. The rich rainforest green backdrops the jewel colors of its many inhabitants. Sit still awhile and the unseen beasts and birds will get used to your presence and emerge from the shadows. Enormous morpho butterflies float by, flashing like bright neon signs. Is that vine really moving? More likely it's a brilliantly costumed tree python, so green it is almost iridescent, draped in sensuous coils on a branch.

Scarlet macaws and lesser parrots plunge and sway in the high branches, announcing their playacting with an outburst of shrieks. Arboreal rodents leap and run along the branches, searching for nectar and insects, while insectivorous birds watch from their vantage points for any movement that will betray a stick insect or leaf-green tree frog to scoop up for lunch. Legions of monkeys, sloths, and fruit- and leaf-eating mammals also live in the green world of the canopy, browsing and hunting, thieving and scavenging, breeding and dying.

Larger hunters live up there, too. In addition to the great eagles plunging through the canopy to grab monkeys, there are also tree-dwelling cats. These superbly athletic climbers are quite capable of catching monkeys and squirrels as they leap from branch to branch and race up trunks. There are also snakes here. Not the great monsters so common in romantic fiction, but much smaller creatures, some twig-thin, such as the chunk-headed snake with catlike eyes, which feasts on frogs and lizards and nestling birds.

Come twilight, the forest soaks in a brief moment of silence. Slowly, the lisping of insects begins. There is a faint rustle as nocturnal rodents come out to forage in the ground litter. And the squabbling of fruit bats replaces that of the birds. All around, myriad beetles and moths take wing in the moist velvet blanket of the tropical night.

The **Rainforest Trust** (6001 SW 63rd Ave., Miami, FL 33143, tel. 305/667-2779, fax 305/665-0691, www.rainforesttrust.com) is a good resource.

TROPICAL DRY FOREST

Before the arrival of the Spanish in the early 16th century, dry forests blanketed the Pacific coastal lowlands from Panamá to Mexico. Fires set by the Spanish and by generations of farmers and ranchers thereafter spread savannas across the province, whose flat alluvial plains and rich volcanic soils are perfect for crops and cattle ranches. Today, the dry forests cling precariously to some 2 percent of their former range—a mere 520 square kilometers of Costa Rica in scattered patches centered on the lower Río Tempisque of Guanacaste. Far rarer than rainforests, they are significantly more endangered, especially by fires, which eviscerate whole forest patches, opening holes in which ecological opportunists—weeds and grasses such as African jaragua—rush in. Eventually savanna comes to replace the forest.

Unlike Costa Rica's rainforests, the rare tropical dry forest is relatively sparsely vegetated, with far fewer tree species and only two strata. Canopy trees have short, stout trunks with large, flat-topped crowns, rarely more than 15 meters above the ground. Beneath is an understory with small, open-top crowns, and a layer of shrubs with vicious spines and thorns. Missing are the great profusion of epiphytes and the year-round lush evergreens of the rainforest.

From November through March, no rain relieves the parching heat. Then, the deciduous dry forests undergo a dramatic seasonal transformation, the purple jacaranda, pink-and-white meadow oak, yellow *corteza amarilla,* scarlet *poró,* and the bright orange flame-of-the-forest exploding in Monet colors in the midst of drought.

The fate of even the preserved dry-forest parcels hinges on the success of two ambitious conservation projects (see the sidebar *Restoring the Dry Forest,* in the *Guanacaste and the Northwest* chapter).

MANGROVE ESTUARIES

Costa Rica's shorelines are home to five species of mangroves. These pioneer land builders thrive at the interface of land and sea, forming a stabilizing tangle that fights tidal erosion and reclaims land from the water.

Mangroves are what botanists call halophytes, plants that thrive in salty conditions. Although they do not require salt (they in fact grow better in fresh water), they thrive where no other tree can. Costa Rica's young rivers have short and violent courses that keep silt and volcanic ash churned up and suspended, so that a great deal of it is carried out of the mountains onto the coastal alluvial plains. The nutrient-rich mud generates algae and other small organisms that form the base of the marine food chain. Food is delivered to the estuaries every day from both the sea and the land so those few plants—and creatures—that can survive here flourish in immense num-

RECYCLING NUTRIENTS IN THE RAINFOREST

One of the most important differences between tropical and temperate environments is what biologists call "species richness." A natural forest patch of a few hundred acres in Michigan, for example, might contain 25–30 species of trees; an equivalent tract of Costa Rican rainforest might contain more than 400. Ohio, at twice Costa's Rica geographical size, has only about 10 species of bats; Costa Rica has more than 100.

Why such complexity, such stupefying abundance of *species* in the neotropics—the tropics of the New World? It all has to do with the rapid pace of nutrient recycling and the way the natural world competes most effectively for nourishment.

In the temperate world, with the warm days and sunlight of spring, plants burst forth with protein-rich buds, shoots, and young leaves, which appear simultaneously in a protein "pulse." Animals bring forth their young during this period of protein abundance: birds return from the south to lay eggs and raise their broods, insect eggs hatch, frogs and toads crawl out of hibernation to reproduce. Come autumn, the same plants produce a second protein glut as tender berries, seeds, and nuts, which critters pack in to sustain themselves through the hardships of impending winter. The synchronized budding and fruiting of foliage is so great that all the hungry mouths gobbling protein hardly threaten a plant species's survival.

In the tropics, by contrast, the seasonal cycle is far less pronounced: sunlight, rain, and warm temperatures are constant, and plants germinate, grow, flower, and seed year-round. Hence, there is no distinct protein surplus. Leaf fall, too, occurs continuously and slowly in the tropical rainforest, unlike the autumnal drops of temperate deciduous forests, and the same tropical conditions of heat and moisture that fuel year-round growth also sponsor fast decomposition of dead leaves. The humus that enriches the soils of more temperate latitudes doesn't have a chance to accumulate in the tropics. Thus, soils are thin and, after millions of years of daily rainfall and constant heat, leached of their nutrient content.

Result? The ecosystem of a tropical rainforest is upside down when compared to forests in the temperate zone, where nutrients are stored in the soil. In the tropics they're stored overhead: in

bers. And their sustained health is vital to the health of other marine ecosystems.

The nutrients the mangrove seeks lie near the surface of the acid mud, deposited by the tides. There is no oxygen to be had in the mud: estuarine mud is so fine-grained that air cannot diffuse through it, and the gases produced by the decomposition of the organic debris within it stay trapped until footsteps release them, producing a strong whiff of rotten eggs. Hence, there is no point in the mangroves sending down deep roots. Instead, the mangroves send out peculiar aerial roots, maintaining a hold on the glutinous mud and giving the mangroves the appearance of walking on water. They draw oxygen from the air through small patches of spongy tissue on their bark.

Up and down the coast, the irrepressible, reddish-barked, shrubby mangroves rise from the dark water on interlocking stilt roots. Small brackish streams and labyrinthine creeks wind among them like snakes, sometimes interconnecting, sometimes petering out in narrow cul-de-sacs, sometimes opening suddenly into broad lagoons. A few clear channels may run through the rich and redolent world of the mangroves, but the trees grow so thickly over much of it that you cannot force even a small boat between them.

Mangrove swamps are esteemed as nurseries of marinelife and as havens for water birds—cormorants, frigate birds, pelicans, herons, and egrets—which feed and nest here by the thousands, producing guano that makes the mangroves grow faster.

---

the densely leafed canopy. Leaves and young shoots represent a major investment of scarce nutrients, which plants cannot afford to have gobbled up by hungry multitudes of animals, insects, and birds. Hence, says one biologist, "It might be said that the plants want to be different from one another in order to avoid being devoured." Intense competition has pressured tropical plants to diversify greatly, to disperse, and to develop defense mechanisms, such as thorns or sickening toxins. Other species stagger their production of shoots and new leaves throughout the year so that they never expose too much new growth to predation at any one time.

Because plant protein is scarce at any given time, and because plants have evolved stratagems to guard it, animals have been forced to compete fiercely. They've diversified like the plants, and competition has resulted in notable examples of specialization, with individual species staking claims to a narrow ecological niche in which other creatures can't compete. One bird species eats only insects driven up from the ground by army ants, while its droppings provide food for a certain species of butterfly.

Through these intricate associations, specific plants and predators become totally dependent on one another. A perfect example is the ant acacia, a tree common along the Pacific coast. The plant is weak and defenseless, a poor competitor in the upward race for sunlight, and easily overshadowed by faster-growing neighbors. Its tiny nectaries (glands that exude sugar) and leaf-tip swellings filled with proteins and vitamins are tempting morsels for hungry insects and birds. None, however, dares steal a nibble, for a species of tiny yet aggressive ants acts as the acacia's praetorian guard. In exchange for the honeylike food that they love, the ants defend their plant fiercely. Any predator foolish enough to touch the acacia is attacked; if a vine threatens to envelop the tree, the ants cut the vine down. If the branches of a neighboring plant threaten to steal the acacia's sunlight, the ants will prune the interloper; if a neighbor's seeds fall to the ground beneath the acacia, the insects will cart them off before they can germinate. If the ants were to become extinct, the plant would never survive. If the plant disappeared, the ants would starve. Each is inextricably in the debt of the other.

A look down into the water reveals luxuriant life: oysters and sponges attached to the roots, small stingrays flapping slowly over the bottom, and tiny fish in schools of tens of thousands. Baby black-tipped sharks and other juvenile fish, too, spend much of their early lives among mangrove roots, out of the heavy surf, shielded by the root maze that keeps out large predators.

High tide brings larger diners—big mangrove snappers and young barracudas hang motionless in the water. Raccoons, snakes, and arboreal creatures also inhabit the mangroves. There is even an arboreal mangrove tree crab *(Aratus pisonii)*, which eats mangrove leaves and is restricted to the very crowns of the trees by the predatory activities of another arboreal crab, *Goniopsis pulcra.*

Mangroves are aggressive colonizers, thanks to one of nature's most remarkable seedlings. The heavy, fleshy mangrove seeds, shaped like plumb bobs, germinate while still on the tree. The flowers bloom for a few weeks in the spring and then fall off, making way for a fruit. A seedling shoot soon sprouts from each fruit and grows to a length of 15–30 cm before dropping from the tree. Falling like darts, at low tide they land in the mud and put down roots immediately. Otherwise, the seedlings—great travelers—become floating scouts and outriders ahead of the advancing roots.

The seaborne seedling can remain alive for as long as a year, during which time it may drift for hundreds of miles. Eventually, it touches the muddy floor and anchors itself, growing as much as 60 cm in its first year. By its third year a young tree starts to sprout its own forest of arching prop roots; in about 10 years it has fostered a thriving colony of mangroves, which edge ever out to sea, forming a great swampy forest. As silt builds up among the roots, land is gradually reclaimed from the sea. Mangroves build up the soil until they strand themselves high and dry. In the end they die on the land they have created.

Fauna

Anyone who has traveled in the tropics in search of wildlife can tell you that disappointment comes easy. But Costa Rica is one place that lives up to its reputation. Costa Rica is nature's live theater—and the actors aren't shy.

My friend Lynn Ferrin wrote, "The birds are like jewels, the animals like creatures in a Rousseau painting." Noisy flocks of oropendolas, with long tails "the color of daffodils," sweep from tree to tree. The scarlet macaws are like rainbows, the toucans and hummingbirds like the green flash of sunset. The tiny poison-dart frogs are bright enough to scare away even the most dimwitted predator. And the electric-blue morphos, the neon narcissi of the butterfly world, make even the most unmoved of viewers gape in awe.

Then there are all the creatures that mimic other things and are harder to spot: insects that look like rotting leaves, moths that look like wasps, the mottled, bark-colored *machaca* (lantern fly), and the giant *Caligo memnon* (cream owl) butterfly whose huge open wings resemble the wide-eyed face of an owl.

Much of the wildlife is glimpsed only as shadows. (Some, like the dreaded fer-de-lance, for example, uncurling in the rotten leaves, you *hope* you don't meet.) Well-known animals that you are *not* likely to see are the cats—pumas, jaguars, margays, and ocelots—and tapirs and white-lipped peccaries. With patience, however, you can usually spot monkeys galore, as well as iguanas, quetzals, and three-fingered sloths that get most of their aerobic exercise by scratching their bellies and look, as someone has said, like "long-armed tree-dwelling Muppets."

The National Institute of Biodiversity (INBio), a private, nonprofit organization formed in 1989, has been charged with the formidable task of collecting, identifying, and labeling every plant and animal species in Costa Rica. "After 100 years of work by the National Museum we still only know 10–20 percent of what we have in the country," says director Rodrigo Gómez. Over the course of the last 110 years, the National Museum collected some 70,000 specimens; in their first 18 months, INBio's hundreds of "parataxonomists" (ordinary citizens trained to gather and preserve specimens) gathered almost two million.

Identifying the species is a prodigious task, which every day turns up something new. Insects, for example, make up about half of the estimated 500,000 to one million plant and animal species in Costa Rica. The country is home seasonally to more than 850 bird species—10 percent of all known bird species (the U.S. and Canada combined have less than half that number). One source reports there are 5,000 different species of grasshoppers, 160 known amphibians, 220 reptiles, and 10 percent of all known butterflies (Corcovado National Park alone has at least 220 different species).

Early Migrations

About three million years ago, the Central American isthmus began to rise from the sea to form the first tentative link between the two Americas. Going from island to island, birds, insects, reptiles, and the first mammals began to move back and forth between the continents. During this period, rodents of North America reached the southern continent, and so did the monkeys, which found the tropical climate to their liking.

In due course, South America connected with North America. Down this corridor came the placental mammals to dispute the possession of South America with the marsupial residents. Creatures poured across the bridge in both directions. The equids used it to enter South America, the opossums to invade North America. A ground sloth the size of an elephant headed north, too, reaching what is now Texas before it died out. Only a few South American mammals, notably armadillos, ground sloths, and porcupines, managed to establish themselves successfully in the north. The greatest migration was in the other direction.

A procession of North American mammals swarmed south, with disastrous effects on native populations. The mammals soon came to dominate the environment, diversifying into forms more appropriate to the tropics. In the course of this rivalry, many marsupial species disappeared, leaving only the tough, opportunistic opossums.

The isthmus has thus served as a "filter bridge" for the intermingling of species and the evolution of modern distinctive Costa Rican biota. Costa Rica's unique location and tropical setting, along with a great variety of local relief and microclimates, have meant that refuge areas for ancient species endangered by changes in environmental conditions have been widely available, and species that have died out elsewhere can still be found here. This, together with generous infusions of plants and animals from both continents, has resulted in a proliferation of species that in many important respects is vastly richer than the biota of either North or South America.

MAMMALS

Given the rich diversity of Costa Rica's ecosystems, it may come as a surprise that only 200 mammal species—half of which are bats—live here. Several species of dolphins and seven species of whales are common in Costa Rican waters, but there are no seals. And the only endemic marine mammal species of any significance is the endangered manatee.

Before man hunted them to extinction, there were many more mammal species. Even today all large- and many small-mammal populations are subject to extreme pressure from hunting or habitat destruction. (Selva and Luna, two young puma cubs orphaned when their mother was shot, are mascots for a national campaign to act against illegal hunting throughout Costa Rica.)

Anteaters

Anteaters are common in lowland and middle-elevation habitats throughout Costa Rica. Anteaters are purists and subsist solely on a diet of ants and termites, plus a few unavoidable bits of dirt. There is no doubt about what the best tool is for the job—a long tongue with thousands of microscopic spines. The anteater's toothless jaw is one long tube. When it feeds, using its powerful forearms and claws to rip open ant and termite

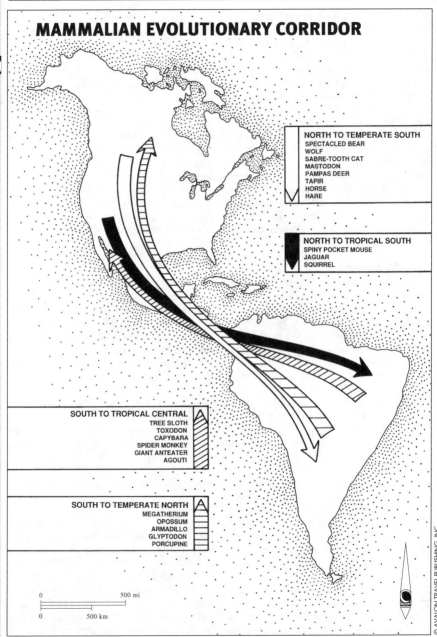

MAMMALIAN EVOLUTIONARY CORRIDOR

NORTH TO TEMPERATE SOUTH
SPECTACLED BEAR
WOLF
SABRE-TOOTH CAT
MASTODON
PAMPAS DEER
TAPIR
HORSE
HARE

NORTH TO TROPICAL SOUTH
SPINY POCKET MOUSE
JAGUAR
SQUIRREL

SOUTH TO TROPICAL CENTRAL
TREE SLOTH
TOXODON
CAPYBARA
SPIDER MONKEY
GIANT ANTEATER
AGOUTI

SOUTH TO TEMPERATE NORTH
MEGATHERIUM
OPOSSUM
ARMADILLO
GLYPTODON
PORCUPINE

0   500 mi

0   500 km

© AVALON TRAVEL PUBLISHING, INC.

nests, its thong of a tongue flicks in and out of its tiny mouth, running deep into the galleries. Each time it withdraws, it brings with it a load of ants, which are scraped off inside the tunnel of its mouth and swallowed, ground down by small quantities of sand and gravel in its stomach.

The most commonly seen of Costa Rica's three anteater species is the tree-dwelling **lesser anteater** (or *tamandua* locally), a beautiful creature with a prehensile tail and the gold-and-black coloration of a panda bear. It can grow to 1.5 meters and weigh up to eight kilograms.

The **giant anteater,** with its huge, bushy tail and astonishingly long proboscis, is now restricted to the less sparsely forested areas of the Osa Peninsula. It can grow to two meters long and when threatened rears itself on its hind legs and slashes wildly with its claws. It also raises its tail over its head. Even machetes cannot cut through its tough bristles; thus the fearsome critter is revered among *campesinos* for its magical abilities.

At night you may with luck see the strictly arboreal, cat-sized **silky anteater,** which can hang from its strong prehensile tail.

Bats

The most numerous mammals by far are the bats (109 species), found throughout Costa Rica. You may come across them slumbering by day halfway up a tree or roosting in a shed, or beneath the eaves of your lodgings. In true Dracula fashion, most bats are lunarphobic: they avoid the bright light. On nights one week before and after the full moon, they suspend foraging completely and stay in their roosts while the moon is at its peak, probably for fear of owls.

Many bat species—like the giant **Jamaican fruit bat** *(murciélago frútero),* with a wingspan of more than 50 cm—are frugivores (fruit eaters) or insectivores, and quite harmless. The Jamaican bat favors figs, taken on the wing.

The three species of **vampire bats** (Ticos call them *vampiros*)—which belong to the neotropics, not Transylvania—are a different matter: they inflict an estimated $100 million of damage on domestic farm animals throughout Central and South America by transmitting rabies and other

diseases. Two species feed on birds; the third on mammals, with a modus operandi almost as frightening as the stuff of Bram Stoker's *Dracula.* It lands on or close to a sleeping mammal, such as a cow. Using its two razor-sharp incisors, it punctures the unsuspecting beast and, with the aid of an anticoagulant saliva, merrily squats beside the wound and laps up the blood while it flows. They're pretty much harmless to humans.

The most interesting of bats, however, and one easily seen in Tortuguero, is the **fishing bulldog bat** *(murciélago pescador),* with its huge wingspan (up to 60 cm across) and great gaff-shaped claws with which it hooks fish. It fishes by sonar. Skimming the water surface, it is able to detect slight ripples ahead. The bat drops its hooked feet at just the right moment and—presto!—supper.

Cats

Costa Rica boasts six endangered members of the cat family. All are active by day and night, but are rarely seen. Although they are legally protected, hunting of cats still occurs in Costa Rica. However, the main threat to the remaining populations is deforestation. Cats are primarily solitary

baby jaguar at San José zoo

and nocturnal and spend the greater part of the day sleeping in trees or hidden in dense vegetation.

One of the most abundant of cats is the **jaguarundi** (called *león breñero* locally), a spotless dark-brown or tawny critter about the size of a large house cat (it can weigh up to nine kg): coloration varies from reddish-brown to grey or black (even siblings may be of different colors). It has a long, slender body, short stocky legs (its hind legs are taller than its forelegs), long tail, and a venal face with yellow eyes suggesting a nasty temperament. It is more diurnal than its cousins and is most active between 4 and 11 A.M., when the jaguarundi is sometimes seen hunting in pairs, preferring lowland habitats.

Pumas *(león)* also inhabit a variety of terrains, though they are rarely seen. This large cat—also called the "mountain lion"—is generally dun-colored, though coloration varies markedly among individuals and from region to region.

The spotted cats include the cute-looking, house-cat-sized **margay** *(caucel)* and its smaller cousin, the **oncilla.** Both wear an ocher coat spotted with black and brown spots, like tiny leopards. Their chests are white. The solitary and strongly nocturnal margay, which can weight up to 6 kg, has a very long tail in relation to its body size, which, combined with its ability to turn its hind feet by 180 degrees, provides monkey-like climbing abilities. It is found only in primary or very little-disturbed forests. The oncilla or tiger cat has black ears and is distinguished from the margay by its face (closely resembling that of a domestic cat), its shorter tail, and more slender body shape. Little is known about the ecology of this solitary animal, which prefers montane cloud forest.

The most commonly seen cat is the **ocelot** *(manigordo),* their larger cousin, which is well-distributed throughout the country and among various habitats. The ocelot is the biggest (males can weigh up to 15 kg; the females up to 11 kg) of Costa Rica's "small" cats and has short, dense fur with brown spots and rosettes with black edges, arranged in parallel rows along its body

© JEAN MERCIER

ocelot

length, with a background of greyish-yellow. It has a characteristic white spot on each ear, and black stripes on both cheeks and forehead.

Worshiped as a god in pre-Columbian civilizations, the **jaguar** is the symbol of the Central American jungle. *Panthera onca* (or *tigre* to locals) was once abundant in the dense forests, coastal mangroves, and lowland savannas of Central America. Today this magnificent and noble beast is an endangered species, rare except in parts of the larger reserves: Santa Rosa, Tortuguero, and Corcovado National Parks, and the Cordillera Talamanca. When roads penetrate the primeval forest, the jaguar is among the first large mammals to disappear. In recent years, jaguar sightings have been more common, suggesting that better preservation of their habitat is paying dividends.

While a few of the famous black "panther" variety exist, most Central American jaguars are a rich yellow, spotted with large black rosettes. Jaguars are the largest and most powerful of the American members of the cat family—a mature jaguar measures over two meters, stands 60 cm at the shoulders, and weighs up to 90 kg. The animal's head and shoulders are massive, the legs relatively short and thick. An adept climber and swimmer, the beast is a versatile hunter, at home in trees, on the ground, and even in water. It feeds on a wide range of arboreal, terrestrial, and aquatic animals and is powerful enough to kill a full-grown cow.

Like all wild cats, jaguars are extremely shy, not particularly dangerous, and attack humans very rarely.

Deer

Costa Rica has two species of deer: the **red brocket deer** (called *cabro de monte*), which favors the rainforests, and the larger, more commonly seen **white-tailed deer** (*venado*), widely dispersed in habitats throughout the country, but especially Guanacaste. The former is slightly hump-backed and bronze. Males have single-prong horns. The latter—a smaller variant of its North American counterpart—varies from gray to red, normally with a white belly and a white dappled throat and face. Males have branched antlers.

Manatees

Anyone venturing to Tortuguero National Park or Gandoca-Manzanillo National Park will no doubt hope to see a West Indian manatee *(manati)*. This herbivorous marine mammal has long been hunted for its flesh, which is supposedly tender and delicious, and for its very tough hide, once used for machine belts and high-pressure hoses. The heavily wrinkled beast looks like a tuskless walrus, with small round eyes, fleshy lips that hang over the sides of its mouth, and no hind limbs, just a large, flat, spatulate tail. Now endangered throughout their former range, these creatures once inhabited brackish rivers and lagoons along the whole coast of Central America's Caribbean shoreline. Today, only a few remain in the most southerly waters of the U.S. and isolated pockets of Central America and the Caribbean Isles. Tortuguero, where the animals are legally protected, has one of the few significant populations.

They are not easy to spot, for they lie submerged with only nostrils showing. Watch for rising bubbles in the water: manatees suffer from flatulence, a result of eating up to 45 kg of water hyacinths and other aquatic flora daily. The animals, sometimes called sea cows, can grow to four meters long and weigh as much as a ton. Interestingly, the manatee is one of few species in which males engage in homosexual activity. Affectionate animals, they kiss each other, sometimes swim with linked flippers, and make solicitous parents.

The **Save the Manatee Club** (500 N. Maitland Ave., Maitland, FL 32751, tel. 407/539-0990 or 800/432-5646, membership@savethemanatee.org, www.savethemanatee.org) is a not-for-profit member-based organization that promotes manatee education/awareness. The **Manatee Survival Foundation** (P.O. Box 50005, Lighthouse Point, FL 33074, tel. 954/943-4391, maryannegray@ellerandco.com) promotes manatee awareness and collects sighting information for regulatory agencies.

Know Costa Rica

CONSERVATION AREAS AND NATIONAL PARKS

Costa Rica has 11 Regional Conservation Area (RCAs). The most important include:

Amistad Conservation Area

The country's largest and least accessible protected area encompasses rugged, mountainous terrain in southern Costa Rica, plus parks of the southern Caribbean littoral. It incorporates several **indigenous reserves,** plus **Las Cruces Biological Station** as well as the following.

Cahuita National Park: Coral reefs and beautiful beaches backed by lowland rainforest replete with wildlife.

Chirripó National Park: Costa Rica's highest peak, spanning diverse ecosystems including cloud forest and tundra *(paramó).*

Gandoca-Manzanillo National Wildlife Refuge: Beautiful shoreline favored for nesting by marine turtles; estuaries protect rare ecosystems plus manatees and a species of freshwater dolphin.

Hitoy-Cerere Biological Reserve: Rugged and remote; mountain slopes and deep valleys smothered with rainforest. Large wildlife population.

La Amistad International Friendship Park Encompasses Chirripó, Hitoy-Cerere, and other mountainous parks of the Talamanca mountains. Much of the park is unexplored. Large population of big cats and other endangered wildlife.

Tapantí-Mecizo De La Muerte National Park: Two life zones—lower montane and premontane rainforest—replete with endangered wildlife and copious birdlife, on northeast side of Talamancas.

Arenal Conservation Area

This conservation area encompasses wildlife-rich environments of the Cordillera de Tilarán, including three private cloud- forest reserves: **Monteverde Cloud Forest Biological Reserve,** the **Children's Eternal Forest,** and the **Santa Elena Cloud Forest Reserve,** plus:

Arenal National Park: Protects the watershed draining into Lake Arenal and includes Arenal Volcano.

Caño Negro National Wildlife Refuge: Vast wetland region replete with birdlife, crocodiles, and other wildlife. A prime sportfishing locale.

Central Volcanic Range Conservation Area

Dramatic topography and a wide range of montane and humid tropical forest types characterize this area flanking the Central Valley. Includes:

Barbilla National Park: Recently inaugurated on the northern side of Turrialba volcano, this rugged park as yet has few trails and minimum facilities.

Braulio Carrillo National Park: Rugged mountain park protects the rainforests on Barva volcano and the Caribbean slopes of the Cordillera Central. Replete with wildlife.

Guayabo National Monument: Protects Costa Rica's most important pre-Columbian site, dating back to 500 B.C.

Irazú Volcano National Park: A drive-up volcano with two craters and good hiking offering stunning views. Little wildlife.

Juan Castro Blanco National Park: Remote mountainous park protecting rainforest on the northeast slopes of the Cordillera Tilarán, west of Poás and east of Arenal Volcano. Bordered by Bosque de la Paz Rainforest/Cloud Forest Reserve.

Poás Volcano National Park: Costa Rica's most visited park, centered on an drive-up volcano that is still active. Hiking trails lead to three craters and varied ecosystems.

Guanacaste Conservation Area

Protects diverse ecosystems in Guanacaste, from shoreline to mountaintop, including:

Bahía Junquillal Wildlife Refuge: Small refuge for crocodiles and other wildlife in the wetland and dry forest habitats north of Santa Rosa.

Guanacaste National Park: Forms a vital biological corridor for migratory animals between the lowland tropical dry forests and montane wet forests and cloud forest atop Orosí and Cacao volcanoes.

Miravalles Volcano National Park: A steep-sided volcano flanked by montane rainforest and cloud forest. Includes several prime hot spring sites.

Rincón de la Vieja National Park: An active

volcano with several craters (good for spotting tapirs), and varied ecosystems, from montane rainforest to tropical dry forest.

Santa Rosa National Park: Wildlife-rich tropical dry forests, important nesting sites for green, leatherback, and ridley turtles, plus La Casona, an important national monument

Tenorio Volcano National Park: Similar to Miravalles.

Nicoya Conservation Area

Covering southern Nicoya, the following parks are being linked by creation of new wildlife refuges and national parks:

Cabo Blanco Absolute Nature Reserve: The first national park in the country protects moist tropical forests and a large population of wildlife, including several endangered species.

Curú Biological Reserve: A private reserve boasting a diversity of habitats and wildlife.

Nicolas Weissenburg Absolute Reserve: Off-limits to visitors, this park, between Tambor and Montezuma, is being reforested.

Osa Conservation Area

This humid region, in the Pacific southwest, comprises some of the largest stands of rainforest in Central America, and includes:

Ballena (Whale) National Marine Park: A protected coastal strip sheltering mangrove and wetland systems and including offshore waters used by whales and other marine mammals

Caño Island Biological Reserve: A remote island covered with rainforest; an important pre-Columbian site. Marine life offshore.

Corcovado National Park: Protects the last significant stand of virgin rainforest in Central America. Boasts one of the most diverse and healthy wildlife populations, including tapirs, jaguars, crocodiles, and scarlet macaws.

Golfito National Wildlife Refuge: Contiguous with Corcovado, protects the watershed of the coastal mountains surrounding Golfito.

Piedras Blancas National Park: Contiguous with Corcovado.

Terraba-Sierpe International Humid Forest Reserve: A vast expanse of coastal mangroves and swamp protecting flocks of wading and other birds, plus crocodiles and mammals.

Tempisque Conservation Area

This RCA unites varied ecosystems protected in:

Barra Honda National Park: A diverse and large cave network with stalagmites and stalactites; deciduous forest up top protects a large wildlife population.

Las Baulas Marine National Park: Protects the preeminent nesting site of the leatherback turtle in Costa Rica.

Lomas Barbudal Biological Reserve: Borders Palo Verde and likewise abounds with waterfowl and other bird species, as well as mammals. Predominantly tropical dry forest. Often called the "insect park" because of the diversity and profusion of its bee, moth, and other insect populations.

Ostional National Wildlife Refuge: A shoreline and offshore refuge for ridley turtles, which nest here en masse.

Palo Verde National Park: Wetlands and rare tropical dry forest predominate in this park encompassing the estuarine ecosystems of the Río Tempisque and its tributaries. Large population of crocodiles and waterfowl.

Tamarindo Wildlife Refuge: Small but vitally important estuarine system behind Las Baulas harbors crocodiles, waterfowl, and a large mammal population.

Tortuguero Conservation Area

Combines vast wetland and forest regions of the northeast Caribbean, most significantly:

Barra del Colorado National Wildlife Refuge: Protecting important tropical humid and wet forests, swamplands, and mangroves bisected by the Ríos Colorado and San Juan and their tributaries. Large populations of crocodiles, birds, and game fish—notably tarpon and snook.

Tortuguero National Park: One of Costa Rica's most important lowland watersheds harboring large wildlife populations, including caimans, manatees, green macaws, river otters. The shoreline is the major nesting site for green turtles in the Caribbean.

Know Costa Rica

CONSERVATION AREAS AND NATIONAL PARKS (cont'd)

Other Areas

On the Central Pacific coast are **Carara National Park,** a vital preserve at the juncture of the dry and wet zones, and protecting species from both habitats; the **Tárcoles estuary,** famous for copious waterfowl and a large crocodile population; and tiny **Manuel Antonio National Park,** famous for its beaches, coral reef, and humid forest, where endangered bird and animal species—including spider monkeys and scarlet macaws—are easily seen.

Cocos Island UNESCO World Heritage Site, about 300 miles southwest of Costa Rica, has rare birds closely related to those of the Galápagos Islands, to which it is geologically related. It is most famous for its large pelagic populations, notably hammerhead sharks.

Monkeys

Costa Rica has four species of monkeys: the cebus (or capuchin), howler, spider, and squirrel. Along with approximately 50 other species, they belong to a group called New World monkeys, which evolved from a single simian group that appeared about 40 million years ago in Africa and Asia. Some of these early primates migrated to North America and then down the land bridge to Central and South America.

Though the North American monkeys gradually died out, their southern cousins flourished and evolved along lines that differ markedly from those of their ancestors in the Old World. While African and Asian monkeys have narrow noses with nostrils that point down (much like human noses), New World monkeys evolved broad, widely spaced nostrils. New World females, too, evolved a singular ability to bear twins. And, perhaps most important, some New World species—notably the cebus, howler, and spider monkeys—developed long prehensile tails for added purchase and balance in the high treetops.

They inhabit a wide range of habitats, from the rainforest canopy to the scrubby undergrowth of the dry forests, though each species occupies its own niche and the species seldom meet. Together, they are the liveliest and most vocal jungle tenants. Beyond the reach of most predators, they have little inhibition in announcing their presence with their roughhousing and howls, chatterings, and screeches.

If you come across a band of monkeys while hiking, stop. Be patient. It may take 30 minutes for them to pass by, one by one. After a while, other animals may appear in their wake—coatis, peccaries, agoutis—feasting on the fruit dropped by the monkeys. Silence is imperative.

The distinctive-looking **capuchin,** or white-faced monkey *(mono cara blanca),* is the smartest and most inquisitive of Central American simians. It derives its name from its black body and monklike white cowl. You've probably seen them dancing at the end of a tether at street fairs in Europe or South America—they're the little guys favored by organ grinders worldwide. Capuchins range widely throughout the wet lowland forests of the Caribbean coast and the deciduous dry

capuchin or white-faced monkey

© JEAN MERCIER

© CHRISTOPHER P. BAKER

baby howler monkey

spider monkey

forests of the Pacific Northwest below 1,500 meters. Two excellent places to see them are Santa Rosa and Manuel Antonio National Parks, where family troops are constantly on the prowl, foraging widely through the treetops and over the forest floor.

These opportunistic feeders are fun to watch as they search under logs and leaves or tear off bark as they seek out insects and small lizards soon after dawn and again in late afternoon. Capuchins also steal birds' eggs and nestlings. Some crafty coastal residents have developed a taste for oysters and other mollusks, which they break open on rocks. The frugal capuchin sometimes hoards his food for "rainy days." While their taste is eclectic, they *are* fussy eaters: they'll meticulously pick out grubs from fruit, which they test for ripeness by smelling and squeezing.

The **howler** *(mono congo)* is the most abundant as well as the largest of Central American monkeys (it can weigh up to five kg). It inhabits both lowland and montane forests throughout Costa Rica. Fortunately, it is less sensitive to habitat destruction than the spider monkey and can be found clinging precariously to existence in many relic patches of forest.

The stentorian males greet each new day with reveille calls that seem more like the explosive roars of lions than those of small arboreal leaf-eaters. The hair-raising vocalizations can carry for almost a mile in even the densest of jungle. The males sing in chorus again at dusk (or whenever trespassers get too close) as a spacing mechanism to keep rivals at a safe distance. Their Pavarotti-like vocal abilities are due to unusually large larynxes and throats that inflate into resonating balloons. Females generally content themselves with loud wails and groans—usually to signal distress or call a straying infant. This noisy yet sedentary canopy browser feeds on leaves and fruit. Although capable of eating anything that grows, howlers are extremely selective feeders.

The smallest and most endangered Costa Rican primate, the **squirrel monkey** *(mono tití)* grows to 25–35 cm, plus a tail up to 45 cm. Less than 2,000 individuals are thought to exist. It is restricted to the rainforests of the southern Pacific lowlands. Always on the go, day and night, they scurry about in the jungle understory and forest floor on all fours, where they are safe from raptor predators. Squirrels are more gregarious than most other monkeys; bands of 40 individuals or more are not uncommon. The golden-orange titi (with its face of white and black) is the arboreal goat of the forest. It will eat almost anything: fruits, insects, small lizards. The titi is well on its way to extinction.

The **Asociación para la Conservación del Mono Titi** (tel. 506/224-5703, monotiti@racsa .co.cr, www.ascomoti.org) accepts donations.

The large, loose-limbed **spider monkey** *(mono colorado)*—the supreme acrobat of the forest—was once the most widespread of the Central American monkeys. Unfortunately, they are very sensitive to human intrusion and are among the first primate species to decline with disturbance. The last few decades have brought significant destruction of spider monkey habitats, and land clearance and hunting have greatly reduced spider monkey populations throughout much of their former range. If you inadvertently come across them you'll soon know it: they often rattle the branches and bark and screech loudly.

These copper-colored acrobats can attain a length of a meter and a half. They have evolved extreme specialization for a highly mobile arboreal lifestyle. Long slender limbs allow spider monkeys to make spectacular leaps. But the spider's greatest secret is its extraordinary prehensile tail, which is longer than the combined length of its head and body. The underside is ridged like a human fingertip for added grip at the end of treetop leaps (it is even sensitive enough for probing and picking). You might see individuals hanging like ripe fruit by their tails.

Gregarious by night (they often bed down in heaps), by day they are among the most solitary of primates. The males stay aloof from the females. While the latter tend to their young, which they carry on their backs, the males are busy marking their territory with secretions from their chest glands.

Peccaries

These myopic, sharp-toothed wild pigs are notoriously fickle and potentially aggressive creatures whose presence in the rainforest may be betrayed by their pungent, musky odor and by the churned-up ground from their grubbing. Gregarious beasts,

they forage in herds and make a fearsome noise if frightened or disturbed. Like most animals, they prefer to flee from human presence. Occasionally, however, an aggressive male may show his bravado by threatening to have a go at you, usually in a bluff charge. Attacks by groups of a dozen or more peccaries sometimes occur. Rangers advise that if attacked, you should climb a tree or stand absolutely still. Don't try to frighten them away—that's a sure way to get gored.

The more common **collared peccary** *(saino)* is marked by an ocher-colored band of hair running from its shoulders down to its nose; the rest of its body is dark brown. The larger **white-lipped peccary** *(cariblanco),* which can grow to one meter long, is all black, or brown, with a white mustache or "beard."

Raccoons

Raccoons, familiar to North Americans, are present throughout Costa Rica, where they are frequently seen begging tidbits from diners at hotel restaurants. The **northern raccoon** *(mapache* to Ticos) is a smaller but otherwise identical cousin of the North American raccoon, and can be found widely in Costa Rica's lowlands, predominantly in moist areas. The white-faced animal is unmistakable with its bandit-like black mask, and its tail of alternating black and white hoops. Don't mistake this animal with its cousin, the darker-colored **crab-eating raccoon,** found only along the Pacific coast.

A relative, the long-nosed **coatimundi** (called *pizote* locally), the most diurnal member of the raccoon family, is found throughout the country. Coatis wear many coats, from yellow to deepest brown, though all are distinguished by faintly ringed tails, white-tipped black snouts, and panda-like eye-rings. The animal is at home both on the ground and in the treetops. They are gregarious critters and often seen in packs. The animal has a fascinating defense technique against predators. When attacked, it raises itself on its hind legs, thrusts its tail between its legs, and waves its tail in front of its face. The attacker goes for the tail, giving the coati a chance to rake the predator in the eyes with its sharp claws.

coati eating human food, Manuel Antonio National Park

© CHRISTOPHER P. BAKER

Another raccoon family member is the small and totally nocturnal **kinkajou** (known to Ticos as the *martilla*), with its large limpid eyes and velvet-soft coat of golden brown. It's a superb climber (it can hang by its prehensile tail) and spends most of its life feeding on fruit, honey, and insects in the treetops. By day it is very drowsy; if picked up, its first instinct is to cuddle against your chest, bury its head to avoid the light, and drop back off to sleep. Its smaller cousins are the much rarer, grayish, bug-eyed **olingo** (*cacomistle*), with its panda-like white spectacled eyes and a bushy white tail ringed with black hoops.

Rodents

The **agouti** (*guatusa* to Ticos) is a brown, cat-size rodent related to the guinea pig. It inhabits the forests up to 6,500 feet elevation, and is often seen by day feeding on the forest floor on fruits and nuts (the wet-forest agoutis are darker than their chestnut-colored dry-forest cousins). It looks like a giant tailless squirrel with the thin legs and tip-toeing gait of a deer, but it sounds like a small dog. They are solitary critters that mark their turf with musk. They form monogamous pairs and produce two or three litters a year.

Agoutis have long been favored for their meat and are voraciously hunted by humans. Their nocturnal cousin, the **paca** (called *tepezcuintle* by locals), also makes good eating, and can grow to a meter long and weigh 10 kg, three times larger than the agouti; it is favored by a wide variety of predators. It is brown with rows of white spots along its side. Both are easily captured because of the strong anal musks they use to scent their territories and because of their habit of running in circles but never leaving their home turf (pacas, at least, are intelligent enough to leap into water and stay submerged for a considerable time). If you disturb one in the forest, you may hear its high-pitched alarm bark before you see it.

Costa Rica also has five squirrel species, including the ubiquitous **variegated squirrel** (*chiza* or *ardilla tricolor* to locals), whose black, white, and red coloration varies in form. The brown and chestnut **red-tailed squirrel** (*ardilla roja*) is also common.

Costa Rica has about 40 species of rats, mice, and gophers.

Sloths

Ask anyone to compile a list of the world's strangest creatures, and the sloth (locally called *perezoso*, which means "lazy"), a creature that moves with the grace and deliberation of a tai chi master, would be right up there with the duck-billed platypus. The sloth, which grows to the size of a medium-size dog, has a small head and flat face with snub nose, beady eyes, and seemingly rudimentary ears (its reputation for poor hearing is entirely incorrect). Its long, bony arms are well developed, with curving claws that hook over and grasp the branches from which it spends almost its entire life suspended upside down. Lulled by its relative tree-top security, the sloth, says naturalist David Attenborough, "has sunken into an existence just short of complete torpor." The creature spends up to 18 hours daily sleeping curled up with its feet drawn close together and its head tucked between the forelimbs.

The arboreal beast, which is actually related to the anteater and armadillo, pays plenty of attention to personal hygiene, despite the fact that its shaggy fur harbors an algae, unique to the beast, that makes the sloth greenly inconspicuous—wonderful camouflage from prowling jaguars and keen-eyed eagles, its chief predators. The sloth also eats the algae; communities of moths live in the depths of its fur and feed on the algae as well.

Costa Rica has two species of sloths: the **three-fingered sloth** *(perezoso de tres dedos)* and the nocturnal, relatively omnivoros **Hoffman's two-fingered sloth** *(perezoso de dos dedos)*. You're more likely to see the three-fingered sloth, which is active by day. The animals are commonly, incorrectly called "three-toed" and "two-toed." In fact, both species have three toes.

At top speed a sloth can barely cover a mile in four hours. On the ground, it is even more awkward and crawls with great difficulty. In fact, there's a very good reason sloths move at a rate barely distinguishable from rigor mortis.

A sloth's digestion works as slowly as its other bodily functions. Its metabolic rate is half that of

CONSERVATION ORGANIZATIONS

The following organizations are active in conservation efforts in Costa Rica and need volunteers and/or contributions to help implement their programs. Most accept volunteers.

The Association for the Conservation of the Mono Titi (tel. 506/224-5703, monotiti@racsa.co.cr, http://ascomoti.org/) works to protect the endangered squirrel monkey.

The Caribbean Conservation Corps (CCC, 4424 NW 13th St. Suite #A1, Gainesville, FL 32609, tel. 352/373-6441 or 800/678-7853, fax 352/375-2449, ccc@cccturtle.org, www.cccturtle.org) works to protect turtle populations and accepts donations and volunteers to assist in research and patrols.

Conservation International (1919 M St., N.W. Suite 600, Washington, D.C. 20036, tel. 202/912-1000 or 800/406-2306, www.conservation.org) supports conservation projects worldwide; in Costa Rica it has been active in supporting La Amistad International Biosphere Reserve.

The Costa Rican Association for the Conservation of Nature, or Asociación Costarricense para la Conservación de la Naturaleza (AS-CONA, Apdo. 8-3790, San José 1000, tel. 506/297-1711), specializes in the investigation of, and legal action against, environmental infringements. Volunteers with appropriate backgrounds are needed.

The Costa Rican Federation for Environmental Conservation, or Federación Costarricense para la Conservación del Ambiente (FECON, Apdo. 1948-1002, San José, tel./fax 506/283-6128, feconcr@racsa.co.cr), is an umbrella organization representing several conservation organizations.

The Cultural Association of Costa Rica (SE-JETKO 1293-2150, Moravia, San José, tel. 506/234-7115) works with indigenous communities to help preserve their cultural integrity and achieve sustainable development.

The Earth Council (P.O. Box 319-6100, San José, tel. 506/205-1600, fax 506/249-3500, ecouncil@terra.ecouncil.ac.cr; in North America, tel. 416/498-3150, fax 416/498-7296 ecsondra@web.ca) works to support and empower communities in building a more secure, equitable, and sustainable future.

The Earth Island Institute (300 Broadway, Suite 28, San Francisco, CA 94133, tel. 415/788-3666 or 800/859-7283, fax 415/788-7324, www.earthisland.org) develops and supports projects that counteract environmental threats and promote sustainable development.

The Earth Justice Legal Defense Fund (426 17th Street, Oakland, CA 94612-2820, tel. 510/550-6700, fax 510/550-6740, eajus@earthjustice.org,

other animals of similar size, and food remains in its stomach for up to a week. Hence, it has evolved a large ruminant-like stomach and intestinal tract to process large quantities of relatively indigestible food. To compensate, it has sacrificed heavy muscle mass—and, hence, mobility—to maximize body size in proportion to weight. Thus, the sloth has evolved as a compromise between a creature large enough to store and process large quantities of food and one light enough to move about in trees without breaking the branches. Sloths need warm weather to synthesize food. During long spells of cold weather, the animals may literally starve to death (they also regulate their body temperature according to the ambient temperature). The sloth's heavy fur coat provides excellent insulation against heat loss. Still, its body temperature drops almost to the temperature of its surroundings at night and, much like cold-blooded reptiles, the sloth needs to take in the sun's rays to bring its temperature to normal mammalian levels.

When nature calls (about once a week), the animal descends to ground level, where it digs

www.earthjustice.org) is a nonprofit law firm for the environment.

The Legal Center for the Environment and Natural Resources (CEDARENA, Apdo. 134-2050 San Pedro, San José, tel. 506/283-7080, fax 506/224-1426, cedarena@racsa.co.cr, www .cedarena.org) is a legal support group that researches and maintains a database on environmental laws and infringements.

The Monteverde Conservation League (Apdo. 10581-1000, San José, tel. 506/645- 5003, fax 506/645-5104, acmmcl@racsa.co.cr, www .acmonteverde.com) promotes reforestation projects and works to assist farmers of the Monteverde region to increase productivity in a sustainable manner. The League also administers the Children's Eternal Cloud Forest Reserve.

Nature Conservancy (4245 N. Fairfax Drive, Suite 100, Arlington, VA 22203-1606, tel. 703/841-5300 or 800/628-6860, fax 703/841-1283, http://nature.org) identifies species in need of protection and acquires land to protect them. Its Latin America division works closely with Fundación Neotrópica and other organizations.

The Neotropic Foundation, or Fundación Neotrópica (Apdo. 236-1002, San José, tel. 506/253-2130, fax 506/253-4210, fneo_cjt@racsa.co .cr, www.neotropica.org), promotes sustainable development and conservation among local communities. It also arranges "debt-for-nature" swaps.

Organization for Tropical Studies (OTS, Apdo. 676-2050, San Pedro, tel. 506/240-6696, fax 506/240-6783, nat.hist@ots.ac.cr, www.ots.ac.cr; in the U.S., P.O. Box 90630, Durham, NC 27708-0630, tel. 919/684-5774, fax 919/684-5661, neo@duke.edu, www.ots.duke.edu) is dedicated to biological research in tropical environments. It offers annual nine-day Rainforest Ecology Workshops in Costà Rica, and maintains research facilities and lodges that are open to the public.

The Rainforest Alliance (665 Broadway, Suite 500, New York, NY 10012, tel. 212/941-1900 or 888/693-2786, fax 212/941-4986, www .rainforest-alliance.org) works to save rainforests worldwide.

The Worldwatch Institute (1776 Massachusetts Ave., N.W., Washington, D.C. 20036-1904, tel. 202/452-1999, fax 202/296-7365, worldwatch@worldwatch.org, www.worldwatch.org) acts as a global environmental watchdog.

The World Wildlife Fund (1250 24th St. N.W., Washington, D.C. 20037, tel. 202/293-4800, fax 202/293-9211, www.wwf.org) works to protect endangered wildlife worldwide. You can make donations earmarked to specific Costa Rica conservation projects.

a small hole with its hind limbs. It defecates into the depression, urinates, covers the broth with leaves, and returns much relieved to its arboreal life. During this 30-minute period, the female "sloth moths" have been busy laying their eggs on the sloth dung. When hatched, the larvae feed and pupate on the feces. The newly emerged adults then fly off to seek a new sloth.

Sloths, which may live up to 20 years or longer, reach sexual maturity at three years, a relatively old age for mammals of their size. Females screech to draw males, which have a bare orange patch on their back with unique sexual markings. Actual copulation has been observed to last as long as 48 hours. Females give birth once a year (the gestation period is about eleven months and is regulated according to environmental conditions) and spend half their adult lives pregnant. Although female sloths are never separated by choice from their offspring, which cling to their mother for the first six months of their lives, they appear peculiarly unsentimental about their young: if a baby tumbles, its plaintive distress calls go unheeded. And when the juvenile reaches six months of age, the mother simply turns tail on her youngster, which inherits her home range of trees.

An easy way to find sloths is to look up into the green foliage of cecropia trees, which form one of the sloth's favorite food staples. The sight of a sloth languishing in open cecropia crowns is a heavenly vision to harpy eagles, which swoop in to snatch the torpid creature much like plucking ripe fruit.

Costa Rica's sloth population is diminishing due to land loss and poaching for the pet trade. To learn more, pay a visit to Aviarios del Caribe Sloth Refuge, near Cahuita (see the *Caribbean* chapter). Aviarios del Caribe, the world's only sloth refuge, is also the premier research station into sloth ecology.

Tapirs

Another symbol of the New World tropics is the strange-looking **Baird's tapir** (*danta* lo-

cally), a solitary, ground-living, plant-eating, forest-dwelling, ungainly mixture of elephant, rhinoceros, pig, and horse. The tapir uses its short, highly mobile proboscis—an evolutionary forerunner to the trunk of the elephant—for plucking leaves and shoveling them into its mouth. This endangered species is the largest indigenous terrestrial land mammal in Central America. Like its natural predator the jaguar, the tapir has suffered severely at the hands of man. The animal was once common in Costa Rica and ranged far and wide in the lowland swamps and forests. Hunters have brought it to the edge of extinction.

Today, tapirs are found only in national parks and reserves where hunting is restricted, with the greatest density in Corcovado National Park, which has a population of fewer than 300, and up to 3,000 meters elevation in the Talamanca mountains. They have learned to be wary of man, and few travelers have the privilege of sighting them in the wild. Tapirs live in dense forests and swamps and rely on concealment for defense. They are generally found wallowing up to their knees in swampy waters, to which they rush precipitously at the first sign of danger. The animals make conspicuous trails in the forest, and because tapirs maintain territories marked with dung or scent, they are easily tracked by dogs.

Weasels

Costa Rica boasts seven members of the weasel family. The most ubiquitous is the skunk (*zorro* in local parlance), one of the most commonly seen mammal species, of which Costa Rica has three species. The black **striped hog-nosed skunk,** with its bushy white tail and white stripe along its rump, will be familiar to North Americans. The smaller **spotted skunk** and **hooded skunk** are more rarely seen. Their defense is a disgusting scent sprayed at predators from an anal gland.

Costa Rica is also home to a badger-like animal called the **grison,** another skunk-like member of the weasel family that can weigh three kg (seven pounds) and is often seen hunting alone or in groups in lowland rainforest during the day.

The grison is gray, with a white stripe running across its forehead and ears, white eye patches, and a black nose, chest, and legs. It looks like a cross between a badger and an otter. Meter-long **otters** (*perro de agua,* or water-dog, to locals) are commonly seen in lowland rivers, especially in Tortuguero.

A cousin, the sleek, long-haired, chocolate-brown **tayra** (locals call it *tolumuco*)—a meter-long giant of the weasel family—resembles a mix of grison and otter. It is often seen in highland habitats throughout Costa Rica. Weighing up to five kg, the tayra habitually preys on rodents but can make quick work of small deer. Tayras can sometimes be seen stalking squirrels in the crowns of deciduous trees with a motion so fluid they seem to move like snakes.

Other Mammals

The mostly nocturnal and near-blind **nine-banded armadillo** *(cusuco),* an armor-plated oddity, and one of only two of the 20 or so species of *edentates* found in Costa Rica, will be familiar to anyone from Texas. The animal can grow to almost one meter long. They are terrestrial dwellers that grub about on the forest floor, feeding on insects and fungi. The female lays a single egg that, remarkably, divides to produce identical triplets. Its smaller cousin, the **naked-tailed armadillo,** is far less frequently seen.

The dog family is represented by the brown-gray **coyote** and nocturnal **gray fox,** both found mostly in the dry northwestern regions.

The marsupials—mammals whose embryonic offspring crawl from the birth canal and are reared in an external pouch—are represented by nine species of opossums, including the black-and-gray-banded, long-legged, **water opossum** and the two-toned, short-legged **common opossum** *(zorro pelón),* a large rat-like critter with a dark brown body and tan underside and a more lively disposition than other opossums—this one defends itself rather than playing dead.

The blunt-nosed, short-spined, **prehensile-tailed porcupine** *(puerco espín)* is nocturnal and arboreal and rarely seen. There are also two species of **rabbits** *(conejos).*

SEALIFE

Costa Rica is as renowned for its marine life as for its terrestrial and avian fauna—most famously, perhaps, for the billfish (marlin and sailfish) that cruise the deep blue waters offshore, and for tarpon and snook, feisty estuarine and wetland game fish. The former swim seasonally in the warm waters off the Golfo de Papagayo and Golfo Dolfo; the latter are concentrated in the waters of the Río Colorado and Caño Negro.

Sharks are forever present in Costa Rican waters. They seem particularly to favor waters in which marine turtles swim. Isla Cocos is renowned for its schools of hammerhead sharks as well as giant whale shark (the world's largest fish), which can also be found hanging out with giant grouper, jewfish, and manta rays in the waters around the Islas Murciélagos, off the Santa Elena peninsula of Guanacaste.

Whales—notably humpbacks—can be seen predictably along the west coast of Costa Rica, Dec.–Oct., when they migrate from both Antarctic and northern Pacific waters to mate and give birth in the warm waters off the Brunca Coast (see the *Central Pacific* chapter).

Small coral reefs exist offshore of Cahuita and Gandoca-Manzanillo, on the Caribbean, and Bahía Ballena, along the Central Pacific shore.

BIRDS

In William Henry Hudson's *Green Mansions,* his great romantic novel of the American tropics, the young hero, Abel, is lured into the jungle by the mysterious call of an unseen bird. So stirred is he by the siren song that he follows the haunting sound deeper and deeper into the forest until he eventually discovers the source: a lovely, half-wild girl called Rima, who has learned to mimic the sounds of the birds. The birds of Costa Rica are so rich and so varied—and often so elusive—that at times it seems as if Rima herself is calling.

With approximately 850 recorded bird species, the country boasts one-tenth of the world's total. More than 630 are resident species; the others are travelers who fly in for the winter. Birds that have all but disappeared in other areas still find tenuous safety in protected lands in Costa Rica, though many species face extinction from deforestation. The nation offers hope for such rare jewels of the bird world as the quetzal and the scarlet macaw, both endangered species, yet commonly seen in protected reserves.

It may surprise you to learn that in a land with so many exotic species the national bird is the relatively drab *yigüirro,* or clay-colored **robin,** a brown-and-buff bird with brick-red eyes. You may hear the male singing during the March–May breeding season when, according to *campesino* folklore, he is "calling the rains."

The four major "avifaunal zones" roughly correspond to the major geographic subdivisions of the country: the northern Pacific lowlands, the southern Pacific lowlands, the Caribbean lowlands, and the interior highlands. Guanacaste's dry habitats (northern Pacific lowlands) share relatively few species with other parts of the country. This is a superlative place, however, for waterfowl: the estuaries, swamps, and lagoons that make up the Tempisque Basin support the richest freshwater avifauna in all Central America, and Palo Verde National Park, at the mouth of the Tempisque, is a birdwatcher's mecca. The southern Pacific lowland region is home to many South American neotropical species, such as jacamars, antbirds, and, of course, parrots. Here, within the dense forests, the air is cool and dank and underwater green and alive with the sounds of birds.

Depending on season, location, and luck, you can expect to see many dozens of species on any one day. Many tour companies offer guided bird-study tours, and the country is well set up with mountain and jungle lodges that specialize in bird-watching programs. But the deep heart of the jungle is not the best place to look for birds: you cannot see well amid the complex, disorganized patterns cast by shadow and light. For best

results, find a large clearing on the fringe of the forest, or a watercourse where birds are sure to be found in abundance.

The sheer size of Costa Rica's bird population has prompted keen competition for food and, consequently, some intriguing food-gathering methods. The **jacamar** snaps up insects on the wing with an audible click of its beak. One species of epicurean kite has a bill like an escargot fork, which it uses to pick snails from their shells. The **attila,** a ruthless killer like its namesake, devours its frog victims whole after bashing them against a tree.

Anhingas and Cormorants

The **anhinga** (*pato aguja* to locals) and its close cousin, the **olivaceous cormorant** *(cormorán),* are sleek, long-necked, stump-tailed waterbirds with the pointy profile of a Concorde. Though they dive for fish in the lagoons and rivers of the lowlands, and are superb swimmers, their feathers lack the waterproof oils of other birds. You can thus often see them after a dousing, perched on a branch, sunning themselves in a vertical position with widespread wings, which are silvered against their sleek black bodies and sinuous necks (tawny in the female) that have earned them the moniker "snake-bird." These birds have kinked necks because they spear fish using the kink as a trigger.

Aracaris and Toucans

The bright-billed **toucans**—"flying bananas"— are a particular delight to watch as they pick fruit off one at a time with their long beaks, throw it in the air, and catch it at the back of their throats. Costa Rica's six toucan species (there are 42 neotropical toucan species) are among the most flamboyant of all Central American birds.

The gregarious **keel-billed toucan** *(tucan pico iris)* inhabits lowland and mid-elevation forests throughout the country except the Pacific southwest. This colorful stunner has a jet-black body, blue feet, a bright yellow chest and face, beady black eyes ringed by green feathers, and a rainbow-hued beak tipped by scarlet, as if it has been dipped in ink. Its similarly colored cousin, Swainson's or **chestnut-mandibled toucan** (Ticos call it *dios tedé,* for the onomatopeic sound it makes), is the largest of the group—it grows to 60 cm long and has a two-tone yellow-and-brown beak. It is found in moist forests below 2,000 feet, notably along the coastal zones, including the Pacific southwest. Listen for a noisy jumble of cries and piercing creaks.

There are also two species of toucanets, smaller cousins of the toucan: the green **emerald toucanet,** a highland bird with a red tail; and the black **yellow-eared toucanet,** found in the Caribbean lowlands.

Aracaris *(tucancillos)* are smaller and sleeker relatives, with more slender beaks. Both the **collared aracari** (a Caribbean bird) and **fiery-billed aracari** (its southern Pacific cousin) boast olive-black bodies, faces, and chests, with a dark band across their rust-yellow underbellies. The former has a two-tone yellow-and-black beak; the latter's beak is also two tone—black and fiery orange.

Birds of Prey

Costa Rica has some 50 raptor species: birds that hunt down live prey seized with their talons. The various species have evolved adaptations to specific habitats. For example, the large **common black hawk** (*gavilán cangrejero,* or "crab-hunting hawk" to Ticos) snacks on crabs and other marine morsels. And the **osprey** is known as *agula pescadora* ("fishing eagle") locally for the skill it applies to scooping fish from rivers or seas while on the wing. It has evolved especially long talons, barbed between the toes, all the better for snatching slippery fish. The bird is found throughout the world and, in Costa Rica, throughout the coastal and inland lowlands.

That lunatic laughter that goes on compulsively at dusk in lowland jungles is the **laughing falcon** (locally called the *guaco* for the repetitive "wah-co" sound it makes), which feeds on lizards and snakes. Its plumage is predominantly white, but with brown wings, a black-and-white banded tail, and black spectacles around its eyes.

© JEAN MERCIER

toucans

Eagles

The endangered neotropical **harpy eagle** *(águila arpía)* at one meter long the largest of all eagles, is renowned for twisting and diving through the treetops in pursuit of unsuspecting sloths and monkeys. Sightings in Costa Rica—where in recent years it has been relegated to the Osa Peninsula and more remote ranges of the Talamancas—are extremely rare.

Costa Rica's two species of caracaras are close cousins to the eagles, though like vultures they also eat carrion. You'll often see these large, fearsomely beaked, goose-stepping, long-legged birds picking at roadkill. The **crested caracara** is named for the black crown atop its bright red face. Its white neck fades into a black-and-white barred body and tail, though the wings and back are charcoal black. The name speaks for its buff-colored cousin, the **yellow-headed caracara.**

Hawks and Kites

Though in many regards identical, hawks are physically robust, with broad wings and short, wide tails, compared to the sleeker kites, which have longer, slender tails and wings.

The most ubiquitous hawk is the small, gray-brown **roadside hawk** *(gavilán chapulinero),* commonly seen perched on telegraph poles and fence posts spying for mice and other potential tasty treats. Like many hawks, it has a yellow beak tipped by black, plus yellow feet and eyes, and is also distinguished by the thin rust-red bands down its chest. Its cousin, the larger, browner, migratory **broad-winged hawk,** wings in for a visit Sept.–May and favors a low perch from which to swoop in for a kill.

The white **black-shouldered kite,** as its name suggests, wears a black shawl across its back of white and light-gray feathers. It favors open habitat and is thus easily seen. You can't confuse it with the **black-chested hawk,** a predominantly black-plumed forest dweller with a white underbelly and telltale white tail band. Its polar opposite is the **white hawk** *(gavilán blanco),* sporting a *black* tail band.

Nor can you mistake the black **double-toothed hawk,** with its white-and-black banded belly and tail, bright-red chest, and white throat, for the graceful, black-and-white **American swallow-tailed kite,** easily recognized by its long, deeply forked black tail. It takes insects in midair, as well as small lizards nabbed from branches.

Owls

Costa Rica's 17 species of owls are nocturnal hunters, more often heard than seen. An exception is the large dark-brown **spectacled owl** (Ticos call it *bujo de anteojos*), which also hunts by day and is conspicuous for its yellow chest and white head with black eye patches and black crown.

Doves and Pigeons

Doves and pigeons—called *palomas* locally—are numerous (Costa Rica has at least 25 species, including endemic neotropical species and migratory visitors familiar to North Americans). The birds belong to the Columbiformes order characterized by the ability, unique in birds, to produce milk for the hatchlings. Remarkably, both genders do so. The secretions gradually diminish, replenished by regurgitated food.

Many neotropical species are far more colorful than their northern counterparts. The large **band-tailed pigeon,** for example, though predominantly gray, has a green nape with white band, blue wings tipped by brown, a yellow bill, and mauve chest and belly. The mauve-gray **red-billed pigeon** has a red nape, bright red feet and forewings, and pale-blue rear quarters fading to a black-and-gray tail. And the **ruddy pigeon** and its ground-dwelling cousin, the **ruddy ground-dove,** are flushed in various shades of rust and red.

Egrets, Herons, and Relatives

Some 25 or so stilt-legged, long-necked wading birds—members of the Ciconiiformes order—are found in Costa Rica. Most common is the snowy white **cattle egret** whose numbers have exploded during the past four decades. Uniquely, its preferred turf is terrestial (it favors cattle pastures) and it can often be seen hitching a ride on the back of cattle, which are happy to have it pick off fleas and ticks. The males have head plumes which, along with the back and chest, turn tawny in breeding season. The species is easily mistaken for the **snowy egret,** a larger though more slender bird wearing "golden slippers" (yellow feet) on its black legs. Largest of the white egrets is the **great egret,** which grows to one meter tall.

There are three species of brown herons—called "tiger herons" *(garza tigre)*—in Costa Rica, most notably the **bare-throated tiger heron.** The **little blue heron,** commonly seen foraging alongside lowland watercourses, is a handsome blue-gray with purplish head plumage (the female is white, with wings tipped in gray). The northern lowlands are also a good place to spot the relatively small **green-backed heron,** fronted by rusty plumage streaked with white. The dun-colored **yellow-crowned night heron** is diurnal, not nocturnal as its name suggests. It is un-

tiger heron, Tortuguero National Park

mistakable, with its black-and-white head crowned with a swept-back yellow plume. Another instantly identifiable bird is the stocky gray **boat-billed heron,** named for the keel shape of its abnormally wide, thick bill. It, too, wears a plumed crown (of black), and has a rust underbelly.

Storks—notable for their fearsomely heavy, slightly upturned bills—also inhabit the lowland wetlands, notably in Caño Negro and Palo Verde National Parks, where the endangered **jabiru** can be seen. This massive bird (it grows to over one meter tall) wears snow-bright plumage, with a charcoal head, and a red scarf around its neck. Its relative, the **wood stork,** is also white, but with black flight feathers and featherless black head.

The **roseate spoonbill** *(espátula rosada)*—also relegated to Caño Negro and Palo Verde National Parks—is the most dramatic of the waders, thanks to its shocking-pink plumage and spatulate bill. Unlike its relatives, it feeds by sight, stirring up the bottom with its feet and disturbing tiny fish and other critters, then *snap!*

Costa Rica also has three species of ibis, recognizable by their long, slender, downturned bills handy for probing muddy watercourses. Nicoya and Guanacaste are good places to spot the **white ibis,** with its startlingly red bill and legs; to see the green-black **green ibis,** head to the Caribbean.

Hummingbirds

Of all the exotically named bird species in Costa Rica, the hummingbirds beat all contenders. Their names are poetry: the **green-crowned brilliant, purple-throated mountaingem, Buffon's plummeteer,** and the bold and strikingly beautiful fiery-throated hummingbird. More than 300 species of New World hummingbirds constitute the family Trochilidae (Costa Rica has 51), and all are stunningly pretty. The **fiery-throated hummingbird,** for example, is a glossy green, shimmering iridescent at close range, with dark blue tail, violet-blue chest, glittering coppery orange throat, and a brilliant blue crown set off by velvety black on the sides and back of the head.

Some males take their exotic plumage one step further and are bedecked with long streamer tails and iridescent mustaches, beards, and visors.

These tiny high-speed machines are named because of the hum made by the beat of their wings. At up to 100 beats per second, the hummingbirds' wings move so rapidly that the naked eye cannot detect them. They are often seen hovering at flowers, from which they extract nectar and often insects with their long, hollow, and extensile tongues forked at the tip. Alone among birds, they can generate power on both the forward and backward wing strokes, a distinction that allows them to also fly backward.

The energy required to function at such an intense pitch is prodigious. The hummingbird has the highest metabolic rate per unit of body weight in the avian world (its pulse rate can exceed 1,200 beats a minute) and requires proportionately large amounts of food. The white-eared hummingbird consumes up to 850 percent of its own weight in food and water each day. At night, it goes into "hibernation," lowering its body temperature and metabolism to conserve energy.

Typically loners, hummingbirds bond with the opposite sex only for the few seconds it takes to mate. Many, such as the fiery-throated hummingbird, are fiercely territorial. With luck you might witness a spectacular aerial battle between males defending their territories. In breeding season, the males "possess" territories rich in flowers attractive to females: the latter gains an ample food source in exchange for offering the male sole paternity rights. Nests are often no larger than a thimble, loosely woven with cobwebs and flecks of bark and lined with silky plant down. Inside, the female will lay two eggs no larger than coffee beans.

Motmots

The motmot is a sickle-billed bird that makes its home in a hole in the ground. Of nine species of motmot in tropical America, six live in Costa Rica. You'll find them from humid coastal southwest plains to the cool highland zone and dry Guanacaste region. Motmots have a pendulous

WHY THE MOTMOT LIVES UNDERGROUND

According to Bribrí legend, the god Sibo asked all the creatures to help him make the world. They all chipped in gladly except the motmot, who hid in a hole. Unfortunately, the bird left his tail hanging out. When the other birds saw this they picked the feathers from the motmot's tail but left the feathers at the tip.

When the world was complete, Sibo gave all the tired animals a rest. Soon the motmot appeared and began boasting about how hard he had labored. But the lazy bird's tail gave the game away, so Sibo, who guessed what had happened, admonished the motmot and banished him to living in a hole in the ground.

twin-feathered tail with the barbs missing three-quarters of the way down, leaving two bare feather shafts with disc-shaped tips resembling oval pendant earrings.

Two commonly seen species are the **blue-crowned motmot** and **turquoise-bowed motmot.** The former has a green-and-brown body with red belly, a scintillating turquoise head, and beady red eyes peeping out between a black Lone Ranger mask. The latter is similarly colored, but with a red back and a large black spot on its chest, plus longer bare "handles" on its racquet-like tail.

Parrots

If ever there were an avian symbol of the neotropics, it must be the parrot. This family of birds is marked by savvy intelligence, an ability to mimic the human voice, and uniformly short, hooked bills hinged to provide the immense power required for cracking seeds and nuts. Costa Rica claims 16 of the world's 330 or so species, including six species of parakeets and two species of macaws, the giants of the parrot kingdom.

The parrots are predominantly green, with short, truncated tails (parakeets and macaws, however, have long tails), and varying degrees of colored markings. All are voluble, screeching raucously as they barrel overhead in fast-flight formation.

Although **macaw** is the common name for any of 15 species of these large, long-tailed birds found throughout Central and South America, only two species inhabit Costa Rica: the scarlet macaw *(lapa roja)* and the great green or Buffon's macaw *(lapa verde)*. Both bird populations are losing their homes to deforestation and poaching. The macaw populations have declined so dramatically that they are now in danger of disappearing completely. (There are far more macaws in captivity than exist in the wild.)

What magnificent creatures these birds are! No protective coloration. No creeping about trying to blend in with the countryside. Instead, they posture like kings and queens. The largest of the neotropical parrots, macaws have harsh, raucous voices that are filled with authority. They fly overhead, calling loudly, their long, trailing tail feathers and short wings making it impossible to confuse them with other birds. They are gregarious and rarely seen alone. They are usually paired male and female—they're monogamous for life—often sitting side by side, grooming and preening each other, and conversing in rasping loving tones, or flying two by two.

Macaws usually nest in softwood trees, where termites have hollowed out holes.

They rarely eat fruit, but prefer seeds and nuts, which they extract with a hooked nutcracker of such strength that it can split that most intractable of nuts, the Brazil nut—or a human finger.

The scarlet macaw can grow to 85 cm in length. It wears a dazzling, rainbow-colored jacket of bright yellow and blue, green, or scarlet. Though the scarlet macaw ranges from Mexico to central South America and was once abundant on both coasts of Costa Rica, today it is found only in a few parks on the Pacific shore, and rarely on the Caribbean side. Only three wild populations of scarlet macaws in Central America have a long-term chance of survival—at Carara National Park and Corcovado National Park in Costa Rica, and Coiba Island in Panamá. The

© CHRISTOPHER P. BAKER

scarlet macaw

bird can also be seen with regularity at Palo Verde National Park, Manuel Antonio National Park, and Santa Rosa National Park, though these populations are below the minimum critical size. An estimated 200 scarlets live at Carara and 1,600 at Corcovado.

It is almost impossible to tell male from female. The scarlet's bright red-orange plumage with touches of blue and yellow does not vary between the sexes or with aging.

The Buffon's macaw, or great green macaw, is slightly smaller than the scarlet. It has a pea-green body, a white face splotched with red, blue wingtips, and a red tail. A few more than 50 breeding pairs of Buffon's macaw are thought to exist in the wild, exclusively in the Caribbean and northern lowlands. The bird relies on the almendro tree—a heavily logged species—for nest sites, and calls have gone out for a ban on logging almendros. Its population is increasing due to environmental efforts.

SAVING THE MACAW

Several conservation groups are working to stabilize and reestablish the scarlet macaw population.

Zoo Ave (tel. 506/433-8989, fax 506/433-9140, zooave@racsa.co.cr, www.zooave.org), at La Garita, west of Alajuela, has an extensive macaw breeding program, and plans to release 10 macaws to the wild each year.

Amigos de las Aves (Apdo. 2306-4050, Alajuela, tel./fax 506/441-2658, richmar @racsa.co.cr, www.hatchedtoflyfree.homestead.com; in the U.S.A., SJO 465, P.O. Box 025216, Miami, FL 33102) is a macaw-breeding program on a three-hectare estate—Flor de Mayo—in Río Segundo de Alajuela. Here, Richard and Margot Frisius, two experienced aviculturists, raise baby macaws using special techniques and cages (in 1997 they succeeded in a first-ever experiment to breed green macaws in captivity). They teach domestically raised macaws how to find native food so that they can be released into the wilds. The first macaws were released in January 1999 at a private reserve in Nicoya. At last visit, dozens of macaws had been released in an experimental program in which congregations of birds are placed for six months in huge release cages to become accustomed to their new surrounds before final release. The birds are then released in pairs. Donations are needed, as are volunteer workers. U.S. tax-deductible donations may be sent to Amigos de las Aves, 317 Thames Dr., Sidwell, LA 70458.

The **Río Colorado Lodge** (Apdo. 5094, San José 1000, tel. 506/710-6879 or 506/232-4063, fax 506/231-5987, tarpon4u@mindspring.com, www.rioco loradolodge.com), at Barra del Colorado, also has a small macaw program.

© CHRISTOPHER P. BAKER

Margot and Richard Frisius with hand-raised macaws at Flor de Mayo, Río Segundo de Alajuela

Seabirds and Shorebirds

Costa Rica has almost 100 species of seabirds and shorebirds, including a wide variety of gulls, with the most common being the **laughing gull** *(gaviota reidora)*. Many are migratory visitors, more abundant in winter months, including the **sanderling,** a small light-gray shorebird that scurries along the surf line in a high-speed jittery gait, like a mechanical toy.

The large, pouch-billed **brown pelican** *(pelicano)* can be seen up and down the Pacific coast (and, in lesser numbers, on the Caribbean), where they can be admired gliding in superb formation over the water, diving for fish, or lazing on fishing boats, waiting for the next catch to come in.

Boobies inhabit several islands off Nicoya, as do **storm petrels, jaegers,** the beautiful red-billed, fork-tailed **royal tern,** and a variety of other seabirds. **Oystercatchers, whimbrels, sandpipers** (often seen in vast flocks), and other shoreline waders frequent the coastal margins.

Frigate birds, with their long scimitar wings and forked tails, hang like sinister kites in the wind all along the Costa Rican coast. They hold a single position in the sky, as if suspended from invisible strings, and from this airborne perch harry gulls and terns until the latter release their

© CHRISTOPHER P. BAKER

frigate bird on Isla Bolaños

catch (bird-watchers have a name for such thievery: kleptoparasitism).

Despite the sinister look imparted by its long hooked beak, the frigate bird is quite beautiful. The adult male is all black with a lustrous faint purplish-green sheen on its back (especially during the courtship season). The female, the much larger of the two, is easily distinguished by the white feathers that extend up her abdomen and breast, and the ring of blue around her eyes.

Second only to a frigate bird's concern for food is its interest in the opposite sex. The females do the conspicuous searching out and selecting of mates. The hens take to the air above the rookery to look over the males, who cluster in groups atop the scrubby mangrove bushes. Whenever a female circles low over the bushes, the males tilt their heads far back to show off their fully inflated scarlet gular pouches (appropriately shaped like hearts), vibrate their wings rapidly back and forth, and attempt to entice the female with loud clicking and drumming sounds.

Once the pair is established, a honeymoon of nest-building begins. In the structured world of the frigate birds, it is the male's job to find twigs for the nest. The piratical frigates will not hesitate to steal twigs from their neighbors' nests, so the females stay home to guard them. The female lays a single egg, and each parent takes turns at one-week shifts during the eight-week incubation. They guard the chick closely against predatory neighbors; hawks and owls make quick feasts of the unwary young. For five months, the dejected-looking youngsters sit immobile beneath the hot sun; even when finally airborne, they remain dependent on their parents for more than a year while they learn the complex trade of air piracy.

Superb stunt flyers, frigate birds often bully other birds on the wing, pulling at the tails of their victims until the latter release or regurgitate a freshly caught meal. Frigate birds also catch much of their food themselves. You may see them skimming the water, snapping up squid, flying fish, and other morsels off the water's surface. (They must keep themselves dry, as they have only a small preen gland, insufficient to oil their feathers; if they get too wet they become waterlogged and drown.)

QUETZAL CULTURE

Early Maya and Aztecs worshiped a god called Quetzalcoatl, the Plumed Serpent that bestowed corn on humans, and depicted him with a headdress of quetzal feathers. The bird's name is derived from *quetzalli,* an Aztec word meaning "precious" or "beautiful." The Maya considered the male's iridescent green tail feathers worth more than gold, and killing the sacred bird was a capital crime (captured quetzals had their tail feathers plucked and were released to grow new ones). Quetzal plumes and jade, which were traded throughout Mesoamerica, were the Maya's most precious objects. It was the color that was significant: "Green—the color of water, the life-giving fluid. Green, the color of the maize crop, had special significance to the people of Mesoamerica," wrote Adrian Digby in his monograph *Mayan Jades,* "and both jade and the feathers of the quetzal were green."

During the colonial period, the indigenous people of Central America came to see the quetzal as a symbol of independence and freedom. Popular folklore relates how the quetzal got its dazzling blood-red breast: in 1524, when the Spanish conquistador Pedro de Alvarado defeated the Maya chieftain Tecun Uman, a gilt and green quetzal lit on Uman's chest at the moment he fell mortally wounded; when the bird took off again, its breast was stained with the brilliant crimson blood of the Maya.

Archaeologists believe that the wearing of quetzal plumes was proscribed, under pain of death, except for Maya priests and nobility. It became a symbol of authority vested in a theocratic elite, much as only Roman nobility was allowed to wear purple silks.

Tanagers and Other Passerines

Costa Rica boasts 50 species of tanagers—small, exorbitantly colored birds that favor dark tropical forests. Tanagers brighten the jungle, and you are likely to spot their bright plumage as you hike along trails. The tanagers' short stubby wings enable them to swerve and dodge at high speed through the undergrowth as they chase after insects.

Among the most astonishing is the **summer tanager,** flame-red from tip to tail. The black male **scarlet-rumped tanager** also has a startlingly flame-red rump (his mate—they travel together—is variegated orange and olive-gray). The exotically plumed **blue-gray tanager** is as variegated in turquoise and teal as a Bahamian sea, while the **silver-throated tanager** is lemon yellow.

Tanagers belong to the order Passerines— "perching birds"—that includes about half of *all* Costa Rica's bird species. It is a taxonomically challenging group, with members characterized by certain anatomical features: notably, three toes pointing forward and a longer toe pointing back. **Sparrows, robins,** and **finches** are Passerines, as are **antbirds** (30 species), **blackbirds** (20 species), **flycatchers** (78 species), **warblers** (52 species), and **wrens** (22 species).

Many tropical Passerines are more exuberantly liveried than their temperate counterparts. Look for the blue-black-and-red **blue-hooded euphonia,** the Day-glo green and yellow **golden-bowed chlorophonia,** and the black-and-flame orange **red-capped manakin.**

Trogons

Costa Rica has 10 of the 40 species of trogons: brightly colored, long-tailed, short-beaked, pigeon-sized, forest-dwelling tropical birds. Most trogons combine bodies of two primary colors—red and blue, blue and yellow, or green and some other color—with a black-and-white striped tail. The **orange-bellied trogon,** for example, is green, with a bright orange belly beneath a sash of white.

Many bird-watchers travel to Costa Rica simply to catch sight of the **quetzal,** or resplendent trogon. What this bird lacks in physical stature it makes up for in audacious plumage: vivid, shimmering green that ignites in the sunshine, flashing emerald to golden and back to iridescent green. The male sports a fuzzy punk hairdo, a scintillating crimson belly, and two brilliant green tail plumes up to 60 cm long, edged in snowy white and sinuous as feather boas. In common with other bird species, the male outshines the female, who lacks the elaborate plumage and has a dun-colored head and only a splotch of crimson.

Its beauty was so fabled and the bird so elusive and shy that early European naturalists believed the quetzal was a fabrication of Central American natives. In 1861, English naturalist Osbert Salvin, the first European to record observing a quetzal, pronounced it "unequaled for splendour among the birds of the New World," and promptly shot it. During the course of the next three decades, thousands of quetzal plumes crossed the Atlantic to fill the specimen cabinets of European collectors and the fashionable milliners' shops of Paris, Amsterdam, and London. Salvin redeemed himself by writing the 40-volume tome *Biología Centrali Americana,* which provided virtually a complete catalog of neotropical species.

The quetzal's territory spans a radius of approximately 300 meters, which the male proclaims each dawn through midmorning and again at dusk with a telltale melodious whistle—a hollow, high-pitched call of two notes, one ascending steeply, the other descending—repeated every 8–10 minutes.

Nest holes (often hollowed out by woodpeckers) are generally about 10 meters from the ground. Within, the female generally lays two light-blue eggs, which take about 18 days to hatch. Both sexes share parental duties. By day, the male incubates the eggs while his two-foot-long tail feathers hang out of the nest. At night, the female takes over.

Although the quetzal eats insects, small frogs, and lizards, it has a penchant for the fruit of the broad-leafed *aguacatillo* (a kind of miniature avocado in the laurel family), which depends on the bird to distribute seeds. The movement of quetzals follows the seasonal fruiting of different laurel species. The quetzal has rather meticulous feeding hours, which you can almost set your watch by. It's fascinating to watch them feeding: an upward swoop for fruit is the bird's aerial signature.

Everywhere throughout its 1,000-mile range (from southern Mexico to western Panamá), the quetzal is endangered by loss of its cloud-forest habitat. This is particularly true of the lower forests around 1,500 to 2,000 meters, to which families of quetzals descend to hollow out nests in dead and decaying trees. This is the best time to see narcissistic males showing off their tail plumes in undulating flight, or launching spiraling skyward flights, which presage a plummeting dive with their tail feathers rippling behind, all part of the courtship ritual.

Despite its iridescence, the bird's plumage offers excellent camouflage under the rainy forest canopy. They also sit motionless for long periods, with their vibrant red chests turned away from any suspected danger. If a quetzal knows you're close by and feels threatened, you may hear a harsh "weec-weec" warning call and see the male's flicking tail feathers betray his presence. Quetzals are easily seen throughout highland Costa Rica at cloud forest elevations.

Waterfowl

Costa Rica lies directly beneath a migratory corridor between North and South America, and in the northern lowland wetlands, the air is always full of **blue-winged teals, shoveler ducks,** and other waterfowl settling and taking off amid the muddy, pool-studded grasslands. Most duck species are winter migrants from North America. Neotropical species include the **black-bellied whistling duck** and **Muscovy ducks.**

The wetlands are also inhabited by 18 species of the order Gruiformes: rails, bitterns, and their relatives, with their large, wide-splayed feet good for wading and running across lily- and grass-choked watercourses. Many are brightly colored, including the **purple gallinule,** liveried in vivid violet and green, with a yellow-tipped red bill, bright yellow legs, and a blue dot on its forehead.

The order includes many migrants, including the charcoal-gray, white-billed **American coot** and **sunbittern,** a long-legged, multihued wader with bright orange legs and bill, and—when in flight—a dramatic sunburst pattern in white, black, and brown beneath the wings, like the markings of a military aircraft.

The widely dispersed *rascón* or **gray-necked wood rail** (common along lowland rivers and lagoons throughout the country) is easily spotted stalking the muddy watercourses in search of frogs and other tidbits. The dark olive-brown bird has a colorful bronze breast, gray neck, orange legs, and red eyes. The black-and-brown, yellow-beaked **northern jacana** is also easy to see, especially in the canals of Tortuguero, hopping about atop water lilies thanks to its long, slender toes—hence its nickname, the "lily-trotter." It has a strange yellow shield atop its bill, and yellow-streaked wing feathers. The female jacana is promiscuous, mating with many males, who take on the task of nest-building and brooding eggs that may have been fertilized by a rival. Tortuguero is also a good place to spot the **sungrebe,** a furtive, brown waterbird with black-and-white striped neck and head and red beak. Males carry young chicks in a fold of skin under their wings.

Vultures

You can't help but be unnerved at the first sight of scrawny black vultures picking at some roadside carcass, or swirling overhead on the thermals as if waiting for your car to break down. They look quite ominous in their undertaker's plumage, with bald heads and hunched shoulders. Costa Rica has four species of vultures (*zopilotes* to Ticos), easily identified by the color of the skin on their heads.

The grotesquely red-headed **turkey vulture** is common in all parts of Costa Rica below 2,000 meters, noticeably so in moister coastal areas where it hops about on the streets of forlorn towns such as Golfito. The stockier **black vulture** has a black head (as do juvenile turkey vultures). Both are otherwise charcoal colored. The two adopt different flying patterns: the turkey vulture flies low, seeking out carrion with its well-developed sense of smell; the black vulture soars higher and uses its eyes to spot carrion and often

© CHRISTOPHER P. BAKER

vultures

drops in to chase off smaller vultures from carcasses it has claimed.

Count yourself lucky to spot the rarer **lesser yellow-headed vulture,** with its namesake yellow head; or the mighty **king vulture,** which wears a handsome white coat with black wing feathers and tail, and a wattled head variegated in vermilion and yellow.

Other Notable Birds

The **three-wattled bellbird,** which inhabits the cloud forests, is rarely spotted in the mist-shrouded treetops, though the male's eerie call, described by one writer as a ventriloqual "bonk!" (or like a hammer clanging on an anvil), haunts the forest as long as the sun is up. It is named for the strange wattles that dangle from its bill. The bellbird is one of the Cotinga family, which includes many of Costa Rica's most exotically liveried species. Its population is declining alarmingly.

In the moist Caribbean lowlands (and occasionally elsewhere) you may spot the telltale pendulous woven nests—often one meter long—of **Montezuma oropendolas,** a large bronze-colored bird with a black neck, head, and belly, a blue-and-orange bill, and bright yellow outer tail feathers. The birds nest in colonies. Their favored trees often look as if they have been hung with cheesesacks. The **chestnut-headed oropendola** is less commonly seen.

Nicoya and Guanacaste are good places to spot the **white-throated magpie jay,** a large and gregarious bird that often begs food from tourists. It is sky-blue above, with a snow-white throat and belly fringed by a dark blue necklace, and—unmistakably—has a tufted crest of black feathers curling forward.

The great **curassow,** growing as tall as one meter, is almost too big for flight and tends to run through the undergrowth if disturbed. You're most likely to see this endangered bird in Corcovado or Santa Rosa National Parks.

All four New World species of kingfishers inhabit Costa Rica: the large red-breasted; the slate-blue **ringed kingfisher,** which can grow to 40 cm; its smaller cousin, the **belted kingfisher;** and the **Amazon kingfisher** and smaller **green kingfisher,** both green with white and red underparts.

The **common pauraque** (or *cuyeo*) is a member of the nightjar family—nocturnal birds that in flight are easily mistaken for bats. They like to sit on the roads at night, where they are well camouflaged (mottled gray, black, and brown), especially on bumpy, dusty roads. The first you know of it is when the bird suddenly decides to lift off as your car approaches, causing you at least a heck of a scare.

Another neotropical nightjar is the odd-looking **great potoo** *(nictibio grande),* a superbly camouflaged bird that perches upright on tree stumps and holds its hawk-like head haughtily aloft. Its squat cousin, the **common potoo,** with its beady yellow-and-black eyes, resembles an owl.

Other birds you might expect to see include the 16 species of **woodpeckers, cuckoos,** any of 11 species of **swifts,** the **tinamou** (a large bird resembling a cross between a hen and a dove), and a host of birds you may not recognize but whose names you will never forget: scarlet-thighed dacnis, violaceous trogons, tody motmots, laneolated monlets, lineated foliage-gleaners, and black-capped pygmy tyrants.

REPTILES

Costa Rica is home to more than 200 species of reptiles, half of them snakes.

Crocodiles and Caimans

Many travelers visit Costa Rica in the hope of seeing American crocodiles and caimans, the croc's diminutive cousins. Both species are easily seen in the wet lowlands. They are superbly adapted for water. Their eyes and nostrils are atop their heads for easy breathing and vision (and smell) while otherwise entirely submerged, and their thick, muscular tails provide tremendous propulsion.

To this reptile, home is a "gator hole" or pond, a system of trails, and a cavelike den linked by a tunnel to the hole. As it moves between its nest

© JEAN MERCIER

crocodile

and its pond and along its trails through the aquatic vegetation, it helps keep the water open and clear. The croc also helps maintain the health of aquatic water systems by weaning out weak and large predatory fish.

Mating season begins in December, when males are overcome with a desire to find a female. The polygamous male (males form harems) will defend his breeding turf from rival suitors with bare-toothed gusto. When estrous females approach, the ardent male gets very excited and goes through a nuptial dance, roaring intensely and even kicking up clouds of spray with his lashing tail. A curtsey by the damsel and the male clasps her ardently with his jaws, their tails intertwine, and the mating takes place, with the union lasting up to one hour.

For all their beastly behavior, crocodiles are devoted parents. A female selects a spot above the high-water mark and exposed to both sunlight and shade, then makes a large nest mound out of sticks, soft vegetation, and mud, which she hollows to make room for her eggs (usually between 30 and 70). Eggs are laid March–May, during dry season. The mother will guard the

nest and keep it moist for several months after laying. The rotting vegetation creates heat, which incubates the eggs. When they are ready to hatch, the hatchlings pipe squeakily and she uncovers the eggs and takes the babies into a special pouch inside her mouth. She then swims away, with the youngsters peering out between a palisade of teeth. The male assists, and soon the young crocs are feeding and playing in a special nursery, guarded by the two watchful parents (only 10 percent of newborn hatchlings survive).

Despite being relics from the age of the dinosaurs, croc brains are far more complex than those of other reptiles. They are sharp learners (in the Tempisque basin, crocs have been seen whacking tree trunks with their tails to dislodge chicks from their nests). They also have an amazing immunology system that can even defeat gangrene.

American crocodiles (not to be confused with the American alligator that inhabits the Florida Everglades) were heavily hunted for their skins until their numbers were so reduced that by the 1960s they were almost extinct. Fortunately, since the 1970s, the American crocodile (called the *cocodrilo* locally) has been protected under the Convention on International Trade in Endangered Species and is making a strong comeback, repopulating many rivers from which it has been absent for years. It can easily be seen in dozens of rivers throughout the lowlands and estuaries along the Pacific coastline. Sections of the Tárcoles River have as many as 240 crocodiles per mile, far higher than anywhere else in Costa Rica.

The creatures, which can live 80 years or more and reach 18 feet (six meters) in length, spend much of their days basking on mudbanks, maintaining an even body temperature, which they regulate by opening their gaping mouths. At night, they sink down into the warm waters of the river for the hunt. The American crocodile—one of four species of New World crocodiles—is generally a fish-eater, but older adults are known to vary their diet with meat... so watch out! Although they are commonly thought to be sluggish, crocodiles, preferring stealth, can run very fast in short bursts. Crocs cannot chew. They simply snap, tear, and swallow. Powerful stomach acids dissolve everything, including bones. A horrible way to go!

One of the smallest of western crocodilians—no more than six feet (two meters) long—and possibly the most abundant in existence today, the speckled **caiman** (*guajipal* locally) is still relatively common in parts of wet lowland Costa Rica on both the Atlantic and Pacific coasts. Palo Verde and Tortuguero are both good places to spot them in small creeks, *playas,* and brackish mangrove swamps, or basking on the banks of streams and ponds.

The scales of the caiman take on the blue-green color of the water it slithers through. Such camouflage and even the ability to breathe underwater, through raised nostrils, have not protected the caiman. Their nests are heavily disturbed by dogs, foxes, lizards, and humans.

Caiman or croc? It's easy to tell. The former is dark brown with darker bands around its tail, and holds its head high when sunning. The much-larger crocodile is an olive color with black spots on its tail.

© CHRISTOPHER P. BAKER

iguana at Hotel Capitán Suizo, Tamarindo

Iguanas and Lizards

The most common reptile you'll see is the dragonlike, tree-dwelling iguana, which seems to have little fear of man and can grow to a meter in length. You'll spot them in all kinds of forest habitats, crawling through the forest leaf litter or basking for long hours on branches that hang over water, its preferred route of escape when threatened. They are most common in drier areas below 2,500 feet elevation.

There's no mistaking this reptile for any other lizard. Its head—the size of a man's fist—is crested with a frightening wig of leathery spines, its heavy body encased in a scaly hide, deeply wrinkled around the sockets of its muscular legs. Despite its menacing *One Million Years B.C.* appearance, it is a nonbelligerent vegetarian.

There are two species in Costa Rica: the **green** and the **spiny-tailed** iguana. The green iguana (*Iguana iguana*), which is a dull to bright green, with a black-banded tail, can grow to two meters long. The males turn a bright orange when they get ready to mate in November or December and choose a lofty perch from which to advertise their showy dewlap, sexual flush, and erect crest of spines (they revert to darker green by night). The horny male will forgo food for weeks to win over the love of his life. Females nest in holes in the ground, then abandon their eggs (fewer than 5 percent of hatchlings will survive to adulthood). Iguanas are territorial and defend their turf aggressively against competitors. The first warning sign is a head bobbing. Often the defending iguana will become lighter in color, like a chameleon.

Campesinos, for reasons you may not wish to know, call the green iguana the "tree chicken." (The iguana population of neighboring countries has been decimated for meat, spurring a cross-border commerce of iguanas; Costa Ricans are not avid consumers of iguana meat.)

The smaller, gray or tan-colored spiny iguana, also called the **ctenosaur** *(Iguana negra)*—known locally as the *garrobo*—has a tail banded with rings of hard spines that it uses to guard against predators by blocking the entrance to holes in trees or the ground.

Another miniature dinosaur is *Basilicus basilicus,* or **Jesus Christ lizard,** a Pacific lowland dweller common in Santa Rosa, Palo Verde, and Corcovado National Parks. These, too, have large crests atop their heads, backs, and tails, and use water as their means of escape, running across it on hind legs (hence their name).

Snakes

The 138 species of snakes make up more than half of all reptile species in the nation. Wherever you are in the country, snakes are sure to be about. They are reclusive, however, and it is a fortunate traveler indeed who gets to see in the wild the fantastically elongated **chunk-headed snake,** with its catlike elliptical eyes, or the slender, beak-nosed, bright green **vine snake.**

Among the more common snake species you are likely to see are the wide-ranging and relatively benign **boas,** which you might spot crawling across a cultivated field or waiting patiently in the bough of a tree in wet or dry tropical forest, savanna, or dry thorn scrub. Boas are aggressive when confronted: though not poisonous, they are quite capable of inflicting serious damage with their large teeth and will not hesitate to bite.

green tree pythons at Grecia's World of Snakes

© CHRISTOPHER P. BAKER

Only 18 species of snakes in Costa Rica are venomous (nine are *very* venomous), including a species of tropical **rattlesnake** found in Guanacaste and a few relic areas of the Meseta Central. It produces a venom considerably more toxic than its North American cousin—blindness and suffocation are typical effects on humans—and it rarely uses its well-developed rattle to warn off the unwary. All Costa Rica's venomous snakes produce the same venom except the coral snake. Hence there are only two anti-venoms: one for the coral snake and a second for all others.

Here are two fascinating tidbits to sink your teeth into. The **coffee palm viper** is a heat-seeking missile that can detect differences of 1/3,000°C per meter! And *Clelia clelia* eats only other snakes and prefers the fearsome **fer-de-lance** (locally called *terciopelo,* Spanish for "velvet"), which is much feared for its aggressiveness—it accounts for 80 percent of all snake bites in Costa Rica—and lethal venom. One of several Central American pit vipers—another is the **bushmaster**—the fer-de-lance can grow to a length of three meters and is abundant throughout the country except Nicoya, particularly in overgrown fields and river courses in drier lowland regions. Juvenile fer-de-lance are arboreal critters that feed on lizards and frogs, which they attract with a yellow-tipped tail. As adults, they come down to earth, where they move about at night and, by daylight, rest in loose coils of burnished brown on the forest floor.

Give the fer-de-lance a wide berth! Unlike other vipers, which usually slither away at the approach of humans and will not strike unless provoked, the fer-de-lance stands its ground and will bite with little provocation. The snake's powerful venom dissolves nerve tissue and destroys blood cells and artery walls; those fortunate enough to survive may suffer paralysis or tissue damage so massive as to require amputation of the bitten limb. The fer-de-lance frequently disgorges venom on the ground, which is said to smell like dog scat—a good warning sign to be aware of when hiking.

Among the more colorful snakes are the four species of **coral snakes,** with small heads, blunt tails, and bright bands of red, black, and yellow or white. These highly venomous snakes (often fatal to humans) exhibit a spectacular defensive display: they flatten their bodies and snap back and forth while swinging their heads side to side and coiling and waving their tails.

In the Pacific Ocean, you may sometimes encounter venomous pelagic **sea snakes,** yellow-bellied and black-backed serpents closely related to terrestrial cobras and coral snakes. This gregarious snake has developed an oarlike tail to paddle its way through the ocean. It tends to drift passively with its buddies among drift-lines of flotsam, where it feeds on small fish.

Turtles

Six of the world's eight species of marine turtles nest on Costa Rica's beaches, and you can see turtles laying eggs somewhere in Costa Rica virtually any time of year.

Tortuguero National Park, in northeastern Costa Rica, is one of fewer than 30 places in the world that the **green turtle** considers clean enough and safe enough to lay its eggs. Although green turtles were once abundant throughout the Caribbean, today there are only three major sites in the region where they nest: one on Aves Island, 62 km west of Montserrat, a second at Gandoca-Manzanillo (and occasionally on beaches north toward Cahuita), and another at Tortuguero.

On the Pacific coast, the most spectacular nestings are at Playa Nancite, in Santa Rosa National Park, and Ostional Wildlife Refuge, where tens of thousands of **olive ridley turtles** come ashore July–Dec. in synchronized mass nestings known as *arribadas.* Giant **leatherback turtles,** which can weigh as much as a ton and reach a length of three meters, nest at Playa Grande, near Tamarindo, Oct.–April. Hawksbills, ridleys, leatherbacks, Pacific greens, and occasionally loggerheads (primarily Caribbean nesters) appear in lesser numbers at other beaches along the Pacific coast.

Terrestrial turtles *(jicoteas)* are also common in Costa Rica, particularly in the Caribbean lowlands. One species—the red turtle, found in northern Pacific lowlands—is particularly easy to spot: its high-domed carapace is gaudily patterned in oranges, reds, yellows, and blacks. Several species of aquatic turtles also frequent the swamps and creeks. Look for them squatting on partially submerged logs.

One hundred years ago, green turtles were as numerous as the bison on the North American plains. They were highly prized for their meat by Central American and Carib Indians, who netted and harpooned them. And British and Spanish fleets, buccaneers, and merchantmen counted on turtle meat to feed their crews while cruising in New World waters. They're easy to catch and easy to keep alive for weeks on their backs in a space no bigger than the turtle itself. ("Turtle turners" patrolled nesting beaches, where they wrestled female turtles onto their backs to be picked up the next day.)

Large-scale green turtle export from Tortuguero was exacerbated in 1912 when turtle soup became a delicacy in Europe. And the recurrent massing of olive ridley turtles at a few accessible beaches fostered intensive human exploitation.

Despite legislation outlawing the taking of turtle eggs or disturbing nesting turtles, nest sites continue to be raided by humans (encouraged by an ancient Mayan legend that says the eggs are aphrodisiacs).

When not nesting in Costa Rica, Pacific ridleys congregate in Mexican and Ecuadorian waters, where commercial exploitation continues in earnest. Turtle oil is used in the manufacture of cosmetics and perfumes, the shells used in jewelry and ornaments, and the offal dried and processed as fertilizer. Hawksbills, which rarely exceed 55 kg, are hunted illegally for the tourist trade: one occasionally still sees stuffed turtle specimens for sale. Only 13 nestings of hawksbills were recorded in 1999 at Tortuguero, a dramatic shortfall for this critically endangered species.

Mother Nature, too, poses her own challenges. Coatis, dogs, raccoons, and peccaries dig up nest sites to get at the tasty eggs. Gulls, vultures, and hungry frigate birds, with their piercing eyes and sharp beaks, pace the beach hungrily awaiting the hatchlings; crabs lie in wait for the tardy; and hungry jacks, barracudas, and sharks come close to shore for the feast.

VOLUNTEER PROGRAMS TO SAVE THE TURTLES

If you're interested in helping save endangered marine turtles, consider volunteering with the following organizations.

The **Caribbean Conservation Corps** (CCC, 4424 NW 13th St. Suite #A1, Gainesville, FL 32609, tel. 352/373-6441 or 800/678-7853, fax 352/375-2449, ccc@cccturtle.org, www.cccturtle .org) enlists volunteers to patrol Tortuguero during nesting season to protect the nests from poaching and help with research and tagging. Enclose $1 and a stamped, self-addressed business-size envelope with your request for information.

The **Earth Island Institute** (300 Broadway, Suite 28, San Francisco, CA 94133, tel. 415/788-3666 or 800/859-7283, fax 415/788-7324, www.earthisland.org) has a "Sea Turtle Restoration Project" in which paying guests count and

tag turtles, take radio-transmitter readings, and perform other duties at Playa Nancite, Punta Banco, and Ostional. Trips usually last eight days.

Earthwatch Institute (3 Clock Tower Place, Suite 100, Box 75, Maynard, MA 01754, tel. 978/461-0081 or 800/776-0188, fax 978/461-2332, info@earthwatch.org, www.earthwatch .org) has 10-day turtle-tagging tours whose participants assist research scientists. Other special-interest trips also focus on natural history.

Save the Turtles of Parismina (www.costricaturtles.com) needs volunteers to assist with turtle research and to help protect the hatcheries at Playa Barra de Matina.

The **Asociación ANAI** (tel. 506/224-3570 or 506/750-0020, anaicr@racsa.co.cr, www.anaircr .org) has similar requirements at Gandoca-Manzanillo National Wildlife Refuge.

Ridley hatchlings have even been found in the stomachs of leatherback turtles. Of the hundreds of eggs laid by a female in one season, only a handful will survive to reach maturity. (As many as 70 percent of the hatchlings are eaten before they reach the water.)

Most of the important nesting sites in Costa Rica are now protected, and access to some is restricted. Still, there is a shortage of undisturbed beaches where turtles can safely nest. Most turtle populations continue to decline because of illegal harvesting and environmental pressures, despite the best efforts of conservationists inspired by Dr. Archie Carr of the University of Florida, who wrote and lectured indefatigably on behalf of turtle protection (see *Tortuguero National Park* in the *Caribbean* chapter).

Turtles have hit on a formula for outwitting their predators, or at least for surviving despite them. Each female turtle normally comes ashore two to six times each season and lays an average of 100 eggs on each occasion.

Most females make their clumsy climb up the beach and lay their eggs under the cover and cool of darkness (loggerheads and ridleys often nest in the daytime, as they seem less timid). They normally time their arrival to coincide with high tide, when they can swim in over the coral reef and when they do not have to drag themselves puffing and panting across a wide expanse of beach. Their great weight, unsupported by water, makes breathing difficult. As a turtle drags her ponderous bulk up the beach, her progress is slow and punctuated by numerous halts to breathe. Some turtles even die of heart attacks brought on by the exertions of digging and laying.

Once she settles on a comfortable spot above the high-tide mark, the female scoops out a large body

WHERE THE TURTLES NEST

Caribbean Coast

Tortuguero: Loggerheads and hawksbills come ashore year-round but especially in August. The major attractions are green turtles, which nest here June to November in vast numbers.

Barra de Matina Beach: Leatherbacks, greens, and hawksbills come ashore at this private sanctuary north of Puerto Limón.

Gandoca-Manzanillo Wildlife Refuge: Four species of turtles lay their eggs on this beautiful beach south of Punta Uva. April and May are the best months to spot leatherbacks. By July, they are gone, replaced by greens, which can be seen in large numbers through September. Hawksbills also come ashore year-round, mostly March to August.

Pacific Coast

Curú Wildlife Refuge: Three species of turtles come ashore at this private refuge, on the eastern coast of the Nicoya Peninsula.

Las Baulas Marine National Park: Playa Grande is Costa Rica's preeminent nesting site for leatherback turtles. It has evolved into perhaps the nation's best-managed site. Leatherbacks come

ashore October to April; up to 100 on any one night. Olive ridley and green turtles can be seen here in small numbers May to August. There's a splendid turtle museum.

Ostional National Wildlife Refuge: This 248-hectare refuge, north of Playa Nosara, protects the major nesting site of olive ridleys (locally called *lora*). It is one of two sites in Costa Rica where synchronized mass nestings *(arribadas)* of the olive ridley occur, at two- to four-week intervals (generally between the third quarter and full moon) April to December, with a peak in July through September. During each *arribada* (which may last four to eight days), up to 120,000 turtles may nest at Ostional. Solitary nesters can be seen on most nights. Leatherbacks and Pacific greens also nest here.

Playa Nancite: Located in Santa Rosa National Park, Nancite—which is off-limits to anyone but scientists—is the second major site for *arribadas*. Some 200,000 ridleys choose Nancite. Leatherbacks and Pacific greens also nest here. Peak arrival for ridleys (called *carpentaria* locally) is midsummer, with a peak in October.

pit with her front flippers. Then her amazingly dexterous hind flippers go to work hollowing out a small egg chamber below her tail and into which white, spongy, golf-ball-size spheres fall every few seconds. After shoveling the sand back into place and flinging sand wildly about to hide her precious treasure, she makes her way back to sea.

The eggs normally take six to eight weeks to hatch, incubated by the warm sand. The sex of the hatchling is determined by the temperature of the sand: males are predominantly produced in cooler sand; a difference of 2–3°C will produce females. Thus, hatchlings from any one nest site are usually siblings of the same gender. Some marvelous internal clock arranges for most eggs to hatch at night when hatchlings can make their frantic rush for the sea concealed by darkness. Often, baby turtles will emerge from the eggs during the day and wait beneath the surface of the beach until nightfall. The young hatch together and dig their way up and out through up to a meter of sand as a kind of "simple-minded, cooperative brotherhood," says Archie Carr, "working mindlessly together to lower the penalties of being succulent on a hostile shore." They are programmed to travel fast across the beach to escape the hungry mouths. Even after reaching the sea they continue to swim frantically for several days—flippers paddling furiously—like clockwork toys.

No one knows where baby turtles go. They swim off and generally are not seen again until they appear years later as adults. Turtles are very slow-growing; most immature turtles of all species increase in carapace length by less than three cm a year. Little, too, is known about the lives of adult marine turtles.

Turtles are great travelers capable of amazing feats of navigation. Greens, for example, navigate across up to 1,500 miles of open sea to return, like salmon, to the same nest site, guided presumably by stars and currents and their own internal compass.

Between females' trips to the nesting beaches, a lot of strenuous romance goes on out in the surf. There is no pair-bonding between individual turtles, and each female may be mated by as many as 10 males. "Sea turtles in love are appallingly in-dustrious," according to Archie Carr. "The male turtle holds himself in the mating position on top of the smooth, curved, wet shell of the wave-tossed female by employing a three-point grappling rig [consisting] of his long, thick, curved, horn-tipped tail and a heavy, hooked claw on each front flipper... The female generally stays coy and resistant for what seems an unnecessarily long while. Other males gather, and all strive together over the female in a vast frothy melee."

When near nesting sites, respect the turtles' need for peace and quiet. Nesting turtles are very timid and extremely sensitive to flashlights, sudden movements, and noise, which will send a female turtle in hasty retreat to the sea without laying her eggs. Sometimes she will drop her eggs on the sand in desperation, without digging a proper nest.

INSECTS

The long history of the rainforest has enabled countless butterflies, moths, ants, termites, wasps, bees, and other tropical insects to evolve in astounding profusion. Ant species alone number in the many thousands. Corcovado National Park boasts at least 220 species of breeding butterflies, plus others that simply pass through. And there are so many species of beetles and

rhinoceros beetle

© CHRISTOPHER P. BAKER

grasshoppers that no one knows the true numbers. Many, many thousands of insect species still await identification.

The most brilliantly painted insects are the butterflies and moths, some quite tiny and obscure, others true giants of the insect kingdom. Many insect species are too small to see. The **hummingbird flower mite,** for example, barely half a millimeter long, is so small it can hitch rides from flower to flower inside the nostrils of hummingbirds.

Many exotic-looking species are immediately recognized. The giant **Guanacaste stick insect** is easily spotted at night on low shrubs. The three-inch **rhinoceros beetle** has an unmistakable long, upward-curving horn on its head.

And the number of spiders ornamented with showy colors is remarkable. Some even double themselves up at the base of leaf stalks, so as to resemble flower buds, and thus deceive the insects on which they prey.

Of course, a host of unfriendly bugs also exist in great numbers: chiggers, wasps and bees (including aggressive African bees), ticks, mosquitoes, fire ants, and the famous "no-see-ums" all can inflict irritating bites on humans.

Ants

Ants are the most abundant insects (one hectare of rainforest contains an average of nine million ants). Though related to bees and wasps, like butterflies they pass through four life stages: egg,

THE UNDERWORLD OF THE LEAFCUTTER ANT

There's something endearing about the leafcutter ant *(Atta cephalotes)*, a mushroom-farming insect that carries upright in its jaws a circular green shard scissored from the leaves of a plant. They are found in lowland forests throughout Costa Rica. At some stage in your travels you're bound to come across an endless troop of "media" workers hauling their cargo along jungle pathways as immaculately cleaned of debris as any swept doorstep.

The nests are built below ground, sometimes extending over an area of 200 square meters, with galleries to a depth of six meters. The largest nests provide homes for single colonies of up to five million insects. Trails span out from the nests, often for 100 meters or more. The worker ants set off from their nests day and night in long columns to demolish trees, removing every shoot, leaf, and stem section by tiny section and transporting them back to their underground chambers (about 15 percent of total leaf harvesting in Costa Rica is the work of leafcutter ants; they are a perpetual pest to commercial crop farmers, who often resort to igniting the nests with petroleum, usually to no avail).

They don't eat this material. Instead, they chew it up to form a compost on which they cultivate a nutritional breadlike fungus whose tiny white fruiting bodies provide them with food. So evolved has this symbiosis become that the fungus has lost its reproductive ability (it no longer produces sexual spores) and relies exclusively on the ants for propagation. When a new queen leaves her parent colony, she carries a piece of fungus with her with which to start a new garden.

The species has evolved different physical castes, each specializing in its own social tasks. At the apex of the leafcutter colony is the queen, which may be five centimeters long. The cutting and carrying are performed by intermediate-size workers ("medias"), guarded by ferocious-looking "majors," or soldier ants, about two centimeters long and with disproportionately large heads and jaws that they use to protect the workers—usually fighting to the death—from even the largest marauder. They also work to keep the trails clear. Most of the workers are tiny minors ("minimas"), which tend the nest and mulch it to feed the fungus gardens. Small "minimas" ride atop the leaves carried by their larger siblings to guard against parasitic phorid flies that attempt to lay their eggs on the leaves so that the eggs may be taken underground, where they will hatch and feed on the ant larvae.

larva, pupae, and adult. They are entirely social creatures, each ant entirely dependent upon its siblings so that the colony (which may contain many million individuals) acts as a single organism. They are also almost entirely blind and rely for communication upon the chemicals—pheromones—that they release to alert each other to danger and food sources.

Each colony is dependent on the queen ant, whose sole task is to produce eggs (thus, most colonies die when the queen, which can live up to 20 years, dies). Only the queen, who may boast a thousand times the body weight of a minor worker, is fertile. Once a year, usually at the beginning of rainy season (around May and June), the queen produces a unique brood of about 50,000 eggs; the approximately one-fifth that are fertilized will become new queens, and the others will become males. The entire colony doubles its efforts to care for and feed the large larva. Upon maturity, males and queens develop wings and, upon a particular weather cue, the progeny from many colonies emerge in synchronicity and swarm in a massive orgy in which queens are mated many times, collecting sperm to be stored and used throughout their lifetime. Males exist only to fertilize the queen and then die.

The queens then rip off their wings and disperse to start their own individual colonies by burrowing into the soil, laying eggs. Only about 1 percent of queens successfully start new colonies. If the colony survives its first year, it may grow large enough to produce soldiers with which to defend itself; after three years it will grow large enough to produce new queens and males.

The most terrifying ants of all are the **army ants,** which march through the forest with the sole intent of turning small creatures into skeletons in a few minutes. They produce a faint hissing sound and distinct ant-army odor. They're like a wolf pack, but with tens of thousands of miniature beasts of prey that merge and unite to form one great living creature. While the ants advance across the forest floor driving small creatures in front of them, humans and other large creatures can simply step aside and watch the column pass by—this can take several hours. Even when the

ants raid human habitations, people can simply clear out with their food stock while the ants clean out the cockroaches and other vermin as thoroughly as any exterminator might.

The army ants' jaws are so powerful that indigenous people have traditionally used them to suture wounds: the tenacious insect is held over a wound and its body squeezed so that its jaws instinctively clamp shut, drawing the flesh back together. The body is then pinched off.

Larvae carried by workers produce pheromones that stimulate the army to keep moving. When the larvae begin to pupate and no longer exude chemical messages, the ants bivouac in a vast ball in a hollow. They actually cling to one another and make a nest of their bodies, complete with passageways and chambers where the eggs are deposited. Once the queen lays her eggs and these hatch as larvae, a new generation of workers and soldiers emerges from the stored pupae. The larvae begin to secrete their characteristic pheromone, and the army is again stimulated to march off and terrorize the bush.

Butterflies

With nearly 1,000 identified species (approximately 10 percent of the world total), Costa Rica

owl-eye butterfly at La Guácima's Butterfly Farm

is a lepidopterist's paradise. You can barely stand still for one minute without checking off a dozen dazzling species: metallic gold riondinidae; delicate black-winged heliconius splashed with bright red and yellow; orange-striped paracaidas; and the deep neon-blue flash of morphos fluttering and diving in a ballet of subaqueous color. The marvelously intricate wing patterns are statements of identity, so that individuals may recognize those with whom mating may be fertile.

Not all this elaboration has a solely sexual connotation. Some butterflies are ornately colored to keep predators at bay. The bright white stripes against black on the **zebra butterfly** (like other members of the Heliconid family), for example, tell birds that the butterfly tastes acrid. There

are even perfectly tasty butterfly species that mimic the heliconid's colors, tricking predators to disdain them. Others use their colors as camouflage so that at rest they blend in with the green or brown leaves or look like the scaly bark of a tree. Among the most intriguing are the **owl-eye butterflies,** with their 13-cm wingspans and startling eye spots. The blue-gray *Caligo memnon,* the cream owl butterfly, is the most spectacular of the owl-eyes: the undersides of its wings are mottled to look like feathers and two large yellow-and-black "eyes" on the hind wing, which it displays when disturbed, give it an uncanny owl's face appearance.

The best time to see butterflies is in the morning, when most species are active. A few

MORPHO BUTTERFLIES

U ndoubtedly the Narcissus of the Costa Rican butterfly kingdom is the famous blue morpho, one of the most beautiful butterflies in the world. There are about 50 species of morphos, all in Central and South America, where they are called *celeste común.* The males of most species are bright neon blue, with iridescent wings that flash like mirrors in the sun. Populations of this magnificent oversized butterfly—it grows to 13–20 cm—are declining due to habitat destruction.

"It used to be a backyard species; now it is found only in reserves," says Maria Sabido, co-founder of the Butterfly Farm, in La Guácima de Alajuela. Still, you can't miss them when they're around and active—particularly in November, when they are extremely common along riverbeds and other moist habitats.

The morpho is a modest, nondescript brown when sitting quietly with wings closed. But when a predator gets too close, it flies off, startling its foe with a flash of its beautiful electric blue wings. (Not that they are always successful. Biologist David Janzen reports that piles of morpho wings are often found under the perches of jacamars and large flycatchers, which are partial to the morpho.)

The subspecies differ in color: in the Atlantic lowlands, the morpho is almost completely iridescent blue; one population in the Meseta Central is almost completely brown, with only a faint hint of electric blue. One species, commonly seen gliding about in the forest canopy, is red on the underside and gray on top.

Showmen have always used mirrors to produce glitter and illusion. The morpho is no exception. Look through a morpho butterfly's wing toward a strong light and you will see only brown. This is because the scales *are* brown. The fiery blue is produced by structure, not by pigment (one consequence is that the color will never fade). Tiny scales on the upper side of the wing are laid in rows that overlap much like roof shingles. These scales are ridged with minute layers that, together with the air spaces between them, refract and reflect light beams, absorbing all the colors except blue. The Atlantic species have additional glassy scales on top of the others to reflect even more light and give the wings a paler, more opalescent quality.

are active at dawn and dusk, and one species is even active by night. In general, butterfly populations are most dense in June and July, corresponding with the onset of the rainy season on the Pacific side. Butterfly migrations are also common. Like birds, higher-elevation species migrate up and down the mountains with changes in local weather. The most amazing migration—unsurpassed by any other insect in the neotropics—is that of the kitelike uranidae (this black and iridescent green species is actually a moth that mimics the swallowtail butterfly), in which millions of individuals pass through Costa Rica heading south from Honduras to Colombia.

AMPHIBIANS

Costa Rica hosts approximately 160 species of amphibians. The amphibians are primarily represented by the dozens of species of frogs and toads, most of which you're probably more likely to hear than to see. That catlike meow? That's Boulenger's hyla, one of Costa Rica's more than 20 kinds of toxic frogs. That sharp *tink, tink* that is usually the most prominent sound on damp nights in Costa Rica's mid-elevation rainforests? That's the tiny tink frog, of course. That insectlike buzz is probably two bright-red poison-arrow frogs wrestling belly-to-belly for the sake of a few square meters of turf. And the deafening choruses of long loud whoops that resound through the night in Nicoya and the adjacent lowlands of Guanacaste? That's an orgiastic band of ugly, orange and purple-black Mexican burrowing toads doing their thing.

Of all Central America's exotic species, none are more colorful—literally and figuratively— than the **poison-arrow frogs,** from which indigenous people extract deadly poisons to tip their arrows. Frogs are tasty little fellows to carnivorous amphibians, reptiles, and birds. Hence, in many species, the mucous glands common in all amphibians have evolved to produce a bitter-tasting poison.

In Central and South America at least 20 kinds of frogs have developed this defense still further: their alkaloid poisons are so toxic that they can paralyze a large bird or small monkey immediately. Several species—the dendrobatids—produce among the most potent toxins known: atelopidtoxin, bufogenin, bufotenidine, and bufotoxin. Pity the poor snake that gobbles up *Dendrobatis granuliferus,* a tiny bright green, red, and black frog that inhabits the lowland forests of the Golfo Dulce region. Another species, *Bufo marinus,* can even squirt its poison in a fine spray. And some species' eggs and tadpoles even produce toxins, making them unpalatable, like bad caviar!

Of course, it's no value to an individual frog if its attacker dies *after* devouring the victim. Hence they have developed conspicuous, striking colors—bright yellow, scarlet, purple, and blue, the colors of poison recognized throughout the animal world—and sometimes "flash colors" (concealed when at rest but flashed at appropriate times to startle predators) that announce, "Beware!" These confident critters don't act like other frogs either. They're active by day, not night, moving boldly around the forest floor, "confident and secure," says one writer, "in their brilliant livery."

April through May, toads go looking for love in the rain pools of scarlet bromeliads that festoon the high branches. Here, high in the trees, tadpoles of arboreal frogs wriggle about. Few Costa Rican frog species breed in permanent bodies of water, where fish predation is intense. Above 1,500 meters, where there are no native fish species, stream breeding is more common, although the introduction in recent years of trout into upland streams already threatens whole frog populations.

The frogs instead have evolved away from dependence on bodies of permanent water. Many species, particularly the 39 species of hylids, spend their entire lives in the tree canopies where they breed in holes and bromeliads. (The hylids have enlarged suction-cup pads on their toes. They often catch their prey in midair leaps: the suction discs guarantee sure-footed landings.) Others deposit their eggs on vegetation over streams; the tadpoles fall when hatched. Others construct frothy foam nests, which they float on pools, dutifully guarded by the watchful male.

Some rainforest species, such as the diminutive and warty eleutherodactylus—its name is longer than its body—live on the ground, where they lay their eggs in moist cups of leaves. The tadpole develops fully within the egg sac before emerging as a perfect, if tiny, replica of its parents. Some tadpole species—the *Hyla* *zeteki,* for example—are cannibalistic: they eat other frogs' tadpoles. The carnivorous smoky frog *(Leptodactylus pentadactylus),* an aggressive giant (adults can grow up to 20 cm long), can eat snakes up to 50 cm long. It, too, can emit a poisonous toxin, to which some snakes are immune. If the smoky frog's loud hissing, inflated body, and poisonous secretions don't manage to scare off its predator, it has another ingenious defense: when captured it emits a loud scream.

Know Costa Rica

Environmental Issues

DEFORESTATION

In the time it takes you to read this page, some 32 hectares of the world's tropical rainforests will be destroyed. The statistics defy comprehension. One hundred years ago, rainforests covered two billion hectares, 14 percent of the earth's land surface. Now only half remains, and the rate of destruction is increasing: an area larger than the U.S. state of Florida is lost every year. If the destruction continues apace, the world's rainforests will vanish within 40 years.

Along the Río San Juan, in the heart of the *llanuras* of the Atlantic lowlands, along the border with Nicaragua, is some of the wildest, wettest, most densely canopied rainforest in Costa Rica. It is a crown jewel of Central American jungle, as shining and sweet-smelling and innocent as it must have been in the first light of Creation. The humid *llanura* is the biggest piece of primeval rainforest left on the Caribbean rim, a tiny enclave of the original carpet that once covered most of lowland Central America. Wet and isolated, these mist-enshrouded waves of green have been relatively untouched by man until recently. Today, the lowland rainforests resound with the carnivorous buzz of chain saws; in the "dry" season, in isolated patches, they are on fire.

It is a story that's been repeated again and again during the past 400 years. Logging, ranching, and the development of large-scale commercial agriculture have transformed much of Costa Rica's wildest terrain. Cattle ranching has been particularly wasteful. Large tracts of virgin forest were felled in the 1930s through 1960s to make way for cattle, stimulated by millions of dollars of loans provided by U.S. banks and businesses promoting the beef industry to feed the North American market. Author Beatrice Blake claims that "Costa Rica loses 2.5 tons of topsoil to erosion for every kilo of meat exported," and that although a "farmer can make 86 times as much money per acre with coffee, and 284 times as much with bananas," cattle ranching takes up more than 20 times the amount of land devoted to bananas and coffee.

Throughout the 1980s, Costa Rica's tropical forest was disappearing at a rate of at least 520 square kilometers a year, and the nation's forests were falling faster than anywhere else in the Western Hemisphere and, as a percentage of national land area, reportedly nine times faster than the rainforests of Brazil. By 1990, less than 1.5 million hectares of primal forest remained (about 20 percent of its original habitat).

By anyone's standards, Costa Rica has since led the way in moving Central America away from the soil-leaching deforestation that plagues the isthmus (when humans cut the forest down, the organic-poor soils are exposed to the elements and are rapidly washed away by the intense rains, and the ground is baked by the blazing sun to leave an infertile wasteland; at lower elevations, humans find their natural

© CHRISTOPHER P. BAKER

logging truck on the Caribbean Coast

water sources diminishing and floods increasing after removal of the protective cover, for when intact the montane rainforest acts as a giant sponge). The country has one of the world's best conservation records: about one-quarter of the country is under some form of official protection. The nation has attempted to protect large areas of natural habitat and to preserve most of its singularly rich biota. But it is a policy marked by the paradox of good intent and poor application.

Despite Costa Rica's achievements in conservation, deforestation continues at an alarming rate... most of it legally under so-called "sustainable" management plans. Many reserves and refuges are poorly managed, and the Forestry Directorate, the government office in charge of managing the country's forest resources, has been accused of failing to fulfill its duties. And the country continues to suffer the kind of environmental degradation and deforestation that plague most tropical countries. In the 1970s, the Costa Rican government banned export of more than 60 diminishing tree species, and national law proscribes cut-ting timber without proper permits. It happens anyway, much of it illegally, with logs reportedly trucked into San José and the coastal ports at night. Wherever new roads are built, the first vehicles in are usually logging trucks. In 1992, the legislature eliminated a key clause in the Forestry Law designed to protect the remaining forests; and a Forestry Law passed in 1996 has favored the loggers. Little effort has been directed toward encouraging private landowners to willingly conserve and rationally manage their forests.

It's a daunting battle. Every year Costa Rica's population grows by 2.5 percent, increasing pressure on land and forcing squatters onto virgin land, where they continue to deplete the forests that once covered 80 percent of Costa Rica. Fires set by ranchers lap at the borders of Santa Rosa National Park. And oil-palm plantations squeeze Manuel Antonio against the Pacific. In the lowlands, fires from slash-and-burn agriculture burn uncontrolled for weeks; in the highlands, forests are logged for timber, roof shingles, and charcoal, while farmers and plantation owners continue to clear mountain slopes.

THE COST OF DEFORESTATION

Many animal and plant species can survive only in large areas of wilderness. Most rainforest species are so highly specialized that they are quickly driven to extinction by the disturbance of their forest homes. Isolation of patches of forest is followed by an exponential decline. The decline of a single species has a domino effect on many dependent species, particularly plants, since tropical plants are far more dependent on individual animal and bird species for seed dispersal than are plants in temperate climates. The reduction of original habitat to one-tenth of its original area means an eventual loss of half its species.

At the current rate of world deforestation, plant and animal species may be disappearing at the rate of 50,000 a year; by the end of the 20th century, an estimated one million species had vanished without ever having been identified, among them many species whose chemical compounds may have held the secrets to cures for a host of debilitating and deadly diseases. The bark of the cinchona tree, for example, has long been the prime source of quinine, an important antimalarial drug. Curare, the vine extract used by South American Indians to poison their arrows and darts, is used as a muscle relaxant in modern surgery. And scientists recently discovered a peptide secreted by an Amazonian frog called Phyllomedusa bicolor that may lead to medicines for strokes, seizure, depression, and Alzheimer's disease. In fact, some 40 percent of all drugs manufactured in the United States are to some degree dependent on natural sources; more than 2,000 tropical rainforest plants have been identified as having some potential to combat cancer.

Costa Rica's National Biodiversity Institute (InBio) recently signed a contract with New Jersey-based pharmaceutical company Merck Co. that calls for the institute to provide Merck with samples of plant and insect species in exchange for royalties from any marketable products. The objective is to finance the conservation of biodiversity and to ensure that Costa Rica receives a small percentage of the massive profits derived from pharmaceutical extracts.

Nonetheless, in 2000 the Ángel Rodríguez administration even authorized oil exploration within an Indian reserve and adjacent to two national parks; while MINAE (the ministry responsible for land welfare and use) proposed a plan to open protected areas for mining, agriculture, and infrastructure development. And just before leaving office, Rodríguez granted a Canadian mining company rights to begin mining gold at Las Crucitas, near the Nicaraguan border; under intense pressure from environmentalists, the Abel Pacheco government rejected the company's environmental impact study.

In April 2003, the government announced a partial ban on logging in 14 cantons most vulnerable to illegal logging (some 35 percent of nationally marketed timber is the result of illegal logging), while setting up a toll-free hotline—tel. 192—for reporting illegal logging.

REFORESTATION AND PROTECTION

Part of the government's answer to deforestation has been to promote reforestation, mostly through a series of tax breaks, leading to tree farms predominantly planted in nonnative species such as teak. These efforts, however, do little to replace the precious native hardwoods or to restore the complex natural ecosystems, which take generations to reestablish. Nonetheless, dozens of dedicated individuals and organizations are determined to preserve and replenish core habitats.

Many of these organizations are attempting to bridge the gap between conservation funding and the nation's massive foreign-debt problems by developing "debt for nature" swaps. Swapping land for debt, for example, the U.S.-based Nature Conservancy has helped swell conservation coffers while curbing the outflow of foreign currency from Costa Rica. Using Nature Conservancy money, for example, the National Parks Foundation bought a share of the nation's debt from a U.S. bank, after the debt was discounted to 17 cents on the dollar. Costa Rica then paid off the National Parks Foundation with bonds in the local currency, with the agreement that the money would be used on conservation projects. Barbilla National Park was created in late 1997 as the first park officially designated to trap greenhouse gases in an effort to promote the sale of "Carbon Bonds" to industrialized nations. The bonds will finance the park.

Privately owned forests constitute the majority of unprotected primary forest remaining in Costa Rica outside the national parks. Scores of private reserves have been created to prove that rainforests can produce more income from such schemes as ecotourism, harvesting ornamental plants, and raising iguanas, pacas, and *tepezcuintles* for food than if cleared for cattle.

Several organizations sponsor voluntary action on the part of landowners. For example, COMBOS, working with CEDARENA and the Nature Conservancy, has written "conservation easements," legal agreements whereby property owners guarantee to restrict the type and amount of development that may take place on the property. Any subsequent owners are bound by the agreement. (Working against these valiant philanthropists is a legal system that grants significant inalienable rights to squatters: if they "improve" the land, they are entitled to just compensation; if they are not ejected in good time, the land becomes theirs. The law has given rise to professional squatters acting on behalf of businesspeople; once the former gains legal title, it is signed over to the sponsor and the squatter moves to another plot.)

National Parks

While much of Costa Rica has been stripped of its forests, the country has managed to protect a larger proportion of its land than any other country in the world. In 1970 there came a growing acknowledgment that something unique and lovely was vanishing, and a systematic effort was begun to save what was left of the wilderness. That year, the Costa Ricans formed a national park system that has won worldwide admiration. Costa Rican law declared inviolate 10.27 percent of a land once compared to Eden; an additional 20 percent or so is legally set aside as forest reserves, "buffer zones," wildlife refuges, and Indian reserves. Throughout the country representative sections of all the major habitats and ecosystems are protected for tomorrow's generations. The National Conservation Areas System (SINAC) protects more than 190 areas—including 34 national parks, eight biological reserves, 13 forest reserves, 56 wildlife refuges, 32 protected zones, and 14 wetlands—in 11 conservation areas.

Besides providing Costa Ricans and foreign travelers with the privilege of admiring and studying the wonders of nature, the national parks and reserves protect the soil and watersheds and harbor an estimated 75 percent of all Costa Rica's species of flora and fauna, including species that have all but disappeared in neighboring countries.

While deforestation continues throughout the country, wildlife preservation in Costa Rica—at least in theory—is only a matter of due process and cash. However, the National Parks Service remains severely hampered by underfunding (MINAE's budget has fallen by 25 percent in the past decade). The government has also found it impossible to pay for land set aside as national parks (15 percent of national parks, 46 percent of biological and nature reserves, and 75 percent of forest reserves are private property with payments outstanding). Costa Rica's Environmental Minister, Carlos Rodríguez, threatened to close the national parks to tourism unless his budget was increased. And budgetary constraints prohibit the severely understaffed Parks Service from hiring more people, or supplying them with uniforms and vehicles (the park service has only eight park officials to patrol Corcovado's 25,000 hectares). Thus, poaching continues inside national parks, often with the connivance of rangers and corrupt NPS officials who receive shares of the booty.

Much of the praise heaped on the National Parks Service actually belongs to individuals (preponderantly foreigners), private groups, and local communities whose efforts—often in the face of bureaucratic opposition—have resulted in many of the wildlife refuges and parks for which the NPS takes credit. (The creation of the National Parks Service itself was the product of lobbying by a foreigner, Olaf Wessberg, as related in David Rains Wallace's *The Quetzal and the Macaw*.)

The current focus is on turning poorly managed forest reserves and wildlife refuges into national parks, and integrating adjacent national parks, reserves, and national forests into Regional Conservation Areas (RCAs) to create corridors where wildlife can move with greater freedom over much larger areas. The premise is that larger parks—more complete ecosystems—are more easily preserved than smaller ones. Each unit is characterized by its unique ecology. There are 11 RCAs: Amistad-Caribe, Amistad-Pacífico, Arenal, Arenal-Huetar Norte, Cordillera Volcánica Central, Guanacaste, Isla del Coco, Osa, Pacífico Central, Tempisque, and Tortuguero.

National parks are under the jurisdiction of the **Sistema Nacional Areas de Conservación** (SINAC, Calle 25, Avenidas 8/10, San José, tel. 506/283-8004, fax 506/223-6963, www.sinac.go .cr; 8 A.M.–4 P.M. Mon.–Fri.), which is responsible to the Ministry of the Environment and Energy (Ministerio de Ambiente y Energia, or MINAE, Apdo. 10094, San José 1000, www .minae.go.cr). Alternately, visit the **Fundación de Parques Nacionales** (Calle 23, Avenida 15, San José, tel. 506/257-2239).

If you need specialized information on scientific aspects of the parks, contact the Conservation Data Center, **Instituto Nacional de Biodiversidad** (INbio, Apdo. 22-3310 Santo Domingo de Heredia, tel. 506/507-8100, www.inbio.ac.cr).

Entrance for walk-in visitors varies from $6 to $10, valid for 24 hours only. No permits are required. You will need permits for a few of the biological reserves; these can be obtained in advance from SINAC.

Many national parks and reserves have campsites ($2 per night), although a few of the more remote wildlife refuges lack even the most rudimentary accommodations. At some parks, you can stay in park ranger housing or at biological research stations if space permits. See regional chapters for details.

Megaparks and Biological Corridors

Wildlife doesn't observe political borders. Birds migrate. Plants grow on each side. "It's not enough to draw lines on a map and call it a park," says Alvaro Ugalde, the former National Parks Service director. "These days, park management is tied into economic issues, war and peace, agriculture, forestry, and helping people find a way to live." Park management increasingly requires international cooperation through the creation of transnational park networks, with neighboring countries viewing the rivers and rainforests along their borders not as dividing lines but as rich tropical ecosystems that they share.

The idea fruited in Central America as the Paseo Pantera, dedicated to preserving biodiversity through the creation of a chain of conservation areas from Belize to Panamá. This cooperative effort, which takes its name from the Path of the Panther (a historical forested corridor that once spanned from Tierra del Fuego to Alaska), has since evolved into the multinational Mesoamerican Biological Corridor project, funded by the World Bank. The intent is creation of a Central American "biogeographic corridor," a contiguous chain of protected areas from Mexico to Colombia. Then the isthmus could once again be a bridge between continents for migrating species.

The most advanced of the transfrontier parks is the La Amistad International Peace Park, created in 1982 when Costa Rica and Panamá signed a pact to join two adjacent protected areas—one in each country—to create one of the richest ecological biospheres in Central America. UNESCO cemented the union by recognizing the binational zone as a biosphere reserve. La Amistad covers 622,000 hectares and includes six Indian reserves and nine protected areas.

History

EARLY HISTORY

When Spanish explorers arrived in what is now Costa Rica at the dawn of the 16th century, they found the region populated by several poorly organized, autonomous tribes living relatively prosperously, if wanton at war, in a land of lush abundance. In all, there were probably no more than 200,000 indigenous people on 18 September 1502, when Columbus put ashore near current-day Puerto Limón. Although human habitation can be traced back at least 10,000 years, the region had remained a sparsely populated backwater separating the two areas of high civilization: Mesoamerica and the Andes. High mountains and swampy lowlands had impeded the migration of advanced cultures. Though these tribes were advanced in ceramics, metalwork, and weaving, there are few signs of large complex communities, little monumental stone architecture lying half-buried in the luxurious undergrowth, and no planned ceremonial centers of comparable significance to those located elsewhere in the isthmus.

The region was a potpourri of distinct cultures divided into chiefdoms. In the east along the Caribbean seaboard and along the southern Pacific shores, the peoples shared distinctly South American cultural traits. These groups—the Caribs on the Caribbean and the Borucas, Chibchas, and Diquis in the southwest—were semi-nomadic hunters and fishermen who raised yucca, squash, *pejibaye* (bright orange palm fruits), and tubers supplemented by crustaceans, shrimp, lobster, and game; chewed coca; and lived in communal village huts surrounded by fortified palisades. One group, the Votos, apparently had female chiefs. The matriarchal Chibchas and Diquis had a highly developed slave system and were accomplished goldsmiths using the lost-wax technique. They were also responsible for the perfectly spherical granite balls *(bolas)* of unknown purpose found in large numbers at burial sites in the Río Terraba valley,

Caño Island, and the Golfito region. Some are the size of grapefruit; others weigh 16 tons. All are as round as the moon. Like other indigenous groups, the people had no written language, and their names are of Spanish origin—bestowed by colonists, often reflecting the names of tribal chiefs.

The most advanced tribes lived in the Central Highlands. The tribes here were the Corobicís, and the Nahuatl, who had recently arrived from Mexico at the time that Columbus stepped ashore. The largest and most significant of Costa Rica's archaeological sites found to date is here, at Guayabo, on the slopes of Turrialba, 56 km east of San José, where an ancient city is being excavated. Dating from perhaps as early as 1000 B.C. to A.D. 1400, Guayabo is thought to have housed as many as 1,000 inhabitants. Rudimentary by the standards of ancient cities elsewhere in the isthmus, it is nonetheless impressive, with wide cobblestone walkways and stone-lined pools and water cisterns fed by aqueducts.

Perhaps more important (little architectural study has been completed) was the Nicoya Peninsula in northwest Costa Rica. In late prehistoric times, trade in pottery from the Nicoya Peninsula brought this area into the Mesoamerican cultural sphere, and a culture developed among the Chorotegas—the most numerous of the region's indigenous groups—that in many ways resembled the more advanced cultures farther north. The Chorotegas were heavily influenced by the Olmec culture, and may have even originated in southern Mexico before settling in Nicoya early in the 14th century (their name means "Fleeing People"). The most advanced of the region's cultures, they developed towns with central plazas, brought with them an accomplished agricultural system based on beans, corns, squash, and gourds, had a calendar, wrote books on deerskin parchment, and produced highly developed ceramics and stylized jade figures depicting animals, humanlike effigies, and men and women with oversized genitals, often making the most of their sexual apparati. Like the Olmecs, they filed their teeth; like the Mayans and Aztecs, the militaristic Chorotegas kept slaves and maintained a rigid class hierarchy dominated by high priests and nobles. Human sacrifice was a cultural mainstay. Little is known of their belief system, though the potency and ubiquity of phallic imagery hints at a fertility-rite religion. Shamans, too, were an important part of each tribal political system; their influence is seen today in the National Museum in San José, where pottery from the region bears unusual symbols believed to have been painted by shamans under the influence of hallucinogens.

Alas, the pre-Columbian cultures were quickly choked by the stern hand of gold-thirsty colonial rule—and condemned, too, that Jehovah might triumph over local idols.

JADE

Ancient Costa Ricans had a love affair with jade. The semiprecious stone first appeared in Costa Rica around 400 B.C., when the Olmecs of Mexico introduced it to the Nicoya Peninsula. It became more prized than gold.

Though early carvings were crude, higher-quality pieces began to appear around A.D. 300, when the indigenous craftsmen developed the "string-saw" carving technique—involving drilling a hole through the selected piece of jade, inserting a string, and sawing back and forth. Pendants, necklaces, and earrings appeared, exquisitely carved with reliefs of human faces and scenes of life. Painstakingly worked figurines of monkeys, crocodiles, anteaters, jaguars, reptiles, and owls (symbol of the underworld) appeared in jade. Most common of all was the eagle, worshipped by indigenous peoples throughout the isthmus.

Costa Rican jade comes in green, black, gray, and—the rarest—blue. Although the quarry for the famous blue jade has never been found, Fidel Tristan, curator of the Jade Museum, believes a local source exists. The nearest known source of green is at Manzanal, in Guatemala.

COLONIALISM

The First Arrivals

When Columbus anchored his storm-damaged vessels—*Captiana, Gallega, Viscaína,* and *Santiago de Palos*—in the Bay of Cariari, off the Caribbean coast on his fourth voyage to the New World in 1502, he was welcomed and treated with great hospitality by indigenous peoples who had never seen white men before.

The tribal dignitaries appeared wearing much gold, which they gave Columbus. "I saw more signs of gold in the first two days than I saw in Española during four years," his journal records. He called the region La Huerta ("The Garden"). Alas, the great navigator struggled home to Spain in worm-eaten ships (he was stranded for one whole year in Jamaica) and never returned. The prospect of vast loot, however, drew adventurers whose numbers were reinforced after Vasco Nuñez de Balboa's discovery of the Pacific in 1513. To these explorers the name Costa Rica would have seemed a cruel hoax. Floods, swamps, and tropical diseases stalked them in the sweltering lowlands. And fierce, elusive Indians harassed them maddeningly.

In 1506, Ferdinand of Spain sent a governor, Diego de Nicuesa, to colonize the Atlantic coast of the isthmus he called Veragua. He ran aground off the coast of Panamá and was forced to march north, enduring a welcome that was less hospitable than the one afforded Columbus. Antagonized indigenous bands used guerrilla tactics to slay the strangers and willingly burnt their own crops to deny them food. Nicuesa set the tone for future expeditions by foreshortening his own cultural lessons with the musket ball. Things seemed more promising when an expedition under Gil González Davila set off from Panamá in 1522 to settle the region. It was Davila's expedition—which reaped quantities of gold—that won the land its nickname of Costa Rica, the "Rich Coast." Alas, the local peoples never revealed the whereabouts of the fabled mines of "Veragua" (most likely it was placer gold found in the gold-rich rivers of the Osa Peninsula).

Davila's Catholic priests also supposedly managed to convert many indigenous people to Christianity with cross and cutlass. But once again, sickness and starvation were the price—the expedition reportedly lost more than 1,000 men. Later colonizing expeditions on the Caribbean failed equally miserably; the coastal settlements dissolved amid internal acrimony, the taunts of the local people, and the debilitating impact of pirate raids. When two years later Francisco Fernández de Córdova founded the first Spanish settlement on the Pacific at Bruselas, near present-day Puntarenas, its inhabitants all died within three years.

For the next four decades Costa Rica was virtually left alone. The conquest of Peru by Pizarro in 1532 and the first of the great silver strikes in Mexico in the 1540s turned eyes away from southern Central America. Guatemala became the administrative center for the Spanish Main in 1543, when the captaincy-general of Guatemala, answerable to the viceroy of New Spain (Mexico), was created with jurisdiction from the Isthmus of Tehuantepec to the empty lands of Costa Rica.

By the 1560s several Spanish cities had consolidated their position farther north and, prompted by an edict of 1559 issued by Philip II of Spain, the representatives in Guatemala thought it time to settle Costa Rica and Christianize the natives. Alas, barbaric treatment and European epidemics—opthalmia, smallpox, and tuberculosis—had already reaped the indigenous people like a scythe, and had so antagonized the survivors that they took to the forests and eventually found refuge amid the remote valleys of the Cordillera Talamanca. Only in the Nicoya Peninsula did there remain any significant indigenous population, the Chorotegas, who soon found themselves chattel on Spanish land under the *encomienda* system whereby Spanish settlers were granted the right to forced indigenous labor.

Settlement

In 1562, Juan Vásquez de Coronado—the true conquistador of Costa Rica—arrived as governor. He treated the surviving indigenous people more humanely and moved the few existing Spanish settlers into the Cartago Valley, where the temperate climate and rich volcanic soils offered the promise of crop cultivation. Cartago was established as the national capital in 1563. The economic and social development of the Spanish provinces was traditionally the work of the soldiers, who were granted *encomiendas,* landholdings that allowed for rights to the use of indigenous serfs. Coronado, however, to the regret of his subordinates, never made use of this system; in response, the indigenous people, led by chief Quitao, willingly subjugated themselves to Spanish rule. Coronado's successor allowed the Spanish to enslave the local population. Soon, there were virtually no indigenous people left alive in the region.

After the initial impetus given by its discovery, Costa Rica lapsed into a lowly Cinderella of the Spanish empire. The gold was soon gone, shipped to Spain. Land was readily available, but there was no indigenous labor to work it. Thus, the early economy lacked the conditions that favored development of the large colonial-style hacienda and feudal system of other Spanish enclaves. The colonists were forced to work the land themselves (even the governor, it is commonly claimed, had to work his own plot of land to survive). Without gold or export crops, trade with other colonies was infrequent at best. The Spanish found themselves impoverished in a subsistence economy. Money became so scarce that the settlers eventually reverted to the indigenous method of using cacao beans as currency.

A full century after its founding, Cartago could boast little more than a few score adobe houses and a single church, which all perished when Volcán Irazú erupted in 1723.

Gradually, however, prompted by an ecclesiastical edict that ordered the populace to resettle near churches, towns took shape. Heredia (Cubujuquie) was founded in 1717, San José (Villaneuva de la Boca del Monte) in 1737, and Alajuela (Villa Hermosa) in 1782. Later, exports of wheat and tobacco placed the colonial economy on a sounder economic basis and encouraged the intensive settlement that characterizes the Meseta Central today.

Intermixing with the native population was not a common practice. In other colonies, Spaniard married native and a distinct class system arose, but mixed-bloods and *ladinos* (mestizos) represent a much smaller element in Costa Rica than they do elsewhere on the isthmus. All this had a leveling effect on colonial society. As the population grew, so did the number of poor families who had never benefitted from the labor of *encomienda* indigenous people or suffered the despotic arrogance of *criollo* (Creole) landowners. Costa Rica, in the traditional view, became a "rural democracy," with no oppressed mestizo class resentful of the maltreatment and scorn of the Creoles. Removed from the mainstream of Spanish culture, the Costa Ricans became individualistic and egalitarian.

Not all areas of the country, however, fit the model of rural democracy. Nicoya and Guanacaste on the Pacific side were administered quite separately in colonial times from the rest of Costa Rica. They fell within the Nicaraguan sphere of influence, and large cattle ranches or haciendas arose. Revisions to the *encomienda* laws in 1542, however, limited the amount of time that indigenous people were obliged to provide their labor; the local people were also rounded up and forcibly concentrated into settlements distant from the haciendas. The large estate owners thus began to import African slaves, who became an important part of the labor force on the cattle ranches that were established in the Pacific northwest. The cattle-ranching economy and the more traditional class-based society that arose persist today.

On the Caribbean of Costa Rica, cacao plantations became well established. Eventually large-scale cacao production gave way to small-scale sharecropping, and then to tobacco as the cacao industry went into decline. Spain closed the Costa Rican ports in 1665 in response to English piracy, thereby cutting off seaborne sources of legal trade. Smuggling flourished, however, for the largely unincorporated Caribbean coast provided a safe haven to buccaneers and smugglers, whose strongholds became 18th-century shipping points for logwood and mahogany. The illicit trade helped weaken central authority.

THE EMERGENCE OF A NATION
Independence

Independence of Central America from Spain on 15 September 1821 came on the coattails of Mexico's declaration earlier in the same year. Independence had little immediate effect, however, for Costa Rica had required only minimal government during the colonial era and had long gone its own way. In fact, the country was so out of touch that the news that independence had been granted reached Costa Rica a full month after the event. In 1823, the other Central American nations proclaimed the United Provinces of Central America, with their capital in Guatemala City, while a Costa Rican provincial council voted for accession to Mexico.

After the declaration, effective power lay in the hands of the separate towns of the isthmus, and it took several years for a stable pattern of political alignment to emerge. The four leading cities of Costa Rica felt as independent as had the city-states of ancient Greece, and the conservative and aristocratic leaders of Cartago and Heredia soon found themselves at odds with the more progressive republican leaders of San José and Alajuela. The local quarrels quickly developed into civic unrest and, in 1823, to civil war. After a brief battle in the Ochomogo Hills, the republican forces of San José were victorious. They rejected Mexico, and Costa Rica joined the federation with full autonomy for its own affairs. Guanacaste voted to secede from Nicaragua and join Costa Rica the following year. In a gesture that set a precedent to be followed in later years, the civilian hero Ramírez relinquished power and retired to his farm, then returned to foil an army coup.

From this moment on, liberalism in Costa Rica had the upper hand. Elsewhere in Central America, conservative groups tied to the church and the erstwhile colonial bureaucracy spent generations at war with anticlerical and laissez-faire liberals, and a cycle of civil wars came to dominate the region. By contrast, in Costa Rica colonial institutions had been relatively weak, and early modernization of the economy propelled the nation out of poverty and laid the foundations of democracy far earlier than elsewhere in the isthmus. While other countries turned to repression to deal with social tensions, Costa Rica turned toward reform. Military plots and coups weren't unknown—they played a large part in determining who came to rule throughout the next century—but the generals usually were puppets used as tools to install favored individuals (usually surprisingly progressive civilian allies) representing the interests of particular cliques.

Juan Mora Fernández, elected the federalist nation's first chief of state in 1824, set the tone by ushering in a nine-year period of progressive sta-

bility. He established a sound judicial system, founded the nation's first newspaper, and expanded public education. He also encouraged coffee cultivation and gave free land grants to would-be coffee growers. The nation, however, was still riven by rivalry, and in September 1835 the War of the League broke out when San José was attacked by the three other towns. They were unsuccessful, and the national flag was planted firmly in San José.

Braulio Carrillo, who seized power as a benevolent dictator in 1835, established an orderly public administration and new legal codes to replace colonial Spanish law. In 1838, he withdrew Costa Rica from the Central American federation and proclaimed independence. The Honduran general Francisco Morazán invaded and toppled Carrillo in 1842. Morazán's extranational ambitions and the military draft and

THE WILLIAM WALKER SAGA

William Walker was 1.65 meters (5 feet, 5 inches) and 55 kg (120 pounds) of cocky intellect and ego. Born in Nashville in 1824, he graduated from the University of Pennsylvania with an M.D. at the age of 19, then went on to study in Paris and Germany. He tried his hand unsuccessfully as a doctor, lawyer, and writer, and even joined the miners and panners in the California Gold Rush. Somewhere along the line, he became filled with grandiose schemes of adventure and an arrogant belief in America's "manifest destiny"—to control other nations. During the next decade the Tennessean freebooter became the scourge of the Central American isthmus.

He dreamed of extending the glory of slavery and forming a confederacy of southern American states to include the Spanish-speaking nations. To wet his feet, he invaded Baja California in 1853 with a few hundred cronies bankrolled by a pro-slavery group called the Knights of the Golden Circle. Forced back north of the border by the Mexican army, Walker found himself behind bars for breaking the Neutrality Act. Acquitted and famous, he attracted a following of kindred spirits to his next wild cause.

During the feverish California Gold Rush, eager fortune hunters sailed down the East Coast to Nicaragua, traveled up the Río San Juan and across Lake Nicaragua, and thence were carried by mule the last 12 miles to the Pacific, where with luck a San Francisco–bound ship would be waiting. In those days, before the Panamá Canal, wealthy North Americans were eyeing southern Nicaragua as the perfect spot to build a passage linking the Pacific Ocean and the Caribbean Sea. The government of Nicaragua decided that both the traffic and the proposed canal were worth a hefty fee.

Backed by North American capitalists and with the tacit sanction of President James Buchanan, Walker landed in Nicaragua in June 1855 with a group of mercenaries—the "fifty-six immortals"—and the ostensible goal of molding a new government that would be more accommodating to U.S. business ventures. Perhaps some of Walker's men thought they were

direct taxes he imposed soon inspired his overthrow. He was executed within the year.

Coffee Is King

The reins of power were taken up by a nouveau elite, the coffee barons, who vied with each other for political dominance. In 1849, the *cafetaleros* announced their ascendancy by conspiring to overthrow the nation's president, José María Castro, an enlightened man who initiated his administration by founding a high school for girls and sponsoring freedom of the press. They chose as Castro's successor Juan Rafael Mora, a powerful *cafetalero*. Mora is remembered for the remarkable economic growth that marked his first term and for "saving" the nation from the imperial ambitions of the American adventurer William Walker during his second term. Still, his countryfolk ousted him from power in 1859;

the masses blamed him for the cholera epidemic that claimed the lives of one in every 10 Costa Ricans, while the elites were horrified when Mora moved to establish a national bank, which would have undermined their control of credit to the coffee producers. After failing in his own coup against his successor, he was executed—a prelude to a second cycle of militarism, for the war of 1856 had introduced Costa Rica to the buying and selling of generals and the establishment of a corps of officers possessing an inflated aura of legitimacy.

The Guardia Legacy

The 1860s were marred by power struggles among the coffee elite, supported by their respective military cronies. General Tomás Guardia, however, was his own man. In April 1870, he overthrew the government and ruled

---

fighting simply to annex Nicaragua to the United States; others may have believed they were part of the great struggle to establish slavery in Central America. But Walker, it seems, had other ambitions—he dreamed of making the five Central American countries a federated state with himself as emperor. After subduing the Nicaraguans, he had himself "elected" president of Nicaragua and promptly legalized slavery there.

Next, Walker looked south to Costa Rica. In March 1856, he invaded Guanacaste. President Mora, backed by the Legislative Assembly, called up an army of 9,000 to join "the loyal sons of Guatemala, El Salvador, and Honduras," who had combined their meager and bickering forces to expel the invaders. President Mora and his brother-in-law, José María Cañas, took personal charge of Costa Rica's band of *campesinos* and makeshift soldiers (Cornelius Vanderbilt, stung by Walker's seizure of his Trans-Isthmian Transit Company steamers, reportedly bankrolled the effort). Armed with machetes and rusty rifles, they marched for Guanacaste and routed Walker and his cronies, who retreated pell-mell. Costa Rica still celebrates its peasant army's victory. The site of the battle—La Casona, in Santa Rosa National Park—is now a museum.

Eventually, the Costa Rican army cornered Walker's forces in a wooden fort at Rivas, in Nicaragua. A drummer boy named Juan Santamaría bravely volunteered to torch the fort, successfully flushing Walker out into the open. His bravery cost Santamaría his life; he is now a national hero and a symbol of resistance to foreign interference.

With his forces defeated, Walker's ambitions were temporarily scuttled. He was eventually rescued by the U.S. Navy and taken to New York, only to return in 1857 with even more troops (*filibusteros*). The Nicaraguan army defeated him again, and Walker was imprisoned. Released three years later and unrepentant, he seized a Honduran customs house. In yet another bid to escape, he surrendered to an English frigate captain who turned him over to the Honduran army, which promptly shot him, thereby bringing to an end the pathetic saga.

for 12 years as an iron-willed military strong-man backed by a powerful centralized government of his own making.

True to Costa Rican tradition, Guardia proved himself a progressive thinker and a bene-factor of the people. His towering reign set in motion forces that shaped the modern liberal-democratic state. Hardly characteristic of 19th-century despots, he abolished capital punishment, managed to curb the power of the coffee barons, and, ironically, tamed the use of the army for political means. He used coffee earnings and taxation to finance roads and pub-lic buildings. And in a landmark revision to the Constitution in 1869, he made "primary edu-cation for both sexes obligatory, free, and at the cost of the Nation."

Guardia had a dream: to make the transport of coffee more efficient and more profitable by forg-ing a railroad linking the Central Valley with the Atlantic coast, and thus with America and Eu-rope. Fulfillment of Guardia's dream was the tri-umph of one man—Minor Keith of Brooklyn, New York—over a world of risks and logistical nightmares.

The shift to democracy was manifest in the election called by President Bernardo Soto in 1889—commonly referred to as the first "honest" election, with popular participation (women and blacks, however, were still excluded from vot-

MINOR KEITH AND THE ATLANTIC RAILROAD

Costa Rica became the first Central American country to grow coffee when seeds were in-troduced from Jamaica in 1808. Coffee flourished and transformed the nation. It was eminently suited to the climate (the dry season made harvest and transportation easy) and volcanic soils of the central highlands. There were no rival products to compete for in-vestments, land, or labor. And the coffee bean—*grano d'oro*—was exempt from taxes. Soon, peasant settlements spread up the slopes of the volcanoes and down the slopes toward the coast.

By 1829, coffee had become the nation's most important product. Foreign money was pouring in. The coffee elite owed its wealth to its control of processing and trade rather than to direct control of land. Small farmers dominated actual production. Thus, no sec-tor of society failed to advance. The coffee bean pulled the country out of its miserable eco-nomic quagmire and placed it squarely on a pedestal as the most prosperous nation in Central America.

In 1871, when President Guardia decided to build his railroad to the Atlantic, coffee for ex-port was still being sent via mule and oxcart 100 km from the Meseta Central to the Pacific port of Puntarenas, then shipped—via a circuitous, three-month voyage—around the southern tip of South America and up the Atlantic to Europe.

Enter Minor Keith, a former stockboy in a Broadway clothing store, lumber surveyor in the American West, and Texas pig farmer. In 1871 at the age of 23, Minor came to Costa Rica at the behest of his brother Henry, who had been commissioned by his uncle, Henry Meiggs (the famous builder of railroads in the Andes), to oversee the construction of the Atlantic Railroad linking the coastal port of Limón with the coffee-producing Meseta Central. By 1873, when the railway should have been completed, only a third had been built and money for the project had run out. (The railroad was to have been financed by a loan of 3.4 million pounds issued by Eng-lish banks; unscrupulous British bankers, however, took advantage of the Costa Ricans by re-taining the majority of the money as commissions.) Henry Keith promptly packed his bags and went home.

The younger brother, who had been running the commissary for railroad workers in Puerto Limón, picked up the standard and for the next 15 years applied unflagging dedication

ing). To Soto's surprise, his opponent José Joaquín Rodríguez won. The Soto government refused to recognize the new president. The masses rose and marched in the streets to support their chosen leader, and Soto stepped down.

During the course of the next two generations, militarism gave way to peaceful transitions to power. Presidents, however, attempted to amend the Constitution to continue their rule and even dismissed uncooperative legislatures.

In 1917, democracy faced its first major challenge. At that time, the state collected the majority of its revenue from the less wealthy. Flores' bill to establish direct, progressive taxation based on income and his espousal of state involvement in the economy had earned the wrath of the elites. They decreed his removal. Minister of War Federico Tinoco Granados seized power. Tinoco ruled as an iron-fisted dictator, but Costa Ricans were no longer prepared to acquiesce in oligarchic restrictions. Women and high-school students led a demonstration calling for his ouster, and Tinoco fled to Europe.

There followed a series of unmemorable administrations culminating in the return of two previous leaders, Ricardo Jiménez and González Víquez, who alternated power for 12 years through the 1920s and 1930s. The apparent tranquility was shattered by the Depression and the social unrest it engendered. Old-fashioned

to achieve the enterprise his brother had botched. He renegotiated the loans and raised new money. He hired workers from Jamaica and China, and drove them—and himself—like beasts of burden.

A direct route to the Caribbean had never been surveyed, and as a result some stretches of railway had to be abandoned when progress turned out to be impossible. The workers had to bore tunnels through mountains, bridge numerous tributaries of the Reventazón River, hack through jungles, and drain the Caribbean marshlands. During the rainy season, mudslides would wash away bridges. And malaria, dysentery, and yellow fever plagued the workers (the project eventually claimed more than 4,000 lives). In December 1890, a bridge high over the turbulent waters of the Birris River finally brought the tracks from Alajuela and Puerto Limón together. It was a prodigious achievement.

For Keith, the endeavor paid off handsomely. He had wrangled from the Costa Rican government a concession of 800,000 acres of land (nearly seven percent of the national territory) along the railway track and coastal plain, plus a 90- year lease on the completed railroad. And the profits from his endeavors were to be tax-free for 20 years.

To help finance the railroad project, Keith planted his lands with bananas, a fruit of Asian origin called *Musa sapientum* (the "muse of wisdom"), which had been brought to the New World by the Spaniards. It was a popular novelty in North America, and Costa Rica became the first Central American country to grow them. Like coffee, the fruit flourished. Exports increased from 100,000 stems in 1883 to more than a million in 1890, when the railroad was completed. By 1899 Keith, who went on to marry the daughter of the Costa Rican president, had become the "Banana King" and Costa Rica the world's leading banana producer.

Along the way, the savvy entrepreneur had wisely entered into a partnership with the Boston Fruit Company, the leading importer of tropical fruits for the U.S. market. Thus was born the United Fruit Company—La Yunai, as Central Americans called it—which during the first half of the 20th century was to become the driving force and overlord of the economies of countries the length and breadth of Latin America.

Know Costa Rica

paternalistic liberalism had failed to resolve social ills such as malnutrition, unemployment, low pay, and poor working conditions. The Depression distilled all these issues, especially after a dramatic communist-led strike against the United Fruit Company, which had attained inordinate political influence, brought tangible gains. Calls grew shrill for reforms.

CIVIL WAR
Calderón

The decade of the 1940s and its climax, the civil war, marked a turning point in Costa Rican history: from paternalistic government by traditional rural elites to modern, urban-focused statecraft controlled by bureaucrats, professionals, and small entrepreneurs. The dawn of the new era was spawned by Rafael Angel Calderón Guardia, a profoundly religious physician and a president (1940–44) with a social conscience. In a period when neighboring Central American nations were under the yoke of tyrannical dictators, Calderón promulgated a series of farsighted reforms. His legacy included a stab at land "reform" (the landless could gain title to unused land by cultivating it), establishment of a guaranteed minimum wage, paid vacations, unemployment compensation, progressive taxation, plus a series of constitutional amendments codifying workers' rights. Calderón also founded the University of Costa Rica.

Calderón's social agenda was hailed by the urban poor and leftists and despised by the upper classes, his original base of support. His early declaration of war on Germany, seizure of German property, and imprisonment of Germans further upset his conservative patrons, many of whom were of German descent. World War II stalled economic growth at a time when Calderón's social programs called for vastly increased public spending. The result was rampant inflation, which eroded his support among the middle and working classes. Abandoned, Calderón crawled into bed with two unlikely partners: the Catholic Church and the communists (Popular Vanguard Party). Together they formed the United Social Christian Party.

The Prelude to Civil War

In 1944, Calderón was replaced by his puppet, Teodoro Picado Michalsky, in an election widely regarded as fraudulent. Picado's uninspired administration failed to address rising discontent throughout the nation. Intellectuals, distrustful of Calderón's "unholy" alliance, joined with businessmen, *campesinos,* and labor activists and formed the Social Democratic Party, dominated by the emergent professional middle classes eager for economic diversification and modernization. In its own strange amalgam, the SDP allied itself with the traditional oligarchic elite. The country was thus polarized. Tensions mounted.

Street violence finally erupted in the run-up to the 1948 election, with Calderón on the ballot for a second presidential term. When he lost to his opponent Otilio Ulate (the representative of *Acción Democrática,* a coalition of anti-calderonistas) by a small margin, the government claimed fraud. The next day, the building holding many of the ballot papers went up in flames, and the calderonista-dominated legislature annulled the election results. Ten days later, on 10 March 1948, the "War of National Liberation" plunged Costa Rica into civil war.

Don Pepe: "Savior of the Nation"

Popular myth suggests that José María ("Don Pepe") Figueres Ferrer—42-year-old coffee farmer, engineer, economist, and philosopher—raised a "ragtag army of university students and intellectuals" and stepped forward to topple the government that had refused to step aside for its democratically elected successor. In actuality, Don Pepe's "revolution" had been long in the planning; the 1948 election merely provided a good excuse.

Don Pepe, an ambitious and outspoken firebrand, had been exiled to Mexico in 1942—the first political outcast since the Tinoco era. Figueres formed an alliance with other exiles, returned to Costa Rica in 1944, began calling for an armed uprising, and arranged for foreign arms to be airlifted in to groups trained by Guatemalan military advisors. In 1946, he participated with a youthful Fidel Castro in an aborted attempt to depose General Trujillo of the Dominican Republic. (Figueres and Castro remained close friends. Years later, following the success of the leftist Sandinistas in Nicaragua, Castro initiated a Costa Rican guerrilla army to topple Costa Rican democracy and prepare for the "Vietnamization" of Central America. Surveying Costa Rica from across the Río San Juan, he is said to have scoffed, "A nurse's strike could bring that down.")

In 1948, back in Costa Rica, Figueres formed the National Liberation Armed Forces in the mountains of Santa María de Dota. Supported by the governments of Guatemala and Cuba, Don Pepe's insurrectionists captured the cities of Cartago and Puerto Limón from calderonistas (the government's army at the time numbered only about 500 men) and were poised to pounce on San José when Calderón, who had little heart for the conflict, capitulated. (The government's pathetically trained soldiers—aided and armed by the Somoza regime in Nicaragua—included communist banana workers from the lowlands; they wore blankets over their shoulders against the cold of the highlands, earning Calderón supporters the nickname *mariachis*.) The 40-day civil war claimed more than 2,000 lives, most of them civilians.

CONTEMPORARY TIMES
Foundation of the Modern State
Don Pepe became head of the Founding Junta of the Second Republic of Costa Rica. As leader of the revolutionary junta, he consolidated Calderón's progressive social reform program and added his own landmark reforms: he banned the press and Communist Party, introduced suffrage for women and full citizenship for blacks, revised the Constitution to outlaw a standing army, established a presidential term limit, and created an independent Electoral Tribunal to oversee future elections. Figueres also shocked the elites by nationalizing the banks and insurance companies.

On a darker note, Don Pepe reneged on the peace terms that guaranteed the safety of the calderonistas: Calderón and many of his followers were exiled to Mexico, special tribunals confiscated their property, and, in a sordid episode, many prominent left-wing officials and activists were abducted and murdered. (Supported by Nicaragua, Calderón twice attempted to invade Costa Rica and topple his nemesis, but was each time repelled. Eventually he was allowed to return, and even ran for president unsuccessfully in 1962.)

Then, by a prior agreement that established the interim junta for 18 months, Figueres returned the reins of power to Otilio Ulate, the actual winner of the 1948 election. Costa Ricans later rewarded Figueres with two terms as president, in 1953–57 and 1970–74. Figueres dominated politics for the next two decades. A socialist, he used his popularity to build his own electoral base and founded the Partido de Liberación Nacional (PLN), which became the principal advocate of state-sponsored development and reform. He died on 8 June 1990, a national hero.

The Contemporary Scene
Social and economic progress since 1948 have helped return the country to stability, and though post–civil war politics have reflected the play of old loyalties and antagonisms, elections have been free and fair. With only two exceptions, the country has ritualistically alternated its presidents between the PLN and the opposition Social Christians. Successive PLN governments have built on the reforms of the *calderonista* era, and the 1950s and 1960s saw a substantial expansion of the welfare state and public school system, funded by economic growth. The intervening conservative governments have encouraged private enterprise and economic self-reliance through tax breaks, protectionism, subsidized credits, and other macroeconomic policies. The combined results were a generally vigorous economic growth and the creation of a welfare state that had grown by 1981 to serve 90 percent of the population, absorbing 40 percent of the national budget in the process and granting the

government the dubious distinction of being the nation's biggest employer.

By 1980, the bubble had burst. Costa Rica was mired in an economic crisis: epidemic inflation, crippling currency devaluation, soaring oil bills and social welfare costs, plummeting coffee, banana, and sugar prices, and the disruptions to trade caused by the Nicaraguan war. When large international loans came due, Costa Rica found itself burdened overnight with the world's greatest per-capita debt. By August 1981, when the nation's foreign debt reached US$4 billion, Costa Rica was forced to cease payment on its international loans, causing an international crisis throughout South America. The U.S. and International Monetary Fund (IMF) stepped in with a massive aid program that injected $3 billion into the economy between 1981 and 1984, equivalent to more than one-third of the Costa Rican government's budget and 10 per-

COSTA RICA AND THE NICARAGUAN REVOLUTION

Costa Rica's relations with neighboring Nicaragua have always been testy. During the 1970s, the Nicaraguan revolution brought these simmering tensions to a boil, threatening to destabilize Costa Rica and plunge the whole of Central America into war. Costa Rica was led to the brink by a myopic U.S. foreign policy. That it was ultimately saved owes much to the integrity of Costa Rican president Oscar Arias Sánchez (1986–90), who earned the 1987 Nobel Peace Prize for bringing peace to the region.

Much of the post-1948 friction between the two nations stemmed from the personal rivalry between Costa Rica's "Don Pepe" Figueres and Nicaragua's strongman dictator, "Tacho" Somoza, who despised Figueres's espousal of social democracy and efforts to rid Central America of tyranny. In 1948, Figueres ousted the *calderonista* government and came to power with the backing of Nicaragua's anti-Somoza opposition. For the next two decades Figueres and the Somoza family conspired against each other.

During Figueres's second term as president (1970–74), relations with Nicaragua briefly improved—enough, in fact, for the Somoza family (now headed by Tacho's son, Anastasio or "Tachito") to acquire three vast properties on the Costa Rican side of the border. (The estates, equipped with airstrips suitable for large aircraft, became training grounds for Cuban exiles planning a military invasion of Cuba; in the 1980s, the lands became training grounds for the contras.)

The Carter administration brought new attitudes toward human rights. U.S. support for rightwing dictatorships temporarily waned, and countries with relatively democratic systems, such as Costa Rica, benefitted from increased aid. Buoyed by the new moral stance, the Nicaraguan church and the Sandinista National Liberation Front (FSLN) stepped up their attacks on the tyrannical Somoza regime. Most Ticos were sympathetic to the Sandinista cause and supported their government's tacit backing of the anti- Somoza revolutionaries who established guerrilla camps in Costa Rica close to the Nicaraguan border. Many Costa Ricans even took up arms alongside the revolutionaries.

As relations worsened, Somoza launched retaliatory air strikes on Costa Rican border towns; Civil Guards came under attack, and the dictator threatened a full-scale invasion, prompting Costa Rica to break off diplomatic relations and seize the Somoza estates. As the Sandinistas became more radical, however, fears were raised that the revolution would have a destabilizing effect throughout the isthmus. President Rodrigo Carazo attempted to rid the northern border of guerrilla camps. Meanwhile, he allowed the FSLN to set up a government-in-exile in San José in the apparent hope that he could influence the Sandinistas into taking a more moderate stance.

The picture was reversed overnight. On 19 July 1979, the Sandinistas toppled the Somoza regime. Thousands of Nicaraguan National Guardsmen and right-wing sympathizers were forced

cent of the nation's gross national product (GNP) for the period (Costa Rica was second only to Israel as the highest per-capita recipient of U.S. aid). Much of the U.S. government aid was tied to Costa Rica's support for the contra cause.

In addition to tens of thousands killed, a decade of war in the region (and then President Luis Alberto Monge's support for U.S. policy) had eroded international confidence in Costa Rica. Regional trade had declined 60 percent.

There had been a capital flight from the country; by 1984, the national debt had almost quadrupled. And as many as 250,000 Nicaraguan exiles and refugees fled into Costa Rica, whose political stability had been seriously undermined.

In May 1984 events took a tragic turn at a press conference on the banks of the Río San Juan held by Edén Pastora, the U.S.-backed leader of the Contras. A bomb exploded, killing foreign journalists (Pastora escaped).

to flee. Many settled in northern Costa Rica, where they were warmly welcomed by wealthy ranchers sympathetic to the right-wing cause. By the summer of 1981, the anti-Sandinistas had been cobbled into the Nicaraguan Democratic Front (FDN), headquartered in Costa Rica; contras roamed throughout the northern provinces, and the CIA was beginning to take charge of events. Costa Rica's foreign policy underwent a dramatic reversal as the former champion of the Sandinista cause found itself embroiled in the Reagan administration's vendetta to oust the Sandinista regime.

Costa Rica was in a bind. In February 1982, Luis Alberto Monge Alvarez was elected president. He originally tried to keep his country neutral. In the face of the Sandinistas' radical shift to the left, however, Monge found himself hostage to U.S. and domestic right-wing pressure to support the contras. As the economy slipped into crisis, he was forced to bow to U.S. demands in exchange for foreign aid. By 1984, when contra raids had begun to prompt Nicaraguan counterstrikes across the border, the CIA, Oliver North, and his cronies in the National Security Council were firmly in command. The Costa Rican Civil Guard was being trained in Honduras by U.S. military advisors; roads and airstrips were being built throughout the northern provinces; and the CIA was running drugs.

By the fall of 1984, Monge's administration, with right-wingers in ascendancy, was giving tacit support to newly formed paramilitary groups that began carrying out acts of domestic terrorism that were intended to implicate the Sandinistas and lead to a militarization of Costa Rica's security forces.

As the prospect of regional war increased, the Costa Rican people "stepped back from the brink" and rallied behind peace advocate Oscar Arias Sánchez in the 1986 presidential elections. Arias had been outraged by U.S. attempts to undermine Costa Rica's neutrality and drag the tiny nation into the conflict. Once inaugurated, he immediately threw his energies into restoring peace to Central America.

In February 1987, Arias presented the leaders of the Central American nations a formal peace plan, which called for suspension of all military aid to insurrectionists, cease-fires to all conflicts, general amnesties for political prisoners and for guerrillas who laid down their arms, negotiations between governments and their opposition, and free and fair elections.

Ronald Reagan called the plan "fatally flawed," but, despite Washington's best efforts to sabotage it, all five Central American presidents—including Nicaragua's Daniel Ortega—signed it in August 1987, rejecting Reagan's military "solution" in favor of a solution in which all concerned committed themselves to fundamental reforms in their political systems.

A general consensus is that the bomb was meant to blame the Sandinistas; the CIA has been implicated.

In February 1986, Costa Ricans elected as their president a relatively young sociologist and economist-lawyer, Oscar Arias Sánchez. Arias' electoral promise had been to work for peace. Immediately, he put his energies into resolving Central America's regional conflicts. Arias' tireless efforts were rewarded in 1987, when his Central American peace plan was signed by the five Central American presidents in Guatemala City—an achievement that earned the Costa Rican president the 1987 Nobel Peace Prize.

In February 1990, Rafael Angel Calderón Fournier, a conservative lawyer and candidate for the Social Christian Unity Party (PUSC), won a narrow victory with 51 percent of the vote. He was inaugurated 50 years to the day after his father, the great reformer, was named president. Restoring Costa Rica's economy to sound health was Calderón's paramount goal. Under pressure from the World Bank and International Monetary Fund, Calderón initiated a series of austerity measures aimed at redressing the country's huge deficit and national debt. Albeit halfheartedly, state-owned enterprises were privatized, elements of social welfare were dismantled, some subsidies and tax exemptions—such as those for *pensionados* (pensioners)—were rescinded, and new taxes were levied on income and savings.

In March 1994, in an intriguing historical quirk, Calderón, son of the president ousted by Don Pepe Figueres in 1948, was replaced by Don Pepe's youthful son, José María Figueres, a graduate of West Point and Harvard. The Figueres administration (1994–98) continued the privatization mandate—though the Legislative Assembly failed to ratify constitutional reforms to privatize state behemoths such as the Banco Nacional. The Figueres period, however, was bedeviled by problems, including the collapse of the Banco Anglo Costarricense in 1994, followed in 1995 by inflation, a massive teachers' strike, and an antigovernment demonstration of

100,000 people. A slump in tourism and Hurricane César, which ripped through the Pacific southwest in July 1996 causing $100 million in damage, worsened the country's plight. A month later the nation was rocked when a female German tourist and her tour guide were kidnapped, generating heaps of unwanted media exposure. Tourism from Europe plummeted. The kidnappers were caught, and the affair took a strange twist when photographs appeared showing the woman kissing one of her captors. Ticos took some solace in the gold medal—the first ever for the country—won at the 1996 Olympics by Costa Rican swimmer Claudia Poll. And President Clinton's visit to Costa Rica in May 1997 during a summit of Central American leaders heralded a new era of free trade and enhanced regional accord.

The Figueres administration was considered a bit of a flop by a majority of the electorate, who in February 1998 voted for the Social Christian Unity Party. Figueres was replaced by Miguel ángel Rodríguez, a wealthy businessman and economist whom Figueres had defeated in a run for president in 1994.

Talks with Nicaragua in 1999–2000 to resolve a flare up over their ongoing border dispute (Nicaragua denies Costa Rica's claim that existing treaties give them rights of usage to the Río San Juan, which is wholly Nicaraguan) proved futile. In April 2000, a series of strikes by government employees erupted into the worst civil unrest since the 1970s, as an attempt by the government to break up the country's 50-year-old power and telecommunications monopoly resulted in nationwide street protests that brought the country to a halt. And two days of mob riots broke out between gangs of youth thugs and the police in October 2000 in San José's drug-and crime-riddled working class Rincón Grande *barrio*.

In April 2002, voters elected a folksy poet and TV personality, Abel Pachecho (Social Christian Unity Party), as president. He pledged to dedicate himself to the poor and disadvantaged. His administration found it difficult to get traction and was beset by a series of ministerial resignations.

President Pacheco took serious flak from Costa Ricans for his support of the U.S. invasion of Iraq; the Ombudsman filed a motion with the Supreme Court charging Pacheco with acting illegally and contrary to the nation's laws. Pacheco has been highly unpopular, garnering only a 19 percent approval rating in an April 2002 poll. Meanwhile, Costa Rica got into a spat with Cuba over the latter's human rights record (about 14,000 Cubans live in Costa Rica, which does not have official relations with Cuba, despite the presence of a Cuban consulate).

In spring 2003, the nation was abuzz with scandalous accusations after the government moved to close down an investment scheme run by two brothers, the Villalobos. Thousands of leading citizens lost money when the government seized all assets. Meanwhile, former president Oscar Arias spearheaded an attempt to overturn the ban on presidential reelection.

Government

Costa Rica is a democratic republic, as defined by the 1949 Constitution. As in the United States, the government is divided into independent executive, legislative, and judicial branches, with separation of powers. In April 2003, the Supreme Court voted to reverse the 1969 law barring presidents and vice presidents from running for office again within an eight-year period following the end of their single term; Oscar Arias (president 1986–90), who led the drive, announced his intention to seek office again.

The executive branch comprises the president, two vice presidents, and a cabinet of 17 members called the Council of Government *(Consejo de Gobierno)*. Legislative power is vested in the Legislative Assembly, a unicameral body composed of 57 members elected by proportional representation. *Diputados* are elected for a four-year term and can be reelected only after four more. Like its U.S. equivalent, the Assembly can override presidential decisions by two-thirds majority vote. The power of the legislature to go against the president's wishes is a cause of constant friction, and presidents have not been cowardly in using such tools as the executive decree to usurp power. The Oduber administration (1974–78), for example, issued 4,709 executive decrees; the legislature enacted just 721 laws in the same period.

The Legislative Assembly also appoints Supreme Court judges for minimum terms of eight years. Twenty-four judges now serve on the Supreme Court. These judges, in turn, select judges for the civil and penal courts. The courts also appoint the three "permanent" magistrates of the Special Electoral Tribunal, an independent body that oversees each election and is given far-reaching powers. The Tribunal appointees serve staggered six-year terms and are appointed one every two years to minimize partisanship (two additional temporary magistrates are appointed a year before each election). Control of the police force reverts to the Supreme Electoral Tribunal during election campaigns to help ensure the integrity of all constitutional guarantees.

The nation is divided into seven provinces—Alajuela, Cartago, Guanacaste, Heredia, Limón, Puntarenas, and San José—each ruled by a governor appointed by the president. The provinces are subdivided into 81 *cantones* (counties), which, in turn, are divided into a total of 421 *distritos* (districts) ruled by municipal councils. The provinces play only one important role: as electoral districts for the Legislative Assembly. The number of deputies for each province is determined by that province's population, with one member for each 30,000 people; seats are allotted according to the proportion of the vote for each party.

Costa Rica is governed through compromise: a tempest may rage at the surface, but a compromise resolution is generally worked out behind the scenes. Says the *Tico Times*: "Most *politicos* are notoriously myopic and selfish, opting to leave tomorrow's problems to the next guy," with the result that the problems become so great that "well-intentioned quick fixes fall flat."

POLITICAL PARTIES

The largest party is the National Liberation Party (Partido de Liberación Nacional, or PLN), founded by the statesman and hero of the Civil War, "Don Pepe" Figueres. The PLN, which roughly equates with European social democracy and American-style welfare-state liberalism, has traditionally enjoyed a majority in the legislature, even when an opposition president has been in power. Its support is traditionally drawn from among the middle-class professionals and entrepreneurs and small farmers and rural *peones*.

PLN's archrival, the Social Christian Unity Party (Partido de Unidad Social Cristiana, or PUSC), formed in 1982, represents more conservative interests.

Between them, the two parties have alternated power since 1949 (in every presidential election

but two, the "ins" have been ousted). The margin is usually narrow. However, in an atypical vote, the PUSC's Abel Pacheco, a psychoanalyst and former TV presenter, won the 2002 election by a landslide.

In addition, a number of less influential parties represent all facets of the political spectrum, notably the Citizen Action Party (PAC), formed in 2002 by former Justice Minister José Miguel Villalobos, who resigned from the Abel Pacheco government in protest of corruption. Most minor parties form around a candidate and represent personal ambitions rather than strong political convictions. (Former president Figueres once accused Ticos of being as domesticated as sheep; they are not easily aroused to passionate defense of a position or cause.)

A small number of families are immensely powerful, regardless of which party is in power, and it is said that they pull the strings behind the scenes. (Just three families have produced 36 of Costa Rica's 51 presidents, and fully three-quarters of congressmen 1821–1970

Election fever! Partisans campaign in San José.

© CHRISTOPHER P. BAKER

were the offspring of this "dynasty of conquistadors.")

ELECTIONS

Costa Rica's national elections, held every four years (on the first Sunday of February), reaffirm the pride Ticos feel for their democratic system. In the rest of Central America, says travel writer Paul Theroux, "an election can be a harrowing piece of criminality; in Costa Rica [it is] something of a fiesta. 'You should have been here for the election,' a woman told me in San José, as if I had missed a party." The streets are crisscrossed with flags, and everyone drives around honking their horns, throwing confetti, and holding up their purple-stained thumbs to show that they voted. (Cynics point out that most of the hoopla is because political favors are dispensed on a massive scale by the victorious party, and that it pays to demonstrate fealty.)

Costa Rican citizens enjoy universal suffrage, and citizens are automatically registered to vote on their 18th birthdays, when they are issued voter identity cards. Since 1959, voting has ostensibly been compulsory—it is a constitutional mandate—for all citizens under 70 years of age. Schoolchildren decked out in party colors usher voters to the voting booths. If the president-elect fails to receive 40 percent of the vote, a special runoff election is held for the two top contenders.

All parties are granted equal airtime on radio and television, and campaign costs are largely drawn from the public purse: any party with 5 percent or more of the vote in the prior election can apply for a proportionate share of the official campaign fund, equal to 0.5 percent of the national budget. If a party fails to get 5 percent of the vote, it is legally required to refund the money, though this rarely happens. The Supreme Electoral Tribunal rules on campaign issues and can prohibit the use of political smears, such as branding an opponent a communist.

Don't expect to buy a drink in the immediate run-up to an election: liquor and beer sales are banned for the preceding three days.

BUREAUCRACY

Little Costa Rica is big on government. Building on the reforms of the *calderonista* era, successive administrations have created an impressive array of health, education, and social-welfare programs while steadily expanding state enterprises and regulatory bodies, all of which spell a massive expansion of the government bureaucracy. In 1949, the state employed only 6 percent of the working population; today the government pays the salaries of approximately one in four employed people. For the nation, this represents a huge financial burden. Public employees are the best paid, most secure, and most highly unionized and vocal workers. Public employees' repetitive demands for higher pay, shorter hours, and greater fringe benefits are so voracious that they eat up a vast proportion of the government benefits intended for the poor. "The state," says one Tican, "is a cow with a thousand teats and everyone wants a teat to suck."

Costa Rica's government employees have nurtured bureaucratic formality to the level of art. The problem has given rise to *despachantes,* people who make a living from their patience and knowledge of the bureaucratic ropes: for a small fee they will wait in line and gather the necessary documents on your behalf.

ARMED FORCES AND POLICE

Costa Rica has no army, navy, or air force. The nation disbanded its military forces in 1949, when it declared itself neutral. Nonetheless, Costa Rica's police force has various powerfully armed branches with a military capability. Throughout the country—especially near the Nicaraguan and Panamanian borders—you'll see "soldiers" in army fatigues touting M-16 rifles.

Costa Rica's police force was until recent years underpaid and its ranks suffered from being little-educated and prone to bribery and corruption (in 2000, the Central American Commission on Human Rights published a report castigating the nation for increased police corruption). The government has made serious efforts in recent years to purge the force of its cancer. Major investment, including new cars and equipment and better training, has resulted in a noticeably more professional police force in recent years.

CORRUPTION AND CRONYISM

Despite the popular image as a beacon of democracy (*El Financiero* published a study in 1997 that found Costa Rica to be the least corrupt of all Latin American countries), nepotism and cronyism are entrenched in the Costa Rican political system, and corruption *is* part of the way things work.

The political system is too weak to resist the "bite," or bribery, locally called *chorizo* (a poor grade of bacon). As a result, most of the nation's governmental authorities are relatively inept. Corruption is so endemic that a board game, suitably called *Chorizo*, was launched in 2000 (the winner is the one who "buys" the most officials, cheats at elections, and connives to grab the most money).

In June 2000, the nation's Ombudswoman charged that the ills in public administration have demoted Costa Rica to a "disillusioned democracy," and warned that radical steps were needed to "re-democratize" the system. At last visit, although only two years old, Abel Pacheco's much-troubled government had witnessed the resignation of 13 ministers, some allegedly due to financial irregularities.

Economy

Costa Rica's economy this century has, in many ways, been a model for developing nations. Highly efficient coffee and banana industries aided by high and stable world prices have drawn in vast export earnings, and manufacturing has grown modestly under the protection of external tariffs and the expanding purchasing power of the domestic market. A recent bright note was the signing of a regional free trade agreement (CAFTA) in 2003 between the U.S. and five central American nations -a culmination of the move, since the late 1970s, progressively toward a more diversified trading economy (coffee, bananas, sugar, and beef, which together represented almost 80 percent of exports in 1980, earn less than 40 percent today).

GDP grew 2.8 percent in 2002 to $16.9 billion, with growth primarily in telecommunications, electronics, and service industries. Nonetheless, the 2002 trade deficit was $1.5 billion; and the country closed 2002 with a $936 million deficit (in 2003, Standard & Poor's lowered Costa Rica's rating from "stable" to "negative" due to the widening budget and central government deficits (which amounted to 5.4 percent of GDP in 2002). Moreover, the *colón* has continued to decline in value, and real wages remain stagnant. One in five of the nation's families are officially below the poverty line, with seven percent in "extreme poverty."

AGRICULTURE

You might be mistaken for thinking that agriculture dominates the Costa Rican economy. Everywhere you go, particularly in the central highlands, a remarkable feature of the land is almost complete cultivation, no matter how steep the slope. Nationwide, some 11 percent of the land area is planted in crops; 46 percent is given to pasture. Agriculture's share of the economy, however, has slipped from 13.3 percent by value in 1992 to only nine percent in 2002.

Despite Costa Rica's reputation as a country of yeoman farmers, land ownership has always been highly concentrated, and there are parts, such as Guanacaste, where rural income distribution resembles the inimical patterns of Guatemala and El Salvador. Today, 71 percent of the economically active rural population is landless. The bottom 50 percent of all landholders own only 3 percent of all land. The top one percent of farm owners own more than one-quarter of the agricultural land. And the multi-national corpora-

© CHRISTOPHER P. BAKER

fruit for sale

tions that today control the plantations are renowned for exploiting their workers (the large hacienda, however, is foreign to the traditions of the Meseta Central).

The mist-shrouded slopes of the Meseta Central and southern highlands are adorned with green undulating carpets of coffee—the *grano d'oro,* or golden bean-that is the most important crop in the highlands. In the higher, more temperate areas, carnations, chrysanthemums, and other flowers grow under acres of plastic sheeting, and dairy farming is becoming more important in a mixed-farming economy that has been a feature of the Meseta since the end of the 19th century. The situation is a far cry from the limited economy of the Altiplano at similar elevations in Guatemala.

Vast banana plantations swathe the Caribbean plains and Golfo Dulce region. Sugarcane is grown by small farmers all over the country but becomes a major crop on plantations as you drop into the lowlands, and west of Ala-

juela; production has been in decline for two decades, however. Cacao, once vital to the 18th-century economy, is on the rise again as a major export crop; the trees, fruit hanging pendulously from their trunks, are everywhere, especially in large plantations of the Caribbean and Northern Zone.

Cassava, papaya, camote (sweet potato), melons, strawberries, chayote (vegetable pear), eggplant, *curraré* (plantain bananas), pimiento, macadamia nuts, ornamental plants, and cut flowers are all fast becoming important export items. And Costa Rica is the world's leading pineapple exporter, with 15,000 hectares of land used for pineapple production (in 2003, pineapple exports -which earned $210 million -surpassed coffee in value).

Bananas

Bananas have been a part of the Caribbean landscape since 1870, when American entrepreneur Minor Keith shipped his first fruit stems to New

Orleans. In 1899, his Tropical Trading & Transport Co. merged with the Boston Fruit Co. to form the United Fruit Co., which soon became the overlord of the political economies of the "banana republics." By the 1920s, much of the jungle south of Puerto Limón had been transformed into a vast sea of bananas. The banana industry continues to expand to meet the demand of a growing international market, and plantations now cover about 50,000 hectares. Most growth is concentrated in the north Atlantic lowlands.

Then, as now in some areas, working conditions were appalling, and strikes were so frequent that when Panamá disease and then *sigatoka* (leaf-spot) disease swept the region in the 1930s and 1940s, United Fruit took the opportunity to abandon its Atlantic holdings and move to the Pacific coast, where it planted around Golfito, Coto Colorado, and Palmar. Violent clashes with the banana workers' unions continued to be the company's nemesis. In 1985, after a 72-day strike,

United Fruit closed its operations in southwestern Costa Rica. Many of the plantations have been replaced by stands of African palms (used in cooking oil, margarine, and soap); others are leased to independent growers and farmers' co-operatives who sell to United Fruit. Labor problems still flare: a telling tale of continued abuse by the banana companies (in 1994, riots ensued when the English company Geest hired illegal immigrants at below minimum wage levels).

The Standard Fruit Co. began production in the Atlantic lowlands in 1956. Alongside AS-BANA (Asociación de Bananeros), a government-sponsored private association, Standard Fruit helped revive the Atlantic coast banana industry. Much of the new acreage, however, has come at the expense of thousands of acres of virgin jungle.

In 2000, the banana companies began cutting back production in Costa Rica due to overproduction. Costa Rican banana exports dropped 25.6 percent from 1999 to 2002, while revenue dropped from $632.2 million to $467.5 million (the country is still the second-biggest exporter of bananas in the world, behind Ecuador). Alas, it has been the independent growers (many of whom were encouraged to expand their acreage by the large banana companies) who have suffered, as the banana conglomerates have cut back on buying from outside growers.

Cattle

By far the largest share of agricultural land (70 percent) is given over to cattle pasture. Costa Rica is today Latin America's leading beef exporter (it accounts for some 5 percent of U.S. meat imports and for about 9 percent of Costa Rica's export earnings). Guanacaste remains essentially what it has been since midcolonial times—cattle country—and three-quarters of Costa Rica's 2.2 million head of cattle are found here. They are mostly humpbacked zebu, originally from India and now adapted over several generations. Low-interest loans in the 1960s and 1970s encouraged a rush into cattle farming for the export market, prompting rapid expansion

banana processing plant and banana fields in the Caribbean lowlands

© CHRISTOPHER P. BAKER

into new areas such as the Valle de El General and more recently the Atlantic lowlands.

The highland slopes are munched upon by herds of Charolais, Hereford, Holstein, and Jersey cattle, raised for the dairy industry.

Coffee

Costa Rica produces 3 percent of the world's coffee and the greatest coffee productivity per acre in the world). Coffee claims about 115,000 hectares of land.

Beans grown here are ranked among the best in the world. Costa Rica's highlands possess ideal conditions for coffee production. The coffee plant loves a seasonal, almost monsoonal climate with a distinct dry season; it grows best in well-drained, fertile soils at elevations between 800 and 1,500 meters with a narrow annual temperature range—natural conditions provided by the Meseta Central. The best coffee—mild coffee commanding the highest prices—is grown near the plant's uppermost altitudinal limits, where the bean takes longer to mature (Costa Rican coffee has an unusually high—86 percent—content of "liqueur," or coffee essence; Brazilian coffee has a meager 29 percent).

The first coffee beans were brought from Jamaica in 1779. Within 50 years coffee had become firmly established; by the 1830s it was the country's prime export earner, a position it occupied until 1991, when coffee plunged to third place in the wake of a precipitous 50 percent fall in world coffee prices. The decline caused widespread distress for small farmers and the 45,000 poorly paid laborers who rely on work in the harvest season. In 1994, however, international coffee prices skyrocketed after large crop losses in Brazil. The 1996-97 harvest increased 9 percent and reaped $376 million. By 2000, prices had waned again, and Costa Rican coffee reserves were destroyed to shore up prices. In 2002, Costa Rica earned only $163 million from coffee.

The plants are grown in nurseries for their first year before being planted in long rows

© CHRISTOPHER P. BAKER

coffee beans picked fresh from the vine

that ramble invitingly down the steep hillsides, their paths coiling and uncoiling like garden snakes. After four years they fruit. In April, with the first rains, the small white blossoms burst forth and the air is laced with perfume not unlike jasmine. By November, the glossy green bushes are plump with shiny red berries—the coffee beans—and the seasonal labor is called into action.

The hand-picked berries are trucked to *beneficios* (processing plants), where they are machine-scrubbed and washed to remove the fruity outer layer and dissolve the gummy substance surrounding the bean (the pulp is returned to the slopes as fertilizer). The moist beans are then blow-dried or laid out to dry in the sun in the traditional manner. The leather skin of the bean is then removed by machine, and the beans are sorted according to size and shape before being vacuum-sealed to retain the fragrance and slight touch of acidity characteristic of the great vintages of Costa Rica.

Multi-national corporations increasingly dominate the scene, while small-time farmers struggle to stay afloat.

The **Costa Rican Coffee Institute** (ICAFE, P.O. Box 37-1000 San José, tel. 506/243-7950, fax 506/223-6025, promo@icafe.go.cr, www.icafe.go.cr) tends to coffee affairs

INDUSTRY

Manufacturing accounts for about 40 percent of GNP, a dramatic rise in recent years. This is due almost entirely to Costa Rica's newfound favor as a darling of high-tech industries. The arrival of Intel, the computer chip manufacturer, whose establishment in 1997 of a $500 million assembly plant in Costa Rica suggested that the country could blossom as a "Silicon Valley South." Motorola, 3COM, and Abbott Laboratories have since built assembly plants. The nation has also staked a claim as a world center for the as-yet-unregulated I-gaming industry (online casinos). Otherwise, there is little to suggest that industrialization is going to transform the essentially agricultural economy in the near future; 95 percent of industry is small-to medium-sized and depends on the small domestic market to sell goods and services.

Local industrial raw materials are restricted to agricultural products, wood, and a small output of mineral ores. Manufacturing is still largely concerned with food processing, although pharmaceutical and textile exports have risen dramatically in recent years. Major industrial projects also include aluminum processing, a petrochemical plant at Moín, a tuna-processing plant at Golfito, and an oil refinery at Puerto Limón.

The state has a monopoly in key economic sectors such as energy, telecommunications, and insurance.

The service sector has increased its share of the economy from 55.8 percent in 1992 to 62.9 percent in 2002.

Hydroelectricity, though well developed and concentrated in the Arenal area, is the only domestic power source of significance.

TOURISM

In 1993, tourism overtook the banana industry to become the nation's prime income earner. In 2002, some 1,113,406 visitors came, generating about US$940 million. The government's goal is a 10 percent annual increase in tourism, attaining 2.3 million tourists by 2012. About 86,000 workers are directly employed in tourism-related activities; another 400,000 are indirectly employed.

The Costa Rican Tourism Institute's annual surveys consistently find that the overwhelming majority of tourists cite natural beauty as one of their main motivations for visiting Costa Rica, and one-third specifically cite ecotourism. Costa Rica practically invented the term—defined as responsible travel that contributes to conservation of natural environments and sustains the well-being of local people by promoting rural economic development. In October 1991, the country was chosen as one of three winners of the first environmental award presented by the American Society of Travel Agents (ASTA) and *Smithsonian* magazine.

Nonetheless, in its haste to boost the influx of tourist dollars, the government of Rafael Calderón began promoting large-scale resort development on the shores of the Pacific northwest. The government decided to position Costa Rica as a comprehensive destination for the whole family, and particularly as a beach resort contender to Mexico and the Caribbean.

Chief among the projects is the Gulf of Papagayo project encompassing several beaches in Guanacaste. The multi-resort complex, constructed by a host of European and Mexican developers, was conceived to be the largest "leisure city" in Central America with more than 20,000 rooms. The development covers 4,942 acres close to several national parks and wildlife reserves, and has stalled since coming under attack from conservation groups.

The country still lacks a model for tourism development and big hotels—and more so, large condominium complexes—are going up all along the Pacific shoreline (residential development around resort hotels is the big money-maker).

Concern about whether Costa Rica is growing too fast and shifting from its ecotourism focus toward mass-market tourism led, in 1993, to a threatened boycott of the country's annual travel trade show, Expotur, by environmentally responsible tour operators. Everyone agreed on one point: the nation was lacking any sort of coherent tourism development plan to control growth. Consequently, developers large and small were pushing up hotels along Costa Rica's 1,227 km (767 miles) of coastline in total disregard of environmental laws. Violations of the Maritime Terrestrial Zone Law, which prohibits construction within 50 meters of the point halfway between high and low tides, are out of control.

Tax credits and other incentives for foreign investors have also pushed the price of land beyond reach of the local population. More than 50 percent of Costa Rica's habitable coastline is now owned by North Americans and Europeans, according to Sergio Guillen, an information officer for the Ministry of Planning. "We are selling our land to the highest bidder," he says. "And the government doesn't seem to care."

Few people were shocked when, in March 1995, 12 ICT officials and even Manuel Chacón, the Minister of Tourism in the Calderón administration, were indicted on a variety of charges relating to violations at Papagayo. The Spanish developer Barceló was taken to court for flagrant breaches of environmental codes during construction of a 400-room resort at Playa Tambor. And Spain's Sol Meliá has been accused of heavy-handedness in the development of its resort at Conchal.

Ecotour operators have warned that without a conscientious national development plan, the government could kill the goose that lays the golden egg. Says Costa Rica Expeditions' founder Michael Kaye: "The [Calderón administration's] policy [was] to use eco-development as a smoke screen to get as much foreign exchange as fast as possible without regard for the long-term consequences... The [Calderón] policy [was] to talk appropriate-scale tourism and to foster mass tourism. People are *already* beginning to see too many other people," says Kaye, who points to the example of Manuel Antonio National Park, where the problem recently reached a crisis.

Defenders of large-scale resorts point out that surging tourism dollars could pull the country out of debt. And the employment opportunities are huge. Chacón claimed the Gulf of Papagayo development alone could provide 30,000 jobs. The government has also poured money into improving road access along the Pacific coast. While many local residents welcome the potential development, others fear that if the roads that lead to more remote natural shrines are paved, more and more tourists will flock, thereby quickening the possible destruction of the very thing they come to worship.

In 1997, the Figueres government initiated a "Certification for Sustainable Tourism" rating system to regulate the environmental impact of hotel development. In March 2003, the government announced creation of the **National Chamber of Ecotourism.**

The People

The 2002 census recorded a population of 3.9 million, more than half of whom lived in the Meseta Central. Approximately 350,000 live in the capital city of San José (about three times that number live in the metropolitan region). Sixty percent of the nation's population is classed as urban. The country's annual population growth rate is 1.56 percent.

DEMOGRAPHY

Costa Rica is unquestionably the most homogeneous of Central American nations in race as well as social class. Travelers familiar with other Central American nations will immediately notice the contrast. The census classifies 94 percent of the population as "white" or "mestizo" and less than three percent as "black" or "Indian." The lighter complexion of Old World immigrants is evident throughout the nation. Exceptions are Guanacaste, where almost half the population is visibly mestizo, a legacy of the

more pervasive unions between Spanish colonists and Chorotega Indians through several generations, and the population of the Atlantic coast province of Puerto Limón which is one-third black, with a distinct culture that reflects its West Indian origins.

Afro-Caribbean People

Costa Rica's approximately 40,000 black people are the nation's largest minority. For many years they were the target of racist immigration and residence laws that restricted them to the Caribbean coast (only as late as 1949, when the new Constitution abrogated apartheid on the Atlantic Railroad, were blacks allowed to travel beyond Siquirres and enter the highlands). Hence, they remained isolated from national culture. Although Afro-Caribbean turtle hunters settled on the Caribbean coast as early as 1825, most blacks today trace their ancestry back to the 10,000 or so Jamaicans hired by Minor Keith to build the Atlantic Railroad, and to later waves

traditional adobe homestead and oxcart, Nicoya

of immigrants who came to work the banana plantations in the late 19th century.

Costa Rica's early black population was "dramatically upwardly mobile" and by the 1920s a majority of the West Indian immigrants worked their own plots of land or had risen to higher-paying positions within the banana industry. Unfortunately, they possessed neither citizenship nor the legal right to own land. In the 1930s, when "white" highlanders began pouring into the lowlands, blacks were quickly dispossessed of land and the best-paying jobs. Late that decade, when the banana blight forced the banana companies to abandon their Caribbean plantations and move to the Pacific, "white" Ticos successfully lobbied for laws forbidding the employment of *gente de color* in other provinces, one of several circumstances that kept blacks dependent on the largesse of the United Fruit Company, whose labor policies were often abhorrent. Pauperized, many blacks migrated to Panamá and the U.S. seeking wartime employment. A good proportion of those who remained converted their subsistence plots into commercial cacao farms and reaped large profits during the 1950s and 1960s from the rise of world cacao prices.

West Indian immigrants played a substantial role in the early years of labor organization, and their early strikes were often violently suppressed. Many black workers, too, joined hands with Figueres in the 1948 civil war. Their reward? Citizenship and full guarantees under the 1949 Constitution, which ended apartheid.

Costa Rica's black population has consistently attained higher educational standards than the national average and many blacks are now found in leading professions throughout the nation. Race relations are harmonious, and blacks are readily accepted as equals by Tico society. On the Caribbean coast, they have retained much of their traditional culture, including religious practices rooted in African belief about transcendence through spiritual possession *(obeah),* their cuisine (codfish and akee, "rundown"), the rhythmic lilt of their slightly antiquated English, and the deeply syncopated funk of their music.

Indigenous People

Costa Rica's indigenous peoples have suffered abysmally. Centuries ago the original tribes were splintered by Spanish conquistadors and compelled to retreat into the vast tracts of the interior mountains (the Chorotegas of Guanacaste, however, were more gradually assimilated into the national culture). Today, approximately 20,000 peoples of the Bribrí, Boruca, and Cabecar tribes manage to eke out a living in remote valleys in the Cordillera Talamanca of southern Costa Rica, where their ancestors had sought refuge from Spanish muskets and dogs. Twenty-four national indigenous communities and eight ethnic groups live on 22 Indian reserves.

In 1939, the government granted every indigenous family an allotment of 148 hectares for traditional farming, and in December 1977 a law was passed prohibiting non-Indians from buying, leasing, or renting land within the reserves. Although various agencies continue to work to promote education, health, and community development, the indigenous people's standard of living is appallingly low, alcoholism is endemic, and they remain subject to constant exploitation. Despite the legislation, many indigenous people have been tricked into selling their allotments or otherwise forced off their lands. Banana companies have gradually encroached, pushing *campesinos* onto marginal land. And mining companies are infiltrating the reserves along newly built roads, which become conduits for contamination, like dirty threads in a wound.

Indigenous peoples complain that the National Commission for Indigenous Affairs (CONAI) has proved ineffective in enforcing protections (in 2002, it had a budget of only $374,345 for all 24 reserves). The Law of Autonomous Development, which would make the indigenous reserves autonomous and eliminate CONAI, has been stalled in Congress since 1992.

The Borucas, who inhabit scattered villages in tight-knit patches of the Pacific southwest, have been most adept at conserving their own language and civilization, including matriarchy, communal land ownership, and traditional

Costa Rican youth

weaving. For most other groups, only a few elders still speak the languages, and interest in traditional crafts is fading. Virtually all groups have adopted elements of Catholicism along with their traditional animistic religions, Spanish is today the predominant tongue.

It is possible in towns such as San Vito and Ciudad Neily, in the Pacific southwest, to see indigenous women and girls in traditional bright-colored garb—a beautiful sight!

Other Ethnic Groups

Immigrants from many nations have been made welcome over the years (between 1870 and 1920, almost 25 percent of Costa Rica's population growth was due to immigration). Jews are prominent in the liberal professions. A Quaker community of several hundred people centers on Monteverde. Germans have for many generations been particularly successful as coffee farmers. Italians have gathered, among other places, in the town of San Vito, on the central Pacific coast. The Chinese man quoted in Paul Theroux's *Old Patagonian Express* is one of several thousand Chinese who call Costa Rica

home. Many are descended from approximately 600 Asians who were imported as contract laborers to work on the Atlantic Railroad; *chinos* and are now conspicuously successful in the hotel, restaurant, and bar trade, and in Limón as middlemen controlling the trade in bananas and cacao.

During the past decade, Costa Rica has become a favorite home away from home for an influx of North Americans and Europeans (predominantly Italian, German, and French, who concentrate in enclaves)—including a large percentage of misfits and malcreants evading the law (Costa Rica has been called the "land of the wanted and the unwanted"). Tens of thousands of Central American refugees from El Salvador, Guatemala, and Nicaragua find safety in Costa Rica, where they provide cheap labor for the coffee fields. The largest group of recent immigrants are *Nicas* (Nicaraguans); as many as 450,000—one seventh of the Costa Rican population—the majority of whom are considered "illegals" not protected by law. They face overt discrimination and are held to blame—unjustifiably—for many of Costa Rica's current social ills.

WAY OF LIFE

Most Costa Ricans—Los Costarricense, or Ticos—insist that their country is a "classless democracy." Ticos lack the volatility, ultranationalism, and deep-seated political divisions of their Latin American brethren. There is considerable social mobility, and no race problem on the scale of the United States'. A so-called middle-class mentality runs deep, including a belief in the Costa Rican equivalent of "the American Dream"—a conviction that through individual effort and sacrifice and a faith in schooling, every Costa Rican can climb the social ladder and better him-or herself.

Still, despite the high value Ticos place on equality and democracy, their society contains all kinds of inequities. For example, the richest one percent of families receive 10 percent of the national income; the poorest 50 percent receive only 20 percent; and at least one-fifth of the population are *marginados* who live in poverty and remain outside the mainstream of progress.

Despite its relative urban sophistication, Costa Rica remains a predominantly agrarian society. Urbanites, like city dwellers worldwide, condescendingly chuckle at rural "hicks." The skewed tenure of a much-diluted feudalism persists in regions long dominated by plantations and haciendas. And the upwardly mobile "elite," who consider menial labor demeaning, prefer to indulge in conspicuous spending and, often, in snobbish behavior.

Though comparatively wealthy compared to most Latin American countries, by developed-world standards most Costa Ricans are poor (the per capita GDP is US$8,500; The average income in the northern lowlands is barely one-seventh of that in San José). Many rural families still live in simple huts of adobe or wood. Shacks made from gasoline tins, old automobile tires, and corrugated tin give a miserable cover to poor urban laborers in *tugurios*—illegally erected slums—on the outskirts and the riverbanks of San José. And a U.N. report on child labor issued in 1997 found that 120,000 Costa Rican minors aged 5–17 are exploited and are paid little or

not at all. Only 56 percent of rural homes receive clean drinking water, while 28.4 percent of urban homes lack clean water. Frequent outbreaks of salmonella and shigella occur.

However, that all paints far too gloomy a picture. In a region where millions starve, the Costa Ricans are comparatively well-to-do. The country has few *desperately* poor, and there are relatively few beggars existing on the bare charity of the world. Most Costa Ricans keep their proud little bungalows tidy and bordered by flowers, and even the poorest are generally well groomed and neatly dressed.

Costa Rica is a class-conscious society. Nonetheless, overt class distinctions are kept within bounds by a delicate balance between "elitism" and egalitarianism unique in the isthmus: aristocratic airs are frowned on and blatant pride in blue blood is ridiculed; even the president is inclined to mingle in public in casual clothing and is commonly addressed in general conversation by his first name or nickname.

The Tican Identity

Costa Ricans' unique traits derive from a profoundly conscious self-image, which orients much of their behavior as both individuals and as a nation. The Ticos—the name is said to stem from the colonial saying "we are all *hermaniticos* " (little brothers)—feel distinct from their neighbors by their "whiteness" and relative lack of indigenous culture. Ticos identify themselves first and foremost as Costa Ricans and only Central Americans, or even Latin Americans, as an afterthought.

In general, Costa Ricans act with humility and judge as uncouth boasting of any kind. Above all, the behavior and comments of most Ticos are dictated by *quedar bien*, a desire to leave a good impression. Like the English, they're terribly frightened of embarrassing themselves, of appearing rude or vulgar (tactless and crude people are considered "badly educated") or unhelpful. As such, they can be exceedingly courteous, almost archaically so (they are prone, for example, to offer flowing compliments and formal greetings).

Ticos are also hard to excite. It is almost impossible to draw a Tico into a spirited debate or argument. They are loath to express or defend a position and simply walk away from arguments. (As such, resentments fester and sneaky retributions—such as arson—are common.) The *notion* of democracy and the ideals of personal liberty are strongly cherished. Costa Ricans are intensely proud of their accomplishments in this arena, and gloss over the glaring inadequacies such as endemic theft, corruption, and fraud.

Ticos are not reflective or analytical, and display limited development of intellectualism, individualism, and applied intelligence. Their Bud-Lite culture has been called the "white bread" for Latin America. Still, they revere education. "We have more teachers than soldiers" is a common boast, and framed school diplomas hang in even the most humble homes. Everyone, too, is eager for the benefits of social progress. Nonetheless, they are also conservative, suspicious of experimentation that is not consistent with a loosely held sense of "*tico* tradition." Many North American and European hoteliers and residents have bemoaned the general passivity that often translates into a lack of initiative.

The cornerstone of society is the family and the village community. Social life still centers on the home. Nepotism—using family ties and connections for gain—is the way things get done in business and government. But traditional values are severely challenged. Drunkenness among the working classes is common. Theft, fraud, and burglary are endemic. Drug abuse, previously unknown in Costa Rica, has intruded (Costa Rica has become a major trading zone for cocaine traffic). And though many Ticos display a genuine concern for conservation (every school has some kind of environmental education program and ecological themes are widely covered in the media), the ethic is still tentative among the population as a whole.

Machismo and the Status of Women

By the standards of many Latin American countries, the nation is progressive and moderately successful in advancing the equal rights of women. That said, legacies of the Spanish Catholic sense of "proper" gender roles are twined like tangled threads through the national fabric. Male and female roles are clearly defined. Machismo, sustained by a belief in the natural superiority of men, is integral to the Costa Rican male's way of life. It "justifies" why he expects to be given due deference by women, why he expects his wife or *novia* (girlfriend) to wait on him hand and foot, why he refrains from household chores, and why he is generally free to do as he pleases, particularly to sleep around. The Latin male expresses his masculinity in amorous conquests, and the faithful husband and male celibate is suspect in the eyes of his friends. But it always takes two to tango. Hip urban Ticas have forsaken old-fashioned romanticism for a latter-day liberalism. Even in the most isolated rural towns, dating in the Western fashion has displaced the *retreta*—the circling of the central plaza by men and women on weekend evenings—and chaperones, once common, are now virtually unknown.

In fact, almost 10 percent of all Costa Rican adults live together in "free unions," one-quarter of all children are *hijos naturales* (born out of wedlock; one in five of such births list the father as "unknown"), and one in five households is headed by a single mother. Many rural households are so-called Queen-bee (all-female) families headed by an elderly matriarch who looks after her grandchildren while the daughters work. Divorce, once a stigma, is now common and easily obtained under the Family Code of 1974, although desertion remains as it has for centuries "the poor man's divorce." *Compañeras,* women in consensual relationships, enjoy the same legal rights as wives.

In theory, the law also forbids gender discrimination in hiring and salaries. Women are entitled to maternity leave and related benefits. And women have attained considerable success in the political and professional arena: women outnumber men in many occupations and notably in university faculties, and the nation has had several female vice-presidents, including both vice-presidents in the 1998-2001 ángel Rodríguez administration.

Nonetheless, low-level occupations especially reflect wide discrepancies in wage levels for men and women. The greater percentage of lower-class women remain chained to the kitchen sink and the rearing of children. And gender relationships, particularly in rural villages, remain dominated to a greater or lesser degree by machismo and *marianismo,* its female equivalent. Women are supposed to be bastions of moral and spiritual integrity, to be accepting of men's infidelities, and to "accept bitter pride in their suffering."

Religion

On the one hand, the country has always been remarkably secular, the link between Christianity and the state always weak. Nonetheless, more than 90 percent of the population is Roman Catholic, the official state religion. Every village has a church and its own saint's day, and every taxi, bus, government office, and home has its token religious icons. The Catholic marriage ceremony is the only church marriage granted state recognition. And the 1949 Constitution even provided for state contributions to the maintenance of the Church, and the salaries of bishops are paid by the state.

Holy Week (the week before Easter) is a national holiday, and communities throughout Costa Rica organize processions beginning on Palm Sunday, when figures dressed as Christ ride through towns on a donkey. Catholics are expected to visit seven churches within the week, leading to long lines of pilgrims walking the roads. On Maundy Thursday, Catholics celebrate the "Last Supper" and men dressed as the disciples have their feet washed in ritual plays. On Easter Friday, the most important day, long processions reenact Christ's march on the Cross, followed on Saturday by effigies of Judas being dragged through the streets. (Ticos get over their maudlin on Sundays with family parties and feasting (the two most famous processions are held at the San Rafael de Oreamuno church in Cartago, and the San Joaquín de Flores, Heredia).

Reruns of classic biblical movies are standard TV fare during Holy Week.

The Catholic church has fiercely protected its turf against Protestant missionaries, and the Protestant evangelism so prevalent in other parts of Central America has yet to make a dent in Costa Rica. A great many sects, however, have found San José the ideal base for proselytizing forays elsewhere in the isthmus. The nation's black population constitutes about half of Costa Rica's 40,000 or so Protestants, though the Archbishop of Canterbury would be horrified at the extent to which "his" religion has been married with African-inspired, voodoo-like *obeah* and *pocomoia* worship.

Superstitions abound in all segments of society, such as the belief that if you climb a tree on Good Friday, you'll grow a tail; and single men refuse to carry the Saint John icon during the procession of the Holy Burial due to the belief that they will never marry. Resignation to God's will is tinged with fatalism. In a crisis Ticos will turn to a favorite saint, one who they believe has special powers or "pull" with God, to demand a miracle. And folkloric belief in witchcraft is still common (Escazú is renowned as a center for *brujos,* witches who specialize in casting out spells and resolving love problems).

Education

Costa Ricans are a relatively highly educated people: the country boasts of 96 percent literacy, the most literate populace in Central America (the literacy figures, however, include many "functional illiterates" counted by their simple ability to sign their own name). In 1869, the country became one of the first in the world to make education both obligatory and free (as early as 1828, an unenforced law made school attendance mandatory). Schooling through the ninth year (age 14) is compulsory.

Nonetheless, according to United Nations statistics, about 40 percent of Costa Rican teenagers drop out of school by the sixth grade or never gain access to secondary education (Panamá and El Salvador both outperform Costa Rica in secondary education). Almost 1,000 schools have only one teacher, often a partially trained *aspirante* (candidate teacher) lacking certification. Plus, there remains a severe shortage of teachers with a sound knowledge of the full panoply of academic subjects, remote rural schools are often difficult to reach in the best of weather, and the Ministry of Education is riven with political appointees who change hats with each administration. (Middle-income and well-to-do families usually send their children to private schools.)

Costa Rica has four state-funded schools of higher learning, and opportunities abound for adults to earn the primary or secondary diplomas they failed to gain as children. The University of Costa Rica (UCR), the largest and oldest university, enrolls some 35,000 students, mostly on scholarships. The main campus is in the northeastern San José community of San Pedro (UCR also has regional centers in Alajuela, Turrialba, Puntarenas, and Cartago). The National University in Heredia (there are regional centers in Liberia and Perez Zeledon) offers a variety of liberal arts, sciences, and professional studies to 13,000 students. Cartago's Technical Institute of Costa Rica (ITCR) specializes in science and technology and seeks to train people for agriculture, industry, and mining. And the State Correspondence University is modeled after the United Kingdom's Open University and has 32 regional centers offering 15 degree courses in health, education, business administration, and the liberal arts.

In addition, there are also scores of private "universities," though the term is applied to even the most marginal cubbyhole college.

Health

Perhaps the most impressive impact of Costa Rica's modern welfare state has been the truly dramatic improvements in national health. Infant mortality has plummeted from 25.6 percent in 1920 to only 10.56 percent in 2002.

And the average Costa Rican today can expect to live to a ripe 76.43 years—about as long as the average U.S.-born citizen. Much of this is thanks to the Social Security system, which provides universal insurance benefits covering medical services, disability, maternity, old-age pensions, and death.

Costa Rica assigns about 10 percent of its GNP to health care. The result? A physician for every 700 people and a hospital bed for every 275. In fact, in some arenas the health-care system isn't far behind that of the U.S. in terms of the latest medical technology, at least in San José, where transplant surgery is now performed. Many North Americans fly here for surgery, including dental work. And the Beverly Hills crowd helps keep Costa Rica's cosmetic surgeons busy.

One key to the nation's success was the creation of the Program for Rural Health in 1970 to ensure that basic health care would reach the furthest backwaters. The program, aimed at the 50 percent of the population living in small communities, established rural health posts attended by paramedics. The clinics are visited regularly by doctors and nurses, and strengthened by education programs stressing good nutrition, hygiene, and safe food preparation.

A major problem continues to be the high incidence of smoking among Ticos—a cherished tradition in Costa Rica.

Language

The Costa Ricans speak Spanish, and do so with a clear, concise dialect littered with phraseology unique to the nation.

The most common Costa Rican phrase is *¡pura vida!*, a popular saying literally meaning "pure life" but used in various contexts, including as a greeting, to express a positive attitude.

The people are correctly called *Costariccense,* or by their nickname, the *Ticos.*

San José is referred to by Ticos as *chepe.*

Arts and Culture

Historically, Costa Rica has been relatively impoverished in the area of native arts and crafts. The country, with its relatively small and heterogeneous pre-Columbian population had no unique cultural legacy that could spark a creative synthesis where the modern and the traditional might merge. And social tensions (often catalysts to artistic expression) felt elsewhere in the isthmus were lacking.

In recent years, however, artists across the spectrum have found a new confidence and are shaking off rigid social norms. The performing arts are flourishing, amply demonstrated by the introduction of an International Art Festival in 1992 (see *Festivals and Holidays,* this chapter), an annual event that has brought inspiration and new ideas while raising the quality of local groups by allowing them to measure themselves against international talent. Ticos now speak proudly of their "cultural revolution."

Costa Rica has a strong *peña* tradition, introduced by Chilean and Argentinian exiles. Literally "circle of friends," *peñas* are bohemian, international gatherings—usually in favored cafes—where moving songs are shared and wine and tears flow.

ART

Santa Ana and neighboring Escazú, immediately southwest of San José, have long been magnets for artists. Escazú in particular is home to many contemporary artists: Christina Fournier; the brothers Jorge, Manuel, Javier, and Carlos Mena; and Dinorah Bolandi, who was awarded the nation's top cultural prize. Here, in the late 1920s, Teodorico Quiros and a group of contemporaries provided the nation with its own identifiable art style—the Costa Rican "Landscape" movement—which expressed in stylized forms the flavor and personality of the drowsy little mountain towns with their cobblestone streets and adobe houses backdropped by volcanoes. The artists, who called themselves the Group of New Sensibility, began to portray Costa Rica in fresh, vibrant colors.

Quiros had been influenced by the French impressionists. In 1994, at age 77, he was awarded the *Premio Magón* award for lifetime achievement in the "creation and promotion of Costa Rican artistic culture." The group also included Luisa Gonzales de Saenz, whose paintings evoke the style of Magritte; the expressionist Manuel de la Cruz, the "Costa Rican Picasso"; as well as Enrique Echandi, who expressed a Teutonic sensibility following studies in Germany.

One of the finest examples of sculpture from this period, the chiseled stone image of a child suckling his mother's breast, can be seen outside the Maternidad Carit maternity clinic in southern San José. Its creator, Francisco Zuñigo (Costa Rica's most acclaimed sculptor), left for Mexico in a fit of artistic pique in 1936 when the sculpture, titled *Maternity,* was lampooned by local critics (one said it looked more like a cow than a woman).

By the late 1950s, many local artists looked down on the work of the prior generation as the art of *casitas* (little houses) and were indulging in more abstract styles. The current batch of young artists have broadened their expressive visions and are now gaining increasing international recognition for their eclectic works.

Isidro Con Wong, a once-poor farmer from Puntarenas, is known for a style redolent of magic realism and has works in permanent collections in several U.S. and French museums (today his paintings sell for about $35,000 each). Roberto Lizano collides Delacroix with Picasso and likes to train his eye on the pomposity of ecclesiastics. Alajuelan artist Gwen Barry is acclaimed for her "Movable Murals"—painted screens populated by characters from Shakespeare and the Renaissance. The works of Rudolfo Stanley seemingly combine those of Toulous Lautrec with Gaugain. Rolando Castellón, who was a director of the New York Mu-

THE OXCARTS OF SARCHÍ

Sarchí is famous as the home of gaily decorated wooden *carretas* (oxcarts), the internationally recognized symbol of Costa Rica. The carts, which once dominated the rural landscape of the central highlands, date back only to the end of the 19th century.

At the height of the coffee boom and before the construction of the Atlantic Railroad, oxcarts were used to transport coffee beans to Puntarenas, on the Pacific coast—a journey requiring 10–15 days. In the rainy season, the oxcart trail became a quagmire. Costa Ricans thus forged their own spokeless wheel—a hybrid between the Aztec disc and the Spanish spoked wheel—to cut through the mud without becoming bogged down. In their heyday, some 10,000 cumbersome, squeaking *carretas* had a dynamic impact on the local economy, spawning highway guards, smithies, inns, teamsters, and crews to maintain the roads.

Today's *carretas* bear little resemblance to the original rough-hewn, rectangular, cane-framed vehicles covered by rawhide tarps. Even then,

Carlos Chaverrí paints a traditional oxcart in Sarchí.

© CHRISTOPHER P. BAKER

though, the compact wheels—about four or five feet in diameter—were natural canvases awaiting an artist. Enter the wife of Fructuoso Barrantes, a cart maker in San Ramón with a paintbrush and a novel idea. She enlivened her husband's cart wheels with a geometric starburst design in bright colors set off by black and white. Soon every farmer in the district had given his aged *carreta* a lively new image.

By 1915, flowers had bloomed beside the pointed stars. Faces and even miniature landscapes soon appeared. And annual contests (still held today) were arranged to reward the most creative artists. The *carretas* had ceased to be purely functional. Each cart was also designed to make its own "song," a chime as unique as a fingerprint, produced by a metal ring striking the hubnut of the wheel as the cart bumped along. Once the oxcart had become a source of individual pride, greater care was taken in their construction, and the best-quality woods were selected to make the best sounds.

The *carretas*, forced from the fields by the advent of tractors and trucks, are almost purely decorative now, but the craft and the art form live on in Sarchí, where artisans still apply their masterly touch at two *fábricas de carretas* (workshops), which are open to view. A finely made reproduction oxcart can cost up to $5,000.

seum of Modern Art before returning to Costa Rica in 1993, translates elements of indigenous life into 3-D art. Escazú artist Katya de Luisa is known for stunning photo collages. And a Cuban aesthetic finds its way into the works of Limonese artist Edgar León, who was influenced by travels in Cuba and Mexico.

CRAFTS

The tourist dollar has spawned a renaissance in crafts. The Boruca peoples are known for their devil masks, and balsa "masks" featuring colorful wildlife and Indian faces. At Guaitil, in Nicoya, not only is the Chorotega tradition of pottery retained, it is booming, so much so that neighboring villages have installed potters' wheels. The women of Drake Bay are famous for *molas,* colorful and decorative hand-sewn appliqué used for blouses, dresses, and wall hangings. Santa Ana, in the Highlands, is also famous for its ceramics: large green ware bowls, urns, vases, coffee mugs, and small *típico* adobe houses fired in brick kilns and clay pits on the patios of some 30 independent family workshops. In Escazú, master craftsman Barry Biesanz skillfully handles razor-sharp knives and chisels to craft subtle, delicate images, bowls as hemispherical as if turned with a lathe, and decorative boxes with tight dovetailed corners from carefully chosen blocks of lignum vitae (ironwood), *narareno* (purple heart), rosewood and other tropical hardwoods.

Many of the best crafts in Costa Rica come from Sarchí, known most notably for its *carretas* (oxcarts). Although an occasional full-size oxcart is still made, today most of the *carretas* are folding miniature trolleys—like little hot-dog stands—that serve as liquor bars or indoor tables, and half-size carts used as garden ornaments or simply to accent a corner of a home. The carts are painted in dazzling white or burning orange and decorated with geometric mandala designs and floral patterns that have found their way, too, onto wall plaques, kitchen trays, and other craft items.

LITERATURE

In literature, Costa Rica has never fielded figures of the stature of Latin American writers such as Gabriel García Márquez, Octavio Paz, Jorge Amado, Pablo Neruda, Isabel Allende, or Jorge Luís Borges. Indeed, the Ticos are not at all well read and lack a passionate interest in literature. Only a handful of writers make a living from writing, and Costa Rican literature is often belittled as the most prosaic and anemic in Latin America. Lacking great goals and struggles, Costa Rica was never a breeding ground for the passions and dialectics that spawned the literary geniuses of Argentina, Brazil, Mexico, Cuba, and Chile, whose works, full of satire and bawdy humor, are clenched fists that cry out against social injustice.

Costa Rica's early literary figures were mostly essayists and poets: Roberto Brenes Mesen and Joaquín García Monge are the most noteworthy. Even the writing of the 1930s and 1940s, whose universal theme was a plea for social progress, lacked the verisimilitude and rich literary delights of other Latin American authors. Carlos Luis Fallas's *Mamita Yunai,* which depicts the plight of banana workers, is the best and best-known example of this genre.

Modern literature still draws largely from the local setting, and though the theme of class struggle has given way to a lighter, more novelistic approach it still largely lacks the mystical, surrealistic, Rabelaisian excesses, the endless layers of experience and meaning, and the wisdom, subtlety, and palpitating romanticism of the best of Brazilian, Argentinean, and Colombian literature. An outstanding exception is Julieta Pinto's *El Eco de los Pasos,* a striking novel about the 1948 civil war.

A compendium of contemporary literature, *Costa Rica: A Traveler's Literary Companion,* edited by Barbara Ras, brings together 26 stories by Costa Rican writers spanning the 20th century.

MUSIC AND DANCE

Ticos love to dance. Says *National Geographic:* "To watch the viselike clutching of Ticos and

Ticas dancing, whether at a San José discotheque or a crossroads cantina, is to marvel that the birthrate in this predominantly Roman Catholic nation is among Central America's lowest." Outside the dance hall, the young prefer to listen to Anglo-American fare, like their counterparts the world over. When it comes to dancing, however, they prefer the hypnotic Latin and rhythmic Caribbean beat and bewildering cadences of *cumbia, lambada, marcado, merengue, salsa, soca,* and the Costa Rican swing, danced with surefooted erotic grace.

Many dances and much of the music of Costa Rica reflect African, even pre-Columbian, as well as Spanish roots. The country is one of the southernmost of the "marimba culture" countries, although the African-derived marimba (xylophone) music of Costa Rica is more elusive and restrained than the vigorous native music of Panamá and Guatemala, its heartland. The guitar, too, is a popular instrument, especially as an accompaniment to folk dances such as the Punto Guanacaste, a heel-and-toe stomping dance for couples, officially decreed the national dance.

The Caribbean coast is the domain of calypso and reggae.

Folkloric Dancing

Guanacaste is the heartland of Costa Rican folkloric music and dancing. Here, even such pre-Columbian instruments as the *chirimia* (oboe) and *quijongo* (a single-string bow with gourd resonator) popularized by the Chorotega are still used as backing for traditional Chorotega dances such as the Danza del Sol and Danza de la Luna. The more familiar Cambute and Botijuela Tamborito usually deal with the issues of enchanted lovers (usually legendary coffee pickers) and are based on the Spanish *paseo,* with pretty maidens in frilly satin skirts and white bodices circled by men in white suits and cowboy hats, accompanied by tossing of scarves, a fanning of hats, and loud lusty yelps from the men.

Vestiges of the indigenous folk dancing tradition linger (barely) elsewhere in the nation. The Borucas still perform their Danza de los Di-

ablitos, and the Talamancas their Danza de los Huelos. But the drums and flutes, including the curious *dru mugata,* an ocarina (a small potato-shaped instrument with a mouthpiece and finger holes which yields soft, sonorous notes), are being replaced by guitars and accordions. Even the solemn indigenous music is basically Spanish in origin and hints at the typically slow and languid Spanish *canción* (song) which gives full rein to the romantic, sentimental aspect of the Latin character.

On the Caribbean, the *cuadrille* is a maypole dance in which each dancer holds one of many ribbons tied to the top of a pole: as they dance they braid their brightly colored ribbons.

Classical Music

Costa Rica stepped onto the world stage in classical music with the formation in 1970 of the National Symphony Orchestra under the baton of an American, Gerald Brown. The orchestra, which performs in the Teatro Nacional, often features world-renowned guest soloists and conductors, such as violinist José Castillo and classical guitarist Pablo Ortíz, who often play together. Its season is April through November. Costa Rica also claims a state-subsidized youth orchestra. The Sura Chamber Choir, founded in 1989 with musicians and vocalists from the country's two state universities, was the first professional choir in Central America, with a repertoire from sacred through Renaissance to contemporary styles.

Festivals

Costa Rica hosts an **International Festival of Music** (P.O. Box 979-1007, tel. 506/282-7724, fax 506/250-5959, antich@costaricamusic.com, www.costaricamusic.com) during the last two weeks of August. The annual six-week-long **Monteverde Music Festival** (tel. 506/645-6121, mvi@mvinstitute.org) is held each January–February.

The **Music Festival of the South Caribbean Coast** (tel. 506/750-0062, fax 506/750-0408, festival@playarchiquitalodge.com), in Feb.–April, features artists from around the country.

THEATER

A nation of avid theater lovers, Costa Rica supports a thriving acting community. In fact, Costa Rica supposedly has more theater companies per capita than any other country in the world. The country's early dramatic productions gained impetus and inspiration from Argentinian and Chilean playwrights and actors who settled here at the turn of the century, when drama was established as part of the standard school curriculum.

The streets of San José are festooned with tiny theaters—everything from comedy to drama, avant-garde, theater-in-the-round, mime, and even puppet theater. Crowds flock every night Tuesday through Sunday. Performances are predominantly in Spanish. The English-speaking Little Theater Group is Costa Rica's oldest theatrical troupe; it performs principally in the Centro Cultural's Eugene O'Neill Theater.

Recreation and Tours

Costa Rica has scores of tour operators. The leading operators offer a complete range of tour options, including one-day and overnight excursions to all the major points of attraction. This gives you the added flexibility of making your own tour arrangements once you've arrived in Costa Rica and have gained a better sense of your options and desires.

The nation boasts scores of bilingual naturalist guides (Costa Rica has more American field biologists than anywhere in the world). Most nature tours are from one to four days; one-day tours typically cost $40–85, including lunch.

I recommend **Costa Rica Expeditions** (P.O. Box 6941-1000, San José, tel. 506/257-0766, fax 506/257-1665, costaric@expeditions.co.cr, www.costaricaexpeditions.com), a pioneer in natural history and adventure travel in Costa Rica. It has a complete range of tour packages nationwide, including from its acclaimed Monteverde Lodge, Tortuga Lodge, and Corcovado Tent Camp.

Other recommended tour operators include **Costa Rica Sun Tours** (Edificio Cerro Chato, La Uruca, San José, tel. 506/296-7757, fax 506/296-4307, info@crsuntours.com, www.crsuntours.com); **Costa Rica Temptations** (P.O. Box 1199-1200, San José, tel. 506/239-9999, fax 506/239-9990, reserv@crtinfo.com, www.crtinfo.com); **Horizontes Nature Tours** (P.O. Box 1780-1002, San José, tel. 506/222-2022, fax 506/255-4513, info@horizontes.com, www.horizontes.com);

and **Swiss Travel Service** (P.O. Box. 7-1970-1000, San José, tel. 506/282-4898, fax 506/282-4890, info@swisstravelcr.com, www.swisstravelcr.com).

Ecole Travel (P.O. Box 11516-1000, San José, tel. 506/223-2240, fax 506/223-4128, info@ecoletravel.com, www.ecoletravel.com) specializes in budget travel, but offers a full tour planning service for all budgets and has online booking and payment.

Several individuals offer private tour services. One who is recommended by a reader is "Chepe" José Morales Corrales, tel./fax 442-1184, a Tico whose driving is "even-tempered." He offers excursions by bus to various spots. Chepe speaks only Spanish; his wife speaks English.

NATURAL HISTORY CRUISE TOURING

Natural-history cruise touring is a splendid way to explore Costa Rica. Normally you'll cruise at night so that each morning when you awake, you're already anchored in a new location. You spend a large part of each day ashore. Options usually include a natural-history tour guided by a professional biologist and perhaps a recreational-cultural excursion. Most vessels cruise the Pacific coast and offer a condensed and comfortable means of reaching a broad combination of remote wilderness sites.

Clipper Cruises (11969 Westline Industrial Dr., St. Louis, MO 63146, tel. 314/655-6700 or 800/325-0010, fax 314/727-6576, clipper @clippercruises.com, www.clippercruise.com) features Costa Rica and Panamá cruises aboard the 138-passenger *Yorktown Clipper.*

Lindblad Expeditions (720 Fifth Ave., New York, NY 10019, tel. 212/765-7740 or 800/425-2724, explore@expeditions.com, www.expeditions .com) offers 8-, 11-, and 15-day itineraries combining Costa Rica and Panamá aboard the 64-passenger *Sea-Voyager.* It has special family expeditions. Rates were from $3,270 (8-day), $3,770 (11-day) and $4,570 (15-day).

Temptress Adventure Cruises (P.O. 1198, San José 1200, tel. 220-1679, fax 220-2103; in the U.S., c/o Cruise West, 2401 4th Av., Suite 700, Seattle, WA 98121-1438, tel. 800/580-0072, fax 206/441-4757, info@cruisewest.com, www.cruisewest.com) operates out of Los Sueños Marina, at Playa Herradura, year-round. Its *Pacific Explorer* comfortably accommodates up to 100 passengers. Per person rates begin at $1,545 for a seven-day program; $1,995 for an eight-day program; and $3,045 for a 10-day cruise including Panamá Canal and San Blas Islands.

Windstar Cruises (300 Elliott Ave. W., Seattle, WA 98119, tel. 206/281-3535 or 800/258-7245, fax 206/286-3229, info@windstarcruises .com, www.windstarcruises.com) uses its luxurious 148-passenger *Wind Song* for seven-day itineraries, Nov.–April, down the Pacific Coast and combining Panamá. Rates began at $2,357 for seven days.

CANOPY TOURS

Hardly a month goes by without *another* "canopy tour" opening in Costa Rica. No experience is necessary for most such treetop explorations, which usually consist of a system of treetop platforms linked by horizontal transverse cables (and/or suspended walkways) that permit you to "fly" through the treetops. The system uses techniques developed by cavers and canyon rappellers and allows you to ascend and explore life amid the canopy from a unique perspective.

It all began at Finca Valverdes in Monteverde, where Canadians Rick Graham and Darren Hreniuk founded a company called Canopy Tour (now The Original Canopy Tour) and created a transverse system through the treetops. The **Original Canopy Tour** (P.O. Box 9797-1000, San José, tel. 506/257-5149, fax 506/256-7626, canopy@canopytour.com, www.canopytour.com) has eight facilities, in Monteverde Cloud Forest Preserve, at Iguana Park, at Isla Tortuga, at Rainmaker, at Tabacón, at Cañon, at Thermales del Bosque near Ciudad Quesada (San Carlos), and at Drake Bay. It charges $45 walk-in, $35 students, $25 children. Package trips from San José are offered. No credit cards.

The success of The Original Canopy Tour company spawned dozens of copycat operations, plus canopy walks via suspension bridges, and even aerial trams through the canopy.

BIRD-WATCHING

Costa Rica is to bird-watchers what Grand Central Station is to pickpockets. Few places in the world can boast so many different bird species in such a small area. However, birding requires some knowledge of where you are going, what you're looking for, and the best season. No self-respecting ornithologist would be caught in the field without his copy of *A Guide to the Birds of Costa Rica* by F. Gary Stiles and Alexander Skutch; *Birds of the Rainforest: Costa Rica* by Carmen Hidalgo; or *A Travel and Site Guide to Birds of Costa Rica,* by Aaron Sekerak. Even with these in hand, your best bet is to hire a qualified guide or to join a bird-watching tour.

The **Birding Club of Costa Rica** (crbirding-club@mailcity.com, http://crbirdingclub.tripod.com) is a useful resource.

In Costa Rica, birding tours are offered through **Horizontes** (P.O. Box 1780-1002, San José, tel. 506/222-2022, fax 506/255-4513, info@horizontes.com, www.horizontes.com) offers one-day and multi-day guided bird-watching trips. It also offers a bird count program in May—the mating and breeding season for many species. Several companies offer one-day quetzal tours.

In North America, **Cheeseman's Ecology Safaris** (20800 Kittredge Rd., Saratoga, CA 95070, tel. 408/867-1371 or 800/527-5330, fax 408/741-0358, info@cheesemans.com, www.cheesemans.com); **Costa Rica Connection** (1124 Nipomo St., Suite C, San Luis Obispo, CA 93401, tel. 805/543-8823 or 800/345-7422, fax 805/543-3626, tours@crconnect.com, www.crconnect.com); **Field Guides** (9433 Bee Cave Road, Bldg., 1, Suite 150, Austin, TX 78733, tel. 512/263-7295 or 800/728-4953, fax 512/263-0117, fieldguides@fieldguides.com, www.fieldguides.com); and **Holbrook Travel** (3540 N.W. 13th St., Gainesville, FL 32609, tel. 800/451-7111, fax 352/371-3710, travel@holbrooktravel.com, www.holbrooktravel.com) offer birding tours to Costa Rica.

In Europe, **Journey Latin America** (14 Devonshire Rd., Chiswick, London W4 2HD, tel. 0181/747-3108, fax 0181/742-1312, tours@journeylatinamerica.com, www.journeylatinamerica.co.uk) offers a 16-day bird-watching tour.

SCUBA DIVING

Costa Rica's diving is for pelagics. If you're looking for coral, you'll be happier in Belize or the Bay Islands of Honduras. Visibility, unfortunately, ranges only 6–24 meters, but water temperatures are a steady 24–29ºC (75–85ºF) or higher.

A wise investment is to join **Divers Alert Network** (The Peter B. Bennett Center, 6 West Colony Place, Durham, NC 27705, tel. 919/684-2948 or 800/446-2671, or 919/684-8111 24-hour emergency line, dan@diversalertnetwork.org, www.diversalertnetwork.org), which provides diving insurance, plus emergency medical evacuation, treatment, and referral services.

National Association of Underwater Instructors (NAUI, PO Box 89789 Tampa, FL 33689-0413, tel. 813/628-6284 or 800/553-6284, fax 813/628-8253, nauihq@nauiww.org, www.naui.org), and the **Professional Association of Diving Instructors** (PADI, 30151 Tomas St., Rancho Santa Margarita, CA 92688-2125, tel. 949/858-7234 or 800/729-7234, fax 949/858-7264, www.padi.com), are handy resources.

The Travelin' Diver's Chapbook (125 E. Sir Francis Drake Blvd., Larkspur, CA 94939, tel. 415/461-5906 or 800/326-1896, editor@undercurrent.org, www.undercurrent.org), offers unbiased resort reviews by divers. Also check out **Scuba Yellow Pages** (www.scubayellowpages.com).

Scuba outfitters are located at the principal beaches; see regional chapters. In San José, **Mundo Aquático** (tel. 506/224-9729, fax 506/234-2982), 25 meters north of Mas X Menos, in San Pedro, rents and sells scuba gear.

The only hyperbaric chamber is at Cuajiniquil, in Guanacaste.

Pacific Coast

Most dive-site development has been along the Pacific coast. You'll see little live coral and few reefs. In their place, divers find an astounding variety and number of fish, soft corals, and invertebrates—a result of the abundant plankton and other marine organisms that thrive in the warm tropical waters. Most diving is around rock formations. Visibility can often be obscured (particularly in rainy season, May–November, where rivers enter the ocean; where rivers are absent, visibility is *enhanced* during this period), but on calm days you may be rewarded with densities of marine life that cannot be found anywhere in the Caribbean.

Favored dive destinations in the Pacific northwest include Islas Murcielagos and the Catalinas. Both locations teem with grouper, snapper, jacks, sharks, and giant mantas, as well as indigenous tropical species. Dozens of morays peer out from beneath rocky ledges. And schools of tang, Cortez angelfish, bright yellow butterflies, hogfish, parrot fish, giant jewfish, turtles, and eagle rays are common. Great bull sharks congregate at a place called "Big Scare." The two island chains are challenging because of their strong currents and surges.

At the Punta Gorda dive site, six km west of Playa Ocotal, thousands of eagle rays have been known to swim by in huge congregations. And divers can drop into select spots where whale sharks bask on the bottom at a depth of 12 meters. Divers also report seeing black marlin cruising gracefully around pinnacle rocks; at Las Corridas, only one kilometer from El Ocotal, you're sure to come face to face with one of the 180-kilogram jewfish that dwell here.

Many hotels have dive shops; see regional chapters.

Bahía Herradura has an area known as El Jardín, famed for its formations of soft coral and sea fans.

Farther south, Caño Island, just off the Osa Peninsula, has a reef that hosts a large variety of tropical fish, as well as groupers, snappers, wahoo, roosterfish, jacks, and tuna. About two km out from Caño is a near-vertical wall and parades of pelagic fish, including manta rays. The island is serviced by dive boats out of Drake Bay and Golfito. Charters can also be arranged out of Quepos.

Cocos Island is the Mt. Everest of dive experiences in Costa Rica. Its reputation for big animal encounters—whale sharks, hammerheads (sometimes schooling 500 at a time), and mantas—have made it renowned. Cocos is 550 km southwest of Costa Rica, necessitating a long sea journey. Several live-aboard dive vessels operate to Cocos.

Caribbean Coast

The Caribbean coast has yet to develop a serious infrastructure catering to sport divers. At Isla Uvita, just offshore from Limón, are tropical fish, sea fans, and a coral reef, plus the wreck of the *Fenix,* a cargo ship that sank about a mile off the island years ago.

Farther south, at Cahuita, is Costa Rica's most beautiful-but much damaged-coral reef, extending 500 meters out from Cahuita Point. The fan-shaped reef covers 593 hectares and has 35 species of coral, including the giant elkhorn. Two old shipwrecks—replete with cannons—lie on the Cahuita reef, seven meters down, playgrounds for more than 500 species of fish.

The Gandoca-Manzanillo Wildlife Refuge protects a southern extension of the Cahuita reef, and one in better condition! If undersea caverns are your thing, check out Puerto Viejo, 20 km south of Cahuita. Best time for diving is during the dry season (February–April), when visibility is at its best. Check with park rangers for conditions, as the area is known for dangerous tides.

FISHING

Fishing expert Jerry Ruhlow (tel. 800/308-3394, info@costaricaoutdoors.com, www.costaricaoutdoors.com) has a column on fishing in the weekly *Tico Times* and also publishes *Costa Rica Outdoors,* a bimonthly dedicated to fishing and outdoor sports.

Carlos Barrantes, the "father of Costa Rican fishing" has a tackle shop, **La Casa del Pescador** (Calle 2, Avenidas 16/18, San José, tel. 506/222-1470).

The **Costa Rican Amateur Fishing Club** (tel. 506/643-3226, clubamateurpesca@racsa.co.cr) is a good resource.

In North America, **Rod & Reel Adventures** (32617 Skyhawk Way

Eugene, OR 97405, tel. 800/356-6982, info @rodreeladventures.com, www.rodreeladventures .com); **Fishing International** (1825 Fourth St., Santa Rosa, CA 95404, tel. 707/542-4242 or 800/950-4242, fax 707/526-3474, eail: fishint @fishinginternational.com, www.fishing international.co); and **Sportfishing Worldwide** (9403 Kenwood Rd., Suite C110, Cincinnati, OH 45242-9921, tel. 513/984-8611 or 800/ 638-7405, fax 513/891-0013, scott@sportfishing worldwide.com, www.sportfishingworldwide .com) offer fishing packages to Costa Rica.

Deep-Sea Fishing

When your fishing-loving friend tells you all about the big one that got away in Costa Rica, don't believe it. Yes, the fish come big in Costa Rica. But *hooking* trophy contenders comes easy; the fish almost seem to line up to get a bite on the hook. The country is the undisputed sailfish capital of the world on the Pacific, the tarpon capital on the Caribbean. Fishing varies from season to season, but hardly a month goes by without some International Game Fish Association record broken.

Boat charters run around $250–400 a half day, and $350–650 for a full day for up to four people, with lunch and beverage included.

No place in the world has posted more "super grand slams"—all three species of marlin and one or more sailfish on the same day—than the Pacific coastal waters of Costa Rica, where it's not unusual to raise 25 or more sailfish in a single day. And in early 1991, an angler out of Guanamar caught the first Pacific blue marlin taken on a fly (at 92 kg, it's also the largest fish ever caught on a fly).

The hard-fighting blue marlin swims in these waters year-round, although this "bull of the ocean" is most abundant in June and July, when large schools of tuna also come close to shore. June–October is best for dorado (another year-round fish). Then, too, yellowfin tuna weighing up to 90 kg offer a rod-bending challenge. Wahoo are also prominent, though less dependable. Generally, summer months are the best in the north; the winter months are best in the south.

Boats out of Puntarenas and resorts near the tip of the Nicoya Peninsula can fish areas protected from the winds year-round. Flamingo and Tamarindo are the two most prominent fishing centers in the northern Pacific. However, northern Guanacaste is largely unfishable Dec.–March because of heavy winds (boat operators at Flamingo and Tamarindo move boats south to Los Sueños and Quepos during the windy season, when the Central Pacific posts its best scores). Quepos is a year-round sportfishing center. The coastal configuration protects these waters from the winds that batter Guanacaste. Many operators offer multi-day trips from Quepos to the waters off Drake Bay and Caño Island, with overnights at one of the local wilderness camps or nature lodges. Golfito is the base for another popular fishing paradise, the Golfo Dulce, with calm seas and light winds the rule.

Inland and Coastal Fishing

Part of the beauty of fishing Costa Rica, says one fisherman, is that "you can fish the Caribbean at dawn, try the Pacific in the afternoon, and still have time to watch a sunset from a mountain stream." Forget the sunset—there are fish in those mountains. A freshwater fishing license is mandatory; the limit is a maximum of five specimens (of any one species) per angler per day. The closed season runs September through December.

Lodges and outfitters provide the permit (license, not fish).

More than a dozen inland rivers provide lots of action on rainbow trout, *machaca* (Central America's answer to American shad), drum, *guapote, mojarra* (Costa Rica's bluegill with teeth), *bobo* (a moss-eating mullet), and other freshwater and tidal species. A good bet is the Río Savegre and other streams around San Gerardo de Dota, Copey and Cañon.

Caño Negro Lagoon and the waters of the Río San Juan present fabulous potential for snook and tarpon. Lake Arenal is famed for its feisty rainbow bass *(guapote)* running 3.5 kg or more (Lake Arenal also boasts the world record for *guapote,* at 5.2 kg).

Costa Rica's northeastern shores, lowland lagoons, and rivers offer the world's hottest tarpon and snook action for the light-tackle enthusiast. At prime fishing spots, tarpon average 35 kg (sometimes reaching up to 70 kg). These silver rockets are caught in the jungle rivers and backwater lagoons, and ocean tarpon fishing just past the breakers is always dependable. Wherever you find them, you'll have your hands full; no other fish jumps, leaps, twists, and turns like the tarpon. When you tire of wrestling these snappy fighters, you can take on snook—another worthy opponent.

Fall, when the rain tapers down and winds swing onshore, flattening the rivermouths, is the best time to get a shot at the trophy snook that return to the beaches around the rivermouths to spawn. Anglers stand knee-deep in the surf and cast at five-to nine-kilogram snook. Snook will hit lures trolled or cast along the riverbanks, but the biggest fish are usually taken from the surf. The all-tackle IGFA record came from Costa Rica, which regularly delivers 14-kilogram fish.

Tarpon are caught year-round. Snook season runs from late August into January, with a peak Aug.–Nov. November through January the area enjoys a run of *calba,* the local name for small snook that average two kilograms and are exceptional sport on light tackle, with 20 or more *calba* per angler in a typical day's catch. Jacks are also common year-round in Caribbean waters. They are voracious predators, and because they are extremely strong and have great endurance, they can be a challenge for any fisher using light tackle.

KAYAKING

Sea kayaking is quickly catching on in Costa Rica, and no wonder. The sea kayak's ability to move silently means you can travel unobtrusively, sneaking close up to wildlife without freaking it out. Dolphins and even turtles have been known to surface alongside to check kayakers out. The long, slender one-and two-man craft provided are remarkably stable and ideally suited for investigating narrow coastal inlets and flatwater rivers larger vessels cannot reach.

Ríos Tropicales (tel. 506/233-6455, fax 506/255-4354, info@riostropicales.com, www.riostropicales.com) and **Serendipity Adventures** (tel. 734/995-0111 or 877/507-1358, fax 734/426-5026, info@serendipityadventures.com, www.serendipityadventures.com) offer kayaking trips.

In North America, **Mariah Wilderness Expeditions** (P.O. Box 70248, Pt. Richmond, CA 94807, tel. 510/233-2303 or 800/462-7424, fax 51-/233-0956, rafting@mariahwe.com, www.mariahwe.com) features sea kayaking as part of a multi-activity trip. **Gulf Islands Kayaking** (S-24, C-34, Galiano Island, BC, Canada V0N 1PO, tel./fax 250/539-2442, info@seakayaking.com, www.seakayak.ca) also has one-week guided kayaking trips.

Anyone planning on kayaking rivers should refer to *The Rivers of Costa Rica: A Canoeing,*

Kayaking, and Rafting Guide by Michael W. Mayfield and Rafael E. Gallo, which provides detailed maps plus a technical description of the entire river system.

In San José, you can rent kayaks, canoes, and camping equipment from **Mundo Aventura** (tel. 506/221-6934, www.maventura.com, 9:30 A.M.–7 P.M. Mon.–Fri., 9:30 A.M.–5 P.M. Saturday).

Costa Sol Rafting (P.O. Box 84390-1000, San José, tel. 293-2150, fax 293-2155, rafting@sol.racsa.co.cr, www.costasol.co.cr and www.costasolrafting.com) has a one-day kayaking school ($100).

Ríos Tropicales (tel. 506/233-6455, fax 506/255-4354, info@riostropicales.com, www.riostropicales.com) offers kayaking trips. **Costa Rica Expeditions** (P.O. Box 6941-1000, San José, tel. 506/257-0766, fax 506/257-1665, costaric@expeditions.co.cr, www.costaricaexpeditions.com) rents kayaks and canoes, plus offers guided programs.

Also *La Virgen de Sarapiquí in the Northern Lowlands chapter.*

In North America, **Canoe Costa Rica** (PMB 567 -3108 Nealwood Ave., Orlando, FL 32806, tel./fax 732/350-3963, canoecr@aol.com, www.canoecostarica.com) and **American Wilderness Experience** (P.O. Box 1486, Boulder, CO 80306, tel. 303/444-2622 or 800/444-0099, fax 303/444-3999, awedave@aol.com, www.awetrips.com) offer canoeing trips, as does **Battenkill Canoe** (6328 Historic Rt. 7A, Arlington, VT 05250, tel. 802/362-2800 or 800/421-5268, fax 802/362-0159, www.battenkill.com).

WHITE-WATER RAFTING

White-water rafting is the ultimate combination of beauty and thrill—an ideal way to savor Costa Rica's natural splendor, diverse ecosystems, and exotic wildlife.

Because the land is so steep, streams pass through hugely varied landscapes within relatively short distances. At high elevations, Costa Rican rivers closely resemble those of California. Farther downstream, the water is warmer and rainforest lines the riverbanks. You'll tumble through a tropical *Fantasia* of feathery bamboo, ferns, and palms, a roller-coaster ride amid glistening jungle. Everything is as silent as a graveyard, except for the chattering monkeys and birds.

Costa Rica regulates its tourist industry, so white-water outfitters are held to strict standards. Rafters are required to wear helmets and life jackets, which are provided by tour operators. Generally, all you need to bring is a swimsuit, a T-shirt, and tennis shoes or sneakers. Sunscreen is a good idea, as you are not only in the open all day, but also exposed to reflections off the water. You'll also need an extra set of clothing, and perhaps a sweater or jacket, as you can easily get chilled if a breeze kicks up when you're wet. And you *will* get wet. Most operators provide a special waterproof bag for cameras. One-day trips start at about $70.

When and Where

Generally, May–June and Sep.–Oct. are the best times for high water. Rivers are rated from class I to VI in degree of difficulty, with V considered for true experts only. The only class V river in the country is the Guayabo section of the Reventazón. Rafting experience is required for this trip; all other trips are generally offered to beginners and intermediates. The following are the most popular runs.

The majestic **Río Chirripó** (class III-IV) runs down the slopes of the southwest Pacific and is recommended for two-to four-day trips. The river, which tumbles from its source on Mt. Chirripó, has been compared to California's Tuolomne and Idaho's Middle Fork of the Salmon, with massive volumes of water and giant waves. It produces more than 100 class III and IV rapids in its first 65 kilometers. The river runs into the Río General. Trips are offered August–December.

The **Río Corobicí** (class II) provides more of a float trip and makes an ideal half-day trip for families, with superb wildlife viewing and calms the whole way. The river flows westward through Guanacaste into the Gulf of Nicoya. It is runnable year-round.

The high-volume **Río General** is famous for its large, challenging rapids and big waves ideal for surfing. Its "outlandish scenery" includes narrow, dramatic gorges and waterfalls. Complex rapids follow in quick succession.

Río Naranjo, in the mountains above Manuel Antonio, on the central Pacific coast, is a corker in high water, with swirling class V action. However, it's inconsistent, with dramatic changes in water level. The upper section runs through rainforest; lower down, it slows as it passes through ranch land before winding through Manuel Antonio National Park and exiting into the Pacific.

For an in-depth immersion in nature, the **Río Pacuare** (class III-IV) is the best choice as it slices through virgin rainforest, plunging through mountain gorges to spill onto the Caribbean plains near Siquirres. Toucans, monkeys, and other animals galore make this journey unforgettable. Overhead loom cliffs from which waterfalls drop right into the river. Black tongues of lava stick out into the river, creating large, technically demanding rapids and making great lunch beaches. And steep drops produce big waves. Though run year-round, the best months are June and October.

White-water rafting enthusiasts will get more than their money's worth of excitement on the **Río Reventazón** (class II-V). The river tumbles out of Lake Angostura and cascades to the Caribbean lowlands in an exciting series of rapids. Stretches of tranquil waters provide the perfect combination of soothing calm and adventure. Beginners can savor class II and III rapids on the "mid-section," the most popular run for one-day trips. The Guayabo section offers class V runs. Constant rainfall allows operators to offer trips year-round; June and July are the best months.

The **Río Sarapiquí** (class III) runs along the eastern flank of the Cordillera Central and drops to the Caribbean lowlands. It is noted for its crystal-clear water, variable terrain, and exciting rapids. Trips are offered May–December.

Tour Companies

In Costa Rica, I recommend **Costa Rica**

Expeditions (P.O. Box 6941-1000, San José, tel. 506/257-0766, fax 506/257-1665, costaric @expeditions.co.cr, www.costaricaexpeditions .com), which offers one-day and multi-day trips on most major rivers. The other preeminent operator is **Ríos Tropicales** (tel. 506/233-6455, fax 506/255-4354, info@riostropicales.com, www.riostropicales.com), which runs the Corobicí, Sarapiquí, Reventazón, General, and Pacuare

Numerous smaller companies offer white-water trips regionally. Also see regional chapters.

In North America, **Mariah Wilderness Expeditions** (P.O. Box 70248, Pt. Richmond, CA 94807, tel. 510/233-2303 or 800/462-7424, fax 51-/233-0956, rafting@mariahwe.com, www .mariahwe.com) offers a nine-day "Tropical Jungle Rafting" trip including four rivers; and rafting is included on an eight-day multi-activity program. **Mountain Travel-Sobek** (1266 66th St., Emeryville, CA 94608, tel. 510/594-6000 or 888/687-6235, fax 510/594-6001, info

@mtsobek.com, www.mtsobek.com) has a 10-day whitewater trip.

WINDSURFING

Despite the strong winds that sweep along the coast of the Pacific northwest in summer, ocean windsurfing in Costa Rica has yet to take off. Bahía Salinas, in the extreme northwest, is recommended and has two windsurfing centers. Inland, Lake Arenal is paradise, with 23–35 kph easterly winds funneling through a mountain corridor year-round. Strong winds rarely cease during the dry season (December–April). The lake has acquired an international reputation as one of the best all-year freshwater windsurfing spots in the world, with two dedicated windsurfing centers. If you rent equipment at Arenal, try negotiating to use the same equipment at the coast, where equipment is in short supply.

Windsport Travel (115 Danforth Ave., Suite 302, Toronto, ON, Canada, tel. 416/520-0688

natural history cruise ship *Pacific Explorer*, Manuel Antonio National Park

© CHRISTOPHER P. BAKER

or 800/640-9530, windsurf@windsport-travel
.com, www.windsport-travel.com) offers windsurfing packages to Costa Rica.

CRUISES/YACHTING

Half-and full-day excursions and sunset cruises
are offered from dozens of beaches along the Pacific
coast. By far the most popular trip is that to Isla
Tortuga, in the Gulf of Nicoya. Several companies
offer daylong excursions from Puntarenas and Los
Sueños, near Jacó (the cruises are also offered as excursions from San José). Larger cruise ships offer
four-day and week-long nature itineraries. See
Natural History Cruise Tours, in this section.

HIKING

Half-day or full-day hiking tours with a professional guide can be arranged through nature
lodges or local tour operators.

Most reserves and national parks maintain
marked trails. The hardy and adventurous might
try a strenuous hike to the peak of Chirripó,
Costa Rica's tallest mountain. Hiking in the more
remote parks may require stamina, a high degree of self-sufficiency, and, says one writer, "a
guide so comfortable with a machete he can pick
your teeth with it." If you plan on hiking in the
Talamancas or other high mountain areas, you're
advised to obtain topographical maps from the
Instituto de Geográfica (*Maps,* in the *Other Practicalities* section, this chapter).

A map, sunscreen, sun hat, insect repellent,
and plenty of water are recommended. Raingear
and a warm sweater or jacket are essential for
hiking at higher elevations.

In Costa Rica, **Coast to Coast Adventures**
(tel./fax 506/280-8054, fax 506/225-6055,
info@ctocadventures.com, www.ctocadventures
.com) specializes in hiking trips.

In North America, **Backroads** (801 Cedar St.,
Berkeley, CA 94710-1800, tel. 510/527-1555 or
800/462-2848, fax 510/527-1444, goactive
@backroads.com, www.backroads.com); **Mountain Travel-Sobek** (1266 66th St., Emeryville,
CA 94608, tel. 510/594-6000 or 888/687-6235,

REDUCING YOUR ENVIRONMENTAL IMPACT

If you're camping, here are some ways to keep
your impact on the environment to a minimum.
• Pick it up, pack it out. In addition, of course,
  to packing out any detritus you've packed in,
  try to leave a convenient pack pocket available
  for carrying out whatever litter you find along
  the trail.
• Give yourself enough time at the end of the
  day to find a camping site that will notice your
  presence the least.
• Bone up on the types of wildlife you're likely to
  meet. The more you know, the better you can
  observe without disrupting them.
• To lessen your visibility, use gear and wear
  clothing that blend in with the landscape.

---

fax 510/594-6001, info@mtsobek.com, www
.mtsobek.com); **Tourtech** (3100 Airway Ave,
Suite 131, Costa Mesa, CA 92626, tel. 714/436-
6561, fax 714/435-4069, info@tourtech.net,
www.tourtech.net); and **Wildland Adventures**
(3516 N.E. 155th St., Seattle, WA 98155, tel.
206/365-0686 or 800/345-4453, fax 206/363-
6615, info@wildad.com, www.wildland.com)
all offer hiking programs in Costa Rica.

For the truly hardy, **Outward Bound** (P.O.
Box 1817-2050 San Pedro, tel. 506/278-6059,
fax 506/676-0486, enrollment@crrobs.org,
www.crrobs.org), the organization that takes
folks into the outdoors to toughen them up and
build self-confidence, offers courses, not "trips,"
that include a hike up Chirripó and have been described by participants as having "fistfuls of experience mashed in your face."

HORSEBACK RIDING

Horseback riding is very popular in Costa Rica,
where the *campesino* culture depends on the horse
for mobility. Wherever you are, horses are sure to
be available for rent. (The native horse of Costa
Rica is the *crillo,* a small, big-chested creature of
good temperament.)

© CHRISTOPHER P. BAKER

riding at Hacienda Los Inocentes

In Santa Ana (about nine km west of San José), **Club Hípico la Caraña** (tel. 506/282-6106, fax 506/282-6754) provide instruction in riding.

Scores of ranches nationwide offer trail rides, notably in Guanacaste, where city slickers longing to be the Marlboro Man can pay perfectly good money to work hard and get coated with dust and manure alongside workaday cowboys. The chorus of mooing and slapping of Levis against leather saddles combines with a rest on the beach as you drive cattle to where the grass is greener to get them ready for the American supermarkets.

In Costa Rica, **Horseback Ride Costa Rica** (P.O. Box 729-1260 Escazú, tel. 506/232-3113, fax 506/220-3797, www.horsebackridecostarica.com) offers eight-day programs.

In North America, **Equitour** (10 Stalnaker St., Dubois, WY 82513, tel. 307/455-3363 or 800/545-0019, fax 307/455-2354, equitour@wyoming.com, www.ridingtours.com) has eight-to 11-day riding adventures in Costa Rica.

In England, **Equitour** (The Bell Hotel, Church St., Charlbury, Oxford OX7 3PP, tel. 0993/849489, llequitour@aol.com) offers horse-riding tours in Costa Rica.

BICYCLING

The occasional sweat and effort make Costa Rica's spectacular landscapes and abiding serenity all the more rewarding from a bicycle saddle. Sure, you'll work for your reward. But you'd never get so close to so much beauty in a car. Away from the main highways, roads are little traveled. However, there are no bike lanes. Potholes are a persistent problem. And traffic can be hazardous on the steep and windy mountain roads. A helmet is a wise investment.

Costa Ricans are fond of cycling, and bicycle racing is a major Costa Rican sport, culminating each December in the 12-day **Vuelta a Costa Rica,** which crisscrosses the mountain chain from sea level to over 3,000 meters. Mountain-bike racing has become very popular, culminating in the **Trofeo Estrella,** the year's biggest race.

Airlines generally allow bicycles to be checked free (properly packaged) with one piece of luggage. Otherwise a small charge may apply. Leave your touring bike at home: bring a mountain bike or rent one once you arrive.

Most group tours are suitable for all levels of competence, but check in advance about the kind of terrain and mileage involved. It helps to ride a bicycle regularly before such a tour. Even so, the pace is as leisurely or demanding as you wish to make it. You'll feel no pressure to conform to anyone else's pace. A support van ("sag wagon") follows in the group's wake to drop off and pick up those wishing to cycle only a part of each day's journey, or those short of breath or energy. And qualified bilingual guides cycle with you to cure any mechanical, physical, or psychological breakdowns. Many hotels and local tour operators also rent mountain bikes.

The following Costa Rican Tour companies offer bicycling tours: **Aventuras Naturales** (tel. 506/225-3939 or 800/514-0411, avenat@racsa .co.cr, www.adventurecostarica.com); **Coast to Coast Adventures**(tel./fax 506/280-8054, fax 506/225-6055, info@ctocadventures.com, www .ctocadventures.com); **Costa Rica Biking Adventure** (P.O. Box 2743-1000 San José, tel. 506/225-6591, info@bikingcostarica.com, www .bikingcostarica.com); and **Ríos Tropicales** (tel. 506/233-6455, fax 506/255-4354, info @riostropicales.com, www.riostropicales.com).

In North America, **Backroads** (801 Cedar St., Berkeley, CA 94710-1800, tel. 510/527-1555 or 800//462-2848, fax 510/527-1444, goactive@backroads.com, www.backroads.com) runs seven-and eight-day mountain-biking tours. **Mariah Wilderness Expeditions** (P.O. Box 70248, Pt. Richmond, CA 94807, tel. 510/233-2303 or 800/462-7424, fax 51-/233-0956, rafting@mariahwe.com, www.mariahwe.com) and **Experience Plus!** (415 Mason Ct. #1, Fort Collins, CO 80526, tel. 970/484-8489 or 800/685-4565, tours@experienceplus.com, www .experienceplus.com) also have guided tours.

MOTORCYCLE TOURING

Motorbike enthusiasts haven't been left out of the two-wheel touring business. Two-wheel touring is growing in popularity. In Costa Rica, **Costa Rica Motorcycle Tours** (P.O. Box 2907-1000 San José, tel. 506/225-6000, fax 506/257-8842, www.crtrails.co.cr; in the U.S., tel. 888/803-3344), offers six-to 12-day tours using BMW F650 Fonduros. **Tour's María Alexandra**

(P.O.Box: 3756-1000 San José, tel. 506/289-5552, fax 506/289-5551, info@costaricamotorcycles.com, www.costaricamotorcycles.com) offers one-day to eight-day trips using Harley Davidsons. **Wild Rider Motorcycles** (tel./fax 506/258-4604, wildrider@ritmo-del-caribe.com, www .wildrider.com) offers one-and three-day tours using Suzuki 350s.

In North America, **Pancho Villa Moto-Tours** (4510 Highway 281 North #3, Spring Branch, TX 78070, tel. 830/438-7744 or 800/233-0564, fax 830/438-7745, info@panchovilla.com, www .panchovilla.com) runs eight-day tours in Costa Rica using BMW F650 Funduros, and four-to 11-day "El Vagabundo"tours, a go-as-you-please program. **Motorcycles Costa Rica** (164 Race Track Rd., Rural Retreat, VA 24368, tel.866/846-4660, fax 276/686-4660, info@motoscostarica .com, www.motoscostarica.com) has six-night trips using dual-sport motorcycles, as does **MotoAdventures** (9660 Creawood Forest, Waite Hill, OH 44094, tel. 440/256-8508, fax 440/ 256-8504, dbowers@motoadventuring.com, www.motoadventuring.com).

GOLFING

Before 1995, the country had just two courses: the championship course at **Meliá Cariari and Country Club** outside San José, and the nine-hole **Hotel Tango Mar,** overlooking the Gulf of Nicoya on the Pacific coast. However, the country is in the midst of a course-building binge.

Recently opened courses include a Robert Trent Jones, Jr. stunner at the Paradisus Playa Conchal, at Playa Conchal, in Nicoya; the **Marriott Los Sueños** course at Playa Herradura, in the Central Pacific; **Los Delfines Golf & Country Club,** at Playa Tambor, in Nicoya; and **Parque Valle del Sol,** at Santa Ana, west of San José. The championship Four Seasons course was due to open in 2004 at Bahía Culebra, in Nicoya.

Three other nine-hole courses are at the **Costa Rica Country Club** in Escazú; the **Los Reyes Country Club** in La Guácima, near Alajuela; and the **El Castillo Country Club** above Heredia.

Costa Rican Golf Adventures (tel. 877/258-2618, www.centralamerica.com/cr/golf) and **Golf in Costa Rica** (tel: 506/290-2704 or 838-5357, golf@golfincostarica.com, www.golfin costarica.com) offer golfing adventures in Costa Rica.

HANG-GLIDING AND AERIAL TOURS

Hang-Glide Costa Rica (tel. 506/778-8710, www.handglidecostarica.com) offers glides in tandem with an instructor. You're towed to 2,000 feet and released (from $69).

Air Jungle Beach Safari (tel. 506/240-5106, fax 506/297-0549, www.ecoescapetours.com) offers an afternoon flight from San José over the northern lowlands, including a jungle river cruise, dinner at Selva Verde, plus nighttime rainforest tour.

Ballooning is offered by **Serendipity Adventures** (tel. 734/995-0111 or 877/507-1358, fax 734/426-5026, info@serendipityadventures.com, www.serendipityadventures.com).

Getting There

BY AIR

About 20 international airlines provide regular service to Costa Rica, which at last visit was served by almost 40 flights weekly. Most flights land at the newly remodeled **Juan Santamaría International Airport** at Alajuela (19 km northwest, and 20 minutes by taxi, from San José). The **Daniel Oduber International Airport,** 12 km west of Liberia in Guanacaste, accepts mostly charters serving the beaches of Nicoya. The **Tobías Bolaños Airport,** four miles southwest of San José, is for domestic flights only.

Reservations and Fares

Airline fares are in constant flux. The cheapest scheduled fares have traditionally been APEX (advance-purchase excursion) fares, which you must buy at least 21 days before departure and which limit your visit to 30 days (from U.S.). From Europe, you must stay a minimum of 14 days and return within 180 days. Penalties usually apply for any changes after you buy your ticket. Generally, the further in advance you buy your ticket, the cheaper it will be. However, the geopolitical uncertainties of recent years—and the blossoming of Internet sites—has diluted previously hard-and-fast rules. Buy your return segment before arriving in Costa Rica, as tickets bought in the country are heavily taxed.

To get the cheapest fares, make your reservations as early as possible (several months is ideal), especially during peak season, as flights often sell out. Central American carriers are usually slightly cheaper than their American counterparts but often stop over at more cities en route. Low-season and midweek travel is often cheaper, as are stays of more than 30 days. Travel during Christmas, New Year, and Easter usually costs more. You can check fares online through **Expedia** (www.expedia.com), *Orbitz* (www.orbitz.com), **Priceline** (www.priceline.com), **Travelocity** (www.travelocity.com), or similar websites. Compare quotations at different sites, as they vary, even for the same flight.

Compare any restrictions on tickets, and check to see what penalties may apply for changes to your ticket. "Open-jaw" tickets permit you to arrive in one city and depart from another; however, they cost considerably more.

Surf the Internet and check with various airlines and charter and tour operators listed below to compare rates. Alternately, use a travel agent. Most travel agents do *not* charge a fee, but derive their income from commissions included in the airlines' fares. It's the agent's responsibility to chase down refunds in the event of overbooking or cancellations (be sure to compare any travel agent's quoted rates with those of specialists in discount tickets).

International specialists in low fares include **STA Travel** (tel. 800/781-4040, go@statravel .com, www.statravel.com), or **Council Travel** (tel. 888/268-6245, globotron@counciltravel .com, www.counciltravelcom), which have offices worldwide.

Always reconfirm your reservation within 72 hours of your departure (reservations are frequently canceled if not reconfirmed, especially during December–January holidays).

From the United States

U.S. flights are either direct or have stopovers in Mexico, Nicaragua, Guatemala, Honduras, and/or El Salvador. **American Airlines** (tel. 800/433-7300, www.aa.com) flies direct to San José daily from Miami and Dallas. **America West Airlines** (tel. 800/235-9292, www.americawest .com) flies daily nonstop between Phoenix and Costa Rica. **Continental** (tel. 800/231-0856, www.continental.com) flies direct to San José daily from Houston and Newark. **Delta** (tel. 800/221-1212, www.delta.com) flies direct to San José daily from Atlanta, and once weekly to Liberia from Atlanta. **Mexicana** (tel. 800/502-2000, www.mexicana.com.mx) flies to San José daily from Los Angeles via Mexico City. **United Airlines** (tel. 800/241-6522, www.united.com) serves San José daily from Chicago and Los Angeles.

TACA (tel. 800/535-8780, www.grupotaca .com) offers daily flights from Los Angeles, Miami, New York, Orlando, and San Francisco, and five flights weekly from New Orleans. TACA, based in El Salvador, was formed by the amalgamation of Costa Rica's national airline, LACSA, and three other Central American carriers. Some flights are nonstop; others make the "milk run" through Central America. Service is aboard Airbus Industries wide-body A310s (240 passengers) and narrow-body A320s (168 passengers). On-board service is usually up to par with U.S. carriers.

In the past, TACA's website has displayed sample round-trip fares in high season as low as $391 from Los Angeles, $260 from Miami, and $418 from New York.

Honduras's **Sol Air** (tel. 786/621-3161 or 866/476-5247) planned to initiate direct service from New Orleans to Costa Rica at press time.

Charters are usually priced for stays of one or two weeks; longer stays usually cost considerably more. Nor are "open-jaw" tickets usually permitted. Charters have an added disadvantage of often leaving at ungodly hours. Departure dates cannot be changed, and heavy cancellation penalties usually apply. Remember to calculate the cost of any savings for accommodations, airport transfers, meals, and other services that may be included in the cost of an air-hotel package.

Apple Vacations (tel. 800/727-3400 East Coast, 800/363-2775 West Coast, www.apple-vacations.com) has weekly charter service to Daniel Oduber Airport in Liberia from Philadelphia and Newark, high season only. **Funjet Vacations** (tel. 800/558-3050, www.funjet.com) offers charter packages.

Martinair (tel. 800/MARTINAIR, www .martinairusa.com) flies from Orlando or Miami four times weekly in high season.

Tico Travel (tel. 800/493-8426, www.ticotravel .com) offers cheap airfares to Costa Rica. **Airfares for Less** (tel. 800/627-8468, www.airfares-for-less.com) is a discount broker. **NOW Voyager** (315 W. 49th St., New York, NY 10019, tel. 212/459-1616, www.nowvoyagertravel.com) specializes in last-minute discount fares.

From Canada

TACA (tel. 888/261-3269, www.taca.com) flies between Toronto and Costa Rica three times weekly. **Air Canada** (tel. 800/869-9000, www .aircanada.com) also flies three times weekly from Toronto via Havana.

Charters may need to be booked through a travel agent. **Signature Vacations** (tel. 416/967-1112 or 866/324-2883, www.signature.ca) flies to San José from Toronto every Thursday (November through late December) and Monday (late December through March) using **Skyservice** (www.skyserviceairlines.com) and **Air Transat** (tel. 514/636-3630 or 800/872-6728, www

.airtransat.com); and to Liberia from Toronto every Thursday using Skyservice. Signature offers flights in conjunction with seven-night (from CAN$1,379) and 14-night packages (from CAN$1,929).

Canadian Universities Travel Service (Travel Cuts, tel. 416/614-2887 or 800-/667-2887 in Toronto, tel. 604/717-7800 in Vancouver, www.travelcuts.com), which has 25 offices throughout Canada, sells discount airfares.

From Latin America and the Caribbean

Mexicana (tel. 800/849-1529, www.mexicana.com.mx; in the U.S.A., tel. 800/531-9321) flies between Mexico City and San José daily, and Guatemala City and San José twice weekly. **TACA** serves Costa Rica from all the Central American nations.

TACA flies between Costa Rica and Argentina, Brazil, Chile, Ecuador, Peru, and Venezuela. Aviateca flies from Colombia; Ladeco links Costa Rica and Chile. And American Airlines, Continental, and United Airlines flights all connect Costa Rica with destinations throughout South America. There are few bargains. If originating in the U.S., it pays to make reservations ahead (airline tickets are heavily taxed and subject to greater restrictions in South America; there are few APEX fares).

There are few flights between Costa Rica and its Caribbean neighbors, except for Cuba. **Cubana** (tel. 06/4877-1330 cubana.aviacion @flashnet.it), TACA, and Air Canada all offer regular scheduled service between San José and Havana.

From the United Kingdom

Costa Rica is served by **British Airways** (tel. 020/8897-4000, www.british-airways.co.uk) from London. American Airlines, British Airways, Continental, United Airlines, USAirways and Virgin Atlantic fly from London to Miami (or New York), where you can connect with an airline serving Costa Rica. **Go,** British Airways' budget wing, has cheap connecting service to other European destinations, as does **Virgin Ex-**

press (tel. 020/7744- 0004), which connects with Madrid, where you can catch flights to Costa Rica. Also consider flying via Havana, which permits a stop-over Cuba.

Typical APEX fares between London and Costa Rica begin at about £600 via the U.S. for stays of less than 30 days. However, you can buy reduced rate fares on scheduled carriers from "bucket shops" (discount ticket agencies), which advertise in leading magazines and Sunday newspapers. One of the most reputable is **Trailfinders** (215 Kensington High St, London W8 7RG, tel. 020/7937-5400, www.trailfinders.co.uk). **STA Travel** (86 Old Brompton Rd., London SW7, tel. 020/7361-6262, www.statravelco.uk) specializes in student fares. STA also has offices throughout the UK. Alternately, try **Council Travel** (28A Poland St., London W1V 3DB, tel. 020/7437-7767).

Another respected operator is **Journey Latin America** (12 Heathfield Terr., London W4 4JE, tel. 020/8747-3108, fax 020/8742-1312, flights @journeylatinamerica.co.uk, www.journeylatinamerica.co.uk), which specializes in cheap fares and tour packages.

Good online resources for discount tickets include www.ebookers.com, www.cheapflights.co.uk, and www.bridgetheworld.com; and for charter flights, **Charter Flight Centre** (www.charterflights.co.uk) and **Dial a Flight** (www.dialaflight.co.uk).

From Continental Europe

From **Germany,** charter carrier **Condor** (tel. 06107/939810, www.condor.com) flies direct from Dusseldorf and Munich in high season. From **the Netherlands,** Costa Rica is served by **Martinair** (tel. 20/60-11-767, fax 20/60-11-303, www.martinair.com) from Amsterdam via Miami (three times weekly) and Orlando. From **Russia, Aeroflot** (tel. 095/753-5555 in Moscow, tel. 812/118-5555 in St. Petersburg, www.aeroflot.ru) flies between Moscow and San José four days weekly via Miami. From **Spain,** Costa Rica is served by **Iberia** (tel. 01/587-8785, www.iberia.com) from Madrid via Puerto Rico or the Dominican Republic.

From Australia and New Zealand

The best bet is to fly to Los Angeles then to Costa Rica. **Air New Zealand** (in Sydney, tel. 02/9223-4666; in Auckland, tel. 09/366-2400), **Delta Airlines** (in Sydney, tel. 02/9262-1777; in Auckland, tel. 09/379-3370), **Qantas** (in Sydney, tel. 02/9957-0111; in Auckland, tel. 09/357-8900), and **United Airlines** (in Sydney, tel. 02/9237-8888; in Auckland, tel. 09/307-9500) offer direct service between Australia, New Zealand, and California. Roundtrip fares from Sydney at press time ranged from A$2,545 to A$2,750. A route via Buenos Aires or Santiago de Chile and then to Costa Rica is also possible.

Specialists in discount fares include **STA Travel** (in Sydney, tel. 02/9212-1255 or 1-800-637444, www.statravel.co.au; in Auckland, tel. 09/309-9723, www.statravel.co.nz), which has regional offices throughout Australia and New Zealand.

Another good online resource for discount airfares is www.flightcentre.com.au.

From Asia

JAL (Japanese Air Lines, tel. 3/100-0006, www.jal.co.jp) offers a weekly charter flight between Tokyo and Havana, from where you can connect to Costa Rica. Otherwise you can take JAL to Paris and connect from there. Otherwise, Asian travelers fly via Europe or the United States. Flying nonstop to Los Angeles is perhaps the easiest route. Alternately, fly United or Malaysia Airlines to Mexico City (20 hours). A roundtrip economy ticket is about HK$16,000, depending on the agent. Hong Kong is a good source for discount plane tickets. From Macau, you can fly with **Iberia** (see *From Spain,* above) nonstop to Madrid and then on to Costa Rica.

STA Travel is a good resource for tickets and has branches in Hong Kong, Tokyo, Singapore, Bangkok, and Kuala Lumpur.

BY LAND

By Bus

The overland route from North America is an attractive alternative for travelers for whom time is no object. Allow at least three weeks (the journey is well over 3,500 km from the U.S.). Obtain all necessary visas and documentation in advance.

Central America is well served by bus. However, buses are often crowded, and you may end up standing for parts of your journey. Rest stops are infrequent. You can travel from San Diego or Texas to Costa Rica by bus for as little as $100 (with hotels and food, however, the cost can add up to more than flying direct). Where possible, book as far ahead as you can—the buses often sell out well in advance.

Watch your baggage; consider keeping it with you on the bus. Passports are often collected by the driver to present en masse to immigration. You will need to provide a passport and visas when buying your ticket.

Buses serve Mexico City from the U.S. border points at Mexicali, Ciudad Juárez, and Laredo. See the sidebar *Crossing into Nicaragua and Panamá* for details on buses between San José and Central American neighbors.

Green Tortoise (494 Broadway, San Francisco, CA 94133, tel. 415/956-7500 or 800/867-8647, fax 415/956-4900, tortoise@greentortoise.com, www.greentortoise.com) is an institution among hardy budget travelers seeking cheap passage down the Central American isthmus. However, it no longer offers regular bus service, having evolved into more of a budget tour operator. It has a 28-day San Francisco–to–Cancún trip, and a 21-day trip from Cancún to Costa Rica. You sleep on bunk beds aboard the bus.

By Car

Many people drive to Costa Rica from the U.S. via Mexico, Guatemala, Honduras, and Nicaragua. It's a long haul, but you can follow the Pan-American Highway all the way from the U.S. to San José. It's 3,700 km minimum, depending on your starting point. Experienced travelers recommend skirting El Salvador and the Guatemalan highlands in favor of the coast road. Allow three weeks at a leisurely pace. Make sure that your vehicle is in tip-top mechanical condition.

You should plan your itinerary to be at each day's destination before nightfall (80 percent of insurance claims are a result of nighttime accidents). Be wary of theft. Always lock your car when parked. Do not leave *any* items in view in the car. Fancy mirrors and other shiny embellishments are likely to be ripped off (take off the license plates and display them *inside* your car).

The American Automobile Association (AAA) publishes a **road map** of Mexico and Central America that's free to AAA members. Also consider the *Traveller's Reference Map of Central America* published by International Travel Map Productions.

You'll need a passport, visas, driver's license, and vehicle registration. It's also advisable to obtain tourist cards (good for 90 days) from the consulate of each country before departing. A U.S. driver's license is good throughout Central America, although an International Driving Permit—issued through AAA—can be handy, too. You'll need to arrange a transit visa for Mexico in advance, plus car entry permits for each country (cars freely pass across international borders without paying customs duty; duty becomes payable, however, if your car is stolen). AAA can provide advice on *carnets* (international travel permits), as well as good area maps. Also check with each country's consulate for latest information.

A separate vehicle liability **insurance policy** is required for each country. Most U.S. firms will not underwrite insurance south of the border. (Insurance sold by AAA covers Mexico only, not Central America.) **Sanborn's** (tel. 800/222-0158, info@sanbornsinsurance. com, www.sanborns insurance.com) specializes in insurance coverage for travel in Mexico and Central America. It publishes a booklet, *Overland Travel,* full of practical information, plus regional guides.

Upon arrival in Costa Rica, foreign drivers must buy insurance stamps for a minimum of three months (approximately $15). There's also a $10 road tax (good for three months) payable upon arrival in Costa Rica. Vehicle permits are issued at the border for stays up to 30 days. You can extend this to six months at the Instituto Costarricense de Turismo (travel agencies in San José can help with paperwork). Don't plan on selling your newer-model car in Costa Rica—you'll be hit with huge import duties.

BY SEA

Costa Rica appears on the itineraries of several cruise ships. However, stops are usually no more than one day, so don't expect more than a cursory glimpse of the country, with excursion tours to popular tourist sites within a day's round-trip drive of the port.

Cruises from Florida usually stop off at various Caribbean islands and/or Cozumel before calling in at Puerto Limón. Cruises from San Diego or Los Angeles normally stop off in Puerto Caldera. Many itineraries include the Panamá Canal and the San Blas Islands.

Contact the **Cruise Line International Association** (CLIA, 500 Fifth Ave. No 1407, New York, NY 10110, tel. 212/921-0066, fax 212/921-0549, info@cruising.org, www.cruising.org) for a complete list of companies that include Costa Rica on their itineraries.

Also see *Natural History Cruise Touring,* in the *Getting Around* section, this chapter.

Freight Ships

At least two freighters that operate regular schedules between North America and Costa Rica take paying passengers. **Freighter World Cruises** (180 South Lake Ave. #335, Pasadena, CA 91101, tel. 818/449-3106, fax 449-9573, www .freighterworld.com) books passage aboard the **M/V** *Americana* (sailing from Houston to Venezuela) and *H. Buss* (sailing from Miami to Panamá); and aboard the *Martime Reederei,* which sails from Hamburg to the Caribbean, calling at Puerto Limón.

Hamburg-Sud Reiseagentur GMBH (Ost-West-Strasse 59, 20457 Hamburg, tel. 040/370-5155, fax 040/370-5242, www.hamburg-sued-reiseagentur.de) books passage aboard Horn Line vessels, sailing from Hamburg to South America.

The semi-annual directory *Ford's Freighter Travel Guide* (19448 Londelius St., Northridge, CA 91342, tel. 818/701-7414) provides comprehensive listings of freighters that take passengers.

Getting Around

BY AIR

Traveling by air in Costa Rica is easy and economical, a quick and comfortable alternative to often long and bumpy road travel. Flights to airstrips around the country are rarely more than 40 minutes from San José. Book well in advance.

The government-subsidized domestic airline **SANSA** (tel. 506/221-9414, fax 506/255-2176, info@flysansa.com, www.flysansa.com) uses 22- to 35-passenger Cessnas. Reservations have to be paid in full and are nonrefundable. Check in at the airport or SANSA's San José office in the basement of Centro Colón (Paseo Colón, Calle 24) at least an hour before departure—it provides a free minibus transfer to Juan Santamaría

Airport. SANSA baggage allowance is 11 kg (22 lbs). Delays and flight cancellations are common. *Schedules change frequently* as well as between seasons.

The privately owned **Nature Air** (tel. 506/220-3054, fax 506/220-0413, info@natureair.com, www.natureair.com), formerly Travelair, flies to 16 destinations from Tobías Bolaños Airport, near Pavas, three km west of downtown San José. Its rates are higher than SANSA's, but the airline is somewhat more reliable. Baggage limit is 12 kg (25 lbs).

Charters

You can charter small planes to fly you to airstrips throughout the country. The going rate is about $300 per hour per planeload (usually for up to four to six people). Most places are within a one-hour reach, but you'll have to pay for the return flight, too, if there are no passengers returning from your destination. Luggage space is limited.

Aero Costa Sol (tel. 506/440-1444, fax 506/441-2671, flyacs@racsa.co.cr; in the U.S., tel. 800/245-8420, fax 305/858-7478) offers charter, ambulance, and executive flights to 23 destinations throughout Costa Rica using twin-engine five-passenger Aztecs, seven-passenger Navajos, and Lear Jets. Other companies are listed in the Yellow Pages.

BY BUS

Buses serve even the most remote towns: generally, if there's a road, there's a bus. They are usually on time. Popular destinations are served by both fast buses *(directo)* and slower buses *(normal* or *corriente),* which make stops en route. Most

Nature Air flight over Tortuguero Canal

© CHRISTOPHER P. BAKER

buses serving major towns from San José use modern air-conditioned Volvos and Mercedes buses, with toilets and sometimes even movies. In the boondocks, local buses are usually old U.S. high-school buses with arse-numbing seats. You can travel to most parts of the country for less than $10. Fares are regulated by the government.

Buy tickets in advance from larger bus companies (with smaller companies, you'll have to pay when getting aboard; don't display wads of money). Get there early or your reservation may not be honored: at least an hour before departure for long-distance buses. Locals pack aboard until there isn't even standing room left, and the rush for seats can be furious. Some buses have storage below; local buses do not. Luggage space inside is usually limited to overhead racks. Travel light; a soft duffel is preferable, so you can tuck it under your seat or carry it on your lap.

Bus stops *(paradas)* nationwide are plain to see; most have shelters. Elsewhere, you can usually flag down rural buses anywhere along their routes. Long-distance buses don't always stop when waved down. To get off, whistle loudly or shout *"¡Pare!"*

Costa Ricans relinquish their seats gladly to pregnant women, the handicapped, elderly people, and mothers with small children. Set a good example: do the same. (Schoolchildren in uniform ride free, so buses are always stopping to pick up and drop off, saving the children long walks between school and home.)

Many buses don't run on Thursday and Friday during Easter week.

See the chart *Buses from San José*, in the *San José* chapter, for a national bus schedule.

Tourist Buses

Interbus (tel. 506/283-5573, fax 506/283-7655, interbus@costaricapass.com, www.interbusonline .com) operates door-to-door shuttles between San José and major tourist destinations, including La Fortuna ($25), Puntarenas ($17), Manuel Antonio ($25), Puerto Viejo de Sarapiquí ($25), Bahía Culebra ($25), Playa Coco ($25), Monteverde ($30), and Tamarindo and Playas Flamingo and Conchal ($25). Complete listings of routes, schedules, and fares are available online.

Grayline Fantasy Bus (tel. 506/232-3681, www.graylinecostarica.com/fantasy_bus.html) offers a similar service to destinations throughout Costa Rica ($21 to $38). It also offers one-day tours from the capital.

Coach Costa Rica (tel. 506/229-4192, info@coachcostarica.com, www.coachcostarica.com) offers transfers throughout the country using modern a/c vans and 4WDs.

BY CAR AND MOTORCYCLE

Nearly half of all foreign tourists to Costa Rica rent a car, which allows total freedom of movement.

Costa Rica has some 30,000 km (18,000 miles) of highway (18 percent paved). The MOPT (Ministry of Public Transport) has invested considerably in road improvements in recent years, particularly in the highlands. Hundreds of miles of new tarmac had been laid at last visit.

However, beyond the Central Highlands, roads generally deteriorate with distance. Even much-traveled roads, such as that to Monteverde Reserve, are still not paved and can shake both a car and its occupants until their doors and teeth rattle. Parts of the country are often impenetrable by road during the rainy season, when flooding and landslides are common and roads get washed out.

Traffic Regulations

You must be at least 21 years old and hold a passport to drive in Costa Rica. Foreign driver's licenses are valid for three months upon arrival. For longer, you'll need a Costa Rican driver's license. Apply at Calle 5, Avenida 18, in San José. The speed limit on highways is 80 kph (50 mph), and 60 kph on secondary roads. Speed limits are vigorously enforced by police with radar guns.

Seat belt use is mandatory, and motorcyclists must wear helmets. Insurance—a state monopoly—is also mandatory; car rental companies sell insurance with rentals.

It is illegal to:
- enter an intersection unless you can exit
- make a right turn on a red light unless indicated by a white arrow
- overtake on the right—you may pass only on the left.

Cars coming uphill have the right of way.

Driving Safety

Costa Rica has traditionally had one of the world's highest auto fatality rates. Tico males live in a macho society and feel the need to assuage their feelings of inadequacy through displays of bravado and unbelievable recklessness, often driving at warp speed, flouting traffic laws, holding traffic lights in disdain, crawling up your tailpipe at 100 kph, and overtaking on blind corners with a total disregard for anyone else's safety. The government's recent efforts to address the problem has begun to have an effect. At last visit, a noticeable improvement in driving habits seemed apparent nationwide—thanks to dramatically higher fines and a vastly expanded and improved police presence. (Nonetheless, fatality statistics remain sobering.)

TIPS FOR DRIVERS

- U.S. license plates are collectors' items—take them off and display them inside your vehicle.
- Good tires are a must, as is a sackful of spare parts.
- Make sure your car is in tip-top condition before leaving.
- Gas stations are few and far between—keep your tank topped up. Have a lock on your gas cap.
- Unleaded gas is hard to come by. Disconnect your catalytic converter.
- Be patient and obliging at customs/immigration posts.
- Never leave anything of value in your car.
- Always secure your parked vehicle with one or more antitheft devices. Apply locking nuts to the wheels.

Roads usually lack sidewalks, so pedestrians—and even livestock—walk the road. Be particularly wary at night. And treat mountain roads with extra caution: they're often blocked by thick fog, floods, and landslides. The two roads from San José to Puntarenas; the road linking San José to Limón; and the Pan-American Highway between the Nicaraguan border and Panamá are notoriously dangerous.

Slow down when you see a *"Vía Adelante!"* sign, indicating that part of the road ahead has collapsed, and whenever you see the sign *topes* or *túmulos,* meaning "road bumps."

Potholes are a particular problem. "Hit a big one," says Bill Baker in *The Essential Road Guide for Costa Rica,* "and it's not unusual to damage a tire or even destroy a wheel . . . Nor is it unusual to have a driver suddenly swerve to avoid one just as you're passing him." And slower-moving vehicles ahead of you often turn on their left-turn indicator to signal that you can overtake—a dangerous practice that is the cause of many accidents with vehicles that really are turning left!

Consider driving with your lights on at *all times* to ensure being seen.

Accidents and Breakdowns

The law states that you must carry fluorescent triangles in case of breakdown. Locals, however, generally pile leaves, rocks, or small branches in the road or at the roadside to warn approaching drivers of a car in trouble. If your car is rented, call the rental agency: it will arrange a tow.

After an accident, *never* move the vehicles until the police arrive. Get the names, license plate numbers, and *cedulas* (legal identification numbers) of any witnesses. Make a sketch of the accident. And call the traffic police *(tráfico)* (tel. 117 or 800/8726-7486).

Do *not* offer statements to anyone other than the police. In case of injury, call the Red Cross (tel. 128 or 911 or 506/221-5818). Try not to leave the accident scene, or at least keep an eye on your car: the other party may tamper with the evidence. And don't let honking traffic—there'll be plenty!—pressure you into moving the cars.

Show the *tráfico* your license and vehicle

Know Costa Rica

© CHRISTOPHER P. BAKER

rough road near Uvita

registration. Make sure you get them back: he is not allowed to keep any documents unless you've been drinking (if you suspect the other driver has been drinking, ask the *tráfico* to administer a Breathalyzer test, or *alcolemia*). Nor can the *tráfico* assess a fine. The police will issue you a green ticket or "summons." You must present this to the nearest municipal office *(alcaldía)* or traffic court *(tribunal de tránsito)* within eight days to make your *declaración* about the accident. Wait a few days so that the police report is on record. Don't skip this! The driver who doesn't show is often found at blame by default. Then take your driver's license, insurance policy, and a police report to the **INS** (Avenida 7, Calles 9/11, San José, tel. 506/223-5800 or 800/800-8000), the state insurance monopoly, to process your claim. Car rental companies will take care of this if your car is rented.

Hitchhiking

Ticos are used to picking up pedestrians in areas where bus service is infrequent, and locals often hitchhike in more remote regions. However, hitchhiking is far from safe and we do not endorse it. Women should never hitchhike alone.

Car Rentals

The leading U.S. car rental companies have franchises in Costa Rica, though not always as reliable as their U.S. parents. There are many local rental companies (some reputable, some not), with slightly cheaper rates. Several agencies have offices at or near Juan Santamaría Airport, plus representatives in popular resort towns.

I highly recommend **Europcar** (tel. 506/257-1158, fax 506/255-4492, info@europcar.co.cr, www.europcar.co.cr) based on my own experiences and that of readers. Their staff have proved consistently professional, trustworthy, and gracious, and their vehicles have always been in good repair.

Regardless of where you plan to go, I recommend you rent a 4WD! If you don't, you'll regret it the first time you hit one of Costa Rica's infamous dirt and/or potholed roads. Four-wheel drives are essential for Nicoya and other off-the-beaten-path destinations. Many rental agencies will *not* insure sedans for travel in certain areas; they may even insist you rent a 4WD for specific regions, especially in rainy season. Don't be like the poor woman who cracked the oil pan on the road up to Monteverde and ended up having to fork out

RIVER FORDINGS

Every year, more bridges are built over rivers that once had to be forded, but in certain parts of the country—notably southwest Nicoya—there are still enough rivers without bridges to add spice to your driving adventure. Usually these are no problem in dry season. But wet season is another matter. Many unwary foreigners misjudge the crossing, swamp the engine, and have to be towed out. Do not expect the car rental agency to be sympathetic; you will have to pay for the damage. It is not unknown for cars to be washed away!

There's a technique to fording rivers successfully. Firstly, *enter the river slowly!* Many drivers charge at the river, causing a huge wave that rides over the hood and drowns the engine. It pays to inch across gently, not least because a shallow crossing often betrays a hidden channel (usually near the bank) where the water runs deep and into which it is easy to plunge nose-first just as you think you've made it across.

If the river is murky, wade across on foot first to gauge the depth. Check for the engine's air filter placement to ensure that it won't swamp. Even if the engine won't swamp, you need to check the height of the door sills. Sure, your car might make it across without stalling, but do you really want six inches of muddy water inside the car?

Look for the tire tracks of other vehicles. It usually pays to follow them. Sometimes you may need to run *along* the riverbed to find the exit, rather than it being a straight-across route. It's often best to wait for a local to arrive and show the way. Be patient!

$6,000. Most agencies offer a range of small to full-size 4WD vehicles.

Minimum age for drivers ranges 21–25, depending on the agency. You'll need a valid driver's license plus a credit card. Without a credit card you'll have to pay a hefty cash deposit. The government fixes a ceiling on rental rates. Most agencies charge the maximum during the high season (Nov.–April) and offer discounts during the low season (May–Oct.). You'll normally get a discount by making your reservations in the U.S. before departure. Stick shift is the norm; you'll pay extra for automatic.

Reserve as far in advance as possible, especially in dry season and for Christmas and holidays. Make sure you clarify any one-way drop-off fees, late return penalties, and other charges. Take a copy of your reservation with you. And be prepared to defend against mysterious new charges that may be tagged on in Costa Rica (I've heard reports of companies charging for a new tire after renters have had a flat tire fixed; you won't know about it until your credit card bill arrives). You must rent for a minimum of three days to qualify for unlimited mileage.

Economy cars such as the Toyota Yaris begin at about $35 daily, $222 weekly low season, $45/$270 high season with unlimited mileage. Compact (midsize) cars such as the Toyota Corolla cost about $40 daily/$240 weekly low season, $52/294 high season with unlimited mileage. Smaller 4WD models such as the Suzuki Sidekick begin at about $60 daily/$360 weekly with unlimited mileage. A midsize 4WD such as the Toyota RAV-4 will cost $57 daily, $342 weekly low season, $75/450 high season. A full-size 4WD such as the Toyota 4-Runner will cost about $72 daily, $432 weekly low season, $110/660 high season. In my opinion, Suzuki Samurai and Sidekicks should be avoided for their detestable springing.

Costa Rica Experts (3166 N. Lincoln Ave. #424, Chicago, IL 60657, tel. 312/935-1009 or 800/827-9046, fax 312/935-9252, info @costaricaexperts.com, www.crexpert.com) and **Costa Rica Temptations** (P.O. Box 1199-1200, San José, tel. 506/239-9999, fax 506/ 239-9990, reserv@crtinfo.com, www.crtinfo .com) offer a 24-day 4WD tour following the "Route of Biodiversity" to remote national parks.

I've heard numerous reports of scams pulled by unscrupulous agencies, including billing extra charges. Always leave one person with the car when you return it to the car rental office, especially if unforeseen billing problems arise (there are numerous examples of renters having their belongings stolen from the vehicle while their attention is distracted). And thieves have been known to slash tires, or deflate them, while you're picking up or dropping off your car; while you're occupied changing the tire, the thieves pounce and strip your vehicle of its contents, then drive off! If you experience a flat shortly after picking up your vehicle, be suspicious; drive to the nearest secure public place.

Fly-Drive Packages

Discover Costa Rica (tel. 506/293-8109, www.allcostaricadestinations.com) is an "open voucher" package that includes hotel, breakfast, and 4WD car rental for $29 daily pp.

TRYING TO TAKE THE ROAD NOT YET TAKEN

How bad can driving conditions be in Costa Rica? Consider this.

"Best turn around now, mate. If you get through I'll buy you a pint—and I'll throw in my missus for free!"

Now, I'm not generally a gambling man. And it wasn't the promise of a beer and another man's woman that made me continue. When a worldly Australian says a road can't be driven, I'm prepared to believe him. He even described the route—a 50-km stretch of Pacific coast midway down the western seaboard of Costa Rica—in several ways, the most polite of which was "a daggy!" (a dirty lump of wool at the back end of a sheep).

But I took a more charitable view. I'd spent the last month perfecting my four-wheel-driving techniques in a Range Rover, going over, around, and across terrain that would have challenged a goat. I reckoned that as long as I could resist being carried off into the mangroves by mosquitoes, I could get through. Sure, it was still the wet season—when, according to all the guidebooks, only horses and tractors could negotiate the track along the jungled shoreline. But my alternative was to follow the Australian over a 240-km detour along the paved road via the banana town of Palmar Sur and the flatlands of the Valle de El General, then back to the coast.

It wasn't long before my pulse began to quicken. Rain had been pelting down for two days, and the mud was inches deep. I encountered two cars and a truck destined to spend the night in a ditch, including a Toyota Tercel full of anguished-looking young surfers outskating Torvill and Dean.

Then there were no more vehicles. No villages or farms. Not another soul for miles. The only sounds were the bellows of howler monkeys, the screechings of toucans and parrots, and the crashing of surf where the track briefly dropped down to the coast. A claustrophobic tangle of rainforest had closed over my head. And for all the world I could have been the only person in it. The level road designed to shake the fillings from my teeth had deteriorated into a trail best described as steeper than a dentist's bill, which would be justified. I soon lost count of the cavities.

Remembering advice I'd been given years before in the Sahara, I pulled out the foot pump stowed in the back and bumped the tire pressures up to what I guessed was around 45 pounds. Hardly ideal for sealed roads but a good precaution on the razor-edged flint that now covered the trail. Grateful for permanent 4WD, and with low ratio still to fall back on, I walked the vehicle up and over the boulder-strewn mountain. It was a case where the argument in favor of a V6 was very persuasive. The car seemed not to notice. I blessed the engineers who had designed the Range Rover. Surely these were the conditions they had in mind when they conceived the car.

Motorcycles

María Alexandra Tours (P.O.Box 3756-1000 San José, tel. 506/289-5552, fax 506/289-5551, info@costaricamotorcycles.com, www.costaricamotorcycles.com) rents Harley-Davidsons ($195 per day, $1,017 per week). A valid motorcycle license is required, and you must be 25 years old.

Wild Rider Motorcycles (tel. 506/258-4604, www.wild-rider.com), at Hotel Ritmo del Caribe, in San José, rents three types of motor-cycles: a Suzuki 350 costs $50 daily, $120 for three days, or $230 weekly; a Kawasaki 650 costs $60/150/280, respectively. Motorcycling in Costa Rica is not recommended except for experienced riders, as road conditions can be challenging. See *Motorcycle Tours,* in the *Recreation and Tours.*

Insurance

Insurance is mandatory and you will need to accept the obligatory CDW (collision damage

© CHRISTOPHER P. BAKER

As tough as it gets!

I inched along the map through more mud. More clifflike hills. More boulders. A small landslide. A fallen tree to manhandle out of the way. More bruising rain. More raging streams to ford. And mile after mile of really wild country that had been barely explored.

"Aaawright! I'm through!" I chimed, looking down into a canyon that seemed to descend into the Stone Age, but which I knew would disgorge me onto the surfaced road, which began at the coast near Uvita.

Instead, the gorge descended into a morass of fathoms-deep, vacuumlike mud. My stomach tightened sickeningly as my vehicle sank until the doors wouldn't open. Yikes! There really was a Shit Creek, and this was it.

I climbed out of the window, sank up to my knees, and began dripping sweat like a faucet. Somewhere beyond the forest canopy the sun heliographed the heavens and sank from view. Blackness descended. The rainforest was suddenly silent. Then the night noises began. I curled up in the back of the Range Rover and groaned miserably as the mosquitoes pressed up against the windows and eyed me greedily.

Fortunately, even atheists have their angels of mercy. Mine was a giant earthmover that miraculously appeared around noon and plucked me from my muddy grave. The giant Cat was one of several tearing up the rainforests for the long-awaited Costanera Sur Highway, a four-year project that when completed, in 1997, provided a final link in communications along the Pacific coast. I retraced my tracks and—tail between my legs—arced around the Fila Costanera mountain range to Dominical.

"Told ya ya'd nivver git through, ya great dill," the Aussie said, as we swigged beer together at a bar called Jungle Jim's.

"You remind me of something Paul Theroux once wrote," I replied, "about how when things were at their most desperate and uncomfortable, he always found himself in the company of Australians, a reminder that he'd touched bottom."

waiver) charged by car rental companies. If you make a reservation through a rental agency abroad and are told the rate includes insurance, or that one of your existing policies—such as American Express auto-rental insurance—will cover it, *get it in writing!* Otherwise, once you arrive in Costa Rica, you may find that you have to pay the *mandatory* insurance fee on top of your quoted rate. The insurance does not cover your car's contents or personal possessions, or a deductible. Each company determines its own deductible—ranging $500–1,000—even though the INS sets this at 20 percent of damages. Rates range from $12 per day for smaller vehicles to $15 daily for larger vehicles.

Inspect your vehicle for damage and marks before departing, or you may be charged for the slightest "damage" when you return. Note even the smallest nick and dent on the diagram you'll be presented to sign. Don't forget the inside, as well as the radio antenna, and check that all the switches and buttons function.

Don't assume the rental agency has taken care of oil, water, brakes, fluids, or tire pressure: check them yourself before setting off. Most agencies provide 24-hour road service.

Gasoline

Unleaded gasoline is called Super and is universally available. Many service stations *(bombas* or *gasolineras)* are open 24 hours; in rural areas they're usually open dawn to dusk only, and they're often far apart—it's a wise idea to fill up whenever you pass a service station. Gasoline costs 250 colones (65 cents) a liter. In the boondocks, there's sure to be someone nearby selling from their backyard stock at a premium.

Maps and Directions

The past few years have seen signposts erected in major cities and along major highways, but don't count on a sign being there when you need it. Many point the wrong way: they were placed by crews who hadn't the foggiest idea which street

Rural gas "station" in Nicoya

was a Calle and which an Avenida (after all, they live in a society that uses landmarks, not street names). Ticos use left-pointing arrows to indicate straight ahead.

Ask directions when in doubt. And check with locals about conditions down the road. Costa Ricans tend to be optimistic about whether roads are passable in excessive rain and fog, so double-check with foreigners if possible.

You'll need the best map you can obtain. I recommend buying a copy of the *Red Guide to Costa Rica* and/or the *Costa Rica Nature Atlas-Guidebook,* which has detailed 1:200,000 road maps; they're not always accurate, but they're the best around.

Traffic Police

Traffic police patrol the highways and pull people over at random to check documentation. In the past they've been fond of rental cars (the TUR on rental car license plates gives the game away) in the hope of extorting bribes, although such instances now seem rare.

If you're stopped, the police will request to see your license, passport, and rental contract. *Tráficos* use radar guns, and you will get no special treatment as a tourist if you're caught speeding. Speeding fines are paid at a bank; the ticket provides instructions. Don't think you can get away with not paying a fine. Delinquent fines are reported to the immigration authorities, and people have been refused exit from the country. Normally, the car rental agency will handle the tickets, although you remain responsible for paying the fine.

Never pay a fine to police on the road. The police cannot legally request payment on site. If he (I've never seen a female traffic cop) demands payment, note the policeman's name and number from his MOPT badge (he is legally required to show his *carnet* upon request). Report the incident to the **Office for the Reception of Complaints** (tel. 506/295-3272 or 506/295-3273, 24 hours).

Oncoming vehicles will often flash their lights at you to warn you of traffic police—or an accident or disabled vehicle—ahead.

BY RAIL

Railway lines, originally built to serve the coffee and banana industry, run from San José to Puntarenas on the Pacific and Puerto Limón on the Caribbean. No scheduled passenger trains run along them. The train to Puntarenas stopped service in October 1991. And the highly popular Jungle Train to Puerto Limón—one of the world's wildest train rides—was discontinued in November 1990.

In 2002, **INCOFER** (tel. 506/233-3300, americatravel@msn.com) introduced a four-hour (each way) train ride from San José to Calderas, on the Pacific, departing at 6 A.M. and returning at 3 P.M. and traveling via San Antonio de Belén, Atenas, and Orotina ($25).

At last visit, the Public Works & Transport Ministry was negotiating with the French government to build a electric light-rail, high-speed system between Alajuela, San José, and Cartago

TAXIS

Costa Rica has a reasonably good nationwide taxi system. Taxis are inexpensive by U.S. standards, so much so that they are a viable means of touring for short trips, especially if you're traveling with two or three others. Generally, taxis will go wherever a road leads. Most taxis are radio dispatched. A white triangle on the front door contains the taxi's license plate number.

Taxi drivers are required by law to use their meters *(marías).* Many drivers don't use them (many will do so in the morning; the later it gets, the less they like to do so). Insist on it being used, as Costa Rican taxi drivers are notorious for overcharging. Don't be afraid to bargain.

Outside San José, you'll usually find taxis around the main square of small towns. Jeep-taxis are common in more remote areas, particularly the Nicoya Peninsula. Outside cities, few taxis are metered and taxi drivers are allowed to negotiate their fare for any journey over 15 kilometers. Check rates in advance with your hotel concierge.

At press time, government-established fares were 240 colones (about $0.60) for the first kilometer and 100 colones (about $0.25) for each additional kilometer in the metropolitan area and 105 elsewhere. The waiting fee is 755 colones per hour (about $1.90). Rates are periodically adjusted. The 20 percent surcharge after 10 P.M. has been ruled illegal and no longer applies.

You can hire a taxi by the hour or half-day; the cost normally compares favorably to renting a car for the day.

You do not have to tip taxi drivers.

FERRIES

Car/passenger ferries link Puntarenas to both Playa Naranjo and Paquera, on the southeastern corner of the Nicoya Peninsula. Water-taxis also operate between key destinations on the Pacific coast.

Visas and Officialdom

DOCUMENTS AND REQUIREMENTS

Passports, Visas, and Tourist Cards

All citizens of the U.S., Canada, Western European nations, plus Australia and New Zealand need a valid passport to enter Costa Rica. No visas are required. Tourist cards are issued during your flight or at the immigration desk upon arrival and permit stays of 90 days.

Citizens of Central and South American nations need a valid passport for stays of 30 days. Extensions are limited to 60 days. Panamanians may stay for 90 days. No visas are required, except for Nicaraguans.

Citizens of most other countries need a passport and a visa, limited to entry for up to 30 days. Citizens of Cuba, former Soviet republics, and other countries with extremist governments may be allowed entry into Costa Rica on a restricted visa subject to approval by a Costa Rican consulate (passports are required).

The law requires that you carry your passport or tourist card with you at all times during your stay. Make photocopies of all documentation and keep them with you, separate from the originals. (A recent attempt to crack down on illegal immigration has resulted in many innocent tourists being carted off to jail to face a bureaucratic minefield of ineptitude and indifference. Police may not be willing to accept a photocopy of your passport as proof of identity; consider carrying the original—well-guarded!—at all times.)

You can request a **tourist card extension** (*prórroga de turismo*) monthly for up to three months from the immigration office (Migración, tel. 506/223-7555, ext. 240 or 276, fax 506/221-2066), near Hospital Mexico, in La Uruca; open 8:30 A.M.–3:30 P.M. weekdays. You'll need three passport-size photos, a ticket out of the country, and adequate funds in cash or traveler's checks to cover your living expenses for the duration of your stay. The extension costs about $30–45. Be sure to begin the process *before* your 30 or 90 days are up. Since you'll need to allow three days minimum—plus an additional four days or more if you are asked to submit to a blood test for AIDS—it may be just as easy to travel to Nicaragua or Panamá for 72 hours and then reenter with a new visa or tourist card.

If you extend your stay illegally beyond the authorized time, anticipate bureaucratic headaches and a heavy toll on your time and patience. If caught, you may be deported (deportees are not allowed back in for 10 years). You will also not be allowed to leave without first obtaining an exit visa ($50), which means a trip back to the immigration office, plus a visit to the Tribunales de Justicia for a document stating you aren't abandoning any offspring or dependents in Costa Rica. Exit visas take 48 hours or more to process; a reputable local travel agent or tour operator can usually obtain what you need for a small fee.

Other Documentation

Tourists staying 30 days or more may be required to demonstrate adequate finances for their proposed stay. In addition, you may be asked to show a return or onward ticket (overland travelers need an onward bus ticket; you can buy one at the border immigration office or from the driver on TICA international buses).

Immunizations

Costa Rican authorities do not require travelers to show proof of immunizations or an international vaccination card (see *Health and Safety*, below). However, if you plan on staying beyond 30 days, you may be required to show proof of being free from AIDS or its precursor, HIV-positive status. If the immigration authorities request that you submit to an AIDS test, the Ministerio de Salud, Ministry of Health, Calle 16, Avenidas 6/8, can oblige.

Check with your travel agent or Costa Rican consulate for the latest updates. Some travelers arriving from Nicaragua report being tested for malarial infection at the border.

EMBASSIES

The following embassies are located in San José: **United States** (tel. 506/290-4114 or 220-3050, Blvd. Rohrmoser), **Canada** (tel. 506/242-4400, fax 506/242-4410, Oficentro Ejecutivo La Sabana, Edificio 5, Sabana Surm behind La Contraloria), and **United Kingdom** (tel. 506/258-2025, fax 506/233-9938, Centro Colón, Paseo Colón, Calles 38/40, britimb@racsa.co.cr).

CUSTOMS

Travelers arriving in Costa Rica are allowed 500 cigarettes or 500 grams of tobacco, plus three liters of wine or spirits. You can also bring in two cameras, binoculars, a personal computer, electrical and video equipment, plus camping, scuba, and other sporting equipment duty-free.

Travelers exiting Costa Rica are charged $26 (or its equivalent in *colones*), including for residents (no tax is imposed for transit stays of less than 12 hours). No departure tax applies if exiting overland or by sea.

Costa Rica prohibits the export of pre-Columbian artifacts.

Returning Home

U.S. citizens can bring in $600 of purchases duty-free. You may also bring in one quart of spirits plus 200 cigarettes (one carton). Live animals, plants, and products made from endangered species will be confiscated by U.S. Customs. Tissue-cultured orchids and other plants in sealed vials are okay. Costa Rica is also listed under the U.S. Customs Service's Generalized System of Preferences (GSP) program, which provides for duty-free importation of arts, handicrafts, and other select items from Third World countries.

Canadian citizens are allowed an "exemption" of C$300 annually (or C$100 per quarter) for goods purchased abroad, plus 1.1 liters of spirits and 200 cigarettes.

U.K. citizens are permitted to import goods worth up to £200, plus 200 cigarettes, 50 cigars, and two liters of spirits.

Australian citizens may import A$400 of goods, plus 250 cigarettes or 50 cigars, and 1.125 liters of spirits. New Zealand citizens can import NZ$700 worth of goods, 200 cigarettes or 50 cigars, and 1.125 liters of spirits.

Drugs

It goes without saying that trying to smuggle drugs through customs is not only illegal, it's stupid. Travelers returning from Central and South America are particularly suspect. Trained dogs are employed to sniff out contraband at U.S. airports as well as at Juan Santamaría Airport in San José. Recent years have seen a concerted effort to stamp out drug trafficking and use within the country.

Know Costa Rica

CROSSING INTO NICARAGUA AND PANAMÁ

You cannot cross into Nicaragua or Panama with a rental car. You can only do so with your own car with Costa Rican plates. You'll need a special permit from the **Registro Nacional** (tel. 506/224-8111, www.registronacional.go.cr). It's good for 15 days and must be obtained in person from the main office in Curridabat, San José (there's also a Registro Nacional in Liberia).

Visa requirements are always in flux, so check in advance with the Nicaraguan or Panamanian embassies. Likewise, borders are open only at specific times and these, too, are subject to change.

NICARAGUA

Officialdom

Citizens of Canada, the U.S., plus most European and Central and South American nations do not need visas to enter Nicaragua. A *tourist visa* is issued at the border ($5, good for three months). Citizens of Colombia and Haiti need *visitor visas*, which cannot be obtained at the border (you have to get them in advance from a Nicaraguan embassy).

You can cross into Nicaragua for 72 hours and renew your 30- or 90-day Costa Rican visa if you want to return to Costa Rica and stay longer. A 72-hour transit visa for Nicaragua costs 75 cents.

Border Crossings

Peñas Blancas: Most people arriving from Nicaragua do so at Peñas Blancas, in northwest Costa Rica. This is a border post, not a town. The Costa Rican and Nicaraguan posts are contiguous. The border is open 6 A.M.–8 P.M. daily. When you arrive at Peñas Blancas, you must get an exit form, which you complete and return with your passport. Then walk 600 meters to the Costa Rican border, where your passport will be validated (it must have at least six months remaining before it expires). On the Nicaraguan side, go to the immigration building, where you'll pay $5 for a 30-day tourist visa, plus $1 municipal stamp. Then

complete a customs declaration sheet, present it with your passport, and proceed to the customs inspection (next building along). Then take your papers to the gate for final inspection.

The wait in line can be several hours. Count on at least an hour for the formalities, and be sure to have all required documents in order or you may as well get back on the bus to San José.

Cross-border buses (70 cents) depart from here every hour for Rivas, a small town about 40 km north of the border. *Colectivo* (shared) taxis also run regularly between the border and Rivas, the nearest Nicaraguan town with accommodations. Buses fill fast—get there early. There's a basic restaurant near the Nicaraguan immigration office.

See *Peñas Blancas*, in the *Guanacaste* chapter, for details of services at Peñas Blancas, plus domestic bus schedules and fares to/from Peñas Blancas.

Southbound, you may be required to pay an exit fee ($2) leaving Nicaragua, plus $1 stamp. (The Costa Rica tourist card is free.) If you're asked for proof of onward ticket when entering Costa Rica, you can buy a bus ticket—valid for 12 months—back to Nicaragua at the bus station at Peñas Blancas; the Costa Rican authorities will normally accept this, though they rarely ask for proof.

Los Chiles: There's also a border post at Los Chiles, in the northern lowlands. The Costa Rican Oficina de Migración (tel. 506/471-1133) is open 8 A.M.–4 P.M. daily. There is no road crossing. You have to hire a boat or take a ferry across the Río San Juan, then take a bus 14 km to San Carlos, on the southeast shore of Lake Nicaragua; or hire a boat to take you downriver to San Carlos.

Buses

Northbound, **Sirca** (tel. 506/223-1464) buses depart for Nicaragua San José Mondays, Wednesdays, Fridays, and Sundays at 5:45 A.M. from Avenida 8, Calles 7/9 (11 hours); **Ticabus** (tel.

506/221-8954, fax 506/255-4771) buses depart daily for Nicaragua, Honduras, and Guatemala at 6 A.M. and 7:30 A.M. from Avenida 4, Calles 9/11 (11 hours); and **Transnica** (tel. 506/256-9072, trannica@racsa.co.cr) offers a deluxe nonstop service to Nicaragua departing the Terminal Caribe in San José daily at 5:30 A.M. ($25; 10 hours).

Southbound, **Sirca** offers service from Managua on Monday, Wednesday, and Friday ($5); **Ticabus** buses depart Managua daily at 6 A.M. and 7 A.M.); and **Transnica Bus** departs Managua daily at 7 A.M. and 10 A.M.

Service on Sirca is reportedly unreliable, and tickets should be bought several days ahead. Buses between Managua and San José are often held up for hours due to border delays.

PANAMÁ

Officialdom

Citizens of Canada, the U.S., plus most European and Central and South American nations do not need visas to enter Panamá. A *tourist visa* is issued at the border ($5, good for 30 days). Citizens of Dominican Republic, Dominica, Haiti, and several other nations outside the Americas need *visitor visas,* which cannot be obtained at the border (you have to get them in advance from a Panamanian embassy).

Border Crossings

Paso Canoas: The main crossing point is on the Pan-American Highway. The border posts have been open 24 hours, but are subject to change (at press time, they were open 6–11 A.M. and 1–6 P.M.). If you don't have a ticket out of the country, you can buy a Tracopa bus ticket in David to Paso Canoas and back. A bus terminal on the Panamanian side offers service to David, the nearest town (90 minutes), every hour or two until 7 P.M. Buses leave from David for Panamá City (last bus 5 P.M.; seven hours).

Sixaola: This rather squalid village on the Caribbean coast sits on the north bank of the Río Sixaola. Its brighter, more lively counterpart is Guabito, a duty-free town on the Panamanian side of the river. The two are linked by a bridge. The Costa Rican Customs and Immigration offices (tel. 506/754-2044) – are open 7 A.M.–5 P.M.; the Panamian office (tel. 507/759-7952) is open 8 A.M.–6 P.M.

Minibuses operate a regular schedule from Guabito to Changuinola (16 km). A narrow-gauge cargo train also runs daily to Almirante (30 km), the end of both rail and road; it leaves at 5 A.M. Taxis are available at all hours ($1 to Changuinola). For access to the rest of Panamá, you can either fly to David from Changuinola or take a boat from Almirante to Bocas del Toro ($2 by ferry; $10 by water taxi) and then Chiriquí Grande, where a road traverses the mountain to David.

Río Sereno: There is another crossing between Costa Rica and Panamá, at the remote mountain border post of **Río Sereno** east of San Vito, in the Pacific southwest, but it is not open to foreigners.

Buses

Southbound, **Alfaro** (tel. 506/222-2666, tracopa@racsa.co.cr) express buses depart San José for David daily at 7:30 A.M. from Avenida 5, Calle 14 ($8.50, eight hours); and via Sixaola to Changuinola on Panamá's Caribbean coast, daily at 10 A.M. ($9, payable to the driver; eight hours). And **Ticabus** (tel. 506/221-8954) buses depart for Panamá City daily at 10 P.M. (20 hours) from Avenida 4, Calles 9/11.

Northbound, **Alfaro** express buses David at 7:30 A.M., and Changuinola at 10 A.M. **Ticabus** (tel. 507/221-8954) buses depart Panamá City at 11 A.M. Panamá time ($25).

Warning: Note that Panamá time is one hour ahead of Costa Rica!

Conduct and Customs

It is a rare visitor to the country who returns home unimpressed by the Costa Ricans' cordial warmth and hospitality.

However, some Tico characteristics can be tiresome. Ticos, for example, have a hard time speaking forthrightly. They can't say "no!" They'd prefer to tell you what they think you might want to hear, rather than the truth. Even other Latin Americans residents in Costa Rica complain about the Ticos' lack of forthrightness and honesty. Thus, when a Tico makes a promise, don't expect him or her to come through, to show up for a date or appointment, or even to return a call. And don't expect an apology! You usually receive an excuse.

Ticos have been called icebergs, for their tendency to conceal the real meaning of what they say or feel below the surface.

Nor should you count on a Tico's punctuality. Most travel businesses are efficient and operate *hora americana*, punctually, but most other Ticos, particularly in government institutions, still tick along on turtle-paced *hora tica*. *"¿Quien sabe?"* ("Who knows?") is an oft-repeated phrase. So too *"¡Tal vez!"* ("Perhaps!") and, of course, *"¡Mañana!"* ("Tomorrow!"). In fact, *mañana* is the busiest day of the week.

Making friends with Ticos usually takes considerably longer than it does in North America or the U.K., for example. Family bonds are so strong that foreigners often find making intimate friendships a challenge. As with many things in Costa Rica, patience is the key.

Young female travelers should be prepared to receive *piropos*—effulgent, romantic, but often vulgar, compliments. A few years ago I had dinner in San José with a young North American friend who was studying for a year at the University of Costa Rica. She was tired, she told me. Tired of the attention-arresting "Ssssst!" of Tico men. Tired of the silent, insistent stares—of *dando cuerva*, "making eyes." Tired of being called *guapa, mi amor,* and *¡machita!* To her, Costa Rica was a land of unbridled and ugly machismo. Everything in life of course is relative. Dressing conservatively can help thwart unwanted advances.

ETHICAL TOURISM

The **Center for Responsible Tourism** (1765-D Le Roy, Berkeley, CA 94709, dodyhd@aol.com) suggests travelers abide by the following Code of Ethics for Tourists:
 • Travel with a spirit of humility and a genuine desire to meet and talk with local people.
 • Be aware of the feelings of others. Act respectfully and avoid offensive behavior, particularly when taking photographs.
 • Cultivate the habit of actively listening and observing rather than merely hearing and seeing. Avoid the temptation to "know all the answers."
 • Realize that others may have concepts of time, and attitudes that are different—not inferior—to those you inherited from your own culture.
 • Instead of looking only for the exotic, discover the richness of another culture and way of life.

 • Learn local customs and respect them.
 • Remember that you are only one of many visitors. Do not expect special privileges.
 • When bargaining with merchants, remember that the poorest one may give up a profit rather than his or her personal dignity. Don't take advantage of the desperately poor. Pay a fair price.
 • Keep your promises to people you meet. If you cannot, do not make the promise.
 • Spend time each day reflecting on your experiences in order to deepen your understanding. Is your enrichment beneficial for all involved?
 • Be aware of why you are traveling in the first place. If you truly want a "home away from home," why travel?

FESTIVALS AND EVENTS

Official Holidays

January 1	*New Year's Day*
March/April	*Easter Week*
April 11	*Juan Santamaría Day*
May 1	*Labor Day*
July 25	*Annexation of Guanacaste Day*
August 15	*Mother's Day*
September 15	*Independence Day*
November 2	*All Soul's Day*
December 25	*Christmas Day*

January

Alajuelita: *Fiesta Patronales.* Parade and pilgrimage (week of January 15).

Palmares: folk dances, music, rodeos (early January).

Santa Cruz: *Fiestas de Santa Cruz.* Folk dances, music, rodeos, bullfights (week of January 15).

February

Boruca: *Fiesta de los Diablitos.* Indian festival, masked dancing, fireworks.

Puntarenas: *Carnival.* Parade floats, music, and dancing (final week).

San Isidro de El General: agricultural fair, bullfights, floral exhibits.

March

Escazú: *Día de los Carretas.* Oxcart parade with music, dancing, and competitions (second Sunday).

Cartago: holy pilgrimage to Ujarrás (mid-month).

San José: cattle show with rodeo, bullfights, and horse races.

San José: book fair.

San José: *International Festival of the Arts.* Dance troupes, theater, experimental music, puppets, jazz, folklore, and classical music (second week).

Tierra Blanca: *Día de los Campesinos* (March 15).

April

Alajuela: *Juan Santamaría Day.* Parade with marching bands (April 11).

San José, *International Festival of the Arts.* Dance troupes, theater, experimental music, puppets, jazz, folklore, and classical music.

San José, *University Week.* Concerts, exhibits, parades (final week).

May

Escazú: oxcart parade (May 15).

Puerto Limón: *May Day.* Cricket matches, music, and dancing (May 1).

San Isidro de El General: oxcart parade (May 15).

RockFest. Rock, punk, ska, and alternative music bands; www.rockfestnews.com

July

Alajuela: *Mango Festival.* Parades, music, craft fairs.

Liberia and Santa Cruz: *Guanacaste Day.* Folkloric dancing, music, rodeos, and bullfights (July 25).

Nationwide: *International Music Festival.* Concerts ranging from classical to jazz.

August

Cartago: *Día del Virgén de los Angeles.* Religious processions (August 2).

Nationwide: *International Music Festival.* Concerts ranging from classical to jazz.

September

Puerto Limón: *Black Culture Festival.* Celebration of Afro-Caribbean culture.

Nationwide: *Noche del Faro* Children make lanterns and parade with drums by night.

Nationwide: *Día de Independencia.* Parades, marching bands, music and dance (September 15).

Upala: *Fiesta del Maía.* Parades and music in celebration of corn (maize).

October

Puerto Limón: *Carnival.* Music, dancing, parades (midmonth).

November

Meseta Central: coffee-picking contests, festivals.

Nationwide: *All Soul's Day.* Church processions (November 2).

San José: *International Theater Festival.* Plays and street theater.

December

Boruca: *Fiesta de los Negritos.* Costumed dancing (December 8).

San José: *Costa Rican International Marathon.*

Nationwide: *Immaculate Conception.* Fireworks (December 8).

Nicoya: *Fiesta de la Yeguita.* Processions, bullfights, fireworks, and concerts (December 12).

Nationwide: *Los Posadas.* Caroling (December 15).

Nationwide: *Topes Caballos.* Horse parades (December 26).

San José: year-end fiestas, with horse procession and parade (December 26).

FESTIVALS, EVENTS, AND HOLIDAYS

Local fiestas called *turnos* are found nationwide, notably in Guanacaste and Nicoya, highlighted by rodeos, fireworks, and firecrackers *(bombetas)*. Often they'll start at dawn. Individual towns also celebrate their patron saint's day: highlights usually include a procession, plus benign bullfights, rodeos, dancing, and secular parades. The *Tico Times* provides weekly listings of festivals and events nationwide.

Costa Rica is a Catholic country, and its holidays *(feriados)* are mostly religious. Most businesses, including banks, close on official holidays. The country closes down entirely during the biggest holiday time, Easter Holy Week *(semana santa)*, Wednesday through Sunday. Buses don't run on Holy Thursday or Good Friday. Banks and offices are closed. And hotels and rental cars are booked solid months in advance as everyone heads for the beach. Avoid the popular beaches during Easter week. Most Ticos now take the whole Christmas *(navidad)* holiday week through New Year as an unofficial holiday.

Easter provides an opportunity to see colorful religious processions.

Accommodations

Costa Rica has about 1,800 hotels and 30,000 hotel rooms. Hardly a week goes by without two or three new hotels springing onto the scene. Accommodations run the gamut from cheap *pensiones,* beachside *cabinas,* and self-catering *apartotels* to rustic jungle lodges, swank mountain lodges, and glitzy resort hotels with casinos. (The term *cabina*—literally "cabins"—is a loose term used throughout Costa Rica to designate accommodations, and as often as not refers to hotel rooms as well as true cabins. And note that the term "suite" is used loosely in Costa Rica and may merely signify that a room has a refrigerator and microwave, sofa, or other accouterment. *Caveat emptor!*)

Don't be afraid of looking at several rooms in a hotel (particularly in budget hotels) before making your decision: this is quite normal and accepted in Costa Rica. Rooms in any one hotel can vary dramatically.

Far too many Costa Rican hoteliers are abusive to guests and fail to rectify faults with their hotels. Guests who complain about very real problems are often treated with disdain, and many readers have written to complain about threatening behavior by hotel owners or their staff. Failure to honor reservations is another common complaint. Discounts or refunds are rarely offered, regardless of circumstances. The problem spans all price levels, although deluxe properties are mostly immune, and foreign-owned properties have a better record.

Most hotels supply towels and soap, but unless you're staying in the upscale hotels, you may need to bring your own shampoos, washcloths, and even a sink plug. The cheapest accommodations usually have communal bathrooms and, especially in hot lowland areas, cold-water showers only; often shower units are powered by electric heating elements, which you switch on for the duration of your shower (don't expect steaming-hot water, however). *Beware!* It's easy to give yourself a shock from any metal object nearby, including the water pipes—hence the nickname "suicide showers." Where trying to flush your waste paper down the toilet may cause a blockage, waste receptacles are provided for paper. Unhygienic, yes, but use the basket unless you fancy a smelly back-up.

Before accepting a room, ensure that the door is secure and that your room can't be entered by someone climbing through the window. Always lock your door. Never leave valuables in your room if you can avoid it, and always lock your possessions in your baggage (many hotel workers are abysmally low-paid and the temptation to steal may be irresistible). Take a padlock to use in cheaper hotels.

If you anticipate carousing until midnight or later, make sure in advance that the hotel provides late access. Many of the better hotels discourage unregistered guests.

The **Certificate for Sustainable Tourism** (CST, tel. 506/257-2264, fax 506/221-1443, info@sustainable-tourism.co.cr, www.turismo-sostenible.co.cr) grades hotels by both environmental and cultural attributes. For hotels to earn acceptance they must have 70 percent native species in their gardens, provide an educational component for guests, contribute to local communities, and meet strict criteria for recycling and energy efficiency.

Reservations

Reservations are strongly advised for dry-season months (Dec.–April). Christmas, Easter week, and weekends are particularly busy. Don't rely on mail to make reservations; it could take several months to confirm. Instead, book online, call direct, send a fax, email, or have your travel agent make reservations for you. It may be necessary to send a deposit, without which your space may be released to someone else. Check on this when you make your reservation. Take a copy of your reservation with you, and reconfirm a few days before arrival.

Rates

Many hotels have separate rates for low ("green") season (May–Oct.) and high season (Nov.–April), often with premium rates during Christmas, New Year, and Easter: low-season discounts average about 20 percent. Upscale properties also have shoulder-season rates. If no single rooms are available, you'll usually be charged the single rate for a double room. And couples requesting a *casa matrimonial* (i.e., wishing to sleep in one bed) will often receive a discount off the normal double rate. A 16.39 percent tax is added to your room bill at most hotels. Some hotels charge extra (as much as 6 percent) for paying by credit card.

Rates are subject to fluctuation. Every attempt has been made to ensure that prices given here are accurate at press time.

ACCOMMODATION TYPES

Apartotels

A hybrid of hotels and apartment buildings, *apartotels* resemble motels on the European and Australian model, and offer rooms with kitchens or kitchenettes (pots and pans and cutlery are provided) and sometimes small suites furnished with sofas and tables and chairs. One- or two-bedroom units are available, and weekly and monthly rates are offered. Most offer daily maid service. Apartotels are particularly economical for families and are popular with Ticos.

Health Spas

Costa Rica offers several health spas. The most complete are **Hotel Martino Med-spa & Resort,** at La Garita; **Tara Resort Hotel & Spa,** above Escazú; **Xandari,** near Alajuela; **El Tucano** near Aguas Zarcas; **Hotel Borinquen,** in Guanacaste; **Villa Caletas,** above Playa Herradura; and **Hotel Si Como No,** at Manuel Antonio, in the Central Pacific.

Homestays and Bed-and-Breakfasts

Many Costa Rican families welcome foreign travelers into their homes as paying guests—an ideal way to experience the legendary Tico hospitality and warmth, and a pleasing opportunity to bone up on your Spanish. "Guesthouse" refers to a bed-and-breakfast hotel in a family-run home where you are made to feel like part of the family, as opposed to hotels that include breakfasts in their room rates. Many local hosts advertise in the *Tico Times.* Also, contact the ICT office (tel. 506/223-1733 or 866/COSTA RICA (866/267-8274), fax 506/355-4997).

Bell's Home Hospitality (P.O. Box 185-1000, San José, tel. 506/225-4752, fax 506/224-5884, homestay@racsa.co.cr, www.homestay.thebells .org; in the U.S., Dept. 1432, P.O. Box 025216, Miami, FL 33102) lists more than 70 host homes in the residential suburbs of San José, plus a few in outlying towns. Rates are $30 s, $45 d (dinners $7 per person). The company arranges accommodations for singles, couples, and families of up to five people, and will match you with an

English-speaking family if you wish. The Bells will also arrange airport transfers and offer a free information service.

Hotels

Costa Rica's hotels run the gamut from beach resorts, mountain lodges, and haciendas-turned-hotels to San José's plusher options. Standards vary greatly. Many upper-end hotels can hold their own on the international hotel scene and live up to expectations. Others can't justify their price: where this is the case, I've said so.

Small Distinctive Hotels of Costa Rica (tel. 506/258-0150, fax 506/258-0153, www.distinctivehotels.com) is an association of six of the finest hotels in the country. **Small Unique Hotels** (www.costa-rica-unique-hotels.com), comprising less stupendous but still worthy hotels, attempts to compete. The **Charming Nature Hotels Group** (oficina@charminghotels.net, www.charminghotels.net) is a consortium of small German-Swiss-owned properties.

Flexi Voucher (tel. 506/232-0400, info @aratours.com, www.flexivoucher-costarica.com) permits you to buy vouchers good for 70 hotels nationwide.

Motels

In Costa Rica, as throughout Latin America, "motels" are explicitly for lovers. Rooms—complete with adult movies and, sometimes, whirlpools and ceiling mirrors—are rented out by the hour. Originally aimed at providing privacy for young couples, today's motels more commonly serve as meeting places for adult trysts. Hence, they're usually hidden behind high walls with private garages for each room to protect guests from inquisitive eyes and chance encounters with the neighbor or spouse.

Nature Lodges

Costa Rica is richly endowed with mountain and jungle lodges, many in private reserves. Most have naturalist guides and arrange nature hikes, horseback riding, and other activities. Some are relatively luxurious; others are basic.

Cooprena (tel. 506/248-2538, fax 506/248-1659, cooprena@racsa.co.cr, www.turismoruralcr .com) is a cooperative of rural community organizations that promotes 10 rustic ecolodges.

Youth Hostels

In Costa Rica, Hostelling International (the U.S. affiliate of the International Youth Hostel Federation, or IYHF) is represented by the Organized Tourist Network, or **RETO** (Apdo. 1355, San José 1002, tel. 506/234-8186, fax 506/224-4085, recajhi@racsa.co.cr, www.hicr.org), based in the Hostel Toruma in San José. Most are standard hotels that honor hostel rates. A few also allow camping.

You can reserve accommodations up to six months in advance through any participating hostel, or via **Hostelling International** (www.iyhf.org).

CAMPING

Several national parks have basic camping facilities (see regional chapters for details), as do a growing number of commercial spots at popular beach sites. Camping is discouraged, and even illegal, on beaches, although that doesn't stop the locals, for whom camping on the beach during national holidays is a tradition.

You'll need a warm sleeping bag and a waterproof tent for camping in the mountains, where you may need permission from local landowners or park rangers before pitching your tent. Generally, a Gore-Tex bivouac bag or even a tarp will suffice in the lowlands. You'll also need a mosquito net and plenty of bug repellent. If you really want the "local" flavor, buy a hammock and sleep between two coconut trees, safely suspended beyond the reach of most creepy crawlies. Avoid grassy pastures: they harbor chiggers and ticks. And don't camp near riverbanks, where snakes congregate and flash floods may be likely.

Bring all your camping gear with you, as quality camping-supply stores are few and far between in Costa Rica.

Theft is a problem. If possible, camp with a group of people so one person can guard the gear.

Food and Drink

COSTA RICAN CUISINE

Costa Rican cuisine is simple and spices are shunned. *Comida típica,* or native dishes, rely heavily on rice and beans, and "home-style" cooking predominates. Meals are generally wholesome and reasonably priced. *Gallo pinto,* the national dish of fried rice and black beans, is ubiquitous, including as a breakfast *(desayuno)* staple. Many meals are derivatives, including *arroz con pollo* (rice and chicken) or *arroz con tuna.* At lunch, *gallo pinto* becomes the *casado* (literally "married"), a cheap set lunch plate of rice and beans supplemented with cabbage-and-tomato salad, fried plantains, and meat. Vegetables do not form a large part of the diet, and when they do, they are usually overcooked.

Food staples include *carne* (beef, sometimes called *bistek*), *pollo* (chicken), and *pescado* (fish). Beef and steaks are quite lean—Costa Rican cattle is grass-fed and flavorful, devoid of injected hormones. Still, don't expect your tenderloin steak *(lomito)* to match its North American counterpart.

Seafoods are popular—especially sea bass (*corvina*), mahi-mahi, shrimp *camarones*), and lobster (*langosto*). Light and flavorful tilapia (African bass) is increasingly popular, especially served with garlic (*al ajillo*). Marlin and sailfish are regional specialties at local restaurants. They are particularly delicious when prepared with a marinated base of fresh herbs and olive oil, and seared over an open grill to retain the moist flavor. Ceviche is also favored throughout Nicoya, using the white meat of *corvina* steeped in lemon juice mixed with dill or cilantro and finely cut red peppers. Guanacaste province is particularly noted for its local specialties, such as *sopa de albondigas* (spicy meatball soup, with chopped eggs) and *pedre* (carob beans, pork, chicken, onions, sweet peppers, salt, and mint), plus foods based on corn, such as tortillas and corn rice.

Sodas, open-air lunch counters, serve inexpensive snacks and meals.

Eating in Costa Rica doesn't present the health problems that plague the unwary traveler elsewhere in Central America, but you need to be cautious. Pesticide use in Costa Rica is unregulated. *Always* wash vegetables in water known to be safe. And ensure that any fruits you eat are peeled yourself; you never know where someone else's hands have been. Otherwise, stick to staples such as bananas and oranges. If on a budget, eat where the locals eat.

There is no shortage of fast-food options—McDonald's, Pizza Hut, KFC, and their local equivalents.

In San José, restaurants serve the gamut of international cuisine at reasonable prices. And though culinary excellence in general declines with distance from the capital city, a growing number of hoteliers and gourmet chefs are opening restaurants worthy of note in even the most secluded backwaters. Take the Caribbean coast, for example, where the local cuisine reflects its Jamaican heritage with mouth-watering specialties such as ackee and codfish (ackee is a small, pink-skinned fruit that tastes like scrambled eggs), johnnycakes, curried goat, curried shrimp, and pepperpot soup, with its subtle, lingering heat.

Many bars in Costa Rica serve *bocas*—savory tidbits ranging from ceviche to *tortillas con queso* (tortillas with cheese)—with drinks. Some provide them free, so long as you're drinking. Others apply a small charge. Turtle *(tortuga)* eggs are a popular dish in many working-class bars.

Most towns have Saturday-morning street markets *(ferias de agricultor).* Even the smallest hamlet has its *pulpería* or *abastacedor*—local grocery store.

Dining in Costa Rica is a leisurely experience. Some restaurants stay open 24 hours. Many close on Sundays.

FRUIT

Costa Rica grows many exotic fruits. The bunches of bright vermilion fruits on the stem found at roadside stalls nationwide are *pejibayes,* teeny relatives of the coconut. You scoop out the boiled avocado-like flesh; its taste is commonly described as falling between that of a chestnut and a pumpkin. The *pejibaye* palm (not to be confused with the *pejibaye*) produces the *palmito* (heart of palm), used in salads. *Guayabas* (guavas) come into season Sept.–Nov.; their pink fruit is used for jams and jellies. A smaller version—*cas*—finds its way into *refrescos* and ice cream. The *marañón,* the fruit of the cashew, is also commonly used in *refrescos. Mamones* are little green spheres containing grapelike pulp. And those yellow-red, egg-size fruits are *granadillas* (passion fruit). One of my favorites—it comes both sweet and sour—is the "star fruit," or *carambeloa,* with the flesh of a grape and the taste of an orange.

Sweet and succulent *sandías* (watermelons) should not be confused with the lookalike *chiverre,* whose "fruit" resembles spaghetti! *Piña* (pineapple) is common. So too are *mélon* (cantaloupe) and mangos. Papayas come in two forms: the round, yellow-orange *amarilla* and the elongated, red-

EATING COSTA RICAN: SOME SPECIALTIES

arreglados—sandwiches or tiny puff pastries stuffed with beef, cheese, or chicken. Greasy!

arroz con pollo—a basic dish of chicken and rice.

casado—*arroz* (rice), frijoles (black beans), *carne* (beef), *repollo* (cabbage), and *plátano* (plantain). Avocado *(aguacates)* or egg may also be included.

ceviche—marinated seafood, often chilled, made of *corvina* (sea bass), *langostinos* (shrimp), or *conchas* (shellfish). Normally served with lemon, chopped onion, garlic, and sweet red peppers.

chorreados—corn pancakes, often served with sour cream *(natilla)*

elote—corn on the cob, either boiled *(elote cocinado)* or roasted *(elote asado)*

empañadas—turnovers stuffed with beans, cheese, meat, or potatoes

enchiladas—pastries stuffed with cheese and potatoes and occasionally meat

gallo—tortilla sandwiches stuffed with beans, cheese, or meat

gallo pinto—the national dish (literally "spotted rooster"), made of lightly spiced rice and black beans. Traditional breakfast *(desayuno)* or lunch dish. Sometimes includes *huevos fritos* (fried eggs).

olla de carne—soup made of squash, corn, *yuca* (a local tuber), chayote (a local pear-shaped vegetable), *ayote* (a pumpkinlike vegetable), and potatoes

palmitos—succulent hearts of palm, common in salads

patacones—thin slices of deep-fried plantain. A popular Caribbean dish. Served like french fries.

pescado ahumado—smoked fish

picadillo—a side dish of fried vegetables and meat

sopa negra—a creamy soup, often with a hard-boiled egg and vegetables soaking in the bean broth

sopa de mondongo—soup made from tripe

tamales—steamed cornmeal pastries stuffed with corn, chicken, or pork, and wrapped in a banana or corn leaf. A popular Christmas dish.

tortillas—Mexican-style corn pancakes or omelettes

Desserts and Sweets (Postres y Dulces)

cono capuchino—an ice-cream cone topped with chocolate

dulce de leche—a syrup of boiled milk and sugar. Also thicker, fudgelike *cajeta*—delicious!

flan—cold caramel custard

mazamorra—cornstarch pudding

melcocha—candy made from raw sugar

milanes—chocolate candies

pan de maíz— sweet cornbread

queque seco—pound cake

torta chilena—multilayered cake filled with *dulce de leche*

orange *cacho*. *Moras* (blackberries) are most commonly used for refrescos.

DRINK

Costa Rica has no national drink, perhaps with the exception of *horchata*, a cinnamon-flavored cornmeal drink, and *guaro*, the *campesino*'s near-tasteless, yet potent, drink of choice. Coffee, of course, is Costa Rica's *grano de oro* (grain of gold). Most of the best coffee is exported. Coffee is traditionally served very strong and mixed with hot milk. When you order coffee with milk *(café con leche)*, you'll generally get half coffee, half milk. If you want it black, you want *café sin leche* or *café negro*.

Milk is pasteurized.

The more popular North American soda pops, such as Pepsi and Coca-Cola, as well as sparkling water (called *agua mineral* or *soda*) are popular and also widely available, as are their *tico* equivalents. *Refrescos* refers to energizing fruit sodas and colas. *Batidos* are fruit shakes served with water *(con agua)* or milk *(con leche)*.

Sugar finds its way into all kinds of drinks, even water: *agua dulce*, another beverage popular with *campesinos* is boiled water with brown sugar—energy for field workers. Roadside stalls also sell *pipas*, green coconuts with the tops chopped off. You drink the refreshing cool milk from a straw.

Imported alcohol is expensive in Costa Rica, so stick with the local drinks. Lovers of beer *(cerveza)* are served locally brewed pilsners and lagers that reflect an early German presence in Costa Rica. Imperial and Bavaria are the two most popular brews. Tropical is a low-calorie "lite" beer. Heineken is also brewed here under license. Bavaria makes a flavorful dark beer *(negra)*. Cheaper bars charge about 60 cents for a local beer; fancy hotels charge about $2.

Even the poorest *campesino* can afford the native red-eye, *guaro*, a harsh, clear spirit distilled from fermented sugarcane. My favorite drink? Guaro mixed with Café Rica, a potent coffee liqueur.

The national liquor monopoly also produces vodka and gin (both recommended), rum (so-so), and whiskey (not recommended). Imported whiskeys—Johnnie Walker is popular—are less expensive than other imported liquors, which are expensive.

Costa Rica even makes its own (unremarkable) wines, sold under the *La Casa Tebar* label, and grown at La Garita by the Vicosa company, which also makes a sparkling wine. Chilean and Argentinian vintages are widely available and inexpensive.

Costa Ricans deplore drunks; it goes against the grain of *quedar bien*. Still, drinking is not restricted to lunch and the evening hours. Don't be surprised to find the Tico at the table next to yours washing down breakfast with a little whiskey. On weekends, in towns, it is not uncommon to have to step over people sprawled across the sidewalks.

Tips for Travelers

ACCESS FOR DISABLED TRAVELERS

Few allowances have been made in infrastructure for travelers with disabilities, although wheelchair ramps are now appearing on sidewalks, and an increasing number of hotels are provisioning rooms and facilities for the physically challenged.

In the U.S., the **Society for Accessible Travel & Hospitality** (347 5th Ave. #610, New York, NY 10016, tel. 212/447-7284, fax 212/725-8253, sathtravel@aol.com, www.sath.org); and the **American Foundation for the Blind** (11 Penn Plaza No 300, New York, NY 10001, tel. 212/502-7600 or 800/232-5463, afbinfo@afb.org, www.afb.org) are good resources.

Flying Wheels Travel (143 W. Bridge St., Owatanna, MN 55060, tel. 507/451-5005, fax 507/451-1685, thq@ll.net, www.flyingwheelstravel.com) is a full-service travel agency for the physically challenged.

In Costa Rica, **Vaya con Silla de Ruedas** (Go with Wheelchairs, Apdo. 54-4150 Sarchí, tel./fax 506/454-4536, vayacon@racsa.co.cr) is a specialized transport service for the ambulatory disabled. It operates a specially outfitted vehicle with three wheelchair stations, has 24-hour service, and offers overnight and multi-day tours ($240 full day, $150 half day, $40 airport transfer).

TRAVELING WITH CHILDREN

Generally, travel with children poses no special problems, and virtually everything you'll need for children is readily available. There are few sanitary or health problems to worry about. However, ensure that your child has vaccinations against measles and rubella (German measles), as well as any other inoculations your doctor advises. Bring cotton swabs, Band-Aids, and a small first-aid kit with any necessary medicines for your child. The **Hospital de Niños** (Children's Hospital, tel. 506/222-0122), is at Paseo Colón, Calle 14, in San José.

Children under two travel free on airlines; children between two and 12 are offered discounts (check with individual airlines). Children are also charged half the adult rate at many hotels; others permit free stays when kids are sharing parents' rooms. Some hotels charge an extra-bed rate. Baby foods and milk (irradiated for longevity) are readily available. Disposable diapers, however, are expensive (consider bringing cloth diapers; they're ecologically more acceptable). If you plan on driving around, bring your child's car seat—they're not offered for rental cars.

The **Tiskita Family Camp** (tel. 506/296-8125; in the U.S., tel. 800/345-7422) is a nine-day package that operates late June through August at Tiskita Jungle Lodge in southwest Costa Rica and features arts and crats, birding, horseback riding, and science projects.

Family Travel Network (www.familytravel-network.com) and *Great Vacations with Your Kids* (New York: E.P. Dutton), by Dorothy Jordan and Marjorie Cohen, are handy reference guides to planning a trip with children.

Family-Friendly Tour Companies

Rascals in Paradise (One Daniel Burnham Ct., Suite 105-C, San Francisco, CA 94109, tel. 415/921-7000, fax 415/775 0900, trips @RascalsInParadise.com, www.rascalsinparadise.com) and **Wildland Adventures** (3516 N.E. 155th St., Seattle, WA 98155, tel. 206/365-0686 or 800/345-4453, fax 206/363-6615, info@wildad.com, www.wildland.com) offer family trips to Costa Rica.

WOMEN TRAVELING ALONE

Most women enjoy traveling in Costa Rica. The majority of Tico men treat foreign women with great respect. Still, Costa Rica *is* a *machismo* society and you may experience certain hassles. The art of gentle seduction is to Ticos a kind of national pastime: a sport and a trial of manhood. They will hiss in appreciation from a distance like serpents, and call out epithets such as *"guapa"* ("pretty one"), *"machita"* (for blondes), or *"mi amor."* Be aware that many Ticos think a gringa is an "easy" *conquista.* The wolf-whistles can grate but, fortunately, sexual assault of female tourists is rare—though it *does* happen. The behavior is usually relegated to lower-class Ticos; middle-class males act more respectfully.

If you welcome the amorous attentions of men, take effusions of love with a grain of salt; while swearing eternal devotion, your Don Juan may conveniently forget to mention he's married. And when he suggests a nightcap at some romantic locale, he may mean one of San José's love motels. On the Caribbean coast are many black "beach boys"—"Rent-a-Rastas"—who earn their living giving pleasure to women looking for love beneath the palms. On the Caribbean, foreign women are expected to open their wallets on their lover's behalf (you're rich, he's poor); less so elsewhere in the country.

Come prepared! Carry condoms; don't rely on the man. And be prepared to encounter resistance from your lover. Although Costa Rica has an admirable anti-AIDS education campaign, there are plenty of macho men who don't get the message.

If you're not interested in love in the tropics, unwanted attention can be a hassle. Pretend not to notice. Avoid eye contact. An insistent stare—*dando cuervo* (making eyes)—is part of their game. You can help prevent these overtures by dressing modestly. Shorts, halter tops, or strapless sundresses in San José invite attention. Wearing a wedding band may help keep the wolves at bay. There have been reports of a few taxi drivers coming on to women passengers. Though this is the exception, where possible take a hotel taxi rather than a street cab. And beware illegal unmarked "taxis" that may be cruising for single women. Avoid deserted beaches, especially at night.

Women Travel: Adventures, Advice, and Experience, by Niktania Jansz and Miranda Davies (Rough Guides), offers practical advice for women travelers, as does *Gutsy Women,* by MaryBeth Bond (Travelers' Tales), a small-format guide with travel tips for women on the road. Likewise, the following magazines may be useful: the quarterly *Journeywoman* (50 Prince Arthur Ave. #1703, Toronto, Canada M5R 1B5, tel. 416/929-7654, editor@journey woman.com, www.journeywoman.com); the quarterly *Maiden Voyages* (109 Minna St. #240, San Francisco, CA 94105, tel. 800/528-8425, info@maiden-voyages.com); and the monthly *Travelin' Woman* (855 Moraga Dr. #14, Los Angeles, CA 90049, tel. 800/871-6409, traveliw @aol.com).

The **Federation of Women's Travel Organizations** (P.O. Box 466, Avenida Palma de Mallorca 15, Spain, tel. 95/205-7060, fax 95/205 -8418, www.ifwto.org; in the U.S., IFWTO, Enterprise, AL 36330, tel. 334/393-4431, fax 530/686-8891, hedegolyers@earthlink.net) is a useful resource.

Mariah Wilderness Expeditions (P.O. Box 70248, Pt. Richmond, CA 94807, tel. 510/233-2303 or 800/462-7424, fax 510/233-0956, rafting@mariahwe.com, www.mariahwe.com) specializes in trips to Costa Rica for women.

In Costa Rica, **CEFEMINA** (Centro Feminista de Información y Acción, Apdo. 5355, San José 1000, tel. 506/224-3986, fax 506/225-4697, www.cefemina.or.cr) is a feminist organization that can provide assistance to women travelers. CEFEMINA publishes the quarterly *Mujer.* The **Women's Club of Costa Rica** (tel. 506/282-6801 or 506/235-6716, www.wccr.org), an English-speaking social forum, is a good resource, as is the **National Institute of Women** (Instituto Nacional de Las Mujeres, tel. 506/253-8066, fax 506/283-0657, info@inamu.go.cr, www.inamu.go.cr).

The **Feminist International Radio Network** (FIRE, tel. 506/249-1319, femintra@hotmail .com, www.fire.or.cr) broadcasts online at its website. And *Pregonera* (pregoner@racsa.co.cr) is a monthly newspaper written by and for women; the name is the feminine version of "town crier."

GAY AND LESBIAN TRAVELERS

On the books, Costa Rica is tolerant of homo-sexuality and has laws to protect gays from dis-crimination; despite being a Roman Catholic nation, homosexual intercourse is legal (the con-sensual age is 17—for heterosexuals it's 15). Still, Costa Rica remains a *machismo* society, and 1999 witnessed violently anti-gay demonstrations. De-spite legal protections, discrimination exists. For the most part, Costa Rican gays remain in the closet. There is even less tolerance of lesbians. Understandably, the climate of abuse and intol-erance has resulted in a high level of alcoholism, drug abuse, and even suicide among Costa Rica's gays. The Costa Rican government is zealous in protecting minors, and gay travelers are advised against fraternizing with anyone under 18.

Gay tourists should feel no discrimination "if you don't indulge in foolish [overt] behavior." These words of advice are from *¡Pura Vida!: A Travel Guide to Gay & Lesbian Costa Rica* by Joseph Itiel (Orchid House, 1993). To understand the so-ciology of Latino homosexuality, readers of Spanish may wish to browse *Hombres que aman hombres,* by Jacobo Schifter Sikora and Johnny Madrigal Pana (San José: Ediciones Illep-Sida, 1992).

Transvestis (transvestites) are part of the gay and prostitution scene. Itiel describes a world of "brutal fights, drugs, unsafe sex, and robberies." A majority of *transvestis,* he says, are involved with drugs. *Beware!*

The "Miss Costa Rica Gay" competition is held mid-June (tel. 506/223-3758 or 506/836-6271, misscostaricagay@hotmail.com).

One of the best resources is www.gaycostar-ica.com. *Gente 10* (www.gente10.com) and *Gay-ness* (P.O. Box 1581-1002 San José, tel. 506/374-2928, gaynesscr@gay.com)s are gay maga-zines published in Costa Rica.

Also see the sidebars *Gay San José,* in the San José chapter, and *Manuel Antonio for Gays and Lesbians,* in the *Central Pacific* chapter.

Organizations

Useful resources include the **International Gay and Lesbian Association** (208 West 13th St., New York, NY 10011, tel. 212/620-7310 or 800/421-1220, info@gaycenter.org, www.gaycenter.org) and the **International Gay & Lesbian Travel Association** (4431 N. Federal Hwy. #304, Fort Lauderdale, FL 33308, tel. 954/776-2626 or 800/448-8550, fax 954/776-3303, iglta@iglta.org, www.iglta.org).

In Costa Rica the most prominent organiza-tion is **Triángulo Rosa** (Apdo. 1619-4050, Ala-juela, tel. 506/258-0214 or 506/223-1370, fax 506/258-0635 or 223-3964, atrirosa@sol.racsa.co.cr), which acts as an information center and provides a gamut of services: safe-sex education, AIDS counseling, and fighting ongoing dis-crimination. It is staffed by volunteers, who can provide recommendations for gay-friendly bars, hotels, and more.

Also try **Asociación Agua Buena** (tel./fax 506/234-2411, rastern@sol.racsa.co.cr, www.aguabuena.org).

Tours

The following specialize in gay travel and offer tours to Costa Rica: **Adventure Tours** (57 Garfield St. #4, Saco, ME 04072, tel. 207/284-2804 or 888/206-6523, info@gayadventuretours.com, www.gayadventuretours.com); **Arco Iris Travel Services** (tel. 619/297-0897 or 800/765-4370, info@arcoiristours.com, www.arcoiris-tours.com); **Colours Destinations** (tel. 954/825-0321 or 877/932-6652, fax 954/825-0322, newcolours@colours.net, www.colours.net); and **Venture Out,** (575 Pierce St. #64, San Francisco, CA 94117, tel. 415/626-5679 or 888/431-6789, rad@venture-out.com, www.venture-out.com).

Mariah Wilderness Expeditions (P.O. Box 70248, Pt. Richmond, CA 94807, tel. 510/233-2303 or 800/462-7424, fax 510/233-0956, rafting @mariahwe.com, www.mariahwe.com) is a gay-friendly, women-owned adventure travel com-pany specializing in Costa Rica.

In France, **Eurogays** (23 Rue du Bourg Ti-bourg, 75004 Paris, tel. 01/48-87-37-77, fax 01/48-87-39-99, info@eurogays.com, www.eurogays.com) is a gay and lesbian travel agency that offers tours to Costa Rica.

Odysseus: The International Gay Travel Planner (P.O. Box 1548, Port Washington, NY 11050, tel. 516/944-5330 or 800/257-5344, fax 516/944-7540, odyusa@odyusa.com, www.odyusa.com) lists worldwide hotels and tours, and publishes travel guides for gays and lesbians. Spartacus International Gay Guide (P.O. Box 37887, Phoenix, AZ 85069, tel. 602/863-2408 or 800/962-2912, fax 602/439-3952, ferrari @q-net.com) is a travel guide.

In Costa Rica, try Gaytours (tel. 506/297-3556, gaytours@costarricense.co.cr, www.gaytourscostarica.com).

Meeting Places

Gay action is centered in San José, where there are several gay bars and clubs.

Hotel Villa Caletas, near Jacó; Hotel Poseidon, in Jacó; and Villa Decary, at Lake Arenal, are among the gay-friendly hotels outside the capital. In Manuel Antonio, Hotel Casa Blanca, La Plantacion and Hotel Villa Roca acept only gay clients.

STUDENTS AND YOUTHS

Student Cards

An International Student Identity Card entitles students 12 years and older to discounts on transportation, entrances to museums, and other savings. When purchased in the U.S. ($20), ISIC (tel. 800/GET-AN-ID) even includes $3,000 in emergency medical coverage, limited hospital coverage, and access to a 24-hour, toll-free emergency hot line. Students can obtain ISICs at any student union. Alternately, contact the Council on International Educational Exchange (CIEE, tel. 212/882-2600 or 888/268-6245, fax 212/822-2699, info@ciee.org, www.ciee.org), which issues ISICs and also arranges study vacations in Costa Rica. In Canada, cards can be obtained from Travel Cuts (tel. 416/614-2887 or 800/667-2887 in Toronto, tel. 604/717-7800 in Vancouver, www.travelcuts.com). In the United Kingdom, students can obtain an ISIC from any student union office.

Know Costa Rica

LANGUAGE STUDY

Costa Rica has dozens of language schools. Most programs include homestays with Costa Rican families—a tremendous (and fun) way to boost your language skills and learn the local idioms. Many also feature workshops on Costa Rican culture, dance lessons, and excursions. Courses run an average of two to four weeks. The norm is three to five hours of instruction daily, more in intensive courses.

The National Registration Center for Study Abroad (P.O. Box 1393, Milwaukee, WI 53201, tel. 414/278-0631, fax 414/271-8884, www.nrcsa.com) evaluates foreign language schools and "chooses the best." It represents three schools in Costa Rica.

The following language schools are recommended:

Centro Panamericano de Idiomas (P.O. Box 151-3007, San Joaquín de Flores, Heredia, tel. 506/265-6306, fax 506/265-6866, info@cpi-edu.com, www.cpi-edu.com).

Costa Rica Language Academy (P.O. Box 1966-2050, San José, tel. 506/280-1685, fax 506/280-2548, spanish@crla.co.cr, www.spanishandmore.com; in the U.S., tel. 866/230- 6361).

Instituto Británico (tel. 506/225-0256, fax 506/253-1894, britanico@amnet.co.cr, www.institutobritanico.com).

Intensa (Apdo. 8110-1000, San José, tel. 506/281-1818, fax 506/253-4337, info@intensa.com, www.intensa.com; in the U.S., tel. 414/278-0631).

Intercultura (Apdo. 1952-3000, Heredia, tel. 506/260-8480, fax 506/260-9243, info @interculturacostarica.com, www.spanish-intercultura.com; in the U.S., tel. 800/205-0642).

Speak Spanish Like a Costa Rican, by Christopher Howard, is a book and 90-minute cassette.

Travel and Work Study

The **University of Costa Rica** offers special *cursos libres* (free courses) during winter break (December–March). It also grants "special student" status to foreigners. Contact the Oficina de Asuntos Internacionales (tel. 506/207-5080, fax 506/225-5822, oauicr@cariari.ucr.ac.cr). The **University for Peace** (PO Box 138-6100, San José, tel. 506/205-9000, fax 506/249-1929, info@upeace.org, www.upeace.org), and **Organization for Tropical Studies** (tel. 506/240-6696, fax 506/240-6783, www.ots.duke.edu; in the U.S., tel. 919/684-5774, fax 919/684-5661) also sponsor study courses. **EcoTeach** (PO Box 737, Suquamish, WA 98392, tel. 360/598-1543 or 800/626-8992, info@ecoteach.com, www.ecoteach.com) places students on environmental projects in Costa Rica.

Work abroad programs are also offered through **CIEE's Work Abroad Department** (Publications Dept., 205 E. 42nd St., New York, NY 10017, books@ciee.org) which publishes a series of reference guides, including *Work, Study, Travel Abroad* and *The High School Student's Guide to Study, Travel, and Adventure Abroad.*

Holbrook Travel (3540 N.W. 13th St., Gainesville, FL 32609, tel. 800/451-7111, fax 352/371-3710, travel@holbrooktravel.com, www.holbrooktravel.com) offers an eight-day "Tropical Education Program" in Costa Rica for students and teachers. The **School for Field Studies** (10 Federal St., Salem, MA 01970, tel. 978/741-3544 or 800/989-4418, fax 978/741-3551, admissions@fieldstudies.org, www.fieldstudies.org) has summer courses in sustainable development.

Transitions Abroad (P.O. Box 1300, Amherst, MA 01004-1300, tel. 413/256-3414 or 800/293-0373, fax 413/256-0373, info@transitionsabroad.com, www.transitionsabroad.com) provides information for students wishing to study abroad; as does **Studyabroad.com** (1450 Edgmont Ave., Suite 140, Chester, PA 19013, tel. 610/499-9200, fax 610/499-9205, studyabroad.com) and **Study Abroad Directory** (8 East First Ave., Suite 102, Denver, CO 80203, tel. 720/570-1702, fax 720/570-1703, www.studyabroaddirectory.com).

In Costa Rica, **Ecole Travel** (P.O. Box 11516-1000, San José, tel. 506/223-2240, fax 506/223-4128, info@ecoletravel.com, www.ecoletravel.com) specializes in student travel, including international student exchange programs focusing on ecology, and includes a visit to Panamá's San Blas islands. It also offers language study.

LIVING IN COSTA RICA

Peter Dickinson, author of *Travel and Retirement Edens Abroad*, considers the quality of life in Costa Rica among the highest in the hemisphere: "It's probably one of the easiest places in the world for Americans to settle." More than 40,000 U.S. citizens share Dickinson's sentiments and have settled here for genteel retirement, the carefree lifestyle, or to escape wrecked marriages or other crises.

The **Association of Residents of Costa Rica** (P.O. Box 1191-1007 Centro Colón, tel. 506/233-8068, fax 506/255-0061, arcr@casacanada.net, www.casacanada.net/arcr), in Casa Canada, at Calle 40 and Avenidas 4, San José, serves the interests of foreign residents as well as those considering living in Costa Rica.

Christopher Howard (Costa Rica Books, Suite 1 SJO 981, P.O. Box 025216, Miami, FL 33102-5216, tel. 506/232-5613, crbooks@racsa.co.cr, www.costaricabooks.com), author of *The Golden Door to Retirement and Living in Costa Rica*, offers fact-finding trips to Costa Rica for would-be retirees. Also see *Living Abroad in Costa Rica*, by Erin Van Rheenen (Avalon Travel Publishing, 2004).

SENIOR TRAVELERS

Useful resources include the **American Association of Retired Persons** (AARP, 601 E. St. West, Washington, D.C. 20049, tel. 202/434-2277 or 800/424-3410, member@aarp.org, www.aarp.or), whose benefits include a "Purchase Privilege Program" offering discounts on airfares, hotels, car rentals, and more. The AARP also offers group tours for seniors.

Another handy resource is *The International Health Guide for Senior Citizen Travelers,* by Robert Lange, M.D. (New York: Pilot Books).

Canadian company **ElderTreks** (597 Markham St., Toronto, Ontario M6G 2L7, tel. 416/588-5000 or 800/741-7956, fax 416/588-9839, eldertreks@eldetreks.com, www.eldertreks.com) offers 14-day trips to Cuba. **Elderhostel** (11 Avenue de Lafayette, Boston, MA 02111, tel. 978/323-4141 or 877/426-8056, fax 617/426-0701, www.elderhostel.org) offers relatively inexpensive educational tours to Costa Rica for seniors, including ecological tours in which participants contribute to the welfare of Mother Nature.

Thinking of retiring in Costa Rica? I recommend the "Live or Retire in Paradise Tour" offered by Christopher Howard (tel. 800/365-2342, crbooks@racsa.co.cr), author of *The Golden Door to Retirement and Living in Costa Rica.*

Health and Safety

Sanitary standards in Costa Rica are high, and the chances of succumbing to a serious disease are rare. As long as you take appropriate precautions and use common sense, you're not likely to incur serious illness. If you do, you have the benefit of knowing that the nation has a good health-care system. There are English-speaking doctors in most cities, and you will rarely find yourself far from medical help.

BEFORE YOU GO

Dental and medical checkups may be advisable before departing home, particularly if you intend to travel for a considerable time or partake in strenuous activities, or if you have an existing medical problem. Take along any medications, including prescriptions for glasses and contact lenses; keep prescription drugs in their original bottles to avoid suspicion at customs. If you suffer from a debilitating health problem, wear a medical alert bracelet. Costa Rican pharmacies can prescribe drugs (be wary of expiration dates, as shelf life of drugs may be shortened under tropical conditions).

A basic health kit is a good idea. Pack the following (as a minimum) in a small plastic container: alcohol swabs and medicinal alcohol, antiseptic cream, Band-Aids, aspirin or painkillers, diarrhea medication, sunburn remedy, antifungal foot powder, calamine and/or antihistamine, water-purification tablets, surgical tape, bandages and gauze, and scissors.

Information on health concerns can be answered by **Intermedic** (777 3rd Ave., New York, NY 10017, tel. 212/486-8900); the **Department of State Citizens Emergency Center** (tel. 202/647-5226, travel.state.gov/medical.html); and the **International Association for Medical Assistance to Travellers** (IAMAT, 417 Center St., Lewiston, NY 14092, tel. 716/754-4883, info @iamat.org, www.iamat.org). In the UK, you can get information, innoculations, and medical supplies from the **British Airways Travel Clinic** (156 Regent St., London W1B 5LB, tel. 020/7439-9584).

An indispensable pocket-sized book is *Staying Healthy in Asia, Africa, and Latin America* (Avalon Travel Publishing), which is packed with first-aid and basic medical information.

The U.S. **Centers for Disease Control and Prevention** (tel. 404/332-4559, travelers' hotline 877/394-8747, fax 888/232-3299, www.cdc .gov) issues the latest health information and advisories by region.

Medical Insurance

Travel insurance is highly recommended; it isn't cheap, but it can be a sound investment. Travel agencies can sell your traveler's health and baggage insurance, as well as insurance against cancellation of a prepaid tour. Travelers should check to see if their health insurance or other policies cover medical expenses while abroad.

The following U.S. companies are recommended for travel insurance: **American Express** (P.O. Box 919010, San Diego, CA 92190, tel. 800/234-0375, www.americanexpress.com); **Travelers** (1 Tower Square, Hartford, CT 06183, tel. 203/277-0111 or 800/243-3174, www.travelers.com); and **TravelGuard International** (1145 Clark St., Stevens Point, WI 54481, tel. 715/345-0505 or 800/826-4919, www.travelguard.com).

The **Council on International Education Exchange** (CIEE, www.ciee.org) offers insurance to students.

In the U.K., the **Association of British Insurers** (51 Gresham St., London BC2V 7HQ, tel. 020/7600-3333, www.abi.org.uk) provides advice for obtaining travel insurance. Inexpensive insurance is offered through **Endsleigh Insurance** (tel. 020/7436-4451, www.endsleigh .co.uk) and **STA Travel** (tel. 020/7361-6262, www.sta.com).

In Australia, **AFTA** (tel. 2/9956-4800, www .afta.com.au) and **Travel Insurance on the Net** (www.travelinsurance.com.au) are good resources.

Costa Rica's social security system (Instituto Nacional de Seguros, or INS; also called the Caja) has a Traveler's Insurance program specifically for foreigners. As well as loss or theft of possessions, it covers emergency medical treatment (hospitalization and surgery, plus emergency dental treatment are covered; services for pre-existing conditions are not), plus repatriation of a body. You can choose coverage between 500,000 and 10 million *colones* for up to 12 weeks. You can buy coverage at travel agencies or the Instituto Nacional de Seguros (tel. 506/223-5800).

Vaccinations

No vaccinations are required to enter Costa Rica.

Epidemic diseases have mostly been eradicated throughout the country. Consult your physician for recommended vaccinations. Travelers planning to rough it should consider vaccinations against tetanus, polio, typhoid, and infectious hepatitis. The latter is endemic throughout Central America, although only infrequently reported in Costa Rica. Main symptoms are stomach pains, loss of appetite, yellowing skin and eyes, and extreme tiredness. Hepatitis A is contracted through unhygienic foods or contaminated water (salads and unpeeled fruits are major culprits). A gamma globulin vaccination is recommended. The much rarer hepatitis B is usually contracted through unclean needles, blood transfusions, or unsafe sex.

MEDICAL SERVICES

In emergencies, call 911. Alternately, call 128 for the Red Cross, which provides ambulance service nationwide. A complete list of emergency numbers is available online at www.ice.go.cr/esp /temas/guias/tel_emer.htm.

The state-run Social Security system (INS, or the Caja) operates full-service hospitals and clinics nationwide. Foreigners receive the same emergency service as Costa Ricans in public hospitals, and no one is turned away in an emergency. Many doctors have trained in the U.S. and are fluent in English.

Private hospitals offer faster and superior treatment. Use public hospitals for life-threatening emergencies only; private clinics and doctors are recommended for all other emergencies and health needs (a large deposit may be requested on admittance). Private office visits usually cost $25–50. Hospitals and clinics accept credit card payment. U.S. insurance is not normally accepted, but you can send your bill to your insurance company for reimbursement. Private doctors are listed by specialty in the Yellow Pages under "Médicos."

Pharmacies are well-stocked. Every community has at least one pharmacy (*farmacia* or *botica*) selling most medications over the counter; only antibiotics and psychotropic drugs require prescriptions.

Medical Evacuation

Membership (from $129 per year) in **Traveler's Emergency Network** (TEN, P.O. Box 668, Millersville, MD 21108, tel. 800/275-4836, www.tenweb.com) or **International SOS Assistance** (2211 Norfolk St., Suite 624, Houston, TX 77098, tel. 713/521-7611 or 800/523-8930, fax 713/521-7655, corpcomm@internationalsos .com, www.internationalsos.com), based in Singapore, provide worldwide ground and air evacuation and medical assistance, plus access to medical facilities around the world.

Several of the insurance companies listed above also provide emergency evacuation and other services.

HEALTH PROBLEMS

Infection

Even the slightest scratch can fester quickly in the tropics. Treat promptly and regularly with antiseptic and keep the wound clean.

Intestinal Problems

Water is safe to drink almost everywhere, although more remote rural areas, as well as Escazú, Santa Ana, Puntarenas, and Puerto Limón, are suspect. To play it safe, drink bottled mineral water *(agua mineral* or *soda)*. Remember, ice cubes are water, too. And don't brush your teeth using suspect water.

Food hygiene standards in Costa Rica are generally high. Milk is pasteurized. However, the change in diet—which may alter the bacteria that are normal and necessary in the bowel— may cause temporary **diarrhea** or **constipation.** (In case of the latter, eat lots of fruit.) Most cases of diarrhea are caused by microbial bowel infections resulting from contaminated food. Common-sense precautions include not eating uncooked fish or shellfish, uncooked vegetables, unwashed salads, or unpeeled fruit. Be fastidious with personal hygiene.

Diarrhea is usually temporary and many doctors recommend letting it run its course. Personally, I like to plug myself up straightaway with Lomotil or a similar "solidifier." Treat diarrhea with rest and lots of liquid to replace the water and salts lost. Avoid alcohol and milk products. If conditions don't improve after three days, seek medical help.

Diarrhea accompanied by severe abdominal pain, blood in your stool, and fever is a sign of **dysentery.** Seek immediate medical diagnosis. Tetracycline or ampicillin is normally used to cure bacillary dysentery. More complex professional treatment is required for amoebic dysentery. The symptoms of both are similar. **Giardiasis,** acquired from infected water, causes diarrhea, bloating, persistent indigestion, and weight loss. Again, seek medical advice. **Intestinal worms** can be contracted by walking barefoot on infested beaches, grass, or earth.

Sunburn and Skin Problems

Don't underestimate the tropical sun! It's intense and can fry you in minutes, particularly at higher elevations. It can burn you through light clothing or while you're lying in the shade. Even if you consider yourself nicely tanned already, *use a suncream or sunblock*—at least SPF 15 or higher. Zinc oxide provides almost 100 percent protection. Use an aloe gel after sunbathing; it helps repair any skin damage. Calamine lotion and aloe gel will soothe light burns; for more serious lobster-pink burns, use steroid creams.

Sun glare—especially prevalent if you're on water—can cause **conjunctivitis** (eye infection). Sunglasses will protect against this. **Prickly heat** is an itchy rash, normally caused by clothing that is too tight and/or in need of washing. This, and **athlete's foot,** are best treated by airing out the body and washing your clothes.

The tropical humidity and heat can sap your body fluids like blotting paper. Drink regularly to avoid dehydration. Leg cramps, exhaustion, and headaches are possible signs of dehydration.

Snakebite

Snakes are common in Costa Rica. Fewer than 500 snakebites are reported each year, and less than 3 percent of these are fatal. The majority of bites occur from people stepping on snakes. Always watch where you're treading or putting your hands. Never reach into holes or under rocks, debris, or forest-floor leaf litter without first checking with a stick to see what might be quietly slumbering there. Be particularly wary in long grass. Avoid streams at night. Many snakes are well-camouflaged arboreal creatures that snooze on branches, so never reach for a branch without looking. If you spot a snake, keep a safe distance, and give the highly aggressive fer-de-lance a *very wide* berth.

If bitten, seek medical attention without delay. Rural health posts and most national park rangers have antivenin kits on-site.

Death from snakebite is extremely rare; fear of the consequences is one of your biggest enemies, so try to relax. Do not move unless absolutely necessary. Commercial snakebite kits are normally good only for the specific species for which they were designed, so it will help if you can definitively identify the critter. But don't endanger yourself further trying to catch it.

If the bite is to a limb, immobilize the limb and apply a tight bandage between the bite and body. Release it for 90 seconds every 15 minutes. Ensure you can slide a finger under the bandage; too tight and you risk further damage. Do *not* cut the bite area in an attempt to suck out the poison unless you are an expert. Many snake poisons are anticoagulants; cutting your blood vessels may cause you to bleed like a hemophiliac. Recommendations to use electric shock as snakebite treatment have gained popular favor recently in Costa Rica; do *not* follow this medically discredited advice.

Insects and Arachnids

Sweet blood or sour blood, at some stage during your visit to Costa Rica, creepy crawlies may get you. Fortunately, only a few people will have fierce reactions. Check your bedding before crawling into bed. Always shake out your shoes and clothing before putting them on. Keep beds away from walls. Repellent sprays and lotions are a must, especially in jungle, marshy areas, and coastal lowlands.

Bites can easily become infected in the tropics, so avoid scratching. Treat with antiseptics or an-

tibiotics. A baking-soda bath can help relieve itching if you're badly bitten, as can antihistamine tablets, hydrocortisone, and calamine lotion. Long-sleeved clothing and full-length pants help keep insects at bay.

Chiggers *(coloradillas)* inhabit grasslands, particularly in Guanacaste. Their bites itch like hell. Mosquito repellent won't deter them. Dust your shoes, socks, and ankles with sulphur powder. Sucking sulphur tablets *(azufre sublimado)* apparently gives your sweat a smell that chiggers find obnoxious. Nail polish apparently works, too (on the bites, not the nails) by suffocating the beasts.

Ticks *(garrapatas)* hang out near livestock. They bury their heads into your skin. Remove them immediately with tweezers—grasp the tick's head parts as close to your skin as possible and pull gently but steadily. Don't try to extract them by holding a lighted match near them or painting them with nail polish remover or petroleum jelly.

Tiny, irritating **no-see-ums** (sandflies about the size of a pinpoint, and known locally as *purrujas*) inhabit many beaches and marshy coastal areas: avoid beaches around dusk, when they appear out of nowhere. They're not fazed by bug repellent with DEET, but Avon's Skin-So-Soft works a treat. Sandflies on the Atlantic coast can pass on leishmaniasis, a debilitating disease: seek urgent treatment for non-healing sores.

Insect larvae, such as that of the botfly, can cause growing boils once laid beneath your skin (you'll see a clear hole in the middle of the boil or pimple). Completely cover with Vaseline and a secure Band-Aid or tape and let it dry overnight; you should be able to squeeze the culprit out the next day.

If stung by a **scorpion** *(alacrán)*—not normally as bad as it sounds—take plenty of liquids and rest. If you're unfortunate enough to contract **scabies** (a microscopic mite) or **lice,** which is possible if you're staying in unhygienic conditions or sleeping with unhygienic bedfellows, use a body shampoo containing gamma benzene hexachloride. You should also wash all clothing and bedding in very hot water, and toss out your underwear. The severe itching caused by scabies infestation appears after three or four weeks (it appears as little dots, often in lines, ending in blisters, especially around the genitals, elbows, wrists, lower abdomen, and nipples).

Avoid **bees'** nests. Africanized bees have infiltrated Costa Rica in recent years. They're very aggressive and will attack with little provocation. Running in a zigzag is said to help in fleeing. If there's water about, take a dunk and stay submerged for a while.

Many bugs are local. The bite of a rare kind of insect found along the southern Caribbean coast and locally called *papalamoya* produces a deep and horrible infection that can even threaten a limb. It may be best to have such infections treated locally (and certainly promptly); doctors back home (or even in San José) might take forever to diagnose and treat the condition.

AIDS and Sexually Transmitted Diseases

AIDS is on the rise throughout Central America. Avoidance of casual sexual contact and/or use of condoms is the best prevention against contracting gonorrhea, syphilis, and other sexually transmitted diseases. Blood transfusions and unclean needles, such as those shared in drug use, are other potential sources of HIV infection. Practice safe sex!

Malaria

Malaria is nonexistent in highland areas, and only a limited risk in the lowlands, although an increase in the incidence of malaria has been reported recently in the Caribbean lowlands, particularly south of Cahuita (the majority of cases are among banana plantation workers). Consult your physician for the best type of antimalarial medication. Begin taking your tablets a few days (or weeks, depending on the prescription) before arriving in an infected zone, and continue taking the tablets for several weeks after leaving the malarial zone. Malaria symptoms include high fever, shivering, headache, and sometimes diarrhea.

Chloroquine (called Alaren in Costa Rica) and Fansidar are both used for short-term pro-

tection. Chloroquine reportedly is still good for Costa Rica, although Panamanian mosquitoes have built up a resistance to the drug. Fansidar may be a safer bet for travel south of Puerto Limón. Fansidar can cause severe skin reactions and is dangerous for people with a history of sulfonamide intolerance. If you take Fansidar and suffer from such skin and mucuous-membrane ailments as itching, rash, mouth or genital sores, or a sore throat, seek medical help immediately.

Avon Skin-So-Soft oil is such an effective bug repellent that U.S. Marines use it by the truckload ("Gee, private, you sure smell nice, and your skin's so soft!"). The best mosquito repellents contain DEET (diethylmetatoluamide). Apply rub-on repellent directly to the skin; use sprays for clothing. DEET is quite toxic; avoid using on small children. And avoid getting this on plastic—it melts it. Use mosquito netting at night in the lowlands; you can obtain good hammocks and "no-see-um" nets in the U.S. from **Campmor** (tel. 800/226-7667, customer-service @campmor.com, www.campmor.com). A fan over your bed and mosquito coils *(espirales)* also help keep mosquitoes at bay. Coils are available from *pulperías* and supermarkets (don't forget the metal stand—*soporte*—for them).

Other Problems

Occasional and serious outbreaks of **dengue fever** have occurred in recent years, notably around Puntarenas and along the Caribbean coast and the Golfito region. Transmitted by mosquitoes, the illness can be fatal (death usually results from internal hemorrhaging). Its symptoms are similar to malaria, with additional severe pain in the joints and bones (it is sometimes called "breaking bones disease") but, unlike malaria, is not recurring. You can spray your clothing with the insecticide *permethrin.*

Rabies, though rare, can be contracted through the bite of an infected dog or other animal. It is always fatal unless treated. You're extremely unlikely to be the victim of a vampire bat, a common rabies vector that preys on cattle. If you're sleeping in the open (or with an unscreened window open)

PROSTITUTION

Prostitution is legal in Costa Rica, drawing male tourists whose presence has earned Costa Rica a controversial reputation as a "New Thailand." Many Costa Rican men use prostitutes as a matter of course, and almost every town and village has a brothel—San José has dozens. The government issues licenses for brothels and provides regular health checks for prostitutes, who are issued *carnets de salud* (health certificates). Statistics suggest, however, that most of the estimated 15,000 prostitutes who work nationwide are not registered.

Most prostitutes are independent (their legal status protects prostitutes from the development of pimping) and work openly out of bars; most are also past the age of consent and do so of free will. Many, however, fall into the profession after a childhood of trauma and sexual abuse—an endemic problem within Costa Rican society (as many as 30 percent of female students at the University of Costa Rica say they have been sexually abused as children).

Sex is legal at the age of 16 in Costa Rica but prostitution under 18 is not, and under Costa Rican and international law, foreigners can be prosecuted for sex with anyone under 18. The issue hit the fan in December 2000 after ABC-TV's *20/20* ran an exposé claiming that Costa Rica had an epidemic of child-sex tourism (estimates suggest that as many as 3,000 prostitutes nationwide may be underage). Several foreigners have been jailed for operating brothels or Internet prostitution rings involving minors.

The Costa Rican Tourism Institute (ICT) has launched a major campaign to attack sex tourism. And in 2003, President Abel Pacheco announced a plan to eradicate the scourge of child prostitution. The **Patronato Nacional de la Infancia** (tel./fax 506/222-7417, www .costaricaenlucha.com) is a government-sponsored organization to fight sexual exploitation of children. And **Casa Alianza** (Covenant House Latin America, tel. 506/253-5439, fax 506/224-5689, info@casa-alianza.org, www.casa-aliazana.org) works to battle child sex exploitation.

Casa Luz (tel. 506/255-3322, casa_luz@hotmail.com) is a home for young mothers who have been physically and/or sexually abused and are at high social risk. By providing shelter, emotional support, educational and vocational development, parental skills, and spiritual counseling, the goal is for the young mothers and their children to be able to live socially healthy lives, with a real hope for the future. It is run by a nonprofit association operated by the owners of the Hotel Grano de Oro, San José. Donations are requested.

The **Center for Responsible Tourism** (1765-D Le Roy Ave., Berkeley, CA 94709, CRTourism@aol.com) publishes a leaflet, "What You Should Know About Sex Tourism Before You Go Abroad."

If you know of anyone who is traveling to Costa Rica with the intent of sexually abusing minors, contact **Interpol** (children@interpol.int, www.interpol.int); the **Task Force for the Protection of Children from Sexual Exploitation in Tourism** (World Tourism Organization, Haya 42, 28020 Madrid, Spain, tel. 91/567-8172, fax 91/571-8219, mdiotallevi@world-tourism .org, www.world-tourism.org); or the **U.S. Customs Service's International Child Pornography Investigation and Coordination Center** (45365 Vintage Park Rd., Suite 250, Sterling, VA 20166, tel. 703/709-9700, icpicc@customs.sprint.com).

© CHRISTOPHER P. BAKER

Police station, Tortuguero

in areas with vampire bat populations, don't leave your flesh exposed. Their bite, containing both anesthetic and anti-coagulant, is said to be painless.

SAFETY CONCERNS

With common sense, you are no more likely to run into problems in Costa Rica than you are in your own back yard. The vast majority of Costa Ricans are honest and friendly. However, burglary is endemic and crimes against tourists have risen alarmingly in recent years, with no part of the country exempt. A liberal judiciary and ineffective policing lead to many offenders being released without charges, or mild sentences that fail to act as deterrents. At last visit, car break-ins had become a pandemic along the Nicoya shoreline, particularly at the most popular surf beaches.

See *Safety Concerns* in the *San José* chapter for information on the capital city. Outside the city, you need to be savvy to some basic precautions. Hikers straying off trails can easily lose their way

amid the rainforests. And don't approach too close to an active volcano, such as Arenal, which may suddenly hiccup lava and breccia far and wide. Atop mountains, sunny weather can turn cold and rainy in seconds, so dress accordingly. And be extra cautious when crossing rivers; a rainstorm upstream can turn the river downstream into a raging torrent without any warning. Ideally, go with a guide.

If things go wrong, contact the **Victims Assistance Office** (tel. 506/295-3271, 7:30 A.M.–noon and 1–4 P.M. Mon.–Fri.), in the OIJ building, in San José You might also contact your embassy or consulate (see the *Embassies and Consulates in Costa Rica* chart). Consulate officials can't get you out of jail, but they can help you locate a lawyer, alleviate unhealthy conditions, or arrange for funds to be wired if you run short of money. They can even authorize a reimbursable loan—the U.S. Department of State hates to admit it—while you arrange for cash to be forwarded, or even lend you money to get home. Don't expect the U.S. embassy to bend over backward; it's notoriously unhelpful. The

Handbook of Consular Services (Public Affairs Staff, Bureau of Consular Affairs, U.S. Department of State, Washington, D.C. 20520) provides details of such assistance. Friends and family can also call the Department of State's **Overseas Citizen Service** (Department of State, 2201 C St. N.W., Washington, D.C. 20520, tel. 202/647-5225) to check on you if things go awry.

The **U.S. State Dept** (tel. 202/647-5225, www.travel.state.gov) publishes travel advisories warning U.S. citizens of trouble spots. The **British Foreign & Commonwealth Office** (Travel Advice Unit, Consular Division, Foreign & Commonwealth Office, 1 Palace St, London SW1E 5HE, tel. 020/7008-0232, www.fco.gov.uk/travel/default.asp) has a similar service.

Theft

Costa Rica's many charms can lull visitors into a false sense of security. Like anywhere else, the country has its share of social ills, with rising street crime among them. An economic crisis and influx of impoverished refugees has spawned a growing band of petty thieves and purse slashers. Violent crime, including armed holdups and muggings, are on the rise (a study by the Inter-American Development Bank suggests that as many as 24,000 Costa Ricans may have met violent deaths in a recent six-year period, prompting a national march in August 2000 to demand government action). Still, most crime is opportunistic, and thieves seek easy targets. Don't become paranoid, but a few common-sense precautions are in order.

The Instituto Costarricense de Turismo publishes a leaflet—*Let's Travel Safe*—listing precautions and a selection of emergency phone numbers. It's given out free at airport immigration counters. The ICT operates a 24-hour toll-free tourist information line (tel. 800/012-3456) for emergencies.

Make photocopies of all important documents: your passport (showing photograph and visas, if applicable), airline ticket, credit cards, insurance policy, driver's license. Carry the photocopies with you, and leave the originals in the hotel safe if possible. If this isn't possible, carry the originals with you in a secure inside pocket. Don't put all your eggs in one basket! Prepare an "emergency kit," to include photocopies of your documents

REPORTING CRIMES

Report theft, assault, and similar crimes to the **Judicial Police** (Organismo de Investigación Judicial, OIJ, tel. 506/222-1365 or 911), in the middle courthouse on Avenida 6/8, Calles 17, in San José.

To report issues relating to drugs, contact the **Policía de Control de Drogas** (tel. 800/376-4266).

Report theft or demands for money by traffic police to the **Ministry of Public Works and Transportation** (Ministerio de Obras Públicas y Transportes, Calle 9, Avenidas 20/22, tel. 506/227-2188). Report similar problems with Radio Patrulla police to the OIJ; then try to identify the police officer at the Radio Patrulla headquarters (tel. 506/226-2242), in front of Centro Comercial del Sur.

For complaints about the police, contact the **Office for the Reception of Complaints** (tel.

506/295-3272 or 506/295-3273, 24 hours), on the first floor of the OIJ building; or to **Victims Assistance Office** (tel. 506/295-3271 or 506/295-3565), on the sixth floor of the OIJ building (7:30 A.M.–noon and 1–9:30 P.M.).

Report complications with restaurants, tour companies, hotels, etc., to the main office of the **Costa Rican Tourism Institute** (ICT, Avenida 4, Calles 5/7, tel. 506/223-1733).

The U.S. State Department maintains a **Citizens' Emergency Center** (tel. 202/647-5225, fax 202/647-3000), as well as a computer bulletin board.

Erin Van Rheenen's *Living Abroad in Costa Rica* (2004, Avalon Travel Publishing's Moon Handbooks series) provides valuable information on finding and dealing with lawyers in Costa Rica, as does the *Legal Guide to Costa Rica*, by Roger Peterson.

and an adequate sum of money to tide you over if your wallet gets stolen. If you're robbed, immediately file a police report. You'll need this to make an insurance claim.

Don't wear jewelry, chains, or expensive watches. They mark you as a wealthy tourist. Wear an inexpensive digital watch. Never carry more cash than you need for the day. The rest should be kept in the hotel safe. If you don't trust the hotel or if it doesn't have a safe, try as best you can to hide your valuables and secure your room. Consider carrying the majority of your money as travelers checks, which can be refunded if lost or stolen.

For credit card security, insist that imprints are made in your presence. Make sure any imprints incorrectly completed are torn up. Don't take someone else's word that it will be done. Destroy the carbons yourself. Don't let store merchants or anyone else walk off with your card. Keep it in sight!

Never leave your purse, camera, or luggage unattended in public places. Always keep a wary eye on your luggage, especially backpacks, on public transportation: sneak thieves love their zippered compartments. And never carry your wallet in your back pocket. Carry your bills in your front pocket beneath a handkerchief. Carry any other money in a money belt, inside pocket, a "secret" pocket sewn into your pants or jacket, or in a body pouch or an elastic wallet below the knee. Spread your money around your person.

Don't carry more luggage than you can adequately manage. Limit your baggage to one suitcase or duffel. And have a lock for each luggage item. Purses should have a short strap (ideally, one with metal woven in) that fits tightly against the body and snaps closed or has a zipper. Always keep purses fully zipped and luggage locked.

Don't trust locals to handle your money. Be particularly wary of credit. And don't exchange money before receiving the services or goods you're paying for—I've heard more than once of locals saying they need money to pay someone in advance to arrange a boat ride or horseback trip, then disappearing.

Be particularly wary after cashing money at a bank. And be cautious at night, particularly if you intend to walk on beaches or park trails, which you should do with someone trusted wherever possible. Stick to well-lit main streets in towns.

Don't leave anything of value within reach of an open window. Make sure you have bars on the window and that your room is otherwise secure (bringing your own lock for the door is a good idea).

Don't leave tents or cars unguarded. If you pick up hitchhikers, *always* take the car keys with you if you get out of the vehicle. Be especially cautious if you have a flat tire, as many robberies involve unsuspecting tourists who are robbed while changing a tire by the roadside. The ICT advises driving to the nearest gas station or other secure site to change the tire. And never permit a Costa Rican male to sit in the back seat of a taxi while you're in the front; there have been several reports of robberies in taxis in which the driver has worked in cahoots with an accomplice, who strangles the victim from behind.

Don't leave anything of value in your car.

A few uniformed policemen are less than honest, and tourists occasionally get shaken down for money. *Never* pay a police officer money. If you are stopped by one who wants to see your passport or to search you, insist on a neutral witness—*"solamente con testigos."* Be wary, too, of "plainclothes policemen." Ask to see identification, and never relinquish your documentation. And be especially wary if he asks a third party to verify his own credentials; they could be in league.

A lot of tourists get ripped off in Costa Rica in all manner of crafty scams. Amorous ladies may approach unsuspecting males and rob them while running their hands over them. Be suspicious of drinks offered by strangers; the beverage may be laced with a knockout drug.

Never allow yourself to be drawn into arguments (the Costa Ricans are so placid that anyone with a temper is immediately to be suspected). And don't be distracted by people spilling things on you. These are ruses meant to distract you while an accomplice steals your valuables. Remain alert to the dark side of self-proclaimed good Samaritans. An acquaintance of mine had her luggage neatly stolen by two men who offered to help as she struggled to cross a street in Puntarenas with two suitcases. Convinced of their good nature, she went off to look for a taxi while they "looked after" her luggage. When she returned, they and her suitcases were gone.

Large-scale scams are common. I know several foreigners who lost huge sums by investing in bogus macadamia farms and other schemes. I've heard cautionary reports that "Newcomers' Seminars" have shills in the audience to inspire attendees to part with their money.

Drugs

Marijuana and cocaine are increasingly available in Costa Rica, which is a transshipment point between South America and the United States. Drug trafficking and laundering of drug money has increased markedly since the ouster of Manuel Noriega from Panamá. And traffickers have been able to entice impoverished farmers into growing marijuana and cocaine, notably in the Talamancas of southern Puntarenas. The dramatic rise in car theft in Costa Rica is believed to be linked to drug trafficking, with stolen cars used to ship goods.

The Costa Rican government and U.S. Drug Enforcement Agency (DEA) has an ongoing anti-narcotics campaign, including a military-style drug eradication program. Penalties for possession or dealing are stiff. If you're offered drugs on the street, be aware that you may be dealing with a plainclothes policeman.

Article 14 of the Drug Law stipulates: "A jail sentence of eight to 20 years shall be imposed upon anyone who participates in any way in international drug dealing." That includes anyone caught distributing, producing, supplying, transforming, refining, extracting, preparing, cultivating, transporting, or storing. The jail sentence also applies to anyone buying or otherwise involved in financial dealings involving drugs. You will receive no special favors because you're foreign. A trial could take many months, in which case you'll be jailed on the premise that you're guilty until proven innocent. Just say no.

Money

Costa Rica's currency is the *colón* (plural *colones*), which is written ¢ and sometimes colloquially called a peso. Notes are issued in the following denominations: 500 (purple; called *cinca teja*), 1,000 (red; called a *rojo*), 2,000 (called *dos rojos*), 5,000 (blue; called a *tucán*), and 10,000 (called a *jaguar*) *colones;* coins come in one, five, 10, 25, 50, 100, and 500 *colones.* Older 20-*colones* notes (brown; called a *teja* colloquially) remain in circulation. The *colón* is divided into 100 *centimos,* though these coins have been taken out of circulation. You may hear money referred to colloquially as *pista* or *plata. Menudo* is loose change.

The five-*colones* bank note is considered obsolete as a form of currency and is popularly sold as a souvenir ($1). It's a beautiful note with a colorful reproduction of the pretty mural on the ceiling of the foyer of the National Theater in San José.

A large quantity of counterfeit bills are in circulation.

Most businesses will accept payment in U.S. dollars, as do taxis. Other international currencies are generally not accepted as direct payment. Many shopkeepers won't accept foreign notes that are torn, however minute the tear. They claim that banks won't process them. They will dispense such notes to you without guilt.

Travelers carrying currency other than U.S. dollars should buy U.S. dollars before arriving in Costa Rica.

CHANGING MONEY

Dollars are widely accepted. You can arrive in

Costa Rica without local currency and function just fine. You can change money at Juan Santamaría Airport upon arrival; the bank is inside the *departure* terminal. Travel with small bills.

Legally, money may be changed only at a bank or hotel cash desk. You are allowed to convert only $50 in *colones* to dollars when departing, so spend all your local currency before leaving.

The value of the *colón* has fallen steadily against the U.S. dollar over the past few years. At press time the official **exchange rate** was approximately 395 *colones* to the dollar. A yearly devaluation of 5–15 percent is expected. All prices in this book are quoted in U.S. dollars unless otherwise indicated.

Banks are normally open 9 A.M.–4 P.M., but hours vary. Foreign-exchange departments are often open longer. There are banks nationwide; many have 24-hour automated teller machines for cash advances using credit cards. Don't expect fast service. At many banks, you'll have to stand in two lines: one to process the transaction, the other to receive your cash. It can sometimes take more than an hour. Ask to make sure you're in the correct line. Banks close during Easter, Christmas, New Year's, and other holidays, so plan accordingly.

Banks are allowed to charge what they wish for foreign-exchange transactions. Shop around if changing a large amount.

Most hotels will exchange dollars for *colones* for guests; some will do so even for nonguests. Hotels offer similar exchange rates to banks. Understandably, hotels will only change small amounts, but at least you'll avoid the long lines that are the plague of banks.

Many hustlers offer illegal money exchange on the street, although this is strictly illegal and dangerous (the Judicial Police say they receive between 10 and 15 complaints a day from people who've been ripped off while changing money on the street). Most victims are tourists. At best, you'll get 5 percent more than the official exchange rate (less for traveler's checks). It isn't worth it!

TRAVELERS CHECKS

At last visit, many businesses were reluctant to take travelers checks due to the prevalence of fraud and following a government decision to place a 30-day hold on processing; some businesses were charging a fee. You'll usually need your passport. You'll receive one or two *colones* less per dollar than if changing cash. Take small-denomination checks, and stick to the well-known international brands, such as **American Express** (www.americanexpress.com), **Citibank** (www.citybank.com), **Barclays** (www.barclays.com), or **Thomas Cook Currency Services** (www.thomascook.co.uk).

CREDIT CARDS

Most larger hotels, car rental companies, and travel suppliers, as well as larger restaurants and stores, will accept credit card payment. Visa is the most widely accepted, followed by MasterCard (American Express is not widely accepted). Conversion is normally at the official exchange rate, although a 6 percent service charge may be added. You can also use your credit cards to get cash advances at banks (minimum $50); some banks will pay cash advances in *colones* only. Most banks accept Visa; very few accept MasterCard.

At least one bank in every major town now has 24-hour ATM (*cajero automatico*) for automatic credit. Note that Plus is the most common international system. You'll need your PIN number. Stick to regular banking hours if possible in case of problems (such as the *cajero* not returning your card).

The **American Express** Express Cash system (tel. 800/227-4669 for information, www.americanexpress.com) links your AmEx card to your U.S. checking account. You can withdraw up to $1,000 in a 21-day period; a $2 fee is charged for each transaction, and the money is usually issued in travelers checks.

You can reach the major credit card companies from within Costa Rica by calling the following numbers:

- American Express, tel. 506/233-0044 or 800/011-0216
- MasterCard, tel. 506/253-2155 or 800/011-0184
- Visa International, tel. 506/223-2211 or 800/011-0030.

MONEY TRANSFERS

You can arrange wire transfers through **Western Union** (tel. 506/283-6336 or 800/777-7777, www.westernunion.com), which has agencies throughout the country, including at convenience stores in small communities. **MoneyGram** (tel. 800/MONEYGRAM [800/666-3947] or 800/926-9400) provides similar service. In either case, funds are transferred almost immediately to be retrieved by the beneficiary with photo ID at any location. You'll be charged a hefty commission on a sliding scale according to the amount sent.

Major banks will arrange cash transfers from the U.S. for a small commission fee. Ask your home bank for the name and details of a "correspondent" bank in San José. If you need money transferred while traveling, simply contact your home bank to arrange a wire transfer to the correspondent bank.

COSTS

Costa Rica is more expensive than the rest of Central and much of South America. However, budget travelers should be able to get by on as little as $30 a day.

Budget hotels will cost $5–15 per night. A breakfast or lunch of *gallo pinto* will cost $1–4, and a dinner with beer at an inexpensive restaurant should cost no more than $5. At the other end of the spectrum, the most expensive restaurants might run you $40 or more per head, and $300-a-night accommodation is available.

Your mode of transportation will make a difference. Day tours featuring sightseeing and first-class hotels average $75–100, all-inclusive. You can fly anywhere in the country for $50 or so, or travel by bus for less than $10. Renting a car will send your costs skyrocketing—a minimum of $40 a day, plus insurance ($12 per day minimum) and gas.

Many tour companies, hotels, and car rental agencies offer discounts to members of Hostelling International. The main ICT information office in San José distributes leaflets and coupons offering discounts at select hotels and other establishments. Also see ad coupons in the *Tico Times*.

Haggling over prices is *not* a tradition in Costa Rica, except at streetside craft stalls.

Restaurants (but not snack bars, or *sodas*), and most service businesses add a 13 percent sales tax. Tourist hotels add a 16.39 percent tax.

Tipping

Taxi drivers do not normally receive tips. Nor is tipping in restaurants the norm—restaurants automatically add both a 15 percent sales tax and a 10 percent service charge to your bill. Don't add an additional tip except as a reward for exceptional service. Bellboys in classy hotels should receive 25 cents to 50 cents per bag. And don't forget your chambermaids ($1 per head per day). Tour guides normally are tipped $1–2 pp per day for large groups, and much more, at your discretion, for small, personalized tours. Again, don't tip if you had lousy service.

Maps and Tourist Information

TOURIST INFORMATION OFFICES

The **Costa Rican Tourism Institute** (Instituto Costarricense de Turismo, or CT) has a 24-hour toll-free tourist information line (tel. 800/343-6332) in the United States. You can request brochures, but anticipate that it will take weeks or months before they arrive. There are no ICT offices abroad.

The ICT head office (tel. 506/223-1733, fax 506/255-4997, promoict@tourism-costarica.com, www.tourism-costarica.com) is at Avenida 4, Calles 5/7, in San José. Word at last visit was that it might relocate.

The **Costa Rica National Chamber of Tourism** (Canatur, tel. 506/296-5314, fax 506/220-4855, www.costarica.tourism.co.cr) can also provide information.

Telephone Information Services

In Costa Rica, a 24-hour, multilingual "Tourist Tele-Info Line" (tel. 506/257-4667) provides information on a wide range of tourist facilities including restaurants, accommodations, and adventures. Only paying business subscribers are listed. The *Tico Times* operates a 24-hour, bilingual **Tourist Information Line** (tel. 506/240-6373).

MAPS

The ICT issues a basic 1:1,000,000 road map (though this is not much use for driving) featuring more detailed inset maps of San José and major cities. The best all-round map is the 1:350,000 scale *National Geographic Adventure Map* (published by the National Geographic Society), but be sure to get the latest edition, as early editions were not entirely accurate. Another good road map is a topographical 1:500,000 sheet published by **ITMB Publishing** (530 W. Broadway, Vancouver BC V5Z 1E9, tel. 604/879-3621, www.itmb.com). And the

Fundación Neotrópica (see the *Conservation Organizations* chart) publishes a superb topographical map with nature reserves and parks emphasized.

The *Red Guide to Costa Rica: National Map Guide* (San José: Guías de Costa Rica) provides detailed regional maps, as does the *Costa Rica Nature Atlas* (San José: Editorial Incafo), which has detailed 1:200,000 scale maps and detailed accounts of national parks and other sites.

The best commercial resource in Costa Rica is **Jiménez & Tanzi, Ltda.** (Apdo. 3553-1000 San José, tel. 506/253-2027, jitanan@jitan.co.cr, www.jitan.co.cr). Topographic maps and detailed city maps can be bought from the **Instituto Geográfica Nacional** (National Geographic Institute, Avenida 20, Calles 9/11, tel. 506/257-7798, ext. 2619, 8:30–11:30 A.M. Mon.–Fri.).

In the U.S., **Omni Resources** (P.O. Box 2096, Burlington, NC 72160, tel. 800/742-2677, fax 336/227-3748, www.omnimap.com) and **Treaty Oak** (P.O. Box 50295, Austin, TX 78763, tel. 512/326-4141, fax 512/443-0973, www.treatyoak .com) both sell a wide variety of maps.

In the UK, try **Stanford's** (12-14 Long Acre, London WC2E 9LP, tel. 020/7836-1321, fax 020/7836-0189, www.stanfords.co.uk) and the **Ordnance Survey International** (Romsey Rd., Southampton SO16 4GU, tel. 08456/050505, fax 023/8079-2615, outside the UK tel. 023/8079-2912, www.ordsvy.gov.uk).

In Australia, try **The Map Shop** (6-10 Peel St., Adelaide, SA 5000, tel. 08/231-2033, www.mapshop.net.au); in New Zealand, try **Specialty Maps** (58 Albert St., Auckland, tel. 09/307-2217, www.specialtymaps.co.nz).

OTHER SOURCES

The **South American Explorer's Club** (126 Indian Creek Rd., Ithaca, NY 14850, tel. 607/277-0488, fax 607/277-6122, explorer@samexplorers .org, www.samexplo.org) publishes the quarterly *South American Explorer* magazine.

Know Costa Rica

In the U.K., the **Latin American Travel Association** (1-7 Windmill Mews, Chiswick, London W4 1RW, tel. 020/8742-1529, fax 020/8742-2025, www.lata.org) promotes Latin American destinations on behalf of its members, most of whom are tour operators and travel suppliers.

The **National Archives** (tel. 506/234-7223, 8 A.M.–3 P.M. Mon.–Fri.), in San José's Barrio Zapote, nine blocks south and one block east of Plaza del Sol, has thousands of documents, maps, and photos dating back to 1539.

542 East Productions (909 Harris Ave., Suite 202C, Bellingham, WA 98225, tel. 360/647-9305 or 877/647-9305, fax 360/647-7756, www.542east.com) sells a series of regional travel DVDs about Costa Rica.

Film and Photography

EQUIPMENT

You are allowed to bring two cameras and six rolls of film into Costa Rica (I've never heard of the official film limit being enforced). Film is susceptible to damage by X-ray machines. Request that film (including your camera loaded with film) be hand-checked by airport security rather than having it go through the X-ray machine.

Digital cameras do away with the hassle of film and have the advantage of being both lightweight and more versatile in high-contrast lighting. Thus, they are particularly advantageous for, say, photographing wildlife in the dark forest.

If you shoot film, I recommend a minimum of one roll per day; much more if you're even halfway serious about your photography. Film is expensive in Costa Rica. If you do need to buy in San José, check the expiration date; the film may be outdated. And the film may have been sitting in the sun for months on end—not good! Kodachrome 64 and Fujichrome 50 give the best color rendition in Costa Rica's bright, high-contrast conditions, but you'll need ASA 200 or 400 for the dark conditions typical within the gloomy rainforest.

Keep your film out of the sun. If possible, refrigerate it. Color emulsions are particularly sensitive to tropical heat and the colors will fade (Kodak film is more likely to fade than Fuji film). Film rolls can also soften with the humidity so that they stretch and refuse to wind in your camera. Pack both your virgin and exposed film in a Ziploc plastic bag with silica gel inside to protect against moisture. You can have Fuji processed in Costa Rica at one of its many outlets; call the central office for information (tel. 506/222-2222). Or buy Kodak film with prepaid processing. It comes with a self-mailer and you can simply pop it in a mailbox; the prints or slides will be mailed to your home. Bear in mind that Costa Rica's mail system is unreliable (professionals should use a private courier service instead).

Bring extra batteries for light meters and flashes. Protect your lenses with a UV or skylight filter, and consider buying "warming," neutral-density, and/or polarizing filters, which can dramatically improve results. Keep your lenses clean and dry when not in use (believe it or not, there's even a tropical mildew that attacks coated lenses). Silica gel packs are essential to help protect your camera gear from moisture; use them if you carry your camera equipment inside a plastic bag.

SHOOTING TIPS

Midday is the worst time for photography. Early morning and late afternoon provide the best light; the wildlife is more active then, too. Use hoods on all your lenses to screen out ambient light. Don't underestimate the intensity of light when photographing in bright sunlight. A good idea is to "stop down" one-third to half an f-stop, or to "push" your film by adjusting your ASA camera setting to the next highest rating to that of your film, to underexpose slightly for better color rendition. In the forest, you'll need as much light as possible. Use a tripod, slow shutter speed, wide-open aperture, and higher-speed film. Use a flash in daytime to "fill in" shaded subjects or dark objects surrounded by bright sunlight.

Photo Etiquette

Ticos enjoy being photographed and will generally cooperate willingly, except in the Caribbean, where many people have a surly response to being photographed. Never assume an automatic right to take a personal photograph, however. Ask permission as appropriate. And respect an individual's right to refuse.

Communications and Media

POSTAL SERVICES

CORTEL, the nation's inefficient mail service, has faced severe criticism for internal fraud and theft. Even when mailing out of Costa Rica, don't enclose anything of value. The Postal Service was made semi-private in 1999, and the new management has set about improving the system, but there is a long way to go. The situation is exacerbated by the lack of street addresses nationwide, although there is a post office in every town and most villages.

Airmail *(correo aereo)* to/from North America averages two weeks, though three or more weeks is not unknown. To/from Europe, anticipate a minimum of three weeks; sea mail *(marítimo)* takes anywhere from six weeks to three months. Postcards cost 95 *colones* (approximately 25 cents) to North America, and 115 *colones* to Europe; letters cost 115 *colones* (about 30 cents) to North America, and 165 *colones* to Europe. Registered mail costs 30 *colones* extra. Opening hours vary; most post offices are open 7 A.M.–6 P.M. Mon.–Fri. and 7 A.M.–noon Saturday.

Mailing packages overseas is expensive. *Don't* seal your package. You must first take it to the central post office for customs inspection. You'll save yourself a lot of headaches by using a courier service.

Incomienda is a system that permits you to send letters and packages with drivers of local buses to anywhere in the country for as little as $1 (you pay by weight). Just take the package to the bus station relevant to the destination. It's efficient and thefts are reportedly rare.

Receiving Mail

Most people rent a post office box *(apartado—* abbreviated Apdo.—but increasingly written as "P.O. Box"). Costa Rican postal codes sometimes appear before the name of the town, or even after the *apartado* number (e.g., Apdo. 890-1000, San José, instead of Apdo. 890, San José 1000).

You can receive international mail c/o "Lista de Correos" at the central post office in San José (Lista de Correos, Correos Central, San José 1000), or any other large town. Each item costs 10 cents. You must pick up your mail in person at window 17 in the hall at the southern end of the building on Calle 2. Bring your passport; you won't get your mail without it.

Incoming letters are filed alphabetically. If the clerk can't find your name under the initial of your surname, try other initials—your first or middle name, for example. Tell anyone you expect to write to you to *print* your surname legibly and to include the words "Central America." Also tell them not to send money or anything else of monetary value, nor to mail parcels larger than a magazine-size envelope. Receiving parcels is a hassle. You'll need to make two or more visits to the Aduana (Customs) in Zapote, on the outskirts of San José; one visit to declare the contents, the second to pay duty. The fee is hefty: at least equal to the value of the goods, however minor they may be.

Private Courier Services

The incidence of mail theft has spawned many private mail services. FedEx and DHL have offices in San José and a few other towns. See the regional chapters for information.

TELEPHONES

Costa Rica has an efficient direct-dial telephone system (including more telephones per capita than any other Latin American nation) under the control of ICE, which has offices in most towns. ICE offers the telephone directory online at www.ice.go.cr or www.superpagescr.com.

Public Phone Booths

Public phone booths are found throughout the nation. In more remote spots, the public phone is usually at the village *pulpería,* or store. Often this is the only phone in a village. They'll dial for you and meter your call; you'll be charged by the minute.

It's a good idea to give your phone booth telephone number (indicated on a yellow sign above the phone) to the person you're calling so he or she can call you back. Phone booths do not have telephone books.

Most public phone booths now use phone cards, not coins. Coin phones accept only five, 10-, and 20-*colones* coins. Wait for the dial tone (similar to that of U.S. phones) before inserting your coin. The coin will drop when your call is connected. Have subsequent coins ready to insert immediately when the beep indicating "time up" sounds, or you'll be cut off. Some phones allow you to stack coins in an automatic feeder.

With phone cards, the cost of your call is automatically deducted from the value of the card. You buy them at ICE telephone agencies, banks, calling card vending machines, and stores.

CHIP cards are sold in units of 1,000 and 2,000 colones and can be used in public phones by inserting in the slot. English-language instructions are provided on the screen. You simply put the card in the telephone slot, dial 199, then 2 for instructions in English; then dial the card number, then 00, the country code, area code, and telephone number.

Tarjeta Viajera Internacionál 199 cards are for touch-tone phones. The card is sold in denominations of $10, $20, and 3,000 colones. **Tarjetas Colibri 197** cards, in Spanish only, are for in-country calls only. They're sold in 500 and 1,000 *colones* denominations. With 199 and 197 cards, you touch in the code on the back of the card.

Local Calls

Local telephone calls within Costa Rica cost 3.25 cents per minute, regardless of distance. Calls from your hotel room are considerably more expensive (and the more expensive the hotel, the more they jack up the fee). There are no area or city codes; simply dial the seven-digit number. In some villages you will reach the local operator, who will connect you with your party.

International Calls

The Costa Rica country code is 506. When calling Costa Rica from North America, dial 011 (the international dial code), then 506, followed by the seven-digit local number. For outbound calls from Costa Rica, dial 00, then the country code and local number. You can dial direct to most countries from public phone booths, or via an English-speaking international operator (dial 116). You'll need to call 116 to make collect calls (reverse the charges) or charge to a telephone credit card. The operator will call you back once he/she has connected you. Hotel operators can also connect you, although charges for calling from hotels are high. The easiest and least costly way, however, to make direct calls is to bill to your credit card or phone card by calling one of the calling assistance operators listed in the accompanying sidebar.

AT&T has a Language Line (tel. 800/843-8420 in North America, tel. 506/648-7174 in Costa Rica) that will connect you with an interpreter. USADirect phones, found at key tourist locations, automatically link you with an AT&T operator.

Direct-dial international calls to North America cost $2–3 per minute, depending on where you're calling. Calls to the U.K. cost $3–4 per minute; to Australia $5 per minute. The first minute costs extra. Cheaper rates apply between 8 P.M. and 7 A.M. and on weekends. Hotels add their own, often exorbitant, charges, plus gov-

INTERNATIONAL CALLING ASSISTANCE

Dictate telegrams and fax	123
Directory Information	113
International information	124
International operator	116
Time	112

Calling into the United States	
AT&T	0800-011-4114
MCI	162 or 0800-012-2222
Sprint	163 or 0800-013-0123
Worldcom	0800-014-4444

Direct dial to foreign operators	
Canada	161 or 0800-015-1161
France	0800-033-1033
Germany	0800-049-1049
Italy	0800-039-1039
Netherlands (Holland)	0800-031-1111
Spain	0800-034-1034
United Kingdom	167 or 0800-044-1044

ernment tax. From a coin box, calls to North America cost 65 cents–$1.60 per minute, depending on where you're calling. Calls to the U.K. cost $1.25–2 per minute; to Australia $1.75–2 per minute.

Cellular Phones
Any number of companies offer cellular phone rentals. See the Yellow Pages (Pápinas Amarillas) under "Telefonia Celular."

FAX AND TELEGRAMS

Most tourist hotels will permit you to use their fax for a small fee. Most post offices permit you to send faxes. You can also send and receive faxes via **Radiográfica Costarricense** (RACSA, www.racsa .co.cr) or ICE (Insituto Costarricense de Electricidad. Most towns have one. The fax must indicate your name and Costa Rican address or telephone number or you'll not be advised of its arrival. Fax transmissions cost $7 per page to Europe, $5 to the United States. ICE also has a telegram service, which you can dictate by telephone (call 123).

INTERNET ACCESS

Costa Rica has scores of cyber cafés nationwide. Many upscale hotels have telephone jacks for laptop plug-in (calls aren't cheap, however, as most hotels add a huge markup).

Most city halls and post offices nationwide are equipped with Internet-connected computers available to the public. RACSA operates the major website servers in Costa Rica through a closely guarded monopoly. The service is inefficient, unreliable, and slow.

KitCom (tel. 506/258-0303, fax 506/258-0606, kitcom@kitcom.net, www.kitcom.net) also has email, fax, voicemail, and online services.

PUBLICATIONS
Local Publications
Costa Rica has three major dailies. *La Nación* (www.nacion.co.cr) is an excellent newspaper, up to international standards, with broad-based coverage of national and international affairs. *La República* and *La Prensa Libre* are lesser alternatives. *El Día,* the other national daily, is a sensationalist rag that prefers to report on sex, mayhem, and gore.

The weekly English-language *Tico Times* (fax 506/233-6378, info@ticotimes.net, www.ticotimes.net) is consistently more analytical than its Costa Rican peers and diligently covers environmental issues and cultural events. It's sold at newsstands and in hotels nationwide ($1). You can order online or contact *Tico Times,* SJO 717, 1601 N.W. 97th Ave. Unit C-101, P.O. Box 025216, Miami, FL 33102-5216.

Costa Rica Traveler (tel. 506/297-0147, www.crtraveler.com) is a glossy bimonthly.

Know Costa Rica

The bimonthly *Costa Rica Outdoors* (Dept. SJO 2316, P.O. Box 025216, Miami, FL 33102; in Costa Rica, P.O. Box 199, Santa Ana 6150, tel. 506/282-6743, info@costaricaoutdoors.com, www.costaricaoutdoors.com) is dedicated to fishing and outdoor sports.

International Publications

International newspapers and magazines are available at a few newsstands, bookstores, and upscale hotels. The *Miami Herald* beams its Latin American edition to Costa Rica, where it is printed as a daily in English. However, Ticos are not passionate readers, and away from large towns you'll be hard-pressed to find magazines, Spanish-language or otherwise.

BROADCASTING

Costa Rica has more than a dozen TV stations. Satellite coverage from the United States is widely available (many hotels that advertise "satellite TV" have access to only a few fuzzy stations) and many hotels provide North American and European programming from C-Span and CNN to ESPN and HBO.

There are about 120 radio stations. The vast majority play Costa Rican music, and finding Western music isn't easy. One of my favorite stations is **Eco 95.9 FM,** which plays classic jazz and has world news and discussions. **Radio Dos,** 99.5 FM, plays "lovers rock" and all-time classics, 24 hours a day. **Radio U,** 101.9 AM, the student-run University of Costa Rica radio station, plays classical, world beat, progressive Spanish-language rock, and jazz fusion. Classical music fans are served by **Radio Universidad,** 870 AM and 96.7 FM (which also plays jazz), and by **Radio FM 96.** For New Age and jazz, tune to **Radio Estereo Azul,** on 99 FM. BBC World Service and Voice of America provide English-language news. The latter offers 24-hour, all-English-language programming, with trivia contests, weather, music, and a Friday-morning segment devoted to tourist information. There's an English-language station—**Radio Paladin**—at 107.5 FM with eclectic programming, including rock and roll in the morning.

Weights, Measures, and Time

WEIGHTS AND MEASURES

Costa Rica operates on the metric system. Liquids are sold in liters, fruits and vegetables by the kilo. Some of the old Spanish measurements still survive in vernacular usage. Street directions, for example, are often given as 100 *varas* (the Spanish "yard," equal to 33 inches) to indicate a city block. See the chart at the back of this book for metric conversions.

TIME

Costa Rica time is equivalent to U.S. Central Standard Time (six hours behind Greenwich mean time, one hour behind New York, two hours ahead of California). Costa Rica has no daylight saving time, during which time it is *seven* hours behind Greenwich and *two* hours behind New York. There is little seasonal variation in dawn (approximately 6 A.M.) and dusk (6 P.M.).

BUSINESS HOURS

Businesses are usually open 8 A.M.–5 P.M. Mon.–Fri. A few also open Saturday morning. Lunch breaks are often two hours; businesses and government offices may close 11:30 A.M.–1:30 P.M. Bank hours vary widely, but in general are open from between 8:15 A.M. or 9 A.M. and 3 P.M. to 3:45 P.M. Most shops open 8 A.M.–6 P.M. Mon.–Sat. Some restaurants close Sunday and Monday. Most businesses also close on holidays.

ELECTRICITY

Costa Rica operates on 110-volts AC (60-cycle) nationwide. Some remote lodges are not connected to the national grid and generate their own power. Check in advance to see if they run on direct current (DC) or a nonstandard voltage. Two types of U.S. plugs are used: flat, parallel two-pins and three rectangular pins. A two-prong adapter is a good idea (most hardware stores in Costa Rica—*ferreterías*—can supply them).

Power surges are common. If you plan on using a laptop computer, use a surge protector. Take a flashlight and spare batteries. A couple of long-lasting candles are also a good idea. Don't forget the matches or a lighter.

Spanish Phrasebook

PRONUNCIATION GUIDE

Consonants

c—as 'c' in "cat," before 'a', 'o', or 'u'; like 's' before 'e' or 'i'

d—as 'd' in "dog," except between vowels, then like 'th' in "that"

g—before 'e' or 'i,' like the 'ch' in Scottish "loch"; elsewhere like 'g' in "get"

h—always silent

j—like the English 'h' in "hotel," but stronger

ll—like the 'y' in "yellow"

ñ—like the 'ni' in "onion"

r—always pronounced as strong 'r'

rr—trilled 'r'

v—similar to the 'b' in "boy" (not as English 'v')

y—similar to English, but with a slight "j" sound. When y stands alone it is pronounced like the 'e' in "me".

z—like 's' in "same"

b, f, k, l, m, n, p, q, s, t, w, x, z as in English

Vowels

a—as in "father," but shorter

e—as in "hen"

i—as in "machine"

o—as in "phone"

u—usually as in "rule"; when it follows a 'q' the 'u' is silent; when it follows an 'h' or 'g' it's pronounced like 'w,' except when it comes between 'g' and 'e' or 'i', when it's also silent

NUMBERS

0—*cero*
1 (masculine)—*uno*, 1 (feminine)*una*
2—*dos*

3—*tres*
4—*cuatro*
5—*cinco*
6—*seis*
7—*siete*
8—*ocho*
9—*nueve*
10—*diez*
11—*once*
12—*doce*
13—*trece*
14—*catorce*
15—*quince*
16—*dieciseis*
17—*diecisiete*
18—*dieciocho*
19—*diecinueve*
20—*veinte*
21—*vientiuno*
30—*treinta*
40—*cuarenta*
50—*cincuenta*
60—*sesenta*
70—*setenta*
80—*ochenta*
90—*noventa*
100—*cien*
101—*cientouno*
200—*doscientos*
1,000—*mil*
10,000—*diez mil*

DAYS OF THE WEEK

Sunday—*domingo*
Monday—*lunes*
Tuesday—*martes*

Wednesday—*miércoles*
Thursday—*jueves*
Friday—*viernes*
Saturday—*sábado*

TIME

What time is it?—*¿Qué hora es?*
one o'clock—*la una*
two o'clock—*las dos*
at two o'clock—*a las dos*
ten past three—*las tres y diez*
six A.M.—*las seis de la mañana*
six P.M.—*las seis de la tarde*
today—*hoy*
tomorrow, morning—*mañana, la mañana*
yesterday—*ayer*
week—*semana*
month—*mes*
year—*año*
last night—*la noche pasada* or *anoche*
next day—*el próximo día* or *al día siguiente*

USEFUL WORDS AND PHRASES

Hello.—*Hola.*
Good morning.—*Buenos días.*
Good afternoon.—*Buenas tardes.*
Good evening.—*Buenas noches.*
How are you?—*¿Cómo está?*
Fine.—*Muy bien.*
And you?—*¿Y usted?* (formal) or *¿Y tú?* (familiar)
So-so.—*Así así.*
Thank you.—*Gracias.*
Thank you very much.—*Muchas gracias.*
You're very kind.—*Usted es muy amable.*
You're welcome; literally, "It's nothing."—*De nada.*
yes—*sí*
no—*no*
I don't know—*no sé* or *no lo sé*
it's fine; okay—*está bien*
good; okay—*bueno*
please—*por favor*
Pleased to meet you.—*Mucho gusto.*
excuse me (physical)—*perdóneme*
excuse me (speech)—*discúlpeme*
I'm sorry.—*Lo siento.*
Goodbye.—*Adiós.*

see you later; literally, "until later"—*hasta luego*
more—*más*
less—*menos*
better—*mejor*
much—*mucho*
a little—*un poco*
large—*grande*
small—*pequeño*
quick—*rápido*
slowly—*despacio*
bad—*malo*
difficult—*difícil*
easy—*fácil*
He/She/It is gone; as in "She left," "He's gone"—*Ya se fue.*
I don't speak Spanish well.—*No hablo bien español.*
I don't understand.—*No entiendo.*
How do you say . . . in Spanish?—*¿Cómo se dice . . . en español?*
Do you understand English?—*¿Entiende el inglés?*
Is English spoken here? (Does anyone here speak English?)—*¿Se habla inglés aquí?*
I'm sorry.—*Lo siento.*
Goodbye.—*Adiós.*
see you later; literally, "until later"—*hasta luego*
more—*más*
less—*menos*
better—*mejor*
much—*mucho*
a little—*un poco*
large—*grande*
small—*pequeño*
quick—*rápido*
slowly—*despacio*
bad—*malo*
difficult—*difícil*
easy—*fácil*
He/She/It is gone; as in "She left," "He's gone"—*Ya se fue.*
I don't speak Spanish well.—*No hablo bien español.*
I don't understand.—*No entiendo.*
How do you say . . . in Spanish?—*¿Cómo se dice . . . en español?*
Do you understand English?—*¿Entiende el inglés?*

Is English spoken here? (Does anyone here speak English?)—*¿Se habla inglés aquí?*

TERMS OF ADDRESS

I—*yo*
you (formal)—*usted*
you (familiar)—*tú*
he/him—*él*
she/her—*ella*
we/us—*nosotros*
you (plural)—*ustedes*
they/them (all males or mixed gender)—*ellos*
they/them (all females)—*ellas*
Mr., sir—*señor*
Mrs., madam—*señora*
Miss, young lady—*señorita*
wife—*esposa*
husband—*marido or esposo*
friend—*amigo (male), amiga (female)*
sweetheart—*novio (male), novia (female)*
son, daughter—*hijo, hija*
brother, sister—*hermano, hermana*
father, mother—*padre, madre*

GETTING AROUND

Where is . . .?—*¿Dónde está . . .?*
How far is it to . . .?—*¿Qué tan lejos está a . . .?*
from . . . to . . .—*de . . . a . . .*
highway—*la carretera*
road—*el camino*
street—*la calle*
block—*la cuadra*
kilometer—*kilómetro*
north—*el norte*
south—*el sur*
west—*el oeste*
east—*el este*
straight ahead—*al derecho or adelante*
to the right—*a la derecha*
to the left—*a la izquierda*

ACCOMMODATIONS

Can I (we) see a room?—*¿Puedo (podemos) ver una habitación?*
What is the rate?—*¿Cuál es el precio?*
a single room—*una habitación sencilla*
a double room—*una habitación doble*

key—*llave*
bathroom—*retrete or lavabo*
bath—*baño*
hot water—*agua caliente*
cold water—*agua fría*
towel—*toalla*
soap—*jabón*
toilet paper—*papel sanitario*
air conditioning—*aire acondicionado*
fan—*abanico, ventilador*
blanket—*cubierta or manta*

PUBLIC TRANSPORT

bus stop—*la parada de la guagua*
main bus terminal—*la central camionera*
airport—*el aeropuerto*
ferry terminal—*la terminal del transbordador*
I want a ticket to . . .- Quiero un tiqué a . . .
I want to get off at . . .- Quiero bajar en . . .
Here, please.—*Aquí, por favor.*
Where is this bus going?—*¿Dónde va este guagua?*
roundtrip—*ida y vuelta*
What do I owe?—*¿Cuánto le debo?*

FOOD

menu—*carta, menú*
glass—*taza*
fork—*tenedor*
knife—*cuchillo*
spoon—*cuchara, cucharita*
napkin—*servilleta*
soft drink—*refresco*
coffee, cream—*café, crema*
tea—*té*
sugar—*azúcar*
drinking water—*agua pura, agua potable*
bottled carbonated water—*club soda*
bottled uncarbonated water—*agua sin gas*
beer—*cerveza*
wine—*vino*
milk—*leche*
juice—*jugo*
eggs—*huevos*
bread—*pan*
watermelon—*patilla*
banana—*plátano*

apple—*manzana*
orange—*naranja*
meat (without)—*carne (sin)*
beef—*carne de res*
chicken—*pollo*
fish—*pescado*
shellfish—*camarones, mariscos*
fried—*frito*
roasted—*asado*
barbecue, barbecued—*barbacoa, al carbón, or a la parilla*
breakfast—*desayuno*
lunch—*almuerzo*
dinner (often eaten in late afternoon)—*comida*
dinner, or a late night snack—*cena*
the check—*la cuenta*

MAKING PURCHASES

I need . . .—*Necesito . . .*
I want . . .—*Deseo . . . or Quiero . . .*
I would like . . . (more polite)—*Quisiera . . .*
How much does it cost?—*¿Cuánto cuesta?*

What's the exchange rate?—*¿Cuál es el tipo de cambio?*
Can I see . . .?—*¿Puedo ver . . .?*
this one—*ésta/ésto*
expensive—*caro*
cheap—*barato*
cheaper—*más barato*
too much—*demasiado*

HEALTH

Help me please.—*Ayúdeme por favor.*
I am ill.—*Estoy enfermo.*
pain—*dolor*
fever—*fiebre*
stomache ache—*dolor de estómago*
vomiting—*vomitar*
diarrhea—*diarrea*
drugstore—*farmacia*
medicine—*medicina*
pill, tablet—*pastilla*
birth control pills—*pastillas contraceptivas*
condoms—*condomes, gomas*

Glossary

abastacedor: small grocery
alacrán: scorpion
a la leña: oven-roasted
albergue: hostel
almuerzo ejecutivo: business lunch (set menu)
apartado: post office box (written Apdo.)
apartotel: self-catering hotel with kitchen units
arribada: mass arrival of marine turtles
arroz con pollo: rice with chicken
autopista: freeway
avenida: avenue
balneario: swimming pool
barrio: district
batido: milkshake
beneficio: coffee processing factory
biblioteca: library
boca: bar snack
bola: ball (refers to the large granite balls from Golfo Dulce)
boyero: oxcart driver

cabina: refers to any budget accommodation
cafelatero: coffee-baron
calle: street
campesino: small-scale farmer or peasant
campo: countryside
canton: county
carreta: traditional ox-cart
carretera: road
casado: set lunch (literally "married")
casita: small house, cottage
cayuco: canoe
cerveza: beer
chorizo: corruption, bribery, a poor grade of bacon
circunvalación: ring-road
cocodrilo: crocodile
colón: local currency
comida típica: local food
cordillera: mountain chain
costeños: coastal people

danta: tapir
empeñada: stuffed turn-over
encomienda: feudal servitude
estero: estuary
fiesta: party
fiesta cívica: civic fiesta
finca: farm
gallo pinto: rice, beans, and fried egg
gasolinera: gas station
grano de oro: coffee bean
guaro: a cheap liquor
guayaba: guava
hacienda: large farmstead, cattle ranch
helado: ice cream
hornilla: geysers
hospedaje: lodging
invierno: "winter" (refers to summer wet season)
lancha: motorized boat, ferry
lapa roja: scarlet macaw
lapa verde: green macaw
lavandería: laundry
manglar: mangrove
manigordo: ocelot
manzanillo: manchineel tree
mapache: northern raccoon
marisquería: seafood restaurant or outlet
mercado: market
mirador: look-out point
mola: stitched appliqué fabric
mono carablanca: capuchin monkey
mono colorado: spider monkey
mono congo: howler monkey
mono tití: squirrel monkey
murciélago: bat

museo: museum
orero: gold-miner
palenque: thatched roof
palmito: heart of palm
panga: small motorized boat
parada: bus stop
páramo: high-altitude savanna
pastelería: bakery
pejibaye: bright orange palm fruit
pensionado: pensioner
perezoso: sloth
pila: mud pond
pizote: coatimundi
plato fuerte: main dish
playa: beach
pulpería: small grocery
purruja: no-see-um, tiny insect
ranchito: open-sided thatched structure
refresco: soda pop or fruit juice
sabanero: cowboy
selva: jungle
soda: simple eatery, usually open to the street
tamandua: lesser anteater
tepezcuintle: a large rodent, also called a *paca*:
terciopelo: fer-de-lance—a fearsome snake
Tico: Costa Rican male
Tica: Costa Rican female
topes: equestrian show
tráfico: traffic police
trapiche: ox-driven sugar mill
venado: deer
verano: "summer" (refers to winter dry season)
vivero: hatchery or nursery

Suggested Reading

General Information

Calderón, Gloria. *Costa Rica: Pura Vida.* San José: Villegas Editores, 2003. This superb, large-format coffee-table book provides a beautiful visual overview of the country.

Chavarría-Aguilar, O.L. *A Bite of Costa Rica: How We Costa Ricans Eat.* Cartago: Ediciones El Castillo, 1993. A small compendium of menus and descriptions of local cuisine.

Jones, Julie. *Between Continents, Between Seas: Pre-Columbian Art of Costa Rica.* Detroit: Detroit Institute of the Arts, 1981.

Mayfield, Michael W., and Rafael E. Gallo. *The Rivers of Costa Rica: A Canoeing, Kayaking, and Rafting Guide.* Birmingham, AL: Menasha Ridge Press, 1988.

Ras, Barbara, ed. *Costa Rica: A Traveler's Literary Companion.* San Francisco: Whereabouts Press, 1994. Twenty-six stories by Costa Rican writers that reflect the ethos of the country.

Schafer, Kevin. *Forests of Eden.* New York: Rizzoli, 2002. A beautifully illustrated coffee-table book celebrating the Central American rainforests.

Nature and Wildlife

Allen, William. *Green Phoenix: Restoring the Tropical Forests of Guanacaste.* Oxford: Oxford University Press, 2001. A wonderful read, this powerfully engaging book tales the story of the remarkable, and successful, efforts to resurrecting Costa Rica's ravaged dry forests.

Alvarado, Guillermo. *Costa Rica: Land of Volcanoes.* Cartago: Editorial Tecnológia de Costa Rica, 1993. A detailed guide to the volcanoes, with science for the layman and a practical bent for the traveler.

Bach, Julie. *Sloths.* Mankato, MN: Creative Education, 2000. This exquisite educational book is lavishly illustrated and was shot mostly on location at Aviarios del Caribe, near Cahuita.

Beletsky, Les. *Ecotravellers Wildlife Guide to Costa Rica.* San Diego: Academia Press, 2002. A superbly illustrated volume for nature lovers.

Boza, Mario, and A. Bonilla. *The National Parks of Costa Rica.* Madrid: INCAFO, 1999. Available in both hardbound coffee-table and less bulky softbound versions, as well as in a handy pocket-size edition. Lots of superb photos. Highly readable, too.

Carr, Archie F. *The Windward Road.* Gainesville: University of Florida Press, 1955. A sympathetic book about the sea turtles of Central America.

Cornelius, Stephen E. *The Sea Turtles of Santa Rosa National Park.* San José: Fundación de Parques Nacionales, 1986.

DeVries, Philip J. *The Butterflies of Costa Rica and Their Natural History.* Princeton, NJ: Princeton University Press, 1987. A well-illustrated and thorough lepidopterist's guide.

Dressler, Robert L. *Field Guide to the Orchids of Costa Rica and Panama.* Ithaca, NY: Comstock Publishing, 1993.

Emmons, Louise H. *Neotropical Rainforest Mammals—A Field Guide.* Chicago: University of Chicago Press, 1997. A thorough yet compact book detailing mammal species throughout the neotropics.

Evans, Sterling. *The Green Republic: A Conservation History.* Amarillo: University of Texas Press, 1999. This academic text reviews the evolution of the nation's conservation ethic and the founding, successes, and failures of the national park system.

Fogden, Michael and Patricia. *Costa Rica Wildlife of the National Parks and Reserves.* San José: Fundación Neotropica, 2003.

Garrison, Ginger. *The Fishes of Cocos Island.* San José: National Biodiversity Institute (INBio): 2000. This illustrated tome catalogs 140 fish species, including several endemic to Cocos Island, in English and Spanish.

Hammel, Barry. *Costa Rica's Native Ornamental Plants.* San José: INBio, 1999. This bilingual field guide offers detailed information on almost 100 ornamentals, from orchids to trees. It features color photography.

Henderson, Carrol L. *Field Guide to the Wildlife of Costa Rica.* Austin: University of Texas Press, 2002. This weighty tome provides a thorough layman's treatment of individual wildlife species, albeit being a bit too bulky for the road. Most species are shown in color photographs.

Herrera, Wilberth. *Costa Rica Nature Atlas-Guidebook.* San José: Editorial Incafo, 1992. A very useful and readable guide to parks, reserves, and other sites of interest. Text is supported by stunning photos and detailed maps showing roads and gas stations.

INBio. *Colección Guías de Campo de Costa Rica.* San José: Instituto Nacional de Biodiversidad (INBio). This series of beautifully illustrated pocket-size nature guides offers 10 titles, including *Mammals of Costa Rica* and *Birds of Costa Rica,* plus separate titles on arboreal ferns; bees, wasps, and ants; beetles; bromeliads; flying insects; mushrooms and fungi; scorpions; and ornamental plants.

Janzen, Daniel, ed. *Costa Rican Natural History.* Chicago: University of Chicago Press, 1983. Weighty, large-format, it's the bible for scien-tific insight into individual species of flora and fauna. 174 contributors.

Johnsgard, Paul A. *Trogons and Quetzals of the World.* Washington: Smithsonian Institute, 2000. A beautifully illustrated guide to these exotic birds.

Kricher, John C. *A Neotropical Companion: An Introduction to the Animals, Plants, and Ecosystems of the New World Tropics.* Princeton, NJ: Princeton University Press, 1989.

Perry, Donald. *Life above the Jungle Floor.* New York: Simon & Schuster, 1986. A fascinating account of life in the forest canopy, relating Perry's scientific studies at Rara Avis.

Rogers, Dennis W. *Costa Rica and Panama: The Best Birding Locations.* San José: Cincus, 1996. Illustrated site guide for serious birders.

Savage, Jay M. *The Amphibians and Reptiles of Costa Rica.* Chicago: University of Chicago Press, 2002. The most comprehensive treatment of amphibian and reptile ecology, with in-depth information on 396 species.

Stiles, F. Gary, and Alexander Skutch. *A Guide to the Birds of Costa Rica.* Ithaca, NY: Cornell University Press, 1989. A superbly illustrated compendium for serious birders.

Wallace, David R. *The Quetzal and the Macaw: The Story of Costa Rica's National Parks.* San Francisco: Sierra Club Books, 1992. An entertaining history of the formation of Costa Rica's national park system.

Wainwright, Mark. *The Natural History of Costa Rica: Mammals.* San José: Zona Tropical, 2003. A splendid companion for naturalists, with identifying charts and lots of esoteric information.

History, Politics, and Social Structure

Ameringer, Charles D. *Don Pepe: A Political Bi-*

ography of José Figueres of Costa Rica. Mexico City: University of Mexico Press, 1978.

Biesanz, Richard, et al. *The Ticos: Culture and Social Change in Costa Rica.* Boulder, CO: Lynne Reinner, 1999. This essential work for understanding Tico culture is an updated version of its popular forerunner, *The Costa Ricans.*

Edelman, Marc, and Joanne Kenen, eds. *The Costa Rican Reader.* New York: Grove Weidenfeld, 1988. An excellent compendium of extracts on politics, history, economics, the contras, etc.

Molina, Iván, and Steven Palmer. *The History of Costa Rica.* San José: Editorial de la Universidad de Costa Rica, 1999. A handy pocket-size, easily digested précis of the country's past.

Palmer, Pauline. *What Happen: A Folk History of Costa Rica's Talamanca Coast.* San José: Ecodesarollos, 1977.

Travel Guides

Agace, Lucy. *Diving and Snorkeling Guide to Cocos Island.* Oakland: Pisces, 1999.

Aritio, Luis Blas, ed. *Costa Rica National Parks Guide.* San José: INCAFO, 2003. Compact and lavishly illustrated pocket guide provides succinct and detailed information on the national parks.

Franke, Joseph. *Costa Rica's National Parks and Preserves: A Visitor's Guide.* Seattle: The Mountaineers, 1993. Excellent guide specifically for those heading into protected zones. Detailed maps and trail routes of most parks and reserves, plus bare-bones information on

preparing for your trip. No hotel or restaurant reviews.

Itiel, Joseph. *Pura Vida! A Travel Guide to Gay & Lesbian Costa Rica.* San Francisco: Orchid House, 1993. An uninhibited, anecdotal account of an experienced gay traveler's time in Costa Rica, including practicalities on accommodations, nightlife, and more.

Pritchard, Audrey, and Raymond Pritchard. *Drive the Pan-Am Highway to Mexico and Central America.* Heredia, Costa Rica: Costa Rica Books. Handy preparatory text with hints on packing, customs, and more.

Red Guide to Costa Rica: National Map Guide. San José: Guias de Costa Rica, 1991. City and regional maps in one book; recommended for self-drive exploration.

Sienko, Walter. *Latin America by Bike: A Complete Touring Guide.* Seattle, WA: The Mountaineers, 1993. Splendidly organized practical guidebook to cycling in the Americas, including a chapter on Costa Rica.

Living in Costa Rica

Van Rheenen, Erin. *Living Abroad in Costa Rica.* Emeryville, CA: Avalon Travel Publishing, 2004. The definitive guide to living in Costa Rica also includes highly useful information for travelers passing through.

Howard, Chris. *The New Golden Door to Retirement and Living in Costa Rica,* 7th ed. San José: C.R. Books, 2004. Another splendid comprehensive guide to making the break.

Internet Resources

Travel

www.centralamerica.com

CentralAmerica.com is one of the largest and best Central America-related travel sites on the Net. Each country—Costa Rica, Nicaragua, Belize, Guatemala, and Panama—is categorized into sections for maps, national parks, recommended hotels, day tours, transportation, activities, etc. It also offers online booking.

www.visitcostarica.com

The official website of the **Costa Rican Tourism Boards** is an excellent resource, covering every facet of travel to and in Costa Rica. Well-organized, offering search capability plus online reservations.

www.costaricapages.com

Costa Rica Pages is another general travel site with direct links to suppliers, institutions, and organizations in a wide range of categories.

www.distinctivehotels.com

For travelers with a taste for elegance, this site represents five of the most endearing hotels in the country, marketed under the umbrella of **Small Distinctive Hotels of Costa Rica.**

www.ahcostarica.com

Ah! Costa Rica is a well-organized online tour reservation center for mainstream travelers. "Recommended" hotels and similarly highlighted properties, tour operators, etc. seems to favor advertisers. *Caveat emptor!*

Activities

www.costaricaexpeditions.com

One of the nation's foremost tour operators, **Costa Rica Expeditions** also has one of the best websites, particularly for choosing personal guides, and for whitewater, nature, and adventure enthusiasts.

www.costaricaoutdoors.com

The first-stop site for anglers, **Costa Rica Outdoors** is also a good resource for travelers interested in other outdoor activities. It permits online reservations.

Ecotourism

www.ecotourism.org

The website of the **International Ecotourism Society** should be the first call for anyone interested in responsible travel to natural areas. It provides ample statistics, valuable links, and a bookstore.

www.planeta.com

Particularly handy for books and travel planning advice, the **"Global Journal of Practical Ecotourism"** provides a directory of links relating to ecotravel worldwide.

www.turismo-sostenible.co.cr

Overseen by the **Costa Rican Tourism Institute (ICT),** this site lets you differentiate tourism sector businesses based on the degree to which they comply with a sustainable model of natural, cultural, and social resource management. It has a search tool for finding individual hotels.

General Information

www.cia.gov/cia/publications/factbook/geos/cs.html

The **U.S. Central Intelligence Agency** provides its thorough statistical and analytical review of Costa Rica here.

www.costarica.com

Packed with practical information, this broad-ranging site offers something for everyone, from classifieds and culture to real estate and retirement living. It has a particularly comprehensive business directory.

www.costaricainternetdirectory.com
The **Costa Rica Internet Directory** offers advertisers in five categories—business, education, health, real estate, and travel—with direct links.

www.costaricaweb.com
Costa Rica Web is another general site covering a wide span of subjects.

www.info.co.cr
Guñas Costa Rica bears a physical resemblance to Yahoo.com and a similar wide-ranging spectrum of subjects, including such esoteric links as the national lottery.

www.infocostarica.com
One of the most comprehensive and visually attractive sites, **Info Costa Rica** provides links that will meet most needs of travelers, businessfolk, and anyone else with a lay interest.

www.ticosearch.com
With more than 1,600 links, **Tico Search** is virtually guaranteed to deliver you to the source of whatever information you need.

Government
www.casapres.go.cr
The official site of the **Costa Rican President,** with links to all of the government ministries, national institutions, government-owned banks.

News and Publications
www.amcostarica.com
The website of **A.M. Costa Rica,** a daily English-language news source for issues relating to Costa Rica. It also has a classified ad section, job listings, restaurant reviews, and an entertainment section.

www.nacion.co.cr
The website of the nation's foremost newspaper, *La Nación*, is the best source for catching up on daily events in Costa Rica. Alas, it's for Spanish speakers only.

www.ticotimes.net
The online edition of *The Tico Times*, the excellent English-language daily published in Costa Rica provides a brief capsule of stories appearing every Friday in the print edition. The mail subscription is more reliable than the online subscription.

Telephone Directories
www.superpagescr.com
Verizon's searchable telephone directory for Costa Rica lets your fingers do the walking.

www.ice.co.cr/principal.html
This telephone directory from **ICE** (Costa Rica Institute of Electricity) also lets you do the walking through the white and yellow pages, if you can stand the annoying flash components.

Index

Beaches

Must-Sees

Acknowledgments

I could not have completed the fifth edition of this book without the support—sometimes minor, often colossal—of a coterie of friends and others to whom thanks are due.

First, no number of words can sufficiently express the thanks due to my friends Eldon and Lori Cooke, who permitted me to use the finest hotel in San José—Hotel Grano de Oro—as my base. Their hospitality and that of Marco, the manager, and the staff added immense pleasure to my capital experience. Likewise, my friend Denis Roy, of Villa Caletas, went out of his way to make my stay at the nation's most resplendent hotel so rewarding; as did friends Glenn and Terry Jampol, at their fabulous coffee-estate-cum-hotel, Finca Rosa Blanca. Special thanks, too, go to Michael Kaye and Natalie Ewing, of Costa Rica Expeditions, for their support with transportation to/from Tortuguero and for hospitality at Tortuga Lodge and Monteverde Lodge; and to Michael for his practical guidance and friendship along the way.

I am also especially grateful to Xinia Novoa Espinoza, of Europcar, for facilitating use of a Toyota RAV-4—a perfectly capable vehicle—to research this edition; to Susan Urza and Isabelle Guerin, of Porter Novelli Public Relations, and Suzana Orozco, of the Instituto Costarricense de Turismo; and to Rob Hodel, of Tico Travel, for his friendship, for the use of a cellphone, and for miscellaneous and always willing assistance.

I'd also like to thank Jim Banks and Cindy Sessoms, of La Paz Waterfall Gardens, for giving of their time. Matís Zeledón, of Down to Earth, deserves special thanks for introducing me to the Terraza de Dota area, and for his gift of premium coffee. And Alexa deserves a special hug for her kind hospitality at Planet Pato.

The following also offered kind hospitality and/or miscellaneous assistance, and credit is due to one and all: Martha Arroyo López and Carolina Sánchez Arias, of Hacienda Guachipelín; John Aspinall and Marco Thomas, of Costa Rica Sun Tours; Peter Aspinall, of Tiskita Lodge; William Aspinall, of Arenal Observatory Lodge; Kimberly Barron, of Makanda; Barry Biesanz, of Biesanz Woodworks; Tessa and Martin Borner, of Posada Mimosa; Mary and Geoff Botosan, of Black Turtle Lodge; Johanna and Michael Bresnan, of Vista del Valle; David Briscoe, of CentralAmerica.com; Sherrill Broudy, of Xandari; Jim Damalis, of Si Como No; Gloria Elena Ferraro, at Rancho San Miguel; Luis Gómez, of Las Cruces Biological Station; Jim Hamilton, of Tilajari; Andrea and Giovanna Holbrook, of Selva Verde Lodge; Christopher Howard, of *Costa Rica Books;* Bradd Johnson, of Aguila de Osa Inn; Gabriel Leyton, of Casa Turire; Daryl Loth, of Casa Marbella B&B; John McKuen, of Seventh Street Books; Barbara MacGregor, of Finca los Caballos; Mauro and Gloria Marchiori, of Escape Caribeño; Sue Moody, of Flor Blanca; Patricia Murillo, of Hacienda los Inocentes; Elizabeth Newton and Terry Newton, of Magellan Inn; Andrzej Nowacki, of Hotel Tres Banderas; Gabriel Rocha, of Villa Caletas; Romy and Lee Rodríguez, of El Cafetal; Ursula Schmidt, of Capitán Suizo; Armando Terzano, of Posada Playa Tortuga; Andreas Veit and Cornelia Neck, of Orosi Lodge; Xavier Vela and Pilar Saavedra-Vela, of Casa de las Tias; Eduardo Villafranca, of Punta Islita; Lana Wedmore, of Luna Lodge; Louis Wilson, of Hotel Tortuga; plus Claude and Sylvia, of Villas del Sueño, and the owners and managers of the Arenal Country Inn and Costa Rica Marriott.

Thanks also to my good friends Michael Valli, Roger Oyama, and Edwin Salem for great times shared on the road.

Above all I wish to thank Lynetta Cornelius, for her selfless support, encouragement, love, and friendship.

I am also indebted to those who contributed in years past to facilitating previous editions of this book. Alas, they are too numerous to mention. Also, readers who kindly contributed comments and updates are too many to name individually, but my deepest appreciation goes to them all.

To all others who lent their support but who through my senility or thoughtlessness have not been acknowledged, a sincere apology and a heartfelt thank you.

I am indebted for the gracious support of Jean Mercier and John Anderson, whose photography graces this book. Those with a commercial interest in Jean's photography should contact him at Apdo. 1798, Alajuela 4050, Costa Rica, tel. 506/441-2897, ledrainois@racsa.co.cr.

This book is dedicated to the memory of Ruedi Schmid.

U.S. ~ Metric Conversion

1 inch	=	2.54 centimeters (cm)
1 foot	=	.304 meters (m)
1 yard	=	0.914 meters
1 mile	=	1.6093 kilometers (km)
1 km	=	.6214 miles
1 fathom	=	1.8288 m
1 chain	=	20.1168 m
1 furlong	=	201.168 m
1 acre	=	.4047 hectares
1 sq km	=	100 hectares
1 sq mile	=	2.59 square km
1 ounce	=	28.35 grams
1 pound	=	.4536 kilograms
1 short ton	=	.90718 metric ton
1 short ton	=	2000 pounds
1 long ton	=	1.016 metric tons
1 long ton	=	2240 pounds
1 metric ton	=	1000 kilograms
1 quart	=	.94635 liters
1 US gallon	=	3.7854 liters
1 Imperial gallon	=	4.5459 liters
1 nautical mile	=	1.852 km

To compute Celsius temperatures, subtract 32 from Fahrenheit and divide by 1.8. To go the other way, multiply Celsius by 1.8 and add 32.

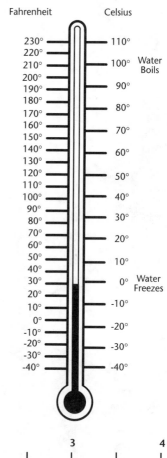